Professional Java Programming

Brett Spell

Wrox Press Ltd. ®

Professional Java Programming

Published by Wrox Press Ltd,
Arden House, 1102 Warwick Road, Acocks Green,
Birmingham, B27 6BH, UK
Printed in the United States
ISBN 186100382X

Trademark Acknowledgements

Credits

Authors
Brett Spell

Additional Material
Grant Palmer

Technical Architect
Craig A. Berry

Technical Editors
Richard Huss
Christian Peak
Andrew Tracey
Mark Waterhouse
Chanoch Wiggers

Managing Editors
Paul Cooper
Viv Emery

Author Agents
Emma Batch
Greg Pearson

Project Manager
Chandima Nethisinghe

Index
Michael Brinkman
Andrew Criddle

Technical Reviewers
Danny Ayers
Thomas Bishop
Carl Burnham
Samir Fernandes
Tony Greening
Ethan Henry
Songmuh Jong
Meeraj Kunnumpurath
Jeff Luszcz
Jim MacIntosh
Vinay Menon
Stephen Potts
Graham Tilbury
Byron Vargas
Tony Wasson
Peter Wikström

Production Project Coordinator
Pip Wonson

Figures
Shabnam Hussain

Cover
Shelley Frazier

Proofreader
Fiona Berryman

The Author

Brett Spell is a native of Westlake, Louisiana and a graduate of Louisiana Tech University. He has been programming professionally in Java since 1996 and is a Sun Certified Java Programmer, Developer, and Architect. Brett lives in Plano, Texas, where he works for Pepsico Business Solutions Group at the Frito-Lay international headquarters.

This book is dedicated to my wife, Shari, who helped make its writing possible. I'd also like to thank my sister, Gwendolyn, for encouraging me to insist on my own title, and my mother, Evelyn, for giving me the confidence to write in the first place.

Professional Java Programmin

Table of Contents

Table of Contents

Table of Contents

Table of Contents

Table of Contents

Table of Contents

Table of Contents

Table of Contents

Table of Contents

Table of Contents

Introduction

Welcome

Welcome to Professional Java Programming. This book shows how you can use the Java language and platform to create great applications, taking advantage of Java's cross-platform nature and the ease of development it offers.

Writing advanced Java applications – crafting robust, well-designed code, making full use of Swing's graphical user interface capabilities, exchanging XML data, or using Java's facilities for distributed computing and accessing native code – can seem intimidating. But there's no need for it to be so, and you'll soon be making full use of these Java features.

This book is by no means a 100% exploration of the topics that you should be familiar with as a professional Java programmer. Instead, the purpose of this book is to introduce you to some of the more common issues that you will need to address and the solutions that are available. Several of these topics such as object-oriented design, Swing components, persistence, threading, and distributed objects are individually the subject of entire books, and rightfully so. The purpose of this book is not to make you an expert in each of these areas, but to introduce topics that you'll face as a professional Java programmer on a regular basis.

Who Should Read This Book

Professional Java Programming is aimed at anyone with some experience of the Java language and platform who wants to improve their programming skills. As Java becomes ever more popular as a choice for professional developers, so more and more people begin to learn the language. This makes your job, as someone who already knows at least some Java, that much harder. However, this book is here to help.

Alternatively, you may well have a fair amount of experience of using and working with Java, and will be looking for something to help give you the edge. You may have encountered situations in which you need a simple solution to a problem, but have been faced with several almost indistinguishable answers with no clear way to choose the best. This book is here to help.

What's Covered in This Book

This book is a comprehensive tour of advanced techniques in the Java language. Although split into twenty chapters, the book can also be divided into five sections:

❑ **Writing Quality Applications**
In the first three chapters, you'll gain further insight into what to do *before* you start writing code: how the Java Virtual Machine (JVM) works, techniques for effective object-oriented class and method design, best practice when dealing with exceptions, and how to handle threading.

❑ **User Interface Components**.
Chapters 4 to 7 cover Event Handling, Layout Managers, JTable and JTree, respectively. Here, you will find out how Java's event model works and how to create custom event types; how to get the most out of the standard layout managers and how to create your own; ways to optimize the use of tables in your applications; and delve into the intricacies of trees.

❑ **Implementing Standard User Interface Behavior**
Chapter 8 looks at issues involved in implementing Cut and Paste functionality in your applications, Chapter 9 follows this up with an examination of Drag and Drop techniques, and Chapter 10 discusses how to use Java's printing facilities in your applications. Chapter 11 rounds off this section by considering how you can create your own custom components

❑ **Creating Distributed Applications**
In Chapters 12 to 15, there is good practical advice on how to tackle key issues in distributed applications. These include using JDBC and XML to store and access data, a good look at persistence, and an examination of distributed object techniques.

❑ **Effective Code**
The final five chapters in the book look at important aspects of delivering an application to the user. Starting with important advice on security for your application in Chapter 16 and tips on performance and memory management in Chapter 17, you then discover all you need to know about providing a help system for your application, documentation for your code, and important issues in preparing your application for an international market. Chapter 20 finishes off by looking at the Java Native Interface.

What You Need to Use This Book

Most of the code in this book was tested with the Java 2 Platform, Standard Edition SDK (JDK 1.3). However, for some of the chapters you need additional software:

❑ A relational database system and a suitable JDBC driver for it – we used Microsoft Access 2000 and the JDBC-ODBC bridge driver supplied with the Java SDK

❑ The Java API for XML Parsing (JAXP), from `http://java.sun.com/xml/`

❑ The Xalan XSLT processor, from `http://xml.apache.org/xalan/`

- ❑ JavaHelp 1.1, from `http://www.java.sun.com/products/javahelp/`
- ❑ A C++ compiler, for the JNI examples in Chapter 20 – we used Microsoft Visual C++ 6.0

The source code from the book is available for download from `http://www.wrox.com/`.

Conventions

To help you get the most from the text and keep track of what's happening, we've used a number of conventions throughout the book.

For instance:

> **These boxes hold important, not-to-be forgotten information which is directly relevant to the surrounding text.**

While the background style is used for asides to the current discussion.

As for styles in the text:

- ❑ When we introduce them, we **highlight** important words.
- ❑ We show keyboard strokes like this: *Ctrl-A*.
- ❑ We show filenames and code within the text like so: `doGet()`
- ❑ Text on user interfaces and URLs are shown as: Menu.

We present example code in two different ways:

```
The code foreground style shows new, important, pertinent code
while code background shows code that's less important in the present
    context, or has been seen before.
```

Professional Java Programmin.

Online discussion at http://p2p.wrox.com

1

Inside Java

According to Sun, Java is "a simple, robust, object-oriented, platform-independent, multithreaded, dynamic, general-purpose programming environment". This relatively simple definition has allowed Java to grow and expand into so many niches that it is almost unrecognizable from how it first started off. Today, you can find Java just about anywhere you can find a microprocessor. It is used in the largest of enterprises to the smallest of devices, from the humble desktop to huge lumbering, super-cooled mainframes. In order for Java to support such a wide range of environments, an almost bewildering array of APIs and versions have been developed, though built around a common set of core classes.

Despite this, in order to become a good Java programmer it is important to be able to do the basics well. Being able to produce a highly complex user interface is all very well, but if your code is bloated, memory hungry, and inefficient your users won't be happy. This book is not about the huge array of development options available to you as a Java developer, but about how to do the common tasks that as a Java developer you will encounter again and again. Over the course of the book we will be concentrating on some of the core language features, such as threading and memory management, that can really make the difference in a professional quality Java application.

At the core of Java's adaptability, and hence popularity, is that it is platform independent. One phrase that has been coined is "Write Once, Run Anywhere" (WORA). This feature is brought about by the way Java itself operates, and in particular the use of an abstract execution environment that allows Java code to be separated from the underlying operating system. Whereas the rest of this book will be about exploring the programming language and APIs of Java, in this chapter we are going to look at the foundations of how Java really operates under the hood, with the Java Virtual Machine. Understanding the inner workings of Java will give you as a programmer a better understanding of the language and should make you a better programmer.

We will be covering:

- ❑   The various components of the Java platform
- ❑   How the Java Virtual Machine allows Java to be platform independent
- ❑   What happens when you run a Java program
- ❑   What a Java class file really contains
- ❑   The key tools needed to work with a Java Virtual Machine

First, then, let's take apart what Java actually is.

Java's Architecture

It is easy to think of Java as merely the programming language with which you develop your applications – writing source files and compiling them into bytecode. However, Java as a programming language is just one component of Java, and it is the underlying architecture that gives Java many of its advantages such as platform independence.

The complete Java architecture is actually the combination of four components:

- ❑   The Java programming language
- ❑   The Java class file format
- ❑   The Java Application Programming Interfaces (APIs)
- ❑   The Java Virtual Machine

So, when you develop in Java you are writing with the Java programming language, which is then compiled into Java class files, which in turn are executed in the Java Virtual Machine.

The combination of the JVM plus the core classes form the **Java platform**, also known as the **Java Runtime Environment (JRE)**, which sits on whatever operating system is being used:

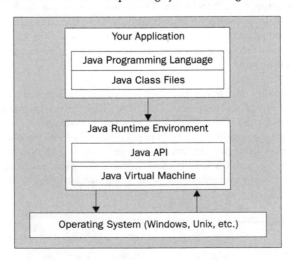

The core classes and supporting file (the JRE) and the interpreter that converts bytecode to native calls (the JVM) used to be separate entities. To run a Java program, the JRE had to be loaded as a separate operation to starting the JVM. However, in the current implementation of the JVM, the JRE has been incorporated into the JVM. So when you start up the JVM, you are also loading the JRE.

The Java Application Programming Interface, or API, is pre-written code organized into packages of similar topics. The Java API is divided into three main platforms:

- The **Java 2 Platform, Standard Edition**, or J2SE for short. This platform contains the core Java classes and the GUI classes.

- The **Java 2 Platform, Enterprise Edition** (J2EE). This package contains the classes and interfaces for developing web-based applications; it contains the servlet, JavaServer Pages and Enterprise JavaBeans classes, amongst others.

- The **Java 2 Platform, Micro Edition** (J2ME). In this package, Java goes back to its roots. It provides an optimized runtime environment for consumer products such as pagers, cellular phones, and car navigation systems.

The Java Virtual Machine

Before we explore the various aspects of writing powerful Java applications, let us spend some time discussing the engine that makes this possible. That engine is called the **Java Virtual Machine**, or **JVM** for short. The Java Virtual Machine is an *abstract* computing machine that interprets compiled Java programs.

With other programming languages such as C or C++, a compiler, which is specific to the processor and often also the operating system, is used to compile the source code into an executable. This executable is then self-sufficient and can then be run on the machine.

One drawback of this is the lack of **portability**. A code compiled under one operating system cannot be run on another operating system. It must be re-compiled on every different system on which it is run. What is more, because of vendor specific compiler features, a code compiled under a certain operating system for a certain processor family (for example, Intel x86, SPARC, Alpha) probably will not be able to run on different type of processor that runs the same operating system. For example, C code compiled on an Alpha workstation running Windows NT will probably not work on an Intel PC that is also running NT.

This problem was particularly acute when people first began to write applications for the Internet. These applications were intended for people running many different operating systems, on many different platforms, through different types of browsers. The only way to resolve this problem was to develop a language that was **platform independent**.

In the early 1990's, developers at Sun Microsystems were working on a platform-independent language for use in consumer electronic devices, which unfortunately was a little too ahead of its time and was therefore shelved. With the advent of the Internet, these developers saw a much greater potential for this language, and Java was born.

The key to the portability of the Java language is that the output of the Java compiler is not standard executable code. Instead, the Java compiler generates an optimized set of instructions called a **bytecode** program. Bytecodes are a sequence of formatted bytes, and we'll look at them in more detail later. The bytecode program is interpreted by the Java runtime system, otherwise known as the Java Virtual Machine. What is more, a bytecode program generated on one platform can be run on any other platform that has a JVM installed.

This is generally true even though some specifics of the JVM may differ from platform-to-platform. In other words, a Java program that is compiled on a UNIX workstation can be run on a PC or a Mac. The source code is written in a standard way, in the Java language and compiled into a bytecode program, and each JVM interprets the bytecode into native calls specific to that platform, that is, into a language that the specific processor can understand. This abstraction is the way various operating systems achieve such operations as printing, file access and handling hardware into a standardized form.

One feature (and some would say drawback) of bytecode is that it is not executed directly by the processor of the machine on which it is run. The bytecode program is run through the JVM, which interprets the bytecode. This is why Java is referred to as an **interpreted language**. Being an interpreted language is what allows Java to be platform independent, but this comes with a performance hit compared to a standard executable-type code. However, the latest release of the Java Development Kit, JDK version 1.3, addressed the performance issue, reducing the speed difference between Java programs and those written using other programming languages.

It is also worth noting that in order to address this, and other perceived problems, there is an API that provides for interfacing Java applications with native applications (applications written in non-java languages, such as C). This API is called JNI and allows developers both to call code written in a non-Java language from Java code and vice versa. This does however negate much of the platform independence of Java, as the native code will suffer from the platform dependence, and so will the Java code by proxy. We will discuss this subject in more detail in Chapter 20.

For machine portability to work, the JVM must be fairly tightly defined. This is achieved by what is known as the **JVM specification**. This specification, developed and controlled by Sun, dictates the format of the bytecode recognized by the JVM as well as features and functionality that must be implemented by the JVM. The JVM specification is what insures the platform independence of the Java language and can be found on the Sun web site at http://java.sun.com/j2se/1.3/docs/index.html.

Therefore, when we talk about a Java Virtual Machine, we can in fact mean three different things:

- ❑   An abstract specification
- ❑   A concrete implementation of the specification
- ❑   A runtime execution environment

Different JVM Implementations

The Sun web site provides a list of companies that are Java technology licensees. These companies support Java on their particular computer and operating system platforms. The companies include IBM, Data General, Sequent Computer Systems, Hewlett-Packard, Silicon Graphics, Blackdown.com, Apple, Novell, Compaq, SCO, Wind River Systems, and Digital Equipment Corporation. These companies embed a version of the JVM into their web browsers, servers, and operating systems.

Why are there different versions of the JVM? Remember that the JVM specification sets down the required functionality for a Java Virtual Machine but does not mandate how that functionality should be implemented. In an attempt to maximize the use of Java, Sun gave third parties some flexibility to be creative with the platform. The important thing is that whatever the implementation, a JVM must adhere to the guidelines set out by the JVM specification. In terms of platform independence, this means that a JVM must be able to interpret bytecode that is correctly generated on any other platform.

The JVM as a Runtime Execution Environment

Every time you run a Java application you are in fact running your application within an instance of the JVM, and each separate application that you run will have its own JVM instance. So far we've seen that Java uses an interpreted form of source code called bytecode, but how do the instructions we code in the Java programming language get translated into instructions that the underlying OS can understand?

The JVM specification defines an abstract internal architecture for this process. We'll look at the components of this internal architecture in a moment, but at a high level, class files (compiled Java files have a `.class` extension and are referred to as class files) are loaded into the JVM where they are then executed by an **execution engine**. When executing the bytecodes, the JVM interacts with the underlying OS through the means of **native methods**, and it is the implementation of these native methods that tie a particular JVM implementation to a particular platform:

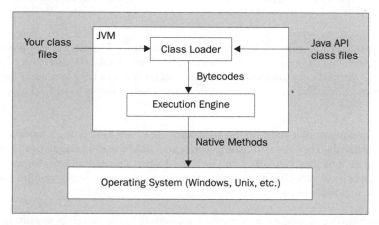

In addition, to the above components, a JVM also needs memory in order to store temporary data related to code execution, such as local variables, which method is executing, and so on. This data is stored within the runtime data areas of the JVM, as explained below.

The Runtime Data Areas of the JVM

While the individual implementations may differ slightly from platform-to-platform, every Java Virtual Machine must supply the following runtime components:

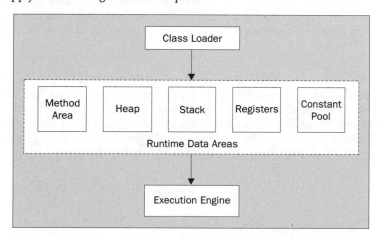

The Heap

The **heap** is a region of free memory that is often used for dynamic or temporary memory allocation. The heap is the runtime data area that provides memory for class and array objects. When class or array objects are created in Java, the memory they require is allocated from the heap, which is created when the JVM starts. Heap memory is reclaimed when references to an object or array no longer exist by an automatic storage management system known as the **garbage collector** – more on this shortly.

The JVM specification does not dictate how the heap is implemented. That is left up to the creativity of the individual implementations of the JVM. The size of the heap may be constant, or it may be allowed to grow as needed or shrink if the current size is unnecessarily large. The programmer may be allowed to specify the initial size of the heap; for example on Win32 and Solaris systems this can be done with the -mx command line options. Heap memory does not need to be contiguous. If the heap runs out of memory and additional memory cannot be allocated to it, an OutOfMemoryError exception will be thrown by the system.

The Stack

A Java **stack frame** is used to store the state of method invocations. The stack frame is used to store data and partial results and includes the method's execution environment, any local variables used for the method invocation, and the method's **operand stack**. The operand stack stores the parameters and return values for most bytecode instructions. The execution environment contains pointers to various aspects of the method invocation.

Frames are the components that make up the JVM stack. They are used to store partial results, data, and return values for methods. They are also used to perform dynamic linking and to issue runtime exceptions. A frame is created when a method is invoked and destroyed when the method exits for any reason. A frame consists of an array of local variables, an operand stack, and a reference to the runtime constant pool of the class of the current method.

When the JVM runs Java code, only one frame, corresponding to the currently executing method, is active at any one time. This is referred to as the current frame. The method it represents is the current method, and the class the method is defined in is the current class. When a thread invokes a method (each thread has its own stack), the JVM creates a new frame, which becomes the current frame, and pushes it onto the stack for that thread.

As with the heap, the JVM specification leaves it up to the specific implementation of the JVM how the stack frames are implemented. The stacks can either be of fixed size or can expand or contract in size as needed. The programmer may be given control over the initial size of the stack and its maximum and minimum sizes. Again, on Win32 and Solaris this is possible through command line options -ss and -oss. If a computation requires a larger stack than is possible, a StackOverflowError exception is thrown.

Method Area

The **method area** is a common storage area shared among all JVM threads. It is used to store such things as the runtime constant pool, method data, field data, and the bytecode for methods and constructors. The JVM specification only details the general features of the method area. It does not mandate the location of the method area, nor does it dictate how the method area is implemented. The method area may be of fixed size, or it may be allowed to grow or shrink. The programmer may be allowed to specify the initial size of the method area. The memory for the method area does not need to be contiguous.

Registers

The **registers** maintained by the JVM are similar to registers on other computer systems. They reflect the current state of the machine and are updated as bytecode is executed. The primary register is the **program counter** (the **pc register**) that indicates the address of the JVM instruction that is currently being executed. If the method currently being executed is native (written in a language other than Java), the value of the pc register is undefined. Other registers in the JVM include a pointer to the execution environment of the current method, a pointer to the first local variable of the currently executing method, and a pointer to the top of the operand stack.

Runtime Constant Pool

The **runtime constant pool** is similar to a symbol table used in other programming languages. As the name suggests, it contains constants including numeric literals and field constants. The memory for each runtime constant pool is allocated from the method area. The runtime constant pool is constructed when the JVM creates the class file for a class or interface.

The Garbage Collector

As was stated previously, when Java class objects are created the memory they require is allocated from the heap. The heap is meant to be an area of *temporary* memory; when the memory is no longer required, it should be returned to the heap and made available for future allocations. If the memory is not properly de-allocates, a situation arises that is known as a **memory leak**. The temporary memory that was allocated but not de-allocated is no longer available for future use. The system will eventually run out of memory, and when this happens it will most likely cause the system to crash.

Java uses what is known as a **garbage collector** to monitor a Java program while it runs and automatically de-allocates memory for objects that no longer exist. Java uses a series of **soft pointers** to keep track of object references. An object table is used to map these soft pointers to the object reference. The soft pointers are called this because they do not point directly to the object but instead point to the object references themselves. The use of soft pointers allows the Java garbage collector to run in the background using a separate thread, and it can examine one object at a time. The garbage collector can mark, remove, move, or examine objects by changing the object table entries.

The garbage collector runs on its own and it is usually not necessary to manipulate it. The garbage collector performs its checking of object references sporadically during the execution of a program. When no references to an object exist, the memory allocated to that object is reclaimed. You can force the garbage collector to run by invoking the static method `gc()` from the `System` class, though there is no guarantee that the object will be garbage collected.

The JVM in Action – Loading, Linking, and Initializing

In order for the JVM to interpret a Java bytecode, it must perform three steps for the required classes and interfaces:

❑ **Loading**
When the JVM loads a class it finds a binary representation of a class or interface and creates a `Class` object from that binary representation (usually a class file created by a Java compiler). A `Class` object encapsulates the runtime state of a class or interface.

❑ **Linking**
Linking is the process of taking the loaded class or interface and combining it with the runtime of the JVM, preparing it for execution.

❑ **Initializing**
Initialization occurs when the JVM invokes the class or interface initialization method.

The First Step

The first thing the JVM does when a stand-alone Java application starts up is to create an initial `Class` object representing the Java class that contains the `public static void main(String args[])` method. The JVM links and initializes this class and invokes the `main()` method. This method starts the ball rolling, so to speak, and drives the loading, linking, and initializing of any additional classes and interfaces that are required.

Loading

The loading process itself is carried out by a **ClassLoader** object or by an object that is a sub-class of `ClassLoader`. The class loader will do some of its own verification checks on the class or interface it is loading. An exception will be thrown if the binary data representing the compiled class or interface is malformed, if the class or interface uses an unsupported version of the class file format, if the class loader could not find the definition of the class or interface, or if there is a class circularity. A class circularity occurs if a class or interface would be its own super-class or super-interface.

There are two general types of class loaders. The one supplied by the JVM is referred to as the **bootstrap class loader**. There can also be **user-defined class loaders**. These are always sub-classes of the `ClassLoader` class. User-defined class loaders can be used to create `Class` objects from non-standard, user-defined sources, perhaps for security purposes. For instance, the `Class` object could be extracted from an encrypted file. A loader may delegate part or all of the loading process to another loader. The loader that ultimately creates the `Class` object is referred to as the defining loader. The loader that begins the loading process is known as the initiating loader.

The loading process using the default bootstrap loader is as follows. First, the loader determines if it has already been recorded as the initiating loader of a class file corresponding to the desired class file. If it has, the `Class` object already exists and the loader stops. (You should note here that loading a class is not the same as creating an instance of it, this step merely makes the class available to the JRE.) If it is not, the loader searches for the class file and, if found, will create the `Class` object from that. If the class file is not found, a `NoClassDefFoundError` exception is thrown.

When a user-defined class loader is used, the process is somewhat different. As with the bootstrap loader, the user-defined loader first determines if it has already been recorded as the initiating loader of a class file corresponding to the desired class file. If it has, the `Class` object already exists and the loader stops. If it is not, the user-defined loader invokes the `loadClass()` method. The return value of this method is the desired class file. The `loadClass()` method assembles the array of bytes representing the class into a `ClassFile` structure. It then calls the `defineClass()` method which creates a `Class` object from the `ClassFile` structure. Alternatively, the `loadClass()` method can simply delegate the loading to another class loader.

Linking

The first step in the linking process is the verification of the class file to be linked.

Java Class File Verification

As the JVM is completely separate from the Java compiler, the JVM, which interprets the class file, has no guarantee that the class file is properly formed or that it was even generated by a Java compiler. Another problem arises with inheritance and class compatibility. If a given class file represents a class that inherits from a super-class represented by another class file, the JVM must make sure that the sub-class class file is compatible with the super-class class file.

The Java Virtual Machine verifies that each class file satisfies the constraints placed on it by the Java language specification, although the Java class verifier is independent of the Java language. Programs written in certain other languages can also be compiled into the class file format, and if everything has been done correctly pass the Java verification process.

The verification process itself is performed in four steps:

❑ In the first step, the class file is loaded by the JVM and checked to make sure it adheres to the basic format of a class file. The class file must be of the correct length. The magic number (which identifies a class file as really being a class) is checked. The constant pool must not contain any unrecognizable information, and the length of each attribute is checked to be sure it is of the correct length.

❑ The second step in the verification process occurs when the file is linked. The actions performed in this step include ensuring that the final keyword constraint is preserved. This means that final classes cannot be sub-classed and final methods cannot be overridden. The constant pool is checked to make sure the elements do not violate any language constraints. All field and method references in the constant pool must be valid. Finally, every class except the Object class is checked to see if it has a direct super-class.

❑ The third verification step also occurs during the linking phase. Every method referenced in the class file is checked to ensure that it adheres to the constraints placed on methods by the Java language. The methods must be invoked with the correct number and type of arguments. The operand stack must always be the same size and contain the same types of values. Local variables must contain an appropriate value before they are accessed. Fields must only be assigned values of the proper type.

❑ The final step in the verification looks at events that occur the first time a method is invoked and ensures that everything is done according to spec. The checks include ensuring that a referenced field or method exists in a given class, verifying that the referenced field or method has the proper descriptor, and ensuring that a method has access to the referenced method or field when it executes.

Preparation

Once the class file has been verified, the JVM prepares the class for initialization by allocating memory space for the class variables and also sets them to default initial values. These are the standard default values, such as 0 for int, false for boolean, etc. These values will be set to their program dependent defaults during the initialization phase.

Resolution

At this (optional) step, the JVM resolves the symbolic references in the runtime constant pool into concrete values.

Initialization

Once the linking process is complete any static fields and static initializers are invoked. Static fields have values that are accessible even when there are no instances of the class; static initializers provide for static initialization that cannot be expressed simply in a single expression. All of these initializers for a type are collected together by the JVM into a special method. For example, the collected initializers for a class become the initialization method <clinit>.

However, when initializing a class, not only must the class initialization method be invoked by the JVM (only the JVM can call it) but in addition, any super-classes must also be initialized (which also involves the invocation of <clinit>). As a result the first class that will always be initialized is Object. The class containing the main() method for an application will always be initialized.

Bytecode Execution

The bytecode from a class file consists of a series of one-byte opcode instructions specifying an operation to be performed. Each opcode may be followed by zero or more operands, which supply arguments or data used by that operation. The JVM interpreter essentially uses a do...while loop that loads each opcode and any associated operands and executes the action represented by the opcode. The bytecode is translated into an action according to the JVM **instruction set**, which maps bytecode to operations represented by the bytecode as specified by the JVM specification. This process continues until all of the opcode has been interpreted.

For reasons of compactness (at the expense of some performance), JVM opcode is constructed of single byte entities. Using one-byte opcode minimizes the required size of the JVM instruction set. Data that requires a size larger than one byte is constructed at runtime from one or more one-byte entities.

The first set of instructions in the JVM instruction set involve basic operations performed on the primitive data types and on objects. The nomenclature used is generally the data type followed by the operation. For instance, the iload instruction (iload is merely a mnemonic representation of the actual instruction) represents a local variable which is an int being loaded onto the operand stack. The fload instruction is for loading a local variable that is a float onto the operand stack, and so on. There are a series of instructions to store a value of a certain data type from the operand stack into a local variable, loading a constant onto the operand stack, and to gain access to more than one local variable.

The second set of instructions in the instruction set concerns arithmetic operations. The arithmetic operation generally involves two values currently on the operand stack. The result of the operation is pushed onto the operand stack. The nomenclature is the same as before. For instance, the iadd operation is for adding two integer values, and the dadd operation is for adding two double values.

Similarly, there are operations representing basic mathematical functions (add, subtract, multiply, and divide), logical operations (bitwise OR, bitwise AND, and bitwise NOT), and some specialized functions including remainder, negate, shift, increment, and comparison.

The JVM adheres to the IEEE 754 standards when it comes to things such as floating point number operations and rounding towards zero. Some integer operations, divide by zero for instance, can throw an ArithmeticException. The floating-point operators do not throw runtime exceptions but instead will return a NaN ("Not a Number" – the result of an invalid mathematical operation) if an overflow condition occurs.

The JVM instruction set includes operations for converting between different types. The JVM directly supports widening conversions, for instance `float` to `double`. The naming convention is the first type, the number 2, and the second type. For example, the instruction `i2l` is for conversion of an `int` to a `long`. The instruction set also includes some narrowing operations, the conversion of an `int` to a `char` for instance. The nomenclature for these operations is the same as for the widening operations.

Instructions exist for the creation and manipulation of class and array objects. The `new` command creates a new class object, and the `newarray`, `anewarray`, and `multinewarray` instructions create an array object. Instructions also exist to access the static and instance variables of classes, load an array component onto the operand stack, store a value from the operand stack into an array component, return the length of an array, and check certain properties of class objects or arrays.

The JVM instruction set provides the `invokevirtual`, `invokeinterface`, `invokespecial`, and `invokestatic` instructions that are used to invoke methods. The `invokevirtual` is the normal method dispatch mode. The other instructions are for methods implemented by an interface, methods requiring special handling such as private or super-class methods, and static methods. There are also method return instructions defined for each data type.

Finally, there is a collection of miscellaneous instructions for doing various other operations. These include instructions for operand stack management, control transfer, exception throwing, implementing the `finally` keyword, and synchronization.

For example, let's take a very simple Java class:

```
class Hello {
  public static void main(String[] args) {
    System.out.println("Hello World!");
  }
}
```

If you compile it and then use the `javap` utility with the –c switch (covered later) to disassemble the class file you can get a mnemonic version of the bytecode:

```
Compiled from Hello.java
class Hello extends java.lang.Object {
    Hello();
    public static void main(java.lang.String[]);
}

Method Hello()
   0 aload_0
   1 invokespecial #1 <Method java.lang.Object()>
   4 return

Method void main(java.lang.String[])
   0 getstatic #2 <Field java.io.PrintStream out>
   3 ldc #3 <String "Hello World!">
   5 invokevirtual #4 <Method void println(java.lang.String)>
   8 return
```

The main set of mnemonics we are interested in is the three lines under the `main()` method which translate the single `System.out.println("Hello World!");` line we wrote in Java.

The first instruction, getstatic, retrieves a PrintStream object from the out field of the java.lang.System object and places it onto the operand stack. The next line, ldc, pushes the String "Hello World!" onto the operand stack. Finally, invokevirtual executes a method in this case println (on the java.io.PrintStream class). For this method to successfully execute it expects there to be a String and an instance of java.io.PrintStream in the stack, in that order. Upon execution these items are removed from the stack.

The Java Class File Format

The JVM cannot interpret the Java programming language directly, so when Java code is compiled the result is one or more class files that it can interpret. The class file contains bytecode, a symbol table, and other information for one class or interface. The class file structure is a precisely defined binary format that ensures that any JVM can load and interpret any class file, no matter where the class file was produced.

The class file itself consists of a stream of 8-bit bytes. All higher bit quantities (16-, 32-, or 64-bits) are created by reading in a combination of 8-bit bytes. Multi-byte quantities are stored in big-endian order (the high bytes come first). The Java language provides I/O streams (supported by the DataInput, DataInputStream, DataOutput, and DataOutputStream interfaces from the java.io package.) that can read and write class files.

> For descriptive purposes, a pseudo-structure format will be used in this section to describe the elements that make up a class file. This is consistent with the nomenclature used in the Java Virtual Machine specification on the Sun web site and in previous publications. In reality, the elements of a class file are stored sequentially, without padding or alignment; however, this would be rather difficult for you to translate into anything meaningful.

The data types in the class file are unsigned one-, two-, or four-byte quantities. These are denoted by the syntax u1, u2, and u4. The class file can also contain a series of contiguous fixed-size items that can be indexed like an array. These are designated using square brackets, [].

The class format contains a single ClassFile structure. This structure contains all the information about the class or interface that the JVM need to know. The general structure of the ClassFile is as follows:

```
ClassFile {
    u4 magic;
    u2 minor_version;
    u2 major_version;
    u2 constant_pool_count;
    cp_info constant_pool[constant_pool_count - 1];
    u2 access_flags;
    u2 this_class;
    u2 super_class;
    u2 interfaces_count;
    u2 interfaces[interfaces_count];
    u2 fields_count;
    field_info fields[fields_count];
    u2 methods_count;
    method_info methods[method_count];
    u2 attributes_count;
    attribute_into attributes[attributes_count];
}
```

The magic parameter is the magic number assigned to the class file format. This will have the value 0xCAFEBABE and identifies the code as being a class file.

The major_version and minor_version are the major and minor versions of the class file format. To the JVM the version numbers indicate the format to which the class file adheres. JVMs can generally only load class files within a certain version range, for example within a single major version but a range of minor versions.

The constant_pool_count is equal to the number of elements contained in the constant pool plus one. This variable is used to determine if a constant_pool index is valid. The constant_pool[ ] item is a table of cp_info structures containing information on the elements in the constant_pool.

The access_flags item is a mask of flags reflecting whether the file is class or interface and the access permissions of the class or interface. The mask will be un-set or a combination of public, final, super, interface, or abstract flags.

The this_class parameter points to a CONSTANT_Class_info structure in the constant_pool representing the class or interface defined by this class file. The super_class item points to a similar element in the constant_pool representing the direct super-class or interface or zero if there is no super-class.

The interfaces_count parameter represents the number of direct super-interfaces for the class or interface. The interfaces[ ] item contains the location of these super-interfaces in the constant_pool table.

The fields_count variable gives the number of field_info structures contained in the ClassFile. The field_info structures represent all fields, both static and instance, declared by the class or interface. The fields[ ] item is a table containing all of the field_info structures for this class or interface.

The methods_count item contains the number of method_info structures in the methods table. A method_info structure provides a description of a method contained in the class or interface. The methods[ ] item is a table containing the method_info structures.

Finally, the attributes_count variable gives the number of attributes in the attributes table of the class or interface. The attributes[ ] item is a table containing the attributes structures.

The Java Programming Language and APIs

All that we have covered so far happens transparently to you the application developer. In fact, you don't really have to know any of the details of Java's internal architecture to program in Java. However, what you do need to know is how to use Java as a programming language and also how to use the various APIs that come with the different platforms to communicate with the underlying software and OS. In fact, this is essentially what the remainder of the book will be about – how to develop effectively with Java.

The Java Programming Language

Although knowledge of the various APIs is essential to really achieving anything with Java, a solid foundation in the core Java language is also highly desirable to make the most effective use of the APIs. In this book we will be exploring the following features of core Java programming:

❑ **Method, Interface, and Class Design**
Writing the main building blocks of your application with Java objects can be simultaneously quite straightforward and hideously complex. However, if you take the time to follow some basic guidelines for creating methods, classes, and libraries, it is not too difficult to develop classes that not only provide the required functionality, but are also reliable, maintainable, and reusable.

❑ **Threading**
Java includes built-in support for multithreaded applications, and you'll often find it necessary or desirable to take advantage of this. To do so, you should be familiar with Java's multi-threading capabilities and know how to implement threads correctly within an application

❑ **Event Handling**
This is a particularly important topic when implementing user interface code, but events are useful in other places as well. Since Java applications are event-driven, you need to know how to use events effectively in Java.

❑ **Performance and Memory Management**
Java is often simplistically described as having no pointers, and is said to handle all memory management automatically. Those statements are only partially true, and it's important to understand what Java can and can't do. A poorly written Java application (and even a well-written one) can easily run out of memory, but there are often ways to prevent this from happening if you understand how references and garbage collection work.

❑ **Controlling Access to Resources**
From its earliest days, Java was always implemented with security built-in at a fundamental level. These features have obviously improved but in many ways the mechanism by which Java controls the access your code can have to valuable system resources, such as the file system and network connections, hasn't changed much. One of the advantages of the current system is that it allows the decoupling of access control from the code itself through the use of policy files.

The Java APIs

As we covered earlier in the chapter, there are in fact three different version of the Java 2 platform, each of which consists of some significantly different APIs. In this book we will mainly be concentrating on some (although not all) of the APIs that form the Standard Edition. More precisely we will be covering:

❑ **Swing Components**
We will be taking an in-depth look at two of the more complex Swing components, JTable and JTree as well as some coverage about how to build your own custom components should the standard set provided with Swing not meet your needs.

❑ **The Data Transfer API**
Closely related to providing the user interface for your application, are the common features of cut-and-paste, and drag-and-drop, each of which rely heavily on the Data Transfer API, for moving data to the clipboard and back.

❑ **The Printing API**
Another common feature often required is the ability to print, which we will be examining through the use of Java 2's printing capabilities.

❑ **JDBC**
All but the most trivial of applications require data to loaded, manipulated and stored in some form or another, and the relational database is one of the most common means of storing such data. The Java Database Connectivity API (JDBC) is the means by which you can use a relational database as your data store.

❑ **Java APIs for XML Parsing**
Although not actually included by default in the Standard Edition, XML is becoming such an important topics for development today that it is worth learning about it as early as possible. The combination of Java's platform independence and XML's language neutrality is a powerful combination indeed.

❑ **Distributed Object APIs**
Although perhaps more suited to the Enterprise Edition platform, we will be looking at some of the APIs that allow you to extend Java's object capabilities across the network. In particular we will compare Sockets, RMI and CORBA as the means to work remotely.

❑ **JavaHelp**
An extension to the core classes, JavaHelp allows you to incorporate help files into your application to help the user out with those less than obvious features.

❑ **Internationalization**
Most commercial applications and those developed for internal use by large organizations are used in more than one country and need to support more than one language. This requirement is often overlooked or treated as an implementation detail, but to be implemented successfully, internationalization usually must be made part of the application design. To create a successful design that includes internationalization support, you need to understand Java's capabilities in that area.

❑ **JNI**
When performance is critical or when Java doesn't provide functionality that's required by your application, you can use "native methods" to execute code written in other programming languages. However, doing so is not trivial and should be a last resort. At a minimum, though, it's necessary to understand how to perform native method calls and how to communicate between Java and non-Java code.

Java Utility Tools – Making the Most of the JVM

The Java 2 Platform, Standard Edition comes with a number of development tools that can be used to compile, execute, and investigate Java programs. Some of the tools that relate to the JVM will be discussed here. A description of all of the utility tools can be found on the Sun website at http://java.sun.com/j2se/1.3/docs/tooldocs/tools.html.

The Java Compiler

The compiler that comes with the J2SE is named `javac`, and reads class and interface definitions and converts these into bytecode files. The command to run the java compiler is:

```
javac [options] [source files] [@file list]
```

The options are command line options. If the number of source files to be compiled is sufficiently short, the files can just be listed one after another. If the number of files is large, a file containing the names of the files to be compiled can be used preceded by the "@" character. Source code file names must end with the `.java` suffix. Execution of `javac` may also be carried out using a script or batch file, or using built-in features of an IDE.

The command line options are used to include additional functionality into the standard compile command. Available options are:

- ❑ -classpath
  This command, followed by a user-specified class path, overrides the system CLASSPATH environment variable.

- ❑ -d
  This command, followed by a directory path, sets the destination directory for the class files generated by the compiler.

- ❑ -deprecation
  Displays a description of any deprecated methods or classes used in the source code.

- ❑ -encoding
  Sets the source file encoding name. Otherwise, the default encoding is used.

- ❑ -g
  Provides more complete debugging information including local variable info.

- ❑ -g:none
  Turns off all debugging information.

- ❑ -g:keyword
  Allows the user to specify the type of debugging information provided. Valid keyword options are *source*, *lines*, and *vars*.

- ❑ -nowarn
  Warning messages will not be provided. Warnings occur when the compiler suspects something is wrong with the source code, but the problem is not catastrophic.

- ❑ -O
  This option is intended to produce optimized code in terms of execution time although in the current implementation of javac this option does nothing.

- ❑ -sourcepath
  This command followed by a source path specifies the path that the compiler will use to search for source code files.

- ❑ -verbose
  This command produces additional information about the classes that are loaded and the source files that were compiled.

The Java Interpreter

The java utility is used to launch a Java application. It does this by loading and running the class file containing the main method of the application. The java utility will interpret the bytecode contained in this file and any other class files that are part of the application. The general command syntax for the java utility is:

```
java [options] class [arguments]
```

or:

```
java [options] -jar file.jar [arguments]
```

The initial class file can be provided as a separate file or as part of a Java Archive (JAR) file. The *options* are command line options for the java utility. The *class* is the name of the class file containing the main() method. The *arguments* are any arguments that need to provided to the main() method.

The standard options for the java utility are:

- ❑ -client
  Specifies that the Java HotSpot Client Virtual Machine will be used. This is the default.

- ❑ -server
  Specifies that the Java HotSpot Server Virtual Machine will be used.

- ❑ -classpath
  This command, followed by a user-specified class path, overrides the system CLASSPATH environment variable.

- ❑ -D property=value
  This command provides a system property with a value.

- ❑ -help or -?
  Prints out information about the java utility.

- ❑ -jar
  Executes a program contained in a JAR file, as shown above.

- ❑ -showversion
  Shows version information and continues running.

- ❑ -verbose
  Provides information about each class that is loaded.

- ❑ -verbose:gc
  Report every garbage collection event.

- ❑ -verbose:jni
  Display information about native methods and other Java Native Interface activity.

- ❑ -version
  Shows version information and then exits.

- ❑ -X
  Displays information about non-standard options and then exits.

On Windows, there is also a utility called javaw that loads and runs the specified class, but does not have an associated console window, for programs that do not require one.

The Java Class Disassembler

The javap utility can be used to look inside a class file. The standard command lists declarations of non-private and non-static fields, methods, constructors, and static initializers for a specified class file. The javap utility can also be used to provide a printout of the JVM instructions that are executed for each method. The basic syntax for the javap command is:

```
javap [options] class
```

The *options* are command line options for the javap utility. These options are:

- ❑ -b
  Ensures backward compatibility with earlier versions of javap.

- ❑ -bootclasspath
  This command, followed by a path, specifies the path from which to load the bootstrap classes. Normally these would be the classes contained in the /lib/rt.jar archive.

- ❑ -c
  Prints out the JVM instructions for the execution of each method. This tells you what the bytecode for each method actually does.

- ❑ -classpath
  This command, followed by a user-specified class path overrides the system CLASSPATH environment variable.

- ❑ -extdirs
  This command followed by a directory overrides the location the system searches for installed extensions. The default location is /lib/ext.

- ❑ -help
  Prints out information about the javap utility.

- ❑ -Jflag
  Passes the specified flag directly to the runtime system.

- ❑ -l
  Displays line and local variables.

- ❑ -package
  Shows only package, protected, and public classes and members. This is the default.

- ❑ -private
  Shows information about all classes and members.

- ❑ -protected
  Displays information about protected and public classes and members only.

- ❑ -public
  Only shows information about public classes and members.

- ❑ -s
  Prints internal type signatures.

- ❑ -verbose
  Prints additional information for each method including stack size, local variable info, and arguments.

Summary

This chapter has been a bit of a whirlwind tour of under the hood of Java, poking in the corners of Java internal architecture that don't get explored all that often. You should now have a better appreciation of what is actually going on when you type `java MyClass` at the command prompt.

We have covered:

- ❑   The components of Java's architecture
- ❑   What the JVM is and how it functions
- ❑   The internals of the JVM architecture
- ❑   The Java class file format

Now we've taken a bit of time to explore the foundations of Java, we are now ready to start the main work of learning how to use all the different components of the Java platform in detail, starting with library, class, and method design.

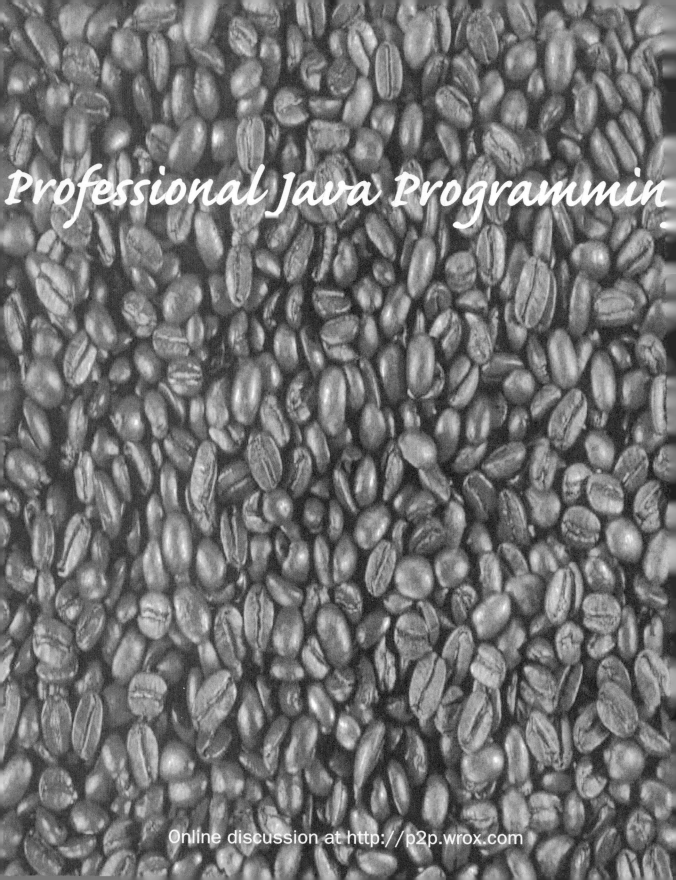

Professional Java Programmin

2

Library, Class, and Method Design

Understanding how to create Java code is relatively easy. However, producing a good **object-oriented design** for your code is much more complex. Good object-oriented design results in code that works correctly, and is reasonably easy to understand, to maintain, to extend, and to reuse. In this chapter we will provide you with some guidelines to help you to produce well-designed code.

One of the primary advantages of using object-oriented programming languages is **reusability**. Creating reusable code saves time and effort by avoiding duplication, which can occur whenever code is created which is similar, or identical, to something that was written previously. Therefore, reusability should be one of the most important aims when designing your code.

While creating reusable code should always be your goal, the reality is that it's sometimes impossible or impractical to make code reusable. Some classes are good candidates for reuse while others are not, and creating reusable software usually requires more work in the short term than creating "throw-away" code. However, as you become more experienced in creating good object-oriented designs, you'll learn to recognize good candidates for reuse, and also how to design classes and methods which are as reusable as possible.

Aside from code reuse, we will cover several other aspects of good design:

- ❑ We will discuss the advantages of inhibiting direct access to class properties using **encapsulation.**

- ❑ We will see how using **immutable** objects and methods can simplify code design.

- ❑ The Object class contains a number of important methods; however, we shall see that there are occasions on which it is beneficial, or necessary, to override these methods.

- ❑ We shall finish the chapter with a look at **exception handling**. The proper use of exceptions is an important part of Java method design, so we will take some time to discuss how to handle exceptions most efficiently.

However, let's start by considering the design of class libraries and packages.

Library Design

Since it's almost certain that some of the code you write will not be reusable, it's a good idea to maintain two sets of packages when building an application. One set should contain reusable code, while the other should contain classes and interfaces that are likely to remain application-specific. By doing this, you can begin to assemble a library of reusable classes, and can easily import them into another application. You should try to treat these reusable classes the same way that most programmers do the Java core classes – as code that can't (or at least shouldn't) be changed. To avoid having to make changes later, you should put a great deal of thought into the initial design of a class. In particular, although you have planned a particular initial use for a class, you should also consider how it could be used differently in the future.

Package Design

Perhaps the first question to be answered concerning packages is: "When do I define them?" Ideally, packages should be defined early in the design phase, prior to creating class definitions. In practice, however, it's usually easier to create packages once your design is at least partially complete. At that point, it's more evident what sort of logical groupings can be created, and those groupings should be the basis for your package design.

A package should be kept reasonably focused and have some type of "theme" or consistency to the classes that are assigned to it. If the package grows very large and contains a subset of classes that can be separated from the main package, you should consider using sub-packages.

For example, the `javax.swing` package contains many classes and interfaces that define visual components, and otherwise provide support for creating Graphical User Interface (GUI) code. A number of classes are defined in the package that is responsible for drawing borders around other components. Instead of adding these border-related classes to `javax.swing`, which would further increase that package's size, the border classes were placed in the `javax.swing.border` sub-package.

This example illustrates that selecting a package is about knowing where a class doesn't belong just as much as knowing where it should reside. An example of a class that should probably not have been included in `javax.swing` is that of `Timer`. This class can be used to send notifications at arbitrary time intervals, or a single notification at some specific point in time. However, this functionality is not inherently tied to visual components, and is also a likely candidate for use by non-visual portions of an application. Therefore, `javax.swing` is arguably a poor location for this class. In fact, a completely new and separate `Timer` class is included in the `java.util` package in JDK 1.3.

Another guideline for package design is that you should prevent your packages from being cluttered with too many small, simple classes that provide little functionality. Doing so can make it difficult for someone who is reviewing the classes in your package to remember the responsibilities of each class.

One way that you can reduce the number of trivial classes visible in a package is to use inner classes. However, their use should be limited to cases where you're reasonably sure that the potential inner class will not need to be referenced outside of the class that defines it. In particular, you should use an anonymous inner class as an event handler when there's a limited amount of functionality in its event handling method(s).

Class Design

An important part of being a professional object-oriented programmer is the ability to create well-designed classes. Practice is an important ingredient in mastering this skill, but there are also some simple principles that can help you become more effective.

Class design is largely a matter of **assigning responsibility**, where you identify the functions that must be implemented and assign each one to the class or classes best suited to perform that function. Alternatively, if there is no existing class that's appropriate, you might decide to create a new class. Some classes are identified in the analysis phase and correspond to real-world entities, while others (known as **pure abstractions**) exist solely to provide needed functionality while allowing you to create a better design. To promote reusability, your classes should have two general characteristics: **loose coupling** and **strong cohesion**. Let's take a closer look at these two properties.

Loose Coupling

Coupling refers to the degree to which classes are dependent upon one another, and two classes that are highly dependent upon each another are considered **tightly** (or **highly**) **coupled**.

Coupling is inevitable in some cases, because classes must maintain references to one another and perform method calls. However, when you implement a class that is also a good candidate for reuse then you should limit its dependencies on other classes as much as you can.

> **In other words, classes that are good candidates for reuse should be as loosely coupled as possible.**

Often it's not obvious how to do this, since you usually can't simply eliminate the interaction between classes. However, in many cases it's possible to create a pure abstraction that handles the interaction between two classes, or to shift the responsibility for the interaction to an existing class that you don't intend to make reusable.

Let's have an example that illustrates this point. Suppose that you need to create a graphical component that allows you to select font properties, enter some sample text, and then have that sample text displayed using the selected font properties. When the font or the sample text changes, the display should also be updated to display the sample text value using the current font settings:

To satisfy these requirements, you might first create a class similar to the one listed below, `FontPropertiesPanel`. This class defines a panel that allows you to select the font properties (name, size, bold, italic):

```java
import java.awt.*;
import java.awt.event.*;
import javax.swing.*;
import javax.swing.event.*;

public class FontPropertiesPanel extends JPanel {

  protected JList nameList;
  protected JComboBox sizeBox;
  protected JCheckBox boldBox;
  protected JCheckBox italicBox;

  protected SampleTextFrame frame;

  public final static int[] fontSizes = {10, 12, 14, 18, 24, 32, 48, 64};

  public FontPropertiesPanel(SampleTextFrame stf) {
    super();
    frame = stf;
    createComponents();
    buildLayout();
  }

  protected void buildLayout() {
    JLabel label;
    GridBagConstraints gbc = new GridBagConstraints();
    GridBagLayout gbl = new GridBagLayout();
    setLayout(gbl);

    gbc.anchor = GridBagConstraints.WEST;
    gbc.insets = new Insets(5, 10, 5, 10);

    gbc.gridx = 0;
    label = new JLabel("Name:", JLabel.LEFT);
    gbl.setConstraints(label, gbc);
    add(label);
    label = new JLabel("Size:", JLabel.LEFT);
    gbl.setConstraints(label, gbc);
    add(label);
    gbl.setConstraints(boldBox, gbc);
    add(boldBox);

    gbc.gridx++;
    nameList.setVisibleRowCount(3);
    JScrollPane jsp = new JScrollPane(nameList);
    gbl.setConstraints(jsp, gbc);
    add(jsp);
    gbl.setConstraints(sizeBox, gbc);
    add(sizeBox);
    gbl.setConstraints(italicBox, gbc);
    add(italicBox);
  }
```

```
protected void createComponents() {
  GraphicsEnvironment ge =
      GraphicsEnvironment.getLocalGraphicsEnvironment();
  String[] names = ge.getAvailableFontFamilyNames();
  nameList = new JList(names);
  nameList.setSelectedIndex(0);
  nameList.setSelectionMode(ListSelectionModel.SINGLE_SELECTION);
  nameList.addListSelectionListener(new ListSelectionListener() {
    public void valueChanged(ListSelectionEvent event) {
      handleFontPropertyChange();
    }
  }
  );
  Integer sizes[] = new Integer[fontSizes.length];
  for (int i = 0; i < sizes.length; i++) {
    sizes[i] = new Integer(fontSizes[i]);
  }
  sizeBox = new JComboBox(sizes);
  sizeBox.addActionListener(new ActionListener() {
    public void actionPerformed(ActionEvent event) {
      handleFontPropertyChange();
    }
  }
  );
  boldBox = new JCheckBox("Bold");
  boldBox.addActionListener(new ActionListener() {
    public void actionPerformed(ActionEvent event) {
      handleFontPropertyChange();
    }
  }
  );
  italicBox = new JCheckBox("Italic");
  italicBox.addActionListener(new ActionListener() {
    public void actionPerformed(ActionEvent event) {
      handleFontPropertyChange();
    }
  }
  );
}

protected void handleFontPropertyChange() {
  frame.refreshDisplayFont();
}

public String getSelectedFontName() {
  return (String)(nameList.getSelectedValue());
}

public int getSelectedFontSize() {
  return ((Integer)(sizeBox.getSelectedItem())).intValue();
}

public boolean isBoldSelected() {
  return boldBox.isSelected();
```

```
    }

    public boolean isItalicSelected() {
      return italicBox.isSelected();
    }

  }
```

Next, you might create a class similar to the one shown below, `SampleTextFrame`. This class contains an instance of `FontPropertiesPanel`, a text field that allows you to type the sample text, and a label that displays that text using the specified font:

```
import java.awt.*;
import javax.swing.*;
import javax.swing.border.*;
import javax.swing.event.*;
import javax.swing.text.*;

public class SampleTextFrame extends JFrame {

  protected FontPropertiesPanel propertiesPanel;
  protected JTextField sampleText;
  protected JLabel displayArea;

  public static void main(String[] args) {
    SampleTextFrame stf = new SampleTextFrame();
    stf.setDefaultCloseOperation(JFrame.EXIT_ON_CLOSE);
    stf.setVisible(true);
  }

  public SampleTextFrame() {
    super();
    createComponents();
    createDocumentListener();
    buildLayout();
    refreshDisplayFont();
    pack();
  }

  protected void createComponents() {
    propertiesPanel = new FontPropertiesPanel(this);
    sampleText = new JTextField(20);
    displayArea = new JLabel("");
    displayArea.setPreferredSize(new Dimension(200, 75));
    displayArea.setMinimumSize(new Dimension(200, 75));
  }

  protected void createDocumentListener() {
    Document document = sampleText.getDocument();
    document.addDocumentListener(new DocumentListener() {
      public void changedUpdate(DocumentEvent event) {
        handleDocumentUpdate();
      }

      public void insertUpdate(DocumentEvent event) {
```

```
        handleDocumentUpdate();
      }

      public void removeUpdate(DocumentEvent event) {
        handleDocumentUpdate();
      }
    }
    );
  }

  protected void buildLayout() {
    Container pane = getContentPane();
    GridBagConstraints gbc = new GridBagConstraints();
    GridBagLayout gbl = new GridBagLayout();
    pane.setLayout(gbl);

    gbc.insets = new Insets(5, 10, 5, 10);
    gbc.fill = GridBagConstraints.HORIZONTAL;
    gbc.weightx = 1;

    gbc.gridx = 0;
    BevelBorder bb = new BevelBorder(BevelBorder.RAISED);
    TitledBorder tb = new TitledBorder(bb, "Font");
    propertiesPanel.setBorder(tb);
    gbl.setConstraints(propertiesPanel, gbc);
    pane.add(propertiesPanel);

    gbl.setConstraints(sampleText, gbc);
    pane.add(sampleText);

    gbl.setConstraints(displayArea, gbc);
    pane.add(displayArea);
  }

  protected void handleDocumentUpdate() {
    displayArea.setText(sampleText.getText());
  }

  public void refreshDisplayFont() {
    displayArea.setFont(getSelectedFont());
  }

  public Font getSelectedFont() {
    String name = propertiesPanel.getSelectedFontName();
    int style = 0;
    style += (propertiesPanel.isBoldSelected() ? Font.BOLD : 0);
    style += (propertiesPanel.isItalicSelected() ? Font.ITALIC : 0);
    int size = propertiesPanel.getSelectedFontSize();
    return new Font(name, style, size);
  }
}
```

As you can see from this code, FontPropertiesPanel maintains a reference to SampleTextFrame, and when a font property changes, it calls the frame's refreshDisplayFont() method.

At first glance this may appear to be an acceptable design for these classes. However, there is a significant drawback: neither class can be used independently of the other. In other words, SampleTextFrame and FontPropertiesPanel are tightly coupled, and as a result are poor candidates for reuse. If you wished to use FontPropertiesPanel as part of some user interface component other than SampleTextFrame, you would be unable to do so in its present form, because the current design allows it to operate only in conjunction with an instance of SampleTextFrame. The relationship between these two classes is illustrated below:

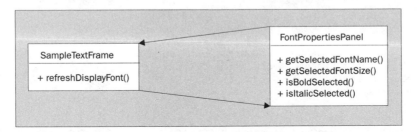

Since it provides functionality that might be useful in another context, FontPropertiesPanel appears to be a good candidate for reuse, if only it can be decoupled from SampleTextFrame. The existing dependence is due to the fact that FontPropertiesPanel calls refreshDisplayFont() directly. Consequently, FontPropertiesPanel is dependent not only upon the existence of SampleTextFrame, but also upon its implementing the refreshDisplayFont() method. In order to decouple FontPropertiesPanel from SampleTextFrame, changes to the font must be communicated to the text display somehow, but in a way that allows FontPropertiesPanel and SampleTextFrame to be loosely coupled.

Also note that when a property changes, SampleTextFrame is responsible for extracting the font properties from FontPropertiesPanel and using that information to construct an instance of Font. This is a poor design not only because it makes the two classes more tightly coupled, but also because it actually requires more code than building a Font instance inside of FontPropertiesPanel, when it has all the information needed to do so. This illustrates another important point related to class design:

> **Functionality should usually be assigned to the class that contains the information needed to perform the function.**

Designing Loosely Coupled Classes

So how can we loosely couple these example classes? Let's consider a few options.

Adding Interfaces

One way is to use a technique that is very simple but also very powerful: couple a class to an interface instead of another class.

For example, we could create an interface for these classes called FontListener. This interface defines a single fontChanged() method which is called by FontPropertiesPanel when the font property value changes.

This means that FontPropertiesPanel is now only dependent upon FontListener, and is not coupled to SampleTextFrame anymore. Any user interface component that needs to incorporate FontPropertiesPanel can do so, if it implements the FontListener interface (and its fontChanged() method) in a class that's responsible for monitoring the font properties.

You should also note that we can use this technique to reduce SampleTextFrame's dependence upon FontPropertiesPanel as well, simply by making it call the interface's fontChanged method too.

The figure below illustrates the relationships between the two classes and the new interface after these changes have been made:

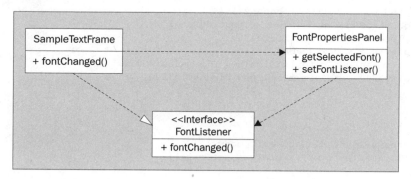

So, to make these two classes more loosely coupled, we'll specify that FontListener's fontChanged() method should be passed a reference to a new font that was built using the newly-selected properties. The implementation of such an interface is shown below:

```
public interface FontListener {
  public void fontChanged(java.awt.Font newFont);
}
```

Next, we'll implement the above interface in SampleTextFrame and have it update the label's font when it receives a message from the FontPropertiesPanel instance:

```
import java.awt.*;
import javax.swing.*;
import javax.swing.border.*;
import javax.swing.event.*;
import javax.swing.text.*;

public class SampleTextFrame extends JFrame implements FontListener {

  protected FontPropertiesPanel propertiesPanel;
  protected JTextField sampleText;
  protected JLabel displayArea;

  public static void main(String[] args) {
    SampleTextFrame stf = new SampleTextFrame();
    stf.setDefaultCloseOperation(JFrame.EXIT_ON_CLOSE);
    stf.setVisible(true);
  }
```

```
   public SampleTextFrame() {
     super();
     createComponents();
     createDocumentListener();
     buildLayout();
     displayArea.setFont(propertiesPanel.getSelectedFont());
     propertiesPanel.setFontListener(this);
     pack();
   }

   protected void createComponents() {
     propertiesPanel = new FontPropertiesPanel();
     sampleText = new JTextField(20);
     displayArea = new JLabel("");
     displayArea.setPreferredSize(new Dimension(200, 75));
     displayArea.setMinimumSize(new Dimension(200, 75));
   }

//...

   protected void handleDocumentUpdate() {
     displayArea.setText(sampleText.getText());
   }

//   public void refreshDisplayFont() {
//     displayArea.setFont(getSelectedFont());
//   }

//   public Font getSelectedFont() {
//     String name = propertiesPanel.getSelectedFontName();
//     int style = 0;
//     style += (propertiesPanel.isBoldSelected() ? Font.BOLD : 0);
//     style += (propertiesPanel.isItalicSelected() ? Font.ITALIC : 0);
//     int size = propertiesPanel.getSelectedFontSize();
//     return new Font(name, style, size);
//   }

   public void fontChanged(Font newFont) {
     displayArea.setFont(newFont);
   }

}
```

Finally, `FontPropertiesPanel` can be modified so that it no longer maintains a reference to `SampleTextFrame`, but instead keeps a reference to a `FontListener`. We'll also implement a `getSelectedFont()` method that can be used to create a new `Font` instance using the currently selected properties:

```
import java.awt.*;
import java.awt.event.*;
import javax.swing.*;
import javax.swing.event.*;
```

```
public class FontPropertiesPanel extends JPanel {

  protected JList nameList;
  protected JComboBox sizeBox;
  protected JCheckBox boldBox;
  protected JCheckBox italicBox;

// protected SampleTextFrame frame;
  protected FontListener listener;

  public final static int[] fontSizes = {10, 12, 14, 18, 24, 32, 48, 64};

// public FontPropertiesPanel(SampleTextFrame stf) {
  public FontPropertiesPanel() {
    super();
// frame = stf;
    createComponents();
    buildLayout();
  }

// ...

  protected void handleFontPropertyChange() {
    listener.fontChanged(getSelectedFont());
  }

  public void setFontListener(FontListener fl) {
    listener = fl;
  }

  public Font getSelectedFont() {
    String name = (String)(nameList.getSelectedValue());
    int style = 0;
    style += (boldBox.isSelected() ? Font.BOLD : 0);
    style += (italicBox.isSelected() ? Font.ITALIC : 0);
    int size = ((Integer)(sizeBox.getSelectedItem())).intValue();
    return new Font(name, style, size);
  }

// public String getSelectedFontName() {
//   return (String)(nameList.getSelectedValue());
// }

// public int getSelectedFontSize() {
//   return ((Integer)(sizeBox.getSelectedItem())).intValue();
// }

// public boolean isBoldSelected() {
//   return boldBox.isSelected();
// }

// public boolean isItalicSelected() {
//   return italicBox.isSelected();
// }

}
```

Although this design is slightly more complex than the original one, it's much more desirable from a reuse standpoint as we have seen – FontPropertiesPanel is now only dependent upon FontListener, and is not coupled to SampleTextFrame at all. In this case, the method was implemented with just a single line of code that refreshes the display so that it uses the updated font properties.

Having decoupled FontPropertiesPanel from SampleTextFrame, let's now see how we can remove SampleTextFrame's dependence upon FontPropertiesPanel too.

Adding Classes

Although SampleTextFrame isn't as strong a candidate for reuse as FontPropertiesPanel, we can make it more reusable by eliminating its dependence upon FontPropertiesPanel. We've already removed one dependency by preventing SampleTextFrame from building a new Font instance based on the properties in the panel, but dependencies still exist. For example, in the createComponents() method, an instance of FontPropertiesPanel is created. In addition, the SampleTextFrame constructor makes calls to the panel's getSelectedFont() and getFontListener() methods. Let's first assume that SampleTextFrame will always contain a JPanel subclass called propertiesPanel, but that we don't want to couple it specifically to FontPropertiesPanel. As well as reducing the coupling between these two classes, this approach also allows us to use other panel types. There's just one problem – how can we achieve this?

A helpful guideline for creating reusable classes is to divide the functionality into two types: functionality that's common and reusable, and functionality that's specific to one application and is not reusable. Dividing up functionality in this way is very useful, because it enables us to:

> **Improve reusability by putting the common functionality in a superclass, and the application-specific logic in a subclass.**

The merits of this approach become clearer if we consider our example classes. We can use this technique to eliminate SampleTextFrame's references to the FontPropertiesPanel class, by moving them all into a subclass of SampleTextFrame, called FontPropertiesFrame. This means that SampleTextFrame becomes dependent upon the FontListener interface only, increasing the reusability of this class.

The next figure illustrates the new relationship between these components:

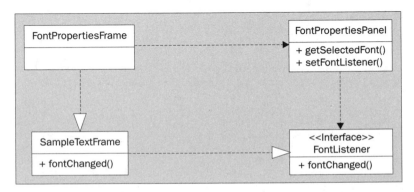

The modified `SampleTextFrame` is shown below:

```java
import java.awt.*;
import javax.swing.*;
import javax.swing.border.*;
import javax.swing.event.*;
import javax.swing.text.*;

public class SampleTextFrame extends JFrame implements FontListener {

//  protected FontPropertiesPanel propertiesPanel;
  protected JPanel propertiesPanel;
  protected JTextField sampleText;
  protected JLabel displayArea;

  public static void main(String[] args) {
    SampleTextFrame stf = new SampleTextFrame();
    stf.setDefaultCloseOperation(JFrame.EXIT_ON_CLOSE);
    stf.setVisible(true);
  }

  public SampleTextFrame() {
    super();
    createComponents();
    createDocumentListener();
    buildLayout();
//    displayArea.setFont(propertiesPanel.getSelectedFont());
//    propertiesPanel.setFontListener(this);
    pack();
  }

  protected void createComponents() {
//    propertiesPanel = new FontPropertiesPanel();
    sampleText = new JTextField(20);
    displayArea = new JLabel("");
    displayArea.setPreferredSize(new Dimension(200, 75));
    displayArea.setMinimumSize(new Dimension(200, 75));
  }

// ...rest of class is unchanged
```

All explicit references to `FontPropertiesPanel` have been removed, and can be added to the new subclass of `SampleTextFrame`:

```java
public class FontPropertiesFrame extends SampleTextFrame {

  public static void main(String[] args) {
    FontPropertiesFrame fpf = new FontPropertiesFrame();
    fpf.setVisible(true);
  }

  public FontPropertiesFrame() {
    super();
    FontPropertiesPanel fontPanel = (FontPropertiesPanel)propertiesPanel;
    displayArea.setFont(fontPanel.getSelectedFont());
```

```
      fontPanel.setFontListener(this);
  }

  protected void createComponents() {
    propertiesPanel = new FontPropertiesPanel();
    super.createComponents ();
  }

}
```

So, to summarize, although it was necessary to create a small class (FontPropertiesFrame) and an interface (FontListener), we've now converted two tightly coupled and practically impossible to reuse classes into good candidates for a reusable code library.

Strong Cohesion

In addition to loosely coupling classes, another characteristic of good class design is a high level of cohesion. For a class to be highly cohesive means that its responsibilities are closely related and that it contains a complete set of related methods. To put it another way:

> **A class is not cohesive if it contains methods that perform unrelated functions, or if some set of closely related functions is split across that class and one or more others.**

An example of lack of cohesion was seen in the example classes we have just used: the original implementation of FontPropertiesPanel did not contain a method to create an instance of Font based on the selected property settings. Therefore, a lack of cohesion is important because it indicates inefficient code design.

Cohesion most commonly becomes a problem when too much functionality is added to a single class. To avoid this problem, a good rule of thumb is to keep the responsibilities of a class limited enough that they can be outlined with a brief description.

For another example of classes that are not cohesive, suppose you're given the code below, which is part of a larger application. First, the StudentReport class is responsible for printing out students' reports:

```
public class StudentReport {

  public void printStudentGrades(Student[] students) {
    TestScore[] testScores;
    TestScore score;
    Student student;
    int total;
    for (int i = 0; i < students.length; i++) {
      student = students[i];
      testScores = student.getTestScores();
      total = 0;
      for (int j = 0; j < testScores.length; j++) {
        score = testScores[j];
        total += score.getPercentCorrect();
      }
      System.out.println("Final grade for " + student.getName() + " is " +
```

```
                              total / testScores.length);
        }
    }
}
```

Second, the `Student` class holds a student's name, and an array containing their test results:

```java
public class Student {

  protected TestScore[] testScores;
  protected String name;

  public String getName() {
    return name;
  }

  public TestScore[] getTestScores() {
    return testScores;
  }

}
```

Finally, the `TestScore` class contains data needed to calculate student grades:

```java
public class TestScore {

  int percentCorrect;

  public int getPercentCorrect() {
    return percentCorrect;
  }

}
```

This code will function correctly. However, note that `StudentReport` is responsible for printing out a list of students and the average of their grades, but it has also been assigned responsibility for calculating the average. It is coupled to both `Student` and to `TestScore`, because `TestScore` contains the information needed to calculate the averages. The figure below illustrates the relationships among these three classes:

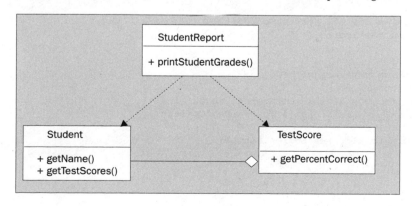

Notice that both StudentReport and Student are dependent upon TestScore. This code is therefore poorly designed, because it violates our guidelines on coupling and cohesion:

❑ The classes are tightly coupled due to an unnecessary dependency, specifically StudentReport's dependency upon TestScore

❑ StudentReport suffers from weak cohesion, because it performs two functions: printing a report, and calculating each student's average

This poor design is a result of the decision to assign StudentReport the responsibility for calculating averages. A better design would involve assigning responsibility for the calculation to Student, and create a method that allows StudentReport to obtain the information from that class. Implementing these changes, we first note that StudentReport's new printStudentGrades() method is therefore much simpler:

```
public class StudentReport {

    public void printStudentGrades(Student[] students) {
        Student student;
        for (int i = 0; i < students.length; i++) {
            student = students[i];
            System.out.println("Final grade for " + student.getName() + " is " +
                                student.getAverage());
        }
    }

}
```

while Student gains a getAverage() method:

```
public class Student {

    protected TestScore[] testScores;
    protected String name;

    public String getName() {
        return name;
    }

    public TestScore[] getTestScores() {
        return testScores;
    }

    public int getAverage() {
        int total = 0;
        for (int i = 0; i < testScores.length; i++) {
            total += testScores[i].getPercentCorrect();
        }
        return total / testScores.length;
    }

}
```

`TestScore` is unchanged. This code is not only more readable, but also more reusable, since there are fewer dependencies, as illustrated below:

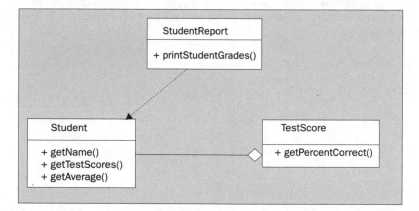

So, in general, you should take the time to assign responsibilities carefully, and minimize the number of dependencies among different classes. As we have seen, you should usually assign responsibility for manipulating data to the class that has access to it. In this case, `Student` had access to all the necessary information while `StudentReport` did not, which made `Student` a better choice for performing the task of calculating an average.

Encapsulation

One of the most basic ways of ensuring good class design is to provide good encapsulation of your data. Encapsulation refers to the hiding of items of data or methods within an object. In other words, to optimize encapsulation you should:

> **Take care to assign the appropriate access attributes to the methods and properties of your classes.**

For example, suppose that we create a class called `Employee` that contains all the information that an application needs to describe an individual:

```
public class Employee {

  public int employeeID;
  public String firstName;
  public String lastName;
}
```

Since the three fields are `public`, it's possible to access them from any other class, such as in the following code segment:

```
Employee emp = new Employee();
emp.employeeID = 123456;
emp.firstName = "John";
emp.lastName = "Smith";
```

Although Java allows you to read and modify fields this way, you should not normally do so. One of the key advantages of objects is that data members can be insulated from modification, but the data member values can also be accessed externally. This is usually achieved by limiting the direct access to these fields, while creating a pair of **accessor** (get) and **mutator** (set) methods for each field that will allow you access to it, as in the following code:

```java
public class Employee {

    protected int employeeID;
    protected String firstName;
    protected String lastName;

    public int getEmployeeID() {
        return employeeID;
    }

    public void setEmployeeID(int id) {
        employeeID = id;
    }

    public String getFirstName() {
        return firstName;
    }

    public void setFirstName(String name) {
        firstName = name;
    }

    public String getLastName() {
        return lastName;
    }

    public void setLastName(String name) {
        lastName = name;
    }

}
```

While, encapsulation and object-oriented "purity" are nice concepts, there are also some very practical advantages to this approach. First, if it becomes necessary for Employee to be made thread-safe (which we'll discuss in detail in Chapter 3), then it's relatively easy to do so if access to its fields is controlled this way; making a class thread-safe is often as simple as adding the synchronized keyword to the method signatures.

Encapsulation also simplifies the task of converting an existing class into a class that is used to create distributed (or "remote") objects, which are covered in more depth in Chapter 15. A distributed object normally resides on a server machine and its methods can be called by applications that reside on different machines (in other words, they can be called "across the network"). Since a distributed object is usually on a separate machine from the caller, the fields that it contains cannot be accessed directly as can be done with a "local" object. However, if you've defined accessor and mutator methods for those fields, the caller can call these remotely, making the location of the object largely transparent.

Hiding Implementation

Another big advantage of using accessor and mutator methods is that they insulate you from changes to a property's implementation. For example, you could change employeeID from an Integer to a String without affecting other classes, as long as you perform the appropriate conversions in the accessor and mutator methods:

```java
public class Employee {

    protected String employeeID;
    protected String firstName;
    protected String lastName;

    public int getEmployeeID() {
        return Integer.parseInt(employeeID);
    }

    public void setEmployeeID(int id) {
        employeeID = Integer.toString(id);
    }

    public String getFirstName() {
        return firstName;
    }

    public void setFirstName(String name) {
        firstName = name;
    }

    public String getLastName() {
        return lastName;
    }

    public void setLastName(String name) {
        lastName = name;
    }

}
```

Although the implementation of employeeID changed, other classes that read or modify it won't see any change in its behavior, because the change in implementation is concealed by the accessor and mutator methods.

Finally, encapsulating the class properties this way allows you to define derived values that can be made accessible. For example, you might define a getFullName() method in Employee that returns the first and last name together as a single string:

```java
public String getFullName() {
    return firstName + " " + lastName;
}
```

Of course, it's possible to obtain derived values without creating an accessor method, but often that means duplicating the code that derives the value. For example, to derive the "full name" property in several places within your application, you'd have to copy the implementation (firstName + " " + lastName) to each of those places. This has the same disadvantage that always accompanies duplicated code: if the implementation ever changes, the change will have to be made to every place in the code that relied upon the old implementation. If you decided to include a middle name, for instance, the use of a `getFullName()` method would allow you to make the change in a single place within your code.

Assigning Access Attributes

In this example, the fields were `protected`, and the methods `public`. As a rule, you should assign fields and methods the most restrictive visibility possible while still providing the functionality you need. The methods in `Employee` are `public` because it's assumed that it should be possible for any other class in any package to be able to access and manipulate the state of an `Employee` instance. What might be less obvious is why the fields were defined as `protected`, since we established that access to them should be controlled through accessor and mutator methods, so `private` might seem like a better choice.

Protected visibility was selected so that subclasses could access these fields directly, which is often necessary. In general, if you're certain that a field or method won't need to be accessed or overridden by a subclass, then you should make it `private`. Otherwise, you should assume that the class will be extended and make the members `protected`. While making a member `protected` also makes it accessible to all classes in the same package, you should not exploit this feature. In other words, only a subclass should ever directly access non-public members within a class. One case where we can relax this rule is in the case of **immutable** fields. Let's now take a closer look at what we mean by "immutable".

Immutable Objects and Fields

To say that an object is immutable means that its state cannot be changed once it has been instantiated. Some examples of immutable objects derive from the **wrapper classes** defined in the `java.lang` package (for example, `Integer`, `Float`, `Boolean`), which are called wrapper classes because they "wrap" functionality around a primitive type.

`String` instances are probably the most commonly used type of immutable object, although it might appear on the surface that you are able to modify them. For example, the following code segment will compile and run successfully as part of a larger application:

```
String myString = "Hi";
System.out.println(myString);

//...

myString = "Hello";
System.out.println(myString);
myString += " there";
System.out.println(myString);
```

Running this code segment would produce the following output:

```
Hi
Hello
Hello there
```

From this example, it may seem that the object instance referenced by `myString` was modified twice after it was initially created: first it was assigned a new value of `"Hello"`, and then `" there"` was appended.

However, in reality, an entirely new `String` instance was created in each case, and the reference was changed to point to the new instance. In other words, the object wasn't modified, but a new object was created and the old one discarded. Any other references to the original string that existed before the two "changes" would still refer to the original Hi text.

Just as the value of an immutable object can't be changed after it is instantiated, the value of an immutable field can't be modified after the object that contains it has been created. To create an immutable field, you must declare it as a **blank final** (in other words, a `final` field that is not assigned a value in its declaration) and initialize its value in each constructor. For example, if you were to decide that it should not be possible to modify an instance of `Employee` after it has been created, you could make all of its fields immutable, as in the following code:

```java
public class Employee {

    public final int employeeID;
    public final String firstName;
    public final String lastName;

    public Employee(int id, String first, String last) {
        employeeID = id;
        firstName = first;
        lastName = last;
    }

}
```

You should note that there is a subtle difference between an immutable field and an immutable object. An immutable field prevents you from changing the object that the field references. It does not prevent you from changing that object's state if the object is mutable.

For example, say we defined the `firstName` and `lastName` fields as instances of `StringBuffer`. This would mean that these fields reference mutable `StringBuffer` objects, so the states of those objects (the contents of the `StringBuffers`) could be changed at any time. However, provided that you had made these fields immutable, you could not store a reference to a different `StringBuffer` into `firstName` or `lastName` after an `Employee` instance is created.

As mentioned earlier, using accessor and mutator methods provide you with an easy way to make access to properties thread-safe. In some cases, however, you may instead choose to provide thread safety by using immutable fields and/or objects; we'll discuss this in more detail in the next chapter.

Overriding Object Methods

The `java.lang.Object` class is the direct or indirect superclass of all Java classes, and it's often necessary or desirable to override some of the methods in `Object`. This section covers the methods that are commonly overridden, providing a description of how each one is used, why you may want to override it, and the information you need to do so.

clone()

This method returns a copy of the object instance, assuming that the class implements the `Cloneable` interface. `Cloneable` is a **tag interface** – that is, an interface that does not define any methods, but is used to mark instances of a class as having some property. In this case, the interface indicates that it is acceptable to create a "clone" (copy) of an instance of the class. The following code checks to see whether the object unknown implements `Cloneable`, and displays a message indicating whether that is the case:

```
Object unknown = getAnObject();
if (unknown instanceof Cloneable) {
  System.out.println("I can create a clone of this object");
} else {
  System.out.println("I can't create a clone of this object");
}
```

Shallow Copies

The default implementation of clone() defined in Object creates a **shallow copy** of the object. A shallow copy is a copy of the object that contains references to the same objects to which the original contained references. For example, suppose that the Employee class defined earlier had implemented Cloneable:

```
public class Employee implements Cloneable {

  public int employeeID;
  public String firstName;
  public String lastName;


}
```

Let's also suppose that an instance of this class is created and initialized, and the clone() method is called to create a copy of it. Note that because Object's implementation of clone() is protected, you must either call it from a subclass or class in the same package, or you must override it and make it public:

```
public Object clone() {
  try {
    return super.clone();
  } catch (CloneNotSupportedException e) {
    System.out.println("Clone failed");
    return this;
  }
}
```

In the following code segment, a shallow copy of the Employee instance is created and a reference to it is stored in myClone.

```
Employee original = new Employee();
original.employeeID = 123456;
original.firstName = "John";
original.lastName = "Smith";
Employee myClone = (Employee)(original.clone());
```

Since it is only a shallow copy, the object references in the clone will point to the same objects – not copies of those objects – that are referenced in the original. This is illustrated graphically below. Both the original and the clone have their own copy of employeeID, since it is a primitive (integer) value and primitives are always copied by value instead of by reference. Note, however, that the other (object) fields contain references to the same object instances:

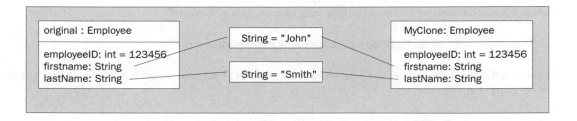

Deep Copies

Shallow copies are sometimes acceptable, but not in all cases. For example, when you create a clone of an object, you'll often do so with the intentions of modifying the contents of the clone later, without changing the original. In that case, a shallow copy may not be sufficient. For example, suppose that you're using the following class:

```
public class MailMessage implements Cloneable {

    protected String sender;
    protected String recipient;
    protected StringBuffer messageText;

    public MailMessage(String from, String to, String message) {
        sender = from;
        recipient = to;
        messageText = new StringBuffer(message);
    }

    public StringBuffer getMessageText() {
        return messageText;
    }

}
```

If you use `clone()` to create a duplicate instance of this class, then you'll have a shallow copy that points to the same object instances as the original. If you then make changes to the `StringBuffer` instance referenced by `messageText`, your changes will affect both the original `MailMessage` instance and its cloned copy. For example:

```
// Create a new instance of MailMessage
MailMessage original = new MailMessage("bspell", "jsmith",
                                "This is the original text");

// Create a shallow copy
MailMessage shallowCopy = (MailMessage)(original.clone());

// Get a reference to the copy's message text
StringBuffer text = shallowCopy.getMessageText();

// Modify the message text using the clone / shallow copy
text.append(" with some additional text appended");

// Now print out the message text using the original MailMessage
System.out.println(original.getMessageText().toString());
```

Running this code segment results in the following message being displayed:

> This is the original text with some additional text appended

To prevent this from happening, you must override the `clone()` method in `MailMessage` so that it creates a **deep copy**. For example:

```
public class MailMessage implements Cloneable {

  protected String sender;
  protected String recipient;
  protected StringBuffer messageText;

  public MailMessage(String from, String to, String message) {
    sender = from;
    recipient = to;
    messageText = new StringBuffer(message);
  }

  public StringBuffer getMessageText() {
    return messageText;
  }

  protected Object clone() {
    try {
      MailMessage mm = (MailMessage)(super.clone());
      mm.messageText = new StringBuffer(messageText.toString());
      return mm;
    } catch (CloneNotSupportedException) {
      System.out.println("Clone Failed");
      return this;
    }
  }

}
```

Note that while it was necessary to create a new `StringBuffer` for `messageText`, it wasn't necessary to create new objects for either `sender` or `recipient`. This is because those two fields point to instances of `String`, which are immutable objects. Since their state can't be changed, it's usually acceptable for the original and the clone to reference the same object instance.

As these examples illustrate, it's generally true that shallow copies are acceptable for objects that contain references to immutable objects and/or to primitives, while more complicated object structures usually require deep copies. When a deep copy is needed, it's your responsibility to implement the functionality yourself.

equals()

This method returns a `boolean` value (`true` or `false`) and determines whether two object instances should be considered equal to one another. What determines equality between two instances is left entirely up to the programmer to decide, and this method can be overridden to perform any type of comparison that's useful to you. The default implementation provided in `Object` tests to see whether the two objects being compared are actually the same object instance, and if so, returns `true`. However, if you define a class for which instances will be compared to one another, you'll often want to use some other criteria.

For example, you might decide that two instances of the class `Employee` we used earlier should be considered equal if the value of `employeeID` is the same in both instances. In that case, you would add a method similar to the following to the class:

```
public boolean equals(Object obj) {
   if ((obj != null) && (obj instanceof Employee)) {
      Employee emp = (Employee)obj;
      if (this.employeeID == emp.employeeID) {
         return true;
      }
   }
   return false;
}
```

This method first checks to ensure that the parameter passed to the `equals()` method is not null and is an instance of `Employee`, and if so, casts it to a reference of that type. It then checks to see whether the `employeeID` field in both instances contain the same value, and if so returns a value of `true`, indicating that the two instances are equal. Although this simple example only uses a single field to determine equality, you can use any criteria that are meaningful to your application when overriding `equals()` in your own classes.

finalize()

This method is called by the garbage collector when it determines that there are no more references to the instance, before the object is destroyed. The most common use of this method is to ensure that any resources held by the instance are released. However, you should note:

> **Java makes no guarantes about when or even if this method will ever be called for an instance, so you should *not* use it for normal cleanup.**

Instead, you should provide a separate method that releases active resources. For example, say you created the class `MyFinalizeTest`, which is outlined below:

```
public class MyFinalizeTest {

   private boolean resourcesInUse;

   public synchronized void allocateResources() {
      performAllocate();
      resourcesInUse = true;
   }

   public synchronized void releaseResources() {
      performRelease();
      resourcesInUse = false;
   }

   /**
    *  If we're still holding resources, release them now
    */
   protected synchronized void finalize() throws Throwable {
      if (resourcesInUse) {
```

```
        releaseResources();
    }
  }

  //  Allocate resources here
  protected void performAllocate() {
  }

  //  Release resources here
  protected void performRelease() {
  }
}
```

You should then encourage programmers who use this class to call the associated finalize() method to perform the cleanup.

hashCode()

An object's hash code value is used primarily to improve the performance of some collection classes, such as java.util.Hashtable. It's not necessary for every instance of a class to return a unique hash code, but you should attempt to make them as unique as possible. This will improve the performance of the classes that use hash codes, since they rely on an object returning a different hash code from most other objects.

There are two requirements for values returned from this method:

❑   Two instances that are considered equal when compared using the equals() method *should* return the same hash code value.

❑   When this method is called for an object two or more times during a single execution of an application, the method should return the same value. However, this requirement need not be met if the object's state changes such that the object would no longer be considered equal to an instance that it was previously equal to.

For example, given our previously defined Employee class, we might choose to simply use the employeeID field as the hash code for each instance. This seems an appropriate choice, since it could be expected to provide a reasonable degree of uniqueness from one instance to the next:

```
public int hashCode() {
  return employeeID;
}
```

This would satisfy the first requirement mentioned above because the value of employeeID would be used to determine equality and as the hash code value. In other words, two instances that have the same employeeID value are considered equal to one another, and they will return the same hash code value. The second requirement is also satisfied, because as long as the employeeID value remains unchanged, the hashCode() method will return the same result each time it is called.

In general, the default implementation of hashCode() will return values that are largely unique and you will not find it necessary to override this method. However, when you override the equals() method, you should normally also override hashCode() to ensure that it meets the two requirements listed above.

toString()

This method returns a string representation of the object instance. You can call this method explicitly whenever it's useful to do so (for instance while debugging), but it is also called implicitly whenever you specify an object reference as part of a string expression. For example, if you create an instance of MailMessage and include it in a string expression, the toString() method is called to obtain its string representation:

```
MailMessage message = new MailMessage("bspell", "jsmith", "This is a test");
System.out.println("Calling toString(): " + message);

// The following line is equivalent to the previous one and would produce
// exactly the same output if it were compiled and executed:
// System.out.println("Calling toString(): " + message.toString());
```

The default implementation of this method in Object simply displays the name of the object's class and the object's hash code value, separated by the "at" symbol (@). For example:

MailMessage@71eaddc4

Since this information usually isn't very helpful, you will normally want to override toString() so that it returns more useful information. Typically, that information should include a partial or complete description of the object's state. For example, you might choose to add the following method to MailMessage:

```
public String toString() {
   return "MailMessage[sender=" + sender + ", recipient=" + recipient +
          ", messageText=" + messageText + "]";
}
```

With this implementation of toString(), running the code segment would result in the following output:

MailMessage[sender=bspell, recipient=jsmith, messageText=This is a test]

This information can be used when debugging, or at any other time when you need to obtain a string representation of an object's state.

Method Design

Many of the design guidelines previously mentioned for classes also apply to methods. For example, methods should be loosely coupled and strongly cohesive, with each method having a single responsibility that can be easily described, and should be independent of other methods as much as possible.

Simplicity

One indication that a method may not be cohesive is the existence of many levels of code blocks. These are easy to identify if the blocks are properly indented. For example:

```
public void doSomethingComplex(int a, int b, Object c, int d) {
   if (a < b) {
```

```
      if (c instanceof Number) {
        for (int i = 0; i < count; i++) {
          if (getSomeData(i) == null) {
            while (d < 5) {
              if (d == 0) {
                handleSpecialCase();
              }
            }
          }
        }
      },
    ]
  }
```

It is sometimes necessary to create such complex logical constructs. However, it's never necessary to include the entire construct in a single method, and splitting it into two or more methods can make the code much easier to understand. Most people find it difficult to follow more than a few levels of logic, and would probably find the following implementation more readable:

```
public void doSomethingComplex(int a, int b, Object c, int d) {
  if (a < b) {
    if (c instanceof Number) {
      for (int i = 0; i < count; i++) {
        doPartOfSomethingComplex(i, d);
      }
    }
  }
}

public void doPartOfSomethingComplex(int i, int d) {
  if (getSomeData(i) == null) {
    while (d < 5) {
      if (d == 0) {
        handleSpecialCase();
      }
    }
  }
}
```

While this may not be the best implementation that can be achieved for these methods, it illustrates that by separating pieces of functionality from a method, you can make its responsibilities simpler and clearer. In addition to greater clarity, structuring your code this way can also make it easier to enhance and debug.

One very basic but extremely important point worth mentioning concerning method design is the use of an obscure, complex algorithm when a simpler alternative exists. Although the more complicated approach may provide minor benefits such as slightly faster execution, that advantage is usually outweighed by the added complexity involved in maintenance and debugging of the code. Stated more simply, readability, extensibility, and reliability are very important, and you should be very hesitant to sacrifice those qualities for an algorithm that seems elegant and clever unless doing so provides some important advantage to your application.

Passing Parameters

When deciding which parameters to pass to a method, you should avoid using "flags" or "control" parameters that tell the method how to perform its function.

We'll use an example to illustrate why this is important. Assume that you are responsible for a `Roster` class that maintains a list of students. In addition, let's assume that a limit exists to the number of students that can normally be included on the roster. However, in some cases, we want to be able to override that maximum. We could create a class like the following one:

```java
import java.util.Vector;

public class Roster {

  protected int capacity;
  protected Vector students;

  public Roster(int max) {
    capacity = max;
    students = new Vector();
  }

  /**
   *  Attempts to add the student name to the Vector that is used to
   *  maintain the list. There is a capacity value that normally will
   *  limit the number of students that can be on the list, but the
   *  caller can override that constraint if the student has been
   *  given permission from their advisor to add the class even though it's
   *  already full.
   *
   *  @param   name      Student to add to the list.
   *  @param   allowExcess  Override capacity check when adding student
   *  @return   true if the student was added to the list, false otherwise
   */
  public boolean addStringToVector(String name, boolean allowExcess) {
    if (!allowExcess) {
      if (students.size() >= capacity) {
        return false;
      }
    }
    students.addElement(name);
    return true;
  }

}
```

At first glance, this method may appear to be reasonably well designed. In fact, it possesses a number of undesirable characteristics. For one thing, it requires callers to pass a parameter that indicates whether the student should be added, which depends upon whether the limit has already been reached. This makes the method less cohesive, because it not only has responsibility for adding the student's name to the `Vector`, but must also determine whether or not it's acceptable to add the student name in the first place.

Given that the method is not cohesive, how can it be improved? First, the `allowExcess` flag should be eliminated, since it's used as a way for the caller to communicate with the method concerning how the method should operate. You should avoid using parameters for that purpose, since they tend to make the purpose of your method less clear and cohesive. In this example, a better solution is to create a separate method that always ignores the capacity value, and remove the `allowExcess` flag:

```java
import java.util.Vector;

public class Roster {
```

```
  protected int capacity;
  protected Vector students;

  public Roster(int max) {
    capacity = max;
    students = new Vector();
  }

  /**
   *  Adds the student name to the Vector that is used to maintain the
   *  list.
   *
   *  @param  name    Student to add to the list.
   */
  public void addStringToVector(String name) {
    students.addElement(name);
  }

  /**
   *  Attempts to add the student name to the Vector that is used to
   *  maintain the list. There is a capacity value that normally will
   *  limit the number of students that can be on the list, but the
   *  caller can override this check if desired.
   *
   *  @param  name    Student to add to the list.
   *  @return  true if the student was added to the list, false otherwise
   */
  public boolean conditionalAddStringToVector(String name) {
    if (students.size() >= capacity) {
      return false;
    }
    addStringToVector(name);
    return true;
  }

}
```

This is an improvement over the original design, as there is more cohesion in these two methods than in the original one. Instead of passing a flag to the method as was done in the previous implementation, the caller can now call the method that provides the desired behavior. Notice that conditionalAddStringToVector() doesn't actually add the student, but instead calls addStringToVector(). Since the "add" operation requires just a single line of code, it might be tempting to copy the contents of addStringToVector() to conditionalAddStringToVector(). However, you should remember that:

> **Code duplication makes the method less cohesive, and the class more difficult to maintain.**

Method Naming

One final point to make about the addStringToVector() and conditionalAddStringToVector() methods in the example above is that they are poorly named. You should avoid names that describe the method implementation, and instead use names that describe what the method does conceptually. For example, these method names imply that the purpose of the method is to add a String to a Vector, which is true in this implementation. However, there are two problems with this approach. First, the names don't provide any useful information that couldn't be obtained from a quick glance at the code. Naming these methods enrollStudentConditionally() and enrollStudent() provides the reader with valuable information about the responsibilities of these methods.

Another reason to avoid choosing a name that describes a method's implementation is that the implementation may change over time. For example, if the student names were to be sorted, you might modify the code so that it stores them in a TreeSet instead of a Vector. In that case, you either must change every occurrence of the method names or resign yourself to having method names that no longer describe the implementation, which is at best confusing to programmers who read your code. An improved version of the Roster class is shown below:

```java
import java.util.Vector;

public class Roster {

  protected int capacity;
  protected Vector students;

  public Roster(int max) {
    capacity = max;
    students = new Vector();
  }

  /**
   *  Enrolls the student in this course.
   *
   *  @param  name    Name of the student to enroll.
   */
  public void enrollStudent(String name) {
    students.addElement(name);
  }

  /**
   *  Attempts to enroll a student in this course. The student is only
   *  added if the capacity limit for the course has not been reached.
   *
   *  @param  name    Name of the student to enroll
   *  @return  true if the student was added to the list, false otherwise
   */
  public boolean enrollStudentConditionally(String name) {
    boolean isEnrolled = false;
    if (students.size() < capacity) {
    enrollStudent(name);
    isEnrolled = true;
    }
    return isEnrolled;
  }

}
```

Minimizing Duplication of Code

In the previous example, we placed the logic for adding a student in one method and called that method from a different one that needed the same functionality. Minimizing duplication is an important step in creating maintainable code, as it prevents you from having to make identical changes to many methods when some implementation detail must be modified. This is particularly important when multiple programmers are involved in creating an application, and applies not only to methods, but also to constructors, since you can call one constructor from another. For example, the following extract from the class DuplicationSample shows an example of how duplication can occur in constructors:

```java
public class DuplicationSample {

  protected int firstValue;
  protected String secondValue;
  protected Integer thirdValue;


  public DuplicationSample(int first, String second, Integer third) {
    firstValue = first;
    secondValue = second;
    thirdValue = third;
  }

  public DuplicationSample(int first, String second) {
    firstValue = first;
    secondValue = second;
    thirdValue = new Integer(0);
  }

}
```

Only the last statement differs in these two constructors, so duplicate code can be eliminated without changing the behavior of the constructors by modifying the class as follows:

```java
public class DuplicationSample {

  protected int firstValue;
  protected String secondValue;
  protected Integer thirdValue;

  public DuplicationSample(int first, String second, Integer third) {
    firstValue = first;
    secondValue = second;
    thirdValue = third;
  }

  public DuplicationSample(int first, String second) {
    this(first, second, new Integer(0));
  }

}
```

Similarly with methods, it's often helpful to use overloading and identify a method implementation that contains a superset of the functionality defined in the other implementations. For example, look at the following code segment:

```
public class AddingMachine {

  /**
   *  Adds two integers together and returns the result.
   */
  public static int addIntegers(int first, int second) {
    return first + second;
  }


  /**
   *  Adds some number of integers together and returns the result.
   */
  public static int addIntegers(int[] values) {
    int result = 0;
    for (int i = 0; i < values.length; i++) {
      result += values[i];
    }
    return result;
  }

}
```

Although there is no code duplication here, there is duplicate functionality – both methods add numbers together. Eliminating this duplication will make the class simpler and more maintainable. The first step is to decide which method should retain the functionality. Note that the first of the methods adds two numbers together, while the other adds the numbers in the values array together. In other words, the first method provides a subset of the functionality of the second one. Since that's the case, we can eliminate the duplication by delegating responsibility for adding the two numbers to the more flexible second method. The alternative implementation is shown below:

```
public class AddingMachine {

  /**
   *  Adds two integers together and returns the result.
   */
  public static int addIntegers(int first, int second) {
    return addIntegers(new int[] {first, second});
  }


  /**
   *  Adds some number of integers together and returns the result.
   */
  public static int addIntegers(int[] values) {
    int result = 0;
    for (int i = 0; i < values.length; i++) {
      result += values[i];
    }
    return result;
  }

}
```

This simplistic example illustrates an important point concerning something that's very common in method design. Specifically, to reduce code duplication, you can often:

> **Identify a method that represents a "special case" of some other method, and then delegate its calls to the more generic implementation.**

Using Exceptions

Exceptions are extremely useful, and the proper use of exceptions is an important part of good method design in Java. However, there are a number of questions related to exception design that arise when designing a class, such as:

- ❑ When should an exception be thrown?
- ❑ What type of exception should be thrown?
- ❑ When should a new exception subclass be created, and what should its superclass be?
- ❑ What information should be included in the exceptions that are thrown?
- ❑ Where should exceptions be caught and handled?

Let's now consider each of these issues in depth.

When to Throw an Exception

In general, your method should throw an exception when a condition is detected that the method can't or shouldn't handle. It's usually obvious when a method can't handle an exception. However, it may seem like circular logic to say that a method should throw an exception when it shouldn't handle some condition. What this really means is that, while the method may be able to handle the condition, it isn't the best candidate for doing so. For example, suppose that you define a simple user interface that allows the user to enter a name and an age. Let's also assume that your interface provides a button that ends the application when pressed, as illustrated below:

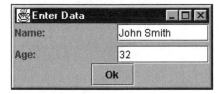

The following two classes provide this functionality. First, the `DataFrame` class displays a frame with a button and an instance of `DataPanel`:

```
import java.awt.*;
import java.awt.event.*;
import javax.swing.*;

public class DataFrame extends JFrame {

  public static void main(String[] args) {
```

```
      DataFrame df = new DataFrame();
      df.setVisible(true);
    }

  public DataFrame() {
    super("Enter Data");
    buildLayout();
    pack();
  }

  protected void buildLayout() {
    Container pane = getContentPane();
    pane.setLayout(new BorderLayout());
    pane.add(new DataPanel(), BorderLayout.CENTER);
    JButton button = new JButton("Ok");
    button.addActionListener(new ActionListener() {
      public void actionPerformed(ActionEvent event) {
        System.exit(0);
      }
    }
    );
    JPanel panel = new JPanel();
    panel.setLayout(new FlowLayout(FlowLayout.CENTER, 0, 0));
    panel.add(button);
    pane.add(panel, BorderLayout.SOUTH);
  }

}
```

Next, the DataPanel class defines the text fields that allow the user to enter a name and age:

```
import java.awt.GridLayout;
import javax.swing.*;

public class DataPanel extends JPanel {

  protected JTextField nameField;
  protected JTextField ageField;

  public DataPanel() {
    buildDisplay();
  }

  protected void buildDisplay() {
    setLayout(new GridLayout(2, 2, 10, 5));
    JLabel label = new JLabel("Name:");
    add(label);
    nameField = new JTextField(10);
    add(nameField);
    label = new JLabel("Age:");
    add(label);
    ageField = new JTextField(10);
    add(ageField);
  }

}
```

Now let's assume that the requirements change after these two classes have been created. Now it's required that the user must have entered valid data before exiting the application. Specifically, the name field should not be blank, and the age field should contain a positive integer. In addition, let's specify that if either of these two conditions is not met, then an error dialog should be displayed, and that the input focus should be set to the field that contains invalid data.

Given these requirements, we must decide where to assign responsibility for the new functionality. The design guidelines that we covered previously would indicate that the responsibility for validation belongs in DataPanel, since it already has access to the data being validated. The other new responsibility that must be assigned is the error message display, and DataFrame stands out as the more desirable choice, because putting the error display logic into DataPanel would make it less cohesive and less flexible. For example, another application might need to reuse DataPanel but it might not want to use dialogs to display validation errors.

This scenario provides an example of what was referred to previously as an error that a method shouldn't handle. The validation method in DataPanel shouldn't be responsible for displaying the error dialog because doing so would make it less cohesive, flexible, and extensible. Instead, it should throw an exception and let its caller in DataFrame display the error.

Choosing the Exception Type

Now that we've determined that an exception will be thrown, what type of exception should be used? There are many subclasses of Exception defined with the Java core classes, and it's acceptable for applications to create and throw instances of those. In fact, nothing prevents you from throwing an exception that's totally unrelated to the problem that has occurred. For example, when the validation routine determines that the user has entered a non-numeric age value, it could throw any type of exception, such as a NullPointerException, a SocketException, or an InterruptedException. However, it should not do so, because these exceptions are normally used to indicate very specific problems that have no relationship to our user interface validation.

While it's possible to use the exception classes defined as part of Java, you should do so only if the exception is an appropriate choice for signaling the type of error that your application experienced. Otherwise, you should create your own Exception subclasses instead and throw instances of those. Besides a situation where no existing exception class accurately describes the condition that has occurred, there is at least one other case where you'll want to create a custom exception class. You'll need to do so when you want to return more information than a simple text message to the caller that's responsible for handling the exception, and we'll see an example of this later in the chapter.

Choosing a Superclass for a Custom Exception Class

When creating your own exception classes, you'll normally want to extend one of two classes: either Exception, or RuntimeException. Most of the time, you'll subclass Exception, which results in your exception being classified as a **checked exception**. You should note that a checked exception must be declared when you create a method that can throw the exception, while **unchecked exceptions** (subclasses of RuntimeException) need not be declared or caught.

For example, the doSomething() method in the following class can throw either MyFirstException or MySecondException, but only MyFirstException must be identified, because it is a checked exception (in other words, it subclasses Exception):

```
public class ExceptionSampler {

    /**
    Not declaring that this method can throw MyFirstException will
```

```
     *  cause the Java compiler to generate an error message when this
     *  class is compiled. However, declaring MySecondException is
     *  optional.
     */
    public void doSomething(boolean throwFirst) throws MyFirstException {
      if (throwFirst) {
        throw new MyFirstException();
      } else {
        throw new MySecondException();
      }
    }

    class MyFirstException extends Exception {
    }

    class MySecondException extends RuntimeException {
    }

  }
```

The factor that determines which type of exception to create is usually the nature of the error or errors that can cause the exception to be thrown.

You normally should throw an unchecked exception when you encounter a condition that seems to indicate some sort of programming error. For example, if you call a method that should only return a positive integer value and it returns a negative or zero value, then it's probably appropriate to throw an unchecked exception. In general, you should throw unchecked exceptions any time you don't want to force callers to handle or declare them.

Keep in mind, however, that using an unchecked exception partially defeats the purpose of throwing an exception in the first place. One of the main benefits of Java's exception handling facility is that it forces programmers to recognize and handle exceptional conditions that can occur. However, this is only strictly true for checked exceptions – by using an unchecked exception, you allow a programmer who's calling a method you created to ignore the error condition, which can decrease the stability of the application. Therefore, you should use unchecked exceptions very sparingly, throwing them only in cases where the condition should theoretically not occur.

There is one case where it's appropriate to violate this guideline, but it doesn't usually apply to applications: an exception that can be thrown from an extremely large number of different places. The exception that's probably thrown more frequently than any other is NullPointerException, which could occur any time you attempt to use an object reference to access a field or method. If NullPointerException were a checked exception, you would be forced to throw it from virtually all methods or to catch it at hundreds or even thousands of places within a single application. Since it is an unchecked exception, you can selectively choose when (or if) to catch it, which makes code less tedious to write and easier to understand.

However, NullPointerException is really something of a special case, and if you find yourself tempted to make an exception unchecked simply to avoid handling it in many places, what may really be needed is a redesign of your application. Most of the time, you'll subclass Exception and throw checked exceptions instead.

In the case of our input validation routine for DataFrame and DataPanel, we'll create a checked exception and call it InputValidationException:

```
public class InputValidationException extends Exception {
}
```

Using a Common Superclass for Different Exception Types

Another issue concerning exceptions occurs when you throw exceptions for different but related types of error conditions.

For example, suppose that you create a method called `attemptLogon()` that can throw a `LogonFailedException` if either the user name or password specified is invalid. Here we have two choices. It's possible to only use a single `LogonFailedException` class in both cases and simply create an appropriate message that describes which type of condition caused the exception to be thrown. Alternatively, you may consider creating subclasses of that exception, (perhaps calling them `InvalidUseridException` and `InvalidPasswordException`) and throwing instances of those subclasses instead of an instance of `LogonFailedException`.

To determine which is the better approach, you need to consider how the exceptions will be handled. If you intend to create error handling for the entry of an invalid password that's different from the handling for an invalid user name, you should create the two subclasses and throw instances of those. However, if your application will simply display the message encapsulated within the exception object and it doesn't care which type of error occurred, you should only create and use a single exception class.

For example, the following code segment illustrates how you might just display the error message contained within the exception class:

```
String userid, password;
// ...
try {
  attemptLogon(userid, password);
} catch (LogonFailedException lfe) {
  System.out.println("Logon failed: " + lfe.getMessage());
}
```

In contrast, the following code segment assumes that the `InvalidPasswordException` is handled differently from other errors (for example, `InvalidUseridException`):

```
String userid, password;
// ...
try {
  attemptLogon(userid, password);
}
// Handle the case where the password was invalid
catch (InvalidPasswordException ipe) {
  // Log the logon attempt and possibly lock the userid
  // to prevent more logon attempts
  recordFailedLogon(userid);
  System.out.println("Logon failed: " + ipe.getMessage());
}
// Handle all other types of errors
catch (LogonFailedException lfe) {
  System.out.println("Logon failed: " + lfe.getMessage());
}
```

You should note that it's not necessary to make `InvalidUseridException` and `InvalidPasswordException` share a single superclass. However, doing so has a significant advantage. Instead of specifying that it throws both types of exception, the `attemptLogon()` method can be defined to throw instances of `LogonFailedException`:

```
    public void attemptLogon(String userid, String password)
        throws LogonFailedException {
```

instead of instances of both `InvalidUseridException` and `InvalidPasswordException`:

```
    public void attemptLogon(String userid, String password)
        throws InvalidUseridException, InvalidPasswordException {
```

Besides making your code slightly simpler, the first approach shown above also makes it possible for you to modify `attemptLogon()` so that it throws additional exception types without also changing the code that calls the method. As long as the new exception type is a subclass of a type that's already declared (for example `LogonFailedException`) you can throw the new type without modifying any other code in your application. For instance, you might change `attemptLogon()` so that it also throws an exception called `AlreadyLoggedOnException`. As long as that new exception type is a subclass of `LogonFailedException`, you're not required to make any changes to the code that calls `attemptLogon()`.

Adding Information to an Exception

When creating your exception, you should include a message that describes the nature of the error that occurred, along with any information that exception handlers will need. Bear in mind that exceptions are a mechanism for communicating with your method's callers, and any information that is needed to process the error should be included.

In the case of our input validation there are two pieces of information that the validation routine should pass back to the handler: an error message, and a reference to the field that contains invalid information. The `Exception` class inherits the ability to store a message from its parent, so the only additional field we need to define is a reference to the component associated with the error. By returning a reference to the component, we make it possible for the frame to move the input focus to that component as a convenience for the user:

```
import java.awt.Component;

public class InputValidationException extends Exception {

  protected Component errorSource;

  public InputValidationException(String message, Component source) {
    super(message);
    errorSource = source;
  }

}
```

Now that the exception class is created, the validation routine in the `DataPanel` class we used earlier can be implemented and made to throw exceptions when it encounters an error:

```
import java.awt.GridLayout;
import javax.swing.*;

public class DataPanel extends JPanel {
```

```
protected JTextField nameField;
protected JTextField ageField;

public DataPanel() {
  buildDisplay();
}

public void validateInput() throws InputValidationException {
  String name = nameField.getText();
  if (name.length() == 0) {
    throw new InputValidationException("No name was specified",
                                      nameField);
  }
  String age = ageField.getText();
  try {
    int value = Integer.parseInt(age);
    if (value <= 0) {
      throw new InputValidationException("Age value must be " +
                                         "a positive integer",
                                         ageField);
    }
  }
  catch (NumberFormatException e) {
    throw new InputValidationException("Age value is missing " +
                                       "or invalid", ageField);
  }
}

protected void buildDisplay() {
  setLayout(new GridLayout(2, 2, 10, 5));
  JLabel label = new JLabel("Name:");
  add(label);
  nameField = new JTextField(10);
  add(nameField);
  label = new JLabel("Age:");
  add(label);
  ageField = new JTextField(10);
  add(ageField);
}

}
```

Note that there are three cases where we throw InputValidationException: when the name field is empty, when the age field is less than or equal to zero, and when the age field is not a valid integer. It's easy to create more than one exception class, such as one for a missing name and one for an invalid age, as shown below:

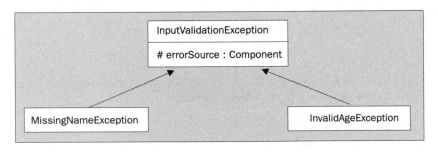

However, as we have already discussed, the only time you should do this is when there are multiple possible error conditions and some of them are handled differently from others. In this example, there are three different error conditions, but they're all handled the same way and by the same caller. Therefore, there's no need to define more than one new Exception subclass.

Finally, DataFrame must be modified so that it catches any validation errors and displays them in a dialog:

```java
import java.awt.*;
import java.awt.event.*;
import javax.swing.*;

public class DataFrame extends JFrame {

    protected DataPanel panel = new DataPanel();

    public static void main(String[] args) {
        DataFrame df = new DataFrame();
        df.setVisible(true);
    }

    public DataFrame() {
        super("Enter Data");
        buildLayout();
        pack();
    }

    protected void buildLayout() {
        Container pane = getContentPane();
        pane.setLayout(new BorderLayout());
        pane.add(panel, BorderLayout.CENTER);
        JButton button = new JButton("Ok");
        button.addActionListener(new ActionListener() {
            public void actionPerformed(ActionEvent event) {
                onOk();
            }
        }
        );
        JPanel panel = new JPanel();
        panel.setLayout(new FlowLayout(FlowLayout.CENTER, 0, 0));
        panel.add(button);
        pane.add(panel, BorderLayout.SOUTH);
    }

    protected void onOk() {
        try {
            panel.validateInput();
            System.exit(0);
        }
        catch (InputValidationException ive) {
            ive.errorSource.requestFocus();
            JOptionPane.showMessageDialog(this, ive.getMessage(),
                                "Validation Error",
                                JOptionPane.ERROR_MESSAGE);
        }
    }
}
```

When to Catch Exceptions

Two final points need to be made concerning where exceptions should be caught and handled. As mentioned earlier, the main factor that will determine where to catch an exception is often simply a matter of good class design. In other words, your choice of where to handle an exception should be one that maintains the cohesiveness and flexibility of the classes involved. However, when no particular class stands out as an appropriate place to handle an exception, the rule of thumb is that you should catch the exception as early as possible.

For example, suppose you have the following nested calls:

```
Method A() calls method B()
  Method B() calls method C()
    Method C() calls method D()
      Method D() calls method E(), which can throw SomeException
```

In this scenario, if method E() can throw SomeException, it's better to catch that exception as far down the call stack as possible. For example, if SomeException can be handled appropriately in method D() while still maintaining cohesion and loose coupling, then do so. This will prevent you from having to declare that SomeException can be thrown from A(), B(), or C(), which simplifies your code. Depending upon the nature of the exception condition and the design of your application, it may be necessary to allow the exception to propagate back to method A(). However, you should only do so if handling the exception earlier would cause you to violate object-oriented design principles such as cohesion and loose coupling.

> **In other words, throw exceptions as often as necessary, but handle them as early as possible.**

Lastly, you'll often find yourself creating a block of code that contains multiple statements that can throw exceptions, either a particular type of exceptions or several different types. In this situation, you should enclose all of the statements within a single try...catch instead of creating a separate one for each statement.

For example, suppose that you've created the following segment of code that creates a database connection and uses it to execute and process the results of a query:

```java
public static void main(String[] args) throws SQLException {
  // ...
  Connection conn = DriverManager.getConnection(url, userid, password);
  Statement stmt = conn.createStatement();
  ResultSet rset = null;
  rset = stmt.executeQuery("SELECT * FROM CUSTOMERS WHERE CUSTID = 123");
  if (rset.next()) {
    String custname = rset.getString("CUSTNAME");
    System.out.println(custname.toUpperCase());
  }
  // ...
  }
```

The majority of the statements in this code segment are capable of throwing an SQLException, but enclosing each one within its own try...catch block would be tedious and result in code that's difficult to read. It may be necessary to do this if your application needs to know specifically which statement caused the exception. However, it's usually appropriate to simply enclose all of the statements in a single try...catch block as shown opposite:

```
try {
    Connection conn = DriverManager.getConnection(url, userid, password);
    Statement stmt = conn.createStatement();
    ResultSet rset = null;
    rset = stmt.executeQuery("SELECT * FROM CUSTOMERS WHERE CUSTID = 123");
    if (rset.next()) {
        String custname = rset.getString("CUSTNAME");
        System.out.println(custname.toUpperCase());
    }
} catch (SQLException sqle) {
    //  Handle exception thrown by one of the statements
}
```

Using a finally Block

One of the more useful features of Java's exception handling facility is the ability to include a `finally` block, which is simply a section of code that is always entered, regardless of what happens within the `try` block.

For example, suppose that you create the following code segment:

```
String value;
// ...
try {
    int intValue = Integer.parseInt(value);
    System.out.println("Is a valid integer value");
}
catch (NumberFormatException nfe) {
    System.out.println("Not a valid integer value");
}
finally {
    System.out.println("This is always executed");
}
```

If the `value` string in the above code represents a valid integer value, the `try` block will complete successfully and the following two messages will be displayed:

    Is a valid integer value
    This is always executed

In contrast, if the `value` string does not represent a valid integer, the `parseInt()` call will cause the `try` block to be exited, the `catch` block entered, and the following messages displayed:

    Not a valid integer value
    This is always executed

The most common reason for using a `finally` block is to ensure that cleanup occurs regardless of what happens within the `try` block. Since most `ResultSet` methods can throw `SQLException`, let's use our database query code segment to illustrate how you might accomplish this:

```
ResultSet rset = null;
Connection conn = DriverManager.getConnection(url, userid, password);
Statement stmt = conn.createStatement();
```

```
try {
  rset = stmt.executeQuery("SELECT * FROM CUSTOMERS WHERE CUSTID = 123");
  if (rset.next()) {
    String custname = rset.getString("CUSTNAME");
    System.out.println(custname.toUpperCase());
  }
} catch (SQLException sqle) {
  System.out.println("Error performing or processing query: " +
                     sqle.getMessage());
}
```

What's missing is a call to the ResultSet object's close() method that will cause the resources associated with that ResultSet to be released. Placing the close() call inside the try block will only work as long as no errors occur, but executeQuery(), next(), and getString() can all throw SQLException. Putting the call to close() inside the catch block is even more inappropriate, since it will then only be invoked if an error does occur. On the surface, it might appear that the best approach is to call close() from outside the try/catch block as shown below:

```
// ...
} catch (SQLException sqle) {
  System.out.println("Error performing or processing query: " +
                     sqle.getMessage());
}
rset.close();
```

While this approach will work in most cases, it doesn't ensure that the close() method will be called. For example, if the getString() method returns a null value, a NullPointerException will be thrown when toUpperCase() is called for the name object. Since NullPointerException is not handled by the try/catch block, execution of this code segment will be terminated, and the call to the ResultSet's close() method will never be executed.

A better approach is to create a finally block that's responsible for closing the ResultSet as shown below:

```
// ...
} catch (SQLException sqle) {
  System.out.println(
      "Error performing or processing query: " +
      sqle.getMessage());
} finally {
  rset.close();
}
```

Note that the close() method will now be called even if the try block terminates prematurely with a NullPointerException. In fact, the finally block will be entered even if a return, break, or continue is placed within the try block (and/or the catch block) as in the following code.

```
try {
  rset = stmt.executeQuery(
      "SELECT * FROM CUSTOMERS WHERE CUSTID = 123");
  if (rset.next()) {
    String name = rset.getString("CUSTNAME");
    System.out.println(name.toUpperCase());
  }
```

```
      return;
   } catch (SQLException sqle) {
     System.out.println("Error performing or processing query: " +
                          sqle.getMessage());
     return;
   } finally {
     rset.close();
   }
```

In practice, you should try to define only a single exit point (a `return` statement) inside a method, which would result in more structured and readable code, but this example illustrates an important point. Specifically, you can ensure that your cleanup code will be executed regardless of what happens within the `try` and `catch` blocks, by placing the code within a `finally` block.

Discarded Exceptions

At this point, it's worth considering what will happen in the above code if the call to `executeQuery()` does not complete successfully but throws an exception. If that occurs, the `catch` block will be executed followed by the `finally` block. Then the `finally` block attempts to call the `ResultSet` object's `close()` method. However, in this scenario, the `rset` variable will contain a `null` value, so the `close()` attempt will result in a `NullPointerException`.

The question then becomes, "What happens to the original `SQLException`?" The answer is that it will be **discarded**, and the code segment will be terminated with a `NullPointerException` with no indication that the original error ever occurred.

One way to avoid this particular problem is to ensure that the `rset` variable contains a reference to a `ResultSet` instead of a `null` value:

```
   } finally {
     if (rset != null) {
       rset.close();
     }
   }
```

Although this minor change allows us to avoid the problem, it's not appropriate in all cases, since you may want take some action if the `close()` call itself throws an exception. Also, the potential for exceptions to be discarded exists even when you're not using `finally`; it can also occur when an exception is thrown from inside a `catch` block.

For example, let's suppose that instead of simply displaying error messages using `System.out.println()` that you instead want to write the messages to a disk file, in which case you might create code like that shown below:

```
try {
  rset = stmt.executeQuery(
    "SELECT * FROM CUSTOMERS WHERE CUSTID = 123");
  if (rset.next()) {
    String name = rset.getString("CUSTNAME");
    System.out.println(name.toUpperCase());
  }
} catch (SQLException sqle) {
```

```
      FileWriter fw = new FileWriter("errors.txt");
      PrintWriter pw = new PrintWriter(fw);
      pw.println("Error performing or processing query: " +
          sqle.getMessage());
      pw.close();
   } finally {
      rset.close();
   }
```

Unfortunately, the FileWriter constructor can throw an IOException, and the original SQLException being handled by the above catch block will be discarded if that occurs. The most obvious solution is to enclose the construction of the FileWriter object within its own try...catch block (in other words, by **nesting** one try...catch block within another):

```
   } catch (SQLException sqle) {
      FileWriter fw = null;
      try {
         fw = new FileWriter("errors.txt");
      } catch (IOException ioe) {
      }
      PrintWriter pw = new PrintWriter(fw);
      pw.println("Error performing or processing query: " +
                sqle.getMessage());
      pw.close();
   } finally {
```

While this approach does prevent the original problem of the SQLException being discarded, the problem of how to handle the second (IOException) error remains an issue. It's likely that you would not want your application to ignore either exception, but it may not be apparent how you can communicate to the caller that both errors occurred.

To understand how this problem can be solved, bear in mind that each exception is nothing more than an object instance, and objects can maintain references to one another. Therefore, to address this problem, we can simply define a new class that allows you to create an exception that maintains a reference to another exception. The LoggingException class shown below is an example of how this can be done:

```
   public class LoggingException extends Exception {

     protected Exception originalException;

     public LoggingException(String message, Exception trigger) {
        super(message);
        originalException = trigger;
     }

     public Exception getOriginalException() {
        return originalException;
     }

   }
```

Notice that in additional to the traditional error message this class also maintains a reference to another `Exception` object. Using this new class, you can throw an instance of `LoggingException` that contains the information from the `IOException` as well as a reference to the exception that describes the original error:

```
public static void main(String[] args) throws SQLException, LoggingException {
// ...
} catch (SQLException sqle) {
  FileWriter fw;
  try {
    fw = new FileWriter("errors.txt");
  } catch (IOException ioe) {
    throw new LoggingException(ioe.getMessage(), sqle);
  }
  PrintWriter pw = new PrintWriter(fw);
  pw.println("Error performing or processing query: " +
      sqle.getMessage());
  pw.close();
} finally {
// ...
```

When the `LoggingException` is thrown, the caller can retrieve information on both exceptions: the `IOException` that occurred when attempting to write the error message, and the `SQLException` that represents the original error.

Nested Exceptions, Stack Traces, and Message Text

When an exception class is instantiated, a **stack trace** is created and associated with the exception object. A stack trace is nothing more than information that describes the path of execution of a thread at some point in time, including the name of each method that was called, the class in which each method is defined, and in most cases the line number within the class.

It's the stack trace information that's displayed when you execute an application that terminates with an exception. For example, suppose that you create a class like the one shown below that attempts to read the contents of a file:

```
import java.io.*;

public class ShowStack {

    public static void main(String[] args) throws IOException {
        ShowStack ss = new ShowStack();
    }

    public ShowStack() throws IOException {
        initialize();
    }

    protected void initialize() throws IOException {
        readFileData();
    }

    protected void readFileData() throws IOException {
        File f = new File("test.txt");
        FileReader fr = new FileReader(f);
```

```
            BufferedReader br = new BufferedReader(fr);
            String line = br.readLine();
    }

}
```

If the file does not exist, this application will terminate by displaying a stack trace like the one shown below:

```
C:\brett\temp>java ShowStack
Exception in thread "main" java.io.FileNotFoundException: test.txt (The system cannot find
the file specified)
        at java.io.FileInputStream.open(Native Method)
        at java.io.FileInputStream.<init>(Unknown Source)
        at java.io.FileInputStream.<init>(Unknown Source)
        at java.io.FileReader.<init>(Unknown Source)
        at ShowStack.readFileData(ShowStack.java:19)
        at ShowStack.initialize(ShowStack.java:14)
        at ShowStack.<init>(ShowStack.java:10)
        at ShowStack.main(ShowStack.java:6)
```

This information indicates that the exception was generated from within the native `open()` method defined in the `FileInputStream` class. Prior to that method being called, several levels of constructors were invoked, which is indicated by the `<init>` entries. The original `FileReader` constructor was called as part of the instantiation that is found on line 19 of the `ShowStack` class, which is a statement within the `readFileData()` method.

By examining the stack trace entries, you can determine the complete execution path of the thread that generated an exception, which in this case began with the execution of the static `main()` method in the `ShowStack` class. The information is obviously extremely useful for debugging purposes, but it raises the question of how to handle the stack trace information in the case of a nested exception. In other words, if a nested exception class like `LoggingException` is thrown, which stack trace should be displayed: the one from the `LoggingException` or the one from the original exception to which it contains a reference?

The answer is that the original exception's stack trace should appear, since it identifies the source of the problem, and to ensure that the correct stack trace is displayed, the `printStackTrace()` method should be overridden in `LoggingException`. As its name implies, `printStackTrace()` is responsible for displaying the stack trace, and it is overloaded with three implementations. Two of those implementations allow you to specify a `PrintStream` or a `PrintWriter` object that indicates where the stack trace output should be sent, while the third simply sends the information to standard output.

The default `printStackTrace()` method displays the class name and message text associated with the exception, followed by the stack trace information. This is appropriate for most exceptions, but not for nested exception classes such as `LoggingException`. Instances of that class should use the default `printStackTrace()` behavior when they don't encapsulate another exception, but when they do, the nested exception's stack trace information should be displayed instead of the trace for the `LoggingException`. This can be done easily by making the following modifications to the custom exception class:

```
public class LoggingException extends Exception {

    protected Exception originalException;
```

```
   public LoggingException(String message, Exception trigger) {
     super(message);
     originalException = trigger;
   }

   public Exception getOriginalException() {
     return originalException;
   }

   public void printStackTrace(java.io.PrintStream ps) {
     if (originalException == null) {
       super.printStackTrace(ps);
     } else {
       ps.println(this);
       originalException.printStackTrace(ps);
     }
   }

   public void printStackTrace(java.io.PrintWriter pw) {
     if (originalException == null) {
       super.printStackTrace(pw);
     } else {
       pw.println(this);
       originalException.printStackTrace(pw);
     }
   }

   public void printStackTrace() {
     printStackTrace(System.err);
   }

}
```

This custom exception class is now largely complete. However there is one problem: the stack trace associated with the original exception will be displayed, but it will be accompanied by a message informing the user that a logging exception had been thrown! This behavior would be extremely confusing for a programmer trying to debug a problem associated with the original exception, because the stack trace would direct the developer to a location in the code that does not throw the type of exception being generated.

For example, if an IOException were the original cause of the exception condition, the programmer would see a LoggingException being thrown but the stack trace associated with that exception would point to code that throws an IOException. Fortunately, there is a simple solution to this problem: modify the LoggingException's getMessage() method so that it indicates that it represents a nested exception and prints both its own message text and that of the original exception. An example of how this can be done is shown below:

```
public class LoggingException extends Exception {

  protected Exception originalException;

  public LoggingException(String message, Exception trigger) {
    super(message);
```

```
      originalException = trigger;
  }

// ...

  public void printStackTrace() {
    printStackTrace(System.err);
  }

  public String getMessage() {
    if (originalException == null) {
      return super.getMessage();
    } else {
      return super.getMessage() + "; nested exception is: \n\t" +
        originalException.toString();
    }
  }

}
```

As we have seen above, creating nested exceptions without overriding the `printStackTrace()` and `getMessage()` methods can make debugging more difficult. Therefore, you should ensure that you provide implementations similar to the ones shown here if you create a custom nested exception class.

Avoiding Exceptions

There are some cases where it's common not to use exceptions at all when an "error" occurs, but to pass back a special value that indicates that such an error occurred. For example, suppose that you define a method that performs a search and returns a value, as in the following case:

```
public Student findStudent(int studentID) {
  // ...
}
```

In this case, if the method could reasonably be expected to fail to find a `Student` instance that matches the specified criteria, it might return a `null` value instead of throwing an exception.

Similarly, if you define a method that returns some integer value that should always be positive or zero, then returning a negative value could be used in place of an exception to indicate an error. For example, the `indexOf()` method in the `String` class does just that, if it can't find an occurrence of the character you specify:

```
String test = "Hello";
// Prints the index of the first occurrence of 'e', in this case 1
System.out.println(test.indexOf('e'));
// Prints -1, since the character 'z' isn't found in the string
System.out.println(test.indexOf('z'));
```

You should only use this technique for a single error condition per method. In other words, do not define a method that returns -1 for one type of error, -2 for another type, and so on. If you find yourself tempted to do this, then you should either rewrite the method, or start using exceptions to signal which error has occurred.

What are the advantages of using this approach instead of throwing an exception? Besides being slightly simpler, it provides faster execution, because there is some overhead associated with throwing an exception. However, the overhead is reasonably small and fast execution is not usually a critical factor when an error has occurred, so exceptions are an appropriate choice in most situations.

In some cases, such as the two described in this section, what constitutes an error can be very subjective. Is it really an error at all when a given character isn't found in a string? Maybe, and maybe not – it depends upon the context. If the application were designed in such a way that the character should be found, most people would classify the results as an error. Otherwise, it's just one possible outcome of the method call, in which case you should avoid throwing exceptions.

Summary

In this chapter, we have covered a number of issues related to the design of packages, classes, and methods including the following:

- ❑ A library of classes can be made more manageable by organizing the classes into packages.

- ❑ Creating classes, interfaces, and packages with loose coupling and strong cohesion tends to make those items more reusable.

- ❑ Encapsulation provides many advantages, including the hiding of implementation details and provides insulation from changes in implementation.

- ❑ Immutable objects and fields can be used to simplify an object-oriented design.

- ❑ The `Object` class contains a number of important methods that it may be necessary or helpful to override.

- ❑ Method design and naming are important parts of a good design. Method design greatly influences the reusability of your code, while naming is an important part of making your code intuitive and easy to understand.

- ❑ Minimizing code duplication not only saves time, but also makes your code more reliable and maintainable.

- ❑ Java's exception handling mechanism is a very powerful, flexible facility that can be used to handle conditions that require attention during the execution of your application.

In the next chapter, we'll look at Java's threading capabilities and how they can be used to create multithread applications.

Professional Java Programmin

3

Using Threads in Your Applications

If you're like most users, you probably have more than one application running on your computer most of the time. In addition, you probably sometimes initiate a long-running task on one application and switch to another application while waiting for that task to complete. For example, you might start downloading a file from the Internet or begin a search that scans your disk drive, and then read your e-mail while the download or search is in progress. This ability to have multiple applications running simultaneously (or at least appear to do so) is called **multitasking**, and each application is usually referred to as a **process**.

In reality, of course, your computer probably has one processor and the operating system makes it appear that the applications are running at the same time by dividing the processor's time between them. One reason that this behavior is useful is that it makes efficient use of processor time that would otherwise be wasted. In both of the examples mentioned above (that is, downloading and searching), the processor would spend much of its time simply waiting for I/O operations to complete unless it has other work that can be done. From a user's perspective, this multitasking behavior is desirable because it allows you to continue to use your computer while some background task is being executed.

Although the above scenario refers to different processes / applications, the same concept is relevant within the context of a single application. For example, a word processor can be made to automatically check your spelling and grammar while it allows you to perform another task such as entering text. Similarly, if your application performs a long-running task such as downloading a large file from the Internet, it's usually desirable to provide a user interface that can respond to a user's request to cancel the download. Java provides built-in support for simultaneous (**concurrent**) tasks within a single application through its threading capabilities, where a **thread** is simply a unit of execution.

In this chapter:

❑ Common reasons for using threads and some of the advantages and disadvantages of doing so will be discussed.

❑ Examples are provided that illustrate how to create threads and manage their execution.

❑ Tips are provided on how to synchronize access to resources that are used by multiple threads, and information on how to prevent problems from occurring is provided.

❑ Changes that occurred to the `Thread` class in Java 2 are explained and sample code is provided that shows how to create or modify your applications to take into account those changes.

❑ Thread pooling, a technique that's used to reduce the overhead associated with creating threads, is explained, and an example of how it can be implemented is provided.

Threading in Java

It's very likely that you've built a multi-threaded application in Java, even if you did not do so explicitly. When you execute a Java application, the `main()` method is executed by a thread, although that fact is largely transparent. In addition, applications that provide a graphical user interface (as most do) will implicitly cause another thread to be created and used: **the AWT event thread**.

Despite its name, the AWT event thread is active for both AWT- and Swing-based user interfaces, and is responsible for painting lightweight components and for performing event notifications. If you create an interface that includes a `JButton` instance, the AWT event thread paints the button when it is made visible, and will call the `actionPerformed()` method for each of the button's listeners when it is pressed.

The fact that the AWT event thread is responsible for both painting and event notification provides the motivation behind one of the more common uses of threads in Java. As long as the thread is busy with event handling, it cannot repaint the user interface, and if you create an event handler that performs some long-running function, the interface may remain unpainted long enough to produce undesirable results.

For example, the code shown below calls the `performDatabaseQuery()` method from `actionPerformed()`. The called method simulates a long-running query by calling the `sleep()` method, causing the currently running thread to pause for five seconds before continuing execution:

```
import java.awt.*;
import java.awt.event.*;
import javax.swing.*;

public class ButtonPress extends JFrame {

  public static void main(String[] args) {
    ButtonPress bp = new ButtonPress();
    bp.setSize(400, 300);
    bp.setVisible(true);
  }

  public ButtonPress() {
    JMenuBar jmb = new JMenuBar();
```

```
    JMenu menu = new JMenu("Execute");
    jmb.add(menu);
    JMenuItem jmi = new JMenuItem("Database Query");
    menu.add(jmi);
    jmi.addActionListener(new ActionListener() {
      public void actionPerformed(ActionEvent event) {
        performDatabaseQuery();
      }
    });
    setJMenuBar(jmb);
  }

  protected void performDatabaseQuery() {

    // Simulate long-running database query
    try {
      Thread.sleep(5000);
    } catch (Exception e) {}
    ;
  }

}
```

Since `actionPerformed()` will be called by the AWT event thread, that thread will be busy until the query completes, which prevents it from repainting the user interface during that time. Therefore, the user interface will appear to "hang" during the query:

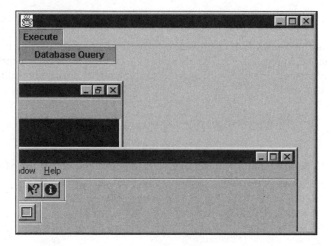

This type of confusing display can occur when one window is temporarily overlaid by another and the first window is not repainted after the second one is hidden or removed.

Creating Threads

Java provides built-in support for multithreaded applications, and creating a new thread is very simple. Each thread is represented by an instance of the `java.lang.Thread` class, and to create a new instance, you simply define a class that extends `Thread` or implements the `java.lang.Runnable` interface.

You'll often want to create a class with code that runs in its own thread, but if that class extends `Thread`, it can't inherit functionality from any other class since Java doesn't support multiple inheritance. Extending `Thread` doesn't provide any functional advantage over implementing `Runnable` and neither approach is significantly easier than the other, so the latter approach (that is, implementing `Runnable`) is usually preferable.

The only method defined in `Runnable` is `run()`, which is called when the thread executes. Once the thread exits `run()` (either normally or due to an uncaught exception), it is considered **dead** and cannot be restarted or reused.

> In effect, the `run()` method serves the same purpose in a thread that the `main()` method does when executing a Java application: it is the initial entry point into your code.

As with the `main()` method, you should not normally call `run()` explicitly. Instead, you'll pass an instance of `Runnable` to a `Thread` constructor and the thread will call `run()` automatically when it is started. For example, to make the `ButtonPress` application multithreaded, you could create a `DatabaseQuery` class like the one shown below that implements `Runnable`:

```
class DatabaseQuery implements Runnable {

  public void run() {
    performDatabaseQuery();
  }


}
```

To use this class, all that's necessary is to create a new instance of `Thread`, passing its constructor a `DatabaseQuery` instance, and call the `Thread's` `start()` method to begin execution. Calling `start()` indicates that the newly created thread should begin execution, and it does so by calling the object's `run()` method as mentioned previously:

```
Thread t = new Thread(new DatabaseQuery());
t.start();
```

An even easier way is to define an anonymous inner class that implements `Runnable` as shown in the following modified `DatabaseQuery` code:

```
public ButtonPress() {
  JMenuBar jmb = new JMenuBar();
  JMenu menu = new JMenu("Execute");
  jmb.add(menu);
  JMenuItem jmi = new JMenuItem("Database Query");
  menu.add(jmi);
  jmi.addActionListener(new ActionListener() {
    public void actionPerformed(ActionEvent event) {
      Thread t = new Thread(new Runnable() {
        public void run() {
          performDatabaseQuery();
        }
      });
      t.start();
```

```
        }
    });
    setJMenuBar(jmb);
}
```

When this code is executed and the menu item activated, the AWT event thread will call the `actionPerformed()` method, create a new thread, and that new thread will call `performDatabaseQuery()`. This allows the AWT event thread to return from `actionPerformed()` very quickly and to repaint the user interface.

In addition to the constructor used here that accepts a single `Runnable` parameter, `Thread` also provides constructors that allow you to specify a name (in the form of a `String`) for the thread and to identify the `ThreadGroup` with which the `Thread` should be associated. Thread groups are described in more detail later in this chapter, and they allow you to create logical groupings of threads. A thread's name has no functional significance, but may allow you to more easily distinguish one thread from another while debugging a multithreaded application.

Disadvantages Of Using Threads

As you can see from the above example, it's extremely easy to create a thread in Java, but you should avoid doing so when possible. Although not obvious from the simple example shown above, there are several disadvantages to using multiple threads within your applications, and they are described below.

Slow Initial Startup

Although not apparent from the above `ButtonPress` class, creating and starting a new thread is a relatively slow operation on some platforms, and in an application where performance is critical, this can be a significant drawback. However, **thread pooling** provides a reasonably simple solution to this problem, and pools are often used by applications that perform many concurrent operations, especially when those operations can be completed quickly. Thread pooling is conceptually very similar to database connection pooling, which is a topic that's described in Chapter 12. Thread pooling is discussed in detail later in this chapter.

Resource Utilization

Each thread is allocated its own **stack**, which is an area of storage used to contain local variable values and other information related to execution. Other system resources are used in addition to the stack, although the specific amount and type of those resources used varies from one Java Virtual Machine to the next. Although it's usually possible to create a very large number of threads, the platform you're using may limit the number that can be created. Even if the platform doesn't explicitly limit the number of threads you can create, there is usually a practical limit determined by the speed of your processor and the amount of available memory on your system.

While this problem cannot be eliminated, it can be controlled through thread pooling. In addition to eliminating the overhead penalty associated with creating a new thread, thread pools can be used to limit the number of threads that are created. This assumes, of course, that your application voluntarily allows a thread pool manager to control when to create threads and how many to create. Java does not include an implementation of a thread pool manager, but as we'll see later in the chapter, it's easy to create one.

Increased Complexity

By far the biggest disadvantage of using threads within your application is the complexity that it adds. For example, if you're debugging a single-threaded application, it's relatively easy to observe your application's flow of execution, but it can be significantly more difficult to do so when using multiple threads.

> **Thread safety usually involves designing the object so that its data can't be read or written by one thread while another thread is in the process of modifying that data. In this context, "data" refers to the information encapsulated by the object, and a single data item can be made up of a field or collection of fields within the object. An example of a data item would be a person's name, which might be contained within a single** `String` **field or within several fields (for example, first, middle, and last names).**

An even more complex problem is the matter of sharing resources among multiple threads. In this context, a **resource** is any entity that can be used by more than one thread simultaneously, and in most cases, you are responsible for coordinating their use by the threads. For example, Swing components are not inherently thread-safe, so you are responsible for coordinating how your application's thread(s) and the AWT event thread use them. This is usually done using the `invokeAndWait()` and `invokeLater()` methods in `SwingUtilities` to delegate modifications to visible components to the AWT event thread.

In general, if you create an object that contains data that can be modified, and the object is accessible by more than one thread, you're responsible for making that object **thread-safe**. Thread safety refers to ensuring that no partial or otherwise inappropriate modifications can be made to an object's state due to two or more threads attempting to update the state simultaneously, and we'll see shortly how this can occur when an object is not thread-safe.

Sharing Resources

Before discussing how to coordinate the use of shared resources among threads, let's first examine which resources are shared. Variables defined locally within a method are not accessible outside that method and are therefore not shared when multiple threads execute the same method for some object. For example, suppose that you run the application listed below which creates two threads that use the same `Runnable` object instance:

```java
public class ThreadShare implements Runnable {

  public static void main(String[] args) {
    ThreadShare ts = new ThreadShare();
    Thread t1 = new Thread(ts);
    Thread t2 = new Thread(ts);
    t1.start();
    t2.start();
  }

  public void run() {
    int nonSharedValue = 100;
    nonSharedValue += 100;
    System.out.println("Value: " + nonSharedValue);
  }

}
```

Since the nonSharedValue variable is defined inside the run() method, it is local to that method and is not shared by the two threads. Since each thread will get its own copy of nonSharedValue, running this application will always produce the following output:

```
Value: 200
Value: 200
```

However, if the application is modified so that the run() method increments an instance variable, that variable will be a shared resource:

```
public class ThreadShare implements Runnable {

    int sharedValue = 100;

    public static void main(String[] args) {
        ThreadShare ts = new ThreadShare();
        Thread t1 = new Thread(ts);
        Thread t2 = new Thread(ts);
        t1.start();
        t2.start();
    }

    public void run() {
        sharedValue += 100;
        System.out.println("Value: " + sharedValue);
    }

}
```

If you modify and execute this application, it will *probably* produce the following results:

```
Value: 200
Value: 300
```

However, it's also possible that the output could match that shown below:

```
Value: 300
Value: 300
```

It's even possible for the program to produce the following results:

```
Value: 300
Value: 200
```

To understand why the output can vary, it's necessary to have some knowledge of how threads are managed by operating systems, since Java's threading support uses the native thread capabilities of the platform on which the Java Virtual Machine executes.

Thread Management

For multiple operations to be executed concurrently by a single microprocessor, it's necessary at some point to transfer control of the processor from one thread to another, which is called **context switching**. Context switching can occur when a thread voluntarily gives up control of the processor, and that approach is known as **cooperative multitasking**. In cooperative multitasking, a thread must execute some instruction or call a method to indicate that it is willing to relinquish control over the processor to another thread. Unfortunately, if a programmer deliberately or accidentally creates a thread that does not periodically give up control of the processor, that thread can easily cause the application to "hang" and/or prevent other threads from running. Windows 3.1 and other older operating systems use cooperative multitasking, and it's possible for one thread to "lock up" an application or even the entire operating system if that thread does not occasionally release control of the processor.

A better approach is **preemptive multitasking**, where control of the processor is arbitrarily transferred from one thread to another, usually after some amount of time has elapsed. Preemptive multitasking has two advantages over cooperative multitasking:

- ❑ It can prevent a thread from monopolizing the processor
- ❑ It removes from the programmer the burden of deciding when to perform a context switch, shifting that responsibility to the operating system

With preemptive multitasking, a programmer need not be concerned with how or when to perform a context switch, but that convenience comes at a price. Although the programmer need not be concerned with the details of context switching, it becomes necessary to *coordinate* the use of resources that are shared by multiple threads.

In the previous example of the `ThreadShare` class, we saw that the results of running the application could vary. The reason for this is that no effort was made to coordinate the use of the shared resource, specifically the `sharedValue` variable. In most cases, the sequence of events will proceed as shown below, where `t1` represents the first thread and `t2` the second:

```
t1 enters the run() method
t1 adds 100 to sharedValue, setting it equal to 200
t1 prints the value of sharedValue
t2 enters the run() method
t2 adds 100 to sharedValue, setting it equal to 300
t2 prints the value of sharedValue
```

However, if the native platform uses preemptive multitasking, it's possible that the sequence of steps can be performed slightly differently. In fact, from an application perspective, it's not possible to predict when a context switch will occur, so you must assume a worst-case scenario. In this case, for example, it's possible for the sequence of steps to occur as shown below:

```
t1 enters the run() method
t1 adds 100 to sharedValue, setting it equal to 200
(Context switch occurs here and t2 is allowed to run)
t2 enters the run() method
t2 adds 100 to sharedValue, setting it equal to 300
t2 prints the value of sharedValue
(Context switch occurs and t1 is allowed to resume execution)
t1 prints the value of sharedValue
```

This is just one of the possible combinations that can occur, which means that the results of the application are **unpredictable**. This type of situation, where the order in which threads execute can affect the results of running an application, is called a **race condition**. Since unpredictability is obviously not desirable in a software application, it's important to avoid race conditions, and the following code illustrates that point. The application creates two instances of CustomerAccount representing a customer's savings and checking accounts. Once the accounts have been created and initialized so that each one contains $1,000, two threads are created which transfer random amounts of money between the two accounts.

In the case of the ThreadShare application, it wasn't clear what the correct output should be because the purpose behind the code's design wasn't stated, but it should be more obvious here. In this case, the intent is clearly to transfer money between two accounts while still maintaining the same total value. To allow us to determine whether that's actually the case, the sum of the two account balances is printed both before and after the transfers take place.

```
public class AccountManager {

  protected CustomerAccount savings;
  protected CustomerAccount checking;

  public final static int SAVINGS_ACCOUNT = 1;
  public final static int CHECKING_ACCOUNT = 2;

  public static void main(String[] args) {
    int transfers = 1000000;
    try {
      transfers = Integer.parseInt(args[0]);
    } catch (Exception e) {}
    AccountManager am = new AccountManager(transfers);
  }

  public AccountManager(int transfers) {
    savings = new CustomerAccount(SAVINGS_ACCOUNT, 1000);
    checking = new CustomerAccount(CHECKING_ACCOUNT, 1000);
    java.text.NumberFormat formatter =
        java.text.NumberFormat.getCurrencyInstance(
        java.util.Locale.US);
    System.out.println("Total balance before transfers: " +
        formatter.format(savings.getBalance() +
        checking.getBalance()));
    TransferManager tm1 = new TransferManager(checking,
        savings, transfers);
    TransferManager tm2 = new TransferManager(savings,
        checking, transfers);
    // Create two threads
    Thread t1 = new Thread(tm1);
    Thread t2 = new Thread(tm2);
    // Initiate execution of the threads
    t1.start();
    t2.start();
    // Wait for both threads to complete execution
    try {
      t1.join();
      t2.join();
    } catch (Exception e) {};
    System.out.println("Total balance after transfers: " +
        formatter.format(savings.getBalance() +
        checking.getBalance()));
  }
```

```
class TransferManager implements Runnable {

  protected CustomerAccount fromAccount;
  protected CustomerAccount toAccount;
  protected int transferCount;

  public TransferManager(CustomerAccount fromacct,
      CustomerAccount toacct, int transfers) {
    fromAccount = fromacct;
    toAccount = toacct;
    transferCount = transfers;
  }

  public void run() {
    double balance;
    double transferAmount;
    for (int i = 0 ; i < transferCount; i++) {
      balance = fromAccount.getBalance();
      transferAmount = (int)(balance * Math.random());
      balance -= transferAmount;
      fromAccount.setBalance(balance);
      balance = toAccount.getBalance();
      balance += transferAmount;
      toAccount.setBalance(balance);
    }
  }

}

class CustomerAccount {

  protected int accountType;
  protected double balance;

  public CustomerAccount(int type, double bal) {
    accountType = type;
    balance = bal;
  }

  public int getAccountType() {
    return accountType;
  }

  public double getBalance() {
    return balance;
  }

  public void setBalance(double newbal) {
    balance = newbal;
  }

}
```

Regardless of how many transfers take place or what the amounts of those transfers are, the total value of the two accounts should be equal to $2,000 once the application completes. In fact, if you compile and execute this application, it will correctly display the following results in *most* cases:

```
Total balance before transfers: $2,000.00
Total balance after transfers: $2,000.00
```

However, it's also possible that it will display results like those below:

Total balance before transfers: $2,000.00
Total balance after transfers: $1,973.00

This variation occurs for exactly the same reason that `ThreadShare`'s output was unpredictable. Specifically, the two threads that are modifying the account balances sometimes produce a conflict as shown below, where `t1` represents one thread and `t2` represents the other:

```
t1 gets the current checking account balance (for example, $1000).
t1 calculates the transfer amount (for example, $15)
t1 subtracts the transfer amount from the checking balance (1000 - 15 = $985)
(Context switch occurs)
t2 calculates the transfer amount (for example, $27)
t2 gets the current savings account balance (for example, $1000).
t2 subtracts the transfer amount from the savings balance (1000 - 27 = $973)
t2 saves the new savings balance (973) in the CustomerAccount object
t2 gets the current checking account balance ($1000)
t2 adds the transfer amount ($27) to the checking balance (1000 + 27 = $1027)
t2 saves the new checking balance ($1027) in the CustomerAccount object
(Context switch occurs)
t1 saves the new checking balance ($985) in the CustomerAccount object
t1 gets the current savings account balance ($973)
t1 adds the transfer amount ($15) to the savings balance (973 + 15 = $988)
t1 saves the new savings balance ($988) in the CustomerAccount object
```

After this sequence of steps, the checking balance is $985 and the savings balance is $988. Although the total of the two account balances should still be $2,000, their total is only $1,973. In effect, $27 was lost due to context switching and the failure to prevent the two threads from making inappropriate updates to the resources they share.

Synchronizing the Use of Shared Resources

In the above example, we saw that it's possible for data to effectively become corrupted when it's modified by more than one thread simultaneously. However, Java's `synchronized` keyword provides an easy way for you to prevent this from happening by allowing you to define methods and blocks of code that can be executed by only one thread at a time. In effect, the `synchronized` keyword *locks* the method or block of code while it's being executed by one thread so that no other threads are allowed to enter until the first thread has exited the method or block.

Each instance of `java.lang.Object` or one of its subclasses (that is, every Java object) maintains a lock (or **monitor**), and the `synchronized` keyword is always implicitly or explicitly associated with an instance of `Object` (primitives cannot be used). Before a thread can enter a `synchronized` method or section of code, it must obtain the monitor of the object associated with that code. If one thread obtains an object's monitor and a second thread attempts to do so, the second thread becomes *blocked* and its execution is suspended until the monitor becomes available.

In addition to the monitor, each object maintains a list of threads that are blocked because they're waiting on the object's monitor. If a thread cannot obtain an object's monitor, it is automatically put on the list, and once the monitor becomes available, one of the threads in the list will be given the monitor and allowed to continue execution. This behavior occurs when you use the `synchronized` keyword, and you do not need to explicitly obtain or release an object's monitor. Instead, it will be automatically obtained (if possible) when a thread enters a `synchronized` method or block of code and released when the thread exits that code block or method.

In the `StudentRoster` code segment shown below (which is just an example – it isn't runnable), a `synchronized` block of code is created that requires a thread to obtain the `studentList` object's monitor before entering the block.

```java
public class StudentRoster {

  protected java.util.Vector studentList;

  public void addStudentToList(Student st) {
    synchronized (studentList) {
      studentList.addElement(st);
    }
    st.setEnrolled(true);
  }

  public void removeStudentFromList(Student st) {
    studentList.removeElement(st);
  }

}
```

In this case, the object that's used for synchronization is an instance of `Vector`, but it can be an instance of any class. As in this example, it's common (but not necessary) for the synchronization to be performed using the object that's accessed or modified within the `synchronized` block. There's no technical requirement that you do so, but this approach provides an easy way for you to remember which object's monitor is used to control access to that object's data.

The `synchronized` keyword can also be used as a method modifier, in which case the entire method is synchronized as shown below:

```java
public class StudentRoster {

  protected java.util.Vector studentList;

  public synchronized void addStudentToList(Student st) {
    studentList.addElement(st);
    st.setEnrolled(true);
  }
}
```

Since it was mentioned earlier that `synchronized` is always associated with an instance of `Object`, you may be wondering which object that is in this case. When `synchronized` is used with an instance (that is, non-`static`) method, the object that will be used is the object against which the method was invoked. For example, if you create an instance of the `StudentList` class and then call its `synchronized` `addStudent()` method, the thread that calls the method must obtain the monitor of the `StudentList` object instance. In other words, the following code is functionally identical to calling `removeStudentFromList()` after adding `synchronized` to that method's definition:

```java
StudentRoster sr = new StudentRoster();
Student st = new Student();
.
.
.
//  Putting the call to removeStudentFromList() in a code block that's
```

```
//  synchronized on the instance of StudentList is functionally equivalent
//  to adding the synchronized keyword to the method definition.
synchronized (sl) {
  sr.removeStudentFromList(st);
}
```

When you define a class (that is, `static`) method that's `synchronized`, calls to that method will be synchronized on the `Class` object associated with the class. For example, suppose that a `static` method is added to `StudentRoster`:

```
public void removeStudentFromList(Student st) {
  studentList.removeElement(st);
}
```

```
public static synchronized StudentRoster getNewInstance() {
  return new StudentRoster();
}
```

```
}
```

Calls to `getNewInstance()` will be synchronized on the `Class` object associated with `StudentRoster`, so specifying `synchronized` with the `getNewInstance()` method definition is equivalent to calling that method using the following code:

```
StudentRoster sr;
.
.
.
//  The following code is equivalent to adding synchronized to the
//  removeStudentFromList() method's definition, because it causes
//  the running thread to attempt to obtain the lock of the Class
//  object associated with StudentList.
synchronized (StudentRoster.class) {
  sr = StudentRoster.getNewInstance();
}
```

Nested Calls to Synchronized Methods and Code Blocks

As mentioned earlier, a thread becomes blocked if it tries to enter a `synchronized` method or section of code while some other thread owns the associated object's monitor. However, you may be wondering what happens if a thread attempts to enter a `synchronized` method when it already owns the associated object's monitor. For example, you might have two synchronized methods in a class where one of them calls the other as shown below:

```
public synchronized void performFirstFunction() {
  //  Some functionality performed here
  .
  performSecondFunction()
}

public synchronized void performSecondFunction() {
  //  Some other functionality performed here
}
```

When a thread enters the `performFirstFunction()` method, it obtains the monitor for the object for which the method is called. Once `performSecondFunction()` is called, there's no need to obtain the object's monitor because the thread is already the owner of that monitor, so the thread is allowed to continue executing normally.

> **Each time a thread successfully enters a method or section of code that's** `synchronized` **on some object, a count value associated with the object is incremented, and when the thread exits that method or block, the value is decremented.**

A thread releases an object's monitor only when the count value associated with the object is zero, which ensures that the thread keeps the monitor until it exits the code that originally caused it to obtain the monitor. In this case, for example, when a thread enters `performFirstFunction()`, it obtains the object's monitor and increments the count value to one. When the call to `performSecondFunction()` occurs, the count value is incremented to two, but will be decremented back to one when the thread exits `performSecondFunction()`. Finally, when the thread exits `performFirstFunction()`, the count value returns to zero and the object's monitor is released by the thread.

Synchronized Blocks Versus Methods

As we've seen, it's possible to synchronize both an entire method and a section of code within a method, and you may wonder which one should be used. To understand which is appropriate in a given situation, it's important to consider what synchronization really provides.

> **Stated simply, synchronization allows you to prevent multi-threaded execution of certain portions of a multi-threaded application.**

In other words, synchronization reduces the concurrency of your application's threads, and if used too extensively, defeats the purpose of using multiple threads.

> **A good rule of thumb is to include as few lines of code as possible within** `synchronized` **methods or blocks, but only to the extent that you have not sacrificed thread safety.**

Adding the `synchronized` keyword to a method definition is a simple, readable way to provide thread safety, but it's sometimes not necessary and may be undesirable. For example, if only one or two lines of code within the method really need to be synchronized, you should enclose that code within its own `synchronized` block instead of synchronizing the entire method. This is particularly true if much of the time devoted to executing that method is spent on code that does not need to be synchronized. In other words, if you synchronize too much of your code, you'll prevent threads from running when they should be able to run.

Deadlocks

Once you have synchronized access to the shared resources within your application, you may encounter a **deadlock**. For example, returning to our `AccountManager` application as an example, let's suppose that we decide to synchronize access to the resources (that is, the `CustomerAccount` objects) that are used by multiple threads:

```
class TransferManager implements Runnable {

  protected CustomerAccount fromAccount;
  protected CustomerAccount toAccount;
  protected int transferCount;

  public TransferManager(CustomerAccount fromacct,
      CustomerAccount toacct, int transfers) {
    fromAccount = fromacct;
    toAccount = toacct;
    transferCount = transfers;
  }

  public void run() {
    double balance;
    double transferAmount;
    for (int i = 0 ; i < transferCount; i++) {
      synchronized (fromAccount) {
        balance = fromAccount.getBalance();
        transferAmount = (int)(balance * Math.random());
        balance -= transferAmount;
        fromAccount.setBalance(balance);
        synchronized (toAccount) {
          balance = toAccount.getBalance();
          balance += transferAmount;
          toAccount.setBalance(balance);
        }
      }
    }
  }
}
```

While these modifications do fix one potential problem, they introduce the possibility of another: specifically deadlock. The first thread that's started in the CustomerAccount application transfers money from the checking account to the savings account, while the second thread transfers money from savings into checking. Therefore, for each of the first thread's iterations through the run() method, it will obtain the checking account object's monitor and then the savings account monitor. The second thread competes for the same two monitors, but it attempts to obtain them in the reverse order.

Now suppose that during an iteration of the run() method that the first thread is interrupted after it obtains the checking account monitor but before it has gotten the savings account monitor. If the second thread then begins executing the loop, it will successfully obtain the savings account monitor, but it will be blocked when it attempts to obtain the checking account monitor. At that point, each thread has successfully obtained one of the two monitors and each will wait indefinitely for the other monitor to become available, which is an example of deadlock.

Deadlock conditions are common in multi-threaded applications and often result in the application becoming "hung". Fortunately, there are at least two ways of preventing this problem, neither of which is terribly complex: high-level synchronization, and lock ordering.

High-Level Synchronization

In the above code, each CustomerAccount's monitor was used to synchronize access to that CustomerAccount instance. Since a transfer operation involved obtaining two locks, it was possible for deadlock to occur if a thread obtained one of the locks but not the other. However, since this form of deadlock cannot occur if only one lock is involved, high-level synchronization offers a potential solution to the problem.

As mentioned earlier, it's customary when adding synchronization to your application to cause an operation to synchronize on the object being accessed or modified, but there is no technical reason that you must do so. In this case, for example, the application synchronizes access to each `CustomerAccount` object using that instance's monitor, but it's entirely acceptable to synchronize access to those objects using some other object.

In high-level synchronization, you simply select a single object that synchronizes access to all shared resources that are involved in some operation. In the case of a transfer operation, for example, you can select an existing object or create a new object that will be used to control access to all instances of `CustomerAccount`. This could be done by creating a new object explicitly for that purpose as shown in the following variable declaration that might be added to `CustomerAccount`:

```
protected final static Object synchronizerObject = new Object();
```

This new object is defined as a class variable because it will be used to synchronize access to all instances of `CustomerAccount` as shown below:

```
public void run() {
  double balance;
  double transferAmount;
  for (int i = 0 ; i < transferCount; i++) {
    synchronized (synchronizerObject) {
      balance = fromAccount.getBalance();
      transferAmount = (int)(balance * Math.random());
      balance -= transferAmount;
      fromAccount.setBalance(balance);
      balance = toAccount.getBalance();
      balance += transferAmount;
      toAccount.setBalance(balance);
    }
  }
}
```

In effect, we have eliminated the deadlock problem by reducing the number of monitors that a thread must own from two to one. However, the problem with this approach is that it reduces the concurrency of the application, since only one transfer can ever be in progress at any given time. In other words, even a transfer involving two completely separate and unrelated `CustomerAccount` objects would be blocked while a thread is executing the code inside this synchronized block.

Lock Ordering

As we saw earlier, the deadlock condition occurred because the two threads attempt to obtain the objects' monitors in a different order. The first thread attempts to obtain the checking account monitor and then the savings account monitor, while the second thread attempts to obtain the same two monitors but in the reverse order. This difference in the order in which the monitors are obtained lies at the root of the deadlock problem, and the problem can be addressed by ensuring that the monitors are obtained in the *same* order by *all* threads.

That can be accomplished by creating an `if` statement that switches the order in which the locks are obtained based on the results of some comparison. In other words, when locking two objects, there must be some way to compare those objects to determine which one's monitor should be obtained first. In this case, the `CustomerAccount` instances provide a convenient way of doing so, since each one maintains an account type (that is, checking or savings) that's stored as an integer value. An example of how this could be implemented in the `TransferManager` class is shown below:

```
    public void run() {
      double balance;
      double transferAmount;
      for (int i = 0 ; i < transferCount; i++) {
        balance = fromAccount.getBalance();
        transferAmount = (int)(balance * Math.random());
        transferFunds(fromAccount, toAccount, transferAmount);
      }
    }

    protected void transferFunds(CustomerAccount account1,
        CustomerAccount account2, double transferAmount) {
      double balance;
      CustomerAccount holder = null;
      //  We want to always synchronize first on the account with the
      //  smaller account type value. If it turns out that the "second"
      //  account actually has a larger type value, we'll simply
      //  switch the two references and multiply the amount being
      //  transferred by -1.
      if (account1.getAccountType() > account2.getAccountType()) {
        holder = account1;
        account1 = account2;
        account2 = holder;
        transferAmount *= -1;
      }
      synchronized (account1) {
        synchronized (account2) {
          balance = account1.getBalance();
          balance -= transferAmount;
          account1.setBalance(balance);
          balance = account2.getBalance();
          balance += transferAmount;
          account1.setBalance(balance);
        }
      }
    }
  }
```

Since the savings account's type value (1) is less than the checking account type (2), a savings account's monitor will always be obtained first by this code, regardless of the type of transfer being performed. In this case, we obtain the monitor of the account with a lower type value, but this code would run equally well if it were modified to first obtain the monitor of the account with the higher type value. In other words, it's not the order in which the monitors are obtained that's important: it's simply necessary to ensure that both threads consistently obtain the monitors in the *same* order.

Thread Priorities

Each Thread is assigned a priority, which is a value between 1 and 10 (inclusive) that is an indication of when a thread should run relative to other threads. In general, a thread's priority determines whether it's given preference by the processor when there are two or more **runnable threads**.

> **A runnable thread is one that is able to execute instructions, which means that it has been started, has not yet died, and is not blocked for any reason.**

When a context switch occurs, the processor typically selects the runnable thread with the highest priority, which means that higher priority threads will usually run before and/or more frequently than lower priority threads. If two or more threads with the same priority are runnable, it's more difficult to predict which one will be allowed to run.

In fact, the factors that determine how long and how often a thread runs are specific to the platform on which it is running and to the Java Virtual Machine implementation in use. One operating system might always select the first available runnable thread with the highest priority, while another system may schedule threads with the same priority in a "round-robin" fashion. In addition, while Java supports ten priorities, the underlying operating system's threading architecture may support a lesser or greater number of priorities. When that is the case, the Java Virtual Machine is responsible for mapping the priority value assigned to the Thread object to an appropriate native priority.

> Given these differences between platforms, Java does not make any guarantees concerning how priority affects a thread's execution. Therefore, you should avoid making assumptions about the effects of thread priorities on your application or at least test its effects on each platform on which your code will be deployed.

When one Thread creates another, that new Thread (sometimes called the **child thread**) is given the same priority value as the one that created it (the **parent thread**). However, you can explicitly set a Thread's priority by calling its setPriority() method and specifying an int parameter value between 1 and 10. The Thread class provides three constants that correspond to low, medium, and high thread priorities: MIN_PRIORITY, NORM_PRIORITY, and MAX_PRIORITY, which correspond to values of 1, 5, and 10, respectively. For example, to create a thread and assign it the lowest possible priority, you could use code similar to that shown below:

```
Runnable myRunnable;
.
.
.
Thread t = new Thread(myRunnable);
t.setPriority(Thread.MIN_PRIORITY);
```

The specific priority you assign to a thread will depend primarily on the nature of the function(s) performed by the thread. For example, if a thread will spend most of its time waiting for input and it performs a task that must be completed quickly, it should normally be assigned a high priority. Conversely, a thread that performs some type of non-critical background task (particularly one that takes a long time to complete) should be given a low priority. The word processor used to create this book, for instance, performs automatic spell checking, but that function is performed in a low-priority thread – at least until the application receives an explicit request to spell check the document.

When selecting thread priorities, be aware that it may be possible for a long-running thread with a high priority to monopolize the processor, even when preemptive multitasking is being used. Therefore, you should use caution in assigning higher priorities, and will usually only do so for threads that can be counted on to periodically relinquish control of the processor voluntarily.

Daemon Threads

Each thread is classified as either a **daemon thread** or a **user thread**, and Thread's setDaemon() method allows you to specify the thread's type. To use setDaemon(), you must call it before a thread is started, and passing a boolean value of true indicates that the thread should be a daemon thread, while false (the default) indicates that it should be a user thread.

The only difference between a daemon thread and a user thread is that one type (user) prevents the Java Virtual Machine from exiting, while the other (daemon) does not. For example, if you compile and execute the application shown below, the JVM will terminate after executing the main() method:

```java
public class Test {

  public static void main(String[] args) {
    Test t = new Test();
  }

  public Test() {
    System.out.println("Hello world.");
  }

}
```

However, if you create a similar application that displays a visual component such as a frame or dialog, the JVM does not exit:

```java
import java.awt.*;
import java.awt.event.*;
import javax.swing.*;

public class Test {

  protected JFrame frame;

  public static void main(String[] args) {
    Test t = new Test();
  }

  public Test() {
    frame = new JFrame("Hello World");
    frame.addWindowListener(new WindowAdapter() {
      public void windowClosing(WindowEvent event) {
        frame.setVisible(false);
        frame.removeWindowListener(this);
        frame.dispose();
        frame = null;
      }
    });
    Container pane = frame.getContentPane();
    pane.setLayout(new FlowLayout());
    pane.add(new JLabel("Hello world."));
    frame.setSize(400, 300);
    frame.setVisible(true);
  }

}
```

Although the modified `Test` class shown above performs all of the appropriate cleanup operations, the JVM does not exit when the window is closed and the resources are released. This is because a JVM will not automatically terminate as long as there are any live user threads, although it may not be obvious which user thread is active. In this case, the user thread preventing the JVM from exiting is the AWT event thread, which is started automatically when the `JFrame` is created so that rendering and event notification services can be provided. If you wish to force the JVM to exit despite the fact that one or more user threads are still executing, you must call the static `exit()` method in the `System` class as shown below:

```
System.exit(0);
```

Daemon threads are often used for background tasks that run continuously and that do not need to perform any cleanup tasks before the JVM terminates execution, and an example of this is the thread that performs garbage collection. If it's important for a thread to perform some cleanup task(s) before the Java Virtual Machine exits, that thread should be made a user thread. Otherwise, it's appropriate for the thread to run as a daemon thread.

Adding Threads to an Application

We'll now create an application that can benefit from the use of threads and examine some of the issues that you'll face when doing so. This application allows you to specify the URL of a file and download it, writing the file to disk. An illustration of how the application will appear during the download is shown here:

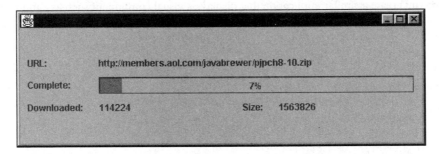

To run this application by itself, you must specify two parameters on the command line: the URL of the file to download, and the output file to which the contents of that URL should be written. When you do so, the component will appear in a frame like the one shown above, and the portion of the file downloaded will be displayed visually through the progress bar. For example, to download the home page from the JavaSoft web site and store its contents in `C:/brett/temp/javahome.html`, you could enter the following command:

```
java Downloader http://www.javasoft.com/index.html C:/brett/temp/javahome.html
```

The initial implementation of this code appears below. The `main()` method defined here creates an instance of the `Downloader` visual component, places it in a frame, displays that frame, and initiates the download by calling `performDownload()`:

```
import java.awt.*;
import java.io.*;
import java.net.*;
import javax.swing.*;
```

```
public class Downloader extends JPanel {

  protected URL downloadURL;
  protected InputStream inputStream;
  protected OutputStream outputStream;
  protected byte[] buffer;

  protected int fileSize;
  protected int bytesRead;

  protected JLabel urlLabel;
  protected JLabel sizeLabel;
  protected JLabel completeLabel;
  protected JProgressBar progressBar;

  public final static int BUFFER_SIZE = 1000;

  protected boolean stopped;

  public static void main(String[] args) throws Exception {
    Downloader dl = null;
    if (args.length < 2) {
      System.out.println("You must specify the URL of the file to download and " +
          "the name of the local file to which its contents will be written.");
      System.exit(0);
    }
    URL url = new URL(args[0]);
    FileOutputStream fos = new FileOutputStream(args[1]);
    try {
      dl = new Downloader(url, fos);
    } catch (FileNotFoundException fnfe) {
      System.out.println("File '" + args[0] + "' does not exist");
      System.exit(0);
    }
    JFrame f = new JFrame();
    f.getContentPane().add(dl);
    f.setSize(600, 400);
    f.setVisible(true);
    dl.performDownload();
  }
}
```

This portion of the code is passed a URL that identifies the file to be downloaded and an `OutputStream` that represents the location to which the file's contents will be written. In this case, it will be a `FileOutputStream`, causing the contents to be written to a local disk file:

```
public Downloader(URL url, OutputStream os) throws IOException {
  downloadURL = url;
  outputStream = os;
  bytesRead = 0;
  URLConnection urlConnection = downloadURL.openConnection();
  fileSize = urlConnection.getContentLength();
  if (fileSize == -1) {
    throw new FileNotFoundException(url.toString());
  }
  inputStream = new BufferedInputStream(
```

```
        urlConnection.getInputStream());
    buffer = new byte[BUFFER_SIZE];
    buildLayout();

    stopped = false;
}
```

This section of the code simply builds the interface that's used to provide feedback to the user on the status of the download, and consists of labels and a JProgressBar:

```
protected void buildLayout() {
    JLabel label;
    setLayout(new GridBagLayout());
    GridBagConstraints gbc = new GridBagConstraints();
    gbc.fill = GridBagConstraints.HORIZONTAL;
    gbc.insets = new Insets(5, 10, 5, 10);

    gbc.gridx = 0;
    label = new JLabel("URL:", JLabel.LEFT);
    add(label, gbc);

    label = new JLabel("Complete:", JLabel.LEFT);
    add(label, gbc);

    label = new JLabel("Downloaded:", JLabel.LEFT);
    add(label, gbc);

    gbc.gridx = 1;
    gbc.gridwidth = GridBagConstraints.REMAINDER;
    gbc.weightx = 1;
    urlLabel = new JLabel(downloadURL.toString());
    add(urlLabel, gbc);

    progressBar = new JProgressBar(0, fileSize);
    progressBar.setStringPainted(true);
    add(progressBar, gbc);

    gbc.gridwidth = 1;
    completeLabel = new JLabel(Integer.toString(bytesRead));
    add(completeLabel, gbc);

    gbc.gridx = 2;
    gbc.weightx = 0;
    gbc.anchor = GridBagConstraints.EAST;
    label = new JLabel("Size:", JLabel.LEFT);
    add(label, gbc);

    gbc.gridx = 3;
    gbc.weightx = 1;
    sizeLabel = new JLabel(Integer.toString(fileSize));
    add(sizeLabel, gbc);
}
```

As its name implies, the performDownload() method shown below is responsible for performing the download. It does this by repeatedly reading a portion of the file into a buffer, writing the contents of that buffer to the output destination, and updating the user interface so that it illustrates the progress of the download:

```
   public void performDownload() {
     int byteCount;
     while ((bytesRead < fileSize) && (!stopped)) {
       try {
         byteCount = inputStream.read(buffer);
         if (byteCount == -1) {
           stopped = true;
           break;
         }
         else {
           outputStream.write(buffer, 0,
               byteCount);
           bytesRead += byteCount;
           progressBar.setValue(bytesRead);
           completeLabel.setText(
               Integer.toString(
               bytesRead));
         }
       } catch (IOException ioe) {
         stopped = true;
         JOptionPane.showMessageDialog(this,
             ioe.getMessage(),
             "I/O Error",
             JOptionPane.ERROR_MESSAGE);
         break;
       }
     }
     try {
       outputStream.close();
       inputStream.close();
     } catch (IOException ioe) {};
   }

 }
```

One problem with this initial implementation of Downloader is that there is no way to control the download process. Downloading starts immediately when the application is executed, and cannot be suspended or canceled. This is particularly undesirable since downloading a large file can be very time consuming, especially when the download occurs over a low-bandwidth network connection.

The first step in allowing a user to control the download process is to create a thread that exists specifically to perform the download. By making this change, it will be possible to integrate an instance of Downloader into a user interface that will allow the download process to be controlled (that is, started, suspended, and stopped) through components such as buttons:

```
import java.awt.*;
import java.io.*;
import java.net.*;
import javax.swing.*;

public class Downloader extends JPanel implements Runnable {

  protected URL downloadURL;
  protected InputStream inputStream;
  protected OutputStream outputStream;
```

```
    protected byte[] buffer;

//...

    protected boolean stopped;

    protected Thread thisThread;

    public static void main(String[] args) throws Exception {
      Downloader dl = null;
      if (args.length < 2) {
        System.out.println("You must specify the URL of the file to download and " +
            "the name of the local file to which its contents will be written.");
        System.exit(0);
      }
      URL url = new URL(args[0]);
      FileOutputStream fos = new FileOutputStream(args[1]);
      try {
        dl = new Downloader(url, fos);
      } catch (FileNotFoundException fnfe) {
        System.out.println("File '" + args[0] + "' does not exist");
        System.exit(0);
      }
      JFrame f = new JFrame();
      f.getContentPane().add(dl);
      f.setSize(600, 400);
      f.setVisible(true);
      dl.thisThread.start();
    }

    public Downloader(URL url, OutputStream os) throws IOException {
      downloadURL = url;
      outputStream = os;
      bytesRead = 0;
      URLConnection urlConnection = downloadURL.openConnection();
      fileSize = urlConnection.getContentLength();
      if (fileSize == -1) {
        throw new FileNotFoundException(url.toString());
      }
      inputStream = new BufferedInputStream(
          urlConnection.getInputStream());
      buffer = new byte[BUFFER_SIZE];
      thisThread = new Thread(this);
      buildLayout();

      stopped = false;
    }

//...

      gbc.gridx = 3;
      gbc.weightx = 1;
      sizeLabel = new JLabel(Integer.toString(fileSize));
      add(sizeLabel, gbc);
    }
```

```
   public void run() {
     performDownload();
   }

   public void performDownload() {
     int byteCount;
//...
```

Although this application appears correct on the surface, there is one small problem with it. Specifically, the AWT event thread and the thread that performs the download share two resources that are not synchronized: the JProgressBar and the JTextField that are updated to provide feedback on the download operation's progress. This is actually a very common problem with multithreaded applications, but Java's SwingUtilities class provides a simple solution. When you create a multithreaded application that needs to modify components after they have been made visible, you can use the invokeLater() and invokeAndWait() methods in SwingUtilities.

These methods allow you to pass a Runnable object instance as a parameter, and they cause the AWT event thread to execute the run() method of that object. The invokeLater() method represents an asynchronous request, which means that it may return before the event thread executes the object's run() method. In contrast, invokeAndWait() represents a synchronous request, meaning that the method waits until the AWT event thread has completed execution of the object's run() method before returning. In the case of Downloader, there is no reason that it should wait for the user interface to be updated before it continues downloading, so invokeLater() can be used.

Making this modification solves the problem of having two different threads sharing the same resources, since only a single thread (that is, the AWT event thread) will access the JProgressBar and JTextField once they have been made visible:

```
   public void performDownload() {
     int byteCount;
     Runnable progressUpdate = new Runnable() {
       public void run() {
         progressBar.setValue(bytesRead);
         completeLabel.setText(
             Integer.toString(
             bytesRead));
       }
     };
     while ((bytesRead < fileSize) && (!stopped)) {
       try {
         byteCount = inputStream.read(buffer);
         if (byteCount == -1) {
           stopped = true;
           break;
         }
         else {
           outputStream.write(buffer, 0,
               byteCount);
           bytesRead += byteCount;
           SwingUtilities.invokeLater(
               progressUpdate);
         }
```

Controlling Threads

It's acceptable in some cases to start a thread and simply allow it to die once it exits the run() method. However, for various reasons, you'll often want to terminate a thread before it exits the run() method or you may simply want to suspend its execution and allow it to resume later. In the latter case, you may wish to suspend its execution for some particular length of time, or you may want it to be suspended until some condition has been met. To provide the functions just described we can create a new subclass of JPanel that defines five buttons:

- A Start button that causes the download thread to begin execution
- A Sleep button that causes the download thread to suspend its execution for a specific length of time, in this case for five seconds
- A Suspend button that causes the thread to suspend its execution indefinitely
- A Resume button that causes the thread to resume execution after the Suspend button was previously pressed
- A Stop button that effectively kills the thread by causing it to exit the run() method

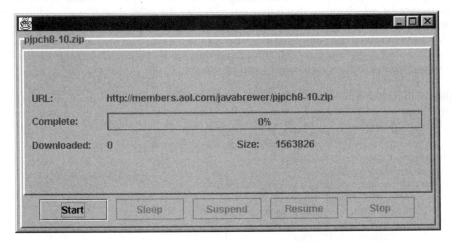

The DownloadManager class shown below displays an instance of Downloader and creates the buttons just described that will be used to control the execution of the Downloader's thread. It takes the same two parameters as the Downloader class, but unlike that class, DownloadManager allows you to interact with the thread performing the download by clicking on one of the buttons that are displayed. It does that by adding action listeners to each of the buttons, and we'll see shortly how to create the code needed for each button to perform the function requested:

```
import java.awt.*;
import java.awt.event.*;
import java.io.*;
import java.net.URL;
import javax.swing.*;
import javax.swing.border.*;

public class DownloadManager extends JPanel {
```

```
    protected Downloader downloader;

    protected JButton startButton;
    protected JButton sleepButton;
    protected JButton suspendButton;
    protected JButton resumeButton;
    protected JButton stopButton;

    public static void main(String[] args) throws Exception {
      URL url = new URL(args[0]);
      FileOutputStream fos = new FileOutputStream(args[1]);
      JFrame f = new JFrame();
      DownloadManager dm = new DownloadManager(url, fos);
      f.getContentPane().add(dm);
      f.setSize(600, 400);
      f.setVisible(true);
    }

    public DownloadManager(URL source, OutputStream os)
        throws IOException {
      downloader = new Downloader(source, os);
      buildLayout();
      Border border = new BevelBorder(BevelBorder.RAISED);
      String name = source.toString();
      int index = name.lastIndexOf('/');
      border = new TitledBorder(border,
          name.substring(index + 1));
      setBorder(border);
    }

    protected void buildLayout() {
      setLayout(new BorderLayout());
      downloader.setBorder(new BevelBorder(BevelBorder.RAISED));
      add(downloader, BorderLayout.CENTER);

      add(getButtonPanel(), BorderLayout.SOUTH);
    }

    protected JPanel getButtonPanel() {
      JPanel outerPanel;
      JPanel innerPanel;

      innerPanel = new JPanel();
      innerPanel.setLayout(new GridLayout(1, 5, 10, 0));

      startButton = new JButton("Start");
      startButton.addActionListener(new ActionListener() {
        public void actionPerformed(ActionEvent event) {
        }
      });
      innerPanel.add(startButton);

      sleepButton = new JButton("Sleep");
      sleepButton.setEnabled(false);
      sleepButton.addActionListener(new ActionListener() {
```

```
      public void actionPerformed(ActionEvent event) {
      }
  });
  innerPanel.add(sleepButton);

  suspendButton = new JButton("Suspend");
  suspendButton.setEnabled(false);
  suspendButton.addActionListener(new ActionListener() {
    public void actionPerformed(ActionEvent event) {
    }
  }),
  innerPanel.add(suspendButton);

  resumeButton = new JButton("Resume");
  resumeButton.setEnabled(false);
  resumeButton.addActionListener(new ActionListener() {
    public void actionPerformed(ActionEvent event) {
    }
  });
  innerPanel.add(resumeButton);

  stopButton = new JButton("Stop");
  stopButton.setEnabled(false);
  stopButton.addActionListener(new ActionListener() {
    public void actionPerformed(ActionEvent event) {
    }
  });
  innerPanel.add(stopButton);

  outerPanel = new JPanel();
  outerPanel.add(innerPanel);
  return outerPanel;
  }

}
```

We'll now proceed to create the functionality needed for each of these buttons, and will then return to the DownloadManager source code to have each button activate the appropriate functionality.

Starting a Thread

As we've seen, starting the execution of a thread is trivial and simply requires that you call the Thread instance's start() method. Calling start() does not necessarily cause the thread to run immediately, but simply makes the thread eligible for execution (that is, makes it **runnable**). Once that occurs, the thread will be executed by the processor at the first available opportunity, although when that occurs is platform-dependent and is affected by many factors. However, unless the processor is very busy executing other applications or other threads within the Java Virtual Machine, the thread will usually begin executing almost immediately when its start() method is called.

The Downloader class can be easily modified to provide a startDownload() method that starts the thread's execution as shown below, and that method will be called when the **Start** button in a DownloaderManager instance is pressed. For now, however, we'll simply define the startDownload() method, and will wait until the methods for all five buttons have been defined before going back and calling those methods from the buttons' action event handlers:

```
    public void startDownload() {
      thisThread.start();
    }
```

Making a Thread "Sleep"

The static sleep() method defined in Thread causes the currently executing thread to temporarily stop executing (that is, to "sleep") for some specific length of time. That length of time can be specified either as a long representing some number of milliseconds or a combination of milliseconds and an int value representing nanoseconds. However, milliseconds provide enough resolution for most situations, so you'll typically be able to use the simpler implementation of sleep(). For example, to cause the current thread to pause for two seconds, you could use the following code:

```
    Thread.sleep(2 * 1000);
```

Similarly, to sleep for 100 nanoseconds, you could use the following code:

```
    Thread.sleep(0, 100);
```

Note that both of these methods can throw an InterruptedException if the sleeping thread is interrupted, a scenario that will be discussed shortly.

Since sleep() affects only the thread that is currently executing, it must be executed by the thread that should sleep, and that thread cannot be "forced" to sleep by any other thread. For example, when the Sleep button is pressed, the actionPerformed() method will be called by the AWT event thread. Since the event thread cannot force the download thread to sleep, it must instead send a sleep request to the download thread, and the code executed by the download thread must be designed to recognize and comply with the request. The easiest way to do so is simply to define a boolean flag inside Downloader that's set to true to signal the download thread that it should sleep, and once the download thread wakes up, it can clear the flag. These steps will be taken each time the Downloader is about to read another portion of the file being downloaded, as shown in the highlighted code of the run() method listed below:

```
    public final static int BUFFER_SIZE = 1000;

    protected boolean stopped;
    protected boolean sleepScheduled;

    public final static int SLEEP_TIME = 5 * 1000;  //  5 seconds

    protected Thread thisThread;

//...

    public Downloader(URL url, OutputStream os) throws IOException {
      downloadURL = url;
      outputStream = os;
      bytesRead = 0;
      URLConnection urlConnection = downloadURL.openConnection();
      fileSize = urlConnection.getContentLength();
      if (fileSize == -1) {
        throw new FileNotFoundException(url.toString());
```

```
      }
   inputStream = new BufferedInputStream(
       urlConnection.getInputStream());
   buffer = new byte[BUFFER_SIZE];
   thisThread = new Thread(this);
   buildLayout();

   stopped = false;
   sleepScheduled = false;
   }

//...

   public void startDownload() {
     thisThread.start();
   }

   public synchronized void setSleepScheduled(boolean doSleep) {
     sleepScheduled = doSleep;
   }

   public synchronized boolean isSleepScheduled() {
     return sleepScheduled;
   }

   public void run() {
     performDownload();
   }

   public void performDownload() {
     int byteCount;
     Runnable progressUpdate = new Runnable() {
       public void run() {
         progressBar.setValue(bytesRead);
         completeLabel.setText(
             Integer.toString(
             bytesRead));
       }
     };
     while ((bytesRead < fileSize) && (!stopped)) {
       try {
         if (isSleepScheduled()) {
           try {
             Thread.sleep(SLEEP_TIME);
             setSleepScheduled(false);
           }
           catch (InterruptedException ie) {
           }
         }
         byteCount = inputStream.read(buffer);
         if (byteCount == -1) {
           stopped = true;
           break;
         }
```

Note that the `setSleepScheduled()` and `isSleepScheduled()` methods are `synchronized`, which is necessary since two threads access a resource. Specifically, that resource is the `sleepScheduled` flag that will be set by the AWT event thread (when the **Sleep** button is pressed) and both set and queried by the download thread.

Suspending a Thread

As we just saw, you can suspend a thread's execution for some length of time using the `sleep()` method. Similarly, you'll often want to suspend a thread for an indefinite length of time, usually until some condition is met and the `wait()` method defined in `Object` allows you to do so. However, before a thread can call an object's `wait()` method, it must own that object's monitor, or an `IllegalMonitorStateException` will be thrown.

The following modifications to `Downloader` illustrate how `wait()` can be used to suspend a thread's execution indefinitely, and we'll later modify the `DownloadManager` class so that it calls the `setSuspended()` method to suspend the download thread. Here, too, a `boolean` flag value is used to provide a way for the AWT event thread to communicate with the download thread when one of the `DownloadManager` buttons (**Suspend**) is pressed:

Add a new member variable:

```
protected boolean stopped;
protected boolean sleepScheduled;
protected boolean suspended;
```

Modify the constructor to set this `suspended` variable to `false`:

```
    stopped = false;
    sleepScheduled = false;
    suspended = false;
}
```

Add accessor and mutator methods that allow the `suspended` flag to be set and queried:

```
public synchronized void setSuspended(boolean suspend) {
   suspended = suspend;
}

public synchronized boolean isSuspended() {
   return suspended;
}
```

Finally, modify the `PerformDownload()` method as appropriate. This code checks the suspended flag, and calls `wait()` if the flag is assigned a value of `true`, causing the thread to be suspended. Later, we'll add the ability to resume a suspended thread, and when the thread is resumed, it will clear the `suspended` flag so that it continues execution unless explicitly suspended again:

```
   } catch (IOException ioe) {
      stopped = true;
      JOptionPane.showMessageDialog(this,
         ioe.getMessage(),
         "I/O Error",
```

```
              JOptionPane.ERROR_MESSAGE);
        break;
      }
      synchronized (this) {
        if (isSuspended()) {
          try {
            this.wait();
            setSuspended(false);
          }
          catch (InterruptedException ie) {
          }
        }
      }
    }
    try {
      outputStream.close();
      inputStream.close();
    } catch (IOException ioe) {};
  }

}
```

In this case, the object that's used for synchronization is the instance of Downloader and that object's wait() method is called to suspend the download thread. The download thread is able to invoke wait() because it will implicitly obtain the object's lock when it enters the synchronized block of code containing the call to wait().

When a thread calls the wait() method and is suspended, it's added to a list of waiting threads that is maintained for each instance of Object.

> In addition, calling wait() causes the thread to release control of the object's monitor, which means that other threads are able to obtain the monitor for that object.

For example, if one thread is blocked because it is waiting to obtain an object's monitor and the thread that owns the monitor calls wait(), the first thread will be given the monitor and allowed to resume execution.

In this case, the wait() method was called with no parameters, which will cause the download thread to wait indefinitely until another thread wakes it up, and the following section describes how to do so. However, you may sometimes wish to have the thread wait for some finite period of time, in which case you can specify that length of time on the wait() method. Like sleep(), wait() provides one method that accepts a long value representing some number of milliseconds and another implementation that also allows you to specify an int nanosecond value. You can take advantage of these methods to cause a thread to "time out" when it's waiting for some resource to become available and that resource does not become available within the desired length of time.

Resuming a Thread

Since calling wait() with no parameters causes a thread to be suspended indefinitely, you may be wondering how you can cause the thread to resume execution. To do so, simply have another thread call either notify() or notifyAll(), both of which are methods defined in Object. As with wait(), a thread must own the object's monitor before it can call notify() or notifyAll(), and if one of those methods is called by a thread that does not own the monitor, an IllegalMonitorStateException is thrown.

In this case, the download thread can be made to "wake up" after it invokes `wait()` by having the AWT event thread call `notify()` or `notifyAll()` when the **Resume** button in `DownloadManager` is pressed. To accommodate this functionality, we can add a `resumeDownload()` method to `Downloader` as shown below:

```
public synchronized void resumeDownload() {
   this.notify();
}
```

Notice that the `resumeDownload()` method is `synchronized`, even though it does not modify any resources that are shared between the AWT event thread and the download thread. This is done so that the event thread will obtain the `Downloader` object's monitor, which is necessary for the event thread to be able to call the object's `notify()` method successfully.

Also note that calling `notify()` or `notifyAll()` does not cause the waiting thread to immediately resume execution. Before any thread that was waiting can resume execution, it must again obtain the monitor of the object on which it was synchronized. In this case, for example, when the AWT event thread calls `notify()` by invoking `resumeDownload()`, the download thread is removed from the `Downloader` object's wait list. However, you should recall that when the download thread invoked the `wait()` method, it implicitly gave up ownership of the monitor, and it must regain ownership of the monitor before it can resume execution. Fortunately, that will happen automatically once the monitor becomes available, which in this case will occur when the AWT event thread exits the `resumeDownload()` method.

Up to this point, it has been implied that `notify()` and `notifyAll()` are interchangeable, which is true in this case, but there is a difference between those two methods that's important for you to understand. In this application, there will only ever be one thread (that is, the download thread) on the object's wait list, but you'll sometimes create applications that allow multiple threads to call `wait()` for a single object instance. Calling `notifyAll()` causes all threads that are waiting to be removed from the wait list, while calling `notify()` results in only a single thread being removed. Java does not specify which thread will be removed when `notify()` is called, and you should not make any assumptions in that respect, since it can vary from one JVM implementation to the next. It may intuitively seem that the first thread that called `wait()` should be removed from the list, but that may or may not be the case. Since you can't cause a specific thread to be resumed using `notify()`, you should only use it when you want to wake up a single waiting thread and don't care which one is awakened.

Stopping a Thread

Most of the code that's needed to stop the download thread is already present, since a `stopped` flag was previously defined. The download thread tests that flag as it performs the download, and once the flag is set to `true`, the download thread exits the `run()` method and dies. However, we're also planning to allow the AWT event thread to set the flag when a `DownloadManager`'s **Stop** button is pressed. Once that change is made, the flag has effectively become a shared resource that can be used by multiple threads, so access to it must be synchronized through accessor and mutator methods, making it thread-safe as shown below:

```
public synchronized void setStopped(boolean stop) {
   stopped = stop;
}

public synchronized boolean isStopped() {
   return stopped;
}
```

```
      public void run() {
        performDownload();
      }

      public void performDownload() {
        int byteCount;
        Runnable progressUpdate = new Runnable() {
          public void run() {
            progressBar.setValue(bytesRead);
            completeLabel.setText(
                Integer.toString(
                  bytesRead));
          }
        };
        while ((bytesRead < fileSize) && (!isStopped())) {
          try {
            if (isSleepScheduled()) {
              try {
                Thread.sleep(SLEEP_TIME);
                setSleepScheduled(false);
              }
              catch (InterruptedException ie) {
              }
            }
            byteCount = inputStream.read(buffer);
            if (byteCount == -1) {
              setStopped(true);
              break;
            }
            else {
              outputStream.write(buffer, 0,
                  byteCount);
              bytesRead += byteCount;
              SwingUtilities.invokeLater(
                  progressUpdate);
            }
          } catch (IOException ioe) {
            setStopped(true);
            JOptionPane.showMessageDialog(this,
                ioe.getMessage(),
                "I/O Error",
                JOptionPane.ERROR_MESSAGE);
            break;
```

While this implementation will work, it has one weakness: the download thread cannot be stopped while it is suspended or sleeping. For example, suppose that you start the download operation and decide to suspend the download. If you then decided to terminate the download completely after having suspended it, you would be forced to resume the download (that is, press the **Resume** button) *and then* stop the download. Ideally, it should be possible to stop a download that was suspended without first resuming the download, and the interrupt() method defined in Thread allows you to do so.

Interrupting a Thread

Each thread maintains a flag that indicates whether the thread has been interrupted, and when you call a thread's interrupt() method, that flag is set to true. In addition, if interrupt() is called while the thread is blocked by a method such as sleep() or wait(), that method will terminate with an InterruptedException. However, in some cases such as when a thread is blocked because it's waiting for an I/O operation to complete, the interrupt flag is set "quietly" (that is, no exception is thrown) and the thread's execution is not affected.

To determine whether `interrupt()` will cause a blocking method to terminate with an exception, you should examine the API documentation for that method. For example, the `read()` method defined in `java.io.InputStream` can block a thread, but it does not throw `InterruptedException`. In contrast, the `waitForAll()` method in `java.awt.MediaTracker` blocks and will result in an `InterruptedException` being thrown if the thread that called `waitForAll()` is interrupted while blocked.

Since some blocking methods throw an `InterruptedException` and others do not, you will sometimes need to explicitly test the interrupted flag to determine whether the thread was interrupted. To accomplish this, you can use either the `static interrupted()` method or the non-static `isInterrupted()`. The `interrupted()` method returns a `boolean` value that identifies the state of the currently executing thread's interrupted flag and clears that flag if it was set. The `isInterrupted()` method similarly returns the value of a thread's interrupted flag but does not change the state of the flag. Therefore, `interrupted()` is appropriate if you want to both test and clear the flag, while `isInterrupted()` is often a better choice, particularly if you prefer to leave the flag unchanged. Either is acceptable in many cases, and the choice of which one to use will depend upon your application.

By making the changes highlighted below, the download thread can be interrupted (and the download canceled) by the AWT event thread, regardless of the state of the download thread:

```java
public void stopDownload() {
   thisThread.interrupt();
}

public void performDownload() {
   int byteCount;
   Runnable progressUpdate = new Runnable() {
     public void run() {
       progressBar.setValue(bytesRead);
       completeLabel.setText(
           Integer.toString(
           bytesRead));
     }
   };
   while ((bytesRead < fileSize) && (!isStopped())) {
     try {
       if (isSleepScheduled()) {
         try {
           Thread.sleep(SLEEP_TIME);
           setSleepScheduled(false);
         }
         catch (InterruptedException ie) {
           setStopped(true);
           break;
         }
       }
       byteCount = inputStream.read(buffer);
       if (byteCount == -1) {
         setStopped(true);
         break;
       }
       else {
         outputStream.write(buffer, 0,
             byteCount);
         bytesRead += byteCount;
         SwingUtilities.invokeLater(
             progressUpdate);
```

```
      }
    } catch (IOException ioe) {
      setStopped(true);
      JOptionPane.showMessageDialog(this,
          ioe.getMessage(),
          "I/O Error",
          JOptionPane.ERROR_MESSAGE);
      break;
    }
    synchronized (this) {
      if (isSuspended()) {
        try {
          this.wait();
          setSuspended(false);
        }
        catch (InterruptedException ie) {
          setStopped(true);
          break;
        }
      }
    }
    if (Thread.interrupted()) {
      setStopped(true);
      break;
    }
  }
  try {
    outputStream.close();
    inputStream.close();
  } catch (IOException ioe) {};
  }

}
```

Completing DownloadManager

We've now added all of the necessary functionality to `Downloader`, and can tie that functionality to the buttons previously defined in `DownloadManager` by making the following changes. With these changes in place, those buttons can be used to start, suspend / sleep, resume, and stop the download that's in progress:

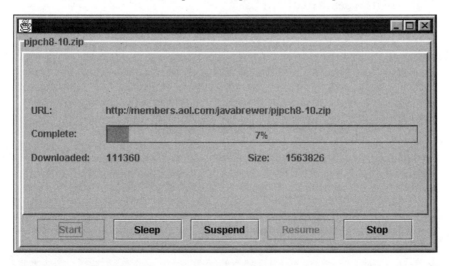

```java
protected JPanel getButtonPanel() {
    JPanel outerPanel;
    JPanel innerPanel;

    innerPanel = new JPanel();
    innerPanel.setLayout(new GridLayout(1, 5, 10, 0));

    startButton = new JButton("Start");
    startButton.addActionListener(new ActionListener() {
      public void actionPerformed(ActionEvent event) {
        startButton.setEnabled(false);
        sleepButton.setEnabled(true);
        resumeButton.setEnabled(false);
        suspendButton.setEnabled(true);
        stopButton.setEnabled(true);
        downloader.startDownload();
      }
    });
    innerPanel.add(startButton);

    sleepButton = new JButton("Sleep");
    sleepButton.setEnabled(false);
    sleepButton.addActionListener(new ActionListener() {
      public void actionPerformed(ActionEvent event) {
        downloader.setSleepScheduled(true);
      }
    });
    innerPanel.add(sleepButton);

    suspendButton = new JButton("Suspend");
    suspendButton.setEnabled(false);
    suspendButton.addActionListener(new ActionListener() {
      public void actionPerformed(ActionEvent event) {
        suspendButton.setEnabled(false);
        resumeButton.setEnabled(true);
        stopButton.setEnabled(true);
        downloader.setSuspended(true);
      }
    });
    innerPanel.add(suspendButton);

    resumeButton = new JButton("Resume");
    resumeButton.setEnabled(false);
    resumeButton.addActionListener(new ActionListener() {
      public void actionPerformed(ActionEvent event) {
        resumeButton.setEnabled(false);
        suspendButton.setEnabled(true);
        stopButton.setEnabled(true);
        downloader.resumeDownload();
      }
    });
    innerPanel.add(resumeButton);

    stopButton = new JButton("Stop");
    stopButton.setEnabled(false);
    stopButton.addActionListener(new ActionListener() {
```

```
        public void actionPerformed(ActionEvent event) {
          stopButton.setEnabled(false);
          sleepButton.setEnabled(false);
          suspendButton.setEnabled(false);
          resumeButton.setEnabled(false);
          downloader.stopDownload();
        }
      });
      innerPanel.add(stopButton);

      outerPanel = new JPanel();
      outerPanel.add(innerPanel);
      return outerPanel;
    }

  }
```

Deprecated Methods in Thread

We've now seen how to add code to an application that will suspend, resume, and stop a running thread, but if you review the API documentation for the Thread class, you'll see that it includes suspend(), resume(), and stop() methods, although they are now deprecated. You can probably guess (correctly) from this fact that those functions were handled "manually" within our application to avoid using the deprecated methods, but it may not be as obvious *why* they are deprecated.

When one thread wishes to stop or suspend another thread, the first thread usually can't know whether the second thread is in a state that's appropriate for it to be suspended. For example, suppose that you're running the AccountManager example that was defined earlier in this chapter, where money is transferred between two accounts. If a thread is stopped after it has removed money from one account but before it has increased the balance in the other account, that money will again be lost. Similarly, if a thread is suspended while it owns the monitor of some object, it will be impossible for other threads to obtain that object's monitor while the owning thread is suspended.

In effect, suspend() and stop() allow a thread to be suspended or stopped even while it is in a state where such an action is inappropriate. Therefore, instead of using those deprecated methods, you should instead send a request to a thread that will cause it to suspend or stop itself at an appropriate point. For example, an AccountManager thread should allow itself to be stopped or suspended before or after a transfer is performed, but not while one is in progress. Similarly, if there are resources that may be needed by other threads, the thread being suspended can release the monitor(s) of those resources before it is suspended. This reduces the likelihood of deadlock, which is a common problem with multithreaded application as we discussed previously.

DownloadFiles

The existing implements of Downloader and DownloadManager provide a great deal of flexibility and functionality, but they have one limitation: you cannot initiate multiple downloads without running each one in a separate Java Virtual Machine process. To address that limitation, we'll now create a new DownloadFiles class that allows you to create instances of DownloadManager by entering URLs in a text field:

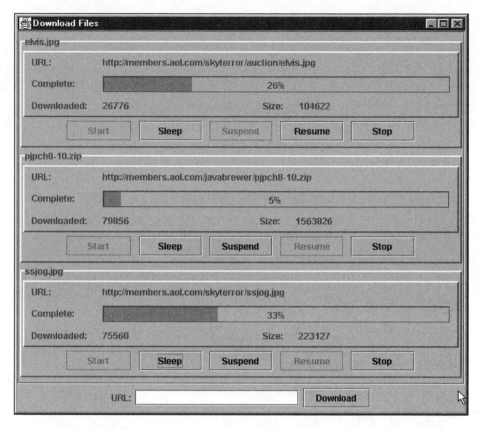

The following code provides the desired functionality. It creates a user interface like the one shown above, and creates a new `DownloadManager` instance when the user enters a URL in the text field and presses *Enter* (or the **Download** button). To use the application, simply compile and execute it and enter the URL of each file that you wish to download into the text field. You can then control the downloads using the buttons that we previously defined in the `DownloadManager` class, and each file will be written to the local drive using the file name portion of its URL:

```java
import java.awt.*;
import java.awt.event.*;
import java.io.*;
import java.net.*;
import javax.swing.*;

public class DownloadFiles extends JPanel {

  protected JPanel listPanel;
  protected GridBagConstraints constraints;

  public static void main(String[] args) {
    JFrame f = new JFrame("Download Files");
    DownloadFiles df = new DownloadFiles();
    for (int i = 0; i < args.length; i++) {
      df.createDownloader(args[i]);
```

```
      }
      f.getContentPane().add(df);
      f.setSize(600, 400);
      f.setVisible(true);
   }

   public DownloadFiles() {
      setLayout(new BorderLayout());
      listPanel = new JPanel();
      listPanel.setLayout(new GridBagLayout());
      constraints = new GridBagConstraints();
      constraints.gridx = 0;
      constraints.weightx = 1;
      constraints.fill = GridBagConstraints.HORIZONTAL;
      constraints.anchor = GridBagConstraints.NORTH;
      JScrollPane jsp = new JScrollPane(listPanel);
      add(jsp, BorderLayout.CENTER);

      add(getAddURLPanel(), BorderLayout.SOUTH);
   }

   protected JPanel getAddURLPanel() {
      JPanel panel = new JPanel();
      JLabel label = new JLabel("URL:");
      final JTextField textField = new JTextField(20);
      JButton downloadButton = new JButton("Download");
      ActionListener actionListener = new ActionListener() {
         public void actionPerformed(ActionEvent event) {
            if (createDownloader(textField.getText())) {
               textField.setText("");
               revalidate();
            }
         }
      };
      textField.addActionListener(actionListener);
      downloadButton.addActionListener(actionListener);
      panel.add(label);
      panel.add(textField);
      panel.add(downloadButton);
      return panel;
   }

   protected boolean createDownloader(String url) {
      try {
         URL downloadURL = new URL(url);
         URLConnection urlConn = downloadURL.openConnection();
         int length = urlConn.getContentLength();
         if (length < 0) throw new Exception(
             "Unable to determine content " +
             "length for '" + url + "'");
         int index = url.lastIndexOf('/');
         FileOutputStream fos = new FileOutputStream(
             url.substring(index + 1));
         BufferedOutputStream bos =
             new BufferedOutputStream(fos);
```

```
              DownloadManager dm = new DownloadManager(
                  downloadURL, bos);
              listPanel.add(dm, constraints);
              return true;
          }
          catch (Exception e) {
            JOptionPane.showMessageDialog(this, e.getMessage(),
                "Unable To Download",
                JOptionPane.ERROR_MESSAGE);
          }
          return false;
      }


  }
```

Although this application provides an easy and convenient way to create instances of DownloadManager, there is currently no way to remove those instances once they have been added. To address that limitation, we might choose to add a button to DownloadFiles that performs the following operations:

❑   Interrupts each active thread, terminating its download

❑   Waits until all threads have died, which may take several seconds depending upon the speed of your network connection

❑   Removes all of the Downloader instances from the user interface display

An easy way to perform the first operation described above (interrupted the active threads) is to use a **ThreadGroup**.

ThreadGroup

Just as packages allow you to organize your Java classes in a hierarchy, the ThreadGroup class allows you to create groups of associated threads and organize them hierarchically. Each ThreadGroup can have one parent and may have child ThreadGroup instances, and you can add a Thread to a particular ThreadGroup when the thread is created by passing a reference to that group to the thread's constructor:

```
Runnable runnable;
ThreadGroup myGroup = new ThreadGroup("My ThreadGroup");
    .
    .
    .
Thread t = new Thread(myGroup, runnable);
```

ThreadGroup wouldn't be very useful if it simply allowed you to create a collection of associated threads, but it also provides a convenient way to control those threads. Specifically, you can use ThreadGroup's interrupt() to interrupt all of its threads with a single method call and you can specify the maximum priority that should be valid for a thread in the group. ThreadGroup also provides suspend(), resume(), and stop() methods that allow you to control the execution of the threads, but those methods have been deprecated for the reasons described earlier, and you should not use them in your application.

As illustrated above, you can add a Thread to a ThreadGroup by passing a reference to the group as a parameter when creating the Thread instance. As the following highlighted code illustrates, Downloader can be easily modified to define a ThreadGroup that will contain all download threads, which will allow us to interrupt them all with a single method call:

```
    public static ThreadGroup downloaderGroup = new ThreadGroup(
        "Download Threads");

  public Downloader(URL url, OutputStream os) throws IOException {
    downloadURL = url;
    outputStream = os;
    bytesRead = 0;
    URLConnection urlConnection = downloadURL.openConnection();
    fileSize = urlConnection.getContentLength();
    if (fileSize == -1) {
      throw new FileNotFoundException(url.toString());
    }
    inputStream = new BufferedInputStream(
        urlConnection.getInputStream());
    buffer = new byte[BUFFER_SIZE];
    thisThread = new Thread(downloaderGroup, this);
    buildLayout();

    stopped = false;
    sleepScheduled = false;
    suspended = false;
  }
```

Now that each thread associated with a Downloader instance is part of the same ThreadGroup, the threads can all be stopped with a single call to the ThreadGroup's interrupt() method. In this case, that will be done by a static method called cancelAllAndWait() within the Downloader class:

```
  public static void cancelAllAndWait() {
    downloaderGroup.interrupt();
  }
```

To obtain a list of the threads that were active before interrupt() was called, it's possible to use the ThreadGroup's activeCount() and enumerate() methods. As its name implies, activeCount() returns the number of active threads in the group, while enumerate() stores a reference to each active thread within a Thread array that's passed to it as a parameter:

```
  public static void cancelAllAndWait() {
    int count = downloaderGroup.activeCount();
    Thread[] threads = new Thread[count];
    count = downloaderGroup.enumerate(threads);
    downloaderGroup.interrupt();
  }
```

To wait for each thread to die, we can use the join() method defined in Thread. When one thread invokes another's join() method, the first thread will be blocked until the second thread dies or until the first thread's interrupt() method is called. In this case, the AWT event thread will call each download thread's join() method once the download threads have been interrupted.

As with wait() and sleep(), it's also possible to specify a particular length of time (in milliseconds and optionally in nanoseconds) that the caller should wait when calling a thread's join() method. However, if you do not do so, the caller waits indefinitely until the thread dies:

```
  public static void cancelAllAndWait() {
    int count = downloaderGroup.activeCount();
    Thread[] threads = new Thread[count];
    count = downloaderGroup.enumerate(threads);
```

```
      downloaderGroup.interrupt();
    for (int i = 0; i < count; i++) {
      try {
        threads[i].join();
      } catch (InterruptedException ie) {};
    }
  }
```

With the `cancelAllAndWait()` method available in `Downloader`, it's easy to add a button to `DownloadFiles` to use that method. When the new **Cancel All** button is pressed, it will call `cancelAllAndWait()`, remove the `DownloadManager` instances, and refresh the user interface display:

```
protected JPanel getAddURLPanel() {
  JPanel panel = new JPanel();
  JLabel label = new JLabel("URL:");
  final JTextField textField = new JTextField(20);
  JButton downloadButton = new JButton("Download");
  ActionListener actionListener = new ActionListener() {
    public void actionPerformed(ActionEvent event) {
      if (createDownloader(textField.getText())) {
        textField.setText("");
        revalidate();
      }
    }
```

```
    };
    textField.addActionListener(actionListener);
    downloadButton.addActionListener(actionListener);
    JButton clearAll = new JButton("Cancel All");
    clearAll.addActionListener(new ActionListener() {
      public void actionPerformed(ActionEvent event) {
        Downloader.cancelAllAndWait();
        listPanel.removeAll();
        revalidate();
        repaint();
      }
    });
    panel.add(label);
    panel.add(textField);
    panel.add(downloadButton);
    panel.add(clearAll);
    return panel;
  }
```

Uncaught Exceptions

As mentioned earlier, a thread dies when it exits the run() method of the Runnable object with which it is associated. In most cases, this will occur when the thread has executed all of the code within that method, but it can also occur if an exception is thrown that is not caught. Perhaps the most common exception that will cause this to occur is NullPointerException, which most Java programmers encounter frequently. If a NullPointerException is thrown from code within your run() method or by code that's called directly or indirectly by that method, it will cause the thread to die unless the exception is caught.

In addition to allowing you to control the associated threads, ThreadGroup also allows you to customize the action that's taken when a thread is stopped because of an uncaught exception. To do so, you must create a subclass of ThreadGroup and override the uncaughtException() method that's passed a reference to a Thread and a reference to a Throwable object. The implementation of uncaughtException() in ThreadGroup simply passes those arguments to the parent ThreadGroup if one exists, or calls the Throwable object's printStackTrace() method if no parent ThreadGroup exists. In other words, the default ThreadGroup implementation is responsible for the stack trace output that you've probably seen when an uncaught exception is thrown.

Voluntarily Relinquishing the Processor

As mentioned earlier, the specific details of how threads share the processor's time vary from one platform to the next. The operating system will sometimes ensure that each thread is eventually given a chance to run, but some platforms are more effective at this than others. Therefore, if you create a multithreaded application, it's possible that one or more threads will not be able to run if other threads of a higher priority are constantly executing. To prevent this from happening, you should be aware of situations where a high-priority thread may run for a long time, and you may wish to cause it to periodically relinquish control of the processor voluntarily.

One way of making a thread give up control of the processor is to call the static yield() method defined in Thread as shown below:

```
  Thread.yield();
```

This method causes the currently executing thread to signal that another thread of the same priority should be allowed to run. Conceptually, you can think of `yield()` as causing the current thread to be moved to the end of the list of runnable threads with the same priority. In theory, this should allow a different thread to run, but as we saw earlier, the mechanism used to select the next thread to run is undefined and platform-specific. Therefore, it's possible that the same thread that yielded control of the processor will be immediately re-selected for execution, even if other runnable threads of the same priority are available. In other words, `yield()` is not a completely reliable way to ensure that one thread does not monopolize the processor.

A more reliable method of ensuring that a thread is temporarily prevented from running is to use the `sleep()` method, but there is a serious drawback to this approach. If you use `sleep()`, you are effectively overriding the native platform's efforts to allocate the processor's time in an efficient and "fair" manner among the threads. For example, suppose that you're given the following simple application:

```
public class Test {

  public static void main(String[] args) {
    Test t = new Test();
  }

  public Test() {
    Runnable runner = new MyRunnable("First");
    Thread t = new Thread(runner);
    t.setPriority(Thread.MIN_PRIORITY);
    t.start();
    runner = new MyRunnable("Second");
    t = new Thread(runner);
    t.setPriority(Thread.MAX_PRIORITY);
    t.start();
  }

  class MyRunnable implements Runnable {

    protected String name;

    public MyRunnable(String tn) {
      name = tn;
    }

    public void run() {
      while (true) {
        System.out.println(name);
      }
    }
  }
}
```

On most platforms, the second thread will be given more of the processor's time because it is assigned a higher priority that the first, which is presumably the desired result. If you were concerned that the first thread might be prevented from ever running on some operating systems, you might modify the `run()` method as shown below:

```
public void run() {
  while (true) {
```

```
      try {Thread.sleep(500);} catch (Exception e) {};
      System.out.println(name);
  }
}
```

The problem with this approach is that it has effectively rendered the two threads' priorities meaningless. Since each thread will sleep for half a second as it loops within the `run()` method, the result on most systems will be that each thread executes for approximately the same length of time.

While it is possible to use `sleep()` to control how threads are run, you should only do so with caution and understand that you may defeat the platform's attempts to execute the threads in an appropriate manner. In addition, using `sleep()` for this purpose may succeed on one platform but fail on another due to differences in the behavior of the operating systems. Fortunately, most operating systems do a reasonably good job of ensuring that each thread is given a chance to run, so you can and should normally use `yield()` instead.

Regardless of whether you use `sleep()` or `yield()`, you should be aware that there is no way in Java to guarantee that low-priority threads will ever be run, at least not while higher-priority threads are also executing. Given this unpredictability and the increased complexity associated with the scheduling of threads of different priorities, you should use priorities with caution.

Thread Pooling

As mentioned earlier, creating and starting a new thread can be a relatively slow process, and creating a large number of threads can seriously degrade the performance of your application. However, thread pooling is a technique that's commonly used to address those problems, particularly in an application that allocates many threads that are used for relatively short amounts of time. To use thread pooling, you must define a **thread pool manager** that maintains a list of threads. As requests are submitted to the manager, it may either create a new thread or allocate an existing one to satisfy the request.

The following `ThreadPool` class illustrates how easily a thread pool manager can be implemented. When you create an instance of this class, it will wait to receive requests in the form of `Runnable` objects passed to the `addTask()` method. If a thread is already available and waiting for work, it is notified when a new task becomes available and will execute the `Runnable` object's `run()` method. If there are no threads already available but the number of active threads is less than some configurable maximum value, a new thread is created to perform the task. Finally, if no threads are available and no additional instances can be created, the task simply remains on the queue until an existing thread becomes available and executes it.

In addition to allowing you to specify a maximum number of threads, the `ThreadPool` class allows you to specify the minimum number that should be running at any given time. If a thread finishes one task and is not given more work within a particular length of time (the "release delay"), that thread will terminate if the number of running threads is greater than the minimum. In other words, if the threads do not continue to receive work, the pool manager will gradually eliminate them until the number of remaining threads is equal to the minimum value:

```
import java.util.Vector;

public class ThreadPool implements Runnable {

  public final static int DEFAULT_MINIMUM_SIZE = 0;
  public final static int DEFAULT_MAXIMUM_SIZE = Integer.MAX_VALUE;
```

```java
public final static long DEFAULT_RELEASE_DELAY = 10 * 1000;

protected int minimumSize;
protected int maximumSize;

protected int currentSize;

protected int availableThreads;

protected long releaseDelay;

protected Vector taskList;

public ThreadPool(int minSize, int maxSize, long delay) {
  minimumSize = minSize;
  maximumSize = maxSize;
  releaseDelay = delay;
  taskList = new Vector(100);
  availableThreads = 0;
}

public ThreadPool() {
  this(DEFAULT_MINIMUM_SIZE, DEFAULT_MAXIMUM_SIZE,
      DEFAULT_RELEASE_DELAY);
}

public synchronized void setMinimumSize(int minSize) {
  minimumSize = minSize;
}

public synchronized int getMinimumSize() {
  return minimumSize;
}

public synchronized void setMaximumSize(int maxSize) {
  maximumSize = maxSize;
}

public synchronized int getMaximumSize() {
  return maximumSize;
}

public synchronized void setReleaseDelay(long delay) {
  releaseDelay = delay;
}

public synchronized long getReleaseDelay() {
  return releaseDelay;
}

public synchronized void addTask(Runnable runnable) {
  taskList.addElement(runnable);
  if (availableThreads > 0) {
```

```
        this.notify();
      }
      else {
        if (currentSize < maximumSize) {
          Thread t = new Thread(this);
          currentSize++;
          t.start();
        }
      }
    }

  public void run() {
    Runnable task;
    while (true) {
      synchronized (this) {
        if (currentSize > maximumSize) {
          currentSize--;
          break;
        }
        task = getNextTask();
        if (task == null) {
          try {
            availableThreads++;
            wait(releaseDelay);
            availableThreads--;
          } catch (InterruptedException ie) {};
          task = getNextTask();
          if (task == null) {
            if (currentSize <= minimumSize) {
              continue;
            }
            currentSize--;
            break;
          }
        }
      }
      try {
        task.run();
      } catch (Exception e) {
        System.err.println("Uncaught exception:");
        e.printStackTrace(System.err);
      }
    }
  }

  protected synchronized Runnable getNextTask() {
    Runnable task = null;
    if (taskList.size() > 0) {
      task = (Runnable)(taskList.elementAt(0));
      taskList.removeElementAt(0);
    }
    return task;
  }

}
```

A thread pool manager class such as this one can be useful to an application that creates and uses many threads and for which performance is an important factor. To use `ThreadPool`, simply create an instance of it using the no-argument constructor or by passing it the three required parameters: the minimum and maximum number of threads to be active, and the amount of time that should pass before an inactive thread is allowed to die. Those values should be set based on an estimate of how many threads your application will use at any given time and the amount of time that you believe will typically elapse before additional work becomes available for an inactive thread.

For example, suppose that you expect that your application will be using an average of five threads at any given point in time. However, let's also assume that your application will at times need to use up to ten threads simultaneously, and that there will be an estimated half-second delay between when one of the ten threads becomes inactive and when a new work request will be received. In that case, you might set the minimum number of threads to five, the maximum to ten, and the "release delay" to one-half of a second or slightly higher as shown below:

```
//  The release delay time is in milliseconds (ms), and 0.5 seconds = 500 ms.
ThreadPool pool = new ThreadPool(5, 10, 500);
```

The initial creation of the minimum number of threads will still generate the same overhead delay that would occur if no thread pool manager were being used. However, once the pool manager has created those threads, they will be reused repeatedly instead of creating new ones each time, which will result in improved execution time for an application that would otherwise create many threads and allow them to die. When the application wishes to assign work to a thread, it can simply call the `addTask()` method, passing it an object that implements `Runnable`:

```
Runnable mytask = new Runnable() {
  public void run() {
    performSomeTask();
  }
};
// When not using a pool manager, you would run the above object in a thread
// by creating code like that shown below:
// Thread t = new Thread(mytask);
// t.start();
// In this case, however, we will pass the object to a ThreadPool for execution
pool.addTask(mytask);
```

When a `Runnable` object is passed to the pool manager, the manager will cause that object's `run()` method to be executed at some point. The specific time at which that occurs will depend upon the minimum and maximum count values that you specified, the number of existing threads, and the number of threads (if any) that are currently available. If an existing thread is currently available, it will be assigned responsibility for executing the `run()` method, or if the current number if threads is less than the maximum number allowed, a new thread will be created. However, if the maximum number of threads has already been created and all of them are busy, the `Runnable` object will remain in the task queue until one of them becomes available.

Besides improving your application's performance, this thread pool manager can provide one other benefit to your application that may not be obvious. By limiting the number of threads that are allowed to be active, it can prevent the application from consuming an excessive amount of the available resources. Although Java does not enforce any limit on the number of threads that can be active, the resources used by each thread impose a practical limit upon the number of threads that can be running at any given time.

For example, while the operating system may theoretically allow many thousands of threads to be executing concurrently, the machine on which your application is executing might only have enough available memory to support hundreds (or only dozens) of threads. As long as your application consistently uses a thread pool manager like the one shown here, you can easily configure the maximum number of threads that will be executing at any given time, and therefore, you can exercise some measure of control over the resources used to support multithreading.

This assumes, of course, that your application doesn't simply create its own threads without using the thread pool manager, since the limit imposed by the manager only applies to threads that it creates, and does not otherwise prevent threads from being created within the JVM. In other words, this ability to control the number of active threads relies on an application's voluntary cooperation with the thread pool manager.

Summary

So we've seen that adding concurrent support to our applications through the astute use of threads is not necessarily a difficult task but we need to be aware of the various possible "bugs" that it can generate if not handled properly.

In this chapter, we've covered the following topics:

- ❑ Common reasons for using threads and some of the advantages and disadvantages of using them.
- ❑ How to create threads and manage their execution.
- ❑ How to synchronize access to resources that are used by multiple threads, and how to prevent problems from occurring.
- ❑ Changes that occurred to the Thread class in Java 2 and how to modify your applications to take into account those changes.
- ❑ Thread pooling, with a sample implementation of a thread pool manager.

In the next chapter, we will move our focus to look at one of the primary functions of the AWT event thread we mentioned at the beginning of the chapter – event handling.

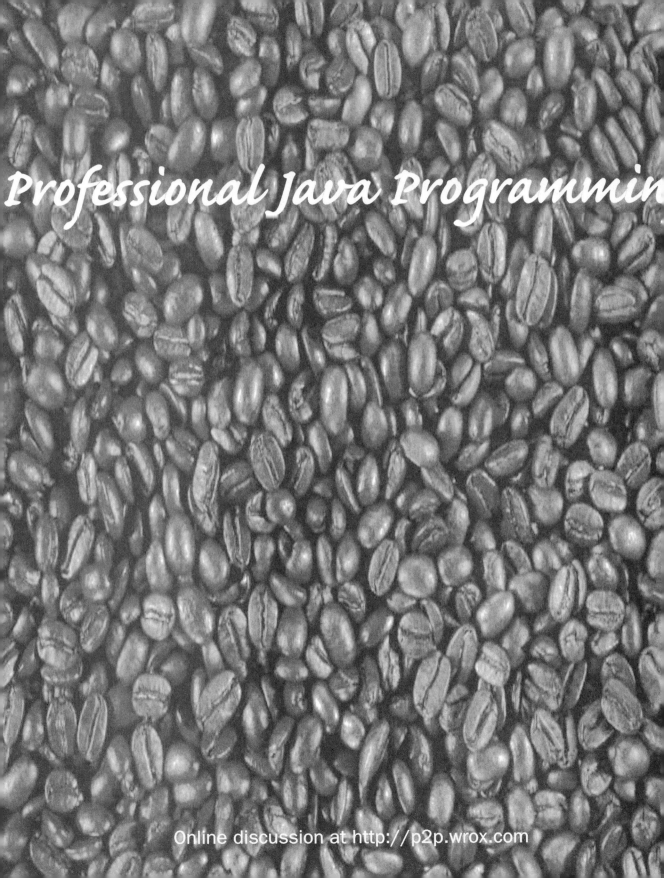

Professional Java Programming

4

Handling Events in Your Applications

If my local library doesn't have a book or some other material that I want to borrow, I can register my interest in that material with the library's computerized notification system. When the material does become available, the system automatically makes a telephone call to notify me of that fact. This approach to notifying people of the availability of materials is an example of the **observer pattern**, which is also known as **publish/subscribe**. In this case, I'm an "observer" of a change to the library material's availability. You could also say that I "subscribed" to the **events** related to the library material's availability and the computerized system "published" information that notified me of a change.

If such a system weren't in place, the only way I could learn about the material becoming available would be to call the library periodically and inquire about the material. This approach, called **polling**, isn't very efficient, because until the material is available, I'm wasting both my own time and that of the librarian when I call to find out the status of the item that I wish to borrow. In addition, I must decide how frequently to call, and there are disadvantages to calling too often or not often enough. Calling too often wastes more of my time and probably annoys the librarian, but not calling often enough can also create a problem: there may be a significant delay after the material is returned before I learn of its availability.

Obviously, observers provide some significant advantages over polling. Observers are much more efficient and provide immediate notification of an event. In fact, **event-driven programming** is fundamental to most modern applications, including those written in Java. Most of the time when you execute an application with a graphical user interface (GUI), it waits for you to trigger an event, where an event is an object that indicates that some type of state change has occurred or is about to occur for a given object. For example, you might need to select a menu item, enter text, press a button, or otherwise indicate in some way that you want the application to perform some task. When started, the word processor that I'm using displays an empty document and waits for me to add text to it. By pressing keys, clicking on a button, or selecting a menu item, I'm generating events that the application responds to. Until then, the application generally sits idle.

Similarly, when creating a Java application, you'll usually design it so that it performs some type of initialization and then waits for an event to occur that will indicate that it should take action. Most often, this means creating a user interface using Swing components, displaying that interface, and waiting until you receive notification of an event from one of the components. This chapter discusses the event handling mechanism in Java, including:

❑   How events are used by Java

❑   How to create custom event types and listeners for those types

❑   The various types of events and subscribers (or **listeners**) used by AWT and Swing components

❑   How the event model changed between Java 1.0 and 1.1

Event Handling Basics

A class that allows listeners to be notified of its events should provide methods for adding and removing listeners from a list. Then, when an event occurs for an instance of that class, it should notify all listeners in its list that the event occurred. This behavior is illustrated in the sequence diagram below, where a JPanel subclass called MyPanel creates a JButton instance, creates an instance of a listener class, and registers the listener with the JButton. Once the button is pressed, the listener is notified that the event occurred.

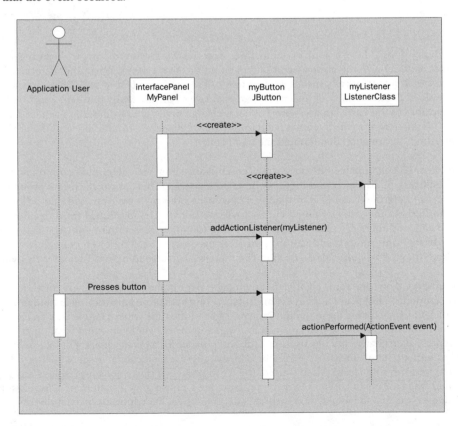

Each listener should implement an interface that's a subclass of `EventListener`, and each such interface will have at least one method that's called when the listeners are to be notified of some event. For example, the interface that's used to send notifications when a component gains or loses the keyboard focus defines two methods:

```
public interface FocusListener extends EventListener {
  public void focusGained(FocusEvent event);
  public void focusLost(FocusEvent event);
}
```

To ensure that a class that will be notified when an object instance gains or loses focus, you must have your class implement this `FocusListener` interface. An instance of the class can then register itself with objects that are able to generate focus events, and they will send notifications to the instance whenever they do so.

It's sometimes inconvenient to implement the interface, as some of the listeners defined in Java require you to implement multiple methods, with each one representing a different type of event. If you're only interested in a single event type, to have to implement all the methods is inconvenient, and creates a degree of unnecessary clutter within your application code, as shown below:

```
import java.awt.event.*;

public class MyFocusLostSubscriber implements FocusListener {

  /**
   *  This method is empty because I don't care about focus gain events.
   *  In fact, the only reason it's implemented here at all is because
   *  this class can't be compiled successfully without it.
   */
  public void focusGained(FocusEvent event) {};

  public void focusLost(FocusEvent event) {
    System.out.println("I care about the focus lost event");
  }

}
```

Adapters are provided for most types of listeners defined in the `java.awt.event` package, and they allow you to reduce the number of methods you define. An adapter implements the listener interface it is associated with by providing empty methods, just as was done in the above `focusGained()` implementation. Instead of implementing the listener interface, you can extend the appropriate adapter and override only the methods you care about, as in the following code:

```
import java.awt.event.*;

public class MyFocusLostSubscriber extends FocusAdapter {

  /**
   *  Even though we didn't implement focusGained() here, the compiler
   *  won't complain because it's implemented in the FocusAdapter
   *  superclass.
   */
  public void focusLost(FocusEvent event) {
```

```
      System.out.println("I care about the focus lost event");
   }

}
```

The following table lists the adapter classes defined in `java.awt.event`, along with the listener interface and event class associated with each one. Notice that adapters are not defined for every type of listener. `ActionListener`, for example, is arguably the most commonly used type, but no adapter is provided because it defines only a single method, and the existance of an adapter class would therefore not be beneficial to programmers:

Listener Interface	Event Class	Adapter Class
ComponentListener	ComponentEvent	ComponentAdapter
ContainerListener	ContainerEvent	ContainerAdapter
FocusListener	FocusEvent	FocusAdapter
KeyListener	KeyEvent	KeyAdapter
MouseListener	MouseEvent	MouseAdapter
MouseMotionListener	MouseMotionEvent	MouseMotionAdapter
WindowListener	WindowEvent	WindowAdapter

Adapters also provide a convenient way to define anonymous inner classes, as in the following code segment:

```
Component myComponent = new JTextField(10);
myComponent.addFocusListener(new FocusAdapter() {
  public void focusLost(FocusEvent event) {
    System.out.println("I care about the focus lost event");
  }
}
);
```

Notice that a parameter of type `FocusEvent` is passed to each of the two methods defined in the `FocusListener` interface.

When a notification is sent to listeners, it should include a reference to an object that provides information describing the event, such as which object instance generated it. This allows the event handler to examine and / or modify the state of the event source without being tightly coupled to that source. For example, you might define an event handler for a text field and assign the event handler responsibility for clearing the field's value when the *Enter* key is pressed. Since a reference to the text field component will be passed to the event handler, it can use that reference to the component instead of explicitly referencing a particular variable name. In other words, you could code something like this:

```
public void actionPerformed(ActionEvent event) {
  JTextField tf = (JTextField)(event.getSource());
  tf.setText("");
}
```

Instead of:

```
public void actionPerformed(ActionEvent event) {
   //  The following is undesirable because it references a particular field,
   //  specifically "firstNameText".
   firstNameText.setText("");
}
```

As is the case with `ActionEvent`, all event objects should be a direct or indirect subclass of `java.util.EventObject`. This simple class extends `java.lang.Object` and adds only a single `getSource()` method that returns a reference to the object that generated the event as illustrated in the above example. `EventObject` also overrides the default `toString()` implementation provided in `Object`, and its implementation displays the name of the event class, along with a string representation of the event source, which can be helpful in debugging. You might, for instance, displays the string representation of an event source to determine the origin of events that are being received by an event handler you've created:

```
public void actionPerformed(ActionEvent event) {
   System.out.println("Received an action event from " + event.getSource());
   // Handle the event here
}
```

AWTEvent

Some event classes directly subclass `EventObject`, while many others subclass `java.awt.AWTEvent`, which is itself a subclass of `EventObject`. In addition to the functionality inherited from its parent, `AWTEvent` provides an additional field called `id`. This field, which is accessible through the `getID()` method, identifies the specific type of event that is represented by the object. For example, in the case of the object sent to the `focusGained()` method, the value of `id` will be set to the `FOCUS_GAINED` constant defined in `FocusEvent`. It may seem redundant to store this information in the object, since the type of event is implicitly defined by which method (`focusGained()` or `focusLost()`) is called. However, this field provides a very useful feature: the ability to filter events, so that not all events are processed for all components.

For example, if you create an object that can generate focus events, but there are no listeners registered to receive those events, then the focus **event mask** will be disabled for that object instance. An event mask is simply a flag that indicates whether events of a particular type are being handled by the object or are being ignored, and event masks are disabled by default. However, when you add a listener to a component, the event mask is automatically enabled, and any future events will be published to the listener. This behavior improves the performance of Java applications by allowing components to ignore events of types for which there are no registered listeners.

To better understand how the `id` field is used to disable event processing, it's necessary to examine the design of the `java.awt.Component` class. Every event that's directly supported by `Component` is sent through its `dispatchEvent()` method. There, the event's category is determined by examining its `id` field. For example, all events with an `id` value equal to either the `FOCUS_GAINED` or `FOCUS_LOST` constants defined in `FocusEvent` are categorized as focus events. Once the category has been established, the logic inside `Component` checks the focus event mask to determine whether it's disabled. If it is disabled (in other words, there are no registered listeners), the event is discarded. Otherwise, it is sent to either the `focusGained()` or `focusLost()` method of each listener, depending upon the specific event type. This ability to filter events adds a degree of complexity to the way that events are handled, but as mentioned earlier, it also improves performance.

In addition to the id field and its associated getID() accessor method, the AWTEvent class also includes a paramString() method that returns a String value describing the event. That value varies from one subclass of AWTEvent to the next, but is generally intended to be used in debugging, and should not be used for any other purpose.

ChangeEvent and ChangeListener

If you examine the documentation on ChangeEvent, it may seem somewhat unusual, since it extends EventObject but does not define any additional properties or methods. The reason for this is that ChangeEvent was deliberately designed not to include any information on the state of the object instance that generated the event. Instead, its use is limited to notifying listeners that some type of change did occur, and the listeners are responsible for retrieving any state information they need directly from the event source. This is called **lightweight notification**, and the lack of state information in the ChangeEvent means that a single instance can be reused repeatedly by a component to notify listeners of different events. For example, an AbstractButton instance can create an instance of ChangeEvent, and use that same instance every time it needs to publish a state change event to its listeners.

The ChangeListener interface is used primarily in cases where a large number of events can be generated during some user input operation. For example, when a user is manipulating the knob on a JSlider as shown below, many events can be generated:

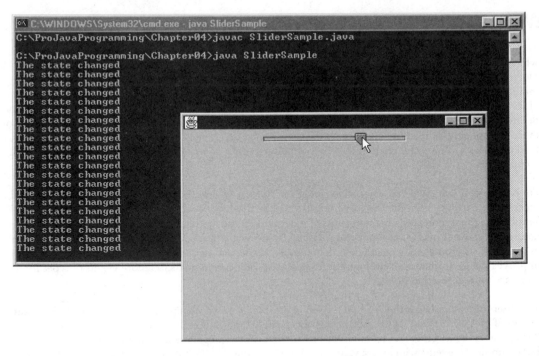

Instead of creating a "heavyweight" event each time, the JSlider instance uses the same ChangeEvent object repeatedly, allowing it to use less memory and avoid the performance penalty associated with the creation of numerous event objects. ChangeListener defines a single method, called stateChanged(), which is called each time the source object's state changes. An example of how to monitor state changes using this interface is shown in the code below:

```
import java.awt.*;
import javax.swing.*;
import javax.swing.event.*;

public class SliderSample extends JFrame {

  public static void main(String[] args) {
    SliderSample ss = new SliderSample();
    ss.setDefaultCloseOperation(JFrame.EXIT_ON_CLOSE);
    ss.setSize(400, 300);
    ss.setVisible(true);
  }

  public SliderSample() {
    Container pane = getContentPane();
    pane.setLayout(new FlowLayout());
    JSlider slider = new JSlider();
    slider.addChangeListener(new ChangeListener() {
      public void stateChanged(ChangeEvent event) {
        System.out.println("The state changed");
      }
    }
    );
    pane.add(slider);
  }

}
```

Events Generated by Component

The java.awt.Component class is the direct or indirect superclass of most visual components defined in the java.awt and javax.swing packages. This class provides support for a substantial number of different events, which means that all of its subclasses inherit the ability to generate these same events.

ComponentEvent and ComponentListener

The ComponentEvent class is a subclass of AWTEvent, and serves two purposes:

❑ First, it is used with the ComponentListener interface to notify subscribers when the visibility, size, or position of a Component changes.

❑ Second, this class serves as the superclass for a number of other event subclasses, which will be discussed later.

ComponentEvent also includes a method called getComponent() that is almost identical to the getSource() method in EventObject. However, as its name implies, getComponent() returns the source as a Component while getSource() returns the source instance as an Object. The getComponent() method is provided simply as a convenience to programmers, who can call this method instead of performing the cast in their own code when the event source must be referenced as a Component.

135

A subscriber should register as a `ComponentListener` when it needs to be notified of changes that occur to a component's visibility, size, or position. When such a change occurs, the appropriate method defined in `ComponentListener` is called for each subscriber. The following table lists the methods defined in `ComponentListener`, the value of the `id` field when each one is called, and a brief description of the component state change that triggers the event:

ComponentListener Method Called	ID Value in ComponentEvent	Component State Change that Triggers Event
componentHidden()	COMPONENT_HIDDEN	Made invisible
componentShown()	COMPONENT_SHOWN	Made visible
componentMoved()	COMPONENT_MOVED	Location changed
componentResized()	COMPONENT_RESIZED	Size changed

An example of how to use `ComponentListener` is shown in the code below, which creates an instance of `JFrame` and registers a `ComponentListener`. If you compile and run this code, it will send a message to standard output each time you resize the frame:

```
import java.awt.event.*;
import javax.swing.JFrame;

public class ComponentList {

  public static void main(String[] args) {
    ComponentList cl = new ComponentList();
  }

  public ComponentList() {
    JFrame f = new JFrame("Hello");
    f.setDefaultCloseOperation(JFrame.EXIT_ON_CLOSE);
    f.setSize(400, 300);
    f.addComponentListener(new ComponentAdapter() {
      public void componentResized(ComponentEvent event) {
        System.out.println("Resize performed");
      }
    }
    );
    f.setVisible(true);
  }
}
```

FocusEvent and FocusListener

In the context of a user interface, the **input focus** is the component that is currently accepting input, and there's usually some visual indication of which component has the focus. For example, in a text field, you'll normally see a blinking **caret** (sometimes incorrectly referred to as a "cursor") when that field has the focus. Other components that can acquire the focus provide different and often more subtle cues. For example, in the following screenshot you can see a faint rectangle around the Has Focus button label:

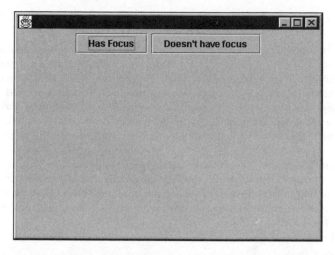

Although the Component class allows you to maintain a list of focus listeners, it's not necessarily the case that instances of its subclasses can always generate focus events. For example, disabled components, and those that do not normally allow any type of input, such as JLabel and JPanel do not normally generate focus events. However, for those that can accept the input focus, you can use the FocusListener interface to detect when a component has gained or lost the focus.

FocusEvent is a subclass of ComponentEvent, and adds a single property and accessor method. When an event is published that indicates that the input focus has been lost, the isTemporary() method can be used to determine if the focus loss is **permanent** or only **temporary**. A permanent loss of focus is the normal scenario, where the focus has been lost because the user pressed the *Tab* key or used the mouse to click on some other component to give it the focus.

A temporary loss is one that occurs only for the duration of some operation such as dragging a scrollbar. In that case, once the drag operation has completed, the input focus is returned to the component that temporarily lost it.

The following table lists the methods defined in FocusListener, the value of the id field when each one is called, and a brief description of when it is called:

FocusListener Method Called	**ID Value in FocusEvent**	**Component State Change that Triggers Event**
focusGained()	FOCUS_GAINED	Gained focus
focusLost()	FOCUS_LOST	Lost focus

The following code segment illustrates how to detect that a component has lost the input focus. In this case, a message is sent to standard output when the JTextField loses the input focus:

```
JTextField myText = new JTextField(10);
myText.addFocusListener(new FocusAdapter() {
  public void focusLost(FocusEvent event) {
    System.out.println("I care about the focus lost event");
  }
}
);
```

InputEvent

This abstract class is not directly associated with a listener, but provides some useful functionality and serves as the superclass of two other event classes that represent user input operations, specifically `KeyEvent` and `MouseEvent`. `InputEvent` provides **modifier flags** that indicate which keys were pressed and / or which mouse button was clicked to generate the event. For example, when a key is pressed, the modifiers identify the other "special" keys that were already pressed, such as the *Shift*, *Control* (*Ctrl*), and *Alt* keys. Similarly, when a mouse button is pressed, those same key modifiers may be set, and a modifier that identifies which mouse button (1, 2, or 3, also known as left, middle, and right) was pressed will be set.

To determine which mouse button was pressed, you should test the modifier flags to determine which one is set when a mouse event occurs. For example, the following code creates a frame and subscribes to mouse press events that occur within its content pane. When a mouse button is clicked, it will send a message to standard output that identifies which button was pressed, along with messages indicating whether the *Shift*, *Control*, and *Alt* keys are down:

```java
import java.awt.*;
import java.awt.event.*;
import javax.swing.*;

public class WhichButton extends JFrame {

  public static void main(String[] args) {
    WhichButton wb = new WhichButton();
    wb.setDefaultCloseOperation(JFrame.EXIT_ON_CLOSE);
    wb.setSize(400, 300);
    wb.setVisible(true);
  }

  public WhichButton() {
    Container pane = getContentPane();
    pane.setLayout(new FlowLayout());
    pane.addMouseListener(new MouseAdapter() {
      public void mousePressed(MouseEvent event) {
        int modifiers = event.getModifiers();
        if ((modifiers & InputEvent.BUTTON1_MASK) != 0)
          System.out.println("Pressed left button");
        else if ((modifiers & InputEvent.BUTTON2_MASK) != 0)
          System.out.println("Pressed center button");
        else if ((modifiers & InputEvent.BUTTON3_MASK) != 0)
          System.out.println("Pressed right button");
        System.out.println("Shift is " +
          (event.isShiftDown() ? "" : "not ") + "pressed");
        System.out.println("Control is " +
          (event.isControlDown() ? "" : "not ") + "pressed");
        System.out.println("Alt is " +
          (event.isAltDown() ? "" : "not " ) + "pressed");
      }
    }
    );
  }

}
```

Finally, InputEvent also includes a timestamp that indicates when the event occurred. This timestamp is a long value that represents the number of milliseconds that have passed between midnight on January 1, 1970 and the point in time when the event occurred. You can use this value to construct an instance of java.util.Date that represents the point in time when the event occurred.

KeyEvent and KeyListener

Key events are generated for a component when the user presses or releases some key on the keyboard. There are two main categories of keys:

- **Character keys**
  Key that have some visual representation and result in a character being displayed when typed

- **Non-character keys**
  Keys that do not have a visual representation

Non-character keys include keys like *Backspace*, *Delete*, *Tab*, *Insert*, and *Delete*, as well as action keys like *F1* and *F2* and modifier keys such as *Control*, *Alt*, and *Shift*. The KeyEvent class defines a large number of constants that correspond to the values used to represent some of the more common keyboard characters, including all of those on standard United States keyboards.

Three types of event can be observed using KeyListener: key press events, key release events, and key type events. Key press and release events are generated for each physical key press and release, respectively, while key type events offer a more "'high-level" representation of the key events. Some characters require you to type a series of keys for the character to be generated, and a key type event is generated once such a sequence is completed. Many international characters require such a sequence of keys to be pressed, since some alphabets are too large for each character to be assigned a unique keyboard key. However, the most common case where sequences are used is in the case of characters that are only accessible when the *Shift* key is pressed.

For example, suppose that you've created an application that displays a message whenever the user presses the *Z* key. On a standard keyboard designed for use in the United States, this is a simple matter of comparing the **key code** with a constant defined in KeyEvent. The key code identifies which physical key was pressed, and is only applicable for key press and release events. An example of how this might be implemented is shown below:

```java
import java.awt.*;
import java.awt.event.*;
import javax.swing.*;

public class WhichKey extends JFrame {

  public static void main(String[] args) {
    WhichKey wk = new WhichKey();
    wk.setDefaultCloseOperation(JFrame.EXIT_ON_CLOSE);
    wk.setSize(400, 300);
    wk.setVisible(true);
  }

  public WhichKey() {
    Container pane = getContentPane();
    pane.setLayout(new FlowLayout());
    JTextField jtf = new JTextField(10);
```

```
    pane.add(jtf);
    jtf.addKeyListener(new KeyAdapter() {
      public void keyPressed(KeyEvent event) {
        //  See if a particular keyboard key was pressed
        if (event.getKeyCode() == KeyEvent.VK_Z)
          System.out.println("Key pressed");
      }
    }
    );
  }
}
```

In this case, it was possible to detect the key in the `keyPressed()` method. However, let's suppose that we want the application to work the same way but with one small modification: instead of the Z key, we want to detect when the asterisk (*) key is pressed. On most keyboards, the asterisk is not a distinct key, but is generated by pressing and holding down the *Shift* key while pressing the *8* key. In other words, the asterisk is a character that is not assigned a unique physical key and is generated through a sequence of key press events. As a result, simply changing the above code to check for a key code equal to `KeyEvent.VK_ASTERISK` is not sufficient, since there is no physical "asterisk key", and therefore, no key pressed event generated for the asterisk character. Instead, we must implement the `keyTyped()` method, which is called for each *logical* key press, as opposed to a physical one.

Since a key type event does not correspond to a physical keyboard key, it does not return a meaningful value when its `getKeyCode()` method is called. To find out which character was typed, it's necessary to call the `getKeyChar()` method, as in the following code. Notice that it returns a `char` value instead of a reference to a keyboard key constant:

```java
import java.awt.*;
import java.awt.event.*;
import javax.swing.*;

public class WhichKey extends JFrame {

  public static void main(String[] args) {
    WhichKey wk = new WhichKey();
    wk.setDefaultCloseOperation(JFrame.EXIT_ON_CLOSE);
    wk.setSize(400, 300);
    wk.setVisible(true);
  }

  public WhichKey() {
    Container pane = getContentPane();
    pane.setLayout(new FlowLayout());
    JTextField jtf = new JTextField(10);
    pane.add(jtf);
    jtf.addKeyListener(new KeyAdapter() {
      public void keyTyped(KeyEvent event) {
        //  See if a particular character was typed
        if (event.getKeyChar() == '*')
          System.out.println("Key pressed");
      }
    }
    );
  }
}
```

The following table lists the methods defined in `KeyListener`, the value of the `id` field when each one is called, and a brief description of when it is called:

KeyListener Method Called	ID Value in KeyEvent	Component State Change that Triggers Event
keyPressed()	KEY_PRESSED	Keyboard key was pressed
keyReleased()	KEY_RELEASED	Keyboard key was released
keyTyped()	KEY_TYPED	Character was typed

MouseEvent, MouseListener, and MouseMotionListener

As you might expect, instances of `MouseEvent` describe events related to the mouse actions, such as movement and button clicks. Each `MouseEvent` contains X and Y coordinate values that indicate where the cursor was located when the event took place, along with a flag that indicates whether or not the event is the platform-dependent "popup trigger" action. In addition, for events generated as the result of a button click, a click count value is included that can be used to detect double-clicks.

Although there is a single `MouseEvent` class that represents the event data, it is used by two different listener interfaces: `MouseListener` and `MouseMotionListener`. `MouseMotionListener` is used solely to subscribe to mouse movement events within a component, while `MouseListener` is used to subscribe to all other mouse events. The motion events were separated from the other types because a high percentage of the `MouseEvents` generated will be motion events. If the listener interfaces were not divided this way, then your application would be forced to subscribe to all types of mouse events in order to be notified of any one type. For example, to detect that a user has clicked on a component, you would also be required to handle motion events, which could degrade the performance of your application. However, with the listener interfaces divided this way, it's possible to have mouse listeners that will be notified of mouse clicks while mouse motion events are not processed.

To see the events that are generated by mouse clicks and movement, compile and run the following application, which displays the text representation of each mouse event in standard output:

```
import java.awt.*;
import java.awt.event.*;
import javax.swing.*;

public class MouseWatcher extends JFrame {

  protected JTextArea textArea = new JTextArea(3, 20);

  public static void main(String[] args) {
    MouseWatcher mw = new MouseWatcher();
    mw.setDefaultCloseOperation(JFrame.EXIT_ON_CLOSE);
    mw.setSize(400, 300);
    mw.setVisible(true);
  }

  public MouseWatcher() {
    Container pane = getContentPane();
    MyMouseListener mml = new MyMouseListener();
    pane.addMouseListener(mml);
    pane.addMouseMotionListener(mml);
```

```
  }

  protected void displayMouseEvent(MouseEvent event) {
    System.out.println(event.toString());
  }

  class MyMouseListener implements MouseListener, MouseMotionListener {

    public void mouseEntered(MouseEvent event) {
      displayMouseEvent(event);
    }

    public void mouseExited(MouseEvent event) {
      displayMouseEvent(event);
    }

    public void mousePressed(MouseEvent event) {
      displayMouseEvent(event);
    }

    public void mouseReleased(MouseEvent event) {
      displayMouseEvent(event);
    }

    public void mouseClicked(MouseEvent event) {
      displayMouseEvent(event);
    }

    public void mouseMoved(MouseEvent event) {
      displayMouseEvent(event);
    }

    public void mouseDragged(MouseEvent event) {
      displayMouseEvent(event);
    }

  }

}
```

The next screenshot shows the output from this program:

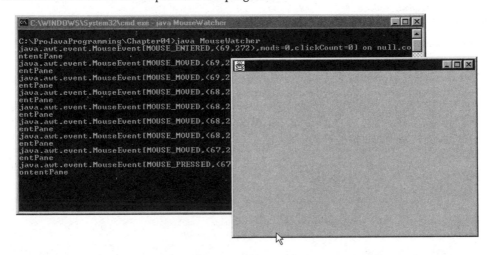

MouseListener

This interface defines methods that are called when the mouse enters or exits the component's display area, along with methods for handling button press events. When the cursor initially enters a component's display area, mouseEntered() is called, and mouseExited() is called when the cursor exits the display area. Pressing one of the mouse buttons generates a call to mousePressed(), and releasing it generates a call to mouseReleased(). A mouse "click" is a conceptual event that consists of a mouse press and release, and mouseClicked() is called each time those two events have occurred.

The following table lists the methods defined in MouseListener, the value of the id field when each one is called, and a brief description of when it is called:

MouseListener Method Called	ID Value in MouseEvent	Component State Change that Triggers Event
mouseClicked()	MOUSE_CLICKED	Mouse button clicked
mouseEntered()	MOUSE_ENTERED	Cursor entered component area
mouseExited()	MOUSE_EXITED	Cursor exited component area
mousePressed()	MOUSE_PRESSED	Mouse button pressed
mouseReleased()	MOUSE_RELEASED	Mouse button released

Detecting Double-Clicks

On some platforms, the double-click of a mouse button (usually the left one) has a special significance, often indicating that the item that was double-clicked should be selected or activated. Although Java doesn't generate a different type of event specifically for a double-click action, you can easily detect one by examining the click count in the mousePressed(), mouseReleased(), or mouseClicked() methods. For example, the following code displays a message when the user double-clicks inside the frame's content pane:

```java
import java.awt.*;
import java.awt.event.*;
import javax.swing.*;

public class DoubleClick extends JFrame {

  public static void main(String[] args) {
    DoubleClick dc = new DoubleClick();
    dc.setDefaultCloseOperation(JFrame.EXIT_ON_CLOSE);
    dc.setSize(400, 300);
    dc.setVisible(true);
  }

  public DoubleClick() {
    final Container pane = getContentPane();
    pane.addMouseListener(new MouseAdapter() {
      public void mouseClicked(MouseEvent event) {
        if (event.getClickCount() == 2) {
          JOptionPane.showMessageDialog(pane, "You double-clicked");
        }
      }
```

```
        }
      );
    }

  }
```

Although `mouseClicked()` will be called twice in this scenario, it will only display the dialog after the second mouse click. You can use this technique to identify double-clicks, triple-clicks, or any number of sequential mouse click operations.

MouseMotionListener

Registering as a component's `MouseMotionListener` causes the subscriber to receive events generated by movement of the mouse. Since `MouseEvent` includes the cursor's position relative to the component origin, you can use the information it contains to determine the cursor's position with respect to the component that generated the event.

To provide support for drag-and-drop operations, Java defines two types of mouse movement events:

- ❑ Normal events
- ❑ Drag events

A drag event occurs when the cursor is moved while one of its buttons is pressed. Mouse drag events have one characteristic that makes them different from every other type of mouse event. Specifically, as long as the mouse button is still pressed, drag events continue to be delivered even after the cursor is moved out of the component's display area. You can see this behavior for yourself by compiling and running the `MouseWatcher` class used in an earlier example. When running that application, move the cursor over the frame's content pane, press a mouse button, and move the cursor away from the frame. Drag events continue to be delivered whenever the mouse moves until you release the mouse button.

The following table lists the methods defined in `MouseMotionListener`, the value of the `id` field when each one is called, and a brief description of when it is called:

MouseMotionListener Method Called	ID Value in HierarchyEvent	Component State Change that Triggers Event
mouseMoved()	MOUSE_MOVED	Cursor moved over component
mouseDragged()	MOUSE_DRAGGED	Cursor moved with a button pressed

InputMethodEvent and InputMethodListener

In most parts of the world, it's possible to use a keyboard that contains a key for each character of the alphabet. However, some alphabets, particularly those in East Asian countries, have thousands of characters, and providing a single keyboard key for each one isn't feasible. Therefore, it's necessary to allow those characters to be generated by a sequence of multiple key presses instead of a single one. Java's **Input Method Framework** provides a mechanism for supporting languages with large character sets as well as input from non-keyboard devices, such as handwriting- and voice-recognition systems.

The InputMethodEvent class and InputMethodListener interface are used to support this functionality, but a detailed description of the input method framework is beyond the scope of this chapter, and it is not normally used by application developers. However, it is mentioned here for the sake of completeness.

HierarchyEvent and HierarchyListener

Newly introduced in Java 1.3, HierarchyEvent and HierarchyListener provide the ability to receive notification of changes to the state of an object that's part of a container hierarchy. For example, when you add a button to a panel and the panel is contained within a frame or dialog, the hierarchy consists of three levels: the frame or dialog window, the panel within that window, and the button within the panel.

As shown in the following table, HierarchyListener defines a single method that's called when a change occurs to one of the components in the hierarchy:

HierarchyListener Method Called	ID Value in MouseEvent	Component State Change that Triggers Event
hierarchyChanged()	HIERARCHY_CHANGED	See description below.

The types of changes for which these notifications will be sent are:

❑   The addition or removal of an ancestor component to or from the hierarchy

❑   The hierarchy's visibility state changes

❑   The hierarchy is shown on the screen or is hidden

The following program can be used to examine the behavior of a component hierarchy when a HierarchyListener is registered. It creates a simply user interface like the one described above and creates and registers a HierarchyListener that displays messages each time it receives an event indicating that the hierarchy's state has changed:

```
import java.awt.event.*;
import javax.swing.*;

public class HierarchyTest extends JFrame {

  public static void main(String[] args) {
    System.out.println("Creating HierarchyTest instance...");
    HierarchyTest ht = new HierarchyTest();
    ht.setDefaultCloseOperation(JFrame.EXIT_ON_CLOSE);
    ht.setSize(600, 300);
    System.out.println("Making the HierarchyTest visible...");
    ht.setVisible(true);
  }

  public HierarchyTest() {
    super("HierarchyTest");
    JPanel panel = new JPanel();
    JButton button = new JButton("Hierarchy Test Component");
    button.addHierarchyListener(new HierarchyListener() {
```

```
        public void hierarchyChanged(HierarchyEvent event) {
          displayHierarchyFlags(event.getChangeFlags());
        }
    });
    System.out.println("Adding button to panel...");
    panel.add(button);
    System.out.println("Adding panel to frame's content pane...");
    getContentPane().add(panel);
  }

  protected void displayHierarchyFlags(long flags) {
    if ((flags & HierarchyEvent.ANCESTOR_MOVED) != 0) {
      System.out.println("Ancestor moved");
    }
    if ((flags & HierarchyEvent.ANCESTOR_RESIZED) != 0) {
      System.out.println("Ancestor resized");
    }
    if ((flags & HierarchyEvent.DISPLAYABILITY_CHANGED) != 0) {
      System.out.println("Ancestor visibility changed");
    }
    if ((flags & HierarchyEvent.PARENT_CHANGED) != 0) {
      System.out.println("Parent changed");
    }
    if ((flags & HierarchyEvent.SHOWING_CHANGED) != 0) {
      System.out.println("Showing changed");
    }
  }
}
```

HierarchyBoundsListener

Like HierarchyListener, HierarchyBoundsListener was introduced in Java 1.3, and as its name implies, HierarchyBoundsListener provides notification of changes to a component hierarchy's bounds. In other words, a HierarchyBoundsListener is notified when the component hierarchy's size or position (i.e., its "bounds") changes, and the methods defined to support the notifications are listed below:

HierarchyBoundsListener Method Called	ID Value in HierarchyEvent	Component State Change that Triggers Event
ancestorMoved()	ANCESTOR_MOVED	An ancestor's position changed
ancestorResized()	ANCESTOR_RESIZED	An ancestor's size changed

By making a small change to the HierarchyTest class defined above, you can observe the HierarchyBoundsListener notifications as well as those of HierarchyListener:

```
public HierarchyTest() {
  super("HierarchyTest");
  JPanel panel = new JPanel();
  JButton button = new JButton("Hierarchy Test Component");
```

```
     button.addHierarchyListener(new HierarchyListener() {
       public void hierarchyChanged(HierarchyEvent event) {
         displayHierarchyFlags(event.getChangeFlags());
       }
     });
     button.addHierarchyBoundsListener(new HierarchyBoundsListener() {
       public void ancestorMoved(HierarchyEvent event) {
         System.out.println("Ancestor moved");
       }
       public void ancestorResized(HierarchyEvent event) {
         System.out.println("Ancestor resized");
       }
     });
     System.out.println("Adding button to panel...");
     panel.add(button);
     System.out.println("Adding panel to frame's content pane...");
     getContentPane().add(panel);
   }
```

With this modification, the sample application will issue a message each time the frame that's displayed is either moved or resized. As with HierarchyListener, the methods defined in HierarchyBoundsListener are passed an instance of HierarchyEvent.

Events Generated by Container

The java.awt.Container class is the superclass of many of the visual components that are available in Java, partly because it is the direct superclass of JComponent; JComponent in turn is the superclass of the majority of the visual Swing components. Containers provide an extremely important function in Java: the ability to combine multiple visual components to create an interface. Any time you use a component that allows you to add other components to its display area, you're using the functionality defined in Container. Some examples of container subclasses include panels, frames, and dialogs. In other words, any component for which you normally use a layout manager is an instance of Container. We'll be learning more about layout managers in the next chapter.

In addition to adding components to a container, it's also possible to remove them, but there's rarely a reason to do so. You're probably already familiar with one or more forms of the add() method that allows you to add components to a container. However, you may not be aware that there is also a remove() method that removes a component from the container, as well as removeAll(), which removes all components that were previously added to the container. In general, it's not necessary to remove components from a container, but you may occasionally find it desirable to do so. The following code segment shows an example of how to use the add() and remove() methods:

```
Container container = new JPanel();
JLabel label = new JLabel("Add me first");
container.add(label, BorderLayout.NORTH);
// ...
container.remove(label);
JTextField textField = new JTextField(10);
container.add(textField);
```

ContainerEvent and ContainerListener

In addition to the event types that are inherited from Component, containers are capable of generating events that allow listeners to be notified when a component is added to or removed from the container. ContainerEvent subclasses ComponentEvent, and provides two additional methods. The getChild() method returns a reference to the "child" component that was added or removed, while getContainer() casts the event source as a Container.

The following table lists the methods defined in ContainerListener, the value of the id field when each one is called, and a brief description of when it is called:

ContainerListener Method Called	ID Value in ContainerEvent	Component State Change that Triggers Event
componentAdded()	COMPONENT_ADDED	Component added to container
componentRemoved()	COMPONENT_REMOVED	Component removed from container

The following code shows an example of how to use ContainerListener to receive notification of components being added and removed from a Container. In this case, the container is the frame's content pane, and a JLabel instance is added to and removed from the container using a pair of buttons. Each time one of the buttons is pressed to add or remove the label, a message dialog is displayed that indicates what type of container event was received:

```java
import java.awt.*;
import java.awt.event.*;
import javax.swing.*;

public class ContainerTest extends JFrame {

  protected Container pane;
  protected JLabel label = new JLabel("Test Label");

  public static void main(String[] args) {
    ContainerTest ct = new ContainerTest();
    ct.setDefaultCloseOperation(JFrame.EXIT_ON_CLOSE);
    ct.setSize(400, 300);
    ct.setVisible(true);
  }

  public ContainerTest() {
    label.setFont(new Font("Dialog", Font.PLAIN, 36));
    pane = getContentPane();
    pane.setLayout(new BorderLayout());
    JPanel panel = new JPanel();
    JButton btn = new JButton("Add");
    btn.addActionListener(new ActionListener() {
      public void actionPerformed(ActionEvent event) {
        pane.add(label, BorderLayout.CENTER);
        refreshDisplay();
      }
    }
    );
```

```
      panel.add(btn);
      btn = new JButton("Remove");
      btn.addActionListener(new ActionListener() {
        public void actionPerformed(ActionEvent event) {
          pane.remove(label);
          refreshDisplay();
        }
      }
      );
      panel.add(btn);
      pane.add(panel, BorderLayout.SOUTH);

      pane.addContainerListener(new ContainerListener() {
        public void componentAdded(ContainerEvent event) {
          JOptionPane.showMessageDialog(pane, "Added component");
        }

        public void componentRemoved(ContainerEvent event) {
          JOptionPane.showMessageDialog(pane, "Removed component");
        }
      }
      );
    }

    protected void refreshDisplay() {
      validate();
      repaint();
    }

  }
```

Events Generated by Window

The java.awt.Window class is a subclass of Container, and is the direct or indirect superclass of all window components in both the AWT and Swing (for example, Frame and JFrame, Dialog and JDialog). It can be used for creating custom window types, but is most frequently used indirectly when an application creates an instance of JFrame or JDialog.

WindowEvent and WindowListener

WindowEvent extends ComponentEvent, and provides a single method called getWindow(), a convenience method that returns the event source as an instance of Window instead of an Object.

The WindowListener interface provides notification of seven different types of events, as illustrated in the following table and described below:

WindowListener Method Called	ID Value in WindowEvent	Component State Change that Triggers Event
windowActivated()	WINDOW_ACTIVATED	Became active window
windowClosed()	WINDOW_CLOSED	Window has been closed
windowClosing()	WINDOW_CLOSING	Close operation requested

Table continued on following page

WindowListener Method Called	ID Value in WindowEvent	Component State Change that Triggers Event
windowDeactivated()	WINDOW_DEACTIVATED	No longer the active window
windowDeiconified()	WINDOW_DEICONIFIED	No longer iconified
windowIconified()	WINDOW_ICONIFIED	Window has been minimized
windowOpened()	WINDOW_OPENED	Made visible for first time

Activated

When this event occurs, it indicates that the window has become the "active" window. Although you may have many windows open at any given time, only one of them can be active, and that window usually is given a slightly different appearance from the others. The specific colors and behavior can vary from one platform to another, but it's usually easy to determine which is the active window. For example, the title bar at the top of the active window might be a bright color, while any inactive windows would have title bars with a dull, often grayed-out appearance.

Closing

This indicates that a request has been generated to close the window. For example, on the Windows operating system, you can click in the upper-right corner of the window on the button that resembles an "X" to close the window. This event is generated prior to the window being closed, and allows you to determine whether the close operation should be allowed to continue. One common use for this capability is to display a dialog that asks the user to confirm that they really want to close the window and terminate the application. This might be appropriate when, for example, the user has changed some data but not saved their changes, and then requests that the window be closed:

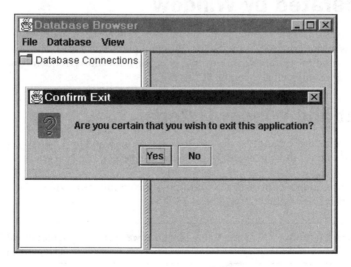

By default, the close does *not* occur automatically after this event is generated for an instance of Window. Instead, you must either hide the window using the setVisible() method, or dispose it using dispose() for the window to be closed. If neither of these operations is performed, then the window remains open. However, both JDialog and JFrame include logic that allows you to specify the default operation that should be performed when this event is received. Specifically, you can indicate that no action should be taken, that the window should be hidden or disposed, or (in the case of a frame) that `System.exit()` should be called. For example, if you create an instance of `JFrame` and want to call `System.exit()` when the user clicks on its close button, you could create code like that shown below:

```
JFrame f = new JFrame("This is a test");
f.addWindowListener(new WindowAdapter() {
  public void windowClosing(WindowEvent event) {
    System.exit(0);
  }
});
```

An easier way to accomplish the same thing is to use `setDefaultCloseOperation()`, a method that's defined in both `JDialog` and `JFrame`. This method requires you to pass an integer value representing the action that should be taken when the dialog or frame is closed, and constants are provided that represent the available options. Those constants are defined in `WindowConstants`, an interface that's implemented by both `JDialog` and `JFrame`, and are listed in the table below:

Constant Name	Action Taken When Close Requested
DO_NOTHING_ON_CLOSE	None
HIDE_ON_CLOSE	Window is hidden/made invisible
DISPOSE_ON_CLOSE	Window is hidden and disposed (that is, its resources released)

For example, if you simply want a frame to be made invisible when its close button is pressed, you could create code like the following:

```
JFrame f = new JFrame("This is a test");
f.setDefaultCloseOperation(JFrame.HIDE_ON_CLOSE);
```

Although none of the three options shown in the above table provides the same functionality as the call to `System.exit()` that was shown earlier, `JFrame` provides a fourth value that does so. Specifically, `JFrame` includes a constant named `EXIT_ON_CLOSE`, and as its name implies, specifying this value will cause the JVM to be terminated when a close operation is requested for the frame. Therefore, the creation of the `WindowAdapter` in the previous code segment could be replaced by a call to `setDefaultCloseOperation()` like the one shown below:

```
JFrame f = new JFrame("This is a test");
f.setDefaultCloseOperation(JFrame.EXIT_ON_CLOSE);
```

Closed

The `dispose()` method has been called for this instance of `Window`. To "dispose" a window means to hide it and to release the resources associated with it. When a window is closed that you expect to be opened and used again, you should simply make it invisible. However, if the window is no longer needed, you should call `dispose()` to free its resources.

Deactivated

The window generating the event is no longer the active window.

Iconified

The window is reduced in size and will be represented by an icon. This is also called "minimizing" and, on the Windows operating system, is accomplished by clicking in the upper-right corner of the window on the button that resembles an underscore character.

Deiconified

This is the opposite of "iconifying", and occurs when the window is restored from an iconified state.

Opened

A window is "opened" when it's made visible for the first time. This event is only generated once for an instance of Window, and is never published again.

Events Generated by JComponent

JComponent is the superclass of most Swing components, and provides a great deal of functionality for its subclasses.

AncestorEvent and AncestorListener

AncestorEvent, which is a subclass of AWTEvent, provides information similar to ComponentEvent. Specifically, it identifies the event source, which can be accessed through the getComponent() method. These events allow you to be notified when the JComponent or one of its ancestors has been made visible or invisible, or has moved. An "ancestor" is a container that the component was added to, either directly or indirectly. AncestorEvent and AncestorListener are used by some Swing components such as JComboBox, but you will not normally need to use them in an application.

Events Generated by AbstractButton

AbstractButton is the superclass of a number of commonly used Swing components, including all of the following:

- ❑   JButton
- ❑   JToggleButton
- ❑   JCheckBox
- ❑   JRadioButton
- ❑   JMenuItem
- ❑   JMenu
- ❑   JRadioButtonMenuItem
- ❑   JCheckBoxMenuItem

Each AbstractButton subclass generates one more of the event types ActionEvent, ChangeEvent, and ItemEvent. However, not every AbstractButton subclass generates each of these three event types, and you should be familiar with which type to use with the component(s) that you're working with.

Each instance of `AbstractButton` maintains a number of different properties, and the state can be modified through user input, such as clicking on the button, or can be modified programmatically. The properties are:

- **Pressed**
  When `true`, indicates that a button press is in progress

- **Armed**
  When `true`, indicates that releasing the mouse button will cause the button to be activated

- **Enabled**
  Indicates whether or not the button's state can change

- **Rollover**
  Set to `true` when the "rollover" behavior is enabled for the button. For example, this allows the button to display one icon when the mouse is over its display area and another one when the mouse is not over the display area

- **Selected**
  Used by most of the subclasses, such as `JRadioButton` and `JCheckBox`, which have an on/off state associated with them

To better understand what the `pressed` and `armed` properties represent, compile and run the following code:

```java
import java.awt.*;
import java.awt.event.*;
import javax.swing.*;
import javax.swing.event.*;

public class ButtonState extends JFrame {

  protected JLabel armedLabel;
  protected JLabel pressedLabel;
  protected Container pane;

  public static void main(String[] args) {
    ButtonState bs = new ButtonState();
    bs.setDefaultCloseOperation(JFrame.EXIT_ON_CLOSE);
    bs.setSize(400, 300);
    bs.setVisible(true);
  }

  public ButtonState() {
    pane = getContentPane();
    pane.setLayout(new BorderLayout());
    JPanel panel = new JPanel();
    panel.setLayout(new GridLayout(2, 2, 10, 5));
    JLabel label = new JLabel("Armed:");
    panel.add(label);
    armedLabel = new JLabel("");
    panel.add(armedLabel);
    label = new JLabel("Pressed:");
    panel.add(label);
    pressedLabel = new JLabel("");
    panel.add(pressedLabel);
```

```
      pane.add(panel, BorderLayout.CENTER);
      panel = new JPanel();
      panel.setLayout(new FlowLayout());
      JButton button = new JButton("Test Me");
      button.addChangeListener(new ChangeListener() {
        public void stateChanged(ChangeEvent event) {
          JButton btn = (JButton)(event.getSource());
          ButtonModel bm = btn.getModel();
          armedLabel.setText(bm.isArmed() ?
              "true" : "false");
          pressedLabel.setText(bm.isPressed() ?
              "true" : "false");
        }
      }
      );
      button.addActionListener(new ActionListener() {
        public void actionPerformed(ActionEvent event) {
          JOptionPane.showMessageDialog(pane,
              "You activated the button");
        }
      }
      );
      panel.add(button);
      pane.add(panel, BorderLayout.SOUTH);
    }

  }
```

This application creates a frame that includes a JButton, and creates a ChangeListener and ActionListener for the button. Whenever the button's state changes, its properties are retrieved and displayed in the frame (see screenshot below), and when the button is activated, a message dialog appears. The term "activated" has been chosen to avoid confusing a button press with the button's pressed property, and as we'll see shortly, defining what's meant by a "button press" isn't quite as simple as it might seem:

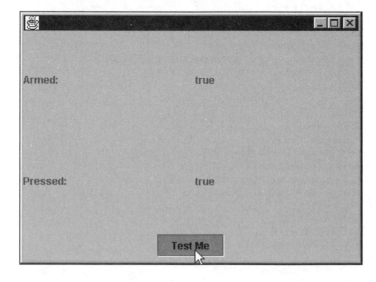

When you run this application and click on the JButton, a message dialog appears. However, to understand the properties that are maintained by an AbstractButton, run the application and try these two variations:

- ❑ Move the cursor over the JButton and press down on the mouse button, but do not release it. Move the cursor so that it's no longer over the JButton and then release the mouse button.

- ❑ Move the cursor over the JButton and press down on the mouse button, but do not release it. Move the cursor so that it's no longer over the JButton, then move it back over the button and release the mouse button.

These scenarios should provide you with some insight into the mechanics of a button press, and particularly the pressed and armed properties.

First, notice that when you pressed down on the mouse button, the JButton's appearance changed, as shown above. At that time, the JButton's pressed and armed properties changed to true. However, when you move the cursor so that it's no longer over the JButton, as illustrated below, the armed property changes to false, while pressed remains true. This is because the pressed property indicates that a button press operation is in progress, while the armed property indicates that button will be activated if the mouse is released. If you release the mouse button when the cursor is no longer over the JButton, then the message dialog does not appear because the JButton will not be activated.

However, if you move the cursor back over the JButton as described in the second scenario and release the mouse button, the message dialog does appear:

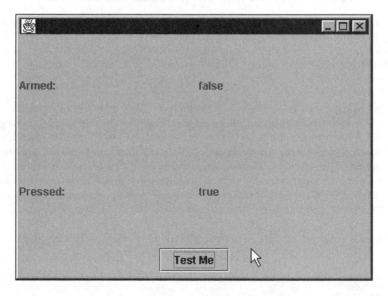

While a button press appears to be a very simple operation, it actually involves four state changes to the JButton instance:

- ❑ Set its armed property to true when the mouse button is pressed
- ❑ Set the pressed property to true when the mouse button is pressed
- ❑ Set the pressed property to false when the mouse button is released
- ❑ Set the armed property to false when the mouse button is released

This examination of how button presses are handled illustrates an important point: that you should choose carefully when deciding what type of listener to add to a component. In the sample code that was used here, we added both a `ChangeListener` and an `ActionListener` to a `JButton`. While both can provide notification of changes to the object's state, `ChangeEvent` is often not an appropriate choice. In this case, four state changes will occur for each button press, causing each `ChangeListener` to be notified four times. If the logic to display the message dialog had been placed in the `stateChanged()` method instead of `actionPerformed()`, the dialog would incorrectly be displayed four times.

ActionEvent and ActionListener

An instance of `ActionEvent` is created and sent to all registered listeners when a button is activated. The `getActionCommand()` method returns the "command string", which is normally the label assigned to the button that generated the event. The `ActionListener` interface defines a single method that is called for each listener registered with a button that is activated:

ActionListener Method Called	ID Value in ActionEvent	Component State Change that Triggers Event
actionPerformed()	ACTION_PERFORMED	Button was pressed/selected

ItemSelectable, ItemEvent, and ItemListener

The `JComboBox`, `JList`, and `AbstractButton` classes are very different from one another, but they do have something in common: they allow the user to select one or more items from a group of items. These components formalize the commonality by implementing the `ItemSelectable` interface. This interface defines methods for adding and removing `ItemEvent` listeners, as well as a method for obtaining a list of the items selected by the component.

`ItemEvent` is published by an `ItemSelectable` component when the item's state changes. Most `AbstractButton` subclasses have an on/off (or selected/deselected) state that can be toggled by selecting that item repeatedly (for example, a `JToggleButton` or `JCheckBox`). In some cases, the state can also be toggled by selecting a different item (for example, a `JRadioButton` that's part of a group of radio buttons). When the state of one of these buttons is modified, an instance of `ItemEvent` is sent to its listeners to notify them of the state change. To determine the state of the item when it publishes an event, the `ItemEvent` class defines a `getStateChange()` method that returns an integer value. This value can be compared to one of two constants (`SELECTED` and `DESELECTED`) that are defined in `ItemEvent`.

For example, the following code displays a message dialog that describes the state of a `JCheckBox` whenever it changes:

```
import java.awt.*;
import java.awt.event.*;
import javax.swing.*;

public class ShowState extends JFrame {

  protected Container pane;

  public static void main(String[] args) {
    ShowState ss = new ShowState();
```

```
        ss.setDefaultCloseOperation(JFrame.EXIT_ON_CLOSE);
        ss.setSize(400, 300);
        ss.setVisible(true);
    }

    public ShowState() {
      pane = getContentPane();
      pane.setLayout(new FlowLayout());
      JCheckBox cb = new JCheckBox("Show my state");
      cb.addItemListener(new ItemListener() {
        public void itemStateChanged(ItemEvent event) {
          int stateValue = event.getStateChange();
          String state = ((stateValue == ItemEvent.SELECTED) ?
              "selected" : "deselected");
          JOptionPane.showMessageDialog(pane,
              "CheckBox is " + state);
        }
      }
      );
      pane.add(cb);
    }

}
```

The `ItemListener` interface defines a single method that is called for each listener registered with a button that is activated:

ItemListener Method Called	ID Value in ItemEvent	Component State Change that Triggers Event
itemStateChanged()	ITEM_STATE_CHANGED	Item selected or deselected

AbstractButton Behavior

Most of the `AbstractButton` subclasses generate both an `ItemEvent` and an `ActionEvent` when the button is pressed, and you could register as either an `ItemListener` or an `ActionListener` to be notified of a button press. However, for those classes that support a selected/deselected state, you'll usually want to know what the new state value is when the button is pressed. `ItemEvent` provides you with that information through its `getStateChange()` method, while `ActionEvent` does not. Of course, you can still determine the object's state by querying it directly instead of obtaining it from the event, but this is not the preferred approach.

For example, compare the following code to the previous implementation. In this case, we created an `ActionListener` instead of an `ItemListener`, and queried the `JCheckBox` directly since its state information was not available through the `ActionEvent` object. Besides being less efficient, this approach makes the event handler code more tightly coupled to the component that generated the event. To avoid these problems, you should use an `ItemListener` when you need to know what the state of an item is when it changes:

```
import java.awt.*;
import java.awt.event.*;
import javax.swing.*;
```

```
public class ActionState extends JFrame {

  protected Container pane;

  public static void main(String[] args) {
    ActionState as = new ActionState();
    as.setDefaultCloseOperation(JFrame.EXIT_ON_CLOSE);
    as.setSize(400, 300);
    as.setVisible(true);
  }

  public ActionState() {
    pane = getContentPane();
    pane.setLayout(new FlowLayout());
    JCheckBox cb = new JCheckBox("Show my state");
    cb.addActionListener(new ActionListener() {
      public void actionPerformed(ActionEvent event) {
        AbstractButton ab = (AbstractButton)(event.getSource());
        String state = (ab.isSelected() ?
            "selected" : "deselected");
        JOptionPane.showMessageDialog(pane,
            "CheckBox is " + state);
      }
    }
    );
    pane.add(cb);
  }

}
```

The ButtonGroup class allows you to identify a set of related AbstractButton instances, and ensures that only one of those instances can ever be selected at any given time. JRadioButtons are most commonly used for this purpose, but you can use any of the AbstractButton subclasses that maintain a selection state. If you click on a button that's part of a group while a different button in the group is selected, then two ItemEvent notifications are sent. The "old" button that was selected sends one, indicating that it is no longer selected, while a second event is sent by the "new" button that was clicked on, indicating that it is now selected.

For example, suppose that you create two JRadioButtons labeled First and Second, add them to a ButtonGroup, and display them both, with neither one selected. If you click on First, it generates both an ActionEvent and a single ItemEvent. After that, clicking on Second causes it to generate one ActionEvent and one ItemEvent, and First generates an ItemEvent to indicate that it is no longer selected. In other words, an ItemEvent is sent both when a button is selected and when it's deselected. This applies whether the button selection change is triggered interactively (for example, by clicking on it) or programmatically (using setSelected()).

To better illustrate this point, compile and run the following code:

```
import java.awt.*;
import java.awt.event.*;
import javax.swing.*;
```

```
public class TwoRadioButtons extends JFrame {

  public static void main(String[] args) {
    TwoRadioButtons trb = new TwoRadioButtons();
    trb.setDefaultCloseOperation(JFrame.EXIT_ON_CLOSE);
    trb.setSize(400, 300);
    trb.setVisible(true);
  }

  public TwoRadioButtons() {
    ButtonGroup group = new ButtonGroup();
    Container pane = getContentPane();
    pane.setLayout(new FlowLayout());
    JRadioButton jrb = new JRadioButton("First");
    group.add(jrb);
    pane.add(jrb);
    registerListeners(jrb, "First");
    jrb = new JRadioButton("Second");
    group.add(jrb);
    pane.add(jrb);
    registerListeners(jrb, "Second");
  }

  protected void registerListeners(JRadioButton jrb, String name) {
    jrb.setName(name);
    jrb.addActionListener(new ActionListener() {
      public void actionPerformed(ActionEvent event) {
        Component comp = (Component)(event.getSource());
        System.out.println("Action performed by " + comp.getName());
      }
    }
    );
    jrb.addItemListener(new ItemListener() {
      public void itemStateChanged(ItemEvent event) {
        Component comp = (Component)(event.getSource());
        System.out.println("Item state changed for " + comp.getName() +
            " to " + (event.getStateChange() == ItemEvent.SELECTED ?
            "selected" : "deselected"));
      }
    }
    );
  }

}
```

This code creates a pair of JRadioButton instances, adds them to a ButtonGroup, and sends a message to the standard output when either one generates an ActionEvent or ItemEvent. When you run this application, it displays a frame with neither button selected, and clicking on the first button generates the following output:

Item state changed for First to selected
Action performed by First

If you then click on the second button, you'll see the following output:

Item state changed for First to deselected
Item state changed for Second to selected
Action performed for Second

Finally, if you click on the second button again despite the fact that it's already selected, you'll see the following:

Item state changed for Second to selected
Action performed for Second

In this last case, the notification related to the item's state change is incorrect and seems to represent a bug in JRadioButton, since a notification was sent despite the fact that the button's state did not actually change. To prevent this problem from affecting your application, you should not assume that an item's state has indeed changed when you receive a notification to that effect. Instead, you should inspect the flag that's provided with the ItemEvent through the getStateChange() method, which currently always provides an accurate indicator of the component's state.

JButton

In general, the behavior previously described is applicable to each of the subclasses of AbstractButton. Unlike the other subclasses, however, JButton does not maintain state and does not publish ItemEvents. To receive notification that a JButton has been pressed, you should register as an ActionListener, since the actionPerformed() method is called whenever the button is activated.

Events Generated by JMenuItem

JMenuItem is a direct subclass of AbstractButton, and has three direct subclasses of its own:

- JMenu
- JCheckBoxMenuItem
- JRadioButtonMenuItem

JMenuItem and its subclasses are used for building menus for Java applications, and they define additional events that can be generated when the classes are used. To build a menu, you create an instance of JMenuBar, add instances of JMenu to it, and add instances of JMenuItem or one of its subclasses to each JMenu. An example of this is shown in the code below:

```
import java.awt.event.*;
import javax.swing.*;

public class MenuSample extends JFrame {

  public static void main(String[] args) {
    MenuSample ms = new MenuSample();
    ms.setDefaultCloseOperation(JFrame.EXIT_ON_CLOSE);
    ms.setSize(400, 300);
    ms.setVisible(true);
  }


  public MenuSample() {
```

```java
    JMenuBar menuBar = new JMenuBar();
    setJMenuBar(menuBar);

    ActionListener actionListener = new ActionListener() {
      public void actionPerformed(ActionEvent event) {
        JOptionPane.showMessageDialog(MenuSample.this, "Menu item '" +
            event.getActionCommand() + "' was activated",
            "Menu Item Activated", JOptionPane.INFORMATION_MESSAGE);
      }
    };

    ItemListener itemListener = new ItemListener() {
      public void itemStateChanged(ItemEvent event) {
        AbstractButton btn = (AbstractButton)(event.getSource());
        JOptionPane.showMessageDialog(MenuSample.this, "A state changed " +
            "occurred for menu item '" + btn.getText() + "'",
            "Menu Item State Changed", JOptionPane.INFORMATION_MESSAGE);
      }
    };

    JMenu menu = new JMenu("First Menu");
    JMenuItem item = new JMenuItem("Menu Item");
    item.addActionListener(actionListener);
    menu.add(item);
    JCheckBoxMenuItem checkItem = new JCheckBoxMenuItem("Check box");
    checkItem.addItemListener(itemListener);
    menu.add(checkItem);

    JMenu subMenu = new JMenu("Submenu");
    JMenuItem subitem1 = new JMenuItem("Submenu item 1");
    subitem1.addActionListener(actionListener);
    subMenu.add(subitem1);
    JMenuItem subitem2 = new JMenuItem("Submenu item 2");
    subitem2.addActionListener(actionListener);
    subMenu.add(subitem2);
    menu.add(subMenu);
    menuBar.add(menu);

    JMenu secondMenu = new JMenu("Second Menu");
    JRadioButtonMenuItem radio1 =
            new JRadioButtonMenuItem("Radio Button 1");
    radio1.addItemListener(itemListener);
    JRadioButtonMenuItem radio2 =
            new JRadioButtonMenuItem("Radio Button 2");
    radio2.addItemListener(itemListener);
    ButtonGroup group = new ButtonGroup();
    group.add(radio1);
    group.add(radio2);
    secondMenu.add(radio1);
    secondMenu.add(radio2);
    menuBar.add(secondMenu);
  }

}
```

This code creates a menu containing the various types of menu item components and adds either an ActionListener or an ItemListener to each one, depending upon which is appropriate. When one of the items is activated, a dialog appears and displays a message indicating which menu item was pressed as shown below:

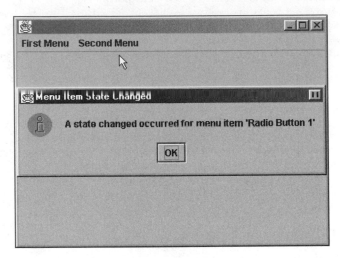

MenuDragMouseEvent and MenuDragMouseListener

MenuDragMouseEvent is a subclass of MouseEvent, and is used to notify listeners of "drag" events that occur within JMenuItem instances. In addition to the functionality that it inherits from MouseEvent, MenuDragMouseEvent also provides a getPath() method that provides the list of menu elements in the hierarchy that generated the event. The first element in this list is typically a JMenuBar, while the last is the JMenuItem element that generated the event.

Menu behavior is handled automatically, so you'll typically not need to use MenuDragMouseListener, but you can do so if you need to be aware of drag events that occur on JMenuItem instances. The MenuDragMouseListener interface defines the following methods:

MenuDragMouseListener Method Called	ID Value in MenuDragMouseEvent (from MouseEvent)	Component State Change that Triggers Event
menuDragMouseDragged()	MOUSE_DRAGGED	Cursor moved
menuDragMouseEntered()	MOUSE_ENTERED	Cursor entered item
menuDragMouseExited()	MOUSE_EXITED	Cursor exited item
menuDragMouseReleased()	MOUSE_RELEASED	Mouse button released

The following code sends messages to standard output when menu drag events occur, and can be used to examine the behavior of menu components with respect to the drag events they generate:

```
import java.awt.Component;
import javax.swing.*;
```

```
import javax.swing.event.*;

public class MenuDragTest extends JFrame {

  public static void main(String[] args) {
    MenuDragTest mdt = new MenuDragTest();
    mdt.setDefaultCloseOperation(JFrame.EXIT_ON_CLOSE);
    mdt.setSize(400, 300);
    mdt.setVisible(true);
  }

  public MenuDragTest() {
    JMenuBar menuBar = new JMenuBar();
    JMenu menu = new JMenu("This is the menu");
    menuBar.add(menu);
    JMenuItem menuItem = new JMenuItem("First item");
    addListener(menuItem);
    menu.add(menuItem);
    menuItem = new JMenuItem("Second item");
    addListener(menuItem);
    menu.add(menuItem);
    setJMenuBar(menuBar);
  }

  protected void addListener(JMenuItem item) {
    item.addMenuDragMouseListener(new MenuDragMouseListener() {
      public void menuDragMouseDragged(MenuDragMouseEvent event) {
        JMenuItem source = (JMenuItem)(event.getSource());

        Component display = source.getComponent();
        System.out.println("Dragged onto " + source.getText());
      }
      public void menuDragMouseEntered(MenuDragMouseEvent event) {
        JMenuItem source = (JMenuItem)(event.getSource());
        Component display = source.getComponent();
        System.out.println("Entered " + source.getText());
      }
      public void menuDragMouseExited(MenuDragMouseEvent event) {
        JMenuItem source = (JMenuItem)(event.getSource());
        Component display = source.getComponent();
        System.out.println("Exited " + source.getText());
      }
      public void menuDragMouseReleased(MenuDragMouseEvent event) {
        JMenuItem source = (JMenuItem)(event.getSource());
        Component display = source.getComponent();
        System.out.println("Released in " + source.getText());
      }
    }
    );
  }
}
```

MenuKeyEvent and MenuKeyListener

Just as `MenuMouseDragEvent` is a menu-specific event that notifies listeners of mouse drag operations, `MenuKeyEvent` provides notification of key events for `JMenuItem` instances. Like its mouse drag equivalent, `MenuKeyEvent` provides an array of menu elements that represent the hierarchy containing the element that generated the event. `MenuKeyListener` defines the following three methods:

MenuKeyListener Method Called	ID Value in MenuKeyEvent (from KeyEvent)	Component State Change that Triggers Event
menuKeyPressed()	KEY_PRESSED	Keyboard key was pressed
menuKeyReleased()	KEY_RELEASED	Keyboard key was released
menuKeyTyped()	KEY_TYPED	Character or characters generated from key(s) pressed

You will rarely find it necessary to use `MenuKeyListener`, since menu behavior is handled for you automatically, including accelerator keys. When you define an accelerator key for a menu item, you can simply use the key to activate the item, and the events generated will be identical to those generated when the mouse is used to activate the menu item. In other words, you do not need to create code to detect and handle accelerator keys because that logic is already provided.

Events Generated by JMenu

`JMenu` is somewhat different from the other `AbstractButton` subclasses, partly because it is not a component that's used on its own. Like the `Container` class and its subclasses, a `JMenu` is used to hold other components, and these are typically other menu components. `JMenu` is also unusual in that unlike the other `JMenuItem` subclasses, it does not generate `ActionEvents`. In any case, there's very rarely any need to add any type of listener to a `JMenu`, since its normal function is to act as a container for other menu objects, and not to initiate operations within your application.

MenuEvent and MenuListener

A `MenuEvent` is generated when a `JMenu` is selected or deselected. `MenuEvent` is a subclass of `EventObject`, but does not provide any additional functionality. Although the `MenuListener` interface defines three methods, only two of them are currently used: `menuSelected()` and `menuDeselected()`.

The following table lists the methods defined by `MenuListener`. Note that there are no values for the ID, because `MenuEvent` does not subclass `AWTEvent`, and does not support an identifier value:

MenuListener Method Called	ID Value in MenuEvent	Component State Change that Triggers Event
menuCanceled()	N/A	N/A
menuDeselected()	N/A	Menu was deselected/deactivated
menuSelected()	N/A	Menu was selected/activated

Events Generated by JTextComponent

The `javax.swing.text.JTextComponent` class is the superclass of text components like `JTextField` and `JTextArea`. These components provide a "caret", which is a visual indicator of where within the text component any inserted text will appear, and is usually represented by a blinking vertical bar. `JTextComponent` generates events that allow you to receive notification of changes to the caret's position or to changes in the text selection.

CaretEvent and CaretListener

`CaretEvent` is a subclass of `EventObject`, and provides two methods: `getDot()`, which identifies the caret's position within the text component, and `getMark()`, which identifies the starting point of a selection block. Note that the starting point value may be equal to, greater than, or less than the caret position. If it's equal to the caret position, then no text is selected. If it's greater than the caret position, this indicates that the user began the selection block and then selected characters to the left of the selection starting point.

For example, the screenshot below illustrates a selection block that started after the letter "e" and ended before the letter "c". Creating this selection would result in a `CaretEvent` being generated that returns a value of 2 when `getDot()` is called, and a value of 5 from `getMark()`:

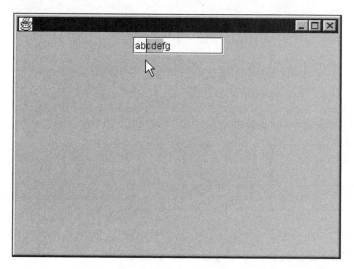

Similarly, if the starting point value is less than the caret position, then the selection was made in a left-to-right manner. To observe this behavior, compile and run the following program, enter some text in the `JTextField`, and select a portion of the text. When you do so, a dialog box appears that displays the values stored in the `CaretEvent` related to the caret position and selection end location:

```
import java.awt.*;
import javax.swing.*;
import javax.swing.event.*;

public class CaretTest extends JFrame {

    protected Container pane;
```

```
public static void main(String[] args) {
  CaretTest ct = new CaretTest();
  ct.setDefaultCloseOperation(JFrame.EXIT_ON_CLOSE);
  ct.setSize(400, 300);
  ct.setVisible(true);
}

public CaretTest() {
  pane = getContentPane();
  pane.setLayout(new FlowLayout());
  JTextField jtf = new JTextField(10);
  pane.add(jtf);
  jtf.addCaretListener(new CaretListener() {
    public void caretUpdate(CaretEvent event) {
      int dot = event.getDot();
      int mark = event.getMark();
      if (dot != mark) {
        JOptionPane.showMessageDialog(pane,
          "Caret location = " + dot +
          ", selection end = " + mark);
      }
    }
  }
  );
}

}
```

The CaretListener interface defines a single method that's called whenever either the caret's position or the selected text changes. Note that because CaretEvent is a subclass of EventObject and not AWTEvent, it does not support an ID value:

CaretListener Method Called	ID Value in CaretEvent	Component State Change that Triggers Event
caretUpdate()	N/A	Caret position or selection text changed

Events Generated by JTextField

In addition to the event types that it inherits, JTextField can generate an ActionEvent to all registered instances of ActionListener whenever the *Enter* key is pressed. This is provided so that you can easily detect when a user presses the *Enter* key, which often is used to indicate that the value entered in the field should be processed in some way.

Events Generated by JEditorPane

JEditorPane is a subclass of JTextComponent that allows you to display different types of text. For example, while JTextField and JTextArea display only plain text, JEditorPane can display Rich Text Format (RTF) and HTML documents as well as plain text.

HyperlinkEvent and HyperlinkListener

HyperlinkEvent instances are generated when some action takes place relative to a hyperlink embedded within a JEditorPane. Specifically, events are generated when the cursor enters and exits the link's display area, as well as when the link is activated, usually by clicking on it.

Three pieces of information are available from a HyperlinkEvent: the type of event that it represents (cursor entry, cursor exit, or activation), an instance of java.net.URL, and a string description of the link.

Although HyperlinkEvent is a subclass of EventObject and does not inherit an ID field from AWTEvent, it provides a similar indication of the type of event (entry, exit, or activation) that it represents. The getEventType() method returns a reference to an instance of an inner class defined within HyperlinkEvent called EventType, and that reference will be to one of three static instances of the EventType object. For example, to determine whether a HyperlinkEvent represents an activation event, you can code something like the following:

```
public void hyperlinkUpdate(HyperlinkEvent event) {
  if (event.getEventType() == HyperlinkEvent.EventType.ACTIVATED) {
    System.out.println("Link was activated");
  }
}
```

In addition to providing the getEventType() method, HyperlinkEvent also provides two other methods. The getURL() method returns an instance of java.net.URL representing the URL that the hyperlink is associated with, and getDescription(), which returns a text description of the link.

The HyperlinkListener interface defines a single method that is called when one of three types of event occurs:

HyperlinkListener Method Called	HyperlinkLister.EventType Instance Referenced	Component State Change that Triggers Event
hyperlinkUpdate()	ACTIVATED	Hyperlink was activated
hyperlinkUpdate()	ENTERED	Cursor moved over link
hyperlinkUpdate()	EXITED	Cursor moved off the link

A common use for the cursor entry and exit notifications is to trigger a change in the cursor type, while an activation event could be used to display the HTML page stored at the specified URL. The code below provides an example of how you might use JEditorPane and the HyperlinkEvent notifications that it generates:

```
import java.awt.*;
import javax.swing.*;
import javax.swing.event.*;

public class SampleTest extends JFrame {

  protected Container pane;
  protected JEditorPane editorPane;
```

```
public static void main(String[] args) {
  SampleTest st = new SampleTest();
  st.setDefaultCloseOperation(JFrame.EXIT_ON_CLOSE);
  st.setSize(400, 300);
  st.setVisible(true);
  try {Thread.sleep(60000);} catch (Exception e) {};
}

public SampleTest() {
  pane = getContentPane();
  pane.setLayout(new GridLayout(1, 1, 0, 0));
  editorPane = new JEditorPane("text/html",
    "Click here to display the JavaSoft web site <p>" +
    "<A HREF=http://www.javasoft.com/>JavaSoft</A>");
  editorPane.setEditable(false);
  editorPane.addHyperlinkListener(new SampleLinkListener());
  pane.add(editorPane);
}

class SampleLinkListener implements HyperlinkListener {

  protected Cursor oldCursor;

  public void hyperlinkUpdate(HyperlinkEvent event) {
    HyperlinkEvent.EventType type = event.getEventType();
    if (type == HyperlinkEvent.EventType.ENTERED) {
      oldCursor = getCursor();
      editorPane.setCursor(Cursor.getPredefinedCursor(
        Cursor.HAND_CURSOR));
    }
    else if (type == HyperlinkEvent.EventType.EXITED) {
      editorPane.setCursor(oldCursor);
    }
    else if (type == HyperlinkEvent.EventType.ACTIVATED) {
      java.net.URL linkURL = event.getURL();
      try {
        editorPane.setPage(linkURL);
      } catch (java.io.IOException ioe) {
        System.out.println("Error occurred:" + ioe);
      }
    }
  }
}
}
```

This code creates a `JEditorPane` that contains text with an embedded hyperlink. It then creates a `HyperlinkListener`, registers it with the pane, and displays the pane in a frame. When mouse movement is detected over the hyperlink, the current cursor type is saved and the cursor is changed to a "hand" icon. A mouse click on the hyperlink will cause the page that the link represents to be displayed, and the cursor will be restored to its original state when it eventually exits the area of the screen occupied by the hyperlink.

Events Generated by Document Implementations

As part of Swing's **Model/View/Controller (MVC)** architecture, the data is displayed in a text component like JTextField, JTextArea, and JEditorPane, and it is separated from the component itself. The text component provides a **view** of the data, while an implementation of the javax.swing.text.Document interface maintains the **model** (the data itself). Document only provides support for plain text with no character attributes (in other words, all characters on a line have the same font, color, etc.), but the StyledDocument interface provides support for assigning attributes on a per-character basis.

Each instance of JTextComponent and its subclasses has a Document implementation associated with it that maintains the data displayed in the component. For example, JTextField and JTextArea use an instance of javax.swing.text.PlainDocument by default, although you can specify your own Document implementation when you create instances of these text components.

DocumentEvent and DocumentListener

Instances of DocumentEvent are generated when some type of change occurs to the document, usually due to user input. For example, when the user enters text in a JTextField or JTextArea, or deletes text from one of these components, then a DocumentEvent is published by the Document implementation associated with the component. The source of most events is a visual component, but DocumentEvent is unusual in that its source is a Document instead of the visual text component that displays the document.

DocumentEvent defines a number of useful capabilities, including the getDocument() method that returns a reference to the event source, and getType(), which identifies the nature of the event (for example, insertion of text, deletion of text, etc.). In addition, it provides the getLength() and getOffset() methods, which identify the number of characters affected by the change, and the offset into the document's text where the change occurred. Finally, for changes to styled text, the getChange() method allows you to obtain information on changes to a particular element or "piece" of a document.

The DocumentListener interface defines three methods, all three of which are used for styled text. However, only the insertion and removal methods are called for PlainDocument instances. In either case, the getType() method returns an instance of the EventType inner class defined within DocumentEvent.

DocumentListener Method Called	Documentevent.Eventtype Instance Referenced	Component State Change that Triggers Event
changedUpdate()	CHANGE	Styled text changed
insertUpdate()	INSERT	Text inserted into document
removeUpdate()	REMOVE	Text deleted from document

The following code illustrates how to use DocumentEvent and DocumentListener with an instance of JTextField. In this case, the interface creates a text field and a button, and the button is only enabled as long as the text field is not empty:

```
import java.awt.*;
import java.awt.event.*;
import javax.swing.*;
import javax.swing.event.*;
import javax.swing.text.*;
```

```java
public class DocumentSample extends JFrame {

  protected JButton exitButton;
  protected Document document;

  public static void main(String[] args) {
    DocumentSample ds = new DocumentSample();
    ds.setDefaultCloseOperation(JFrame.EXIT_ON_CLOSE);
    ds.setSize(400, 300);
    ds.setVisible(true);
  }

  public DocumentSample() {
    Container pane = getContentPane();
    pane.setLayout(new BorderLayout());
    JTextField textField = new JTextField(10);
    pane.add(textField, BorderLayout.NORTH);
    exitButton = new JButton("Exit Sample Application");
    exitButton.addActionListener(new ActionListener() {
      public void actionPerformed(ActionEvent event) {
        System.exit(0);
      }
    }
    );
    JPanel panel = new JPanel();
    panel.add(exitButton);
    pane.add(panel, BorderLayout.SOUTH);
    // The following line returns an instance of PlainDocument
    document = textField.getDocument();
    document.addDocumentListener(new DocumentListener() {

      public void changedUpdate(DocumentEvent event) {};

      public void insertUpdate(DocumentEvent event) {
        exitButton.setEnabled(document.getLength() != 0);
      }

      public void removeUpdate(DocumentEvent event) {
        exitButton.setEnabled(document.getLength() != 0);
      }
    }
    );
    exitButton.setEnabled(document.getLength() != 0);
  }

}
```

This program works by creating a DocumentListener and registering it with a text component. Each time a modification is made to the component (that is, text is inserted or deleted), the DocumentListener examines the length of the text in the text component. The application's exit button is disabled if the length of the text is zero and is enabled if the length is greater than zero.

Input Validation

Applications commonly need to validate or restrict input as it's being generated. For example, you might wish to create a text field that only allows numeric characters to be entered, or you may want to limit the number of characters that can be entered into the field. It may appear that you can implement these features using document events, but that is not the preferred method.

To perform input validation, you should create a subclass of PlainDocument and override the insertString() method to implement the desired behavior. For example, the NumericDocument class shown below allows only numeric digits (0-9) to be entered, and allows the user to specify how many digits are allowed. If an attempt is made to enter a non-digit character in the field, an audible "beep" is generated, and the text is not added:

```java
import java.awt.Toolkit;
import javax.swing.text.*;

public class NumericDocument extends PlainDocument {

  protected int maxDigits = -1;

  protected static Toolkit toolkit = Toolkit.getDefaultToolkit();

  public NumericDocument(int digits) {
    super();
    maxDigits = digits;
  }

  public NumericDocument() {
    this(-1);
  }

  public int getMaxDigits() {
    return maxDigits;
  }

  public void insertString(int offset, String text, AttributeSet attributes)
      throws BadLocationException {
    int count = text.length();
    for (int i = 0; i < count; i++) {
      if (!(Character.isDigit(text.charAt(i)))) {
        toolkit.beep();
        return;
      }
    }
    if ((maxDigits > 0) && ((getLength() + count) > maxDigits)) {
      toolkit.beep();
      return;
    }
    super.insertString(offset, text, attributes);
  }

}
```

To use this `NumericDocument` class, you can create an instance of it and pass that instance to the `JTextComponent` subclass when it's created, or you can override the `createDefaultModel()` in the class you're using it with. For example, the following class extends `JTextField` and overrides its `createDefaultModel()` method to return an instance of `NumericDocument` instead of `Document`:

```
import javax.swing.JTextField;
import javax.swing.text.Document;

public class NumericTextField extends JTextField {

    public NumericTextField(String text, int columns) {
        super(text, columns);
    }

    protected Document createDefaultModel() {
        return new NumericDocument(getColumns());
    }

}
```

UndoableEditEvent and UndoableEditListener

Even the most primitive text editors usually have **undo** and **redo** capabilities that allow you to reverse the effects of changes that you've made to text you're editing. For example, if you delete a block of text and then decide that you want it restored to the document, the undo operation normally provides you with that capability. After performing an undo operation, if you decide that you really did want the text deleted, the redo function causes the text to be deleted again.

Swing provides this capability for text components by generating instances of `UndoableEditEvent`. These events are generated for `Document` instances whenever the user makes a change that can be undone. There are three simple steps that you should take to implement undo/redo capabilities:

❑ Create an instance of `javax.swing.undo.UndoManager`, which is used to maintain information on how to undo and redo edits.

❑ Create user interface elements (usually menu items) that allow the user to request undo and redo operations. These requests are delegated to the `UndoManager`, which then performs the appropriate operation.

❑ Register with the text component's `Document` as an `UndoableEditListener`. When an `UndoableEditEvent` is received, you should add its edit information to the `UndoManager` so that it can undo or redo the edit if requested.

The `UndoableEditListener` interface defines a single method that is called whenever an edit is performed that can be undone and redone. Note that `UndoableEditEvent` is a subclass of `EventObject`, and does not include an `ID` value.

UndoableEditListener Method Called	ID Value in UndoableEditEvent	Component State Change that Triggers Event
undoableEditHappened()	N/A	Edit occurred that can be undone and redone

The following code creates a user interface with a single text field, along with Undo and Redo menu items. It also creates an UndoableEditListener that sends the edit information along to the UndoManager when an UndoableEditEvent is received. When an undo or redo request is received from the user interface via a menu item selection, the request is delegated to the UndoManager, which modifies the text field appropriately. After each undo or redo operation, the menu items are enabled or disabled based on which operations the UndoManager indicates that it is capable of performing:

```java
import java.awt.*;
import java.awt.event.*;
import javax.swing.*;
import javax.swing.event.*;
import javax.swing.text.*;
import javax.swing.undo.*;

public class UndoTest extends JFrame {

  protected Container pane;
  protected UndoAction undoAction = new UndoAction();
  protected RedoAction redoAction = new RedoAction();
  protected UndoManager undoManager = new UndoManager();

  public static void main(String[] args) {
    UndoTest ut = new UndoTest();
    ut.setDefaultCloseOperation(JFrame.EXIT_ON_CLOSE);
    ut.setSize(400, 300);
    ut.setVisible(true);
  }

  public UndoTest() {
    JMenuBar jmb = new JMenuBar();
    setJMenuBar(jmb);
    JMenu jm = new JMenu("Edit");
    jmb.add(jm);
    jm.add(undoAction);
    jm.add(redoAction);

    JTextField textField = new JTextField(10);
    createUndoListeners(textField.getDocument());
    pane = getContentPane();
    pane.setLayout(new FlowLayout());
    pane.add(textField);

    undoAction.refreshUndoState();
    redoAction.refreshRedoState();
  }

  protected void createUndoListeners(Document document) {
    document.addUndoableEditListener(new UndoableEditListener() {
      public void undoableEditHappened(UndoableEditEvent uee) {
        undoManager.addEdit(uee.getEdit());
        undoAction.refreshUndoState();
        redoAction.refreshRedoState();
      }
    }
    );
  }
```

```java
class UndoAction extends AbstractAction {

  public UndoAction() {
    super("Undo");
  }

  public void actionPerformed(ActionEvent event) {
    try {
      undoManager.undo();
    } catch (CannotUndoException cue) {
      JOptionPane.showMessageDialog(pane, "Unable to undo: " + cue);
    }
    refreshUndoState();
    redoAction.refreshRedoState();
  }

  protected void refreshUndoState() {
    if (undoManager.canUndo()) {
      setEnabled(true);
      putValue(Action.NAME, undoManager.getUndoPresentationName());
    }
    else {
      setEnabled(false);
      putValue(Action.NAME, "Undo");
    }
  }

}

class RedoAction extends AbstractAction {

  public RedoAction() {
    super("Redo");
  }

  public void actionPerformed(ActionEvent event) {
    try {
      undoManager.redo();
    } catch (CannotRedoException cre) {
      JOptionPane.showMessageDialog(pane, "Unable to redo: " + cre);
    }
    refreshRedoState();
    undoAction.refreshUndoState();
  }

  protected void refreshRedoState() {
    if (undoManager.canRedo()) {
      setEnabled(true);
      putValue(Action.NAME, undoManager.getRedoPresentationName());
    } else {
      setEnabled(false);
      putValue(Action.NAME, "Redo");
    }
  }

}

}
```

Events Generated by JList

The JList component provides a visual representation of a group of items, and allows you to select one or more of the items in the list. Information on which items in the list are selected is stored in an implementation of ListSelectionModel, although this is usually transparent when using JList instances. The list can be programmed to allow only a single item to be selected, a single range of items, or multiple ranges of items (in other words, any arbitrary groups) to be selected. This setting is modified by calling the setSelectionMode() method, which is passed one of these three constant values defined in ListSelectionModel: MULTIPLE_INTERVAL_SELECTION, SINGLE_INTERVAL_SELECTION, or SINGLE_SELECTION.

ListSelectionEvent and ListSelectionListener

The ListSelectionModel interface allows listeners to be notified when changes are made to the selections maintained by the model. These listeners must implement the ListSelectionInterface and will receive notification of any changes that occur to the selections.

When a change is made to the selection list, each listener's valueChanged() method is called twice: once while the selection is being changed, and again after the change is complete. If you create code that performs some operation when the selection changes, you'll typically only want it to execute once for each change. Therefore, you need some way to distinguish between the first ("change in progress") call and the second ("change complete") one. Fortunately, the ListSelectionEvent class provides a getValueIsAdjusting() method that returns a boolean value of true for the first message, and false for the second one.

While the ListSelectionEvent does not identify which specific items were selected or deselected, it does provide you with a range that includes both. The getFirstIndex() method returns an integer value that identifies the first row in the list that was either selected or deselected, while getLastIndex() returns the value of the last row for which the selection state changed.

Most of the time when a selection event occurs, your application is only interested in finding out which row or rows have been selected, but this information is not provided in the event object. Instead, you must query the JList instance using either getSelectedIndices() or getSelectedValues(). The getSelectedIndices() method returns an array of index values identifying which rows are selected, while getSelectedValues() returns an array containing the values stored in those rows.

JList also provides the getSelectedIndex() and getSelectedValue() methods as a convenience for cases where you only allow a single item to be selected, or only want to retrieve the index or value of the first row that's selected.

ListSelectionListener defines a single method that's called whenever a change occurs to its selections. ListSelectionEvent is a subclass of EventObject, and does not contain an ID value.

ListSelectionListener Method Called	ID Value in ListSelectionEvent	Component State Change that Triggers Event
valueChanged()	N/A	One or more items were selected or deselected

Events Generated by ListModel Implementations

Just as the items selected within a JList are maintained by a ListSelectionModel, the data displayed in the JList is stored in a ListModel implementation. The DefaultListModel is used by default to maintain data in a JList, and it's often possible to use a JList without interacting with the ListModel at all. However, it's sometimes useful to define your own model, and you should be aware of the events that are supported by ListModel.

ListDataEvent and ListDataListener

ListDataEvent objects are sent to listeners of a ListModel whenever data is added to, removed from, or modified in the model. ListDataEvent provides a getType() method that indicates which of these occurred and returns an integer equal to one of three constants defined in ListDataEvent: CONTENTS_CHANGED, INTERVAL_ADDED, or INTERVAL_REMOVED. In addition, the event object provides getIndex0() and getIndex1() methods that indicate the beginning and ending index values of the affected data.

The ListDataListener interface defines a method for each of the three types of changes, as shown below.

ListDataListener Method Called	ListDataEvent Constant Returned from getType()	Component State Change that Triggers Event
contentsChanged()	CONTENTS_CHANGED	List data was modified
intervalAdded()	INTERVAL_ADDED	Data added to model
intervalRemoved()	INTERVAL_REMOVED	Data deleted from model

Events Generated by JComboBox

The JComboBox is a combination of a drop-down list of items and a display/edit area that can be used to enter a value that is not in the list. When an item is selected or the *Enter* key is pressed when typing in the editable area, an ActionEvent is generated. In addition, if the item selected is not the same one that had previously been selected, two ItemEvent messages are generated. One message is sent for the previously selected item with an ID of ItemEvent.DESELECTED, and another for the newly selected item with an ID of ItemEvent.SELECTED. In both cases, the ItemEvent instance's getItem() method returns a reference to the object stored in the JComboBox that is associated with the event.

Events Generated by JTable

Swing's JTable does not generate any events directly, but uses a number of support interfaces that do. Specifically, these are the CellEditor, TableModel, TableColumnModel, and ListSelectionModel. JTable is covered in more detail in Chapter 6, and in general, it's not necessary for you to register as a listener of events generated by the support classes. However, it may be helpful to do so in some cases, so they're discussed briefly here.

CellEditorListener

The CellEditor interface defines the set of methods that must be implemented for a class to support editing of a cell, and JTable uses the TableCellEditor interface, which extends CellEditor and defines an additional table-specific method. Two of the methods defined in CellEditor are cancelCellEditing() and stopCellEditing(), and listeners can register to receive notification when these methods are called. Editing is stopped, for example, when the user presses *Enter* or the *Tab* key, while the *Esc* (*Escape*) key causes editing to be canceled.

When a cell editor's cancelCellEditing() method is called, any changes made to the cell's value are discarded, and the value is restored to its original state. The stopCellEditing() is similar to cancelCellEditing(), but allows changes that have been made to the cell's value to be saved. Unlike cancelCellEditing(), a call to stopCellEditing() is considered a conditional request, and the editor may choose to ignore it. If the request will be ignored, stopCellEditing() should return a boolean value of false, while it should return true if editing was stopped. For example, if a cell is used to represent a date value and the user has only partially entered a valid date, the cell editor might decline to stop the editing by returning a value of false to the caller.

A class can be notified when the editing of a cell is stopped or canceled by adding itself as a listener to a CellEditor. It must implement the CellEditorListener, which defines two methods: one that's called when editing is canceled, and another that's called when editing is stopped. Both methods are passed an instance of ChangeEvent, which contains no state information, and there is no CellEditorEvent associated with the CellEditorListener interface:

CellEditorListener Method Called	ID Value	Component State Change that Triggers Event
editingCanceled()	N/A	Editing was canceled
editingStopped()	N/A	Editing was stopped

TableModelEvent and TableModelListener

The TableModel interface defines a set of methods that are used to provide data to a JTable instance. The JTable component is discussed in more detail in Chapter 6, but some of the items returned by a TableModel are:

- ❑ The number of rows and columns in the table
- ❑ The value of a given table cell
- ❑ Whether or not a given cell should be editable
- ❑ The header to display over each column
- ❑ The type (class) of data stored in each column

TableModelEvent instances are sent to listeners to notify them of changes to the model data. Usually the only listener is an instance of JTable, since it needs to be notified of changes to the underlying data that it displays. It's rarely necessary for you to subscribe to events generated by a TableModel, but if you wish to be notified of changes, you can create a class that implements TableModelListener and register an instance of that class with the TableModel. For example, you might create a graphing component that uses charts to display the data in a TableModel at the same time that the data is displayed in a JTable.

TableModelEvent provides a getType() method that identifies the type of change that occurred, as well as methods that identify the rows and column that were affected by the change. TableModelListener implements a single tableChanged() method that's called whenever data is inserted, updated, or modified in the associated model:

TableModelListener Method Called	TableModelEvent Constant Returned from getType()	Component State Change that Triggers Event
tableChanged()	INSERT	Table data was inserted
tableChanged()	UPDATE	Table data was updated
tableChanged()	DELETE	Table data was deleted

TableColumnModelEvent and TableColumnModelListener

Information on the columns within a JTable is maintained in an instance of a class that implements the TableColumnModel interface, and the TableColumnModelListener allows you to receive notifications of changes to the column model. TableColumnModelListener is unusual in that it defines five different methods, and in two cases, the type of event object passed to the method is different from the type sent to the other methods.

As with TableModelListener, the only registered listener of column events is usually a JTable, and it's not usually necessary or appropriate for your application to handle these events, but it is sometimes useful to do so. For example, you might create a user interface that contains two instances of JTable and wish to allow each table to receive notification when the width of one of the other table's columns changes.

The following table lists the method name, the class of event object passed to the method, and a description of how the event is triggered:

TableColumnModel Listener Method Called	EventObject Parameter Class	Component State Change that Triggers Event
columnAdded()	TableColumnModelEvent	Column added to table
columnMarginChanged()	ChangeEvent	Column's margin changed
columnMoved()	TableColumnModelEvent	Column was moved to a different position within table
columnRemoved()	TableColumnModelEvent	Column removed from the table
ColumnSelection Changed()	ListSelectionEvent	Column selection has changed

Events Generated by JTree

Swing's JTree component is used primarily to provide a user interface mechanism for displaying and navigating hierarchical data. For example, a tree is commonly used when displaying file system objects such as files and directories. The JTree class itself is defined in the javax.swing package, but most of its support classes are defined in the javax.swing.tree subpackage.

Each item in a JTree is called a **node**, and a node can have **child** nodes that are below it in the hierarchy. In that case, the upper node is called a **parent** node, and Swing's JTree implementation provides the ability to navigate from a parent to its children and vice versa. In addition, a node can be either **expanded**, which means that its children are visible, or **collapsed**, in which case the children are not visible. Each child has an **index value** with respect to its parent, with the first child added to the parent assigned an index of 0, the second an index of 1, etc.

The top-level node in a JTree is referred to as the root node, and all other nodes in the tree are direct or indirect ancestors of that node. The TreePath class is used to represent a navigation path from the root node to some node in the tree.

TreeExpansionEvent and TreeExpansionListener

You can receive notification that a node within a JTree has been expanded or collapsed by defining a class that implements TreeExpansionListener and calling the JTree's addTreeExpansionListener() method. Then, when a node in the tree is collapsed or expanded, the appropriate listener method is called and passed an instance of TreeExpansionEvent. The TreeExpansionEvent class is a subclass of EventObject, and provides a single method called getPath() that returns an instance of TreePath, and this path represents the node that was collapsed or expanded.

The TreeExpansionListener interface defines two methods: one that's called when a node is expanded, and the other is called when a node is collapsed:

TreeExpansionListener Method Called	ID Value	Component State Change that Triggers Event
treeCollapsed()	N/A	Tree node was collapsed
treeExpanded()	N/A	Tree node was expanded

TreeWillExpandEvent and TreeWillExpandListener

The TreeWillExpandListener interface is very similar to TreeExpansionListener, but there is an important difference. As its name implies, the methods associated with TreeWillExpandListener are called before the expansion or collapse occurs, and listeners have the option of preventing (or **vetoing**) the change. More often, TreeWillExpandListener is used to provide applications with a form of **lazy instantiation**, which can improve an application's performance and reduce the amount of memory that it uses. Lazy instantiaton involves waiting until data is actually needed before loading or creating it. In this context, for example, if you create a JTree that displays the contents of a file system, you might wait until a given directory node is about to expand before reading the contents of that directory and creating the child nodes representing the subdirectories and files it contains.

Vetoable events are common when using JavaBeans, but it's not necessary to understand JavaBeans to take advantage of this feature. To prevent the tree node from expanding or collapsing, the method should veto the change by simply throwing an ExpandVetoException.

Like TreeExpansionListener, the TreeWillExpandListener methods are passed instances of TreeExpansionEvent, which provides a method that identifies the path to the affected node. TreeWillExpandListener provides one method that's called for expansions, and another that's called when a node is to be collapsed:

TreeWillExpandListener Method Called	ID Value	Component State Change that Triggers Event
treeWillCollapse()	N/A	Collapse requested for tree node
treeWillExpand()	N/A	Expansion requested for tree node

The screenshot below shows an application that creates a simple tree structure and two check boxes, and then adds a TreeWillExpandListener to the JTree instance:

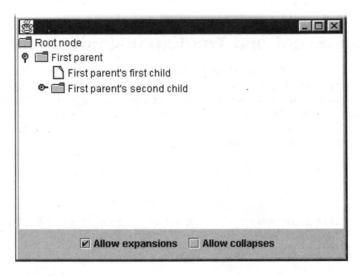

When a request is made to collapse or expand a node, the state of the check box associated with the operation is tested to determine whether it should be allowed. If the check box is checked, the collapse or expansion is allowed, but if not, an ExpandVetoException is thrown. Notice that unlike most exceptions, the ExpandVetoException constructors require you to pass a TreeExpansionEvent instance as a parameter:

```
import java.awt.*;
import java.awt.event.*;
import javax.swing.*;
import javax.swing.event.*;
import javax.swing.tree.*;

public class ExpansionTest extends JFrame {

  JCheckBox allowExpansions;
  JCheckBox allowCollapses;

  public static void main(String[] args) {
    ExpansionTest et = new ExpansionTest();
    et.setDefaultCloseOperation(JFrame.EXIT_ON_CLOSE);
    et.setSize(400, 300);
    et.setVisible(true);
  }
```

```
public ExpansionTest() {
  DefaultMutableTreeNode root, parent, child;
  Container pane = getContentPane();
  pane.setLayout(new BorderLayout());
  allowExpansions = new JCheckBox("Allow expansions");
  allowCollapses = new JCheckBox("Allow collapses");
  JPanel panel = new JPanel();
  panel.add(allowExpansions);
  panel.add(allowCollapses);
  pane.add(panel, BorderLayout.SOUTH);

  root = new DefaultMutableTreeNode("Root node");
  parent = new DefaultMutableTreeNode("First parent");
  root.add(parent);
  child = new DefaultMutableTreeNode("First parent's first child");
  parent.add(child);
  child = new DefaultMutableTreeNode("First parent's second child");
  parent.add(child);
  parent = child;
  child = new DefaultMutableTreeNode("Second child's only child");
  parent.add(child);
  JTree tree = new JTree(root);

  tree.addTreeWillExpandListener(new TreeWillExpandListener() {
    public void treeWillCollapse(TreeExpansionEvent event)
        throws ExpandVetoException {
      if (!(allowCollapses.isSelected()))
        throw new ExpandVetoException(event,
            "Collapses not allowed");
    }

    public void treeWillExpand(TreeExpansionEvent event)
        throws ExpandVetoException {
      if (!(allowExpansions.isSelected()))
        throw new ExpandVetoException(event,
            "Expansions not allowed");
    }
  }
  );

  pane.add(tree, BorderLayout.CENTER);
  }

}
```

TreeSelectionEvent and TreeSelectionListener

The nodes in a JTree can be selected and deselected, and its addTreeSelectionListener() method is used to register a list that is notified when nodes are selected or deselected. TreeSelectionListener defines a single method that's passed a TreeSelectionEvent, and this object contains information on the changes that were made to the tree node selections.

The getPaths() method in TreeSelectionEvent returns an array of TreePath objects that represent the nodes that are selected or deselected. The getPath() method is provided as a convenience for cases where only a single node can be selected or when you only want to access the first node for which the selection status changed.

Since the `TreePath` objects can represent either selected or deselected nodes, `TreeSelectionEvent` provides an `isAddedPath()` method that returns a `boolean` value indicating whether or not the specified `TreePath` was selected (`true`) or deselected (`false`). For example, the following code segment obtains the list of `TreePath` objects for which the selection state changed, loops through each one, and prints a message indicating whether or not it was selected or deselected:

```
public void valueChanged(TreeSelectionEvent event) {
   TreePath[] paths = event.getPaths();
   for (int i = 0; i < paths.length; i++) {
     System.out.println(paths[i] + " was " +
         (event.isAddedPath(paths[i]) ? "selected" : "deselected"));
   }
}
```

Besides the implementation that requires a `TreePath` parameter, `TreeSelectionEvent` provides another `isAddedPath()` method as a convenience that takes no parameters, and returns the selection state of the first path for which the state changed. This is useful when the tree only allows a single node to be selected, or when you only need to determine the selection state of the first changed node:

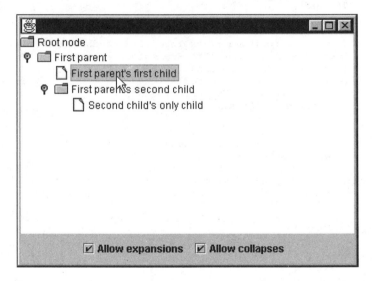

Like other components such as `JList` and `JTable`, the `JTree` allows you to select a range of items that should be selected. For example, suppose that the node labeled First Parent is selected by clicking on it as shown in the screenshot above. To select a range of nodes, you can then hold down the *Shift* key and click on the First Parent's Second Child node. This selects all nodes between the already-selected node and the one that was clicked on (inclusive). In this case, three nodes are selected: First Parent, First Parent's First Child, and First Parent's Second Child, as shown in the next screenshot.

In the context of a `JTree`, the **lead selection path** refers to the path representing the selected node at the highest point in the hierarchy. In this example, the lead selection path represents the First Parent node, since it is the highest selected node in the hierarchy:

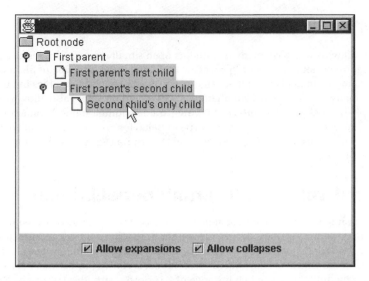

As we've seen, the `TreeSelectionEvent` class provides a list of `TreePath` objects that represent the nodes whose selection states have changed and methods to determine whether or not a node was selected or deselected. In addition, it also allows you to identify the old and new lead selection path. The new one is the lead selection path after the selection changes were made, while the old one was the lead selection path prior to the selection changes having been made. These can be identified by calling the `getNewLeadSelectionPath()` and `getOldLeadSelectionPath()` methods of the `TreeSelectionEvent` object:

`TreeSelectionListener` Method Called	ID Value	Component State Change that Triggers Event
`valueChanged()`	N/A	Tree nodes were selected or deselected

TreeModelEvent and TreeModelListener

Just as `JTable` uses the `TableModel` interface to define the methods for accessing its data, the `JTree` uses `TreeModel` to define the methods for accessing and maintaining the data it displays. The `addTreeModelListener()` method allows an object to register as a subscriber to changes that occur in the tree's data, although this is normally only used by the `JTree` class. However, you can create your own `TreeModelListener` implementations that will be notified whenever such changes occur, in which case a `TreeModelEvent` is passed as a parameter.

The `getTreePath()` method in `TreeModelEvent` identifies the path of the node that generated the event, and the path can represent a node that was inserted, deleted, or modified in some way. To obtain a list of the nodes that are children of the affected node, you can call the `getChildren()` method, which returns an array of objects representing each child node. The `getChildCount()` method identifies the total number of children the affected node has, while `getChildAt()` returns a reference to the node's child at the specified index. Conversely, the `getIndex()` method is passed a reference to a child node and returns its index value relative to the parent.

Events Generated by JInternalFrame

Some applications allow you to have many documents open simultaneously. In this case, "documents" is used in a generic sense to refer not only to word processor files, but also to any type of file that's managed by an application. For example, an application that can display, create, and edit graphics images would probably allow you to have many images opened simultaneously. It would probably also allow you to switch between those images simply by clicking on an **internal frame** ("frame within a frame") containing the document you wish to work with. Applications that support this type of behavior are sometimes called **Multiple Document Interface (MDI)** applications, and Swing provides the JInternalFrame component to allow you to create such applications in Java.

InternalFrameEvent and InternalFrameListener

To receive notification of events related to instances of JInternalFrame, you should use the InternalFrameListener interface. It provides methods that have names and functions that correspond to those in the WindowListener interface. Specifically, you can be notified when a window is opened for the first time, is activated, deactivated, iconified, deiconified, is closing, or has been closed. Also, just as WindowListener methods are passed an instance of WindowEvent, the InternalFrameListener methods are passed references to InternalFrameEvent objects. The names of the methods defined in InternalFrameListener are listed below, but for more detailed information on when each one is called, you should refer to the WindowListener documentation earlier in this chapter:

InternalFrameListener Method Called	ID Value in InternalFrameEvent	Component State Change that Triggers Event
internalFrameActivated()	INTERNAL_FRAME_ACTIVATED	Became active frame
internalFrameClosed()	INTERNAL_FRAME_CLOSED	Frame has been disposed
internalFrameClosing()	INTERNAL_FRAME_CLOSING	Close operation requested
InternalFrame Deactivated()	INTERNAL_FRAME_ DEACTIVATED	No longer the active frame
InternalFrame Deiconified()	INTERNAL_FRAME_ DEICONIFIED	No longer iconified
internalFrameIconified()	INTERNAL_FRAME_ICONIFIED	Frame has been minimized
internalFrameOpened()	INTERNAL_FRAME_OPENED	Made visible for first time

Events Generated by JPopupMenu

Unlike the JMenuItem and its subclasses that are associated with a menu bar, a JPopupMenu can be displayed anywhere on the screen. The appearance of a popup menu is often triggered by a click of the right mouse button, and the operation that's performed by activating one of the popup menu items is often context-dependent. In other words, the specific action taken will depend upon what item (if any) is selected at the time that the popup menu is displayed.

PopupMenuEvent and PopupMenuListener

The PopupMenuEvent class extends EventObject, and does not include any additional functionality. An instance is passed to the methods defined by PopupMenuListener, which are listed below.

Note that as of Java 1.3, the popupMenuCanceled() *method is never called, although this could change in a later release.*

PopupMenuListener Method Called	ID Value	Component State Change that Triggers Event
popupMenuCanceled()	N/A	Not currently used
popupMenuWillBecomeInvisible()	N/A	Menu will become invisible
popupMenuWillBecomeVisible()	N/A	Menu will become visible

Notice that these events are related to the state of the popup menu itself and are not used to provide a notification that a particular menu item was selected. To detect the activation of an item that's part of a popup menu, you must register a listener for that item just as you would for a standard "pull-down" menu. For more information on this subject, refer to the section that describes the events generated by JMenuItem.

The following code provides an example of how to create and display a popup menu, which it does when the user right-clicks on the JTable:

```java
import java.awt.*;
import java.awt.event.*;
import javax.swing.*;
import javax.swing.event.*;
import javax.swing.table.*;

public class PopupTest extends JFrame {

  protected Object[][] values = {{"First", new Integer(1)},
          {"Second", new Integer(2)},
          {"Third", new Integer(3)}};

  public static void main(String[] args) {
    PopupTest pt = new PopupTest();
    pt.setDefaultCloseOperation(JFrame.EXIT_ON_CLOSE);
    pt.setSize(400, 300);
    pt.setVisible(true);
  }

  public PopupTest() {
    Container pane = getContentPane();
    JTable table = new JTable(new MyTableModel());
    table.addMouseListener(new MouseAdapter() {
      public void mousePressed(MouseEvent event) {
        if ((event.getModifiers() & InputEvent.BUTTON3_MASK) != 0) {
          JPopupMenu jpm = new MyPopupMenu();
          jpm.addPopupMenuListener(new PopupMenuListener() {
            public void popupMenuCanceled(PopupMenuEvent event) {
              System.out.println("Menu canceled");
            }
```

```
             public void popupMenuWillBecomeInvisible(PopupMenuEvent event) {
               System.out.println("Menu will become invisible");
             }

             public void popupMenuWillBecomeVisible(PopupMenuEvent event) {
               System.out.println("Menu will become visible");
             }
           });
           jpm.show(event.getComponent(), event.getX(), event.getY());
         }
       }
     }
     );
   pane.setLayout(new FlowLayout());
   pane.add(table);
}

class MyTableModel extends AbstractTableModel {

  public int getRowCount() {
    return values.length;
  }

  public int getColumnCount() {
    return values[0].length;
  }

  public Object getValueAt(int row, int column) {
    return values[row][column];
  }

}

class MyPopupMenu extends JPopupMenu {

  public MyPopupMenu() {
    add("Update");
    add("Insert");
    add("Delete");
  }

}
}
```

The screenshot adjacent shows this program in use:

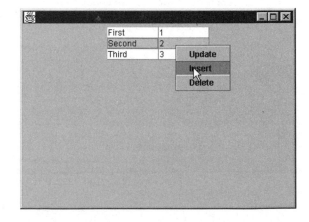

Events Generated by JScrollBar

The JScrollBar is not usually used as a standalone component, but is typically a part of another component such as a JScrollPane. Scroll bars are normally used when an application needs to display some information, but there's too much data to include all of it on the screen at once. In that case, a scroll bar is used to allow the user to select which portion of the data to display. Visually, a scroll bar consists of either a vertical or a horizontal rectangle with arrow buttons at each end and contains a slider (also called a "knob" or "thumb"). The scroll bar is assigned a numeric range, and the slider's position corresponds to a value within that range.

In addition to being assigned a range of values, each scroll bar is assigned a **unit increment** and a **block increment**. The unit increment is used to move the display forward and backward by one unit, although the meaning of 'unit' depends on the type of data displayed. For example, when displaying text, a 'unit' would typically be one line of text. To scroll forward or 'down' by one unit causes the display to change so that the next line in the document would appear and the line that had been at the top of the display would disappear.

The block increment, also called the **page increment**, refers to some number of units that's meaningful in the context of the data being displayed. If text data is displayed and 20 lines of text are visible, the block increment might be set to a value such that a block represents 19 lines. It's customary with text displays to leave one line on the screen, so that in a forward scroll, for example, the line that had been the last line on the screen becomes the first one after the display moves down.

AdjustmentEvent and AdjustmentListener

Although JScrollBar is usually part of some other component, you may find it useful to integrate it into your own custom components and receive notification of any changes that are made to its value. When that's the case, you can create a class that implements AdjustmentListener and that registers itself as a subscriber that should be notified of changes to the scroll bar.

The AdjustmentEvent class extends AWTEvent, and provides a method that indicates the scroll bar's value after it has been changed. It also defines a getType() method that the API documentation suggests should indicate which type of adjustment took place, but due to the design of JScrollBar, the method always returns a value equal to the TRACK constant defined in AdjustmentEvent:

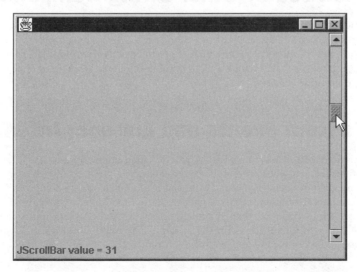

AdjustmentListener defines a single method that's called whenever the scroll bar's knob changes position, and an example of how you can use this to monitor the scroll bar is illustrated above. The code listed below creates a label and a scroll bar, and when the scroll bar's value is adjusted, it is displayed in the label:

```java
import java.awt.*;
import java.awt.event.*;
import javax.swing.*;
import javax.swing.event.*;

public class ScrollBarTest extends JFrame {

    protected JLabel label;

    public static void main(String[] args) {
        ScrollBarTest sbt = new ScrollBarTest();
        sbt.setDefaultCloseOperation(JFrame.EXIT_ON_CLOSE);
        sbt.setSize(400, 300);
        sbt.setVisible(true);
    }

    public ScrollBarTest() {
        Container pane = getContentPane();
        pane.setLayout(new BorderLayout());
        label = new JLabel("JscrollBar value = 0");
        pane.add(label, BorderLayout.SOUTH);
        JScrollBar jsb = new JScrollBar();
        jsb.addAdjustmentListener(new AdjustmentListener() {
            public void adjustmentValueChanged(AdjustmentEvent event) {
                label.setText("JScrollBar value = " + event.getValue());
            }
        }
        );
        pane.add(jsb, BorderLayout.EAST);
    }
}
```

Events Generated by Other Swing Components

Other Swing components generate events, but in many cases, these are ChangeEvent instances. For example, JProgressBar, JSlider, JTabbedPane, and JViewport support the ChangeListener interface for notifying interested parties when their state changes. As mentioned earlier, ChangeEvent is typically used by components that generate a large number of events when used, and the component must be queried directly to determine its state.

Creating Custom Events and Listener Interfaces

In Chapter 2, we created a FontPropertiesPanel that maintained a reference to an implementation of a FontListener interface, and generated an event by calling the fontChanged() method defined in that interface. Generating custom events is a trivial task, and is often desirable when you've created a component with state information that is of interest to external classes. For example, in the case of FontPropertiesPanel, it generated an event whenever one of the font property selections (name, size, or style) changed. We'll now modify FontPropertiesPanel to make it more consistent with other classes that generate events, and examine the issues related to doing so.

Designing Event Objects

When creating an event object, you should define a class that's a subclass of `EventObject` or one of its subclasses. Refer to the information earlier in this chapter on `AWTEvent`, `ComponentEvent`, and the other types defined in Java to determine whether it's appropriate to subclass one of these. In general, if your component needs the functionality provided by one of these classes, you should subclass the appropriate one instead of implementing it yourself. For example, to create an event object for the `FontPropertiesPanel` that records the type of font property changed, you might decide to use the `ID` value that's provided by `AWTEvent`. In addition, since the class that generates these events is a subclass of `Component`, it may be desirable to inherit the `getComponent()` method defined in `ComponentEvent`.

Once you've determined which class your event object should extend, you should consider what information to provide to the listeners. In the case of `FontPropertiesPanel`, we'll add a field that maintains a reference to an instance of `java.awt.Font` that was constructed using the newly selected font properties. Finally, to make the information available to the listeners, you must define accessor methods that return references to the properties encapsulated within the event object, which in this case means creating a `getNewFont()` method. The resulting event object is shown below:

```java
import java.awt.Component;
import java.awt.Font;
import java.awt.event.ComponentEvent;

public class FontEvent extends ComponentEvent {

  protected Font newFont;

  public final static int FONT_FIRST = 0;
  public final static int FONT_NAME_CHANGED = 0;
  public final static int FONT_SIZE_CHANGED = 1;
  public final static int FONT_STYLE_CHANGED = 2;
  public final static int FONT_LAST = 2;

  public FontEvent(Component source, int id, Font font) {
    super(source, id);
    newFont = font;
  }

  public Font getNewFont() {
    return newFont;
  }

}
```

The `FONT_FIRST` and `FONT_LAST` constants do not actually represent event types, but instead identify the bounds of the valid event identifiers. Although not strictly required, it's customary to include constants like these so that an event identifier can be validated easily.

Designing Listeners

To design the listener interface, you should consider the number of different types of event that can occur, and depending upon the number of different types, you will want to choose between one of two approaches. You'll either create a separate method in the listener interface for each type or define a single method and require the listeners to distinguish between the types based on the event object's identifier value.

To contrast these two approaches, let's examine two existing listener interfaces. For example, WindowListener defines a method for each of seven different types of event, while TableModelListener defines a single method that is called for three different types of events (inserts, updates, and deletes).

Creating a separate method for each type of event can make implementation of a listener interface more tedious, and may be frustrating if the programmer is only interested in one type of event. If your listener interface does declare multiple methods, you may choose to simplify its implementation by creating an adapter similar to the ones supplied with the Java core classes.

In any case, using a single method for multiple types of events makes your code less readable and the handler method less cohesive. Therefore, you should avoid this approach when there are different event types that are of interest to listeners.

However, the most important factor to be considered when determining how many methods to define in a listener interface is how the different event types will be handled by listeners. For example, there are four different components in FontPropertiesPanel that can be modified:

- ❑ The name list
- ❑ The size combo box selection
- ❑ Check boxes for boldstyles
- ❑ Check boxes for italic styles

While a case could be made for creating a separate method for each of these, or at least one for each font property (name, size, and style), it's probably not useful to do so. That's because regardless of which property changes, the change is likely to be handled by listeners in the same way – by updating the font of some component or components. In other words, it's not useful to identify which property changed, because the resulting behavior is the same in any case.

When you do create a listener, it should extend the EventListener interface defined in the java.util package. EventListener does not define any methods, but is a tag interface, and is necessary if you plan to use the EventListenerList class as described in the next section.

Given all these guidelines, the following listener can be created for use with the FontPropertiesPanel to notify objects when a change has been made to the font properties:

```
public interface FontListener extends java.util.EventListener {

  public void fontChanged(FontEvent event);

}
```

Maintaining Listener Lists

In the previous implementation of FontPropertiesPanel in Chapter 2, it maintained a reference to a single listener, and notified that listener of changes to the font properties. However, it's often desirable to allow multiple listeners to be registered to receive events, and Swing provides an easy way to do so with the EventListenerList class included in the javax.swing.event package.

Any class that generates events should include addXXXListener() and removeXXXListener() methods for each type of event that it can generate. In the case of FontPropertiesPanel, we'll define addFontListener() and removeFontListener() methods that add to and remove from a listener to the list, respectively. Inside those methods, we'll add the listener to the EventListenerList instance by calling its add() and remove() methods, as in the following code segment:

```
public void addFontListener(FontListener listener) {
    listenerList.add(FontListener.class, listener);
}

public void removeFontListener(FontListener listener) {
    listenerList.remove(FontListener.class, listener);
}
```

Note that in both the add() and remove() methods, the EventListenerList requires you to specify the Class instance associated with the listener interface. This is needed because a single instance of EventListenerList is able to maintain references to different types of listeners, which makes it necessary to identify the listener type for each entry.

For example, if FontPropertiesPanel also generated action events, then it would be possible for the listener list to contain references to ActionListener implementations and FontListener implementations. By recording the listener interface type for each registered listener, it's possible to later identify which listeners should be notified for a given event type, as you'll see below.

Publishing Events

The final step needed to complete FontPropertiesPanel is to create the code that notifies registered listeners when the font changes. All that's necessary is to create an instance of the event object, loop through the list of registered listeners, and call the appropriate method for each one.

```
protected void fireFontChangedEvent(FontEvent event) {
    Object[] list = listenerList.getListenerList();
    for (int i = 0; i < list.length; i += 2) {
        Class listenerClass = (Class)(list[i]);
        if (listenerClass == FontListener.class) {
            FontListener listener = (FontListener)(list[i + 1]);
            listener.fontChanged(event);
        }
    }
}
```

There are two important points to be made concerning this code. First, notice that the list returned from getListenerList() contains pairs of entries, which is why a value of 2 is added to the iteration variable instead of the traditional value of 1. Each pair of entries represents the two parameters that were passed to addFontListener() method: a reference to the listener object, and a Class instance that identifies the listener interface that the object implements.

The other important point to be aware of concerning this code is that it examines the Class associated with each entry to ensure that the entry really represents a FontListener. That verification isn't necessary in this case because only one type of listener is supported by FontPropertiesPanel. However, it's a good idea to include the test anyway to avoid invalid casts if you later add support for another event type to the component and record its listeners in the same list.

The final version of `FontPropertiesPanel` that implements the improved event broadcasting is shown below:

```java
import java.awt.*;
import java.awt.event.*;
import javax.swing.*;
import javax.swing.event.*;

public class FontPropertiesPanel extends JPanel {

    protected JList nameList;
    protected JComboBox sizeBox;
    protected JCheckBox boldBox;
    protected JCheckBox italicBox;

    protected EventListenerList listenerList;

    public final static int[] fontSizes = {10, 12, 14, 18, 24, 32, 48, 64};

    public FontPropertiesPanel() {
        super();
        createComponents();
        buildLayout();
        listenerList = new EventListenerList();
    }

    protected void buildLayout() {
        JLabel label;
        GridBagConstraints gbc = new GridBagConstraints();
        GridBagLayout gbl = new GridBagLayout();
        setLayout(gbl);

        gbc.anchor = GridBagConstraints.WEST;
        gbc.insets = new Insets(5, 10, 5, 10);

        gbc.gridx = 0;
        label = new JLabel("Name:", JLabel.LEFT);
        gbl.setConstraints(label, gbc);
        add(label);
        label = new JLabel("Size:", JLabel.LEFT);
        gbl.setConstraints(label, gbc);
        add(label);
        gbl.setConstraints(boldBox, gbc);
        add(boldBox);

        gbc.gridx++;
        nameList.setVisibleRowCount(3);
        JScrollPane jsp = new JScrollPane(nameList);
        gbl.setConstraints(jsp, gbc);
        add(jsp);
        gbl.setConstraints(sizeBox, gbc);
        add(sizeBox);
        gbl.setConstraints(italicBox, gbc);
        add(italicBox);
    }
```

```java
protected void createComponents() {
  GraphicsEnvironment ge =
      GraphicsEnvironment.getLocalGraphicsEnvironment();
  String[] names = ge.getAvailableFontFamilyNames();
  nameList = new JList(names);
  nameList.setSelectedIndex(0);
  nameList.setSelectionMode(ListSelectionModel.SINGLE_SELECTION);
  nameList.addListSelectionListener(new ListSelectionListener() {
    public void valueChanged(ListSelectionEvent event) {
      if (!(event.getValueIsAdjusting())) {
        fireFontNameChangeEvent();
      }
    }
  }
  );
  Integer sizes[] = new Integer[fontSizes.length];
  for (int i = 0; i < sizes.length; i++) {
    sizes[i] = new Integer(fontSizes[i]);
  }
  sizeBox = new JComboBox(sizes);
  sizeBox.addActionListener(new ActionListener() {
    public void actionPerformed(ActionEvent event) {
      fireFontSizeChangeEvent();
    }
  }
  );
  boldBox = new JCheckBox("Bold");
  boldBox.addActionListener(new ActionListener() {
    public void actionPerformed(ActionEvent event) {
      fireFontStyleChangeEvent();
    }
  }
  );
  italicBox = new JCheckBox("Italic");
  italicBox.addActionListener(new ActionListener() {
    public void actionPerformed(ActionEvent event) {
      fireFontStyleChangeEvent();
    }
  }
  );
}


public void addFontListener(FontListener listener) {
  listenerList.add(FontListener.class, listener);
}

public void removeFontListener(FontListener listener) {
  listenerList.remove(FontListener.class, listener);
}

protected void fireFontNameChangeEvent() {
  fireFontChangedEvent(new FontEvent(
      this, FontEvent.FONT_NAME_CHANGED, getSelectedFont()));
}
```

```
   protected void fireFontSizeChangeEvent() {
     fireFontChangedEvent(new FontEvent(
         this, FontEvent.FONT_SIZE_CHANGED, getSelectedFont()));
   }

   protected void fireFontStyleChangeEvent() {
     fireFontChangedEvent(new FontEvent(
         this, FontEvent.FONT_STYLE_CHANGED, getSelectedFont()));
   }

   protected void fireFontChangedEvent(FontEvent event) {
     Object[] list = listenerList.getListenerList();
     for (int i = 0; i < list.length; i += 2) {
       Class listenerClass = (Class)(list[i]);
       if (listenerClass == FontListener.class) {
         FontListener listener = (FontListener)(list[i + 1]);
         listener.fontChanged(event);
       }
     }
   }
```

```
  public Font getSelectedFont() {
     String name = (String)(nameList.getSelectedValue());
     int style = 0;
     style += (boldBox.isSelected() ? Font.BOLD : 0);
     style += (italicBox.isSelected() ? Font.ITALIC : 0);
     int size = ((Integer)(sizeBox.getSelectedItem())).intValue();
     return new Font(name, style, size);
  }

}
```

General Guidelines for Event Handling

When an event is triggered by some user input such as a mouse button click or a key press, the appropriate listeners are usually called from the **event dispatch thread**. The event thread is created for you automatically, and in addition to calling listener methods, it is responsible for **painting** the user interface components. To illustrate this behavior, compile and run the following application:

```
import java.awt.*;
import java.awt.event.*;
import javax.swing.*;

public class EventThreadTest extends JFrame {

  public static void main(String[] args) {
    EventThreadTest ett = new EventThreadTest();
    ett.setDefaultCloseOperation(JFrame.EXIT_ON_CLOSE);
    ett.setSize(400, 300);
    ett.setVisible(true);
  }

  public EventThreadTest() {
```

```
     Container pane = getContentPane();
     pane.setLayout(new FlowLayout());
     JButton button = new JButton("Click Here");
     button.addActionListener(new ActionListener() {
       public void actionPerformed(ActionEvent event) {
         doSomethingThatTakesAWhile();
       }
     }
     );
     pane.add(button);
   }

   protected void doSomethingThatTakesAWhile() {
     try {
       Thread.sleep(10000);
     }
     catch (InterruptedException ie) {};
   }

 }
```

When the button is pressed, the event thread calls the `actionPerformed()` method of the listener registered with the button, and "sleeps" for 10,000 milliseconds (10 seconds). As illustrated below, the button is not repainted in its 'raised' state until that time expires, because the sleeping event thread is responsible for the repaint operation. Although this is a very artificial example, it's quite common to have long-running operations that are initiated from an event handler method. However, since the same thread handles user interface event notifications and screen painting, the repaint operation may be stalled until the completion of a potentially very lengthy event.

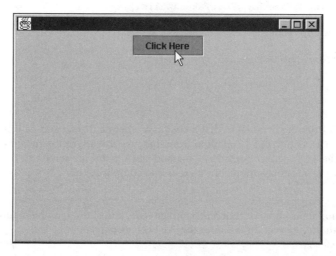

One way to address this is to create a separate thread and perform any operation that may take longer than one or two seconds in that thread, allowing the event thread to perform its other responsibilities, specifically repainting and other event notifications. An example of this is illustrated in the code below:

```
import java.awt.*;
import java.awt.event.*;
import javax.swing.*;
```

```
public class EventThreadTest extends JFrame {

  public static void main(String[] args) {
    EventThreadTest ett = new EventThreadTest();
    ett.setDefaultCloseOperation(JFrame.EXIT_ON_CLOSE);
    ett.setSize(400, 300);
    ett.setVisible(true);
  }

  public EventThreadTest() {
    Container pane = getContentPane();
    pane.setLayout(new FlowLayout());
    JButton button = new JButton("Click Here");
    button.addActionListener(new ActionListener() {
      public void actionPerformed(ActionEvent event) {
        Thread t = new Thread(new Runnable() {
          public void run() {
            doSomethingThatTakesAWhile();
          }
        }
        );
        t.start();
      }
    }
    );
    pane.add(button);
  }

  protected void doSomethingThatTakesAWhile() {
    try {
      Thread.sleep(10000);
    }
    catch (InterruptedException ie) {};
  }

}
```

This approach differs from the first one in that it creates a separate thread and calls the doSomethingThatTakesAWhile() method from that new thread. In the meantime, the event thread is able to return from the actionPerformed() method and repaint the screen or dispatch other events. In many cases, this approach is appropriate, but there is one complication:

> **The Swing components are not inherently thread-safe, and should not be modified from a thread other than the event thread once they've been displayed.**

The reason for this is to prevent the event thread from attempting to modify a component at the same time that some other thread does, which can have negative consequences. The following class provides an example of how this can happen. One button adds data to a JList, while the other removes data from the list. The "add" operation is deliberately slow, and runs in its own thread. The "clear list" operation, however, is run from the event handler thread:

```java
import java.awt.*;
import java.awt.event.*;
import javax.swing.*;
import javax.swing.event.*;

public class UpdateList extends JFrame {

  protected JList sampleList;
  protected DefaultListModel listModel;

  public final static String[] values = {"First", "Second", "Third"};

  public static void main(String[] args) {
    UpdateList ul = new UpdateList();
    ul.setDefaultCloseOperation(JFrame.EXIT_ON_CLOSE);
    ul.setSize(400, 300);
    ul.setVisible(true);
  }

  public UpdateList() {
    Container pane = getContentPane();
    pane.setLayout(new BorderLayout());
    JPanel panel = new JPanel();
    JButton button = new JButton("Populate List");
    button.addActionListener(new ActionListener() {
      public void actionPerformed(ActionEvent event) {
        Thread t = new Thread(new Runnable() {
          public void run() {
            populateListModel();
          }
        }
        );
        t.start();
      }
    }
    );
    panel.add(button);
    button = new JButton("Clear List");
    button.addActionListener(new ActionListener() {
      public void actionPerformed(ActionEvent event) {
        listModel.removeAllElements();
      }
    }
    );
    panel.add(button);
    pane.add(panel, BorderLayout.SOUTH);

    listModel = new DefaultListModel();
    sampleList = new JList(listModel);
    pane.add(sampleList, BorderLayout.CENTER);
  }

  protected void populateListModel() {
    for (int i = 0; i < values.length; i++) {
      //  Make the operation arbitrarily slow
      try {Thread.sleep(5000);} catch (Exception e) {};
      listModel.addElement(values[i]);
    }
  }
}
```

The problem with this approach is that two different threads can modify the JList component simultaneously, and since it's not thread-safe, the object can wind up in an inconsistent state.

The solution to this problem is to allow the event thread to perform both updates to the list, although it's probably not obvious how to do this without introducing the original problem of blocking the repainting of the components. The SwingUtilities class provides two methods that allow you to request that the event thread perform some operation: invokeLater() and invokeAndWait(). Both these methods are static methods that require a single Runnable object be passed to them, and both will cause the event thread to queue a request to execute the object's run() method. However, the invokeLater() is asynchronous, while invokeAndWait() is synchronous. In other words, a call to invokeLater() may return before the Runnable object's run() method is executed, while invokeAndWait() is guaranteed not to return until the run() method has completed.

In this case, we'll modify the populateListModel() method so that the code that populates the button is called from the event thread:

```
protected void populateListModel() {
  for (int i = 0; i < values.length; i++) {
    final Object value = values[i];
    //  Make the operation arbitrarily slow
    try {Thread.sleep(5000);} catch (Exception e) {};
    try {
        SwingUtilities.invokeAndWait(new Runnable() {
          public void run() {
            listModel.addElement(value);
          }
        }
        );
    } catch (Exception e) {};
  }
}
```

With this implementation, the repainting isn't blocked, because the population logic is processed in its own thread. However, it waits for the event thread to perform the modifications to the JList by using the invokeAndWait() method.

Java 1.0 Event Model

Java's approach to event handling changed dramatically when release 1.1 became available. Although you should not use the Java 1.0 event model when writing new code, it's helpful to be somewhat familiar with it in case you must support code that uses the old model. In addition, some older browsers only support the 1.0 event model, so you may need to understand it if you're writing applets.

In Java 1.0, java.awt.Event is the only type of event object, and is used for all types of events: key press and release events, mouse events, focus events, etc. Each specific type of event is identified by an ID value, similar to the one that is still used by java.awt.AWTEvent. When an event is generated, it's sent to the handleEvent() defined in java.awt.Component, and this method delegates processing of the event to a convenience method that provides more type-specific parameters. For example, when the cursor enters a component's display area, the handleEvent() method receives an Event. If it determines that the event is a MOUSE_ENTER event, it calls the component's mouseEnter() method, passing it a reference to the event, and the X and Y coordinates of the cursor obtained from the event object.

Both `handleEvent()` and the type-specific event handler methods like `mouseEnter()` return a `boolean` value, and this value indicates whether the event has been handled or not. If the event was not handled, then it propagates up the containment hierarchy. For example, if an instance of `java.awt.Button` generates an `ACTION_EVENT`, the event is first sent to the `Button` object and processed by its `action()` method. If that method returns `false`, indicating that the event was not handled, the event is next sent to the button's `Container` "parent", if any. This process continues until one of the parent containers handles the event (returns `true`) or until there are no more parent containers to which to pass it. The following code illustrates this behavior by creating a `Frame` that contains a `Panel`, and adding a `Button` instance to the panel, although it generates deprecation warnings when compiled:

```java
import java.awt.*;

public class ButtonTest extends Frame {

  public static void main(String[] args) {
    ButtonTest bt = new ButtonTest();
    bt.setSize(400, 300);
    bt.setVisible(true);
  }

  public ButtonTest() {
    setLayout(new BorderLayout());
    Panel panel = new Panel();
    Button button = new Button("Click Here");
    panel.add(button);
    add(panel);
  }

  public boolean handleEvent(Event event) {
    if (event.id == Event.ACTION_EVENT) {
      System.out.println("This method is called first");
    }
    return super.handleEvent(event);
  }

  public boolean action(Event event, Object source) {
    System.out.println("This one is called second");
    return true;
  }

}
```

When this application is run and the button pressed, the following sequence of events occurs:

❑ The button's `handleEvent()` method is passed an `Event` of type `ACTION_EVENT`, and `handleEvent()` delegates the event processing to the `action()` method.

❑ The `action()` method is defined in `java.awt.Component` and is not overridden in the `Button` subclass, so the `Component` implementation is called, which simply returns a value `false`, indicating that the event was not handled.

❑ Since the event was not handled by the `Button` instance, it is propagated up the containment hierarchy. In this case, it is sent to the parent `Container`'s `handleEvent()` method and the above steps are repeated.

❑ The Container also does not handle the event, so the event is then passed to the container's parent (the ButtonTest instance defined above).

❑ The handleEvent() method in ButtonTest receives the event, prints a message, and then passes the event to the superclass implementation of handleEvent(), which sends the message to action().

❑ The action() method displays a second message and then returns the value true, indicating that it handled the event and that it should not be propagated any further up the containment hierarchy.

Note that in the last step, it wasn't necessary to return true from the action() method, because the ButtonTest class represents the top of the containment hierarchy, and the event could not be propagated further anyway.

This event model created two problems for programmers. First, it becomes necessary to create many subclasses of the components that generate events, such as Button, so that those events can be handled at an appropriate location within the code. Second, many events are processed by components that aren't "interested" in them. Therefore, this architecture provided a model that was not flexible or scalable, and was deprecated in Java 1.1. Although this event model still functions in the current version of Java, it may be eliminated at some time in the future, and should not be used when writing new code.

Summary

In this chapter, we have examined how events are supported in Java and looked at many of the existing listener interfaces and events used with those interfaces. The various AWT and Swing components can generate a large number of possible events so it pays to have a good idea of how they all work, especially as some can be a bit counterintuitive.

We've also seen how it's possible to create your own custom listener types and seen how easily those types can be supported.

The next chapter will look at another important topic when creating Swing-based GUIs: using layout managers.

Professional Java Programmin

5

Using Layout Managers

In Java, the `java.awt.Container` class and its subclasses can be used to display groups of components. For example, you might use a `JPanel` to display a related set of buttons or add components to the content pane of a `JFrame`. **Layout managers** are classes used to control the size and location of each component that's added to a container, and in most cases, a layout manager is also responsible for determining the sizes returned from the container's `getMinimumSize()`, `getPreferredSize()`, and `getMaximumSize()` methods. Layout managers are important because they simplify the task of positioning and sizing components and because they allow you to create flexible user interfaces.

Java provides a number of different layout managers that you should be familiar with, and each one has advantages and disadvantages. Some are easy to use but provide limited flexibility, while others are very flexible but also much more difficult to use. When none of the layout managers provided with Java suits your needs, you can easily create your own, although it's not often necessary to do so if you're familiar with those that are already available.

In this chapter we will see:

❑   How to use layout managers to organize your GUI

❑   The different types of layout manager that you can use and how to use them effectively

❑   How to combine different layout managers within the same GUI

❑   How to build your own custom layout manager

Layout Managers and GUI Construction

To assign a layout manager to a container, you must create an instance of the manager and pass it to the setLayout() method defined in Container. For example, the following code provides an example of how to create an instance of BorderLayout and assign it to a JPanel:

```
JPanel panel = new JPanel();
panel.setLayout(new BorderLayout());
```

The overloaded add() method defined in Container is used to add a Component to a container, which then becomes known as the component's **parent container**. Similarly, the component added is referred to as a **child component** of the container.

Although Container defines a number of different implementations of add(), the two used most often are:

- ❑ add(Component comp)
- ❑ add(Component comp, Object constraints)

In both cases, a reference to the child component is sent to the Container. However, the second implementation also includes a **constraints** parameter that provides information normally used by the layout manager to determine where the component should be placed and/or what its size should be. The specific subclass of Object used for this parameter depends upon what type of layout manager is involved. For example, if you're using a GridBagLayout, the constraints parameter must be an instance of the java.awt.GridBagConstraints class, while other layout managers require you to pass a String value.

Some layout managers do not support constraints and use the order in which components are added to their parent container to determine their positions. When you're using a layout manager that does not accept constraints, you should use the simpler add() method shown above that takes only a single Component parameter. Doing so is equivalent to passing a null value for the constraint parameter, which means that the two lines of code shown below are functionally identical to one another:

```
myContainer.add(someComponent);
```

```
myContainer.add(someComponent, null);
```

On the other hand, using code like that shown above with a layout manager that does support constraints will cause the layout manager to assign some default constraint information to the component. Therefore, unless you're certain that the default information will produce the results you want, you should always explicitly specify a constraint parameter when using a layout manager that supports constraints.

When add() is called, the container adds the component to a list that it maintains and calls the layout manager's addLayoutComponent() method. That method is passed references to the component being added and to the constraints object specified, and this allows the layout manager to save the constraint information and associate it with the component for later use.

When a layout manager's layoutContainer() method is called, it is passed a reference to the container for which components should be arranged. The layout manager obtains the list of child components by calling the container's getComponents() method and sets the size and location for each visible child using `Component` methods such as `setSize()`, `setLocation()`, and `setBounds()`. If the layout manager supports constraints, it will use them to determine each component's size and location, but if it does not, it will arrange the components based on the order in which they occured in the list returned by `getComponents()`.

To determine what a component's size should be, the layout manager usually also considers the container's size and may call each component's `getPreferredSize()`, `getMinimumSize()`, or `getMaximumSize()` methods. However, the layout manager is not required to respect the values returned by those methods, and in some cases, Java's layout managers do ignore them.

Each container has inset values that indicate the number of pixels around the container's edges that are reserved and cannot be used to display child components. Those values are encapsulated by an instance of `java.awt.Insets`, which defines four `int` values, each corresponding to one side of the container: `top`, `left`, `bottom`, and `right`. Those values usually describe the width of the border on the sides of the container, but in some cases, there may be additional space reserved. For example, `JDialog` and `JFrame` both include a title bar along their top edges, and that space is reserved by setting the `top` inset value appropriately.

When a layout manager calculates the amount of space available in a container, it subtracts the container's left and right insets from its width and the top and bottom insets from the height. In addition, when the layout manager arranges the child components, it will position them inside the container's inset area so that none of the components overlay the reserved portion of space around the container's edges.

Java's Layout Managers

It's possible to create your own layout manager class and this chapter describes how to do so, but the Java core classes include a number of layout managers that are flexible enough to meet the needs of most applications. The following list identifies the layout manager classes that are provided with Java, which are listed in what is arguably their order of complexity starting with the least complex and ending with the most complicated one:

- ❑ CardLayout
- ❑ FlowLayout
- ❑ GridLayout
- ❑ BorderLayout
- ❑ GridBagLayout
- ❑ BoxLayout (Java 2)

When you create an instance of a `Container` subclass that's provided with Java (for example, `JPanel`, `JFrame`, `JDialog`, etc.), that object will automatically be assigned a layout manager. The following table lists some of the classes that you might use and identifies the default layout manager type for each one:

Component	Default Layout Manager
JPanel	FlowLayout
JFrame (content pane)	BorderLayout

Table continued on following page

Component	Default Layout Manager
JDialog (content pane)	BorderLayout
JApplet (content pane)	BorderLayout
Box	BoxLayout

This chapter examines the capabilities of the layout managers that are provided with Java, and specifically examines the following characteristics of each one:

❑   How a layout manager instance is constructed.

❑   The constraints that can be specified when adding a child component.

❑   How each child component's size is calculated.

❑   How each child component's position is calculated.

❑   What happens when the container has more or less space than it needs to display its child components. The emphasis here is on what happens when the container has less space than it needs, since that's usually when problems occur.

❑   How the values returned by a container's getMinimumSize(), getPreferredSize(), and getMaximumSize() methods are calculated by the layout manager.

CardLayout

The CardLayout layout manager allows you to add multiple components to a container, and each component is added and displayed in the same location. However, only one of the components is made visible at any given time, and you can specify which one that should be by calling the first(), last(), next(), and previous() methods defined in CardLayout. Those methods refer to the components added to the container, and display the component that was added in the order corresponding to the method name. For example, first() causes the component added first to appear, last() causes the most recently added one to appear, while next() and previous() allow you to iterate through the components in either a forward or backward direction. In addition, the show() method allows you to specify that a particular component should be displayed, regardless of the order in which it was added to the container relative to the other components.

The CardLayout class is arguably the least useful of the layout managers included with Java. Prior to the introduction of Swing, CardLayout was envisioned as a way to create a tabbed user interface, but the JTabbedPane provides a much better mechanism for doing so. However, CardLayout may still be useful in some cases, such as when constructing a Windows-style "wizard" interface that displays a series of panels one at a time.

Constructing a CardLayout

You can specify horizontal and vertical gap values when you create a new instance of CardLayout and these gaps will be placed around the edges of the component displayed in the container. Specifically, the horizontal gap appears on the left and right sides of the component, and the vertical gap is used at the top and bottom of the component to separate it from the edge of the container.

Constraints

When adding components to a container that uses a CardLayout, you should assign a unique name represented by a String value to each component (in other words, no two of the components in the container should be assigned the same name). This allows you to select which component in the container to display by passing that component's name to the show() method. For example, the following code segment creates a frame that uses a CardLayout for its content pane. Three panels (or "tabs") are added to the content pane, each with a different background color and each assigned a unique name. Once the frame is constructed, the displayTab() method is called, passing it the name of the second (green) tab. That method calls CardLayout's show() method, which causes the specified component to be made visible. After this, the next() method is used to cycle through the tabs one at a time:

```java
import java.awt.*;
import javax.swing.*;

public class CardTest extends JFrame {

  protected CardLayout layout;

  public static void main(String[] args) {
    CardTest ct = new CardTest();
    ct.setDefaultCloseOperation(JFrame.EXIT_ON_CLOSE);
    ct.displayTab("Green Tab");
    ct.setSize(400, 300);
    ct.setVisible(true);
    while (true) {
      try {
        Thread.sleep(3000);
      } catch (Exception e) {}
      ;
      ct.cycle();
    }
  }

  public CardTest() {
    JPanel tab;
    Container pane = getContentPane();
    layout = new CardLayout();
    pane.setLayout(layout);
    tab = new JPanel();
    tab.setBackground(Color.red);
    pane.add(tab, "Red Tab");
    tab = new JPanel();
    tab.setBackground(Color.green);
    pane.add(tab, "Green Tab");
    tab = new JPanel();
    tab.setBackground(Color.blue);
    pane.add(tab, "Blue Tab");
  }

  public void cycle() {
    layout.next(this.getContentPane());
  }
```

```
public void displayTab(String name) {
    layout.show(this.getContentPane(), name);
}

}
```

Child Component Sizes

Only a single child component is ever visible when a CardLayout is used, and that component's size is set to the container's available display area. The available display area is defined as the container's dimensions minus its insets and any horizontal and vertical gaps that should be placed around the edges of the child components.

Child Component Locations

The single visible child component always fills the entire available display area of the parent container, so its location is implicitly defined to be the upper-left corner of the parent.

Resizing Behavior

The size of the component displayed is set to the container's available display area. If the container's size increases or decreases, a corresponding change occurs to the size of the displayed component.

Container Size

CardLayout identifies the preferred size of its container as the largest preferred width and largest preferred height of any child component. Similarly, the minimum size is equal to the largest minimum width and height values returned by any of the container's child components. The maximum size is effectively set to infinity, since CardLayout's maximumLayoutSize() method returns Integer.MAX_VALUE for both the maximum width and maximum height, where Integer.MAX_VALUE is a constant that represents the largest possible integer (that is, int or Integer) value.

FlowLayout

The FlowLayout arranges the components in rows from left-to-right and top-to-bottom order based on the order in which they were added to the container, allowing each component to occupy as much or as little space as it needs. This layout manager is useful when you wish to create a collection of adjacent components that are all allowed to be displayed using their default sizes.

Constructing a FlowLayout

When creating a new FlowLayout instance, you can specify the alignment that should be used when positioning the child components. The alignment value should correspond to one of the constants defined in FlowLayout, specifically LEFT, CENTER, or RIGHT. As mentioned previously, FlowLayout arranges components in rows, and the alignment specifies the alignment of the rows. For example, if you create a FlowLayout that's left aligned, the components in each row will appear next to the left edge of the container.

The FlowLayout constructors allow you to specify the horizontal and vertical gaps that should appear between components, and if you use a constructor that does not accept these values, they both default to 5. Note that unlike the gaps used by some other layout managers, the gaps generated by a FlowLayout appear not only between adjacent components, but also between components and the edge of the container.

To construct a FlowLayout that's right aligned and uses a horizontal gap of 10 pixels and vertical gap of 5 pixels between components, you can use the following code:

```
FlowLayout fl = new FlowLayout(FlowLayout.RIGHT, 10, 5);
```

Constraints

FlowLayout does not use any constraints to determine a component's location or size, and you should use the simple add(Component) method when adding components to a FlowLayout-managed container.

Child Component Sizes

Components managed by a FlowLayout are always set to their preferred size (both width and height), regardless of the size of the parent container.

Child Component Locations

Components added to a FlowLayout-managed container are displayed in rows in left-to-right and top-to-bottom order based on when each component was added to the container relative to the others. For example, the first component appears at the top of the container to the left of other components in the row.

A component's specific location depends upon three factors: the alignment value used by the FlowLayout, the size of the component, and the size of the other components that were added to the layout before it. A FlowLayout includes as many components as it can on each row until the width of the row would exceed the size of the container. In the screenshot below, five components have been added to a container that uses a FlowLayout:

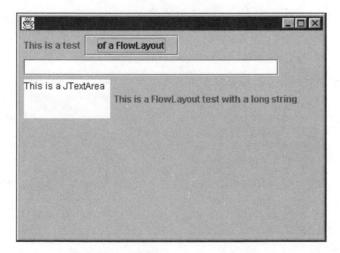

The code that creates this display is as follows:

```java
import java.awt.*;
import javax.swing.*;

public class FlowTest extends JFrame {

  public static void main(String[] args) {
    FlowTest ft = new FlowTest();
    ft.setDefaultCloseOperation(JFrame.EXIT_ON_CLOSE);
    ft.setSize(400, 300);
    ft.setVisible(true);
  }

  public FlowTest() {
    super();
    Container pane = getContentPane();
    pane.setLayout(new FlowLayout(FlowLayout.LEFT));
    pane.add(new JLabel("This is a test"));
    pane.add(new JButton("of a FlowLayout"));
    pane.add(new JTextField(30));
    pane.add(new JTextArea("This is a JTextArea", 3, 10));
    pane.add(new JLabel("This is a FlowLayout test with a long string"));
  }

}
```

In this case, the container is sufficiently wide to allow the first two components to be placed on the first row. However, the third component is placed on the next row by itself, and the fourth and fifth components appear together on another row. The first row appears at the top of the container, and each subsequent row occurs immediately below the previous one, with the height of a row determined by the height of the tallest component in that row. Each component within a row is centered vertically within the row, as shown above.

A component's horizontal position within a row is determined partly by when it was added to the container and is affected by the alignment value used by the FlowLayout. In the screenshot above, the components are left aligned, but below you can see the displays that are generated when the components are right aligned:

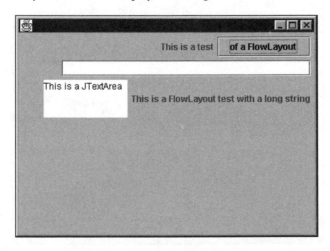

and center aligned:

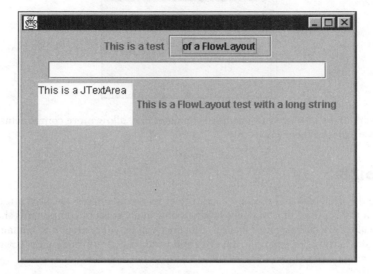

As you can see, the alignment value is used to determine how to distribute extra space that's available when a row's components do not occupy the entire width of the container.

Resizing Behavior

Reducing the width of a container managed by a FlowLayout causes the rows to shrink in size, which may cause some components to be moved to a new or different row. If the width of the frame is reduced further, then portions of the wider components begin to disappear, as shown below:

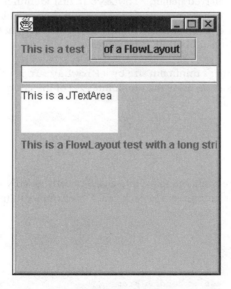

Similarly, if the frame's vertical size is reduced so that there's not enough vertical space to display all rows, some of the components will become partially or completely inaccessible:

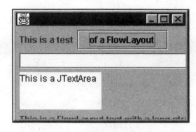

Increasing the width of a FlowLayout-managed container may allow more components to appear on a single row than were placed there previously.

Container Size

When calculating the preferred and minimum size values for a container, FlowLayout can't make any assumptions about the width of the container or about how many rows of components should be created. Instead, the size values are calculated so that the container will be wide enough to contain *all* child components in a single row. For example, the preferred width value returned by a FlowLayout is determined by adding three values:

- ❑ The left and right inset values of the container
- ❑ The amount of space needed to provide horizontal gaps
- ❑ The sum of all child components' preferred widths

In other words, a FlowLayout's preferred width is the amount of horizontal space needed to display all its child components from end-to-end on a single row using their preferred sizes.

To determine the container's preferred height, FlowLayout first identifies the preferred height of the tallest component in the container. The container's preferred height is then calculated as the sum of largest component height, the number of pixels needed to provide vertical gaps at the top and bottom edges of the container, and the container's top and bottom inset values.

The value returned for a container's minimum size by a FlowLayout is calculated in essentially the same way as the preferred size, but is done using the minimum sizes of the components in the container instead of their preferred sizes.

GridLayout

This layout manager divides the available space into a grid of **cells**, evenly allocating the space among all the cells in the grid and placing one component in each cell. For example, in the following code, four buttons are added to a container that uses a GridLayout:

```
import java.awt.*;
import javax.swing.*;

public class GridSizeTest extends JFrame {

  public static void main(String[] args) {
    GridSizeTest gst = new GridSizeTest();
```

```
      gst.setDefaultCloseOperation(JFrame.EXIT_ON_CLOSE);
      gst.pack();               // pack() makes the window the right
      gst.setVisible(true);     // size for all it's components to fit
   }

   public GridSizeTest() {
      Container pane = getContentPane();
      pane.setLayout(new GridLayout(2, 2));
      JButton button = new JButton("First");
      pane.add(button);
      button = new JButton("Second with a very long name");
      pane.add(button);
      button = new JButton("Hi");
      button.setFont(new Font("Courier", Font.PLAIN, 36));
      pane.add(button);
      button = new JButton("There");
      pane.add(button);
   }

}
```

When this code is compiled and executed, it produces a display like the one shown below. Notice that all of the buttons are allocated the same amount of space, even though one button's label is wider than the others and another has a label that's much taller than the rest:

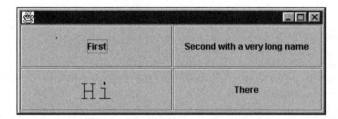

As this example illustrates, GridLayout is useful when some rectangular portion of your interface contains adjacent components that should all be assigned the same size and when the amount of space between those components is consistent. For instance, you might use a GridLayout to create a panel that contains a row of buttons that are all the same size and which have the same amount of space between one another.

Constructing a GridLayout

When you create an instance of GridLayout, you normally will specify the number of rows and columns that you want it to provide, and you may choose to specify the amount of horizontal and vertical space that should appear between adjacent components. However, you can choose to set any of these values after construction using the setRows(), setColumns(), setHgap(), and setVgap() methods. An example of creating a GridLayout and assigning it to a container is shown in the code below. This application parses the command line parameters to determine how many rows and columns should be available, creates 20 JButton instances, and adds each button to the container:

```
import java.awt.*;
import javax.swing.*;
```

```
public class GridTest extends JFrame {

  public static void main(String[] args) {
    if (args.length < 2) {
      System.out.println("You must enter a row count and a column count");
      return;
    }
    int rows = Integer.parseInt(args[0]);
    int cols = Integer.parseInt(args[1]);
    GridTest gt = new GridTest(rows, cols);
    gt.setDefaultCloseOperation(JFrame.EXIT_ON_CLOSE);
    gt.pack();
    gt.setVisible(true);
  }

  public GridTest(int rows, int cols) {
    Container pane = getContentPane();
    pane.setLayout(new GridLayout(rows, cols));
    for (int i = 0; i < 20; i++) {
      JButton button = new JButton(Integer.toString(i + 1));
      pane.add(button);
    }
  }
}
```

When you create a GridLayout, you can specify a value of 0 for either the row or column count, but not both. If you set the number of rows to 0, GridLayout creates as many rows as it needs to display all the components using the specified number of columns. For example, the screenshot below illustrates what will be displayed when 0 is specified for the number of rows and 3 for the number of columns:

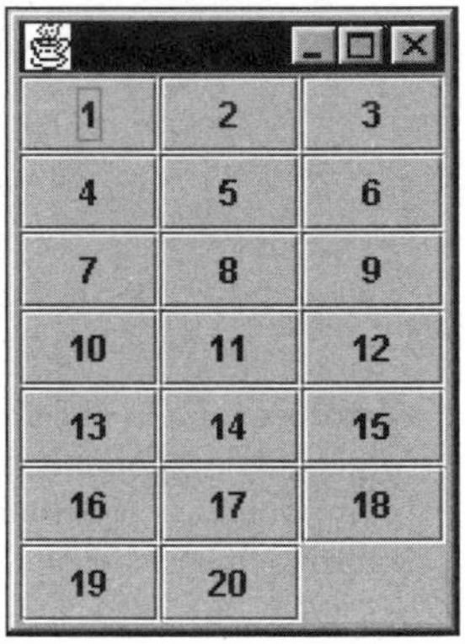

Similarly, if you set the number of columns to 0, the layout manager creates as many columns as it needs to display the child components using the specified number of rows. In the next screenshot, the row count was set to 3 and the column count to 0:

It's important to understand that the row and column counts you specify are considered *suggestions*, and the `GridLayout` may not actually create the number you request. In most cases it will, but there are some exceptions. For example, if you specify a non-zero value for both the row and column count, the column count is effectively ignored, and the layout manager creates as many columns as it needs to, using the requested number of rows.

> **In other words, specifying both a row and column count produces the same result as specifying 0 for the column count.**

When a value of 3 is specified for the number of rows and 100 for the number of columns using the `GridTest` class, the result is the same as shown above for 3 rows and 0 columns.

This behavior might seem undesirable, but there is a reason for it. Specifically, it allows the layout manager to handle cases where the number of components in the container is greater than the product of the row count by the column count. For example, if you specify a row count of 2 and a column count of 2 but then proceed to add six components to the container, `GridLayout` simply adds another column to the grid so that it can display all six components.

As you can see, the number of rows and columns created by a `GridLayout` is not necessarily equal to the number that you request. In fact, the number actually created is calculated with a simple formula that uses the number of child components in the container (which we'll call **childComponentCount**), the requested number of rows (**requestedRows**), and the requested number of columns (**requestedColumns**). If the requested number of rows is non-zero, the `GridLayout` determines the number of rows and columns using the following equations:

```
actualRows = requestedRows
actualColumns = (childComponentCount + requestedRows - 1) / requestedRows
```

Note that this formula can lead to a situation where more rows are created than are needed to display all the components. When that happens, an empty space will appear at the bottom of the container that represents the unused rows. Since that's not usually the desired behavior, you should be aware of this possibility when deciding how many rows to request when creating a `GridLayout`. On the other hand, if the requested number of rows (**requestedRows**) is zero, then `GridLayout` uses the following equations instead of the ones shown above:

```
actualColumns = requestedColumns
actualRows = (childComponentCount + requestedColumns - 1) / requestedColumns
```

In most cases, these equations result in the `GridLayout` creating the number of rows and columns you specified, but as we've seen, that's not always the case.

Constraints

`GridLayout` does not use any constraints to determine a component's location or size, and you should use the `add(Component)` method when adding components to a `GridLayout`-managed container.

Child Component Sizes

Each cell in a `GridLayout` is assigned the same width and height, and each child component is compressed or stretched to fill a single cell. The specific height and width values for the cells are determined by calculating the available display area and dividing the width by the actual column count and the height by the actual row count. The available display area is defined as the dimensions of the container minus its insets and any space needed for the horizontal and vertical component gaps, as shown in the following equations:

```
availableWidth = totalWidth - leftInset -
                 rightInset - ((actualColumns - 1) * horizontalGap)
componentWidth = availableWidth / actualColumns
```

For example, if a component has a width of 400, right and left insets of 5, a horizontal gap value of 10 between the components in a row, and contains 4 columns, the width of each component will be:

```
availableWidth = 400 - 5 - 5 - ((4 - 1) * 10) = 400 - 10 - 30 = 360
componentWidth = 360 / 4 = 90 pixels
```

In this case, every component in the container will be made 90 pixels wide, and a similar equation is used to calculate the components' heights. Note that `GridLayout` does not respect the values returned by a component's `getMinimumSize()` and `getMaximumSize()` method. In other words, a `GridLayout` may cause a component to be smaller than its "minimum" size or larger than its "maximum" size. You can see an example of this behavior by running the `GridTest` application defined earlier and resizing the frame that contains the buttons. As the frame's dimensions change, the button sizes will be increased or decreased to fill the available display area.

Child Component Locations

`GridLayout` divides the container into a grid using the actual number of rows and columns that it calculates are needed. As components are added to the container, they are placed in the grid from left to right and from top to bottom based on when they were added to the container relative to one another. For example, the first component added to the container appears in the upper-left corner of the screen and the second one to the right of the first (if the grid provides at least two columns). That continues until an entire row in the grid has been filled. After that, adding another component will cause it to appear on the second row in the first column, the next one is placed in the second row and second column, etc.

Resizing Behavior

Since `GridLayout` forces all child components to fit within the container's display area, the component sizes may become very small if the container is allocated less space than it requests through its `getPreferredSize()` method. For example, the screenshot below illustrates what happens when the `GridTest` application is run and its window's height is reduced. In this case, the button labels have become vertically very small and are almost unreadable, illustrating the point made earlier that `GridLayout` does not respect a component's minimum size:

Similarly, if a GridLayout-managed container is made larger than its requested size, the components within the container will be made sufficiently large to fill the container, regardless of their maximum size.

Container Size

GridLayout calculates the size of its associated container by examining the dimensions of each child component within the container and recording the largest width and height values it finds. For example, when a GridLayout is asked for the container's preferred size, it calls getPreferredSize() for each child component and records the largest preferred height value returned by a component. That maximum preferred component height is then multiplied by the number of rows to be displayed and added to the container's top and bottom insets, along with the number of pixels needed to provide the vertical spacing between component rows. A similar calculation occurs for the container's width, as shown below:

```
containerHeight = (largestComponentHeight * actualRows) +
                  ((actualRows - 1) * verticalGap) +
                  (containerTopInset + containerBottomInset)

containerWidth = (largestComponentWidth * actualColumns) +
                 ((actualColumns - 1) * horizontalGap) +
                 (containerLeftInset + containerRightInset)
```

The same equation is used to calculate a container's minimum size, but the largestComponentWidth and largestComponentHeight values are obtained by calling the getMinimumSize() instead of getPreferredSize().

BorderLayout

A BorderLayout divides the container into five areas, and a component can be added to each area. The five regions correspond to the top, left, bottom, and right sides of the container, along with one in the center, as illustrated:

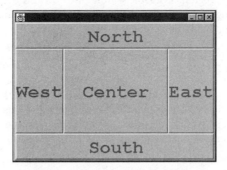

The code that produced this display appears below. As the code and the button labels illustrate, each of the five areas is associated with a constant value defined in BorderLayout: NORTH, SOUTH, EAST, WEST, and CENTER for the top, bottom, right, left, and center regions, respectively:

```
import java.awt.*;
import javax.swing.*;
```

```
import javax.swing.border.BevelBorder;

public class BorderSample extends JFrame {

  public static void main(String[] args) {
    BorderSample bs = new BorderSample();
    bs.setDefaultCloseOperation(JFrame.EXIT_ON_CLOSE);
    Container pane = bs.getContentPane();
    pane.setLayout(new BorderLayout());
    Font f = new Font("Courier", Font.BOLD, 36);
    JLabel label = new JLabel("North", JLabel.CENTER);
    label.setFont(f);
    label.setBorder(BorderFactory.createBevelBorder(BevelBorder.RAISED));
    pane.add(label, BorderLayout.NORTH);
    label = new JLabel("South", JLabel.CENTER);
    label.setFont(f);
    label.setBorder(BorderFactory.createBevelBorder(BevelBorder.RAISED));
    pane.add(label, BorderLayout.SOUTH);
    label = new JLabel("East", JLabel.CENTER);
    label.setFont(f);
    label.setBorder(BorderFactory.createBevelBorder(BevelBorder.RAISED));
    pane.add(label, BorderLayout.EAST);
    label = new JLabel("West", JLabel.CENTER);
    label.setFont(f);
    label.setBorder(BorderFactory.createBevelBorder(BevelBorder.RAISED));
    pane.add(label, BorderLayout.WEST);
    label = new JLabel("Center", JLabel.CENTER);
    label.setFont(f);
    label.setBorder(BorderFactory.createBevelBorder(BevelBorder.RAISED));
    pane.add(label, BorderLayout.CENTER);
    bs.setSize(400, 300);
    bs.setVisible(true);
  }

}
```

Note that although there are five regions available within a BorderLayout, it's not necessary to add a component to each one. Leaving an area empty does not affect the BorderLayout's behavior, but it may result in the CENTER component being made larger than it would have been otherwise.

Constructing a BorderLayout

The only parameters that may be passed to a BorderLayout constructor are the horizontal and vertical gaps that are used to separate adjacent components. The vertical gap is inserted below the NORTH component and above the SOUTH component, while the horizontal gap appears to the right of the WEST component and to the left of the EAST component. If you use the constructor that does not accept any parameters, no gaps are inserted.

Constraints

When adding a component to a container that's using a BorderLayout, you should supply a constraint that identifies which area should contain the component. The constraint should be a reference to one of five constants defined in BorderLayout: NORTH, SOUTH, EAST, WEST, or CENTER. An example of adding a component to a container that uses a BorderLayout is shown below, where a JLabel instance is added to the NORTH (top) area of the container:

```
myContainer.add(new JLabel("Hello"), BorderLayout.NORTH);
```

You can use the simpler form of add() that only accepts a single Component parameter with no constraints, in which case, the component will be added as if you had specified the CENTER area. However, since this form of add() does not explicitly identify which area the component is added to and may be confusing to someone reading your code, you should explicitly specify CENTER instead.

The last component you add to a region is the only one that will be displayed, so if you add a component and specify an area that's already occupied, the component that was previously added will not appear. However, you'll normally add a single component to a particular region, so you will usually only encounter this behavior with code that has a mistake.

Child Component Sizes

The size assigned to a child component by a BorderLayout depends upon a number of factors, including the following: the component's preferred size, the region of the container in which the component is displayed, the preferred size of the other components within the container, and the size of the container:

❑   **North Component**
    The component displayed in the NORTH area is assigned a height equal to its preferred height, and a width equal to the available width of the container. The available width is defined as the container's total width minus its right and left inset values.

❑   **South Component**
    Like the NORTH component, the component displayed in the SOUTH area is assigned a height equal to its preferred height, and a width equal to the available width of the container.

❑   **East Component**
    The component displayed in the EAST area is assigned a width equal to its preferred width and a height equal to the available height of the container minus the vertical space occupied by the NORTH and SOUTH components. The available height of the container is defined as the container's total height minus its top and bottom inset values.

❑   **West Component**
    Like the EAST component, the component displayed in the WEST area is assigned a width equal to its preferred width. Its height is set to the available height of the container minus the vertical space occupied by the NORTH and SOUTH components.

❑   **Center Component**
    The CENTER component is allocated any space that's left over inside the container after the other four components have been allocated space as described above. As a result, the CENTER component shrinks and expands to fill the remaining area, so its size depends upon the size of the container and how much of that space is taken up by the other components in the container.

Child Component Locations

The location of each child component managed by a BorderLayout is explicitly identified when it's added to the container. That is, the NORTH component appears at the top of the container, the SOUTH component at the bottom, the EAST component on the right, and WEST component on the left. The CENTER component occupies any remaining area in the center of the container.

Resizing Behavior

When a container's components are managed by BorderLayout, reducing the container's vertical size causes the EAST, CENTER, and WEST components to become "shorter" (smaller vertically) until there is only enough vertical space to display the NORTH and SOUTH components. Reducing the container's height by resizing the window manually so that it is smaller than the combined height of the NORTH and SOUTH components (which are always displayed using their preferred height values) causes those two components to overlap one another, as shown below:

Reducing the width of a container managed by a BorderLayout initially causes the widths of the NORTH, CENTER, and SOUTH components to become smaller until the CENTER component eventually disappears completely. At that point, reducing the container's width further causes the EAST and WEST components to overlap:

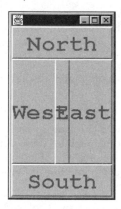

Increasing the size of a BorderLayout-managed container causes the CENTER component to become larger, and can increase the widths of the NORTH and SOUTH components and the heights of the EAST and WEST components.

Container Size

The minimum size defined for a container managed by a BorderLayout is calculated by calling the getMinimumSize() method for all components in the container. The minimum widths of the WEST, CENTER, and EAST components are added together (if they are present) along with the value needed to create a horizontal gap, and that sum is treated as a single value. The value is then compared to the minimum width of the NORTH component and the minimum width of the SOUTH component, and the largest value of the three is chosen as the container's minimum width. The minimum height of the container is selected using a similar approach, but the sequence of steps is slightly different. The minimum heights of the WEST, CENTER, and EAST components are compared and the largest of those three values is selected. It is then added to the minimum height of the NORTH and SOUTH components along with the space needed for vertical gaps and that value is used as the container's minimum height.

The preferred size of a `BorderLayout`-managed container is calculated using exactly the same approach described above, except that the `getPreferredSize()` method is called for each component instead of `getMinimumSize()`.

GridBagLayout

The `GridBagLayout` layout manager is by far the most flexible layout manager that's included with Java, but it does not enjoy widespread popularity among Java programmers due to its complexity and its sometimes non-intuitive behavior.

> However, **GridBagLayout is often the only layout manager flexible enough to arrange components in a particular manner, and is used frequently in spite of the difficulty involved.**

As its name implies, `GridBagLayout` bears some similarity to `GridLayout`, but only at a very superficial level. Both divide the container's available display area into a grid of cells, but beyond that, `GridBagLayout` and `GridLayout` don't have much in common. Some of the important differences between them include the following:

❑ When using a `GridLayout`, a component's position within the grid is determined by the order in which it is added to the container relative to other components. With a `GridBagLayout`, you can explicitly define the component's location within the grid.

❑ Each component in a `GridLayout` occupies exactly one cell in the grid, but components managed by a `GridBagLayout` can span multiple rows and/or columns within the grid.

❑ `GridLayout` assigns each row the same height and each column the same width, which causes every cell in the grid to have exactly the same dimensions. In contrast, `GridBagLayout` allows each row to have a separate height and every column its own width, so every cell in the grid can theoretically have a unique size.

❑ `GridLayout` does not support any constraints, while `GridBagLayout` allows you to specify a different set of constraint values for each component, and those constraints allow you to customize the component's size and position within the grid.

If you're not already familiar with it, you may be wondering why `GridBagLayout` is considered so difficult to use by many Java programmers. Some of the possible reasons are:

❑ **The number of constraints and their interactions**
`GridBagConstraints` encapsulates eleven different constraint values, and each child component is assigned its own instance of `GridBagConstraints`. Although no single constraint is particularly difficult to understand, the way in which the constraints interact with one another and with the constraints of other components is somewhat complex.

❑ **Row height and column widths**
`GridBagLayout`'s ability to provide a separate height for each row and width for each column is one of its primary advantages, but that capability also adds a great deal of complexity to its use. In some cases, especially with complex layouts containing many components, it can be difficult to predict what a component's size or position will be, and it's easy to make mistakes that produce results different from what you expected.

❑ **Component location**
When you see a component inside a GridLayout, it's usually easy to identify which cell the component occupies without examining the source code. That's because all cells (and components) are the same size, and the cells are aligned with one another. In the case of a GridBagLayout, identifying which cell or cells a component occupies can be difficult, since cell widths and heights can vary and since a component can span multiple cells.

❑ **Component size**
Most other layout managers have simple rules that determine the size that a component is set to, but GridBagLayout provides much greater flexibility in this area, as well as more complexity.

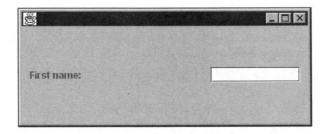

The screenshot above provides a simple example of the type of problem that can be difficult to diagnose when using a GridBagLayout. In this case, a frame was created and a JLabel and a JTextField have been added to it. However, a large gap exists between the label and text field, and since JLabel instances are transparent by default, there's no indication of whether or not the gap is due to the label's size or exists for some other reason. Most of the time, a component includes a border that is drawn around its edges, and that border provides you with an easy way to estimate the component's size. However, some frequently used components such as JLabel and JPanel do not include a border by default, and it can be more difficult to determine their sizes visually.

When you're designing a user interface using a GridBagLayout, this type of problem can cause a great deal of frustration. However, there are some simple ways that you can modify your code so that it provides you with visual feedback on the size of your components and/or the cells that they occupy.

For example, when working with a JLabel or JPanel, it can be helpful to temporarily add a border or set the component's background color so that you can easily identify its edges. The following code sets the background color for the JLabel used in the previous example, as shown below:

```
label.setBackground(Color.green);
label.setOpaque(true);
```

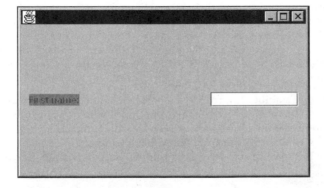

In this case, the color was set to green, although you can use any color that contrasts with the background color of parent the container. Note also that it was necessary to call the setOpaque() method, since a JLabel normally has a transparent background. Although setting the label's background color did establish that the label itself does not occupy the space between its text and the JTextField, it's still not clear why there is such a large gap between the two components.

Another way to provide helpful visual information is to create a JPanel subclass that overrides the paintComponent() method and uses information provided by GridBagLayout to draw the borders of each cell within the grid. The getLayoutDimensions() method returns a two-dimensional array of integer values that identify the height of each row and width of each column in the grid. Here is an example of such a JPanel subclass, which should work fine with any program that uses GridBagLayout.

```java
import java.awt.*;
import javax.swing.*;

public class GridBagCellPanel extends JPanel {

  public void paintComponent(Graphics g) {
    super.paintComponent(g);
    LayoutManager manager = getLayout();
    if ((manager != null) && (manager instanceof GridBagLayout)) {
      GridBagLayout layout = (GridBagLayout) manager;
      g.setColor(getForeground());
      Point p = layout.getLayoutOrigin();
      int[][] sizes = layout.getLayoutDimensions();
      int[] colWidths = sizes[0];
      int[] rowHeights = sizes[1];
      int width, height;
      int xpos = p.x;
      int ypos;
      for (int x = 0; x < colWidths.length; x++) {
        ypos = p.y;
        width = colWidths[x];
        for (int y = 0; y < rowHeights.length; y++) {
          height = rowHeights[y];
          g.drawRect(xpos, ypos, width - 1, height - 1);
          g.drawRect(xpos + 1, ypos + 1, width - 3, height - 3);
          ypos += height;
        }
        xpos += width;
      }
    }
  }
}
```

If the user interface is added to an instance of the GridBagCellPanel class, a dark border appears around the edge of each cell in the grid, as shown below. This illustrates that the column containing the label is very large, and the gap exists because the component is positioned on the left side of its cell.

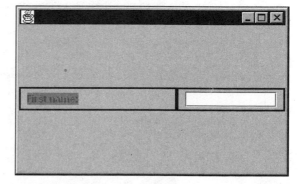

This example illustrates another important point related to GridBagLayout: a component does not necessarily expand to completely fill the cell or cells that it occupies. A component's size is normally set to its preferred or minimum size, and in this case, the component's preferred width is considerably smaller than the width of the cell that it occupies. It's important to keep in mind this distinction between a component's actual size and its **display area**, or the area of the container reserved for that component. A component's display area is the rectangular region defined by the cell or cells assigned to the component. In this case, only a single cell was assigned to each component, but as mentioned earlier, a cell can span multiple rows and/or columns.

Constructing a GridBagLayout

GridBagLayout provides only a single, no-argument constructor so it's very simple to create one, as shown in the following code:

```
GridBagLayout gbl = new GridBagLayout();
```

Constraints

Each component that's added to a container managed by a GridBagLayout has an associated set of constraint values, and those values are encapsulated by an instance of the GridBagConstraints class.

GridBagConstraints provides two constructors: one that accepts no parameters, and another that accepts the eleven constraint values that are supported. Although you can use either constructor, code that passes many parameter values to a constructor can be difficult to understand, even for someone who's familiar with GridBagLayout, so you should avoid using that form. GridBagConstraints represents one of the few cases in Java where it's acceptable to access the fields within an object without using accessor and mutator methods. In fact, because GridBagConstraints doesn't provide accessor or mutator methods for its properties, you must set those properties directly by assigning them values as shown below:

```
GridBagConstraints gbc = new GridBagConstraints();
gbc.gridx = 0;
gbc.gridy = 3;
```

When you add a component to a container managed by a GridBagLayout, you can use the add() method that accepts a Component and a constraints Object, or you can use the simpler form that accepts only a Component reference. However, if you do use the simpler form, you must call the setConstraints() method in GridBagLayout to associate the Component with a set of constraint values. For example, suppose you've created the following code:

```
GridBagLayout layout = new GridBagLayout();
setLayout(layout);
GridBagConstraints constraints = new GridBagConstraints();
JButton button = new JButton("Testing");
```

You can add the button to the container after first associating it with the set of constraints, as in the following code:

```
layout.setConstraints(button, constraints);
add(button);
```

Alternatively, you can use the form of the add() method that accepts a parameter representing constraint information:

```
add(button, constraints);
```

Both of these approaches are valid, but the second one is probably somewhat more intuitive for most people and requires slightly less code.

Although you'll typically add more than one component to a container and each component will usually have different constraint values from the others, you can use the same instance of GridBagConstraints for all components. That's because when you add a component to a container managed by a GridBagLayout, the layout manager uses the clone() method in GridBagConstraints to make a "deep copy" of the constraints. In other words, when you add a component, a copy is made of its associated GridBagConstraints object, and that copy is saved by the GridBagLayout for later reference. Therefore, you can use a single GridBagConstraints object repeatedly, since the layout manager uses it just long enough to create a copy of it.

Fields Defined in GridBagConstraints

The following fields are defined in GridBagConstraints, most of which are int values. However, the insets field is a reference to an instance of the java.awt.Insets class, and weightx and weighty are double (floating-point) values.

gridx

This constraint allows you to identify the first/left-most column within the grid that should be assigned to the component's display area. The first column (the one at the left edge of the container) corresponds to a value of 0, the next column to a value of 1, and so on. For example, to specify that a component should begin in the first column, you can add the following code to your application:

```
GridBagConstraints constraints = new GridBagConstraints();
constraints.gridx = 0;
```

By default, the gridx constraint value is set to GridBagConstraints.RELATIVE, which is discussed below.

gridy

This constraint allows you to identify the first/top row within the grid that should be assigned to the component's display area. The first row (the one at the top edge of the container) corresponds to a value of 0, the next row to a value of 1, and so on. For example, to specify that a component should begin in the third row, you can add the following code to your application:

```
GridBagConstraints constraints = new GridBagConstraints();
constraints.gridy = 2;
```

By default, the gridy constraint value is set to GridBagConstraints.RELATIVE.

Relative Positioning

The two examples shown above both use absolute position values. However, you can set gridx and/or gridy to the value defined by the RELATIVE constant in GridBagConstraints to indicate that the component should be positioned relative to some other component. If you specify RELATIVE for gridx and an absolute value for gridy, the component you add will be placed at the end of the row identified by the gridy value. For example, the following code will create five JButton instances, adding three of them to the second row using relative positioning:

```
import java.awt.*;
import javax.swing.*;

public class RelativeX {

  public static void main(String[] args) {
    JFrame f = new JFrame();
    f.setDefaultCloseOperation(JFrame.EXIT_ON_CLOSE);
    Container pane = f.getContentPane();
    pane.setLayout(new GridBagLayout());
    GridBagConstraints gbc = new GridBagConstraints();
    gbc.gridy = 0;
    pane.add(new JButton("First row"), gbc);
    gbc.gridx = GridBagConstraints.RELATIVE;
    gbc.gridy = 1;
    pane.add(new JButton("Second row, first column"), gbc);
    pane.add(new JButton("Second row, second column"), gbc);
    pane.add(new JButton("Second row, third column"), gbc);
    gbc.gridy = 2;
    pane.add(new JButton("Third row"), gbc);
    f.setSize(600, 300);
    f.setVisible(true);
  }

}
```

The display produced by this program is as follows:

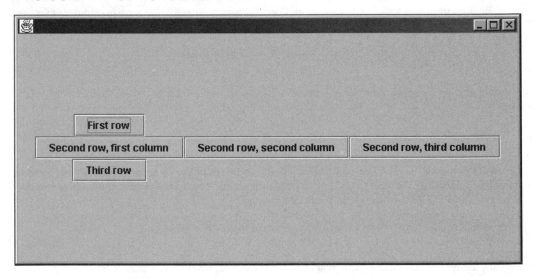

Similarly, specifying an explicit column/gridx value and RELATIVE for the row/gridy value causes components to be added on a top-to-bottom basis to the specified column. For example, the following code will create five JButton instances, adding three of them to the second column using relative positioning:

```
import java.awt.*;
import javax.swing.*;
```

```
public class RelativeY {

  public static void main(String[] args) {
    JFrame f = new JFrame();
    f.setDefaultCloseOperation(JFrame.EXIT_ON_CLOSE);
    Container pane = f.getContentPane();
    pane.setLayout(new GridBagLayout());
    GridBagConstraints gbc = new GridBagConstraints();
    gbc.gridx = 0;
    pane.add(new JButton("First column"), gbc);
    gbc.gridx = 1;
    gbc.gridy = GridBagConstraints.RELATIVE;
    pane.add(new JButton("Second column, first row"), gbc);
    pane.add(new JButton("Second column, second row"), gbc);
    pane.add(new JButton("Second column, third row"), gbc);
    gbc.gridx = 2;
    pane.add(new JButton("Third column"), gbc);
    f.setSize(600, 300);
    f.setVisible(true);
  }

}
```

This version produces the following display:

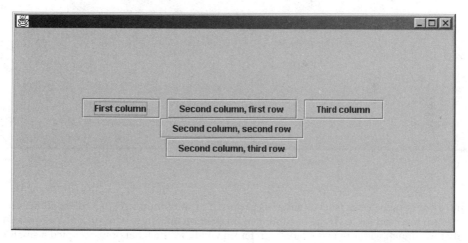

You can also specify RELATIVE for both gridx and gridy when adding a component to a container. If you do so, the component will be added to the end of the top row (row 0) in the grid, as in the following code:

```
import java.awt.*;
import javax.swing.*;

public class RelativeXY {

  public static void main(String[] args) {
    JFrame f = new JFrame();
    f.setDefaultCloseOperation(JFrame.EXIT_ON_CLOSE);
```

```
        Container pane = f.getContentPane();
        pane.setLayout(new GridBagLayout());
        GridBagConstraints gbc = new GridBagConstraints();
        gbc.gridx = 1;
        gbc.gridy = GridBagConstraints.RELATIVE;
        pane.add(new JButton("First row, first column"), gbc);
        pane.add(new JButton("Second row"), gbc);
        pane.add(new JButton("Third row"), gbc);
        gbc.gridx = GridBagConstraints.RELATIVE;
        pane.add(new JButton("First row, second column"), gbc);
        f.setSize(600, 300);
        f.setVisible(true);
    }

}
```

That code results in the following display:

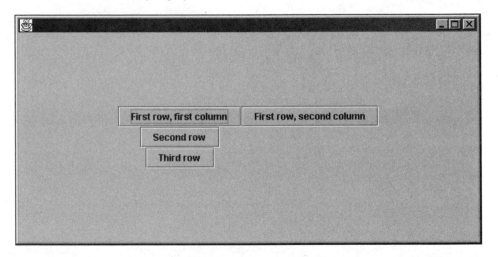

fill

By default, a component's size is set to either its preferred or minimum size, regardless of the size of the cell or cells that are reserved for it. At the beginning of this section on GridBagLayout, we saw a JLabel in a column that was much wider than the label's preferred width, so the label only occupied a small portion of its available display area. However, you can use the fill constraint to indicate that the component should be stretched to fill its available display area horizontally, vertically, or both. For example, the following code creates three buttons, and the first two are displayed using their preferred sizes. However, the third button is made to expand horizontally to fill the width of its column:

```
import java.awt.*;
import javax.swing.*;

public class Fill {

  public static void main(String[] args) {
    JFrame f = new JFrame();
```

```
    f.setDefaultCloseOperation(JFrame.EXIT_ON_CLOSE);
    Container pane = f.getContentPane();
    pane.setLayout(new GridBagLayout());
    GridBagConstraints gbc = new GridBagConstraints();
    gbc.gridx = 0;
    gbc.gridy = GridBagConstraints.RELATIVE;
    pane.add(new JButton("This button's preferred width "
                        + "is large because its text is long"), gbc);
    pane.add(new JButton("Small centered button"), gbc);
    gbc.fill = GridBagConstraints.HORIZONTAL;
    pane.add(new JButton("Expands to fill column width"), gbc);
    f.setSize(400, 300);
    f.setVisible(true);
  }

}
```

The display produced by this example is as follows:

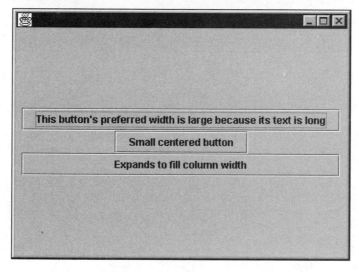

There are four constants defined in `GridBagConstraints` that you can use to set the `fill` value:

- HORIZONTAL
  Expand the component horizontally to fill its display area

- VERTICAL
  Expand the component vertically to fill its display area

- BOTH
  Expand the component both horizontally and vertically to fill its display area

- NONE
  The component should be allowed to remain at its natural (preferred or minimum) size; this is the default value

gridwidth

This constraint identifies the number of columns that the component spans, and its default value is 1. For example, in the screenshot below, the button in the third row spans both columns:

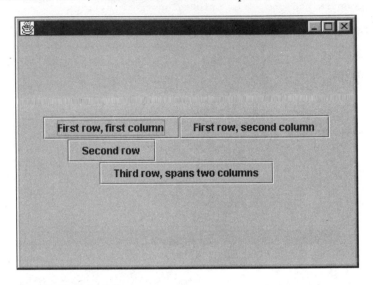

The code to create this display is as follows:

```java
import java.awt.*;
import javax.swing.*;

public class ColumnSpan {

  public static void main(String[] args) {
    JFrame f = new JFrame();
    f.setDefaultCloseOperation(JFrame.EXIT_ON_CLOSE);
    Container pane = f.getContentPane();
    pane.setLayout(new GridBagLayout());
    GridBagConstraints gbc = new GridBagConstraints();
    gbc.gridx = 1;
    gbc.gridy = GridBagConstraints.RELATIVE;
    pane.add(new JButton("First row, first column"), gbc);
    pane.add(new JButton("Second row"), gbc);
    gbc.gridwidth = 2;
    pane.add(new JButton("Third row, spans two columns"), gbc);
    gbc.gridwidth = 1;
    gbc.gridx = GridBagConstraints.RELATIVE;
    pane.add(new JButton("First row, second column"), gbc);
    f.setSize(400, 300);
    f.setVisible(true);
  }

}
```

In this case, the button's size is set to its preferred width, and the button is centered horizontally within its display area. However, it can be made to fill both columns by setting the fill value:

```
import java.awt.*;
import javax.swing.*;

public class ColumnSpan {

  public static void main(String[] args) {
    JFrame f = new JFrame();
    f.setDefaultCloseOperation(JFrame.EXIT_ON_CLOSE);
    Container pane = f.getContentPane();
    pane.setLayout(new GridBagLayout());
    GridBagConstraints gbc = new GridBagConstraints();
    gbc.gridx = 1;
    gbc.gridy = GridBagConstraints.RELATIVE;
    pane.add(new JButton("First row, first column"), gbc);
    pane.add(new JButton("Second row"), gbc);
    gbc.gridwidth = 2;
    gbc.fill = GridBagConstraints.HORIZONTAL;
    pane.add(new JButton("Third row, spans two columns"), gbc);
    gbc.gridwidth = 1;
    gbc.fill = GridBagConstraints.NONE;
    gbc.gridx = GridBagConstraints.RELATIVE;
    pane.add(new JButton("First row, second column"), gbc);
    f.setSize(400, 300);
    f.setVisible(true);
  }

}
```

With these alterations, the second being to reset the `fill` value, the display now becomes:

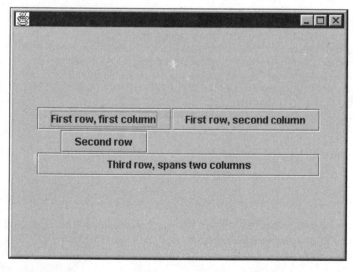

In addition to specifying an explicit number of columns to span, you can use the REMAINDER constant defined in `GridBagConstraints`. This indicates that the component's display area should begin with the column specified by the `gridx` value and that it should fill all the remaining columns to the right of that column. An example is shown overleaf:

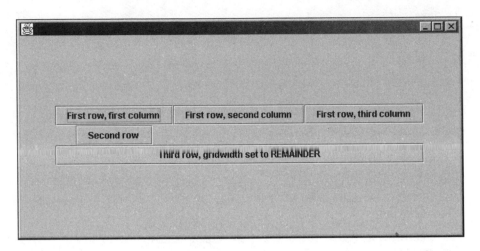

This display was produced by the following code:

```java
import java.awt.*;
import javax.swing.*;

public class Remainder {

    public static void main(String[] args) {
        JFrame f = new JFrame();
        f.setDefaultCloseOperation(JFrame.EXIT_ON_CLOSE);
        Container pane = f.getContentPane();
        pane.setLayout(new GridBagLayout());
        GridBagConstraints gbc = new GridBagConstraints();
        pane.add(new JButton("First row, first column"), gbc);
        pane.add(new JButton("First row, second column"), gbc);
        pane.add(new JButton("First row, third column"), gbc);
        gbc.gridx = 0;
        pane.add(new JButton("Second row"), gbc);
        gbc.gridwidth = GridBagConstraints.REMAINDER;
        gbc.fill = GridBagConstraints.HORIZONTAL;
        pane.add(new JButton("Third row, gridwidth set to REMAINDER"), gbc);
        f.setSize(600, 300);
        f.setVisible(true);
    }

}
```

You can also set a `gridwidth` value to `RELATIVE`, which is similar to `REMAINDER`. However, `RELATIVE` causes the component to span all remaining columns *except* the last one in the grid. For example, you might make the modifications shown below to the `Remainder` class defined earlier:

```java
pane.add(new JButton("Second row"), gbc);
gbc.gridwidth = GridBagConstraints.RELATIVE;
gbc.fill = GridBagConstraints.HORIZONTAL;
pane.add(new JButton("Third row, gridwidth set to RELATIVE"), gbc);
```

If you compile and execute the code, it will produce a display like this one:

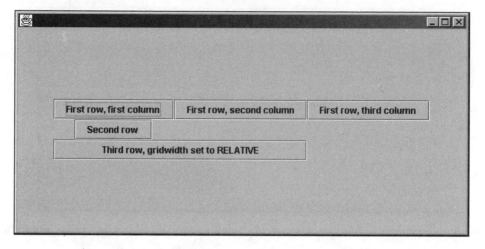

gridheight

Just as gridwidth defines the number of columns that a component's display area spans, this constraint defines the number of rows allocated. As with gridwidth, you can specify RELATIVE, REMAINDER, or an absolute value. The following code provides an example of this:

```java
import java.awt.*;
import javax.swing.*;

public class GridHeight {

  public static void main(String[] args) {
    JFrame f = new JFrame();
    f.setDefaultCloseOperation(JFrame.EXIT_ON_CLOSE);
    Container pane = f.getContentPane();
    pane.setLayout(new GridBagLayout());
    GridBagConstraints gbc = new GridBagConstraints();
    pane.add(new JButton("First row, first column"), gbc);
    pane.add(new JButton("First row, second column"), gbc);
    gbc.gridheight = GridBagConstraints.REMAINDER;
    gbc.fill = GridBagConstraints.VERTICAL;
    pane.add(new JButton("First row, third column"), gbc);
    gbc.gridx = 0;
    gbc.gridheight = 1;
    gbc.fill = GridBagConstraints.NONE;
    pane.add(new JButton("Second row"), gbc);
    pane.add(new JButton("Third row"), gbc);
    f.setSize(600, 300);
    f.setVisible(true);
  }

}
```

The following screen shot illustrates the behavior of this new class:

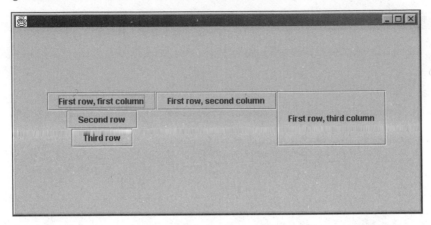

The default value for `gridheight` is 1, which causes the component to occupy a single row in the grid.

anchor

You can use this constraint to identify how a component should be positioned within its display area when its size is smaller than that area. The `anchor` constraint should be set to one of the following nine values: CENTER, NORTH, NORTHEAST, EAST, SOUTHEAST, SOUTH, SOUTHWEST, WEST, or NORTHWEST. The default value (CENTER) causes the component to be centered both vertically and horizontally within its display area, while the other values define a corner or side of the area. For example, NORTHEAST causes the component to be placed in the upper-right corner of its display area, EAST causes it to be centered vertically and placed against the right side of its display area, and so on. To illustrate an example of this behavior, suppose that you make the following additions to the `GridHeight` class defined earlier:

```
gbc.fill = GridBagConstraints.NONE;
gbc.anchor = GridBagConstraints.EAST;
pane.add(new JButton("Second row"), gbc);
gbc.anchor = GridBagConstraints.CENTER;
pane.add(new JButton("Third row"), gbc);
```

This modification causes the button on the second row to appear in the east/right side of its display area as shown below. However, once that button has been added to the panel, the `anchor` property is changed back to CENTER (the default value), so the button on the third row appears centered:

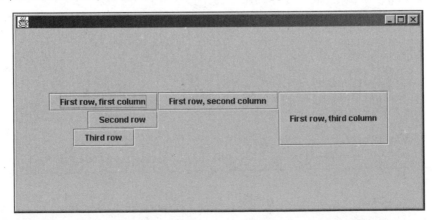

insets

This constraint is a reference to an instance of the Insets class, and allows you to define some number of pixels that should be reserved around the four edges (top, left, bottom, and right) of the component's display area. You'll typically use this to provide white space between components in adjacent rows and columns, just as horizontal and vertical gap values are used by other layout managers. However, GridBagLayout's approach is much more flexible, because not only can you specify a different gap size for every component, but you can also specify a unique size for each side of the component.

To set the inset values for a component, you can create an instance of Insets or modify the one that's created automatically when a GridBagConstraints object is created. The following code segment illustrates how to set these values:

```
GridBagConstraints gbc = new GridBagConstraints();
gbc.insets = new Insets(5, 10, 5, 10);
```

or:

```
GridBagConstraints gbc = new GridBagConstraints();
gbc.insets.top = 5;
gbc.insets.left = 10;
gbc.insets.bottom = 5;
gbc.insets.right = 10;
```

If you insert one of these two code segments into the GridHeight class defined earlier, compile and execute the code, it will produce a display like the one that follows:

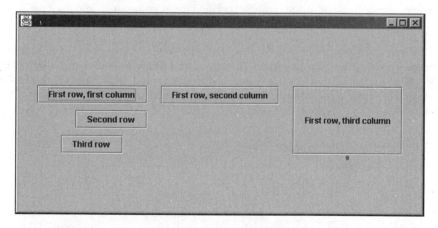

One final point worth noting relative to insets is that a component is never allowed to overlay the inset portions of its display area, even if the fill constraint causes the component be stretched.

ipadx

This value is added to the component's preferred or minimum size to determine the width of the component, and the "i" refers to the fact that the pad value is added to the component's "internal" (that is, preferred or minimum) width as opposed to its current (displayed) width. For example, if a component has a preferred width of 40 pixels and you specify a value of 10 for this constraint, the component will be 50 pixels wide when components are displayed using preferred widths.

You can also make components smaller than their preferred or minimum sizes by specifying negative pad values, so if you were to specify a value of −10 for this constraint in the above example, the component would be assigned a width of 30 pixels instead of its preferred width of 40. The default value of this constraint is 0.

ipady

Just as `ipadx` represents some number that's added to a component's preferred or minimum width, this value is added to the component's height before it is displayed. The default value of this constraint is 0.

weightx

This value is used to determine how to resize the columns in the grid when the container is either wider or narrower than the area needed to display the components at their preferred or minimum widths. If all components in a grid have a `weightx` value of 0.0 (the default), any extra horizontal space is divided evenly between the left and right edges of the container. A detailed description of how weights are used and how they interact with other constraints is provided later.

weighty

This value is used to determine how to resize the rows within the grid when the container's height is larger or smaller than the size needed to display the components using their preferred or minimum heights. If all components in a grid have a `weighty` value of 0.0 (the default), any extra vertical space is divided evenly between the top and bottom edges of the container.

Calculating Row Heights and Column Widths

The initial calculation of the height of a row is done by determining the amount of space that's needed to display the tallest component in the row. The height of a particular component is the sum of its preferred or minimum height, the vertical pad value (`ipady`) specified for its constraints, and the `top` and `bottom` insets that should appear around the component.

Similarly, when calculating the width of a column, the width needed for each component is calculated, and the largest value is used as the column's width. A component's width is defined as the sum of its preferred or minimum width, its horizontal pad (`ipadx`) value, and its `right` and `left` inset values. For example, suppose that you've created a container with nine child components, and those components have the following width values:

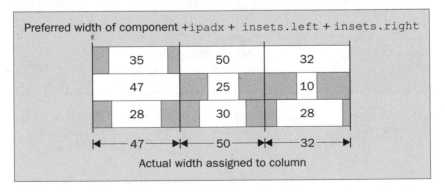

Calculating Sizes when Components Span Multiple Cells

The process of calculating a row height or column width is slightly more complex when it involves a component that spans multiple rows or columns. When calculating row heights and column widths, GridBagLayout processes the components in order of their gridwidth (for column widths) and gridheight (for row heights) values. For example, to calculate column widths, the layout manager will first examine the components that have a gridwidth of 1, then those with a gridwidth of 2, etc.

When GridBagLayout needs to determine the size of a column and it encounters a component that spans multiple columns, it attempts to distribute the component's preferred width across those columns. The distribution occurs in left-to-right order, and any remaining width is distributed to the last column that the component occupies. For example, suppose that you have the same components described earlier, but with a component on the second row that has a gridwidth value of 2 (that is, it fills the first two columns). In that case, the column widths will be calculated as follows:

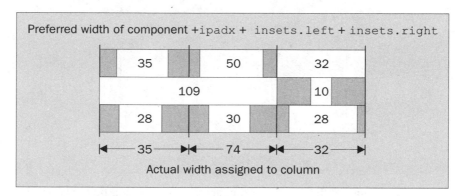

When the layout manager examines the components with a gridwidth value of 1, it establishes preliminary widths of 35, 50, and 32 for the three columns. However, when it examines components with a gridwidth of 2, it determines that the existing column widths are not adequate to allow the components to be displayed properly. This is due to the component on the second row that spans the first two columns and has a width of 109 pixels. Since that component's width exceeds the sum of the preliminary widths for the columns it occupies (35 + 50 = 85), the width of the second column is increased to 74 (109 − 35 = 74) so that the component's size can be accommodated.

Weight Values, Row Heights, and Column Widths

One of the more confusing aspects of GridBagLayout is how components' weightx values affect column widths and how weighty values affect row heights. When a GridBagLayout attempts to organize the components in its container, it compares the amount of space it needs to the actual size of the container. If the two sizes are not exactly the same, the layout manager must decide where and by how much to increase or reduce the size of rows and columns, and it uses weight values for this purpose. Stated simply, the weight values you specify through GridBagConstraints are used to assign each row and column a weight and the amount of space taken from or added to a row or column is determined by its weight value.

Distributing Extra Space

The following example is provided as an illustration of how space is distributed, but for the sake of simplicity, only involves weightx values and column width adjustments. However, the calculation of row heights using weighty values is done in exactly the same way, so the concepts are relevant to both column widths and row heights.

Let's assume that a container has been created that uses a GridBagLayout to manage the size and position of its child components, and that a width of 400 pixels is needed to display the components using their minimum sizes. However, let's also assume that when the layout manager prepares to arrange the components, it determines that the container is 600 pixels wide. In this case, the GridBagLayout must determine how to distribute the extra 200 pixels to its columns.

Calculating Column Weights

The first step that the GridBagLayout must take is to calculate a weight for each column, and that weight will determine how much of the extra 200 pixels will be distributed to the column. In the simplest case where each component has a gridwidth value of 1 (in other words, no component spans multiple columns), the weight of a column is defined as the largest weightx value of any component within that column. For example, suppose that the following table represents the weightx values of components in a container:

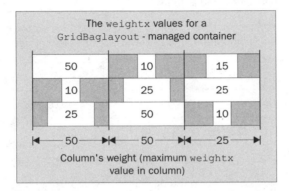

The weightx values for a
GridBaglayout - managed container

Column's weight (maximum weightx
value in column)

Since the weight of a column is defined as the maximum weightx value in that column, the weights of the three columns in this grid are 50, 50, and 25, respectively. As we'll see shortly, neither the weights' absolute values nor their sum is particularly important, but you may find it easier to work with round numbers.

In the case where a component spans multiple columns, the calculation of a column's weight value is slightly more complex. Using a different set of components in some other container, let's suppose that there are three rows of components in the grid, and that the second row contains a component that spans the second and third columns as shown below. It's easy to guess the weight of the first column, since it's simply the maximum weightx value found in that column (1.0). However, it's probably not as obvious how the weight values of the remaining two columns are calculated:

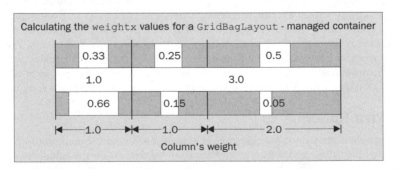

Calculating the weightx values for a GridBagLayout - managed container

Column's weight

To understand how the weight values were derived for the second and third columns, it's important to know that when GridBagLayout calculates column weights, it processes components in order based on their gridwidth values. In other words, GridBagLayout first examines the weightx values of all components that have a gridwidth value of 1, then those that have a value of 2, and so on. In this case, the layout manager's first iteration will process 7 of the 8 components in the container, initially ignoring the component on the second row that has a gridwidth of 2. In the process of doing so, it calculates a preliminary column weight of 0.25 for the second column and 0.5 for the third column.

On the GridBagLayout's next iteration, it processes the weightx of the component that spans the second and third columns, and must distribute that value (3.0) across the two columns. It does this by distributing the amount proportionally based upon the preliminary weight values of the columns. Specifically, it adds together the preliminary column weight values and divides the weight value of each column by that sum to determine a percentage of the spanning component's weightx value that should be distributed to the column.

For example, in this case, the preliminary weight values of the second and third columns are 0.25 and 0.5, respectively, and the sum of these two values is 0.75. Dividing the preliminary weight of the second column by 0.75 produces a value of 0.33, and dividing the third column's preliminary weight by the same 0.75 produces a value of 0.67. These values represent the percentage of the spanning component's weightx value that will be distributed to each column. Specifically, one-third (33%) will be assigned to the second column, and the remaining two-thirds (67%) will be assigned to the third column. Since the weight of the component that spans the two columns is 3, it represents a weight of 1 (3.0 * 0.33 = 1.0) for the second column and 2 (3.0 * 0.67 = 2.0) for the third.

Since the component in the second row represents a weightx value of 1 for the second column and 2 for the third column, the second column's final weight value is 1 and the third column's final weight is 2.

Converting Weights to Percentages

Now that a weight value has been assigned to each column, those values can be used to determine the amount of extra space that should be allocated to each column. This is done by first calculating the sum of all column weight values and dividing each column's weight by that sum. In this case, the sum of all the weights is 4 (1.0 + 1.0 + 2.0 = 4), and the first column is given one-fourth (25%) of the extra space. Similarly, the second column is allocated one-fourth (25%) of the space, and the third and final column receives the remaining two-fourths (50%). For the first example (with column weights fo 50, 50, and 25, with a sum of 125), the first two columns receive two-fifths of the extra space each (50 / 125 = 0.4 or 40%), while the last column receives the remaining one-fifth (20%).

Distributing the Extra Space

Having calculated the percentage of extra space that should be added to the width of each column, it's easy to determine the number of pixels that will be distributed in our example. Since there are 200 extra pixels, the first and second columns will be made wider by 50 pixels (200 * 0.25 = 50), while the third column becomes 100 pixels wider (200 * 0.5 = 100).

Although this example describes a situation where extra space was being added to columns, the same principles apply when space needs to be taken away. For example, if the container had been 200 pixels smaller than it needed to be instead of 200 larger, the three columns would have been reduced in size by 50, 50, and 100 pixels, respectively.

General Guidelines for Setting Weights

As you can see, GridBagLayout's behavior with respect to weight values is somewhat complex. However, you can reduce the complexity in some cases by assigning weightx values only to the components in a single row and weighty values to those in a particular column. If you do so, you're effectively setting the weight value for the entire row or column when you specify it for the component, which makes it easier to predict how space will be added or taken away.

In addition, you may find it easier to use weight values that add up to some round number such as 1.0 or 100.0, allowing you to easily associate a weight value with a percentage. For example, given the previous grid, you could specify the weightx values only on the components in the first row as shown below:

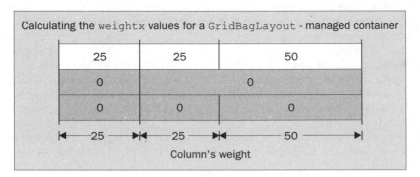

Calculating the weightx values for a GridBagLayout - managed container

In this case, only the components in the first row were assigned weightx values and the sum of those values is 100, making it much more obvious how space will be added or removed from the columns. Specifically, the first and second columns are allocated 25% of any extra space, while the third one is given the remaining 50%.

You may have noticed that in some examples, relatively large weight values (for example, 50, 10, 15, etc.) were used, while smaller ones were specified at other times. This was done deliberately to illustrate a point: the absolute size of weight values used is unimportant. What matters is how large those values are *relative to one another*. In other words, you can produce the same results using fractional values as you can by using very large numbers. For example, three columns with weights of 0.25, 0.25, and 0.50 have space distributed to them in exactly the same amounts that they would if the columns had weights of 100, 100 and 200.

It's also important to remember that weights do not necessarily represent the relative sizes of the cells, but rather the relative amount of space that will be added to or taken away from those cells. For example, if you create a grid with two columns and the second column is assigned a weight that's twice as large as the first, you should not expect the second column to be twice as large. However, you can correctly assume that the second column will be given twice as much extra space as the first if excess space is distributed to them.

GridBagTester

Even with a good understanding of GridBagLayout, it can be difficult to assign constraint values so that your user interface is displayed correctly, and you may find it necessary to repeatedly modify, compile, and execute your code. However, the GridBagTester utility provided here can be used to test your user interface classes that use GridBagLayout and to modify the constraint values graphically until they produce the desired results. This utility was written for the purposes of this book, so that you can see the effects of changing the various constraints without having to recompile the code after each modification.

To use `GridBagTester`, you simply create an instance of it by passing its constructor a `Container` that's managed by a `GridBagLayout` and `GridBagTester` will create a `JFrame` that displays the container. In addition, it provides other information that describes the components, their constraint values, and the rows and columns defined in the container grid:

❑   A table at the top of the frame displays the width and weight of each column in the grid. It also displays a value that identifies what percentage of space will be added to or taken away from the column's width if the container is made wider or narrower than its current width.

❑   A table on the left side of the frame displays the height and weight of each row in the grid. It also displays a value that identifies what percentage of space will be added to or taken away from the row's height if the container is made taller or shorter than its current height.

❑   A table at the bottom of the frame displays information about each component in the container. Specifically, that information includes the component's name, location within the container, actual/current size, preferred size, minimum size, and the constraint values assigned to the component. With the exception of the preferred and minimum size values, all of the cells in this table are editable. You can dynamically change a component's constraints and immediately see the effect of your change upon its size and position, as well as the weight and size of any rows and columns it occupies.

The `GridBagTester` source code is somewhat long, but if you find it helpful to have when working with a `GridBagLayout`, you can find it all in Appendix B. You'll also need `NumericTextField` from Chapter 4.

As an example of how `GridBagTester` may be useful, suppose that you've created a layout similar to the one below that allows a first and last name to be entered, along with an address:

```java
import java.awt.*;
import javax.swing.*;

public class SimplePanel extends JPanel {

  public static void main(String[] args) {
    JFrame f = new JFrame();
    f.setDefaultCloseOperation(JFrame.EXIT_ON_CLOSE);
    f.getContentPane().add(new SimplePanel());
    f.setSize(400, 300);
    f.setVisible(true);
  }

  public SimplePanel() {
    super();
    GridBagConstraints constraints = new GridBagConstraints();
    GridBagLayout layout = new GridBagLayout();
    setLayout(layout);

    constraints.anchor = GridBagConstraints.WEST;

    constraints.gridy = 0;
    JLabel label = new JLabel("First name:");
    add(label, constraints);

    JTextField tf = new JTextField(8);
    add(tf, constraints);
```

```
        label = new JLabel("Last name:");
        add(label, constraints);

        tf = new JTextField(8);
        add(tf, constraints);

        constraints.gridy = 1;
        label = new JLabel("Address:");
        add(label, constraints);

        tf = new JTextField(10);
        add(tf, constraints);
    }

}
```

Initially, it produces a display like that shown below:

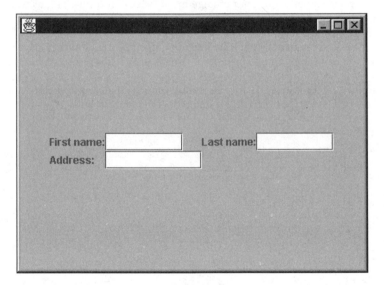

Although this display is functional, it's not very user-friendly. You can improve it by repeatedly modifying, compiling, and executing your code, but doing so is tedious and time-consuming. Alternatively, you can make a slight modification to the main() method that will allow you to view and modify the component's constraint information:

```
public static void main(String[] args) {
    // JFrame f = new JFrame();
    // f.setDefaultCloseOperation(JFrame.EXIT_ON_CLOSE);
    // f.getContentPane().add(new SimplePanel());
    // f.setSize(400, 300);
    // f.setVisible(true);
    GridBagTester gbt = new GridBagTester(new SimplePanel());
}
```

When the program is run now, the display is as follows:

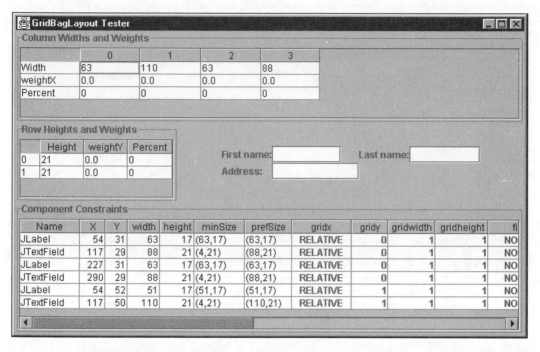

For example, you might change the `gridwidth` value of the `JTextField` on the second row to `REMAINDER` and its fill value to `HORIZONTAL`, which produces the display shown below:

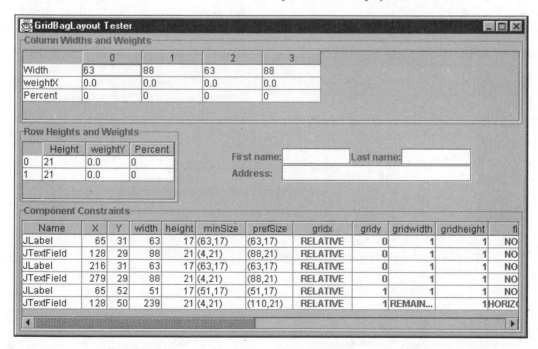

This improves the appearance of the display, although it still appears somewhat cluttered because there are no gaps between the components. To add space between them, you could change the inset values for all of the components so that there are 5 pixels above and below, and 10 to the left and the right of each component:

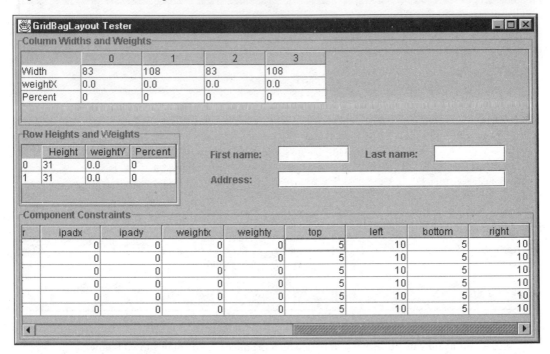

You may also find it helpful to use `GridBagTester` in addition to the `GridBagCellPanel` class defined earlier, so that you can easily identify the edges of a cell:

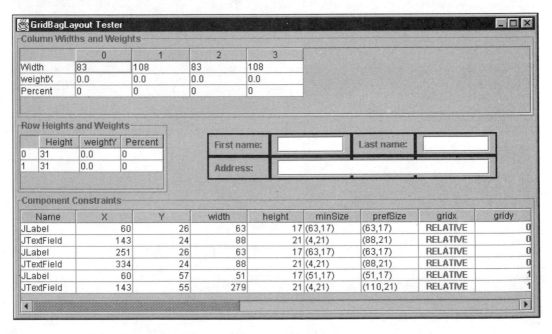

For example, changing the superclass of `SimplePanel` from `JPanel` to `GridBagCellPanel` causes a border to be drawn around each cell in the grid:

```
public class SimplePanel extends GridBagCellPanel {
```

Child Component Sizes

The size of a child component in a `GridBagLayout` depends upon the constraint values specified for the child component as well as the size of the parent container. Specifically, the `ipadx` and `ipady` values are added to the component's preferred or minimum width and height, respectively, and the `fill` constraint can cause the component to be expanded to fill its available display area.

It has been stated a number of times that `GridBagLayout` uses a component's preferred size *or* its minimum size without explaining the circumstances in which one is used and the other is not. Very simply, `GridBagLayout` attempts to use the preferred sizes of the child components, but it only does so if the container is large enough to display all of the child components using their preferred sizes. Otherwise, the `GridBagLayout` reformats the display using the components' minimum sizes. However, `GridBagLayout`, respects minimum sizes, and will never make a component smaller than that size unless you specify a negative value for either the `ipadx` or `ipady` properties. In addition, it always adds the `ipadx` and `ipady` values to either the preferred or the minimum size, depending upon which one is being used.

To illustrate this behavior, let's first review the components' sizes in the screenshot below, paying particular attention to the `JTextField` instances:

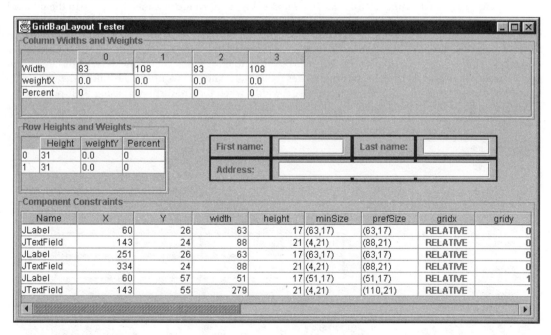

Notice that with the exception of the `JTextField` on the second row, which has been stretched to fill three columns, each of the components is displayed using its preferred size. You should also note that while the `JLabel` instances have the same values for preferred and minimum sizes, the `JTextField` instances do not. The `JTextField` minimum width values are much smaller than the preferred widths (a minimum width of 4 pixels, and a preferred width of 88 pixels). Since that is the case, you can expect that if the panel becomes too small to display the components using their preferred widths, the text fields will shrink to their minimum sizes. As shown below, that's exactly what happens when the dialog is made slightly narrower, reducing the container's width as well. The second and fourth columns have been reallocated 24 pixels wide each, since they both contain a `JTextField` with a minimum width of 4 and left and right inset values of 10.

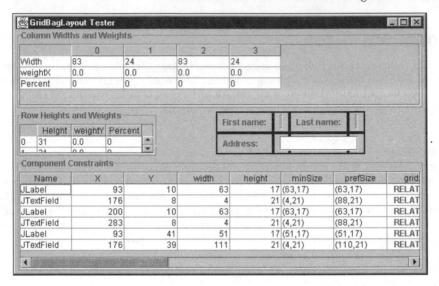

This behavior is somewhat undesirable, since the text fields can shrink dramatically in size to the point of being unusable. One solution to the problem is to set the `weightx` values of the text fields so that they do not shrink as much. For example, if we set the `weightx` for both of the `JTextField` instances in the first row to 0.5 and set their `fill` values to `HORIZONTAL`, they'll grow and shrink as the width of the container changes (see below). You could also use the `ipadx` values to ensure that the `JTextField` instances don't become unusable when set to their minimum sizes. However, doing so would also result in the specified number of pixels being added to the `JTextField` widths when they're displayed using their preferred sizes, causing them to be larger than necessary in that case and wasting screen space.

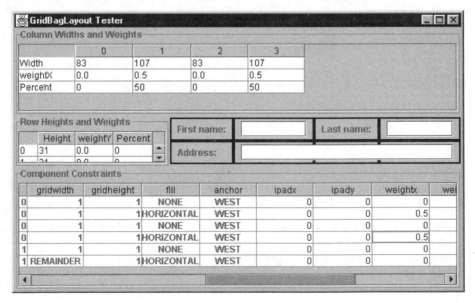

The `fill` value also can affect a component's size, but it is applied only after the grid's row and column sizes have been calculated. In other words, the `fill` value can affect the size of a component within its display area, but unlike constraints such as `ipadx`, `ipady`, and `insets`, it is not used in calculating the size of that area. Similarly, the weight values are applicable only after the initial cell sizes have been calculated using the component sizes, pads, and inset values.

Child Component Locations

The location of each child component in a `GridBagLayout`-managed container is determined primarily by the component's display area, which is identified by its `gridx`, `gridy`, `gridwidth`, and `gridheight` values. Those values define the rectangular region within the grid that makes up the component's display area, and the component will be displayed somewhere inside that area.

In addition to the number and location of cells that the component occupies, its `anchor` constraint affects where a component is located within those cells. By default, a component is centered both vertically and horizontally within its display area.

Resizing Behavior

If you shrink a container managed by a `GridBagLayout` so that it can no longer display its components using their preferred sizes, it reformats the display using their minimum sizes. If the container continues to shrink until the components cannot be displayed using their minimum sizes, then portions of the display will disappear from the panel:

Container Size

To calculate the preferred width of a container, `GridBagLayout` adds the widths of all grid columns in the container, and those widths are calculated using the preferred width of each component in the column. The sum of those width values is added to the container's left and right inset values to obtain the container's preferred width, and its preferred height is calculated in the same manner using the components' preferred heights.

The container's minimum size is calculated in the same manner, except that it uses the components' minimum size values instead of their preferred sizes. `GridBagLayout` does not impose any maximum size limit on the container.

BoxLayout

Each of the five layout managers discussed so far is defined in the `java.awt` package and has been available since Java 1.0. However, `BoxLayout` is a more recent addition to Java and is included in the `javax.swing` package. `BoxLayout` is an attempt to provide some of the flexibility of `GridBagLayout` without the complexity involved in its use.

A `BoxLayout` allows you to create either a single row or a single column of components. In other words, the components you add to a `BoxLayout` are arranged vertically from top-to-bottom, or horizontally from left-to-right.

`BoxLayout` is different from the other layout managers in a number of ways, and uses some properties defined in `Component` that the other layout managers ignore. For example, `BoxLayout` respects a component's maximum size, and will never make the component larger than the dimensions specified by that property. In addition, a `BoxLayout` that arranges its components vertically (or a "vertical `BoxLayout`") uses each component's alignment along the X axis, which is available through the `getAlignmentX()` method in `Component`. Similarly, `BoxLayout` uses the components' alignments along the Y axis (and the corresponding `getAlignmentY()` method) when it arranges them horizontally.

`BoxLayout` is different from the other layout managers in one other important way: it uses a component's *maximum* size to determine the amount of space that the component should occupy. In many cases, a component's maximum size is the same as or is close to its preferred size. However, as we'll see later, some components have very large maximum size values, which can produce unexpected or undesirable results when used with a `BoxLayout`.

Alignment Values, Ascents and Descents

Component alignment values play a major role in determining how components are positioned within a `BoxLayout`-managed container, but before we can examine how alignment values are used, it's necessary to define some terms.

A component's alignment is represented by a float value that can range from 0.0 to 1.0, and you may find it helpful to think of this number as a percentage value, with 0.0 representing 0% and 1.0 representing 100%. By default, a component's X and Y alignment values are both set to 0.5. The component's **ascent value** is calculated by multiplying one of its dimensions by one of its alignment values. For example, if you're using a horizontal `BoxLayout`, you could calculate the **preferred height ascent** for a component by multiplying the component's preferred height by its Y alignment value, as in the following equation:

```
Dimension prefSize = comp.getPreferredSize();
int ascent = (int)(prefSize.height * comp.getAlignmentY());
```

Similarly, a component's **descent value** is calculated by subtracting the component's ascent value from the size that was used to calculate the ascent, as shown below:

```
int descent = prefSize.height - ascent;
```

In other words, the sum of the ascent and descent values is equal to the dimension that was used to calculate them, and they represent the portions of the component that lie on either side of an imaginary line. For example, suppose that the above code was executed for a component with a preferred height of 400 pixels, and that the component's Y alignment value is 0.25. The ascent value would be 100 (400 * 0.25 = 100), while the descent value would be 300 (400 - 100 = 300).

Note that ascent and descent values can be calculated from a component's preferred, minimum, or maximum sizes, and as we'll see, each one plays a role in BoxLayout's behavior. In addition, the "ascent" and "descent" concepts apply to both a component's horizontal size as well as its vertical size, although only one (either vertical or horizontal) is used in a given BoxLayout. A component's horizontal ascent and descent are used when it's added to a vertical BoxLayout, while its vertical ascent and descent are used when it is in a horizontal BoxLayout.

If this seems somewhat confusing, keep in mind that the horizontal placement of components in a horizontal box is simple – they appear next to one another from left to right. Similarly, for a vertical box, components are simply "stacked" from top to bottom. In either case, the alignment, ascent, and descent values are used to calculate the component's position in the remaining dimension.

You can see an example of this behavior by compiling the following code, which uses a vertical BoxLayout:

```java
import java.awt.*;
import javax.swing.*;

public class BoxTest {

  public static void main(String[] args) {
    JFrame f = new JFrame("Vertical BoxLayout-managed container");
    f.setDefaultCloseOperation(JFrame.EXIT_ON_CLOSE);
    Container pane = f.getContentPane();
    pane.setLayout(new BoxLayout(pane, BoxLayout.Y_AXIS));
    for (float align = 0.0f; align <= 1.0f; align += 0.25f) {
      JButton button = new JButton("X Alignment = " + align);
      button.setAlignmentX(align);
      pane.add(button);
    }
    f.setSize(400, 300);
    f.setVisible(true);
  }

}
```

When executed, this code produces a display like the one shown below:

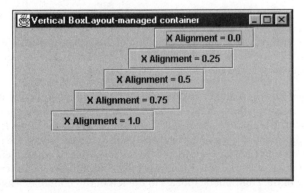

In addition to the alignment values assigned to each component, an alignment value is calculated for a container when it's managed by a BoxLayout. The container's horizontal alignment is calculated by a vertical BoxLayout, while the vertical alignment is used by a horizontal BoxLayout. These are accessible through LayoutManager2's getLayoutAlignmentX() and getLayoutAlignmentY() methods, although BoxLayout is currently the only layout manager that returns a meaningful value from those methods.

Layout Alignment Calculations

For a vertical BoxLayout, the container's X alignment is used to position components within the container, and its value is derived from the X alignment values of those components. The layout manager first examines each component and identifies the largest **minimum width ascent** and **minimum width descent** (that is, ascent and descent values calculated using the components' minimum widths) of any component. Once it has identified those two values, it calculates their sum, divides the largest minimum width ascent by that sum, and the result of that calculation becomes the container's alignment.

For example, let's assume that the following table describes the components in a container managed by a vertical BoxLayout. As mentioned before, the ascent value is calculated by multiplying the dimension (in this case, the width) by the alignment value, and the descent is the dimension value minus the ascent:

Minimum Width	X Alignment	Ascent	Descent
90	0.2	18	72
36	0.75	27	9
80	0.25	20	60
72	0.5	36	36
28	1.0	28	0
Maximum ascent/descent value:		36	72

In this case, the largest ascent value is 36 and the largest descent is 72. Therefore, the container's alignment value is 0.33, as calculated using the formula below:

```
alignment = max(ascent) / ( max(ascent) + max(descent) )
```

or:

```
alignment = 36 / (36 + 72) = 0.33
```

Note that although this example examines the calculation of the X alignment for a vertical BoxLayout, the calculations are done exactly the same way for a horizontal BoxLayout, although the components' Y alignments and height values are used instead.

Now that we've examined how a container's alignment is calculated, you may be wondering why it's important. Conceptually, you can think of the container's alignment as defining an imaginary line (or **axis**) inside the container around which the components are positioned. For example, for a vertical BoxLayout, a component with an X alignment of 0.0 will normally be placed completely to the right of the axis. Similarly, a component with an alignment of 1.0 appears entirely to the left, while a component with an alignment of 0.5 is centered on the axis. In other words, you can think of the component's alignment as a value that determines what portion of the component appears to the left of the container's axis.

To identify the location of a container's axis, you can multiply the appropriate alignment value by the corresponding dimension. For example, if you were using a horizontal container, you would multiply the container's actual/current height by its Y alignment value. In the screenshot below, the container's axis is represented graphically by a thick, dark-colored line, although you will not normally see such an indication of its location when using a BoxLayout:

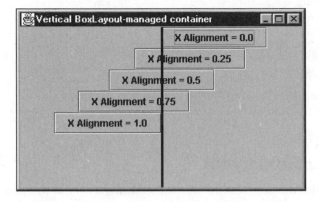

However, it's easy to implement this functionality, which serves a purpose similar to that of the
`GridBagCellPanel` class defined earlier:

```java
import java.awt.*;
import javax.swing.*;

public class BoxPanel extends JPanel {

  public void paintChildren(Graphics g) {
    super.paintChildren(g);
    Dimension size = getSize();
    LayoutManager manager = getLayout();
    if ((manager != null) && (manager instanceof BoxLayout)) {
      BoxLayout layout = (BoxLayout) manager;

      // There's currently no accessor method that allows
      // us to determine the orientation (vertical or
      // horizontal) used by a BoxLayout, so we'll hard-code
      // this class to assume vertical orientation
      boolean vertical = true;
      if (vertical) {
        int axis = (int) (layout.getLayoutAlignmentX(this) * size.width);
        g.fillRect(axis - 1, 0, 3, size.height);
      } else {
        int axis = (int) (layout.getLayoutAlignmentY(this) * size.height);
        g.fillRect(0, axis - 1, size.width, 3);
      }
    }
  }

}
```

Once you've compiled `BoxPanel`, you can easily modify the `BoxTest` application defined earlier so that it
uses `BoxPanel`:

```java
public static void main(String[] args) {
  JFrame f = new JFrame("Vertical BoxLayout-managed container");
  f.setDefaultCloseOperation(JFrame.EXIT_ON_CLOSE);
  Container pane = new BoxPanel();
  f.setContentPane(pane);
```

```
      pane.setLayout(new BoxLayout(pane, BoxLayout.Y_AXIS));
      for (float align = 0.0f; align <= 1.0f; align += 0.25f) {
        JButton button = new JButton("X Alignment = " + align);
        button.setAlignmentX(align);
        pane.add(button);
      }
      f.setSize(400, 300);
      f.setVisible(true);
  }
```

Constructing a BoxLayout

BoxLayout is somewhat different from the other layout managers in that its constructor must be passed a reference to the Container instance that uses it. In addition, you must specify how the BoxLayout should arrange its components: vertically (in a column) or horizontally (in a row), specifying either the BoxLayout.Y_AXIS or BoxLayout.X_AXIS constant, respectively. For example, you can use the following code to create a BoxLayout that will display its components in a column:

```
JPanel panel = new JPanel();
BoxLayout bl = new BoxLayout(panel, BoxLayout.Y_AXIS);
panel.setLayout(bl);
```

In addition to creating a BoxLayout this way, there is an alternative that's provided by the Box class. Specifically, it includes static getVerticalBox() and getHorizontalBox() factory methods that return an instance of Box that uses a BoxLayout to arrange its components. As you might expect, getVerticalBox() returns a container that arranges its components vertically, while getHorizontalBox() returns one that arranges its components horizontally. The Box class is discussed in more detail shortly.

Constraints

BoxLayout does not support constraints in the traditional sense, and you should use the simple form of add() when adding a component to a parent container. However, a component's alignment values effectively act as constraints by defining how the component should be placed within its parent container. In addition, JComponent defines setAlignmentX() and setAlignmentY() mutator methods that allow you to set those values instead of creating a subclass that overrides the accessor methods.

Child Component Sizes

Before setting the widths of components in a vertical box, BoxLayout calculates an ascent and descent value for the container using its current/actual width and its derived alignment value. In other words, the BoxLayout determines how much space is available on each side of the container's axis.

When setting the size of a component in a vertical box, BoxLayout calculates the component's maximum width ascent and maximum width descent. It then compares the component's ascent to the container's ascent, and the component's descent to the container's descent, selecting the smaller value in each case. In other words, BoxLayout tries to use the component's maximum width, but if that width exceeds the size available within the container, it uses the container's preferred width instead.

For many components, this behavior is acceptable because the maximum width is the same as or is close to the preferred width, but in some cases, the results may not be what you intended. For example, the existing implementation of BoxTest displays buttons with different alignment values using the buttons' preferred sizes. This behavior is consistent with the way that most other layout managers handle button instances, and is appropriate for most situations. However, suppose that you modify the code so that it creates instances of JTextField instead of instances of JButton:

```java
import java.awt.*;
import javax.swing.*;

public class BoxTest {

    public static void main(String[] args) {
        JFrame f = new JFrame("Vertical BoxLayout-managed container");
        f.setDefaultCloseOperation(JFrame.EXIT_ON_CLOSE);
        Container pane = new BoxPanel();
        f.setContentPane(pane);
        pane.setLayout(new BoxLayout(pane, BoxLayout.Y_AXIS));
        for (float align = 0.0f; align <= 1.0f; align += 0.25f) {
//        JButton button = new JButton("X Alignment = " + align);
//        button.setAlignmentX(align);
//        pane.add(button);
          JTextField tf = new JTextField("X Alignment = " + align, 10);
          tf.setAlignmentX(align);
          pane.add(tf);
        }
        f.setSize(400, 300);
        f.setVisible(true);
    }

}
```

As the following screen shot illustrates, making these changes to the code does indeed cause text fields to appear in place of the buttons, but unlike the buttons, the text fields are stretched to fill the parent container:

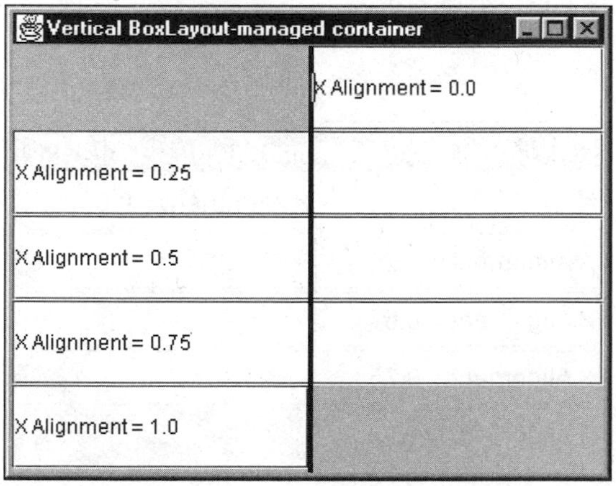

This occurs because unlike JButton, the JTextField class returns an extremely large value for its maximum width and height, and BoxLayout uses each component's maximum width to determine its size.

Notice that in this example, the container is also filled vertically. When managing a vertical box, `BoxLayout` attempts to stretch components to fill the container vertically, although it respects the components' maximum size values. If the components cannot be stretched to fill the area vertically, then whitespace appears at the bottom (or the right for a horizontal box), as shown earlier.

When components must be stretched vertically because the container is larger than their combined heights, `BoxLayout` first calculates how much space remains to be filled. It then stretches each component vertically by comparing the component's maximum height to its preferred height, and allocates the extra space based on that difference. In other words, the closer a component's maximum size is to its preferred size, the less that component will be stretched. Components that have the same value for their maximum and preferred sizes will not be stretched at all, and no component is ever made larger than its maximum size by `BoxLayout`.

Although this discussion examines how a `BoxLayout` sets the sizes for child components in vertical boxes, the same concepts are applicable to horizontal boxes, but their width values are used instead of their heights.

Child Component Locations

The exact location of a child component within a `BoxLayout` is determined by a complex interaction between the child's size values, its alignment, and the size and alignment values of the other children in the container. In addition, the order in which a component is added to the container affects its location, since child components are displayed in top-to-bottom order for a vertical box and left-to-right order for a horizontal one.

In general, a child component's position is determined by its alignment values and the parent container's alignment value. If the child has an alignment value of 0.0, it is placed to the right of or below the container's axis. Similarly, an alignment of 0.5 causes it to be centered on the axis, and a value of 1.0 causes it to appear left of or above the axis.

Resizing Behavior

Increasing and reducing the size of the parent container causes the absolute position of the container's axis to change, but the child components remain at the same position relative to the axis. If the child components were compressed, their sizes will increase as the container grows, or they may shrink if the container shrinks. For example, the screenshot below shows the results of running the modified `BoxTest` application and reducing the size of the frame:

Container Size

The container's minimum, preferred, and maximum sizes returned by a `BoxLayout` are the sizes needed to display the components using their minimum, preferred, and maximum sizes, respectively. For example, when using a vertical box, each child component's size is calculated using the techniques described earlier, and the height of the container will be the sum of the child components' heights, while the container's width will be equal to the width of the widest child component.

Swing's Box Class

In addition to `BoxLayout`, Swing includes the `Box` class, which provides functionality that's used to support `BoxLayout`. `Box` is a subclass of `java.awt.Container`, and you can use an instance of it as a visual component if it's convenient to do so. However, you should keep in mind that as a direct subclass of `Container`, `Box` does not inherit the functionality of `JComponent`, which you will often need. That functionality, and when you will need, is explained in Chapter 11.

In addition to acting as a visual component, `Box` provides a number of static "factory methods" that can be used to create instances of components that make using `BoxLayout` easier. For example, the `createHorizontalBox()` and `createVerticalBox()` methods return instances of `Box` that use a horizontal and a vertical `BoxLayout`, respectively.

`Box` also provides factory methods that create transparent components that you can add to a `BoxLayout`-managed container to provide space between the other components. The three types of components provided by `Box` are **rigid areas**, **glue** components, and **struts**.

Rigid Areas

A rigid area is simply a component with no visual representation that has the same dimensions for its minimum, and maximum sizes. You must specify the dimensions to be used when you create a rigid area, which is done by calling the static `createRigidArea()` method in the `Box` class. In the example below, a rigid area with a height of 15 has been added between each button in the original `BoxTest` class:

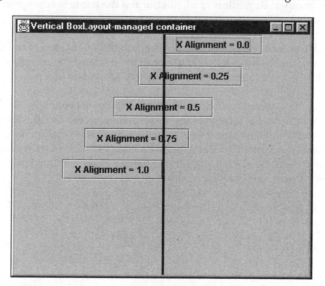

This is achieved by modifying the code as follows:

```
import java.awt.*;
import javax.swing.*;

public class BoxTest {

  public static void main(String[] args) {
    JFrame f = new JFrame("Vertical BoxLayout-managed container");
    f.setDefaultCloseOperation(JFrame.EXIT_ON_CLOSE);
    Container pane = new BoxPanel();
    f.setContentPane(pane);
    BoxLayout bl = new BoxLayout(pane, BoxLayout.Y_AXIS);
    pane.setLayout(bl);
    for (float align = 0.0f; align <= 1.0f; align += 0.25f) {
      JButton button = new JButton("X Alignment = " + align);
      button.setAlignmentX(align);
      pane.add(button);
      pane.add(Box.createRigidArea(new Dimension(0, 15)));
    }
    f.setSize(400, 300);
    f.setVisible(true);
  }
}
```

Glue

Like a rigid area, a glue component is simply a component with no visual representation, but unlike a rigid area, you are not allowed to specify a size when creating an instance of a glue component. That's because while rigid areas occupy some fixed amount of space within containers, glue components expand and contract based on the amount of space that's left unused by other (non-glue) components. If you feel that this brief description doesn't describe behavior that's conceptually similar to real-life glue, you're not alone. While "real" glue causes things to "stick together", Swing's glue components actually allow other components to be spread apart from one another. Regardless of whether or not the name is appropriate, "glue" is the term that we're stuck with (pun intended).

Which method you call to create a glue object depends upon the orientation of the BoxLayout that you're using. For a vertical box, you should call the static createVerticalGlue() method, while createHorizontalGlue() is intended to be used with a horizontal box.

Glue objects are used to fill any extra vertical or horizontal space in a container so that the space won't appear at the bottom or right side of the container. Instead, the space is usually distributed evenly to the glue components, and an example of how glue is used appears below. Note that unlike a rigid area, glue components expand and contract to fill the area between components when the container's size increases or decreases. An example of how to use glue is illustrated below, where the BoxTest application has been modified to add a glue component below each button:

```
import java.awt.*;
import javax.swing.*;

public class BoxTest {

  public static void main(String[] args) {
```

```
   JFrame f = new JFrame("Vertical BoxLayout-managed container");
   f.setDefaultCloseOperation(JFrame.EXIT_ON_CLOSE);
   Container pane = new BoxPanel();
   f.setContentPane(pane);
   pane.setLayout(new BoxLayout(pane, BoxLayout.Y_AXIS));
   for (float align = 0.0f; align <= 1.0f; align += 0.25f) {
     JButton button = new JButton("X Alignment = " + align);
     button.setAlignmentX(align);
     pane.add(button);
     pane.add(Box.createVerticalGlue());
   }
   f.setSize(400, 300);
   f.setVisible(true);
  }

}
```

Executing this code produces results like those shown below, where the extra vertical space is distributed evenly to each of the glue components:

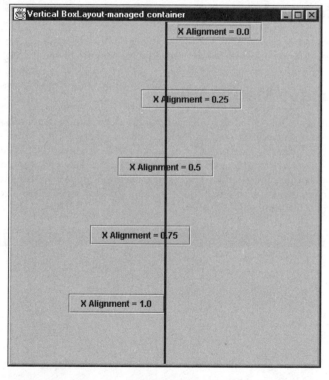

As mentioned earlier, extra vertical space is distributed by a vertical BoxLayout based on the difference between a component's maximum vertical size and its preferred vertical size. As you might guess, glue components are simply "dummy" components with a large maximum size and a minimum size of 0, so in many cases, all extra space will be assigned to them. However, as we saw earlier with JTextField instances, it's possible for other components with large maximum sizes to accidentally be made inappropriately large by a BoxLayout, and this can occur even when glue components are used.

Struts

One definition of the word "strut" in Webster's New World dictionary is, "a brace fitted into a framework to resist pressure in the direction of its length", and unlike glue components, struts are appropriately named. Struts are similar to rigid areas, but with an important difference: instead of specifying both the width and height of the component, you only specify a strut's size in *one* dimension.

Specifically, you specify the width when you call `createHorizontalStrut()` and the height when calling `createVerticalStrut()`. The strut uses the value you specify for its minimum, preferred, and maximum size in that dimension, and uses 0 for the other dimension when setting its minimum and preferred size. However, when setting the maximum size, Bun uses a very large value for the remaining dimension (width for a vertical box, height for a horizontal box), and this can cause undesirable results. Specifically, the presence of a very large strut component in the `BoxLayout` can result in its container being assigned a size that's larger than what was intended.

Since rigid areas can provide the same functionality and because there is a potential problem associated with the use of struts, you should avoid struts and use rigid areas instead.

Guidelines for Using Layout Managers

Now that we've examined the advantages and disadvantages of the layout managers included with Java, it's appropriate to discuss some more general topics related to how to use layout managers.

Combining Layout Managers

In the previous discussions of layout managers, each one was treated independently of the other, but it's common practice for a user interface to use multiple layout managers. In fact, you'll often find it necessary or desirable to create a container that uses one type of layout manager and add child containers to that parent which use different types of layout managers. For example, suppose that you want to create a user interface like the one shown below. In this case, the component at the top is displayed using its preferred height and fills the width of the container. In addition, a row of buttons that are equal in size occupies the bottom, and a component in the center fills the remaining area.

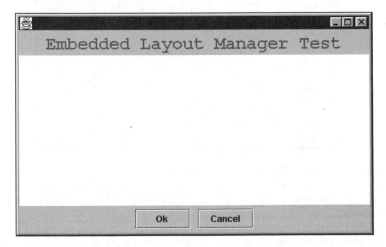

To some extent, BorderLayout provides the functionality needed to create this component, but you cannot use it directly to create the bottom row of buttons. That's because BorderLayout allows only a single component to be added to a location, such as the SOUTH portion of its container. This problem can be resolved by adding the two buttons to a container such as a JPanel and adding that panel to the parent managed by a BorderLayout. Since the buttons should be given the same size, GridLayout is the obvious choice for the container that the buttons will be added to, and the code to implement this is shown below:

```java
import java.awt.*;
import javax.swing.*;

public class Embedded extends JFrame {

  public static void main(String[] args) {
    Embedded e = new Embedded();
    e.setDefaultCloseOperation(JFrame.EXIT_ON_CLOSE);
    e.setSize(400, 300);
    e.setVisible(true);
  }

  public Embedded() {
    Container pane = getContentPane();
    pane.setLayout(new BorderLayout());
    pane.add(getHeader(), BorderLayout.NORTH);
    pane.add(getTextArea(), BorderLayout.CENTER);
    pane.add(getButtonPanel(), BorderLayout.SOUTH);
  }

  protected JComponent getHeader() {
    JLabel label = new JLabel("Embedded Layout Manager Test",
                             JLabel.CENTER);
    label.setFont(new Font("Courier", Font.BOLD, 24));
    return label;
  }

  protected JComponent getTextArea() {
    return new JTextArea(10, 10);
  }

  protected JComponent getButtonPanel() {
    JPanel inner = new JPanel();
    inner.setLayout(new GridLayout(1, 2, 10, 0));
    inner.add(new JButton("Ok"));
    inner.add(new JButton("Cancel"));
    return inner;
  }

}
```

As shown below, this code doesn't quite achieve the desired results, since the buttons have been stretched to fill the width of the container:

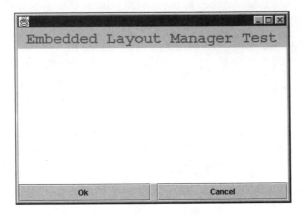

That's because the buttons' parent container is stretched by the BorderLayout so that its width is equal to the width of the frame, and that in turn causes the GridLayout to stretch the buttons to fill their parent container. To fix this problem, it's necessary to put the panel managed by the GridLayout into another container that won't stretch it. Since FlowLayout always displays components using their preferred size, we can use it to provide this behavior, so we'll define an additional FlowLayout-managed JPanel, add the button panel to it, and add the button panel to the content pane:

```
protected JComponent getButtonPanel() {
    JPanel inner = new JPanel();
    inner.setLayout(new GridLayout(1, 2, 10, 0));
    inner.add(new JButton("Ok"));
    inner.add(new JButton("Cancel"));
    JPanel outer = new JPanel();
    outer.setLayout(new FlowLayout());
    outer.add(inner);
    return outer;
    // return inner;
}
```

Finally, running this modified code produces the desired interface that was illustrated at the start of this section.

You'll often find it necessary to embed containers within other containers and to use different layout managers when doing so. If you're creating a complex user interface, it's often helpful to conceptually break the interface down into smaller, simpler portions that can be created using the existing layout managers. Those smaller pieces can then be created and combined into the large, complex interface instead of trying to produce the desired results with a single layout manager.

Absolute Positioning Without a Layout Manager

Although there's rarely a reason to do so, you can completely avoid using a layout manager when designing an interface. However, if you don't use a layout manager, you are responsible for explicitly setting the size and position of each component within a container using Component methods such as setSize(), setLocation(), and setBounds(). This approach is rarely desirable, because it usually results in an interface that must be revised to appropriately handle even minor changes.

Although using absolute positioning without a layout manager can prevent using a more complicated mixture of layout managers, since Java is so portable the application could well be run on a device with a display smaller than that on which it was originally designed. If you know the smallest likely size of the screen the application will run on, you can use absolute positioning with a non-resizable window

If you wish to remove the layout manager from a container and explicitly set the size and position of the components in that container, you can call the setLayout() method and specify a null value, as shown below:

```
JPanel panel = new JPanel();
panel.setLayout(null);
```

When a container displays its child components, it does so using the position and size values assigned to those components, which are usually set by a layout manager. If you add a component to a container and do not set the component's location, it will appear at the container's origin (in other words, at coordinates 0, 0). However, if you add a component to a container and do not specify the component's size, it will not appear at all, because its width and height values will both be 0. The preferred, minimum, and maximum size values are used by layout managers to determine the size that should be used for a component, but components are not automatically set to any of those three sizes when created.

Invisible Components

Components that have their visibility flag set to false do not appear when their parent container is displayed, and you can query and modify the visibility flag using Component's isVisible() and setVisible() methods. In general, layout managers ignore invisible components inside their layoutContainer() method, causing the container to be formatted as though the invisible components had not been added.

You'll most often use invisible components when some portion of your user interface should not always be displayed. For example, your interface might have a menu item that allows the user to toggle the display status of some element such as a tool bar or status bar. In that case, you could add the element to the container when the container is being constructed, but make it invisible until it should be displayed.

Depending upon the superclass of the component that's made visible or invisible, it may be necessary for you to use revalidate() to cause the layout manager to reposition and resize the components in the container. JComponent subclasses automatically trigger this behavior, but others do not.

Specifying an Index when Adding a Component

Earlier, we saw that each Container maintains a list of child components and that the components are listed in the order in which they were added to the container. Normally when a component is added to a container, that component is added to the end of the container's list. However, if you prefer to insert the component at a particular position within the list, you can use one of two additional forms of the add() method that were not previously mentioned in this chapter. They are:

- ❑   add(Component comp, int index)
- ❑   add(Component comp, Object constraints, int index)

As we've seen, some layout managers position child components within the container based on when they were added. In reality, that behavior is based on the component's index value (its position within the parent container's list), which is assumed to reflect the sequence in which the components were added to the container. In most cases where the index value is significant, you'll simply add components in the order that you want them to appear. However, for various reasons, it's not always possible or desirable to do so and you'll want to explicitly specify an index value when adding a child component.

A component's place in the list is sometimes significant for another reason as well, since its index value (also called its **Z-order**) defines its position on the Z axis. In other words, the order in which two components appear in their parent container's list determines which component appears "in front of" the other. When a container receives a `paint()` request, it paints its children in reverse order (from last to first), so that the most recently added child appears "behind" the others, and the first one appears "in front". It's like putting a pile of papers on your desk, then turning the pile upside down.

Z-order isn't usually important because layout managers normally don't allow components to occupy the same coordinates within their parent container. However, if you're not using a layout manager or if you're using one that allows components to overlap one another, Z-order can become significant. For example, the following application defines two JButton instances that partially overlap.

```java
import java.awt.*;
import javax.swing.*;

public class ZOrder extends JPanel {

  public static void main(String[] args) {
    JFrame f = new JFrame();
    f.setDefaultCloseOperation(JFrame.EXIT_ON_CLOSE);
    f.setContentPane(new ZOrder());
    f.setSize(400, 300);
    f.setVisible(true);
  }

  public ZOrder() {
    setLayout(null);
    JButton first = new JButton("This button is added first");
    first.setBounds(20, 50, 200, 30);
    add(first);
    JButton second = new JButton("This button is added second");
    second.setBounds(120, 65, 200, 30);
    add(second);
  }

}
```

If you compile and run this application, it displays the first button in front of the second one as shown below, which is the expected result based on the behavior described:

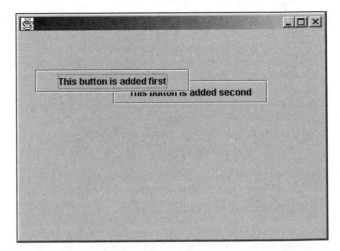

However, if you move the cursor over the second button, that button will appear in front of the first one, which may seem to contradict the statements that have been made concerning Z-order:

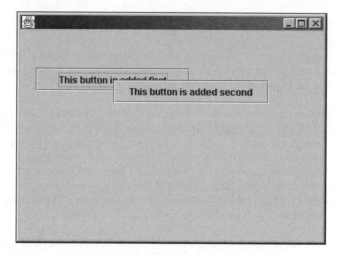

In reality, the second button is still behind the first one in those cases, but it has been repainted while the first one was not, so the second one *seems* to be in front. Moving the mouse over a component causes the component to be repainted so that it will repair the "damage" done when the cursor was painted over part of the component, which is why this behavior occurs. You can prove that the first button is still in front by moving the mouse over the portion of the interface where the two buttons overlap one another, at which time the first button will be repainted and again appear in front of the second one.

> *Note that unlike a component's X and Y coordinates, Z-order can only be set when a component is added to a container. Therefore, if you wish to change a component's Z-order, you must remove it from the container and add it again, explicitly specifying the new index value when you call the* `add()` *method.*

Creating your own Layout Manager

The layout managers that we've examined so far are a standard part of Java, and provide enough functionality to allow you to create very complex and flexible layouts. However, the existing layout managers are sometimes not capable of setting the size or position of components the way you'd like, and in that situation, you may choose to create your own layout manager.

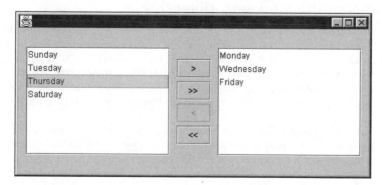

For example, suppose that you wish to create a component that allows you to select items from a list like the one shown above, and that you have the following requirements that must be met:

❑ The column of buttons in the middle of the component should always be displayed using its preferred size.

❑ The two JList components should both be the same size vertically and horizontally, and they should shrink or expand to fill the container's remaining horizontal space after the center component has been allocated its preferred size.

Given these requirements, none of the layout managers that we've already seen are appropriate for this custom component, primarily because of the requirement that the two JList components be the same size. Only GridLayout allows you to ensure that two components have the same horizontal and vertical size, but using that layout manager would also cause the button column in the center to have the same size as the JList instances. GridBagLayout allows you to assign all components in a row the same height or all components in a column the same width, but it does not provide you with a way to make components the same size in both dimensions. In this case, it's necessary for us to create a layout manager to support this component, and we'll name this new layout manager class DividerLayout.

As it turns out, creating a custom layout manager is very simple. All that you need to do is create a class which implements the LayoutManager2 interface defined in the java.awt package. We'll begin by examining the methods defined in LayoutManager2 that your custom layout manager class must implement, and then examine those in the LayoutManager class, since it is the superclass of LayoutManager2.

When considering how you will implement these methods, keep in mind that a layout manager instance is associated with and used by a Container, and that these methods should not normally be called directly by your application code.

With the exception of removeLayoutComponent() and the overloaded addLayoutComponent(), all methods defined in LayoutManager and LayoutManager2 are passed a reference to the parent container associated with the layout manager instance.

LayoutManager2 Methods

This interface defines five methods, three of which will normally contain little or no code. LayoutManager2 did not exist in Java 1.0, but was added in 1.1 to provide support for new features like alignment values, maximum sizes (Java 1.0 only supported minimum and preferred sizes), and a more generic add() method.

addLayoutComponent(Component, Object)

This method is called by the layout manager's container when its add() method is invoked, indicating that a component should be added to the container. The container passes the request along to the layout manager so that the manager can take whatever action is necessary, such as creating a copy of the constraint information and defining a relationship between the component and the constraint data. For example, GridBagLayout creates a clone of the GridBagConstraints object that's passed to it and associates that GridBagConstraints clone with the component by adding an entry to a Hashtable.

As mentioned earlier in this chapter, the layout manager *is not* responsible for maintaining a list of the components that have been added to the container. That task is performed by the container itself, and the list of components maintained by the container is accessible through its getComponents() method. In fact, FlowLayout and GridLayout do not maintain references to the components added to the layout, since they don't support any constraint information. Instead, they position each component based on when it was added to the `Container`, and they're able to do this because the array returned by `getComponents()` lists the components in the order in which they were added to the container. Only when a layout manager needs to associate constraint information with a component will it normally maintain references to the components.

When you create a custom layout manager, you'll need to decide whether any constraint information should be specified when a component is added. If the layout manager doesn't need constraint information, then the application can simply call the `add()` method in `Container` that accepts a single component instance.

If your layout manager does need constraint information, you can create a custom class like `GridBagConstraints` that encapsulates the information, or if the constraint information is simple, you can use an existing class. For example, the `DividerLayout` requires some type of constraint information that identifies which position (left, center, or right) the component should occupy. Since `DividerLayout` is somewhat similar to `BorderLayout`, we'll define three `String` constants called WEST, CENTER, and EAST that correspond to the three positions available within the container:

```
import java.awt.*;

public class DividerLayout implements LayoutManager2 {

  public final static String WEST = "WEST";
  public final static String EAST = "EAST";
  public final static String CENTER = "CENTER";

  protected Component westComponent;
  protected Component centerComponent;
  protected Component eastComponent;

  // Methods go here ...
}
```

In addition, `DividerLayout` needs to associate a component with its constraint value so that the component's position can be selected when the time comes to set the sizes and positions of the container's child components:

```
public void addLayoutComponent(Component comp, Object constraints) {
  if (WEST.equalsIgnoreCase((String)constraints)) {
    westComponent = comp;
  }
  else if (CENTER.equalsIgnoreCase((String)constraints)) {
    centerComponent = comp;
  }
  else if (EAST.equalsIgnoreCase((String)constraints)) {
    eastComponent = comp;
  }
}
```

maximumLayoutSize()

This method is called by a container when its `getMaximumSize()` method is called. The layout manager is responsible for calculating the amount of space that the container needs to display all of its components using their maximum sizes.

In the case of `DividerLayout`, it identifies the largest height value from the three components and determines which of the two outer components has a larger width value. That width value is multiplied by 2 since there are two "outer" components that will be assigned identical widths and the result is added to the width of the center component, as shown below:

```
public Dimension maximumLayoutSize(Container target) {
  Dimension size;
  int width = 0;
  int height = 0;
  if ((westComponent != null) && (westComponent.isVisible())) {
    size = westComponent.getMaximumSize();
    width = Math.max(width, size.width);
    height = Math.max(height, size.height);
  }
  if ((eastComponent != null) && (eastComponent.isVisible())) {
    size = eastComponent.getMaximumSize();
    width = Math.max(width, size.width);
    height = Math.max(height, size.height);
  }
  width *= 2;
  if ((centerComponent != null) && (centerComponent.isVisible())) {
    size = centerComponent.getPreferredSize();
    width += size.width;
    height = Math.max(height, size.height);
  }
  return new Dimension(width, height);
}
```

getLayoutAlignmentX() and getLayoutAlignmentY()

These methods are provided for layout managers such as `BoxLayout` that use an alignment value to position the components within the container. Like most layout managers, however, `DividerLayout` does not use alignment values, so the value returned isn't important, and "dummy" implementations are shown below:

```
public float getLayoutAlignmentX(Container target) {
  return 0.0f;
}

public float getLayoutAlignmentY(Container target) {
  return 0.0f;
}
```

invalidateLayout()

This method is called to indicate to the layout manager that it should clear any cached information related to the size and position of the container's components. This is *only* related to information that has been derived by the layout manager itself, and a call to this method *does not* indicate that constraint information that was explicitly passed to the layout manager should be discarded. For example, if your layout manager performs computations that are slow and complex, it may be worthwhile to cache the results of those computations. Like most layout managers, no action needs to be taken in `DividerLayout`'s implementation of this method:

```
public void invalidateLayout(Container target) {
}
```

LayoutManager Methods

This is the interface originally included in Java 1.0 for creating a layout manager. It defines basic methods related to managing the components added to a container.

addLayoutComponent (String, Component)

This is the method that was originally used for adding a child component to a parent container, but this method has effectively been deprecated. It is not marked as deprecated by a javadoc-style @deprecated tag, but it is deprecated conceptually, because another, more flexible method exists and should be used instead. In fact, as you'll see shortly, the implementation of this method in DividerLayout does nothing more than call its replacement, which is the addLayoutComponent() method defined in LayoutManager2.

This method was provided to allow String constraint values to be passed to CardLayout and BorderLayout instances. However, because this method only accepts a String value, you cannot pass any other type of object to represent the constraints. For example, since an instance of GridBagConstraints is not a subclass of String, you could not use it as an argument with the add() method in Java 1.0. Instead, it was necessary to call GridBagLayout's setConstraints() method to associate the GridBagConstraints with a component, as shown in the following code:

```
GridBagLayout gbl = new GridBagLayout();
setLayout(gbl);
GridBagConstraints gbc = new GridBagConstraints();
Button btn = new Button("Testing");
gbl.setConstraints(btn, gbc);
add(btn);
```

With the addition of the more generic addLayoutComponent() method in LayoutManager2, it's now possible to pass any type of Object to the layout manager when you call add(). In Java 1.1, GridBagLayout was modified to extend LayoutManager2, so you can now add a component to a container and specify that component's constraints at the same time, as shown below:

```
GridBagLayout gbl = new GridBagLayout();
setLayout(gbl);
GridBagConstraints gbc = new GridBagConstraints();
Button btn = new Button("Testing");
//  gbl.setConstraints(btn, gbc);
//  add(btn);
add(btn, gbc);
```

As mentioned before, you'll normally implement this method by delegating the call to the addLayoutComponent() method defined in LayoutManager2, which can be done by simply reversing the order of the parameter values as shown below. Alternatively, you may simply choose to ignore a call to this method completely if your custom layout manager doesn't accept a String instance for a constraint parameter:

```
public void addLayoutComponent(String name, Component comp) {
   // The following line can be commented out without
   // affecting this layout manager
   addLayoutComponent(comp, name);
}
```

removeLayoutComponent()

This method is called when a component is removed from the container. Your custom layout manager should remove any references to the component, as well as any data it maintains that's related to the component, such as constraint information. The implementation of this method in `DividerLayout` is shown below:

```java
public void removeLayoutComponent(Component comp) {
  if (comp == westComponent) {
    westComponent = null;
  }
  else if (comp == centerComponent) {
    centerComponent = null;
  }
  else if (comp == eastComponent) {
    centerComponent = null;
  }
}
```

preferredLayoutSize() and minimumLayoutSize()

`preferredLayoutSize()` is similar to the `maximumLayoutSize()` method described earlier, and in fact its implementation will often differ only in that it calls the `getPreferredSize()` method for each component instead of `getMaximumSize()`. The purpose of this method is to calculate the preferred size of the `Container` instance associated with this layout manager. The implementation of this method in `DividerLayout` is shown below:

```java
public Dimension preferredLayoutSize(Container parent) {
  Dimension size;
  int width = 0;
  int height = 0;
  if ((westComponent != null) && (westComponent.isVisible())) {
    size = westComponent.getPreferredSize();
    width = Math.max(width, size.width);
    height = Math.max(height, size.height);
  }
  if ((eastComponent != null) && (eastComponent.isVisible())) {
    size = eastComponent.getPreferredSize();
    width = Math.max(width, size.width);
    height = Math.max(height, size.height);
  }
  width *= 2;
  if ((centerComponent != null) && (centerComponent.isVisible())) {
    size = centerComponent.getPreferredSize();
    width += size.width;
    height = Math.max(height, size.height);
  }
  return new Dimension(width, height);
}
```

Similarly, `minimumLayoutSize()` differs only in that it calls the `getMinimumSize()` method instead of `getPreferredSize()` or `getMaximumSize()`; the purpose of this method is to calculate the minimum size of the `Container` instance associated with this layout manager:

```
public Dimension minimumLayoutSize(Container parent) {
  Dimension size;
  int width = 0;
  int height = 0;
  if ((westComponent != null) && (westComponent.isVisible())) {
    size = westComponent.getMinimumSize();
    width = Math.max(width, size.width);
    height = Math.max(height, size.height);
  }
  if ((eastComponent != null) && (eastComponent.isVisible())) {
    size = eastComponent.getMinimumSize();
    width = Math.max(width, size.width);
    height = Math.max(height, size.height);
  }
  width *= 2;
  if ((centerComponent != null) && (centerComponent.isVisible())) {
    size = centerComponent.getPreferredSize();
    width += size.width;
    height += Math.max(height, size.height);
  }
  return new Dimension(width, height);
}
```

layoutContainer()

This is the method that's responsible for setting the size and position of the child components within a container, and is called when the container's doLayout() method is invoked.

Within this method, you'll typically use the preferred, minimum, or maximum component sizes, or some combination of those, and you should use methods defined in Component such as setSize(), setLocation(), and setBounds() to modify each component's size and/or position.

When implementing layoutContainer(), you should keep in mind that the size of the container may or may not be the same size that your class returned from minimumLayoutSize(), preferredLayoutSize(), or maximumLayoutSize(). In other words, you may have to allocate excess space or shrink your components, depending upon what you decide is appropriate for your layout manager. For example, in the case of DividerLayout, the two outer components are expected to shrink or expand to fill the space that remains after the middle component is allocated its preferred size.

Finally, you should be aware that it's standard practice to ignore components that are invisible, which can be determined by calling the isVisible() method. The reasons for making components invisible were discussed in more detail earlier, but you should keep this guideline in mind when designing a custom layout manager.

```
public void layoutContainer(Container container) {
  Insets insets = container.getInsets();
  Dimension westSize = new Dimension(0, 0);
  Dimension centerSize = new Dimension(0, 0);
  Dimension eastSize = new Dimension(0, 0);
  Rectangle centerBounds = new Rectangle(0, 0, 0, 0);
  Dimension containerSize = container.getSize();
  int centerX = containerSize.width / 2;
  int centerY = containerSize.height / 2;
  if ((centerComponent != null) && (centerComponent.isVisible())) {
    centerSize = centerComponent.getPreferredSize();
```

```
        centerSize.width = Math.min(centerSize.width,
            containerSize.width - insets.left - insets.right);
        centerSize.height = Math.min(centerSize.height,
            containerSize.height - insets.top - insets.bottom);
        centerComponent.setBounds(centerX - (centerSize.width / 2),
                                  centerY - (centerSize.height / 2),
                                  centerSize.width, centerSize.height);
        centerBounds = centerComponent.getBounds();
      }
      if ((westComponent != null) && (westComponent.isVisible())) {
        westSize = westComponent.getPreferredSize();
      }
      if ((eastComponent != null) && (eastComponent.isVisible())) {
        eastSize = eastComponent.getPreferredSize();
      }
      int maxWidth = Math.min(westSize.width, eastSize.width);
      maxWidth = Math.max(maxWidth, (containerSize.width -
          centerBounds.width - insets.left - insets.right) / 2);
      int maxHeight = Math.min(westSize.height, eastSize.height);
      maxHeight = Math.min(maxHeight, containerSize.height -
          insets.top - insets.bottom);
      if (westComponent != null) {
        westComponent.setBounds(centerBounds.x - maxWidth,
            centerY - (maxHeight / 2), maxWidth, maxHeight);
      }
      if (eastComponent != null) {
        eastComponent.setBounds(centerBounds.x + centerBounds.width,
            centerY - (maxHeight / 2), maxWidth, maxHeight);
      }
    }
```

Using a Custom Layout Manager

Now that a layout manager exists that can provide the appropriate user interface behavior, it's easy to implement the selector component mentioned earlier, and the source for `SelectorPanel` is shown below:

```
import java.awt.*;
import java.awt.event.*;
import javax.swing.*;
import javax.swing.event.*;
import java.util.*;

public class SelectorPanel extends JPanel {

  protected SelectorListModel unselectedModel;
  protected SelectorListModel selectedModel;
  protected JList unselectedList;
  protected JList selectedList;

  protected JButton addSelections;
  protected JButton addAll;
  protected JButton removeSelections;
  protected JButton removeAll;
```

```java
public SelectorPanel(Object[] values, int[] selections) {
  super();
  unselectedModel = new SelectorListModel(values);
  selectedModel = new SelectorListModel(null);
  if (selections != null) {
    selectedModel.takeEntriesFrom(unselectedModel, selections);
  }
  buildLayout();
}

public SelectorPanel(Object[] values) {
  this(values, null);
}

protected void buildLayout() {
  SelectionListener listener = new SelectionListener();
  setLayout(new DividerLayout());
  unselectedList = new JList(unselectedModel);
  unselectedList.addListSelectionListener(listener);
  add(new JScrollPane(unselectedList), DividerLayout.WEST);
  add(getButtonPanel(), DividerLayout.CENTER);
  selectedList = new JList(selectedModel);
  selectedList.addListSelectionListener(listener);
  add(new JScrollPane(selectedList), DividerLayout.EAST);

  addButtonListeners();
  enableButtons();
}

protected Component getButtonPanel() {
  JPanel innerPanel = new JPanel();
  innerPanel.setLayout(new GridLayout(4, 1, 0, 5));
  addSelections = new JButton(">");
  innerPanel.add(addSelections);
  addAll = new JButton(">>");
  innerPanel.add(addAll);
  removeSelections = new JButton("<");
  innerPanel.add(removeSelections);
  removeAll = new JButton("<<");
  innerPanel.add(removeAll);

  JPanel outerPanel = new JPanel();
  outerPanel.setLayout(new GridBagLayout());
  GridBagConstraints gbc = new GridBagConstraints();
  gbc.insets = new Insets(0, 10, 0, 10);
  outerPanel.add(innerPanel, gbc);

  return outerPanel;
}

protected void addButtonListeners() {
  addSelections.addActionListener(new ActionListener() {
    public void actionPerformed(ActionEvent event) {
      addSelectedItems();
    }
```

```
    });
    addAll.addActionListener(new ActionListener() {
      public void actionPerformed(ActionEvent event) {
        addAllItems();
      }
    });
    removeSelections.addActionListener(new ActionListener() {
      public void actionPerformed(ActionEvent event) {
        removeSelectedItems();
      }
    });
    removeAll.addActionListener(new ActionListener() {
      public void actionPerformed(ActionEvent event) {
        removeAllItems();
      }
    });
  }

  protected void addSelectedItems() {
    int[] selections = unselectedList.getSelectedIndices();
    selectedModel.takeEntriesFrom(unselectedModel, selections);
    enableButtons();
  }

  protected void addAllItems() {
    selectedModel.takeAllEntriesFrom(unselectedModel);
    enableButtons();
  }

  protected void removeSelectedItems() {
    int[] selections = selectedList.getSelectedIndices();
    unselectedModel.takeEntriesFrom(selectedModel, selections);
    enableButtons();
  }

  protected void removeAllItems() {
    unselectedModel.takeAllEntriesFrom(selectedModel);
    enableButtons();
  }

  protected void enableButtons() {
    ListModel model;
    int[] selections;

    selections = unselectedList.getSelectedIndices();
    addSelections.setEnabled(selections.length > 0);
    model = unselectedList.getModel();
    addAll.setEnabled(model.getSize() > 0);

    selections = selectedList.getSelectedIndices();
    removeSelections.setEnabled(selections.length > 0);
    model = selectedList.getModel();
    removeAll.setEnabled(model.getSize() > 0);
  }
```

```java
    public Object[] getSelectedValues() {
      return selectedModel.getValues();
    }

    public Object[] getUnselectedValues() {
      return unselectedModel.getValues();
    }

    class SelectorListModel extends AbstractListModel {

      protected TreeMap map;

      public SelectorListModel(Object[] values) {
        map = new TreeMap();
        if (values != null) {
          for (int i = 0; i < values.length; i++) {
            map.put(new Integer(i), values[i]);
          }
        }
      }

      public Object getElementAt(int index) {
        Set keys = map.keySet();
        return map.get(keys.toArray()[index]);
      }

      public int getSize() {
        return map.size();
      }

      public void takeEntriesFrom(SelectorListModel source, int[] rows) {
        Object key;
        Object[] keys = source.map.keySet().toArray();
        for (int i = 0; i < rows.length; i++) {
          key = keys[rows[i]];
          map.put(key, source.map.remove(key));
        }
        source.fireIntervalRemoved(source, 0, keys.length - 1);
        fireIntervalAdded(this, 0, getSize() - 1);
      }

      public void takeAllEntriesFrom(SelectorListModel source) {
        map.putAll(source.map);
        int count = source.getSize();
        source.map.clear();
        source.fireIntervalRemoved(source, 0, count - 1);
        fireIntervalAdded(this, 0, getSize() - 1);
      }

      public Object[] getValues() {
        return map.values().toArray();
      }

    }
```

```
class SelectionListener implements ListSelectionListener {

  public void valueChanged(ListSelectionEvent event) {
    JList list = (JList) (event.getSource());
    int[] selections = list.getSelectedIndices();
    if (selections.length > 0) {
      int[] indices = {};
      list = (list == selectedList ? unselectedList : selectedList);
      list.setSelectedIndices(indices);
    }
    enableButtons();
  }

}
}
```

Finally, you can easily test out this new class by compiling and executing the following code:

```
import java.awt.*;
import javax.swing.*;

public class SelectorTest extends JPanel {

  public static void main(String[] args) {
    JFrame f = new JFrame();
    f.setDefaultCloseOperation(JFrame.EXIT_ON_CLOSE);
    Container pane = f.getContentPane();
    pane.setLayout(new BorderLayout());
    Object[] values = {
      "Sunday", "Monday", "Tuesday", "Wednesday", "Thursday", "Friday",
      "Saturday"
    };
    SelectorPanel sp = new SelectorPanel(values);
    sp.setBorder(BorderFactory.createEmptyBorder(5, 10, 5, 10));
    pane.add(sp);
    f.setSize(400, 300);
    f.setVisible(true);
  }

}
```

Which should look like this:

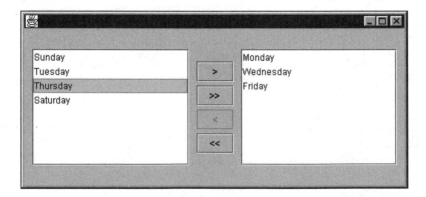

Summary

In this chapter we have examined the following topics related to layout managers:

- ❑ The layout managers that are provided with the Java core classes and how they work
- ❑ How and when to create a custom layout manager class
- ❑ How to use layout managers together to build complex user interfaces
- ❑ How and when to use absolute positioning instead of a layout manager
- ❑ The behavior of layout managers with respect to invisible components
- ❑ The importance of Z-order and how to control it

In the next chapter we will look at a particular Swing component – JTable.

Professional Java Programmin

Online discussion at http://p2p.wrox.com

6

Swing's JTable Component

Many applications need to display data in a tabular form, and Swing provides a table component (also sometimes called a "grid") that allows you to do so. The JTable class, defined in the javax.swing package, provides a great deal of functionality that you can use to create a user interface for viewing and updating data. This chapter examines some of the functionality that's commonly needed when using a table component, and illustrates how to implement it using JTable. In the process, you'll learn a great deal about how JTable works, how to make use of its existing capabilities, and how to extend its capabilities.

In this chapter, we'll cover a variety of topics related to JTable, including the following:

- ❑ How to create a data model for a table
- ❑ How column widths are assigned
- ❑ Data models
- ❑ Cell rendering and editing
- ❑ Handling cell selections
- ❑ Working with table headers
- ❑ Implementing sort functionality for table rows

The following screen shot shows an example of how a JTable component appears:

Besides the obvious ability to display information, JTable also allows you to easily edit the information, set column headers and widths, and to control how information is displayed within the table. However, the most basic function is that of displaying the data, and before you can display information in a JTable, you must encapsulate the data in a data model and make the model available to the table.

The Data Model

In addition to the JTable class, which represents the visual table component, Swing provides a number of support classes and interfaces that are used by JTable, and they are defined in the javax.swing.table package. Perhaps the most important is the **TableModel** interface, which defines the interface between a JTable and its **data model**. Like other Swing components, JTable uses a model/view/controller design that separates the visual component (a JTable instance) from its data (a TableModel implementation). This provides greater flexibility and reusability, but can also make JTable more complex to work with. Fortunately, programmers can be insulated from much of the complexity by using some of the default implementations provided with Swing.

As you might expect, the TableModel associated with a JTable is responsible for providing the table with the data that it displays, but the model is also responsible for providing some information that may not be as obvious, including the following:

- ❑ The dimensions of the table (the number of rows and columns in the table)
- ❑ The type of data contained within each column within the table
- ❑ The column headers that should be displayed
- ❑ Whether the value in a given cell can be edited

Although somewhat contrived, we'll use the data that's hard-coded in the class listed below for most of the chapter. In reality, the data displayed in a JTable is usually retrieved from some external source such as a relational database table. However, the TableValues class is convenient because it can be created easily and allows us to create sample JTable code without also writing JDBC code, which makes the examples easier to follow:

```
import java.util.Calendar;
import java.util.GregorianCalendar;

public class TableValues {
```

```
public final static int FIRST_NAME = 0;
public final static int LAST_NAME = 1;
public final static int DATE_OF_BIRTH = 2;
public final static int ACCOUNT_BALANCE = 3;
public final static int GENDER = 4;

public final static boolean GENDER_MALE = true;
public final static boolean GENDER_FEMALE = false;

public Object[][] values = {
    {
      "Clay", "Ashworth",
      new GregorianCalendar(1962, Calendar.FEBRUARY, 20).getTime(),
      new Float(12345.67), new Boolean(GENDER_MALE)
    }, {
      "Jacob", "Ashworth",
      new GregorianCalendar(1987, Calendar.JANUARY, 6).getTime(),
      new Float(23456.78), new Boolean(GENDER_MALE)
    }, {
      "Jordan", "Ashworth",
      new GregorianCalendar(1989, Calendar.AUGUST, 31).getTime(),
      new Float(34567.89), new Boolean(GENDER_FEMALE)
    }, {
      "Evelyn", "Kirk",
      new GregorianCalendar(1945, Calendar.JANUARY, 16).getTime(),
      new Float(-456.70), new Boolean(GENDER_FEMALE)
    }, {
      "Belle", "Spyres",
      new GregorianCalendar(1907, Calendar.AUGUST, 2).getTime(),
      new Float(567.00), new Boolean(GENDER_FEMALE)
    }
};

}
```

At this point, the class contains only data and no executable code, but as we'll see shortly, it can easily be transformed into a `TableModel` implementation that can be used to expose the data to a `JTable`. Before doing so, you may want to briefly study the following class diagram that describes the `TableModel` interface and its methods:

<<Interface>> TableModel
◆getRowCount() : int
◆getColumnCount() : int
◆getValueAt(row : int, column : int) : Object
◆setValueAt(value : Object, row : int, column : int) : void
◆getColumnName(column : int) : String
◆getColumnClass(column : int) : Class
◆isCellEditable(row : int, column : int) : boolean
◆addTableModelListener(listener : TableModelListener) : void
◆removeTableModelListener(listener : TableModelListener) : void

With nine methods to implement, the interface might appear complex and tedious to someone who wants to create a table quickly. However, Java also provides the AbstractTableModel and DefaultTableModel classes, which both implement the TableModel interface, and can be used with minimal effort. In fact, the AbstractTableModel can be extended by implementing three simple methods:

- One that returns the row count

- Another that returns the column count

- A third that returns the value associated with a particular cell

An example of how to implement this is shown in the following code, which modifies the TableValues class to extend AbstractTableModel and implements its three abstract methods:

```java
import java.util.Calendar;
import java.util.GregorianCalendar;
import javax.swing.table.AbstractTableModel;

public class TableValues extends AbstractTableModel {

    public final static int FIRST_NAME = 0;
    public final static int LAST_NAME = 1;
    public final static int DATE_OF_BIRTH = 2;
    public final static int ACCOUNT_BALANCE = 3;
    public final static int GENDER = 4;

    public final static boolean GENDER_MALE = true;
    public final static boolean GENDER_FEMALE = false;

    public Object[][] values = {
        {
          "Clay", "Ashworth",
          new GregorianCalendar(1962, Calendar.FEBRUARY, 20).getTime(),
          new Float(12345.67), new Boolean(GENDER_MALE)
        }, {
          "Jacob", "Ashworth",
          new GregorianCalendar(1987, Calendar.JANUARY, 6).getTime(),
          new Float(23456.78), new Boolean(GENDER_MALE)
        }, {
          "Jordan", "Ashworth",
          new GregorianCalendar(1989, Calendar.AUGUST, 31).getTime(),
          new Float(34567.89), new Boolean(GENDER_FEMALE)
        }, {
          "Evelyn", "Kirk",
          new GregorianCalendar(1945, Calendar.JANUARY, 16).getTime(),
          new Float(-456.70), new Boolean(GENDER_FEMALE)
        }, {
          "Belle", "Spyres",
          new GregorianCalendar(1907, Calendar.AUGUST, 2).getTime(),
          new Float(567.00), new Boolean(GENDER_FEMALE)
        }
    };

    public int getRowCount() {
      return values.length;
    }
```

```
    public int getColumnCount() {
      return values[0].length;
    }

    public Object getValueAt(int row, int column) {
      return values[row][column];
    }

  }
```

Creating a TableModel implementation is a trivial matter when using AbstractTableModel, and in this case, required just a single line for each of the three methods implemented. Although the DefaultTableModel provides a way to create a TableModel that's sometimes even easier, its use is not recommended, primarily because it creates its own references to the cell data. Besides being less scalable and less flexible, that approach complicates the issue of editing, which we'll examine later. To understand why DefaultTableModel isn't scalable, it's necessary to have some understanding of how JTable works.

As we've seen, the TableModel is responsible for indicating how many rows and columns the table contains, and getRowCount() and getColumnCount() are called immediately when a table is created and displayed. However, the table never maintains references to the data from the TableModel, but simply accesses the information long enough to render it when needed.

For example, suppose that you create a model that returns a value of 100 from getRowCount(), but that your table is inside a JScrollPane and that the display area is large enough to display only ten rows at once. When the table is displayed, it will initially access the first ten rows of data in the TableModel, and will access the data for the other rows only when (or if) you scroll down so that they are displayed within the JScrollPane's viewport. Why is this behavior important? Because it allows you to display extremely large amounts of data within a JTable without having all the data loaded into memory simultaneously. Instead, your TableModel can load the data it needs in an "on demand" (or if you prefer, "just in time") fashion, which allows you to minimize the amount of memory used.

With this point in mind, let's return to the discussion of DefaultTableModel and consider the implications of its creating a reference to each of the data items that it encapsulates. Since it requires a reference to each item, all its data must be in memory for as long as the model is in use, and it can't respond to data retrieval requests on an "as needed" basis. Therefore, since DefaultTableModel does have potentially serious drawbacks and is only slightly easier to use, you should generally use AbstractTableModel instead. You may still choose to use DefaultTableModel if your table will only contain a small amount of data, since it's always faster to have data cached in memory. However, if your table will contain a large amount of data and memory utilization is a concern, you'll want to use AbstractTableModel.

When you create a subclass of AbstractTableModel, that class is completely responsible for accessing the data that's needed by the table. Your implementation might cache data in memory the way that DefaultTableModel does, or you might leave the data in some external location such as a relational database and access it only when it's needed. In the case of the TableValues class, we hard-coded data into a class for the sake of convenience, but a more realistic scenario would be to have the data retrieved from a database or a disk file.

Now that we've created a TableModel implementation, it's possible to create a JTable and populate it with the data stored in the TableValues class, as shown in the following code:

```java
import java.awt.*;
import javax.swing.*;

public class SimpleTableTest extends JFrame {

  protected JTable table;

  public static void main(String[] args) {
    SimpleTableTest stt = new SimpleTableTest();
    stt.setDefaultCloseOperation(JFrame.EXIT_ON_CLOSE);
    stt.setSize(400, 300);
    stt.setVisible(true);
  }

  public SimpleTableTest() {
    Container pane = getContentPane();
    pane.setLayout(new BorderLayout());
    TableValues tv = new TableValues();
    table = new JTable(tv);
    pane.add(table, BorderLayout.CENTER);
  }

}
```

This application provides a simple table that displays the `TableValues` data:

Clay	Ashworth	Tue Feb 20 ...	12345.67	true
Jacob	Ashworth	Tue Jan 06 ...	23456.78	true
Jordan	Ashworth	Thu Aug 31...	34567.89	false
Evelyn	Kirk	Tue Jan 16 ...	-456.7	false
Belle	Spyres	Fri Aug 02 ...	567.0	false

However, there are several problems. For example, if the frame is resized so that it's smaller than the table, portions of the data are invisible and inaccessible :

In addition, several of the columns format their data in a way that's not appropriate or not ideal. For example, the `Gender` column displays "true" or "false" instead of "Male" or "Female," while the `Account Balance` column correctly displays the numeric value, but does not use currency conventions.

Using JScrollPane with JTable

As in any case where there may be too much information to display at one time, the `JScrollPane` class can be used to allow large amounts of data to be viewed. In fact, instances of `JTable` should almost always be displayed inside a `JScrollPane`, because as well as allowing you to view large tables in a small area, `JScrollPane` also provides support for column headers.

You can supply the column headers by implementing the `getColumnName()` method in your `TableModel`, or they will default to a letter of the alphabet, with a header of "A" for the first column, "B" for the second, and so on. A modified version of `TableValues` that returns the column names is shown below:

```java
import java.util.Calendar;
import java.util.GregorianCalendar;
import javax.swing.table.AbstractTableModel;

public class TableValues extends AbstractTableModel {

  public final static int FIRST_NAME = 0;
  public final static int LAST_NAME = 1;
  public final static int DATE_OF_BIRTH = 2;
  public final static int ACCOUNT_BALANCE = 3;
  public final static int GENDER = 4;

  public final static boolean GENDER_MALE = true;
  public final static boolean GENDER_FEMALE = false;

  public final static String[] columnNames = {
    "First Name", "Last Name", "Date of Birth", "Account Balance", "Gender"
  };

  public Object[][] values = {
    {
      "Clay", "Ashworth",
      new GregorianCalendar(1962, Calendar.FEBRUARY, 20).getTime(),
      new Float(12345.67), new Boolean(GENDER_MALE)
    }, {
      "Jacob", "Ashworth",
      new GregorianCalendar(1987, Calendar.JANUARY, 6).getTime(),
      new Float(23456.78), new Boolean(GENDER_MALE)
    }, {
      "Jordan", "Ashworth",
      new GregorianCalendar(1989, Calendar.AUGUST, 31).getTime(),
      new Float(34567.89), new Boolean(GENDER_FEMALE)
    }, {
      "Evelyn", "Kirk",
      new GregorianCalendar(1945, Calendar.JANUARY, 16).getTime(),
      new Float(-456.70), new Boolean(GENDER_FEMALE)
    }, {
```

```
      "Belle", "Spyres",
      new GregorianCalendar(1907, Calendar.AUGUST, 2).getTime(),
      new Float(567.00), new Boolean(GENDER_FEMALE)
    }
  };

  public int getRowCount() {
    return values.length;
  }

  public int getColumnCount() {
    return values[0].length;
  }

  public Object getValueAt(int row, int column) {
    return values[row][column];
  }

  public String getColumnName(int column) {
    return columnNames[column];
  }

}
```

We'll now modify the `SimpleTableTest` constructor so that it encloses the table within a `JScrollPane`:

```
  public SimpleTableTest() {
    Container pane = getContentPane();
    pane.setLayout(new BorderLayout());
    TableValues tv = new TableValues();
    table = new JTable(tv);
    // pane.add(table, BorderLayout.CENTER);
    JScrollPane jsp = new JScrollPane(table);
    pane.add(jsp, BorderLayout.CENTER);
  }
```

Now that the table is displayed inside a `JScrollPane`, the column headers appear:

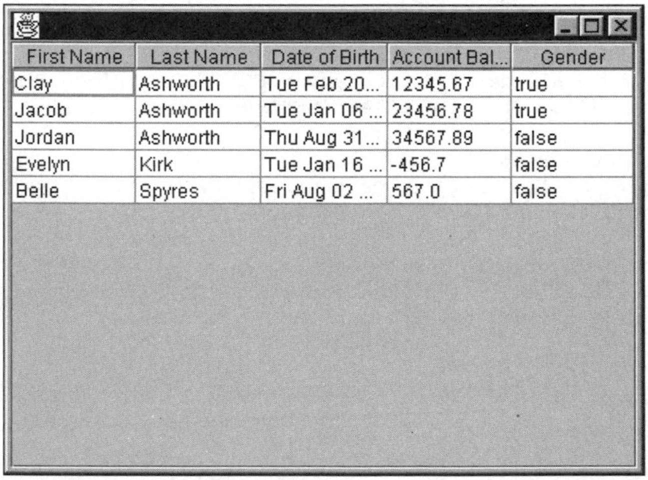

First Name	Last Name	Date of Birth	Account Bal...	Gender
Clay	Ashworth	Tue Feb 20...	12345.67	true
Jacob	Ashworth	Tue Jan 06 ...	23456.78	true
Jordan	Ashworth	Thu Aug 31...	34567.89	false
Evelyn	Kirk	Tue Jan 16 ...	-456.7	false
Belle	Spyres	Fri Aug 02 ...	567.0	false

You might also expect that resizing the frame (and as a result, the table) would cause scroll bars to appear when there's not enough space to display all of the data. As the following screenshot shows, a vertical scroll bar does appear when the table is reduced in size, but instead of a horizontal scroll bar appearing, each column shrinks and expands along with the table:

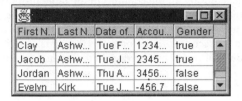

To understand why this occurs, it's necessary to examine the design of JTable and how some of its support classes function.

JTable's Column-Oriented Design

The design of the JTable component is very much column-oriented, and each JTable contains a reference to an implementation of the TableColumnModel interface. A TableColumnModel, such as DefaultTableColumnModel defined in javax.swing.table, describes a set of columns displayed by a JTable, and represents each column with an instance of the TableColumn class. For example, suppose that you define a TableModel that contains five columns of data. If you then create an instance of JTable using that model, the table creates an instance of DefaultTableColumnModel, retrieves the column count from the TableModel and creates and adds five TableColumn instances to the DefaultTableColumnModel.

Each instance of TableColumn contains information such as the column header, the current, minimum, maximum, and preferred width values for the column, and a flag that indicates whether the column can be resized. When created, a column's current and preferred width values are initially set to 75, the minimum to 15, and the maximum width is effectively set to infinity (Integer.MAX_VALUE).

After a column is created, its width values can be changed explicitly by the setWidth(), setMinWidth(), setMaxWidth(), and setPreferredWidth() methods for the current, minimum, maximum, and preferred widths, respectively. In addition, a column's current width can be modified if the size of the table that it's a part of changes.

Each JTable instance has an **auto resize mode** setting, which can be one of five values that correspond to constants defined in JTable:

- ❑ AUTO_RESIZE_ALL_COLUMNS

- ❑ AUTO_RESIZE_LAST_COLUMN

- ❑ AUTO_RESIZE_NEXT_COLUMN

- ❑ AUTO_RESIZE_OFF

- ❑ AUTO_RESIZE_SUBSEQUENT_COLUMNS

The value of this setting determines how or if the table's columns are resized when the width of the table or one of the columns changes.

Table Resizing

If the table's auto resize mode is set to AUTO_RESIZE_OFF, changing the size of the table *does not* affect the current size of the columns within the table. When it is set to any of the other four values, however, a change to the table's width is distributed among all the columns in the table proportionally based on their preferred sizes. For example, suppose that a table contains two columns and that one of the columns has a preferred width of 200 and the other a preferred width of 100. In that case, the first column occupies two-thirds of the table's horizontal space, while the second column occupies the remaining one-third. If the table is then made 30 pixels wider, 20 of the additional pixels will be distributed to the first column, and 10 to the second one. This allows the column sizes to remain proportionally the same relative to one another, regardless of changes to the table's actual size.

If a table's mode is AUTO_RESIZE_OFF and the sum of all the column widths is greater than the table's width, then a horizontal scrollbar appears. To see this behavior, let's make another minor change to the SimpleTableTest constructor:

```
public SimpleTableTest() {
   Container pane = getContentPane();
   pane.setLayout(new BorderLayout());
   TableValues tv = new TableValues();
   table = new JTable(tv);
   table.setAutoResizeMode(JTable.AUTO_RESIZE_OFF);
   // pane.add(table, BorderLayout.CENTER);
   JScrollPane jsp = new JScrollPane(table);
   pane.add(jsp, BorderLayout.CENTER);
}
```

Each column maintains its default width (75), and when the table is made too narrow to display all of the columns, a horizontal scrollbar appears. Any other auto resize mode cause the columns to expand or contract when the table is resized:

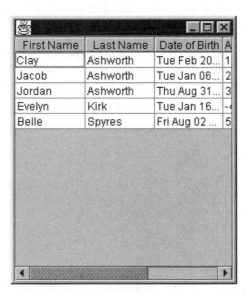

Column Resizing

Now that we've seen how changing the width of a table can affect the width of the columns within that table, it's also important to examine how changing the width of one column can change the widths of the others. A column's width can be changed programmatically via the mutator methods for the four width values (current, minimum, maximum, and preferred) or it can be modified through the user interface provided by JTable:

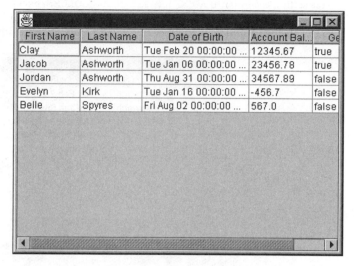

When one column's size is changed, its effect on the widths of the other columns depends upon the table's auto resize mode setting, and the behavior associated with each setting is described below.

AUTO_RESIZE_OFF

When auto resizing is disabled, changing the width of one column has no effect on the size of the other columns in the table. This may result in the table being too small to display all the columns, in which case a horizontal scroll bar appears (if the table is contained within a JScrollPane). Alternatively, resizing a column may result in the table being larger than the combined width of all the columns, in which case some amount of white space appears inside the table.

AUTO_RESIZE_NEXT_COLUMN

With this setting, when a change is made to the width of a column, the column to the right of that column (the "next column") gains or loses horizontal space. Here the Date of Birth column has been increased in size, which results in the column to its right (Account Balance) becoming narrower:

AUTO_RESIZE_SUBSEQUENT_COLUMNS

This setting is similar to AUTO_RESIZE_NEXT_COLUMN, except that when a column is resized, *all* the other columns to its right gain or lose width. In this case, the Date of Birth column has been made wider, which causes the two columns that follow it (Account Balance and Gender) to become narrower:

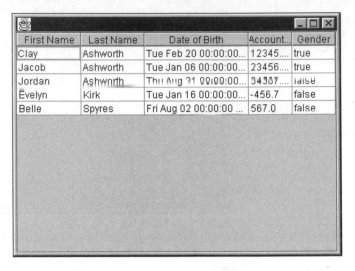

The difference between the original width of the resized column and its new width is referred to as the **delta value,** and this amount is distributed proportionally among the columns to the right of the resized column.

AUTO_RESIZE_LAST_COLUMN

When this setting is used and a column is resized, the delta value is applied to the last column in the table to make it wider or narrower than it was. Here the Date of Birth column has been made wider, causing the Gender column to become narrower by the same amount:

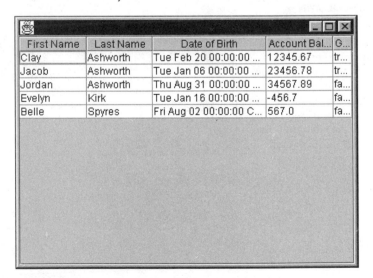

AUTO_RESIZE_ALL_COLUMNS

This is the default setting for a new instance of JTable, and causes any changes to one column's width to be proportionally distributed among all other columns in the table. When the **Date of Birth** column becomes larger, the delta value is divided among the other columns in the table, causing them to become narrower:

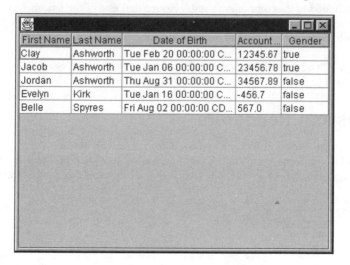

Cell Rendering

As mentioned earlier, the data in several of the columns isn't displayed in an ideal fashion. Specifically, three things can be improved:

❑ The **Date of Birth** column displays both a date and time, but should only display a date, and that date should be in a format that does not include the day of the week.

❑ **Account Balance** displays a simple numeric value, but should use currency-formatting conventions.

❑ The **Gender** column displays a somewhat non-intuitive value of "true" or "false" instead of "Male" or "Female."

JTable cells are drawn by **cell renderers**, which are classes that implement the TableCellRenderer interface. That interface defines a single getTableCellRendererComponent() method that returns a reference to the Component that will perform the drawing operation. However, since it's often convenient to define a single class that implements TableCellRenderer and that can perform the rendering, a TableCellRenderer will often simply return a reference to itself. The parameters passed to getTableCellRendererComponent() are:

❑ A reference to the JTable that contains the cell being drawn

❑ A reference to the cell's value

❑ A boolean flag that indicates whether or not the cell is selected

❑ A boolean flag that indicates whether or not the cell has the input focus

- ❑   The row index of the cell being drawn

- ❑   The column index of the cell being drawn

In addition to returning a reference to the rendering component, `getTableCellRendererComponent()` is responsible for initializing the component's state. Notice that one of the parameters listed above is a reference to the value stored in the cell that's about to be rendered, and some representation of that value is usually stored in the rendering component before a reference to it is returned.

As we'll see shortly, `JTable` provides predefined renderers that you can use to have your data displayed properly, but first we'll look at how easily custom renderer classes can be defined.

Creating Custom Renderers

The following class provides an example of a custom renderer, and it will be used to display the values in the Gender field in our sample application's table. Those values currently appear as a text string of "true" or "false" depending upon the cell's value, but this renderer will cause them to be drawn by a `JComboBox`:

```java
import java.awt.Component;
import javax.swing.JComboBox;
import javax.swing.JTable;
import javax.swing.table.TableCellRenderer;

public class GenderRenderer extends JComboBox
        implements TableCellRenderer {

  public GenderRenderer() {
    super();
    addItem("Male");
    addItem("Female");
  }

  public Component getTableCellRendererComponent(JTable table,
          Object value, boolean isSelected, boolean hasFocus, int row,
          int column) {

    if (isSelected) {
      setForeground(table.getSelectionForeground());
      super.setBackground(table.getSelectionBackground());
    } else {
      setForeground(table.getForeground());
      setBackground(table.getBackground());
    }

    boolean isMale = ((Boolean) value).booleanValue();
    setSelectedIndex(isMale ? 0 : 1);
    return this;
  }

}
```

When an instance of this class is created, it adds two items to its list: a "Male" selection, and a "Female" selection. The `getTableCellRendererComponent()` performs some simple color selection for the foreground and background, and then selects the appropriate gender based on the cell's value ("Male" for `true`, "Female" for `false`). Once this renderer class has been created, you can specify that it should be used for the Gender column by making the following changes to `SimpleTableTest`:

```java
import java.awt.*;
import javax.swing.*;
import javax.swing.table.*;

public class SimpleTableTest extends JFrame {

  protected JTable table;

  public static void main(String[] args) {
    SimpleTableTest stt = new SimpleTableTest();
    stt.setDefaultCloseOperation(JFrame.EXIT_ON_CLOSE);
    stt.setSize(400, 300);
    stt.setVisible(true);
  }

  public SimpleTableTest() {
    Container pane = getContentPane();
    pane.setLayout(new BorderLayout());
    TableValues tv = new TableValues();
    table = new JTable(tv);
    TableColumnModel tcm = table.getColumnModel();
    TableColumn tc = tcm.getColumn(TableValues.GENDER);
    tc.setCellRenderer(new GenderRenderer());
    JScrollPane jsp = new JScrollPane(table);
    pane.add(jsp, BorderLayout.CENTER);
  }

}
```

When you compile and execute the modified version of the application, it produces a display like the one shown below. Notice that the "true" and "false" strings that previously appeared in the Gender column now seem to have been replaced by instances of JCheckBox:

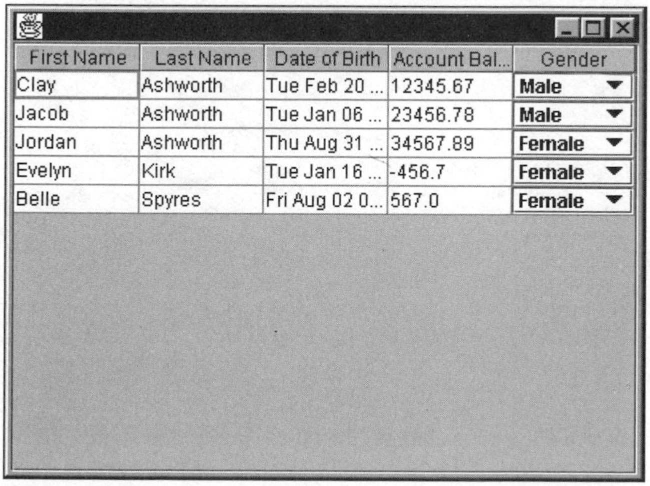

It's important to realize that renderers are *not* really added to JTable instances the way that visual components are added to a Container, which in this case means that the table doesn't contain any instances of JCheckBox. Instead, when the table is painted, each cell delegates responsibility for drawing its contents, which is done by passing a Graphics object to a renderer component's paint() method, and the drawing region is set to correspond to the area occupied by the cell. In other words, no instances of JCheckBox were added to the JTable in this example, but rather a single instance of JCheckBox drew itself onto the area occupied by each cell in the Gender column. This approach may seem unnecessarily complex, but it allows a single component to draw most or all of a table's cells instead of requiring the table to allocate a component for each cell, which would consume far more memory.

In many cases, the easiest way to define a custom cell renderer is to extend Swing's DefaultTableCellRenderer, which as its name implies is the default renderer for cells in a JTable. DefaultTableCellRenderer extends JLabel and it displays cell values using their String representations. An object's String representation is obtained by calling its toString() method, and DefaultTableCellRenderer passes that representation to the setText() method it inherits from JLabel. This behavior is implemented in the setValue() method, which is passed a reference to the value of the cell that's about to be rendered:

```
protected void setValue(Object value) {
   setText((value == null) ? "" : value.toString());
}
```

In effect, DefaultTableCellRenderer is simply a JLabel that sets its own text based on the value of the cell being rendered.

In many cases, calling toString() isn't an appropriate way to obtain a representation of the cell's value, and an example of this is the **Account Balance** column in our sample application. The values displayed in that column are technically correct, but they're not formatted in a manner that makes it obvious that they represent currency values. However, this can easily be addressed by creating a custom TableCellRenderer and assigning it responsibility for drawing the cells in that column.

```
import java.text.NumberFormat;
import javax.swing.table.DefaultTableCellRenderer;

public class CurrencyRenderer extends DefaultTableCellRenderer {

  public CurrencyRenderer() {
    super();
    setHorizontalAlignment(javax.swing.SwingConstants.RIGHT);
  }

  public void setValue(Object value) {
    if ((value != null) && (value instanceof Number)) {
      Number numberValue = (Number) value;
      NumberFormat formatter = NumberFormat.getCurrencyInstance();
      value = formatter.format(numberValue.doubleValue());
    }
    super.setValue(value);
  }

}
```

This simple class does just two things: it changes the label's horizontal alignment during construction, and it overrides the setValue() method defined in DefaultTableCellRenderer. Since we know that this renderer class will only be used to render the cells containing numeric values, we can cast the cell's value to a Number and then format the value as a currency using Java's NumberFormat class.

Now that we've created a custom renderer for the **Account Balance** column, we need to have the table use the renderer when drawing the cells in that column, which could be done by explicitly assigning it to the `TableColumn` as we did in the previous example. However, there is another way to accomplish this that's worth mentioning and which is more appropriate in many cases. Besides associating a renderer with a particular column, you can also associate it with a particular type of data, and the renderer will then be used to draw all cells in columns that contain that type of data.

When a `JTable` is initialized, it creates a map that defines associations between classes and renderers, and it uses that map to select a cell renderer when drawing cells in columns for which no renderer was explicitly set. In other words, if you have not explicitly assigned a renderer to a column as we did earlier, `JTable` will select a renderer based upon the type of data stored in that column. It determines the column's data type by calling the `getColumnClass()` method in the `TableModel`, and that method returns an instance of `Class`. However, the implementation of `getColumnClass()` in `AbstractTableModel` simply indicates that all its columns contain instances of `Object` as shown below:

```
public Class getColumnClass(int columnIndex) {
   return Object.class;
}
```

Since `AbstractTableModel` can't know what kind of data its subclasses will contain, the only assumption that it can safely make is that each cell contains an instance of `Object`, although in practice, the cells will almost certainly contain instances of some *subclass* of `Object` such as `Float`, `Date`, etc. Therefore, if you want the table to be able to determine the specific type of data its columns contain, you must override `getColumnClass()` in your `TableModel` class. For example, since all of the values in the **Account Balance** column are instances of `Float`, we could add the following `getColumnClass()` implementation to the `TableValues` class:

```
public Class getColumnClass(int column) {
   Class dataType = super.getColumnClass(column);
   if (column == ACCOUNT_BALANCE) {
     dataType = Float.class;
   }
   return dataType;
}
```

Now that our JTable is able to determine that the `Account Balance` column contains `Float` data, we need to associate our `CurrencyRenderer` class with that data type, which can easily be done by calling `setDefaultRenderer()` as shown below:

```
public SimpleTableTest() {
   Container pane = getContentPane();
   pane.setLayout(new BorderLayout());
   TableValues tv = new TableValues();
   table = new JTable(tv);
   TableColumnModel tcm = table.getColumnModel();
   TableColumn tc = tcm.getColumn(TableValues.GENDER);
   tc.setCellRenderer(new GenderRenderer());
   table.setDefaultRenderer(Float.class, new CurrencyRenderer());
   JScrollPane jsp = new JScrollPane(table);
   pane.add(jsp, BorderLayout.CENTER);
}
```

This new addition to `SimpleTableTest` causes `CurrencyRenderer` to become the default renderer for all columns containing `Float` data. Therefore, `CurrencyRenderer` will be used to draw the cells in the **Account Balance** column because no renderer was assigned to the column and because `getColumnClass()` now indicates that the column contains `Float` data. An example of how the interface will appear when the program is executed with these modifications is shown below:

At this point, you may be wondering what happens when no renderer has been explicitly assigned to a column and there is no entry in the table's class-to-renderer map that matches the column's data type. You're correct if you've guessed that the rendering is handled by `DefaultTableCellRenderer`, but it's important to understand exactly how that occurs.

When no renderer has been explicitly assigned to a column and no entry for the column's `Class` is found in the table's class-to-renderer map, `JTable` traverses the inheritance hierarchy of the column's `Class`, searching the class-to-renderer map for an entry corresponding to each superclass until it locates one. For example, if `getColumnClass()` indicates that the column contains `Float` data but no entry for `Float` is found in the class-to-renderer map, `JTable` next attempts to locate a map entry that corresponds to `Float`'s immediate superclass, which is `Number`. If it does not find an entry for `Number`, it will attempt to retrieve an entry for `Object` (`Number`'s immediate superclass), which will always succeed because the map automatically contains an entry that associates `Object` columns with `DefaultTableCellRenderer`.

To summarize `JTable`'s behavior, the steps for locating a renderer are listed below:

- ❑ If a renderer has been set for the cell's `TableColumn`, use that renderer
- ❑ Obtain a reference to a `Class` instance by calling the `TableModel`'s `getColumnClass()` method
- ❑ If a renderer has been mapped to that `Class`, use that renderer
- ❑ Obtain a reference to the `Class` instance of the type's superclass and repeat the previous step until a match is found

This approach provides a great deal of flexibility in assigning renderers to table cells, since it allows you to create a renderer and have it handle rendering for columns with a specific data type, along with any subclasses of that type.

JTable's Default Renderers

We've now seen how to create custom renderers and how to associate a renderer with a given type of data. However, it's often not necessary to do either one, since JTable includes a number of predefined renderers for commonly used data types, and entries for those renderers are automatically included in its class-to-renderer map.

For example, it was already mentioned that an entry exists in the map that associates Object columns with DefaultTableCellRenderer, but other, more sophisticated renderers are provided as well. This means that if one of the predefined renderers is appropriate for your application, the only coding you need to do is to identify your columns' data types in an implementation of getColumnClass() so that JTable will use the appropriate renderers. To illustrate this point, we'll use JTable's predefined renderer for instances of java.util.Date by simply modifying TableValues so that it indicates that the **Date of Birth** column contains instances of Date:

```
public Class getColumnClass(int column) {
  Class dataType = super.getColumnClass(column);
  if (column == ACCOUNT_BALANCE) {
    dataType = Float.class;
  }
  else if (column == DATE_OF_BIRTH) {
    dataType = java.util.Date.class;
  }
  return dataType;
}
```

As we saw earlier, the date values displayed by DefaultTableCellRenderer were lengthy and included a time (since Java's Date class represents both a date and a time). However, JTable's predefined date renderer produces a shorter, more appropriate representation of each date value as shown below:

First Name	Last Name	Date of Birth	Account Bal...	Gender
Clay	Ashworth	Feb 20, 1962	$12,345.67	Male ▼
Jacob	Ashworth	Jan 6, 1987	$23,456.78	Male ▼
Jordan	Ashworth	Aug 31, 1989	$34,567.89	Female ▼
Evelyn	Kirk	Jan 16, 1945	($456.70)	Female ▼
Belle	Spyres	Aug 2, 1907	$567.00	Female ▼

In addition to java.util.Date, JTable includes predefined renderers for a number of other classes, including the following:

java.lang.Number

This is the superclass of the numeric wrappers such as `Integer`, `Float`, `Long`, etc. The renderer that's defined for `Number` is a subclass of `DefaultTableCellRenderer` that simply sets its alignment value to `RIGHT` as we did in `CurrencyRenderer`. In other words, the `Number` renderer displays the `toString()` representation of the cell values, but it displays the text adjacent to the right side of the cell instead of the left (the default). An example of how this would appear if used with the **Account Balance** column in `SampleTableTest` class is shown here:

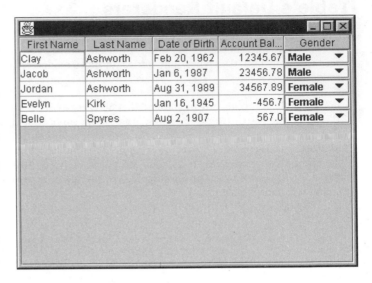

javax.swing.ImageIcon

The renderer associated with this class allows you to display instances of `ImageIcon` within a table. The renderer is simply an instance of `DefaultTableCellRenderer` that takes advantage of the fact that a `JLabel` can contain both text and an icon. Instead of rendering the cell by setting its text value, this renderer sets its icon instead.

java.lang.Boolean

When this renderer is used, it displays the value for the cell as a `JCheckBox` that is either checked (when the cell's value is `true`) or unchecked (when the value is `false`). An example of how it would appear if used with the `Gender` column `SimpleTableTest` is shown here:

First Name	Last Name	Date of Birth	Account Bal...	Gender
Clay	Ashworth	Feb 20, 1962	$12,345.67	☑
Jacob	Ashworth	Jan 6, 1987	$23,456.78	☑
Jordan	Ashworth	Aug 31, 1989	$34,567.89	☐
Evelyn	Kirk	Jan 16, 1945	($456.70)	☐
Belle	Spyres	Aug 2, 1907	$567.00	☐

Editing Table Cells

Although each cell in the Gender column now appears to be a JComboBox, it's not possible to change the gender that's selected. In fact, none of the cells in the table is editable, and clicking on them merely causes the row to be selected. To change this behavior, you must override the isCellEditable() method, because the implementation in DefaultTableModel always returns false. However, this can be changed easily by adding the following code to TableValues:

```
public boolean isCellEditable(int row, int column) {
   if (column == GENDER) {
     return true;
   }
   return false;
}
```

This indicates that the cells in the Gender column are now editable. However, if you click on a cell in that column intending to select a gender from a JComboBox, you may be surprised to find that nothing happens except that the row you clicked on becomes selected. If you double-click on the cell, a JTextField appears that is initialized with the string equivalent of the cell's Boolean value ("true" or "false") and you can edit the data in the text field:

First Name	Last Name	Date of Birth	Account Bal...	Gender
Clay	Ashworth	Feb 20, 1962	$12,345.67	Male ▼
Jacob	Ashworth	Jan 6, 1987	$23,456.78	Male ▼
Jordan	Ashworth	Aug 31, 1989	$34,567.89	false
Evelyn	Kirk	Jan 16, 1945	($456.70)	Female ▼
Belle	Spyres	Aug 2, 1907	$567.00	Female ▼

You may be surprised that a text field appears when you edit the cell, because the cell seems to contain a JComboBox, but remember that table cells don't actually *contain* any components. The cells are simply drawn by components (the renderers), and in this case, the component happens to be a JComboBox. However, editing is a completely separate process that may or may not be handled by the same type of component that performed the rendering. For example, the default rendering component used by JTable is a JLabel, while the default editing component is a JTextField, which is why a text field appeared in this case.

Regardless of which type of component is used, it may seem that the cells are finally editable, which is partly true, but if you enter a value into one of these cells, the value you type is discarded once you complete the editing. To understand why this occurs and what to do about it, you should be familiar with cell editors and how JTable handles the editing of its cells.

Cell Editors

Just as cell renderers control the way that a cell's values are drawn, **cell editors** handle cell value editing. Editors are slightly more complex than renderers, but have many similarities to renderers:

❑ An editor can be assigned to one or more `TableColumn` instances.

❑ An editor can be associated with one or more data types (classes), and will be used to display that type of data when no editor is associated with a cell's column.

❑ Existing visual components are used to provide editing capabilities, just as they are used by renderers to draw cell values. In fact, the same type of visual component that's used as a cell's renderer is often used for its editor as well. For example, a cell might be assigned a renderer that uses a `JComboBox` and an editor that uses the same component.

You can assign an editor to one or more `TableColumn` instances or object types using the `setCellEditor()` method in `TableColumn` and `setDefaultEditor()` in `JTable`, respectively. However, the implementation of the `TableCellEditor` interface is more complex than `TableCellRenderer`, and to understand the methods defined in `TableCellEditor`, it's useful to examine how editors interact with `JTable` instances.

When a `JTable` detects a mouse click over one of its cells, it calls the `isCellEditable()` method in the `TableModel`. That method returns a value of `false` if the cell should not be editable, in which case processing terminates and no further action is taken. However, if the method returns `true`, then the table identifies the cell editor for that cell and calls the `CellEditor`'s `isCellEditable()` method as well.

Although `TableModel` and `CellEditor` both define methods called `isCellEditable()`, there is an important difference between the two. Specifically, the `TableModel` method is only passed row and column index values, while the `CellEditor` method is also passed the `EventObject` representing the mouse click. This can be used, for example, to check the "click count" stored in the event. A cell must be double-clicked before it is edited, as observed earlier when editing the **Gender** column values. In other words, the `isCellEditable()` method returns a value of `false` when the click count is 1, while it returns `true` if the count is greater than 1. This behavior allows the cell editor to distinguish between a request to select the cell (a single-click) and a request to edit the cell (a double-click).

The edit operation is allowed to proceed only if *both* the `TableModel`'s *and* the `CellEditor`'s `isCellEditable()` method return a value of `true`. When that's the case, the editing is initiated by calling the `getTableCellEditorComponent()` method, which is passed the following parameters:

❑ A reference to the `JTable` that contains the cell being edited

❑ A reference to the cell's current value

❑ A `boolean` flag that indicates whether or not the cell is selected

❑ The row index of the cell being edited

❑ The column index of the cell being edited

If these parameters look familiar, it's because they're almost identical to those passed to the `getTableCellRendererComponent()` method in `TableCellRenderer`. The only difference is that this method is not passed a `boolean` value indicating whether or not the cell has the input focus, since that is implied by the fact that the cell is being edited.

Before returning a reference to the component that's responsible for handling editing, getTableCellEditorComponent() should prepare the editor by initializing its value appropriately so that it matches the current cell value. For example, let's assume that we're creating an editor that allows users to select either "Male" or "Female" from a JComboBox that represents the Gender column value in TableValues. In that case, the JComboBox that performs the editing should be prepared by selecting the item it contains that corresponds to the cell's gender value: "Male" if the cell's value is true, "Female" if the value is false.

Once the editing component has been prepared and returned from the getTableCellEditorComponent() method, the JTable sets the size and location of that component so that it's directly "over" the cell being edited. This makes it appear that the cell is edited in place, when in fact, a component that supports editing (such as a JTextField or in this case, a JComboBox) has been superimposed over the cell.

With the editing component positioned over the cell being edited, the event that originally triggered the edit processing is posted to the editing component. For example, in the case of a JComboBox-based editor, the same mouse event that initiated the editing is passed to the combo box, possibly causing it to display its drop-down menu when editing starts. Finally, the CellEditor's shouldSelectCell() method is passed the same mouse event object, and if it returns true, the cell (and possibly others, depending upon the table's selection settings) is selected.

Each CellEditor is required to implement the addCellEditorListener() and removeCellEditorListener() methods, and the CellEditorListener interface defines two methods: editingStopped() and editingCanceled(). In practice, the only listener is usually the JTable itself, which is notified when editing is stopped or canceled. In addition, the CellEditor must implement the cancelCellEditing() and stopCellEditing() methods, which call the editingStopped() and editingCanceled() methods of registered listeners.

A request to end editing can come either from the JTable that contains the cell, or from the editor component itself. For example, suppose that you click on one cell and begin editing its value. If you then click on a different cell, the JTable calls the stopCellEditing() method of the first cell's editor before it initiates editing of the second cell. Alternatively, the editor component may stop the editing when some event occurs that implies that editing is complete. For example, when using a JComboBox as an editor, and it receives an ActionEvent message indicating that a selection was made, then it's appropriate to terminate the edit. Similarly, a JTextField might signal that editing has ended when it detects that the *Return* key was pressed.

Regardless of where the request originates to end editing, the JTable's editingStopped() method is called since it is a registered CellEditorListener. Inside this method, the table calls the editor's getCellEditorValue() method to retrieve the cell's new value and passes that value to the setValueAt() method in the JTable's TableModel. That is, it retrieves the cell's new value from the editor and sends it to the data model so that it can be stored "permanently".

The following class defines a component that can be used to provide editing of the rows in the Gender column defined in TableValues. It defines a subclass of JComboBox that initializes itself with "Male" and "Female" entries and listens for changes to its state (waits for a selection to be made).

When editing is initiated for one of the cells in the Gender column, the getTableCellEditorComponent() method is called, giving the editor a chance to initialize its state before it is made visible. In this case, the editor simply makes either "Male" or "Female" the selected entry based on the value stored in the cell being edited. When the user selects an item in the JComboBox, fireEditingStopped() is called, which signals to the table that the edit session has ended. The table will then call getCellEditorValue() to retrieve the new value that should be stored in the cell and will pass that value to the TableModel's setValueAt() method.

```java
import java.awt.Component;
import java.util.EventObject;
import java.awt.event.*;
import javax.swing.*;
import javax.swing.event.*;
import javax.swing.table.*;

public class GenderEditor extends JComboBox implements TableCellEditor {

  protected EventListenerList listenerList = new EventListenerList();
  protected ChangeEvent changeEvent = new ChangeEvent(this);

  public GenderEditor() {
    super();
    addItem("Male");
    addItem("Female");
    addActionListener(new ActionListener() {
      public void actionPerformed(ActionEvent event) {
        fireEditingStopped();
      }
    });
  }

  public void addCellEditorListener(CellEditorListener listener) {
    listenerList.add(CellEditorListener.class, listener);
  }

  public void removeCellEditorListener(CellEditorListener listener) {
    listenerList.remove(CellEditorListener.class, listener);
  }

  protected void fireEditingStopped() {
    CellEditorListener listener;
    Object[] listeners = listenerList.getListenerList();
    for (int i = 0; i < listeners.length; i++) {
      if (listeners[i] == CellEditorListener.class) {
        listener = (CellEditorListener) listeners[i + 1];
        listener.editingStopped(changeEvent);
      }
    }
  }

  protected void fireEditingCanceled() {
    CellEditorListener listener;
    Object[] listeners = listenerList.getListenerList();
    for (int i = 0; i < listeners.length; i++) {
      if (listeners[i] == CellEditorListener.class) {
        listener = (CellEditorListener) listeners[i + 1];
        listener.editingCanceled(changeEvent);
      }
    }
  }

  public void cancelCellEditing() {
    fireEditingCanceled();
  }
```

```
    public boolean stopCellEditing() {
      fireEditingStopped();
      return true;
    }

    public boolean isCellEditable(EventObject event) {
      return true;
    }

    public boolean shouldSelectCell(EventObject event) {
      return true;
    }

    public Object getCellEditorValue() {
      return new Boolean(getSelectedIndex() == 0 ? true : false);
    }

    public Component getTableCellEditorComponent(JTable table, Object value,
            boolean isSelected, int row, int column) {
      boolean isMale = ((Boolean) value).booleanValue();
      setSelectedIndex(isMale ? 0 : 1);
      return this;
    }
  }
```

Now that the editor component has been defined, it needs to be associated with the Gender column, as shown in the following code:

```
    public SimpleTableTest() {
      Container pane = getContentPane();
      pane.setLayout(new BorderLayout());
      TableValues tv = new TableValues();
      table = new JTable(tv);
      TableColumnModel tcm = table.getColumnModel();
      TableColumn tc = tcm.getColumn(TableValues.GENDER);
      tc.setCellRenderer(new GenderRenderer());
      tc.setCellEditor(new GenderEditor());
      table.setDefaultRenderer(Float.class, new CurrencyRenderer());
      JScrollPane jsp = new JScrollPane(table);
      pane.add(jsp, BorderLayout.CENTER);
    }
```

When this code is compiled and run, a JComboBox correctly appears, is initialized with the appropriate gender value, and allows you to select either "Male" or "Female":

However, selecting a different value from the one already stored in the cell does not result in the cell's value being modified. That's because the value is never changed in the `TableModel`, which is done by implementing the `setValueAt()` method in the `TableValues` class:

```
public void setValueAt(Object value, int row, int column) {
  values[row][column] = value;
}
```

DefaultCellEditor

It's not necessary in every case to build a completely new cell editor. In fact, the `DefaultCellEditor` class allows you to easily create editor components using a `JCheckBox`, `JComboBox`, or `JTextField`. All that's necessary is to create an instance of `DefaultCellEditor` and pass it an instance of one of these three components. However, the `DefaultCellEditor` is not very flexible, and you'll often need to create your own editor as was done in this case.

Table Selection Settings

From a selection perspective, `JTable` is a two-dimensional component: each selected cell has both a row and column index. In contrast, `JList` selections are one-dimensional, since only a row index value is associated with each cell. Due to its two-dimensional nature, a `JTable`'s selection information can't be maintained by a single `ListSelectionModel`, because that interface only supports one-dimensional selection information. To address this issue, `JTable` uses two `DefaultListSelectionModel` instances:

❑ One that's maintained directly by the `JTable` itself for row selection information

❑ Another that's maintained through the `TableColumnModel` for column selections

For the most part, however, this "trick" is concealed from `JTable` programmers.

It was mentioned earlier that when a cell is selected, other cells might also become selected, depending upon the table's selection settings. In fact, the `JTable` component is very flexible in terms of the types of selections that can be made, and supports a number of different settings related to selection behavior. To manage its selection behavior, `JTable` uses the `ListSelectionModel` interface and its `DefaultListSelectionModel` implementation:

❑ **Row Selections**
If enabled, **row selection mode** indicates that when a cell is selected, all other cells in its row should become selected as well. This is the default behavior for a `JTable`, where an entire row is selected when a single cell in that row was clicked. `JTable` provides accessor and mutator methods called `getRowSelectionAllowed()` and `setRowSelectionAllowed()` respectively, and these methods allow you to query and enable or disable row selection mode.

❑ **Column Selections**
Just as `JTable` supports a row selection mode, it also supports a **column selection mode**, where selecting one cell causes all cells in its column to become selected. The `getColumnSelectionAllowed()` and `setColumnSelectionAllowed()` accessor and mutator methods allow you to query and modify this mode.

❑   **Cell Selections**
In **cell selection mode**, selecting a cell *does not* cause any other cells in the table to become selected. The `getCellSelectionEnabled()` and `setCellSelectionEnabled()` methods query and modify the cell selection mode for a `JTable`. Enabling cell selection mode effectively disables the row and column selection modes.

Combining Row, Column, and Cell Selection Modes

The row and column selection modes can be used together, so that clicking on a cell causes all other cells in the same row or column to be selected:

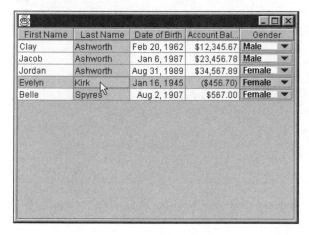

However, enabling cell selection mode overrides the row and column selection modes, causing them to be ignored as if they were both disabled. For example, suppose you create the following code segment:

```
JTable table;
    .
    .
    .
table.setRowSelectionAllowed(true);
table.setColumnSelectionAllowed(true);
table.setCellSelectionEnabled(true);
```

As long as cell selection mode is enabled, the row and column selection modes are effectively disabled, and only cell selections are allowed. Therefore, although there are three selection settings, there are only five meaningful combinations of those three settings:

❑   Only row selection mode is enabled

❑   Only column selection mode is enabled

❑   Both row and column selection modes are enabled

❑   Cell selection mode is enabled (the other two are ignored)

❑   All three (row, column, and cell) selection modes are disabled

In this last case, the behavior is what you would probably expect; with all three modes disabled, no cells can be selected.

List Selection Modes

When some type of cell selection occurs, one or both of the `ListSelectionModel` instances are updated to reflect the selection(s) made, although the specific changes to those models will depend on the selection mode or modes enabled. By default, each model can maintain multiple value ranges (or **intervals**). For example, given the selections shown in the following screenshot, the selection model that's responsible for recording row selections might record that items 0 through 1 and 3 through 4 are selected (a total of four rows):

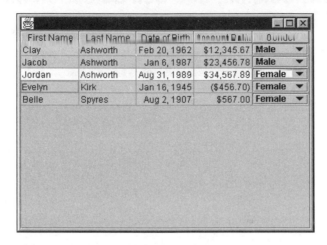

To select two intervals like this, perform the following steps using the most recent version of `SimpleTableTest`:

- ❑ Click on the top row
- ❑ Press and hold down the *Shift* key, and click on the second row. At this point, the first range (0 through 1) of rows has been selected
- ❑ Release the *Shift* key, press and hold down the *Ctrl* key and click on the fourth row
- ❑ Release the *Ctrl* key, press and hold down the *Shift* key and click on the last row – the second range of rows (3 through 4) has now been selected

As you can see, pressing down the *Shift* key while making a selection indicates that you wish to select the second in a pair of values that defines a range of values (that is, a set of consecutive rows). Pressing down the *Ctrl* key while making a selection indicates that any previous selections should not be cleared before making another selection. An alternative approach to using the *Shift* key to select a range of values is to drag the mouse (press and hold down the left mouse button while moving the cursor) from one cell to another. For example, in this case, you could click on a cell in the top row and drag the mouse to the second row to select the first range of rows.

This example illustrates the default mode, known as **multiple interval selection**, which is one of three modes that the `ListSelectionModel` supports. The other two modes are **single interval selection** and **single selection**.

As its name implies, single interval selection mode allows a model to maintain a single interval instead of multiple intervals. For example, if you repeat the above steps with single interval selection, the first range of values (rows 0 through 1) become deselected when you attempt to select the second interval (rows 3 through 4).

In single selection mode, a `ListSelectionModel` allows only a single item to be selected, and no range of items is allowed. Any attempt to select another item will cause the previously selected item to be deselected. For example, when column selection mode is enabled in conjunction with single selection mode, only a single column at a time can be selected.

As mentioned earlier, each `JTable` maintains two `ListSelectionModel` instances, and provides a `setSelectionMode()` method that sets the selection mode for both instances. Each selection mode is represented by a constant value defined in `ListSelectionModel`:

- ❑   MULTIPLE_INTERVAL_SELECTION

- ❑   SINGLE_INTERVAL_SELECTION

- ❑   SINGLE_SELECTION

Note, however, that `JTable` does *not* provide a `getSelectionMode()` method, and to determine the current mode, you must retrieve that information from one of the `ListSelectionModel` instances, as illustrated in the code below:

```
JTable table;
 .
 .
 .
int oldSelectionMode = table.getSelectionModel().getSelectionMode();
table.setSelectionMode(ListSelectionModel.SINGLE_INTERVAL_SELECT);
```

Selection Mode Combinations

As mentioned earlier, there are five combinations of row, column, and cell selection modes available. In addition, three `ListSelectionModel` modes are available, which results in 15 different combinations. While this provides you with a great deal of flexibility in how table cells are selected, it also results in a somewhat confusing array of choices. However, by temporarily making the following modifications to `SimpleTableTest`, you can select the table and list selection modes used, which allows you to experiment with the behavior of different combinations:

```
import java.awt.*;
import java.awt.event.*;
import javax.swing.*;
import javax.swing.table.*;
import javax.swing.border.*;

public class SimpleTableTest extends JFrame {

  protected JTable table;

  public static void main(String[] args) {
    SimpleTableTest stt = new SimpleTableTest();
    stt.setDefaultCloseOperation(JFrame.EXIT_ON_CLOSE);
    stt.setSize(400, 300);
    stt.setVisible(true);
  }

  public SimpleTableTest() {
```

```
Container pane = getContentPane();
pane.setLayout(new BorderLayout());
TableValues tv = new TableValues();
table = new JTable(tv);
TableColumnModel tcm = table.getColumnModel();
TableColumn tc = tcm.getColumn(TableValues.GENDER);
tc.setCellRenderer(new GenderRenderer());
tc.setCellEditor(new GenderEditor());
table.setDefaultRenderer(Float.class, new CurrencyRenderer());
JScrollPane jsp = new JScrollPane(table);
pane.add(jsp, BorderLayout.CENTER);

JPanel outerPanel = new JPanel();
outerPanel.setLayout(new GridLayout(1, 2, 0, 0));
JPanel innerPanel = new JPanel();
innerPanel.setLayout(new FlowLayout());
JCheckBox modeBox = new JCheckBox("Row", true);
modeBox.addItemListener(new ItemListener() {
  public void itemStateChanged(ItemEvent event) {
    JCheckBox box = (JCheckBox) (event.getSource());
    table.setRowSelectionAllowed(box.isSelected());
  }
});
innerPanel.add(modeBox);
modeBox = new JCheckBox("Column");
modeBox.addItemListener(new ItemListener() {
  public void itemStateChanged(ItemEvent event) {
    JCheckBox box = (JCheckBox) (event.getSource());
    table.setColumnSelectionAllowed(box.isSelected());
  }
});
innerPanel.add(modeBox);
modeBox = new JCheckBox("Cell");
modeBox.addItemListener(new ItemListener() {
  public void itemStateChanged(ItemEvent event) {
    JCheckBox box = (JCheckBox) (event.getSource());
    table.setCellSelectionEnabled(box.isSelected());
  }
});
innerPanel.add(modeBox);

BevelBorder bb = new BevelBorder(BevelBorder.RAISED);
TitledBorder tb = new TitledBorder(bb, "Table Selection Types");
innerPanel.setBorder(tb);
outerPanel.add(innerPanel);
innerPanel = new JPanel();
innerPanel.setLayout(new FlowLayout());
JComboBox listModes = new JComboBox();
listModes.addItem("Single Selection");
listModes.addItem("Single Interval Selection");
listModes.addItem("Multiple Interval Selections");
listModes.setSelectedIndex(2);
listModes.addItemListener(new ItemListener() {
```

```
    public void itemStateChanged(ItemEvent event) {
      JComboBox box = (JComboBox) (event.getSource());
      int index = box.getSelectedIndex();
      switch (index) {
      case 0:
        table.setSelectionMode(ListSelectionModel.SINGLE_SELECTION);
        break;
      case 1:
        table
          .setSelectionMode(ListSelectionModel.SINGLE_INTERVAL_SELECTION);
        break;
      case 2:
        table
          .setSelectionMode(ListSelectionModel
            .MULTIPLE_INTERVAL_SELECTION);
        break;
      }
    }
  });
  innerPanel.add(listModes);
  bb = new BevelBorder(BevelBorder.RAISED);
  tb = new TitledBorder(bb, "List Selection Modes");
  innerPanel.setBorder(tb);
  outerPanel.add(innerPanel);

  pane.add(outerPanel, BorderLayout.SOUTH);
  }
}
```

As shown in the following screenshot, this code adds a pair of panels to the bottom of the SimpleTableTest interface. The panel on the left allows you to enable and disable row, column, and cell selections, while the panel on the right contains a JComboBox that allows you to choose a selection mode. The selections you make in the check boxes and the combo box are detected and used to update the selection state of the JTable, which provides you with the ability to experiment with different selection modes.

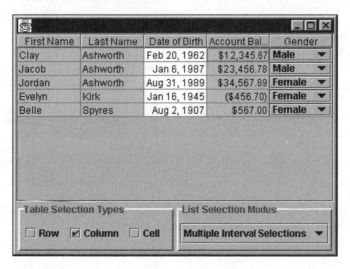

Setting Selections Programmatically

In addition to user-generated events that change which cells are selected within a table, it's also possible to set and query a JTable's selections programmatically, and the following table illustrates the methods available for doing so:

Method	Behavior
getSelectedRowCount()	Returns the number of rows in the table that are currently selected.
getSelectedRows()	Returns an array of integers, each one representing the index value of a currently selected row in the table.
getSelectedRow()	Returns an integer index value that identifies the first row (the row closest to the top of the table) that's selected. This is useful when only a single row can be selected.
SetRowSelectionInterval (int index0, int index1)	Each row within the range of values (inclusive) is selected. Any rows not in that range that were selected prior to this method call are deselected.
AddRowSelectionInterval (int index0, int index1)	Each row within the range of values (inclusive) is selected.
getSelectedColumnCount()	Returns the number of columns in the table that are currently selected.
getSelectedColumns()	Returns an array of integers, each one representing the index value of a currently selected column in the table.
getSelectedColumn()	Returns an integer index value that identifies the first column (the row closest to the left side of the table) that's selected. This is useful when only a single column can be selected.
SetColumnSelectionInterval (int index0, int index1)	Each column within the range of values (inclusive) is selected. Any columns not in that range that were selected prior to this method call are deselected.
addColumnSelectionInterval()	Two integer values are passed to this method, and each column within the range of values (inclusive) is selected.

All these methods are defined in JTable, but each of them delegates the request to a ListSelectionModel. Specifically, the row selection method calls are delegated to the model maintained by the JTable itself (the row model), while the column selection calls are handled by the selection model maintained by the table's TableColumnModel implementation.

Table Headers

As implemented by JTable, the column headers don't provide much functionality. They don't seem to respond when clicked on, and only display a single row of text that can be used to describe the columns.

However, when designing your user interface, you may want to add functionality to the headers. For example, you might wish to provide a tool tip for each header, to allow a column to be selected or sorted when its header is clicked, and to allow multiple lines of text to be displayed in the header. By understanding how JTable headers function, you can provide these capabilities and more.

Drawing Headers

Just as a table's data cells are drawn using renderers that are instances of JLabel by default, so are the table's header cells. The renderer for a given column's header is accessible through the TableColumn instance for that column, and can be obtained by calling the getHeaderRenderer() method. For example, the following code obtains a reference to the renderer for the second column in a table:

```
JTable table;
.
.
.
TableColumnModel tcm = table.getColumnModel();
TableColumn tc = tcm.getColumn(1);
TableCellRenderer tcr = tc.getHeaderRenderer();
```

In addition to retrieving the header renderer, it's also possible to set it. For example, you might wish to create a renderer that displays multiple rows of header text, since JLabel does not provide this functionality. Multi-line column headers can be useful because they allow you to display longer header text without wasting precious horizontal space in the table's display area, and an example of how a multi-line header renderer might be implemented is shown below:

```
import java.awt.*;
import java.util.StringTokenizer;
import javax.swing.*;
import javax.swing.table.TableCellRenderer;

public class MultiLineHeaderRenderer extends JPanel
  implements TableCellRenderer {

  public Component getTableCellRendererComponent(JTable table,
          Object value, boolean isSelected, boolean hasFocus, int row,
          int column) {
    JLabel label;
    removeAll();
    StringTokenizer strtok = new StringTokenizer((String) value, "\r\n");
    setLayout(new GridLayout(strtok.countTokens(), 1));
    while (strtok.hasMoreElements()) {
      label = new JLabel((String) strtok.nextElement(), JLabel.CENTER);
      LookAndFeel.installColorsAndFont(label, "TableHeader.background",
                                       "TableHeader.foreground",
                                       "TableHeader.font");
      add(label);
```

```
    }
    LookAndFeel.installBorder(this, "TableHeader.cellBorder");
    return this;
  }


}
```

This renderer requires that the column header contained an embedded carriage return or linefeed character where the text should be split, so we'll make such a modification to the Account Balance header as defined in TableValues:

```
public final static boolean GENDER_MALE = true;
public final static boolean GENDER_FEMALE = false;

public final static String[] columnNames = {"First Name", "Last Name",
    "Date of Birth", "Account\nBalance", "Gender"};
```

When the MultiLineHeaderRenderer is called to prepare the rendering component, it parses the header text, creates a separate JLabel for each line, and adds the label to a JPanel. It also sets the colors and font used by each label so that it matches the values normally used by a JTable header renderer. Finally, the renderer adds a border to the JPanel so that its appearance matches that of other table column headers:

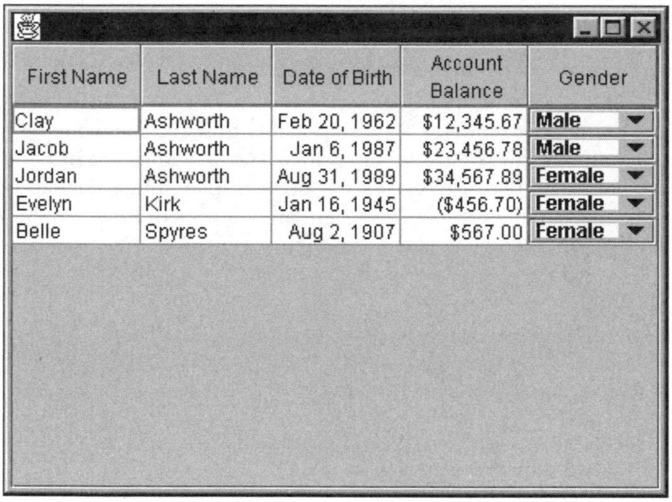

The final step is to assign an instance of MultiLineHeaderRenderer to the Account Balance's TableColumn instance, so that the header fits within the horizontal space allocated for the column:

```
public SimpleTableTest() {
  Container pane = getContentPane();
  pane.setLayout(new BorderLayout());
  TableValues tv = new TableValues();
  table = new JTable(tv);
  TableColumnModel tcm = table.getColumnModel();
  TableColumn tc = tcm.getColumn(TableValues.GENDER);
  tc.setCellRenderer(new GenderRenderer());
  tc.setCellEditor(new GenderEditor());
```

```
MultiLineHeaderRenderer mlhr = new MultiLineHeaderRenderer();
tc = tcm.getColumn(TableValues.ACCOUNT_BALANCE);
tc.setHeaderRenderer(mlhr);
table.setDefaultRenderer(Float.class, new CurrencyRenderer());
JScrollPane jsp = new JScrollPane(table);
pane.add(jsp, BorderLayout.CENTER);
}
```

Tool Tips and Renderer Reuse

Now that we've examined how to access and create header renderers, it's easy to add tool tips to headers. Assuming that the renderer component is a subclass of JComponent, all that's necessary is to access the header renderer and call the setToolTipText() method. For example, the following change results in a tool tip being set for the **Account Balance** column:

```
public SimpleTableTest() {
    Container pane = getContentPane();
    pane.setLayout(new BorderLayout());
    TableValues tv = new TableValues();
    table = new JTable(tv);
    TableColumnModel tcm = table.getColumnModel();
    TableColumn tc = tcm.getColumn(TableValues.GENDER);
    tc.setCellRenderer(new GenderRenderer());
    tc.setCellEditor(new GenderEditor());
    MultiLineHeaderRenderer mlhr = new MultiLineHeaderRenderer();
    mlhr.setToolTipText("This is the person's current account balance");
    tc = tcm.getColumn(TableValues.ACCOUNT_BALANCE);
    tc.setHeaderRenderer(mlhr);
    table.setDefaultRenderer(Float.class, new CurrencyRenderer());
    JScrollPane jsp = new JScrollPane(table);
    pane.add(jsp, BorderLayout.CENTER);
}
```

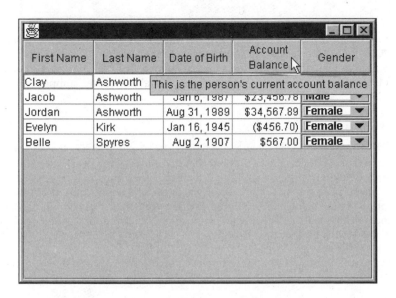

There is one potential problem that you should be aware of when specifying tool tips, and the problem is related to the way that cell renderers are used. Although we've assigned our header renderer responsibility for rendering only one column header, it's common for a single renderer to handle the rendering for all the columns in a table. In other words, just as we saw earlier that a single renderer can be used to draw many (or all) of the data cells in a table, the same is true of a column header renderer.

For example, a single instance of `MultiLineHeaderRenderer` could be used to draw the headers for both the Account Balance and Date of Birth columns. However, in the above case where the tool tip text was set, it would not be appropriate to use the same renderer to draw more than one column header. That's because the renderer was assigned information that's related to a specific column (the tool tip for the Account Balance column) and using it to render another column will have undesirable consequences. Specifically, the incorrect tool tip text is displayed for the Date of Birth column when the same `MultiLineHeaderRenderer` instance is used for both it and the Account Balance column:

First Name	Last Name	Date of Birth	Account Balance	Gender
Clay	Ashworth	This is the person's current account balance		
Jacob	Ashworth	Jan 6, 1987	$23,456.78	Male ▼
Jordan	Ashworth	Aug 31, 1989	$34,567.89	Female ▼
Evelyn	Kirk	Jan 16, 1945	($456.70)	Female ▼
Belle	Spyres	Aug 2, 1907	$567.00	Female ▼

This problem could be addressed in a number of ways, with the most obvious being to assign a different instance of the `MultiLineHeaderRenderer` class to each table column, each of which could have its own tool tip. However, assigning a different renderer to each column isn't really an ideal solution, and as we'll see shortly, there's a better way to address this problem using the table's header component.

JTableHeader

As you may recall, running the implementation of `SimpleTableTest` defined at the beginning of this chapter resulted in a table being displayed with no column headers. However, when the `JTable` was added to a `JScrollPane`, headers appeared that displayed the labels returned by the `getColumnName()` method. Column headers are automatically created whenever a table is displayed within a `JScrollPane` and they are displayed in the scroll pane's **column header viewport**. The column header viewport is an area above the main display portion of a `JScrollPane`, and the component stored in that area can be accessed and modified using the `getColumnHeader()` and `setColumnHeader()` methods.

For example, to store an instance of `JButton` in the column header, you could temporarily modify the `SimpleTableTest` class as shown here:

```
public SimpleTableTest() {
  Container pane = getContentPane();
  pane.setLayout(new BorderLayout());
  TableValues tv = new TableValues();
  table = new JTable(tv);
  TableColumnModel tcm = table.getColumnModel();
  TableColumn tc = tcm.getColumn(TableValues.GENDER);
  tc.setCellRenderer(new GenderRenderer());
  tc.setCellEditor(new GenderEditor());
  MultiLineHeaderRenderer mlhr = new MultiLineHeaderRenderer();
  mlhr.setToolTipText("This is the person's current account balance");
  tc = tcm.getColumn(TableValues.ACCOUNT_BALANCE);
  tc.setHeaderRenderer(mlhr);
  table.setDefaultRenderer(Float.class, new CurrencyRenderer());
  JScrollPane jsp = new JScrollPane(table) {
    public void setColumnHeaderView(Component comp) {
      super.setColumnHeaderView(new JButton("This is a JButton"));
    }
  };
  pane.add(jsp, BorderLayout.CENTER);
}
```

This code overrides the setColumnHeaderView() method in the scroll pane and instead of setting it to the parameter passed to that method, stores a JButton instance as the column header:

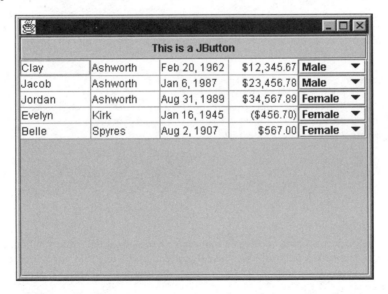

Although you won't often need to use this method, it illustrates that any component can be used as a row header. The obvious question, however, is what type of component is used by default, and the answer is that the column header is normally an instance of JTableHeader.

JTableHeader is a visual component that provides most of the user interface behavior related to moving and resizing columns. For example, when you resize a column using mouse drags, you're interacting with a JTableHeader instance. In addition, you can re-order columns in a table by moving the cursor over a table header, pressing the left-mouse button, and dragging the column to a different position within the table. That functionality is also provided through the JTableHeader class.

Another responsibility of JTableHeader is to return tool tip text, which usually occurs when the cursor lingers over one of the table's column headers. This may surprise you, since we saw earlier that setting the tool tip text for the header renderer allowed us to modify the tool tip, which would seem to indicate that it's the header renderer and not the JTableHeader that's responsible for providing a tool tip. In fact, the JTableHeader is responsible for doing so, but it normally delegates requests for tool tip text to the header renderers.

When getToolTipText() is called, it's passed a MouseEvent that allows the JTableHeader to determine which column header is underneath the cursor. It then selects the header renderer for that column and returns the tool tip text provided by the renderer. This approach works fine if each column has its own header renderer, because you can then set a separate tool tip for each column, but it's not as appropriate when a single renderer is responsible for drawing multiple column headers. To address this limitation, we can easily create a subclass of JTableHeader that maintains an array of tips and returns one from that array instead of obtaining it from a header renderer:

```java
import java.awt.event.MouseEvent;
import javax.swing.table.*;

public class JTableHeaderToolTips extends JTableHeader {

  protected String[] toolTips;

  public JTableHeaderToolTips(TableColumnModel tcm) {
    super(tcm);
  }

  public void setToolTips(String[] tips) {
    toolTips = tips;
  }

  public String getToolTipText(MouseEvent event) {
    String tip = super.getToolTipText(event);
    int column = columnAtPoint(event.getPoint());
    if ((toolTips != null) && (column < toolTips.length)
            && (toolTips[column] != null)) {
      tip = toolTips[column];
    }
    return tip;
  }

}
```

When this JTableHeader subclass receives a request for a tool tip, it determines which column is under the mouse and attempts to return a tip from its own array instead of the one that's provided by the column's header renderer. You can use an instance of this class by making the following changes to SimpleTableTest:

```java
public SimpleTableTest() {
  Container pane = getContentPane();
  pane.setLayout(new BorderLayout());
  TableValues tv = new TableValues();
  table = new JTable(tv);
  TableColumnModel tcm = table.getColumnModel();
  TableColumn tc = tcm.getColumn(TableValues.GENDER);
  tc.setCellRenderer(new GenderRenderer());
```

```
        tc.setCellEditor(new GenderEditor());
        MultiLineHeaderRenderer mlhr = new MultiLineHeaderRenderer();
        //mlhr.setToolTipText("This is the person's current account balance");
        tc = tcm.getColumn(TableValues.ACCOUNT_BALANCE);
        tc.setHeaderRenderer(mlhr);
        JTableHeaderToolTips jthtt = new
            JTableHeaderToolTips(table.getColumnModel());
        jthtt.setToolTips(new String[] {"Customer's First Name",
            "Customer's Last Name", "Customer's Date of Birth",
            "Customer's Account Balance", "Customer's Gender"});
        table.setTableHeader(jthtt);
        table.setDefaultRenderer(Float.class, new CurrencyRenderer());
        JScrollPane jsp = new JScrollPane(table);
        pane.add(jsp, BorderLayout.CENTER);
    }
```

With this code in place, moving the mouse over each column header results in that column's tool tip text being displayed:

The key to providing this functionality was our ability to determine which column was underneath the cursor when the tool tip text was requested, which we did using the columnAtPoint() method defined in JTableHeader. You could use the same technique to display tool tips on a per-cell basis within the JTable's data area by overriding JTable's getToolTipText() method and using its rowAtPoint() and columnAtPoint() methods to identify which cell is underneath the cursor.

Another way in which you might use JTableHeader is to detect and handle mouse events that occur over the headers. For example, suppose that your application allows a user to select a table column and you find that users instinctively tend to click on column headers in an attempt to cause the column to become selected.

However, JTable does not provide this behavior by default, so if you want a mouse click on a column header to result in the column being selected, you must implement the behavior yourself by detecting the click and performing the selection. Unlike requests for tool tips, which are delegated to the appropriate header renderer, mouse events are not sent to the renderers. Therefore, if you want to be notified of mouse events, you must register as a listener of the JTableHeader.

The code below disables row selection, enables column selection mode, and adds a mouse listener to the table header. When a click event occurs on a header, the listener determines which column the event is associated with and selects that column:

```java
import java.awt.*;
import java.awt.event.*;
import javax.swing.*;
import javax.swing.table.*;

public class SimpleTableTest extends JFrame {

  protected JTable table;

  public static void main(String[] args) {
    SimpleTableTest stt = new SimpleTableTest();
    stt.setDefaultCloseOperation(JFrame.EXIT_ON_CLOSE);
    stt.setSize(400, 300);
    stt.setVisible(true);
  }

  public SimpleTableTest() {
    Container pane = getContentPane();
    pane.setLayout(new BorderLayout());
    TableValues tv = new TableValues();
    table = new JTable(tv);
    table.setRowSelectionAllowed(false);
    table.setColumnSelectionAllowed(true);
    TableColumnModel tcm = table.getColumnModel();
    TableColumn tc = tcm.getColumn(TableValues.GENDER);
    tc.setCellRenderer(new GenderRenderer());
    tc.setCellEditor(new GenderEditor());
    MultiLineHeaderRenderer mlhr = new MultiLineHeaderRenderer();
    tc = tcm.getColumn(TableValues.ACCOUNT_BALANCE);
    tc.setHeaderRenderer(mlhr);
    JTableHeaderToolTips jthtt =
        new JTableHeaderToolTips(table.getColumnModel());
    jthtt.setToolTips(new String[] {
      "Customer's First Name", "Customer's Last Name",
      "Customer's Date of Birth", "Customer's Account Balance",
      "Customer's Gender"
    });
    table.setTableHeader(jthtt);
    table.setDefaultRenderer(Float.class, new CurrencyRenderer());
    JScrollPane jsp = new JScrollPane(table);
    pane.add(jsp, BorderLayout.CENTER);
    addHeaderListener();
  }

  public void addHeaderListener() {
    table.getTableHeader().addMouseListener(new MouseAdapter() {
      public void mousePressed(MouseEvent event) {
        JTableHeader header = (JTableHeader) (event.getSource());
        int index = header.columnAtPoint(event.getPoint());
        table.setColumnSelectionInterval(index, index);
      }
    });
  }

}
```

Creating Row Headers

For many displays, column headers are sufficient, but you'll sometimes want to create row headers for the data in a JTable. As it turns out, this is very easy to do, since the JScrollPane provides not only a viewport for column headers, but also one for row headers. Unlike the column header viewport, the row viewport is empty by default, but it's trivial to create your own header and have it displayed.

The following class can be used as a row header, and is simply a JTable that displays a single column with the index value (starting at 1 instead of 0) of each row displayed in that column. The class is very simple, and in fact, much of its code exists simply to make minor adjustments to its appearance and behavior, such as preventing its cells from being selected:

```java
import javax.swing.*;
import javax.swing.table.*;

public class RowNumberHeader extends JTable {

  protected JTable mainTable;

  public RowNumberHeader(JTable table) {
    super();
    mainTable = table;
    setModel(new RowNumberTableModel());
    setPreferredScrollableViewportSize(getMinimumSize());
    setRowSelectionAllowed(false);
    JComponent renderer = (JComponent) getDefaultRenderer(Object.class);
    LookAndFeel.installColorsAndFont(renderer, "TableHeader.background",
                                     "TableHeader.foreground",
                                     "TableHeader.font");
    LookAndFeel.installBorder(this, "TableHeader.cellBorder");
  }

  public int getRowHeight(int row) {
    return mainTable.getRowHeight();
  }

  class RowNumberTableModel extends AbstractTableModel {

    public int getRowCount() {
      return mainTable.getModel().getRowCount();
    }

    public int getColumnCount() {
      return 1;
    }

    public Object getValueAt(int row, int column) {
      return new Integer(row + 1);
    }

  }

}
```

After defining this class, it can be used by making a temporary change to the `SimpleTableTest` class:

```
public SimpleTableTest() {
   Container pane = getContentPane();
   pane.setLayout(new BorderLayout());
   TableValues tv = new TableValues();
   table = new JTable(tv);
   table.setRowSelectionAllowed(false);
   table.setColumnSelectionAllowed(true);
   TableColumnModel tcm = table.getColumnModel();
   TableColumn tc = tcm.getColumn(TableValues.GENDER);
   tc.setCellRenderer(new GenderRenderer());
   tc.setCellEditor(new GenderEditor());
   MultiLineHeaderRenderer mlhr = new MultiLineHeaderRenderer();
   tc = tcm.getColumn(TableValues.ACCOUNT_BALANCE);
   tc.setHeaderRenderer(mlhr);
   JTableHeaderToolTips jthtt = new
       JTableHeaderToolTips(table.getColumnModel());
   jthtt.setToolTips(new String[] {"Customer's First Name",
       "Customer's Last Name", "Customer's Date of Birth",
       "Customer's Account Balance", "Customer's Gender"});
   table.setTableHeader(jthtt);
   table.setDefaultRenderer(Float.class, new CurrencyRenderer());
   JScrollPane jsp = new JScrollPane(table);
   JViewport jvp = new JViewport();
   jvp.setView(new RowNumberHeader(table));
   jsp.setRowHeader(jvp);
   pane.add(jsp, BorderLayout.CENTER);
   addHeaderListener();
}
```

When executed, each table row includes a number on the left side:

	First Name	Last Name	Date of Birth	Account Balance	Gender
1	Clay	Ashworth	Feb 20, 1962	$12,345.67	Male ▼
2	Jacob	Ashworth	Jan 6, 1987	$23,456.78	Male ▼
3	Jordan	Ashworth	Aug 31, 1989	$34,567.89	Female ▼
4	Evelyn	Kirk	Jan 16, 1945	($456.70)	Female ▼
5	Belle	Spyres	Aug 2, 1907	$567.00	Female ▼

Frozen Columns

In addition to displaying row headers, it's sometimes desirable to "freeze" one or more columns in the table so that they're visible even when the user scrolls right or left horizontally. For example, in the case of this data, it might be desirable to freeze the first column (First Name) so that it's always visible. This can be done, but it is slightly more complex than creating simple row labels.

The steps for doing this are:

- ❑ Create a JTable that we'll call the **main table** and enclose it in a JScrollPane. This table will display the non-frozen data.

- ❑ Create a second JTable that we'll call the **header table**, and add it to a JScrollPane as well. This table should use the same TableModel as the main table, but will display the frozen column(s).

- ❑ Create an empty TableColumnModel that will later be assigned to the header table.

- ❑ Remove the TableColumn instances from the main table's TableColumnModel for each column to be frozen and add them to the column model created in the previous step.

- ❑ Assign the column model that now contains the frozen TableColumn instances to the header table using setColumnModel().

- ❑ The JScrollPane that contains the header table should now also contain a JTableHeader in its column header viewport. Obtain a reference to it, and move it to the upper-left corner of the JScrollPane that contains the main table. This can be done using the scroll pane's setCorner() method.

- ❑ Set the header table's preferred scrollable viewport width so that it's just large enough to display the frozen columns. Its default width is 450, which is usually larger than necessary.

In effect, to freeze columns, you split the JTable into two separate tables, display the table containing the frozen columns as the JScrollPane's row header, and move that table's column headers to the upper-left corner of the outer scroll pane. This behavior is implemented in the following class:

```
import java.awt.*;
import javax.swing.*;
import javax.swing.table.*;

public class FrozenColumnHeader extends JScrollPane {

  protected JTable mainTable;
  protected JTable headerTable;
  protected int columnCount;

  public FrozenColumnHeader(JTable table, int columns) {
    super();
    mainTable = table;
    headerTable = new JTable(mainTable.getModel());
    getViewport().setView(headerTable);
    columnCount = columns;
  }

  public void addNotify() {
    TableColumn column;
```

```
    super.addNotify();
    TableColumnModel mainModel = mainTable.getColumnModel();
    TableColumnModel headerModel = new DefaultTableColumnModel();
    int frozenWidth = 0;
    for (int i = 0; i < columnCount; i++) {
      column = mainModel.getColumn(0);
      mainModel.removeColumn(column);
      headerModel.addColumn(column);
      frozenWidth += column.getPreferredWidth()
                    + headerModel.getColumnMargin();
    }
    headerTable.setColumnModel(headerModel);
    Component columnHeader = getColumnHeader().getView();
    getColumnHeader().sctView(null);
    JScrollPane mainScrollPane =
      (JScrollPane) SwingUtilities.getAncestorOfClass(JScrollPane.class,
            mainTable);
    mainScrollPane.setCorner(JScrollPane.UPPER_LEFT_CORNER, columnHeader);
    headerTable
      .setPreferredScrollableViewportSize(new Dimension(frozenWidth, 0));
  }

}
```

This class can be used by creating an instance of it and passing a reference to a JTable to the constructor, along with the number of columns from that table to freeze. For example, the following modification to SimpleTableTest causes the **First Name** column to be frozen:

```
public SimpleTableTest() {
  Container pane = getContentPane();
  pane.setLayout(new BorderLayout());
  TableValues tv = new TableValues();
  table = new JTable(tv);
  table.setRowSelectionAllowed(false);
  table.setColumnSelectionAllowed(true);
  TableColumnModel tcm = table.getColumnModel();
  TableColumn tc = tcm.getColumn(TableValues.GENDER);
  tc.setCellRenderer(new GenderRenderer());
  tc.setCellEditor(new GenderEditor());
  MultiLineHeaderRenderer mlhr = new MultiLineHeaderRenderer();
  tc = tcm.getColumn(TableValues.ACCOUNT_BALANCE);
  tc.setHeaderRenderer(mlhr);
  JTableHeaderToolTips jthtt = new
      JTableHeaderToolTips(table.getColumnModel());
  jthtt.setToolTips(new String[] {"Customer's First Name",
      "Customer's Last Name", "Customer's Date of Birth",
      "Customer's Account Balance", "Customer's Gender"});
  table.setTableHeader(jthtt);
  table.setDefaultRenderer(Float.class, new CurrencyRenderer());
  JScrollPane jsp = new JScrollPane(table);
  JViewport jvp = new JViewport();
  jvp.setView(new FrozenColumnHeader(table, 1));
  //  The following line isn't necessary, but is done
  //  to illustrate that the "frozen" columns remain
  //  visible even when the main table is scrolled
```

```
        table.setAutoResizeMode(JTable.AUTO_RESIZE_OFF);
        jsp.setRowHeader(jvp);
        pane.add(jsp, BorderLayout.CENTER);
        addHeaderListener();
    }
```

When you execute this code, you can resize the frame so that it's too narrow to display all of the columns in the table. However, regardless of which portion of the table is displayed, the "frozen" column on the left will remain visible as shown below:

Although this example illustrates how to freeze a single column, you can apply this same technique if you wish to freeze multiple columns. This approach can also be used to freeze rows of data simply by adding a table containing the rows to the JScrollPane's column header viewport.

Sorting Table Rows

When displaying information in a JTable, you'll sometimes want to sort the rows in the table based on the values in one or more of the columns. Since sorting is a slow and potentially complex task, you should try to have the data sorted by some external application. For example, if you're displaying data from a relational database, you can have the database present the rows to you in sorted order by indicating that fact in the SELECT statement you issue. However, for various reasons, it's sometimes necessary for you to take responsibility for sorting the data in a table, and since JTable doesn't directly support sorting, you must implement the code that will provide this behavior.

To sort the data displayed in a table, you can use one of two approaches: sort the data "in place", or add a sorting layer between the JTable and the TableModel that contains the data. To sort the data in place means that you logically change the position of the data in the arrays or collection objects that contain the data. For example, in the case of the data defined in TableValues, the values would be rearranged within the array so that they occur in sorted order.

A somewhat more flexible approach is to add a sorting layer between the table and its data model. Specifically, this would involve creating a second `TableModel` that we'll call the **sort model**, and this model would contain a reference to the original model (such as an instance of `TableValues`) that we'll call the **source model**. In this case, the source model's data need not ever be moved or changed in any way. Instead, the sort model can create a list of index values that reference the source model data in sorted order. For example, given three string values stored in the source model:

```
Kirk
Ashworth
Spyres
```

The sort model can sort these strings and build a set of index values that references them in sorted (ascending) order. In this case, the index values would be:

```
1
0
2
```

By using this list of index values to reference the rows in the source model, the data can appear to be sorted, when in reality, it's still stored in its original unsorted order. The following class implements a sorted model and uses the `java.util.TreeSet` collection object to perform the sorting.

`SortedTableModel` is a very simple class, consisting mainly of the `sortRows()` method, an inner class used to perform the sorting, and `TableModel` methods that delegate their functionality to the source model. Notice, however, that `getValueAt()` and `setValueAt()` perform a sort of translation on the row index value, so that the caller (usually a `JTable` instance) sees the model data in sorted order:

```java
import javax.swing.table.*;
import java.util.*;

public class SortedTableModel extends AbstractTableModel {

    protected TableModel sourceModel;
    protected int[] indexValues;

    public SortedTableModel(TableModel model) {
        super();
        sourceModel = model;
    }

    public int getRowCount() {
        return sourceModel.getRowCount();
    }

    public int getColumnCount() {
        return sourceModel.getColumnCount();
    }

    public Object getValueAt(int row, int column) {
        if (indexValues != null) {
            row = getSourceIndex(row);
        }
        return sourceModel.getValueAt(row, column);
```

```java
  }

  public void setValueAt(Object value, int row, int column) {
    if (indexValues != null) {
      row = getSourceIndex(row);
    }
    sourceModel.setValueAt(value, row, column);
  }

  public boolean isCellEditable(int row, int column) {
    return sourceModel.isCellEditable(row, column);
  }

  public String getColumnName(int column) {
    return sourceModel.getColumnName(column);
  }

  public Class getColumnClass(int column) {
    return sourceModel.getColumnClass(column);
  }

  public int getSourceIndex(int index) {
    if (indexValues != null) {
      return indexValues[index];
    }
    return -1;
  }

  public void sortRows(int column, boolean ascending) {
    SortedItemHolder holder;
    TreeSet sortedList = new TreeSet();
    int count = getRowCount();
    for (int i = 0; i < count; i++) {
      holder = new SortedItemHolder(sourceModel.getValueAt(i, column), i);
      sortedList.add(holder);
    }
    indexValues = new int[count];
    Iterator iterator = sortedList.iterator();
    int index = (ascending ? 0 : count - 1);
    while (iterator.hasNext()) {
      holder = (SortedItemHolder) (iterator.next());
      indexValues[index] = holder.position;
      index += (ascending ? 1 : -1);
    }
    refreshViews();
  }

  public void clearSort() {
    indexValues = null;
    refreshViews();
  }

  public void refreshViews() {
    fireTableDataChanged();
  }
```

```
class SortedItemHolder implements Comparable {

  public final Object value;
  public final int position;

  public SortedItemHolder(Object value, int position) {
    this.value = value;
    this.position = position;
  }

  public int compareTo(Object parm) {
    SortedItemHolder holder = (SortedItemHolder) parm;
    Comparable comp = (Comparable) value;
    int result = comp.compareTo(holder.value);
    if (result == 0) {
      result = (position < holder.position) ? -1 : 1;
    }
    return result;
  }

  public int hashCode() {
    return position;
  }

  public boolean equals(Object comp) {
    if (comp instanceof SortedItemHolder) {
      SortedItemHolder other = (SortedItemHolder) comp;
      if ((position == other.position) && (value == other.value)) {
        return true;
      }
    }
    return false;
  }

  }

}
```

Using this class, you can display table data in sorted order. The sortRows() method takes each item in the column it is given, and puts it into a TreeSet as a SortedItemHolder. After this, it sorts the items into the desired order, and returns the results and refreshes the view. The following code sorts the table data in ascending order based on the values in the **Account Balance** column:

```
public SimpleTableTest() {
  Container pane = getContentPane();
  pane.setLayout(new BorderLayout());
  TableValues tv = new TableValues();
  SortedTableModel stm = new SortedTableModel(tv);
  stm.sortRows(TableValues.ACCOUNT_BALANCE, true);
  table = new JTable(stm);
  table.setRowSelectionAllowed(false);
  table.setColumnSelectionAllowed(true);
  TableColumnModel tcm = table.getColumnModel();
  TableColumn tc = tcm.getColumn(TableValues.GENDER);
  tc.setCellRenderer(new GenderRenderer());
```

```
        tc.setCellEditor(new GenderEditor());
        MultiLineHeaderRenderer mlhr = new MultiLineHeaderRenderer();
        tc = tcm.getColumn(TableValues.ACCOUNT_BALANCE);
        tc.setHeaderRenderer(mlhr);
        JTableHeaderToolTips jthtt = new
            JTableHeaderToolTips(table.getColumnModel());
        jthtt.setToolTips(new String[] {"Customer's First Name",
            "Customer's Last Name", "Customer's Date of Birth",
            "Customer's Account Balance", "Customer's Gender"});
        table.setTableHeader(jthtt);
        table.setDefaultRenderer(Float.class, new CurrencyRenderer());
        JScrollPane jsp = new JScrollPane(table);
        pane.add(jsp, BorderLayout.CENTER);
        addHeaderListener();
    }
```

First Name	Last Name	Date of Birth	Account Balance	Gender
Evelyn	Kirk	Jan 16, 1945	($456.70)	Female ▼
Belle	Spyres	Aug 2, 1907	$567.00	Female ▼
Clay	Ashworth	Feb 20, 1962	$12,345.67	Male ▼
Jacob	Ashworth	Jan 6, 1987	$23,456.78	Male ▼
Jordan	Ashworth	Aug 31, 1989	$34,567.89	Female ▼

Dynamic Sort Column Selection

In the previous example, a specific sort column was "hard-coded" into the application, and could not be changed once the application was executed. However, it's very easy to create a user interface that allows the sort column to be selected dynamically. We can simply create a header renderer that detects mouse clicks, determines which column header the cursor was over, and sorts the table based on the values in that column:

```java
import java.awt.*;
import javax.swing.*;
import javax.swing.table.*;
import javax.swing.plaf.basic.BasicArrowButton;

public class SortedColumnHeaderRenderer implements TableCellRenderer {

  protected TableCellRenderer textRenderer;
  protected SortedTableModel sortedModel;
```

```
    protected int sortColumn = -1;
    protected boolean sortAscending = true;

    public SortedColumnHeaderRenderer(SortedTableModel model,
                                      TableCellRenderer renderer) {
      sortedModel = model;
      textRenderer = renderer;
    }

    public SortedColumnHeaderRenderer(SortedTableModel model) {
      this(model, null);
    }

    public Component getTableCellRendererComponent(JTable table,
            Object value, boolean isSelected, boolean hasFocus, int row,
            int column) {
      Component text;
      JPanel panel = new JPanel();
      panel.setLayout(new BorderLayout());

      if (textRenderer != null) {
        text = textRenderer.getTableCellRendererComponent(table, value,
              isSelected, hasFocus, row, column);
      } else {
        text = new JLabel((String) value, JLabel.CENTER);
        LookAndFeel.installColorsAndFont((JComponent) text,
                                    "TableHeader.background",
                                    "TableHeader.foreground",
                                    "TableHeader.font");
      }
      panel.add(text, BorderLayout.CENTER);

      if (column == sortColumn) {
        BasicArrowButton bab = new BasicArrowButton((sortAscending
              ? SwingConstants.NORTH : SwingConstants.SOUTH));
        panel.add(bab, BorderLayout.WEST);
      }
      LookAndFeel.installBorder(panel, "TableHeader.cellBorder");
      return panel;
    }

    public void columnSelected(int column) {
      if (column != sortColumn) {
        sortColumn = column;
        sortAscending = true;
      } else {
        sortAscending = !sortAscending;
        if (sortAscending) {
          sortColumn = -1;
        }
      }
      if (sortColumn != -1) {
        sortedModel.sortRows(sortColumn, sortAscending);
      } else {
        sortedModel.clearSort();
      }
    }
  }
}
```

There are three important points to be made concerning this renderer. First, it can be passed a reference to another renderer that will be delegated responsibility for drawing the column header text. That allows you to combine the functionality of this renderer with that of some other renderer, such as the `MultiLineHeaderRenderer`. In other words, you can create a table with headers that both display multi-line text and allow you to dynamically select the sort column.

Another point to be made concerning this class is that it maintains a variable that identifies which column is sorted. Since that is the case, a single instance of this class should be used to render all columns that can be selected for sorting.

Thirdly, there are limitations to what type of data it can sort. See the section *Using Comparable* below for further details, and a way around this problem.

When you assign this renderer to the header cells, it allows you to sort on a particular column by clicking on that column's header. The first time you click on a column header, the table rows are sorted in ascending order based on that column's values. If you click again on the same column header, the rows are resorted, this time in descending order, and clicking a third time causes the table data to be displayed in its original unsorted order. When the table data is sorted, a visual indicator appears that illustrates how the data is sorted: an up arrow for ascending order, and a down arrow for descending:

An example of how to use the renderer can be found in the following code:

```
import java.awt.*;
import java.awt.event.*;
import javax.swing.*;
import javax.swing.table.*;

public class SimpleTableTest extends JFrame {

  protected JTable table;
  protected SortedColumnHeaderRenderer renderer;

  public static void main(String[] args) {
    SimpleTableTest stt = new SimpleTableTest();
```

```
      stt.setDefaultCloseOperation(JFrame.EXIT_ON_CLOSE);
      stt.setSize(400, 300);
      stt.setVisible(true);
    }

    public SimpleTableTest() {
      Container pane = getContentPane();
      pane.setLayout(new BorderLayout());
      TableValues tv = new TableValues();
      SortedTableModel stm = new SortedTableModel(tv);

      // stm.sortRows(TableValues.ACCOUNT_BALANCE, true);
      table = new JTable(stm);
      table.setRowSelectionAllowed(false);
      table.setColumnSelectionAllowed(true);
      TableColumnModel tcm = table.getColumnModel();
      TableColumn tc = tcm.getColumn(TableValues.GENDER);
      tc.setCellRenderer(new GenderRenderer());
      tc.setCellEditor(new GenderEditor());
      MultiLineHeaderRenderer mlhr = new MultiLineHeaderRenderer();

      // tc = tcm.getColumn(TableValues.ACCOUNT_BALANCE);
      // tc.setHeaderRenderer(mlhr);
      renderer = new SortedColumnHeaderRenderer(stm, mlhr);
      int count = tcm.getColumnCount();
      for (int i = 0; i < count; i++) {
        tc = tcm.getColumn(i);
        tc.setHeaderRenderer(renderer);
      }
      JTableHeaderToolTips jthtt =
          new JTableHeaderToolTips(table.getColumnModel());
      jthtt.setToolTips(new String[] {
        "Customer's First Name", "Customer's Last Name",
        "Customer's Date of Birth", "Customer's Account Balance",
        "Customer's Gender"
      });
      table.setTableHeader(jthtt);
      table.setDefaultRenderer(Float.class, new CurrencyRenderer());
      JScrollPane jsp = new JScrollPane(table);
      pane.add(jsp, BorderLayout.CENTER);
      addHeaderListener();
    }

    public void addHeaderListener() {
      table.getTableHeader().addMouseListener(new MouseAdapter() {
        public void mousePressed(MouseEvent event) {
          JTableHeader header = (JTableHeader)(event.getSource());
          int index = header.columnAtPoint(event.getPoint());
          renderer.columnSelected(index);
          table.setColumnSelectionInterval(index, index);
        }
      });
    }

  }
```

In addition to the changes shown above, the other column headers in TableValues could be modified to
display multiple lines of text by embedding linefeed characters in them:

```
public final static String[] columnNames = {"First\nName", "Last\nName",
    "Date of\nBirth", "Account\nBalance", "Gender"};
```

Using Comparable

One limitation of this approach to sorting that you should be aware of is that it uses the Comparable interface to determine the value of one object relative to another (less than, greater than, or equal to). However, this usually isn't a problem, because in Java 2, that interface is implemented by most classes that can be sorted in a meaningful way. For example, the numeric wrapper classes (Integer, Float, Long, etc.), String, Date, and several others all implement Comparable. However, Boolean does not, because although it's obvious that a value of true isn't equal to a value of false, it's unclear which value should be considered greater than or less than the other one. In fact, if you click on the header of the **Gender** column, the program generates a ClassCastException when trying to cast the Boolean values in that column to instances of Comparable.

One way to address this problem is to have the code that initiates sorting examine the type of data in the column to ensure that the values can be sorted. As we've seen, the column's data type can be obtained by calling the TableModel's getColumnClass() method, and we can use the Class object returned from that method to determine whether or not the objects in the column are instances of a class that implements Comparable. This can easily be done by making the following changes to the addHeaderListener() method defined in SimpleTableTest:

```
public void addHeaderListener() {
   table.getTableHeader().addMouseListener(new MouseAdapter() {
     public void mousePressed(MouseEvent event) {
       JTableHeader header = (JTableHeader)(event.getSource());
       int index = header.columnAtPoint(event.getPoint());
       Class dataType = table.getModel().getColumnClass(index);
       Class[] interfaces = dataType.getInterfaces();
       for (int i = 0; i < interfaces.length; i++) {
         if (interfaces[i].equals(java.lang.Comparable.class)) {
           renderer.columnSelected(index);
           break;
         }
       }
       table.setColumnSelectionInterval(index, index);
     }
   });
}
```

As the adjacent screenshot illustrates, this code does indeed prevent the application from attempting to sort the Boolean values in the **Gender** column. Instead, the column is simply selected:

First Name	Last Name	Date of Birth	Account Balance	Gender
Evelyn	Kirk	Jan 16, 1945	($456.70)	Female
Belle	Spyres	Aug 2, 1907	$567.00	Female
Clay	Ashworth	Feb 20, 1962	$12,345.67	Male
Jacob	Ashworth	Jan 6, 1987	$23,456.78	Male
Jordan	Ashworth	Aug 31, 1989	$34,567.89	Female

However, there is still one problem remaining: while it's true that clicking on the Gender column doesn't result in that column being resorted, clicking on the First Name and Last Name column headers also does not seem to have any effect. This is because the only two columns for which our TableModel (specifically, the TableValues class) returns a meaningful value are Date of Birth and Account Balance, and it indicates that all other columns contain Object values. In other words, our application won't sort on the First Name, Last Name, or Gender columns because it only knows that those columns contain Object instances, and Object doesn't implement the Comparable interface. However, this can easily be addressed by simply updating the getColumnClass() method in TableValues so that it more accurately describes the data types of all the columns it encapsulates:

```
public Class getColumnClass(int column) {
    Class dataType = super.getColumnClass(column);
    if (column == ACCOUNT_BALANCE) {
        dataType = Float.class;
    }
    else if (column == DATE_OF_BIRTH) {
        dataType = java.util.Date.class;
    }
    else if ((column == FIRST_NAME) || (column == LAST_NAME)) {
        dataType = String.class;
    }
    else if (column == GENDER) {
        dataType = Boolean.class;
    }
    return dataType;
}
```

With this modification, you can now sort on all of the columns except for Gender, which is the correct behavior. In this case, all of the classes we used for sorting were part of the Java core classes, but you may wish to sort on some user-defined class that's specific to your application. Fortunately, implementing the Comparable interface is trivial, and an example of how to do so is provided in the SortedItemHolder inner class shown above.

Adding and Removing Table Rows

In all of the examples we've looked at so far, no JTable data was changed, added, or removed programmatically. However, you will sometimes want to dynamically change the data in a JTable after it is displayed, and all that's necessary is to make the changes to your TableModel and then notify its listeners (the JTable instance) that the data was modified.

For example, the following application provides a simple one-column table and a text field that allows you to add lines of text to the table:

```
import java.awt.*;
import java.awt.event.*;
import javax.swing.*;
import javax.swing.event.*;
import javax.swing.table.*;
import java.util.Vector;

public class RowAdder extends JFrame {
```

```
    protected SimpleModel tableData;
    protected JTable table;
    protected JTextField textField;

    public static void main(String[] args) {
      RowAdder ra = new RowAdder();
      ra.setDefaultCloseOperation(JFrame.EXIT_ON_CLOSE);
      ra.setSize(400, 300);
      ra.setVisible(true);
    }

    public RowAdder() {
      Container pane = getContentPane();
      pane.setLayout(new BorderLayout());
      tableData = new SimpleModel();
      table = new JTable(tableData);
      table.getColumnModel().getColumn(0).setPreferredWidth(300);
      JScrollPane jsp = new JScrollPane(table);
      pane.add(jsp, BorderLayout.CENTER);
      textField = new JTextField();
      textField.addActionListener(new ActionListener() {
        public void actionPerformed(ActionEvent event) {
          addLineToTable();
        }
      });
      pane.add(textField, BorderLayout.SOUTH);
    }

    protected void addLineToTable() {
      tableData.addText(textField.getText());
      textField.setText("");
    }

    class SimpleModel extends AbstractTableModel {

      protected Vector textData = new Vector();

      public void addText(String text) {
        textData.addElement(text);
        fireTableDataChanged();
      }

      public int getRowCount() {
        return textData.size();
      }


      public int getColumnCount() {
        return 1;
      }

      public Object getValueAt(int row, int column) {
        return textData.elementAt(row);
      }

    }

  }
```

This code creates a JTable, and allows you to enter text in a text field and press the *Return* key to add that text to the table:

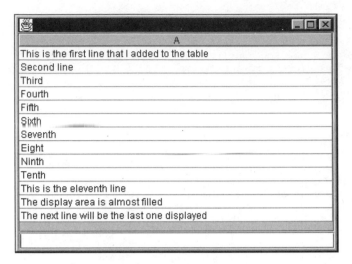

When that occurs, the data is added to the TableModel and the fireTableDataChanged() method is called. This method is provided by AbstractTableModel as a convenience.

Even if your TableModel isn't a subclass of AbstractTableModel, it's still trivial to refresh the table display when your data changes, for instance when you want to remove a row. All that's necessary is to construct an instance of TableModelEvent and pass it as the parameter to the tableChanged() method of all listeners that are registered with the TableModel through its addTableModelListener() method. The following code segment illustrates how this can be done:

```
protected EventListenerList listenerList = new EventListenerList();
    .
    .
    .

public void notifyListenersOfDataChange() {
  TableModelEvent event = new TableModelEvent(this);
  Object[] listeners = listenerList.getListenerList();
  for (int i = 0; i < listeners.length; i++) {
    if (listeners[i] == TableModelListener.class) {
      TableModelListener listener = (TableModelListener)(listeners[i + 1]);
      listener.tableChanged(event);
    }
  }
}
```

This code illustrates how easily you can notify listeners (in practice, usually a single JTable instance) of a change to a TableModel's data. However, as mentioned before, AbstractTableModel implements this functionality for you. It also includes a number of fireTable() methods that create a TableModelEvent containing information about specifically what type of change (insert, update, or delete) occurred, along with the rows and columns that were affected by the change. You can use those methods to cause your table to be refreshed when you have made insertions, updates, or deletions to the data in the table's model.

Displaying a Particular Table Row

In the RowAdder class just defined, a row is added to the table each time the *Return* key is pressed in a text field. The first dozen or so rows appear immediately in the table, but eventually, there's not enough room to display all of the table rows, and a vertical scroll bar appears. At that point, since new rows are added to the end of the table, they will not be visible unless you manually scroll to the bottom of the table. However, when you're adding data to a table like this, it's often helpful to scroll the table automatically so that it always shows the most recently added row. This can be done by accessing the JViewport instance that's associated with the table's scroll pane, and changing the view position so that the bottom row appears at the scroll pane. The RowAdder class previously defined can easily be modified to perform this operation, as shown below:

```java
public RowAdder() {
  Container pane = getContentPane();
  pane.setLayout(new BorderLayout());
  tableData = new SimpleModel();
  table = new JTable(tableData);
  table.getColumnModel().getColumn(0).setPreferredWidth(300);
  table.addComponentListener(new TableScroller());
  JScrollPane jsp = new JScrollPane(table);
  pane.add(jsp, BorderLayout.CENTER);
  textField = new JTextField();
  textField.addActionListener(new ActionListener() {
    public void actionPerformed(ActionEvent event) {
      addLineToTable();
    }
  });
  pane.add(textField, BorderLayout.SOUTH);
}

class TableScroller extends ComponentAdapter {

  public void componentResized(ComponentEvent event) {
    int lastRow = tableData.getRowCount() - 1;
    int cellTop = table.getCellRect(lastRow, 0, true).y;
    JScrollPane jsp = (JScrollPane)SwingUtilities.getAncestorOfClass(
        JScrollPane.class, table);
    JViewport jvp = jsp.getViewport();
    int portHeight = jvp.getSize().height;
    int position = cellTop - (portHeight - table.getRowHeight() -
        table.getRowMargin());
    if (position >= 0) {
      jvp.setViewPosition(new Point(0, position));
    }
  }
}
```

The componentResized() method obtains the last row's size and coordinates by calling the table's getCellRect() method. It then uses the row's vertical position, the size of the viewport, and the height of the row to adjust the view position so that the last row is displayed at the bottom of the table. By using functionality similar to this, you can ensure that any given table row is visible, such as in this case where a new row was added to the table and should be displayed.

Summary

In this chapter, we've examined the functionality provided by JTable and how it provides those capabilities. Specifically, we've discussed:

- How to create a TableModel
- Column resizing modes
- Rendering and editing of table cells
- Selection modes
- JTableHeader and how it can be used to provide an improved user interface
- Creating numbered rows and frozen columns
- Sorting
- Handling dynamic updates to the table data

In the next chapter we will be looking at another of Swing's more complex components – JTree.

Professional Java Programmin

Online discussion at http://p2p.wrox.com

7

Swing's JTree Component

The `JTree` component defined in the `javax.swing` package is a component that's commonly used to display hierarchical data such as the contents of a file system. Even if you've never used `JTree` before, you've almost certainly seen a component like the one that appears on the left side of the Windows Explorer application:

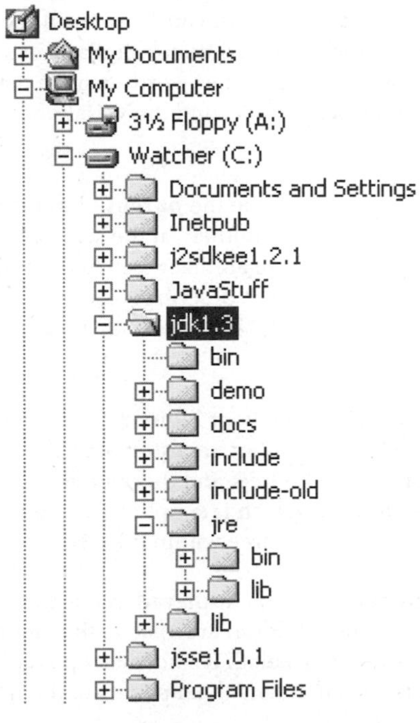

This chapter describes how to use `JTree` and illustrates how to provide some functionality that's often needed. In this chapter we will cover:

❑   Terminology related to tree structures and the data that they display

❑   `JTree`'s support classes and interfaces

❑   How to construct and manipulate the data model associated with a tree

❑   Controlling how the items in a tree are drawn (rendered) and edited

❑   How to select items in a tree and detect when selections change

❑   How to control which portions of a tree's data are displayed (expanded) or concealed (collapsed)

JTree Terminology

Before discussing how to use `JTree`, it's necessary to define the terminology that will be used to describe the different parts of a tree and its behavior. Each item that's displayed in the tree is referred to as a **node**, and every `JTree` contains a single **root node** that resides at the top of the node hierarchy:

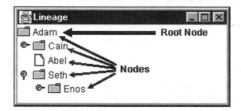

Each node is either a **branch node** or a **leaf node**, although the exact meanings of those terms can vary. "Leaf node" can refer to a node that *does not* contain other nodes, or it can refer to a node that *cannot* contain other nodes. In the example above, "Abel" is a "Leaf node". "Branch node" similarly can mean a node that *does* contain other nodes or one that *can* contain other nodes. In other words, a node that does not contain other nodes can be described as either a leaf node or a branch node, and the variation in meaning is discussed in more detail later.

When a branch node does contain other nodes, it is said to be the **parent** of those nodes, and they are referred to as **children** of that branch and **siblings** of one another. In the screenshot above, the "Adam" node is the parent of "Cain", "Abel", and "Seth", and those three are likewise children of "Adam" and siblings of one another. Since the parent/child relationship is relative (it describes one node's relationship to another), a single node can be both a parent and a child. For example, "Seth" is both a parent (relative to "Enos") and a child (relative to "Adam").

All nodes that are contained by a branch node either directly or indirectly are referred to as the branch's **descendents**, and the branch itself is likewise referred to as an **ancestor** of its descendents. In the case above, the "Adam" node is the ancestor of all other nodes in the tree, and those nodes are all descendents of "Adam". A closely related concept is that of a **subtree**, which is simply a tree node and all of its descendents, since that collection of nodes effectively forms a separate "tree within the tree".

The `JTree` component normally allows a parent node to be displayed in one of two states: with its children visible, or with its children concealed. When a node's children are visible, that node is **expanded**, while a **collapsed** node is one for which its descendents are concealed. It's normally possible for you to toggle this state by clicking on the node's **handle**, which is a small image that appears to the left of the node.

The screenshot below contains two instances of JTree that contain the same data, but two of the three non-root nodes ("colors" and "food") in the left tree are expanded, while all three of those in the right tree are collapsed. Note that the appearance of the handle varies slightly based upon the state (expanded or collapsed) of the node with which it's associated:

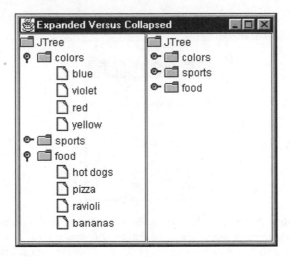

When a node is collapsed, all of its descendents are **hidden**, because those nodes cannot be seen, while a node for which all ancestors are expanded is considered **viewable**. The term "viewable" correctly implies only that a node is *eligible* to be seen, but not that it is currently visible. The reason for this distinction is that like JTable components, JTree instances often contain too much data to be able to display all of their nodes simultaneously, and for that reason, trees are often contained inside instances of JScrollPane. Only when a node is actually visible is it considered **displayed**, which means that the node is positioned within the portion of the tree that's currently visible in the JScrollPane.

Creating a JTree

Creating a JTree instance is easy to do, and many different constructors are provided. Although the no-argument constructor populates the tree with dummy data like that shown above, several others accept a list of items in the form of an object array, a Vector, or a Hashtable, for example:

```
import javax.swing.*;

public class SimpleTreeTest extends JFrame {

  public static void main(String[] args) {
    SimpleTreeTest stt = new SimpleTreeTest();
    stt.setDefaultCloseOperation(JFrame.EXIT_ON_CLOSE);
    stt.setSize(400, 300);
    stt.setVisible(true);
  }

  public SimpleTreeTest() {
    Object[] genealogy = {"Jeff", "Joseph", "Pearl", "Owen", "Sarah",
        "John"};
    JTree tree = new JTree(genealogy);
```

```
        JScrollPane jsp = new JScrollPane(tree);
        getContentPane().add(jsp);
    }

}
```

This results in a display like that shown below:

It may appear at first glance that there is no root node, or that each of the six nodes in the array passed to the JTree constructor is somehow a root node. In reality, this constructor produces a JTree instance that has a concealed root node, and each of the objects in the array parameter is made a child of that invisible root. To view the root node, add an additional line of code that calls the setRootVisible() method:

```
    public SimpleTreeTest() {
        Object[] genealogy = {"Jeff", "Joseph", "Pearl", "Owen", "Sarah",
            "John"};
        JTree tree = new JTree(genealogy);
        tree.setRootVisible(true);
        JScrollPane jsp = new JScrollPane(tree);
        getContentPane().add(jsp);
    }
```

This results in a display like the one below:

Here the node values are all instances of the String class, but any type of object can be used as a node. JTree's default behavior is to display the value returned by each object's toString() method, which in this case is simply the String value itself.

In this example, each of the six nodes is assumed to be a leaf node since there are no children defined, but it is possible to use this technique to create more complex tree structures. For example, a second level of nodes could be added by modifying the code as shown below:

```
public SimpleTreeTest() {
    Object[] genealogy = {"Jeff", "Joseph", "Pearl", "Owen", "Sarah",
        "John"};
    genealogy[0] = new Object[] {"Jerry", "Selma", "Joe", "Evelyn"};
    JTree tree = new JTree(genealogy);
    tree.setRootVisible(true);
    JScrollPane jsp = new JScrollPane(tree);
    getContentPane().add(jsp);
}
```

With this modification, the first element in the `genealogy` array was changed from a `String` into another array, and when this code is compiled and executed, it produces a tree like the one below:

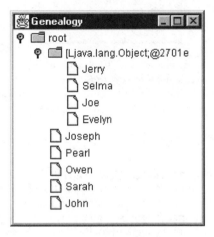

Although this does display the data in a way that's largely appropriate, the `toString()` method of the second object array returns a value (`[Ljava.lang.Object;@2701e`) that's not meaningful. There are several ways of addressing this problem, but one easy way is to use either `Vector` or `Hashtable` instead of an array and override the object's `toString()` method so that it returns the desired value. An illustration of how this might be done is shown in the following code segment:

```
public SimpleTreeTest() {
    Object[] genealogy = {"Jeff", "Joseph", "Pearl", "Owen", "Sarah",
        "John"};
    java.util.Vector v = new java.util.Vector() {
      public String toString() {
        return "Jeff";
      }
    };
    v.addElement("Jerry");
    v.addElement("Selma");
    v.addElement("Joe");
    v.addElement("Evelyn");
    genealogy[0] = v;
    JTree tree = new JTree(genealogy);
```

```
        tree.setRootVisible(true);
        JScrollPane jsp = new JScrollPane(tree);
        getContentPane().add(jsp);
    }
```

As expected, this modified version of the code displays the name "Jeff" for the first child node's label instead of the cryptic value returned by the Object array:

However, this approach is less than ideal, and as we'll see later in this chapter the classes and interfaces in the javax.swing.tree package provide a better way to define the nodes in a tree and their parent/child relationships. Prior to that discussion, it's useful to examine the TreeModel interface, which defines the methods that are invoked by JTree to retrieve the data it displays.

TreeModel

Like other Swing components, an instance of the JTree class defined in javax.swing represents the component **view**, while some other object represents the **model**. In other words, the model is the object that encapsulates the data to be displayed, while the view (a JTree instance) is the visual representation of that data. For a class to serve as a JTree model, it must implement TreeModel, an interface that's defined in the javax.swing.tree package. Each of the methods defined in TreeModel is described below, although you will not normally call these methods yourself. Instead, they are typically used by an instance of JTree to obtain the data it displays.

There will be further discussion of the topics raised in each of these sections at a later point. This is intended as an overview; details will be looked at later.

addTreeModelListener(), removeTreeModelListener()

An instance of a TreeModelListener implementation is passed to these methods, which are used to add and remove listeners to and from a list of objects that wish to be notified of changes to the tree data. Each listener is notified when a node is added or removed from the tree and when the tree's structure otherwise changes. In practice, the only registered listener of a given TreeModel instance will be the JTree instance associated with the model, and by registering as a listener, the tree can be notified of changes to the data that it displays.

getRoot()

This method returns the object representing the tree's root node. In the previous examples, a root node was constructed automatically and the objects in the array or Vector passed to the JTree constructor were made children of that root node. In most cases, however, you'll construct your own root node, add children to it, and pass it to a JTree constructor. We'll see how to do this shortly.

getChildCount()

An object representing one of the previously identified tree nodes (the root node or one of its descendents) is passed to this method, which returns an integer value that identifies the number of children associated with that node.

getChild()

An object representing one of the previously identified tree nodes is passed to this method along with an integer index value, and a reference to the appropriate child node is returned. The specific node returned is based on the value of the index parameter and corresponds to the child's position within its parent's list of children. For example, if the index value is zero (0), the first child node (the one that appears directly below its parent) is returned, while a value of one (1) returns the second child node, and so on. In the code segment below, the third child of the node represented by parent is returned:

```
TreeModel model;
Object childNode, parentNode;
// ...

Object childNode = model.getChild(parentNode, 2);
```

getIndexOfChild()

This method provides functionality that's essentially the opposite of that provided by getChild(). While getChild() returns a child node given an index, getIndexOfChild() returns the index associated with a specific child node. Two parameters representing tree nodes are passed to this method: one that's a parent and another representing one of that parent's children, and getIndexOfChild() returns an integer that identifies the child's position within the parent's list of children. For example, if getIndexOfChild() is called and passed a reference to a node that is the third child of the specified parent node, it returns a value of two (2). If a parent/child relationship does not exist between the two nodes, a value of –1 is returned. The following code illustrates the behavior of this method:

```
Object parentNode, firstChild, secondChild, thirdChild;
TreeModel model;
// ...

//  This code assumes that the nodes have been created and the
//  children added to their parent
//  The following line prints "0"
System.out.println(model.getIndexOfChild(parentNode, firstChild));
//  The following line prints "1"
System.out.println(model.getIndexOfChild(parentNode, secondChild));
//  The following line prints "2"
System.out.println(model.getIndexOfChild(parentNode, thirdChild));
```

isLeaf()

This method is passed an object that has previously been identified by the TreeModel as one of the nodes in the tree, and it should return a boolean value of true if that object represents a leaf node. As mentioned earlier, it's possible for "leaf node" to refer either to a node that cannot have children or to one that simply does not currently have children, which is why it's necessary to define both this method and getChildCount(). Depending upon which definition of "leaf node" is applied it may or may not be possible to identify leaf nodes based solely upon a node's child count.

valueForPathChanged()

This method is passed an instance of `TreePath` and an `Object` representing the new value that is to be associated with the node identified by the `TreePath`, and is called when the node's value has changed. For example, when the editing of a tree node is completed and the new value should be saved, this method is called to cause the `TreeModel` to update its data accordingly. `TreePath`, which identifies a specific node within the tree, is discussed later in the chapter.

Creating Tree Nodes

Now that we've seen how `TreeModel` is used to encapsulate the data displayed in a `JTree`, we'll examine the interfaces and class provided in the `javax.swing.tree` package that allow you to easily create and manipulate tree nodes. The class most commonly used to represent a tree node is `DefaultMutableTreeNode`, an implementation of the `MutableTreeNode` interface, which is in turn a subinterface of `TreeNode`. Although you won't often find it necessary to create your own `TreeNode` or `MutableTreeNode` implementations, a familiarity with those interfaces and some knowledge of how they can be implemented is helpful when using `JTree`.

TreeNode

One thing that should be apparent from the description of `TreeModel` is that a model is responsible for providing information such as whether a given node is a leaf or a branch, and a list of each node's children. While it might be technically possible to store that information in the `TreeModel` itself, doing so would be difficult and complex at best. A better approach is to allow each node to maintain its own information, and `TreeNode` provides an interface that a `TreeModel` can use to retrieve the data from the node.

In fact, of the seven `TreeNode` methods, four of them map directly to methods in `TreeModel`. The `DefaultTreeModel` class described later in this chapter takes advantage of that by only supporting objects that implement `TreeNode`, allowing it to delegate responsibility for the four methods listed below to the nodes themselves:

TreeModel Method	Corresponding Method In TreeNode
getChild()	getChildAt()
getChildCount()	getChildCount()
getIndexOfChild()	getIndex()
isLeaf()	isLeaf()

Although the names vary slightly in two cases, the only difference between the parameter lists of the methods in a pair is the presence or absence of an `Object` that represents the node for which the information should be provided. For example, the `TreeModel`'s `getChildCount()` method accepts a single `Object` parameter that identifies the parent node for which the child count should be returned:

```
public int getChildCount(Object parent);
```

In contrast, the `getChildCount()` method in `TreeNode` is defined to return the child count of the object for which the method is called (the `"this"` object), so no identifying node parameter is required:

```
public int getChildCount();
```

Since all nodes in a `DefaultTreeModel` must be instances of `TreeNode`, the implementation of `getChildCount()` in that model implementation is trivial:

```java
public class DefaultTreeModel implements TreeModel {

  public int getChildCount(Object parent) {
    return ((TreeNode)parent).getChildCount();
  }
  // ...
```

getChildCount()

This method returns an integer value that identifies the number of children that the node has, and it is called by the method of the same name in `TreeModel`.

getChildAt()

A single integer index value is passed to `getChildAt()`, and it returns the `TreeNode` corresponding to the child node at the specified index. For example, a parent's first child corresponds to a value of zero (0), the second to a value of one (1), etc. This method can be used by a `TreeModel` to delegate responsibility for identifying a child's index by calling `getChildAt()` from the `getChild()` method in the `TreeModel` implementation.

getIndex()

The functionality of this method is essentially the opposite of that found in `getChildAt()`, and while `getChildAt()` returns a `TreeNode` given an index, this method is passed a `TreeNode` and returns that node's index. By calling this method from the `getIndexOfChild()` method in `TreeModel`, a model can delegate responsibility for that function to the node itself.

children()

This method returns an instance of `java.util.Enumeration` containing the `TreeNode` objects that are the children of this node.

getParent()

This method returns a reference to the `TreeNode` that is the parent of this node, unless this node represents the root node, in which case `getParent()` returns a value of `null`.

isLeaf()

A value of `true` should be returned by this method if the node represents a leaf node, or `false` if it represents a branch node. `JTree`'s normal behavior is to display an icon for leaf nodes that's different from the one it displays for branch nodes, and this method is used to determine which icon is associated with the node.

getAllowsChildren()

As its name implies, this method returns a `boolean` value that indicates whether the node is eligible to have children. If the node supports children, it should return a value of `true`, while nodes that do not support children should return `false`.

Nodes Without Children: Leaf or Branch?

As previously mentioned, the terms "leaf" and "branch" can be used in one of two ways:

❑ Leaf nodes are those that *do not* have any children, while branch nodes are those that *do* have children.

❑ Leaf nodes are those that *cannot* have children, while branch nodes are those that *can*, which may include some nodes without children.

This ambiguity can be confusing and it may seem unnecessarily so, but the reason for this vagueness is that you may want the first meaning to be used in some cases and the second to apply in others. For example, suppose that you're using JTree to display genealogy/lineage information (a "family tree"). In that situation, it's probably reasonable to apply the first set of definitions to the JTree: leaf nodes represent individuals who do (or did) not have any children, while branch nodes are people who do (or did) have children.

However, let's also consider the case where you're using a JTree to represent the contents of a file system. In that case, you would probably want each directory displayed as a branch node, *even if the directory does not contain any children* (files or other directories). In other words, empty directories should be represented by the same icon as those that are not empty, meaning that the node type (leaf or branch) should be determined by a node's *ability* to contain children instead of whether it actually does.

You've probably guessed that JTree supports both sets of definitions, which is indeed the case, but you may be wondering how to control which one is used. The answer is that it's ultimately the responsibility of the TreeModel to make that determination, since its isLeaf() method is responsible for classifying a node as a leaf or branch. The TreeModel can determine which value should be returned from that method, or it can delegate responsibility to the node itself. For example, if you've created a TreeModel implementation that contains a set of objects that all implement TreeNode, there are many ways that you could implement the model's isLeaf() method. For example, the following implementation simply leaves it up to each node to determine whether the node is a branch or a leaf node:

```
public class MyTreeModel implements TreeModel {

  public boolean isLeaf(Object node) {
    return ((TreeNode)node).isLeaf();
  }
  // ...
```

You'll more commonly want the model itself to determine whether a node is a leaf or a branch so that all the nodes in the tree are classified consistently. The implementation below uses the first definition given earlier, returning true from isLeaf() if the node does not have any children and false if it does have children:

```
public boolean isLeaf(Object node) {
  return ((TreeNode)node).getChildCount() == 0;
}
```

Similarly, the following implementation uses the second definition of a "leaf" node, returning true from isLeaf() if the node is *capable* of having children (regardless of whether it currently *does* have children):

```
public boolean isLeaf(Object node) {
   return ((TreeNode)node).getAllowsChildren();
}
```

Another approach is to create a `TreeModel` that can use either definition. For example, you might create an implementation like the one below that allows you to set a `boolean` value called `asksAllowsChildren`. When that value is `true`, the node's `getAllowsChildren()` method is used to determine whether the node is a leaf or branch node (using the second definition). However, when the value of `asksAllowsChildren` is `false`, the node's type (leaf or branch) is determined by the presence or absence of children (the first definition):

```
public class MyTreeModel implements TreeModel {

   protected boolean asksAllowsChildren;

   public void setAsksAllowsChildren(boolean asks) {
      asksAllowsChildren = asks;
   }

   public boolean isLeaf(Object node) {
      boolean result;
      TreeNode treenode = (TreeNode)node;
      if (asksAllowsChildren) {
         result = treenode.getAllowsChildren();
      }
      else {
         result = (treenode.getChildCount() == 0);
      }
      return result;
   }

   // ...
```

The above approach is very similar to that used by `DefaultTreeModel`, which is the only `TreeModel` implementation supplied with Swing. In fact, the only difference is that instead of calling the `TreeNode`'s `getChildCount()` method if `asksAllowChildren` is `false`, `DefaultTreeModel` calls the node's `isLeaf()` method. When using `DefaultTreeModel`, therefore, choosing a definition of "leaf" and "branch" is as easy as calling `setAsksAllowsChildren()`. The default behavior is to classify all nodes without children as leaf nodes, but by passing a value of `true` to `setAsksAllowsChildren()`, you can cause the alternative definition to be used instead.

MutableTreeNode

Examples were given at the beginning of this chapter on how to create a `JTree`, and in those cases, a single object instance (a `String`) was used to represent both a node and the value associated with that node. As we've seen, however, it can be helpful to create a class that implements `TreeNode`, in which case it's necessary to separate the value associated with a node from the class that implements `TreeNode`.

For example, you could not create a subclass of `java.lang.String` that implements `TreeNode` because `String` is a `final` class, and even if it were possible, it wouldn't be desirable from an object-oriented design standpoint. A better solution is to create an interface that extends `TreeNode` and that adds support for a **user object**, which is simply a value that's associated with the node, and the `MutableTreeNode` interface does just that. The "mutable" portion of this interface's name refers to the fact that it defines methods that can be called to modify the state of the node, specifically its parent, list of child nodes, and the associated user object value. The following are descriptions of the methods defined in `MutableTreeNode`, and examples are given in each case of how the method might be implemented.

setUserObject()

Use `setUserObject()` to specify the value of the user object for this node. A single `Object` parameter is passed to this method, and a class that implements this interface should normally save a reference to that object. This can be done with a simple mutator method as shown in the code segment listed below:

```
public class MyMutableTreeNode implements MutableTreeNode {

  protected Object userObject;

  public void setUserObject(Object value) {
    userObject = value;
  }
}
```

setParent()

You should use `setParent()` to store a reference to the node's parent, passing it a reference to a `MutableTreeNode`. A class that implements this interface will typically choose to save a reference to the parent node as in the following code:

```
public class MyMutableTreeNode implements MutableTreeNode {

  protected MutableTreeNode parent;

  public void setParent(MutableTreeNode newParent) {
    parent = newParent;
  }
}
```

This is useful for moving a node from one position in the tree to another.

remove()

There are two versions of this overloaded method: one that is passed an integer index value that identifies the child to be removed, and another that is passed a reference to the `MutableTreeNode` to be removed. When called, `remove()` should set the child node's parent to `null` and remove the child from this parent node's list of child nodes, as in the following code:

```
public class MyMutableTreeNode implements MutableTreeNode {

  protected java.util.Vector children = new java.util.Vector();

  public void remove(MutableTreeNode child) {
    remove(children.indexOf(child));
  }

  public void remove(int index) {
```

```
      MutableTreeNode child = (MutableTreeNode)(children.remove(
                  index));
      child.setParent(null);
   }
```

removeFromParent()

As its name suggests, this method is responsible for removing the node from its parent, and an example of how this might be implemented is shown below.

```
public class MyMutableTreeNode implements MutableTreeNode {

   protected java.util.Vector children = new java.util.Vector();

   public void removeFromParent() {
     //  Obtain a reference to this node's parent
     MutableTreeNode parent = (MutableTreeNode)getParent();
     //  If it has a parent, remove it from that parent node
     if (parent != null) {
       parent.remove(child);
     }
   }
}
```

insert()

Two parameters are passed to this method: a reference to an instance of MutableTreeNode and an index value that identifies where the node should be inserted relative to the parent node's existing children. For example, if the index value is zero (0), the node being inserted is made the first child of this node, and the index values of the other children are incremented by one (1).

If you create your own implementation of MutableTreeNode, you should ensure that the setParent() method of the node being inserted is called and passed a reference to this node, as shown in the sample code below. You should also ensure that the node being added is removed from any parent to which it had previously been assigned so that the child is not referenced by more than one parent. An example of how this might be implemented appears in the following code segment:

```
public class MyMutableTreeNode implements MutableTreeNode {

   protected java.util.Vector children = new java.util.Vector();

   public void insert(MutableTreeNode child, int index) {
     // If node has a parent, remove it from that parent first
     child.removeFromParent();
     // Insert the child into the list at the specified location
     children.insertElementAt(child, index);
     // Now set its parent to this node
     child.setParent(this);
   }
```

DefaultMutableTreeNode

It should be obvious from the descriptions of the methods in `TreeNode` and `MutableTreeNode` that it's very easy to create your own implementations of those interfaces. As mentioned earlier, however, it's rarely necessary to do so because the `javax.swing.tree` package also includes `DefaultMutableTreeNode`, and the behavior of this class is appropriate for most applications. In addition to its many methods, `DefaultMutableTreeNode` contains four fields, although each of them exists solely to support implementation of the `TreeNode` and `MutableTreeNode` methods:

- ❑ A reference to a parent `MutableTreeNode`, the value of which is returned by `getParent()`.

- ❑ A collection of child nodes that are all instances of `MutableTreeNode`. The child nodes are accessible through a variety of methods, including `children()`, `getChildAt()`, and many others.

- ❑ A reference to a user object that is accessible through the `getUserObject()` and `setUserObject()` accessor and mutator methods. As mentioned earlier, the user object allows you to associate a value with a node, and any type of `Object` can be used. Note, however, that the reference to the user object is `transient`, which means that the user object will not be marshaled along with the node that references if the node is serialized. For more information on transient fields, serialization and marshaling, refer to chapter 13.

- ❑ A flag named `allowsChildren` that you can use to specify whether this node is allowed to have children. That flag is accessible through the `getAllowsChildren()` and `setAllowsChildren()` methods.

Creating DefaultMutableTreeNode Instances

Instances of `DefaultMutableTreeNode` can be created and used very easily, and only three constructors are defined. One constructor accepts no parameters, another expects a user object (`Object`) value, and the third allows you to specify a user object and a `boolean` value that indicates whether the node allows children to be added. The first two constructors result in an instance that allows children, so to create a node with an initial value of a user object with a value of "Hello" that accepts children, you could use the following code:

```
DefaultMutableTreeNode node = new DefaultMutableTreeNode("Hello");
```

It's equally simple to add children to a node, since in addition to the `insert()` method defined in `MutableTreeNode`, `DefaultMutableTreeNode` also includes a method called `add()` which appends the specified node to the end of the list of children:

```
DefaultMutableTreeNode parent = new DefaultMutableTreeNode("Adam");
DefaultMutableTreeNode child = new DefaultMutableTreeNode("Cain");
parent.add(child);
```

Note that before a node is added as a child of some other node, it is first removed from the child list of any existing parent that it may have. For example, suppose that you execute the following code:

```
DefaultMutableTreeNode parent = new DefaultMutableTreeNode("Adam");
DefaultMutableTreeNode child = new DefaultMutableTreeNode("Cain");
```

```
parent.add(child);
DefaultMutableTreeNode otherParent = new DefaultMutableTreeNode("Eve");
otherParent.add(child);
```

The first three lines shown above are identical to those of the previous code segment, so they obviously will produce exactly the same results. However, when otherParent's add() method is called, the child node will first be removed from its existing parent ("Adam") and only then will it be added to otherParent's list of children. This behavior ensures that a child node only ever has a single parent, and that no parent node has references to children that have been added to some other parent.

Using DefaultMutableTreeNode

DefaultMutableTreeNode contains many methods in addition to those needed to implement the TreeNode and MutableTreeNode interfaces and most of the methods have names that should be self-explanatory. For example, getFirstChild() and getLastChild() return references to the node's first and last child nodes, respectively.

In fact, a large portion of the methods in DefaultMutableTreeNode are used to retrieve some node or group of nodes that have some relationship to the node for which the method is called. A handful of the remaining methods (such as isNodeXXX()) are used to determine whether some specific type of relationship exists between this node and another.

For example, isNodeRelated() is passed a reference to a TreeNode and returns a value of true if *any* type of relationship exists between that node and the one for which the method is called. In other words, it returns true if the two nodes are contained within the same tree.

While the purpose of most of the methods should be obvious from their names, others may be less intuitive, and some of the methods likely to fall into that latter category are described below.

getLevel(), getDepth()

A node's "level" refers to the number of parent nodes that must be traversed to reach the root node, while a node's "depth" represents the maximum number of levels that currently exist below the node. In other words, the level value is derived by counting the number of levels that must be traveled "up" the tree until the root node is reached, so the root node has a level of zero. In contrast, the depth is the maximum number of levels that *can* be traversed "down" the tree from that node:

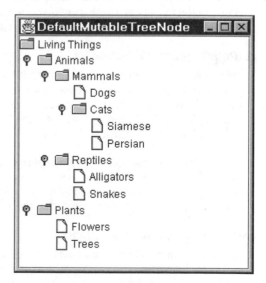

The table below shows, for each node in the fully expanded tree above, the level and depth of each node in the tree:

Node Name	Level	Depth
Living Things	0	4
Animals	1	3
Mammals	2	2
Dogs	3	0
Cats	3	1
Siamese	4	0
Persian	4	0
Reptiles	2	1
Alligators	3	0
Snakes	3	0
Plants	1	1
Flowers	2	0
Trees	2	0

getSharedAncestor()

To use this method, you must pass a reference to another DefaultMutableTreeNode, and getSharedAncestor() returns a reference to the first node that is a common ancestor of that parameter node and the one for which this method was called. For example, if you passed a reference to the "Persian" node in the tree above to the getSharedAncestor() method of the "Alligators" node (or vice versa), a reference to the "Animals" node would be returned.

getPath(), getUserObjectPath()

When you call the getPath() method, it returns an array of TreeNode objects that represent the nodes that must be traversed from the root node to reach the node for which the method is called. For example, if this method is called for the "Reptiles" node in the tree above, it will return references to three nodes: "Living Things", "Animals", and "Reptiles" nodes. Note that the first entry in the array is always the root node, while the last is always the node for which this method was called.

The getUserObjectPath() method is very similar to getPath(), but instead of returning references to the TreeNode objects, it instead returns an Object array representing the user object associated with each node in the path. If the path includes nodes that have not been assigned user object values, null values will appear in the appropriate places within the array returned by getUserObjectPath().

pathFromAncestorEnumeration()

To use this method, you must pass it a TreeNode representing an ancestor of the node for which the method is called. Like getPath(), this method returns a list of nodes, but there are two differences. First, pathFromAncestorEnumeration() returns an Enumeration instead of an array, and second, the list of nodes begins with the ancestor you identified instead of the tree's root node. Therefore, the first node in the list will always be the ancestor node parameter, and the last node will (as in the case of getPath()) always be the node against which the method was invoked.

For example, if you call `pathFromAncestorEnumeration()` for the "Siamese" node in the tree above and pass it a reference to the "Mammals" node, it will return an enumeration containing references to three nodes: "Mammals", "Cats", and "Siamese" (in that order).

This method throws an IllegalArgumentException if the node passed to it is not an ancestor of the node against which the method is invoked. Therefore, you should be prepared to handle the exception or you should ensure that the argument node is indeed an ancestor before calling this method.

Obtaining a List of Nodes

The last four `DefaultMutableTreeNode` methods that we'll examine are all used to obtain a list of the nodes in a tree or the subtree defined by the node for which the method is invoked. For example, if you call one of these methods for the root node shown in the tree above, it will return a list that contains an entry for each of the nodes in the tree. However, if you were to call the method for the "Reptiles" node, the list would only contain entries for the "Reptiles", "Alligators", and "Snakes" nodes.

Since these four methods all return an `Enumeration` containing a node and all of its descendent nodes, the obvious question is how these methods differ. As you might expect, the difference is in the order in which the nodes occur in the list that's returned.

depthFirstEnumeration(), postorderEnumeration()

These two methods are effectively synonyms for one another, since they both produce the same results, returning a list generated using a "depth-first" or "postorder" traversal of the appropriate tree nodes. When a node is being processed using this approach, it is first examined to determine whether it has any children. If it does, each child is processed before the parent node is added to the list, and this behavior is repeated recursively until a node is reached that does not have children. A parent is only added to the list that's being built after any child nodes have been processed, and it's that behavior that gives postorder traversal its name. Since children are added before their parents, the node for which this method is called is always the last node in the list returned.

To illustrate this technique, let's assume that you call `depthFirstEnumeration()` or `postorderEnumeration()` for the "Cats" node shown in the tree above. Since that node has two children, they will be processed before it is added to the list, and since those two children do not have any descendents, they are simply added to the list without additional recursive calls. Once the two child nodes have been processed, the parent "Cats" node is added to the list and an `Enumeration` is returned that contains references to the three nodes in the following order:

- Siamese
- Persian
- Cats

The sequence in which the nodes are traversed is represented graphically in the following diagram:

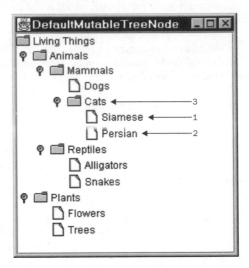

Similarly, if one of these methods is called for the "Mammals" node, the "Dog" node will be the first in the list, because it is the first node found that does not have any children. After that, the next three nodes processed will be the same ones added to the list in the previous example, and finally the "Mammals" node itself is added, resulting in the following entries in the list returned:

- ❑ Dog
- ❑ Siamese
- ❑ Persian
- ❑ Cats
- ❑ Mammals

Again, the sequence is represented visually in the following illustration:

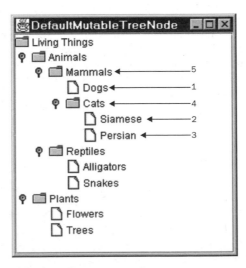

Since these two methods (depthFirstEnumeration() and postorderEnumeration()) produce exactly the same results, which one should be used is largely a matter of personal preference. For instance, you may find it easier to remember that this technique involves processing nodes in a "depth first" order, in which case you might be more inclined to use depthFirstEnumeration().

breadthFirstEnumeration()

This type of enumeration is easier to visualize, since it traverses the nodes in order of their level, and nodes that are at the same level are listed in order from top to bottom. For example, if you were to call this method for the "Animals" node of the tree above, it would first add that node to the list, since it is the top node. The next two nodes added would be "Mammals" and "Reptiles" (which are both children of "Animals") followed by "Dogs", "Cats", "Alligators", and "Snakes", and finally "Siamese" and "Persian". In other words, this method starts with the node specified and works its way through the tree from the closest descendents to the most distant ones. The name is derived from the fact that this technique results in the tree's breadth/width being traversed before its depth when the tree is visualized with the root node at the top and the most distant descendants at the bottom. A visual representation of this sequence is shown below:

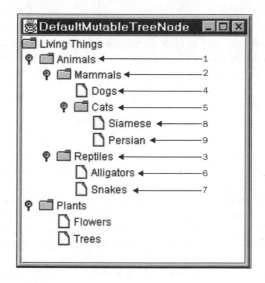

preorderEnumeration()

This technique most closely resembles the depthFirstEnumeration() and postorderEnumeration() methods described above, but each parent is added to the list *before* its children are processed recursively instead of afterwards. The resulting order of the nodes is the same order that they appear from top to bottom in the JTree. In the case of the tree above, calling preorderEnumeration() for the root node would cause the nodes to appear in the list in the order shown below:

❑   Living Things

❑   Animals

❑   Mammals

❑   Dogs

- ❑ Cats
- ❑ Siamese
- ❑ Persian
- ❑ Reptiles
- ❑ Alligators
- ❑ Snakes
- ❑ Plants
- ❑ Flowers
- ❑ Trees

TreePath

When working with a `Vector` or array of values, you can reference each value by using its index, as illustrated in the following code segment where the second value in a `Vector` and third value in an array are printed:

```
Vector v;
Object[] array;
// ...

System.out.println(v.elementAt(1));
System.out.println(array[2]);
```

This simple index approach can be used for an array or `Vector`, because those objects represent linear (one-dimensional) data structures. In other words, each value is assigned a position that can be uniquely identified by a simple whole number (0, 1, 2, 3, etc.). However, the hierarchical structure of nodes in a `JTree` makes it somewhat more difficult to define a technique for identifying a particular node within the tree.

`JTree` does use index values to identify visible nodes within a tree, assigning each node a value based on its vertical position within the tree. The root node is always at the top of the tree, so its position (when it's visible) corresponds to an index value of zero (0), and each node below it is assigned a unique value as shown in the figure below:

Although some of the methods in `JTree` allow you to reference nodes in this manner, you should keep in mind that a node's index value is dependent upon the state of the tree.

To illustrate this point, suppose that the tree above is partially collapsed, so that the children of the "Jeff" node are not visible. As the following diagram shows, most of the visible rows' index values have changed, which shows that a given index cannot be relied upon to consistently identify a particular node:

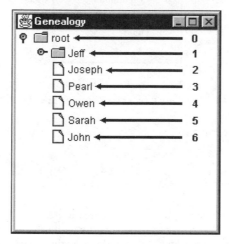

In addition, adding or deleting nodes or even changing the position of a node within the tree can cause a node's index value to change, as shown in the next diagram where one of the nodes has been deleted. Therefore, you should *only* use index values to refer to the node at a given vertical position within the tree, and not as a means of identifying a specific node. For that purpose, you should use an instance of `TreePath`, which is a class defined in the `javax.swing.tree` package.

As its name implies, a `TreePath` encapsulates a node's **path**, which is simply a list of nodes that must be traversed (usually starting from the root node) to reach the node identified by the path. For example, the `TreePath` associated with the "soccer" node in the next screenshot could be constructed by creating a three-element array containing references to the "JTree", "sports", and "soccer" nodes in that order:

As we saw earlier, the getPath() method in DefaultMutableTreeNode can be used to obtain such an array, and you can use it to create an instance of TreePath using code like that shown below:

```
DefaultMutableTreeNode myNode;
// ...

// This code assumes that the node has been added to the tree
TreePath path = new TreePath(myNode.getPath());
```

Unlike an index value, a path can always be used to identify a specific node regardless of which portions of a tree are collapsed or expanded. For that reason, most of the methods in JTree that perform some operation related to a specific node allow you to identify that node through a TreePath. Some JTree methods are overloaded, providing one implementation that allows you to specify a TreePath and another that allows you to specify an index value that identifies a visible node based on its vertical position (as described above). In general, you should use the TreePath implementation instead of the index implementation, since TreePath values are less sensitive to changes in the tree's state.

TreeModelListener

TreeModelListener is an interface that can be implemented by classes that will register as listeners of TreeModel events, such as the addition, deletion, or modification of nodes in the model. In practice, the only listener registered with a model is usually the JTree that uses the model, and it uses this interface to receive notification of changes to the data it displays. Only four methods are defined in TreeModelListener, and they are described below.

treeNodesChanged()

This method is called when one or more of the nodes within the model has experienced a state change (the user object value associated with the node changes). Note that this method *should not* be called to notify listeners of structural changes to the tree (insertion, deletion, or change in position of nodes) because other TreeModelListener methods are provided for that purpose.

treeNodesInserted()

The treeNodesInserted() method is called for each registered listener after nodes have been inserted into the tree.

treeNodesRemoved()

Just as `treeNodesInserted()` is called after nodes have been added to the model/tree, this method is called after nodes have been removed. This method is only called once for each removal, even if a node with descendents is removed, which effectively means that multiple nodes have been eliminated from the tree.

treeStructureChanged()

When this method is called, it indicates that a significant change (something more complex than the simple addition, modification, or deletion of nodes) was made to the tree or to some portion of the tree below a particular node. For example, `treeStructureChanged()` may be called if the current root node is replaced with a different one, which results in the entire tree structure being replaced.

TreeModelEvent

Each of the methods defined in `TreeModelListener` is passed a reference to a `TreeModelEvent` object that can be used to obtain information about the source and nature of the event that occurred. The following are brief descriptions of the methods defined in `TreeModelEvent`, and each one includes an explanation of when and how to use the methods.

getTreePath(), getPath()

These methods are used to identify the parent node of the nodes that have been modified, inserted, or deleted. When `getTreePath()` is called, it returns an instance of `TreePath` which identifies the parent of the affected nodes, while `getPath()` returns the array of `Object` values that are encapsulated by the `TreePath`. In other words, these methods provide essentially the same information in two different forms.

getChildren()

Just as `getPath()` and `getTreePath()` identify the parent of the nodes that were inserted, updated, or deleted, this method can be used to obtain references to the specific nodes that triggered the event. It returns an array of `Object` values and each entry in the array represents one of the nodes that was modified, added, or removed.

getChildIndices()

This method can be used within calls to `treeNodesChanged()`, `treeNodesRemoved()`, and `treeNodesInserted()` to identify the nodes that were changed, removed, or inserted. An array of integer values is returned, and each integer represents the index into a parent's list of children. In the case of a deletion, the index identifies the position that the node held in the parent's list *before* the node was deleted, while the index represents the node's *current* position when an update or insertion has occurred. For example, if the second and fourth children of some node are modified, this method returns an `int` array with two elements: the first with a value of one and the second entry a value of three.

DefaultTreeModel

The `DefaultTreeModel` class defined in `javax.swing.tree` is the only `TreeModel` implementation supplied with Java, but it is easy to use and is appropriate for most applications. However, it only supports nodes that are instances of `DefaultMutableTreeNode`, so you must ensure that your nodes are all instances of that class or create your own `TreeModel` implementation.

It's very easy to create an instance of DefaultTreeModel, although you won't normally do so explicitly, but will instead allow a JTree to create one automatically. For example, the code segments at the beginning of this chapter that created String arrays and passed them to a JTree constructor resulted in the creation of a DefaultTreeModel. To access a JTree's existing model, simply call its getModel() method, which returns an instance of TreeModel that you can cast to DefaultTreeModel (or some other class) if you know which type of model is being used.

If you do wish to create a model, simply use the constructor that accepts an instance of a TreeNode as in the example below, and that node will be used as the root node of your tree. Once the model has been created, it can be passed to a JTree constructor or specified as the model of an existing tree by calling JTree's setModel() method:

```
TreeNode myRoot;
JTree myTree;
// ...

DefaultTreeModel myModel = new DefaultTreeModel(myRoot);
myTree = new JTree(myModel);
```

or:

```
TreeNode myRoot;
JTree myTree = new JTree();
// ...

DefaultTreeModel myModel = new DefaultTreeModel(myRoot);
myTree.setModel(myModel);
```

In addition to implementing the TreeModel methods, DefaultTreeModel also provides pairs of methods that make it easy for you to modify the structure of the tree and to notify listeners of changes. Each pair consists of a method that performs the modification (inserting a node, say) and another method that creates an appropriate TreeModelEvent and notifies any registered listeners of the modification. The following table lists those methods, along with a description of when to use each one:

Update Method	Notification Method	Typical Use
setRoot()	nodeStructureChanged()	Setting a new root node
valueForPathChanged()	nodesChanged()	Modifying a node's value
insertNodeInto()	nodesWereInserted()	Inserting a node
removeNodeFromParent()	nodesWereRemoved()	Deleting a node

It is not necessary for you to invoke both methods when you make a change to the tree's structure, since each of the update methods listed in the above table will call the corresponding notification method for you. However, if you make changes to a node (modify its value, insert or delete children, etc.) directly instead of through the model's update method, you should call the appropriate notification method.

For example, suppose that you wish to insert several nodes into the tree and that you have a reference to the parent to which they should be added. You can either use the insertNodeInto() method (which is the preferred approach) or you can perform the insertion "manually" and then call the notification method.

The following example illustrates how to use `insertNodeInto()` given an array of nodes to be inserted:

```
MutableTreeNode parentNode;
MutableTreeNode[] childrenToAdd;
JTree tree;
// ...

DefaultTreeModel model = (DefaultTreeModel)(tree.getModel());
for (int i = 0; i < childrenToAdd.length; i++) {
  model.insertNodeInto(childrenToAdd[i], parentNode, i);
}
```

This is a convenient approach because it prevents you from having to construct your own `TreeModelEvent` object and explicitly request that registered listeners be notified. However, one problem with this approach is that it will generate a separate `TreeModelListener` notification for each node inserted, which can be undesirable from a performance standpoint if you're inserting a larger number of nodes. In that case, it may be preferable to perform the insertions directly and then request that a notification be sent, as in the following segment:

```
MutableTreeNode parentNode;
MutableTreeNode[] childrenToAdd;
JTree tree;
// ...

DefaultTreeModel model = (DefaultTreeModel)(tree.getModel());
int[] indices = new int[childrenToAdd.length];
for (int i = 0; i < childrenToAdd.length; i++) {
  parentNode.insert(childrenToAdd[i], i);
  indices[i] = i;
}
model.nodesWereInserted(parentNode, indices);
```

Although this example only illustrates how `insertNodeInto()` and `nodesWereInserted()` are used, the other methods function in essentially the same way. For example, `valueForPathChanged()` simply sets the user object of the node you identify with a `TreePath` and then calls the `nodeChanged()` method (which in turn calls `nodesChanged()` to notify listeners that the node changed). In most cases, these notification methods will simply cause the `JTree` to refresh its appearance so that it reflects the modified state of its `TreeModel`.

Another `DefaultTreeModel` method worth mentioning is `reload()`, which is overloaded with two implementations: one that does not accept any parameters and another that accepts a single `TreeNode` reference. Like `setRoot()`, the `reload()` methods call `nodeStructureChanged()`, and these methods are useful when the tree or some portion of it has changed significantly. However, `reload()` also causes all nodes with children to be collapsed, so you should not call it if you wish to maintain the visual state of your `JTree`.

Rendering Tree Nodes

Responsibility for drawing the nodes within a tree (also sometimes called **cells**) is assigned to an implementation of `TreeCellRenderer`, an interface defined in `javax.swing.tree`. That interface defines a single `getTreeCellRendererComponent()` method which is responsible for preparing and returning a `Component` that's used to draw the cell.

In other words, for each visible node in a JTree, the paint() method of the renderer associated with the tree is used to draw the node. TreeCellRenderer implementations often extend an existing visual component (JLabel), which allows the renderer to be created easily. For example, a renderer is easy to create by extending JLabel because that class already contains painting/rendering logic that's appropriate in many cases for displaying tree nodes.

When called, the getTreeCellRendererComponent() method is passed the following parameters:

❑   A reference to the JTree that the node is associated with

❑   An Object representing the node's value

❑   A boolean value that indicates whether the node is currently selected

❑   A boolean value that indicates whether the node is currently expanded

❑   A boolean value that indicates whether the node is a leaf

❑   An int that identifies the node's vertical position within the tree

❑   A boolean value indicating whether the node currently has the input focus

Before getTreeCellRendererComponent() returns a reference to the renderer, it should first use the above parameter values to modify the state of the component appropriately. At a minimum, the parameter representing the node's value should be used to initialize the renderer component so that it displays that value when its paint() method is called. You'll also typically want to initialize the component based on the state of the node being rendered, such as using a different background color to identify selected nodes as opposed to those that are not selected.

By default, JTree instances create and use an instance of DefaultTreeCellRenderer, which is a subclass of JLabel. When its getTreeCellRendererComponent() method is called, this class first converts the node's value into a String by passing a reference to the value to the tree's convertValueToText() method. That method simply calls the value object's toString() method and returns the result (see figure below), although you can modify that behavior by creating your own JTree subclass and overriding convertValueToText():

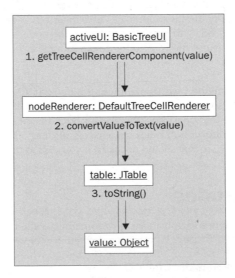

Once the `DefaultTreeCellRender` has obtained a text representation of the node's value, it sets foreground and background colors appropriately based upon whether the node is selected and then obtains an icon. The specific icon displayed is based upon whether the node is a leaf or a branch and if a branch, whether it is currently expanded or contracted. If you prefer to use icons other than those provided with the active look-and-feel, you can modify the appropriate properties in a `DefaultTreeCellRenderer`. Accessor and mutator methods are provided for each of the properties listed in the following table and you can easily customize a `JTree`'s appearance through these methods:

DefaultTreeCellRenderer Property	Description
`backgroundNonSelectionColor`	Background color used when node not selected
`backgroundSelectionColor`	Background color used when node is selected
`borderSelectionColor`	Color used to draw the component's border
`leafIcon`	Icon used for leaf nodes
`closedIcon`	Icon used for collapsed branch nodes
`openIcon`	Icon used for expanded branch nodes
`textNonSelectionColor`	Text color used when node not selected
`textSelectionColor`	Text color used when node is selected

For example, suppose that you wish to use your own icon for leaf nodes instead of the default icon. To do so, you simply need to obtain a reference to the `DefaultTreeCellRenderer` and call the appropriate mutator method as shown in the following code:

```
javax.swing.JTree myTree;
javax.swing.Icon myCustomLeafIcon =
    new ImageIcon("D:/brett/temp/myicon.gif");
// ...

DefaultTreeCellRenderer renderer = (DefaultTreeCellRenderer)
    (myTree.getCellRenderer());
renderer.setLeafIcon(myCustomLeafIcon);
```

Creating a Custom Renderer

Although the `DefaultTreeCellRenderer` class is appropriate in many cases, you'll sometimes need to create a custom renderer when you wish to display node(s) in a manner that's not possible when using the default renderer. Creating a custom renderer for use with a `JTree` is very easy to do, and the process is almost identical to that used for creating renderers for `JTable` cells. Simply create an implementation of `TreeCellRenderer` and specify that the `JTree` should use that renderer to draw its nodes.

For example, let's suppose that you have defined a class similar to the one shown below that encapsulates a true/false test question and the answer given to it:

```
public class TrueFalseQuestion {
```

```
  protected final String question;
  protected boolean answer;

  public TrueFalseQuestion(String quest) {
    question = quest;
  }

  public String getQuestion() {
    return question;
  }

  public boolean getAnswer() {
    return answer;
  }

  public void setAnswer(boolean ans) {
    answer = ans;
  }

  public String toString() {
    return question + " = " + answer;
  }

}
```

Since this class encapsulates a single immutable (unchangeable) String value and a mutable boolean value, it is an ideal candidate to be rendered by a JCheckBox. Let's further assume that you wish to create a user interface that displays a group of these objects in a JTree. We could attempt to do so using the default renderer, with code like that shown below:

```
import javax.swing.*;
import javax.swing.tree.*;

public class TreeTest extends JFrame {

  protected final static String[] questions = {
    "Green Kryptonite is only deadly "
    + "to beings from Krypton with superpowers",
            "Red Kryptonite's effects are permanent",
            "Gold Kryptonite permanently enhances superpowers",
            "Blue Kryptonite affects only Bizarros",
            "White Kryptonite affects only marine life",
            "Jewel Kryptonite was formed from Krypton's "
            + "Jewel Mountains"
  };

  public static void main(String[] args) {
    TreeTest tt = new TreeTest();
    tt.setDefaultCloseOperation(JFrame.EXIT_ON_CLOSE);
    tt.setSize(400, 300);
    tt.setVisible(true);
  }

  public TreeTest() {
```

```
        super("Smallville University Final Exam");
        JTree tree = new JTree(getRootNode());
        JScrollPane jsp = new JScrollPane(tree);
        getContentPane().add(jsp);
    }

    protected MutableTreeNode getRootNode() {
        DefaultMutableTreeNode root, child;
        TrueFalseQuestion question;
        root = new DefaultMutableTreeNode("Kryptonite Questions -- Check all "
                                    + "of the following that are true "
                                    + "statements");
        for (int i = 0; i < questions.length; i++) {
            question = new TrueFalseQuestion(questions[i]);
            child = new DefaultMutableTreeNode(question);
            root.add(child);
        }
        return root;
    }

}
```

In this case, however, the display will not produce the desired results:

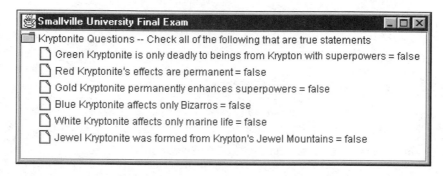

As described earlier, the default renderer is a JLabel which renders a node's value by displaying its text representation (the String returned by the object's toString() method) and an appropriate icon. In this case, the test questions should be represented by instances of JCheckBox, and no icons should appear. That could be accomplished by simply creating a TreeCellRenderer implementation that extends JCheckBox, but we'll instead extend the existing DefaultTreeCellRenderer. The reason for this is that it's not appropriate to render all tree nodes as check boxes, but only those that are instances of TrueFalseQuestion.

For example, the branch node labeled "Kryptonite Questions" should continue to be rendered as a label, but its children (which are instances of TrueFalseQuestion) should be rendered as check boxes. By extending DefaultTreeCellRenderer, we can create a class that handles TrueFalseQuestion nodes but delegates rendering responsibilities to its superclass for other node types.

The following code does just that: it examines the value parameter passed to getTreeCellRendererComponent(), and if that value does not encapsulate a TrueFalseQuestion instance, it allows the superclass code to render the node. If, on the other hand, the node is a TrueFalseQuestion, the text and selection status of a JCheckBox are updated appropriately and that component is allowed to perform the rendering operation:

```java
import java.awt.*;
import javax.swing.*;
import javax.swing.tree.*;

public class QuestionCellRenderer extends DefaultTreeCellRenderer {

  protected JCheckBox questionRenderer = new JCheckBox();

  public Component getTreeCellRendererComponent(JTree tree, Object value,
          boolean selected, boolean expanded, boolean leaf, int row
          boolean hasFocus) {
    if (value instanceof DefaultMutableTreeNode) {
      DefaultMutableTreeNode node = (DefaultMutableTreeNode) value;
      Object userObject = node.getUserObject();
      if (userObject instanceof TrueFalseQuestion) {
        TrueFalseQuestion question = (TrueFalseQuestion) userObject;
        prepareQuestionRenderer(question, selected);
        return questionRenderer;
      }
    }
    return super.getTreeCellRendererComponent(tree, value, selected,
                                              expanded, leaf, row,
                                              hasFocus);

  }

  protected void prepareQuestionRenderer(TrueFalseQuestion tfq,
                                         boolean selected) {
    questionRenderer.setText(tfq.getQuestion());
    questionRenderer.setSelected(tfq.getAnswer());
    if (selected) {
      questionRenderer.setForeground(getTextSelectionColor());
      questionRenderer.setBackground(getBackgroundSelectionColor());
    } else {
      questionRenderer.setForeground(getTextNonSelectionColor());
      questionRenderer.setBackground(getBackgroundNonSelectionColor());
    }
  }
}
```

To use this renderer, simply create an instance of it and assign that object to the JTree. An example of how to do this is provided below, showing a modified version of the TreeTest constructor defined earlier:

```java
public TreeTest() {
  super("Smallville University Final Exam");
  JTree tree = new JTree(getRootNode());
  QuestionCellRenderer renderer = new QuestionCellRenderer();
  tree.setCellRenderer(renderer);
  JScrollPane jsp = new JScrollPane(tree);
  getContentPane().add(jsp);
}
```

When this code is compiled and executed, it renders the TrueFalseQuestion objects as instances of JCheckBox as illustrated opposite:

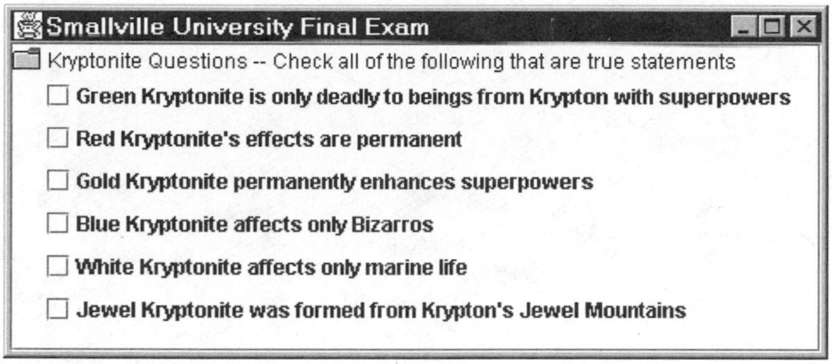

Smallville University Final Exam

Kryptonite Questions -- Check all of the following that are true statements

☐ Green Kryptonite is only deadly to beings from Krypton with superpowers

☐ Red Kryptonite's effects are permanent

☐ Gold Kryptonite permanently enhances superpowers

☐ Blue Kryptonite affects only Bizarros

☐ White Kryptonite affects only marine life

☐ Jewel Kryptonite was formed from Krypton's Jewel Mountains

At this point, the tree's appearance is appropriate, but its behavior is not. If you attempt to check one of the checkboxes that appear in the frame, nothing will happen, which is due to the fact that JTree does not allow you to edit its cells by default. However, you can control that behavior by calling the tree's setEditable() method as shown below:

```
public TreeTest() {
    super("Smallville University Final Exam");
    JTree tree = new JTree(getRootNode());
    QuestionCellRenderer renderer = new QuestionCellRenderer();
    tree.setCellRenderer(renderer);
    tree.setEditable(true);
    JScrollPane jsp = new JScrollPane(tree);
    getContentPane().add(jsp);
}
```

After making this change, you will be able to initiate editing of a node's value by clicking on the node three times or by clicking once on a node that is already selected. However, when you do attempt to edit a node, the results will probably not be what you expected. Instead of the JCheckBox's state changing, a text representation of the TrueFalseQuestion appears in a JTextBox and it will remain there if you press *Enter* to complete the edit. To understand why this occurs and how to provide more appropriate behavior, it's necessary to understand the editing mechanism used by instances of JTree.

Editing Tree Nodes

Tree cell editing is conceptually similar to rendering, although there are some important differences. Just as a renderer is associated with each JTree, a TreeCellEditor is also assigned to every tree. TreeCellEditor is an interface defined in javax.swing.tree and is a subclass of the CellEditor interface (which is also the superinterface of the TableCellEditor interface used by JTable instances). The figure overleaf illustrates the relationships between these interfaces and classes, as well as the DefaultCellEditor class discussed below:

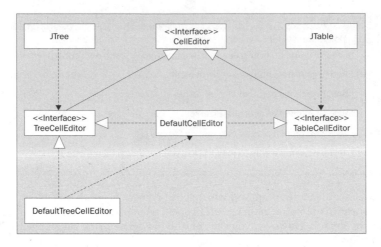

By default, each JTree creates and uses an instance of DefaultTreeCellEditor to manage the editing of its nodes, although you can create your own TreeCellEditor implementation or create a subclass of DefaultTreeCellEditor. Just as a tree's renderer provides a method that returns a rendering component, each TreeCellEditor provides a getTreeCellEditorComponent() method that returns an editing component.

In addition, just as the DefaultTreeCellRenderer is a JLabel subclass that displays each node's value as a text string, the DefaultTreeCellEditor uses a JTextField to allow editing of those values. Before describing the behavior of the DefaultTreeCellEditor class, it's helpful to understand how a determination is made that a tree node/cell should be edited.

When a JTree is created, it uses a subclass of BasicTreeUI (defined in javax.swing.plaf.basic) to provide the tree's appearance. The BasicTreeUI creates listeners that will be notified of events that occur such as mouse clicks, since those events can trigger behavior such as the selection or editing of a tree node. When a mouse click event is detected by the listener and the click occurred over a node, the BasicTreeUI's startEditing() method is called, which is responsible for determining whether or not the mouse click should cause editing to begin. If so, editing is initiated and startEditing() returns a value of true.

On the other hand, if startEditing() determines that the mouse event should *not* cause an edit to be performed, it returns a value of false, which will cause the BasicTreeUI's selectPathForEvent() to be invoked, allowing the mouse event to be interpreted as a request to select the node instead of a request to begin editing it. In other words, the tree first attempts to interpret a mouse click as an attempt to edit a node, and then as an attempt to select the node.

When deciding whether or not the mouse event should cause an edit operation to occur, BasicTreeUI's startEditing() method first determines whether the tree considers the cell eligible for editing by calling the JTree's isPathEditable() method. That method returns the value of the boolean flag called editable which is controlled by the setEditable() method in JTree that we used earlier to allow our tree nodes to be edited. As we'll see later, you can control whether or not individual nodes are editable by creating a JTree subclass that overrides isPathEditable(). That approach can be used when you wish to allow only some of the tree's nodes to be edited, as opposed to the above technique, which makes all nodes eligible for editing.

Assuming that the JTree allows its nodes to be edited, the startEditing() method in BasicTreeUI next calls the cell editor's getTreeCellEditorComponent() method and then its isCellEditable() method. If the cell editor also gives its permission to initiate editing (in other words, its isCellEditable() method returns true), the editor component is added to the JTree at the position of the node being edited and editing is allowed to begin. The collaboration diagram below graphically illustrates most of the behavior just described:

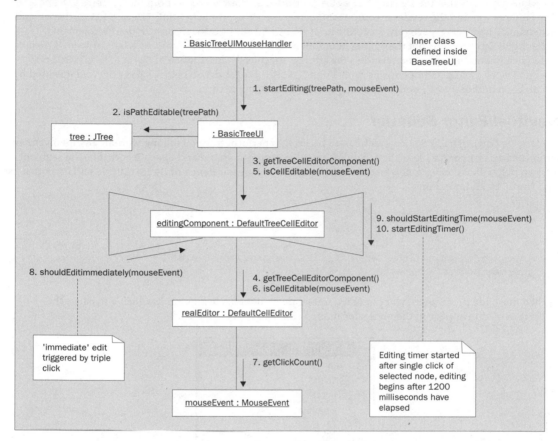

When it is determined that the editing of a cell should be ended, the CellEditor's stopCellEditing() or cancelCellEditing() method is called. For editing to be "stopped" means that changes made during the edit session should be saved, while "canceling" an edit means to discard any changes and restore the node's value to its original state. In the case of a JTextField-based editor, for example, editing ends when the *Enter* key is pressed (which generates an ActionEvent for the text field), when a node other than the one being edited is selected with the mouse, or when the *Escape* key is pressed. The first scenario described (when the *Enter* key is pressed) causes editing to be stopped, while the other two are examples of how editing can be canceled. In other words, pressing the *Enter* key causes your changes to be saved, while selecting a different node or pressing *Escape* causes them to be discarded.

When editing ends (is stopped or canceled), the editor component is removed from the JTree and the editor's getCellEditorValue() method is called to retrieve the node's new value. That value is then passed to the valueForPathChanged() method of the TreeModel associated with the JTree, causing the value returned by the editor to be propagated to the model (in other words, the modified value is saved in the tree's data model).

With an understanding of how cell editing occurs, we can now return to our discussion of the `DefaultTreeCellEditor` class mentioned earlier.

DefaultTreeCellEditor And DefaultCellEditor

Previously we saw that the `DefaultTreeCellRenderer` class serves as both the `TreeCellRenderer` implementation and the renderer component, which it does by implementing `TreeCellRenderer` and by extending `JLabel`, respectively. In contrast, while `DefaultTreeCellEditor` does implement `TreeCellEditor`, it is not the editing component (it does not extend `JTextField`). Instead, it maintains a reference to another object that handles the editing, specifically an instance of `DefaultCellEditor`. `DefaultCellEditor` implements both `TreeCellEditor` and `TableCellEditor`, and it is used by `JTable` in addition to `JTree` as the default cell editor component.

DefaultCellEditor Behavior

In fact, `DefaultCellEditor` can be used by itself to perform tree cell editing without any involvement from `DefaultTreeCellEditor`. To illustrate this, simply compile and execute code like the segment shown below that creates a new tree and sets its editor to a new instance of `DefaultCellEditor` that uses a `JTextField` for editing:

```
JTree tree = new JTree();
// ...

tree.setCellEditor(new DefaultCellEditor(new JTextField()));
tree.setEditable(true);
```

When this code is executed, you can edit a tree node by double-clicking on it, which will cause the `JTextField` to appear in the node's location:

The problem with this behavior, that `DefaultTreeCellEditor` is designed to address, is that the editing component (in this case the `JTextField`) covers all of the node's display area including its icon. Notice, for example, that no icon is displayed for the node being edited ("Baseball"). Recall that by default, nodes are rendered by a `JLabel` (which includes both an icon and a text area) but edited by a `JTextField` (which does not support icons). `DefaultTreeCellEditor` overcomes this problem by creating an editing container that's made up of an icon extracted from the `TreeCellRenderer` and the editing component itself (a `JTextField`).

In addition to providing a single class that can be used for both table and tree editing, `DefaultCellEditor` allows you to perform the editing with a `JTextField`, `JComboBox`, or `JCheckBox`. In addition, since mouse clicks are the traditional way of initiating the edit of a cell, `DefaultCellEditor` maintains a value that you can set to control the number of clicks that are required to begin an edit operation. For example, setting the value to two (2) will make it necessary for the user to double-click on a cell to initiate an edit session. This allows you to easily distinguish between a request to select a cell (a single click) and a request to edit (a double click).

DefaultTreeCellEditor Behavior

Continuing our discussion of `DefaultTreeCellEditor`, recall that its `isCellEditable()` method is called by the `BasicTreeUI` to determine whether editing should begin. When `DefaultTreeCellEditor`'s `isCellEditable()` method is called, it in turn calls the implementation of `isCellEditable()` in the `DefaultCellEditor` to which it maintains a reference. The `DefaultCellEditor` will return a value of `true` if the click count associated with the mouse event is at least as great as the number of clicks it has been programmed to require and will return `false` otherwise. If it does return `false`, the `DefaultTreeCellEditor` will likewise return that value, and editing will not be started, although the `JTree` sets the click count to 1, so this method will normally always return `true`.

Once the `DefaultTreeCellEditor` has queried the `DefaultCellEditor` to determine whether editing should be started, it next checks for a special case: three or more mouse clicks. When this occurs, it triggers an "immediate edit" that causes editing of the node to begin immediately. Finally, if you single-click on a node that is already selected, a timer is started, and a "delayed edit" will occur 1.2 seconds later as long as you do not select a different node before that time elapses. Stated simply, the behavior of a `DefaultTreeCellEditor` is such that a "triple-click" (three quick, successive mouse clicks) causes editing to begin immediately, while a "single-click" of an already selected node causes editing to begin 1.2 seconds later.

`DefaultTreeCellEditor` also allows you to perform the editing with a `JTextField`, `JComboBox`, or `JCheckBox`, just like `DefaultCellEditor` does.

Creating a Custom Editor

We'll now create a custom editor that can be used to edit `TrueFalseQuestion` nodes that are rendered by the `QuestionCellRenderer` class defined earlier. It's appropriate in some cases to use one type of component for drawing nodes and a different type for editing their values (`JLabel` for rendering and `JTextField` for editing). In this case, however, `JCheckBox` is an appropriate choice for both rendering *and* editing, so this custom editor class will use a `JCheckBox` just as the previously defined custom renderer class did.

Before creating the custom editor, an obvious question that must be answered is which existing class (if any) should be used as the superclass. Although `DefaultTreeCellEditor` might seem like an obvious choice, it is moderately complex and is somewhat coupled to the use of a `JTextField` for editing. In contrast, `DefaultCellEditor` is more generic and includes a constructor that accepts a single parameter representing the `JCheckBox` to be used for editing. Therefore, we can begin the implementation of our custom editor class by extending `DefaultCellEditor` and providing a no-argument constructor that creates a new `JCheckBox` and passes it to the superclass constructor:

```
import java.awt.*;
import javax.swing.*;
import javax.swing.tree.*;
```

```
public class QuestionCellEditor extends DefaultCellEditor {

  public QuestionCellEditor() {
    super(new JCheckBox());
  }

  // More methods and member variables here ...

}
```

Since `DefaultCellEditor` already implements `TreeCellEditor`, it's not necessary to explicitly specify that interface in `QuestionCellEditor`, but it is necessary to override the `getTreeCellEditorComponent()` method. Although `DefaultCellEditor` already supports the use of a `JCheckBox` instance for editing, it assumes that the value being edited is a `Boolean` value. In this case, however, the value being edited is an instance of `TrueFalseQuestion`, and `getTreeCellEditorComponent()` must be implemented accordingly. Doing so is very much like implementing `getTreeCellRendererComponent()` in a renderer class. Specifically, all that must be done is to initialize the component used for editing so that it will contain the appropriate initial value when it is made visible to the user. For the `QuestionCellEditor` class, that means setting the `JCheckBox`'s text and selection state values to match the question and answer values encapsulated by the `TrueFalseQuestion` object. Note that the `TrueFalseQuestion` instance is encapsulated within an instance of `DefaultMutableTreeNode` when it's passed to `getTreeCellEditorComponent()`, and it is the responsibility of `getQuestionFromValue()` to extract it:

```
protected TrueFalseQuestion question;

public Component getTreeCellEditorComponent(JTree tree, Object value,
      boolean selected, boolean expanded, boolean leaf,
      int row) {
  JCheckBox editor = null;
  question = getQuestionFromValue(value);
  if (question != null) {
    editor = (JCheckBox)(super.getComponent());
    editor.setText(question.getQuestion());
    editor.setSelected(question.getAnswer());
  }
  return editor;
}

public static TrueFalseQuestion getQuestionFromValue(Object value) {
  if (value instanceof DefaultMutableTreeNode) {
    DefaultMutableTreeNode node = (DefaultMutableTreeNode)value;
    Object userObject = node.getUserObject();
    if (userObject instanceof TrueFalseQuestion) {
      return (TrueFalseQuestion)userObject;
    }
  }
  return null;
}
```

The only other change that must be made to this class is to override the `getCellEditorValue()` method. That method is called when editing is completed so that the modified value can be stored in the `TreeModel` associated with the tree. In this case, the object being edited was a `TrueFalseQuestion`, so `getCellEditorValue()` should return an instance of that class. Since a reference to the object being edited is maintained in `QuestionCellEditor`, it can simply update that object based on the results of the edit and return a reference to it from `getCellEditorValue()`. However, it would be equally valid to create a new instance of `TrueFalseQuestion` and return a reference to that object instead:

```
    public Object getCellEditorValue() {
      JCheckBox editor = (JCheckBox)(super.getComponent());
      question.setAnswer(editor.isSelected());
      return question;
    }
```

Since the `TrueFalseQuestion` object passed to `getTreeCellEditorComponent()` is encapsulated within a `DefaultMutableTreeNode`, you might have expected it to also be necessary to return a `DefaultMutableTreeNode` from `getCellEditorValue()`. However, this is not required because the `DefaultTreeModel` class automatically encapsulates the objects passed to its `valueForPathChanged()` method inside instances of `DefaultMutableTreeNode`. In other words, the `value` object passed to `getTreeCellEditorComponent()` is normally a `DefaultMutableTreeNode` that encapsulates the "real" data (the user object), but you *should not* wrap data in a `DefaultMutableTreeNode` before returning it from `getCellEditorValue()`.

Finally, with the editor class defined, you can create an instance of it, assign that object responsibility for the editing a `JTree`'s nodes and enable the nodes for editing as shown below:

```
    public TreeTest() {
      super("Smallville University Final Exam");
      JTree tree = new JTree(getRootNode());
      QuestionCellRenderer renderer = new QuestionCellRenderer();
      tree.setCellRenderer(renderer);
      QuestionCellEditor editor = new QuestionCellEditor();
      tree.setCellEditor(editor);
      tree.setEditable(true);
      JScrollPane jsp = new JScrollPane(tree);
      getContentPane().add(jsp);
    }
```

Unfortunately, a problem exists with this code: because it enables editing for all cells and because the root node doesn't represent a `TrueFalseQuestion`, an exception will occur if you attempt to edit that node.

Limiting Edits to Certain Nodes

To complete this application, you may want to allow some nodes to be edited while preventing others from being modified. In the case of the `TreeTest` application, simply setting the `JTree`'s editable property to `true` will allow all nodes to be edited, including the header/root node that is simply a `String` instead of `TrueFalseQuestion`. As mentioned earlier, a node's ability to be edited is controlled by the `isPathEditable()` method in `JTree`, and by creating a subclass and overriding that method, you can modify the default behavior. The code segment shown below does just that, returning a value of `true` for nodes that represent `TrueFalseQuestion` instances and `false` for all other nodes:

```
    public TreeTest() {
      super("Smallville University Final Exam");
      JTree tree = new JTree(getRootNode()) {
        public boolean isPathEditable(TreePath path) {
          Object comp = path.getLastPathComponent();
          if (comp instanceof DefaultMutableTreeNode) {
            DefaultMutableTreeNode node =
                (DefaultMutableTreeNode)comp;
            Object userObject = node.getUserObject();
            if (userObject instanceof TrueFalseQuestion) {
              return true;
            }
          }
```

```
            return false;
        }
    };
    QuestionCellRenderer renderer = new QuestionCellRenderer();
    tree.setCellRenderer(renderer);
    QuestionCellEditor editor = new QuestionCellEditor();
    tree.setCellEditor(editor);
    tree.setEditable(true);
    JScrollPane jsp = new JScrollPane(tree);
    getContentPane().add(jsp);
}
```

Customizing Branch Node Handles

When customizing the nodes' appearance earlier, you may have noticed that creating a custom renderer had no effect upon the handle icons used to indicate whether branch nodes are expanded or collapsed. That's because the handle icon is drawn by the tree's user interface (UI) object instead of the cell renderer. For a JTree, that object is a subclass of BasicTreeUI (such as the MetalTreeUI class that's used when the Java or "Metal" look-and-feel is active), and BasicTreeUI maintains two icons: one for collapsed branch nodes and another for expanded nodes.

There are two ways that you can modify these icons, although the approach you take will depend upon whether you wish to modify them for all JTree instances or for a single instance. To modify them for a single JTree instance, obtain a reference (using the getUI() method of your JTree instance) to the instance of BasicTreeUI that's associated with the tree and call its setCollapsedIcon() and setExpandedIcon() methods as shown below:

```
import javax.swing.plaf.basic.*;
// ...
javax.swing.Icon customExpandedIcon;
javax.swing.Icon customCollapsedIcon;
// ...

JTree myTree = new JTree();
// Obtain a reference to the BasicTreeUI used by this tree
BasicTreeUI ui = (BasicTreeUI)(myTree.getUI());
// Now set the icons it uses for branch node handles
ui.setExpandedIcon(customExpandedIcon);
ui.setCollapsedIcon(customCollapsedIcon);
```

If, on the other hand, you wish to change the icons for *all* instances of JTree, you can use the UIManager's put() method. When a new BasicTreeUI is created, it retrieves the pair of icons maintained by the UIManager, so by changing those two icons, you will effectively be changing the icons used by each new JTree instance that's created. An illustration of how this can be done is shown below:

```
javax.swing.Icon customExpandedIcon;
javax.swing.Icon customCollapsedIcon;
// ...

UIManager.put("Tree.expandedIcon", customExpandedIcon);
UIManager.put("Tree.collapsedIcon", customCollapsedIcon);
```

It's also possible to eliminate the handle icons completely by creating a BasicTreeUI subclass that returns false from its shouldPaintExpandControlMethod(). As its name implies, that method's purpose is to determine whether a handle icon should be displayed at all. It's normally used to prevent handles from being displayed next to leaf nodes and the root node, which does not display a handle unless you call the JTree's setShowsRootHandles() method and pass it a value of true. Here, however, we can create an implementation of shouldPaintExpandControlMethod() that always returns false, which prevents handles from appearing next to any of the nodes. The easiest way to override the method is to create an anonymous inner class as shown below, where the appropriate BasicTreeUIClass is extended:

```
JTree myTree = new JTree();
javax.swing.plaf.metal.MetalTreeUI customUI =
new javax.swing.plaf.metal.MetalTreeUI() {
  protected boolean shouldPaintExpandControl(TreePath path, int row,
      boolean isExpanded, boolean wasExpanded, boolean leaf) {
    return false;
  }
};
myTree.setUI(customUI);
```

As the screenshot to the right shows, this code causes the branch nodes within the tree to be drawn without handles, although the nodes can still be expanded and collapsed by double clicking on them (if editing is not enabled) or by using the right and left arrow keys:

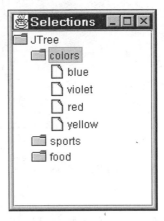

Line Style with the Java/Metal Look-and-Feel

All the examples shown in this chapter so far have used the Java (or "Metal") look-and-feel, but the following two screenshots illustrate how JTree instances are drawn when using the "Motif" and "Windows" look-and-feels, respectively:

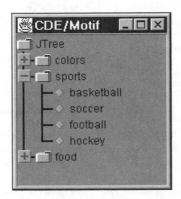

As these figures show, the Java look-and-feel is the only one that does not draw lines between the nodes in a JTree, although it is possible to modify this behavior. To do so, call the JTree's putClientProperty() method to modify the JTree.lineStyle property as shown below, specifying one of three line styles: "None" (the default), "Horizontal", or "Angled".

```
JTree myTree = new JTree();
myTree.putClientProperty("JTree.lineStyle", "Horizontal");
```

The "Angled" style draws lines between the parent nodes and their children while the "Horizontal" style results in a line being drawn above each node that has children. The following two screenshots illustrate the "Angled" and "Horizontal" styles, respectively:

Note that this technique only works with the Java/Metal look-and-feel, and you cannot use it to modify the lines drawn between nodes by the Motif or Windows look-and-feels.

Node Selection

Many applications allow users to select one or more nodes within a JTree for some purpose. For example, suppose that you want users to be able to select nodes graphically using only a mouse so that some operation (such as deletion from the tree) can be performed on the selected nodes. It's easy to make selections when using JTree, and this can be done by simply moving the cursor over the node you wish to select and pressing the left mouse button. As illustrated below, DefaultTreeCellRenderer highlights selected nodes by rendering them with colors that are different from those used for unselected nodes:

The selection of a JTree's nodes is controlled by an implementation of TreeSelectionModel, and the DefaultTreeSelectionModel class is used by default. Although it's possible to create your own selection model implementation, there's rarely any reason to do so, since DefaultTreeSelectionModel is very flexible. In any case, you can specify which model should be used or retrieve a reference to the existing model using the setSelectionModel() and getSelectionModel() methods defined in JTree. If you want to prevent any tree nodes from being selected, simply pass a null value to setSelectionModel() as shown in the following code segment:

```
JTree myTree = new JTree();
// The following code will prevent the user from selecting nodes in the tree
myTree.setSelectionModel(null);
```

Selection Modes

`TreeSelectionModel` supports three selection modes, each of which is represented by a constant value defined in that interface. Those constants are identified below, and the behavior associated with each one is described:

- ❑ SINGLE_TREE_SELECTION
  When this selection mode is active, only a single node can ever be selected at any given time. Each time you select a node, any node that was previously selected becomes deselected.

- ❑ CONTIGUOUS_TREE_SELECTION
  This mode allows you to define a single range of nodes (a set of "contiguous" nodes), and all the nodes within that range become selected.

- ❑ DISCONTIGUOUS_TREE_SELECTION
  With this selection mode, which is the default, there are no restrictions on how many nodes can be selected or on where the nodes that are selected must be positioned relative to one another. Any group of nodes within the tree can be selected at any time.

To set the selection mode, simply call the `TreeSelectionModel`'s `setSelectionMode()` method, passing it the value of one of the three constants defined above. For example, to set the selection mode for a given `JTree`, you could use code like the following:

```
JTree myTree = new JTree();
TreeSelectionModel model = myTree.getSelectionModel();
model.setSelectionMode(TreeSelectionModel.CONTIGUOUS_TREE_SELECTION);
```

For the most part, the selection modes are simple and easy to understand, but we'll briefly illustrate how contiguous selections work. As mentioned above, a contiguous selection is simply a group of adjacent (or "contiguous") nodes. Given the tree shown below, suppose that you wish to select all of the nodes in the tree beginning with "February" and ending with "October":

One way of doing this would be to press and hold down the *Ctrl* key while clicking on each of the nodes separately, but a quicker way is to select the appropriate range of nodes. For example, you might first click on the "February" node and then press and hold down the *Shift* key while clicking on the "October" node, resulting in the desired range of nodes being selected as shown. In this case, the "February" node is referred to as the **anchor selection**, since it's the first node used to define the range of contiguous nodes, and the "October" node is referred to as the **lead selection**:

Two important points should be made concerning the behavior of `JTree` and `DefaultSelectionModel` concerning which nodes are selected when you use the mouse in this manner. First, selecting a branch node such as the "colors", "sports", or "food" nodes in the next screenshot *will not* cause that node's children to be selected:

Second, be aware that mouse-initiated selections only apply to viewable nodes, recalling that a "viewable" node is one for which all ancestors are expanded. To illustrate this point, suppose that you select a range of nodes displayed by the tree in the first screenshot below, by first selecting "yellow" and then "hot dogs". This will result in exactly four nodes being selected: "yellow", "sports", "food", and "hot dogs". Note that although the "sports" node is selected, its children remain unselected, which can be seen by expanding that node (the second screenshot) and noting that its children are not selected:

TreeSelectionListener

You'll sometimes want to be notified when tree selection changes have been made, and by creating an instance of `TreeSelectionListener` and registering it with the `JTree`, you can receive such notification. This interface defines a single `valueChanged()` method that is called when the selection state of one or more nodes has changed. In other words, registered listeners are notified when unselected nodes become selected, as well as when selected nodes become unselected. For example, to create a listener using an anonymous inner class, you could write code similar to that shown below:

```
import javax.swing.event.*;
// ...
JTree myTree = new JTree();
myTree.addTreeSelectionListener(new TreeSelectionListener() {
  public void valueChanged(TreeSelectionEvent event) {
    //  Add code here to handle selection changes
  }
});
```

TreeSelectionEvent

As the above code segment illustrates, the `valueChanged()` method defined in `TreeSelectionListener` is passed an instance of `TreeSelectionEvent`. You can use the following methods in `TreeSelectionEvent` to obtain information that describes the type of selection change that occurred, and to determine which nodes were involved in the change.

getPaths(), getPath()

You can use these methods to determine which path or paths were involved in the selection change that occurred. The `getPaths()` method returns an array of `TreePath` objects, each of which identifies a node that experienced a selection state change. The `getPath()` method returns a single `TreePath` object, and is provided as a convenience for those times when you're using `SINGLE_TREE_SELECTION` mode and only need to obtain a reference to a single `TreePath` object. If you're using either of the other selection modes, `getPath()` returns the first path in the array that's provided by `getPaths()`.

isAddedPath()

There are three implementations of this overloaded method, each of which returns a `boolean` value that indicates whether or not some specific node/path became selected (as opposed to deselected). One implementation accepts a `TreePath` which should be equal to one of those returned by `getPaths()`, while another accepts an integer index value that should be greater than 0 and less than the number of paths returned by `getPaths()`. In both cases, the parameter value identifies a specific node/path for which the selection state changed, and this method returns a value of `true` if the node was selected or `false` if it was deselected. The third implementation of `isAddedPath()` does not accept parameters, and like `getPath()` it is provided as a convenience for cases where only a single path can be selected at any given time.

getNewLeadSelectionPath(), getOldLeadSelectionPath()

Each of these methods returns a reference to a `TreeNode` representing the new (after the selection state change occurs) and old (before the change occurs) lead selection paths. In most cases, your application will not need to be concerned with lead (or anchor) paths, so these methods are not normally used.

Selection Methods in JTree

While the methods defined in `TreeSelectionEvent` are useful for identifying nodes that are newly selected or deselected, you'll often want to retrieve a list of all selected nodes. In addition, it's often desirable to select nodes programmatically, and `JTree` contains methods that allow you to do all these things. For example, `getSelectionPaths()` returns an array of `TreePath` objects that identifies all paths/nodes that are currently selected, while `setSelectionPaths()` allows your code to specify which paths should be selected. If you wish to identify paths using their index (vertical position) values instead of `TreeNode` instances, you can use the `getSelectionRows()` and `setSelectionInterval()` methods instead.

The following code provides an example of how you might use `getSelectionPaths()` to create an application that displays a popup menu that can be used to delete the currently selected nodes, as illustrated below:

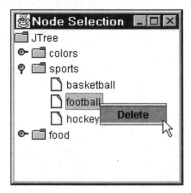

This application displays a `JTree` and adds a `MouseListener` that will cause a `JPopupMenu` to appear when a right mouse click occurs. If the user activates the **Delete** menu item in that popup menu, the `deleteSelectedItems()` method is called, which deletes the currently selected nodes from the tree:

```java
import java.awt.event.*;
import javax.swing.*;
import javax.swing.tree.*;

public class DeleteNodes extends JFrame {

  protected JTree tree;

  public static void main(String[] args) {
    DeleteNodes dn = new DeleteNodes(new JTree());
    dn.setDefaultCloseOperation(JFrame.EXIT_ON_CLOSE);
    dn.setSize(400, 300);
    dn.setVisible(true);
  }

  public DeleteNodes(JTree jt) {
    super("Node Selection");
    tree = jt;
    getContentPane().add(tree);
    tree.addMouseListener(new MouseAdapter() {
      public void mousePressed(MouseEvent event) {
        if (((event.getModifiers() &
            InputEvent.BUTTON3_MASK)
```

```
                        != 0) &&
                    (tree.getSelectionCount() > 0)) {
                showMenu(event.getX(), event.getY());
            }
        }
    });
}

protected void showMenu(int x, int y) {
    JPopupMenu popup = new JPopupMenu();
    JMenuItem mi = new JMenuItem("Delete");
    TreePath path = tree.getSelectionPath();
    Object node = path.getLastPathComponent();
    if (node == tree.getModel().getRoot()) {
        mi.setEnabled(false);
    }
    popup.add(mi);
    mi.addActionListener(new ActionListener() {
        public void actionPerformed(ActionEvent event) {
            deleteSelectedItems();
        }
    });
    popup.show(tree, x, y);
}

protected void deleteSelectedItems() {
    DefaultMutableTreeNode node;
    DefaultTreeModel model =
        (DefaultTreeModel)(tree.getModel());
    TreePath[] paths = tree.getSelectionPaths();
    for (int i = 0; i < paths.length; i++) {
        node = (DefaultMutableTreeNode)(
            paths[i].getLastPathComponent());
        model.removeNodeFromParent(node);
    }
}
```

Notice that this application is designed to only allow you to perform the deletion when the root node is not one of the nodes selected, which is necessary because DefaultTreeModel requires the presence of a root node. If you select the root node and then press the right mouse button, the popup menu will still appear, but the Delete menu item will be disabled, preventing you from performing the operation.

Collapsing and Expanding Nodes

In most cases, you'll leave the responsibility for collapsing and expanding nodes to the user, who will do so graphically with the mouse. However, there are times when it's convenient or necessary to expand or collapse nodes programmatically, which can be done very easily. To do so, use the expandPath() and collapsePath() methods or the expandRow() and collapseRow() methods defined in JTree.

As their names imply, the first pair of methods require that you specify a TreePath parameter which identifies the node to be expanded or collapsed. In contrast, the second pair allows you to identify the node by specifying its position index (an integer value representing its vertical position within the tree).

For example, given the following tree:

To collapse the "sports" node you could execute the following code:

```
JTree myTree = new JTree();
// ...
myTree.collapseRow(2);
```

Similarly, to expand the "food" node, you might execute the following statement:

```
myTree.expandRow(7);
```

Detecting Collapses and Expansions

In addition to being able to expand and collapse nodes programmatically, it's also sometimes useful to be notified when those operations occur. Fortunately, JTree supports two types of listeners that allow you to receive such notification, one of which notifies you before the operation occurs and another that notifies listeners after the change has occurred.

TreeExpansionListener

By implementing this interface, you can create an object that can register with a JTree to receive notifications after one of the tree's nodes has been expanded or collapsed. TreeExpansionListener defines two methods, both of which are passed instances of TreeExpansionEvent. That event class provides a single getPath() method that returns an instance of TreePath identifying the node that was expanded or collapsed.

To register an object so that it will receive these notifications, simply call the JTree's addTreeExpansionListener() method, passing a reference to the object that implements TreeExpansionListener. You can also use the tree's removeTreeExpansionListener() to prevent the listener from receiving further notifications.

treeCollapsed()

This method is called for all registered listeners after one of the tree's nodes has been collapsed. You can use the TreeExpansionEvent parameter's getPath() method to obtain access to a TreePath object that identifies the node that was collapsed.

treeExpanded()

This method is called for all registered listeners after one of the tree's nodes has been expanded. You can use the `TreeExpansionEvent` parameter's `getPath()` method to obtain access to a `TreePath` object that identifies the node that was expanded.

TreeWillExpandListener

Like `TreeExpansionListener`, this interface is used to create listeners that will be notified of requests to collapse and expand nodes. However, as its name implies, this interface identifies listeners that are notified of those operations *before* they occur instead of afterwards. This allows you to populate a tree's data in an "on-demand" fashion, creating a node's children (and loading the data associated with those children) only when the node is about to be expanded and its children displayed.

In addition, this interface allows you to actually prevent (or "veto") the pending operation by throwing an exception from the notification method. To do so, create and throw an instance of the `ExpandVetoException` class defined in `javax.swing.tree` package. That class provides two constructors, both of which require that you pass a reference to a `TreeExpansionEvent` object. One of the two constructors also allows you to specify an error message that will be passed to the exception object's constructor and used as its message text.

The following code illustrates how a `TreeWillExpandListener` can be implemented using an anonymous inner class, and this listener will allow all expansions but prevent/veto all attempts to collapse the tree's nodes:

```
import javax.swing.event.*;
// ...
JTree myTree = new JTree();
myTree.addTreeWillExpandListener(new TreeWillExpandListener() {
  public void treeWillExpand(TreeExpansionEvent event)
      throws ExpandVetoException {
    System.out.println("Expanding path " + event.getPath());
  }

  public void treeWillCollapse(TreeExpansionEvent event)
      throws ExpandVetoException {
    throw new ExpandVetoException(event, "Collapses not allowed");
  }
});
```

Note that it's never necessary for you to handle an `ExpandVetoException`, even if an expansion or collapse operation you initiate programmatically (through JTree's `collapseXXX()` and `expandXXX()` methods) is vetoed. However, if you want your code to determine whether the operation was successful, the `expandXXX()` or `collapseXXX()` call can be followed by a call to JTree's `isExpanded()` or `isCollapsed()` methods. These return `boolean` values that will allow you to determine whether the node's expansion state matches what it should be if the requested operation succeeded, and an example of how they might be used appears below:

```
JTree myTree;
TreePath somePath;
// ...

myTree.expandPath(somePath);
```

```
if (myTree.isExpanded(somePath)) {
  System.out.println("Expansion succeeded");
}
else {
  System.out.println("Expansion failed");
}
```

treeWillExpand()

This method is called for all registered listeners before one of the tree's nodes is expanded. You can use the `TreeExpansionEvent` parameter's `getPath()` method to obtain access to a `TreePath` object that identifies the node that will be expanded, and throwing an `ExpandVetoException` from this method will prevent the expansion from occurring.

treeWillCollapse()

This method is called for all registered listeners before one of the tree's nodes is collapsed. You can use the `TreeExpansionEvent` parameter's `getPath()` method to obtain access to a `TreePath` object that identifies the node that will be collapsed, and throwing an `ExpandVetoException` from this method will prevent the collapse from occurring.

Summary

This chapter has considered the terminology related to tree structures and the data that they display, while looking closely at `JTree`'s support classes and interfaces. We have also seen how to construct and manipulate the data model associated with a tree.

As we moved further into our examination of `JTree`, we looked at ways of controlling how the items in a tree are drawn (rendered) and edited. After this, we considered how to select items in a tree and detect when selections change and finally how to control which portions of a tree's data are displayed (expanded) or concealed (collapsed).

We now move on to examine how to add cut and paste capabilities to your Swing applications.

Professional Java Programmin

8

Adding Cut and Paste Functionality

The phrase "cut and paste" actually refers to three different operations. When data is "cut", it is removed from the entity that contained it, while a "copy" operation duplicates the data but leaves it intact in its original location. When a "paste" is performed, data that was previously cut or copied is inserted either into some other location or at the same location to duplicate the data.

It's common for an application to allow you to initiate cut and paste operations in several ways, such as through menu items or by pressing certain combinations of keys. On Windows, for example, most applications allow you to copy the selected data by pressing *Ctrl-C*, cut with *Ctrl-X*, and paste with *Ctrl-V*.

Swing components currently do not provide automatic support for cut and paste operations, and their absence may come as an unpleasant surprise to your application's users. However, it is possible to add these capabilities to Java applications using the `java.awt.datatransfer` package, and this chapter explains how to do so. Some of the topics we'll cover include the following:

- ❑ Clipboards and their relevance to cut and paste operations
- ❑ The classes and interfaces Java provides that support these operations
- ❑ How to cut, copy, and paste various data types

Unfortunately, the material presented here is partly academic, as at the time of writing, problems exist with Sun's Java implementations for Windows and Solaris that prevent the transfer of data from one application to another. Although you can transfer any type of data within a single Java application, you can only transfer text data between different Windows applications, and cross-application transfers are largely broken on Solaris 2.6 and 2.7 as well.

Even if you don't intend to provide cut and paste functions, it's still a good idea to understand how to implement them, particularly if your application needs to support drag and drop operations. Java's drag and drop capabilities are examined in the next chapter, but much of the information covered here is relevant to that discussion as well.

Where Cut and Copied Data is Stored

Normally when you cut or copy data from an application and then terminate the application, the data you extracted can still be pasted to another location. For example, if you copy text from a word processor, you'll be able to paste that text to another application even after the word processor is no longer running. As you might expect, that's possible because the data is copied to a location outside the application from which it was extracted. The resource provided for that purpose is called a **clipboard**, and in Java, a clipboard is represented by an instance of the Clipboard class defined in java.awt.datatransfer. Although you can create your own instances of Clipboard in Java, you won't normally need or want to do so. Instead, you'll use the **system clipboard** that represents the underlying operating system's clipboard, and you can obtain a reference to it through an instance of Toolkit.

The Toolkit class defined in java.awt provides a variety of utility functions related to user interface behavior. You can access an instance of Toolkit by calling the getToolkit() method in Component, or by using the static getDefaultToolkit() method defined in Toolkit:

```
JButton btn = new JButton("Hello");
Toolkit tk = btn.getToolkit();
```

or:

```
Toolkit tk = Toolkit.getDefaultToolkit();
```

Once you've obtained a reference to a Toolkit, you can access the system clipboard by calling getSystemClipboard():

```
Clipboard scb = Toolkit.getDefaultToolkit().getSystemClipboard();
```

Using the System Clipboard

The system clipboard should theoretically allow you to cut or copy data from a Java application and paste that data into a Java or non-Java application, but unfortunately, it isn't that simple. The object returned by getSystemClipboard() is only a *representation* of the underlying operating system's clipboard and the data stored in Java's "system clipboard" may or may not propagate to the operating system clipboard. Currently in most cases, it does not, but later in this chapter, we'll see what kinds of data you can successfully store there. First, however, we'll examine Clipboard and the classes associated with it.

Clipboard

The Clipboard class includes three methods: getContents(), setContents(), and getName(). There's rarely any reason to access the clipboard's name, so the only two methods of interest are setContents() and getContents(). As their names imply, those methods are used to set and retrieve the clipboard's contents, so we'll use setContents() for cut and copy operations and getContents() when pasting data.

setContents()

The `setContents()` method is passed two parameters:

- ❑ A reference to an implementation of the `Transferable` interface
- ❑ A reference to an implementation of the `ClipboardOwner` interface

The `Transferable` parameter represents the data you wish to store in the clipboard, while the `ClipboardOwner` is an object that should be notified when the data being stored is later overwritten.

getContents()

This method returns an instance of `Transferable` to the caller, and that object represents the contents of the clipboard. If the clipboard is empty or contains a type of data that Java cannot process, `getContents()` returns a `null` value.

Transferable

To store data in the clipboard, you must wrap it in an instance of a `Transferable` implementation, and data is similarly encapsulated when you read it from the clipboard. In addition to serving as a container for clipboard data, a `Transferable` provides methods that allow you to determine the type of data it contains.

Many different applications can store data in the clipboard, and many different data formats are used by those applications. For example, information cut or copied from a text editor is very different from data stored by an application that allows you to edit image files. In addition, the image editor's data is probably not meaningful to the text editor and vice versa. As you might expect, when information is stored in the clipboard, the type of data that it represents is recorded as well. This allows an application to determine whether the data represents a type that it's able to process, and if so, the user may be able to paste the data into that application.

In many cases, it's oversimplifying matters to associate data with a single, specific type, because information can often be represented in more than one way. If you create an instance of Java's `Integer` wrapper class, you'll normally think of it as an `Integer` object, and rightly so. However, if you examine the API documentation for `Integer`, you'll see that it has a large number of methods that allow you to extract the value it encapsulates in many different forms. For example, you can call the `intValue()`, `longValue()`, and `floatValue()` methods to obtain a reference to an `int`, `long`, or `float` primitive instead of an `Integer`. In addition, you can call `toString()` to obtain a `String` representation of the numeric value, as well as `toBinaryString()`, `toHexString()`, and so on. The point is that even this simple piece of information can be retrieved in many different (but equally valid) forms, and that's often true of data in the clipboard as well.

This is why one of the responsibilities of a `Transferable` is to identify the different formats in which the data it encapsulates can be retrieved. Each type is represented by an instance of `DataFlavor`, which we'll examine in detail shortly. First, however, we'll look at `Transferable`'s methods and then at the `ClipboardOwner` interface.

getTransferDataFlavors()

This method returns an array of `DataFlavor` objects that identify the different data formats ("flavors") that are supported by the `Transferable`. For example, if you cut or copy text from a `StyledDocument` in Java, it may be possible to read the clipboard contents in more than one format. One flavor could represent text with its style information (for example, colors, fonts, etc.) intact, and that representation might be used to insert the text into a `StyledDocument`. However, to allow the text to be pasted into a `JTextField`, you would use a flavor that represents the text data stripped of its style information.

The DataFlavor instances returned by getTransferDataFlavors() are ordered based on which format provides the most detailed (or "richest") version of the data. This allows an application to select the best flavor by identifying the first one in the list that it can accept. In the example given above, the flavor representing styled text would appear first in the list, since it provides the most detailed representation of the data in the clipboard.

isDataFlavorSupported()

This method can be used to determine whether a specific DataFlavor is supported by the Transferable. It accepts a DataFlavor as a parameter and returns a boolean value of true if the specified flavor is supported.

When isDataFlavorSupported() is called, it should compare the DataFlavor that was passed as a parameter to the flavors in the list of those it supports. In other words, if the DataFlavor parameter is equal to one of the flavors that would be returned by getTransferDataFlavors(), this method should return true.

> Note that when comparing **DataFlavor** instances, you should be sure to use the **equals()** method instead of the equality (==) operator. It's usually not important whether or not two **DataFlavor** references point to the same object instance. Instead, your code should establish whether or not two instances describe the same type of data, and that can be determined using **DataFlavor**'s implementation of the **equals()** method.

getTransferData()

This method returns the data encapsulated by the Transferable, and as you might expect, an instance of DataFlavor must be specified as a parameter. If that parameter represents a flavor that's not supported, an UnsupportedFlavorException is thrown. Otherwise, the data is returned to the caller in the requested format.

Note that you must also declare java.io.IOException as a checked exception that can be thrown by this method.

ClipboardOwner

In addition to Transferable, an instance of a ClipboardOwner implementation is passed as a parameter to the setContents() method. The ClipboardOwner interface defines a single lostOwnership() method that's called when the data being stored in the clipboard is later overwritten by another call to setContents(). In other words, the ClipboardOwner object is temporarily registered as a listener of the clipboard data, and that owner will receive a notification when the clipboard is next modified.

You're free to use the ClipboardOwner in any way that's helpful, but you often won't need to take any action when data you stored in the clipboard has been overwritten. When that's the case, you can pass a null value to setContents() for the ClipboardOwner or you can implement a "dummy" lostOwnership() method that contains no code. However, as we'll see, ClipboardOwner can sometimes play an important role in maintaining clipboard data.

The StringSelection class defined in java.awt.datatransfer implements both Transferable and ClipboardOwner and it allows you to store and retrieve text data. Although Java's Data Transfer API may appear somewhat complex, it is very easy to cut and paste text. For example, the following code segment stores "Hello" in the clipboard using the StringSelection class:

```
Clipboard cb = Toolkit.getDefaultToolkit().getSystemClipboard();
StringSelection ss = new StringSelection("Hello");
cb.setContents(ss, ss);
```

Note that in this case, the `StringSelection` instance was used for both parameter values passed to `setContents()` method. That's possible because `StringSelection` implements both the `Transferable` and `ClipboardOwner` interfaces, although its `lostOwnership()` method currently does not contain any code.

When you encapsulate data in a `Transferable` and store that `Transferable` in the clipboard, you should not modify the data until after `lostOwnership()` is called. Java's Data Transfer specification allows a "lazy data model" to be used, which means that calling `setContents()` may or may not result in the data being copied from the `Transferable` into the clipboard.

> In some cases, the data is not retrieved until a request is made to read the contents of the clipboard, so you should leave the data intact, at least until `lostOwnership()` is called.

For example, suppose that your application uses a `Transferable` that encapsulates an array of integer values and an instance of that class is stored in the clipboard. For the original data to be accessible, the values in the array must remain unchanged even after you call the `setContents()` method. Only when the `ClipboardOwner`'s `lostOwnership()` notification occurs can your application safely make changes to the array. Later in the chapter, we'll see how you can design your code with this behavior in mind. However, you should be aware that if your application terminates before the data it stored in the clipboard is retrieved, the information will not be available to other applications via the clipboard.

DataFlavor

As mentioned earlier, an instance of `DataFlavor` identifies a specific type of data supported by a `Transferable` implementation. `DataFlavor` defines three properties that are used to describe the data type:

- **A human-readable name**
  The human-readable name is provided as a convenience, and its use is optional. It does allow you to associate a user-friendly name with a data flavor, so you may choose to use it in your application.

- **A representation class**
  A `DataFlavor`'s representation class identifies the type of Java object returned from a `Transferable` when its `getContents()` method is passed a reference to that `DataFlavor`. The representation class is maintained in `DataFlavor` as an instance of `java.lang.Class`.

- **A MIME type**
  The third property stored in a `DataFlavor` is a MIME type, which is represented as a `String` value.

MIME Types

If you only ever needed to transfer data between Java applications, then the representation class maintained in `DataFlavor` would be sufficient to describe the type of data in the clipboard. For example, if you were to store text information in the clipboard, you could associate the data with the `java.lang.String` class, but that association would only be meaningful to Java programs.

However, to transfer data between Java and non-Java applications, it's necessary to assign each data type a name that's not specific to Java. In addition, since Java applications can run on many platforms, the data type's name should not be tied to a particular application or platform. In other words, what's needed is a set of platform-independent, language-neutral names that are associated with different types of data (for example, text, graphics, audio, etc.). Fortunately, such names have already been defined, and are used by DataFlavor.

MIME is an acronym derived from **Multipurpose Internet Mail Extensions**, an Internet standard that allows different types of data to be embedded within electronic mail documents. This is accomplished partly through the definition of **content types** (or simply **MIME types**) which are names associated with commonly used data types.

A MIME type consists of a **top-level media type** that describes the general category of the data and a **subtype** that defines a more specific type of data, with the two types separated by a forward slash ("/"). For example, simple character data with no attributes (that is, font, color, or formatting information) is defined as text/plain. Other top-level types include image, audio, video, and application, so some examples of other MIME types are image/gif, image/jpeg, text/html, and video/mpeg. A large number of data types are registered with the Internet Assigned Numbers Authority (IANA), including those just mentioned. Applications that read and write those data types are encouraged to use and recognize the MIME types, and a process exists for registering a new MIME type when one does not already exist.

You can also define custom MIME types for use by your application, in which case you should use a top-level type of application. You can use any subtype name that you'd like, but it should begin with "x-" to indicate that it's an unregistered type. In addition, application/octet-stream is used as a generic type to describe binary data of an unknown format.

In addition to the type and subtype, a MIME type can include additional parameters that describe the data. For example, while text/plain might seem adequate to identify simple text data, the issue is complicated by the existence of a large number of different character sets. To address this, you can use parameters to provide an even more detailed description of the type of data a MIME type represents. A parameter consists of a type / value pair separated by an equals ("=") sign, and parameters are delimited by semicolon (";") characters. For example, the following MIME types describe three different varieties of text data:

```
text/plain; charset=unicode
text/plain; charset=ascii
text/plain; charset=iso-8859-1
```

Creating an Instance of DataFlavor

You can create a new DataFlavor using the constructor that takes a single String parameter representing a MIME type. For example, the following creates an instance of DataFlavor that represents Rich Text Format (RTF) data:

```
DataFlavor rtfFlavor = new DataFlavor("text/rtf; charset=ascii");
```

When you use this constructor, the representation class for the DataFlavor is set to java.io.InputStream, which has a special significance with respect to transferable data. A variation of this constructor is also provided that allows you to specify the human-readable name that should be assigned to the DataFlavor. If you wish to assign the name, you can use that constructor, or you can call the setHumanPresentableName() method after the DataFlavor has been created.

Depending upon the type of data contained within your application, you may sometimes want to store an instance of a serializable Java object in the clipboard instead of raw data, and a different constructor is provided for that purpose. It requires you to pass an instance of `java.lang.Class` that identifies the representation class and a `String` that identifies the human-readable name, as shown below:

```
DataFlavor myFlavor = new DataFlavor(MySerial.class, "A class I created");
```

When you use this constructor, the MIME type for the `DataFlavor` is set to `application/x-java-serialized-object`. Since a serialized Java object is only meaningful to a Java Virtual Machine, this type of `DataFlavor` is only useful when transferring information between Java applications.

We've now looked at the two categories of `DataFlavor` instances: those that are associated with a particular MIME type, and those that are related to a particular Java class. When creating your own `DataFlavor`, the type of flavor you create will depend on the type of data being cut and pasted, as well as the type of applications involved in the transfer. For example, if you only intend to cut and paste data between Java applications, you should define flavors that are class-based and use serialized object instances. However, if you intend to transfer between Java and non-Java (or "native") applications, you should use a MIME-based `DataFlavor` that has a representation class of `InputStream`. Doing so allows the Java Virtual Machine to transfer the clipboard data to a native application as a stream of binary data that conforms to some agreed-upon protocol (that is, a MIME type).

Storing and Retrieving Serialized Java Objects

To illustrate how to store and retrieve serialized Java objects, we'll now create a crude image editing application. The application will allow you to select portions of an image and cut, copy, or paste selections to and from the clipboard.

The `ImageEditor` class displays the contents of an image file in a `JFrame` and allows you to select a rectangular portion of the image by dragging the mouse. The selected area is identified by a brightly-colored rectangle that's drawn as the mouse is dragged:

Once you've selected a portion of the image, you can press the right-mouse button to display a popup menu that allows you to cut or copy the selection. The following listing provides this functionality, although the `performCut()`, `performCopy()`, and `performPaste()` methods are not complete yet. Specifically, this application uses an `ImageIcon` and a `JLabel` to display the contents of an image file, and it listens for mouse events, drawing a selection square around the selected area as the mouse is dragged. In addition, it creates a popup menu that is displayed when the right-mouse button is pressed:

```java
import java.awt.*;
import java.awt.datatransfer.*;
import java.awt.event.*;
import java.awt.image.*;
import javax.swing.*;

public class ImageEditor extends JPanel {

  public final static int LINE_WIDTH = 2;

  protected ImageIcon icon;
  protected Point start = new Point(0, 0);
  protected Point finish = new Point(0, 0);
  protected Point pastePoint;

  protected JPopupMenu popupMenu;
  protected AbstractAction cutAction;
  protected AbstractAction copyAction;
  protected AbstractAction pasteAction;

  public static void main(String[] args) {
    if (args.length == 0) {
      System.out.println("You must specify the name of an image file");
      return;
    }
    ImageEditor editor = new ImageEditor(args[0]);
    JFrame f = new JFrame(args[0]);
    f.setDefaultCloseOperation(JFrame.EXIT_ON_CLOSE);
    f.setContentPane(editor);
    f.setSize(400, 300);
    f.setVisible(true);
  }

  public ImageEditor(String name) {
    super();
    buildPopupMenu();
    setBackground(Color.black);
    setLayout(new GridLayout(1, 1, 0, 0));
    icon = new ImageIcon(name);
    JLabel label = new JLabel(icon);
    label.setHorizontalAlignment(SwingConstants.LEFT);
    label.setVerticalAlignment(SwingConstants.TOP);
    label.addMouseListener(new MouseAdapter() {
      public void mousePressed(MouseEvent event) {
        handleMouseDown(event);
      }
    });
    label.addMouseMotionListener(new MouseMotionAdapter() {
```

```
      public void mouseDragged(MouseEvent event) {
        handleMouseDrag(event);
      }
    });
    JScrollPane jsp = new JScrollPane(label);
    add(jsp);
  }


  protected void handleMouseDown(MouseEvent event) {
    if ((event.getModifiers() & InputEvent.BUTTON1_MASK) != 0) {
      start = event.getPoint();
      finish = event.getPoint();
    }
    else if ((event.getModifiers() & InputEvent.BUTTON3_MASK) != 0) {
      displayPopupMenu(event.getPoint());
      pastePoint = event.getPoint();
    }
  }

  protected void handleMouseDrag(MouseEvent event) {
    finish = event.getPoint();
    repaint();
  }

  protected void buildPopupMenu() {
    popupMenu = new JPopupMenu();
    copyAction = new AbstractAction("Copy") {
      public void actionPerformed(ActionEvent event) {
        performCopy();
      }
    };
    popupMenu.add(copyAction);
    cutAction = new AbstractAction("Cut") {
      public void actionPerformed(ActionEvent event) {
        performCut();
      }
    };
    popupMenu.add(cutAction);
    pasteAction = new AbstractAction("Paste") {
      public void actionPerformed(ActionEvent event) {
        performPaste();
      }
    };
    popupMenu.add(pasteAction);
  }

  protected void displayPopupMenu(Point p) {
    Clipboard cb = getToolkit().getSystemClipboard();
    Transferable t = cb.getContents(this);
    boolean isSelected = !(start.equals(finish));
    cutAction.setEnabled(isSelected);
    copyAction.setEnabled(isSelected);
    popupMenu.show(this, p.x, p.y);
  }
```

```
protected void performCopy() {
}

protected void performCut() {
}

protected void performPaste() {
}

protected Rectangle getSelectedArea() {
  int width = finish.x - start.x;
  int height = finish.y - start.y;
  return new Rectangle(start.x, start.y, width, height);
}

protected int[] getPixels(Rectangle area) {
  int[] pixels = new int[area.width * area.height];
  PixelGrabber pg = new PixelGrabber(icon.getImage(), area.x,
                                     area.y, area.width,
                                     area.height, pixels, 0,
                                     area.width);
  try {
    pg.grabPixels();
  } catch (Exception e) {}
  ;
  return pixels;
}

protected void setPixels(int[] newPixels, Rectangle area) {
  int pixel;
  Image image = icon.getImage();
  int imageWidth = icon.getIconWidth();
  int imageHeight = icon.getIconHeight();
  int[] oldPixels = new int[imageWidth * imageHeight];
  PixelGrabber pg = new PixelGrabber(image, 0, 0, imageWidth,
                                     imageHeight, oldPixels, 0,
                                     imageWidth);
  try {
    pg.grabPixels();
  } catch (Exception e) {}
  ;
  for (int y = 0; y < area.height; y++) {
    if (imageHeight <= area.y + y) {
      break;
    }
    for (int x = 0; x < area.width; x++) {
      if (imageWidth <= area.x + x) {
        break;
      }
      oldPixels[((area.y + y) * imageWidth) + area.x + x] =
        newPixels[(area.width * y) + x];
    }
  }
  MemoryImageSource mis = new MemoryImageSource(imageWidth,
```

```
                imageHeight, oldPixels, 0, imageWidth);
    icon.setImage(createImage(mis));
    repaint();
  }

  public void paint(Graphics g) {
    super.paint(g);
    int width = finish.x - start.x;
    int height = finish.y - start.y;
    if ((width > 0) && (height > 0)) {
      g.setColor(Color.blue);
      for (int i = 0; i < LINE_WIDTH; i++) {
        g.drawRect(start.x + i, start.y + i, width, height);
      }
    }
  }
 }
}
```

To support the cut and paste operations, we must define a Java class that can be used to encapsulate a portion of the image that's cut or copied. In addition, it's necessary to define an implementation of Transferable that can be stored in and retrieved from the clipboard. Although these two functions could easily be combined in a single class, we'll implement them separately to provide a more cohesive design for the application.

The ImageData class defined below can be used to store part of an image that's cut or copied, along with the width and height of that area. Note that it implements the Serializable interface, which allows instances of ImageData to be serialized:

```
public class ImageData implements java.io.Serializable {

  protected int width;
  protected int height;
  protected int[] pixelData;

  public ImageData(int width, int height, int[] pixels) {
    this.width = width;
    this.height = height;
    pixelData = pixels;
  }

  public int getWidth() {
    return width;
  }

  public int getHeight() {
    return height;
  }

  public int[] getPixelData() {
    return pixelData;
  }

 }
```

The next task is to define the Transferable implementation that can be used to store image data in the clipboard. We'll also have this class implement ClipboardOwner so that it can be notified when its data is no longer stored in the clipboard. In this case, however, the lostOwnership() implementation does not do anything when that occurs.

397

```
import java.awt.datatransfer.*;

public class ImageSelection implements Transferable, ClipboardOwner {

  public void lostOwnership(Clipboard cb, Transferable t) {}

}
```

Since `ImageSelection` encapsulates an instance of `ImageData`, a constructor should be defined that accepts an `ImageData` object and stores a reference to the object:

```
import java.awt.datatransfer.*;

public class ImageSelection implements Transferable, ClipboardOwner {

  protected ImageData imageData;

  public ImageSelection(ImageData data) {
    imageData = data;
  }

  public void lostOwnership(Clipboard cb, Transferable t) {
  }

}
```

In addition, it's necessary for `ImageSelection` to identify the data formats it supports. To provide that capability, we'll define a single `DataFlavor` with a representation class of `ImageData` and a MIME type of `application/x-java-serialized-object`. In other words, this flavor represents serialized `ImageData` instances:

```
import java.awt.datatransfer.*;

public class ImageSelection implements Transferable, ClipboardOwner {

  protected ImageData imageData;

  public final static DataFlavor IMAGE_DATA_FLAVOR =
      new DataFlavor(ImageData.class, "Image Data");

  public ImageSelection(ImageData data) {
    imageData = data;
  }

  public void lostOwnership(Clipboard cb, Transferable t) {
  }

}
```

Although the `DataFlavor` was defined inside the `Transferable` class in this case, you may or may not choose to use this approach when creating your own `Transferable` implementations. The issue of where to define a `DataFlavor` is strictly one of good object-oriented design, and has no affect on the flavor's usability.

To complete the `ImageSelection` class, we must implement the `Transferable` methods. We'll first write the code for `getTransferDataFlavors()`, which can be done by defining a static array of `DataFlavor` objects and returning a reference to that array:

```java
import java.awt.datatransfer.*;

public class ImageSelection implements Transferable, ClipboardOwner {

  protected ImageData imageData;

  public final static DataFlavor IMAGE_DATA_FLAVOR =
      new DataFlavor(ImageData.class, "Image Data");

  protected final static DataFlavor[] flavors = {
    IMAGE_DATA_FLAVOR
  };

  public ImageSelection(ImageData data) {
    imageData = data;
  }

  public DataFlavor[] getTransferDataFlavors() {
    return flavors;
  }

  public void lostOwnership(Clipboard cb, Transferable t) {
  }

}
```

The `isDataFlavorSupported()` method is equally simple, and all that's necessary is to loop through the flavors in the array and compare each one to the parameter value:

```java
import java.awt.datatransfer.*;

public class ImageSelection implements Transferable, ClipboardOwner {

  protected ImageData imageData;

  public final static DataFlavor IMAGE_DATA_FLAVOR =
    new DataFlavor(ImageData.class, "Image Data");

  protected final static DataFlavor[] flavors = {
    IMAGE_DATA_FLAVOR
  };

  public ImageSelection(ImageData data) {
    imageData = data;
  }

  public DataFlavor[] getTransferDataFlavors() {
    return flavors;
  }

  public boolean isDataFlavorSupported(DataFlavor flavor) {
```

```
      for (int i = 0; i < flavors.length; i++) {
        if (flavor.equals(flavors[i])) {
          return true;
        }
      }
      return false;
    }

    public void lostOwnership(Clipboard cb, Transferable t) {}

}
```

Finally, getTransferData() must be implemented, which is responsible for returning data in the requested flavor. In this case, only IMAGE_DATA_FLAVOR is supported, and that flavor can be provided simply by returning a reference to the encapsulated data object:

```
import java.awt.datatransfer.*;

public class ImageSelection implements Transferable, ClipboardOwner {

  protected ImageData imageData;

  public final static DataFlavor IMAGE_DATA_FLAVOR =
    new DataFlavor(ImageData.class, "Image Data");

  protected final static DataFlavor[] flavors = {
    IMAGE_DATA_FLAVOR
  };

  public ImageSelection(ImageData data) {
    imageData = data;
  }

  public Object getTransferData(DataFlavor flavor)
        throws java.io.IOException, UnsupportedFlavorException {
    if (flavor.equals(IMAGE_DATA_FLAVOR)) {
      return imageData;
    }
    throw new UnsupportedFlavorException(flavor);
  }

  public DataFlavor[] getTransferDataFlavors() {
    return flavors;
  }
```

Now that the Transferable implementation is complete, all that's left is to write the code in ImageEditor to perform the cut, copy, and paste operations. Since most of the needed functionality is already present, there's very little work to do.

In the case of the performCopy() method, we can create an instance of ImageSelection and store it in the clipboard using the setContents() method, as shown below:

```
protected void performCopy() {
  Rectangle r = getSelectedArea();
  int[] pixels = getPixels(r);
  ImageData data = new ImageData(r.width, r.height, pixels);
  ImageSelection selection = new ImageSelection(data);
  Clipboard cb = getToolkit().getSystemClipboard();
  cb.setContents(selection, selection);
}
```

The cut operation is almost identical but has one additional step. After the image data is copied to the clipboard, the pixels that were copied are set to 0 in the original image (that is, they are "removed" from the image):

```
protected void performCut() {
  Rectangle r = getSelectedArea();
  int[] pixels = getPixels(r);
  ImageData data = new ImageData(r.width, r.height, pixels);
  ImageSelection selection = new ImageSelection(data);
  Clipboard cb = getToolkit().getSystemClipboard();
  cb.setContents(selection, selection);
  for (int i = 0; i < pixels.length; i++) {
    pixels[i] = 0;
  }
  setPixels(pixels, r);
}
```

Finally, the performPaste() method can be completed. It must obtain a reference to the Transferable stored in the clipboard (if any), ensure that the data can be retrieved in the supported format, and overwrite a portion of the image with that data:

```
protected void performPaste() {
  Clipboard cb = getToolkit().getSystemClipboard();
  try {
    Transferable t = cb.getContents(this);
    if (t.isDataFlavorSupported(
        ImageSelection.IMAGE_DATA_FLAVOR)) {
      ImageData data = (ImageData)(t.getTransferData(
          ImageSelection.IMAGE_DATA_FLAVOR));
      Rectangle area = new Rectangle(start.x, start.y,
          data.getWidth(), data.getHeight());
      int[] pixels = data.getPixelData();
      setPixels(pixels, area);
    }
  }
  catch (Exception e) {
    JOptionPane.showMessageDialog(this,
        "Unable to paste clipboard data");
  }
}
```

Finally, we can also make a minor change to ImageEditor that causes the **Paste** menu item to be disabled when the clipboard does not contain the supported data flavor:

```
protected void displayPopupMenu(Point p) {
  Clipboard cb = getToolkit().getSystemClipboard();
```

```
        Transferable t = cb.getContents(this);
        boolean isSelected = !(start.equals(finish));
        cutAction.setEnabled(isSelected);
        copyAction.setEnabled(isSelected);
        boolean canPaste = ((t != null) &&
            (t.isDataFlavorSupported(
            ImageSelection.IMAGE_DATA_FLAVOR)));
        pasteAction.setEnabled(canPaste);
        popupMenu.show(this, p.x, p.y);
    }
```

To execute this application, compile and run it, specifying the name of a GIF or JPEG file as the first command-line parameter. For example:

```
    java ImageEditor Vacation.gif
```

To select an area of the image to cut or paste, move the mouse to the upper-left corner of the region and press and hold down the left-mouse button. As you drag the cursor, a brightly colored rectangle appears that identifies the selected area. Once a selection is made, you can click on the right-mouse button to access a JPopupMenu with Cut, Copy, and Paste menu items.

Select Cut or Copy and then move the mouse to the location where you wish to paste the image data. Press the left-mouse button to select the location where the image data should be pasted and then press the right button to bring up the popup menu again and perform the paste operation.

Although this application may appear correct, there is a problem with it. If you perform a cut and paste instead of a copy and paste, the area you paste the selection into is cleared. For example, as shown here an area of the image has been selected and cut, and is about to be pasted to a different location:

However, pasting the data causes the area to be cleared instead of overwritten with the selection:

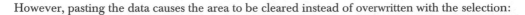

This problem illustrates a point made earlier related to modifying data after it is stored in the clipboard. In this case, the data that's cut is stored in an int array, and ImageEditor uses that array *after* the data is stored in the clipboard but *before* the data is pasted. Intuitively, you might expect that storing data in the clipboard creates a copy of the data, and that making changes to the array after it has been stored will not affect the clipboard contents. However, as you can see from this example, that is not always the case.

Fortunately, the problem is easy to fix, and can be addressed by modifying the ImageData class so that it creates a copy of the array instead of maintaining a reference to the original data. This prevents ImageEditor from modifying the data in the clipboard, since it no longer has a reference to the same array that's stored there:

```
public class ImageData implements java.io.Serializable {

    protected int width;
    protected int height;
    protected int[] pixelData;

    public ImageData(int width, int height, int[] pixels) {
        this.width = width;
        this.height = height;
        pixelData = (int[])(pixels.clone());
    }

    public int getWidth() {
        return width;
    }
```

```
    public int getHeight() {
      return height;
    }

    public int[] getPixelData() {
      return pixelData;
    }

  }
```

Storing and Retrieving Other Types of Data

So far, we've only looked at storing Java objects in the clipboard. However, in some cases, it's useful to be able to transfer data between Java and non-Java applications.

It might seem that Java's MIME-based approach to identifying the content type of a `Transferable`'s data would make it easy to transfer data between Java and non-Java applications. However, this is not the case, primarily because each operating system's clipboard supports its own proprietary data types instead of standard MIME types. For example, Windows defines the `CF_TEXT`, `CF_DIB`, and `CF_HDROP` clipboard types for text, bitmap (image), and file selection data, respectively.

Although native clipboards don't use MIME types, it is possible in some cases to define a mapping between a native platform's clipboard type and a MIME type. In fact, that's exactly what occurs when you use the `StringSelection` class provided with Java. When you call the `setContents()` method to store a `StringSelection` in the clipboard, the text is automatically converted to an appropriate native clipboard format (for example, `CF_TEXT`) so that it is readable by non-Java applications. Similarly, when `getContents()` is called, the data is translated from the native format such as `CF_TEXT` into a `String` encapsulated by an instance of `StringSelection`. In the future, there may be other `Transferable` types that are translated automatically for you this way, but text data is the only type currently supported for clipboard operations.

In Java 1.2, `StringSelection` supports two flavors, both of which are represented by constants defined in `DataFlavor`: `stringFlavor` and `plainTextFlavor`. While `stringFlavor` is used to transfer serialized `String` instances between Java programs, `plainTextFlavor` was created for text transfers between Java and non-Java applications. However, due to problems in the design and implementation of `StringSelection`, `plainTextFlavor` is deprecated in Java 1.3. `StringSelection`'s problems are primarily related to its use in drag and drop operations, and as of this writing, both flavors work correctly for clipboard transfers, at least within the limits described at the beginning of this chapter. In spite of that fact, you should avoid using `plainTextFlavor` since it is now deprecated.

Writing Arbitrary Binary Data

To store binary data in the clipboard, you must define a `DataFlavor` which represents the MIME type associated with the data and which has a representation class of `InputStream`. A `Transferable` that supports the flavor should provide an `InputStream` that returns a stream of bytes in the appropriate format for the MIME type.

Normally when you write binary data to the clipboard, it will be necessary to write it using a format that one or more other applications are able to interpret. In some cases, this can be done through a **codec**, which is software that performs data conversions between two or more formats. For example, Sun provides a codec with the Java 2D API that allows you to convert data representing a JPEG image to and from an instance of Java's `BufferedImage` class.

We'll now modify the ImageSelection class so that it supports an additional DataFlavor representing the image/jpeg MIME type. When that flavor is requested on a call to getTransferData(), an InputStream is returned that can be used to read a stream of bytes in JPEG format:

```java
import java.awt.*;
import java.awt.datatransfer.*;
import java.awt.image.*;
import java.io.*;
import com.sun.image.codec.jpeg.*;

public class ImageSelection implements Transferable, ClipboardOwner {

  protected ImageData imageData;

  public final static DataFlavor IMAGE_DATA_FLAVOR =
    new DataFlavor(ImageData.class, "Image Data");

  public final static DataFlavor JPEG_MIME_FLAVOR =
    new DataFlavor("image/jpeg", "JPEG Image Data");

  protected final static DataFlavor[] flavors = {
    JPEG_MIME_FLAVOR, IMAGE_DATA_FLAVOR
  };

  public ImageSelection(ImageData data) {
    imageData = data;
  }

  public Object getTransferData(DataFlavor flavor)
          throws java.io.IOException, UnsupportedFlavorException {
    if (flavor.equals(IMAGE_DATA_FLAVOR)) {
      return imageData;
    } else if (flavor.equals(JPEG_MIME_FLAVOR)) {
      return getJPEGInputStream();
    }
    throw new UnsupportedFlavorException(flavor);
  }

  protected InputStream getJPEGInputStream() throws IOException {
    int width = imageData.getWidth();
    int height = imageData.getHeight();
    MemoryImageSource mis = new MemoryImageSource(width, height,
            imageData.getPixelData(), 0, width);
    BufferedImage bi =
      new BufferedImage(width, height, BufferedImage.TYPE_3BYTE_BGR);
    Graphics2D g2d = bi.createGraphics();
    Image img = Toolkit.getDefaultToolkit().createImage(mis);
    g2d.drawImage(img, 0, 0, null);
    ByteArrayOutputStream baos = new ByteArrayOutputStream();
    JPEGImageEncoder jie = JPEGCodec.createJPEGEncoder(baos);
    jie.encode(bi);
    baos.close();
    return new ByteArrayInputStream(baos.toByteArray());
  }

  public DataFlavor[] getTransferDataFlavors() {
```

```
      return flavors;
    }

    public boolean isDataFlavorSupported(DataFlavor flavor) {
      for (int i = 0; i < flavors.length; i++) {
        if (flavor.equals(flavors[i])) {
          return true;
        }
      }
      return false;
    }

    public void lostOwnership(Clipboard cb, Transferable t) {}

  }
```

Note that in this example, the binary data corresponds to a specific MIME format, specifically that of a JPEG image. If you wish to write binary data that doesn't correspond to an existing MIME type, you can create a custom type (for example, `application/x-mybinary`) or simply use the generic `application/octet-stream` type.

Once the problems with Java's Data Transfer API have been resolved, you'll be able to transfer data between Java and non-Java applications by storing the data as a stream of binary data as we did in this example. In the meantime, however, you can test the functionality added to `ImageSelection` by adding a popup menu item to `ImageEditor`. That menu item should allow you to retrieve the contents of the clipboard as a stream of JPEG data and save the data to a disk file. In other words, you can cut or copy a portion of an image and save the selection to disk as a new JPEG file by making the following changes. To do this, first define an `AbstractAction` that corresponds to the new menu item:

```
  protected JPopupMenu popupMenu;
  protected AbstractAction cutAction;
  protected AbstractAction copyAction;
  protected AbstractAction pasteAction;
  protected AbstractAction saveAction;
```

Next, add a new menu item to the popup menu:

```
  protected void buildPopupMenu() {
    popupMenu = new JPopupMenu();
    copyAction = new AbstractAction("Copy") {
      public void actionPerformed(ActionEvent event) {
        performCopy();
      }
    };
    popupMenu.add(copyAction);
    cutAction = new AbstractAction("Cut") {
      public void actionPerformed(ActionEvent event) {
        performCut();
      }
    };
    popupMenu.add(cutAction);
    pasteAction = new AbstractAction("Paste") {
      public void actionPerformed(ActionEvent event) {
        performPaste();
```

```
      }
    };
    popupMenu.add(pasteAction);
    saveAction = new AbstractAction("Save") {
      public void actionPerformed(ActionEvent event) {
        performSave();
      }
    };
    popupMenu.add(saveAction);
  }
```

Finally, implement the method that will perform the save operation, and update the code that sets the state of the menu items so that the **Save** menu item is only enabled when there is data in the clipboard:

```
protected void displayPopupMenu(Point p) {
  Clipboard cb = getToolkit().getSystemClipboard();
  Transferable t = cb.getContents(this);
  boolean isSelected = !(start.equals(finish));
  cutAction.setEnabled(isSelected);
  copyAction.setEnabled(isSelected);
  boolean canPaste = ((t != null) &&
      (t.isDataFlavorSupported(
      ImageSelection.IMAGE_DATA_FLAVOR)));
  pasteAction.setEnabled(canPaste);
  saveAction.setEnabled(canPaste);
  popupMenu.show(this, p.x, p.y);
}
```

```
protected void performSave() {
  JFileChooser jfc = new JFileChooser();
  jfc.showSaveDialog(this);
  java.io.File f = jfc.getSelectedFile();
  Clipboard cb = getToolkit().getSystemClipboard();
  Transferable t = cb.getContents(this);
  DataFlavor flavor = ImageSelection.JPEG_MIME_FLAVOR;
  if ((!(f == null)) && (!(t == null))
        && (t.isDataFlavorSupported(flavor))) {
    try {
      java.io.FileOutputStream fos =
        new java.io.FileOutputStream(f);
      java.io.InputStream is =
        (java.io.InputStream) (t.getTransferData(flavor));
      int value = is.read();
      while (value != -1) {
        fos.write((byte) value);
        value = is.read();
      }
      fos.close();
      is.close();
    } catch (Exception e) {}
  }
}
```

Cutting and Pasting Text

At the beginning of the chapter, a statement was made that Swing components do not provide automatic support for cut, copy, and paste operations, which is true. However, it's also true that JTextComponent (the superclass of JTextField and JTextArea) contains cut(), copy(), and paste() methods that cut, copy, and paste text onto the system clipboard, respectively. As we saw earlier, the StringSelection class that's provided with Java makes it easy to store text in the clipboard, but the presence of these methods in JTextComponent makes it even easier.

For example, suppose that you wish to create a popup menu that appears when the right-mouse button is pressed, and you would like for that menu to display Cut, Copy, and Paste items and allow the appropriate function to be executed when the user selects one. Since the methods already exist that provide those functions, this behavior can be easily implemented by simply creating code that displays a popup menu.

The following class extends MouseAdapter, which allows it to be registered with a Component and to receive notification when a mouse click occurs over that component, although the implementation of the mousePressed() method is not yet complete. This class also creates an instance of JPopupMenu and adds menu items to it in the form of AbstractAction implementations. Notice that when one of the menu items is called, it simply delegates the call (for example, a cut operation) to the corresponding method in a JTextComponent instance:

```
import java.awt.datatransfer.*;
import java.awt.*;
import java.awt.event.*;
import javax.swing.*;
import javax.swing.text.*;

public class TextComponentCutPaste extends MouseAdapter {

  protected JTextComponent textComponent;
  protected JPopupMenu popupMenu;
  protected AbstractAction cutAction;
  protected AbstractAction copyAction;
  protected AbstractAction pasteAction;

  public TextComponentCutPaste() {
    popupMenu = new JPopupMenu();
    cutAction = new AbstractAction("Cut") {
      public void actionPerformed(ActionEvent event) {
        onCut();
      }
    };
    popupMenu.add(cutAction);
    copyAction = new AbstractAction("Copy") {
      public void actionPerformed(ActionEvent event) {
        onCopy();
      }
    };
    popupMenu.add(copyAction);
    pasteAction = new AbstractAction("Paste") {
      public void actionPerformed(ActionEvent event) {
        onPaste();
```

```
        }
    };
    popupMenu.add(pasteAction);
}

public void onCut() {
    textComponent.cut();
}

public void onCopy() {
    textComponent.copy();
}

public void onPaste() {
    textComponent.paste();
}

public void mousePressed(MouseEvent event) {
}
```

Finally, we'll complete the `mousePressed()` method, which is where most of the important functionality is found. When called, it obtains a reference to the `JTextComponent` over which the mouse click occurred and sets the popup menu's item states appropriately. Specifically, Cut and Copy are enabled only if some text is selected within the text component, while Paste is only enabled if the clipboard contains text data. Finally, once the states of the menu items have been initialized appropriately, the popup menu is displayed at the position where the mouse press took place:

```
public void mousePressed(MouseEvent event) {
    if ((event.getModifiers() & InputEvent.BUTTON3_MASK) != 0) {
        textComponent = (JTextComponent)(event.getSource());
        String selected = textComponent.getSelectedText();
        // Only enable cut, copy when some text is selected
        boolean canCut = ((selected != null) && (selected.length() > 0));
        cutAction.setEnabled(canCut);
        copyAction.setEnabled(canCut);
        Clipboard cb = Toolkit.getDefaultToolkit().getSystemClipboard();
        Transferable t = cb.getContents(this);
        // Only enable paste if the component has the focus and the
        // clipboard contains text data
        pasteAction.setEnabled((t.isDataFlavorSupported(DataFlavor.stringFlavor)) &&
            textComponent.hasFocus());
        popupMenu.show(textComponent, event.getX(), event.getY());
    }
}
```

This completes the implementation of our `TextComponentCutPaste` class. Its design allows a single instance of this class to handle cut and paste operations for multiple `JTextComponent` instances within an interface. Therefore, you can create a test application similar to the one shown below that creates a `JTextField` and a `JTextArea` and uses the same instance of `TextComponentCutPaste` to provide cut and paste support for both:

```
import java.awt.*;
import javax.swing.*;

public class TextTest extends JFrame {

  public static void main(String[] args) {
    TextTest tt = new TextTest();
    tt.setDefaultCloseOperation(JFrame.EXIT_ON_CLOSE);
    tt.setSize(400, 300);
    tt.setVisible(true);
  }

  public TextTest() {
    Container pane = getContentPane();
    pane.setLayout(new FlowLayout());
    JTextField tf = new JTextField(10);
    JTextArea ta = new JTextArea(10, 10);
    pane.add(tf);
    pane.add(new JScrollPane(ta));
    TextComponentCutPaste tccp = new TextComponentCutPaste();
    tf.addMouseListener(tccp);
    ta.addMouseListener(tccp);
  }

}
```

If you compile and execute this code, it produces an interface like the one shown below. By typing text into one or both of the text fields, you can test the cut, copy, and paste functionality that's included in JTextComponent. In fact, depending upon whether or not transfer between applications is functional on the platform you're using, you may be able to use this program to transfer text between Java and native applications.

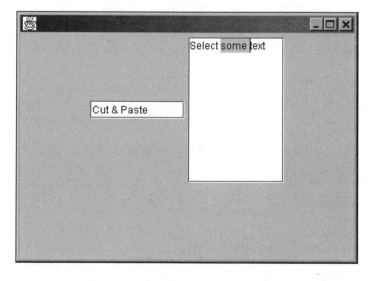

Summary

In this chapter, we've examined Java's cut and paste capabilities, and how to use them in conjunction with the clipboard. We've developed an image manipulation program with a basic cut and paste implementation. Although the facility is not fully functional, we've seen how easily you can perform cut and paste functions.

We've also amended the application to include a means of saving clipboard contents to disk.

In the next chapter we'll go on to looking at another method of manipulating the placement of data – drag and drop.

Professional Java Programmin

9

Adding Drag and Drop Functionality

In a drag and drop operation, data is moved ("dragged") from one location and stored ("dropped") in another. For example, most operating systems provide a utility similar to Windows Explorer, which allows you to perform drag and drop operations on the list of available files. Drag and drop provides an intuitive visual representation of the moving or copying of data from one location to another, and is an important part of most modern operating systems. It can be used by many applications and in a variety of ways, so it's helpful to be familiar with the functionality that's available in Java 2.

Most of the classes associated with drag and drop are defined in the `java.awt.dnd` package, but some parts of the Data Transfer API defined in `java.awt.datatransfer` are also used. The classes defined in `java.awt.dnd` may seem complex and confusing, but the truth is that it's not difficult to add drag and drop capabilities to your applications. In fact, once the data to be dragged is wrapped in a `Transferable`, there's usually not much more code to write.

The `Transferable` interface in the `java.awt.datatransfer` package serves the same purpose in a drag and drop operation that it does when used to cut and paste. Specifically, a `Transferable` encapsulates the data that's dragged and provides `DataFlavor` instances that identify the formats in which the data can be retrieved.

In this chapter we will examine the following issues:

- ❑   The fundamental concepts associated with drag and drop operations

- ❑   Adding drag support to components so that they can be used to initiate drag and drop operations

- ❑   Adding drop support to components so that they can be used to terminate drag and drop operations

- ❑ Issues related to different types of transfers (for example, those between a Java and native application, as opposed to a transfer within a single Java Virtual Machine)

- ❑ How to implement autoscroll support for drop targets contained within a scroll pane

- ❑ Issues related to the transfer of text data between Java and native applications

While Java's cut and paste capabilities are currently somewhat limited, its drag and drop functionality is much more reliable and complete. That might seem surprising since the two facilities perform similar functions and since some of the same classes and interfaces are involved. Despite the similarities, Java's implementation of drag and drop is completely separate from its cut and paste facility, which is why one set of operations works well even though the other does not. However, bug reports on the JavaSoft web site indicate that the cut and paste functionality will be revised in a future release so that it uses the more robust code provided by drag and drop, so both should be functioning equally well at some future date.

Drag and Drop Operation Types

Just as cut, copy, and paste functions are collectively referred to as "cut and paste", the phrase "drag and drop" refers to several different operations. In a **move** operation, the data that's dragged is removed from its original location and stored in some other location. A **copy** operation is similar to a move, except that the original data remains intact and a copy of it is created and stored in the drop location. Finally, a **link** or **reference** operation results in the creation of a representation of or reference to the original data. For example, the terminology varies across platforms, but most operating systems allow you to create file "shortcuts" or "aliases".

The way in which drag and drop operations are started and ended varies from one operating system to the next, because each platform defines its own set of **gestures** for that purpose. Those gestures are usually a combination of mouse button and key presses, and the buttons and keys involved are referred to as **modifiers**.

For example, on Windows, you can initiate a move operation by pressing the left-mouse button and then dragging the cursor. A copy operation is initiated by performing the same steps while also holding down the *Ctrl* key. Finally, a link operation requires you to press and hold down both the *Shift* and *Ctrl* keys while dragging the mouse. In each case, the object that's dragged is usually either the component that was underneath the cursor when the left button was initially pressed, or is some data item that the component represents.

When the appropriate drag gestures have been performed, the drag operation is initiated by an object called a **drag source**, and the drop is handled by an object called a **drop target**. You'll write code to control the behavior of the drag source and drop target and that code can take any action that's appropriate for the application. In some cases, your code may choose to perform an operation (copy, move, or link) other than the one associated with the user's gestures. For example, if a Windows user requests a copy operation by pressing the *Ctrl* key while dragging, your application might choose to perform a move instead if the copy operation isn't appropriate in the context of that application.

The individual drag and drop operations (and some combinations) are represented by int values defined in the DnDConstants class. Specifically, those constants are:

- ❑ ACTION_MOVE

- ❑   `ACTION_COPY`
- ❑   `ACTION_REFERENCE`
- ❑   `ACTION_LINK`
- ❑   `ACTION_COPY_OR_MOVE`

"Reference" and "link" are synonyms for the same operation, so their associated constants are assigned the same value. The `ACTION_COPY_OR_MOVE` constant is provided as a convenience, since it represents a commonly used combination.

Predefined Cursors

During drag and drop operations, it's common practice to provide visual feedback to the user concerning the state of the operation, and one way that this is done is through the cursor that's displayed. A pair of cursors exists for each of the three operation types, and those cursors are accessible through constants defined in `DragSource`. Each pair includes a **drop cursor** that is normally displayed when the cursor is over a component that can accept a drop and a **nodrop cursor** when the cursor is over components that cannot:

Cursor Constants Defined in DragSource and Sample Cursors		
	Drop Cursor	**NoDrop Cursor**
Move	DefaultMoveDrop	DefaultMoveNoDrop
Copy	DefaultCopyDrop	DefaultCopyNoDrop
Link/Reference	DefaultLinkDrop	DefaultLinkNoDrop

You won't normally find it necessary to use these constants, because in most cases, Java's drag and drop facility will change the cursor for you automatically to reflect the status of the drag and drop operation. In general, the only time you need to select one of these cursors is when initiating a drag event, in which case you'll specify the initial cursor that should be displayed. As you'll see later, that cursor should normally be one of the nodrop cursors identified in the above table.

File Selection Drops from Native Applications

In the previous chapter, we saw that each `DataFlavor` contains a MIME type used to identify the specific data format the flavor represents. However, each operating system defines its own proprietary data types, and to transfer data between a Java and native application, a `DataFlavor`'s MIME type must be mapped to an equivalent native type. For example, to transfer text information between Java and native Windows applications, Java automatically converts a `StringSelection` in the clipboard to the `CF_TEXT` type, and vice versa.

While text information is the type of data most commonly involved in cut and paste operations, file selections represent the most frequently used data type in drag and drop operations.

In the same way that Java provides an automatic conversion of clipboard text data, it also performs a translation that allows you to drag and drop file selections between Java and native applications.

Those selections are represented by a `Transferable` that supports a `DataFlavor` with a MIME type of `application/x-java-file-list` and a representation class of `java.util.List`. The `List` object returned by this type of `Transferable` contains a collection of `java.io.File` objects that identify the files selected. If you drop files from a native application onto a Java program, Java automatically creates an instance of `java.util.List` containing `File` objects and wraps that list in a `Transferable`.

Adding Drop Support

Although it might seem more logical to begin with support for dragging, we'll first look at how to handle drops in Java. Drop support is somewhat easier to implement, and this approach provides a good opportunity to illustrate how Java can accept data that's dropped from a native application, such as the Windows Explorer.

To demonstrate how to implement drop support, we'll create a subclass of `JPanel` called `ImageViewer` that accepts image file selection drops. For each file that's dropped, `ImageViewer` creates an `ImageIcon` and displays the icon in a `JLabel`:

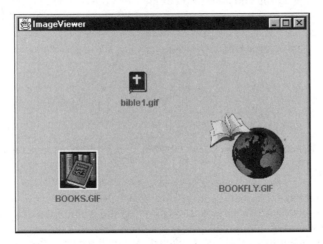

The following code represents the initial implementation of `ImageViewer`. The `getLabelFromFile()` method is passed an instance of `File` and attempts to use that file to create and return a `JLabel`. Since we want to be able to add `JLabel` instances to any point in the container, `ImageViewer` does not use a layout manager. Therefore, it's necessary to explicitly set the size and position of each component added, and `addNewComponent()` is provided for that purpose:

```
import java.awt.*;
import java.awt.datatransfer.*;
import java.awt.dnd.*;
import java.io.*;
import javax.swing.*;

public class ImageViewer extends JPanel {

  public static void main(String[] args) {
    JFrame f = new JFrame("ImageViewer");
    f.setDefaultCloseOperation(JFrame.EXIT_ON_CLOSE);
    f.setContentPane(new ImageViewer());
```

```
      f.setSize(400, 300);
      f.setVisible(true);
   }

   public ImageViewer() {
      super();
      setLayout(null);
   }

   protected JLabel getLabelFromFile(File f) {
      ImageIcon icon = new ImageIcon(f.getAbsolutePath());
      JLabel label = new JLabel(icon);
      label.setText(f.getName());
      label.setHorizontalTextPosition(JLabel.CENTER);
      label.setVerticalTextPosition(JLabel.BOTTOM);
      return label;
   }

   protected void addNewComponent(Component comp, Point location) {
      comp.setLocation(location);
      comp.setSize(comp.getPreferredSize());
      add(comp);
      repaint();
   }

}
```

With the basic functionality implemented, we can begin to add drop support to our custom component, and the first step in doing so is to associate it with a drop target.

DropTarget

Before you can perform drops on a Component, you must create an instance of DropTarget and associate it with the component, which can be done in several different ways. However, the easiest approach in most cases is to provide a reference to the component when you create the DropTarget. Once it has been created, you can enable and disable a DropTarget by calling its setActive() method and its state can be queried using isActive().

The DropTarget receives notification of events related to the drag and drop operation, and provides support for a single listener that is also notified of those events. To handle drops, you must define a DropTargetListener implementation and associate it with a DropTarget just as you did for the drop component.

DropTargetListener

A DropTargetListener has two primary responsibilities: providing **drag under effects** during a drag and drop operation, and handling the recipient's side of a drop when it occurs.

> **Drag under effects are changes made to the drop component's appearance that provide feedback to the user during the drag operation.**

For example, if you create a `DropTargetListener` for use with a `JTable`, you might implement code that highlights the cell underneath the cursor as it moves across the table. An example of this will be provided later in the chapter, but for now, drag under effects are treated as an advanced topic and in practice are often not needed.

In addition to the drag under effects, a `DropTargetListener` is responsible for handling the drop operation, which typically involves storing the data that's dropped or a reference to the data. How and where the data is stored is application-specific and usually depends on the operation type (move, copy, or link), the type of data dropped, and the type of component onto which it's dropped. In the case of `ImageViewer`, the `DropTargetListener` uses the file selections to create `JLabel` instances, and the labels are added to the panel at the drop location.

`ImageViewer` contains an inner class that provides an implementation of `DropTargetListener`, and that class is shown below. Each of the five methods defined in `DropTargetListener` is examined in detail in this chapter, but in many cases, you will only need to write code for `drop()`, which (as its name implies) is called when a drop occurs. To use this inner class, insert it into the `ImageViewer` class after the last method that's defined there:

```
class MyDropListener implements DropTargetListener {

  public void dragEnter(DropTargetDragEvent event) {
  }

  public void dragExit(DropTargetEvent event) {
  }

  public void dragOver(DropTargetDragEvent event) {
  }

  public void dropActionChanged(DropTargetDragEvent event) {
  }

  public void drop(DropTargetDropEvent event) {
  }

}
```

It's now possible to create a `DropTarget`, which we'll do using a constructor that is passed a reference to the drop component (that is, the `ImageViewer` instance), the operations the target supports, and a reference to a `DropTargetListener`:

```
public ImageViewer() {
  super();
  setLayout(null);
  DropTarget dt = new DropTarget(this,
      DnDConstants.ACTION_COPY_OR_MOVE,
      new MyDropListener());
}
```

Events Passed to DropTargetListener Methods

Now that we've created the `DropTarget`, it's necessary to complete the implementation of the methods within `MyDropListener`. To better understand how those methods are used, we need to examine the event objects that are passed to them.

DropTargetEvent

This is the superclass of the `DropTargetDragEvent` and `DropTargetDropEvent` classes discussed below, and an instance of this class is passed to `dragExit()`. However, `DropTargetEvent` does not define any methods or properties that you'll normally use.

DropTargetDragEvent

An instance of `DropTargetDragEvent` is passed to the `dragEnter()`, `dragOver()`, and `dropActionChanged()` methods. `DropTargetDragEvent` allows those methods to identify the type of data being dragged, as well as the specific location of the cursor and other information regarding the current operation. In addition, this event object provides methods that allow the drag operation to be accepted or rejected, and the reasons for doing so and consequences of those actions are discussed later.

getCurrentDataFlavors()
getCurrentDataFlavorsAsList()
isDataFlavorSupported()

These methods allow you to determine which `DataFlavor`(s) can be used to transfer data if a drop occurs. While `getCurrentDataFlavors()` returns an array of `DataFlavor` instances, `getCurrentDataFlavorsAsList()` returns a `java.util.List` containing the valid flavors. When you need to determine whether the data can be retrieved using a specific flavor, you should use `isDataFlavorSupported()`. That method returns a `boolean` value of `true` if the flavor you pass to it as a parameter is supported.

These methods are often used by a `DropTargetListener` to determine whether the data being dragged can be represented in a form that the drop target can process. If not, it's common for the drop target to reject the drag operation, the implications of which are discussed later.

getLocation()

You can use this method to determine where the cursor was located when the event occurred. An instance of `java.awt.Point` is returned that identifies the cursor's position within the component across which it's being dragged, and the position is relative to the component's origin (coordinates 0, 0).

This method is most commonly used to provide drag under effects. For example, if data is dragged across a `JTable`, the drop target may use the cursor's location to determine which table cell is underneath the cursor and select or highlight that cell appropriately.

getSourceActions()

A drop target may need to determine what operations are supported by the drag source, and this method makes it possible to obtain that information.

acceptDrag()

This method indicates that the drop target is prepared to accept a drop, and you should specify the operation type that the target will perform if a drop does occur. That type should be one of the types supported by the drag source, which can be identified by calling `getSourceActions()`.

You are *not* required to call this method within the `DropTargetListener` methods. However, you should call `acceptDrag()` if your drop target wishes to perform an operation other than the one selected by the user.

rejectDrag()

A call to `rejectDrag()` indicates that your drop target is not prepared to accept a drop, and the reasons for that can vary from one application to the next. You'll often reject a drag when the type of data being dragged cannot be processed by the drop target or when the cursor is over an area of the component that cannot accept drops. For example, `ImageViewer` rejects drags when the data being dragged cannot be retrieved using the `javaFileListFlavor` data flavor.

getDropAction()

This method identifies the operation type that the user currently has selected, and returns an `int` value that corresponds to one of the action constants defined in `DragSource`: `ACTION_MOVE`, `ACTION_COPY`, or `ACTION_LINK` / `ACTION_REFERENCE`.

If your drop target can support more than one type of operation, it should normally use this method to select the operation that was requested by the user.

DropTargetDropEvent

An instance of `DropTargetDropEvent` is passed to the `drop()` method when a drop occurs. Many of the methods in this class are identical in name and function to those in `DropTargetDragEvent`, so only those that are unique to `DropTargetDropEvent` are discussed here.

acceptDrop()

This method is essentially the same as `acceptDrag()` and indicates to the caller which operation is to be performed on the data that's transferred. This method should be called *before* the data is accessed using `getTransferable()` or that call may fail.

rejectDrop()

You should call this method if your drop target cannot perform the requested operation.

getTransferable()

This method can be called to retrieve a `Transferable` that encapsulates the data that was dropped. Note that it should only be called *after* your drop target has invoked `acceptDrop()`.

isLocalTransfer()

Use this method to find out if the drag and drop operation has taken place within a single Java Virtual Machine (i.e. this is a **local transfer**). It's sometimes important to distinguish local from **remote transfers**, and the reasons for doing so are described in detail later in this chapter.

dropComplete()

Once your drop processing is finished, you should call the `dropComplete()` method to signal completion of the drop operation. A parameter value of `true` indicates that the transfer was successful, while `false` indicates that it was not.

Drag Sessions

Several of the methods in `DropTargetListener` are called as a result of cursor movement, and to accurately determine when they're invoked, it's necessary to identify what we'll call a **drag session**. A drag session begins when the cursor enters the component's display area and ends when it exits the display area or when a drop occurs. In most cases, only one drag session occurs per component in a single drag and drop operation. However, the user may choose to repeatedly move the cursor over a component and then away from it for some reason. In general, you won't need to concern yourself with drag sessions, but the concept is relevant to some of the `DropTargetListener` behavior described below.

Rejecting Drags and Drops

When your drop target wishes to indicate that it will not accept a drop, it can call `rejectDrag()` from within the `dragEnter()`, `dragOver()`, and `dropActionChanged()` methods. When a drag is rejected, the cursor changes to a nodrop cursor and if a drop occurs *during that drag session*, it is ignored (that is, the `drop()` method is not called).

> *Note that a drag rejection is effective only for the current drag session, and if the cursor exits and re-enters the component's display area, any previous rejection is effectively canceled. This isn't a problem in most cases, because the same conditions that caused your code to reject the drag in one drag session normally will still exist in another. However, you should realize that rejecting a drag does not* permanently *prevent the drop from completing.*

It's also important to know that rejecting a drag does not prevent further `DropTargetListener` notifications. For example, if you reject a drag operation from the `dragEnter()` method, `dragOver()` will still be called as the cursor moves over the component, and `dragExit()` will be called when the cursor exits the component area. As we'll see later, it's even possible to accept a drag after you had rejected a previous one in the same drag session.

Given the choice between rejecting a drop request or rejecting a drag operation and preventing the drop request from occurring, you may be wondering which should you choose. In most cases, it's appropriate to reject the drag operation, because you'll usually know at that time (that is, before the drop actually occurs) whether or not you intend to allow the drop to take place. However, there may be cases in which the state of the drop target can change while the drag is taking place, which in turn may affect its ability to accept the drop. In other words, if you can't be certain whether or not a drop target will accept the drop until it actually occurs, you should accept the drag requests and reject the drop if necessary.

DropTargetListener Method Descriptions

Now that we've examined the event objects that are passed to the `DropTargetListener` methods, we'll see when those methods are called and how you should use them.

dragEnter()

During a drag and drop operation, this method is called when the cursor enters the display area of the component associated with the `DropTarget`. You may wish to use this method to initiate drag under effects for the component, or you may choose to accept or reject the drag operation. `ImageViewer` uses `dragEnter()` to reject the drag operation when the data being dragged is not a list of files:

```
public void dragEnter(DropTargetDragEvent event) {
   if (event.isDataFlavorSupported(
       DataFlavor.javaFileListFlavor)) {
     return;
   }
   event.rejectDrag();
}
```

dragOver()

This method is passed an instance of `DropTargetDragEvent` and is called when the cursor moves after it has previously entered the display area of the drop component. If you are providing drag under effects, you may need to update them each time `dragOver()` is called. However, if you're not providing drag under effects, you will not need to implement this method, which is the case with our `ImageViewer` application.

dragExit()

An instance of `DropTargetEvent` is passed to this method, which is called when the cursor exits the display area of the drop component. If you are providing drag under effects, you normally should discontinue them when `dragExit()` is invoked. As with `dragOver()`, you'll not normally implement this method if you're not providing drag under support.

drop()

This method is called when a drop occurs, and it is responsible for accepting or rejecting the drop and for processing the dropped data. When a drop takes place over an instance of `ImageViewer`, for example, the file selections that were dropped must be converted into `JLabel` instances and added to the container as shown below:

```
import java.awt.*;
import java.awt.datatransfer.*;
import java.awt.dnd.*;
import java.io.*;
import javax.swing.*;

public class ImageViewer extends JPanel {

  public static void main(String[] args) {
    JFrame f = new JFrame("ImageViewer");
    f.setDefaultCloseOperation(JFrame.EXIT_ON_CLOSE);
    f.setContentPane(new ImageViewer());
    f.setSize(400, 300);
    f.setVisible(true);
  }

  public ImageViewer() {
    super();
    setLayout(null);
    DropTarget dt = new DropTarget(this,
        DnDConstants.ACTION_COPY_OR_MOVE,
        new MyDropListener());
  }

  protected JLabel getLabelFromFile(File f) {
    ImageIcon icon = new ImageIcon(f.getAbsolutePath());
    JLabel label = new JLabel(icon);
    label.setText(f.getName());
    label.setHorizontalTextPosition(JLabel.CENTER);
    label.setVerticalTextPosition(JLabel.BOTTOM);
    return label;
  }

  protected void addNewComponent(Component comp, Point location) {
    comp.setLocation(location);
```

```
        comp.setSize(comp.getPreferredSize());
        add(comp);
        repaint();
    }

    class MyDropListener implements DropTargetListener {

        public void dragEnter(DropTargetDragEvent event) {
            if (event.isDataFlavorSupported(
                DataFlavor.javaFileListFlavor)) {
                return;
            }
            event.rejectDrag();
        }

        public void dragExit(DropTargetEvent event) {
        }

        public void dragOver(DropTargetDragEvent event) {
        }

        public void dropActionChanged(DropTargetDragEvent event) {
        }

        public void drop(DropTargetDropEvent event) {
            if (event.isDataFlavorSupported(
                DataFlavor.javaFileListFlavor)) try {
                event.acceptDrop(DnDConstants.ACTION_COPY);
                Transferable t = event.getTransferable();
                java.util.List list = (java.util.List)(
                    t.getTransferData(
                    DataFlavor.javaFileListFlavor));
                java.util.Iterator i = list.iterator();
                while (i.hasNext()) {
                    JLabel label = getLabelFromFile(
                        (File)(i.next()));
                    addNewComponent(label, event.getLocation());
                }
                event.dropComplete(true);
            } catch (Exception e) {
                event.dropComplete(false);
            }
        }
    }
}
```

The first action this drop() implementation takes is to determine whether javaFileListFlavor can be used to retrieve the data. That test isn't really needed because a similar test was already performed in dragEnter(), and drop() will not be called if the drag was rejected. However, we'll leave the code in place because ImageViewer will later be modified to accept an additional DataFlavor. When that change is made, the drop() method must distinguish between the two flavors so that it can handle each of them differently.

After the data type has been verified, acceptDrop() is called and is passed the type of operation to be performed. As you may recall, the drop target is able to support both move and copy (ACTION_COPY_OR_MOVE) operations, but a single operation should be specified when calling `acceptDrop()`. In many cases, the copy and move operations are handled the same way by a drop target, but it's still important to select the appropriate operation. That's because the drag source is notified of which operation was selected, and the drag source processing often *does* vary based on that selection.

After accepting the drop operation, the method shown above retrieves the `Transferable` data, extracts the file list from it, creates a `JLabel` for each file, and adds the labels to the container. Once the data has been successfully retrieved and processed, `dropComplete()` is called and is passed a parameter value of `true`, indicating that the drop was successful.

In addition to identifying the type of operation accepted by the drop target, a drag source is also able to determine whether the drop operation completed successfully. That information is needed so that the drag source can take appropriate action based on the outcome of the drop. For example, if a move operation was requested and the drop was successful, the drag source often must remove the dragged data from its original location.

dropActionChanged()

Earlier we saw that the type of operation to perform is determined by the status of keyboard and mouse modifier keys and buttons. However, it's possible for the user to change the selected drop action after a drag has been initiated by changing the state of those modifiers. For example, if you begin a copy operation on Windows and then release the *Ctrl* key while dragging the data, you have effectively changed the requested drop action. When such a change does occur, this method is called to notify the `DropTargetListener` of the modification. You will only need to implement this method is your application needs to take some action when the drop action changes, which is not the case with `ImageViewer`.

Drop-Enabling ImageViewer

We've now created all the code that's necessary to allow `ImageViewer` to display image files that are dropped on it, and the complete listing is included below. If you compile and run this application, you will be able to drop image file selections onto the window. For example, once this application's user interface appears, you should start the Windows Explorer (or a similar application) and use that application to drag `GIF` and `JPEG` files and drop them into the frame created by `ImageViewer`:

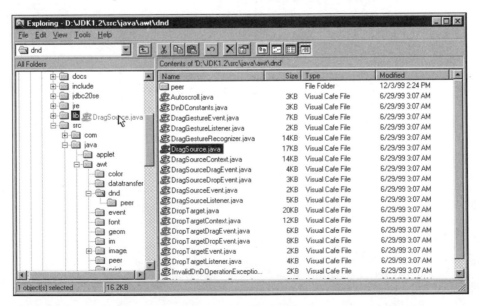

Adding Drag Support

Now that `ImageViewer` is able to process file selection drops, we'll add drag support so that it's possible to drag and drop the `JLabel` objects that were created. Once that's done, it will be possible to move the labels around within a single `ImageViewer` and to move a label from one instance of `ImageViewer` to another.

Defining a Transferable

Before data can be dragged, it must be wrapped in a `Transferable` implementation, just as we did in the previous chapter for cut and paste operations. To support the `Transferable` implementation for `JLabel` instances we'll first define a `DataFlavor` that describes the type of data encapsulated by the `Transferable`:

```
public class ImageViewer extends JPanel {

    public final static DataFlavor LABEL_FLAVOR =
        new DataFlavor(JLabel.class, "Label Instances");
```

The `DataFlavor` constructor used here allows us to create flavors that describe serialized Java objects and this data flavor's MIME type is set to `application/x-java-serialized-object` accordingly. `JLabel` instances are serializable because `Component` (which `JLabel` inherits from) implements the `Serializable` interface.

With the `DataFlavor` defined, we can create a `Transferable` implementation, which in this case is defined as an inner class of `ImageViewer` named `LabelSelection`:

```
class LabelSelection implements Transferable {

  private DataFlavor[] flavors = {
    LABEL_FLAVOR
  };

  protected JLabel label;

  public LabelSelection(JLabel lbl) {
    label = lbl;
  }

  public DataFlavor[] getTransferDataFlavors() {
    return flavors;
  }

  public boolean isDataFlavorSupported(DataFlavor flavor) {
    for (int i = 0; i < flavors.length; i++) {
      if (flavors[i].equals(flavor)) {
        return true;
      }
    }
    return false;
  }

  public Object getTransferData(DataFlavor flavor)
        throws UnsupportedFlavorException, IOException {
```

```
    if (flavor.equals(LABEL_FLAVOR)) {
      return label;
    }
    throw new UnsupportedFlavorException(flavor);
  }

}
```

Now that we've created a `Transferable` that encapsulates a `JLabel`, we can write the code that initiates a drag operation.

Obtaining a Drag Source

Earlier we saw that an instance of `DropTarget` is created for each component that should be able to receive drops. In contrast, there is normally only one drag source per application. That's because although many drop targets can exist simultaneously, only one drag operation can be in progress at any given time, since you only have one mouse with which to control an operation.

As you might expect, a drag source in Java is represented by an instance of the `DragSource` class, and a singleton instance of that class is accessible through the static `getDefaultDragSource()` method:

```
DragSource source = DragSource.getDefaultDragSource();
```

As you'll see, there are many similarities between `DragSource` and `DropTarget`, and one of those similarities is that, like `DropTarget`, a `DragSource` can support a listener.

In the case of `ImageViewer`, we want to be able to drag each `JLabel` that's added to the container. To accomplish this, we'll first modify the `addNewComponent()` method so that the default drag source is accessed each time a `JLabel` is added:

```
protected void addNewComponent(Component comp, Point location) {
  DragSource source = DragSource.getDefaultDragSource();
  comp.setLocation(location);
  comp.setSize(comp.getPreferredSize());
  add(comp);
  repaint();
}
```

At this point, it may not be obvious what to do with the `DragSource`. There is no `DragSource` constructor to which we can pass a reference to the label being added, nor is there an `addDragSourceListener()` method available. Instead, your application should register a listener indirectly by creating a `DragGestureRecognizer`.

Drag Gesture Recognizers

The gestures that are used to initiate drag and drop operations can vary from one operating system to the next. For example, a move operation is initiated on Windows by pressing the left-mouse button and then dragging the cursor. However, other operating systems may use different key and/or button combinations to initiate the same operation.

Ideally, a Java application should be able to recognize the gestures that are appropriate for the platform on which it's running, but at the same time, an application should not contain code that's specific to any one platform. `DragGestureRecognizer` allows you to satisfy both requirements by providing a level of abstraction between your application and the recognition of gestures that should initiate a drag and drop operation.

Just as you create a `DropTarget` for each component that can accept drops, it's necessary to create a `DragGestureRecognizer` for each component that can be used to initiate a drag. The parameters passed to the `DragGestureRecognizer` constructor are very similar to those passed to a `DropTarget`: a `Component` instance, the operations supported, and a listener. In this case, however, the listener is an implementation of `DragGestureListener`:

```
protected void addNewComponent(Component comp, Point location) {
    DragSource source = DragSource.getDefaultDragSource();
    source.createDefaultDragGestureRecognizer(comp,
        DnDConstants.ACTION_COPY_OR_MOVE,
        new MyGestureListener());
    comp.setLocation(location);
    comp.setSize(comp.getPreferredSize());
    add(comp);
    repaint();
}

class MyGestureListener implements DragGestureListener {

    public void dragGestureRecognized(DragGestureEvent event) {}

}
```

Although you can create your own `DragGestureRecognizer` class, there's rarely a reason to do so. Instead, you'll normally obtain an instance of the default `DragGestureRecognizer` class that's provided by the singleton `DragSource`. When you do so, the `DragGestureRecognizer` registers itself as a listener of the component's events so that it can determine when a drag operation should be started. It accomplishes this by monitoring the component events, and when it detects that the user has taken the appropriate action(s) to begin dragging, it sends a notification to the `DragGestureListener` by calling its `dragGestureRecognized()` method.

DragGestureListener

The `DragGestureListener` interface defines a single method that's called when a `DragGestureRecognizer` determines that a drag operation has been requested.

dragGestureRecognized()

This method is called when a `DragGestureRecognizer` determines that the user has requested a drag operation using the standard gestures for the current platform. It is the responsibility of `dragGestureRecognized()` to initiate the drag operation once it has determined that the drag should be allowed to take place.

Many times, such as in the `ImageViewer` application, the drag can be allowed to start unconditionally when `dragGestureRecognized()` is called. However, if the drag component is a more sophisticated control such as a `JTable` or `JTree`, you may wish to be more selective. In the case of a `JTree`, you might allow the user to drag nodes around within the tree but only allow certain nodes to be dragged (for example, only leaf nodes). In that case, you might ignore gestures that occur over nodes that cannot be dragged or you may display an error message when the user attempts to drag an ineligible node.

DragGestureEvent

Among other things, an instance of DragGestureEvent describes the events that were detected by the DragGestureRecognizer. A number of methods within DragGestureEvent allow you to access the InputEvent objects that describe those events, although there's almost never a reason for you to do so. In fact, if you create code that's dependent upon platform-specific event information, you will have defeated the purpose of using a DragGestureRecognizer.

In many cases, the only method you'll use in DragGestureEvent is startDrag(). However, there are some other methods that can be helpful, and we'll examine each of them briefly.

getComponent()

This method returns a reference to the component associated with the DragGestureRecognizer. In the case of ImageViewer, this would be an instance of JLabel.

getDragAction()

The specific operation type requested (move, copy, or link/reference) is returned by this method. It is represented as an int value, and will be one of the following: ACTION_MOVE, ACTION_COPY, or ACTION_LINK (which is equivalent to ACTION_REFERENCE).

getDragOrigin()

You can use this method to determine where the cursor was located when the drag was started. It returns an instance of java.awt.Point that identifies the cursor's position relative to the component origin (that is, coordinates 0, 0).

getDragSource()

This returns a reference to the DragSource that created the DragGestureRecognizer.

getSourceAsDragGestureRecognizer()

This method returns a reference to the DragGestureRecognizer.

startDrag()

In many cases, startDrag() is the only method you'll call from your dragGestureRecognized() implementation, and as its name implies, it initiates the drag operation. The parameters that you can specify when calling startDrag() are:

- ❑ The initial Cursor to display during the operation.
- ❑ An Image used to visually represent the data while it is being dragged. Some operating systems (including Windows) do not support drag images and will ignore this parameter value. To determine whether or not drag image support is available, your application can call the static isDragImageSupported() method in DragSource.
- ❑ The location (represented by an instance of java.awt.Point) relative to the cursor's "hotspot" where the drag image will be displayed if it is supported.
- ❑ A Transferable that encapsulates the data to be moved, copied, or linked.
- ❑ An instance of a DragSourceListener implementation that is used to track the progress of the operation and to perform tasks that are the responsibility of the initiator of the operation.

There are two implementations of the `startDrag()` method, one of which accepts all five of the parameters just described. However, we'll use the simpler version that allows the drag image and coordinate parameters to be omitted. A partial listing of the modified `ImageViewer` class is shown below:

```java
public class ImageViewer extends JPanel {

  public final static DataFlavor LABEL_FLAVOR =
      new DataFlavor(JLabel.class, "Label Instances");

  protected DragSourceListener sourceListener;
  protected JLabel draggedComponent;

  public static void main(String[] args) {
    JFrame f = new JFrame("ImageViewer");
    f.setDefaultCloseOperation(JFrame.EXIT_ON_CLOSE);
    f.setContentPane(new ImageViewer());
    f.setSize(400, 300);
    f.setVisible(true);
  }

  public ImageViewer() {
    super();
    setLayout(null);
    DropTarget dt = new DropTarget(this,
        DnDConstants.ACTION_COPY_OR_MOVE,
        new MyDropListener());
    sourceListener = new MySourceListener();
  }

  protected JLabel getLabelFromFile(File f) {
    ImageIcon icon = new ImageIcon(f.getAbsolutePath());
    JLabel label = new JLabel(icon);
    label.setText(f.getName());
    label.setHorizontalTextPosition(JLabel.CENTER);
    label.setVerticalTextPosition(JLabel.BOTTOM);
    return label;
  }

  protected void addNewComponent(Component comp, Point location) {
    DragSource source = DragSource.getDefaultDragSource();
    source.createDefaultDragGestureRecognizer(comp,
        DnDConstants.ACTION_COPY_OR_MOVE,
        new MyGestureListener());
    comp.setLocation(location);
    comp.setSize(comp.getPreferredSize());
    add(comp);
    repaint();
  }

  class MyGestureListener implements DragGestureListener {

    public void dragGestureRecognized(DragGestureEvent event) {
      Cursor cursor = null;
      draggedComponent = (JLabel)(event.getComponent());
      switch (event.getDragAction()) {
        case DnDConstants.ACTION_MOVE:
          cursor = DragSource.DefaultMoveNoDrop;
```

```
        break;
      case DnDConstants.ACTION_COPY:
        cursor = DragSource.DefaultCopyNoDrop;
        break;
      case DnDConstants.ACTION_LINK:
        cursor = DragSource.DefaultLinkNoDrop;
        break;
    }
    event.startDrag(cursor,
      new LabelSelection(draggedComponent),
      sourceListener);
  }
}

class MySourceListener implements DragSourceListener {

  public void dragEnter(DragSourceDragEvent event) {};
  public void dragExit(DragSourceEvent event) {};
  public void dragOver(DragSourceDragEvent event) {};
  public void dropActionChanged(DragSourceDragEvent event) {};
  public void dragDropEnd(DragSourceDropEvent event) {};
}
```

The dragGestureRecognized() method defined here selects an appropriate nodrop cursor based on the operation type. A nodrop cursor is chosen because it's standard practice to prevent the drop from occurring until after the cursor exits the display area of the component being dragged. Stated more simply, you must move the data somewhere before you can drop it.

The second parameter passed to startDrag() in the above code is an instance of the LabelSelection class that was defined earlier. That class implements Transferable and maintains a reference to the JLabel that will be dragged.

Finally, startDrag() is passed as a reference to a DragSourceListener that can be used to track the drag operation. In most cases, it's possible to use a single DragSourceListener for all of the DragGestureRecognizers since only a single drag and drop operation can be in progress at any given time.

We've now done everything that's necessary to begin the drag operation. At this point, all that's left to do is to handle the drop, and most of the code necessary to do so is similar to code we've already written. In fact, we'll simply add another block of code to the existing drop() method so that it can process Transferable instances that encapsulate labels:

```
public void drop(DropTargetDropEvent event) {
  if (event.isDataFlavorSupported(DataFlavor.javaFileListFlavor)) {
    try {
      event.acceptDrop(DnDConstants.ACTION_COPY);
      Transferable t = event.getTransferable();
      java.util.List list = (java.util.List)
              (t.getTransferData(DataFlavor.javaFileListFlavor));
      java.util.Iterator i = list.iterator();
      while (i.hasNext()) {
        JLabel label = getLabelFromFile((File)(i.next()));
        addNewComponent(label, event.getLocation());
      }
      event.dropComplete(true);
```

```
        } catch (Exception e) {
          event.dropComplete(false);
        }
      else if (event.isDataFlavorSupported(LABEL_FLAVOR))
      try {
        event.acceptDrop(DnDConstants.ACTION_MOVE);
        Transferable t = event.getTransferable();
        JLabel label = (JLabel)(t.getTransferData(LABEL_FLAVOR));
        addNewComponent(label, event.getLocation());
        event.dropComplete(true);
      } catch (Exception e) {
        event.dropComplete(false);
      }
    }
  }
```

As you may recall, the original implementation of MyDropListener's dragEnter() method rejects drags when the data cannot be accessed using javaFileListFlavor. However, since we now also provide support for LABEL_FLAVOR, the dragEnter() method should be modified to allow that flavor as well:

```
class MyDropListener implements DropTargetListener {

  public void dragEnter(DropTargetDragEvent event) {
    if ((event.isDataFlavorSupported(
        DataFlavor.javaFileListFlavor)) ||
        (event.isDataFlavorSupported(
        LABEL_FLAVOR))) {
      return;
    }
    event.rejectDrag();
  }
```

At this point, ImageViewer supports both drag and drop operations, although if you execute the application in its current state, you'll see that something is still missing. Each time you drag and drop a JLabel, the original remains intact and a duplicate of it appears at the drop location:

This occurs in spite of the fact that the move operation is selected by the drop target, and to understand why this happens, it's necessary to understand why the object serialization facility is used to transfer Java objects.

An object reference is only meaningful within the Java Virtual Machine in which it exists, so an object can't really be moved when data is dragged from one JVM instance and dropped onto another. However, it is possible to create a *copy* of an object by sending a representation of it to the target JVM, which can then create a duplicate. That's exactly what Java's object serialization provides, and is the reason why it's necessary for the drag source to delete the original JLabel. Serialized objects are never really moved but are copied; so to simulate a move in a drag and drop operation, the original object must be deleted after its copy is created.

Later we'll see how you can transfer an object reference when a drag and drop operation occurs within a single JVM instance. However, any time you use a DataFlavor with a MIME type of application/x-java-serialized-object, your drop target receives a copy of the original object instead of a reference to it.

We've now established why the drag source in ImageViewer must delete the original label after it's dropped, but we have not yet implemented any code to do so. To identify the appropriate place for that logic, it's necessary to be familiar with the DragSourceListener interface, its methods, and the event objects passed to those methods.

DragSourceListener

The drag source has two primary responsibilities: removing the source data from its previous location in a move operation, and providing **drag over effects**. As you may recall, *drag under* effects are provided by the drop target and are used to modify the appearance of the drop component. In contrast, *drag over* effects are related to the cursor's appearance and are provided by the drag source. For example, when a drag occurs over a component that cannot accept a drop, the drag source is responsible for displaying a nodrop cursor.

You won't normally find it necessary to provide drag over effects because in most cases the appropriate cursor appears automatically. If you move the cursor over a component that's not able to accept the drop or if a drag is rejected, a nodrop cursor appears. However, there may be cases where you wish to customize the appearance of the cursor so that it's different from what is displayed by default.

To change the cursor, you must obtain a reference to the DragSourceContext using the getDragSourceContext() defined in DragSourceEvent and inherited by its subclasses. Once you have a DragSourceContext reference, you can call the setCursor() method as shown below:

```
public void dragOver(DragSourceDragEvent event) {
   //  Normally some condition logic would go here
   DragSourceContext dsc = event.getDragSourceContext();
   dsc.setCursor(DragSource.DefaultCopyNoDrop);
}
```

Now that we've seen what the DragSourceListener interface is responsible for, we'll examine each of the methods it defines.

dragEnter()

This method is called when the cursor enters the display area of a drop component, and you may remember that a method by this same name is defined in the DropTargetListener interface. When the cursor enters a drop component's display area, the drop target's dragEnter() method is called first, followed by that of the drag source. However, that latter call only occurs if the first drop target's dragEnter() method does not reject the drag operation.

dragOver()

This method is called when the cursor is moved after it has previously entered the drop component's display area. There is a method by the same name as this one defined in `DropTargetListener`, and this one is called only after that one has executed. In other words, `dragOver()` is first called for the drop target, and then for the drag source. However, if the drop target rejects the operation, the drag source's method is not called.

dragExit()

This method is called when the cursor exits the display area of a drop component.

dropActionChanged()

A call to `dropActionChanged()` indicates that the status of a modifier used to select the drop action (for example, the *Ctrl* or *Shift* key) has changed. There is a method by the same name as this one defined in `DropTargetListener`, and this one is called only after that one has executed. In other words, `dropActionChanged()` is first called for the drop target, and then for the drag source. However, if the drop target rejects the operation, the drag source's method is not called.

dragDropEnd()

After a drop has occurred and the `DropTargetListener`'s `drop()` method is invoked, `dragDropEnd()` is called to notify the drag source that the drop has completed. As you'll see shortly, the event object passed to this method allows it to determine the type of operation selected by the drop target and to determine the value specified when the drop target called `dropComplete()`. In other words, this method can determine whether the drop completed successfully.

Since this method is called once the drop has completed and because it allows you to determine the final status of the operation, you should use `dragDropEnd()` to perform the `DragSourceListener`'s cleanup-related tasks.

Event Objects Passed to DragSourceListener Methods

Now that we've covered the methods defined by `DragSourceListener`, it's appropriate to examine the event objects passed to those methods.

DragSourceEvent

This is the superclass of the `DragSourceDragEvent` and `DragSourceDropEvent` classes defined below. However, `DragSourceEvent` does not provide any methods that you'll use.

DragSourceDragEvent

An instance of `DragSourceDragEvent` class is passed to the `dragEnter()`, `dragOver()`, and `dropActionChanged()` methods. Unlike a drop target, a drag source cannot accept or reject a drag, so the methods provided by this event object are purely informational.

getTargetActions()

This method identifies the intersection of the actions supported by the drag source and those supported by the drop target. For example, suppose that the drag source supports move, copy, and link operations but the drop target supports only move and link. In that case, the value returned by `getTargetActions()` would equal the combined values of the `ACTION_MOVE` and `ACTION_LINK` constants. In other words, this method identifies the operations that both the drag source and the drop target support.

getUserAction()

The operation requested by the user is identified by this method, and is based on the current state of the modifier keys and buttons.

getDropAction()

This identifies the **effective drop action**, which is defined as the intersection of the target actions and the current user action. If the user has selected an action that the drag source or the drop target does not support, this value will be equal to the ACTION_NONE constant defined in DnDConstants.

getGestureModifiers()

You can use this method to determine the state of the modifiers that determine the type of operation requested. For example, this value identifies the state of the mouse buttons, Shift, Alt, and Ctrl keys. For more information on how to interpret the value returned by this method, see the modifier constants defined in java.awt.event.InputEvent.

DragSourceDropEvent

An instance of this class is passed to dragDropEnd(), which is called after the drop has been processed by the drop target.

getDropAction()

You can use this method to determine which operation the drop target selected. In other words, this identifies the action specified when the DropTargetListener's drop() method called acceptDrop().

You'll normally use this value to determine what action your DragSourceListener should take. If a move operation was selected, the data that was dropped usually must be removed from its original location by the drag source.

getDropSuccess()

While the getDropAction() method identifies the action selected by the drop target, this method provides an indication of the value specified by the target when dropComplete() was called. In other words, this method returns a value of true if the drop completed successfully or false otherwise.

Drag Source Handling of Drop Completion

Now that we've reviewed the events and methods associated with DragSourceListener, it should be obvious how to fix the problem with ImageViewer that was identified earlier. When a JLabel is moved, the drag source is responsible for removing the label from its original location, and that should be done in the dragDropEnd() method.

The modifications to dragDropEnd() are highlighted below. Note that most of the cleanup performed in that method is dependent upon both the successful completion of the drop and the type of operation selected by the drop target. If the target selects an operation other than ACTION_MOVE, the original JLabel component will not be removed:

```
class MySourceListener implements DragSourceListener {

    public void dragEnter(DragSourceDragEvent event) {};
    public void dragExit(DragSourceEvent event) {};
```

```
      public void dragOver(DragSourceDragEvent event) {};
      public void dropActionChanged(DragSourceDragEvent event) {};

      public void dragDropEnd(DragSourceDropEvent event) {
        if ((event.getDropSuccess())
              && (event.getDropAction() == DnDConstants.ACTION_MOVE)) {
          remove(draggedComponent);
          repaint();
        }
        draggedComponent = null;
      }
    }
```

Local Transfers

When dragging and dropping Java objects, as `ImageViewer` now allows us to do, there are two categories of transfer operations. In a **local transfer**, the drag source and drop target (and the data transferred) reside in a single Java Virtual Machine instance, while a **remote transfer** involves moving data from one JVM instance to a different one.

The `DataFlavor` used by `ImageViewer` has a representation class of `JLabel` and its MIME type defaults to `application/x-java-serialized-object`. As mentioned earlier, using that MIME type always results in the drop target receiving a *copy* of the original object instead of a reference to it, even in a local transfer. However, it is sometimes desirable in local transfers to pass a reference to the original data instead of a copy. For example, you might wish to do so if the data can't be serialized or if you want to improve the performance of local transfers, since serialization can be relatively slow. To illustrate how to pass object references, `ImageViewer` will now be modified to do so when a local transfer takes place.

Local Object Data Flavors

To perform reference transfers, you must define a `DataFlavor` that has a representation class corresponding to the type of object to be transferred, which in this case is `JLabel`. In addition, the flavor's MIME type should be set to the `javaJVMLocalObjectMimeType` string constant defined in `DataFlavor`. However, it may not be immediately obvious how to create a flavor that fulfills these two requirements.

We saw earlier that `DataFlavor` provides two types of constructors: one that allows you to specify the flavor's MIME type, and another that allows you to identify its representation class. In this case, we want to specify both items, but there does not appear to be a constructor that allows us to do so. In addition, there are no mutator methods for either the MIME type or the representation class, so it's not possible to modify those values after construction.

In fact, it is possible to specify both values using the `DataFlavor` constructor that accepts a MIME type `String`. This can be done by specifying the representation class as a parameter that's appended to the MIME type, as shown below:

```
    public class ImageViewer extends JPanel {

      public final static DataFlavor LABEL_FLAVOR =
        new DataFlavor(JLabel.class, "Label Instances");
```

```
public final static DataFlavor LOCAL_LABEL_FLAVOR = new DataFlavor(
    DataFlavor.javaJVMLocalObjectMimeType +
    "; class=javax.swing.JLabel", "Local Label");
```

The LOCAL_LABEL_FLAVOR will be created with a MIME type of application/x-java-jvm-local-objectref (the value stored in javaJVMLocalObjectMimeType), a representation class of JLabel, and a human-readable name of 'Local Label'.

Since this new DataFlavor will be used with LabelSelection to transfer JLabel references, it's necessary to update LabelSelection appropriately. In addition to adding LOCAL_LABEL_FLAVOR to the list of flavors supported by LabelSelection, a block of code must be created in getTransferData():

```
class LabelSelection implements Transferable {

  private DataFlavor[] flavors = {LABEL_FLAVOR, LOCAL_LABEL_FLAVOR};

  protected JLabel label;

  public LabelSelection(JLabel lbl) {
    label = lbl;
  }

  public DataFlavor[] getTransferDataFlavors() {
    return flavors;
  }

  public boolean isDataFlavorSupported(DataFlavor flavor) {
    for (int i = 0; i < flavors.length; i++) {
      if (flavors[i].equals(flavor)) return true;
    }
    return false;
  }

  public Object getTransferData(DataFlavor flavor) throws
      UnsupportedFlavorException, IOException {
    if (flavor.equals(LABEL_FLAVOR)) {
      return label;
    }
    else if (flavor.equals(LOCAL_LABEL_FLAVOR)) {
      return label;
    }
    throw new UnsupportedFlavorException(flavor);
  }
```

It may seem strange that the code in getTransferData() is the same for LABEL_FLAVOR and LOCAL_LABEL_FLAVOR. After all, LABEL_FLAVOR is used to retrieve a serialized copy of the object, while LOCAL_LABEL_FLAVOR is intended to provide a reference to the original object. The reason that this code will work as expected is that Java's drag and drop facility treats the application/x-java-serialized-object MIME type used by LABEL_FLAVOR as a special case. When data is retrieved using that type, the drag and drop facility ensures that a serialized copy of the object is returned, *even in a local transfer*.

In other words, if you use application/x-java-serialized-object, you *always* get a copy of the data and never a reference to the original when calling getTransferData(). In contrast, when other MIME types are used (e.g., LOCAL_LABEL_FLAVOR), no special processing occurs and getTransferData() is allowed to return a reference to the original object.

Handling the Reference Transfer

Now that we've defined a DataFlavor for transferring object references and added support for it to the Transferable implementation, it's easy to modify ImageViewer to support reference transfers. All that's needed is a change to the drop() method so that it uses the new LOCAL_LABEL_FLAVOR when possible:

```
public void drop(DropTargetDropEvent event) {
  if (event.isDataFlavorSupported(DataFlavor.javaFileListFlavor)) {
    try {
      event.acceptDrop(DnDConstants.ACTION_COPY);
      Transferable t = event.getTransferable();
      java.util.List list = (java.util.List)
            (t.getTransferData(DataFlavor.javaFileListFlavor));
      java.util.Iterator i = list.iterator();
      while (i.hasNext()) {
        JLabel label = getLabelFromFile((File)(i.next()));
        addNewComponent(label, event.getLocation());
      }
      event.dropComplete(true);
    } catch (Exception e) {
      event.dropComplete(false);
    }
  } else if (event.isDataFlavorSupported(LABEL_FLAVOR)) {
    try {
      event.acceptDrop(DnDConstants.ACTION_MOVE);
      Transferable t = event.getTransferable();
      boolean doLocal = (event.isLocalTransfer() &&
          (t.isDataFlavorSupported(LOCAL_LABEL_FLAVOR)));
      DataFlavor flavor = (doLocal ? LOCAL_LABEL_FLAVOR : LABEL_FLAVOR);
      JLabel label = (JLabel)(t.getTransferData(flavor));
      addNewComponent(label, event.getLocation());
      event.dropComplete(true);
    } catch (Exception e) {
      event.dropComplete(false);
    }
  }
}
```

Potential Problem Areas

Several changes have now been made to ImageViewer that should allow it to correctly process reference transfers. However, if you run the application and try to drag and drop JLabel instances within a single ImageViewer application, you may be surprised by the results. Instead of moving to the drop location, the labels disappear from the panel when they are dropped.

You may recall that the DropTargetListener's drop() method is called when the drop occurs, and that method adds the label that's dropped to the ImageViewer container. Once drop() has executed, the DragSourceListener's dragDropEnd() method is called to allow the drag source to remove the original data as shown below:

```
public void dragDropEnd(DragSourceDropEvent event) {
  if ((event.getDropSuccess()) &&
```

```
        (event.getDropAction() ==
        DnDConstants.ACTION_MOVE)) {
    remove(draggedComponent);
    repaint();
  }
  draggedComponent = null;
}
```

In this case, the drop target adds the dropped label to its new container and the drag source removes it from its old container. In a local transfer using ImageViewer, the "old" and "new" containers are actually the same object, but that fact isn't relevant to the problem. What is important, however, is the order in which the drag source and drop target processing takes place.

Since drop() is called before dragDropEnd(), the component is added to its new container before being removed from the old one. When it is added, logic in the java.awt.Container class causes the label to be removed from its old container, which is done to ensure that a Component can only ever reside within a single parent container at any given time. After drop() completes, dragDropEnd() is called, and being unaware that the label was already removed from its old container, proceeds to remove the component from its container. The result of this second removal is the effective deletion of the label, since no more references to it exist.

It might seem that one way to address this problem it is to have the drag source determine the type of transfer (local or remote) and handle the drop differently for each type. For example, the drag source could be designed so that it does not remove the JLabel from its parent container when a local transfer takes place. Unfortunately, the DragSourceDropEvent object passed to dragDropEnd() provides just two items of information: the type of operation selected by the drop target, and an indication of the success or failure of the transfer. Therefore, a drag source cannot distinguish local transfers from remote transfers.

On the other hand, the drop target *can* distinguish between local and remote transfers, and that capability provides a solution to this problem. Since the drag source only removes the label from its old container when a move occurs, we can address the problem by changing the drop target so that it selects an operation other than move.

Link/Reference Operations

It has been mentioned that Java"s drag and drop support defines a link or reference operation in addition to move and copy. However, the purpose of the link/reference operation may not be obvious, since there is no consistent meaning associated with the terms "link" or "reference." Although, "move" and "copy" mean the same thing on all platforms, Windows may define a "reference" operation that"s completely different from the Solaris "reference" operation.

Since the meaning of the reference operation is vague, you should not use it to drag and drop data between Java and native applications. However, when transferring data between Java applications, the link/reference operation has been assigned a very specific meaning. In the context of a local transfer, the reference operation is used to transfer a reference to some object, just as ImageViewer is now capable of doing. Similarly, when you are performing remote transfers between Java applications, the data that's transferred should be some representation of the original object but not a copy of it. For example, you might pass a reference to a remote object defined using Java's Remote Method Invocation (RMI) facilities if the data that's being dragged represents some remote resource.

Given this definition of the reference operation, we can make a small change to ImageViewer that accomplishes two things. First, it correctly identifies a local transfer within ImageViewer as a reference operation instead of a move. Second, it prevents the drag source from incorrectly deleting the component that's dragged in a local transfer:

```java
public void drop(DropTargetDropEvent event) {
  if (event.isDataFlavorSupported(DataFlavor.javaFileListFlavor)) {
    try {
      event.acceptDrop(DnDConstants.ACTION_COPY);
      Transferable t = event.getTransferable();
      java.util.List list = (java.util.List)
              (t.getTransferData(DataFlavor.javaFileListFlavor));
      java.util.Iterator i = list.iterator();
      while (i.hasNext()) {
        JLabel label = getLabelFromFile((File)(i.next()));
        addNewComponent(label, event.getLocation());
      }
      event.dropComplete(true);
    } catch (Exception e) {
      event.dropComplete(false);
    }
  } else if (event.isDataFlavorSupported(LABEL_FLAVOR)) {
    try {
      int operation = (event.isLocalTransfer()
                       ? DnDConstants.ACTION_REFERENCE
                       : DnDConstants.ACTION_MOVE);
      event.acceptDrop(operation);
      Transferable t = event.getTransferable();
      boolean doLocal = (event.isLocalTransfer() &&
          (t.isDataFlavorSupported(LOCAL_LABEL_FLAVOR)));
      DataFlavor flavor = (doLocal ? LOCAL_LABEL_FLAVOR : LABEL_FLAVOR);
      JLabel label = (JLabel)(t.getTransferData(flavor));
      addNewComponent(label, event.getLocation());
      event.dropComplete(true);
    } catch (Exception e) {
      event.dropComplete(false);
    }
  }
}
```

Local transfers have other implications that you must consider as well, including how to support the copy operation. That operation is easy to support in a remote transfer, because the drop target always receives a copy of the data, but for local transfers, there must be some way to create a copy of the data that's dropped. Some classes simplify this for you by overriding the clone() method defined in java.lang.Object, but many (including JLabel) do not.

Advanced Drop Support

Adding drop support to ImageViewer required very little effort, partly due to the simplicity of its behavior. However, we'll now create a JTable subclass called DropTable that provides support for drag under effects and automatic scrolling. It will be possible to drag a JLabel instance from ImageViewer and drop it onto a DropTable, at which time the table will extract the label's icon and display that icon in the table cell underneath the cursor.

The initial implementation of the DropTable is shown below. The table contains 5 columns and 15 rows, but initially does not display any data:

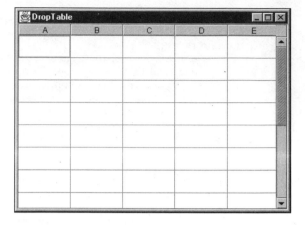

A large portion of its code is contained within the drop() method, which is similar to the drop() implementation found in ImageViewer:

```java
import java.awt.*;
import java.awt.datatransfer.*;
import java.awt.dnd.*;
import javax.swing.*;
import javax.swing.event.*;
import javax.swing.table.*;

public class DropTable extends JTable {

  public final static DataFlavor LABEL_FLAVOR =
      new DataFlavor(JLabel.class, "JLabel Instances");

  public static void main(String[] args) {
    JFrame f = new JFrame("DropTable");
    f.setDefaultCloseOperation(JFrame.EXIT_ON_CLOSE);
    f.getContentPane().add(new JScrollPane(new DropTable()));
    f.setSize(400, 300);
    f.setVisible(true);
  }

  public DropTable() {
    super();
    setModel(new DefaultTableModel(15, 5) {
      public Class getColumnClass(int column) {
        return ImageIcon.class;
      }
    });
    setCellSelectionEnabled(true);
    setAutoResizeMode(JTable.AUTO_RESIZE_OFF);
    setRowHeight(32);
    new DropTarget(this, DnDConstants.ACTION_MOVE,
        new DropTableListener());
  }

  class DropTableListener implements DropTargetListener {
```

```java
      public void dragEnter(DropTargetDragEvent event) {
      }

      public void dragOver(DropTargetDragEvent event) {
      }

      public void dragExit(DropTargetEvent event) {
      }

      public void dropActionChanged(DropTargetDragEvent event) {};

      public void drop(DropTargetDropEvent event) {
        Point p = event.getLocation();
        int row = rowAtPoint(p);
        int column = columnAtPoint(p);
        if (event.isDataFlavorSupported(LABEL_FLAVOR)) {
          event.acceptDrop(DnDConstants.ACTION_MOVE);
          try {
            Transferable t = event.getTransferable();
            JLabel label = (JLabel)(t.getTransferData(
                ImageViewer.LABEL_FLAVOR));
            ImageIcon icon = (ImageIcon)(
                label.getIcon());
            setValueAt(icon, row, column);
          } catch (Exception e) {
            event.dropComplete(false);
            return;
          }
          event.dropComplete(true);
          tableChanged(new TableModelEvent(getModel()));
        }
        else {
          event.rejectDrop();
        }
      }
    }
  }
```

To use this class, you must first execute the ImageViewer application in a separate Java Virtual Machine
and use the Windows Explorer (or an equivalent application) to drop some images onto the frame created by
ImageViewer. You should recall that ImageViewer is both a drag source and a drop target, which means
that after you have dropped an image onto it, you can drag that same image from the ImageViewer frame
and drop it somewhere else, such as into the DropTable window.

In the screen shot below, three separate GIF files were dropped onto the ImageViewer window, and
one of them was then dragged from that window and dropped into the first row of the middle column of
the DropTable:

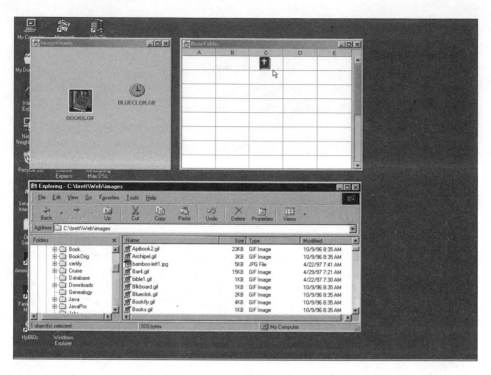

Now that the basic functionality needed is present, we'll make some improvements to the `DropTable` class. The first enhancement we'll make to this class is the addition of drag under effects, which are provided by highlighting the cell underneath the cursor as data is dragged across the table:

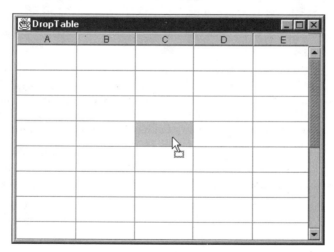

This is accomplished by selecting the cell when `dragEnter()` and `dragOver()` are called. In addition, `JTable`'s `clearSelection()` method is invoked from `dragExit()` to discontinue drag under effects when the cursor exits the table's display area:

```
protected void displayDragUnderEffects(Point p) {
    int row = rowAtPoint(p);
```

```
        int column = columnAtPoint(p);
        setRowSelectionInterval(row, row);
        setColumnSelectionInterval(column, column);
        repaint();
    }

    class DropTableListener implements DropTargetListener {

      public void dragEnter(DropTargetDragEvent event) {
        displayDragUnderEffects(event.getLocation());
      }

      public void dragOver(DropTargetDragEvent event) {
        displayDragUnderEffects(event.getLocation());
      }

      public void dragExit(DropTargetEvent event) {
        clearSelection();
      }
```

Next, we'll modify the code so that drops are accepted only when the cursor is over the middle ("C") table column. That's done by defining a constant that identifies the valid drop column and comparing the constant to the cursor's column location when the drop occurs:

```
import java.awt.*;
import java.awt.datatransfer.*;
import java.awt.dnd.*;
import javax.swing.*;
import javax.swing.event.*;
import javax.swing.table.*;

public class DropTable extends JTable {

    public final static DataFlavor LABEL_FLAVOR =
        new DataFlavor(JLabel.class, "JLabel Instances");

    public final static int DROP_COLUMN = 2;

    public static void main(String[] args) {
      JFrame f = new JFrame("DropTable");
      f.setDefaultCloseOperation(JFrame.EXIT_ON_CLOSE);
      f.getContentPane().add(new JScrollPane(new DropTable()));
      f.setSize(400, 300);
      f.setVisible(true);
    }

    public DropTable() {
      super(new DefaultTableModel(15, 5) {
        public Class getColumnClass(int column) {
          return ImageIcon.class;
        }
      });
      setCellSelectionEnabled(true);
      setAutoResizeMode(JTable.AUTO_RESIZE_OFF);
      setRowHeight(32);
```

```
      new DropTarget(this, DnDConstants.ACTION_MOVE,
          new DropTableListener());
  }

  protected void displayDragUnderEffects(Point p) {
    int row = rowAtPoint(p);
    int column = columnAtPoint(p);
    setRowSelectionInterval(row, row);
    setColumnSelectionInterval(column, column);
    repaint();
  }

  class DropTableListener implements DropTargetListener {

    public void dragEnter(DropTargetDragEvent event) {
      displayDragUnderEffects(event.getLocation());
    }

    public void dragOver(DropTargetDragEvent event) {
      displayDragUnderEffects(event.getLocation());
    }

    public void dragExit(DropTargetEvent event) {
      clearSelection();
    }

    public void dropActionChanged(DropTargetDragEvent event) {};

    public void drop(DropTargetDropEvent event) {
      Point p = event.getLocation();
      int row = rowAtPoint(p);
      int column = columnAtPoint(p);
      if ((event.isDataFlavorSupported(LABEL_FLAVOR)) &&
          (column == DROP_COLUMN)) {
        event.acceptDrop(DnDConstants.ACTION_MOVE);
        try {
          Transferable t = event.getTransferable();
          JLabel label = (JLabel)(t.getTransferData(
              ImageViewer.LABEL_FLAVOR));
          ImageIcon icon = (ImageIcon)(
              label.getIcon());
          setValueAt(icon, row, column);
        } catch (Exception e) {
          event.dropComplete(false);
          return;
        }
        event.dropComplete(true);
        tableChanged(new TableModelEvent(getModel()));
      }
      else {
        event.rejectDrop();
      }
    }
  }
}
```

Although this code does prevent data from being dropped on the outer columns, there is one problem with it. Specifically, while the data is being dragged over those outer columns, there is no visual indication that a drop cannot be performed. Instead, the drop cursor is always displayed while the cursor is over the table, even when it's over a column that cannot accept a drop:

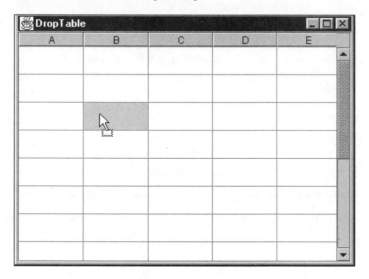

Instead of simply ignoring drops as the above code does, a better approach is to reject a drag operation that occurs over an invalid column. Not only will that cause the cursor to change to a nodrop cursor, but it will also prevent the drop() method from being called when the cursor is dragged over the outer columns. We can also use this opportunity to ensure that the data being dragged is in fact a JLabel and to reject the drag if that's not the case:

```
protected void handleDrag(DropTargetDragEvent event) {
  int column = columnAtPoint(event.getLocation());
  if ((column != DROP_COLUMN) || (!(
      event.isDataFlavorSupported(
      LABEL_FLAVOR)))) {
    event.rejectDrag();
  }
}

class DropTableListener implements DropTargetListener {

  public void dragEnter(DropTargetDragEvent event) {
    displayDragUnderEffects(event.getLocation());
    handleDrag(event);
  }

  public void dragOver(DropTargetDragEvent event) {
    displayDragUnderEffects(event.getLocation());
    handleDrag(event);
  }
```

DropTable will now reject drag events that occur over the outer columns, but a new problem has been introduced. Once a drag has been rejected, the user will be unable to complete a drop in that session, even after the cursor is moved to the center column:

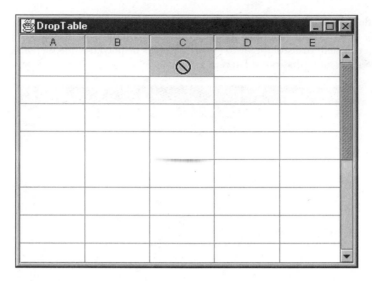

To address this problem, drag events that occur over the center column must be accepted to re-enable drops, as shown below:

```
protected void handleDrag(DropTargetDragEvent event) {
   int column = columnAtPoint(event.getLocation());
   if ((column != DROP_COLUMN) || (!(
       event.isDataFlavorSupported(
       LABEL_FLAVOR)))) {
     event.rejectDrag();
   }
   else {
     event.acceptDrag(DnDConstants.ACTION_MOVE);
   }
}
```

Autoscrolling

There is one final enhancement that needs to be made to DropTable. As is often the case, this application's JTable is displayed inside a JScrollPane that allows only a portion of the table's rows to be displayed at any given time. When the DropTable is first displayed, for example, a handful of the top rows are displayed, and you must use the scrollbar to adjust the viewport position before you can view the bottom rows. Adjusting the viewport position is normally done by dragging the scrollbar knobs or clicking on the arrow buttons, but neither of these is possible while you're performing a drag operation.

In theory, you should be able to drag and drop a label into any row in a DropTable, but in practice, you currently can only drop the label on a row that was already visible when the drag operation started. Fortunately, Java's drag and drop facility includes support for a feature called **autoscrolling** that allows you to scroll components while dragging data over them.

> *Note that Java's autoscroll facility does not perform the scrolling for you, but it does provide the events and information that you need to have your application do so.*

Autoscroll Support

To support autoscrolling, your drop component must implement the `java.dnd.Autoscroll` interface and provide the appropriate behavior for the two methods it defines. When those methods are implemented correctly, you can cause a component such as a `JTable` to scroll by moving the cursor to the visible edge of the component. For example, to make a `DropTable` scroll downward, you would move the cursor close to the bottom visible portion of the table:

Once you've made the following change to `DropTable`, you should implement the `getAutoscrollInsets()` and `autoscroll()` methods.

```
public class DropTable extends JTable implements Autoscroll {
```

getAutoscrollInsets()

You must return an instance of `java.awt.Insets` from this method, and those insets define the autoscroll areas of the component. The `Insets` class encapsulates four values that are used to define a border area, which in this case defines the area in which the cursor must appear to generate an autoscroll event. The four values passed to the `Insets` constructor indicate the size of the area relative to the top, left, bottom, and right edges of the container (in that order). The following code segment illustrates how to create an instance of Insets that has borders of 10, 20, 30, and 40 pixels on a container's top, left, bottom, and right edges, respectively:

```
Insets myInsets = new Insets(10, 20, 30, 40);
```

By creating an instance of `Insets` and returning it from this method, you are identifying the portion of the component that should cause autoscroll events to be generated. When the cursor lingers over an autoscroll area during a drag operation, Java automatically calls your `autoscroll()` method to indicate that you should adjust the position of the viewport:

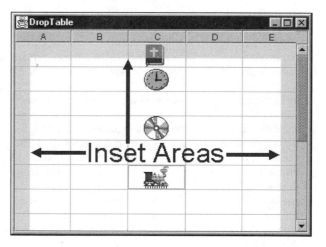

The shaded areas illustrate the inset areas that will be active if you provide inset values of 20 pixels on each side of the `JTable` using code similar to the following:

```
public Insets getAutoscrollInsets() {
   return new Insets(20, 20, 20, 20);
}
```

Adjusting Insets

Notice that there is no shaded area at the bottom of the table, since the bottom autoscroll area is not visible. As that area is defined as the twenty rows of pixels adjacent to the table's bottom edge, the scrollable area is inaccessible when the top of the table is displayed:

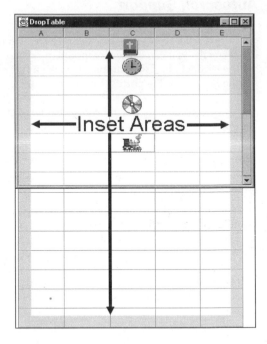

Since the whole point of autoscrolling is to *make* other portions of the table accessible, the insets should always be set so that some portion of the autoscroll area on each side of the table is always visible. Instead of using fixed values as is done in the above code segment, you should design your `getAutoscrollInsets()` method to dynamically increase and decrease the size of the autoscroll insets based on the position of the viewport.

For example, suppose that you wish to have a bottom autoscroll area that's twenty pixels in height and that you want the bottom autoscroll area to always be visible, regardless of the viewport's position. To accomplish that, you must calculate the number of pixels rows that are not visible because they're "below" the viewport, add twenty to that value, and use the result as your bottom autoscroll inset value. In other words, when the top of the table is displayed, you must make the bottom autoscroll inset value very large so that it "overflows" into the displayed area:

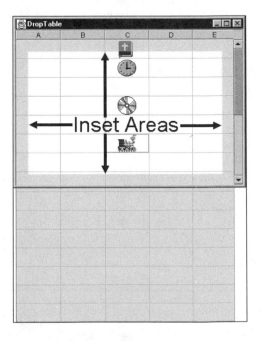

To determine how much of the table component is below the viewport area, you must obtain a reference to the table's `JViewport` parent container, which can easily be done using the static `getAncestorOfClass()` method in `SwingUtilities`. The following method returns a `Rectangle` instance that identifies the size and coordinates of the viewport rectangle:

```
protected Rectangle getTableRect() {
   JViewport jvp = (JViewport)(SwingUtilities.getAncestorOfClass(
      JViewport.class, this));
   return (jvp == null ? null : jvp.getViewRect());
}
```

By determining the viewport's size and position relative to the `JTable`, we can easily calculate how large the autoscroll insets should be. For example, to create a 20-pixel autoscroll inset area at the top of the table, you can simply add 20 to the Y position of the viewport. The other inset values can be similarly calculated using the table size and the viewport information as shown below:

```
public Insets getAutoscrollInsets() {
   Insets insets = new Insets(0, 0, 0, 0);
   Rectangle rect = getTableRect();
   if (rect != null) {
      insets.top = rect.y + 20;
      insets.left = rect.x + 20;
      insets.bottom = getHeight() - (rect.y + rect.height) + 20;
      insets.right = getWidth() - (rect.x + rect.width) + 20;
   }
   return insets;
}
```

autoscroll()

This method is called at regular intervals when Java's drag and drop facility detects that the cursor has lingered over an autoscroll area during a drag operation. In other words, a call to this method represents a notification to your application that it may need to scroll the component by adjusting the viewport position.

An instance of `Point` is passed as an argument to `autoscroll()`, and that parameter identifies the cursor's position relative to the component origin. You can use the cursor position to determine which component edge(s) the cursor is near, which in turn identifies the direction(s) in which to scroll the component.

In addition to the scroll direction, you must also determine how many pixels the viewport should move in that direction. That value will depend on the type of component and the size of the elements it contains. For example, when scrolling a `JTable` horizontally, you will normally want to scroll the table one column at a time, while each vertical scroll operation should move the table up or down a row. Therefore, to scroll a table, your code must determine how many pixels are in a row or column. Fortunately, it's easy to do so for the components that you'll scroll most often, such as `JTable`, `JTree`, and `JList`, because those classes all implement the `javax.swing.Scrollable` interface. One of the methods defined in `Scrollable` is `getScrollableUnitIncrement()`, which returns a value representing the number of pixels in a "unit" (that is, a row or column).

Once you've determined how many pixels to move the viewport, you must calculate its new position and modify it appropriately, although you should not perform that modification from the thread that calls `autoscroll()`. In an earlier chapter, we saw that Swing components are not inherently thread-safe, and because of that, you should defer component changes to the event dispatching thread. This can be done easily using the `invokeAndWait()` and `invokeLater()` methods defined in `SwingUtilities`, which causes the event dispatching thread to execute the `Runnable` implementation of the object you use as a parameter.

In the case of `DropTable`, `autoscroll()` is allowed to calculate the viewport's new position, but it does not reposition the component. Instead, the new position value is stored in a field called `viewLocation` that is an instance of `Point`:

```
public class DropTable extends JTable implements Autoscroll {

  public final static DataFlavor LABEL_FLAVOR =
      new DataFlavor(JLabel.class, "JLabel Instances");

  public final static int DROP_COLUMN = 2;

  protected Point viewLocation;
```

When the new viewport position has been selected, `scheduleViewportUpdate()` is called to create a request for the event dispatch thread that will cause it to modify the viewport location. The method providing that functionality is shown below:

```
protected void scheduleViewportUpdate() {
   SwingUtilities.invokeLater(new Runnable() {
     public void run() {
       JScrollBar scrollBar;
       Point p;
       synchronized (this) {
         p = viewLocation;
       }
       JScrollPane jsp = (JScrollPane)(
             SwingUtilities.getAncestorOfClass(
             JScrollPane.class, DropTable.this));
// Due to an apparent painting problem in JTable, we'll use the somewhat
// unusual technique of modifying the scrollbar values instead of setting
// the viewport's position.
//       JViewport jvp = jsp.getViewport();
//       jvp.setViewPosition(p);
       scrollBar = jsp.getHorizontalScrollBar();
       scrollBar.setValue(p.x);
       scrollBar = jsp.getVerticalScrollBar();
       scrollBar.setValue(p.y);
     }
   });
 }
```

Finally, the `autoscroll()` method must be implemented. It uses the `Point` parameter value to determine the scrolling direction(s), calculates the viewport's new position, and calls `scheduleViewportUpdate()` so that the event dispatch thread will perform the scrolling:

```
public synchronized void autoscroll(Point p) {
   int offset;
   Insets insets = getAutoscrollInsets();
   Rectangle rect = getTableRect();
   JViewport jvp = (JViewport)(SwingUtilities.getAncestorOfClass(
       JViewport.class, this));
   if (jvp != null) {
     Point oldLocation = jvp.getViewPosition();
     if (p.y < insets.top) {
       offset = getScrollableUnitIncrement(rect,
```

```
                    SwingConstants.VERTICAL, -1);
        viewLocation = new Point(oldLocation.x,
            oldLocation.y - offset);
    }
    if (p.x < insets.left) {
      offset = getScrollableUnitIncrement(rect,
          SwingConstants.HORIZONTAL, -1);
      viewLocation = new Point(oldLocation.x - offset,
          oldLocation.y);
    }
    if (p.y > getHeight() - insets.bottom) {
      offset = getScrollableUnitIncrement(rect,
          SwingConstants.VERTICAL, 1);
      viewLocation = new Point(oldLocation.x,
          oldLocation.y + offset);
    }
    if (p.x > getWidth() - insets.right) {
      offset = getScrollableUnitIncrement(rect,
          SwingConstants.HORIZONTAL, 1);
      viewLocation = new Point(oldLocation.x + offset,
          oldLocation.y);
    }

    if (!(oldLocation.equals(viewLocation))) {
      scheduleViewportUpdate();
    }
  }
}
```

With this code in place, you can drop a label into any row in a `DropTable` by using its autoscroll capabilities.

Transfers Between Java and Native Applications

We've already seen that it's possible to drop file selections made from a native application into a Java application. Those selections are represented by a `Transferable` that returns an instance of `java.util.List`, and that list contains `java.io.File` objects that identify the files selected. In reality, of course, the native platform doesn't use any Java classes when it allows users to make file selections. However, Java's drag and drop facility automatically converts the native type (for example, `CF_HDROP` on Windows) into a form that your Java application can use easily, just as the clipboard facility does with text data.

In some cases, you may wish to transfer data between a Java application and a native application in a format that is not converted automatically (for example, image data). However, for your application to perform some sort of processing of data dropped from a native application, it usually must convert the information into a more convenient format. For example, if **Device Independent Bitmap (DIB)** data is dragged from a native Windows application and dropped onto your Java program, you'll probably want to convert the information to a more useable format such as an instance of `java.awt.Image`. Similarly, when dragging data from a Java application and dropping onto a native application, it's necessary to provide the information in a format that the native program can process (for example, DIB). In the previous chapter, an application was created that could convert pixel data from an instance of `Image` into a JPEG-compatible byte string using a codec that's provided with the Java 2D API.

Once you're able to perform data conversions, you must complete one other task before you can drag and drop that type of data between Java and native applications. Specifically, you must define the mapping between the MIME type you'll use and the corresponding platform-specific data type, and you define the mapping by adding an entry to the flavormap.properties file. That file is located in the /jre/lib/ subdirectory of your JDK / JRE installation.

If you edit the file, you'll see entries for some of the data types that can already be transferred between Java and native applications, such as file selections (HDROP on Windows) and text. The format for entries in flavormap.properties is:

```
NATIVE=MIME Type
```

Where "NATIVE" is the name of the native data type that you intend to use (for example, HDROP), and "MIME Type" is the MIME type that a compatible DataFlavor encapsulates. For example, to add an entry for DIB data, you could specify the following entry:

```
DIB=image/x-win-bmp; class=java.io.InputStream
```

With this entry added to the file, you will be able to drag and drop DIB information between Java and non-Java applications. When you drop DIB information onto a Java application, it is automatically wrapped in a Transferable that returns an InputStream, and you can use that stream to read the raw DIB data. To support the dragging of DIB data from a Java application to a Windows program, you must first define a DataFlavor that uses the above MIME type, as in the following example:

```
DataFlavor DIBFlavor = new DataFlavor("image/x-win-bmp", "DIB Data");
```

Note that it is not necessary to identify the representation class as InputStream, since the DataFlavor constructor used here selects that value by default.

The next step is to create a Transferable that supports this flavor by returning an InputStream that produces a sequence of bytes conforming to the DIB format. Converting data between the DIB and Java Image formats is a non-trivial exercise, and is beyond the scope of this book.

The FlavorMap Interface

The FlavorMap interface in java.awt.datatransfer is used to define a mapping between native data types and MIME types. A default map is created using the entries in flavormap.properties, and that map is accessible through the SystemFlavorMap class. When performing drag and drop operations, you can specify the map that should be used to translate data types, but if you do not do so, the default map is used instead.

When you drag Transferable data from a Java application and drop it onto a native program, the MIME types that the Transferable supports are extracted from its DataFlavor list. For each MIME type that has a matching entry in the FlavorMap, a corresponding native type is identified to the native application, which uses that information to process the data that's dropped.

A similar conversion takes place when you drag data from a native application and drop it onto a Java program. In that case, Java's drag and drop facility wraps the data from the native application in a Transferable and provides a DataFlavor for each native type corresponding to a MIME type in the FlavorMap.

Text Data Transfers

In the previous chapter on cut and paste operations, we saw that text information can be transferred with minimal effort using the clipboard facility and the `StringSelection` class that implements `Transferable`. Unfortunately, dragging and dropping text information is somewhat more complex.

Before exploring the issues involved in the transfer of text information, let's briefly review `StringSelection`. You may recall that it encapsulates a `String` and is able to return the text in one of two flavors, each of which is represented by a constant in `DataFlavor`. The `stringFlavor` constant has a representation class of `java.lang.String`, a MIME type of `application/x-java-serialized-object`, and represents a serialized `String` object. That flavor can only be used to transfer text between Java applications since a serialized Java object is not meaningful to a native application.

In contrast, the `plainTextFlavor` was specifically intended to provide the ability to transfer text data between Java and native applications and has a representation class of `java.io.InputStream` and a MIME type of `text/plain`. In other words, passing this flavor to a `StringSelection`'s `getTransferData()` method should return an `InputStream` that produces a stream of text data.

Text Transfers Between Java Applications

You can successfully use `StringSelection` to transfer data between Java applications as long as the drop target uses `stringFlavor` when calling `getTransferData()`. However, attempts to use `plainTextFlavor` fail due to a bug in `StringSelection` that causes it to return a `StringReader`. That behavior is incorrect since `plainTextFlavor`'s representation class is `InputStream`, and `StringReader` is not a subclass of `InputStream`.

Text Transfers Between Java and Native Applications

Transferring text data between Java and native applications is more complicated than Java-to-Java transfers, mostly due to the fact that no single character set is used on all platforms, or even by all applications on a single platform. For example, Java applications maintain text information using Unicode, but native applications can and frequently do use other character sets, such as ASCII and ISO 8859-1. Therefore, it's often necessary to perform conversions when transferring text data between Java and native applications.

In the previous chapter, we saw that it's possible to transfer text data between Java and native applications using the clipboard (that is, cut and paste), and it was not necessary to perform any sort of character set conversions. In reality, they were performed, but are handled automatically and transparently by Java's clipboard facility. In contrast, you are responsible for performing such conversions when transferring text using drag and drop operations.

Text Transfers from Java to Native Applications

If you wrap text data in a `StringSelection` and drag it over a native application, the application will probably not accept a drop of that data. That's because most applications cannot process either of the two flavors supported by `StringSelection` (that is, `stringFlavor` and `plainTextFlavor`). It shouldn't be surprising that native applications can't accept `stringFlavor` data, since that flavor represents an instance of a serialized Java object. However, you might expect that `plainTextFlavor` could be used since it has a MIME type of `text/plain`.

To understand why `plainTextFlavor` can't be used in a Java-to-native transfer of text information, it's necessary to review the definition of that flavor, which is shown below:

```
text/plain; class=java.io.InputStream; charset=unicode
```

As you can see, `plainTextFlavor` represents an `InputStream` that returns a sequence of bytes representing Unicode character data. Unfortunately, this prevents it from being used by programs that cannot process Unicode data, and is the reason why most native applications will not allow you to drop text that's encapsulated in an instance of `StringSelection`.

> Note that because it fails when used with `StringSelection` and since it cannot be used to transfer data from Java to native applications, the `plainTextFlavor` constant defined in `DataFlavor` is deprecated in JDK 1.3, so you should avoid using it.

Text Transfers from Native Applications to Java

As mentioned earlier, dragging data from a native program and dropping it onto a Java application causes the data to be wrapped in a generic `Transferable` object. That object will also contain a list of `DataFlavor` instances that were created by mapping native types to MIME types using the entries in a `FlavorMap`.

In the case of text data transfers, the `DataFlavor` will normally have a MIME type of `text/plain` and includes a parameter that identifies the character set associated with the data. For example:

```
text/plain; charset=ascii
text/plain; charset=iso-8859-1
```

As these definitions imply, the `InputStream` provided by the `Transferable` will produce a stream of bytes representing the text information as it was stored by the native application. For example, in the case of the first definition listed above, the `InputStream` would return a sequence of ASCII characters. Therefore, if your application needs to process the information as an instance of `String`, the data must first be converted from ASCII to Unicode.

In Java 1.3, a method was added to `DataFlavor` that makes it easy for you to perform character set conversions. The `getReaderForText()` method requires that you pass a `Transferable` instance as a parameter, and it returns an appropriate subclass of `java.io.Reader` that will convert the native character data into Unicode. If you're using an earlier version of Java, you'll need to implement functionality similar to that found in `getReaderForText()`, but it's not difficult to do so, and an example of how to accomplish this is shown below:

```java
public static Reader getReaderForText(Transferable trans)
      throws IOException, UnsupportedFlavorException {
  DataFlavor[] flavors = trans.getTransferDataFlavors();
  for (int i = 0; i < flavors.length; i++) {
    if ((!(flavors[i].isMimeTypeEqual("text/plain")))
          || (!(flavors[i].getRepresentationClass()
             .equals(java.io.InputStream.class)))) {
      continue;
    }
    InputStream stream =
      (InputStream) (trans.getTransferData(flavors[i]));
    String encoding = flavors[i].getParameter("charset");
    return new InputStreamReader(stream, encoding);
  }
  throw new IllegalArgumentException("No text/plain flavor found " +
    "with an InputStream representation class");
}
```

The `getReaderForText()` method shown here locates a `DataFlavor` with a MIME type of `text/plain` and a representation class of `InputStream`. It then retrieves a reference to the `InputStream` that can be used to provide the data and extracts the character set (also called a character encoding) name from the `DataFlavor`. Using the `InputStream` and character set name, a new instance of `InputStreamReader` is created that can be used to convert the text data from its native representation into Unicode characters.

When handling text data that was dropped from a native application, you can use `getReaderForText()` to convert the data into a `String` using code similar to the following:

```
public void drop(DropTargetDropEvent event) {
   StringBuffer result = new StringBuffer();
   event.acceptDrop(DnDConstants.ACTION_COPY);
   DataFlavor[] flavors = event.getCurrentDataFlavors();
   Transferable t = event.getTransferable();
   try {
     Reader r = getReaderForText(t);
     int nextChar = r.read();
     while (nextChar != -1) {
       result.append((char)nextChar);
       nextChar = r.read();
     }
     event.dropComplete(true);
   } catch (Exception e) {
     event.dropComplete(false);
   }
   System.out.println("String '" + result + "' was dropped");
}
```

Creating a New Transferable for Text Data

As we've seen, `StringSelection` has some significant limitations when used in drag and drop operations. Specifically, it often can't be used to transfer text data from Java to non-Java applications because it can only provide the data as a stream of Unicode characters. In addition, transfers from one Java application to another fail if the recipient attempts to use `plainTextFlavor`, which `StringSelection` claims to support.

The easiest way to address these problems is to create a new `Transferable` that provides the ability to transfer text data, but which does not have the limitations of `StringSelection`. The `TextSelection` class shown below fulfills those requirements:

```
import java.awt.datatransfer.*;
import java.io.*;

public class TextSelection implements Transferable {

  protected String text;

  public final static DataFlavor UNICODE_FLAVOR = new DataFlavor(
      "text/plain; charset=unicode; " +
      "class=java.io.InputStream", "Unicode Text");
  public final static DataFlavor LATIN1_FLAVOR = new DataFlavor(
      "text/plain; charset=iso-8859-1; " +
      "class=java.io.InputStream", "Latin-1 Text");
  public final static DataFlavor ASCII_FLAVOR = new DataFlavor(
```

```
              "text/plain; charset=ascii; " +
              "class=java.io.InputStream", "ASCII Text");


    public static DataFlavor[] SUPPORTED_FLAVORS = {DataFlavor.stringFlavor,
        UNICODE_FLAVOR, LATIN1_FLAVOR, ASCII_FLAVOR};

    public TextSelection(String selection) {
      text = selection;
    }

    public DataFlavor[] getTransferDataFlavors() {
      return SUPPORTED_FLAVORS;
    }

    public boolean isDataFlavorSupported(DataFlavor flavor) {
      for (int i = 0; i < SUPPORTED_FLAVORS.length; i++) {
        if (SUPPORTED_FLAVORS[i].equals(flavor)) return true;
      }
      return false;
    }

    public Object getTransferData(DataFlavor flavor) throws
        IOException, UnsupportedFlavorException {
      if (flavor.equals(DataFlavor.stringFlavor)) {
        return text;
      }
      else if ((flavor.isMimeTypeEqual("text/plain")) &&
          (flavor.getRepresentationClass().equals(
          java.io.InputStream.class))) try {
        String encoding = flavor.getParameter("charset");
        if ((encoding != null) && (encoding.length() > 0)) {
          return new ByteArrayInputStream(
             text.getBytes(encoding));
        }
        return new ByteArrayInputStream(text.getBytes());
      } catch (Exception e) {};
      throw new UnsupportedFlavorException(flavor);
    }

}
```

You can use this class when you want to drag text from a Java application to a native application, and to do so, simply encapsulate the String in an instance of TextSelection by passing it to the constructor as shown below:

```
String transferText;
   .
   .
   .
TextSelection ts = new TextSelection(transferText);
```

In other words, this class can be used in exactly the same way that you would use Java's StringSelection, but it does not have the limitations that exist with that class.

The only part of this class that might require explanation is the getTransferData() method, specifically the code block that returns a ByteArrayInputStream. However, it's easily understood when you know that getBytes() provides functionality that's essentially the opposite of what StringReader was used for earlier. In other words, while StringReader converts native character data to Unicode, getBytes() can be used to convert Unicode text into some other format such as ASCII or ISO-8859-1.

Depending upon the platform and applications you're using, you may find it necessary to include additional DataFlavor definitions in TextSelection for it to function properly.

Adding Drag and Drop Support to JTextComponent Subclasses

Now that we've defined a Transferable that can be used to encapsulate text data, we'll see how to add drag and drop support to Swing's JTextComponent subclasses, such as JTextField and JTextArea. Once this support is completed, you will be able to drag text from a Java application and drop it onto a native program, and vice versa.

The first thing we'll do is define the class listed below that accepts a JTextComponent parameter in its constructor, and saves a reference to that component:

```
import javax.swing.text.*;

public class DragNDropTextSupport {

  protected JTextComponent component;

  public DragNDropTextSupport(JTextComponent comp) {
    component = comp;
  }

}
```

Once again, we'll add drop support first, since it's easier to implement than dragging. To provide drop capabilities, we must create a DropTarget instance, passing it a reference to the drop component, flags indicating which transfer types are allowed, and a reference to a DropTargetListener implementation. That last parameter will be supplied by defining an inner class called TextDropTargetListener that is shown below:

```
import java.awt.dnd.*;
import javax.swing.text.*;

public class DragNDropTextSupport {

  protected JTextComponent component;

  public DragNDropTextSupport(JTextComponent comp) {
    component = comp;
    DropTarget dt - new DropTarget(component,
      DnDConstants.ACTION_COPY_OR_MOVE,
      new TextDropTargetListener());
  }
```

```
class TextDropTargetListener implements DropTargetListener {

    public void dragEnter(DropTargetDragEvent event) {};
    public void dragExit(DropTargetEvent event) {};
    public void dragOver(DropTargetDragEvent event) {};
    public void dropActionChanged(DropTargetDragEvent event) {};
    public void drop(DropTargetDropEvent event) {};

}
}
```

Since we only want to allow a drop to occur when the data being dragged represents text information, we should add functionality to dragEnter() that will reject drags of any other type of data across the component:

```
import java.awt.datatransfer.*;
import java.awt.dnd.*;
import javax.swing.text.*;

public class DragNDropTextSupport {

  protected JTextComponent component;

  public DragNDropTextSupport(JTextComponent comp) {
    component = comp;
    DropTarget dt = new DropTarget(component,
        DnDConstants.ACTION_COPY_OR_MOVE,
        new TextDropTargetListener());
  }

  class TextDropTargetListener implements DropTargetListener {

    public void dragEnter(DropTargetDragEvent event) {
      DataFlavor[] flavors = event.getCurrentDataFlavors();
      for (int i = 0; i < flavors.length; i++) {
        if (flavors[i].isMimeTypeEqual("text/plain")) {
          return;
        }
      }
      event.rejectDrag();
    }

    public void dragExit(DropTargetEvent event) {};
    public void dragOver(DropTargetDragEvent event) {};
    public void dropActionChanged(DropTargetDragEvent event) {};
    public void drop(DropTargetDropEvent event) {};

  }

}
```

The last step in implementing drop support is to provide the implementation of the drop() method. This implementation first determines which DataFlavor to use by calling selectBestTextFlavor(), and that method returns the first flavor it finds that contains a MIME type with a primary type of "text". You should remember that when a Transferable returns an array of DataFlavor instances, the entries in the array are listed in order from most detailed flavor to the least. Therefore, selectBestTextFlavor() will choose the text flavor that provides the most information by returning the first flavor that contains a MIME type of "text".

Once it has obtained a `DataFlavor`, the `drop()` method uses `getReaderForText()` to access a `Reader` instance that can be used to read the text that's encapsulated by the `Transferable`. If the data being dropped was transferred from a native application that uses a character set other than Unicode, the `Reader` automatically performs the conversion from that character set.

After reading all of the characters that were transferred, `drop()` simply calls the `replaceSelection()` method of the `JTextComponent`, which will cause the currently selected text (if any) to be replaced with the string that was dropped. If nothing is selected, the string will be appended to the end of the component's text:

```java
import java.awt.datatransfer.*;
import java.awt.dnd.*;
import java.io.*;
import javax.swing.text.*;

public class DragNDropTextSupport {

  protected JTextComponent component;

  public DragNDropTextSupport(JTextComponent comp) {
    component = comp;
    DropTarget dt = new DropTarget(component,
        DnDConstants.ACTION_COPY_OR_MOVE,
        new TextDropTargetListener());
  }

  class TextDropTargetListener implements DropTargetListener {

    public void dragEnter(DropTargetDragEvent event) {
      DataFlavor[] flavors = event.getCurrentDataFlavors();
      for (int i = 0; i < flavors.length; i++) {
        if (flavors[i].isMimeTypeEqual("text/plain")) {
          return;
        }
      }
      event.rejectDrag();
    }

    public void dragExit(DropTargetEvent event) {};
    public void dragOver(DropTargetDragEvent event) {};
    public void dropActionChanged(DropTargetDragEvent event) {};

    public void drop(DropTargetDropEvent event) {
      event.acceptDrop(event.getDropAction());
      Transferable t = event.getTransferable();
      DataFlavor[] flavors = event.getCurrentDataFlavors();
      DataFlavor flavor = DataFlavor.selectBestTextFlavor(flavors);
      if (flavor != null) try {
        Reader r = flavor.getReaderForText(t);
        StringBuffer text = new StringBuffer("");
        int inputChar = r.read();
        while (inputChar > 0) {
          text.append((char)inputChar);
          inputChar = r.read();
        }
        component.replaceSelection(text.toString());
        event.dropComplete(true);
```

```
        } catch (Exception e) {
          event.dropComplete(false);
        }
      }

    }

  }
```

Our support for dropping text on instances of `JTextComponent` is now complete, and you can test it by creating a simple application like the one shown below which creates and displays a `JTextArea`:

```java
import java.awt.*;
import javax.swing.*;

public class TextTest extends JFrame {

  public static void main(String[] args) {
    TextTest tt = new TextTest();
    tt.setDefaultCloseOperation(JFrame.EXIT_ON_CLOSE);
    tt.setSize(400, 300);
    tt.setVisible(true);
  }

  public TextTest() {
    super("TextTest");
    Container pane = getContentPane();
    pane.setLayout(new FlowLayout());
    JTextArea tf = new JTextArea(10, 30);
    DragNDropTextSupport support = new DragNDropTextSupport(tf);
    pane.add(new JScrollPane(tf));
  }

}
```

To test this application, simply compile and execute it, and then execute an application such as WordPad on Windows. WordPad allows you to select a block of text and then drag that selection to some other location, including a different application. In this case, you'll be able to drop the text into the `JTextArea` defined by `TextTest`.

Adding Drag Support to JTextComponents

As we've just seen, adding drop support to instances of `JTextComponent` can be done very easily. Unfortunately, adding drag support is somewhat more complicated for reasons that have nothing to do with the design or complexity of Java's drag and drop facilities. Instead, the complexity is introduced by the normal behavior of `JTextComponent` instances and how they interpret mouse events. To understand this, it's helpful to first review the behavior of the WordPad application that we just used to test our drop support. Normally when the cursor is over a block of text within WordPad, the "text" cursor is displayed as shown opposite:

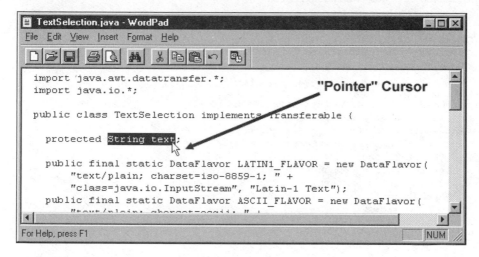

However, when you select a block of text within WordPad and move the cursor over that selection, the cursor changes to the "pointer" cursor to indicate that the text can be dragged:

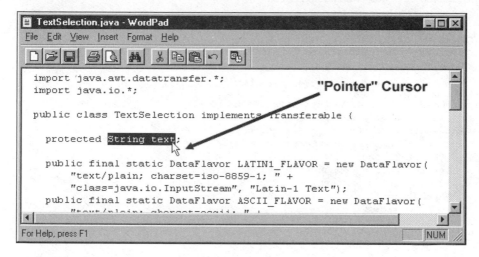

Obviously, if we're going to provide the ability to drag text from a `JTextComponent`, we need to provide similar visual feedback to the user to make dragging intuitive. In addition, we'll need to modify the way that a `JTextComponent` reacts to some mouse events if we want to be able to drag selected text from an instance of that class.

To understand the issue, execute the `TextTest` application again, type (or drop) some text into the `JTextArea` and select a portion of that text. If you then move the cursor over your selection, the cursor does not change to the pointer cursor as it would in WordPad, and clicking on the selection to begin the drag operation causes the selected text to be de-selected and the caret inserted at the place where you clicked. In short, `JTextComponent`'s behavior was not designed with drag operations in mind, so if we want it to function in an intuitive manner, it will be necessary to modify that behavior slightly.

The first functionality we'll implement is a `boolean` flag that's used to indicate whether or not a drag operation is in progress, since it will be important to know when that's the case. In addition, the `isOverSelection()` method shown below will be used later to determine whether or not the mouse is over a portion of the selected text (if any) when certain mouse events occur:

```
import java.awt.*;
import java.awt.datatransfer.*;
import java.awt.dnd.*;
import java.awt.event;
import java.io.*;
import javax.swing.text.*;

public class DragNDropTextSupport {

  protected JTextComponent component;

  protected boolean dragInProgress;

  public DragNDropTextSupport(JTextComponent comp) {
    component = comp;
    DropTarget dt = new DropTarget(component,
        DnDConstants.ACTION_COPY_OR_MOVE,
        new TextDropTargetListener());
  }

  protected boolean isDragInProgress() {
    return dragInProgress;
  }

  protected void setDragInProgress(boolean dragging) {
    dragInProgress = dragging;
  }

  protected boolean isOverSelection(Point p) {
    boolean result = false;
    int start = component.getSelectionStart();
    int end = component.getSelectionEnd();
    if (start != end) {
      int location = component.viewToModel(p);
      if ((location > start) && (location <= end)) {
        result = true;
      }
    }
    return result;
  }

  class TextDropTargetListener implements DropTargetListener {

    public void dragEnter(DropTargetDragEvent event) {
      DataFlavor[] flavors = event.getCurrentDataFlavors();
      for (int i = 0; i < flavors.length; i++) {
        if (flavors[i].isMimeTypeEqual("text/plain")) {
          return;
        }
      }
      event.rejectDrag();
    }

    public void dragExit(DropTargetEvent event) {};
    public void dragOver(DropTargetDragEvent event) {};
    public void dropActionChanged(DropTargetDragEvent event) {};
```

```
public void drop(DropTargetDropEvent event) {
  event.acceptDrop(event.getDropAction());
  Transferable t = event.getTransferable();
  DataFlavor[] flavors = event.getCurrentDataFlavors();
  DataFlavor flavor = DataFlavor.selectBestTextFlavor(flavors);
  if (flavor != null) try {
    Reader r = flavor.getReaderForText(t);
    StringBuffer text = new StringBuffer("");
    int inputChar = r.read();
    while (inputChar > 0) {
      text.append((char)inputChar);
      inputChar = r.read();
    }
    component.replaceSelection(text.toString());
    event.dropComplete(true);
  } catch (Exception e) {
    event.dropComplete(false);
  }
}

}

}
```

Next, we must create a `DragGestureRecognizer` that will detect when a drag gesture has occurred over the text field. When the recognizer is created, an instance of a class called `TextDragGestureRecognizer` is registered with the recognizer, and will be sent notification of any drag gestures that are detected.

```
public DragNDropTextSupport(JTextComponent comp) {
  component = comp;
  DropTarget dt = new DropTarget(component,
      DnDConstants.ACTION_COPY_OR_MOVE,
      new TextDropTargetListener());
  DragSource source = DragSource.getDefaultDragSource();
  source.createDefaultDragGestureRecognizer(component,
      DnDConstants.ACTION_COPY_OR_MOVE,
      new TextDragGestureRecognizer());
}
```

The implementation of `TextDragGesture` is shown below, and as you can see, it only initiates the drag operation if the drag gesture took place when the cursor was over some portion of selected text:

```
class TextDragGestureRecognizer implements DragGestureListener {

  public void dragGestureRecognized(DragGestureEvent event) {
    MouseEvent trigger = (MouseEvent)(event.getTriggerEvent());
    if (isOverSelection(trigger.getPoint())) {
      Cursor cursor = null;
      switch (event.getDragAction()) {
        case DnDConstants.ACTION_COPY:
          cursor = DragSource.DefaultCopyNoDrop;
          break;
        case DnDConstants.ACTION_MOVE:
          cursor = DragSource.DefaultMoveNoDrop;
```

```
            break;
        }
        TextSelection selection = new TextSelection(
            component.getSelectedText());
        event.startDrag(cursor, selection, new TextSourceListener());
        setDragInProgress(true);
    }
}
```

Notice that the `TextDragGestureRecognizer` in turn references yet another class called `TextSourceListener`. That class monitors the progress of the drag operation, and when a drop is performed, it removes the selected text from the `JTextComponent` if the operation was a move (as opposed to a copy):

```
class TextSourceListener implements DragSourceListener {

    public void dragEnter(DragSourceDragEvent event) {};
    public void dragExit(DragSourceEvent event) {};
    public void dragOver(DragSourceDragEvent event) {};
    public void dropActionChanged(DragSourceDragEvent event) {};

    public void dragDropEnd(DragSourceDropEvent event) {
        if ((event.getDropSuccess()) && (event.getDropAction() ==
            DnDConstants.ACTION_MOVE)) {
            component.replaceSelection("");
        }
        setDragInProgress(false);
    }
}
```

Most of the code we've implemented so far is very simple and is essentially identical to the code that was implemented earlier in this chapter. In fact, we now have all of the drag and drop functionality that's needed to drag text from a `JTextField`, but one thing is still missing: code that modifies the way that the `JTextComponent` will react to mouse events. In other words, we're now able to distinguish between a drag that occurs over selected text and one that does not, but we haven't modified the component's behavior so that it distinguishes between them. In other words, if you were to compile this code and test it with the `TextTest` application defined earlier, the `JTextArea` would behave exactly the same way that it did before.

It's important to realize that we only want to change `JTextComponent`'s behavior under certain very specific conditions. For example, it should still be possible to select text by clicking with the left-mouse button and dragging it across the text that's to be selected. However, once a selection has been made, a mouse press should not cause the text to be unselected as it normally would, and a mouse drag that occurs over the selected text should not affect the selection. Instead, a mouse drag that occurs over selected text should be interpreted as the beginning of a drag operation by our `DragGestureRecognizer`, but should be ignored by the `JTextComponent` itself. This may sound like a complicated task, but `JTextComponent`'s robust design makes it easy to implement.

To understand how to do so, you simply need to be aware that `JTextComponent`'s reaction to mouse and focus events is controlled by an object that's an implementation of the `Caret` interface defined in the `javax.swing.text` package. By default, an instance of the `DefaultCaret` class is used, but we can easily define a subclass of `DefaultCaret` and modify its behavior slightly. The following inner class defined in `DragNDropTextSupport` does just that:

```
class DragSupportCaret extends DefaultCaret {

  public void mouseMoved(MouseEvent event) {
    super.mouseMoved(event);
    Cursor newCursor = null;
    if (isOverSelection(event.getPoint())) {
      newCursor = Cursor.getPredefinedCursor(Cursor.DEFAULT_CURSOR);
    }
    else {
      newCursor = Cursor.getPredefinedCursor(Cursor.TEXT_CURSOR);
    }
    if (!(newCursor.equals(component.getCursor()))) {
      component.setCursor(newCursor);
    }
  }

  public void mouseExited(MouseEvent event) {
    if (!(isDragInProgress())) {
      super.mouseExited(event);
    }
  }

  public void mouseDragged(MouseEvent event) {
    if (!(isOverSelection(event.getPoint()))) {
      super.mouseDragged(event);
    }
  }

  public void mousePressed(MouseEvent event) {
    if (!(isOverSelection(event.getPoint()))) {
      super.mousePressed(event);
    }
  }

}
```

This simple class does just two things: first, it only forwards some mouse events to the JTextComponent, which will prevent the component from responding to events that should only be interpreted as initiating or performing a drag. Second, as the mouse moves over the component, DragCaretSupport displays a pointer cursor (indicating that it is prepared to initiate a drag) when the cursor is over a text selection. However, when the mouse is moved and the cursor is *not* over a selection, the normal "pointer" cursor is displayed instead, as would normally be shown. Finally, we must add code to replace the default Caret used by the JTextComponent with our own custom subclass, and the final portion of DragNDropTextSupport appears below:

```
public DragNDropTextSupport(JTextComponent comp) {
  component = comp;
  DragSupportCaret caret = new DragSupportCaret();
  caret.setBlinkRate(component.getCaret().getBlinkRate());
  component.setCaret(caret);
  DropTarget dt = new DropTarget(component,
      DnDConstants.ACTION_COPY_OR_MOVE,
      new TextDropTargetListener());
  DragSource source = DragSource.getDefaultDragSource();
  source.createDefaultDragGestureRecognizer(component,
```

```
                DnDConstants.ACTION_COPY_OR_MOVE,
                new TextDragGestureRecognizer());
    }
```

With this code in place, you can now run the `TextTest` application and drag and drop text from its `JTextArea` into a native application such as WordPad and vice versa.

Summary

In this chapter, we've covered issues related to Java's drag and drop support, including the following:

- ❑ The fundamental concepts associated with drag and drop operations
- ❑ How to add drag support to components so that they can be used to initiate drag and drop operations
- ❑ How to add drop support to components so that they can be used to terminate drag and drop operations
- ❑ Issues related to different types of transfers (for example, those between a Java and native application, as opposed to a transfer within a single Java Virtual Machine)
- ❑ How to implement autoscroll support for drop targets contained within a scroll pane
- ❑ Issues related to the transfer of text data between Java and native applications

In the next chapter, we'll examine another type of functionality you may want to add to your Swing applications – printing.

Professional Java Programmin.

10
Printing

One of the most basic functions of a software application is the ability to send output to a printer. In its earliest releases, Java provided no support for printing at all, although a crude printing facility was introduced in Java 1.1 that used the `PrintJob` class defined in `java.awt`. Unfortunately, the capabilities provided by `PrintJob` were somewhat limited and unreliable, so the `java.awt.print` package was created and it is included in the Java 2 platform.

In this chapter, we'll examine the capabilities of this new printing facility, and we'll discuss the following related topics:

- ❑   Some basic concepts related to printing
- ❑   The various classes that are used by the new printing facility
- ❑   Selecting printer options such as the orientation (portrait or landscape)
- ❑   Starting and stopping printer jobs
- ❑   Providing standard printing features such as print preview

Printing in Java 2

The new printing facility is much more robust and uses `java.awt.print.PrinterJob`, which should not be confused with the older `java.awt.PrintJob` class that is still available. `PrinterJob` allows you to set parameters, display dialogs, and start and cancel printing, and you can easily obtain a reference to an instance of `PrinterJob` using the static `getPrinterJob()` factory method:

```
PrinterJob job = PrinterJob.getPrinterJob();
```

Before starting a job, you must identify the object responsible for producing the output to be printed. That object must implement `Printable` and/or `Pageable`, where `Pageable` simply represents a collection of `Printable` instances.

`Printable` defines a single `print()` method that's called when a page should be drawn (or "**rendered**"), and is passed a reference to a `Graphics` object that represents the page being rendered. If you're already familiar with `Graphics`, it's probably because an instance is passed to the `paint()` method of AWT and Swing components when they are displayed as part of a user interface. As you may suspect, the fact that components are already able to render themselves onto a `Graphics` object makes it easy to print them, and we'll see how to do so later in the chapter.

The new printing facility supports a resolution of 72 dots per inch (DPI), which means that each pixel that you draw onto a `Graphics` object will occupy 1/72 of an inch (approximately 0.3528 millimeters) on the printed page. That unit of measure (that is, 1/72 of an inch) is called a **point**, and is used by Java's new printing facility to represent locations and size values. So for example, a sheet of letter size paper (8.5 inches wide and 11 inches long) is 612 (8.5 * 72 = 612) points wide and 792 (11 * 72 = 792) points long.

Based on this information, it might seem that you could produce printed output up to 612 points wide and 792 points long on letter size paper. However, most printers can only print on a subset (although usually a very large one) of the total area available on the paper. The portions of a page that are unusable (which we'll call the **hardware margins**) vary from one model of printer to the next, but the shaded area in the figure provides an example of the area that may be unavailable:

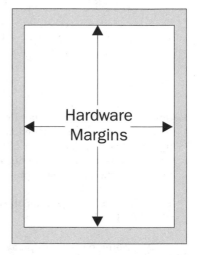

Hardware margins aren't normally important because most applications use margin sizes that are greater than those imposed on them by the hardware. For example, you might wish to have one-inch margins on each side of a printed text document to improve readability, and the approximate area of a letter-size page that's available with margins of that size is illustrated here. The area inside the margins available for printing is known as the **imageable area** and you'll need to take the size and position of that area into consideration during printing:

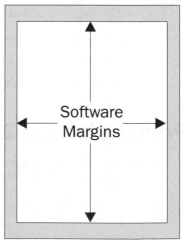

Support Classes

Before performing an in-depth examination of Java's printing capabilities, it's necessary to review the classes that support `PrinterJob`:

Name	Type	Description
Paper	class	Describes the physical characteristics of a certain type of paper
PageFormat	class	Describes the size and orientation of a page that is to be printed
Book	class	A convenient implementation of the `Pageable` interface
Printable	interface	Represents a single printable page
Pageable	interface	Represents a collection of printable pages

Specifically, we'll examine the `Paper`, `PageFormat`, and `Book` classes and the `Printable` and `Pageable` interfaces.

Paper

The `java.awt.print.Paper` class encapsulates two pieces of information:

❑   The physical size of the paper you're printing on

❑   The size and position of the imageable area

`Paper` includes a single no-argument constructor that initializes its properties to correspond to U.S. letter size paper with one-inch margins on each side (top, left, bottom, and right) of the page.

It's actually somewhat misleading to suggest that instances of `Paper` maintain margin information, because they do not, at least not explicitly. However, margin sizes can be derived using the paper size and imageable area information. For example, if the imageable area is located 144 points from the left-edge of the paper, the paper effectively has a two-inch $(144/72 = 2)$ left margin. The right margin can be similarly calculated by subtracting the width of the imageable area and the width of the left margin from the total width of the paper.

For the most part, the methods defined in `Paper` are simple accessor and mutator methods that allow you to reference the encapsulated information.

getWidth(), getHeight(), setSize()

These methods allow you to modify and query the physical dimensions of the paper. Those values are maintained as `double` primitives that identify the paper size in points. For example, since `Paper`'s values default to those of a letter size piece of paper, the initial width value of a `Paper` instance is 612 ($8.5 * 72 = 612$) and the initial height is 792 ($11 * 72 = 792$).

setImageableArea(), getImageableX(), getImageableY(), getImageableWidth(), getImageableHeight()

These methods allow you to modify and query the size and location of the imageable area. The `setImageableArea()` method requires four `double` parameter values: the X position, Y position, width, and height of the paper's imageable area.

For example, to set the imageable area for a letter-size piece of paper that should have one-inch left and right margins and 1.5-inch top and bottom margins, you could use the following code:

```
double paperWidth = 8.5 * 72;
double paperHeight = 11 * 72;
double xMargin = 1.0 * 72;
double yMargin = 1.5 * 72;
double areaWidth = paperWidth - (xMargin * 2);
double areaHeight = paperHeight - (yMargin * 2);
Paper p = new Paper();
p.setImageableArea(xMargin, yMargin, areaWidth, areaHeight);
```

Note that these are point values, so the margin sizes must be converted from inches to points before calling `setImageableArea`.

clone()

`Paper` implements the `Cloneable` interface and overrides the `clone()` method inherited from `java.lang.Object`. This allows you to easily create copies of a `Paper` object.

Using Paper with Alternative Paper Sizes

As we saw above, it's easy to set the imageable area size for an instance of `Paper`. Similarly, you'll sometimes want to adjust the paper size and margins to correspond to some type of paper other than U.S. letter size. For example, you could use code like that shown below to create an instance of `Paper` that will be used to print to A4-sized pages (210 millimeters wide and 297 millimeters long) with 25 millimeter margins around each edge:

```
Paper paperA4 = new Paper();
double inchesPerMillimeter = 0.0394;
double widthInInches = inchesPerMillimeter * 210;
double heightInInches = inchesPerMillimeter * 297;
double marginSizeInInches = inchesPerMillimeter * 25;
double widthInPoints = widthInInches * 72;
double heightInPoints = heightInInches * 72;
double marginSizeInPoints = marginSizeInInches * 72;
double availableWidth = widthInPoints - (marginSizeInPoints * 2);
double availableHeight = heightInPoints - (marginSizeInPoints * 2);
paperA4.setImageableArea(marginSizeInPoints, marginSizeInPoints,
        availableWidth, availableHeight);
```

PageFormat

While `Paper` describes the physical attributes of the paper used in printing, the `PageFormat` class describes the logical characteristics of one or more printed pages. Depending upon the orientation (portrait or landscape) used when printing, the physical attribute values may be identical to the logical attributes.

An instance of `PageFormat` is passed to the `print()` method when it's called so that the `Printable` implementation can determine the size and location of the imageable area on the page and confine its rendering to that region accordingly.

setOrientation(), getOrientation()

These methods allow you to modify and query the orientation value for the page(s) printed using this `PageFormat` object. The orientation is maintained as an `int` value that corresponds to one of the following constants defined in `PageFormat`: PORTRAIT, LANDSCAPE, or REVERSE_LANDSCAPE. The default value is PORTRAIT, which produces output similar to that shown below:

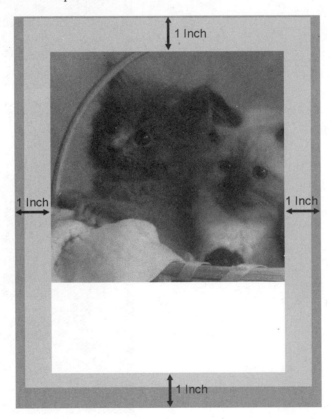

The figures below show examples of output produced using LANDSCAPE:

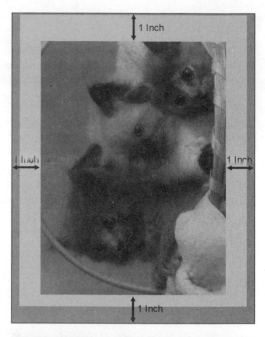

and REVERSE_LANDSCAPE:

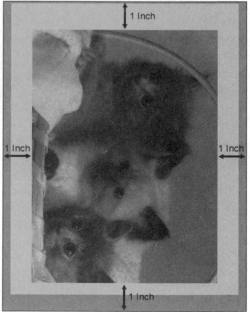

getPaper(), setPaper()

PageFormat maintains a reference to a Paper object, and these methods allow you to obtain a copy of that object and to replace it. The default Paper object corresponds to US letter size paper with one-inch margins on each side.

> It's important to understand that **getPaper()** returns a *copy* of the **PageFormat's Paper** object instead of a reference to the original.

Therefore, if you wish to modify the paper's size or imageable area values, you must call getPaper(), modify the object returned, and then call setPaper() to update the PageFormat's reference.

An example of this is shown in the code below:

```
PageFormat pf = new PageFormat();
Paper p = pf.getPaper();
p.setImageableArea(0, 0, p.getWidth(), p.getHeight());
pf.setPaper(p);
```

getMatrix()

This method returns a matrix that can be used to rotate an image appropriately so that its orientation is correct when it's printed. However, such rotations are performed automatically and transparently based on the orientation value you select, and you will not normally use this method directly.

getWidth(), getHeight()

These methods return the logical size of the paper, as opposed to the physical size returned by the methods of the same name in Paper. The physical size identifies the actual size of the paper and always produces the same value for a certain type of paper (for example, US letter size). On the other hand, the logical size represents the paper size that's adjusted based on the selected orientation. If you use portrait orientation, the logical width and height are the same as the physical width and height.

However, if you select landscape orientation, you've effectively rotated the paper, although in reality the data itself is logically rotated before it's printed. When either LANDSCAPE or REVERSE_LANDSCAPE is specified for the orientation value, the paper's logical width equals its physical height, and its logical height equals its physical width.

getImageableX(), getImageableY(), getImageableWidth(), getImageableHeight()

In much the same way that getWidth() and getHeight() translate the physical paper size into a logical size, these methods convert Paper's imageable area values based on the selected orientation.

clone()

This method is overridden from the Object implementation to allow you to easily create copies of a PageFormat instance.

Printable

As mentioned earlier, the Printable interface identifies an object capable of producing printed output, and defines a single method.

print()

This method is called one or more times during printing so that the Printable implementation can render a page of output. Three parameter values are passed to print() that allow it to perform the rendering appropriately:

- ❑ A `Graphics` object representing the page being rendered.

- ❑ A `PageFormat` object that describes the logical characteristics of the paper onto which printing will occur.

- ❑ An integer value that identifies the page to render. This is necessary because a single `Printable` instance may be responsible for printing multiple pages.

Some printer jobs produce output that's easy to render, while others may be very complex and involve a large number of rendering operations. For the more complicated printer jobs, it may not be practical to determine in advance how many pages will be printed. For that reason, `print()` is required to return a value that indicates whether it was able to render the requested page. The value should correspond to one of two constants defined in `Printable`:

- ❑ `PAGE_EXISTS` if the page was successfully rendered

- ❑ `NO_SUCH_PAGE` if the `Printable` could not render the requested page

When you identify a `Printable` implementation to `PrinterJob` and initiate printing, the `print()` method is called repeatedly until it returns a value of `NO_SUCH_PAGE`. Therefore, you would typically include logic similar to the following in your `print()` method to cause the print job to end after printing a single page:

```
public int print(Graphics g, PageFormat pageFormat, int pageNumber) {
   if (pageNumber == 0) {
      // Rendering logic would normally go here
      return Printable.PAGE_EXISTS;
   }
   else {
      return Printable.NO_SUCH_PAGE;
   }
}
```

In effect, your `print()` method is responsible for identifying the printing equivalent of an "end-of-file" condition, and until it does so, `PrinterJob` will continue to print pages rendered by your `Printable`.

Note that the page number passed to `print()` is zero-indexed, meaning that a value of 0 represents the first page, 1 represents the second page, and so on.

Sample Printing Application

It's now possible to create a simple printing application using the classes described above. The following application requires the user to specify the name of an image (for example, GIF or JPEG) file as the first command line parameter and the constructor uses that file to create an instance of `java.awt.Image`. Although this example only illustrates how to print an image, we'll see later in the chapter that it's just as easy to print Swing components:

```
import java.awt.*;
import java.awt.print.*;

public class ImagePrint {

   protected Image printImage;
```

```
   public static void main(String[] args) {
     ImagePrint ip = new ImagePrint(args[0]);
     System.exit(0);
   }

   // Constructor and inner class will go here ...

}
```

To print the loaded image, an implementation of `Printable` must be defined that will print the image. In this case, an inner class is used to provide the `Printable` implementation; the `print()` method is implemented as outlined a moment ago, and simply uses the `Graphics` class's `drawImage()` method to print the image specified on the command line:

```
class MyPrintable implements Printable {

  public int print(Graphics g, PageFormat pf, int pageIndex) {
    if (pageIndex == 0) {
      g.drawImage(printImage, 0, 0, null);
      return Printable.PAGE_EXISTS;
    }
    return Printable.NO_SUCH_PAGE;
  }

}
```

In the constructor, we'll obtain an `Image` using the filename passed on the command line, and then create a `PageFormat` to define the margins that should be used, and that `PageFormat` will be passed to the `print()` method in `MyPrintable` when it's called. In this case, the margins are set to one inch on the left and right sides and 1.5 inches on the top and bottom edges:

```
public ImagePrint(String fileName) {
  printImage = new javax.swing.ImageIcon(fileName).getImage();
  Paper p = new Paper();
  p.setImageableArea(1 * 72,     // Left margin 1 inch
                     1.5 * 72,   // Top margin 1.5 inches
                     6.5 * 72,   // Width 6.5 inches
                     8 * 72);    // Height 8 inches
  PageFormat format = new PageFormat();
  format.setPaper(p);
```

Finally, we can obtain an instance of `PrinterJob` and use it to initiate the printing operation by calling `setPrintable()`, which is passed a reference to the `Printable` object and the `PageFormat` that should be used:

```
  format.setPaper(p);
  PrinterJob pj = PrinterJob.getPrinterJob();
  pj.setPrintable(new MyPrintable(), format);
  try {
    pj.print();
  } catch (PrinterException pe) {
```

```
            System.out.println("Printing failed: " + pe.getMessage());
        }
    }
```

If you compile and execute this application, you may be somewhat surprised by the results. Instead of the image being printed inside the imageable area, it is aligned at the upper-left corner of the page and a section is missing from both the top and left sides of the image:

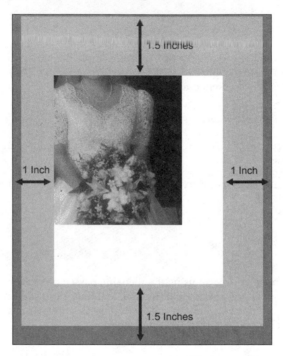

This occurs because the Graphics object passed to print() is "clipped" to prevent you from drawing outside the imageable area even though the origin (coordinates 0, 0) of the Graphics object corresponds to the upper-left edge of the paper.

Perhaps the most obvious solution to this problem is to change the coordinates specified on the call to drawImage(). However, a better solution is to adjust the Graphics object's origin so that it corresponds to the corner of the imageable area, instead of the corner of the page. That can be accomplished using translate(), which causes all subsequent drawing operations to be offset by the specified number of pixels. Conceptually, you may find it easier to think of translate() as moving the rendered output down and/or to the right when positive translation values are specified, or up and to the left for negative values:

```
public int print(Graphics g, PageFormat pf, int pageIndex) {
    g.translate((int)(pf.getImageableX()),
        (int)(pf.getImageableY())));
    if (pageIndex == 0) {
      g.drawImage(printImage, 0, 0, null);
        return Printable.PAGE_EXISTS;
    }
    return Printable.NO_SUCH_PAGE;
}
```

If you make this modification and execute the `ImagePrint` application, the image will correctly appear within the imageable area as shown below:

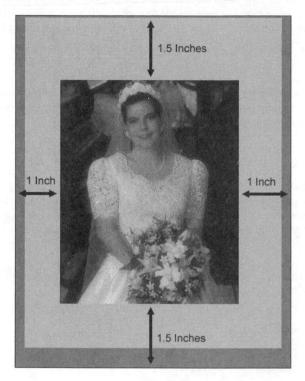

Pageable

The `setPrintable()` method in `PrinterJob` allows you to specify a single `Printable`/`PageFormat` pair, and those two objects are used to render all pages that are printed. That limitation isn't significant as long as you're only printing a single page or as long as all the pages you're printing can be rendered by a single `Printable`/`PageFormat` pair. In some multi-page printer jobs, however, it may not be feasible for a single `Printable` to render all of the pages, or for the same `PageFormat` to be used when rendering them.

The `Pageable` interface defines a set of methods that can be used to create a collection of `Printable`/`PageFormat` pairs, with each pair corresponding to a printed page.

getPrintable()

Given a page number, this method returns the `Printable` implementation responsible for rendering the page.

getPageFormat()

Given a page number, this method returns the `PageFormat` that describes the logical characteristics of the page.

getNumberOfPages()

This method should return an int value that identifies the number of pages encapsulated by this Pageable object. Sometimes, however, it may not be possible to provide the page count before the printing occurs. In that case, you should return the UNKNOWN_NUMBER_OF_PAGES constant defined in Pageable.

Book

Book is an implementation of the Pageable interface and defines methods that allow you to add pairs of Printable/PageFormat objects to the collection. In addition to the three methods defined in the Pageable interface, Book implements the methods described below.

append()

This overloaded method has two implementations, although both of them require a Printable parameter and a PageFormat parameter. One implementation assumes that the Printable/PageFormat pair will be used to print a single page, while the other implementation allows you to specify the number of pages that the pair should render. For example, if you have already initialized a number of Printable and PageFormat objects, you could use code similar to the following to encapsulate those objects in an instance of Book:

```
Printable myPrintable1, myPrintable2, myPrintable3;
PageFormat myFormat1, myFormat2, myFormat3;
// ...

Book myBook = new Book();
myBook.append(myPrintable1, myFormat1);
myBook.append(myPrintable2, myFormat2, 5);
myBook.append(myPrintable3, myFormat3);
```

This code segment creates a Book that can print seven pages. The first page will be rendered by myPrintable1, the next five by myPrintable2, and the last page by myPrintable3. When a particular page is to be rendered, the print() method of the associated Printable object is called and is passed a reference to the PageFormat object that was added to the book along with the Printable.

setPage()

While append() adds a Printable/PageFormat pair to the end of the Book's list, this method stores a pair at a specific page location. For example:

```
Book myBook = new Book();
MyBook.append(myPrintable1, myFormat1, 5);
MyBook.setPage(2, myPrintable2, myFormat2);
```

This code segment initializes a Book that can print five pages, with myPrintable1 and myFormat1 used for pages 1, 2, 4, and 5, and myPrintable2 and myFormat2 used for page 3. As is the case with the print() method, the page index values specified on setPage() calls are zero-indexed, meaning that the first page corresponds to a value of 0 so the parameter 2 in the arguments to setPage() above refers to the third page.

PrinterJob

Some of the methods defined in `PrinterJob` have already been described briefly, but there are many other methods available, and each of them is described below:

setPrintable()

Calling this method allows you to identify the object that should be responsible for rendering the pages of printed output, and that object must implement the `Printable` interface. One version of this overloaded method accepts a `PageFormat` instance, while the other does not. If you do not specify a `PageFormat` parameter, a default instance is created using the no-argument `PageFormat` constructor.

setPageable()

When multiple pages are to be printed, it's helpful to create pairs of `Printable` and `PageFormat` objects and store them in a `Pageable` object. When you do so, you can use `setPageable()` to identify the object to the `PrinterJob`, and it will use the `Printable`/`PageFormat` pairs encapsulated by that `Pageable` to perform the rendering operations.

print()

This method initiates the printing operation, and should only be invoked after either `setPrintable()` or `setPageable()` is called to identify the object responsible for rendering pages. This is a synchronous call, which means that `print()` does not return until after all pages have been rendered and submitted for printing.

It's important to understand that the rendering and submission process is separate from the actual printing. In fact, after a job has been rendered and submitted, a large amount of time may pass before it's actually printed. This could happen because the printer is powered off, is busy printing some other job, or is otherwise unavailable.

Once a job is submitted for printing, it's usually stored in a buffer, and that buffer may be provided by the printer itself or by the operating system on the machine to which the printer is physically attached. In either case, `print()` returns once the job has been submitted, and your Java application has no control over the job after that occurs. Prior to the completion of the `print()` method, however, you can call the `PrinterJob`'s `cancel()` method.

cancel()

When a printer job is being rendered/submitted (during a call to `print()`), you can use this method to cancel the job, although pages that have already been submitted may still be allowed to print. As the `print()` method does not return until the job has been submitted and because `cancel()` must be called before the submission occurs, this method can only be called by a thread other than the one that is initiating printing. However, as we'll see later in the chapter, this can be done quite easily.

isCanceled()

You can use this method to determine whether a request is pending to cancel the current printer job. If a job is in progress and a request was made to cancel it, this method returns `true`.

setJobName(), getJobName()

These methods allow you to modify and retrieve the name of the printer job. That name can be used to identify a particular printer job, and may be displayed by utilities that allow you to view the files in the printer queue, such as the one shown overleaf:

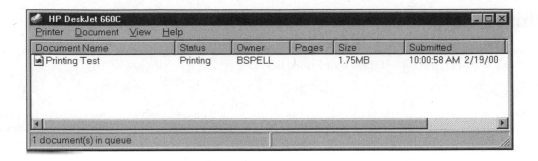

getUserName()

You can call getUserName() to retrieve the name of the user associated with the printer job.

setCopies(), getCopies()

Using these methods, you can set and retrieve an integer value indicating how many copies of the output should be printed.

defaultPage()

This method returns a PageFormat with settings that should correspond to the system's default settings. However, the settings returned currently always correspond to a U.S. letter size (8.5- by 11-inch) page.

validatePage()

This method is passed an instance of PageFormat and it returns a modified copy of the object that reflects the limitations of the printer. For example, if the page's imageable area is defined so that it would extend beyond the hardware margins, the imageable area values will be modified so that they're within the bounds that are supported by the printer. To create a PageFormat object that allows print() to use all available space on a page, you could use code similar to the following:

```
Paper paper = new Paper();
paper.setImageableArea(0, 0, 8.5 * 72, 11 * 72);
PageFormat pageFormat = new PageFormat();
pageFormat.setPaper(paper);
pageFormat = PrinterJob.getPrinterJob().validatePage(pageFormat);
```

Note that validatePage() *does not modify or return the original* PageFormat *instance that's passed to it as a parameter. Instead, it creates a clone of that object and the clone is then modified appropriately and returned to the caller.*

pageDialog()

You can use this method to allow a user to modify the PageFormat properties, such as the margin sizes and orientation value. When pageDialog() is invoked, a dialog appears like the one shown below that allows the user to edit those values. If the **Cancel** button is used to dismiss the dialog, this method returns a reference to the original PageFormat object and that object remains unchanged. However, if **OK** is pressed, pageDialog() returns a *copy* of the original PageFormat object, and the copy is modified to reflect the values selected by the user through the dialog:

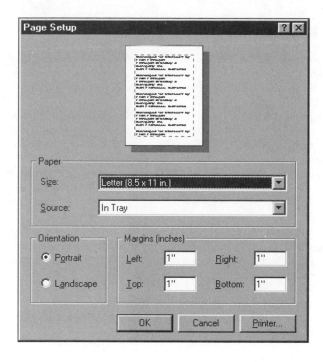

printDialog()

This method causes a dialog like the one below to appear, and that dialog can be used to change the job's properties. A `boolean` value of `true` is returned by `printDialog()` if the user closed the dialog by pressing the OK button, while a value of `false` indicates that Cancel was pressed:

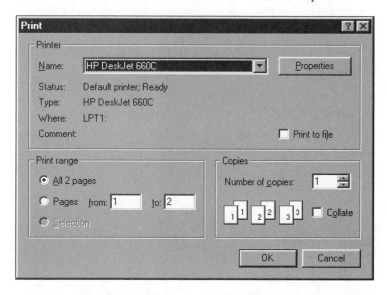

You'll normally invoke `printDialog()` after calling `setPrintable()` or `setPageable()` and immediately before initiating printing, and start the job only if this method returns a value of `true`.

Printing Components

The `ImagePrint` application defined earlier illustrates how easy it is to print images in Java, but in practice, you'll often want to print components instead. As we'll see, it's very easy to print Swing components, although the results may not be suitable for your needs in some cases.

When a Swing component is displayed, its `paint()` method is called and the component renders itself using the `Graphics` object passed to `paint()`. In contrast, the appearance of an AWT component is provided by its **peer** and not by the component itself. For example, `javax.swing.JButton` instances render their representation, but `java.awt.Button` objects do not. In fact, `Button` doesn't even override the empty `paint()` method that it inherits from `Component`. When you create a Button, its appearance is provided by an instance of the native platform's button object, and the Java `Button` instance simply acts as a wrapper for that native peer object.

This difference in the way that AWT and Swing components are drawn is relevant to the new printing facility, because the new printing API relies on rendering that's done using an instance of `Graphics`. Since AWT components do not draw themselves using a `Graphics` object, you can't print them unless you implement the code to do so.

> **Therefore, you'll normally want to confine the printing of components to Swing classes whenever possible.**

As you might expect, the printing facility's use of `Graphics` makes it easy to print Swing components. In fact, sometimes all that's necessary is for your `print()` method to call the `paint()` method of the Swing component(s), passing the `Graphics` object as a parameter.

For example, the following application creates a display and when the Print button is pressed, it creates an instance of the `MyPrintable` inner class and identifies that object to a `PrinterJob`:

```java
import java.awt.*;
import java.awt.event.*;
import java.awt.print.*;
import javax.swing.*;

public class PrintComponents extends JFrame {

  public static void main(String[] args) {
    PrintComponents pc = new PrintComponents();
    pc.setDefaultCloseOperation(JFrame.EXIT_ON_CLOSE);
    pc.setSize(400, 300);
    pc.setVisible(true);
  }

  public PrintComponents() {
    super("Print Components");
    JLabel label;
    JTextField textField;

    Container pane = getContentPane();
    pane.setLayout(new GridBagLayout());
    GridBagConstraints gbc = new GridBagConstraints();
```

```
      gbc.anchor = GridBagConstraints.WEST;
      gbc.fill = GridBagConstraints.HORIZONTAL;
      gbc.insets = new Insets(5, 10, 5, 10);

      gbc.gridy = 0;
      label = new JLabel("Last Name:", JLabel.LEFT);
      pane.add(label, gbc);
      textField = new JTextField(8);
      pane.add(textField, gbc);

      label = new JLabel("First Name:", JLabel.LEFT);
      pane.add(label, gbc);
      textField = new JTextField(8);
      pane.add(textField, gbc);

      gbc.gridy++;
      label = new JLabel("Address:", JLabel.LEFT);
      pane.add(label, gbc);
      textField = new JTextField(8);
      gbc.gridwidth = GridBagConstraints.REMAINDER;
      pane.add(textField, gbc);

      gbc.gridy++;
      gbc.gridwidth = 1;
      label = new JLabel("Phone:", JLabel.LEFT);
      pane.add(label, gbc);
      textField = new JTextField(8);
      pane.add(textField, gbc);

      label = new JLabel("Postal Code:", JLabel.LEFT);
      pane.add(label, gbc);
      textField = new JTextField(8);
      pane.add(textField, gbc);

      gbc.gridy++;
      gbc.fill = GridBagConstraints.NONE;
      gbc.anchor = GridBagConstraints.CENTER;
      gbc.gridwidth = GridBagConstraints.REMAINDER;
      JButton btn = new JButton("Print");
      btn.addActionListener(new ActionListener() {
        public void actionPerformed(ActionEvent event) {
          performPrint();
        }
      });
      pane.add(btn, gbc);
    }

  protected void performPrint() {
      PrinterJob job = PrinterJob.getPrinterJob();
      job.setPrintable(new MyPrintable());
      try {
        job.print();
      } catch (PrinterException pe) {};
    }

    // MyPrintable inner class goes here...

}
```

The display will look like this:

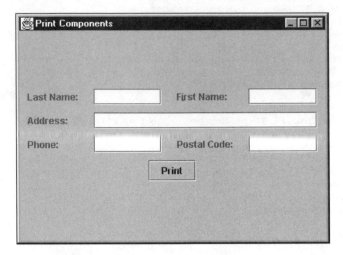

Almost all of the code in this application is devoted to creating the user interface; all that's needed to print that interface is contained in the `MyPrintable` inner class:

```
class MyPrintable implements Printable {

  public int print(Graphics g, PageFormat pf, int index) {
    if (index == 0) {
      g.translate((int)(pf.getImageableX()),
          (int)(pf.getImageableY()));
      Container pane = getContentPane();
      pane.paint(g);
      return Printable.PAGE_EXISTS;
    }
    return Printable.NO_SUCH_PAGE;
  }

}
```

The `print()` method simply obtains a reference to the frame's content pane and calls that component's `paint()` method, passing it a reference to the `Graphics` object representing the page being rendered.

It's not much more difficult to print the individual components without including the parent container in the output. You can obtain a list of the components by calling the container's `getComponents()` method, and then simply print each one individually. We'll first attempt to do so using the following code:

```
public int print(Graphics g, PageFormat pf, int index) {
  if (index == 0) {
    g.translate((int)(pf.getImageableX()),
        (int)(pf.getImageableY()));
    Container pane = getContentPane();
    // pane.paint(g);
    Component[] comps = pane.getComponents();
    for (int i = 0; i < comps.length; i++) {
      comps[i].paint(g);
```

```
        }
      return Printable.PAGE_EXISTS;
    }
    return Printable.NO_SUCH_PAGE;
  }
```

If you compile and execute this application, the printed output will appear similar to that shown below. This occurs because each component renders itself relative to the origin (coordinates 0, 0) of the graphics context. Therefore, all components are drawn at the same location, causing each component to overwrite those that were previously rendered:

When a container's `paint()` method is called, it calls the `paint()` method of each child component and ensures that the child is rendered at the appropriate location. However, since the container's `paint()` method is not used in this case, we must provide the same functionality in our `print()` method. That can be done using `translate()` to temporarily modify the origin of the `Graphics` object so that each component draws itself at the correct location:

```
public int print(Graphics g, PageFormat pf, int index) {
  if (index == 0) {
    g.translate((int)(pf.getImageableX()),
        (int)(pf.getImageableY()));
    Container pane = getContentPane();
```

```
        // pane.paint(g);
        Component[] comps = pane.getComponents();
        for (int i = 0; i < comps.length; i++) {
          g.translate(comps[i].getX(), comps[i].getY());
          comps[i].paint(g);
          g.translate(0 - comps[i].getX(), 0 - comps[i].getY());
        }
        return Printable.PAGE_EXISTS;
      }
      return Printable.NO_SUCH_PAGE;
    }
```

Notice that two translate() calls were added: one to modify the Graphics object's origin, and another to restore its value after the component is painted. That's necessary because calls to translate() are cumulative, and if the second translate() call were removed, each component would be positioned relative to the previously rendered component instead of relative to the container origin. In other words, each successive component that's drawn would incorrectly appear below and to the right of the previous one. However, as long as the Graphics object's origin is restored each time, the components appear at the appropriate locations:

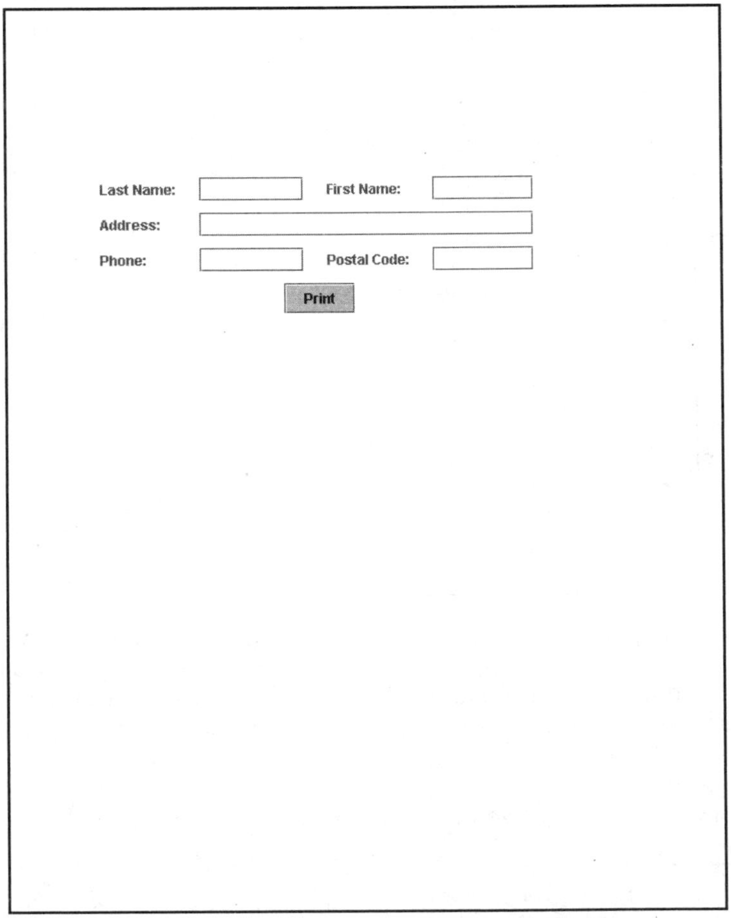

Last Name: [   ]   First Name: [   ]

Address: [   ]

Phone: [   ]   Postal Code: [   ]

Print

Summary of Component Painting

As you can see, it's extremely easy to print Swing components. Unfortunately, while this "What-You-See-Is-What-You-Get" (WYSIWYG) or "screenshot" approach provides a simple way to print, the output that it produces often isn't acceptable for professional-quality report printing. Fonts and borders that are appropriate in a graphical user interface often aren't as attractive in printed form, especially when the printer produces black-and-white output as most laser printers do. Unfortunately, there is no easy solution to this problem, and your only options are to provide your own `print()`/`paint()` implementations or to obtain a third-party package that does so. However, in some cases, you may be able to produce printed output that's acceptable by changing a component's font, borders, colors, and so on.

When Output Exceeds a Single Page

The examples provided up to this point all illustrate cases where the output could be printed on a single page. In practice, however, you'll often need to print data that won't fit on one sheet of paper, and when that's the case, you'll need to know what options are available.

For example, suppose that you wish to print the `JTable` shown below, which is both wider and longer than one piece of paper:

	Address	Phone	Postal Code	Date
	1117 Sampson Street	3184397030	70669-0531	2009/10/3
on	3420 Davis Road	3184941888	70669-0645	1999/7/18
Mark Borel	415 Walcot Road	3188826432	70669-0790	2000/3/3
Brigette Brown	904 Shafer Street	3184365577	70669-0390	2001/11/21
Tami Buchart	222 Walcot Road	3188820204	70669-0790	2000/9/27
Natalie Chaisson	1601 Sampson Street	3184398972	70669-0401	2002/7/5
John Christian	1016 Guillory Street	3184363622	70669-0511	2005/10/31
Teresa Cole	1119 Sampson Street	3184339334	70669-0531	2003/2/15
Laura Davis	330 Walcot Road	3188821313	70669-0790	2002/4/20
Daniel Douglas	704 Goss Road	3184368176	70669-0200	2010/12/1
Christine Eastman	3366 Charlotte Avenue	3184971990	70669-0641	2001/6/13
Troy Evans	1093 Columbia Southern Road	3188820480	70669-3960	1998/3/30
Allen Fanta	3393 Bayou Dinde Road	3188826481	70669-0810	1997/9/19
Jim Farley	929 Sampson Street	3184338335	70669-0531	2000/4/2
Edward Feagin	901 Shady Lane	3184330901	70669-0399	2008/12/15
Gary Gentry	1121 Sampson Street	3184395363	70669-0531	2003/2/9
David Guillory	912 John Stine Road	3184361125	70669-0260	2007/11/22
Sonya Hall	1008 Sampson Street	3184395328	70669-0531	2014/11/30
Stephanie Hebert	1213 Miller Avenue	3184337898	70669-0481	2010/1/16
Keith Henson	3416 Highway 90	3188826086	70669-0791	2012/8/18
Johnny Johnson	400 Sulphur Avenue	3184369657	70669-0544	1997/4/5
Kody Kay	3500 Houston River Road	3184398604	70669-0549	2003/9/23
Don Kelly	940 John Stine Road	3184940926	70669-0260	2000/1/2
Joanna Kile	713 Johnson Street	3184919379	70669-0550	2003/12/31
Joe King	1547 Miller Avenue	3184392794	70669-0480	2001/11/24
Kelli Koskela	507 John Stine Road	3184333179	70669-0281	2009/2/14
Wade Kemp	1124 Garfield Street	3184399263	70669-0500	2007/5/17
Derek LaLanne	804 Columbia Southern Road	3188826550	70669-0238	2003/8/18
Shawn Liles	1010 Shady Lane	3184335100	70669-0381	1996/4/22
Kelly Lovett	2301 Sampson Street	3184330875	70669-0271	2004/7/21
Rhonda Lovett	3919 Houston River Road	3184339922	70669-0661	2020/9/18
Dino Lucius	1601 Sampson Street	3184391486	70669-0401	2018/11/3
John Montalbano	109 Walcot Road	3188820630	70669-0790	1999/12/20
Scott Peterson	510 Lake Street	3184335880	70669-0542	1997/10/12
Keith Reed	801 Sampson Street	3184391744	70669-0530	1996/7/3
Herman Roessler	Pete Manena Road	3188820304	70669-1039	2001/5/5
Robin Ross	3300 Old Spanish Trail	3188820234	70669-0770	2003/8/3
Robin Rougeau	3300 Shady Lane	3188820234	70669-0399	2007/9/12
Ross Tuttle	713 Johnson Street	3184919379	70669-0550	2008/8/3
Teri White	2516 Westwood Road	3184940263	70669-0201	2005/6/12

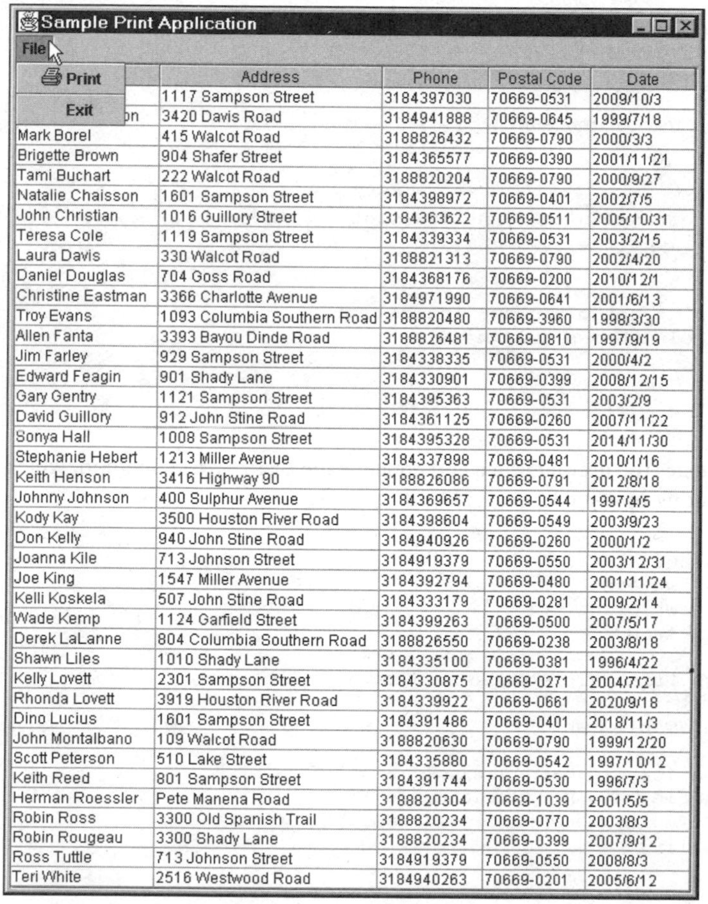

This table and user interface can be created using the following code. `SampleTableModel` contains the data itself:

```java
import javax.swing.table.*;

public class SampleTableModel extends AbstractTableModel {

  public final static String[] columnNames = {"Name", "Address", "Phone",
      "Postal Code", "Date"};

  public final static Object[][] values = {
      {"Janet Abul",
      "1117 Sampson Street",
      "3184397030", "70669-0531", "2009/10/3"},

      {"Debbie Anderson",
      "3420 Davis Road",
      "3184941888", "70669-0645", "1999/7/18"},

      // Many more entries...

      {"Teri White",
      "2516 Westwood Road",
      "3184940263", "70669-0201", "2005/6/12"}
  };

  public int getRowCount() {
    return values.length;
  }

  public int getColumnCount() {
    return 5;
  }

  public Object getValueAt(int row, int column) {
    return values[row][column];
  }

  public String getColumnName(int column) {
    return columnNames[column];
  }

}
```

`PrintSample` creates the user interface and contains the `onPrint()` method, which creates a new thread to perform the printing operation:

```java
import java.awt.*;
import java.awt.event.*;
import java.awt.print.*;
import javax.swing.*;

public class PrintSample extends JFrame {

  protected JTable table;

  public static void main(String[] args) {
    PrintSample ps = new PrintSample();
    ps.setDefaultCloseOperation(JFrame.EXIT_ON_CLOSE);
    ps.pack();
```

```
      ps.setVisible(true);
    }

  public PrintSample() {
    super("Sample Print Application");
    table = new JTable(new SampleTableModel());
    table.setAutoResizeMode(JTable.AUTO_RESIZE_OFF);
    setContentPane(new JScrollPane(table));
    buildMenuBar();
  }

  protected void buildMenuBar() {
    JMenuBar menuBar = new JMenuBar();
    JMenu menu = new JMenu("File");
    menu.add(new AbstractAction("Print",
        new ImageIcon("print.gif")) {
      public void actionPerformed(ActionEvent event) {
        onPrint();
      }
    });
    menu.addSeparator();
    menu.add(new AbstractAction("Exit",
        new ImageIcon("empty.gif")) {
      public void actionPerformed(ActionEvent event) {
        System.exit(0);
      }
    });
    menuBar.add(menu);
    setJMenuBar(menuBar);
  }

  protected void onPrint() {
    Thread t = new Thread(new Runnable() {
      public void run() {
        PrinterJob pj = PrinterJob.getPrinterJob();
        Paper paper = new Paper();
        paper.setImageableArea(72, 144, 6.5 * 72, 7 * 72);
        PageFormat pageFormat = new PageFormat();
        pageFormat.setPaper(paper);
        TablePrinter tablePrinter = new TablePrinter(table);
        pj.setPrintable(tablePrinter, pageFormat);
        try {
          pj.print();
        } catch (PrinterException pe) {
          JOptionPane.showMessageDialog(
              PrintSample.this,
              "Printing error:" +
              pe.getMessage());
        }
      }
    });
    t.start();
  }
}
```

PrintSample also uses the TablePrinter class listed below, which implements Printable and is responsible for printing the table:

```
import java.awt.*;
import java.awt.print.*;
```

```
import javax.swing.*;
import javax.swing.table.*;

public class TablePrinter implements Printable {

  protected JTable table;

  public TablePrinter(JTable tbl) {
    table = tbl;
  }

  public int print(Graphics g, PageFormat pf, int index) {
    if (index == 0) {
      g.translate((int)(pf.getImageableX()),
          (int)(pf.getImageableY()));
      table.paint(g);
      return Printable.PAGE_EXISTS;
    }
    return Printable.NO_SUCH_PAGE;
  }

}
```

When the Print item on the File menu is activated, this application prints the table on a single page of paper with one-inch left and right and two-inch top and bottom margins. The column widths on the printed page(s) will correspond to the widths of the columns that are displayed on the screen:

Janet Abel	1117 Sampson Street	3184397030	70669-0531	20
Debbie Anderson	3420 Davis Road	3184941888	70669-0645	19
Mark Borel	415 Walcot Road	3188826432	70669-0790	20
Brigette Brown	904 Shafer Street	3184365577	70669-0390	20
Tami Buchart	222 Walcot Road	3188820204	70669-0790	20
Natalie Chaisson	1601 Sampson Street	3184398972	70669-0401	20
John Christian	1016 Guillory Street	3184363622	70669-0511	20
Teresa Cole	1119 Sampson Street	3184339334	70669-0531	20
Laura Davis	330 Walcot Road	3188821313	70669-0790	20
Daniel Douglas	704 Goss Road	3184368176	70669-0200	20
Christine Eastman	3366 Charlotte Avenue	3184971990	70669-0641	20
Troy Evans	1093 Columbia Southern Road	3188820480	70669-3960	19
Allen Fanta	3393 Bayou Dinde Road	3188826481	70669-0810	19
Jim Farley	929 Sampson Street	3184338335	70669-0531	20
Edward Feagin	901 Shady Lane	3184330901	70669-0399	20
Gary Gentry	1121 Sampson Street	3184395363	70669-0531	20
David Guillory	912 John Stine Road	3184361125	70669-0260	20
Sonya Hall	1008 Sampson Street	3184395328	70669-0531	20
Stephanie Hebert	1213 Miller Avenue	3184337898	70669-0481	20
Keith Henson	3416 Highway 90	3188826086	70669-0791	20
Johnny Johnson	400 Sulphur Avenue	3184369657	70669-0544	19
Kody Kay	3500 Houston River Road	3184398604	70669-0549	20
Don Kelly	940 John Stine Road	3184940926	70669-0260	20
Joanna Kile	713 Johnson Street	3184919379	70669-0550	20
Joe King	1547 Miller Avenue	3184392794	70669-0480	20
Kelli Koskela	507 John Stine Road	3184333179	70669-0281	20
Wade Kemp	1124 Garfield Street	3184399263	70669-0500	20
Derek LaLanne	804 Columbia Southern Road	3188826550	70669-0238	20
Shawn Liles	1010 Shady Lane	3184335100	70669-0381	19
Kelly Lovett	2301 Sampson Street	3184330875	70669-0271	20
Rhonda Lovett	3919 Houston River Road	3184339922	70669-0661	20
Dino Lucius	1601 Sampson Street	3184391498	70669-0401	20

Although most of the table does appear, there are several problems:

- ❑ Part of the table data is missing because the table is too large to fit on one page
- ❑ The table header does not appear at all
- ❑ No border is drawn around the top and left edges of the table

These last two problems are actually normal behavior for a table that's not drawn by a `JScrollPane` parent container. A table header normally only appears when a `JTable` is inside a `JScrollPane`, so for the header to appear, the `print()` method in `TablePrinter` must draw it along with the table itself.

The missing border on the left and top edges is related to the way that table cell borders are drawn. Specifically, the borders are normally only drawn on the right and bottom edges, although this isn't usually apparent because a `JTable` typically appears inside a `JScrollPane` that provides its own border.

The header problem will be addressed later in the chapter, but for now we'll focus on what can be done to ensure that the entire table is printed. You have four options available to you for increasing the amount of data printed:

- ❑ Use a different orientation (landscape) to make better use of the space available on the paper
- ❑ Reduce the margin sizes
- ❑ Scale the output (make it smaller) so that it fits on a single page
- ❑ Produce multiple pages of output

We'll now examine each of these four options and provide an example of how to implement them using the `PrintSample` application.

Changing Orientation

You'll often wish to print output that takes up more space horizontally than it does vertically. When doing so, you may choose to rotate the output by using landscape or reverse landscape orientation. That can be accomplished by modifying the `PageFormat` instance that's created in `PrintSample`:

```
protected void onPrint() {
  Thread t = new Thread(new Runnable() {
    public void run() {
      PrinterJob pj = PrinterJob.getPrinterJob();
      Paper paper = new Paper();
      paper.setImageableArea(72, 144, 6.5 * 72, 7 * 72);
      PageFormat pageFormat = new PageFormat();
      pageFormat.setPaper(paper);
      pageFormat.setOrientation(PageFormat.LANDSCAPE);
      TablePrinter tablePrinter = new TablePrinter(table);
      pj.setPrintable(tablePrinter, pageFormat);
      try {
        pj.print();
      } catch (PrinterException pe) {
        JOptionPane.showMessageDialog(
            PrintSample.this,
            "Printing error:" +
            pe.getMessage());
```

```
            }
        }
    });
    t.start();
}
```

Unfortunately, changing the orientation actually produces less output in this case, because the table's height is greater than its width:

Janet Abel	1117 Sampson Street	3184397030	70669-0531	2009/10/
Debbie Anderson	3420 Davis Road	3184941888	70669-0645	1999/7/1
Mark Borel	415 Walcot Road	3188826432	70669-0790	2000/3/3
Brigette Brown	904 Shafer Street	3184365577	70669-0390	2001/11/
Tami Buchart	222 Walcot Road	3188820204	70669-0790	2000/9/2
Natalie Chaisson	1601 Sampson Street	3184398972	70669-0401	2002/7/5
John Christian	1016 Guillory Street	3184363622	70669-0511	2005/10/
Teresa Cole	1119 Sampson Street	3184339334	70669-0531	2003/2/1
Laura Davis	330 Walcot Road	3188821313	70669-0790	2002/4/2
Daniel Douglas	704 Goss Road	3184368176	70669-0200	2010/12/
Christine Eastman	3366 Charlotte Avenue	3184971990	70669-0641	2001/6/1
Troy Evans	1093 Columbia Southern Road	3188820480	70669-3960	1998/3/3
Allen Fanta	3393 Bayou Dinde Road	3188826481	70669-0810	1997/9/1
Jim Farley	929 Sampson Street	3184338335	70669-0531	2000/4/2
Edward Feagin	901 Shady Lane	3184330901	70669-0399	2008/12/
Gary Gentry	1121 Sampson Street	3184395363	70669-0531	2003/2/9
David Guillory	912 John Stine Road	3184361125	70669-0260	2007/11/
Sonya Hall	1008 Sampson Street	3184395328	70669-0531	2014/11/
Stephanie Hebert	1213 Miller Avenue	3184337898	70669-0481	2010/1/1
Keith Henson	3416 Highway 90	3188826086	70669-0791	2012/8/1
Johnny Johnson	400 Sulphur Avenue	3184369657	70669-0544	1997/4/5
Kody Kay	3500 Houston River Road	3184398604	70669-0549	2003/9/2
Don Kelly	940 John Stine Road	3184940926	70669-0260	2000/1/2
Joanna Kile	713 Johnson Street	3184919379	70669-0550	2003/12/
Joe King	1547 Miller Avenue	3184392794	70669-0480	2001/11/
Kelli Koskela	507 John Stine Road	3184333179	70669-0281	2009/2/1
Wade Kemp	1124 Garfield Street	3184399263	70669-0500	2007/5/1
Derek LaLanne	804 Columbia Southern Road	3188826550	70669-0238	2003/8/1
Shawn Liles	1010 Shady Lane	3184335100	70669-0381	1996/4/2

Modifying Margins

Another way to make better use of the space on a page is to decrease the margin sizes, although very small margins tend to make your output less attractive. However, when it's important to make maximum use of the available space on the page and/or appearance is of secondary importance, you may choose to reduce the margin sizes.

Although you can design your application to arbitrarily select margin sizes, you generally should not do so. In fact, your application should also not arbitrarily select the orientation as PrintSample now does, but should instead allow the user to select the orientation and the page margins. That functionality can be provided through the pageDialog() method in PrinterJob, which displays a dialog that allows the user to edit PageFormat settings:

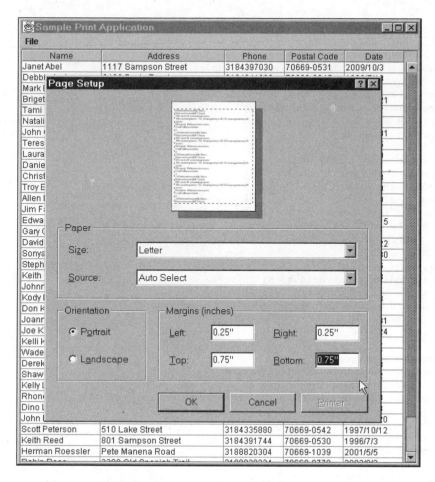

The following modifications to `PrintSample` provide a **Page Setup** menu item, and when that item is activated, a page setup dialog appears as shown above, allowing the user to select the orientation and margin sizes.

```java
import java.awt.*;
import java.awt.event.*;
import java.awt.print.*;
import javax.swing.*;

public class PrintSample extends JFrame {

  protected JTable table;
  protected PageFormat pageFormat;

  public static void main(String[] args) {
    PrintSample ps = new PrintSample();
    ps.setDefaultCloseOperation(JFrame.EXIT_ON_CLOSE);
    ps.pack();
    ps.setVisible(true);
  }
```

```
  public PrintSample() {
    super("Sample Print Application");
    table = new JTable(new SampleTableModel());
    table.setAutoResizeMode(JTable.AUTO_RESIZE_OFF);
    setContentPane(new JScrollPane(table));
    pageFormat = new PageFormat();
    buildMenuBar();
  }

  protected void buildMenuBar() {
    JMenuBar menuBar = new JMenuBar();
    JMenu menu = new JMenu("File");
    menu.add(new AbstractAction("Page Setup",
        new ImageIcon("empty.gif")) {
      public void actionPerformed(ActionEvent event) {
        onPageSetup();
      }
    });
    menu.add(new AbstractAction("Print",
        new ImageIcon("print.gif")) {
      public void actionPerformed(ActionEvent event) {
        onPrint();
      }
    });
    menu.addSeparator();
    menu.add(new AbstractAction("Exit",
        new ImageIcon("empty.gif")) {
      public void actionPerformed(ActionEvent event) {
        System.exit(0);
      }
    });
    menuBar.add(menu);
    setJMenuBar(menuBar);
  }

  protected void onPageSetup() {
    Thread t = new Thread(new Runnable() {
      public void run() {
        PrinterJob pj = PrinterJob.getPrinterJob();
        pageFormat = pj.pageDialog(pageFormat);
      }
    });
    t.start();
  }

  protected void onPrint() {
    Thread t = new Thread(new Runnable() {
      public void run() {
        PrinterJob pj = PrinterJob.getPrinterJob();
        // Paper paper = new Paper();
        // paper.setImageableArea(72, 144, 6.5 * 72, 7 * 72);
        // PageFormat pageFormat = new PageFormat();
        // pageFormat.setPaper(paper);
        // pageFormat.setOrientation(PageFormat.LANDSCAPE);
```

```
                TablePrinter tablePrinter = new TablePrinter(table);
                pj.setPrintable(tablePrinter, pageFormat);
                try {
                  pj.print();
                } catch (PrinterException pe) {
                  JOptionPane.showMessageDialog(
                      PrintSample.this,
                      "Printing error:" +
                      pe.getMessage());
                }
              }
            });
          t.start();
        }

      }
```

Scaling

The Java 2D API was introduced in Java 2 and it provides a great deal of functionality that was not available in previous releases. Part of the Java 2D API is the `Graphics2D` class, which is a subclass of `Graphics` and which provides many methods that allow you to perform sophisticated rendering operations.

The `print()` methods implemented in this chapter have so far used only the methods defined in `Graphics`, but in fact, you're not limited to the capabilities of that class. In Java 2, the object passed to `print()` (and components' `paint()`) methods is actually an instance of `Graphics2D`, so you're able to take advantage of the enhanced capabilities of Java's 2D API. To do so, simply cast the `Graphics` object passed to your `print()` method, as shown below:

```
public int print(Graphics g, PageFormat pf, int page) {
  Graphics2D g2d = (Graphics2D)g;
  if (page == 0) {
    // Perform rendering here
    return Printable.PAGE_EXISTS;
  }
  return Printable.NO_SUCH_PAGE;
}
```

One of the capabilities provided by `Graphics2D` is the ability to perform **scaling**, which changes the size of the output that you render. For example, suppose that you modify the scale factor so that it renders your output at half its normal size. In that case, an image that's 100 pixels wide and 50 pixels in height will be only 50 pixels wide and 25 in height when rendered and printed. In other words, scaling allows you to shrink or enlarge your output, and you can use this technique to ensure that your data will fit on a printed page.

When you set a scale factor for a `Graphics2D` object, you normally should use the same value for both the width and the height. This causes your output to have the same proportions that it would have if it had not been scaled, while using two different scale values will distort your output. For example, if you're rendering a square but you use one value to scale the width and a different value to scale the height, the shape will be rendered as a rectangle instead of a square.

You'll typically select a scale factor by calculating the value that can be used to make the output as large as possible while still fitting within a single page, and the calculations for doing so are simple. For example, you could make the following changes to `TablePrinter` to make the `JTable` shrink or expand so that it fills a page of output:

```java
import java.awt.*;
import java.awt.print.*;
import javax.swing.*;
import javax.swing.table.*;

public class TablePrinter implements Printable {

  protected JTable table;

  public TablePrinter(JTable tbl) {
    table = tbl;
  }

  public int print(Graphics g, PageFormat pf, int index) {
    if (index == 0) {
      g.translate((int)(pf.getImageableX()),
          (int)(pf.getImageableY()));
      Graphics2D g2d = (Graphics2D)g;
      double pageWidth = pf.getImageableWidth();
      double pageHeight = pf.getImageableHeight();
      double tableWidth = table.getWidth();
      double tableHeight = table.getHeight();
      // Find out what scale factor should be applied
      // to make the table's width small enough to
      // fit on the page
      double scaleX = pageWidth / tableWidth;
      // Now do the same for the height
      double scaleY = pageHeight / tableHeight;
      // Pick the smaller of the two values so that
      // the table is as large as possible while
      // not exceeding either the page's width or
      // its height
      double scaleFactor = Math.min(scaleX, scaleY);
      // Now set the scale factor
      g2d.scale(scaleFactor, scaleFactor);
      table.paint(g);
      return Printable.PAGE_EXISTS;
    }
    return Printable.NO_SUCH_PAGE;
  }

}
```

Multi-Page Printing

Although we've now seen three ways to include more information on a single printed page, none of these options is entirely acceptable. Modifying margins and changing the page orientation provides only a small amount of additional space. Scaling can be used to print a very large amount of information on a single page, but shrinking your output by a large amount can make it unreadable and therefore useless. Ultimately, it's often necessary to produce more than one page of output when printing data.

Unfortunately, generating multiple pages of output adds a new level of complexity to the rendering process. Instead of simply calling a component's paint() method, you will sometimes find it necessary to "split" a large component across multiple pages, drawing a different portion of the component on each page. This can be accomplished using a technique mentioned earlier called **clipping**.

Clipping

Clipping involves reducing the portion of a Graphics object's drawing area that can be modified. For example, when print() is called, the Graphics object passed to that method is clipped so that you can't modify any pixels outside the imageable area.

To print only a portion of a component, you'll use translate() to (conceptually) position the component over the imageable area and clip the Graphics object so that only a subset of the component's visual representation is rendered.

For example, let's assume that you wish to render a JTable that's many hundreds or even thousands of pixels in height, and that you plan to render 500 rows of pixels per printed page. The following application illustrates how you can split the table across multiple pages:

```java
import java.awt.*;
import java.awt.print.*;
import javax.swing.*;

public class ClipTest {

  protected JTable table;

  public static void main(String[] args) {
    ClipTest ct = new ClipTest();
  }

  public ClipTest() {
    table = new JTable(new SampleTableModel ());
    table.setSize(table.getPreferredSize());
    PrinterJob job = PrinterJob.getPrinterJob();
    job.setPrintable(new MyPrintable());
    try {
      job.print();
    } catch (PrinterException pe) {};
    System.exit(0);
  }

  class MyPrintable implements Printable {

    public int print(Graphics g, PageFormat pf, int index) {
      int positionX = (int)(pf.getImageableX());
      int positionY = (int)(pf.getImageableY());
      int width = (int)(pf.getImageableWidth());
      g.clipRect (positionX, positionY, width, 500);
      g.translate(positionX, positionY);
      int pixelIndex = index * 500;
      if (pixelIndex < table.getHeight()) {
        g.translate(0, -pixelIndex);
        table.paint(g);
        return Printable.PAGE_EXISTS;
```

```
      }
      return Printable.NO_SUCH_PAGE;
   }


 }


}
```

This application does split a table vertically when its height makes it too large to fit on a page. However, it does not split a table horizontally when it's too wide to fit on a page, which is one limitation of this simple implementation. In addition, it splits the table into 500-pixel blocks, even if the split occurs in the middle of a row. In other words, a single row of table cells can be partially printed at the end of one page with the remainder of that row printed at the beginning of the next page. Ideally, the `Printable` should split the table at row boundaries. Finally, this sample application does not print the table's header, which makes the output more difficult to interpret.

The `TablePrinter` class listed below addresses all the limitations just described. Although it may appear complex, it simply uses techniques that have already been identified in this chapter.

The table's header is rendered after a reference to it is obtained via the `getTableHeader()` method in `JTable`, and the determination of where to split the table is made using `rowAtPoint()`, `columnAtPoint()`, and `getCellRect()`:

```java
import java.awt.*;
import java.awt.print.*;
import javax.swing.*;
import javax.swing.table.*;

public class TablePrinter implements Printable, Pageable {

  protected JTable table;
  protected PageFormat pageFormat;
  protected int headerStatus = ALL_PAGES;

  /**
   * These constants indicate which pages should include column headers
   */
  public final static int ALL_PAGES = 0;
  public final static int FIRST_PAGE_ONLY = 1;
  public final static int NO_PAGES = 2;

  public TablePrinter(JTable tbl, PageFormat pf) {
    table = tbl;
    pageFormat = pf;
  }

  /**
   * Perform the printing here
   */
  public int print(Graphics g, PageFormat pf, int index) {
    Dimension size = null;
    //  Get the table's preferred size
    if ((table.getWidth() == 0) || (table.getHeight() == 0)) {
      table.setSize(table.getPreferredSize());
```

```
    }
    int tableWidth = table.getWidth();
    int tableHeight = table.getHeight();
    int positionX = 0;
    int positionY = 0;

    //  Loop until we have printed the entire table
    int pageIndex = 0;
    while (positionY < tableHeight) {
      positionX = 0;
      while (positionX < tableWidth) {
        size = getPrintSize(positionX, positionY);
        if (pageIndex == index) {
          //  Paint as much of the table as will fit on a page
          paintTable(g, positionX, positionY, size);
          return Printable.PAGE_EXISTS;
        }
        pageIndex++;
        positionX += size.width;
      }
      positionY += size.height;
    }
    return Printable.NO_SUCH_PAGE;
}

/**
 * Calculate how much of the table will fit on a page without
 * causing a row or column to be split across two pages
 */
protected Dimension getPrintSize(int positionX, int positionY) {
  Rectangle rect;
  int printWidth;
  int printHeight;
  int firstCol = table.columnAtPoint(
      new Point(positionX, positionY));
  int firstRow = table.rowAtPoint(
      new Point(positionX, positionY));
  int maxWidth = (int)(pageFormat.getImageableWidth());
  int maxHeight = (int)(pageFormat.getImageableHeight());
  if (displayHeaderOnPage(positionY)) {
    maxHeight -= table.getTableHeader().getHeight();
  }

  int lastCol = table.columnAtPoint(
      new Point(positionX + maxWidth, positionY));
  if (lastCol == -1) {
    printWidth = table.getWidth() - positionX;
  }
  else {
    rect = table.getCellRect(0, lastCol - 1, true);
    printWidth = rect.x + rect.width - positionX;
  }

  int lastRow = table.rowAtPoint(new Point(
      positionX, positionY + maxHeight));
```

```
      if (lastRow == -1) {
        printHeight = table.getHeight() - positionY;
      }
      else {
        rect = table.getCellRect(lastRow - 1, 0, true);
        printHeight = rect.y + rect.height - positionY;
      }
      return new Dimension(printWidth, printHeight);
    }

    /**
     * Paint / print a portion of the table
     */
    protected void paintTable(Graphics g, int positionX, int positionY,
        Dimension size) {
      int offsetX = (int)(pageFormat.getImageableX());
      int offsetY = (int)(pageFormat.getImageableY());
      if (displayHeaderOnPage(positionY)) {
        JTableHeader header = table.getTableHeader();
        if ((header.getWidth() == 0) ||
            (header.getHeight() == 0)) {
          header.setSize(header.getPreferredSize());
        }
        int headerHeight = header.getHeight();
        g.translate(offsetX - positionX, offsetY);
        g.clipRect(positionX, 0,
            size.width, size.height + headerHeight);
        header.paint(g);
        g.translate(0, headerHeight - positionY);
        g.clipRect(positionX, positionY, size.width, size.height);
      }
      else {
        g.translate(offsetX - positionX,
            offsetY - positionY);
        g.clipRect(positionX, positionY,
            size.width, size.height);
      }
      table.paint(g);
    }

    /**
     * Determine whether or not to paint the headers on the current page
     */
    protected boolean displayHeaderOnPage(int positionY) {
      return ((headerStatus == ALL_PAGES) ||
          ((headerStatus == FIRST_PAGE_ONLY) &&
          positionY == 0));
    }

    /**
     * Calculate the number of pages it will take to print the entire table
     */
    public int getNumberOfPages() {
      Dimension size = null;
      int tableWidth = table.getWidth();
```

```
      int tableHeight = table.getHeight();
      int positionX = 0;
      int positionY = 0;

      int pageIndex = 0;
      while (positionY < tableHeight) {
        positionX = 0;
        while (positionX < tableWidth) {
          size = getPrintSize(positionX, positionY);
          positionX += size.width;
          pageIndex++;
        }
        positionY += size.height;
      }
      return pageIndex;
    }

    public Printable getPrintable(int index) {
      return this;
    }

    public PageFormat getPageFormat(int index) {
      return pageFormat;
    }

}
```

An example of how to use this modified class is provided by updating the onPrint() method in PrintSample:

```
protected void onPrint() {
  Thread t = new Thread(new Runnable() {
    public void run() {
      PrinterJob pj = PrinterJob.getPrinterJob();
      TablePrinter tablePrinter = new TablePrinter(table,
          pageFormat);
      pj.setPageable(tablePrinter);
      try {
        pj.print();
      } catch (PrinterException pe) {
        JOptionPane.showMessageDialog(
            PrintSample.this,
            "Printing error:" +
            pe.getMessage());
      }
    }
  });
  t.start();
}
```

Print Preview

A standard part of many applications is the facility that provides a preview of how your output will appear if printed, and you may wish to add this capability to your Java applications. One easy way to do so is to create a visual component class that uses a `Printable` and a `PageFormat` to render itself.

For example, the component's size should correspond to the page dimensions identified by the `PageFormat` object. Similarly, when `paint()` is called, the rendering operation should be delegated to the `Printable` object. An implementation of such a component is shown below:

```java
import java.awt.*;
import java.awt.geom.*;
import java.awt.print.*;
import javax.swing.*;
import javax.swing.border.*;

public class PrintComponent extends JPanel {

  /**
   * The item to be printed
   */
  protected Printable printable;

  /**
   * PageFormat to use when printing
   */
  protected PageFormat pageFormat;

  /**
   * The page that is currently displayed
   */
  protected int displayPage;

  /**
   * The scale factor (1.0 = 100%)
   */
  protected double scaleFactor;

  public PrintComponent(Printable p, PageFormat pf) {
    setPrintable(p);
    setPageFormat(pf);
    setDisplayPage(0);
    setScaleFactor(100);
    setBackground(Color.white);
  }

  public void setPrintable(Printable p) {
    printable = p;
    revalidate();
  }

  public void setPageFormat(PageFormat pf) {
    pageFormat = pf;
    revalidate();
  }

  public void setDisplayPage(int page) {
    displayPage = page;
    revalidate();
```

```
    }

    public void setScaleFactor(double scale) {
      scaleFactor = scale;
      revalidate();
    }

    public double getScaleFactor() {
      return scaleFactor;
    }

    /**
     * Calculate the size of this component with the specified scale factor
     */
    public Dimension getSizeWithScale(double scale) {
      Insets insets = getInsets();
      int width = ((int)(pageFormat.getWidth() *
          scale / 100d)) +
          insets.left + insets.right;
      int height = ((int)(pageFormat.getHeight() *
          scale / 100d)) +
          insets.top + insets.bottom;
      return new Dimension(width, height);
    }

    public Dimension getPreferredSize() {
      return getSizeWithScale(scaleFactor);
    }

    public Dimension getMinimumSize() {
      return getPreferredSize();
    }

    /**
     * Paint this component, taking the scale factor into account and
     * sizing it appropriately.
     */
    public void paintComponent(Graphics g) {
      super.paintComponent(g);
      Graphics2D g2 = (Graphics2D)g;
      Rectangle clipRect = g2.getClipBounds();
      AffineTransform at = g2.getTransform();
      int x = (int)(pageFormat.getImageableX() *
          scaleFactor / 100d);
      int y = (int)(pageFormat.getImageableY() *
          scaleFactor / 100d);
      int w = (int)(pageFormat.getImageableWidth() *
          scaleFactor / 100d);
      int h = (int)(pageFormat.getImageableHeight() *
          scaleFactor / 100d);
      g2.clipRect(x, y, w, h);
      g2.scale(scaleFactor / 100, scaleFactor / 100);
      try {
        printable.print(g, pageFormat, displayPage);
      } catch (PrinterException pe) {};
      g2.setTransform(at);
      g2.setClip(clipRect);
    }

}
```

Note that since a `Printable` can print more than one page, this class also allows you to identify which page the `Printable` should render when its `paint()` method is called. In addition, `PrintComponent` supports a "scale factor" property that can be used to increase or decrease the component's size. A scale factor of 100 corresponds to its normal size, which is the paper size identified by the `PageFormat` object.

With `PrintComponent` defined, implementing print preview functionality can be accomplished easily, and an example of how to do so appears below. In fact, the following code merely creates a simple Swing-based interface that provides the user with the ability to easily interact with the `PrintComponent` class we just defined. It provides **Previous** and **Next** buttons that allow you to select which page of the specified `Pageable` is currently displayed, a **Size To Fit** button that sets the scale factor to the largest value that will allow the current page to be completely displayed, and a text field that allows you to enter a specific scale factor:

```java
import java.awt.*;
import java.awt.event.*;
import java.awt.print.*;
import javax.swing.*;
import javax.swing.border.*;

public class PrintPreviewer extends JPanel {

  protected Pageable pageable;
  protected PrintComponent printComponent;
  protected int pageIndex;

  protected JScrollPane scrollPane;
  protected JButton previousButton;
  protected JButton nextButton;
  protected JButton sizeButton;
  protected JTextField scaleText;

  public PrintPreviewer(Pageable p, int page) {
    pageable = p;
    pageIndex = page;
    printComponent = new PrintComponent(null, null);
    printComponent.setBorder(BorderFactory.createBevelBorder(
        BevelBorder.RAISED));
    buildLayout();
    displayPage(pageIndex);
  }

  /**
   * Adds the appropriate components to this panel
   */
  protected void buildLayout() {
    setLayout(new BorderLayout());
    JPanel panel = new JPanel();
    panel.setLayout(new FlowLayout(FlowLayout.CENTER, 10, 10));
    panel.add(printComponent);
    scrollPane = new JScrollPane(panel);
    add(scrollPane, BorderLayout.CENTER);
    add(getBottomPanel(), BorderLayout.SOUTH);
    addListeners();
  }

  /**
   * Returns a panel that contains the buttons supported by this interface
   */
  protected JPanel getBottomPanel() {
```

```java
        JPanel outer = new JPanel();
        outer.setLayout(new FlowLayout(FlowLayout.CENTER, 10, 0));
        JPanel inner = new JPanel();
        inner.setLayout(new GridLayout(1, 2, 10, 0));
        previousButton = new JButton("Previous");
        inner.add(previousButton);
        nextButton = new JButton("Next");
        inner.add(nextButton);
        outer.add(inner);
        scaleText = new JTextField(3);
        outer.add(scaleText);
        sizeButton = new JButton("Size To Fit");
        outer.add(sizeButton);
        return outer;
    }

    /**
     * Adds listeners to the buttons and the text field
     */
    protected void addListeners() {
      previousButton.addActionListener(new ActionListener() {
        public void actionPerformed(ActionEvent event) {
          displayPage(pageIndex - 1);
        }
      });
      nextButton.addActionListener(new ActionListener() {
        public void actionPerformed(ActionEvent event) {
          displayPage(pageIndex + 1);
        }
      });
      sizeButton.addActionListener(new ActionListener() {
        public void actionPerformed(ActionEvent event) {
          sizeToFit();
        }
      });
      scaleText.addActionListener(new ActionListener() {
        public void actionPerformed(ActionEvent event) {
          try {
            int scale = Integer.parseInt(
                scaleText.getText());
            printComponent.setScaleFactor(scale);
          } catch (NumberFormatException nfe) {};
        }
      });
    }

    /**
     * Displays the specified page within the panel
     */
    protected void displayPage(int index) {
      pageIndex = index;
      printComponent.setPrintable(pageable.getPrintable(pageIndex));
      printComponent.setPageFormat(pageable.getPageFormat(pageIndex));
      printComponent.setDisplayPage(index);
      previousButton.setEnabled(pageIndex > 0);
      nextButton.setEnabled(pageIndex <
          (pageable.getNumberOfPages() - 1));
      repaint();
    }

    /**
     * Determine the largest scale factor that can be used that will
```

```
 * allow the current page to be displayed completely. In other words,
 * make the page as large as possible without making it necessary for
 * the user to use scroll bars to view the entire page. This is
 * accomplished by calculating the ratios that represent the actual
 * width of the page relative to the available width, and the actual
 * height of the page to the available height. The smaller of the two
 * values will dictate how large the ratio can be set while still
 * allowing the entire page to be displayed.
 */
protected void sizeToFit() {
  int newScaleFactor;
  Dimension compSize = printComponent.getSizeWithScale(100d);
  Dimension viewSize = scrollPane.getSize();

  int scaleX = (viewSize.width - 25) * 100 / compSize.width;
  int scaleY = (viewSize.height - 25) * 100 / compSize.height;
  newScaleFactor = Math.min(scaleX, scaleY);

  printComponent.setScaleFactor(newScaleFactor);
  scaleText.setText(Integer.toString(newScaleFactor));
  repaint();
}

}
```

Most of the code in `PrintPreviewer` either creates or supports the user interface, which is shown below. For example, the interface allows you to type in a numeric value into a text field at the bottom of the screen, and when you do so the `PrintComponent`'s scale factor is set to that value:

Name	Address	Phone	Postal Code	Date
Janet Abel	1117 Sampson Street	3184397030	70669-0531	2009/10/3
Debbie Anderson	3420 Davis Road	3184941888	70669-0645	1999/7/18
Mark Borel	415 Walcot Road	3188826432	70669-0790	2000/3/3
Brigette Brown	904 Shafer Street	3184365577	70669-0390	2001/11/21
Tami Buchart	222 Walcot Road	3188820204	70669-0790	2000/9/27
Natalie Chaisson	1601 Sampson Street	3184398972	70669-0401	2002/7/5
John Christian	1016 Guillory Street	3184363622	70669-0511	2005/10/31
Teresa Cole	1119 Sampson Street	3184339334	70669-0531	2003/2/15
Laura Davis	330 Walcot Road	3188821313	70669-0790	2002/4/20
Daniel Douglas	704 Goss Road	3184368176	70669-0200	2010/12/1
Christine Eastman	3366 Charlotte Avenue	3184971990	70669-0641	2001/6/13
Troy Evans	1093 Columbia Southern Road	3188820480	70669-3960	1998/3/30
Allen Fanta	3393 Bayou Dinde Road	3188826481	70669-0810	1997/9/19
Jim Farley	929 Sampson Street	3184338335	70669-0531	2000/4/2
Edward Feagin	901 Shady Lane	3184330901	70669-0399	2008/12/15
Gary Gentry	1121 Sampson Street	3184395363	70669-0531	2003/2/9
David Guillory	912 John Stine Road	3184361125	70669-0260	2007/11/22
Sonya Hall	1008 Sampson Street	3184395328	70669-0531	2014/11/30
Stephanie Hebert	1213 Miller Avenue	3184337898	70669-0481	2010/1/16
Keith Henson	3416 Highway 90	3188826086	70669-0791	2012/8/18
Johnny Johnson	400 Sulphur Avenue	3184369657	70669-0544	1997/4/5
Kody Kay	3500 Houston River Road	3184398604	70669-0549	2003/9/23
Don Kelly	940 John Stine Road	3184940926	70669-0260	2000/1/2
Joanna Kile	713 Johnson Street	3184919379	70669-0550	2003/12/31
Joe King	1547 Miller Avenue	3184392794	70669-0480	2001/11/24
Kelli Koskela	507 John Stine Road	3184333179	70669-0281	2009/2/14
Wade Kemp	1124 Garfield Street	3184399263	70669-0500	2007/5/17
Derek LaLanne	804 Columbia Southern Road	3188826550	70669-0238	2003/8/18
Shawn Liles	1010 Shady Lane	3184335100	70669-0381	1996/4/22
Kelly Lovett	2301 Sampson Street	3184330875	70669-0271	2004/7/21
Rhonda Lovett	3919 Houston River Road	3184339922	70669-0661	2020/9/18
Dino Lucius	1601 Sampson Street	3184391486	70669-0401	2018/11/3

Previous | Next | 84 | Size To Fit

The `sizeToFit()` method is called when the button at the bottom of the screen is pressed, and that method makes the `PrintComponent` as large as possible without exceeding the width or height of its parent container.

Finally, `PrintSample` must be modified to support the new print preview facility:

```java
import java.awt.*;
import java.awt.event.*;
import java.awt.print.*;
import javax.swing.*;

public class PrintSample extends JFrame {

  protected JTable table;
  protected PageFormat pageFormat;

  public static void main(String[] args) {
    PrintSample ps = new PrintSample();
    ps.setDefaultCloseOperation(JFrame.EXIT_ON_CLOSE);
    ps.pack();
    ps.setVisible(true);
  }

  public PrintSample() {
    super("Sample Print Application");
    table = new JTable(new SampleTableModel());
    table.setAutoResizeMode(JTable.AUTO_RESIZE_OFF);
    setContentPane(new JScrollPane(table));
    pageFormat = new PageFormat();
    buildMenuBar();
  }

  protected void buildMenuBar() {
    JMenuBar menuBar = new JMenuBar();
    JMenu menu = new JMenu("File");
    menu.add(new AbstractAction("Page Setup",
        new ImageIcon("empty.gif")) {
      public void actionPerformed(ActionEvent event) {
        onPageSetup();
      }
    });
    menu.add(new AbstractAction("Print Preview",
        new ImageIcon("preview.gif")) {
      public void actionPerformed(ActionEvent event) {
        onPrintPreview();
      }
    });
    menu.add(new AbstractAction("Print",
        new ImageIcon("print.gif")) {
      public void actionPerformed(ActionEvent event) {
        onPrint();
      }
    });
    menu.addSeparator();
    menu.add(new AbstractAction("Exit",
        new ImageIcon("empty.gif")) {
      public void actionPerformed(ActionEvent event) {
        System.exit(0);
      }
    });
```

```
      menuBar.add(menu);
      setJMenuBar(menuBar);
   }

   protected void onPageSetup() {
     Thread t = new Thread(new Runnable() {
       public void run() {
         PrinterJob pj = PrinterJob.getPrinterJob();
         pageFormat = pj.pageDialog(pageFormat);
       }
     });
     t.start();
   }

   protected void onPrintPreview() {
     Thread t = new Thread(new Runnable() {
       public void run() {
         TablePrinter tp = new TablePrinter(table,
             pageFormat);
         PrintPreviewer pp = new PrintPreviewer(
             tp, 0);
         JDialog dlg = new JDialog(PrintSample.this,
             "Print Preview");
         dlg.getContentPane().add(pp);
         dlg.setSize(400, 300);
         dlg.setVisible(true);
       }
     });
     t.start();
   }

   protected void onPrint() {
     Thread t = new Thread(new Runnable() {
       public void run() {
         PrinterJob pj = PrinterJob.getPrinterJob();
         TablePrinter tablePrinter = new TablePrinter(table,
             pageFormat);
         pj.setPageable(tablePrinter);
         try {
           pj.print();
         } catch (PrinterException pe) {
           JOptionPane.showMessageDialog(
               PrintSample.this,
               "Printing error:" +
               pe.getMessage());
         }
       }
     });
     t.start();
   }

}
```

Printer Job Status Dialog and Cancel Button

`PrintSample` now provides a complete and functional set of printing-related functions, as reflected on the menu shown below:

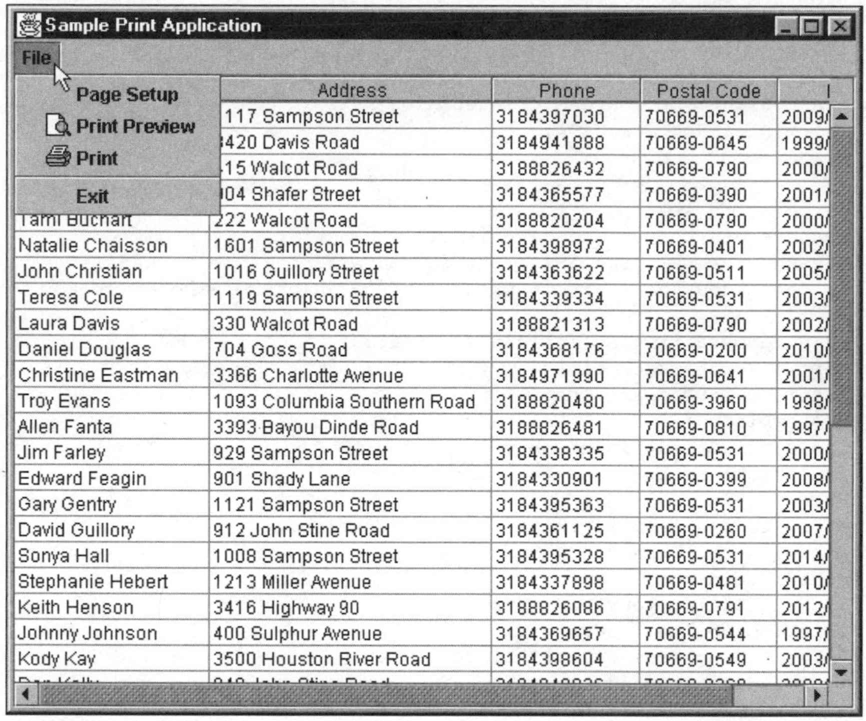

However, there is one final enhancement that can be made. Many applications display a status dialog during printing, and that dialog typically identifies the page currently being rendered and provides a button that allows the print request to be canceled. This functionality can be implemented easily by defining a class similar to the one below:

```java
import java.awt.print.*;
import javax.swing.*;

/**
 * Creating an instance of this class and printing it allows it to
 * add a status dialog during printing. The print requests are
 * simply delegated to the Pageable that actually contains the
 * data to be printed, but by intercepting those calls, we can update
 * the page number displayed in our dialog so that it indicates
 * which page is currently being displayed.
 */
public class PrintMonitor implements Pageable {

  protected PrinterJob printerJob;
  protected Pageable pageable;
  protected JOptionPane optionPane;
  protected JDialog statusDialog;
```

```java
public PrintMonitor(Pageable p) {
    pageable = p;
    printerJob = PrinterJob.getPrinterJob();
    String[] options = {"Cancel"};
    optionPane = new JOptionPane("",
        JOptionPane.INFORMATION_MESSAGE,
        JOptionPane.CANCEL_OPTION,
        null, options);
    statusDialog = optionPane.createDialog(null,
        "Printer Job Status");
}

/**
 * Create a new thread and have it call the print() method.
 * This ensures that the AWT event thread will be able to handle
 * the Cancel button if it is pressed, and can cancel the print job.
 */
public void performPrint(boolean showDialog)
        throws PrinterException {
    printerJob.setPageable(this);
    if (showDialog) {
        boolean isOk = printerJob.printDialog();
        if (!isOk) return;
    }
    optionPane.setMessage("Initiating printer job...");
    Thread t = new Thread(new Runnable() {
        public void run() {
            statusDialog.setVisible(true);
            if (optionPane.getValue() !=
                JOptionPane.UNINITIALIZED_VALUE) {
                printerJob.cancel();
            }
        }
    });
    t.start();
    printerJob.print();
    statusDialog.setVisible(false);
}

public int getNumberOfPages() {
    return pageable.getNumberOfPages();
}

/*
 * Update our dialog message and delegate the getPrintable() call
 */
public Printable getPrintable(int index) {
    optionPane.setMessage("Printing page " + (index + 1));
    return pageable.getPrintable(index);
}

public PageFormat getPageFormat(int index) {
    return pageable.getPageFormat(index);
}
}
```

To use this class, simply create an instance of it, passing a `Pageable` object to its constructor. When you call the `performPrint()` method, `PrintMonitor` displays a print dialog that allows the user to select job options, and if the user dismisses the dialog using the OK button, the job is printed. During printing, a dialog is displayed that includes a **Cancel** button:

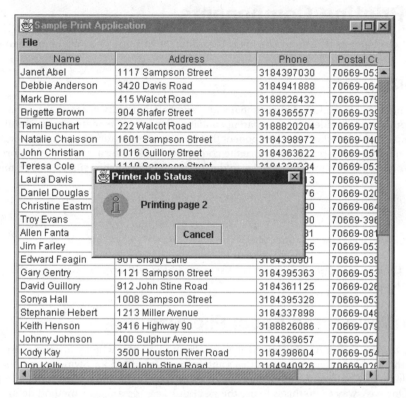

If the button is pressed, the rendering/submission process is discontinued. By making a small modification to its `onPrint()` method, `PrintSample` can be updated to take advantage of this new functionality:

```
protected void onPrint() {
   Thread t = new Thread(new Runnable() {
      public void run() {
         TablePrinter tp = new TablePrinter(table,
            pageFormat);
         PrintMonitor pm = new PrintMonitor(tp);
         try {
            pm.performPrint(true);
         } catch (PrinterException pe) {
            JOptionPane.showMessageDialog(
               PrintSample.this,
               "Printing error:" +
               pe.getMessage());
         }
      }
   });
   t.start();
}
```

Unfortunately, canceling the submission of a print job currently causes the `print()` method to throw a `PrinterException` with no message text, so as of Java 1.3, the dialog will display a message that reads, "Printing error: null" instead of including meaningful message text.

Tips for Printing Components

There are two more points that should be made regarding the printing of Swing components.

Default Size

When components are instantiated, their initial width and height usually are both set to zero and it's normally only after a component is added to some parent container that its size is set to a meaningful value. Therefore, if you call the `paint()` method of a component that has never been added to a container, it usually will result in no rendering being performed since the component's size is zero. If you wish to print such a component, you should execute code similar to the following before calling its `paint()` method:

```
Component comp;
// ...

comp.setSize(comp.getPreferredSize());
```

This will set the component to its preferred size so that it will appear when rendered by its `paint()` method.

Double Buffering and Spool File Size

You may find that Java's printing facility creates very large spool files when you print components, which is partly due to the double buffering support that's automatically enabled for Swing components. You'll rarely want to disable double buffering completely, but you may wish to disable it long enough to print a component. One easy way to do this is to use the `setDoubleBuffered()` method defined in `JComponent` as shown below:

```
Graphics g;
JTable table;
// ...

boolean wasEnabled = table.isDoubleBuffered();
table.setDoubleBuffered(false);
table.paint(g);
table.setDoubleBuffered(wasEnabled);
```

However, a better solution is to disable double buffering for the entire thread, which can be done using the `RepaintManager`:

```
Graphics g;
JTable table;
// ...

RepaintManager manager = RepaintManager.currentManager(table);
```

```
boolean wasEnabled = manager.isDoubleBufferingEnabled();
manager.setDoubleBufferingEnabled(false);
table.paint(g);
manager.setDoubleBufferingEnabled(wasEnabled);
```

If you still encounter problems with the size of spool files after disabling double buffering and you're using Java 1.2x, you may wish to consider migrating to Java 1.3, where the printing capabilities have been improved somewhat and tend to use less memory.

Summary

In this chapter we have covered the basics of printing in Java and examined the following topics:

- ❑ The classes defined in the `java.awt.print` package, how to use them, and how they interact with one another to provide printing capabilities

- ❑ How to print images and components, including components that are too large to fit onto a single page

- ❑ Printing options (for example, orientation) and how to control print jobs

- ❑ How to add support for a print preview and status dialog

In the next chapter, we will consider how we can create custom GUI components in Java.

Professional Java Programmin

Online discussion at http://p2p.wrox.com

11

Creating Custom GUI Components

Java contains a large assortment of very flexible visual components, and in many cases a user interface can be designed using only those components. However, in some cases, the existing components are not adequate for an application's needs, and you'll find it necessary to create a "custom" component. For example, some applications need a component that can display a calendar representation and that allows the user to select a date from the calendar. However, Java does not include such a control, so when one is needed, it must either be created or obtained from some external source.

Although it may sound complex and intimidating, almost every Java programmer who has created all or part of an application's user interface has created custom components. Adding labels, text fields, buttons, and other components to a frame or dialog that's displayed by an application is an example of creating a custom control, but one that's very simple and specialized. In contrast, the creation of more complex components requires a deeper understanding of the issues covered in this chapter, including:

- ❑   Factors that influence whether to build a new component or buy an existing one
- ❑   The classes that are typically extended when creating a custom component and the properties associated with those classes
- ❑   How to associate specific properties and behavior with a custom component that you create
- ❑   How to create a non-rectangular component

Build vs. Buy

The issue of "build versus buy" isn't specific to Java or to components, but in some cases, this issue must be addressed at an application level. For example, your organisation may be faced with choosing between building a new software application or purchasing an existing one. An existing application that's commercially available is often referred to as "**3rd-party**", "**off-the-shelf**" (**OTS**), "**commercial off-the-shelf**" (**COTS**), or sometimes as **"shrink-wrapped"** software, particularly if it's sold in relatively large quantities.

In the case of a component such as a calendar control, you'll often find both commercial components that must be purchased, and others that are freely available. Free components can often be found on web sites such as Gamelan (http://www.gamelan.com/) or Code Guru (http://www.codeguru.com/), but are usually offered on an "as-is" basis without any guarantee of support or future enhancement. For example, before Swing was widely used, a number of different software vendors sold table (or "grid") and tree components. They provided functionality similar to what is available now with `JTable` and `JTree`, and some of those commercial components are still sold.

There are many issues that you should consider when evaluating OTS components. Obviously, the component must provide the desired functionality, but many other factors may be involved, including the following:

- Cost
- Performance
- Extensibility
- Ease of use
- Reliability
- Documentation
- Quality and cost of support

As you can see, these are the same issues usually considered when evaluating a complete software application.

Another important factor that's sometimes overlooked is the availability of source code. In the past, it was rare for vendors to provide their product's source code, but many now do so, although usually at an additional cost. Access to the component's source code can be very helpful when attempting to understand, extend, or debug a component, and the additional cost is sometimes small.

Developing Custom Components

You'll often find that no component is available that provides the functionality you need, and this is often due to the specialized nature of software applications. At other times, components may be available, but the time and effort saved by purchasing one is outweighed by its cost. When you've determined that it's necessary to create a custom component, one of the first tasks you'll deal with is the selection of a superclass for the component. However, before you make that selection, it's important to be aware of the capabilities provided by the classes that are commonly used for this purpose.

java.awt.Component

`Component` is the simplest superclass used for creating custom components, and all visual components should subclass it either directly or indirectly. `Component` provides support for a number of frequently used properties, such as foreground and background colors, the font used when drawing text and so on. In most cases, those property values are maintained by fields in the `Component` instance, and simple accessor and mutator methods are available that allow you to retrieve and set their values.

Some properties exhibit a form of "inheritance" from the component's parent container when those properties have not been explicitly set for the component. For example, suppose that you create an instance of a `Component` subclass, add it to a parent container, and never explicitly set the component's font. If you then call the accessor method to retrieve the component's font (`getFont()`), the component will recognize that its font has not been set (that is, it is `null`), and will return the value returned by its parent container's `getFont()` method. The parent container may do the same thing, which can result in the request propagating up the containment hierarchy until a non-`null` value is found or until the last parent container is reached.

This behavior is very useful, because it allows you to assign a property value to a single component at the top of the containment hierarchy (for example, a `JFrame`) and have all the components that it contains "inherit" that value. The properties that support this behavior include the component's font, cursor, orientation, background and foreground colors.

The following table provides a partial list of properties maintained by `Component` and includes a brief explanation of what each one represents:

Property	Property Type	Description
location	java.awt.Point	Position relative to the upper-left corner of the parent container
size	java.awt.Dimension	Size in pixels
bounds	java.awt.Rectangle	Combination of location and size
enabled	boolean	Able to accept user input
visible	boolean	Will appear if all ancestor containers are visible on the screen
background	java.awt.Color	Color used to draw background
foreground	java.awt.Color	Color used to draw foreground details (for example, text information)
cursor	java.awt.Cursor	Icon that appears when the cursor moves over the component
font	java.awt.Font	Font used to draw text that appears within the component
preferredSize	java.awt.Dimension	The "ideal" size to allocate for this component
minimumSize	java.awt.Dimension	The minimum size this component needs
maximumSize	java.awt.Dimension	The maximum size for this component
focusTraversable	boolean	Indicates whether or not the component will accept the input focus when the focus is moved using the *Tab* key
parent	java.awt.Container	The parent container that this component has been added to (if any)

java.awt.Container

Container is a subclass of Component, and adds the ability to aggregate or "contain" other components, which are added and removed using add() and remove() respectively. You should use this class or one of its subclasses when your custom component will need to contain other components.

Layout Manager

When a component is added to a parent container, its size and position are usually controlled by a layout manager, represented by an implementation of the java.awt.LayoutManager (or LayoutManager2) interface. You can assign a layout manager to a container by calling its setLayout() method and retrieve a reference to it using getLayout(). By default, a Container is not assigned any layout manager, and adding a component to a container without a layout manager causes the component to be displayed using its current location and dimension values.

Insets

Containers frequently don't make all of their visible space available for child components to occupy. There are usually areas around the outer edges of the container that are used to enhance the container's graphical appearance, and child components are not allowed to overlay that portion of the container. For example, many components display a border, and the JDialog and JFrame classes provide title bars as well:

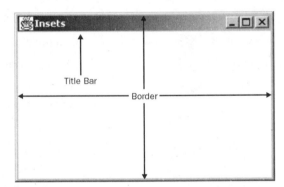

A container's insets are used to identify the number of reserved pixels on each side of the component: the top, left, bottom, and right edges. A set of inset values are encapsulated by an instance of the java.awt.Insets class, which provides an integer value for each side that identifies the number of reserved pixels on that edge. This information is used by layout managers to ensure that child components are positioned within the valid display area for the container.

The insets can be retrieved by calling getInsets(), but Container does not provide a corresponding setInsets() method. Therefore, you may need to override getInsets() when you create a custom component so that you can return insets that identify the component's border area.

javax.swing.JComponent

JComponent is a subclass of Container, and is the direct or indirect superclass of almost all of the visual components that are part of Swing. When defining a custom component, JComponent is usually a better superclass choice than Component or Container, since it provides additional useful properties such as double buffering and opacity. These and some of the other JComponent properties that you'll often find useful are described below:

Border

As previously mentioned, it's common for a component to have a border drawn around its edges. A Swing border is represented by an implementation of the `javax.swing.border.Border` interface, and `JComponent` allows you to assign a border to each component instance. The component's border is accessible through the `getBorder()` and `setBorder()` methods. Swing includes a number of predefined border types that are adequate in most cases, although you can create your own `Border` implementation if you wish to do so.

Tool Tip

A tool tip is a string associated with a component that usually provides a description of the component's purpose or function. A component's tool tip is typically displayed in a small window when the cursor moves over the component and remains there for some short period of time. The tool tip text can be modified and retrieved using the `setToolTipText()` and `getToolTipText()` methods, respectively.

Minimum, Maximum, and Preferred Size Mutators

`Component` provides accessor methods for the minimum, maximum, and preferred size properties, but does not provide mutators for them. However, `JComponent` includes the `setMinimumSize()`, `setMaximumSize()`, and `setPreferredSize()` methods that allow you to set those values.

When the accessor method for one of these size properties is called, `JComponent` first checks to see whether the size has been explicitly set by a call to the corresponding mutator method. If it was set to some value, then that value is returned to the caller, but if not, the `ComponentUI` associated with the component is called to provide the size information. A `ComponentUI` is an instance of a class that's responsible for providing much of a Swing component's functionality, but there sometimes is no `ComponentUI` associated with a component. When that's the case and no size was explicitly set, this method returns the size provided by the corresponding method in the (`Container`) superclass.

Double Buffering

Double buffering is a technique that's used to reduce screen "flicker". Flickering can occur during animation when a frame of animation (not to be confused with a `Frame` or `JFrame` component) is created on-screen. Animation is normally done by clearing a frame, redrawing the display elements, and making the frame visible. However, if the clear and redraw operations are performed where they can be seen (that is, on-screen), the user may briefly observe the frame in an intermediate state, causing flicker.

When double buffering is used, each animation frame is drawn to an **off-screen image**, and once it's complete the frame is copied to the display. Since the image is never visible in an intermediate state, this approach produces smoother animation that's free of flickering. Prior to Swing, double buffering was only available when implemented by the application developer. However, `JComponent` subclasses automatically include support for this feature, which can be enabled or disabled using the `setDoubleBuffered()` method and its state queried using `isDoubleBuffered()`.

When double buffering is enabled for a parent container, it's used while drawing all of the parent's child components and their children, grandchildren, and so on. Since double buffering is automatically enabled for `JRootPane`, it's effectively enabled for all Swing-based user interface components unless explicitly disabled by your application. In other words, it's not normally necessary for you to enable this feature, and there's rarely a reason to disable it.

Transparency and Opacity

A **transparent** component is one for which you can 'see through' all or part of its display area to the parent container underneath it, while an **opaque** component completely covers its display area. In general, you should design custom components so that they are opaque, but there may be cases where it's appropriate not to do so. For example, if you wish to define a component that does not have a rectangular appearance, such as a round button, you may choose to make it transparent and not paint the area outside the button.

JComponent supports an opacity property that can be queried and modified, and it serves two purposes. First, for Swing components, it's used to indicate whether the component's background should be cleared before drawing it. In addition, the isOpaque() accessor method is used by Swing to improve painting performance.

For example, suppose that you create a custom component that's added to a parent container, after which the container needs to be repainted for some reason. If your custom component identifies itself as opaque (it completely paints its display area), then Swing need not request that the parent container repaint the area underneath your component. However, if your component is partially or completely transparent, then the parent container must repaint itself underneath the transparent area to ensure that the display is correct.

Choosing a Superclass

There are different categories of custom components, although a component rarely fits neatly within a single category:

- ❑ Components with a low-level superclass, such as Component or JComponent, where you must implement most of the desired behavior. You'll often create this type of component when one does not exist that provides functionality similar to what is needed by your application.

- ❑ Components with a high-level superclass, such as JTable or JFrame, where your custom class inherits more complex behavior from its parent and modifies or extends the parent's capabilities. Components of this type are frequently created when an existing one provides most of the functionality you need, and only minor changes or additions are required, such as in the ShadowLabel class defined later.

- ❑ A variation on the previous category, where your custom component is mostly a collection of existing components and may or may not provide a significant amount of user interface behavior. The scenario mentioned at the beginning of this chapter is an example of this category, where you create a frame for your application that contains a collection of components. In that situation, the code that you write is often largely the 'glue' (or 'mediator') that defines how those components interact with one another, but does not modify or extend their behavior.

Even when an existing component appears to provide a good starting point for your custom component, it's sometimes not obvious how to extend it simply by looking at the API information. For example, suppose that you wish to create a component that displays text with a 'shadow':

Although you can do so by creating a subclass of JComponent, you might suspect (correctly) that the functionality could be implemented much more easily by extending JLabel. However, browsing the API documentation for JLabel doesn't immediately reveal how to do so, since there's no obvious way to override a method that will allow you to accomplish the desired goal.

A detailed exploration of Swing's **pluggable look-and-feel** facility is beyond the scope of this chapter, but it's sufficient to know that most Swing components are drawn by an associated ComponentUI. In the case of JLabel, it's drawn by an implementation of the abstract LabelUI class defined in the javax.swing.plaf package. Specifically, the LabelUI implementation used is normally an instance of the BasicLabelUI class (defined in javax.swing.plaf.basic) or one of its subclasses, depending upon which "look-and-feel" is active.

The ComponentUI subclasses are similar in purpose and function to the TableCellRenderer implementations used by JTable to draw or "render" its cells. Just as a TableCellRenderer is delegated responsibility for drawing table cells, a ComponentUI draws Swing components, and one ComponentUI can be used to draw many component instances. For example, if you create many instances of JLabel and add them to your user interface, a single LabelUI instance will normally be used to draw all the labels.

By browsing the documentation for BasicLabelUI, we find that its paintEnabledText() method is responsible for drawing the label's text. Since our goal is to customize the appearance of the JLabel so that it contains a "shadow", we can create a subclass of BasicLabelUI that performs that function by overriding paintEnabledText():

```java
class ShadowLabelUI extends javax.swing.plaf.basic.BasicLabelUI {

  protected void paintEnabledText(JLabel l, Graphics g, String s,
                                  int textX, int textY) {
    int accChar = l.getDisplayedMnemonic();
    g.setColor(getAverageColor(l.getBackground(), l.getForeground()));
    BasicGraphicsUtils.drawString(g, s, accChar, textX + offsetX,
                                  textY + offsetY);
    super.paintEnabledText(l, g, s, textX, textY);
  }

  protected Color getAverageColor(Color first, Color second) {
    Color result = new Color((first.getRed() + second.getRed()) / 2,
                             (first.getGreen() + second.getGreen())
                             / 2, (first.getBlue() + second.getBlue()) / 2);
    return result;
  }

}
```

ShadowLabelUI cannot be compiled independently, but it can be successfully compiled when added as an inner class to our custom component that we'll define below. In addition to overriding paintEnabledText(), this simple class provides a getAverageColor() method that's used to calculate the shadow text color by averaging the values from the label's background and foreground colors.

With the ComponentUI subclass defined, we can now create a JLabel subclass that uses that new ComponentUI class to draw its text, as in the following code:

```
import java.awt.*;
import javax.swing.*;
import javax.swing.plaf.basic.BasicGraphicsUtils;
import javax.swing.plaf.metal.MetalLabelUI;

public class ShadowLabel extends JLabel {

  protected int offsetX;
  protected int offsetY;

  public static void main(String[] args) {
    JFrame frame = new JFrame();
    Container pane = frame.getContentPane();
    pane.setLayout(new FlowLayout());
    ShadowLabel sl =
      new ShadowLabel("This component displays \"shadowed\" text", 15, 10);
    pane.add(sl);
    Font f = sl.getFont();
    sl.setFont(new Font(f.getFontName(), f.getStyle(),
                        f.getSize() + 10));
    frame.setSize(500, 100);
    frame.setVisible(true);
  }

  public ShadowLabel(String text, int offx, int offy) {
    super(text);
    offsetX = offx;
    offsetY = offy;
    setUI(new ShadowLabelUI());
  }

  public Dimension getPreferredSize() {
    Dimension preferred = super.getPreferredSize();
    return new Dimension(preferred.width + offsetX * 2,
                         preferred.height + offsetY * 2);
  }

  // Inner class ShadowLabelUI ...

}
```

Notice that in addition to setting its ComponentUI to the new ShadowLabelUI, this component also overrides the getPreferredSize() method. That's necessary because the getPreferredSize() method in JLabel only ensures that the label is large enough to display the normal text that it draws. Since the shadow text is displayed at some offset relative to the normal text, the label may not be large enough to completely display the shadow text unless getPreferredSize() takes the shadow text offsets into account.

In the above scenario, JLabel provided a good starting point for creating our custom component because it provides functionality very similar to what was needed. In some cases, however, the component you're creating may be too different from any existing high-level Java component for you to benefit from using that component as the superclass. In that case, you should choose a more low-level superclass for your custom component, such as JComponent or JPanel. If your component will contain other components, then you'll normally want to use JPanel, but if it will not, JComponent is an appropriate choice.

Custom Component Properties and Behavior

For your custom component to interact properly within a user interface, you must define its appearance and behavior. Some of the specific details that you'll need to address are the component's painting behavior, size, and its handling of the input focus.

Painting

Painting (or "rendering") refers to the act of drawing a component's representation on the screen, and for most Swing components, is done by a `ComponentUI` subclass. Painting is handled somewhat differently for AWT's mostly "**heavyweight**" components as opposed to Swing's "**lightweight**' components. However, since Swing provides a superset of the AWT's functionality and is the preferred mechanism for creating a user interface, this discussion focuses primarily on painting in Swing.

> *A heavyweight component is one that is associated with a component created by the underlying operating system, in which case the Java code for that component simply delegates most of its functionality to the native component or "peer".*
>
> *For example, if you create an instance of AWT's `Button` class while executing a Java program on Windows, the Java Virtual Machine will create an instance of the Windows operating system's component that's equivalent to `Button` and associate the Java `Button` object with that peer. In contrast to an instance of `JButton`, where all of the component's functionality is provided through Java code, a `Button`'s functionality (including painting) is handled by its peer and the underlying operating system.*

Three things will normally cause a component to be painted:

- ❑ When the component is first displayed on the screen
- ❑ When a change occurs to the component's internal state that should be reflected in its visual representation
- ❑ When its display is "damaged" and needs to be "repaired"

Component "damage" occurs when a component becomes partially obscured and is then exposed. For example, if a component in one window is covered up by a second window and that window is then closed, the component must be repainted.

When a component is first displayed or has been damaged, a request to paint the component is generated for you automatically. However, the component itself is responsible for generating a paint request when a change occurs to its internal state that should result in it being repainted. For example, if you modify the text assigned to a `JLabel`, the label generates a paint request so that the new text will appear.

A paint request can be made for a component by calling its `repaint()` method. The call is referred to as a "request" because calling `repaint()` doesn't immediately cause the component to be redrawn. Instead, it queues a request on the event dispatching thread's event queue to paint the object, and that thread will eventually call the component's `paint()` method. In other words, you cannot assume that a component has been painted once a call to `repaint()` completes. In some cases, the operation *may have* already been performed, but in most cases, the paint operation actually occurs later.

For both AWT and Swing components, a component is responsible for drawing itself when its paint()
method is called, and that method is passed a java.awt.Graphics object. The Graphics instance is
effectively a drawing board, and it provides methods that the component can use to render its visual
representation. For example, Graphics provides methods that allow you to specify the color that
should be used when drawing. In addition, it provides methods for drawing text, empty or filled shapes
(lines, rectangles, ovals, etc.), and images. Graphics uses a simple X-Y coordinate system, with the
origin (0, 0) representing the upper-left corner of the component's display area.

In many cases, you won't need to concern yourself with painting at all. For example, if you create a
component that has a high-level superclass, you'll usually allow component painting to be handled by
the class you extended. In other cases, however, you'll need to implement the painting code such as
when you customize the appearance of a component (for example, ShadowLabel) or when you create a
new component using a low-level superclass like JComponent.

As mentioned earlier, the paint() method is called to paint both Swing and AWT components, but
when creating a JComponent subclass, you should not normally override that method. JComponent's
paint() method contains moderately complex logic, including some related to double buffering, so
overriding this method can have undesirable side-effects. However, paint() also breaks the drawing
operation down into three smaller steps, and it's this design that provides you with a safe and easy way
to control painting behavior.

Specifically, the three steps are the painting of the component itself, the painting of its border, and the
painting of its children. These operations are handled by JComponent's paintComponent(),
paintBorder(), and paintChildren() methods, respectively, and by overriding the
paintComponent() method, you can define custom painting code without interfering with the
component's normal functions.

If your component is intended to be opaque, the first thing you'll typically do when painting it is to clear
the background, as shown in the following code:

```
protected void paintComponent(Graphics g) {
  g.setColor(getBackground());
  g.fillRect(0, 0, getWidth(), getHeight());
}
```

In some cases, you may want to call the superclass paintComponent() method instead of or in
addition to clearing the background yourself:

```
protected void paintComponent(Graphics g) {
  super.paintComponent(g);
}
```

The paintComponent() method in JComponent simply calls the update() method in the
ComponentUI associated with the component. That update() method clears the component's
background if its opaque flag is enabled, and then calls the paint() method, which is usually
overridden by the ComponentUI subclass (for example, BasicLabelUI) and coordinates the drawing
of the component.

After clearing the background, you should add the code needed to perform the remainder of the
painting necessary to render your custom component. This painting is often done using the component's
foreground color, but you may choose to use other colors.

Color Selection

When selecting the color to use for painting a particular area of a custom component, you should determine whether or not that area is represented by one of the constants defined in `java.awt.SystemColor`. Most modern operating systems allow you to select or create a color "scheme" that defines which colors should be used for various types of components.

For example, one scheme might assign a dark blue color to the title bar of an active dialog or frame and dark gray to inactive title bars. `SystemColor` provides you with access to the operating system's current color scheme by providing constants that correspond to various components and component elements, such as the title bar. Instead of "hard-coding" a particular color within your custom component logic, you can ensure that your component has an appearance that's consistent with other components, regardless of the color scheme in use.

For example, if you create a custom `Window` subclass and want its appearance to be similar to that of other windows, you could code something like the following when clearing your custom component's background:

```
protected void paintComponent(Graphics g) {
  Dimension size = getSize();
  g.setColor(SystemColor.window);
  g.fillRect(0, 0, size.width, size.height);
}
```

When creating a custom component, it's important to use `SystemColor` to ensure that your component's appearance is consistent with other portions of the display in which it's included, and failure to do so can result in your component's appearance being very inappropriate.

Size

Another important part of a component's appearance is its size. When you create a custom component, particularly one that has a low-level superclass like `JComponent` or `JPanel`, you'll need to identify a way to calculate and return meaningful size values from the `getMinimumSize()`, `getMaximumSize()`, and `getPreferredSize()` methods.

Preferred Size

This is the component's "ideal" size, and should be sufficiently large to display the component in an optimal manner. In other words, it should provide enough space to show all of the information the component is responsible for displaying, as well as enough white space to make the component's appearance user-friendly. For example, in the `ShadowLabel` example, the `getPreferredSize()` method was overridden to ensure that sufficient space was available to display the shadow text.

If that method had been omitted, the preferred size could result in a label that displays a truncated shadow. This illustrates that a component's preferred size is often dependent upon a variety of factors related to its state. For example, in the case of a `JLabel`, its preferred size is related to the text that it is assigned to display, as well as the font that it uses when displaying that text.

It's also important to note that a component's preferred size should include sufficient space to paint its border or other details that are added to its edges, such as the title bar in the case of a frame or dialog. The amount of space needed for this is accessible through the `getInsets()` method, which identifies the component's "border" area. The inset values for the left and right edges should be used when calculating the component's preferred width, while the values for the top and bottom edges should be used to determine its preferred height.

For example, the following code indicates that the component needs 100 pixels of horizontal space and 50 pixels of vertical space *in addition to* any space used for its insets, such as space around its edges for painting a `Border`:

```
public Dimension getPreferredSize() {
  Insets insets = getInsets();
  int width = 100 + insets.left + insets.right;
  int height = 50 + insets.top + insets.bottom;
  return new Dimension(width, height);
}
```

Minimum Size

This is the minimum size that should be allocated for the component, and for many components is identical to the preferred size. However, it may be possible in some cases to allow the component to be displayed in a manner that's not ideal but still provides all the information and functionality that is expected. In that case, you can return a value from `getMinimumSize()` that differs from the component's preferred size.

Maximum Size

This is the maximum size that should be allocated for the component, and for many components is identical to the preferred size. In some cases, you may choose to return a maximum width and height equal to the largest value supported by the `int` type (that is, `Integer.MAX_VALUE`).

Handling Dynamic Size and Location Changes

For various reasons, a component's size or location may change after it has been displayed. For example, suppose that we add the following method to `ShadowLabel` so that the shadow's offset values can be modified after an instance has been created:

```
public void setOffsets(Point offsets) {
  offsetX = offsets.x;
  offsetY = offsets.y;
}
```

When the offsets are changed, it's important to ensure that the component's size is updated so that it can display the shadow text correctly. As you may recall, the component's preferred size was dependent upon the shadow offset values, since it's important to ensure that the component is sufficiently large to prevent the shadow text from being "clipped. For example, if we temporarily remove the `getPreferredSize()` method that was implemented earlier, the display will appear similar to the one shown below:

invalidate()

An "invalid" component is one that has had a change made to its state, but which has not had its size and/or position updated to reflect the change. You can specify that a `Component` is invalid by calling its `invalidate()` method, although in most cases you won't have to invoke this explicitly.

Invalidating a component causes all of its "ancestors" to become invalidated as well. In other words, if you invalidate an instance of ShadowLabel that is contained by a JRootPane, and that root pane is contained by a JFrame, all three components (the ShadowLabel, JRootPane, and JFrame) are marked as invalid. This reflects the fact that changes to a component's state can affect not only the appropriate size of that component, but also the size of its parent container. That's because a parent container's size is often based in large part on the size of its child components.

In the case of ShadowLabel, a call to setOffsets() causes a change to the component's state (that is, the shadow offset values), so a call to invalidate() should be added to that method:

```
public void setOffsets(Point offsets) {
  offsetX = offsets.x;
  offsetY = offsets.y;
  invalidate();
}
```

validate()

Once you've marked a component as invalid, you'll usually want the layout manager that controls its size and location to refresh the layout. For example, if the offset values of a ShadowLabel change, the layout manager should resize the label so that it's sufficiently large to display the shadow text. To refresh a layout, you can call validate() for the Container that should be updated. Although validate() is defined in Component, it's normally only meaningful when called for a Container instance. When validate() is called, the container's doLayout() method is executed, which in turn sends a request to the container's layout manager to update the size and position of the child components.

When a ShadowLabel's offset values have changed and the component has been invalidated, the next step is to validate the label's parent container so that it updates the layout based on the label's new state. This can be done by obtaining a reference to the label's parent and calling its validate() method:

```
public void setOffsets(Point offsets) {
  offsetX = offsets.x;
  offsetY = offsets.y;
  invalidate();
  Container parent = getParent();
  if (parent != null) {
    parent.validate();
  }
}
```

Now if we make one small modification to the main() method to display the label using offsets of 3 horizontal and 2 vertical pixels, wait five seconds, and then change the horizontal and vertical offsets to 20 and 10, respectively, you can see how the calls to invalidate(), validate(), and repaint() in the setOffsets() method allow the component to be dynamically resized after it has been displayed:

```
public static void main(String[] args) {
  JFrame frame = new JFrame();
  Container pane = frame.getContentPane();
  pane.setLayout(new FlowLayout());
  ShadowLabel sl =
    new ShadowLabel("This component displays \"shadowed\" text", 3, 2);
  pane.add(sl);
  Font f = sl.getFont();
```

```
    sl.setFont(new Font(f.getFontName(), f.getStyle(),
                  f.getSize() + 10));
    frame.setSize(500, 100);
    frame.setVisible(true);
    try {
      Thread.sleep(5000);
    } catch (Exception e) {};
    sl.setOffsets(new Point(20, 10));
  }
```

revalidate()

While this modified version of ShadowLabel works well in this simple case, it doesn't work as well in a more complex scenario. For example, let's add a ShadowLabel to a JPanel, add that panel to the side of a BorderLayout, and observe the label's behavior when the offset values change. This can be performed by making the following modifications to ShadowLabel:

```
public static void main(String[] args) {
  JFrame frame = new JFrame();
  Container pane = frame.getContentPane();
  // pane.setLayout(new FlowLayout());
  pane.setLayout(new BorderLayout());
  pane.add(new JButton("Center Button"), BorderLayout.CENTER);
  ShadowLabel sl = new ShadowLabel(
      "This component displays \"shadowed\" text", 3, 2);
  // pane.add(sl);
  JPanel panel = new JPanel();
  panel.add(sl);
  pane.add(panel, BorderLayout.WEST);
  Font f = sl.getFont();
  sl.setFont(new Font(f.getFontName(), f.getStyle(), f.getSize() + 5));
  frame.setSize(500, 100);
  frame.setVisible(true);
  try {Thread.sleep(5000);} catch (Exception e) {};
  sl.setOffsets(new Point(20, 10));
}
```

When this code is run, it initially displays something similar to this:

After five seconds have elapsed and the label's shadow offsets have changed, the display changes to something like this:

This behavior might not be what you'd expect from a `BorderLayout`. Normally, the `EAST` and `WEST` components (such as the `ShadowLabel` in this case) are displayed using their preferred sizes and the center component is given only the space that's left over. In other words, when the label's shadow offsets increased, its size should have increased as well, reducing the space available for the button display.

In this case, the button remained at its original size after the offsets changed, while the `ShadowLabel`'s size did not change. This resulted in the `ShadowLabel` being too small to render the shadow text, causing the text being clipped. To understand why this happened, let's examine the `setOffsets()` method again and determine what effect it will have upon the display:

```
public void setOffsets(Point offsets) {
  offsetX = offsets.x;
  offsetY = offsets.y;
  invalidate();
  Container parent = getParent();
  if (parent != null) {
    parent.validate();
  }
}
```

Notice that the parent container of the `ShadowLabel` (now a `JPanel`) is validated when the offsets are changed, and in fact, this method *does* cause the label's size to be updated. However, if its size did change, why did it appear to remain the same? The answer has to do with how `validate()` is handled.

While `invalidate()` propagates *up* the containment hierarchy from a child to its parent (and grandparent, etc.), a call to `validate()` propagates *down* the containment hierarchy. In other words, the container itself is first validated, after which each child component is validated, followed by its grandchildren, and so on. In this case, the `JPanel` is validated and its layout manager reformats the display. However, since the validation doesn't propagate up the containment hierarchy, the `JPanel`'s parent container (that is, the frame's content pane) never updates the sizes of its components. In other words, the `BorderLayout` is never notified of the validation request, so the `JPanel` and `JButton` that it contains are never resized.

This problem can be solved by calling `validate()` for the container at the top of the containment hierarchy (the `JFrame`) instead of the component's immediate parent (the `JPanel`). This would ensure that each `Container` "ancestor" of the invalid component is updated correctly. Although the logic for doing this is trivial, it's usually not necessary to implement it because `JComponent` provides a method called `revalidate()`. When `revalidate()` is called for a component, that component is invalidated and added to a list of components that need to be validated by Swing's `RepaintManager`.

When the `RepaintManager` validates a component, it ascends the component's containment hierarchy until it locates a container that returns a value of `true` from the `isValidateRoot()` method (defined in `JComponent`) or until it reaches the top component in the hierarchy. In this case, for example, when the `RepaintManager` is called for the `ShadowLabel`, it will first examine the `ShadowLabel`, followed by its parent `Container` and then the `JRootPane` "grandparent". Since instances of `JRootPane` return `true` from `isValidateRoot()`, the `RepaintManager` will stop ascending the containment tree at that point and invoke the `JRootPane`'s `validate()` method:

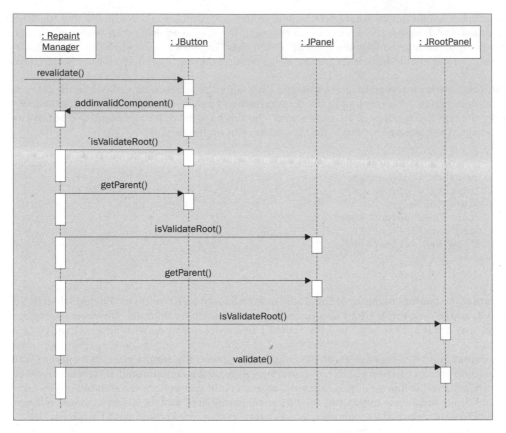

In other words, `revalidate()` provides all the functionality needed to cause the `ShadowLabel` component's display to be updated appropriately, and the `validate()` and `invalidate()` logic in `setOffsets()` can be replaced with a call to `revalidate()` as shown below:

```
public void setOffsets(Point offsets) {
  offsetX = offsets.x;
  offsetY = offsets.y;
  // invalidate();
  // Container parent = getParent();
  // if (parent != null) {
  //   parent.validate();
  // }
  revalidate();
}
```

After the 5-second delay, the label is redrawn with the larger offsets, and space is reallocated from the center `JButton` to the `ShadowLabel`, allowing it to correctly display the shadow text:

As you can see, `revalidate()` provides a simple mechanism for ensuring that changes to your component's state generate the appropriate changes in its display. You'll normally want to call `revalidate()` from any mutator method you define that causes a change to your component's state that should trigger a change to its external appearance.

Focus Assignment

Components that accept user input are usually capable of being assigned the input focus, which identifies the component that will receive keyboard events. If your custom component accepts user input as many do, you should ensure that its behavior with respect to the input focus is appropriate, and this section provides the information that you'll need to make that assessment.

Focus assignment can be done either programmatically using the `requestFocus()` method, or can occur as a result of user input, such as clicking on a particular field or pressing the *Tab* key. In reality, the distinction is a subtle one, since user input that affects the focus assignment (for example, pressing the *Tab* key or clicking on a component) is eventually translated into a call to `requestFocus()`.

Calling `requestFocus()` for a component is a simple operation, and doing so explicitly identifies the component that should receive the input focus. Somewhat more complex is the handling of the *Tab* key, since pressing *Tab* indicates that the input focus should move from its current location to the "next" component in the tab traversal path. Similarly, pressing *Shift-Tab* indicates that the focus should move to the "previous" component in the traversal path. Identifying the "next" and "previous" components in the tab traversal path is a potentially very complex operation, and in fact, Swing provides the `javax.swing.FocusManager` and its `DefaultFocusManager` subclass specifically for that purpose.

The behavior provided by `DefaultFocusManager` is very simple and is suitable for many applications. However, you can modify its behavior by creating your own subclass and assigning it focus management responsibility by calling the static `setCurrentManager()` method in `FocusManager`. It's hardly ever necessary to do so, because you can achieve a significant degree of customization more easily by using the methods that are provided in `Component` and `JComponent` which affect how the input focus is managed.

hasFocus()

This method, which is defined in `Component`, returns a `boolean` value indicating whether the component is currently assigned the input focus.

requestFocus()
isRequestFocusEnabled()
setRequestFocusEnabled()

The `java.awt.Component` class defines a `requestFocus()` method that can be called when the focus should be assigned to that component. In addition, Swing's `JComponent` overrides this method and provides an additional layer of functionality. Specifically, `JComponent` makes the call to `requestFocus()` conditional upon the value of a flag (`REQUEST_FOCUS_DISABLED`) that can be set and queried using `setRequestFocusEnabled()` and `isRequestFocusEnabled()` respectively.

If the flag is set to `false` when a call is made to `JComponent`'s `requestFocus()` method, the request is ignored, but if the flag is set to `true`, the request is passed to the superclass (`Component`) `requestFocus()` method.

grabFocus()

This method in JComponent makes an unconditional call to the requestFocus() method in the Component superclass. In other words, it does not test the REQUEST_FOCUS_DISABLED flag to determine whether to call the superclass requestFocus() method. This method is used by Swing to control the input focus and should not normally be used by application code.

transferFocus()

Calling this method for a component causes the input focus to move to the next item in the focus traversal path after that component. For example, suppose that the traversal path causes the focus to move between components A, B, and C in that order. If transferFocus() is called for component B the input focus moves to component C, regardless of where it had been previously located.

getNextFocusableComponent()
setNextFocusableComponent()

The setNextFocusableComponent() method allows you to explicitly identify the component that should follow this one in the focus traversal path. Similarly, getNextFocusableComponent() is called by DefaultTraversalManager when it is about to transfer the input focus to the "next" component in the traversal path.

If getNextFocusableComponent() returns a null value, the traversal manager selects the component that is to the right of and at roughly the same vertical position as this component. If no such component exists, DefaultTraversalManager normally selects the left-most component that's below this one. In other words, if getNextFocusableComponent() does not identify the "next" component in the traversal path, the traversal manager will select a component based on its position, and that selection is done in a left-to-right and top-to-bottom manner.

isFocusTraversable()

This method is similar to the isRequestFocusEnabled() method, although there are two important differences. First, this accessor method does not have a corresponding mutator method, so you must override this method to changes the value it returns. In addition, this method indicates whether the component can receive the focus as the result of *Tab* or *Shift-Tab* being pressed. In contrast, isRequestFocusEnabled() method identifies the component's ability to receive the input focus when its requestFocust() method is called.

To prevent a component from ever getting the input focus, you should return false from this method and disable the requestFocus() method by calling setRequestFocusEnabled() with a parameter value of false.

isManagingFocus()

By default, this method returns a value of false, which indicates that the component is not responsible for handling *Tab* key events. In that case, the focus-related keyboard events are processed by the focus manager, and they are not sent to the component or its listeners. When this method returns true and the *Tab* key is pressed while the component has the input focus, the key events generated are sent to the component and its listeners, just as is normally done when a key is pressed. You may choose to override this method if you wish to have your component customize the functionality associated with the *Tab* key, such as in a text editor.

isFocusCycleRoot()

By overriding this method to return a value of `true`, a container can prevent *Tab* and *Shift-Tab* from being used to move the input focus to a component outside the container. For example, the code below creates two `JPanel` instances, each containing three text fields:

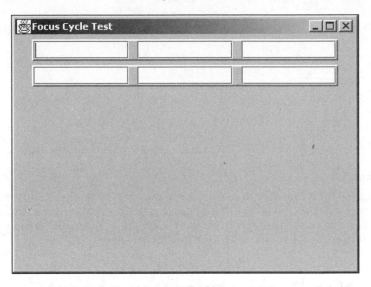

Normally, you would be able to use *Tab* and *Shift-Tab* to move among all of the six text fields. However, because each panel identifies itself as a "cycle root", pressing the tab key only moves the input focus among the three components within that panel. To move the focus to a component outside the cycle root, you must click on the component or programmatically change the focus using `requestFocus()`:

```java
import java.awt.*;
import javax.swing.*;
import javax.swing.border.BevelBorder;

public class FocusCycleTest extends JFrame {

  public static void main(String[] args) {
    FocusCycleTest fct = new FocusCycleTest();
    fct.setSize(400, 300);
    fct.setVisible(true);
  }

  public FocusCycleTest() {
    super("Focus Cycle Test");
    Container pane = getContentPane();
    pane.setLayout(new FlowLayout());
    pane.add(new ThreeFieldPanel("First Cycle Root"));
    pane.add(new ThreeFieldPanel("Second Cycle Root"));
  }

  class ThreeFieldPanel extends JPanel {

    public ThreeFieldPanel(String title) {
      setLayout(new GridLayout(1, 3, 10, 0));
```

```
        JTextField tf = new JTextField(10);
        add(tf);
        tf = new JTextField(10);
        add(tf);
        tf = new JTextField(10);
        add(tf);
        setBorder(BorderFactory.createBevelBorder(BevelBorder.RAISED));
    }

    public boolean isFocusCycleRoot() {
        return true;
    }

  }

}
```

requestDefaultFocus()

This method is called for a container to request that input focus be assigned to the first component within the container that's able to accept it. It returns `true` if a component was found that could accept the focus, or `false` otherwise. The logic for identifying the first "focusable" component is defined in `JComponent`, and you should not normally override this method.

Creating a Non-Rectangular Component

As we saw earlier, a component's position is represented by a pair of coordinates, while its size is represented by another pair of numeric values, and this approach effectively makes each component rectangular in nature. In other words, each component is effectively a rectangle with its upper-left corner at the position identified by its location, while the lower-right corner is implicitly defined by the component's size. In most cases, this doesn't present a problem because a rectangle is an appropriate shape for many components. However, you'll sometimes want to define a component that is not rectangular, and this section describes how that can be done.

For example, suppose that you want to create a component class called `Triangle` that (as its name implies) represents a triangle. The following listing provides an example of how such a class might be created:

```
import java.awt.*;
import javax.swing.*;

public class Triangle extends JComponent {

  protected Polygon activeRegion;

  public Triangle() {
    setPreferredSize(new Dimension(100, 100));
  }

  public void setBounds(int x, int y, int width, int height) {
    super.setBounds(x, y, width, height);
    int[] xpoints = new int[3];
```

```
      int[] ypoints = new int[3];

      // The top coordinate that defines the triangle
      xpoints[0] = (width - 1) / 2;
      ypoints[0] = 0;

      // The bottom left coordinate that defines the triangle
      xpoints[1] = 0;
      ypoints[1] = height - 1;

      // The bottom right coordinate that defines the triangle
      xpoints[2] = width - 1;
      ypoints[2] = height - 1;
      activeRegion = new Polygon(xpoints, ypoints, 3);
   }

   public void paintComponent(Graphics g) {
      g.setColor(getForeground());
      g.fillPolygon(activeRegion);
   }

}
```

In addition, you could create a class like the one shown below to test this new component and an example of how it might appear is shown here:

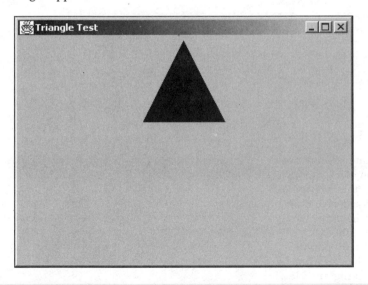

```
public class TriangleTest extends javax.swing.JFrame {

   public static void main(String[] args) {
      TriangleTest tt = new TriangleTest();
      tt.setSize(400, 300);
      tt.setVisible(true);
   }
```

```
   public TriangleTest() {
      super("Triangle Test");
      getContentPane().setLayout(new java.awt.FlowLayout());
      Triangle t = new Triangle();
      getContentPane().add(t);
   }

}
```

It may seem that the `Triangle` component is complete, which may in fact be the case, although it depends on how you want the component to respond to user input. For example, let's suppose that you add a `MouseListener` to the `Triangle` and print a message each time a mouse button is pressed:

```
import java.awt.event.*;

public class TriangleTest extends javax.swing.JFrame {

   public static void main(String[] args) {
      TriangleTest tt = new TriangleTest();
      tt.setSize(400, 300);
      tt.setVisible(true);
   }

   public TriangleTest() {
      super("Triangle Test");
      getContentPane().setLayout(new java.awt.FlowLayout());
      Triangle t = new Triangle();
      getContentPane().add(t);
      t.addMouseListener(new MouseAdapter() {
         public void mousePressed(MouseEvent event) {
            System.out.println("You clicked on the triangle");
         }
      });
   }
}
```

If you compile and execute this modified version of `TriangleTest`, the message will indeed be displayed each time you click inside the triangular region. However, the component will also exhibit some behavior that may not be as desirable: clicking outside the *triangular* area but inside the component's *rectangular* area still generates a message:

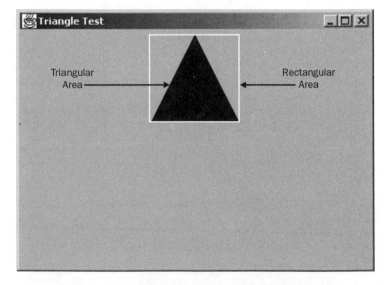

In other words, although the component looks like a triangle, it still behaves like a rectangle. Fortunately, `Component`'s `contains()` method provides a simple solution to this problem.

A `boolean` value is returned from `contains()`, and that value indicates whether a given point is considered to be inside the component for which the method is called. The implementation of this method in `Component` returns `true` if the coordinates are greater than or equal to zero but less than the width (for the X coordinate) or height (for the Y coordinate):

```
return (x >= 0) && (x < width) && (y >= 0) && (y < height);
```

In other words, the default implementation assumes that the component is rectangular in nature, although you can change this behavior very easily. `Polygon` (which is not a subclass of `Component`) contains its own `contains()` method, and that method performs essentially the same function as the `Component` equivalent. In the case of the `Polygon`, however, the method is much more sophisticated, and can determine whether a point falls within the region defined by the `Polygon`'s coordinates. Therefore, the same `Polygon` object that's already used for drawing the rectangle can also be used to determine whether a given point falls within the rectangular area:

```
public class Triangle extends JComponent {

    protected Polygon activeRegion;

    public Triangle() {
        setPreferredSize(new Dimension(100, 100));
    }

    public boolean contains(int x, int y) {
        return activeRegion.contains(x, y);
    }

    // ...
```

To understand what affect this code will have on the component's ability to receive the mouse events, it's important to understand how event recipients are identified.

You may have wondered how Java determines which specific component should be notified of a mouse event when one occurs. It does this by calling the `contains()` method of every visible component until it locates one that returns a value of `true`, at which time that component is notified of the event. In other words, by overriding `contains()` to modify its behavior as we just did, you can reduce a component's active region from its rectangular area to some subset of that area (for example, a triangular region). In effect, we've created a component that not only looks like a triangle, but actually behaves like one despite the fact that its size and position are still represented by X and Y coordinates and width and height values.

539

Summary

In this chapter, we've examined the following topics related to components in Java:

- ❑ Some of the factors involved in deciding whether or not to build a new component or buy (or use) one that is already available

- ❑ The more commonly used properties associated with some frequently used component superclasses

- ❑ How to implement a custom component

In the next chapter, we move on to look at accessing relational databases using JDBC.

Professional Java Programmin

Online discussion at http://p2p.wrox.com

12

Java Database Connectivity (JDBC)

When your application creates or uses large amounts of data, it's usually necessary for that information to be stored in a database. The most widely used type is the relational database, and some examples of relational database products are Oracle, DB2, Sybase, Informix, and Microsoft SQL Server. A **relational database** product is sometimes referred to as a **Relational Database Management System** (**RDBMS** or simply **DBMS**), while a "database" usually refers to a collection of data managed by a DBMS.

Java's support for relational databases is provided through the **Java Database Connectivity API (JDBC)** that is largely contained in the `java.sql` package and consists of some interfaces and a handful of simple classes. Just as Java programs are intended to work on many different platforms, JDBC is designed to allow your application to communicate with many different database systems.

In this chapter, we'll examine each of the following topics related to using JDBC:

- ❑ Driver types and how to select and obtain a driver
- ❑ Obtaining a connection to a database
- ❑ Executing SQL statements and stored procedures
- ❑ Data types defined in JDBC and how they are related to "native" types
- ❑ How to manage transactions
- ❑ Database connection pooling
- ❑ Processing errors and warnings generated by JDBC functions
- ❑ Debugging database applications

Using JDBC

Using JDBC is very simple, and you only need to take a few steps to add database functionality to your application. The steps involved are:

❑ Select/obtain a JDBC driver or use the JDBC-ODBC bridge driver described later that's included in Java's core classes. If you do not use the bridge driver, you must add the driver code to your CLASSPATH just as you would any other third-party library.

❑ Obtain a database connection using DriverManager or a DataSource and a URL that's appropriate for the driver you're using.

❑ Create a Statement or an instance of one of its subinterfaces (PreparedStatement or CallableStatement) and use it to execute SQL commands.

For example, the following code uses the bridge driver mentioned above to create a connection to an ODBC data source called projava, performs a query, and sends the data returned by that query to standard output:

```java
import java.sql.*;

public class TestJDBC {
  public static void main(String args[]) throws Exception {
    String userid = "bspell";
    String password = "brett";
    // Register the driver with DriverManager
    new sun.jdbc.odbc.JdbcOdbcDriver();
    // Get a connection
    Connection conn = DriverManager.getConnection("jdbc:odbc:projava",
                                                  userid, password);
    // Create a statement for executing SQL
    Statement stmt = conn.createStatement();
    // Execute a query / SELECT statement
    ResultSet rset = stmt.executeQuery("SELECT * FROM TESTTABLE");
    ResultSetMetaData rsmd = rset.getMetaData();
    // Find out how many columns were returned by the query
    int count = rsmd.getColumnCount();
    // Loop until all rows have been processed
    while (rset.next()) {
      // Loop until all columns in current row have been processed
      for (int i = 1; i <= count; i++) {
        // Print out the current value
        System.out.print(rset.getObject(i));
        // Put a comma between each value
        if (i < count) {
          System.out.println(",");
        }
      }
      // Start the next row's values on a new line
      System.out.println("");
    }
    // Close the database objects
    rset.close();
    stmt.close();
    conn.close();
  }
}
```

SQL Standards and JDBC Versions

Providing a single interface to many DBMS products is difficult because each product supports a unique collection of features and data types. For example, while SQL Server supports a `boolean` data type Oracle does not, although you can simulate boolean data using numeric fields. Even when two DBMS products provide the same functionality, the way that you use that functionality on one DBMS can be very different from the way it's used on the other. Fortunately, JDBC provides a layer of abstraction between your application and the specific details of how to perform a particular task.

Variation between DBMS products has been limited somewhat by organizations that have established standards for the **Structured Query Language (SQL)**. The most widely adopted and well-known standard is the SQL2 standard (also known as SQL92), although a more recent standard called SQL3 has emerged. SQL3 is partly an attempt to address what is perceived as a serious limitation of SQL2: its lack of support for object-oriented concepts. When SQL2 was designed, object-oriented programming was not yet widely adopted, and the result is that the SQL language as defined by SQL2 is poorly suited to object persistence. In fact, an entire category of products has emerged to address this problem using technology called **object-relational mapping**, and we'll examine that topic in more detail in the next chapter.

The original JDBC specification (1.x) defines functionality that is based on the SQL2/SQL92 standard, and support for that specification was included in the Java 1.1 core classes. However, the JDBC 2.x specification has since been released and it provides support for many of the SQL3's new features. While all JDBC 1.x classes and interfaces are defined in the `java.sql` package, some of the JDBC 2.x components are stored in `javax.sql`, which is called the **JDBC 2.x Optional Package** or "**Standard Extension API**". That separation was done to keep the core classes small, and because most of the functionality defined in the optional package is related to other standard extensions such as **JNDI (Java Naming and Directory Interface)**. Unlike `java.sql`, the `javax.sql` package is not included in the Java core classes, so if you wish to use the functionality defined in the optional package, you must download it separately from the JavaSoft website and add it to your `CLASSPATH`.

JDBC Drivers

The most important part of the `java.sql` package is its collection of interfaces, because they define how your application interacts with a relational database. One of those interfaces is `Driver`, and it includes a method that's used to obtain database connections, although you won't normally invoke that method directly. The phrase **JDBC driver** is sometimes used to refer specifically to a `Driver` implementation, but more often it refers to a group of related files that provide access to a particular type of DBMS. Those files typically include implementations of the `java.sql` interfaces (including `Driver`), along with other support classes that are needed to provide database access.

A JDBC driver is usually packaged as a ZIP or JAR file, and drivers can be obtained from a variety of sources. Most DBMS vendors supply at least one driver for use with their own database, usually at no cost. However, drivers are also sold by third parties, and those often provide better performance and/or reliability than the database vendor implementations. A list of known drivers is available at `http://industry.java.sun.com/products/jdbc/drivers`, and includes information such as the DBMS product(s) each driver supports, the driver type, and the specific JDBC features it supports. Note that it's not necessary for a driver to support all features defined in the JDBC specification for the driver to be considered JDBC-compliant, although most drivers do support most features.

> **If there is a specific feature that your application is or will be dependant upon, you should test the driver in advance before choosing it or contact the vendor that supplies the driver before purchasing it to ensure that it supports the desired functionality.**

Like any other third-party library, a JDBC driver that you obtain for use within your application must be added to your CLASSPATH when the application is executed. For example, if you have downloaded a driver that's packaged as a ZIP file called CLASSES111.ZIP stored in the C:/brett/temp directory, you could use the following statement to execute an application called MyDatabaseApp and include the driver in your CLASSPATH:

```
java -classpath=C:/brett/temp/CLASSES111.ZIP MyDatabaseApp
```

Driver Types

JDBC drivers are divided into four categories or "types" based on how they provide a connection to the database. Each category has unique advantages and disadvantages, and it's common for driver vendors to provide more than one type of JDBC driver for a database. For example, Oracle Corporation provides both a type-2 and a type-4 driver for their DBMS.

Type 1 – Connection through an ODBC Data Source

Microsoft's **Open Database Connectivity (ODBC)** is conceptually very similar to JDBC and is widely used to provide relational database connectivity. In fact, ODBC is provided with the Windows operating system, and you can define an ODBC **data source** through the Control Panel window:

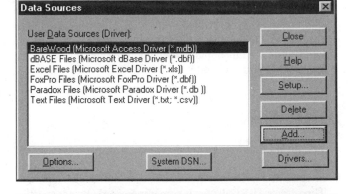

A data source is simply a way of associating a name with a particular database, and when creating a new data source, you must select the ODBC driver used to access the database:

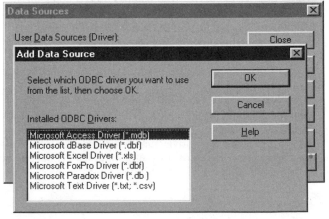

The only Java JDBC driver supplied with the Java core classes is a type-1 driver that's commonly referred to as the **JDBC-ODBC bridge driver**. Although this driver is not very robust, it's usually sufficient for performing simple tests and for development of small applications. A type-1 JDBC driver is simply a driver that accesses a database through an ODBC data source. To obtain a database connection from a type-1 driver, you must identify the name of the ODBC data source to which you wish to connect. The JDBC driver then satisfies your application's requests by converting JDBC operations into the equivalent ODBC operations and returning the results.

This type of driver is useful because it allows you to use any database that's accessible through ODBC, but it requires that ODBC be installed on each client machine. That's usually not a problem if your application's database code will only run on Windows, since ODBC is included in Windows by default, but if your client will run on other platforms, the absence of ODBC may be an issue. In addition, type-1 drivers suffer from poor performance because each operation must be processed by two different drivers: a JDBC driver and an ODBC driver.

Type 2 – Connection through Native Client Networking Code

Most DBMS products provide a client interface that allows you to interact with the database server. For example, Oracle provides the SQL*Plus application that allows you to connect to a database, issue SQL statements, and view the results of those statements (the rows returned from a query). However, before you can use SQL*Plus, you must install Oracle's networking software that allows a client to communicate with the database server.

A type-2 JDBC driver includes both Java and native code, and it communicates with the client-side network software of a particular DBMS. It provides better performance than a type-1 driver does, but it can make distributing your application more difficult since you must ensure that each client has the networking software installed.

Type 3 – Connection through Middleware

This type of driver is written entirely in Java, and it sends database requests to a server component. Those requests are transmitted using a protocol that's not specific to any database, and the server component is responsible for converting it into the appropriate format before forwarding the request to a particular DBMS.

A type-3 driver has the disadvantage of requiring a server-side component, but it does allow you to change the DBMS being used on the server without affecting your client code.

Type 4 – Direct Connection to DBMS

A type-4 driver is written entirely in Java and communicates directly with a DBMS server using the appropriate protocol for that type of server. For example, in the case of Oracle's type-4 driver, a socket connection is opened between the JDBC application and the database server.

This type of driver is easy to use because the only component needed is the driver itself, which can easily be packaged with a Java application. No other client- or server-side software is required, which simplifies distributing your application.

Obtaining a Database Connection

As mentioned earlier, an implementation of the Driver interface can be used to obtain a database connection, although you should not call the methods in that class directly. Instead, you should request a connection from the DriverManager singleton through its static getConnection() methods.

When you call `getConnection()`, `DriverManager` passes the parameter values specified to each registered driver until it finds one that is able to establish a connection using those values. Although you can explicitly register a driver by calling the `registerDriver()` method, you don't have to do so. When an instance of a `Driver` implementation is created, it automatically registers itself with the `DriverManager`, so you can register a driver implicitly by instantiating it as shown below:

```
new oracle.jdbc.driver.OracleDriver();
```

or:

```
Class.forName("oracle.jdbc.driver.OracleDriver");
```

Alternatively, you can have drivers loaded automatically by setting the value of the `jdbc.drivers` system property when starting a Java Virtual Machine. The `jdbc.drivers` property should contain the names of the `Driver` classes to be loaded, and can be set using the `-D` option available on most JVM implementations. The following command executes the `main()` method of the Java class named `Test` after loading the JDBC-ODBC bridge driver. You can specify multiple drivers by separating the fully qualified `Driver` class names (the package *and* class names) with the colon (`":"`) character:

```
java -Djdbc.drivers=sun.jdbc.odbc.JdbcOdbcDriver Test
```

JDBC URL Formats

At a minimum, you must specify a **JDBC URL** when calling `getConnection()`, although a userid and password are often provided as well. The URL identifies the specific database that you wish to connect to, while the userid and password provide the authentication information that the database may require before a connection can be created.

The JDBC URL is not a traditional URL that can be represented by an instance of `java.net.URL`, but is a `String` value that identifies a particular JDBC driver and database. The general format of a JDBC URL is `jdbc:<subprotocol>:<subname>`, where the values of `<subprotocol>` and `<subname>` vary based on the database you wish to connect to and the driver being used. For example, to use the JDBC-ODBC bridge driver to connect to an ODBC data source named `projava`, you would specify the URL `jdbc:odbc:projava`.

This example is actually somewhat simplistic, because JDBC URLs are usually slightly more complex than the one shown above. For example, to use Oracle's type-4 (or "thin-client") driver, you must create a `<subname>` that includes three items: the host name of the machine that the DBMS server is running on, the port number that it uses to listen for incoming connections, and the name of the database to which you wish to connect. To use Oracle's thin-client driver to connect to a database called `projava` maintained on a server named `oraserve` that uses port 1521, you would specify URL `jdbc:oracle:thin:@oraserver:1521:projava`.

To use Oracle's type-2 (or "OCI") driver to connect to the same database, you must use a URL of the form `jdbc:oracle:oci8:@projava`. Since the format of the URL is driver-specific, you should review the documentation associated with the driver you're using to determine the correct format of a URL.

A database connection is represented in JDBC by an instance of the `Connection` class, and as you might expect, an instance of that class is returned by `DriverManager`'s `getConnection()` methods. The following code segment loads an Oracle driver (which will register itself with the `DriverManager`) and then obtains a database connection:

```
Class.forName("oracle.jdbc.driver.OracleDriver");
String url = "jdbc:oracle:thin:@oraserver:1521:projava";
Connection connect = DriverManager.getConnection(url, "bspell", "brett");
```

Obtaining Connections from a DataSource (JDBC 2.x Optional Package)

The technique just described for obtaining a database connection is easy to use, but it does have one drawback. Since you must load a driver and construct a driver- and database-specific URL, this approach causes your application to be tightly coupled to a specific driver and database. Although there are ways to address those weaknesses, no standard solution was defined until JDBC 2.x, when the DataSource interface was introduced as part of the optional package.

A DataSource is simply a class that provides a layer of abstraction between your application and the information needed to connect to a database. That information may include the "identity" of the Driver class, the information needed to construct a valid URL, and a userid and password. Like DriverManager, DataSource provides getConnection() methods that can be used to obtain database connections.

As of this writing, most DataSource implementations are not in widespread use, but the JavaSoft documentation suggests that a DataSource will most commonly be accessed through the Java Naming and Directory Interface (JNDI). JNDI is an API that defines methods used to associate names with resources and provide access to those resources through a "directory". In this case, the resource would be a DataSource that is able to obtain a connection to a particular database, and an example of how JNDI and the DataSource might be used is shown below:

```
Context ctx = new InitialContext();
DataSource source = (DataSource)(ctx.lookup("jdbc/projava"));
Connection connect = source.getConnection();
```

With this approach, your application code is only coupled to the name assigned to the database (projava) instead of a particular driver and URL. In fact, this technique allows both the driver and the information used to connect to the database to be modified without requiring any changes to your source code.

Although DataSource is described in the DriverManager API documentation as "the preferred means of connecting to a data source", DataSource implementations are currently rare. If one is not provided for you with the driver you're using, your only options are to continue to use DriverManager for obtaining connections, or to create your own DataSource implementation. Since DriverManager is not deprecated, it's still appropriate to use that class, and in many cases this will be the easiest approach. However, you can create a DataSource like the one shown below that can be used with either of the JDBC drivers provided by Oracle. When executing the application, you should ensure that one of the two drivers is included in your application's CLASSPATH as described earlier.

Two constructors are provided in this class, and the one that you should use will depend upon which driver you're using: one that only accepts a "system ID" parameter, which is the only value needed for the type-2 driver, and another that also accepts a host name and port number, which you should use with the type-4 driver. The getConnection() method returns a Connection given a userid and password, while getSubname() is responsible for building the "subname" portion of the URL that's used to obtain the connection:

```java
import java.io.PrintWriter;
import java.sql.*;
import javax.sql.*;

public class OracleDataSource implements DataSource {

  static {
    new oracle.jdbc.driver.OracleDriver();
  }

  protected boolean usingThinDriver;

  protected String description = "Oracle Data Source";
  protected String serverName;
  protected int portNumber;
  protected String databaseName;

  public OracleDataSource(String host, int port, String sid) {
    setServerName(host);
    setPortNumber(port);
    setDatabaseName(sid);
    usingThinDriver = true;
  }

  public OracleDataSource(String sid) {
    setDatabaseName(sid);
    usingThinDriver = false;
  }

  public boolean isUsingThinDriver() {
    return usingThinDriver;
  }

  public void setUsingThinDriver(boolean thin) {
    usingThinDriver = thin;
  }

  public String getDescription() {
    return description;
  }

  public void setDescription(String desc) {
    description = desc;
  }

  public String getServerName() {
    return serverName;
  }

  public void setServerName(String name) {
    serverName = name;
  }

  public int getPortNumber() {
    return portNumber;
  }
```

```java
    public void setPortNumber(int port) {
      portNumber = port;
    }

    public String getDatabaseName() {
      return databaseName;
    }

    public void setDatabaseName(String name) {
      databaseName = name;
    }

    public Connection getConnection() throws SQLException{
      return getConnection(null, null);
    }

    public Connection getConnection(String userid, String password)
        throws SQLException {
      String url = "jdbc:oracle:" + getSubname();
      return DriverManager.getConnection(url, userid, password);
    }

    protected String getSubname() {
      return (isUsingThinDriver()
            ? "thin:@" + getServerName() + ":" + getPortNumber() + ":" +
              getDatabaseName()
            : "oci8:@" + getDatabaseName());
    }

    public int getLoginTimeout() throws SQLException {
      return DriverManager.getLoginTimeout();
    }

    public PrintWriter getLogWriter() throws SQLException {
      return DriverManager.getLogWriter();
    }

    public void setLoginTimeout(int timeout) throws SQLException {
      DriverManager.setLoginTimeout(timeout);
    }

    public void setLogWriter(PrintWriter writer) throws SQLException {
      DriverManager.setLogWriter(writer);
    }

  }
```

There are several important points to be made concerning this DataSource implementation. First, the property names (description, serverName, portNumber, databaseName) were not selected arbitrarily, but are defined in the JDBC 2.x specification. When creating a DataSource property, you should use the name documented in the specification when one has been defined for the type of property you're creating.

It's also worth noting that some of the methods defined in DataSource are identical to those implemented in DriverManager, and in the case of OracleDriver, those methods simply call their DriverManager equivalent. This duplication of methods is due to DataSource having effectively superceded DriverManager as the preferred mechanism for creating connections, although as mentioned earlier, it's still appropriate in most cases to use DriverManager.

Finally, although it was not done in this case, you may wish to include userid and password values when creating a DataSource instance so that those values need not be specified each time your application requests a database connection.

DatabaseMetaData

The DatabaseMetaData interface defines a large number of methods that allow you to identify the capabilities of the DBMS and the JDBC driver, as well as allowing you to obtain a description of the contents of the database. For example, you can retrieve the list of schemas defined in the database, the tables within each schema, the columns within each table, and the characteristics of those columns, such as their size and data types. In addition, you can use DatabaseMetaData to identify primary and foreign keys, indices, and many other items.

In general, the methods in DatabaseMetaData can be broken down into two categories:

❑ Those that are used to describe DBMS features/functionality, and which typically return a boolean, an int, or a String. For example:

- supportsOuterJoins() returns a boolean that indicates whether or not the database supports outer joins

- getMaxConnections() returns an int that identifies the maximum number of simultaneous connections that can be open to the database

- getDatabaseProductName() returns the name of the DBMS product

❑ Those that describe the contents of the database to which the connection is established, which it returns within a ResultSet, an interface described later in the chapter that's normally used in JDBC to represent the results of a query. Examples of this category of method include getSchemas(), which returns a list of schemas defined in the database, and getTables(), which as its name implies returns a list of the tables defined.

Once you've successfully connected to the database, it's possible to obtain a reference to an instance of DatabaseMetaData using code similar to the following:

```
Connection connect = DriverManager.getConnection(url, "bspell", "brett");
DatabaseMetaData dmd = connect.getMetaData();
```

Statement

Once you've obtained a database connection through DriverManager or through a DataSource, you can create a Statement object. A Statement allows you to execute SQL commands, and an instance of Statement can be created by calling Connection's createStatement() method:

```
Connection connect = DriverManager.getConnection("jdbc:odbc:projava");
Statement stmt = connect.createStatement();
```

In JDBC 1.x, the `Statement` interface defines three methods for executing SQL commands, and JDBC 2.x adds a fourth. The specific methods used will depend upon the type of statements you're executing and the type of results returned by those statements.

A single instance of `Statement` can be reused repeatedly to execute SQL statements, and simple applications usually need to create only one `Statement`. However, each instance allows only a single SQL command to be active at any given time, so you may sometimes need to create multiple `Statement` objects. For example, if your application needs to perform a query while the results of a previous query are still being processed, the two queries must be issued from different `Statement` instances.

executeUpdate()

This method allows you to execute most **Data Manipulation Language (DML)** statements (`INSERT`, `UPDATE`, and `DELETE`) and **Data Definition Language (DDL)** statements (`CREATE TABLE`, `CREATE VIEW`, etc.). It accepts a single `String` parameter that represents the SQL statement to be executed, and returns an integer value identifying the number of rows that were modified by the statement. Examples of how to use `executeUpdate()` are shown below:

```
Statement stmt = connect.createStatement();
int rowsChanged = stmt.executeUpdate(
    "UPDATE MYTABLE SET ACCTSTATUS = 0 WHERE CUSTID = 123");
rowsChanged = stmt.executeUpdate(
    "UPDATE HERTABLE SET ACCTBAL = 0 WHERE CUSTID = 123");
```

For DDL commands, a value of zero is always returned by `executeUpdate()`.

executeQuery()

When you wish to perform a query (issue a `SELECT` statement), you can do so using the `executeQuery()` method. This method requires a `String` parameter representing the statement to be executed and it returns a `ResultSet` that can be used to process the results of the query:

```
ResultSet rset = stmt.executeQuery("SELECT * FROM MYTABLE");
```

A detailed description of how to use `ResultSet` is provided later in this chapter.

execute()

In some unusual cases, a single SQL statement can return multiple update counts or `ResultSet` instances, and you should use this method when you expect that to be the case. Like `executeUpdate()` and `executeQuery()`, this method is passed a `String` parameter representing the statement to be executed, but `execute()` returns a `boolean` value instead of an `int` or a `ResultSet`. That `boolean` value identifies the data type of the first return value, and will be `true` if the first value is a `ResultSet` or `false` if it is an integer.

You can iterate through the return values by calling `getMoreResults()`, which returns a `boolean` value with the same meaning as the value returned by `execute()`. `ResultSet` instances and integer update counts can be retrieved from the queue using `getResultSet()` and `getUpdateCount()`, respectively, but when `getUpdateCount()` returns a value of –1, the end of the result queue has been reached.

addBatch(), executeBatch() (JDBC 2.x)

The `executeUpdate()` method described above is simple and easy to use, but has one disadvantage: each SQL statement executed is immediately sent to the database. While that is not a problem as long as a small number of updates are being executed, it can result in poor performance when making many changes to a database. The DBMS server and the client application typically reside on different machines, which means that each invocation of `executeUpdate()` will incur the overhead associated with a network call. That overhead is usually substantial, and it's much more efficient to transfer a large amount of data in a single network call than it is to transfer smaller amounts of data using many calls.

The `addBatch()` method can be called multiple times for a `Statement` and allows you to create a group (or "batch") of update (`INSERT`, `UPDATE`, `DELETE`) statements. Once you've added the statements that you wish to include in the batch, `executeBatch()` will send those statements to the DBMS using a single network call and the results are returned as an array of `int` values. Since batch updates greatly reduce network overhead, they can significantly improve an application's performance. A simple example of how to use batch updates is provided below:

```
Statement stmt = connect.createStatement();
stmt.addBatch("UPDATE MYTABLE SET STATUS = 5 WHERE CUSTID = 123");
stmt.addBatch("UPDATE HISTABLE SET FIRSTNAME = 'John' WHERE CUSTID = 456");
int[] results = stmt.executeBatch();
```

When all of the updates in a batch complete normally, `executeBatch()` returns an array of integer values, and there will be an array element for each update statement. Like the integer value returned by `executeUpdate()`, each integer identifies the number of rows the statement changed, or will be -2 if that number could not be determined.

A JDBC driver may or may not continue executing batch update statements after one of them fails. When an error does occur, a `BatchUpdateException` is thrown that can be used to retrieve the integer values for the statements that were executed. If the driver continued to execute updates after a failure, the `BatchUpdateException`'s `getUpdateCounts()` method will return an array of integers for every statement in the batch, including a count value of -3 as the array element for a statement that was not executed successfully. If the driver stopped executing statements once a failure occurred, the integer array will only contain count values for the statements prior to the one that failed. Regardless of the outcome, the list of SQL commands in the `Statement`'s batch is cleared once `executeBatch()` completes. You can also clear the list of statements without executing them by calling the `clearBatch()` method.

PreparedStatement

When you call one of `Statement`'s `execute()` methods, the SQL statement specified is "compiled" by the JDBC driver before being sent to the DBMS. In many cases, you'll wish to execute multiple statements that are very similar and may only differ by a single parameter value. For example, you might execute SQL statements like those shown below:

```
Statement stmt = connect.createStatement();
stmt.executeUpdate(
    "UPDATE MYTABLE SET FNAME = 'Jacob' WHERE CUSTID = 123");
stmt.executeUpdate(
    "UPDATE MYTABLE SET FNAME = 'Jordan' WHERE CUSTID = 456");
stmt.executeUpdate(
    "UPDATE MYTABLE SET FNAME = 'Jeffery' WHERE CUSTID = 789");
```

Compiling each SQL statement can result in poor performance if a large number of statements are executed. However, this example illustrates the usefulness of `PreparedStatement`, which is a subclass of `Statement`. `PreparedStatement` allows you to compile a statement one time and use **substitution parameters** to modify the final SQL statement that's executed. In this case, for example, you might create a `PreparedStatement` using code like that shown below:

```
PreparedStatement pstmt = connect.prepareStatement(
    "UPDATE MYTABLE SET FNAME = ? WHERE CUSTID = ?");
```

The two question marks (?) in the statement represent substitution parameters, and you can use the `setXXX()` methods defined in `PreparedStatement` to specify values for those fields. For example, the following code is functionally equivalent to the group of statements used earlier:

```
PreparedStatement pstmt = connect.prepareStatement(
    "UPDATE MYTABLE SET FNAME = ? WHERE CUSTID = ?");
```

```
pstmt.setString(1, "Jacob");
pstmt.setInt(2, 123);
pstmt.executeUpdate();

pstmt.setString(1, "Jordan");
pstmt.setInt(2, 456);
pstmt.executeUpdate();

pstmt.setString(1, "Jeffery");
pstmt.setInt(2, 789);
pstmt.executeUpdate();
```

This approach is much more efficient because the statement is only compiled once, although it's executed several times.

> Note that the substitution field index values are 1-based instead of 0-based, meaning that the first question mark corresponds to field 1, the second to field 2, and so on.

Another advantage of using a `PreparedStatement` instead of a `Statement` is that it partially insulates your application from the details of creating a valid SQL statement. For example, suppose that you attempt to execute the following code:

```
Statement stmt = connect.createStatement();
String insertText = "This won't work";
String sqlText = "UPDATE MYTABLE SET FNAME = '" + insertText + "' " +
                 "WHERE CUSTID = 123";
stmt.executeUpdate(sqlText);
```

The SQL statement that's constructed in the code segment listed above will fail because of the embedded single quote/apostrophe character in the word `"won't"`. In other words, the SQL statement will contain the text shown below:

```
UPDATE MYTABLE SET FNAME = 'This won't work' WHERE CUSTID = 123
```

It is possible to solve this problem (and use a `Statement`) by changing each embedded apostrophe into a pair of apostrophes. However, that approach is moderately complex and requires you to perform a conversion on any string that may have embedded apostrophes before using the string in an SQL statement.

A related problem occurs when embedding date values in an SQL statement, since each DBMS can define its own date format. For example, the following statement may be valid for one DBMS but not another:

```
UPDATE ACCTINFO SET DATEOFSALE = '09-FEB-2001' WHERE ACCTNUM = 456
```

A third problem occurs when you wish to store binary data in a database. SQL supports text, numeric, and date information, but does not define a way for you to embed a series of byte values in an SQL statement.

Fortunately, `PreparedStatement` provides an easy solution for all three of these problems. Instead of embedding the data value directly inside the SQL statement, you can simply define a substitution parameter and use a `setXXX()` method to store the appropriate value. When you do so, the JDBC driver assumes responsibility for creating a valid SQL statement, which insulates your application from the details of embedding a particular type of data. For example, you can store a `String` value (with or without embedded quotation marks) in a `PreparedStatement` using code like that shown below:

```
String insertText = "This won't work";
PreparedStatement pstmt = connect.prepareStatement(
    "UPDATE MYTABLE SET FNAME = ? WHERE CUSTID = 123");
pstmt.setString(1, insertText);
pstmt.executeUpdate();
```

A `Date` value can be specified the same way, as illustrated below. Note, however, that an instance of `java.util.Date` must first be converted into an instance of `java.sql.Date`:

```
java.util.Date dateValue = new java.util.Date();
java.sql.Date sqlDate = new java.sql.Date(dateValue.getTime());
PreparedStatement pstmt = connect.prepareStatement(
    "UPDATE ACCTINFO SET DATEOFSALE = ? WHERE ACCTNUM = 456");
pstmt.setDate(1, sqlDate);
pstmt.executeUpdate();
```

Finally, an array of byte values can be stored by encapsulating them in a `ByteArrayInputStream` and storing a reference to that stream using `setBinaryStream()`:

```
byte[] pixelValues;
// ...
PreparedStatement pstmt = connect.prepareStatement(
    "UPDATE APPIMAGES SET IMAGEDATA = ? WHERE IMAGEID = 789");
ByteArrayInputStream bais = new ByteArrayInputStream(pixelValues);
pstmt.setBinaryStream(1, bais, pixelValues.length);
```

CallableStatement

`CallableStatement` is a subclass of `PreparedStatement`, and this class allows you to execute **stored procedures**, or programs stored inside a database. Stored procedures are usually written in a proprietary language such as Oracle's PL/SQL, and they typically contain a combination of SQL statements and structured programming instructions. The simplest version of a stored procedure call is shown below, where `myProcedure` is a stored procedure that performs a query:

```
String procedureCall = "{call myProcedure}";
CallableStatement cstmt = connect.prepareCall(procedureCall);
ResultSet rset = cstmt.executeQuery();
```

Note that the string used to call the stored procedure is enclosed in braces. This is done because the syntax for calling stored procedures is not a standard part of SQL, so JDBC supports these calls through its **escape syntax**. The escape syntax is used for nonstandard SQL extensions that are supported by JDBC and it indicates to the driver that the escape text must be converted into a form that's appropriate for the DBMS.

Like Java methods, stored procedures may allow you to pass parameter values (in stored procedure terminology, an **IN parameter**) and may provide a return value (or **result parameter**). Unlike Java methods, however, stored procedures can return multiple values through **OUT parameters**, and a parameter can be an IN parameter, an OUT parameter, or both (INOUT). Parameters are identified by question marks in CallableStatement commands the same way that substitution fields are identified for PreparedStatement commands. For example, to call myProcedure and indicate that it returns a result parameter, you could execute the following:

```
String procedureCall = "{?= call myProcedure}";
```

IN and OUT parameters can be specified inside parenthesis as illustrated in the following example, where three parameters are specified for myProcedure:

```
String procedureCall = "{?= call myProcedure(?, ?, ?)}";
```

Before calling a stored procedure, you must provide a value for each IN parameter and identify the type of data that will be returned by each OUT parameter. Providing a value for an IN parameter is done in exactly the same way that you set values for PreparedStatement instances, namely by using the setXXX() methods:

```
String procedureCall = "{?= call myProcedure(?, ?, ?)}";
CallableStatement cstmt = connect.prepareCall(procedureCall);
cstmt.setString(2, "Hello");
cstmt.setInt(3, 123);
cstmt.setBoolean(4, true);
```

Identifying the type of data returned by each OUT parameter is equally simple, and is done using CallableStatement's registerOutParameter() method. When calling that method, you must specify the index of the parameter and an integer value that corresponds to one of the data types defined in java.sql.Types, which is described below. In this example, the result parameter is expected to return a numeric value, and the second of the three IN parameters is also declared as an OUT (or more accurately, as an INOUT) parameter that returns character data:

```
String procedureCall = "{?= call myProcedure(?, ?, ?)}";
CallableStatement cstmt = connect.prepareCall(procedureCall);
cstmt.setString(2, "Hello");
cstmt.setInt(3, 123);
cstmt.setBoolean(4, true);
cstmt.registerOutParameter(1, Types.NUMERIC);
cstmt.registerOutParameter(3, Types.VARCHAR);
```

Once the stored procedure has been executed, you can retrieve values from the result, OUT, and INOUT parameters using the getXXX() methods defined in CallableStatement:

```
String procedureCall = "{?= call myProcedure(?, ?, ?)}";
CallableStatement cstmt = connect.prepareCall(procedureCall);
cstmt.setString(2, "Hello");
cstmt.setInt(3, 123);
cstmt.setBoolean(4, true);
cstmt.registerOutParameter(1, Types.NUMERIC);
cstmt.registerOutParameter(3, Types.VARCHAR);
cstmt.execute();
java.math.BigDecimal bd = cstmt.getBigDecimal(1);
String str = cstmt.getString(3);
```

JDBC Data Types

SQL defines a number of standard data types, and those types are represented in Java by integer constants defined in the java.sql.Types class. As indicated below, JDBC defines a mapping between each SQL data type and a Java class that's able to encapsulate values of that type. The following table lists each SQL type/Types constant, its associated Java class, and an indication of the release (JDBC 1.x or 2.x) in which the type was introduced:

SQL Type/Types Constant	Associated Java Type	JDBC Version
ARRAY	java.sql.Array	2.x
BIGINT	long	1.x
BINARY	byte[]	1.x
BIT	boolean	1.x
BLOB	java.sql.Blob	2.x
CHAR	String	1.x
CLOB	java.sql.Clob	2.x
DATE	java.sql.Date	1.x
DECIMAL	java.math.BigDecimal	1.x
DISTINCT	(See below)	2.x
DOUBLE	double	1.x
FLOAT	double	1.x
INTEGER	int	1.x
JAVA_OBJECT	(See below)	2.x
LONGVARBINARY	byte[]	1.x
LONGVARCHAR	String	1.x

SQL Type/Types Constant	Associated Java Type	JDBC Version
NULL	null	1.x
NUMERIC	java.math.BigDecimal	1.x
OTHER	(See below)	1.x
REAL	float	1.x
REF	java.sql.Ref	2.x
SMALLINT	short	1.x
STRUCT	java.sql.Struct	2.x
TIME	java.sql.Time	1.x
TIMESTAMP	java.sql.Timestamp	1.x
TINYINT	byte	1.x
VARBINARY	byte[]	1.x
VARCHAR	String	1.x

Most of these types should be self-explanatory, but some that may not be are described below.

ARRAY

Most database columns can contain only a single value of a simple data type in each row. However, the SQL3 standard provides support for an ARRAY type that allows you to define columns that contain an array of values in each row.

To store an array in a database column, you can use code like that shown below:

```
String[] names = {"Jacob", "Jordan", "Jeffery"};
PreparedStatement ps = connect.prepareStatement(
    "UPDATE NAMETABLE SET NAMECOL = ? WHERE EMPLOYEE = 123");
ps.setObject(1, names);
ps.executeUpdate();
```

To read an array of values from a database row, you can use the getArray() method in ResultSet:

```
String[] names;
Statement stmt = connect.createStatement();
ResultSet rset = stmt.executeQuery(
    "SELECT * FROM NAMETABLE WHERE EMPLOYEE = 123");
if (rset.next()) {
  Array sqlArray = rset.getArray("NAMECOL");
  names = (String[])(sqlArray.getArray());
  for (int i = 0; i < names.length; i++) {
    System.out.println(names[i]);
  }
}
```

Alternatively, you can use the getResultSet() method defined in Array instead of getArray(). The following code segment will produce the same output as the one shown above, but it retrieves the values through a ResultSet instead of an array of String instances:

```
Statement stmt = connect.createStatement();
ResultSet rset = stmt.executeQuery(
    "SELECT * FROM NAMETABLE WHERE EMPLOYEE = 123");
if (rset.next()) {
  Array sqlArray = rset.getArray("NAMECOL");
  ResultSet arraySet = sqlArray.getResultSet();
  while (arraySet.next()) {
    System.out.println(arraySet.getObject(2));
  }
}
```

BLOB, CLOB

When you perform a query and access a value stored in a table row, you normally must retrieve the entire value. For example, if you perform a query that returns table rows containing character data, the full text value is returned when you call getString() or getObject(). That behavior is acceptable in most cases, but it can be a problem when reading data from columns that contain extremely large values. For example, if a column contains binary data that represents a large audio or video "clip", it may be undesirable or even impossible to read the entire clip into memory at one time due to its size.

SQL3 defines the BLOB (Binary Large Object) and CLOB (Character Large Object) types that are represented by the Blob and Clob interfaces in java.sql. These new types allow you to retrieve specific portions of a database column's value instead of requiring that the entire value be read into memory. In addition, the Blob and Clob interfaces define methods that allow you to search for a particular sequence of byte values (for Blobs) or characters (for Clobs) without first retrieving the data you're searching against from the database. For example, the following code performs a query, obtains a Clob from the ResultSet, and searches for "Professional Java Programming" in the text stored in the database. If that string is found, up to one hundred characters are read from the database starting at the position where the search text was located:

```
Statement stmt = connect.createStatement();
ResultSet rset = stmt.executeQuery(
    "SELECT * FROM MYBOOK WHERE TEXTID = 123");
Clob myClob = rset.getClob("CHAPTERTEXT");
long index = myClob.position("Professional Java Programming", 0);
if (index != -1) {
  String theText = myClob.getSubString(index, 100);
}
```

DATE, TIME, TIMESTAMP

The DATE type defined by SQL represents a date (day, month, and year) value only, TIME represents a time (hours, minutes, and seconds) only, and TIMESTAMP is a combination of a date and a time. Each of these is represented by a java.util.Date subclass defined in java.sql such as the java.sql.Timestamp class.

The java.util.Date class could not be used directly to represent a TIMESTAMP because SQL's definition of that type requires that it support nanosecond values, while java.util.Date supports nothing smaller than milliseconds.

DISTINCT

SQL3 supports **user-defined types** (UDTs) that allow users to define new data types based on existing types. A **distinct data type** is a user-defined type that's based on a single existing SQL data type. For example, you might wish to create a new type to represent the two-character language codes used by Java's `Locale` object, which can be accomplished with the following SQL command:

```
CREATE TYPE LANGUAGECODE AS CHAR(2);
```

Once a distinct type has been created, it can be used when defining the columns that make up tables within the database. You can retrieve the value of a distinct data type from a `ResultSet` by using the `getXXX()` method that's appropriate for the underlying type. In this case, for example, you would use `getString()` to retrieve the value stored in a `LANGUAGECODE` column.

STRUCT

Structured types are similar to distinct types, but structured types allow you to create more complex data types. Although conceptually similar to Java classes, an SQL structured type contains only data, while classes typically contain both data and logic. For example, suppose that you have a Java class like the one shown below:

```
public class Student {

  public String name;
  public int studentID;
  public java.util.Date dateOfBirth;
  public float testScore;

}
```

In practice, this class would normally contain accessor and mutator methods for its properties, although those are omitted here for the sake of simplicity. In any case, given this `Student` class, an equivalent structured type could be created using an SQL command similar to the one below:

```
CREATE TYPE STUDENT {
    STUDENTNAME   VARCHAR(20),
    STUDENTID     NUMERIC(10),
    DATEOFBIRTH   DATE,
    TESTSCORE     NUMERIC(5, 2)
}
```

Once a structured type has been created, it can be used when defining the columns that make up database tables.

Since they are conceptually very similar to classes, structured types can be very useful for providing object persistence, and that topic is discussed in detail in the next chapter.

REF

Just as SQL3's structured types are similar to classes, its new REF type provides functionality similar to that of an object reference, and an SQL3-compliant DBMS will allow you to create columns containing references to structured type instances. For example, if you define the STUDENT structured type described above, you can define table columns that contain references to instances of STUDENT.

Although conceptually very similar to one another, an instance of SQL's REF type does not map directly to a Java object reference. You cannot, for example, create an instance of the Student class and store a reference to that object in a database. It is possible to obtain access to a REF using ResultSet's getRef() method that returns an instance of java.sql.Ref. However, Ref does not currently provide any useful functionality. Intuitively, you might expect a Ref to allow you to access the values stored in the structured type/object instance, but that is not the case. To access those values, you must perform a query/SELECT and specify the Ref value in a WHERE clause just as you would a traditional primary key.

JAVA_OBJECT

A DBMS may provide direct support for storing Java objects in the database, and this type identifies columns that contain some type of Java object.

OTHER

This value represents columns that have a type that the JDBC driver was unable to map to a known SQL type.

ResultSet

An instance of ResultSet is returned from executeQuery(), and one or more instances may be returned from execute(). A ResultSet is a representation of the data returned by your query, and it allows you to process the results one row at a time. Before you can process a row, you must move the ResultSet's **cursor** (pointer) to that row, and the row that's pointed to by the cursor is called the **current row**. When a ResultSet is created, the cursor is initially positioned before the first row.

You should be aware that the data returned by your query is not usually stored in the ResultSet object. In most cases, the data remains on the database server and only when the cursor moves to a particular row is that row read from the server and cached by the ResultSet. This allows you to perform queries that return a much larger volume of data than can be cached in your machine's memory.

Instances of ResultSet are sometimes returned by methods in java.sql when no query has been issued explicitly. For example, some of the methods defined in DatabaseMetaData return data in the form of a ResultSet.

It's helpful to review some ResultSet properties before describing the methods defined in that interface, because its properties determine which of a ResultSet's methods you're able to use for a particular instance, and how they function.

Forward-Only Versus Scrollable (Scrollability Type)

Scrollability describes the type of cursor movement that's allowed, and a **forward-only** ResultSet only allows the cursor to be moved forward one row at a time using the next() method. However, with a **scrollable** ResultSet, you can use a variety of methods to position the cursor. It can be moved forward or backward, and can be moved in those directions by any number of rows. In addition, it's possible to move the cursor to a specific row (in other words, to use absolute instead of relative positioning), including the first and last rows in the ResultSet.

> Only the **next()** method is defined in JDBC 1.x, and the other cursor positioning methods were added to **ResultSet** as part of the JDBC 2.x enhancements. Even if a JDBC driver is compliant with the 2.x specification, it may not allow you to create a scrollable **ResultSet**.

You can determine which ResultSet types are supported by calling the supportsResultSetType() method in DatabaseMetaData.

Read-Only Versus Updatable (Concurrency Mode)

ResultSet defines a large number of getXXX() methods that allow you to read column values from the current row (for example, getString(), getFloat(), etc.), and it includes a corresponding updateXXX() method for each getXXX(). While it's always possible to call the read/get methods, a ResultSet's **concurrency mode** determines whether you can use the write/update methods. As its name implies, a **read-only** ResultSet allows you only to read the data, while an **updatable** ResultSet allows you both to read the data and to modify it through the ResultSet.

> The **updateXXX()** methods were added to **ResultSet** as part of the enhanced functionality of JDBC 2.x, but even some JDBC 2.x-compliant drivers may not support updatable result sets.

However, your application can determine which concurrency modes are supported by calling the supportsResultSetConcurrency() method in DatabaseMetaData.

Update Sensitivity

While you're using a ResultSet to process the results of a query, it's usually possible for other users/applications to modify the rows in the database that were returned by your query. Update sensitivity indicates whether the ResultSet will reflect changes that are made to the underlying data *after* the ResultSet is created. Those updates are known as "changes by others" to distinguish them from changes made to the data using an updatable ResultSet's updateXXX() methods. If you call a getXXX() method to read data from the current row, a **sensitive** ResultSet will return the data stored in the underlying database even if the data was changed by another user after the ResultSet was created. However, an **insensitive** ResultSet does not detect such changes, and may return outdated information which may not match the search criteria.

Update sensitivity does not imply that a ResultSet is sensitive to all types of changes. For example, a ResultSet might be sensitive to row deletions but not to row updates or insertions. In addition, a ResultSet's sensitivity to "changes by others" can be different from its sensitivity to its own changes (modifications to the data made through the updateXXX() methods). However, DatabaseMetaData provides methods that allow you to determine which types of changes are visible for a given ResultSet type.

Selecting ResultSet Properties

To set the scrollability, concurrency, and sensitivity properties, you must specify the appropriate values when creating a Statement. The code segments shown earlier used the createStatement() method that does not accept any parameter values, but another version of createStatement() allows you to specify two integer values representing ResultSet properties:

```
int resultSetType, resultSetConcurrency;
// ...

Statement stmt = connect.createStatement(resultSetType,
                                    resultSetConcurrency);
```

- ❑   The `resultSetType` parameter represents a combination of the scrollability and sensitivity properties, and it should be assigned one of the following constants defined in `ResultSet`: `TYPE_FORWARD_ONLY`, `TYPE_SCROLL_INSENSITIVE`, or `TYPE_SCROLL_SENSITIVE`.

- ❑   The `resultSetConcurrency` value represents the concurrency mode for `ResultSet` instances created by this statement, and should be assigned the value of either `CONCUR_READ_ONLY` or `CONCUR_UPDATABLE`.

You can use these constants and the `createStatement()` method shown above to create a `Statement` that will produce `ResultSet` instances with the desired properties. For example, you can use code similar to the following to create a `Statement` and request that the `ResultSet` instances it creates be scrollable, sensitive to others' changes, and updatable:

```
Statement stmt = connect.createStatement(ResultSet.TYPE_SCROLL_SENSITIVE,
                                    ResultSet.CONCUR_UPDATABLE);
```

> **Note that if you specify a type of `ResultSet` that's not supported by the driver, it will not generate an error when `createStatement()` is called.**

Instead, the `Statement` will produce `ResultSet` instances that match the type you requested as closely as possible. In this case, for example, if the driver supports updatable `ResultSet` instances but not scrolling, it will create forward-only instances that are updatable.

Performance Hints (JDBC 2.x)

For drivers that support JDBC 2.x, it's possible to provide information that can improve the performance of a `ResultSet`. As mentioned earlier, a row is normally retrieved from the database only after it becomes the `ResultSet`'s current row, but JDBC 2.x allows buffering or "pre-fetching" of rows by a `ResultSet`.

The **fetch size** specifies the number of rows that the `ResultSet` should retrieve from the database each time it needs to read new rows, and that value is set using the `setFetchSize()` method. In other words, when the driver is capable of buffering database records, this value identifies the maximum number of records that should be buffered. For example, suppose that you execute the following code:

```
ResultSet rset = stmt.executeQuery("SELECT * FROM MYTABLE");
rset.setFetchSize(10);
```

If you execute the `ResultSet`'s `next()` method, it should retrieve ten records from the database and store them in a buffer. As your application executes the `next()` method again to process more records, the `ResultSet` will not request more data from the database until all ten of the original records have been processed. Once that occurs, the `ResultSet` will retrieve up to ten more records, and the process will be repeated. Just as performing updates in a batch improved performance by reducing network calls, this type of record buffering can improve performance for the same reason.

You can also suggest a **fetch direction** to the driver, and doing so may improve its performance by identifying the direction in which you plan to process the records in a ResultSet. The fetch direction is specified using the setFetchDirection() method, and that method requires an integer parameter value that should be equal to FETCH_FORWARD or to FETCH_REVERSE, both of which are constants defined in ResultSet.

Note that the fetch size and fetch direction settings are described as "hints" because the driver may choose to ignore one or both of those values. In fact, a driver may not even support pre-fetching/buffering of rows at all.

Using ResultSet

Almost all of the methods defined in ResultSet fall into one of three categories: cursor positioning, data retrieval, and data modification.

Cursor Positioning

The positioning methods allow you to change the position of the cursor so that you can select which row to process. As mentioned earlier, JDBC 1.x supports only the next() method, which moves the cursor forward one row, and even some JDBC 2.x drivers may not support scrollable ResultSet instances.

The next() method does not accept any parameter values, and returns a boolean value that indicates whether another row was found. In other words, the value returned from next() is the ResultSet equivalent of an end-of-file indicator. If it returns true, the cursor points to valid row that can be processed, but if it returns false, the cursor has moved beyond the last row in the ResultSet.

The following code segment shows how to iterate through the rows in a ResultSet using next():

```
ResultSet rset = stmt.executeQuery("SELECT * FROM MYTABLE");
while (rset.next()) {
  // Process the current row here
}
```

The other positioning methods that we mentioned earlier are not described in detail here, but they are equally simple to use and allow you to move the cursor to any row in the ResultSet. You can use relative positioning to move the cursor forward or back a specified number of rows, or you can use absolute positioning to move the cursor to a specific row. For example, to move the cursor back five rows from its current position, you could execute the following code:

```
ResultSet rset;
// ...

rset.relative(-5);
```

In addition, positioning methods are provided that move the cursor to (or before) the first row in the ResultSet and to (or after) the last row.

Data Retrieval

The getXXX() methods defined in ResultSet allow you to retrieve data from the current row, and the specific method used determines the type of value returned. For example, getBytes() returns an array of bytes, getString() returns a String instance, getInt() an int value, and so on. In most cases you will know in advance which data type is stored in a particular column, but if you do not know, you may wish to use the getObject() method. When getObject() is called, it returns an Object that's appropriate for the type of data stored in the column, such as a String for character data, a byte array for raw binary data, an appropriate wrapper object for primitive types (for example, a BigDecimal for numeric data), and so on.

Two implementations are provided for each data retrieval getXXX() method defined in ResultSet: one that accepts an integer parameter, and another that requires a String. The integer value represents the position within the ResultSet of the column from which the data should be retrieved, and is 1-based. For example, to retrieve a String value from the second column, you could use code similar to the following:

```
ResultSet rset;
// ...

String columnValue = rset.getString(2);
```

The getXXX() methods that accept a String parameter require that the String be equal to the name of one of the columns in the ResultSet:

```
ResultSet rset;
// ...

String columnValue = rset.getString("FIRSTNAME");
```

Note that some drivers may not allow you to retrieve a column's value more than once, and/or require that you must access the columns in left-to-right order. If your application's design makes it necessary to access the data repeatedly, you may need to read the data from the ResultSet and cache it in memory to allow your code to function properly.

Data Modification

When a ResultSet is updatable, you can use its updateXXX() methods to modify the data in the current row, while insertRow() and deleteRow() insert a new row and delete the current row, respectively.

The updateXXX() methods are similar to the getXXX() methods, in that you can specify either a column's name or its index in the ResultSet. For example, to update the third column with a float value, you could execute code like that shown here:

```
ResultSet rset;
// ...

rset.updateFloat(3, 123.45f);
```

> Modifications that you make to the ResultSet's data are not immediately propagated to the underlying database. Calling updateRow() causes any changes made to the current row to be saved, while cancelRowUpdates() causes your changes to be discarded.

The refreshRow() method also causes any updates to be discarded, but there is an important difference between it and cancelRowUpdates(). While cancelRowUpdates() causes the row's original values to be restored, refreshRow() actually re-reads the row from the database. This can be useful if the information may have changed in a way that can affect the behavior of your application.

Determining the Number of Rows Returned

You'll often wish to determine the number of rows returned by a query before processing the ResultSet data, but JDBC 1.x does not provide any way to do so directly. There are at least two ways of doing so indirectly, but both of them require you to execute an extra SELECT statement, and neither of them is acceptable in all situations.

One option is to issue a SELECT statement that uses the aggregate COUNT(*) function to determine the number of records. This approach is easy to implement, but it does require you to effectively perform the same query twice, which can significantly degrade the performance of your application, since queries are often very time-consuming. However, this approach may be acceptable with smaller databases, and an example of how to use COUNT() is shown below:

```
int recordCount = 0;
Statement stmt = connect.createStatement();

// Get the number of records matching the search criteria
ResultSet rset = stmt.executeQuery(
  "SELECT COUNT(*) FROM EMPLOYEE WHERE SALARY < 50000");
if (rset.next()) {
  recordCount = rset.getInt(1);
}

// Now get the real data
rset = stmt.executeQuery("SELECT * FROM EMPLOYEE WHERE SALARY < 50000");
```

The only other approach available with JDBC 1.x is to perform the same query twice, iterating through the records returned the first time to obtain a count. This technique may be appropriate when the number of records returned in the ResultSet is small, but is usually not acceptable for larger amounts of data:

```
int recordCount = 0;
Statement stmt = connect.createStatement();
// Get the number of records matching the search criteria
ResultSet rset = stmt.executeQuery(
    "SELECT * FROM EMPLOYEE WHERE SALARY < 50000");
while (rset.next()) {
  recordCount++;
}
// Now get the real data
rset = stmt.executeQuery("SELECT * FROM EMPLOYEE WHERE SALARY < 50000");
```

JDBC 2.x does provide an easier and more efficient way to determine the number of rows encapsulated by a ResultSet, but only when the ResultSet is scrollable. Specifically, you can use the last() method defined in JDBC 2.x to move the cursor to the last row in the ResultSet and then call getRow() to retrieve the index of the current row:

```
int recordCount;
Statement stmt = connect.createStatement();
// Get the data
ResultSet rset = stmt.executeQuery(
    "SELECT COUNT(*) FROM EMPLOYEE WHERE SALARY < 50000");
// Move the cursor to the last row
```

```
rset.last();
// Get the current row's index (i.e., the number of rows in the ResultSet)
recordCount = rset.getRow();
// Restore the cursor to its previous position
rset.beforeFirst();
```

ResultSetMetaData

As described earlier, DatabaseMetaData can be used to determine the capabilities of the DBMS and the JDBC driver, as well as to examine the contents of the database. Similarly, ResultSetMetaData can be used to obtain information that describes the columns returned by a query, such as each column's name and the type of data that it contains. ResultSetMetaData can also be used to determine the number of columns returned by a query, so you could use a code segment like the one below to display the column names and values returned by a query:

```
public void printResultSet(ResultSet rset) throws SQLException {
  ResultSetMetaData rsmd = rset.getMetaData();
  int count = rsmd.getColumnCount();
  for (int i = 0; i < count; i++) {
    System.out.print((i == 0 ? "" : "\t") +
    rsmd.getColumnName(i + 1));
  }
  System.out.println();
  while (rset.next()) {
    for (int i = 0; i < count; i++) {
      System.out.print((i == 0 ? "" : "\t") +
      rset.getObject(i + 1));
    }
    System.out.println();
  }
}
```

Rowset (JDBC 2.x Optional Package)

The RowSet interface extends ResultSet and provides some potentially very useful functionality. Unlike a ResultSet, which is returned by methods that are used to execute query statements, your application can create instances of RowSet directly. After creating an instance of RowSet, you must provide it with the information needed to connect to a database, specifically a userid, password, and a URL or a DataSource name. In addition, you must specify a **command string**, which is simply a String representing a SELECT statement that produces the data that the RowSet encapsulates.

As mentioned earlier, a row represented by a ResultSet generally remains in the database until it becomes the current row (in other words, until the cursor is moved to that row). However, a **cached RowSet** may choose to read the records it encapsulates into memory, which provides several benefits:

❑ The RowSet needs to connect to the database just long enough to retrieve all of its records, while a ResultSet maintains an open connection to the database until the ResultSet is closed. This type of RowSet that does not normally have an open connection to the database is known as a **disconnected RowSet**, while a **connected RowSet** maintains a connection as long as it is open.

❑ The cached RowSet and its contents can be serialized and stored in a disk file or transmitted across a network.

❑ A cached RowSet can simulate JDBC 2.x features such as scrolling and updatability even if the underlying JDBC driver does not support those features. Since the rows from the database are stored in memory, they can be accessed in any order to simulate a scrollable ResultSet. Simulating an updatable ResultSet is even easier, since the RowSet only needs to provide updateXXX() implements that modify the cached data.

RowSet provides one other very useful feature that ResultSet does not. Specifically, RowSet generates events that allow listeners to be notified when the RowSet is changed in some way. For example, notifications are sent when the RowSet is populated with data, when the cursor moves, and when the RowSet's data is changed.

Although you can create your own RowSet implementations, an example is provided by Sun, and at the time of this writing it is available on the Java Developer Connection web site (http://developer.java.sun.com/developer/earlyAccess/crs/). Sun's sun.jdbc.rowset.CachedRowSet is a cached, disconnected RowSet that can be used to retrieve small amounts of data from a database and transfer them between different machines. Although it can theoretically be used to read larger amounts of data, memory constraints generally make it impossible or at least undesirable to do so.

An example of how to use the CachedRowSet is shown in the code segment below. This segment creates a RowSet that encapsulates the data in the TEST database table and stores a serialized representation of the RowSet in a disk file named rowset.ser.

```
CachedRowSet rowSet = new CachedRowSet();
rowSet.setCommand("SELECT * FROM TEST");
rowSet.setUrl("jdbc:odbc:mytestdb");
rowSet.setUsername("bspell");
rowSet.setPassword("brett");
rowSet.execute();
FileOutputStream fos = new FileOutputStream("rowset.ser");
ObjectOutputStream oos = new ObjectOutputStream(fos);
oos.writeObject(rowSet);
oos.close();
```

Transactions

Applications often need to make related changes to more than one database table, and it's usually important that either all of the changes succeed or that none of them do. The classic example of this is an application that transfers money from one bank account to another, perhaps from a savings account to a checking account or vice versa. If the two account balances are stored in separate table, it's necessary to issue two UPDATE statements: one that subtracts the appropriate amount from the first table, and another that adds the appropriate amount to the second table:

```
import java.sql.*;

public class TransTest {

  protected String url = "jdbc:odbc:banktest";
```

```
    protected String userid = "bspell";
    protected String password = "brett";

    public static void main(String args[]) throws Exception {
      new TransTest();
    }

    public TransTest() throws Exception {
      Class.forName("sun.jdbc.odbc.JdbcOdbcDriver");
      transferFunds(90000, 46229, "TABLE1", "TABLE2");
    }

    public void transferFunds(float transferAmount, int accountNumber,
        String fromTable, String toTable) throws SQLException,
        InvalidTransferException {
      Statement stmt = null;
      ResultSet rset = null;
      Connection conn = DriverManager.getConnection(url, userid,
          password);
      try {
        stmt = conn.createStatement();
        rset = stmt.executeQuery("SELECT BALANCE FROM " + fromTable +
            " WHERE ACCOUNTID = " + accountNumber);
        rset.next();
        float fromBalance = rset.getFloat(1);
        if (fromBalance < transferAmount) {
          throw new InvalidTransferException("Insufficient funds available");
        }
        rset.close();
        rset = null;

        rset = stmt.executeQuery("SELECT BALANCE FROM " + toTable +
            " WHERE ACCOUNTID = " + accountNumber);
        rset.next();
        float toBalance = rset.getFloat(1);
        rset.close();
        rset = null;

        fromBalance -= transferAmount;
        toBalance += transferAmount;
        stmt.executeUpdate("UPDATE " + fromTable + " SET BALANCE = " +
            fromBalance + " WHERE ACCOUNTID = " + accountNumber);
        if(true) throw new SQLException();  // NOTE THIS!
        stmt.executeUpdate("UPDATE " + toTable + " SET BALANCE = " +
            toBalance + " WHERE ACCOUNTID = " + accountNumber);
      } finally {
        if (rset != null) rset.close();
        if (stmt != null) stmt.close();
        conn.close();
      }
    }

    class InvalidTransferException extends Exception {

      public InvalidTransferException(String message) {
```

```
        super (message);
    }

  }

}
```

Unfortunately, there is a potential problem with this code. It's possible for the application to be interrupted after it has deducted the transfer amount from the checking account but before that amount is added to the savings account balance. If such an interruption does occur, the customer will lose money, which is not desirable for the customer. Similarly, if the order of the updates is reversed and an interruption occurs, the customer's accounts will collectively contain more money than they did before the transfer was initiated, and that outcome is even less desirable for the bank.

A **transaction** is a collection of related updates that should either fail or succeed as a group. Updates that are part of a transaction are issued in the same way that non-transactional updates are issued, and there is no batch-like facility in JDBC for defining the updates in a transaction. However, methods are available that allow you to define the beginning and end of a transaction, and you must use those methods to make updates part of a transaction.

At any point during a transaction, you can end the transaction and discard (or **rollback**) the changes that have occurred, which you'll frequently do if one of the updates generates an error. However, if the updates all complete successfully, you'll normally end the transaction and save (or **commit**) the changes that were made.

When using JDBC, it's not necessary to explicitly identify the start of a transaction because all updates are considered part of a transaction. However, a commit operation is performed by default after each update, which effectively disables transaction processing since a transaction is only useful when it includes multiple updates. You can disable the default behavior (and enable transactions) by passing a value of `false` to the `setAutoCommit()` method in `Connection`.

`Connection` also defines `commit()` and `rollback()` methods that end the current transaction and save or discard the changes that were part of the transaction.

> Only a single transaction can be active for a `Connection` at any given time, so if your application needs to have multiple transactions active simultaneously, you must obtain a connection for each transaction.

The class shown earlier can be easily updated to use transactions to ensure that either both balances are updated or that neither one is changed:

```
import java.sql.*;

public class TransTest {

  protected String url = "jdbc:odbc:banktest";
  protected String userid = "bspell";
  protected String password = "brett";

  public static void main(String args[]) throws Exception {
    new TransTest();
```

```
    }

    public TransTest() throws Exception {
      Class.forName("sun.jdbc.odbc.JdbcOdbcDriver");
      transferFunds(90000, 46229, "TABLE1", "TABLE2");
    }

    public void transferFunds(float transferAmount, int accountNumber,
        String fromTable, String toTable) throws SQLException,
        InvalidTransferException {
      Statement stmt = null;
      ResultSet rset = null;
      Connection conn = DriverManager.getConnection(url, userid,
          password);
      conn.setAutoCommit(false);
      try {
        stmt = conn.createStatement();
        rset = stmt.executeQuery("SELECT BALANCE FROM " + fromTable +
            " WHERE ACCOUNTID = " + accountNumber);
        rset.next();
        float fromBalance = rset.getFloat(1);
        if (fromBalance < transferAmount) {
          throw new InvalidTransferException("Insufficient funds available");
        }
        rset.close();
        rset = null;

        rset = stmt.executeQuery("SELECT BALANCE FROM " + toTable +
            " WHERE ACCOUNTID = " + accountNumber);
        rset.next();
        float toBalance = rset.getFloat(1);
        rset.close();
        rset = null;

        fromBalance -= transferAmount;
        toBalance += transferAmount;
        stmt.executeUpdate("UPDATE " + fromTable + " SET BALANCE = " +
            fromBalance + " WHERE ACCOUNTID = " + accountNumber);
        if(true) throw new SQLException();   // NOTE THIS!
        stmt.executeUpdate("UPDATE " + toTable + " SET BALANCE = " +
            toBalance + " WHERE ACCOUNTID = " + accountNumber);
        conn.commit();
      } catch (SQLException sqle) {
        conn.rollback();
        throw sqle;
      } finally {
        if (rset != null) rset.close();
        if (stmt != null) stmt.close();
        conn.close();
      }
    }

    class InvalidTransferException extends Exception {

      public InvalidTransferException(String message) {
```

```
        super(message);
    }

  }

}
```

Note that this code differs from the original implementation in two ways:

❑   First, it disables the autocommit feature so that the first account update won't be permanently
     saved until/unless commit() is called explicitly.

❑   Second, it intercepts any SQLException before it's returned to the caller and performs a
     rollback() on the connection, which will ensure that the data in the database is restored to
     its original condition when an error occurs. This is important to do because the second update
     might fail even though the first one had succeeded.

Read-Only Transactions

Up to this point, transactions have been discussed only in the context of update operations. While they are often
most useful when performing updates, transactions can be used with query operations as well. For example,
issuing a SELECT statement twice within the same transaction should result in the query returning the same
results the second time as it did originally, even if the underlying data is modified between the two queries. In
other words, transactions can be used with query operations to ensure that they return consistent results.

It's important to realize that regardless of the type of SQL statements used, transaction support is provided by
the DBMS and not by the JDBC driver. In addition, depending upon how the DBMS implements transaction
support, there are a number of problems that can occur when multiple transactions access the same data and
those problems are described below. Later, we'll see how you can avoid these scenarios, or at least select
which ones your application will allow to occur.

Dirty Reads

A **dirty read** occurs when a table row is modified as part of one transaction and a second transaction
performs a query that returns the modified row in spite of the fact that the modification has not been
committed. This behavior is inappropriate since the first transaction may choose to roll back the update, in
which case the second transaction has effectively read invalid (or "dirty") data.

Non-Repeatable Reads

As mentioned above, performing the same query multiple times in a single transaction should produce the
same results each time. In some cases, however, the updates or deletions made by one transaction can affect
the query results of another transaction. For example, suppose that transaction "A" performs a query that
returns ten rows, after which transaction "B" deletes one of those rows from the database. If transaction "A"
then executes the same query and only nine rows are returned, a **non-repeatable read** has occurred.

Phantom Reads

This type of problem is similar to the non-repeatable read, but is related to rows that are inserted. For
example, suppose that transaction "A" performs a query that returns five rows, after which transaction 'B'
inserts a new row that meets the criteria specified by transaction "A". If "A" then re-issues the query and sees
the newly inserted row, a **phantom read** has occurred.

Transaction Isolation Levels

Many applications do not support multiple transactions and will not experience the problems just described. However, for some database-intensive applications where the integrity of the data is very important, it's necessary to eliminate these problems or at least control which ones can occur. Most DBMS products do provide some degree of control over these problems, and they usually do so through data **locking**. Locking is a technique that makes some or all of the data in a table unavailable while it is being read or updated by a transaction. If other transactions attempt to access locked data, their requests will fail, or more frequently, they will be made to wait until the transaction that caused the lock to occur has ended.

In the simplest case, an entire table can be locked as long as its data is referenced by an active transaction, which will prevent any of the three problems just described from occurring. However, that approach has the disadvantage of making the table's data unavailable to other applications for what could be a large amount of time, and that behavior may be unacceptable. In other words, dirty reads, non-repeatable reads, and phantom reads can be avoided, but only by sacrificing accessibility to the data to some extent.

In practice, the ideal balance between data integrity and data accessibility varies from one application to another. Some applications are more concerned with accessibility to the data, while others are primarily concerned with data integrity, and still others may seek a middle ground between the two extremes. Since application needs vary, **transaction isolation levels** are provided to allow an application to select an appropriate balance between accessibility and transaction integrity.

Four transaction isolation levels exist, and each one is represented in JDBC by a constant defined in `Connection`. A given DBMS product may not support all four levels, but you can determine which ones are supported using the `supportsTransactionIsolationLevel()` method defined in `DatabaseMetaData`.

The four isolation levels are described below, with the first one representing maximum accessibility and minimum data integrity, while the last one represents the opposite extreme:

- ❑ **Read Uncommited**
  This transaction isolation level is represented by the `TRANSACTION_READ_UNCOMMITTED` constant, and it allows dirty, non-repeatable, and phantom reads to occur.

- ❑ **Read Committed**
  This level is represented by `TRANSACTION_READ_COMMITTED`, and it only allows non-repeatable and phantom reads to occur, while dirty reads are prevented.

- ❑ **Repeatable Read**
  This level is represented by `TRANSACTION_REPEATABLE_READ` and only allows phantom reads to occur, while prevent dirty and non-repeatable reads.

- ❑ **Serializable**
  Dirty, non-repeatable, and phantom reads are all prevented from occurring when this level is used, which is represented by the `TRANSACTION_SERIALIZABLE` constant.

The default isolation level that's in effect will vary from one DBMS product to the next, although you can determine which one is active for a given `Connection` by calling its `getTransactionIsolationLevel()` method. That method returns an integer value equal to one of the four constants mentioned above that represent the different isolation levels.

Once you've selected an appropriate isolation level and ensured that it is available with the DBMS your application uses, you can easily specify the desired level by calling the `setTransactionIsolation()` method in `Connection`:

```
connect.setTransactionIsolation(Connection.TRANSACTION_REPEATABLE_READ);
```

Distributed Transactions

The transaction capabilities discussed up to this point are applicable to changes made to tables in a single database. In some cases, however, you may wish to make related changes to tables stored in databases residing on different machines, perhaps involving two completely different DBMS products. For example, you might wish to make an update to an Oracle database on one server and a Sybase database on a different machine and need those updates to be made as a single unit. That type of operation is known as a **distributed transaction**, and is supported in Java through the **Java Transaction API (JTA)** and the **Java Transaction Service (JTS)**. However, a detailed discussion of distributed transactions is beyond the scope of this book.

Connection Pooling

Creating a database connection is a relatively slow process, and if an application repeatedly opens and closes many connections, it may have a serious negative impact on the speed of the application, and thus on its value. However, you can improve performance by using **connection pooling**, a technique that allows existing connections to be reused. Connection pooling is conceptually very similar to **thread pooling**, a topic we covered in Chapter 3.

A **connection pool manager** can be implemented as part of a JDBC driver or as a separate component if the driver does not support pooling. The JDBC 2.x optional package includes interfaces used to perform connection pooling and partially describes how a connection pool manager should be implemented. If the driver you're using supports JDBC 2.x-style connection pooling, you can get an instance of a `PooledConnection` from a `DataSource` by calling the `getPooledConnection()` method. Once you've done so, you can obtain a database connection by calling the `PooledConnection` object's `getConnection()` method as shown below:

```
String url = "jdbc:oracle:thin:@myserver:1521:mydata";
String userid = "bspell";
String password = "brett";
OracleConnectionPoolDataSource ocpds = new OracleConnectionPoolDataSource();
ocpds.setURL(url);
ocpds.setUser(userid);
ocpds.setPassword(password);
PooledConnection pool = ocpds.getPooledConnection();
// ...
Connection conn = pool.getConnection();
```

When a database connection is requested from a pool manager, the manager attempts to provide one from its pool of existing connections, but if that pool is empty, a new connection is created and returned instead. Once an application has finished using a connection, the connection is returned to the pool manager instead of being closed, which allows the manager to avoid the overhead of creating a new connection the next time one is needed.

This description is somewhat misleading, because it implies that a true database connection is returned by the pool manager and that the application using the connection is aware of and cooperates with the pool manager by "giving back" connections. In reality, the manager returns a **proxy** object that maintains a reference to a real database connection created by a JDBC driver. Most of the proxy's methods simply delegate their functionality to the real connection, but the proxy's `close()` method returns the real database connection to the pool manager instead of closing the connection. The following code segment illustrates how such a proxy might be implemented:

```
import java.sql.*;

public class ProxyConnection implements Connection {

  protected Connection realConnection;

  public ProxyConnection(Connection connect) {
    realConnection = connect;
  }

  public void clearWarnings() throws SQLException {
    realConnection.clearWarnings();
  }

  public void close() throws SQLException {
    // Don't close the real connection. Return it to the pool
    // manager instead. This example assumes the existance of
    // a class named PoolManager that's reponsible for connection
    // pool management.
    PoolManager.connectionClosed(realConnection);
  }

  public void commit() throws SQLException {
    realConnection.commit();
  }

  public Statement createStatement() throws SQLException {
    return realConnection.createStatement();
  }

  // etc.
```

In other words, the proxy object maintains a reference to a "real" Connection and intercepts the calls that are made. This design makes connection pooling transparent to your application, because a pooled connection behaves exactly the same way that a non-pooled connection does.

Errors and Warnings

Errors can occur for many reasons when performing database operations, and most of the methods defined in the java.sql package can throw SQLException, which is described below.

SQLException

Like other Exception subclasses, SQLException includes a message that describes the nature of the error, and it can be retrieved by calling getMessage(). However, SQLException also provides other properties that you may find helpful, and the methods used to access them are described below.

getNextException(), setNextException()

These methods allow you to modify or retrieve the reference to the next instance of SQLException in a chain of exceptions. Multiple errors can occur during a single operation in some cases, and this chaining technique allows an instance of SQLException to be created for each error.

getErrorCode()

This method returns an integer value that describes the error, although the meaning of that value is driver-specific. To interpret the meaning of this value, you should consult the documentation associated with the driver and/or the DBMS.

getSQLState()

The SQLState value is a five-character String that identifies the nature of the error that occurred. This value is defined by the X/OPEN SQL standard, and is common to all DBMS implementations that have adopted the standard. Since the SQLState provides a very specific indication of the type of problem that occurred, your application may be able to use it to recover from an error or otherwise handle (or ignore) it appropriately.

The SQLState consists of two parts: the first two characters, which are unfortunately called the "class", and the last three characters, known as the "subclass". A class effectively identifies a high-level type of error, while a subclass identifies a more specific error. Classes and subclasses can be either standard (defined as part of the X/OPEN specification) or implementation-defined (specific to a particular DBMS product). Standard classes and subclasses begin with one of the characters 0-4 or A-H. Subsequent characters and the first character of an implementation-defined class or subclass can be any letter or digit (0-9, A-Z).

A listing of some standard classes and subclasses is shown in the table below, along with the associated condition (description of the class) or subcondition (description of the subclass). Note that some classes do not have subclasses because the class itself is sufficient to describe in detail the type of problem that occurred:

Class	Condition	Subclass	Subcondition
00	Successful	000	
01	Warning	000	
		001	Cursor operation conflict
		002	Disconnect error
		003	Null value eliminated in set function
		004	String data right truncation
		005	Insufficient item descriptor areas
		006	Privilege not revoked
		007	Privilege not granted
		008	Implicit zero-bit padding
		009	Search condition too long for schema
		00A	Query expression too long for schema
02	No data	000	
07	Dynamic SQL error	000	

Table continued on following page

Class	Condition	Subclass	Subcondition
		001	Using clause does not match parameters
		002	Using clause does not match target
		003	Cursor specification cannot be executed
		004	Using clause required for parameters
		005	Prepared statement not a cursor spec.
		006	Restricted data type attribute violation
		007	Using clause required for result fields
		008	Invalid descriptor count
		009	Invalid descriptor index
08	Connection exception	000	
		001	Client unable to establish connection
		002	Connection name already in use
		003	Connection does not exist
		004	Server rejected connection request
		006	Connection failure
		007	Transaction resolution unknown
0A	Feature not supported	000	
		001	Multiple server transactions
21	Cardinality violation	000	
22	Data exception	000	
		001	String data right truncation
		002	Null value without indicator
		003	Numeric value out of range
		005	Assignment error
		007	Invalid DATETIME format
		008	DATETIME field overflow
		009	Invalid time zone displacement value
		011	Substring error

Class	Condition	Subclass	Subcondition
		012	Division by zero
		015	Interval field overflow
		018	Invalid character value for cast
		019	Invalid escape character
		021	Character not supported
		022	Indicator overflow
		023	Invalid parameter value
		024	Unterminated C string
		025	Invalid escape sequence
		026	String data length mismatch
		027	Trim error
23	Integrity constraint violation	000	
24	Invalid cursor state	000	
25	Invalid transaction state	000	
26	Invalid SQL statement name	000	
27	Triggered data change violation	000	
28	Invalid authorization specification	000	
2A	Syntax error or access rule violation in SQL statement	000	
2B	Dependent privilege descriptors still exist	000	
2C	Invalid character set name	000	
2D	Invalid transaction termination	000	
2E	Invalid connection name	000	
33	Invalid SQL descriptor name	000	
34	Invalid cursor name	000	
35	Invalid condition number	000	
37	Syntax error or access rule violation in dynamic SQL statement	000	
3C	Ambiguous cursor name	000	

Table continued on following page

Class	Condition	Subclass	Subcondition
3D	Invalid catalog name	000	
3F	Invalid schema name	000	
40	Transaction rollback	000	
42	Syntax error or access rule violation	000	
44	Check option violation	000	
HZ	Remote database access	UUU	

SQLWarning

SQLException is somewhat unusual in that it's used by JDBC in two different ways. First, as previously noted, it can be thrown by many of the java.sql methods and in that way it is similar to other exception classes. However, there are many types of errors that can occur which are not critical and which will not cause your application's execution to be interrupted. For example, if you read a floating-point value into an integer field using ResultSet's getInt() method, a portion of the original value may be lost. That type of problem may be of interest to your application but in many cases should be ignored, so it does not result in an exception being thrown. Instead, an instance of SQLWarning (a subclass of SQLException) is created and appended to a list maintained by the object that generated the warning, which in this example would be a ResultSet.

However, Connection, Statement, and ResultSet can all generate warnings, and each of those classes provides a getWarnings() method accordingly. That method returns the first SQLWarning instance in the object's list, and the list effectively serves as an error log. In other words, when any event generates a warning, an instance of SQLWarning is quietly (without being thrown or otherwise interrupting your application) added to the list of warnings maintained for the object that generated it. In addition to the getWarnings() methods, Connection, Statement, and ResultSet each provide a clearWarnings() method that can be used to remove all warnings currently chained.

Debugging

JDBC provides a logging facility that driver classes can use to display diagnostic information. For example, the driver may generate a message each time one of its classes' methods are called, and/or it may display the SQL statements that are actually sent to the DBMS. Those statements are sometimes different from the ones that your code specifies, because the driver often modifies statements before forwarding them to the database, such as when it fills in the parameter values specified for a PreparedStatement. In addition, the message log may contain SQL statements that were issued by the driver itself that do not correspond to any statements explicitly executed by your application.

This logging facility first appeared in JDBC 1.x, and can be used by passing a reference to a PrintStream to the static setLogStream() method in DriverManager. For example, you might execute the following code to have the messages sent to standard output:

```
DriverManager.setLogStream(System.out);
```

The following listing provides an example of the output that may be produced by this code:

```
Fetching (SQLFetch), hStmt=5312212
End of result set (SQL_NO_DATA)
Free statement (SQLFreeStmt), hStmt=5312212, fOption=1
*Connection.createStatement
Allocating Statement Handle (SQLAllocStmt), hDbc=5311148
hStmt=5312212
Registering Statement sun.jdbc.odbc.JdbcOdbcStatement@63cb330d
*Statement.executeQuery (SELECT * FROM Attribute)
*Statement.execute (SELECT * FROM Attribute)
Free statement (SQLFreeStmt), hStmt=5312212, fOption=0
Executing (SQLExecDirect), hStmt=5312212, szSqlStr=SELECT * FROM Attribute
Number of result columns (SQLNumResultCols), hStmt=5312212
value=8
Number of result columns (SQLNumResultCols), hStmt=5312212
value=8
*ResultSet.getMetaData
*ResultSetMetaData.getColumnName (1)
Column attributes (SQLColAttributes), hStmt=5312212, icol=1, type=1
value (String)=AttributeKey
```

In JDBC 2.x, the setLogStream() method was deprecated and replaced by setLogWriter(), which is passed an instance of PrintWriter. The code listed below creates an instance of PrintWriter using System.out and calls setLogWriter() to direct messages to standard output:

```
OutputStreamWriter osw = new OutputStreamWriter(System.out);
PrintWriter pw = new PrintWriter(osw);
DriverManager.setLogWriter(pw);
```

However, currently there is a bit of a bug with using the setLogWriter() method in that if used in conjunction with a JDBC 1.0 driver, you are unlikely to get any debugging information. See the Java docs for more detail.

Releasing Resources

One of the characteristics of Java that makes it easy to use is its automatic garbage collection. In most cases, it's acceptable to release a resource simply by eliminating references to the object that represents it, and the same is true to some degree of database resources (for example, instances of Connection, Statement, and ResultSet). For example, if you create a connection to a database, you can release it by simply de-referencing it as shown in the code below:

```
String url = "jdbc:oracle:thin:@oraserver:1521:projava";
Connection connect = DriverManager.getConnection(url, "bspell", "brett");
// ...

connect = null;
```

Although this approach should eventually result in the connection being closed, that will not occur until the garbage collector reclaims the Connection object. However, the garbage collector may never run, and even if it does, this code could result in the connection remaining open (but unused) for a long time. To avoid this problem, you should always explicitly release database resources by calling the close() method that is defined in Connection, Statement, and ResultSet:

```
String url = "jdbc:oracle:thin:@oraserver:1521:projava";
Connection connect = DriverManager.getConnection(url, "bspell", "brett");
// ...

connect.close();
connect = null;
```

Not only will failure to explicitly release resources prevent other applications from using those resources, but it may also degrade the performance of your application if a large number of connections are created. It's particularly important to close connections when connection pooling is in use, since a failure to do so will usually prevent the Connection from being returned to the pool manager until the garbage collector runs.

A Database Browser Application

Let's finish off by seeing how all these bits of JDBC fit together by building an application that allows you to browse the tables in a database using the JDBC-ODBC bridge. When the application is started, a dialog is presented into which a JDBC URL, together with a username and password, can be entered:

Once connected to the database, a JTable is used to display the data; three JComboBox components at the top of the window allow the user to select the catalog, schema, and table to be displayed:

ProductID	SupplierID	CategoryID	UnitPrice	UnitsInStock	UnitsOnOrd...	Discontinued	ReorderL
1	1	1	18.0000	39	0	false	10
2	1	1	19.0000	17	40	false	25
3	1	2	10.0000	13	70	false	25
4	2	2	22.0000	53	0	false	0
5	2	2	21.3500	0	0	true	0
6	3	2	25.0000	120	0	false	25
7	3	7	30.0000	15	0	false	10
8	3	2	40.0000	6	0	false	0
9	4	6	97.0000	29	0	true	0
10	4	8	31.0000	31	0	false	0
11	5	4	21.0000	22	30	false	30
12	5	4	38.0000	86	0	false	0
13	6	8	6.0000	24	0	false	5
14	6	7	23.2500	35	0	false	0
15	6	2	15.5000	39	0	false	5
16	7	3	17.4500	29	0	false	10
17	7	6	39.0000	0	0	true	0
18	7	8	62.5000	42	0	false	0

Catalog: Northwind Schema: dbo Table: Products

Exit

```
import java.awt.*;
import java.awt.event.*;
import java.sql.*;
import java.util.Vector;
import javax.swing.*;
import javax.swing.table.*;

public class DatabaseBrowser extends JFrame {
```

In addition to the various GUI components required, we need to hold a reference to the `Connection` to the database. The `main()` method simply makes sure that the JDBC-ODBC driver class is loaded, and creates a new `DatabaseBrowser` object:

```
protected Connection connection;
protected JComboBox catalogBox;
protected JComboBox schemaBox;
protected JComboBox tableBox;
protected JTable table;

public static void main(String[] args) throws Exception {
  new sun.jdbc.odbc.JdbcOdbcDriver();
  DatabaseBrowser db = new DatabaseBrowser();
}
```

The constructor and related methods, build the GUI layout. Before the main window is displayed, a connection dialog is shown requesting that the user enter the username, password, and database URL:

```
public DatabaseBrowser() throws Exception {
  super("Database Browser");
  ConnectionDialog cd = new ConnectionDialog(this);
  connection = cd.getConnection();
  buildFrameLayout();
  setSize(600, 450);
  setVisible(true);
}

protected void buildFrameLayout() {
  Container pane = getContentPane();
  pane.add(getSelectionPanel(), BorderLayout.NORTH);
  table = new JTable();
  table.setAutoResizeMode(JTable.AUTO_RESIZE_OFF);
  refreshTable();
  pane.add(new JScrollPane(table), BorderLayout.CENTER);
  pane.add(getFrameButtonPanel(), BorderLayout.SOUTH);
}

protected JPanel getFrameButtonPanel() {
  JPanel panel = new JPanel();
  JButton button = new JButton("Exit");
  button.addActionListener(new ActionListener() {
    public void actionPerformed(ActionEvent event) {
      System.exit(0);
    }
  });
```

```
    panel.add(button);
    return panel;
}

protected JPanel getSelectionPanel() {
  JLabel label;
  JPanel panel = new JPanel();
  panel.setLayout(new GridBagLayout());
  GridBagConstraints gbc = new GridBagConstraints();
  gbc.gridy = 0;
  gbc.insets = new Insets(5, 10, 5, 10);
  label = new JLabel("Catalog", JLabel.RIGHT);
  panel.add(label, gbc);
  label = new JLabel("Schema", JLabel.RIGHT);
  panel.add(label, gbc);
  label = new JLabel("Table", JLabel.RIGHT);
  panel.add(label, gbc);

  gbc.gridy = 1;
  catalogBox = new JComboBox();
  populateCatalogBox();
  panel.add(catalogBox, gbc);
  schemaBox = new JComboBox();
  populateSchemaBox();
  panel.add(schemaBox, gbc);
  tableBox = new JComboBox();
  populateTableBox();
  panel.add(tableBox, gbc);
```

At this point, event listeners are registered for the three JComboBoxes that call the relevant methods to update the display:

```
    catalogBox.addItemListener(new ItemListener() {
      public void itemStateChanged(ItemEvent event) {
        String newCatalog = (String)(
            catalogBox.getSelectedItem());
        try {
          connection.setCatalog(newCatalog);
        } catch (Exception e) {};
        populateSchemaBox();
        populateTableBox();
        refreshTable();
      }
    });

    schemaBox.addItemListener(new ItemListener() {
      public void itemStateChanged(ItemEvent event) {
        populateTableBox();
        refreshTable();
      }
    });

    tableBox.addItemListener(new ItemListener() {
      public void itemStateChanged(ItemEvent event) {
        refreshTable();
```

```
      }
    });
    return panel;
}
```

`populateCatalogBox()`, `populateSchemaBox()`, and `populateTableBox()` update the JComboBoxes from which the user can select the desired catalog, schema, and table, by obtaining and querying a `DatabaseMetaData` object:

```
protected void populateCatalogBox() {
  try {
    DatabaseMetaData dmd = connection.getMetaData();
    ResultSet rset = dmd.getCatalogs();
    Vector values = new Vector();
    while (rset.next()) {
      values.addElement(rset.getString(1));
    }
    rset.close();
    catalogBox.setModel(new DefaultComboBoxModel(values));
    catalogBox.setSelectedItem(connection.getCatalog());
    catalogBox.setEnabled(values.size() > 0);
  } catch (Exception e) {
    catalogBox.setEnabled(false);
  }
}

protected void populateSchemaBox() {
  try {
    DatabaseMetaData dmd = connection.getMetaData();
    ResultSet rset = dmd.getSchemas();
    Vector values = new Vector();
    while (rset.next()) {
      values.addElement(rset.getString(1));
    }
    rset.close();
    schemaBox.setModel(new DefaultComboBoxModel(values));
    schemaBox.setEnabled(values.size() > 0);
  } catch (Exception e) {
    schemaBox.setEnabled(false);
  }
}

protected void populateTableBox() {
  try {
    String[] types = {"TABLE"};
    String catalog = connection.getCatalog();
    String schema = (String)(schemaBox.getSelectedItem());
    DatabaseMetaData dmd = connection.getMetaData();
    ResultSet rset = dmd.getTables(catalog, schema, null,
        types);
    Vector values = new Vector();
    while (rset.next()) {
      values.addElement(rset.getString(3));
    }
    rset.close();
```

```
        tableBox.setModel(new DefaultComboBoxModel(values));
        tableBox.setEnabled(values.size() > 0);
    } catch (Exception e) {
        tableBox.setEnabled(false);
    }
}
```

refreshTable() is called when the selected catalog, schema, or table has been changed. It builds a query string from these, performs the query, and creates a new ResultSetTableModel (an inner class we will consider in a moment) encapsulating these results:

```
protected void refreshTable() {
    String catalog = (catalogBox.isEnabled() ?
        catalogBox.getSelectedItem().toString() :
        null);
    String schema = (schemaBox.isEnabled() ?
        schemaBox.getSelectedItem().toString() :
        null);
    String tableName = (String)tableBox.getSelectedItem();
    if (tableName == null) {
        table.setModel(new DefaultTableModel());
        return;
    }
    String selectTable = (schema == null ? "" : schema + ".") +
        tableName;
    if (selectTable.indexOf(' ') > 0) {
        selectTable = "\"" + selectTable + "\"";
    }
    try {
        Statement stmt = connection.createStatement();
        ResultSet rset = stmt.executeQuery("SELECT * FROM " +
            selectTable);
        table.setModel(new ResultSetTableModel(rset));
    } catch (Exception e) {};
}
```

The ConnectionDialog inner class creates the dialog displayed when the program is started:

```
class ConnectionDialog extends JDialog {

    protected JTextField useridField;
    protected JTextField passwordField;
    protected JTextField urlField;

    protected boolean canceled;
    protected Connection connect;

    public ConnectionDialog(JFrame f) {
        super(f, "Connect To Database", true);
        buildDialogLayout();
        setSize(300, 200);
    }

    public Connection getConnection() {
```

```java
      setVisible(true);
      return connect;
   }

   protected void buildDialogLayout() {
      JLabel label;

      Container pane = getContentPane();
      pane.setLayout(new GridBagLayout());
      GridBagConstraints gbc = new GridBagConstraints();
      gbc.anchor = GridBagConstraints.WEST;
      gbc.insets = new Insets(5, 10, 5, 10);

      gbc.gridx = 0;
      gbc.gridy = 0;
      label = new JLabel("Userid:", JLabel.LEFT);
      pane.add(label, gbc);

      gbc.gridy++;
      label = new JLabel("Password:", JLabel.LEFT);
      pane.add(label, gbc);

      gbc.gridy++;
      label = new JLabel("URL:", JLabel.LEFT);
      pane.add(label, gbc);

      gbc.gridx = 1;
      gbc.gridy = 0;

      useridField = new JTextField(10);
      pane.add(useridField, gbc);

      gbc.gridy++;
      passwordField = new JTextField(10);
      pane.add(passwordField, gbc);

      gbc.gridy++;
      urlField = new JTextField(15);
      pane.add(urlField, gbc);

      gbc.gridx = 0;
      gbc.gridy = 3;
      gbc.gridwidth = GridBagConstraints.REMAINDER;
      gbc.anchor = GridBagConstraints.CENTER;
      pane.add(getButtonPanel(), gbc);
   }

   protected JPanel getButtonPanel() {
      JPanel panel = new JPanel();
      JButton btn = new JButton("Ok");
      btn.addActionListener(new ActionListener() {
         public void actionPerformed(ActionEvent event) {
            onDialogOk();
         }
      });
```

```
    panel.add(btn);
    btn = new JButton("Cancel");
    btn.addActionListener(new ActionListener() {
      public void actionPerformed(ActionEvent event) {
        onDialogCancel();
      }
    });
    panel.add(btn);
    return panel;
}

protected void onDialogOk() {
  if (attemptConnection()) {
    setVisible(false);
  }
}

protected void onDialogCancel() {
  System.exit(0);
}
```

attemptConnection() is called when the dialog's OK button is activated, and attempts to connect to the specified database using the username and password given:

```
protected boolean attemptConnection() {
  try {
    connect = DriverManager.getConnection(
        urlField.getText(),
        useridField.getText(),
        passwordField.getText());
    return true;
  } catch (Exception e) {
    JOptionPane.showMessageDialog(this,
        "Error connecting to " +
        "database: " + e.getMessage());
  }
  return false;
}
```

Finally, the ResultSetTableModel inner class is used to encapsulate the ResultSet containing the table data. The column names are obtained by getting the ResultSetMetaData for the results, and stored in a Vector; the data itself is stored as a Vector of Vectors:

```
class ResultSetTableModel extends AbstractTableModel {

  protected Vector columnHeaders;
  protected Vector tableData;

  public ResultSetTableModel(ResultSet rset)
      throws SQLException {
    Vector rowData;
    ResultSetMetaData rsmd = rset.getMetaData();
```

```java
      int count = rsmd.getColumnCount();
      columnHeaders = new Vector(count);
      tableData = new Vector();
      for (int i = 1; i <= count; i++) {
        columnHeaders.addElement(rsmd.getColumnName(i));
      }
      while (rset.next()) {
        rowData = new Vector(count);
        for (int i = 1; i <= count; i++) {
          rowData.addElement(rset.getObject(i));
        }
        tableData.addElement(rowData);
      }
    }

    public int getColumnCount() {
      return columnHeaders.size();
    }

    public int getRowCount() {
      return tableData.size();
    }

    public Object getValueAt(int row, int column) {
      Vector rowData = (Vector)(tableData.elementAt(row));
      return rowData.elementAt(column);
    }

    public boolean isCellEditable(int row, int column) {
      return false;
    }

    public String getColumnName(int column) {
      return (String)(columnHeaders.elementAt(column));
    }

  }

}
```

Summary

In this chapter, we've looked at each of the following topics:

- ❑ Driver types and how to select and obtain a driver
- ❑ Obtaining a connection to a database
- ❑ Executing SQL statements and stored procedures
- ❑ Data types defined in JDBC and how they related to "native" types
- ❑ How to manage transactions
- ❑ Database connection pooling
- ❑ Processing errors and warnings generated by JDBC functions
- ❑ Debugging guidelines for database applications

In the next chapter, we'll examine the options available to Java applications for providing persistence (in other words, storing data), including how to apply the information contained in this chapter.

Professional Java Programmin

13
Persisting Data

Persistence refers to the ability to store (and usually retrieve) data that's created by your application, and is an important part of all but the most trivial programs. The persistent data can be as simple as the userid associated with the last successful logon to an application, or it might be very complex and require a great deal of space, such as the information in an airline reservation system. Persistent data may be read immediately (or shortly) after it's stored, or it may simply linger for quite some time (perhaps after the application that stored it has terminated) before it is used/read again.

In this chapter, we will:

- ❑ Examine some of the different persistence techniques available in Java
- ❑ Provide examples of how to use them
- ❑ Give guidelines that describe when each is appropriate

When adding persistence capabilities to your application, you must determine where to store the data, and in most cases you'll select from one of two options: a disk file or a database. In reality, storing information in a database is simply a special case of writing it to disk, because DBMS products usually store the information they manage in a disk file. However, from a programming and conceptual perspective, the two approaches are very different, and are covered separately in this chapter.

An Overview of java.io

Before discussing persistence, it's helpful to examine the large and somewhat confusing collection of input and output stream classes defined in the `java.io` package, because all the information we store or retrieve from storage will have to travel by way of those streams.

Note that most of them do not allow you to create a new stream, but instead add functionality to an existing stream.

The following diagram illustrates the relationships of some of these classes to one another, although it only includes classes that are used to read data. However, an equivalent diagram showing the classes used to write data would have a very similar structure:

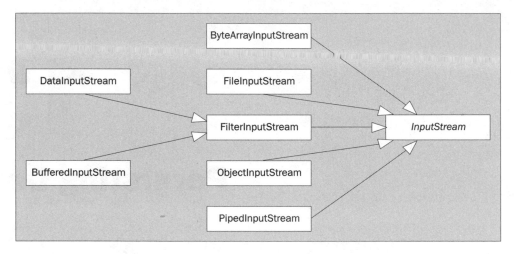

Reading and Writing Binary Data

In this context, "binary data" refers to any type of data, which could be data that represents some particular object, or may simply be a sequence of "raw" numeric values. For example, binary data might represent a serialized object, numbers representing the pixels values that make up some image, or numbers representing a test score.

Input and Output Streams

Input and output streams represent the lowest-level classes provided in Java, and they provide only the most basic functionality accordingly. However, as we'll see shortly, subclasses of these two do provide more sophisticated functionality that makes it easy for you to read and write data.

InputStream, OutputStream

The abstract InputStream and OutputStream classes define methods that allow you to read and write streams of raw binary data (for example, methods for reading and writing one or more bytes of data, usually as blocks of data).

InputStream and OutputStream Subclasses

The abstract input and output streams do not provide methods for converting that data to or from a more useful form, such as an object instance or a primitive value, but that capability is included in some of the subclasses described below.

FileInputStream, FileOutputStream

You can use these concrete subclasses of `InputStream` and `OutputStream` to create a new input or output stream that reads from or writes to a file, respectively. You'll typically create an instance of one of these classes with the constructor that accepts the `String` name of a file (and optionally, its directory) or the constructor that accepts an instance of `java.io.File`. For example, to read from a file named `myoutput.txt` in the `/testfile` subdirectory, you could use either of the following:

```
FileInputStream fis = new FileInputStream("./testfile/myoutput.txt");
```

or:

```
File f = new File("./testfile/myoutput.txt");
// ...

FileInputStream fis = new FileInputStream(f);
```

Note that like their superclasses, `FileInputStream` and `FileOutputStream` only provide methods for reading and writing bytes of data.

FilterInputStream, FilterOutputStream

Although you won't normally use these classes directly, it's important to understand the functionality they provide, since it's the basis for some of the other classes described here. `FilterInputStream` and `FilterOutputStream` allow you to insert a layer of logic between your application and the source or destination of the data being read or written (for example, a disk file). That additional layer can be used to modify the data in some useful way or to provide other functionality. For example, as we'll see later, Java provides classes that will perform conversions between Unicode and other character encodings as text data is being read or written.

BufferedInputStream, BufferedOutputStream

`BufferedInputStream` and `BufferedOutputStream` are subclasses of `FilterInputStream` and `FilterOutputStream`, respectively. These classes provide buffering capability that can reduce the number of **Input/Output (I/O)** operations performed, which often improves an application's performance. When buffering is not used, each read operation you perform causes data to be retrieved from your data source (for example, from a disk file). If you read one byte at a time from a disk file, the number of read operations performed will equal the number of bytes in the file. Unfortunately, I/O operations usually incur a large amount of overhead, and it's more efficient to read groups of bytes instead of one byte per operation.

Note that these classes do not allow you to create a new stream, but instead provide buffering functionality for existing streams. For example, you can create a `BufferedOutputStream` that writes to a disk file using code similar to that shown below:

```
FileOutputStream fos = new FileOutputStream("myoutput.txt");
BufferedOutputStream bos = new BufferedOutputStream(fos, 1000);
```

This code creates a `BufferedOutputStream` with a 1000-byte buffer area in memory, and as you write bytes to that stream, they will be stored in the buffer until it is full. Once the buffer is filled, it is written to the disk file and the process can be repeated. Since only one output operation occurs for every 1000 bytes written, this approach is much more efficient than writing each individual byte to the disk file. In practice, the specific buffer size you choose will depend upon a variety of factors that are specific to your application, such as the amount of memory you can afford to allocate to buffering, the overhead associated with I/O operations performed against the device being read from or written to, the relative importance of performance, and so on.

Similarly, a `BufferedInputStream` reads groups of bytes and fulfills read requests using the data in its buffer until all the data has been read from the buffer (the buffer is "empty"). If a read request occurs while the buffer is empty, another group of bytes is read into the buffer and the process is repeated until the entire file has been read.

One important point to keep in mind when using a `BufferedOutputStream` is that you should call the `flush()` method when you're finished writing data to it. This will cause any data that is currently stored in the buffer to be written immediately instead of waiting until the buffer becomes full, which in this scenario will never happen because there is no more data to be written. Technically, it's not strictly necessary to ever call `flush()` explicitly because it will be called by the `close()` method before the stream is closed, but it is good programming practice to do so anyway.

DataInputStream, DataOutputStream

The classes that have been described so far only allow you to read and write streams of bytes. While you may sometimes wish to provide persistence for raw binary data, you'll more commonly want to store and retrieve objects such as instances of `java.lang.String` and primitive (for example, `int`, `boolean`, `float`, `char`) values. To allow you to do so, there must be a way to represent those data types as a stream of bytes, and `DataInputStream` and `DataOutputStream` provide that capability. They include methods such as `writeInt()` in `DataOutputStream` which converts an `int` value into four bytes of data that are written to the stream. Similarly, the `readInt()` method in `DataInputStream` reads four bytes of data from the stream and uses those bytes to construct an `int` value.

These classes are used by Java's object serialization facility to read and write primitive types and `String` values, but they do not use human-readable formats. For example, if you write data to a disk file using a `DataOutputStream`, you should not edit that file using a word processor or text editor and expect to see meaningful data. This is even true for `String` values, which can be read and written using the `readUTF()` and `writeUTF()` methods. To write data in a human-readable format, you should use `PrintStream` or one of the `Writer` classes described later.

ObjectInputStream, ObjectOutputStream

`ObjectInputStream` and `ObjectOutputStream` extend `DataInputStream` and `DataOutputStream` respectively, and these subclasses provide the ability to read and write objects using Java's object serialization protocol. Serialization is described in detail later in this chapter.

ByteArrayInputStream, ByteArrayOutputStream

When reading or writing data, the source or destination of your data will typically be an external source such as a disk file, but you'll sometimes want to read or write from a buffer in memory instead. These classes allow you to create an `InputStream` that returns the values in an array of bytes or an `OutputStream` that creates a byte array as data is written to it. For example, you might wish to view the stream of bytes created when an instance of `java.util.Date` is written to an `ObjectOutputStream` using serialization. To do so, you could use a `ByteArrayOutputStream` in code similar to the following:

```
import java.io.*;

public class ByteArrayTest {

  public static void main(String[] args) throws Exception {
    ByteArrayOutputStream baos = new ByteArrayOutputStream();
    ObjectOutputStream oos = new ObjectOutputStream(baos);
    oos.writeObject(new java.util.Date());
```

```
      oos.close();
      byte[] values = baos.toByteArray();
      for (int i = 0; i < values.length; i++) {
        System.out.print(values[i] + " ");
      }
    }
}
```

This class serializes an instance of `java.util.Date`, writes a stream of bytes representing that object to a `ByteArrayOutputStream`, and prints the value of each byte. If you compile and run the application, it will produce output similar to that shown below:

```
-84 -19 0 5 115 114 0 14 106 97 118 97 46 117 116 105 108 46 68 97 116 101 104 106
-127 1 75 89 116 25 3 0 0 120 112 119 8 0 0 0 -35 -83 -86 -29 108 120
```

PipedInputStream, PipedOutputStream

When your application creates two threads that transfer large amounts of data between each other, input and output streams provide a convenient mechanism for performing the transfers, and these classes are provided specifically for that purpose. As you would expect, a `PipedOutputStream` is used by the thread sending data (the 'source'), while a `PipedInputStream` is used by the receiver (or "sink"). Before a data transfer can take place, the input stream and output stream must be connected, which is done through their constructors (as shown below) or by calling the `connect()` method for either stream:

```
// This stream will be used by the sender of the data
PipedOutputStream pos = new PipedOutputStream();

// This stream will be used by the receiver of the data
PipedInputStream pis = new PipedInputStream(pos);
```

Reading and Writing Text Data

Text information is one of the most commonly used types of data in software applications, and a single character is represented in Java by the primitive `char` type. Each `char` is stored in memory as a two-byte Unicode character, and groups of characters are encapsulated by instances of `java.lang.String` (and `StringBuffer`).

When writing text information to some external source such as a disk file, you may want to be able to edit that information with a native application such as a word processor. However, if text information is stored using its Unicode representation, applications that do not use Unicode will not be able to read the text correctly. For example, suppose that you compile and run the following application that writes a short `String` to a disk file. Note that the `writeChars()` method does not perform any conversion on the data, but simply writes each character's two-byte Unicode value:

```
import java.io.*;

public class WriteText {

  public static void main(String[] args) throws IOException {
    String stuff = "Howdy";
    FileOutputStream fos = new FileOutputStream("test.out");
```

```
        DataOutputStream dos = new DataOutputStream(fos);
        dos.writeChars(stuff);
        fos.close();
    }
}
```

If you edit the contents of the test.out file, you'll probably see something like the following:

```
H o w d y
```

Depending upon your platform and the application that you use to view the data, a blank space or a "garbage" character will probably appear before each of the five letters. That will not occur if the application you use supports Unicode, but many applications do not. In effect, this output isn't truly human-readable because it was written using a character encoding that's probably not supported by the applications available to you, and it cannot easily be edited.

As mentioned earlier, the DataInput and DataOutput classes also support methods for reading and writing String values through the readUTF() and writeUTF() methods, respectively. However, those methods perform conversions between Unicode and a variation of an encoding called **UTF-8**.

UTF is an acronym for **Unicode Transformation Format**, and is used to store Unicode character data. However, instead of each character occupying two bytes, a single character can be represented in UTF-8 by as few as one byte or as many as three. In addition, UTF-8 has a very useful characteristic: all characters defined in the ASCII character set are represented by exactly the same value in UTF-8. For example, a capital "A" corresponds to a single byte with a (decimal) value of 65 in both ASCII and in UTF-8. In other words, the same byte sequence that is used to represent a sequence of ASCII characters can be interpreted as a sequence of UTF-8 characters, and a sequence of single-byte UTF-8 characters can be interpreted as ASCII data.

It may seem that this mapping between UTF-8 and ASCII makes writeUTF() appropriate for creating human-readable output, and you might modify the previously defined WriteText class to use writeUTF() as shown below:

```
import java.io.*;

public class WriteText {

    public static void main(String[] args) throws IOException {
        String stuff = "Howdy";
        FileOutputStream fos = new FileOutputStream("test.out");
        DataOutputStream dos = new DataOutputStream(fos);
        // sdos.writeChars(stuff);
        dos.writeUTF(stuff);
        fos.close();
    }
}
```

If you now examine the contents of the test.out file, you'll see something similar to the following:

```
Howdy
```

The first two characters in the file will appear either as blank spaces or as garbage characters. This occurs because `writeUTF()` precedes the UTF characters with two bytes that identify the number of bytes that the data occupies. For example, the hexadecimal values written in this case would be `00 05 48 6F 77 64 79`.

The first two bytes represent the length of the output, while each of the remaining bytes represents one of the characters in the string. In this case, the value in the two header bytes is equal to the number of characters in the string, but that is only because each character is represented in UTF-8 by a single byte. If the string included characters that required a two- or three-byte UTF-8 representation, the header value would be larger than the number of characters. In other words, the header value represents the length of the output data but not necessary the length of the original string.

> *Note that since only two bytes are used for the length, you can only write out strings that can be represented in 65535 characters or less, and attempting to write a longer string with `writeUTF()` results in a `UTFDataFormatError` being thrown.*

Due to the presence of the header field and its use of UTF-8 encoding, `writeUTF()` should not be used to create output that's intended for viewing or editing by native applications.

Readers and Writers

Each operating system typically supports a single character encoding for its own use, but an application running on that system is not required to use that same encoding. For example, Windows supports the `Cp1252` encoding and most Windows applications use that encoding, but Java Virtual Machines running on Windows use Unicode. However, when an application does use an encoding different from that of the native platform, the application must assume responsibility for performing conversions between the two encodings when appropriate.

As we've seen, neither `writeChars()` nor `writeUTF()` is appropriate for creating text output that can be read by native applications. The `writeChars()` method is inappropriate because it produces a stream of Unicode characters, while `writeUTF()` produces a stream of UTF-8 characters that's preceded by a header value. What's needed is an easy way to perform translations between Unicode characters and the native platform's character encoding, and that's exactly what the `Reader` and `Writer` classes defined in `java.io` provide.

Reader, Writer

These abstract classes define methods for reading and writing one or more characters of data. Just as `InputStream` and `OutputStream` are byte-oriented and are used to process raw binary data, the `Reader` and `Writer` classes are character-oriented and are used to process text information. By default, readers and writers perform conversions to and from the native platform's encoding, although in some cases, you can explicitly specify the encoding that should be used. You can determine the default encoding for your platform by executing the following line of code:

```
System.out.println(System.getProperty("file.encoding"));
```

InputStreamReader, OutputStreamWriter

These classes act as "bridges" between `InputStream` and `Reader` and between `OutputStream` and `Writer`. In other words, `InputStreamReader` allows you to create a `Reader` that uses an `InputStream` as the source of its data, while `OutputStreamWriter` allows you to create a `Writer` that writes its data to an `OutputStream`. For example, you can use the following code to write a `String` to a file using the platform's default character encoding:

```
import java.io.*;

public class WriteText {

  public static void main(String[] args) throws IOException {
    String stuff = "Howdy";
    FileOutputStream fos = new FileOutputStream("test.out");
    OutputStreamWriter osw = new OutputStreamWriter(fos);
    for (int i = 0; i < stuff.length(); i++) {
      osw.write(stuff.charAt(i));
    }
    osw.close();
  }
}
```

When `write()` is called, the `OutputStreamWriter` converts the two-byte Unicode character into a sequence of one or more bytes using the platform's default encoding and writes the data to the `FileOutputStream`. Conversely, an `InputStreamReader` processes the incoming stream of bytes as characters encoded using the default encoding and converts them into Unicode `char` values.

A characteristic of these two classes that's very useful is that they allow you to specify which character encoding should be used to interpret the input (from an `InputStreamReader`) or how to convert the output (for an `OutputStreamWriter`). For example, suppose that you wish to read character data from an `InputStream`, and you know that the incoming data is encoded using UTF-8. To ensure that the data will be converted correctly into Unicode text, you could create an `InputStreamReader` that would perform the conversion for you using code like that shown below:

```
FileInputStream sourceStream = new FileInputStream("mytest.txt");
InputStreamReader textReader = new InputStreamReader(sourceStream, "UTF-8");
```

In this case, `sourceStream` represents the `InputStream` that provides the UTF-8 encoded data, but you can use `textReader` to read the text as Unicode characters. Similarly, you can use `OutputStreamWriter` to convert Java's Unicode characters into some other encoding before writing the data to an `OutputStream`. The following code segment produces an `OutputStreamWriter` that will encode any text that's written using the ISO-8859-1 encoding:

```
FileOutputStream targetStream = new FileOutputStream("mytest.txt");
OutputStreamWriter textWriter = new OutputStreamWriter(targetStream,
    "ISO-8859-1");
```

As we saw in the earlier examples, `InputStreamReader` and `OutputStreamWriter` will default to some character encoding that's appropriate for the platform you're using if you construct instances of those classes without explicitly specifying an encoding.

Reader and Writer Subclasses

Equivalent `Reader` and `Writer` implementations are provided for many of the `InputStream` and `OutputStream` classes defined in `java.io`, and they are listed in the tables opposite:

InputStream	Reader
BufferedInputStream	BufferedReader
ByteArrayInputStream	CharArrayReader
FileInputStream	FileReader
FilterInputStream	FilterReader
PipedInputStream	PipedReader

OutputStream	Writer
BufferedOutputStream	BufferedWriter
ByteArrayOutputStream	CharArrayWriter
FileOutputStream	FileWriter
FilterOutputStream	FilterWriter
PipedOutputStream	PipedWriter

PrintStream, PrintWriter

Like `ObjectOutputStream`, `PrintStream` and `PrintWriter` provide methods that allow you to write a primitive value or object to an output stream, but with an important difference. While `ObjectOutputStream` converts the primitive or object into a machine-readable stream of bytes, these classes convert the information into a human-readable text representation of the value. You're probably already familiar with `PrintStream` from having used methods such as `System.out.println()`, where `out` is an instance of `PrintStream` that represents "standard output", and an example of its use is shown below:

```
java.util.Date curdate = new java.util.Date();
// Print the date in human-readable form
System.out.println(curdate);
```

File-Based Persistence

Now that most of the `InputStream`, `OutputStream`, `Reader` and `Writer` classes have been covered, it's possible to examine the file-based persistence options that are available.

Flat Files

One approach is to use a **flat file**, which is simply a text file that can be viewed and edited using the native platform's text editors and word processors. This approach is convenient when working with small amounts of data that can be easily represented using text, because it allows you to examine and modify data without using the application that originally created it. For example, suppose that your application displays a dialog that prompts the user to enter a valid userid, password, and host name combination before access to the application is granted. In that situation, it may be helpful to store default values for those properties in a flat file and have the dialog read the file and populate its fields appropriately. This would allow the user to avoid entering the same values during each logon, but would also allow the default values to be modified easily with a text editor.

Flat files are appropriate for small amounts of text information, but are usually not appropriate for larger volumes of data. When working with large amounts of data, you'll typically want to be able to perform searches, and flat files can only be searched sequentially. In addition, true insertions and deletions are not possible, although these operations can be simulated by creating a new copy of the file with the appropriate changes made.

The following code segment attempts to read a userid and host name from a file called logon.txt using the readLine() method in BufferedReader. Note that since a Reader is used, the text will automatically be converted from the native platform's default encoding type to Unicode characters:

```java
import java.io.*;

public class ReadHostData {

  public static void main(String[] args) throws IOException {
    String userid = "";
    String hostName = "";
    File file = new File("logon.txt");
    if (file.exists()) {
      String value;
      FileReader fileReader = new FileReader(file);
      BufferedReader reader = new BufferedReader(fileReader);
      value = reader.readLine();
      if (value != null) {
        userid = value;
      }
      value = reader.readLine();
      if (value != null) {
        hostName = value;
      }
      fileReader.close();
      System.out.println("Logging on to host '" + hostName +
          "' as user '" + userid + "'");
    }
  }
}
```

Similarly, the following code segment can be used to write the userid and host values to the file:

```java
import java.io.*;

public class WriteHostData {

  public static void main(String[] args) throws IOException {
    String userid = "bspell";
    String hostName = "myserver";
    File file = new File("logon.txt");
    FileWriter fileWriter = new FileWriter(file);
    BufferedWriter writer = new BufferedWriter(fileWriter);
    writer.write(userid);
    writer.newLine();
    writer.write(hostName);
    writer.close();
  }
}
```

Note that the `newLine()` method is called in this segment so that the userid and host name will be separated by a carriage return (CR) and/or linefeed (LF) character. When writing multiple items of data (or "records") to a flat file, you'll typically use a character or combination of characters to separate ("delimit") the items. This makes it easy to parse the different items when the file's contents are read, and the CR and LF characters are normally used in text files to separate lines of text.

Although you can explicitly write a carriage return and/or linefeed character, you should not normally do so. For example, you could modify the code shown above to include delimiter characters in the `String` passed to the `write()` method:

```
writer.write(userid + "\r\n");
// writer.newLine();
```

The problem with this approach is that it's not appropriate for all platforms, since some operating systems use only CR or LF to indicate the end of a line in a text field. To ensure that your application writes the appropriate delimiter character(s), you should use a method such as `BufferedWriter`'s `newLine()`. However, if the class you're using doesn't provide a method like `newLine()`, you can obtain the platform-specific line delimiter character(s) using the following code:

```
String delimiter = System.getProperty("line.separator");
```

Storing Object Instances

Storing and retrieving text data is very simple once you're familiar with the `Reader` and `Writer` classes. However, you'll often want to store the state of objects so that they can be retrieved later, which is a much more complex problem. For example, suppose that you want to be able to save instances of the following class to disk. In practice, a class like this would have accessor and mutator methods defined for each of its properties, but they are omitted here for the sake of simplicity:

```java
import java.io.*;

public class AccountInfo {

  protected String lastName;
  protected String firstName;
  protected int age;
  protected float accountBalance;

  public AccountInfo(String last, String first, int years,
      float balance) {
    lastName = last;
    firstName = first;
    age = years;
    accountBalance = balance;
  }
}
```

It's easy to create a method that will write the contents of this class to an `OutputStream` as shown in the following listing. This listing also includes a `main()` method that can be used to test the new functionality:

```
import java.io.*;

public class AccountInfo {

    protected String lastName;
    protected String firstName;
    protected int age;
    protected float accountBalance;

    public static void main(String[] args) throws Exception {
        AccountInfo ai = new AccountInfo("Smith", "John", 34, 1234.56f);
        FileOutputStream fos = new FileOutputStream("persist.txt");
        ai.saveState(fos);
    }

    public AccountInfo(String last, String first, int years,
        float balance) {
        lastName = last;
        firstName = first;
        age = years;
        accountBalance = balance;
    }

    public void saveState(OutputStream stream) throws IOException {
        OutputStreamWriter osw = new OutputStreamWriter(stream);
        BufferedWriter writer = new BufferedWriter(osw);
        writer.write(lastName);
        writer.newLine();
        writer.write(firstName);
        writer.newLine();
        writer.write(Integer.toString(age));
        writer.newLine();
        writer.write(Float.toString(accountBalance));
        writer.close();
    }
}
```

If you compile and run this application, it will create a file called persist.txt with the following contents:

```
Smith
John
34
1234.56
```

Similarly, it's easy to create a restoreState() method that can be used to restore the state of an object from a file:

```
import java.io.*;

public class AccountInfo {

    protected String lastName;
    protected String firstName;
    protected int age;
```

```
    protected float accountBalance;

    public static void main(String[] args) throws Exception {
      AccountInfo account = new AccountInfo();
      InputStream input = new FileInputStream("persist.txt");
      account.restoreState(input);
    }

    public AccountInfo() {
    }

    public AccountInfo(String last, String first, int years,
        float balance) {
      lastName = last;
      firstName = first;
      age = years;
      accountBalance = balance;
    }

    public void saveState(OutputStream stream) throws IOException {
      OutputStreamWriter osw = new OutputStreamWriter(stream);
      BufferedWriter writer = new BufferedWriter(osw);
      writer.write(lastName);
      writer.newLine();
      writer.write(firstName);
      writer.newLine();
      writer.write(Integer.toString(age));
      writer.newLine();
      writer.write(Float.toString(accountBalance));
      writer.close();
    }

    public void restoreState(InputStream stream) throws IOException {
      InputStreamReader isr = new InputStreamReader(stream);
      BufferedReader reader = new BufferedReader(isr);
      lastName = reader.readLine();
      firstName = reader.readLine();
      age = Integer.parseInt(reader.readLine());
      accountBalance = Float.parseFloat(reader.readLine());
      reader.close();
    }

  }
```

Although this approach will work for very simple cases, there are several reasons why it's not ideal. Perhaps the most obvious problem is that the saveState() and restoreState() are tightly coupled to the structure of the AccountInfo class. If a field is added, removed, renamed, or if its data type changes, corresponding changes must be made to the saveState() and restoreState() fields. In addition, storing an object's state in a flat file is only convenient as long as the class contains simple data types that can be easily represented as text. If AccountInfo contained arrays and/or more complex property types, such as an instance of java.awt.Image or some user-defined class, it might be difficult to represent the value of those properties using plain text. What's needed is a more robust mechanism for storing the state of objects, and Java's object serialization provides such a mechanism.

Object Serialization

Java's object serialization allows you to convert the state of an object into a stream of byte values (called **marshaling**) and it allows you to create a duplicate object (one with the same state) using those values (called **unmarshaling**). For example, a distributed application can transmit marshaled data across a network and effectively create a copy of an object on another machine. In the context of persistence, serialization is useful because it allows you to store an object's state and recreate a copy of the object later, even in a different application.

An object that is **serializable** can be written (marshaled) using ObjectOutputStream's writeObject() method, and read (unmarshaled) using ObjectInputStream's readObject(). For example, the following code creates an instance of Date and writes it to a disk file. This is possible because Date is serializable, as are many of the other Java core classes:

```java
import java.io.*;

public class StoreDate {

  public static void main(String[] args) throws IOException {
    java.util.Date curDate = new java.util.Date();
    FileOutputStream fos = new FileOutputStream("myobject.ser");
    ObjectOutputStream oos = new ObjectOutputStream(fos);
    oos.writeObject(curDate);
    oos.close();
  }
}
```

You can easily determine which classes are serializable by examining their API information, and those that implement either java.io.Serializable or java.io.Externalizable can normally be serialized. When creating a class of your own that you wish to serialize you must implement one of those interfaces, and in most cases you should use Serializable.

java.io.Serializable

You should implement this interface when you want Java to assume responsibility for marshaling and unmarshaling object instances. For example, suppose that you have created the following class and wish to make it serializable:

```java
import java.util.Date;

public class Person {

  protected String fullName;
  protected Date dateOfBirth;

  public Person(String name, Date dob) {
    fullName = name;
    dateOfBirth = dob;
  }

}
```

If you attempt to serialize an instance of `Person`, an exception will be thrown that indicates that the class is not serializable. This can be illustrated by creating a `main()` method that attempts to write an instance of `Person` to a disk file:

```java
import java.io.*;
import java.util.Date;

public class Person {

  protected String fullName;
  protected Date dateOfBirth;

  public static void main(String[] args) throws Exception {
    FileOutputStream fos = new FileOutputStream("output.ser");
    ObjectOutputStream oos = new ObjectOutputStream(fos);
    oos.writeObject(new Person("John Smith", new Date()));
    oos.close();
  }

  public Person(String name, Date dob) {
    fullName = name;
    dateOfBirth = dob;
  }

}
```

If you compile and execute this code, it will throw a `NotSerializableException` and generate output like that shown below:

```
Exception in thread "main" java.io.NotSerializableException: Person
    at java.io.ObjectOutputStream.outputObject(ObjectOutputStream.java:1148)

    at java.io.ObjectOutputStream.writeObject(ObjectOutputStream.java:366)
    at Person.main(Person.java:12)
```

However, making this class serializable is as easy as implementing the `Serializable` interface. It's not even necessary to implement any methods, because `Serializable` is a **tag interface** that simply indicates to `ObjectOutputStream` that you wish to allow it to serialize instances of the class:

```java
import java.io.*;
import java.util.Date;

public class Person implements Serializable {

  protected String fullName;
  protected Date dateOfBirth;

  public static void main(String[] args) throws Exception {
    FileOutputStream fos = new FileOutputStream("output.ser");
    ObjectOutputStream oos = new ObjectOutputStream(fos);
    oos.writeObject(new Person("John Smith", new Date()));
    oos.close();
  }
```

```
      public Person(String name, Date dob) {
        fullName = name;
        dateOfBirth = dob;
      }

    }
```

If you compile and execute this modified code, it will create a file called `output.ser` that contains a representation of an instance of `Person`. If you view the contents of that file, you'll see many garbage characters, but you'll also find readable text, such as the name of the class ("Person") and the names and types of its fields (for example, "dateOfBirth" and "java.util.Date").

> *Note that although there's no technical reason why you must do so, it's common practice to use an extension of `.ser` for files containing serialized Java objects.*

In this case, the `defaultWriteObject()` method in `ObjectOutputStream` was allowed to assume responsibility for marshaling the data, which is the approach you'll normally use. That method examines the structure of the object being serialized and marshals all of its fields that are not marked `static` or `transient`. By not serializing `transient` fields, `ObjectOutputStream` provides an easy way for you to exclude fields from the marshaled output. For example, if you wish to exclude the `dateOfBirth` field from the marshaled data, you can make the following modification to `Person`:

```
public class Person implements Serializable {

    protected String fullName;
    protected transient Date dateOfBirth;
```

Reading an instance of a serialized object is just as easy as writing one, and can be done using code like that shown below:

```
import java.io.*;

public class ReadPerson {

    public static void main(String[] args) throws Exception {
        FileInputStream fis = new FileInputStream("output.ser");
        ObjectInputStream ois = new ObjectInputStream(fis);
        Person person = (Person)(ois.readObject());
        System.out.println(person.fullName + " was born on " +
            person.dateOfBirth);
    }

}
```

In this case, the data is unmarshaled by `ObjectInputStream`'s `readObject()` method and a new instance of `Person` is created and its state initialized using the data in `output.ser`.

Serializing Complex Objects

The `Person` class is very simple, consisting of references to just two other objects (a `String` and a `Date`), and does not inherit any properties from a superclass. However, classes often have a much more complex structure that can include fields inherited from a superclass, primitives, arrays, and references to other objects.

The figure below illustrates a more complex set of classes, and the corresponding Java source code is shown below. The accessor and mutator methods that would normally be defined are again omitted for the sake of simplicity:

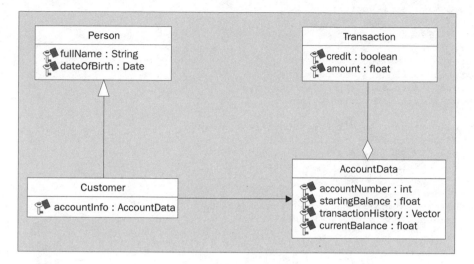

`Person` represents a fairly generic person, with a name and date of birth:

```
import java.util.Date;

public class Person implements java.io.Serializable {

  protected String fullName;
  protected Date dateOfBirth;

  public Person(String name, Date dob) {
    fullName = name;
    dateOfBirth = dob;
  }

}
```

`Customer` extends `Person`, and stores a reference to an `AccountData` object:

```
public class Customer extends Person {

  protected AccountData accountInfo;

  public Customer(String name, java.util.Date dob, int acctnum,
      float startbal) {
    super(name, dob);
    accountInfo = new AccountData(acctnum, startbal);
  }

  public AccountData getAccountInfo() {
    return accountInfo;
  }

}
```

AccountData stores data about the Customer's bank account: account number, starting balance, current balance, and a Vector containing Transaction objects:

```java
import java.util.Vector;

public class AccountData {

  protected int accountNumber;
  protected float startingBalance;
  protected Vector transactionHistory;
  protected float currentBalance;

  public AccountData(int acctnum, float startbal) {
    accountNumber = acctnum;
    startingBalance = startbal;
    transactionHistory = new Vector();
  }

  public void addTransaction(Transaction trans) {
    transactionHistory.addElement(trans);
  }

}
```

Finally, Transaction represents a single transaction:

```java
public class Transaction {

  protected boolean credit;
  protected float amount;

  public Transaction(boolean cr, float amt) {
    credit = cr;
    amount = amt;
  }

}
```

As you can see, serializing an instance of Customer is considerably more complicated than serializing a Person object. For the state of a Customer object to be saved, all fields in Customer and its Person superclass must be marshaled, along with all other objects referenced by the Customer instance. In this case, those objects include instances of AccountData, java.util.Vector, and Transaction in addition to the String and Date fields inherited from Person.

The following code creates an instance of Customer, adds a Transaction to the customer's history information, and attempts to write the customer data to a disk file:

```java
import java.io.*;

public class WriteCustomer {

  public static void main(String[] args) throws IOException {
    Customer cust = new Customer("John Smith", new java.util.Date(),
        1234, 100.00f);
```

```
        cust.getAccountInfo().addTransaction(new Transaction(true, 50.00f));
        FileOutputStream fos = new FileOutputStream("test.ser");
        ObjectOutputStream oos = new ObjectOutputStream(fos);
        oos.writeObject(cust);
    }

}
```

However, if you run this code, an exception will be thrown and output will appear similar to the following:

```
Exception in thread "main" java.io.NotSerializableException: AccountData
    at java.io.ObjectOutputStream.outputObject(ObjectOutputStream.java:1148)
    at java.io.ObjectOutputStream.writeObject(ObjectOutputStream.java:366)
    at java.io.ObjectOutputStream.outputClassFields
(ObjectOutputStream.java:1841)
    at java.io.ObjectOutputStream.defaultWriteObject
(ObjectOutputStream.java:480)
    at java.io.ObjectOutputStream.outputObject(ObjectOutputStream.java:1214)
    at java.io.ObjectOutputStream.writeObject(ObjectOutputStream.java:366)
    at Test.main(Test.java:13)
```

The exception indicates that serialization failed because the AccountData is not serializable, which illustrates an important point. To serialize an object, all objects that it references (either directly or indirectly) through fields that are not static or transient must also be serializable. In other words, Customer must be serializable along with all of the classes to which it contains references. In this case, those classes are String, Date, AccountData, Vector, and Transaction.

All primitive types (for example, int and float) are serializable, as are many of Java's core classes, including String, Date, and Vector. In addition, Customer is already serializable because the class it inherits from (Person) implements Serializable. Therefore, AccountData and Transaction are the only remaining types that need to be made serializable, which can be done by modifying them so that they implement Serializable:

```
import java.io.*;
import java.util.Vector;

public class AccountData implements Serializable {
    // ...
```

and:

```
import java.io.Serializable;

public class Transaction implements Serializable {
    // ...
```

Once these changes have been made, you can successfully execute the code segment shown earlier that attempts to store an instance of Customer in a file.

> It's important to understand that Java's serialization mechanism does not store the definition of an object's class when the object is marshaled. For example, if you write an instance of Customer to a disk file, that object's state is saved, but the Customer.class file must still be accessible for the instance to later be unmarshaled.

Given the following code segment, you can use it to read an instance of Customer from the test.ser file created by the previous sample code:

```
import java.io.*;

public class ReadCustomer {

  public static void main(String[] args) throws Exception {
    FileInputStream fis = new FileInputStream("test.ser");
    ObjectInputStream ois = new ObjectInputStream(fis);
    Customer cust = (Customer)(ois.readObject());
  }

}
```

However, if you execute this code after erasing the Customer.class file, an exception will be thrown and output will appear like that shown below:

```
Exception in thread "main" java.lang.ClassNotFoundException: Customer
    at java.io.ObjectInputStream.inputObject(ObjectInputStream.java:981)
    at java.io.ObjectInputStream.readObject(ObjectInputStream.java:369)
    at java.io.ObjectInputStream.readObject(ObjectInputStream.java:232)
    at CustomerTest.main(CustomerTest.java:8)
```

This exception indicates that unmarshaling could not take place because the Customer class definition (the Customer.class file) was not found. This is not usually a problem when a serialized object is read by the same application that wrote it, but it can sometimes cause problems when you are creating distributed applications. Therefore, if you're transporting objects from one Java Virtual Machine to another, you must ensure that the class definition is available in both places.

Modifying Classes after Serializing Instances

After using the code segment defined earlier to store an instance of Customer in a file, we can make a minor modification to Customer to see what effect the change has on our ability to unmarshal the file's data. For example, a toString() method can be defined that does nothing but call the superclass method it overrides:

```
public class Customer extends Person {

  protected AccountData accountInfo;

  public Customer(String name, java.util.Date dob, int acctnum,
      float startbal) {
    super(name, dob);
    accountInfo = new AccountData(acctnum, startbal);
  }

  public AccountData getAccountInfo() {
    return accountInfo;
  }

  public String toString() {
    return super.toString();
  }

}
```

From a purely functional standpoint, the Customer class has not changed at all. It will behave exactly the same way that it did before this modification was made, and no fields in it or its superclass have been affected in any way. However, if you attempt to run the code segment defined previously that reads a serialized Customer instance, you'll receive messages like those shown below:

```
Exception in thread "main" java.io.InvalidClassException: Customer; Local class
not compatible: stream classdesc serialVersionUID=-6363704609801339457 local class
serialVersionUID=5621265845502133341
   at java.io.ObjectStreamClass.validateLocalClass(
ObjectStreamClass.java:438)
   at java.io.ObjectStreamClass.setClass(ObjectStreamClass.java:482)
   at java.io.ObjectInputStream.inputClassDescriptor(
ObjectInputStream.java:785)
   at java.io.ObjectInputStream.readObject(ObjectInputStream.java:353)
   at java.io.ObjectInputStream.readObject(ObjectInputStream.java:232)
   at java.io.ObjectInputStream.inputObject(ObjectInputStream.java:978)
   at java.io.ObjectInputStream.readObject(ObjectInputStream.java:369)
   at java.io.ObjectInputStream.readObject(ObjectInputStream.java:232)
   at CustomerTest.main(CustomerTest.java:8)
```

Although these messages appear somewhat cryptic, you may suspect from the "Local class not compatible" message that readObject() has somehow detected that the class was modified. Since we've established that the class definition itself is not stored with a serialized object instance, the obvious question is how the change was detected.

Another question is how to prevent this exception from being thrown, since there's no reason that the serialized instance of Customer should not be compatible with the current implementation (the **local class**). The only change that was made to Customer was the addition of a toString() method that has no effect on the state of a Customer instance. Therefore, it ought to be possible to unmarshal an instance of Customer using the modified local class.

A clue to the answers to these two questions is provided in the exception's message, where two serialVersionUID values are listed.

Stream Unique Identifiers

A **stream unique identifier** (**SUID** or "serialVersionUID") is a 64-bit value that Java's object serialization facility uses to determine whether a serialized object instance is compatible with the local class of the same name. The SUID is calculated using the class definition, such as the name of the class, its modifiers (for example, public, final, etc.), the interfaces implemented, the methods defined, etc. In other words, the SUID is a hash code designed specifically to detect changes to a class. This is done to prevent problems that could occur if you attempted to unmarshal a serialized object instance using an incompatible local class. In this case, however, we've established that the local Customer class *is* compatible with the serialized instance, so it should be possible to use that class to unmarshal the Customer object.

When comparing the SUID of a serialized object instance with the local class, ObjectInputStream calculates the local class SUID *unless you explicitly specify a value for it.* In other words, if you define a value for the SUID of the local class, ObjectInputStream will use that value for the comparison instead of calculating one at runtime. By defining a Customer SUID value that's equal to the one in the serialized instance, you'll be able to unmarshal the serialized object because its SUID will match the one in the local class.

To explicitly define a value for the SUID, you must create a field like the one highlighted below:

```
public class Customer extends Person {

  protected AccountData accountInfo;

  private final static long serialVersionUID = -6363704609801339457L;

  public Customer(String name, java.util.Date dob, int acctnum,
      float startbal) {
    super(name, dob);
    accountInfo = new AccountData(acctnum, startbal);
  }

  public AccountData getAccountInfo() {
    return accountInfo;
  }

  public String toString() {
    return super.toString();
  }

}
```

In this case, the SUID value was taken from the error message listed earlier that identified the SUID of the serialized instance. In practice, however, you should use the SUID that's calculated for a class using the `serialver` utility provided with the Java (Software) Development Kit. For example, you could prevent errors like the one shown earlier by specifying `Customer`'s SUID *before* making changes to it, and the best way to select a value for the SUID is to use `serialver`. To run the utility, simply specify the name of that class for which it should calculate an SUID value:

```
serialver Customer
```

This would produce output similar to that shown below, and you could copy the displayed field declaration directly into the class, as we did above:

```
Customer:    static final long serialVersionUID = -6363704609801339457L;
```

Once the SUID has been specified for a class, that value will be stored with any serialized instances of the class, and you can modify the class without causing an `InvalidClassException` to occur during unmarshaling. Note that this behavior applies to any superclass(es) of the class being unmarshaled, so that if the `Person` class had changed, we would need to take the same steps illustrated here, except that we would instead explicitly define a SUID for `Person` instead of `Customer`.

Customizing Serialization

As mentioned earlier, you can prevent the fields in a class from being serialized by making them `transient`. However, Java 2 provides an additional way to control which fields to save and restore as part of an object's state. Specifically, you can define a field called `serialPersistentFields` that is an array of `ObjectStreamField` instances.

Each `ObjectStreamField` identifies a field that should be included when marshaling and unmarshaling an instance of the class. To create an instance of `ObjectStreamField`, you must use its constructor that requires a `String` representing the name of the field and an instance of `Class` that identifies the field's data type. For example, you could modify `AccountData` so that the `currentBalance` field would not be saved and restored:

```
import java.io.*;
import java.util.Vector;

public class AccountData implements Serializable {

  protected int accountNumber;
  protected float startingBalance;
  protected Vector transactionHistory;
  protected float currentBalance;

  private final static ObjectStreamField[] serialPersistentFields = {
      new ObjectStreamField("accountNumber", Integer.TYPE),
      new ObjectStreamField("startingBalance", Float.TYPE),
      new ObjectStreamField("transactionHistory", Vector.class)
  };

  public AccountData(int acctnum, float startbal) {
    accountNumber = acctnum;
    startingBalance = startbal;
    transactionHistory = new Vector();
  }

  public void addTransaction(Transaction trans) {
    transactionHistory.addElement(trans);
  }

}
```

At first glance, the usefulness of `serialPersistentFields` may not appear obvious. In fact, it's slightly more tedious to use than simply adding the `transient` keyword to the fields that should not be serialized. However, as we'll see shortly, you can use `serialPersistentFields` to ensure that a local class remains compatible with older serialized instances of that class.

Defining readObject() and writeObject()

Another way to control which fields are stored and retrieved is to define `readObject()` and/or `writeObject()` methods in your serializable class. Using these methods, you can exercise a great deal of control over how objects' states are marshaled and unmarshaled. There are three primary uses of the `readObject()` and `writeObject()` methods:

❑ Store extra information describing the object's state that would not normally be written during marshaling

❑ Implement customized save and restore processing

❑ Change values before marshaling and/or after unmarshaling

When you implement `writeObject()` in a class that's serializable, `ObjectOutputStream` will detect its presence and delegate responsibility to that method for writing the object's contents to an output stream. Similarly, creating a `readObject()` method in your serializable class will cause `ObjectInputStream` to allow that method to handle reading the data when an instance is being instantiated from serialized information.

An important point to be made concerning readObject() and writeObject() is that each class is only responsible for reading and/or writing its own properties and not those defined in its superclass or subclasses (if any). In other words, if you were to implement readObject() and writeObject() in the Person class, the AccountData property information in Customer would still be saved and restored automatically by ObjectInputStream and ObjectOutputStream. To control the reading and writing of the properties in both Person and its Customer subclass, you must provide readObject() and writeObject() implementations in both classes.

Storing Extra Information

You can use readObject() and writeObject() to store information in the serialized data stream that would not be included by the default serialization processing. The following code doesn't add any useful functionality to the AccountData class, but it does illustrate how you can add data to the serialized representation of an object instance. In this case, a message is appended to the serialized data to indicate when the object was marshaled, and when the object is unmarshaled, the message is read from the InputStream and printed:

```java
import java.io.*;
import java.util.Vector;

public class AccountData implements Serializable {

  // ...

    private void writeObject(ObjectOutputStream stream)
        throws IOException {
      stream.defaultWriteObject();
      stream.writeObject("This instance was marshaled at " +
          new java.util.Date().toString());
    }

    private void readObject(ObjectInputStream stream) throws IOException {
      try {
        stream.defaultReadObject();
        String message = (String)(stream.readObject());
        System.out.println(message);
      } catch (ClassNotFoundException cnfe) {};
    }

}
```

Note that the first action taken in each method is to invoke defaultXXXObject() method of the stream parameter. That causes the fields to be marshaled and unmarshaled just as if the writeObject() and readObject() methods had not been defined, and once that's completed, the extra information can be read or written. In other words, defaultWriteObject() and defaultReadObject() will marshal all fields (or only those referenced in serialPersistentFields if it is present) that are not defined as static or transient.

Implementing Custom Save and Restore Logic

In the above example, the defaultWriteObject() and defaultReadObject() methods were used to invoke the default save and restore behavior for marshaling and unmarshaling an object instance. However, you may instead choose to allow your writeObject() and readObject() methods to take full responsibility for saving and restoring object states. For example, you might decide that an account's history information should not be stored when an instance of AccountData is serialized. In reality, the easiest way to accomplish this would be to make transactionHistory a transient field, but the following code illustrates how you can use readObject() and writeObject() to control which information is saved and restored:

```
import java.io.*;
import java.util.Vector;

public class AccountData implements java.io.Serializable {

  // ...

    private void writeObject(ObjectOutputStream stream)
        throws IOException {
      stream.writeInt(accountNumber);
      stream.writeFloat(startingBalance);
      stream.writeFloat(currentBalance);
    }

    private void readObject(ObjectInputStream stream) throws IOException {
      accountNumber = stream.readInt();
      startingBalance = stream.readFloat();
      currentBalance = stream.readFloat();
    }

}
```

In this case, only the three fields that we read and write will be marshaled and unmarshaled, regardless of how many fields are defined in the object and regardless of what fields (if any) are referenced in serialPersistentFields.

Changing Values Before and After Marshaling

Another use of the writeObject() and readObject() methods is to modify the values stored in an object's fields before they're written or after they're read. The most common use for this technique is to assign values to objects that were not included in the marshaled output. For example, fields that are transient or that were deliberately excluded for some other reason may need to be initialized as part of the readObject() processing.

In the above example, the transactionHistory field is not saved or restored with the rest of the fields in an AccountData object. That has the undesirable effect of causing transactionHistory to be assigned a value of null when an AccountData instance is created from serialized data. Since transactionHistory is null, calling addTransaction() will result in a NullPointerException being thrown.

To avoid this problem, you can simply add a line to the readObject() method that initializes transactionHistory when an instance of AccountData is created from serialization data:

```
    private void readObject(ObjectInputStream stream) throws IOException {
      accountNumber = stream.readInt();
      startingBalance = stream.readFloat();
      currentBalance = stream.readFloat();
      transactionHistory = new Vector();
    }
```

Handling Class Incompatibilities

Earlier we examined how you can use a local class that's different from the definition used to create a serialized object instance. That was done by explicitly specifying the SUID value for the class, but is only appropriate as long as the new class definition is compatible with the old one. In some cases, however, you may wish to make changes that *are not* compatible with the old class definition. For example, suppose that you create an instance of Customer and write it to disk using the WriteCustomer class defined earlier. After doing so, you may decide to change the Person class so that the first and last names are maintained in separate String variables as shown below:

```java
import java.util.Date;

public class Person implements java.io.Serializable {

    // protected String fullName;
    protected String lastName;
    protected String firstName;
    protected Date dateOfBirth;

    private final static long serialVersionUID = -8151523381735922859L;

    public Person(String name, Date dob) {
        setName(name);
    //     fullName = name;
        dateOfBirth = dob;
    }

    protected void setName(String name) {
        int index = name.indexOf(' ');
        if (index != -1) {
            firstName = name.substring(0, index);
            lastName = name.substring(index + 1);
        }
        else {
            firstName = name;
            lastName = "";
        }
    }
}
```

Unfortunately, this change is not compatible with the data that was previously stored using the original implementation of Person. That data contains the value of a variable called fullName that no longer exists in Person. If you make the changes shown above and execute the ReadCustomer application defined earlier, an instance of Customer will be created, but its lastName and firstName fields will both be null.

Fortunately, Java 1.2 provides a way to define a mapping between fields in different versions of a class when the class definition changes. To do so, you must first create a serialPersistentFields list that identifies the fields to be saved during serialization. Note that a String field named fullName is defined in the serialPersistentFields shown below, although that field no longer exists in the Person class:

```java
import java.io.*;
import java.util.Date;
```

```
public class Person implements java.io.Serializable {

//  protected String fullName;
   protected String lastName;
   protected String firstName;
   protected Date dateOfBirth;

   private final static long serialVersionUID = -8151523381735922859L;

   private final static ObjectStreamField[] serialPersistentFields = {
       new ObjectStreamField("fullName", String.class),
       new ObjectStreamField("dateOfBirth", Date.class)
       };

   // ...

}
```

The next step is to implement writeObject() and call the ObjectOutputStream's putFields() method, which returns an instance of PutField. PutField is an inner class defined in ObjectOutputStream that allows you to specify the names of the fields that should be marshaled and the value associated with each field. If a class uses PutField instead of writing its properties directly to an ObjectOutputStream, that class can remain compatible with older versions of itself, even when fields are added, changed, or removed. In this case, for example, Person will use a PutField to write a single fullName property that's derived from its firstName and lastName fields.

To use a PutField, you must create a key/value pair for each field in the class that should be serialized, where the key is the String name of a field identified in serialPersistentFields. The value of each pair should correspond to the value associated with the field, which can be a derived value. In this case, for example, a derived value is obtained by concatenating the firstName and lastName fields, and that value is associated with a field called fullName. Once you have added an entry to the PutField for each field and its associated value, you must call writeFields() to write the data to the output stream:

```
private void writeObject(ObjectOutputStream stream)
    throws IOException {
  ObjectOutputStream.PutField fields = stream.putFields();
  fields.put("fullName", firstName + " " + lastName);
  fields.put("dateOfBirth", dateOfBirth);
  stream.writeFields();
}
```

To allow Person instances to be correctly initialized from the data that was written, you must also implement the readObject() method and perform the reverse operation. Specifically, you'll obtain access to a GetField instance, extract values from it, and use those values to initialize the fields within the Person object. In this case, a fullName value is accessible through the GetField object, and that value which must be split into first and last names:

```
private void readObject(ObjectInputStream stream) throws IOException {
    try {
      ObjectInputStream.GetField fields = stream.readFields();
      setName((String)(fields.get("fullName", null)));
```

```
        dateOfBirth = (Date)(fields.get("dateOfBirth", null));
    } catch (ClassNotFoundException e) {};
}
```

Note that this processing does not override the stream unique identifier checking that's normally performed by `ObjectOutputStream`. In other words, you must ensure that the serialized `Person`'s SUID is equal to that of the local class, or an exception will be thrown when you attempt to read the serialized object.

Serializable Classes with Non-Serializable Superclasses

It was mentioned earlier that implementing `Serializable` in one class means that each of its subclasses effectively "inherits" that interface and the subclasses' fields will automatically be serialized when appropriate:

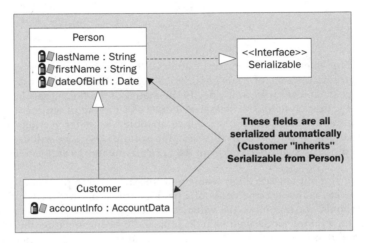

However, it *is not* the case that implementing `Serializable` in a subclass will cause the superclass fields to automatically be serialized. For example, suppose that you were to modify `Customer` so that it implements `Serializable` and change `Person` so that it does not:

```
import java.io.*;
import java.util.Date;

public class Person {

    // protected String fullName;
    protected String lastName;
    protected String firstName;
    protected Date dateOfBirth;
    // . . .
```

And:

```
import java.io.*;

public class Customer extends Person implements Serializable {

    protected AccountData accountInfo;
    // . . .
```

With these changes in place, the properties in Person will *not* automatically be marshaled when an instance of Customer is serialized:

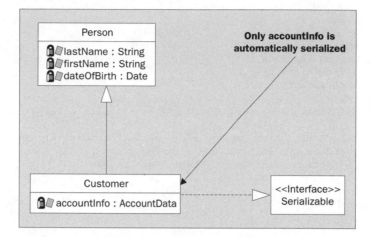

You can cause those properties to be saved and restored by implementing readObject() and writeObject() in Customer to save and restore the properties inherited from Person, and an example of this is shown below:

```java
import java.io.*;

public class Customer extends Person implements Serializable {

    protected AccountData accountInfo;

    public Customer(String name, java.util.Date dob, int acctnum,
            float startbal) {
        super(name, dob);
        accountInfo = new AccountData(acctnum, startbal);
    }

    public AccountData getAccountInfo() {
        return accountInfo;
    }

    private void writeObject(ObjectOutputStream oos) throws IOException {
        oos.defaultWriteObject();
        oos.writeObject(super.firstName);
        oos.writeObject(super.lastName);
        oos.writeObject(super.dateOfBirth);
    }

    private void readObject(ObjectInputStream ois) throws IOException,
            ClassNotFoundException {
        ois.defaultReadObject();
        super.firstName = (String)(ois.readObject());
        super.lastName = (String)(ois.readObject());
        super.dateOfBirth = (java.util.Date)(ois.readObject());
    }

}
```

There is one other change that must be made for this approach to work correctly. Specifically, the Person class must provide a no-argument constructor that's accessible from Customer:

```
public class Person {

    // protected String fullName;
    protected String lastName;
    protected String firstName;
    protected Date dateOfBirth;

    private final static long serialVersionUID = -8151523381735922859L;

    private final static ObjectStreamField[] serialPersistentFields = {
        new ObjectStreamField("fullName", String.class),
        new ObjectStreamField("dateOfBirth", Date.class)
        };

    public Person() {
    }
```

Any time you create a class that implements Serializable, it must be able to access a no-argument constructor of its first non-serializable superclass. This ensures that the serialization code is able to create an instance of the parent class during unmarshaling.

java.io.Externalizable

Like Serializable, this interface identifies a class that can be serialized. However, an implementation of Externalizable must take full responsibility for saving and restoring its state, including properties inherited from a superclass. The Externalizable interface is not widely used, and is not described in detail here.

writeExternal()

This method is called to save the state of the object, and is passed an instance of ObjectOutput as a parameter.

readExternal()

This method is called to initialize the state of an object instance, and is passed an instance of ObjectInput as a parameter.

Documentation Comment Tags

A number of documentation comment tags are defined that allow you to document the fields that will be serialized, and those tags are described below.

@serial description

You should include this tag in the documentation comments for each field that will be serialized by default (all non-static, non-transient fields). The *description* portion of this tag should describe how the field is used and identify its possible values.

@serialField name type description

When `serialPersistenceFields` is defined, you should use this tag to document each of the `ObjectStreamField` instances in the array as shown below:

```
/**
 * Explicitly identify the fields that should be serialized in this class.
 *
 * @serialField fullName    String            This is the person's full name
 * @serialField dateOfBirth java.util.Date  This is the person's birthdate
 */
private final static ObjectStreamField[] serialPersistentFields = {
    new ObjectStreamField("fullName", String.class),
    new ObjectStreamField("dateOfBirth", Date.class)
};
```

@serialData description

This tag should be used when `writeObject()` is implemented for a class that implements `Serializable` and for the `writeExternal()` method in an implementation of `Externalizable`. The tag describes the sequence and types of data items written to the output streams passed to those methods. For example:

```
/**
 * Saves the state of this class by writing the fields
 * that should be preserved as part of its state.
 *
 * @serialData  The <code>defaultWriteObject()</code> method is called
 *              to write the AccountData object associated with this
 *              instance. After that, a String name value is written to
 *              the stream, followed by a Date representing the customer's
 *              date of birth.
 */
private void writeObject(ObjectOutputStream oos) throws IOException {
  oos.defaultWriteObject();
  oos.writeObject(super.fullName);
  oos.writeObject(super.dateOfBirth);
}
```

Relational Database Persistence

Like flat files, serialization is an acceptable persistence mechanism for relatively small amounts of data. However, when your application uses or creates large volumes of data, it's usually necessary to store that information in a database. The previous chapter described the mechanics of using JDBC but did not illustrate how it can be used to store and retrieve objects.

To save and restore object states, there are three approaches you can take:

- ❑ Storing serialized representations of objects as raw binary data
- ❑ Traditional object-relational mapping
- ❑ Mapping structured types to Java classes

The first two options are available in both JDBC 1.x and 2.x, but mapping structured types to Java classes requires a DBMS that supports structured types and a JDBC 2.x-compliant driver.

Storing Serialized Objects

Most database columns store a specific type of data, such as character, numeric, or date values. However, DBMS products usually also provide a data type that allows you to store binary data (that is, an arbitrary collection of bytes), and you can use a column of that type to store and retrieve representations of serializable objects. For example, suppose that you have defined a database table named MYTABLE that contains a column called BINDATA, and that column is used for storing binary data. The following code segment illustrates how you can store an instance of a Vector (or any other serializable object) in the BINDATA column:

```java
import java.io.*;
import java.sql.*;
import java.util.*;

public class WriteBinary {

  public static void main(String[] args) throws Exception {
    Connection connect = DriverManager.getConnection("jdbc:odbc:mytest");

    Vector v = new Vector();
    v.addElement("Professional");
    v.addElement("Java");
    v.addElement("Programming");
    v.addElement(new java.util.Date());

    PreparedStatement pstmt = connect.prepareStatement(
        "UPDATE MYTABLE SET BINDATA = ? WHERE ITEMKEY = 123456");

    // Create an output stream that will generate a byte array
    ByteArrayOutputStream baos = new ByteArrayOutputStream();
    // Wrap an ObjectOutputStream around it
    ObjectOutputStream oos = new ObjectOutputStream(baos);
    // Create a serialized representation of the Vector and its data
    oos.writeObject(v);
    // Close the stream
    oos.close();

    // Get the byte array from the stream
    byte[] binaryData = baos.toByteArray();

    // Store the byte array in the BINDATA column
    pstmt.setBytes(1, binaryData);
    pstmt.executeUpdate();
  }

}
```

You can also unmarshal the binary data and effectively recreate the Vector using code like that shown below. This code reads the Vector from the database and prints the string representation of each of its elements:

```java
import java.io.*;
import java.sql.*;
import java.util.*;

public class ReadBinary {

  public static void main(String[] args) throws Exception {
    Connection conn = DriverManager.getConnection("jdbc:odbc:mytest");
    Vector v = null;
    PreparedStatement pstmt = conn.prepareStatement(
        "SELECT BINDATA FROM MYTABLE WHERE ITEMKEY = 123456");
    ResultSet rset = pstmt.executeQuery();

    if (rset.next()) {
      InputStream is = rset.getBinaryStream(1);
      ObjectInputStream ois = new ObjectInputStream(is);
      v = (Vector)(ois.readObject());
    }
    rset.close();

    Enumeration enum = v.elements();
    while (enum.hasMoreElements()) {
      System.out.println(enum.nextElement());
    }
  }

}
```

This approach to storing objects in a relational database is acceptable for simple objects, but it does have some limitations. First, you may wish to perform searches based on a field in the object, but this technique does not allow you to do so. For example, suppose that you had stored instances of the Person class shown below as serialized objects in a database:

```java
import java.io.Serializable;
import java.util.Date;

public class Person implements Serializable {

  protected int socialSecurityNumber;
  protected String firstName;
  protected String lastName;
  protected Date dateOfBirth;

  public Person(int ssn, String fname, String lname, Date dob) {
    socialSecurityNumber = ssn;
    firstName = fname;
    lastName = lname;
    dateOfBirth = dob;
  }

}
```

You might wish to perform a query (SELECT) that locates a row containing a Person object with a particular first, last name, or date of birth. However, you cannot do so when each Person object is stored as a stream of bytes that's meaningless to the DBMS. Another disadvantage to this approach is that each object stored in the database must be retrieved in its entirety before any fields in the object can be referenced. While that may not be a problem for the simple Person class defined above, it can be undesirable if you store objects that can include large amounts of data.

Storing a serialized representation of an object in a database is easy and may be acceptable for some simple objects, especially if the object's state can't be represented by a data type that's directly supported by the DBMS (for example, ImageIcon). However, if the object consists of fields that can be mapped to existing DBMS data types (for example, character, numeric, or date/time values), a different approach is usually more appropriate.

Object-Relational Mapping

A better way of providing object persistence for a Java class is to map the fields in that class to the columns of a database table. For example, you could use the following SQL command to create a database table called PERSON that contains a column for each field defined in the Person class:

```
CREATE TABLE PERSON (
   SOCIALSECURITYNUMBER   NUMERIC(9) PRIMARY KEY,
   FIRSTNAME              VARCHAR(20),
   LASTNAME               VARCHAR(20),
   DATEOFBIRTH            DATE
)
```

Note that aside from being all uppercase letters, the database column names are identical to the names of the fields in the associated Java class. This is not strictly necessary, but does make it easier to see which table column corresponds to a given field in the Java class.

With the PERSON table defined, methods can be created that will build the statements needed to insert, update, or delete a row using an instance of the Person class. These are shown below, along with a main() method that creates a new instance of Person, inserts it into the database and then updates and deletes it:

```
import java.io.Serializable;
import java.sql.*;
import java.util.Date;
import java.util.GregorianCalendar;

public class Person implements Serializable {

   protected int socialSecurityNumber;
   protected String firstName;
   protected String lastName;
   protected Date dateOfBirth;

   public static void main(String[] args) throws SQLException {
      GregorianCalendar gc = new GregorianCalendar(1966,
         GregorianCalendar.FEBRUARY, 9);
      Person p = new Person(123456789, "Brett", "Spell", gc.getTime());
      Connection conn = DriverManager.getConnection(
         "jdbc:odbc:people");
      conn.setAutoCommit(true);
      //  Insert the Person into the database
      p.performInsert(conn);
      p.dateOfBirth = new java.util.Date();
      //  Update the Person's database information
      p.performUpdate(conn);
      //  Delete the Person's database information
```

```
      p.performDelete(conn);
      conn.close();
   }

   public Person(int ssn, String fname, String lname, Date dob) {
      socialSecurityNumber = ssn;
      firstName = fname;
      lastName = lname;
      dateOfBirth = dob;
   }

   public void performInsert(Connection connect) throws SQLException {
      PreparedStatement pstmt = connect.prepareStatement(
          "INSERT INTO PERSON (SOCIALSECURITYNUMBER, " +
          "FIRSTNAME, LASTNAME, DATEOFBIRTH) " +
          "VALUES (?, ?, ?, ?)");
      pstmt.setInt(1, socialSecurityNumber);
      pstmt.setString(2, firstName);
      pstmt.setString(3, lastName);
      pstmt.setDate(4, new java.sql.Date(dateOfBirth.getTime()));
      pstmt.execute();
      pstmt.close();
   }

   public void performUpdate(Connection connect) throws SQLException {
      PreparedStatement pstmt = connect.prepareStatement(
          "UPDATE PERSON SET FIRSTNAME = ?, LASTNAME = ?, " +
          "DATEOFBIRTH = ? WHERE SOCIALSECURITYNUMBER = " +
          socialSecurityNumber);
      pstmt.setString(1, firstName);
      pstmt.setString(2, lastName);
      pstmt.setDate(3, new java.sql.Date(dateOfBirth.getTime()));
      pstmt.executeUpdate();
      pstmt.close();
   }

   public void performDelete(Connection connect) throws SQLException {
      Statement stmt = connect.createStatement();
      stmt.executeUpdate("DELETE FROM PERSON " +
          "WHERE SOCIALSECURITYNUMBER = " +
          socialSecurityNumber);
      stmt.close();
   }

}
```

It's also possible to define a method that returns an instance of Person given a ResultSet that contains rows from the PERSON table:

```
   public static Person getPerson(ResultSet rset) throws SQLException {
      int ssn = rset.getInt("SOCIALSECURITYNUMBER");
      String fname = rset.getString("FIRSTNAME");
      String lname = rset.getString("LASTNAME");
      Date dob = rset.getDate("DATEOFBIRTH");
      return new Person(ssn, fname, lname, dob);
   }
```

If you wish to test this new method, simply ensure that one or more rows have been added to the `Person` table in the database, perform a query against the table, and use `getPerson()` to create an instance of `Person` for each row that's returned. An example of how this can be done is shown below, where the `main()` method is modified to insert a row and then immediately read all rows from the database and display the name of the person described by that row:

```
public static void main(String[] args) throws SQLException {
    GregorianCalendar gc = new GregorianCalendar(1966,
        GregorianCalendar.FEBRUARY, 9);
    Person p = new Person(123456789, "Brett", "Spell", gc.getTime());
    Connection conn = DriverManager.getConnection(
        "jdbc:odbc:people");
    conn.setAutoCommit(true);
    // Insert the Person into the database
    p.performInsert(conn);
    p.dateOfBirth = new java.util.Date();
    // Update the Person's database information
//    p.performUpdate(conn);
    // Delete the Person's database information
//    p.performDelete(conn);
    Statement stmt = conn.createStatement();
    ResultSet rset = stmt.executeQuery("SELECT * FROM PERSON");
    while (rset.next()) {
      p = getPerson(rset);
      System.out.println("Read data for " + p.firstName + " " +
          p.lastName);
    }
    rset.close();
    stmt.close();
    conn.close();
  }
```

This technique of defining a method for each type of SQL statement works reasonably well, but it does require that you add similar methods to every Java class that you wish to store in the database. In addition, the `Person` class is now tightly coupled not only to the persistence mechanism (mapping its fields to columns in a database table), but also to the database table itself. If one of the database columns is renamed, the `Person` class must be updated accordingly.

Those issues can be resolved by creating a class that uses reflection and metadata to map the fields defined in an object to the columns in a database table. An example of how this could be done is shown in the following code, where the `SimplePersistence` class dynamically builds an `INSERT` statement using the field names that are identified through reflection:

```
import java.lang.reflect.*;
import java.sql.*;

public class SimplePersistence {

  public static void insertRow(Object object, Connection connect)
      throws SQLException, IllegalAccessException {
    Class objectClass = object.getClass();
    String fullName = objectClass.getName();
    String className = fullName.substring(
        fullName.lastIndexOf('.') + 1);
```

```
      Field[] fields = objectClass.getDeclaredFields();
      StringBuffer columnNames = new StringBuffer();
      StringBuffer columnValues = new StringBuffer();
      for (int i = 0; i < fields.length; i++) {
        columnNames.append((i == 0 ? "" : ", ") +
            fields[i].getName());
        columnValues.append((i == 0 ? "" : ", ") + "?");
      }
      String sql = "INSERT INTO " + className +
          " (" + columnNames + ")" +
          " VALUES (" + columnValues + ")";
      PreparedStatement pstmt = connect.prepareStatement(sql);
      for (int i = 0; i < fields.length; i++) {
        Object value = fields[i].get(object);
        if (value instanceof java.util.Date) {
          java.util.Date dateval = (java.util.Date)value;
          value = new java.sql.Date(dateval.getTime());
        }
        pstmt.setObject(i + 1, value);
      }
      pstmt.executeUpdate();
      pstmt.close();
    }

  }
```

Performing an UPDATE or DELETE is slightly more complex, because those statements should ideally use only the primary key to select the row to update or delete. For example, since the social security number is the primary key in this case, the statements should contain WHERE clauses like the ones shown below:

```
DELETE FROM PERSON WHERE SOCIALSECURITYNUMBER = ?
UPDATE PERSON SET FIRSTNAME = ?, LASTNAME = ?, DATEOFBIRTH = ?
WHERE SOCIALSECURITYNUMBER = ?
```

Since our SimplePersistence class builds SQL statements dynamically, it must somehow determine which table columns are part of the primary key, and DatabaseMetaData will allow us to do just that. The getKeyFieldNames() method listed below creates a Hashtable that contains an entry for each column that's part of the primary key:

```
import java.lang.reflect.*;
import java.sql.*;
import java.util.*;

public class SimplePersistence {

  public final static int COLUMN_NAME = 4;

  // ...

  protected static Hashtable getKeyFieldNames(Connection connect,
      String table) throws SQLException {
    Hashtable results = new Hashtable();
    DatabaseMetaData dmd = connect.getMetaData();
    String catalog = (dmd.supportsCatalogsInTableDefinitions() ?
```

```
        connect.getCatalog() : null);
    String schema = (dmd.supportsSchemasInTableDefinitions() ?
        dmd.getUserName() : null);
    ResultSet rset = dmd.getPrimaryKeys(catalog, schema, table);
    while (rset.next()) {
      results.put(rset.getString(COLUMN_NAME).toUpperCase(), "");
    }
    rset.close();
    return results;
  }

}
```

With the getKeyFieldNames() method defined, we can create the methods that will perform updates and deletes. The updateRow() method obtains a list of the fields that are declared in the class being updated and builds an UPDATE command that can be used with a PreparedStatement. That statement will contain a parameter for each field in the class, and the parameter values will be filled in using the values within the fields of the object passed to the method. In addition, a WHERE clause will be constructed using the list of primary key columns that was obtained from getKeyFieldNames():

```
    public static void updateRow(Object object, Connection connect)
        throws SQLException, IllegalAccessException {
      String fieldName;

      Class objectClass = object.getClass();
      String fullName = objectClass.getName();
      String className = fullName.substring(fullName.lastIndexOf('.') + 1);
      Field[] fields = objectClass.getDeclaredFields();
      StringBuffer valClause = new StringBuffer();
      StringBuffer keyClause = new StringBuffer();
      Vector valValues = new Vector();
      Vector keyValues = new Vector();
      Hashtable keyFields = getKeyFieldNames(connect,
                                        className.toUpperCase());
      for (int i = 0; i < fields.length; i++) {
        Object value = fields[i].get(object);
        if (value instanceof java.util.Date) {
          java.util.Date dateval = (java.util.Date)value;
          value = new java.sql.Date(dateval.getTime());
        }

        fieldName = fields[i].getName().toUpperCase();
        if (keyFields.get(fieldName) != null) {
          keyClause.append((keyClause.length() == 0 ? "" : " AND ")
                        + fieldName + " = ?");
          keyValues.addElement(value);
        }
        else {
          valClause.append((valClause.length() == 0 ? "" : ", ")
                        + fieldName + " = ?");
          valValues.addElement(value);
        }
      }
      String sql = "UPDATE " + className + " SET " + valClause +
                " WHERE " + keyClause;
```

```
    PreparedStatement pstmt = connect.prepareStatement(sql);
    int index = 1;
    Enumeration values = valValues.elements();
    while (values.hasMoreElements()) {
      pstmt.setObject(index++, values.nextElement());
    }
    values = keyValues.elements();
    while (values.hasMoreElements()) {
      pstmt.setObject(index++, values.nextElement());
    }
    pstmt.executeUpdate();
    pstmt.close();
  }
```

The deleteRow() method is simpler than updateRow(), since only the primary key columns and their values must be included in the statement that's executed. Here, too, the getKeyFields() method is used to identify the primary key columns, and a WHERE clause is constructed that will ensure that only the row corresponding to the specified object will be deleted:

```
public static void deleteRow(Object object, Connection connect)
    throws SQLException, IllegalAccessException {
  String fieldName;

  Class objectClass = object.getClass();
  String fullName = objectClass.getName();
  String className = fullName.substring(fullName.lastIndexOf('.') + 1);
  Field[] fields = objectClass.getDeclaredFields();
  StringBuffer sql = new StringBuffer("DELETE FROM " + className +
                                      " WHERE ");
  Hashtable keyFields = getKeyFieldNames(connect,
                                    className.toUpperCase());
  Object[] values = new Object[keyFields.size()];
  boolean useAnd = false;
  Enumeration fieldList = keyFields.keys();
  for (int i = 0; i < keyFields.size(); i++) {
    fieldName = (String)(fieldList.nextElement());
    for (int j = 0; j < fields.length; j++) {
      if (fieldName.equalsIgnoreCase(fields[j].getName())) {
        sql.append((useAnd ? " AND " : "") + fieldName + " = ?");
        useAnd = true;
        Object value = fields[j].get(object);
        if (value instanceof java.util.Date) {
          java.util.Date dateval = (java.util.Date)value;
          value = new java.sql.Date(dateval.getTime());
        }
        values[i] = value;
        break;
      }
    }
  }
  PreparedStatement pstmt = connect.prepareStatement(sql.toString());
  for (int i = 0; i < values.length; i++) {
    pstmt.setObject(i + 1, values[i]);
  }
  pstmt.executeUpdate();
}
```

You can now use the `SimplePersistence` class to insert, update, and delete instances of a Java class into a database. The ability to read objects from the database can be added by implementing the `getObjectFromRow()` method shown below:

```
protected static Object getObjectFromRow(ResultSet rset,
    Class objectClass) throws Exception {
  Class fieldClass;
  int index;
  Class[] classes = {};
  Object[] args = {};
  Constructor construct = objectClass.getConstructor(classes);
  Object objectInstance = construct.newInstance(args);
  Field[] fields = objectClass.getDeclaredFields();
  for (int i = 0; i < fields.length; i++) {
    index = rset.findColumn(fields[i].getName());
    if (index > 0) {
      fieldClass = fields[i].getType();
      Object value = rset.getObject(index);
      if (value instanceof Number) {
        Number num = (Number)value;
        if (fieldClass.equals(Byte.TYPE)) {
          value = new Byte(num.byteValue());
        }
        else if (fieldClass.equals(Short.TYPE)) {
          value = new Short(num.shortValue());
        }
        else if (fieldClass.equals(Integer.TYPE)) {
          value = new Integer(num.intValue());
        }
        else if (fieldClass.equals(Long.TYPE)) {
          value = new Long(num.longValue());
        }
        else if (fieldClass.equals(Float.TYPE)) {
          value = new Float(num.floatValue());
        }
        else if (fieldClass.equals(Double.TYPE)) {
          value = new Double(num.doubleValue());
        }
      }
      fields[i].set(objectInstance, value);
    }
  }
  return objectInstance;
}
```

The `getObjectFromRow()` method requires that the class being instantiated has a no-argument constructor, and one can easily be added to the `Person` class as shown below:

```
import java.io.Serializable;
import java.util.Date;

public class Person implements Serializable {

  protected int socialSecurityNumber;
  protected String firstName;
```

```
   protected String lastName;
   protected Date dateOfBirth;

   public Person() {
   }

   public Person(int ssn, String fname, String lname, Date dob) {
     socialSecurityNumber = ssn;
     firstName = fname;
     lastName = lname;
     dateOfBirth = dob;
   }

}
```

To test the `SimplePersistence` out, you can use code like that shown in the `main()` method below, which will insert, update, delete, and retrieve entries from the PERSON table:

```
public class SimplePersistence {

   public final static int COLUMN_NAME = 4;

   public static void main(String[] args) throws Exception {
     GregorianCalendar gc = new GregorianCalendar(1966,
         GregorianCalendar.FEBRUARY, 9);
     Person p = new Person(123456789, "Brett", "Spell", gc.getTime());
     Connection conn = DriverManager.getConnection(
         "jdbc:odbc:people");
     //  Insert the Person we just created into the database
     insertRow(p, conn);
     //  Modify the date of birth
     p.dateOfBirth = new java.util.Date();
     //  Update the database record
     updateRow(p, conn);
     Statement stmt = conn.createStatement();
     //  Query the PERSON table
     ResultSet rset = stmt.executeQuery("SELECT * FROM PERSON");
     while (rset.next()) {
       //  Create a Person object from the current row
       p = (Person)(getObjectFromRow(rset, Person.class));
       System.out.println("Found " + p.firstName + " " + p.lastName);
     }
     rset.close();
     stmt.close();
     //  Delete the last row in the table
     deleteRow(p, conn);
     conn.close();
   }
```

While `SimplePersistence` does solve the problems identified earlier, and is more flexible than the previous approach, it does not provide a robust persistence mechanism. For example, it cannot correctly process properties inherited from a superclass and will not work correctly with classes that define references to other user-defined classes. In addition, each field in the class being processed must map to a column of the same name and appropriate type in the database, and the database table must have the same name as the class. Although `SimplePersistence` may be sufficient for simple classes like `Person`, it is not appropriate for relatively complex objects such as instances of the `Employee` class defined earlier in this chapter.

Despite its limitations, SimplePersistence provides an example of how to perform a very complex function: mapping objects to relational database tables. More advanced object-relational mapping capabilities are often provided with application server products, including those that support Enterprise JavaBeans. However, if using an application server is undesirable or impossible, you may find it convenient to take advantage of the ability of JDBC 2.x to map objects to structured database types.

Object Persistence with Structured Types

The getObject() method in ResultSet and setObject() method in PreparedStatement automatically perform conversions between database types and certain Java classes. For example, an instance of String is returned when getObject() is called for a column that represents character data stored in the database.

JDBC 2.x extends this capability by allowing you to map structured types to Java classes so that you can retrieve an instance of a user-defined class from getObject(). It also allows you to store an instance of the class using PreparedStatement's setObject() method, providing a simple but powerful form of persistence. To use this facility, you must do two things: map a structured type to a Java class, and implement the SQLData interface in the class.

To illustrate how to map structured database types to Java class, we'll create a structured type called FULLNM using a SQL command like the one below:

```
CREATE TYPE FULLNM (
   FIRSTNM     VARCHAR(20),
   MIDDLENM    VARCHAR(20),
   LASTNM      VARCHAR(20)
)
```

The new FULLNM structured type will be mapped to the Java class shown here:

```
public class FullName {

  protected String firstName;
  protected String middleName;
  protected String lastName;

  public FullName() {
  }

  public FullName(String first, String middle, String last) {
    firstName = first;
    middleName = middle;
    lastName = last;
  }

}
```

Mapping a Structured Type to a Class

To map a structured type to a class, you must first obtain a reference to the type map for the Connection that you're using. The map is represented by an instance of java.util.Map, and can be retrieved using code similar to the following:

```
Connection connect;
// Obtain a connection to the database here
// ...

java.util.Map typeMap = connect.getTypeMap();
```

Once you have a reference to the map, you can add an entry to it that identifies a structured type and its associated Java class. Since each structured type is associated with a specific schema, you must include the schema name when adding a map entry. For example, in this case we'll define a mapping between the FullName class and the FULLNM type in the database. If FULLNM was created in the BSPELL schema, the following code could be used to create a map entry:

```
typeMap.put("BSPELL.FULLNM", FullName.class);
```

The new map entry's key is a String that contains the schema-qualified name of the database type, while the entry's value is an instance of java.lang.Class that identifies the class that corresponds to the database type.

Implementing SQLData

With the FULLNM structured type mapped to the Name class, the only remaining step is to modify FullName so that it implements SQLData. This interface defines three methods, each of which is described below:

readSQL()

This method is called when an instance of a Java class is being created from a structured type stored in the database. It is passed an instance of SQLInput and a String representing the name of the structured type being read. SQLInput provides a group of readXXX() methods (readArray(), readBlob(), readDate(), readString(), etc.) that are similar to ResultSet's getXXX() methods. The SQLInput object represents an input stream that contains the values of the individual elements of the structured SQL type, and those values must be read in the same order that they were specified on the structured type definition. For example, when an instance of FullName is created, it must read the first, middle, and last name strings in that order, which is the same order in which they were defined on the CREATE TYPE command.

An example of how the readSQL() might be defined for FullName is shown below:

```
import java.sql.*;

public class FullName implements SQLData {

  protected String firstName;
  protected String middleName;
  protected String lastName;

  protected String typeName;

  public FullName() {
  }

  public FullName(String first, String middle, String last) {
    firstName = first;
```

```
        middleName = middle;
        lastName = last;
    }

    public void readSQL(SQLInput sqlInput, String type)
        throws SQLException {
        typeName = type;
        firstName = sqlInput.readString();
        middleName = sqlInput.readString();
        lastName = sqlInput.readString();
    }

    // ... More new methods ...

}
```

writeSQL()

While readSQL() is used to read structured type data into a Java object, writeSQL() is used to write the object's properties into a structured type. Just as it's necessary to read the fields in the order in which they were defined, they must also be written in that same order:

```
    public void writeSQL(SQLOutput sqlOutput) throws SQLException {
        sqlOutput.writeString(firstName);
        sqlOutput.writeString(middleName);
        sqlOutput.writeString(lastName);
    }
```

getSQLTypeName()

This method is called to determine the name of the structured type that should be mapped to this object, and usually can simply return the String specified when readSQL() was called:

```
    public String getSQLTypeName() {
        return typeName;
    }
```

Storing and Retrieving Instances of Mapped Classes

Since the FullName class now implements SQLData, instances of that class can be read from and written to database columns that are defined using the FULLNM structured type. For example, suppose that you have created a table using the following SQL command:

```
CREATE TABLE EMPLOYEE (
    EMPLOYEEID  NUMERIC(10),
    EMPNAME     FULLNM,
    STARTDATE   DATE,
    SALARY      NUMERIC(6)
)
```

Notice that the EMPNAME column contains instances of the FULLNM structured type defined earlier. With this table defined, you could use the following code to insert a row:

```
import java.sql.*;

public class WriteFullName {
```

```java
    public static void main(String[] args) throws SQLException {
        Connection connect = DriverManager.getConnection(
            "jdbc:odbc:people");
        java.util.Map typeMap = connect.getTypeMap();
        typeMap.put("BSPELL.FULLNM", FullName.class);

        int employeeID = 123456;
        FullName fullName = new FullName("Jeff", "Davis", "Kirk");
        java.util.Date sd = new java.util.Date();
        java.sql.Date startDate = new java.sql.Date(sd.getTime());
        int salary = 250000;
        PreparedStatement pstmt = connect.prepareStatement(
            "INSERT INTO EMPLOYEE (EMPLOYEEID, EMPNAME, STARTDATE, SALARY) " +
            " VALUES (?, ?, ?, ?) ");
        pstmt.setInt(1, employeeID);
        pstmt.setObject(2, fullName);
        pstmt.setDate(3, startDate);
        pstmt.setInt(4, salary);
        pstmt.executeUpdate();
    }

}
```

Note that the `PreparedStatement`'s `setObject()` method was used to store a reference to the instance of `FullName` being inserted. When `executeUpdate()` is called, the `FullName` object's `writeSQL()` method is invoked and will write the object's fields into the structured type column.

Reading an instance of `FullName` from the database is even easier, as illustrated by the highlighted code below:

```java
import java.sql.*;

public class ReadFullName {

    public static void main(String[] args) throws SQLException {
        Connection connect = DriverManager.getConnection(
            "jdbc:odbc:people");
        java.util.Map typeMap = connect.getTypeMap();
        typeMap.put("BSPELL.FULLNM", FullName.class);
        Statement stmt = connect.createStatement();
        ResultSet rset = stmt.executeQuery("SELECT * FROM EMPLOYEE");
        while (rset.next()) {
            FullName fn = (FullName)(rset.getObject("EMPNAME"));
        }
    }

}
```

References to Other Mapped Classes

As you may recall, one of the limitations of the `SimplePersistence` class was that it did not handle references from one user-defined class to another. Since such references are common, that limitation greatly reduced the usefulness of `SimplePersistence`. Fortunately, JDBC's structured type-to-class mapping suffers from no such limitation, and you can embed references from one class/type to another. For example, suppose that you create the following structured type:

```
CREATE TYPE STUDENT (
  STUDENTID     NUMERIC(10),
  STUDENTNAME   FULLNM,
  TESTSCORE     NUMERIC(5, 2)
)
```

A corresponding Java class that implements SQLData can be created easily, as shown below. Note that the writeSQL() method calls writeObject() to write the FullName object to the database, which is possible since that object maps to the FULLNM structured type:

```java
import java.sql.*;

public class Student implements SQLData {

  protected int idNumber;
  protected FullName fullName;
  protected float testScore;

  protected String typeName;

  public Student() {
  }

  public Student(int id, FullName fn, float score) {
    idNumber = id;
    fullName = fn;
    testScore = score;
  }

  public void writeSQL(SQLOutput sqlOutput) throws SQLException {
    sqlOutput.writeInt(idNumber);
    sqlOutput.writeObject(fullName);
    sqlOutput.writeFloat(testScore);
  }

  public void readSQL(SQLInput sqlInput, String type)
      throws SQLException {
    typeName = type;
    idNumber = sqlInput.readInt();
    fullName = (FullName)(sqlInput.readObject());
    testScore = sqlInput.readFloat();
  }

  public String getSQLTypeName() {
    return typeName;
  }

}
```

When writeObject() is passed an object that implements SQLData as FullName does, it will call that object's writeSQL() method. In effect, writeSQL() is called recursively until the states of all objects have been completely written to the SQLOutput stream.

Just as it was possible to use the FULLNM structured type when creating tables, the new STUDENT type can also be used for that purpose as shown opposite:

```
CREATE TABLE ENROLLMENT (
   COURSEID          NUMERIC(8),
   STUDENTINFO       STUDENT,
   ENROLLMENTDATE    DATE
)
```

The following code illustrates how you can create an instance of the Student class and use it to update a row in the database, assuming that data has previously been added to the ENROLLMENT table:

```
import java.sql.*;

public class WriteStudent {

   public static void main(String[] args) throws SQLException {
      Connection connect = DriverManager.getConnection(
            "jdbc:cloudscape:survivor");
      java.util.Map typeMap = connect.getTypeMap();
      typeMap.put("BSPELL.STUDENT", Student.class);
      typeMap.put("BSPELL.FULLNM", FullName.class);
      FullName fn = new FullName("Jeff", "Davis", "Kirk");
      Student st = new Student(12345, fn, 95.0f);
      PreparedStatement pstmt = connect.prepareStatement(
            "UPDATE ENROLLMENT SET STUDENTINFO = ? WHERE COURSEID = 123");
      pstmt.setObject(1, st);
   }

}
```

Summary

In this chapter, we've discussed a number of important topics related to persistence, including the following:

- ❑ The classes defined in the java.io package and when and how to use them to read binary data

- ❑ How to read character data in a platform-independent manner

- ❑ Using flat files to save the state information

- ❑ Java's object serialization and how it works

- ❑ How to overcome some common problems related to serialization

- ❑ Customizing the behavior of serialization through the use of readObject() and writeObject()

- ❑ Storing object instances in a relational database

- ❑ How to use object/relational mapping to store individual property values in corresponding database table columns

- ❑ Using the SQLData interface to easily achieve object persistence

As we've seen, persistence is moderately complex unless you use some existing facility such as serialization or a relational database, so it's not usually desirable to implement your own persistence mechanism. Serialization is usually a very acceptable option for simple application, that will store and retrieve small amounts of data, but relational database products offer a more robust and scalable solution.

In the next chapter, we'll take a look at XML, a relatively new technology for describing data that is becoming highly important for developing applications today.

14

XML

Although Java and XML are not inherently tied together, XML is often discussed in the context of Java. This chapter explains why this is the case and provides an overview of XML, along with a description of some of the tools available, and when and how to use them. We will look at:

- ❑ What XML is, and how to create an XML document
- ❑ Using Document Type Definitions (DTDs) to define XML "grammar"
- ❑ Parsing and validating XML documents using both the Simple API for XML (SAX) and the Document Object Model (DOM)
- ❑ Using XML namespaces to eliminate ambiguities where a document uses multiple DTDs
- ❑ Transforming XML documents with XSLT

eXtensible Markup Language (**XML**) is, like the **HyperText Markup Language** (**HTML**), derived from the **Standard Generalized Markup Language** (**SGML**), a language designed to describe and define data so that information can be managed as objects rather than merely a series of characters. Although SGML is extremely flexible and powerful, it's also very complex and difficult to use, and XML is an attempt to provide much of SGML's functionality without its complexity. The "extensible" part of XML refers to the fact that, unlike HTML, you're free to define your own tags, which as we'll see is a very useful feature.

XML was designed in order to provide a means to express data in a platform independent, extensible, self-descriptive and self-consistent way, that is, to provide additional metadata that puts the information in context. This is done by surrounding the data with tags that define the data's structure and by providing additional information as attributes. HTML is a language also loosely based on SGML that most people should be aware of, if not familiar with. Unlike SGML and XML, though, HTML is concerned solely with the presentation of data in a specific context – that of the Internet. HTML provides information on how to present the information in such a way that a browser can interpret it.

The underlying problem is that storing information in HTML format limits the uses that we can put this information to, its focus on the presentation of data rather than the data itself makes it difficult to extract information. We can create arbitrary rules that will describe where information can be found, for example, the fourth line of the document contains the subject of the information, the last line contains copyright information etc. However, this makes our information inflexible.

XML does not concern itself with the way that information should be displayed. It simply provides information about the data and its structure so that we can process and evaluate the data and leaves the display of the data to the software that processes it. This additional information on the data is both human readable and machine-readable and all contained in HTML-like tags, as we will see below.

The following listing provides a very simple example of an XML document, and one of the first things you should notice is how much it resembles HTML:

```xml
<?xml version="1.0" ?>

<book>
  <title>Professional Java Programming</title>
  <author>Brett Spell</author>
  <publisher>Wrox Press</publisher>

  <tableOfContents showPageNumbers="Yes">
    <tocEntry>Printing</tocEntry>
    <tocEntry>Cut And Paste</tocEntry>
    <tocEntry>Drag And Drop</tocEntry>
  </tableOfContents>
</book>
```

Any blank lines and indentation (white space) present for readability in the document content will be preserved by the parser and passed to the application for processing; white space within element tags and attribute values may be removed. Also unlike HTML, XML is case-sensitive, so be sure to use the appropriate case when creating a document; `<Author>`, `<author>` and `<AUTHOR>` are three distinct elements.

XML vs. HTML

In order to further explain the benefits of XML, it's helpful to compare it to HTML, and to review some of HTML's weaknesses as a medium for storing information. For example, suppose that we construct an HTML document that's similar to the above XML document:

```html
<html>
<body>
<center><h1>Professional Java Programming</h1></center>
<h4>Brett Spell</h4>
<b>
<h3>Table Of Contents</h3>
<ul>
  <li>Printing</li>
  <li>Cut and Paste</li>
  <li>Drag and Drop</li>
</ul>
</b>
```

```
<h4>Wrox Press</h4>
<img src="http://www.wrox.com/images/wrox_logo100.gif" alt="Wrox Logo" />
</body>
</html>
```

When viewed in a web browser, this document produces a display like the following:

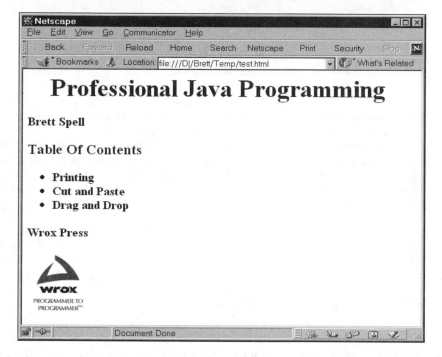

Although the data contained in the document is identical, a very important difference emerges when you compare the HTML document with its XML equivalent. The HTML version is a combination of data (a book's name, author, and publisher) and instructions on how to display the data given by the <center>, <h1>, <h4> tags, etc. In other words, the data in an HTML document is tightly coupled to the tags used to control how the data is displayed and, as in the case of object-oriented design, this tight coupling is undesirable because it limits reusability and extensibility.

For example, suppose that you want to print the information contained in the above HTML document instead of displaying it in a web browser. You may wish to produce printed output that's similar (or identical in effect) to the output produced by displaying the document in a browser. However, you might want to create printed documentation that has a different format from the browser display. In either case, printed output obviously has different characteristics from a browser display, and it may be inappropriate or impossible to use the same characteristics in both cases. For one thing, it's common to use a black-and-white printer, while browsers normally assume that they're used with a color monitor.

Therefore, the use of different colors to highlight some portion of a document may be appropriate for a browser but inappropriate for printed output. Similarly, while hyperlinks are commonly embedded in HTML documents to provide easy navigation between documents, they're not applicable when viewing printed output. In the following example, the HTML document contains a reference to another chapter that can be accessed by clicking on the hyperlink text:

```
The DataFlavor class is covered more thoroughly in the chapter on <a
href="http://www.wrox.com/projava/cutpaste.html">cut and paste</a>
```

When printing this information, it might be more appropriate to refer to a page number, or perhaps to include endnotes that describe the URLs referenced within the document:

> The DataFlavor class is covered more thoroughly in the chapter on cut and paste[1]
> .
> .
> .
> [1]http://www.wrox.com/books/projava/cutpaste.html

In addition to printing, there are many different media that can be used for representing data besides a web browser. You might prefer to display the data on a device with a less powerful user interface such as that provided by a mobile phone or an organizer such as a Palm device. Alternatively, you may want to display the data using an interface that's *more* flexible than the one offered by a browser, such as a Swing-based "thick client" application interface. In addition, if we need to filter the data for relevant parts, for example to display only the table of contents, this would require an in-depth knowledge of the information itself.

The important thing to realize is that you'll often need to present more than one view of your data, but HTML makes this difficult at best. On the surface, it may seem that the data within an HTML document could be displayed in other forms by parsing the document and converting its contents. Unfortunately, there are at least two reasons why it often isn't practical to do so:

- ❑ HTML documents do not contain information that describes their data
- ❑ HTML documents are not required to be **well-formed** documents

We'll first examine the significance of having information that describes the data (also referred to as **metadata**), and then we'll see what it means for a document to be "well-formed" and why it's important.

Describing Data

Let's assume that you attempt to create code that parses the HTML document defined earlier. In order to display the data in some arbitrary format, the parsing code must be able to identify specific portions of the data within the document such as the author, publisher, and so on. Unfortunately, this is difficult to do reliably because there is no information in the document indicating that a particular piece of data represents some specific type of information. Although a human reader might easily guess that "Wrox Press" refers to the publisher, it's not feasible to expect a software application to make the same deduction.

As mentioned previously, you could "hard-code" an application so that it assumes that the second <h4> tag in a document identifies the book publisher, but that approach is very inflexible and unreliable. If the order of the tags changes, or if an additional <h4> tag is inserted prior to the existing ones, the technique would no longer work correctly. In other words, scanning for <h4> tags is inappropriate because that tag doesn't describe the type of data that follows it; it simply describes how the data is to be displayed.

In contrast, XML describes only the data, and does not include information that specifies how the data is to be displayed. For example, the <publisher> tag defined in the sample XML document earlier indicates what type of data follows it without specifying how that information should appear. By building an application that *understands* the significance of a <publisher> tag you can create code that reliably interprets the contents of XML documents structured as the document above, even if their contents change.

More importantly, you can define a structure for your documents so that potential consumers of your data can reliably process and interpret it. In addition this defined structure allows other parties to create structured documents that you, and other data consumers, can process using the same software that processes your own documents. In essence, XML defines a document creation, processing and exchange format.

Well-Formed Documents

Although the HTML document defined earlier qualifies as a well-formed document, it's not necessary for this be true for the HTML to be considered acceptable. To some extent this is as a result of the software that processes it, which seeks to minimize processing errors by compensating for errors in processed documents. For example, the two leading web browsers, Internet Explorer and Netscape Navigator, both allow documents that are not well-formed.

XML, however, requires well-formed documents as they are much easier to parse correctly and are easier for applications to represent internally. It is also easier, as a result, to maintain the integrity of data. The following list summarizes the characteristics of a well-formed document:

❑ Each start tag must have a corresponding end tag, except for **empty elements** (which are described below)

❑ Attribute values must be enclosed in quotes

❑ Special characters used to define tags, called **reserved characters**, must be represented by their equivalent escape sequences (described later)

❑ The document cannot contain any overlapping tags (the most recently opened tag must be the first to be closed)

Unlike HTML, XML documents must always be well-formed. This means they're easy to parse and to represent in memory using collections of objects. Before discussing how this is done, however, it's important to understand each of the four characteristics listed above so you will know how to create a valid XML document.

Matching Start and End Tags

In most cases, each start tag (for example, <html>, <center>, <h1>, etc.) in the HTML document has a corresponding end tag (</html>, </center>, </h1>) that identifies the tag's effective range. Each pair of start and end tags is collectively referred to as an **element**, an important term that we'll use frequently through this chapter. XML requires that each start tag have an end tag, with the exception of empty elements.

While it may appear that the <img> tag in the HTML document violates this rule and therefore prevents the document from being well-formed, that is not the case. This is an example of an empty element, or an element for which it is not necessary or meaningful to put information between the start and end tags. Since the **attributes** (src and alt) within the <img> tag contain all the information needed in the element, there is no need to provide a corresponding </img> tag. Instead, in XML the start tag is identified as defining an empty element by ending it with a combination of the forward slash and greater than characters (/>) as shown below. In contrast, start tags are usually terminated with the greater than character only:

```
<img src="http://www.wrox.com/images/wrox_logo100.gif" alt="Wrox Logo" />
```

Attribute Values and Quotation Marks

Some HTML tags allow you to specify attributes, where an attribute/value pair consists of an attribute name and a value that's assigned to the attribute, separated by an equals sign (=). For example, the `<img>` element shown below contains two attributes named `src` and `alt`:

```
<img src="http://www.wrox.com/images/wrox_logo100.gif" alt="Wrox Logo" />
```

As this example illustrates, attribute values can be enclosed within quotation marks, and you must do so for each attribute value that contains embedded spaces (as in the case of the above `alt` attribute). In contrast, when the value does not contain spaces, it's not only possible to omit the quotation marks, but excluding them is common practice. For example, the following variation of the `<img>` tag (in which the quotation marks around the `src` attribute's value have been removed) would be considered valid HTML:

```
<img src=http://www.wrox.com/images/wrox_logo100.gif alt="Wrox Logo" />
```

Unfortunately, this causes those documents to be more difficult to parse, since it complicates the task of identifying the end of an attribute value. XML documents also allow you to specify attributes, but to ensure that the elements and their attributes can be parsed easily, you *must* place quotation marks around each attribute value. Therefore, while the above `<img>` tag may be valid as part of an HTML document, it would not be acceptable in XML.

Representing Reserved Characters

Some characters such as the less than sign (<), greater than sign (>), and ampersand (&) have special meanings in the context of an XML document and cannot be used directly in the document. For example, if you were to modify the "Cut and Paste" and "Drag and Drop" text from the sample HTML document above to read "Cut & Paste" and "Drag & Drop" as shown below, a parser will fail to process the document correctly:

```
<ul>
  <li>Printing</li>
  <li>Cut & Paste</li>
  <li>Drag & Drop</li>
</ul>
```

In fact, one of the things the ampersand is used for is to allow you to embed these special characters into documents indirectly by providing an abbreviated name for each one that can be used in place of the character. To use the abbreviated name, place an ampersand before the name and a semicolon after it, and each sequence will be replaced with the character that it represents when the document is loaded. The following table provides a list of some of the characters for which abbreviated names have been defined, and the sequences you should use to represent those characters in XML documents:

Name	Character	Equivalent Sequence
Less than sign	<	&lt;
Greater than sign	>	&gt;

Name	Character	Equivalent Sequence
Apostrophe	'	'
Quotation mark	"	"
Ampersand	&	&

For example, if you wish to embed a less than sign in a document, you would use the < string instead of the less than sign (<). Similarly, to embed ampersands into a document, you would use & instead, as shown below:

```
<ul>
  <li>Printing</li>
  <li>Cut &amp; Paste</li>
  <li>Drag &amp; Drop</li>
</ul>
```

When a document containing the above sequences is loaded, each occurrence of "&" will be replaced with "&" during processing of the document. As we'll see, these sequences are examples of **entity references**, and they are described in more detail later in this chapter.

Overlapping Elements

Two elements overlap when one element "contains" a start tag but does not contain the associated end tag. For example in the following HTML:

```
<ul>
  <li>Printing</li>
  <li>Cut and Paste</li>
  <b>
  <li>Drag and Drop</li>
</ul>
</b>
```

Instead of the unordered list (<ul>) element being contained entirely within the bold (<b>) element, the two now overlap, and the bold property only applies to some of the items in the unordered list instead of all of them. Although overlapping tags are often created accidentally and are confusing at best, most browsers tolerate them. Unfortunately, they not only make parsing of an HTML document more difficult, but they also greatly increase the complexity of creating a representation of such a document.

To better understand this point, suppose that you've created a set of classes that are used to represent the structure of an HTML document you're parsing. For example, you might create a class called UnorderedList that contains a collection of ListItem objects, and those objects might be maintained in a Vector or Hashtable. As long as there are no overlapping tags, creating such a representation of the document's contents and characteristics is reasonably simple and can be accomplished by creating an object hierarchy:

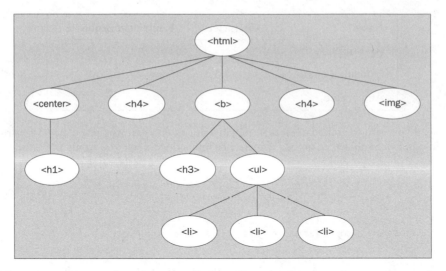

An XML document represented as above is called a **node tree**, where a node represents each element, its contents, and parameters, comments, entities and other node types. We will cover each of these in the remainder of the book.

Of course, when a document contains overlapping nodes, this hierarchical tree structure representation would not be possible.

When and Why to Use XML

Now that you understand some of the deficiencies associated with HTML as a storage format, you may still be wondering when and why you would use XML. It's obviously easier to parse and to represent internally than HTML, but when is it useful to take advantage of those characteristics? One use for XML that's already been mentioned is for providing multiple views of data. In effect, the XML document defines the data model, and you can create more than one view of that model based upon the needs of your application. We'll examine this capability more in-depth later in the chapter when we discuss the **eXtensible Stylesheet Language** (**XSL**), and specifically, **eXtensible Stylesheet Language for Transformations (XSLT)**, which allows you to transform an XML document's content into some other form such as HTML or another XML document.

Another significant application of XML is for representing data that is to be transferred between different applications. Since XML describes data and is easy to parse but is not tied to a particular programming language, it allows you to transfer information between applications easily in a platform and language independent way. In fact, it is often said that just as Java provides interoperability across platforms for programmatic code, XML provides the same type of interoperability for data. Many relational database products now incorporate XML support.

An important variation of this is the use of XML for businesses to submit various types of electronic documents to one another such as purchase orders, invoices, etc. In the past, the preferred technology for doing this was Electronic Document Interchange (EDI) and the X12 standards. X12 defines a number of electronic documents and a specific format for each one, and it is used by many organizations. However, those documents are somewhat inflexible and complex, and EDI has not been as widely adopted as many had predicted. In contrast, XML allows companies to easily create their own formats for electronic documents that can be changed without requiring the company's business partners (or a standards organization) to first update their application code, as XSLT provides an easy means for data to be transformed to and from an agreed standardized DTD or Schema understood by all parties.

One common use of XML is for creating configuration files. In the early days of Windows, it was common for applications to create and use their own initialization (.ini) file containing configuration information. Although simple to implement and easy to edit, those files are somewhat restrictive, and have been largely abandoned by Windows applications in favor of the Windows registry, which contains a hierarchical collection of configuration information, allowing each application to reference values stored in its "branch" of the registry tree:

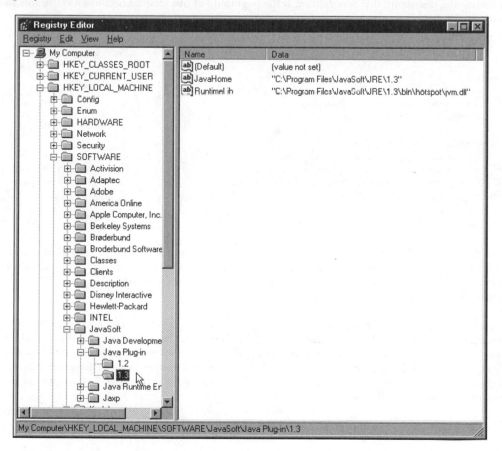

Since an XML document represents a collection of hierarchical data, it is a good candidate for the type of configuration information that's stored in the Windows registry. In fact, version 1.1 of the Enterprise JavaBeans specification requires **deployment descriptors** to be written in XML instead of the serialized object representation required by the 1.0 specification. A deployment descriptor is essentially a configuration file that describes how an Enterprise JavaBean is to be used and includes information such as which users are allowed to access the bean and their associated privileges.

While the serialized object approach was very convenient for the Enterprise JavaBeans server, it complicates the editing of the deployment descriptor by users. However, since XML is both human-readable and can be parsed easily, it provides a format that's convenient for both humans and software. Similarly Java-based web applications using servlets and JavaServer Pages use an XML deployment descriptor for configuration.

Creating an XML Document

Although the creation and editing of XML documents is currently done primarily with simple text editor/word processor applications, it's very easy to create a new document. Aside from the requirement that it be well-formed, there are almost no restrictions on what an XML document must contain. However, let's review the document that was defined at the beginning of this chapter because it illustrates some important points:

```
<?xml version="1.0" ?>

<book>
  <title>Professional Java Programming</title>
  <author>Brett Spell</author>
  <publisher>Wrox Press</publisher>

  <tableOfContents showPageNumbers="Yes">
    <tocEntry>Printing</tocEntry>
    <tocEntry>Cut and Paste</tocEntry>
    <tocEntry>Drag and Drop</tocEntry>
  </tableOfContents>

</book>
```

Unlike the rest of the file, the first line does not describe the data in the document. Instead, it is a **processing instruction**; processing instructions can be used to provide special information to applications that process the document's contents in some way. In this case, the instruction identifies the file as an XML document and specifies which version of XML was used to create the document.

Although only the `version` attribute is specified in this example, the instruction actually supports two other attributes: `encoding` and `standalone`. As its name implies, `encoding` indicates which character set was used to construct the document, while `standalone` (which must be assigned a value of "yes" or "no") indicates whether the document contains references to other files. For example, a file that does not contain external references and that was created using the UTF-8 character set might contain the following instruction:

```
<?xml version="1.0" encoding="UTF-8" standalone="yes" ?>
```

Root Elements

One other point to make concerning the structure of an XML document is that it must have only one element at the outermost level, known as the **root element**. In the document above, the <book> element contains all of the other data elements, and only the <?xml> processing instruction lies outside that element, so <book> is the root element. Since there may only be one root element, it would not be valid, for example, to include another element at the same level in the document as in the following listing:

```
<?xml version="1.0" ?>

<book>
  <title>Professional Java Programming</title>
...
</book>
```

```
<tableOfContents>
...
</tableOfContents>
```

In general, the prolog (the part of an XML document before the root element's start tag) consists of an optional <?xml> declaration, zero or more comments, processing instructions, and whitespace characters, followed by an optional Document Type Declaration (see later).

Components of an XML Document

Like HTML, XML allows you to use elements (with or without attributes) within the root element, and those elements can contain text or other elements. For example, the `<tableOfContents>` element contains a `showPageNumber` attribute with a value of `"Yes"`, together with three other elements, each of which contains text data:

```
<tableOfContents showPageNumbers="Yes">
   <tocEntry>Printing</tocEntry>
   <tocEntry>Cut and Paste</tocEntry>
   <tocEntry>Drag and Drop</tocEntry>
</tableOfContents>
```

Empty elements are valid in XML, so both of the following elements are acceptable:

```
<exampleElement></exampleElement>
```

and:

```
<exampleElement/>
```

XML also allows you to specify comments within your documents in the same way that you do within HTML:

```
<!-- This is a comment -->
<title>Professional Java Programming</title>
<author>Brett Spell</author>
<publisher>Wrox Press</publisher>
```

XML also supports CDATA ("character data") sections, which are portions of the document that are never parsed. The beginning of such a section is identified by `<![CDATA[` and terminated with `]]>`; Everything between those character sequences is ignored by an XML parser:

```
<title>Professional Java Programming</title>
<![CDATA[
The <title> element identifies the title of this book. I can put open tags
without close tags (or vice versa) here because this entire block will be
ignored by XML parsers.
]]>
<author>Brett Spell</author>
<publisher>Wrox Press</publisher>
```

On the surface, it may appear that a CDATA section is functionally identical to a comment, but there's an important difference. Some parsers may examine the text in a comment block, and although the text is generally ignored using reserved characters (for example, <, >, and &) in a comment may cause the parser to fail. However, the information in a CDATA block is always ignored by a parser, so you can include literally any information between the <! [CDATA[and]]> delimiters without affecting the parsing of the document. In fact, you can even include text that would normally be interpreted as XML tags without being concerned about the parser attempting to parse and validate the information.

Defining a Grammar Through a DTD

Any document that does not violate the four guidelines described earlier is considered well-formed, but in the context of XML it means something else entirely to say that a document is **valid**.

It is often useful to define the set of elements that can be used within a document (or within a group of documents) and to define the way in which those tags may be used. Such a set of rules is referred to as the document "grammar", and most XML parsers allow you to ensure that a document follows those rules (in other words, that the document is "valid").

By defining the set of tags, and the relationships between those tags, we make two things possible. Firstly, we can validate that information to check that all required information is present to make the data complete and that no extraneous information is present. Secondly, we also make it possible for consumers of the data, such as a third party or another department to process that information by describing what data is present and the format the information is in.

To define a grammar, you must create a **Document Type Definition** (**DTD**), a set of instructions that specify what elements are allowed in the document, what they can contain and what attributes they may have, and in what order they are allowed to occur.

Where to Define a DTD

Although it's technically possible to include a DTD in the document that it defines, it's not normally a good idea to do so. This is only advisable where we know the document is the only one of its kind. As you can imagine the likelihood of this is very small, it is much more likely that we will have multiple document of the same format. In this case, you should create a separate file for the DTD. This prevents the DTD from being coupled to a specific document.

As mentioned earlier, however, the purpose of the DTD is to allow an XML parser to ensure that a document is valid (as defined by the DTD), so there must be some way to associate a document with a DTD. This is done using the DOCTYPE declaration, which requires that you specify the following values:

❑   The name of the root element to which the DTD is to be applied, such as book

❑   Either SYSTEM or PUBLIC, the meanings of which will be defined shortly

❑   A URI that identifies the location from which the DTD can be loaded

For example, suppose that the DTD for the previously constructed booktest.xml XML document is stored in a file named book.dtd on the local hard drive in a subdirectory called /dtds. In that case, an XML document might contain a DOCTYPE instruction like the one shown opposite:

```
<?xml version="1.0" ?>
<!DOCTYPE book SYSTEM "./dtds/book.dtd">

<book>
```

In this case, only the DTD's **system identifier** (./dtds/book.dtd) was specified, although you can also include a **public identifier** using the PUBLIC keyword. The system identifier represents a URI that describes the "physical" location of the DTD, while a public identifier is essentially a name that an XML parser may be able to use to locate the DTD. When a DTD is well recognized, it is possible that software will have a local copy of it; the public keyword specifies the identifier for the DTD.

Of course, well recognized is a relative term; therefore, the XML specification allows us to also include the physical location where the DTD may be found. This allows programs to make optimizations by saving the round trip to the server to retrieve the DTD if it is available locally.

Public identifiers are not discussed in detail in this chapter, but an example of how one might be used appears below:

```
<?xml version="1.0" ?>
<!DOCTYPE html PUBLIC "-//W3C//DTD XHTML 1.0 Transitional//EN"
                "http://www.w3.org/TR/xhtml1/DTD/xhtml1-transitional.dtd">
```

Defining Elements

In DTDs, the ELEMENT tag is used to declare an element, and consists of the ELEMENT keyword, the name of the element, and a content specification. The element name can contain letters, digits, and the colon (:), underscore (_), hyphen (-), and period (.) characters. It must start with a letter, underscore, or colon.

The content specification for the element describes what sort of content may occur between the element's start and end tags, and falls into four categories:

- ❑ **Empty:** the element may not have any content
- ❑ **Element:** the element may contain specified child elements
- ❑ **Mixed:** the element may contain a mixture of child elements and parsed character data (#PCDATA)
- ❑ **Any:** the element may contain any well-formed content

"Empty" and "any" content are declared using the EMPTY and ANY keywords:

```
<!ELEMENT SomeData  EMPTY>
<!ELEMENT AnyOldThing  ANY>
```

You may want to specify an element as an empty element if it has no reason for content. For example, you should recall the earlier discussion of the <img> tag used by HTML and the fact that all of the information needed by that element is included inside the start tag's attributes. When you want to prevent the document author from embedding information between the open and close tags of an element, you can specify that using the EMPTY keyword on the element definition as shown below:

```
<!ELEMENT myEmptyElementType #EMPTY>
```

With this definition for the myEmptyElementType, the following represent valid uses of that element:

```
<book>
  <myEmptyElementType/>
  <!-- ... -->
  <myEmptyElementType></myEmptyElementType>
</book>
```

However, it would *not* be valid to put data between the start and end tags as shown below:

```
<myEmptyElementType>Hello world</myEmptyElementType>
```

Element and mixed content, however, are declared using a **content model** that describes the internal structure of the element's content. For example, to create a DTD that allows a <book> to contain <title>, <author>, and <publisher> elements, you could code the following:

```
<!ELEMENT book (title, author, publisher)>
```

This entry indicates that a <book> consists of exactly one <title>, one <author>, and one <publisher> in that order. We must also define each of these elements. If each of those elements must contain text data (for example, "Professional Java Programming" between the <title> and </title> tags), you might define them as shown below. #PCDATA is derived from "parsed character data", and indicates that any arbitrary text can appear:

```
<!ELEMENT book (title, author, publisher)>
<!ELEMENT title (#PCDATA)>
<!ELEMENT author (#PCDATA)>
<!ELEMENT publisher (#PCDATA)>
```

In the example above, there must be exactly one of each of the three elements contained within a <book>, but it's often possible for the number of elements to vary. For example, if you wish to specify that a book can have zero or more authors, this could be expressed in the DTD by placing an asterisk (*) character after the element reference:

```
<!ELEMENT book (title, author*, publisher)>
<!ELEMENT title (#PCDATA)>
<!ELEMENT author (#PCDATA)>
<!ELEMENT publisher (#PCDATA)>
```

Given this modified version of the DTD, the following would represent a valid <book> element (note the presence of multiple <author> elements):

```
<book>
  <title>Professional Java Programming</title>
  <author>Brett Spell</author>
  <author>George Gongo</author>
  <publisher>Wrox Press</publisher>
</book>
```

You would probably decide that a book must have at least one author. In that case, you could use the plus sign (+) instead of the asterisk. This characters specifies that one or more <author> tags be present:

```
<!ELEMENT book (title, author+, publisher)>
<!ELEMENT title (#PCDATA)>
<!ELEMENT author (#PCDATA)>
<!ELEMENT publisher (#PCDATA)>
```

Finally, the question mark (?) indicates that an element can occur at most one time (either it does not occur at all or it occurs only once). If you wanted to specify that a book has either no publisher or a single publisher, you might make the following change:

```
<!ELEMENT book (title, author, publisher?)>
<!ELEMENT title (#PCDATA)>
<!ELEMENT author (#PCDATA)>
<!ELEMENT publisher (#PCDATA)>
```

The use of these characters is summarized in the following table:

Character	Number of Times Element can Occur
* (asterisk)	Zero or more
+ (plus sign)	One or more
? (question mark)	Zero or one

Using this information, we can complete the DTD for our <book> element by defining a <tableOfContents> element that contains one or more <tocEntry> elements:

```
<!ELEMENT book (title, author, publisher, tableOfContents)>
<!ELEMENT title (#PCDATA)>
<!ELEMENT author (#PCDATA)>
<!ELEMENT publisher (#PCDATA)>
<!ELEMENT tableOfContents (tocEntry+)>
<!ELEMENT tocEntry (#PCDATA)>
```

Using Parentheses

Note that up to this point, the "repeat" characters have been appended to the names of the tags they're associated with and are included inside the parenthesis. However, you can also use the characters outside the parenthesis to indicate that a sequence of elements can, or must be, repeated. For example, suppose that the definition of the <tableOfContents> element is expanded so that it consists of pairs of <tocEntry> and <pageNumber> elements:

```
<tableOfContents>
  <tocEntry>Printing</tocEntry> <pageNumber>123</pageNumber>
  <tocEntry>Cut &amp; Paste</tocEntry> <pageNumber<456</pageNumber>
  <tocEntry>Drag &amp; Drop</tocEntry> <pageNumber>789</pageNumber>
</tableOfContents>
```

In other words, it is actually a *pair* of elements that should be repeated one or more times instead of a single element as defined in the DTD above. In this case the definition can be easily modified to accommodate this new grammar, as shown below. Note the presence of the plus sign outside the parenthesis instead of immediately adjacent to an element name:

```
<!ELEMENT book (title, author, publisher, tableOfContents)>
<!ELEMENT title (#PCDATA)>
<!ELEMENT author (#PCDATA)>
<!ELEMENT publisher (#PCDATA)>
<!ELEMENT tableOfContents (tocEntry, pageNumber)+>
<!ELEMENT tocEntry (#PCDATA)>
<!ELEMENT pageNumber (#PCDATA)>
```

Using the Vertical Bar Character

Up until now, it has been assumed that elements in an XML document always follow sequentially. For example, a <book> contains a <title>, which is followed by an <author>, and that element is in turn followed by a <publisher> element. In practice, however, it's more common to allow a given element to be followed by one of several possible other elements. You may want to allow a <title> to be followed by an <author> *or* a <publisher> or some entirely new type of element such as an <overview>.

Fortunately, it is possible to specify this type of rule using a DTD, and an example of how it might be done appears below. Note that the vertical bar (|) is used to indicate that one element or another can appear in a given position:

```
<!ELEMENT book (title, (author | publisher | tableOfContents | overView))>
```

Given this modified DTD definition, each of the following represents a valid <book> element:

```
<book>
  <title>Professional Java Programming</title>
  <author>Brett Spell</author>
</book>
```

or:

```
<book>
  <title>Professional Java Programming</title>
  <publisher>Wrox Press</publisher>
</book>
```

or:

```
<book>
  <title>Professional Java Programming</title>
  <tableOfContents showPageNumbers="yes">
    <tocEntry>Printing</tocEntry>
    <tocEntry>Cut &amp;Paste</tocEntry>
    <tocEntry>Drag &amp; Drop</tocEntry>
  </tableOfContents>
</book>
```

Defining Element Attributes

In addition to using a DTD to specify which elements can appear and in what order they may occur, you can also indicate which attributes can be used with those elements. For example, if you wish to allow a `<tableOfContents>` element to contain an attribute named `showPageNumbers` that has a default value of `"yes"`, you could make the following addition:

```
<!ELEMENT book (title, author, publisher, tableOfContents)>
<!ELEMENT title (#PCDATA)>
<!ELEMENT author (#PCDATA)>
<!ELEMENT publisher (#PCDATA)>
<!ELEMENT tableOfContents (tocEntry, pageNumber)+>
<!ATTLIST tableOfContents showPageNumbers CDATA "yes">
<!ELEMENT tocEntry (#PCDATA)>
<!ELEMENT pageNumber (#PCDATA)>
```

Note that while PCDATA (which is used for element definitions) refers to *parsed* character data, CDATA simply indicates that the attribute supports character data. In other words, the text located between elements' start and end tags is parsed, because other elements can be embedded within that text. However, the value of an attribute is not parsed because it does not contain any embedded information relevant to the structure of the XML document.

ATTLIST defines an attribute. It takes as parameters, the element that this attribute belongs to, the name of the attribute, its contents, and any default value.

It's possible to specify multiple attributes in a single attribute definition, so that if the tableOfContents element supported an additional entry called showSections, the above entry might be modified slightly:

```
<!ATTLIST tableOfContents showPageNumbers CDATA "yes" showSections CDATA
"no">
```

Since white space is ignored, attributes are often placed on separate lines with each parameter aligned with those of the other attributes as shown below. This approach is functionally identical to the above entry, but represents a more readable format.

```
<!ATTLIST tableOfContents  showPageNumbers  CDATA  "yes"
                           showSections     CDATA  "no">
```

The #FIXED, #REQUIRED, and #IMPLIED Keywords

If you wish to prevent the default attribute value you specify from being overridden by the creator of an XML document specifying a different value, you can precede the value with #FIXED in your DTD as shown below:

```
<!ATTLIST tableOfContents showPageNumbers CDATA #FIXED "yes">
```

On the other hand, if you want to force the creator to specify a value for the attribute, you can use the #REQUIRED keyword. Note that since the document writer must specify a value for the attribute, a default value is not meaningful and therefore is not included:

```
<!ATTLIST tableOfContents showPageNumbers CDATA #REQUIRED>
```

Sometimes a default value for an element is not meaningful and whether the author needs to specify a value is dependant on the use of the document. In this case you can use the #IMPLIED keyword.

Specifying #IMPLIED indicates that some default value is implied by the absence of an explicit value, but that the default should be selected by the software processing the document instead of the document author or DTD creator:

```
<!ATTLIST tableOfContents showPageNumbers CDATA #IMPLIED>
```

The use of the #FIXED, #REQUIRED, and #IMPLIED keywords is summarized in the following table:

Keyword	Meaning	Default Value in DTD
#FIXED	The attribute cannot be specified in the document; it always has the default value given in the DTD	Must be specified
#REQUIRED	A value must be specified in the document; there cannot be a default value	Must not be specified
#IMPLIED	There is no default value, but use of the attribute in the document is optional	Must not be specified

Attribute Types

CDATA allows any arbitrary text to be specified by the creator of an XML document unless the #FIXED keyword is specified for the attribute's value. There are, however, several other attribute types; the available types are summarized in the table below:

Attribute Type	Meaning
CDATA	Character data (a string)
ID	A name unique within the document – the value must follow the rules for names in XML, and the attribute must be #IMPLIED or #REQUIRED
IDREF	Reference to an element with an ID attribute with the same value as this IDREF attribute
IDREFS	A series of IDREFs, separated by white space
ENTITY	The name of a predefined external entity
ENTITIES	A series of ENTITY names separated by white space
NMTOKEN	A name – the value must be composed as per element names, except that it may start with any allowed character
NMTOKENS	A series of NMTOKENs separated by whitespace
NOTATION	The value must be one of a set of names indicating notation types declared in the DTD
Enumerated values	The value must be one of a series of user-defined values specified in the DTD – see below

If you wish to specify a list of valid values, you should use an enumerated type, to specify the values that are acceptable for an attribute. For example, if valid values for an attribute named `userResponse` are `"yes"`, `"no"`, and `"cancel"` (and the default is `"no"`), you can represent this rule with the following entry:

```
<!ATTLIST userResponse (yes|no|cancel) "no">
```

Entities

Before leaving the topic of DTDs, it's important to examine how entities are defined and used. An entity represents some piece of information that can be embedded within an XML document or a DTD – they associate a name with some other document fragment.

Each entity is either an **internal entity** or an **external entity**. The value of an internal entity is defined explicitly inside the DTD, while the data associated with an external entity is stored separately from the DTD, usually in a file on a local drive or on the network.

Entities are also classified based on whether they are defined for use within the DTD (**parameter entities**) or in XML documents (**general entities**), and each entity must be one or the other but cannot be both. In fact, the syntax for defining a parameter entity is slightly different from that of a general entity, as is the notation used to reference them in a DTD or XML document.

Internal Entities

Internal entities are defined by creating `<!ENTITY>` entries in the DTD and by specifying a name and value for each entity. As the following examples illustrate, the definition of a parameter entity differs from that of a general entity only in that a percent sign (%) is specified before a parameter entry's name:

```
<!-- The following is an example of a general entity definition, for use
     in the document itself -->
<!ENTITY currentYear "2000">

<!-- The following is an example of a parameter entity definition, for use
     within the DTD -->
<!ENTITY % yesNoCancel "(yes|no|cancel)">
```

Since the values of both of these entities (`"2000"` and `"(yes|no|cancel)"`) are defined in the DTD, they are examples of internal entities. Defining an external entity is slightly more complex, and is discussed later in the chapter.

Creating Internal Entity References

Once we have defined them, entity references are simple to use, although again there is a minor difference between general entity references and parameter entity references. To reference a general entity reference, simply precede the name of the entity with an ampersand (&) character and follow it with a semicolon (;):

```
<tocEntry>Year &currentYear; summary</tocEntry>
```

Parameter entity references are very similar, but use the percent sign (%) instead of the ampersand. In the following example, an entity named `yesNoCancel` has been defined and is referenced in an attribute list entry in a DTD:

```
<!ATTLIST response %yesNoCancel; "cancel">
```

Using Internal Entity References

Entities are often used as simple substitution parameters that allow you to embed references to an entity in a document and have those references automatically replaced with the entity's value when the document is processed. We already saw an example of this previously where the ampersand (&) character was embedded within an XML document using a special sequence that represents that character (&). That was nothing more than a reference to an entity named amp which has been assigned a value of &, and when the document was processed each entity reference was replaced with the entity's actual value.

It is possible to use entities to define sophisticated entities that can be used repeatedly throughout your DTD. For example, suppose that you define a set of attributes that are shared by many of the elements described in the DTD. Instead of putting multiple copies of those attributes inside the DTD, you could define an entity like the one shown below and reference it in the attribute entries that follow:

```
<!ENTITY % sharedAttrs
"fontName   CDATA   #IMPLIED
 fontSize   CDATA   #IMPLIED
 color      CDATA   #IMPLIED"
 >
```

Given this entity definition, you might code the following two attribute list definitions:

```
<!ATTLIST textInfo %sharedAttrs; alignment (left|center|right) "left">

<!ATTLIST introduction %sharedAttrs;>
```

Since the reference to the sharedAttrs entity will effectively be replaced with its value, the above entries are equivalent to the following:

```
<!ATTLIST textInfo
   fontName   CDATA           #IMPLIED
   fontSize   CDATA           #IMPLIED
   color      CDATA           #IMPLIED
   alignment  (left,center,right)      "left">

<!ATTLIST introduction
   fontName   CDATA           #IMPLIED
   fontSize   CDATA           #IMPLIED
   color      CDATA           #IMPLIED>
```

External Entities

The discussion of entities up to this point has focused upon internal entities, which are entities with values defined inside the DTD, while external entities are those that have values stored in some external location. When you define an external entity, you must specify the entity's system identifier and you may choose to specify a public identifier. However, the simplest type of external entity definition consists of only a system identifier as shown below:

```
<!ENTITY % symbols SYSTEM "symbol.ent">
```

In this case, a parameter entity named symbols is defined and its value corresponds to the contents of a file named symbol.ent. To specify a public identifier in addition to the system identifier, you should use the PUBLIC keyword instead of SYSTEM and specify the public identifier before the system identifier as shown below:

```
<!ENTITY % symbols PUBLIC "-//W3C//ENTITIES XHTML symbols//EN" "symbol.ent">
```

Although it may not be apparent, this example illustrates what is probably the most common use of external parameter entities: including the contents of one DTD file inside another. To understand why this is useful, suppose that you wish to define some entity values that will be used in many different DTD files. To prevent duplication and for the sake of convenience, it would be helpful to define those values in a single file and include the file in each of the DTD files which need to reference the values. For example, let's assume that you've created a file named `myvalues.dtd` that contains the following entries:

```
<!ENTITY % yesNoCancel    "(yes|no|cancel)">
<!ENTITY % yesNo          "(yes|no)">
<!ENTITY % okCancel       "(ok|cancel)">
```

In addition, suppose that you're creating a new DTD file in which you wish to use the entity values defined in `myvalues.dtd`. Instead of copying those entity definitions into the new DTD, you can define an external entity that has a value equal to the contents of `myvalues.dtd` and then reference the entity in the new DTD as shown below:

```
<!ENTITY % types  "author | publisher | tableOfContents">
<!ENTITY % notes  "footnote | endnote">

<!-- The following line creates an external entity named "getValues" -->
<!ENTITY % getValues SYSTEM "myvalues.dtd">

<!-- Now pull the contents of "myvalues.dtd" into this file -->
<!-- In effect, this performs an "include" operation         -->
%getValues;

<!-- Other DTD information goes here -->
```

In other words, the above approach is functionally identical to the following:

```
<!ENTITY % types      "author | publisher | tableOfContents">
<!ENTITY % notes      "footnote | endnote">

<!ENTITY % yesNoCancel  "(yes|no|cancel)">
<!ENTITY % yesNo    "(yes|no)">
<!ENTITY % okCancel     "(ok|cancel)">

<!-- Other DTD information goes here -->
```

Note that this technique can be used with both parameter and general entities, so you can also use this approach to include one XML document inside another.

Embedding Binary Data in XML Documents

Using the technique just described, you can accomplish another task that's sometimes useful: embedding binary data in an XML document. In the above example, the external entity's value corresponded to the contents of a file that contained text information. However, you can just as easily create an entity that maps to a file containing some other type of data such as an image (for exmaple, GIF or JPEG) or audio file. Although there's no reason to do so for a parameter entity (since binary data isn't useful anywhere within a DTD), you may want to create a general entity that maps to a binary file. In effect, this allows you to embed any type of data within an XML document.

There is one important difference between including text and including binary data. When you include text, that text will often represent information that should be processed by parsers as part of the document in which it is included. In other words, from the parser's point of view, the included text appears to be part of the document that's processed. However, when you include binary content inside an XML document, it's obviously not useful to try to have a parser interpret the binary data as a collection of XML elements. In fact, doing so would almost certainly cause the parser to generate an error and fail to process the document. For this reason, it's possible to define external **unparsed entities** representing data that is ignored by parsers.

To create an unparsed entity, you must first add a NOTATION entry for the entity's data type to the DTD. Multiple entities can refer to a single notation/data type, but you should create a separate notation entry for each different type of data that's embedded within your documents. A notation entry consists of nothing more than a name and a public identifier for the notation, as shown below:

```
<!NOTATION gifImage PUBLIC "+//WROX//IMAGES Image types//EN">
```

Once a notation is defined, you can create an unparsed entity in the same way that you would a parsed entity, which is done by including the NDATA keyword and the name of the appropriate notation:

```
<!ENTITY logoImage SYSTEM "wroxlogo.gif" NDATA gifImage>
```

With these entries included in the DTD, you can create an XML document that contains one or more embedded images by creating references to the logoImage entity defined above:

```
<publisher>
  <publisherName>Wrox Press</publisherName>
  <publisherLogo>&logoImage;</publisherLogo>
</publisher>
```

Conditional Sections

One final thing you can do with DTDs is to instruct the parser either to include or to ignore a section of declarations. Conditional sections consist of <![, followed by either INCLUDE or IGNORE, followed by a block of declarations within square brackets, and a final]>, for example:

```
<![INCLUDE
  [<!ELEMENT WillBeIncluded (#PCDATA)>
   <!ATTLIST WillBeIncluded isInteresting (yes|no) #REQUIRED>
]]>
```

or

```
<![IGNORE
  [<!ELEMENT IsBoring (#PCDATA)>
]]>
```

Conditional sections are useful when used in conjunction with parameter entities that expand to either INCLUDE or IGNORE; which allows us, for example, to write a DTD which includes extra elements while we are debugging (maybe for logging purposes) while being easily switched over to exclude such elements in a production environment.

Schemas

Although DTDs are fairly comprehensive, they have one or two drawbacks. The first is that DTDs are not themselves XML compliant. In addition, there is limited type checking available in the DTD specification making it more difficult to check documents for type errors. The first problem is worth exploring further, why is the fact that DTDs are not XML compliant a problem?

Well, firstly, they are not extensible, and are therefore inflexible. In order to add or modify the document structure, a new DTD must be written. Secondly, programmatic processing of their metadata is difficult. It is possible to parse them of course; however, it is yet another specification to learn, and it would be handy to be able to apply XML knowledge to processing them. In addition, they are vulnerable to name collisions. We will see later what possible actions we can take to avoid name collisions; however, it is again limited. There is a requirement for specifying identity in a flexible way.

Finally, there is no way to express inheritance, and as XML is being used in programmatic situations where data is handled in an object-oriented way this can be another limitation.

An alternative way of defining document structure, contents and semantics has been proposed called **XML Schemas** and at the writing of this book, this specification has reached Candidate Recommendation. Unfortunately, schemas are out of scope for this book; to find out more refer to `http://www.w3.org/XML`.

Parsing and Validation

It has been mentioned before that one of XML's most important features is that it can be parsed and validated easily, but no mention has been made of how this can be done. In fact, XML parsers are available for free from a variety of sources, one of which is JavaSoft's **Java API for XML Parsing (JAXP)** technology. As of this writing, version 1.0.1 of JAXP is available for download at `http://java.sun.com/xml/`, and it includes classes and interfaces that allow you to easily parse, validate, and in some cases modify XML documents.

In other words, a class that is capable of parsing XML documents (a **parser**) may also be able to verify that those documents are valid (in which case it is called a **validating parser**). In addition, some parsers allow you to load a document into memory and modify its contents programmatically. However, the term "parser" is used here in a generic sense to refer to any software that is at least capable of parsing documents (interpreting their contents in a meaningful manner). The two main standards that have emerged for creating XML parsers are the **Simple API for XML (SAX)** and the **Document Object Model (DOM)**, and although these two technologies both define XML parsers, they do so in different ways and therefore have very different strengths and weaknesses:

- ❑ DOM was defined by the World Wide Web Consortium (W3C) and is the more powerful of the two technologies, allowing you to parse, validate, and update XML documents. DOM processing involves reading the entire document into memory, where it is maintained as a hierarchical collection of objects. By modifying that collection of objects you can change the structure and content of the document in memory, after which the updated document can be saved again to some external location.

- ❑ In contrast, SAX was created as a result of a mailing list discussion, and provides sequential, read-only access to the document's contents. In other words, SAX does not provide any facility for modifying a document, and it does not allow you to examine an arbitrary portion of the document (it does not provide "random access" to the document's contents).

Instead, it allows you to register various types of listeners with a parser and the parser will notify the appropriate listener for each portion of the document it processes. This approach is sometimes referred to as "event-based" because it treats each portion of the document as an event for which it sends a notification. Although some programmers may not find this approach intuitive, SAX is simple to use and has the advantage of not requiring that the entire document be loaded into memory at once. While that may not be a significant advantage for smaller documents, it can be a very important factor when processing extremely large XML files.

SAX processors are used in order to extract information from XML documents in a memory efficient way. By setting handlers for appropriate events, we are able to extract information relating to that event as the XML document is streamed past the parser. This contrasts with DOM where the entire document resides in memory. For the main, SAX parsers are used in any read-only operations relating to XML documents for their minimal use of system resources.

DOM, on the other hand, is used for the generation and manipulation of XML documents. As we can add elements, and manipulate the content and structure of XML documents, this is a very versatile, though memory intensive technique.

JavaSoft's JAXP download contains implementations of both SAX and DOM parsers, and we'll now examine the classes and interfaces associated with each and see how they can be used to process XML documents. Those classes and interfaces are divided into several different packages based partially upon the type of parser (SAX or DOM) each one is associated with and also based upon whether or not the class or interface represents proprietary code. In other words, the classes and interfaces that are part of the SAX or DOM standard are stored in separate packages (`org.xml.sax` and `org.w3c.dom`) from those that are specific to JAXP, which are found in `javax.xml.parsers`.

Note that in this chapter, "DOM" refers to W3C's DOM Level 1 recommendation, where a recommendation is simply a completed standard. As of this writing, the Level 3 DOM is still a works in progress, and Level 2 is now also a recommendation. As you might expect, each subsequent level adds functionality to the specification, but due to space constraints and a lack of completed specifications, only Level 1 is described here. For full details of DOM, see `http://www.w3.org/DOM/`. *Similarly, "SAX" refers to version 1.0 of the SAX standard, which is the version used by JAXP's current SAX parser implementation, although the SAX 2.0 specification is now available at* `http://www.megginson.com/SAX/index.html`.

Parsing with the SAX Implementation in JAXP

To create an instance of a SAX parser from the JAXP download, you must obtain an instance of `SAXParserFactory` and use that object to create an instance of a `SaxParser`, as shown below:

```
javax.xml.parsers.SAXParserFactory factory;
javax.xml.parsers.SAXParser parser;
// ...
factory = SAXParserFactory.newInstance();
parser = factory.newSAXParser();
```

If you're not familiar with the factory pattern, it may not be obvious why these classes are designed in such a way as to require two steps to create a parser instance. By forcing you to use the SAXParserFactory, instead of creating a new parser directly, this design makes it possible to have the factory generate instances of an entirely new class without requiring changes to your source code. In other words, the newSaxParser() method can return an instance of some other parser implementation (as long as the object is a SAXParser) without affecting this code.

A SAXParserFactory may create non-validating parsers by default, but you can request that it instead return instances of validating parsers by calling its setValidating() method as shown below:

```
factory = SAXParserFactory.newInstance();
factory.setValidating(true);
parser = factory.newSAXParser();
```

Although it may seem that a validating parser should always be used when one is available, that is not necessarily the case. Validation can be a relatively slow process, and in many instances, you'll already know that the document being parsed is valid. When that is the case and/or when performance is an important consideration for your application, you may choose to use a non-validating parser even when a validating version is available.

Parser

As suggested by the package in which they're located, both SAXParser and SAXParserFactory are specific to JavaSoft's SAX implementation and are not part of the SAX standard. However, SAXParser is little more than a thin wrapper around an implementation of Parser, an interface defined in org.xml.sax that *is* part of the SAX standard:

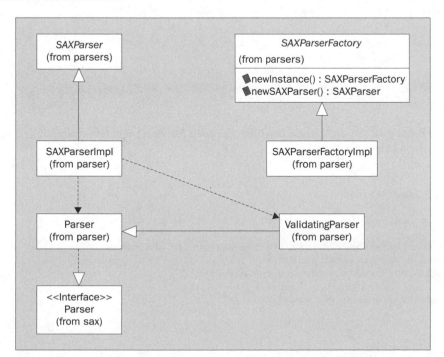

Since almost all of the relevant processing takes place in the methods defined by `Parser`, we will temporarily suspend our discussion of JavaSoft's `SAXParser` class and return to it later. In the meantime, it's helpful to examine the methods that `Parser` defines to understand how they're used.

The main method in the `Parser` interface is the `Parse()` method. Calling this method causes a `Parser` implementation to begin parsing the XML document, identified through the parameter value passed to it. The `parse()` method is overloaded and allows you to specify either an `InputSource` as a parameter or a `String` representing a URI. As mentioned above, you can create an instance of `InputSource` by passing an instance of `Reader` or `InputStream`, or by passing a `String` that represents a URI, and an example of each approach is provided below:

```java
import java.io.*;
import javax.xml.parsers.*;
import org.xml.sax.*;

public class SAXTest {

  public static void main(String[] args) throws Exception {
    org.xml.sax.InputSource source;
    String fileName = "D:/brett/temp/SaxTest.xml";

    // Create an InputSource using an InputStream (specifically,
    // a FileInputStream)
    FileInputStream inputStream = new FileInputStream(fileName);
    source = new InputSource(inputStream);
    // Create an InputSource using a Reader (specifically, a FileReader)
    FileReader reader = new FileReader(fileName);
    source = new InputSource(reader);
    // Create an InputSource by specifying a URI/system identifier
    source = new InputSource("file://localhost/" + fileName);

    // ...

  }
}

// ...
```

Once you've created an `InputSource` that identifies the XML document, you can call the `parse()` method to cause it to begin parsing:

```java
// ...
public class SAXTest {

  public static void main(String[] args) throws Exception {
    // ...
    SAXParserFactory factory = SAXParserFactory.newInstance();
    factory.setValidating(true);
    SAXParser parser = factory.newSAXParser();

    parser.parse(source, new MyHandler());
  }
}
```

```
class MyHandler extends HandlerBase {
  // ...
}
```

The above examples of how to create an InputSource assumed that the file to be parsed was located on the local hard drive. However, since a URI allows you to also specify files that are stored in a remote network location, the additional implementation of the parse() method is provided for convenience.

The parser allows you to receive notifications as it processes each portion of an XML document, but we must first register a listener for these events, which we can do using the setDocumentHandler() method.

This method is passed a reference to an implementation of DocumentHandler, an interface defined in the org.xml.sax package. The DocumentHandler interface defines the notification methods that are called.

In addition we can listen for errors, registering an error handler using the following method, setErrorHandler(). An implementation of the ErrorHandler interface is passed to this method, and just as the parser notifies a DocumentHandler as it scans the document content, the ErrorHandler receives notification of any errors that occur. Like DocumentHandler, ErrorHandler is defined in org.xml.sax.

However, to examine the document's contents and to handle errors that may occur, you will need to be familiar with DocumentHandler and ErrorHandler, both of which we will discuss in just a moment.

Before we do that, we will look at the last three methods provided in this interface setLocale(), setDTDHandler() and setEntityResolver().

As its name implies, setLocale(), allows you to specify the Locale that should be used for messages generated during the parsing of a document. If the Parser implementation does not support the Locale specified, this method will throw a SAXException. Applications must not call this method during parsing.

setDTDHandler() is passed an object that implements the DTDHandler interface defined in org.xml.sax. That interface defines two methods called notationDecl() and unparsedEntityDecl() which are called when the parser encounters notation and unparsed entity references in a DTD. You should recall that notations are used to define data types, and that unparsed entities are simply embedded binary data of some specific type. The DTDHandler methods are each passed the notation's name, public identifier, system identifier, and (in the case of unparsedEntityDecl()) the entity's name when NOTATION and unparsed ENTITY entries are encountered in a DTD.

Finally, setEntityResolver() is called with an object that implements the EntityResolver interface, which defines a single method called resolveEntity() called before the parser attempts to retrieve the value of an external entity. The entity's public and system identifiers are passed to resolveEntity(), which returns an instance of InputSource, a class defined in org.xml.sax.

As its name implies, an InputSource is simply an object that provides access to some information, which in this case is the entity's value. InputSource constructors exist that allow you to pass a reference to a java.io.Reader, a java.io.InputStream, or a String that represents the entity's system identifier (for example, a URI).

If the application does not register an entity resolver, the SAX parser will resolve system identifiers and open connections to entities itself. It is rarely necessary to create an EntityResolver, since the parser will normally be able to locate the appropriate resource based on the entity's public and/or system identifier values, so this interface is not discussed in detail in this chapter.

The DocumentHandler Interface

As mentioned above, this interface defines the methods that are called by a SAX parser as it processes each item in an XML document. This is the main interface that most SAX applications implement; the parser calls this instance's methods to report basic document-related events.

The methods defined in this interface include the `startDocument()` and `endDocument()` methods, which are called once at the beginning and end of the document respectively. These methods give you an opportunity to perform any initialization that's needed before the parser generates messages (method calls) related to the document's content, and to perform any cleanup needed by your application when parsing has completed. Such cleanup may include closing files or network connections, releasing resources, etc.

The `startElement()` is called each time a parser encounters a start tag for an element in the document being processed, and is passed a reference to the element's name and an `AttributeList` object that encapsulates its attribute values.

> *If the element name has a namespace prefix (discussed later), the prefix will still be attached to the name passed to this method.*

`AttributeList`, like the other interfaces discussed in this section, is defined in the `org.xml.sax` package and includes a method called `getLength()` that returns an integer value of the number of attributes defined for the element. In addition, `AttributeList` provides the `getName()`, `getType()`, and `getValue()` methods that allow you to access the elements explicitly specified attribute name, type, and value respectively, where an attribute's "type" is a `String` name such as "CDATA", "ENTITY", or "NOTATION". `#IMPLIED` attributes are omitted.

To illustrate how `startElement()` can be used to handle the parsing of elements, suppose that you have defined the following XML file:

```xml
<?xml version="1.0"?>

<rootElement>
  <firstNested someAttr="Hello" anotherAttr="Howdy"/>
  <secondNested>This is a test</secondNested>
</rootElement>
```

In addition, let's assume that you create a `startElement()` implementation like the one shown below. It obtains the number of attributes in each element, displays that number along with the attribute's name, and prints the characteristics of each attribute:

```java
// ...

class MyHandler extends HandlerBase {

    public void startElement(String name, AttributeList attrs) {
        int count = attrs.getLength();
        System.out.println("Processing element '" +
                            name + "' with " +
                            count +  " attributes");
        for (int i = 0; i < count; i++) {
            System.out.println("Attribute name='" + attrs.getName(i) +
                                "', type='" + attrs.getType(i) +
```

```
                              "', value='" + attrs.getValue(i) + "'");
        }
    System.out.println();
  }

}
```

Given the above XML document and the `startElement()` implementation just defined, the output produced by parsing the document is shown below:

    Processing element 'rootElement' with 0 attributes

    Processing element 'firstNested' with 2 attributes
    Attribute name='someAttr', type='CDATA', value='Hello'
    Attribute name='anotherAttr', type='CDATA', value='Howdy'

    Processing element 'secondNested' with 0 attributes

There is also a corresponding `endElement()` method. Note that every call to `startElement()` will result in a corresponding call to `endElement()`, even if the element being parsed is empty. In other words, the following element would result in a call to both `startElement()` and this method:

```
<myEmptyElement/>
```

As with `startElement()`, any namespace prefix will still be attached to the element name.

processingInstruction()

Each time a SAX parser encounters a processing instruction in the XML document, it calls this method and passes the information contained within the instruction. Note that although an XML declaration like the one shown below is a processing instruction, it does not result in this method being invoked:

```
<?xml version="1.0" ?>
```

However any other instructions in the document will result in a call to `processingInstruction()`. When `processingInstruction()` is called, it is passed two `String` parameters. The first parameter is the **instruction target**, which is the string that immediately follows the first question mark, and the second is the **instruction data**, which is the remainder of the text defined within the instruction. For example, suppose that you create and parse an XML document that contains the following:

```
<?xml version="1.0" ?>
<!-- ... -->

<?firstInstruction Hello world?>
<?secondInstruction?>
```

This document fragment contains three processing instructions, but as mentioned above, the XML declaration is effectively ignored by the parser, so the `processingInstruction()` method will only be invoked twice by the parser. The first time it is called, a value of `"firstInstruction"` will be passed for the target value and the instruction data will be equal to `"Hello world"`. Similarly, the second invocation will occur with a target value of `"secondInstruction"` and an empty `String` for the instruction data.

ignorableWhitespace()

As its name implies, this method may be called when the SAX parser encounters white space (for example, blank lines, tags, and spaces) that is not relevant to the document's content. This type of white space is generally added to make an XML document more readable, such as the indentations that are used to make the element hierarchy obvious and blank lines to separate groups of related elements. Contiguous blocks of white space may be returned as a single block, or may be split into a number of blocks.

Three parameters are passed to `ignorableWhitespace()` that allow you to determine the specific text data that makes up the white space: a character array, a starting index value, and a length value (both `int`s). The character array may contain "extra" data in addition to those characters that make up the white space, so you should use the starting index and length values to access only the appropriate data. For example, to obtain a `String` representation of the white space characters, you might create code like that shown below:

```
// ...

class MyHandler extends HandlerBase {
    public void ignorableWhitespace(char[] data, int start, int length) {
        String whitespace = new String(data, start, length);
        System.out.println("Whitespace: \"" + whitespace + "\"");
    }
}
```

Note that only validating parsers are required to call this method when they encounter white space, while non-validating parsers may alternately report through the `characters()` method.

characters()

This method notifies the `DocumentHandler` of any character data (text) that's parsed which does not correspond to one of the previously described types of information (for example, an element or processing instruction). For example, the text information found between an element's start and end tags may be passed to the `characters()` method, allowing the `DocumentHandler` to process that information appropriately. As mentioned earlier, white space may also be passed to this method by a non-validating parser, so your `DocumentHandler` should be able to ignore white space characters if you wish to omit them from its processing.

While it's often true that a collection of adjacent characters in an XML document will be passed in a single call to `characters()`, there is no guarantee that this will occur. It is considered acceptable for a parser to pass a given sequence of text to the `characters()` method in multiple "chunks" instead of passing the entire string in one call. To illustrate this point, you could use the following implementation of `characters()` which converts the unprintable characters (tab, carriage return, and linefeed) into printable text (for example, a tab character is converted to /t):

```
// ...

class MyHandler extends HandlerBase {

    public void characters(char[] data, int start, int length) {
        String text = replaceNonprintables(new String(data, start, length));
        System.out.println("Got characters '" + text + "'");
    }
}
```

```
    protected String replaceNonprintables(String text) {
      String[][] replacements = {{"\r", "\\r"},
                                 {"\n", "\\n"},
                                 {"\t", "\\t"}};
      char findChar;
      String replaceWith;
      int index;
      for (int i = 0; i < replacements.length; i++) {
        findChar = replacements[i][0].charAt(0);
        replaceWith = replacements[i][1];
        index = text.indexOf(findChar);
        while (index >= 0) {
          text = text.substring(0, index) + replaceWith +
                 text.substring(index + 1);
          index = text.indexOf(findChar);
        }
      }
      return text;
    }

  }
```

If this code is used to parse the XML file defined earlier in the discussion of `startElement()`, it will produce results similar to those shown below:

```
Got characters ''
Got characters '\n'
Got characters '\t'
Got characters ''
Got characters '\n'
Got characters '\t'
Got characters 'This is a test'
Got characters ''
Got characters '\n'
```

There are several points to be made concerning this output. First, notice that several calls to `characters()` are made with what amounts to an empty string (zero characters are identified as having been parsed). Second, although the linefeed and tab characters are adjacent to one another inside the document, each one is passed in a separate call to `characters()`. Finally, note that both white space (tabs and line feeds) and the text between start and end tags (`"This is a test"`) are passed to `characters()`, which indicates that the parser being used is a non-validating parser.

setDocumentLocator()

An object that implements the `Locator` interface may be passed to this method by the parser before it begins parsing a document. Once parsing begins, the `Locator` can be used by the `DocumentHandler` methods to determine which portion of the current document is being parsed. This is done using the `Locator`'s `getLineNumber()` and `getColumnNumber()` methods to retrieve the line and column position that were last processed. In addition, you can obtain the document's public and system identifiers by calling the `Locator`'s `getPublicId()` and `getSystemId()` methods.

Although the SAX specification recommends that parsers create and maintain a `Locator` (in which case it should use this method to pass a reference to your `DocumentHandler` implementation), it is not required that parsers do so. In other words, if you intend to use `setDocumentLocator()` you should check that the parser you are using supports a locator.

Indicating Errors During Parsing

Although it's common practice to leave enforcement of the document's structure and element content to a validating parser, you may want to perform additional validation on a document's data. For example, you might wish to compare the text between the start and end tags of some element to a list of valid values, which could be done by examining the text when it is passed to the characters() method. In addition, a situation can arise where some sort of error prevents you from completing the processing needed to perform the comparison.

In either case, you'll typically want to indicate that an error has occurred and that processing should be discontinued, and as is normally the case in Java, you can indicate this by throwing an exception. Although it was not mentioned previously, each of the methods in the previously described interfaces (except for setDocumentLocator()) is capable of throwing an instance of SAXException, which is described below. If you want your DocumentHandler to cause parsing to be stopped due to some error or other condition, simply have it throw a SAXException from the method that's responsible for detecting that condition.

SAXException

Like other exception classes, SAXException provides a constructor that can be passed a String representing a message that describes why the error occurred, and the message is accessible via the getMessage() method. However, SAXException also provides constructors that allow you to pass a reference to an Exception object instead of or in addition to a message string. This alternative is useful because it's common to throw a SAXException simply because some other exception occurred during your processing of the SAX parsing events.

In other words, SAXException can encapsulate not only a message but also a reference to another exception that caused your code to throw the SAXException. The subclass SAXParseException (covered shortly) can be used if it is necessary to include information about a specific location in the XML document. For example, the following code segment provides an example of how a RemoteException can be wrapped in a SAXException if a network error occurs during the processing of a startElement() message from the parser:

```
import java.rmi.*;
// ...

class MyHandler extends HandlerBase {

    public void startElement(String name, AttributeList attrs)
            throws SAXException {
      if (name.equals("doRemoteStuff")) {
        try {
          callMyRemoteMethod();
        } catch (RemoteException remote) {
          throw new SAXException("Error occurred on remote method call",
                                  remote);
        }
      }
    }

    public void callMyRemoteMethod() throws RemoteException {
      throw new RemoteException();
    }
}
```

ErrorHandler

The last SAX interface to be covered in this chapter is ErrorHandler, and it allows you to control how errors that occur during parsing are processed and to log those errors. When the parser determines that some type of error has occurred, it calls the appropriate method for the ErrorHandler instance that has registered an interest in such events. Depending upon the nature of the error that occurred, the parser may attempt to continue to parse the document, but you can throw a SAXException if you wish to ensure that parsing does not continue. Throwing an exception from one of the ErrorHandler methods will always cause parsing of the document to be stopped.

The method called will reflect the severity of the error that has occurred. warning() is called to indicate a relatively minor error that will not prevent the parser from continuing and may not even prevent the document from being parsed correctly.

The error() method is called if a serious problem is encountered to notify the ErrorHandler of the problem and allow it to determine whether parsing should be continued. An XML document that does not conform to the grammar defined in its associated DTD (an "invalid" document) is an example of the type of situation that will cause this method to be invoked.

As in the case of a warning, the parser will attempt to continue processing the document after calling your error() method unless that method throws a SAXException.

Finally, fatalError() will be called in case of a severe problem, such as finding that the document is not well-formed. The parser may or may not attempt to continue processing the document, but in most cases, a fatal error will cause parsing of a document to stop even if your fatalError() implementation does not throw an exception. If the parser does continue parsing the document it will only do so in order to note any consequent errors in the document.

SAXParseException

Each of the ErrorHandler methods just described is passed an instance of SAXParseException, which is a direct subclass of SAXException. In addition to the functionality provided by its superclass, SAXParseException encapsulates a reference to a Locator object or to the information available through such an object. In either case, SAXParseException provides the four methods defined below that allow you to retrieve information that describes the location of the document and the location within the document where the error was encountered:

Method Name	Return Value
getColumnNumber()	Column number where the error was encountered
getLineNumber()	Line number where the error was encountered
getPublicId()	Public identifier of file being parsed when the error occurred
getSystemId()	System identifier of file being parsed when the error occurred

HandlerBase

HandlerBase is a convenience class that implements the EntityResolver, DTDHandler, DocumentHandler, and ErrorHandler interfaces described above:

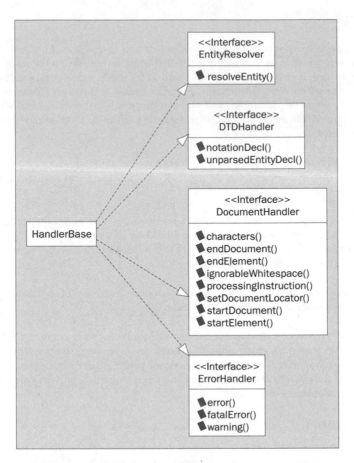

HandlerBase does not contain any useful functionality, but like AWT's adapter classes it can be convenient to use when you want to implement a subset of the methods in one or more of the four interfaces.

Since it provides "dummy" implementations for each of the methods defined in the four interfaces, you can create a HandlerBase subclass that includes only implementations of the methods that you're interested in using.

Using HandlerBase with SAXParser

Near the beginning of our discussion of parsing with SAX, we created some code that used the SAXParser class provided with the JAXP download. Now that we've examined the standard SAX classes and interfaces, it's possible to complete the discussion of how SAXParser is used. Recall that SAXParser maintains a reference to an object that implements Parser, and that both Parser and SAXParser define an overloaded parse() method. The parse() method in Parser only allows you to identify the document to be parsed, but the SAXParser implementation also allows you pass a reference to a HandlerBase object.

The SAXParser object delegates responsibility for parsing to the Parser object it maintains a reference to, but it only does so after registering the HandlerBase object as the listener of the four types of parsing events. This may be somewhat confusing given the similarity of the names, but it should be easier to understand by examining the following code segment, which is similar to the code found in SAXParser:

```
public class SAXParser {

  protected Parser parser;

  public void parse(InputSource is, HandlerBase hb) throws SAXException {
    if (hb != null) {
      parser.setDocumentHandler(hb);
      parser.setEntityResolver(hb);
      parser.setErrorHandler(hb);
      parser.setDTDHandler(hb);
    }
    parser.parse(is);
  }
}
```

SAX Parsing Example

We'll now see how to use the classes and interfaces that have been discussed to parse an XML document and print out the results.

To use the JAXP classes, you must add the appropriate JAR files to your classpath, specifically jaxp.jar (which contains the javax.xml.parser package) and parser.jar (which contains org.xml.sax and org.w3c.dom). You can now create an instance of SAXParser and pass it an InputSource or a String representing a URI, along with a reference to a HandlerBase object.

The following code provides an initial implementation of a Java application that allows you to specify a URI and passes it to an instance of Parser:

```
import javax.xml.parsers.*;
import org.xml.sax.*;

public class ParseTest {

  public static void main(String[] args) throws Exception {
    if ( args.length == 1) {
      ParseTest pt = new ParseTest(args[0]);
    } else {
      System.out.println("usage: parsetest <inputfile>");
    }
  }

  public ParseTest(String uri) throws Exception {
    SAXParserFactory factory = SAXParserFactory.newInstance();
    factory.setValidating(true);
    SAXParser parser = factory.newSAXParser();
    parser.parse(uri, new MyHandler());
  }

  class MyHandler extends HandlerBase {

    // ...

  }

}
```

Note that this class also contains an inner class called `MyHandler` that's a subclass of `HandlerBase`, although it currently does not override any of its inherited methods. However, we can cause `MyHandler` to simply echo the document information it receives to standard output by adding implementations for some of those methods. For example, `startElement()` and `endElement()` can be made to generate start and end tags for the elements that are parsed as shown below:

```
public void startElement(String name, AttributeList attrs) {
  System.out.print("<" + name);
  int count = attrs.getLength();
  for (int i = 0; i < count; i++) {
    System.out.print(" " + attrs.getName(i) + "=\"" +
                       attrs.getValue(i) + "\"");
  }
  System.out.print(">");
}

public void endElement(String name) {
  System.out.print("</" + name + ">");
}
```

It's also necessary to provide an implementation of `characters()` to ensure that text data that appears between start and end tags is displayed, and an example of how this might be implemented appears below:

```
public void characters(char[] data, int start, int length) {
  String text = new String(data, start, length);
  System.out.print(text);
}
```

Finally, to ensure that the appearance of the output is similar to that of the XML source file, we can also display any white space that the parser processes. The easiest way to do this is simply to pass the white space data to the `characters()` method just implemented, which can be done very easily because both methods have the same signature (expect the same type of parameters):

```
public void ignorableWhitespace(char[] data, int start, int length) {
  characters(data, start, length);
}
```

With this application completed, you can use it to parse a copy of the XML file defined at the beginning of this chapter. To do so, execute the `main()` method in `ParseTest`, passing it a URI that identifies the XML file to be parsed. In this case, the file is named `booktest.xml`, and if it's stored in the `C:/brett/temp` directory of the local hard drive, you would enter:

```
java ParseTest file:/C:/brett/temp/booktest.xml
```

When executed, the program displays output that is almost identical to the source file, although it does not include the XML identifier at the top of the file:

```
<book>
  <title>Professional Java Programming</title>
  <author>Brett Spell</author>
  <publisher>Wrox Press</publisher>
```

```
    <tableOfContents showPageNumbers="Yes">
      <tocEntry>Printing</tocEntry>
      <tocEntry>Cut and Paste</tocEntry>
      <tocEntry>Drag and Drop</tocEntry>
    </tableOfContents>
  </book>
```

Although DocumentHandler does include a method that is notified when processing instructions are encountered, creating an implementation of that method would not be helpful in this case. That's because as mentioned earlier, the <?xml> declaration is ignored by SAX parsers although it is technically a processing instruction.

Now, the example above is not entirely useful. All we have done with this ingenious program is to produce a not-quite-compliant copy of our XML file. I think you can see, however, that we can extract any required information from the file using a combination of handlers and conditional constructs. Queries can be executed against XML files in this way to extract required information much like database queries.

XML Validation Using a DTD

Now let's suppose that you wish to define the following DTD and have the parser use it to validate your document:

```
<!ELEMENT book (title, author, publisher, tableOfContents)>
<!ELEMENT title (#PCDATA)>
<!ELEMENT author (#PCDATA)>
<!ELEMENT publisher (#PCDATA)>
<!ELEMENT tableOfContents (tocEntry+)>
<!ATTLIST tableOfContents showPageNumbers CDATA "yes">
<!ELEMENT tocEntry (#PCDATA)>
```

To associate the XML document with this DTD, simply create a DOCTYPE instruction in the XML file as shown below. This assumes that the DTD is defined in a file called bookgram.dtd that is stored in the same directory as the XML document:

```
<?xml version="1.0" ?>
<!DOCTYPE book SYSTEM "./bookgram.dtd">

<book>
  <!-- ... -->
```

No errors will occur if you again execute the ParseTest application with this modified version of the XML file because the document is well-formed and conforms to the grammar rules defined in the DTD.

We can test out the validation, however, by making a change like the one shown below:

```
<?xml version="1.0" ?>
<!DOCTYPE book SYSTEM "./bookgram.dtd">

<book>
  <title>Professional Java Programming</title>
  <author>Brett Spell</author>
  <publisher>Wrox Press</publisher>
```

```
    <tableOfContents showPageNumbers="Yes">
      <tocEntry>Printing</tocEntry>
      <tocEntry>Cut and Paste</tocEntry>
      <badEntry>Drag and Drop</badEntry>
    </tableOfContents>
  </book>
```

If you rerun the application, however, you will still not see any indication that an error has occurred. Why is this? You should recall from our discussion of the ErrorHandler interface that while fatal errors may cause a parser to stop processing a document, warnings and errors do not – at least not automatically.

To force processing to stop (or even receive any indication that a problem occurred) when an invalid document is detected, you must create an implementation of the error() method of the ErrorHandler that's registered with the parser. In this case, an instance of the MyHandler inner class is used as the ErrorHandler implementation, so we must add the error() method to that class:

```
public void error(SAXParseException spe) throws SAXException {
  System.out.println();
  throw new SAXException(spe.getMessage());
}
```

If you compile and execute ParseTest again after adding the above method to the MyHandler class, the parse() method will throw an exception when the inappropriate tag is encountered and produce output like that shown below:

```
C:\brett\temp>java ParseTest file:/C:/brett/temp/booktest.xml
<book>
  <title>Professional Java Programming</title>
  <author>Brett Spell</author>
  <publisher>Wrox Press</publisher>

  <tableOfContents showPageNumbers="Yes">
    <tocEntry>Printing</tocEntry>
    <tocEntry>Cut and Paste</tocEntry>

Exception in thread "main" org.xml.sax.SAXException: Element
"tableOfContents" does not allow "badEntry" here.
        at ParseTest$MyHandler.error(ParseTest.java:48)
        at com.sun.xml.parser.Parser.error(Parser.java:2780)
        at com.sun.xml.parser.ValidatingParser$ChildrenValidator.consume
          (ValidatingParser.java:310)
        at com.sun.xml.parser.Parser.maybeElement(Parser.java:1280)
        at com.sun.xml.parser.Parser.content(Parser.java:1498)
        at com.sun.xml.parser.Parser.maybeElement(Parser.java:1399)
        at com.sun.xml.parser.Parser.content(Parser.java:1498)
        at com.sun.xml.parser.Parser.maybeElement(Parser.java:1399)
        at com.sun.xml.parser.Parser.parseInternal(Parser.java:491)
        at com.sun.xml.parser.Parser.parse(Parser.java:283)
        at javax.xml.parsers.SAXParser.parse(SAXParser.java:155)
        at javax.xml.parsers.SAXParser.parse(SAXParser.java:100)
        at ParseTest.<init>(ParseTest.java:18)
        at ParseTest.main(ParseTest.java:8)
```

Parsing with the DOM Implementation in JAXP

As described earlier, DOM is more powerful than SAX in some ways and can be more intuitive, especially if you're already familiar with hierarchical tree structures such as those used by Swing's JTree component. In fact, although there is no direct relationship between JTree and DOM, you may find it helpful to review Chapter 7 (which covers JTree in depth) since much of the terminology defined there relating to tree structures applies to DOM as well. In addition, DOM is provided for document creation and manipulation.

As we've seen, a SAX parser scans an XML document sequentially and reports the contents of the document through handler interfaces. In contrast, a DOM parser creates a collection of objects in memory that represents the document's contents. These objects are implementations of the interfaces defined in the org.w3c.dom package:

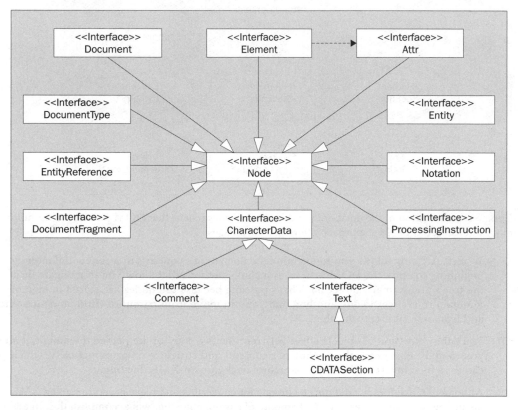

With a few exceptions, each interface represents some particular type of information found in an XML document, and using a hierarchical collection of these objects, DOM is able to create a structure that mimics the document's contents. For example, suppose that you process the following XML data with a DOM parser:

```
<tableOfContents showPageNumbers="Yes">
   <tocEntry>Printing</tocEntry>
   <tocEntry>Cut and Paste</tocEntry>
   <tocEntry>Drag and Drop</tocEntry>
</tableOfContents>
```

DOM would represent the `<tableOfContents>` element with an object that implements the `Element` interface. That object will contain a reference to a single `Attr` representing the `showPageNumbers` attribute. In addition, the `Element` object will contain a child node for each of the `<tocEntry>` items, and each of these will in turn contain a single `Text` node representing the text between the start and end tags of each element.

The figure below provides a simplified illustration of how this would appear, although it omits what can be an important detail – that nodes are also created for white space such as carriage returns, line feeds, tabs and spaces. It's possible in many cases to ignore the nodes that represent white space, although as we'll see later in the chapter, it's important to be aware of their existence:

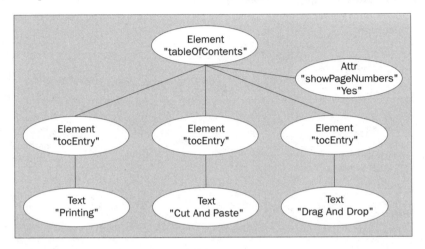

Creating a representation of the document in this manner does means that DOM parsers are far more memory intensive, but DOM's approach offers two advantages:

- While SAX only allows you to examine the document's contents in a sequential manner (from beginning to end), the DOM interfaces include methods that allow you to navigate through the tree's nodes in any direction. That's possible because the nodes are stored in memory and maintain references to one another, and you can move from parent to child (and vice versa) and from one sibling to another.

- Since the collection of objects effectively represents a copy of the parsed document, it allows you to make changes to the document's contents and structure programmatically, which you can save by converting the object structure back into an XML document.

  Although DOM does not define a technique for converting an object structure into an XML document, it's easy to create a small amount of custom code that will accomplish this. In addition, some DOM implementations (including the one provided with the JAXP download) provide proprietary mechanisms for converting a collection of objects back into an XML document.

The steps for creating an instance of the DOM parser implementation that's supplied with JAXP are almost identical to those associated with the SAX parser. Specifically, you must create an instance of a factory class, use the factory to create an instance of a parser object before calling its `parse()` method:

```
DocumentBuilderFactory factory = DocumentBuilderFactory.newInstance();
factory.setValidating(true);
DocumentBuilder builder = factory.newDocumentBuilder();
```

Like the SAXParserFactory and SAXParser classes, DocumentBuilderFactory and DocumentBuilder are not part of the DOM standard but are specific to JAXP and are defined in the javax.xml.parsers package. DocumentBuilder, like SAXParser, also provides a parse() method that accepts an instance of File, InputStream, InputSource, or a String representing a URI. Any of those objects can be passed to the method to identify the file to be parsed.

Unlike a SAX parser, the DOM equivalent does not use listeners and does not send any notifications as it parses the document, although it may throw an exception if an error occurs during parsing. Once that is done you can examine the document's contents using the following interfaces defined in org.w3c.dom.

The Node Interface

This interface is the superinterface of many of the other DOM interfaces, and, as you would expect, Node defines methods that are shared by many of the different types of objects used to represent portions of an XML document.

Using the methods defined in this interface, we can determine various things about the current node. The first of these methods, getNodeType() allows you to easily determine which type of XML document item is represented by this node. It returns a short value corresponding to one of the constants defined in Node listed in the table below:

Node Constant	Associated Interface Name
ATTRIBUTE_NODE	Attr
CDATA_SECTION_NODE	CDATASection
COMMENT_NODE	Comment
DOCUMENT_FRAGMENT_NODE	DocumentFragment
DOCUMENT_NODE	Document
DOCUMENT_TYPE_NODE	DocumentType
ELEMENT_NODE	Element
ENTITY_NODE	Entity
ENTITY_REFERENCE_NODE	EntityReference
NOTATION_NODE	Notation
PROCESSING_INSTRUCTION_NODE	ProcessingInstruction
TEXT_NODE	Text

The following code segment illustrates how you could use this method to determine what action to take for the document item a given Node represents:

```
protected void displayTree(Node node) {
   short nodeType = node.getNodeType();
   switch (nodeType) {
     case Node.DOCUMENT_NODE:
```

```
      printDocument((Document)node);
      break;
   case Node.ELEMENT_NODE:
      printElement((Element)node);
      break;
   case Node.TEXT_NODE:
      printText((Text)node);
      break;
   default:
   }
}
```

In addition to determining the type of node, we can also discover its name. The relevance of this varies from node to node; while an element has a name, a text node does not, and so the returned value will depend on the element's type. In cases where it is not meaningful to request the node's name, this will often describe the type of node; for example, a text node would return the value "#text". The remainder also return information that relates to their function.

An element node will return its tag name (for exmaple, "book" for a <book> element), attributes will return their name, as will notations and entities, etc. It should follow that there is no setNodeName() method defined in Node.

Some of the Node subinterfaces listed in the above table define an additional accessor method that returns the same value as getNodeName(), to provide a more intuitive way to access the value. For example, you can call getTarget() to retrieve the instruction target of a ProcessingInstruction object instead of calling the more generic and less intuitive getNodeName().

There are also methods defined to retrieve node values, any child nodes, attributes and any sibling nodes (nodes at the same level as the current node with the same parent node). You should remember that Elements' content is encapsulated by relevant objects such as Text, Comment, etc. and therefore does not have a "value". These objects are usually represented as child nodes of the relevant element.

These methods are summarized in the table below:

Method Name	Returns
getNodeValue() and setNodeValue()	Gets or sets the content, value or data for that node. The get method returns null in many cases.
getAttributes()	This returns a NamedNodeMap of the attributes for an element node. Returns null for all other nodes.
appendChild(), insertBefore(), removeChild() and replaceChild()	As their names imply, these methods are used to add, replace, and remove child nodes from the node for which the method is called.
getChildNodes(), getFirstChild() and getLastChild()	Obtain the first or last child, or a NodeList of all the child nodes for this node.
getNextSibling() and getPreviousSibling()	Get the next sibling and previous sibling respectively.

Method Name	Returns
hasChildNodes()	Returns a Boolean indicating the presence of child nodes.
getOwnerDocument()	Each Node object is associated with a particular Document, and this method returns a reference to that Document instance unless this Node is itself a Document, in which case it returns null.
cloneNode()	A copy of this node is returned by cloneNode(). You can specify a deep or shallow copy depending upon the value of the boolean parameter that's passed. A value of true, will cause the entire subtree defined by this node to be copied, while false indicates that only this node should be copied.

NodeList is an object much like the Vector class though simpler. It defines just two methods: getLength(), which indicates how many objects are in the collection, and item(), which returns a reference to the Node items referenced by an index value.

For example, the following code segment obtains a list of children from a Node, uses the NodeList object to retrieve a reference to each one, and prints their String representations:

```
org.w3c.dom.Node parentNode;
org.w3c.dom.NodeList nodeList;
// ...

nodeList = parentNode.getChildNodes();
int count = nodeList.getLength();
for (int i = 0; i < count; i++) {
  node = nodeList.item(i);
  System.out.println(node.toString());
}
```

Document

As mentioned earlier, the Document interface is implemented by an object that represents an entire XML document. A Document is returned by the DOM parser's parse() method. In other words, the object returned by parse() is the starting point from which you can begin to examine (or update) the document.

The Document provides the getDocumentElement() method to obtain access to the Node that represents the XML document's root element. You can then begin to process document:

```
DocumentBuilderFactory factory = DocumentBuilderFactory.newInstance();
factory.setValidating(true);
DocumentBuilder builder = factory.newDocumentBuilder();
Document doc = builder.parse(uri);
Element rootElement = (doc.getDocumentElement());
```

If you were to execute this code using the XML document defined at the beginning of this chapter, for example, the getDocumentElement() method would return a reference to the object representing the <book> element.

Just as a Document represents an XML document, a DocumentType represents a DTD, which can be retrieved using the getDocType() method. Each Document can maintain a reference to a DocumentType object, and this method allows you to access that object. If there is no DTD associated with the object, getDocType() returns a null value. Note that although the Level 1 DOM specification does allow you to retrieve some of a document's DTD information, it does not allow you to modify that data or create a new DTD.

Creating Nodes

The document element also provides methods to create instances of each type of node, including the createAttribute(), createElement(), and createTextNode() methods. Once you have created a node, you must assign it a value if applicable, or otherwise initialize it, before attaching it to the document.

These all represent factory methods that allow you to create nodes without coupling your code to any particular DOM implementation.

The getElementsByTagName() method

You can use this method to obtain a NodeList that encapsulates all Element nodes in the document with a particular name or a list of all Element nodes in the document regardless of their names. You can also obtain a list of all elements by passing a String value of "*". Examples of how this method might be used are listed below:

```
Document document;
NodeList list1, list2;
// ...

// Obtain a list of elements representing all of the elements in the
// document.
list1 = document.getElementsByTagName("*");
// Obtain a list of all elements with a tag/node name of "tocEntry".
list2 = document.getElementsByTagName("tocEntry");
```

You will probably find that you use this method often, as the examples in the remainder of the chapter do.

Element

As already mentioned, objects that represent elements within the XML document implement this interface. As you might expect, most of the methods defined in Element provide functionality that allows you to create, update, remove, and retrieve attribute values.

This interface also provides the getTagName() method as a convenience method, that is functionally identical to the getNodeName() method inherited from the Node interface.

normalize()

The normalize() method causes the parser to combine adjacent Text nodes that are descendents of this element, which can make processing simpler and more efficient. In addition, some operations may be sensitive to changes in the tree's structure, which can occur if a document is stored and reloaded without first being normalized. For example, suppose that you create two new Text nodes and add them to an element as shown below:

```
Document document;
Text text1, text2;
Element element;
```

```
// ...

text1 = document.createTextNode("Pepsico Business ");
text2 = document.createTextNode("Solutions Group");
element.appendChild(text1);
element.appendChild(text2);
```

If this document is saved and reloaded, it's likely that the text will be stored in a single node that contains a value of `"Pepsico Business Solutions Group"`. However, you can force the nodes to be merged immediately by calling the `normalize()` method:

```
element.appendChild(text1);

element.appendChild(text2);
element.normalize();
```

One final method that should be mentioned for this interface is the `getElementsByTagName()` method. This method performs the same task as the method of the same name in the `Document` interface, but in this case only elements that are descendents of this one are included in the search.

Attr

The Attr interface is implemented by objects that are used to represent attributes, and it defines methods for accessing and modifying the attribute's value and for retrieving its name. Note that `Attr` instances are not child nodes of the element they belong to.

getName()

Like `getTagName()`, this method is provided as a convenience, and is functionally equivalent to `getNodeName()`. It includes a `getValue()` and corresponding `setValue()` methods.

In addition, the `getSpecified()` method returns a `boolean` value that allows you to distinguish between attribute values that were actually specified in the XML document and those that are default values specified in the document's DTD. A value of `true` is returned if the value was specified in the XML document or if the value has been set/modified by a call to the `Attr` object's `setValue()` method. If the attribute's value was derived from its definition in a DTD and its `setValue()` has not been called, `getSpecified()` returns `false`. Note that if `setValue()` is called, this method will return `true` even if the value passed to the `setValue()` method is the same value that was already assigned to the attribute.

CharacterData

`CharacterData` is a subclass of `Node`, and like `Node`, `CharacterData` is used to define methods that are shared by other interfaces used to represent portions of an XML document. Specifically, `CharacterData` is the superclass of the `Text`, `Comment`, and `CDATASection` interfaces. Each `CharacterData` subclass is used to encapsulate text ("character data") information, and this interface defines methods for setting, retrieving, and modifying that text. In fact, many of the methods described below are similar to methods defined in Java's `StringBuffer` class.

`CharacterData` defines the following methods: `getLength()`, which returns an integer value that represents the number of characters in the text string associated with this node, `setData()` sets the text value associated with this node with the value of the `String` object passed to it.

There are also methods to return, append to, insert into, replace and delete the data in the node.

Text

It is worth examining this interface. Text is one of the subinterfaces of CharacterData, and is used to represent text within an XML document. Objects that implement this interface can be added as children to an Element node to describe the data between the element's start and end tags. For example, suppose that you create an XML document that contains the following elements:

```
<outer>Java and <keyword>XML</keyword> are good</outer>
```

When a DOM parser has processed this portion of the document, the <outer> element will contain three child nodes in the following order:

- ❑ An instance of Text containing the first portion of the text ("Java and ")

- ❑ An Element representing <keyword> that in turn contains one child – a Text object with a value of "XML"

- ❑ Another Text object containing the remainder of the text (" are good.")

These nodes are illustrated in the figure below:

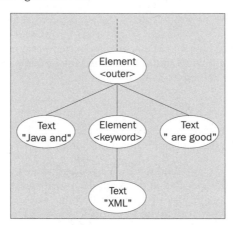

It's important to realize that from a DOM parser's perspective, there is no difference between text that represents meaningful information (for example, "Java and") and text that represents white space (line feed and character return characters, tabs, and spaces). If you were to create an <example> element like the one below, it too would have three child nodes. The second child would represent the empty <myInner> element, while the first and third children would represent the white space that precede and follow that element in the document text, respectively:

```
<example>
   <myInner/>
</example>
```

splitText()

This is the only method defined in the Text interface and is essentially the opposite of the "normalization" operation described previously that's available through the Element interface. In other words, while Element's normalize() method combines adjacent Text entries into a single entry, this method causes the Text object to be split into two separate (adjacent) instances of Text.

The only parameter passed to this method is an integer that indicates the position at which the Text object's character data should be split. The characters up to and including the character at the position you specify will remain in the existing node, and any characters after that will be added to a new Text node. That new node will then be inserted into the parent node's list of children so that it immediately follows the original Text node:

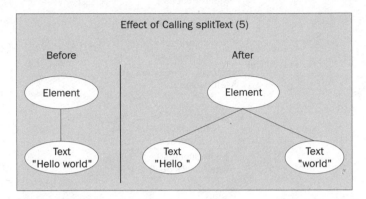

You'll use this method when you wish to insert new elements or other data between two portions of text in an XML document. Once you've called splitText(), you can insert child nodes between the original Text node and its newly created sibling.

DocumentFragment

No methods are defined in this interface and it does not correspond to a specific portion of an XML document, but DocumentFragment has a property that can be very useful. Like all Node subclasses, it can contain child nodes and it can be added as a child to other nodes. However, when a DocumentFragment is added as a child of some other node the DocumentFragment's children, rather than the DocumentFragment itself, will be added. Therefore, DocumentFragment provides a convenient container object for a collection of nodes that you wish to make children of some other node – for example, when rearranging a document, or implementing cut-and-paste type functionality. Using DocumentFragment avoids the overhead of using a Document to hold the nodes.

For the remainder of the interfaces defined in this package you should refer to the documentation; they should not give you too many surprises in any case and like most classes, you may find that you use a section of the available methods in most cases, with an occasional requirement for the more esoteric methods.

Parsing and Traversing a Document with DOM

Now that we've examined the DOM interfaces, we'll see how they can be used to examine an XML document that has been parsed and used to create a hierarchical collection of objects in memory. Each Element node can contain its own child nodes that can be other Element nodes, and those children may have their own child nodes, and so on for a theoretically infinite number of levels:

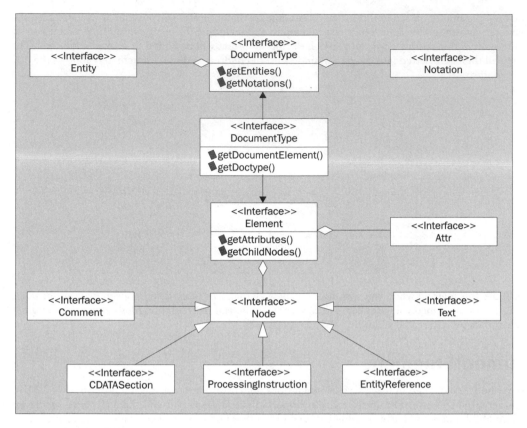

As mentioned earlier, the DocumentBuilder class is the DOM parser that's included with the JAXP download, and like the SAXParser, it includes a parse() method. In addition, the DocumentBuilder's parse() method returns a Document object that represents your entry point to the object structure that it created. Once you have access to the Document object, you can call getDocumentElement() to obtain a reference to the XML document's root element or getDocumentType() if you intend to examine the document's DTD. The following code segment provides an illustration of how you might use the JAXP classes to create a DOM parser, load and parse a document, and obtain access to its root element:

```
String uri;
// ...

DocumentBuilderFactory factory = DocumentBuilderFactory.newInstance();
factory.setValidating(true);
DocumentBuilder builder = factory.newDocumentBuilder();
Document doc = builder.parse(uri);
Element rootElement = doc.getDocumentElement();
```

As we've seen, the Node interface includes methods that allow you to access a node's parent, children, or siblings, and it's easy to use them to navigate through a document structure. For example, suppose that you're given an Element node and you wish to display the subtree that it represents as it appeared in the original XML document.

This means not only examining the object structure but actually reversing the parsing process and converting the objects back into an XML document. You can do this quite easily by creating code that traverses the tree, identifies which type of item each Node represents, and processes the node accordingly. An outline of such an application is shown below:

```java
import javax.xml.parsers.*;
import org.w3c.dom.*;

public class DOMTest {

  public static void main(String[] args) throws Exception {
    DOMTest dt = new DOMTest(args[0]);
  }

  public DOMTest(String uri) throws Exception {
    DocumentBuilderFactory factory =
        DocumentBuilderFactory.newInstance();
    factory.setValidating(true);
    DocumentBuilder builder = factory.newDocumentBuilder();
    Document doc = builder.parse(uri);
    displayTree(doc.getDocumentElement());
  }

  protected void displayTree(Node node) {
    short nodeType = node.getNodeType();
    switch (nodeType) {
      case Node.ELEMENT_NODE:
        printElement((Element)node);
        break;
      case Node.TEXT_NODE:
        printText((Text)node);
        break;
      case Node.COMMENT_NODE:
        printComment((Comment)node);
        break;
      case Node.CDATA_SECTION_NODE:
        printCDATA((CDATASection)node);
        break;
      case Node.ENTITY_REFERENCE_NODE:
        printEntityReference((EntityReference)node);
        break;
      case Node.PROCESSING_INSTRUCTION_NODE:
        printProcessingInstruction(
            (ProcessingInstruction)node);
        break;
      default:
    }
  }

  protected void printElement(Element node) {
    // ...
  }

  protected void printText(CharacterData node) {
    // ...
```

```
    }

    protected void printComment(Comment node) {
      // ...
    }

    protected void printCDATA(CDATASection node) {
      // ...
    }

    protected void printEntityReference(EntityReference node) {
      // ...
    }

    protected void printProcessingInstruction(ProcessingInstruction node) {
      // ...
    }

}
```

Except for Element instances, each type of Node subclass object can be converted into an appropriate text representation very easily. In fact, all of the above printXXX() methods except printElement() can be completed with a single statement that wraps the node data in an appropriate character string:

```
    protected void printText(CharacterData node) {
      System.out.print(node.getData());
    }

    protected void printComment(Comment node) {
      System.out.print("<!--" + node.getData() + "-->");
    }

    protected void printCDATA(CDATASection node) {
      System.out.print("<![CDATA[" + node.getData() + "]]>");
    }

    protected void printEntityReference(EntityReference node) {
      System.out.print("&" + node.getNodeName() + ";");
    }

    protected void printProcessingInstruction(ProcessingInstruction node) {
      System.out.print("<?" + node.getTarget() + " " + node.getData() + "?>");
    }
```

Processing Element nodes is slightly more complex because they can have attributes and child nodes that must be included in the output, but the start and end tags can easily be generated as shown below:

```
    protected void printElement(Element node) {
      // ...
      System.out.print("<" + node.getNodeName());
      // ...
      System.out.print(">");
      // ...
      System.out.print("</" + node.getNodeName() + ">");
    }
```

To include an element's attribute values inside its start tag, you must retrieve a reference to its attribute list by calling the getAttributes() method. After that, iterate through the list, and generate output for each one, placing quotes around its value:

```
protected void printElement(Element node) {
  Attr attr;
  System.out.print("<" + node.getNodeName());
  NamedNodeMap attrs = node.getAttributes();
  int count = attrs.getLength();
  for (int i = 0; i < count; i++) {
    attr = (Attr)(attrs.item(i));
    System.out.print(" " + attr.getName() + "=\"" + attr.getValue() +
                    "\"");
  }
  System.out.print(">");
  // ...
  System.out.print("</" + node.getNodeName() + ">");
}
```

You must also ensure that all of an element's child nodes are included in the generated output, but this is even easier to accomplish. Simply obtain a reference to the list of children by calling getChildNodes() and call the displayTree() method for each one. This causes the entire tree structure to be processed using preorder traversal, a term that's described in the JTree chapter of this book. Stated simply, however, it means that a node is processed/displayed before its children instead of afterwards:

```
protected void printElement(Element node) {
  Node child;
  Attr attr;
  System.out.print("<" + node.getNodeName());
  NamedNodeMap attrs = node.getAttributes();
  int count = attrs.getLength();
  for (int i = 0; i < count; i++) {
    attr = (Attr)(attrs.item(i));
    System.out.print(" " + attr.getName() + "=\"" + attr.getValue() +
                    "\"");
  }
  System.out.print(">");
  NodeList children = node.getChildNodes();
  count = children.getLength();
  for (int i = 0; i < count; i++) {
    child = children.item(i);
    displayTree(child);
  }
  System.out.print("</" + node.getNodeName() + ">");
}
```

With the printElement() method in place, you can now use the DOMTest application to print the contents of an XML document's root element. To do so simply compile the code and execute it, passing a string that represents a URI to the main() method as shown below:

```
C:\brett\temp>java DOMTest file:/c:/brett/temp/booktest.xml
<book><title>Professional Java Programming</title><author>Brett Spell</autho
r><publisher>Wrox Press</publisher><tableOfContents showPageNumbers="Yes"><t
ocEntry>Printing</tocEntry><tocEntry>Cut and Paste</tocEntry><tocEntry>Drag
and Drop</tocEntry></tableOfContents></book>
```

Although this application provided a reason for us to see how to traverse a DOM tree, it really wasn't necessary to implement this functionality at all. That's because the DOM implementation supplied with the JAXP download contains `toString()` methods that do essentially the same thing as our `printXXX()` methods. In fact, the following simplified version of `DOMTest` will produce exactly the same output as the code we just created:

```
import javax.xml.parsers.*;
import org.w3c.dom.*;

public class DOMTest2 {

  public static void main(String[] args) throws Exception {
    DOMTest2 dt = new DOMTest2s(args[0]);
  }

  public DOMTest2(String uri) throws Exception {
    DocumentBuilderFactory factory =
        DocumentBuilderFactory.newInstance();
    factory.setValidating(true);
    DocumentBuilder builder = factory.newDocumentBuilder();
    Document doc = builder.parse(uri);
    System.out.println(doc.getDocumentElement());
  }

}
```

It may be tempting to take advantage of this functionality if you're using the JAXP parser, but you should keep in mind that this behavior is not part of the Level 1 DOM standard. Therefore, to ensure that your application code can work with different parsers, you must implement a custom solution as was done here or wait for a parser that supports DOM Level 3. That specification will define the interface for an "XML writer", or code that writes a DOM document as XML source.

Editing Documents with DOM

Using DOM to edit a document can be done in essentially the same way as using it to scan the document. In other words, iterate through every child element of the root determine whether it meets our criteria and process it accordingly. In order to achieve this, DOM also provides methods that allow you to add, modify, and delete nodes from the tree.

If we are trying to access a certain element, we can also use the `getElementsByTagName()` method of the `Document` class. This will return a `NodeList` that contains all the elements whose name is the same as the `String` passed as a parameter.

For example, given the following XML document, suppose that you wish to assign a value of "no" to the `showPageNumbers` attribute value in the `<tableOfContents>` element:

```
<?xml version="1.0" ?>

<book>
  <title>Professional Java Programming</title>
  <author>Brett Spell</author>
  <publisher>Wrox Press</publisher>
```

```
      <tableOfContents showPageNumbers="yes">
        <tocEntry>Printing</tocEntry>
        <tocEntry>Cut &amp; Paste</tocEntry>
        <tocEntry>Drag &amp; Drop</tocEntry>
      </tableOfContents>
    </book>
```

We initialize a Document with the relevant XML document (booktest.xml) as before. We then obtain a NodeSet of all the elements with the name tableOfContents and once that's done, we call setAttribute() to set the showPageNumbers value to "no" as shown below:

```java
import javax.xml.parsers.*;
import org.w3c.dom.*;

public class DOMTest3 {

  public static void main(String[] args) throws Exception {
    DOMTest3 dt = new DOMTest3(args[0]);
  }

  public DOMTest3(String uri) throws Exception {
    DocumentBuilderFactory factory =
        DocumentBuilderFactory.newInstance();
    factory.setValidating(true);
    DocumentBuilder builder = factory.newDocumentBuilder();

    Document doc = builder.parse(uri);
    NodeList children = doc.getElementsByTagName("tableOfContents");

    Element current;

    int count = children.getLength();
    for (int i = 0; i < count; i++) {
      current = (Element)children.item(i);
      current.setAttribute("showPageNumbers", "no");
    }
    System.out.println(doc.getDocumentElement());
  }
}
```

Let's look at another example. If, for whatever reason, you wish to delete the <tableOfContents> tag completely rather than modifying its attribute, you can use the removeChild() method of the Node interface as shown below:

```java
import javax.xml.parsers.*;
import org.w3c.dom.*;

public class DOMTest4 {

  public static void main(String[] args) throws Exception {
    DOMTest4 dt = new DOMTest4(args[0]);
  }

  public DOMTest4(String uri) throws Exception {
```

```
DocumentBuilderFactory factory =
    DocumentBuilderFactory.newInstance();
factory.setValidating(true);
DocumentBuilder builder = factory.newDocumentBuilder();

Document doc = builder.parse(uri);

NodeList children = doc.getElementsByTagName("tableOfContents");

Element current;
Element parentElement;

int count = children.getLength();
System.out.println("There " + (count==1?"is ":"are ") + count +
                    " tableOfContents element"+ (count==1?"":"s"));

for (int i = 0; i < count; i++) {
    System.out.println("Deleting child element number " + (I+1));

    current = (Element)children.item(i);

    parentElement = (Element)element.getParentNode();
    parentElement.removeChild(current);
}

System.out.println(doc.getDocumentElement());
    }
}
```

In this example, we retrieve all the nodes whose name is tableOfContents, as before. This time, however, we remove the element. We do this using the removeChild() method of the Node interface by first obtaining the parent element of the current node, and then removing the current child.

When removing nodes like this, keep in mind that you're removing not only the node that you specify on the call to removeChild() but all of its descendents as well. In this case, for example, removing the <tableOfContents> element results in the removal of the three <tocEntry> elements that are its children, those three nodes' children, and so on.

> Keep in mind that removeChild() effectively eliminates the entire subtree defined by the node that you pass as a parameter value.

Creating and Adding New Nodes

Creating and adding new nodes is equally simple, using the Node interface's appendChild(), insertBefore(), and replaceChild() methods. Creating a new node is something that we've not done before, although you may remember that the Document interface includes factory methods that return instances of the different types of Node objects. In most cases, these methods require a single parameter that represents the name of the node to be created, and an example of how you might create a new Element node is shown below:

```
Document doc = builder.parse(uri);
// ...

Element myNewElement = doc.createElement("tocEntry");
```

Once the new element is created, you can call its mutator methods to modify its state, and once it is properly initialized, you can add it to the object structure. The following code creates a new `Element` representing a `<tocEntry>` and a new `Text` node containing the value `"Help"`. It then makes the `Text` node a child of the new element, and inserts that element before the second child of the `<tableOfContents>` node:

```java
import javax.xml.parsers.*;
import org.w3c.dom.*;

public class DOMTest5 {

  public static void main(String[] args) throws Exception {
    DOMTest5 dt = new DOMTest5(args[0]);
  }

  public DOMTest5(String uri) throws Exception {
    DocumentBuilderFactory factory = DocumentBuilderFactory.newInstance();
    factory.setValidating(true);
    DocumentBuilder builder = factory.newDocumentBuilder();

    Document doc = builder.parse(uri);

    NodeList children = doc.getElementsByTagName("tableOfContents");

    Element current = null;
    int count = children.getLength();
    for (int i = 0; i < count; i++) {
      current = (Element)children.item(i);

      // Get the list of <tocEntry> items
      NodeList tocItems = current.getElementsByTagName("tocEntry");

      // Obtain a reference to the second one
      Node secondChild = tocItems.item(1);
      // Create a new <tocEntry> element
      Element newTOCItem = doc.createElement("tocEntry");

      // Create a new "Help" text node
      Text newText = doc.createTextNode("Help");

      // Make it a child of the new <tocEntry> element

      // <tocEntry>Help</tocEntry>
      newTOCItem.appendChild(newText);

      // Add the new <tocEntry> element to <tableOfContents>
      current.insertBefore(newTOCItem, secondChild);
    }
    System.out.println(doc.getDocumentElement());
  }

}
```

In effect, this is equivalent to making the following addition to the original XML document:

```
<tableOfContents showPageNumbers="Yes">
  <tocEntry>Printing</tocEntry>
  <tocEntry>Help</tocEntry>
  <tocEntry>Cut &amp; Paste</tocEntry>
  <tocEntry>Drag &amp; Drop</tocEntry>
</tableOfContents>
```

This illustrates an important point that may not be obvious. While it may appear that the original `<tableOfContents>` node had only three children, it has at least seven – four `Text` nodes representing white space in addition to the three `<tocEntry>` `Element` nodes. If the tree has been normalized (which it typically will be after it is first constructed) there will be exactly seven child nodes. However, it's possible that one "section" of white space is made up of two sequential `Text` nodes (for exmaple, a line feed followed by a tab).

In any case, when adding data nodes to a tree as was done here, you may also want to add a `Text` node representing white space as well. Although white space has no impact upon a parser's ability to process the document or upon the logical organization of the document, you want to add it for the sake of readability. In order to decouple this class from the XML file, you should do this dynamically by examining white space before and after the other nodes at the same level as this one.

Creating a New Document

All of the `Document` instances we've used so far were created when the `parse()` method read and processed an existing document, but you'll sometimes want to create a new object collection that is not associated with an existing XML document. Although the DOM Level 1 specification does not define how this should be done, JAXP's `DocumentBuilder` class contains a `newDocument()` method that you can use to obtain a new (and empty) `Document` object:

```java
import javax.xml.parsers.*;
import org.w3c.dom.*;

public class DOMTest6 {

  public static void main(String[] args) throws Exception {
    DOMTest6 dt = new DOMTest6();
  }

  public DOMTest6() throws Exception {
    DocumentBuilderFactory factory =
        DocumentBuilderFactory.newInstance();
    factory.setValidating(true);
    DocumentBuilder builder = factory.newDocumentBuilder();
    Document document = builder.newDocument();

    // ...
  }

}
```

Once you've created a new `Document` object, the first `Element` child that you add to it will become the document's root element and you can add other nodes as described above:

```java
import javax.xml.parsers.*;
import org.w3c.dom.*;

public class DOMTest6 {
```

```
public static void main(String[] args) throws Exception {
  DOMTest6 dt = new DOMTest6();
}

public DOMTest6() throws Exception {
  DocumentBuilderFactory factory =
      DocumentBuilderFactory.newInstance();
  factory.setValidating(true);
  DocumentBuilder builder = factory.newDocumentBuilder();

  Document document = builder.newDocument();
  // Create a new Element object
  Element rootElement = document.createElement("book");
  // Make it the root element of this new document
  document.appendChild(rootElement);

  System.out.println(document.getDocumentElement());
}

}
```

You can then continue in this way to create a full XML document. This is one way to create XML documents from data extracted, perhaps, from a database or other data source.

> You should note that unless some intelligent programming is done, the resultant class would be irretrievably bound to the current DTD (assuming validated XML files).

Namespaces

Earlier in the chapter, we saw that it's possible to include the contents of one DTD file within another by defining an external parameter entity and creating a reference to that entity. Although very useful, this capability also introduces a potential problem. Specifically, it's possible for an element name to be used in both DTDs, and when the two are combined it may become unclear which element is referenced in an XML document. For example, you might create the following DTD in a file called `snacks.dtd` and define elements and attributes related to snack foods:

```
<!ELEMENT cookies (#PCDATA)>
<!ATTLIST cookies haveChocolate CDATA "yes">
<!ELEMENT pretzels (#PCDATA)>
<!ATTLIST pretzels haveSalt CDATA "yes">
```

In addition, you could create another DTD similar to the one shown below in a file called `browser.dtd` that contains definitions for browser-related elements and attributes:

```
<!ELEMENT JavaScript (#PCDATA)>
<!ATTLIST JavaScript isEnabled CDATA "no">
<!ELEMENT cookies (#PCDATA)>
<!ATTLIST cookies areAccepted CDATA "no">
```

Now let's assume that you use both of these in a third DTD called `preferences.dtd` by defining external entities and creating references to them:

```
<!ENTITY snacks SYSTEM "snacks.dtd">
<!ENTITY browser SYSTEM "browser.dtd">
%snacks;
%browser;
```

Finally, you might create an XML document that uses `preferences.dtd` and which contains a `<cookies>` element:

```
<cookies>I really like these</cookies>
```

It's unclear at this point which DTD element is referenced. Is it the one defined in `snacks.dtd` or the one defined in `browser.dtd`? Which attribute can be specified with the element: `areAccepted` or `haveChocolate`? As it turns out, this type of naming "collision" is potentially very common, so the World Wide Web Consortium has created the **namespace** standard to provide a solution.

Before examining this standard, it's worth pointing out that this problem is very similar to the problem of naming Java classes. In other words, if you have more than one person creating new classes and assigning them names, it's likely that two or more people will create a class with the same name, which can lead to ambiguity. In fact, even within the Java 2 core classes, there are at least two pairs of classes with the same name. There is a `List` collection interface as well as an AWT component called `List`, and there are two separate classes named `Date`. However, these collisions do not present a problem because in each case the two classes with the same name are defined in separate packages.

By associating each class with a specific package, it only becomes necessary to avoid collisions within a single package, since each class name is qualified (either implicitly or explicitly) with the name of the package in which it's defined. In other words, it's perfectly acceptable to have a `java.util.Date` class and a `java.sql.Date` class, as long as your code makes it clear which one you mean.

The namespace standard uses essentially the same solution to the problem of element and attribute name collisions in DTDs, although each element is associated with a URI rather than a package. Assigning a URI to an element is as easy as defining an attribute named `xmlns` (derived from "XML namespace") to the element and assigning it a value that corresponds to the URI, as shown below. In practice you would associate every element in your DTD with a namespace, but it has only been done for the `cookies` element here:

```
<!ELEMENT cookies (#PCDATA)>
<!ATTLIST cookies
  hasChocolate  CDATA          "yes"
  xmlns         CDATA  #FIXED  "http://members.aol.com/javabrewer/snacks/">
<!ELEMENT pretzels (#PCDATA)>
<!ATTLIST pretzels hasSalt CDATA "yes">
```

Similarly, for the `browser.dtd` file:

```
<!ELEMENT JavaScript (#PCDATA)>
<!ATTLIST JavaScript isEnabled CDATA "no">
<!ELEMENT cookies (#PCDATA)>
<!ATTLIST cookies
  areAllowed  CDATA          "no"
  xmlns       CDATA  #FIXED  "http://members.aol.com/javabrewer/browser/">
```

Once this is done, you can combine DTDs without fear of collision problems as long as no two elements are assigned the same name *and* URI. In addition, you can qualify element references in XML documents as shown below, where the first reference is to a snack and the second to a browser artifact:

```
<cookie xmlns="http://members.aol.com/javabrewer/snacks/">
  I like this kind of cookie.
</cookie>
<cookie xmlns="http://members.aol.com/javabrewer/browser/">
  I don't like this kind of cookie.
</cookie>
```

Note that the namespace specification applies not only to the element for which it is specified, but also to any elements contained within that element. For example, suppose that you were to define the following element:

```
<cookie xmlns="http://members.aol.com/javabrewer/snacks/">
I like this kind of cookie.
  <chips>Chocolate</chips>
</cookie>
```

In this case, the `<chips>` element is contained within the `<cookie>` element, and since no namespace was specified for `<chips>`, it effectively "inherits" the one used with `<cookie>`. Therefore, if more than one `<chips>` element is defined, this element would be interpreted as a reference the one associated with the /snacks/ URI.

To make it clear which elements are referenced in your documents, you can specify the namespace for each one. However, entering the same URI repeatedly for each element is tedious and error-prone, and it could complicate the task of changing the URI if it becomes necessary to do so. Fortunately, it's possible to define a **namespace prefix**, which is essentially an alias you can define and associate with the URI. Once that's done, you can simply specify the alias instead of the full URI, which makes your documents much more readable and easier to create.

For example, the following element defines an alias called snacks, and that alias is used to indicate that each of the elements with that alias is associated with the /snacks/ URI:

```
<snacks:cookie xmlns:snacks="http://members.aol.com/javabrewer/snacks/">
I like this kind of cookie.
  <snacks:chips>Chocolate</snacks:chips>
</snacks:cookie>
```

As this example illustrates, the snacks alias is defined by following the xmlns attribute name with a colon (:) and the name of the alias. With the alias defined, you can qualify each element name by preceding it with the alias and a colon. In other words, the following two elements are equivalent:

```
<snacks:chips>Chocolate</snacks:chips>
```

and:

```
<chips xmlns="http://members.aol.com/javabrewer/snacks/">Chocolate</chips>
```

The first entry is more readable and easier to type, and you'll commonly see this notation in XML documents. In most cases, the alias is defined in the root element, and each of the elements below that will contain a reference to that alias.

Transforming XML Documents

It has already been pointed out that XML allows you to separate your data from instructions that describe how the data is displayed. However, no mention has been made so far of how to convert an XML document into some format that's appropriate for display, such as an HTML document.

For example, you should recall that an HTML document and a similar XML document were defined at the beginning of this chapter. Since the HTML version contains information that describes how to format the data, it's possible to view that document in a browser and have it display the data appropriately. In contrast, the XML document does not contain any such display guidelines.

One option for converting an XML document into some other format is to use a SAX or DOM parser to examine the document's contents and write out an appropriate representation. In other words, you could create code that uses SAX to identify the elements in a document and produces the appropriate HTML for each type of element. For example, if you wanted to convert a `<title>` element in an XML document into `<center>` and `<h1>` elements, you might create code like that shown below:

```
public void startElement(String name, AttributeList attrs) {
  if (name.equalsIgnoreCase("title")) {
    System.out.print("<center><h1>");
  }
}

public void endElement(String name) {
  if (name.equals("title")) {
    System.out.print("</h1></center>");
  }
}

public void ignorableWhitespace(char[] chars, int start, int length) {
  characters(chars, start, length);
}

public void characters(char[] chars, int start, int length) {
  System.out.print(new String(chars, start, length));
}
```

Now let's assume that the code is used when processing the following element:

```
<title>Professional Java Programming</title>
```

The code would convert the element into the HTML code shown below:

```
<center><h1>Professional Java Programming</h1></center>
```

This example provides only a very simple example of how to convert XML into HTML, but in reality, it can be a very complex and difficult task. There is an alternative to this called **eXtensible Stylesheet Language Transformations (XSLT)**. XSLT is part of a standard created by the World Wide Web Consortium called XSL that allows you to create **stylesheets** for XML documents, where a style sheet is simply a file that describes how information should be presented.

XSL allows you to do two things that are distinct from one another: rearranging the structure of your document's nodes also known as XSLT, and describing how the nodes should be displayed, **eXtensible Stylesheet Language, Formatting Objects** (**XSL-FO**). In other words, you can convert a document from one XML grammar to another or even from one XML format to some non-XML format such as HTML, RTF, PDF, etc. using XSLT. (XSLT and XSL are sometimes used interchangeably, and this section focuses on XSLT.) XSL-FO has not been greatly adopted so far and is not relevant to this discussion.

The separation of transformation from generating or parsing XML documents offered by XSLT helps us, once again, to keep our application loosely coupled. Of course, the main advantage to using XSL/XSLT here is that it is non-compiled. The transformation can be re-written outside of the Java code, and still work to perform different formatting. This allows some of the "programming" tasks to be devolved to non-coders. XSLT is an XML language itself so it should look familiar to you.

We'll now see how to create an XSLT file that will transform the XML document at the beginning of this chapter into the equivalent HTML document. First, you should create a file called booktran.xsl that contains the following three lines. The first line is the XML declaration that you've already seen, while the next line is the stylesheet declaration that identifies the namespace that will be used to refer to XSLT instructions:

```
<?xml version="1.0"?>
<xsl:stylesheet xmlns:xsl="http://www.w3.org/1999/XSL/Transform"
                version="1.0">
</xsl:stylesheet>
```

To specify how XML data is formatted, you must create **templates**, elements containing transformation instructions and data. The template element has one attribute match that specifies the element to transform. Any element content is copied into the output.

In the following stylesheet, for example, when a <book> element is encountered, we want an HTML document to be generated that contains the same data found in <book>, but with HTML tags that describe how to format the data. Therefore, we can create a template like the one shown below that will generate the <html> and </html> tags when a <book> is encountered:

```
<?xml version="1.0"?>
<xsl:stylesheet xmlns:xsl="http://www.w3.org/1999/XSL/Transform" version="1.0">

<xsl:template match="book">
<html>
...
</html>
</xsl:template>

</xsl:stylesheet>
```

We can copy the content of that element into the output using <value-of>. This element evaluates the value given in its select attribute and assigns the value of the resultant node to the output. In the following XSLT stylesheet, the select attribute has been assigned with a value of "title". This indicates to the XSLT processor that it should look for a child node of the current (<book>) element called "title" and copy its content to the output. In addition the code also extracts the book's author and publisher:

```
<?xml version="1.0"?>

<xsl:stylesheet xmlns:xsl="http://www.w3.org/1999/XSL/Transform" version="1.0">
```

```
<xsl:template match="book">
<html>
   <center>
     <h1>
        <xsl:value-of select="title"/>
     </h1>
   </center>
   <h4>
     <xsl:value-of select="author"/>
   </h4>
   <h4>
     <xsl:value-of select="publisher"/>
   </h4>
</html>
</xsl:template>

</xsl:stylesheet>
```

The above XSLT document would create the following output when applied to the `booktest.xml` created earlier in the chapter:

```
<html>
   <center>
     <h1>
        Professional Java Programming
     </h1>
   </center>
   <h4>
     Brett Spell
   </h4>
   <h4>
     Wrox Press
   </h4>
</html>
```

XSLT also offers tags for conditional execution of sections of template, iteration through selected nodes, and sorting those nodes, to name but a few. In combination, these elements can be used to transform any XML file to your desired output format.

A full examination of the elements provided is unfortunately outside the scope of the book; however, we will explain any additional tags as we encounter them. Those interested should refer to Professional XML, WROX Press for more information on this fascinating subject.

Performing an XSL Transformation

Like SAX and DOM, you must obtain an XSLT processor before you can use this technology, but again, free implementations are available for download. For example, the Apache XML Project **Xalan** processor is available at `http://xml.apache.org/xalan/`, and that download includes the Apache XML parser (**Xerces**), which is used by Xalan. Once you've downloaded them, simply add `xalan.jar` and `xerces.jar` (both located in the root installation directory) to your classpath.

After adding the two JAR files to your classpath, performing a transformation is as simple as executing the `main()` method of the `Process` class defined in the `org.apache.xalan.xslt` package. When you do so, you should specify three parameter values:

- ❑   in: The name of the XML file that you wish to transform.
- ❑   xsl: The name of the XSL transformation file to use.
- ❑   out: The name of the file to be created by the transformation.

For example, if your XML file is named booktest.xml, your XSL file is booktran.xsl, and you wish to store the transformed output in booktest.html, you would enter a command like the one highlighted below:

```
java org.apache.xalan.xslt.Process -in booktest.xml -xsl booktran.xsl
    -out booktest.html
```

This command will generate the booktest.html file shown earlier.

Introducing XPath

Before continuing, it's helpful to closely examine the values of the select attributes associated with the value-of instructions we created a moment ago. Although it may not be apparent, these are examples of **XPath** (XML Path Language) values. XPath is an expression language used to express nodes in an XML document tree, specify conditions for different ways of processing a node, and generating text from the tree. Here it simply provides a way to refer to specific nodes in the XML document.

XPath is a separate standard to XSL/XSLT, but as this example illustrates, it is used to identify document nodes referenced during transformations. XPath uses the concepts of a context node (the current node being processed) to allow relative references, as well as allowing absolute references (from the document root). This includes ways of referencing a child node, whether by name as done in the code above, or by number, a nodes attributes, text values, any comments present in the node etc.

We can also evaluate expressions for Boolean results, and include a function library for anything from string manipulation to discovering the position of the node in relation to its siblings. Fortunately, XPath is somewhat intuitive, since the notation used is very similar to what you're probably already accustomed to using when referring to directories in a file system, although it is definitely worth referring to the aforementioned Professional XML book for further information. Again, I will attempt to explain its usage as it appears in the remaining text.

At this point, two things need to be added to the application: the table of contents information and the publisher's logo image. The table of contents header can easily be produced using the techniques already described:

```
<?xml version="1.0"?>

<xsl:stylesheet xmlns:xsl="http://www.w3.org/1999/XSL/Transform"
                version="1.0">

<xsl:template match="book">
<html>
  <body>
    <center><h1><xsl:value-of select="title"/></h1></center>
    <h4><xsl:value-of select="author"/></h4>
    <b>
    <h3>Table Of Contents</h3>
    </b>
```

```
        <h4><xsl:value-of select="publisher"/></h4>
    </body>
</html>
</xsl:template>
```

On the other hand, including the `<tocItem>` entries in the output is slightly more complex because there are several such entries and because they are not directly below the `<book>` element being processed. That isn't really a difficult problem to solve because XPath allows us to refer to the `<tocItem>` entries from the `<book>` template. However, since there are multiple such entries, we can use the `<for-each>` tag, which works much like Java's `if...else` construct, to define a loop that will process each one of them as shown below:

```
<xsl:template match="book">
<html>
    <body>
        <center><h1><xsl:value-of select="title"/></h1></center>
        <h4><xsl:value-of select="author"/></h4>
        <b>
        <h3>Table Of Contents</h3>
        <ul>

    <xsl:for-each select="tableOfContents/tocEntry">

    </xsl:for-each>

        </ul>
        </b>
        <h4><xsl:value-of select="publisher"/></h4>
    </body>
</html>
</xsl:template>
```

With this loop in place, we can easily generate output for each `<tocEntry>` element. Note the use of the single period (`.`) for the select value, which selects the content of the specified node, which in the context of the loop refers to the value of the `<tocEntry>` element:

```
<xsl:for-each select="tableOfContents/tocEntry">
    <li><xsl:value-of select="."/></li>
</xsl:for-each>
```

Finally, we can add the `<img>` tag that will display the publisher's logo, although there are at least two ways to accomplish this. One approach is to explicitly embed the information in the document as you would in an HTML document:

```
<img src="http://www.wrox.com/images/wrox_logo100.gif" alt="Wrox Logo" />
```

However, if you prefer to avoid explicitly identifying the file in your XSL document, you could use entity references instead:

```
<?xml version="1.0"?>
<!DOCTYPE xsl:stylesheet SYSTEM "pubinfo.dtd">
<!-- remainder of XSLT stylesheet snipped for the sake of brevity-->
<h4><xsl:value-of select="publisher"/></h4>
<img src="&logoFile;" alt="&logoText;" />
```

This latter approach would also require that a `pubinfo.dtd` file be created with the following contents:

```
<!-- pubinfo.dtd -->
<!ENTITY logoFile "http://www.wrox.com/images/wrox_logo100.gif">
<!ENTITY logoText "Wrox Logo">
```

Alternatively, you can include this information in the XML file and extract it using appropriately placed `<value-of>` tags. The completed stylesheet is included below:

```
<?xml version="1.0"?>
<!DOCTYPE xsl:stylesheet SYSTEM "pubinfo.dtd">

<xsl:stylesheet xmlns:xsl="http://www.w3.org/1999/XSL/Transform" version="1.0">

<xsl:template match="book">
<html>
  <body>
    <center><h1><xsl:value-of select="title"/></h1></center>
    <h4><xsl:value-of select="author"/></h4>
    <b>
    <h3>Table Of Contents</h3>
   <xsl:for-each select="tableOfContents/tocEntry">
    <li><xsl:value-of select="."/></li>
   </xsl:for-each>
    </b>
    <h4><xsl:value-of select="publisher"/></h4>
    <img src="&logoFile;" alt="&logoText;" />
  <body>
</html>
</xsl:template>

</xsl:stylesheet>
```

The output produced by this stylesheet is as follows (format for readability):

```
<html>
  <body>
    <center>
      <h1>Professional Java Programming</h1>
    </center>
    <h4>Brett Spell</h4>
    <b>
      <h3>Table Of Contents</h3>
      <li>Printing</li>
      <li>Cut and Paste</li>
      <li>Drag and Drop</li>
    </b>
    <h4>Wrox Press</h4>
    <img alt="Wrox Logo"
         src="http://www.wrox.com/images/wrox_logo100.gif">
  </body>
</html>
```

Creating and Using Additional Templates

Although the above approach is acceptable for relatively simple XML documents, it has one significant design flaw. Specifically, all processing takes place inside a single template, and if your document's structure is complex, you will be forced to put a large amount of code inside that template. This is roughly equivalent to creating a single large, "monolithic" method in Java to perform a complex algorithm with many steps. Such a method becomes difficult to understand and maintain, so it's usually desirable to separate the functions by placing them in different methods (or templates in this case).

A good candidate for such a change is the code that handles the <tableOfContents> elements and its <tocItem> sub-elements, since that code accounts for roughly half of the logic inside the existing template.

A new template that only handles <tableOfContents> elements can be created easily as shown below, and it contains essentially the same instructions that were present in <book>. The only exception is that the <tocEntry> items are referenced from a location relative to the <tableOfContents> entry instead of the <book> element. Therefore, the path used in the <for-each> instruction to reference each <tocEntry> must be changed from "tableOfContents/tocEntry" to "tocEntry":

```
<?xml version="1.0"?>
<!DOCTYPE xsl:stylesheet SYSTEM "pubinfo.dtd">

<xsl:stylesheet xmlns:xsl="http://www.w3.org/1999/XSL/Transform" version="1.0">

<xsl:template match="book">
<html>
<center><h1><xsl:value-of select="title"/></h1></center>
<h4><xsl:value-of select="author"/></h4>
<h4><xsl:value-of select="publisher"/></h4>
<img src="&logoFile;" alt="&logoText;"/>
</html>
</xsl:template>
```

```
<xsl:template match="tableOfContents">
<b>
<H3>Table Of Contents</H3>
<xsl:for-each select="tocEntry">
<li><xsl:value-of select="."/></li>
</xsl:for-each>
</b>
</xsl:template>
```

```
</xsl:stylesheet>
```

Although you might expect the template associated with the <tableOfContents> element to be called automatically, that is not the case. Only the template that handles the root element will be called automatically, and to use any other templates, you must explicitly "call" them using the <apply-templates> element. This instruction causes the XSLT processor to handle the specified child element(s) of the current element and embed the results in the output being created.

For example, to include the <tableOfContents> element output between the text created for the <author> and <publisher> elements you would need to make the following modification:

```
<!-- ... -->

<xsl:template match="book">
<html>
<center><h1><xsl:value-of select="title"/></h1></center>
<h4><xsl:value-of select="author"/></h4>
<xsl:apply-templates select="tableOfContents"/>
<h4><xsl:value-of select="publisher"/></h4>
<img src="&logoFile;" alt="&logoText;"/>
</html>
</xsl:template>
<!-- ... -->
```

This command will again generate a file `booktest.html` containing the following content:

```
<html>
<center>
<h1>Professional Java Programming</h1>
</center>
<h4>Brett Spell</h4>
<b>
<H3>Table Of Contents</H3>
<li>Printing</li>
<li>Cut and Paste</li>
<li>Drag and Drop</li>
</b>
<h4>Wrox Press</h4>
<img alt="Wrox Logo" src="http://www.wrox.com/images/wrox_logo100.gif"></html>
```

Although the white space is not quite the same as that of the HTML document defined earlier in the chapter, the two documents are functionally identical from a browser's perspective.

Transforming from your own Code

Obviously, a lot of the time running an XSLT processor from the command line is not going to be ideal, and a way of invoking the processor from within your Java code is necessary. This is not yet standardized (though an XSLT invocation mechanism is planned for JAXP 1.1), so the way to do this will depend on your particular XSLT processor.

With Xalan, you need to use an instance of the `org.apache.xalan.xslt.XSLTProcessor` class. Xalan can use Java streams (for example, files), DOM trees, or SAX events for both input and output, and also provides a facility to "compile" a frequently used stylesheet to speed up processing. The code below shows a simple example of performing an XSLT transformation where the original XML document and the stylesheet are again in `booktest.xml` and `booktran.xsl`, and the generated file is `booktest.html`:

```
import org.apache.xalan.xslt.*;

public class XSLTTest {

  public static void main(String args[]) throws org.xml.sax.SAXException {

    // Instantiate an XSLTProcessor
```

```
        XSLTProcessor processor = XSLTProcessorFactory.getProcessor();

        // Prepare the XML and XSL files and the destination file
        XSLTInputSource xmlFile = new XSLTInputSource("booktest.xml");
        XSLTInputSource xslFile =  new XSLTInputSource("booktran.xsl");
        XSLTResultTarget outputFile = new XSLTResultTarget("booktest.html");

        // Transform the document
        processor.process(xmlFile, xslFile, outputFile);
    }
}
```

Unfortunately it's not possible to cover all the possible ways of invoking Xalan from your own code here (and the method will be different for other XSLT processors, in any case) but there are extensive examples at `http://xml.apache.org/xalan/`.

Getting More Information

We have covered just a very small sample of the functionality that's included in XSLT, which is a large and somewhat complex language. Due to its size and complexity, it's not possible to cover it in depth in this chapter, but if you wish to learn more, you can find the complete specification at `http://www.w3.org/TR/xslt/`, or see *XSLT Programmer's Reference* by Michael Kay, Wrox Press, 2000, ISBN 1861003129.

Summary

In this chapter, we have looked at:

- ❑ HTML and why it is not a suitable medium for data storage.

- ❑ What XML is and its benefits as a storage medium. We have looked at the benefits of XML for transmitting data between applications. Being a text format it is both OS and programming language independent and is therefore invaluable in cross platform applications. We have seen that it can be a useful alternative/complement to traditional storage mediums, such as database techniques, because of the additional metadata provided.

- ❑ We looked at the structure of XML documents.

- ❑ Using DTDs to define the structure of an XML document. We have seen that, by defining a DTD, we are defining a new data markup language. This allows us to share data with other parties, and to extract data in a reliable and simple way. We can express data in a data centric way and leave interpretation and display to other systems in a way that leaves data storage loosely coupled to data consumption applications.

- ❑ We have seen how we can parse XML documents using the SAX and DOM APIs. We have seen their relative benefits, and drawbacks, and discussed when it is appropriate to use each parsing standard.

- ❑ We have discussed namespaces as a means to preventing name collisions. We have also mentioned Schemas; this is the emerging standard for specifying XML standards and you should certainly find out more if you intend to do much work in this area.

❑ We briefly examined transforming XML documents using XSLT. This is a vast subject and is also worth further examination. XSLT can be used as a means to providing content to multiple data consumers including applications and content browsers. We do this by transforming the data from its XML format to another format, XML or other. We saw how we can use XSLT to transform XML to HTML. You should note that XSLT can also be used to extract data from XML sources.

The next chapter looks at the issue of using distributed objects in Java.

Professional Java Programmin

15

Distributed Objects

In recent years, the approach used for most application development has shifted from client/server to three- or n-tier applications. In a multi-tiered design, the application is usually broken down into three components or "tiers": a presentation/user interface component, a business logic component, and a data storage and retrieval component, typically represented by a database. This type of architecture is usually more flexible and reusable than a similar client/server design, but it does increase the complexity of the application. One of the issues that must be addressed is how to allow the user interface and business logic components to communicate with one another, since it's common (but not necessary) for those two components to reside on separate machines. In addition, it's sometimes desirable for different parts of the business logic (or parts of the database) to reside on separate machines.

When different pieces of an application reside on separate physical machines, the program is known as a **distributed application**, and a **distributed object** is simply an object that allows its methods to be called by processes running on different machines, or communicating across different process spaces (such as different JVMs running on the same machine). This chapter examines the different technologies that are available for creating distributed objects in Java.

We will look in detail at:

- ❑   Sockets
- ❑   CORBA
- ❑   RMI
- ❑   Enterprise JavaBeans

Many books have been written on the topic of distributed objects and application design, and this chapter is not intended to provide in-depth information on the subject. Instead, it is intended to provide an introduction to the options that are available for creating distributed objects in Java and compare and contrast them at a high level.

For a more thorough study of distributed objects, especially in the enterprise arena, I would recommend you take a look at Professional Java Server Programming (1-861004-65-6), also from Wrox Press.

Terminology

Before looking at the options that are available for creating distributed objects, it's important to define some relevant terms. A **transport service** is a low-level mechanism for communicating over a network and the transport service that's used most commonly is TCP/IP, which stands for **Transmission Control Protocol/Internet Protocol**. To simplify TCP/IP programming, a **socket**-based API is often used, and a socket implementation is provided in Java's core classes, in the java.net package. In this context, a "socket" is simply one endpoint of a connection that's made between two processes, and each process uses its socket to communicate with the other process. As we'll see, sockets allow the processes to send and receive streams of binary data, and are not object-oriented in nature.

For two processes to communicate effectively they must agree upon the format and content of data that's sent between themselves through the transport service (sockets). The results that describe what data is sent (and when) are referred to as a **communications protocol** or simply a "protocol", and some examples of protocols are HyperText Transfer Protocol (HTTP, used primarily by web servers and browsers) and Internet Inter-Orb Protocol (IIOP) used by CORBA.

A **distributed object framework** refers to technology that can be used to create distributed objects, and examples of this are the Common Object Request Broker Architecture (CORBA) and Java's Remote Method Invocation (RMI). A distributed object framework may be tied to a particular communications protocol, as in the case of CORBA, which uses IIOP. However, frameworks can be independent of the protocol, as in the case of RMI, which can also use IIOP in addition to its default Java Remote Method Protocol (JRMP).

The Chat Application

To understand the different options that are available for creating distributed objects in Java, we'll implement three different versions of a crude chat application. The chat application server reads a list of userid/password combinations from a flat file, and each client must specify a valid combination when connecting to the server. If an invalid userid and/or password is specified, a LogonFailedException is thrown and an error dialog is displayed:

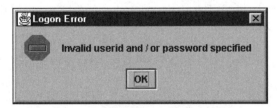

Once a user has logged on to the chat application, a client interface is displayed that allows the user to enter messages and view the messages entered by the chat users. When the user enters a message, that message is sent to the server component, and the server in turn forwards the message to each user that's logged on:

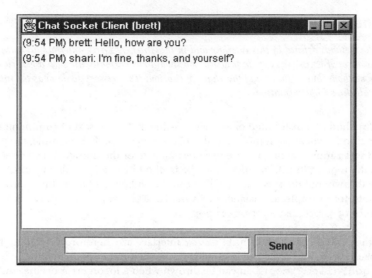

The basic functionality required for this chat application is provided in the classes described below. Later in the chapter, we'll see how to complete the application using three different approaches: sockets, CORBA and RMI.

ChatClient

This interface defines the one method that must be provided by each client implementation. Specifically, the client must provide a displayMessage() method that can be called by the server when the server broadcasts a message that was sent by one of the chat users:

```
package chat;

public interface ChatClient {

  public void displayMessage(ChatMessage message) throws Exception;

}
```

ChatServer

The server interface is also simple and defines just two methods that can be called by clients once they have logged on. The broadcastMessage() method sends a message to all active chat users, while getHistory() allows the client to retrieve the list of messages that were previously sent. Clients will invoke getHistory() immediately after logging on to the chat application so that they can see the messages that were sent before they logged on:

```
package chat;

public interface ChatServer {

  public void broadcastMessage(String message) throws Exception;

  public ChatMessage[] getHistory() throws Exception;

}
```

Exceptions When Calling Distributed Objects

Notice that the methods defined in this interface and in the ChatClient *interface all declare that they can throw instances of* Exception. *In practice, you should not normally use such a generic class when defining your methods, but in the case of this chat application, it's necessary to do so as the interface is to be used with all three implementations.*

When you call a method of a distributed object, it's possible that some sort of communications error can occur since the method invocation involves a call across the network. For example, the process that the distributed object was running in might have been terminated, or there might be some sort of network error that would cause the request to fail. In either case, the method invocation will fail, and some type of exception will be thrown, but the specific type of exception will depend upon the approach being used. If you're using sockets, for example, an instance of java.io.IOException will be thrown, while RMI would generate an instance of java.rmi.RemoteException.

The methods in the ChatClient and ChatServer interface are therefore defined to throw instances of Exception because those interfaces will be used with the different implementations of the chat application. In addition, a LogonFailedException can be thrown when a logon error occurs, and that exception is defined below:

```java
package chat;

public class LogonFailedException extends Exception {

  public LogonFailedException(String message) {
    super(message);
  }

}
```

ChatMessage

Instances of ChatMessage are passed to the client interface's displayMessage() method and an array of ChatMessage objects is returned from the server's getHistory() method. As shown below, each instance of ChatMessage includes message text along with an instance of java.util.Date that identifies when the message was sent. By sending the date/time of the message to the client, the chat application allows each client to display the message time according to the client locale's time formatting conventions:

```java
package chat;

import java.util.Date;

public class ChatMessage {

  public Date messageDate;
  public String messageText;

  public ChatMessage(Date date, String text) {
    messageDate = date;
    messageText = text;
  }

}
```

BaseClient

This code provides the basic functionality needed for the client portion of the chat application. These classes are to be extended by subclasses that will implement the specific communications methods later in this chapter. It maintains some user interface components that allow it to display the chat messages and to provide the user with the ability to enter new messages to be sent. In addition, it maintains a reference to a `ChatServer` implementation and the userid that was used to log on to the chat application:

```java
package chat;

import java.awt.*;
import java.awt.event.*;
import java.text.DateFormat;
import java.util.StringTokenizer;
import javax.swing.*;

public class BaseClient extends JPanel {

  protected JList messageList;
  protected DefaultListModel listModel;
  protected JTextField messageField;

  protected ChatServer server;

  protected String userid;

  public BaseClient() {
    buildLayout();
  }

  public BaseClient(String user, ChatServer s) {
    this();
    userid = user;
    server = s;
  }

  protected void buildLayout() {
    setLayout(new BorderLayout());
    listModel = new DefaultListModel();
    messageList = new JList(listModel);
    JScrollPane scrollPane = new JScrollPane(messageList);
    add(scrollPane, BorderLayout.CENTER);

    ActionListener listener = new ActionListener() {
      public void actionPerformed(ActionEvent event) {
        String message = messageField.getText();
        try {
          server.broadcastMessage(userid + ": " + message);
        } catch (Exception e) {}
        ;
        messageField.setText("");
      }
    };
    JPanel commandPanel = new JPanel();
    messageField = new JTextField(20);
```

```
    messageField.addActionListener(listener);
    commandPanel.add(messageField);

    JButton sendButton = new JButton("Send");
    sendButton.addActionListener(listener);
    commandPanel.add(sendButton);
    add(commandPanel, BorderLayout.SOUTH);
  }

  public void displayMessage(ChatMessage message) {
    DateFormat formatter = DateFormat.getTimeInstance(DateFormat.SHORT);
    java.util.Date msgDate = message.messageDate;
    String msgText = message.messageText;
    String line = "(" + formatter.format(msgDate) + ") " + msgText;
    listModel.addElement(line);
    int count = listModel.getSize();
    messageList.ensureIndexIsVisible(count - 1);
  }

  public void displayHistory() throws Exception {
    ChatMessage[] messages = server.getHistory();
    for (int i = 0; i < messages.length; i++) {
      displayMessage(messages[i]);
    }
  }
}
```

BaseServer

This class provides the functionality needed to support the server portion of the chat application. It maintains a list of valid userid/password combinations that are read from a disk file, a list of currently logged on clients, and a list of messages that have been sent (the message "history"):

```
package chat;

import java.io.*;
import java.util.*;

public class BaseServer {

  public final static String USER_LIST_FILE = "userlist.txt";

  public final static int HISTORY_LENGTH = 100;

  protected Hashtable userList = new Hashtable();
  protected Vector clientList = new Vector();
  protected Vector messageHistory = new Vector();

  public BaseServer() throws IOException {
    readUserList();
  }

  protected void readUserList() throws IOException {
    String userid;
    String password;
```

```
      File f = new File(USER_LIST_FILE);
      if (!(f.exists())) {
        return;
      }
      FileReader fileReader = new FileReader(f);
      BufferedReader reader = new BufferedReader(fileReader);
      String fileText = reader.readLine();
      while (fileText != null) {
        int index = fileText.indexOf(' ');
        if (index != -1) {
          userid = fileText.substring(0, index);
          password = fileText.substring(index + 1);
          userList.put(userid.toLowerCase(), password);
        }
        fileText = reader.readLine();
      }
      reader.close();
    }


    public synchronized boolean isValidUserInfo(String user,
                                                String password) {
      String actualPassword = (String) (userList.get(user.toLowerCase()));
      return ((actualPassword != null)
              && actualPassword.equalsIgnoreCase(password));
    }


    public synchronized void addClient(ChatClient client) {
      clientList.addElement(client);
    }


    public synchronized void broadcastMessage(String text) {
      ChatClient client;
      java.util.Date curdate = new java.util.Date();
      ChatMessage message = new ChatMessage(curdate, text);
      Enumeration clients = clientList.elements();
      while (clients.hasMoreElements()) {
        client = (ChatClient) (clients.nextElement());
        try {
          client.displayMessage(message);
        } catch (Exception e) {}
        ;
      }
      addMessageToHistory(message);
    }


    protected synchronized void addMessageToHistory(ChatMessage message) {
      messageHistory.addElement(message);
      while (messageHistory.size() > HISTORY_LENGTH) {
        messageHistory.removeElementAt(0);
      }
    }


    public ChatMessage[] getHistory() {
      int count = messageHistory.size();
      ChatMessage[] messages = new ChatMessage[count];
```

```
    for (int i = 0; i < count; i++) {
      messages[i] = (ChatMessage) (messageHistory.elementAt(i));
    }
    return messages;
  }

}
```

You may be wondering why neither `BaseClient` nor `BaseServer` implement the `ChatClient` and `ChatServer` interfaces we defined earlier. Once we've discussed sockets and what we'll need to do to implement the application properly, we'll return to these interfaces.

Client vs. Server

Although the files and interfaces defined above are called `ChatClient`, `BaseClient`, `ChatServer`, and `BaseServer`, the distinction between a "client" and a "server" may not be as obvious as it seems. In one context, a "client" is simply a user of some application, while the "server" is a software component that provides services to the client(s). In this case, for example, the client can be thought of as `ChatClient` and `BaseClient`, and/or as the human user who enters and reads messages. Similarly, "server" may refer to the `ChatServer` and `BaseServer` code and/or to the physical machine on which the code executes.

As mentioned earlier, however, in the context of distributed objects, "client" usually refers simply to the process that calls the method of a distributed object, while "server" refers to the distributed object being called. In that context, the `ChatClient` and `ChatServer` implementations each represent both a client and a server. For example, `ChatClient` acts as a client when it invokes the server"s `broadcastMessage()` method, but the `ChatClient` acts as a server when its `displayMessage()` method is called by the `ChatServer`.

Sockets

As mentioned earlier, sockets provide an API that allows you to use TCP/IP to communicate between two processes running on different machines, and the socket classes are defined in the `java.net` package. For a connection to be established one of the processes must be waiting for connections using a `ServerSocket` and the other process must create a connection by instantiating a (client) `Socket`.

Establishing a Connection

For the client to establish the connection, an **address** and a **port** must be passed to the `Socket` constructor.

Address

To connect to another process, you must identify the machine on which that process exists, and an address can be specified using an instance of `InetAddress`. Each `InetAddress` encapsulates an **Internet Protocol (IP) address**, and an instance can be obtained by using the static `getByName()` factory method, passing that method either an IP address or a **host name**.

Each machine connected to the Internet is assigned a unique IP address that consists of four eight-bit numeric values (for example, 204.148.170.3). However, since such identifiers are difficult for people to remember, each machine is also usually assigned at least one "domain" or host name that maps to its IP address. The host name is translated into the corresponding IP address by the **Domain Name System (DNS)**. For example, if you wish to browse the Wrox web site, you don't have to remember the web server's IP address, but can simply specify its host name when entering the URL. To create an instance of `InetAddress` that corresponds to the Wrox web server, you could use either of the following:

```
InetAddress wroxAddress = InetAddress.getByName("204.148.170.161");
```

or:

```
InetAddress wroxAddress = InetAddress.getByName("www.wrox.com");
```

Note that "localhost" and the IP address 127.0.0.1 have a special meaning: they are both used to represent the local machine. For example, one process can connect to another process running on the same physical machine by specifying a host name of "localhost" or an IP address of 127.0.0.1. You can use `InetAddress.getByName(null)` to get a reference to localhost.

Port

To connect to a particular process on some machine, you must specify that machine's address, along with the port on which the process you wish to connect to is listening. To understand ports, it may be helpful to compare them to telephone extensions used by large organizations and in buildings where many individuals are located. You're often able to reach an operator or automated system by calling some central number (which corresponds to an IP address) and can then connect to an individual (the process) by entering an extension (the port number).

Since it's necessary for a client to know the port number that a server is listening on, you normally must decide in advance which port number will be used for incoming connections. In general, that number should be a value between 1025 and 5000 (inclusive) that's not already used by some other application, since port numbers below 1025 are reserved for well-known services such as FTP and TELNET.

ServerSocket

To create a `ServerSocket`, you must specify the port number on which it should listen for incoming connections, or you can specify zero (0) to have a port number selected automatically. For example, you could use the following code to create a `ServerSocket` to listen on port 1234 for incoming connections:

```
ServerSocket ss = new ServerSocket(1234);
```

Once the `ServerSocket` is created, you can use its `accept()` method to wait for an incoming connection, and that method returns an instance of `Socket`:

```
ServerSocket ss = new ServerSocket(1234);
Socket s = ss.accept();
```

The `accept()` method blocks until an incoming connection has been created, at which time it returns a `Socket` instance that can be used to communicate with the client that created the connection.

Note that when a `Socket` is returned from `accept()`, that socket does not use the same port number that the `ServerSocket` listens on for incoming connections. Instead, the new `Socket` is automatically assigned a different port number, which allows a single `ServerSocket` instance to be used repeatedly to accept incoming connections.

Socket

An instance of `Socket` represents one side of a connection between two processes, and when a connection is complete, both the client and the server will use instances of `Socket`. As we saw previously, the server's socket is normally created by calling `accept()`, and that method will return a `Socket` when a client creates a connection.

For a client to connect to a server that's waiting for connections, the client must explicitly create an instance of `Socket`, passing to its constructor an `InetAddress` or a `String` containing the host name, and a port number. The `InetAddress` instance or host name must identify the host machine to which the connection should be made, while the port number must identify the port on which the server is listening for connections. For example, to connect to the Wrox web server at port 80, you could use the following code:

```
Socket s = new Socket("www.wrox.com", 80);
```

or:

```
InetAddress wroxAddr = InetAddress.getByName("www.wrox.com");
Socket s = new Socket(wroxAddr, 80);
```

When a `Socket` is created this way, it's automatically assigned to one of your machine's ports, and you do not normally need to be concerned with which one is selected.

Once a connection is established, you can retrieve instances of `java.io.OutputStream` and `java.io.InputStream` from the `Socket` and use those to send and receive data, respectively. For example, the following code connects to the Wrox web server, requests that it return the contents of the default HTML page, and prints the data returned by the web server:

```
Socket s = new Socket("www.wrox.com", 80);
OutputStream os = s.getOutputStream();
PrintStream ps = new PrintStream(os);
ps.print("GET / HTTP/1.0\r\n\r\n");
InputStream is = s.getInputStream();
InputStreamReader isr = new InputStreamReader(is);
BufferedReader br = new BufferedReader(isr);
String line = br.readLine();
while (line != null) {
  System.out.println(line);
  line = br.readLine();
}
```

Implementing a ChatServer Using Sockets

Now that we've seen how information can be sent and retrieved using sockets, we can begin to construct a class that uses them to handle the server portion of the chat application. First, there must be a way for a client to connect to the chat server, which can be done by having the server code create a `ServerSocket` and wait for incoming connections:

```
package chat.socket;

import chat.*;

import java.io.*;
import java.net.*;

public class SocketServer extends BaseServer {

  public final static int PORT_NUMBER = 1234;

  public static void main(String[] args) throws IOException {
    SocketServer ss = new SocketServer();
  }

  public SocketServer() throws IOException {
    Socket client;
    ServerSocket ss = new ServerSocket(PORT_NUMBER);
    while (true) {
      client = ss.accept();
      // ...
    }
  }

  // ...

}
```

This code loops continuously, waiting for incoming connections and creating `Socket` instances for each one, but does nothing when a connection is created. By definition, the chat application is only useful if multiple users can be logged on to it simultaneously, and for the server to support multiple users, it must be able to wait for messages from each of those users. The best way to accomplish this is to create a separate thread for each user and allow that thread to wait for incoming messages:

```
  public SocketServer() throws IOException {
    Socket client;
    ServerSocket ss = new ServerSocket(PORT_NUMBER);
    while (true) {
      client = ss.accept();
      SocketSkeleton skel = new SocketSkeleton(client);
      addClient(skel);
      skel.start();
    }
  }

  class SocketSkeleton extends Thread implements ChatClient {

    protected Socket receiveSocket;

    public SocketSkeleton(Socket client) {
      receiveSocket = client;
    }

    public void run() {
      // ...
```

```
        }

        public void displayMessage(ChatMessage message) throws IOException {
            // ...
        }

    }

}
```

The inner class called SocketSkeleton will serve as a client's **proxy** on the server machine. In other words, calls to the displayMessage() method of a SocketSkeleton will be transmitted across the network to the client code on a user's machine. Similarly, calls from a chat client to the chat server's broadcastMessage() and getHistory() methods will be received by the thread executing the run() method of the SocketSkeleton instance, forwarded to the chat server, and the results returned to the client:

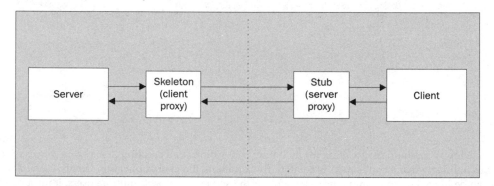

Sockets represent a primitive send/receive mechanism for communication, and do not explicitly provide the ability for one process to call another's methods. However, we can simulate this capability by defining a protocol that allows the client code to send data to the server that indicates which server method should be called. For example, an integer value can be arbitrarily selected for each server method, and the client code can transmit an integer value to the server to indicate which method should be called.

In the code shown below, the initialize() method creates an InputStream and OutputStream pair that will be used to read incoming command/method invocations from the client and to return the results of the method call to the client. The thread then waits for an int value to be received from the client, compares that value to the INVOKE_GET_HISTORY and INVOKE_BROADCAST constants, and calls the appropriate method. If the method requires parameter values, those values will be read from the InputStream, and if any return value is provided by the method, it is written to the OutputStream:

```
package chat.socket;

import chat.*;

import java.io.*;
import java.net.*;

public class SocketServer extends BaseServer {
```

```
public final static int PORT_NUMBER = 1234;
public final static int INVOKE_GET_HISTORY = 0;
public final static int INVOKE_BROADCAST = 1;

// ...

class SocketSkeleton extends Thread implements ChatClient {

// ...

  public void run() {
    int methodID;
    try {
      initialize();
      while (true) {
        methodID = inInput.readInt();
        switch (methodID) {
          case INVOKE_BROADCAST:
            handleBroadcast();
            break;
          case INVOKE_GET_HISTORY:
            handleGetHistory();
            break;
        }
      }
    } catch (Exception ioe) {}
  }

  protected void handleBroadcast() throws IOException {
    String message = inInput.readUTF();
    broadcastMessage(message);
  }

  protected void handleGetHistory() throws IOException {
    ChatMessage message;
    java.util.Date msgDate;
    String msgText;

    int count = messageHistory.size();
    inOutput.writeInt(count);
    for (int i = 0; i < count; i++) {
      message = (ChatMessage)
        (messageHistory.elementAt(i));
      msgDate = message.messageDate;
      msgText = message.messageText;
      inOutput.writeLong(
        msgDate.getTime());
      inOutput.writeUTF(msgText);
    }
  }

  protected void initialize() throws IOException, LogonFailedException {
    InputStream is;
    OutputStream os;
```

```
        is = receiveSocket.getInputStream();
        inInput = new DataInputStream(is);
        os = receiveSocket.getOutputStream();
        inOutput = new DataOutputStream(os);
      }

  // ...

    }

  }
```

Although this does address the issue of calls from the client to the server, there are two problems with the existing application. First, there is no user validation/logon processing that ensures that the user has the authorization to use the chat application. In addition, while it is possible for the client to call the server's methods, it is not possible for the server to invoke the client's `displayMessage()` method. The logon problem can be addressed easily by requiring that the client send a valid userid and password using the incoming socket connection prior to any server method invocations. After reading the userid and password, the server sends a response to the client indicating whether the logon attempt was successful. The response is represented by an integer value equal to one of two constants defined in `SocketServer`: LOGON_SUCCESSFUL or LOGON_FAILED:

```
package chat.socket;

import chat.*;

import java.io.*;
import java.net.*;

public class SocketServer extends BaseServer {

  // ...

    public final static int LOGON_SUCCESSFUL = 0;
    public final static int LOGON_FAILED = -1;

  // ...

    class SocketSkeleton extends Thread implements ChatClient {

      protected DataInputStream inInput;
      protected DataOutputStream inOutput;

      // ...

      protected void initialize() throws IOException, LogonFailedException {
        InputStream is;
        OutputStream os;

        is = receiveSocket.getInputStream();
        inInput = new DataInputStream(is);
        os = receiveSocket.getOutputStream();
        inOutput = new DataOutputStream(os);
        String userid = inInput.readUTF();
```

```
      String password = inInput.readUTF();
      if (isValidUserInfo(userid, password)) {
        inOutput.writeInt(LOGON_SUCCESSFUL);
      }
      else {
        inOutput.writeInt(LOGON_FAILED);
        throw new LogonFailedException("Invalid userid / password");
      }
    }
```

The remaining problem of allowing the server to invoke the client's methods is somewhat more complex. Although the receiveSocket can be used to both send and receive data, it's not possible to use it for server-to-client invocations when it is also used for client-to-server calls. If one thread attempts to transmit data over a socket while another thread is blocked waiting to receive data from that socket, the first thread will also become blocked. What's needed is a second socket connection between the client and the server that can be used exclusively for server-to-client calls.

One way to accomplish this is to have the client code create a ServerSocket and wait for an incoming connect after it has successfully obtained a connection to the server. The following code modifies the initialize() method so that it reads an additional int value from the newly created socket connection and uses that value as the port number to create a second connection to the client. That connection can then be used to transmit displayMessage() calls to the client, as shown below:

```
class SocketSkeleton extends Thread implements ChatClient {

  protected DataInputStream inInput;
  protected DataOutputStream inOutput;

  protected DataOutputStream outOutput;

  protected Socket receiveSocket;
  protected Socket sendSocket;

  // ...

  protected void initialize() throws IOException {
    InputStream is;
    OutputStream os;
    InetAddress addr;

    is = receiveSocket.getInputStream();
    inInput = new DataInputStream(is);
    os = receiveSocket.getOutputStream();
    inOutput = new DataOutputStream(os);
    String userid = inInput.readUTF();
    String password = inInput.readUTF();
    int sendPort = inInput.readInt();
    addr = receiveSocket.getInetAddress();
    if (isValidUserInfo(userid, password)) {
      inOutput.writeInt(LOGON_SUCCESSFUL);
      sendSocket = new Socket(addr, sendPort);
      os = sendSocket.getOutputStream();
      outOutput = new DataOutputStream(os);
    }
```

```
        else {
          inOutput.writeInt(LOGON_FAILED);
          throw new IOException("Logon failure");
        }
      }

    public void displayMessage(ChatMessage message)
        throws IOException {
      java.util.Date msgDate = message.messageDate;
      long timeValue = msgDate.getTime();
      String msgText = message.messageText;
      outOutput.writeLong(timeValue);
      outOutput.writeUTF(msgText);
    }

  }

}
```

Implementing a ChatClient Using Sockets

With the SocketServer class completed, we can now create the SocketClient class as well. Given the functionality that's defined in the server, the client must perform the following tasks when initialized:

❑   Create a connection to the server using the port number on which the server listens. This connection will be used by the server to process calls from the client to the server and to return the results of those calls to the client.

❑   Transmit a valid user and password to the server using the socket connection.

❑   Create a ServerSocket that will be used to create a second connection between this client and the server. This connection will be used to allow the server to call the client's displayMessage() method.

Just as the SocketServer defined a client proxy called SocketSkeleton, the SocketClient defines a server proxy called SocketStub. That class will be used to convert calls to the server's methods into data that can be sent across a socket connection, and will read the results of those calls from the connection. Its run() method also allows a thread to loop continuously, waiting for data from the server that represents calls to the client's displayMessage() method:

```
package chat.socket;

import chat.*;

import java.awt.*;
import java.io.*;
import java.net.*;
import javax.swing.*;

public class SocketClient extends BaseClient {

  public static void main(String[] args) throws Exception {
    String userid = (args.length > 0 ? args[0] : "brett");
    String password = (args.length > 1 ? args[1] : "bspell");
```

```
    String host = (args.length > 2 ? args[2] : "localhost");

    SocketClient sc = new SocketClient(userid, password, host);
    JFrame f = new JFrame("Chat Socket Client (" + userid + ")");
    f.getContentPane().add(sc, BorderLayout.CENTER);
    f.setSize(400, 300);
    f.setVisible(true);
  }

  public SocketClient(String user, String password,
                      String host) throws Exception {
    userid = user;
    try {
      server = new SocketStub(user, password, host);
      displayHistory();
    } catch (Exception e) {
      JOptionPane.showMessageDialog(this, e.getMessage(), "Logon Error",
                                    JOptionPane.ERROR_MESSAGE);
      System.exit(0);
    }
  }
}

class SocketStub extends Thread implements ChatServer {

  protected ServerSocket serverSocket;

  protected Socket sendSocket;
  protected Socket receiveSocket;

  protected DataOutputStream outOutput;
  protected DataInputStream outInput;

  protected DataInputStream inInput;

  public SocketStub(String userid, String password, String host)
          throws IOException, LogonFailedException {
    serverSocket = new ServerSocket(0);
    setPriority(Thread.MAX_PRIORITY);
    start();
    performLogon(userid, password, host);
  }

  public void performLogon(String user, String password, String host)
          throws IOException, LogonFailedException {
    InputStream is;
    OutputStream os;

    InetAddress addr = InetAddress.getByName(host);
    sendSocket = new Socket(addr, SocketServer.PORT_NUMBER);
    is = sendSocket.getInputStream();
    outInput = new DataInputStream(is);
    os = sendSocket.getOutputStream();
    outOutput = new DataOutputStream(os);
    outOutput.writeUTF(user);
    outOutput.writeUTF(password);
```

```
      outOutput.writeInt(serverSocket.getLocalPort());
      int status = outInput.readInt();
      if (status == SocketServer.LOGON_FAILED) {
        throw new LogonFailedException("Invalid userid and/or password "
                                    + "specified");
      }
  }

  public void run() {
    ChatMessage message;
    long timeValue;
    java.util.Date msgDate;
    String msgText;
    try {
      initialize();
      while (true) {
        timeValue = inInput.readLong();
        msgText = inInput.readUTF();
        msgDate = new java.util.Date(timeValue);
        message = new ChatMessage(msgDate, msgText);
        displayMessage(message);
      }
    } catch (Exception ioe) {}
    ;
  }

  protected void initialize() throws IOException {
    InetAddress sendaddr;
    InetAddress recvaddr;
    InputStream is;
    Socket s = serverSocket.accept();
    sendaddr = sendSocket.getInetAddress();
    recvaddr = s.getInetAddress();
    if (sendaddr.equals(recvaddr)) {
      receiveSocket = s;
      is = receiveSocket.getInputStream();
      inInput = new DataInputStream(is);
    }
  }

  public void broadcastMessage(String message) throws IOException {
    outOutput.writeInt(SocketServer.INVOKE_BROADCAST);
    outOutput.writeUTF(message);
  }

  public ChatMessage[] getHistory() throws IOException {
    ChatMessage[] messages = null;

    int count;
    long timeValue;
    java.util.Date msgDate;
    String msgText;

    outOutput.writeInt(SocketServer.INVOKE_GET_HISTORY);
    count = outInput.readInt();
```

```
        messages = new ChatMessage[count];
        for (int i = 0; i < count; i++) {
          timeValue = outInput.readLong();
          msgText = outInput.readUTF();
          msgDate = new java.util.Date(timeValue);
          messages[i] = new ChatMessage(msgDate, msgText);
        }
        return messages;
      }
   }
}
```

Executing the Socket-Based Chat Application

To execute the application, you must do the following:

❑ Define a list of valid userid/password combinations in a file named `userlist.txt`. That file should contain a line for each valid userid/password combination that can be used to log on to the chat application. An example of the contents you might place in this file is shown below:

```
bspell brett

someuser mypassword

dschales secret
```

❑ Execute the `SocketServer` application:

```
java chat.socket.SocketServer
```

❑ Execute one or more instances of the `SocketClient` application, specifying a userid/password combination that's defined in the `userlist.txt` file:

```
java chat.socket.SocketClient bspell brett
```

Socket Summary

As this example illustrates, it is possible to create distributed objects using sockets, but you should not normally do so. Distributed object frameworks such as CORBA and RMI will handle many of the details easily or automatically that you must write code for yourself when using sockets. For example, it was necessary in this case to manually implement the client proxy ("stub") and server proxy ("skeleton") classes used to convert a method invocation and its parameter values into streams of bytes. However, when you use CORBA or RMI, those classes are created for you, and they provide much more robust implementations than the ones created here.

CORBA

CORBA, which stands for **Common Object Request Broker Architecture**, was created by the Object Management Group (http://www.omg.org/), an industry consortium with hundreds of members. Like Java, CORBA provides a form of cross-platform compatibility, but in a much more limited sense. CORBA makes it possible for a distributed object on one platform to be used by applications that may reside on other platforms and which may be written in different programming languages from that used to create the distributed object.

CORBA does use a language called the **Interface Definition Language (IDL)**, but it does not allow you to create distributed object implementations, at least not directly. Instead, IDL is simply used to define the methods available with a given distributed object, along with the types of data that are passed to and returned from those methods. To create a distributed object using CORBA, you must first create the IDL code that defines the object's methods, compile this IDL, and use the source code generated by the IDL compiler (also called stubs) to create the object implementation. We will look at each of these stages in turn.

Defining Distributed Object Methods in IDL

For the most part, IDL is simple and somewhat intuitive for Java programmers, and we'll now use IDL to define the methods provided by implementations of the `ChatClient` and `ChatServer` interfaces. To begin defining the methods an object provides, you must first specify the package in which the object is located, using the `module` keyword. In this case, for example, we'll eventually create `CORBAClient` and `CORBAServer` classes that will be stored in a package named `chat.corba`, so the IDL could begin with the following two `module` statements. The indention is not required, but makes the IDL more readable and is common practice:

```
module chat {
  module corba {

  };
};
```

As mentioned earlier, we'll eventually use an IDL compiler to generate some Java source code files using this IDL, and that source code will be used to build the distributed objects. In effect, the IDL will generate the interfaces and some other related classes, and we'll create implementation classes called `CORBAClient` and `CORBAServer` that implement those interfaces. The keyword used to define an interface in IDL is called (intuitively enough) `interface` and so we define our interfaces as shown below:

```
module chat {
  module corba {

    interface CORBAChatClient {
    };

    interface CORBAChatServer {
    };

  };
};
```

We've now created `CORBAChatClient` and `CORBAChatServer` interfaces, although no methods have been defined in either one yet. The `broadcastMessage()` method can easily be mapped to IDL, since it is passed a single `String` parameter and does not return a result. In this case, that parameter is mapped to a `String` variable named `message` and closely resembles a method declaration in a Java interface:

```
interface CORBAChatServer {
  void broadcastMessage(in string message);
};
```

The void keyword in CORBA maps directly to the void keyword in Java: both indicate that no value is returned from the method. IDL method signatures are very similar to those in Java, and include comma-delimited argument descriptions, but broadcastMessage() accepts only a single argument. Unlike Java, however, IDL supports three types of parameters: in, out, and inout parameters. An in parameter represents a pass-by-value argument, which is the only type of argument that Java supports directly. For example, suppose that you're given the following Java code:

```java
public void callerMethod() {
    String mine = "Hello";
    calledMethod(mine);
    System.out.println(mine);
}

public void calledMethod(String parm) {
    parm = "Goodbye";
}
```

Since calledMethod() is given its own reference to the String value that's passed as an argument, it cannot modify the reference to the text maintained by callerMethod(), and executing this code will cause "Hello" to be printed. However, we can simulate a call by reference using a **holder class** as shown below:

```java
class StringHolder {

    public StringHolder(String ref) {
        stringReference = ref;
    }

    public String stringReference;
}
```

```java
public void callerMethod() {
    StringHolder holder = new StringHolder("Hello");
    calledMethod(holder);
    System.out.println(holder.stringReference);
}

public void calledMethod(StringHolder holder) {
    holder.stringReference = "Goodbye";
}
```

By passing a reference to an object that maintains a reference to another object, it's possible for calledMethod() to modify the caller's reference, and executing this code will cause it to display the "Goodbye" message. In effect, by using a holder class, we've simulated call-by-reference functionality that allows the called method to modify the caller's reference, and that's exactly what CORBA's out and inout argument types imply. In fact, as we'll see later, IDL compilers generate holder classes automatically for interfaces and data types that you define within your IDL.

Data Types in CORBA

As we saw earlier, the broadCastMessage() method was defined in the CORBAChatServer interface with a type of string, as shown below:

```java
void broadcastMessage(in string message);
```

The `string` type is one of a number of data types defined in CORBA that map directly to a Java data type, and some of the other types are listed in the table below:

Java Type	CORBA Type
String	wstring
boolean	boolean
char	wchar
byte	octet
short	unsigned short
int	unsigned long
long	unsigned long long
float	float
double	double

The Java data types that map to existing CORBA types can be passed to and/or returned from methods defined in a CORBA interface. However, before you can pass a reference to some user-defined type such as `ChatMessage`, you must include a definition to that type in the IDL file.

User-Defined Data Types

In addition to `broadcastMessage()`, the `ChatServer` interface also defines a `getHistory()` method that returns an array of `ChatMessage` objects. As defined earlier in this chapter, `ChatMessage` is a simple class that encapsulates two data items: an instance of `java.util.Date` and a `String` representing message text. The message text field can be mapped directly to an existing CORBA type, since Java `String` instances correspond to the CORBA string type, but there is no CORBA equivalent for Java's `Date` class.

To create an IDL equivalent of the `ChatMessage` class, it's necessary to represent a `Date` instance using one of the types that CORBA does support. Fortunately, the date/time value encapsulated by a `Date` instance can be represented as a single (Java) `long` value. That value can be retrieved from a `Date` instance using its `getTime()` method, and a `Date` constructor is available that creates an instance of `Date` using a `long` value. Therefore, a user-defined type can be created in IDL that encapsulates a `string` and a `long long` (the CORBA equivalent of Java's `long` type), and that type can be used to transport `ChatMessage` data.

To create a user-defined data type in CORBA, you can use the `struct` keyword to define a **structure** that encapsulates multiple data items. In this case, we'll define a structure in IDL that corresponds to the `ChatMessage` class, as shown below:

```
module chat {
  module corba {

    struct ChatMessageStruct {
      long long messageTime;
      string messageText;
    };
```

```
      interface CORBAChatClient {
      };

      interface CORBAChatServer {
        void broadcastMessage(in string message);
      };

    };
  };
```

We've now defined a data type that can be used to return history data from the server's `getHistory()` method, but there's one more step that must be taken before we can include that method's definition in the `CORBAChatServer` interface. CORBA does not allow you to define a method that is passed or returns an array of items, which `getHistory()` is designed to do. However, you can create a user-defined data type that represents an array and use that type as the method's return type or as an argument type as shown below:

```
typedef ChatMessageStruct messages[100];
interface CORBAChatServer {
  messages getHistory();
};
```

The problem with this approach is that the number of `ChatMessageStruct` objects isn't known at compilation time, and it could theoretically exceed the 100-instance limit that's imposed by this IDL. Fortunately, CORBA also allows you to define a **sequence**, which is simply a one-dimensional array of undetermined size, and we can easily define a sequence using code like that shown below:

```
typedef sequence<ChatMessageStruct> messages;
```

The above line of code defines a new data type called `messages` that represents a sequence (an array of `ChatMessageStruct` objects of unspecified size). With this new type defined, we can complete the implementation of the `CORBAChatServer` interface by defining the `getHistory()` method:

```
module chat {
  module corba {

    struct ChatMessageStruct {
      long long messageTime;
      string messageText;
    };

    typedef sequence<ChatMessageStruct> messages;

    interface CORBAChatClient {
    };

    interface CORBAChatServer {
      void broadcastMessage(in string message);
      messages getHistory();
    };

  };
};
```

Next, the CORBAChatClient interface can be completed as well. That interface includes only a single displayMessage() method that's passed an instance of ChatMessageStruct representing a message that was received from the server:

```
// ...

    interface CORBAChatClient {
      void displayMessage(in ChatMessageStruct message);
    };

// ...
```

Finally, we can complete the IDL for the chat application by defining an interface that will allow a client to log on to the server. This interface will include a performLogon() method that accepts three parameters: a userid, a password, and a reference to a CORBAChatClient instance. The CORBAChatClient must be passed to the server during logon so that the server can send messages that are broadcast by the chat users to the user who is logging on.

If the client passes an invalid userid/password combination to the logon manager, the logon manager should throw an exception. You can define exceptions in IDL in much the same way that user-defined types are generated, although you must use the exception keyword as shown below:

```
exception LogonFailed {
  string message;
};
```

This IDL segment defines an exception named LogonFailed that contains a reference to a String value, and in this case, that value will contain the message text associated with the exception.

With the LogonFailed exception defined, the IDL for the chat application can be completed by defining the LogonManager interface and its performLogon() method as shown below. Note that the raises keyword is used to identify exceptions that can be generated when a method is called:

```
module chat {
  module corba {

    struct ChatMessageStruct {
      long long messageTime;
      string messageText;
    };

    typedef sequence<ChatMessageStruct> messages;

    interface CORBAChatClient {
      void displayMessage(in ChatMessageStruct message);
    };

    interface CORBAChatServer {

      void broadcastMessage(in string message);

      messages getHistory();

    };

    exception LogonFailed {
```

```
        string message;
    };

    interface LogonManager {

        CORBAChatServer performLogon(in string userid,
            in string password,
            in CORBAChatClient client)
            raises (LogonFailed);

    };
  };
};
```

On the surface, it might appear that the performLogon() method should be added to the CORBAChatServer interface instead of being defined in its own interface, but that is not the case. For a client to call performLogon(), the client must obtain a reference to the distributed object that implements that method. If performLogon() were included in the CORBAChatServer interface, giving the client the ability to access the performLogon() method would also allow the client to call broadcastMessage() and getHistory() before logging on. Instead, the application is designed so that only the LogonManager object is directly accessible to the client, and to obtain access to the CORBAChatServer, the client must pass a valid userid and password to performLogon().

Compiling IDL

With the chat application's IDL completed, we can now compile the IDL file, which will generate many Java source files. To compile IDL, you must have access to an IDL compiler that corresponds to the language that you're using to create the distributed object(s). In this case, for example, we're using Java, so we need an IDL-to-Java compiler, and one is included with the Java 2 Software Development Kit 1.3.

The name of the utility is idlj, and it can be used to generate the Java **bindings** for an IDL file. Bindings are simply the Java source code files that correspond to the IDL, and those files can be used to create a distributed CORBA object. To compile the IDL created for the chat application, you could use the following command if the IDL is stored in a file called CORBAChat.idl:

```
idlj -fall CORBAChat.idl
```

The -f option is used to identify which bindings (client and/or server) should be created, and in this case, both the client and server ("all") bindings are generated. When this command is executed, it will create a large number of files in the chat/corba subdirectory, including the following:

Helpers

The idlj utility generates a "helper" source file for each interface, struct, and typedef defined within the IDL, and that file provides convenience methods for the associated type of entity; the class name has Helper appended.

For example, the helper class associated with an interface definition includes a narrow() method that allows you to cast an instance of org.omg.CORBA.Object to the specific class associated with the interface. As we'll see, most CORBA-related methods that return an object reference simply return a reference to an instance of org.omg.CORBA.Object. Before that object's methods can be used, you must cast it to a specific subclass, which is done using the narrow() method in the helper for that subclass.

Holders

As mentioned earlier, Java supports only pass-by-value method calls (in parameters) directly, but CORBA supports pass-by-reference through `out` and `inout` parameters. Holder classes allow Java code to simulate `out` and `inout` parameters by passing a reference to a holder on a method call, while the holder object maintains a reference to the actual parameter value; their names have `Holder` appended. In other words, the holder classes provide the same functionality as the `StringHolder` class defined earlier in this chapter.

Operations

An operations interface is generated for each interface defined in the IDL, and each is assigned the name of the interface with `Operations` appended to it. The operations classes simply define the interfaces implemented by the distributed object as shown below.

```
package chat.corba;


/**
 * chat/corba/CORBAChatServerOperations.java
 * Generated by the IDL-to-Java compiler (portable), version "3.0"
 * from corbachat.idl
 * Wednesday, September 27, 2000 4:00:20 PM GMT+01:00
 */

public interface CORBAChatServerOperations
{
  void broadcastMessage (String message);
  chat.corba.ChatMessageStruct[] getHistory ();
} // interface CORBAChatServerOperations
```

Interfaces

The interfaces generated by `idlj` are similar to the operations classes and actually extend those interfaces, but they also extend other interfaces that must be implemented to create a distributed object instance. As shown below, the `CORBAChatServer` interface generated by the IDL compiler extends not only `CORBAChatServerOperations`, but also the `org.omg.CORBA.Object` and `org.omg.CORBA.portable.IDLEntity` interfaces:

```
package chat.corba;


/**
 * chat/corba/CORBAChatServer.java
 * Generated by the IDL-to-Java compiler (portable), version "3.0"
 * from corbachat.idl
 * Wednesday, September 27, 2000 4:00:20 PM GMT+01:00
 */

public interface CORBAChatServer extends CORBAChatServerOperations,
org.omg.CORBA.Object, org.omg.CORBA.portable.IDLEntity
{
} // interface CORBAChatServer
```

Stubs

A "stub" is generated for each interface, and is used by a CORBA client to invoke the methods of a server object.

ImplBase Classes

An `ImplBase` class is created for each interface defined in your IDL, and you should extend that class to complete the implementation of your distributed CORBA objects. For example, the `CORBAServer` class that we'll define shortly will extend the `ImplBase` class generated by the IDL compiler.

User-Defined Types

The IDL compiler will also generate source files for the structures defined in your IDL, such as the `ChatMessageStruct` type described previously, and these files define simple data encapsulation classes like the one shown below:

```
package chat.corba;


/**
 * chat/corba/ChatMessageStruct.java
 * Generated by the IDL-to-Java compiler (portable), version "3.0"
 * from corbachat.idl
 * Wednesday, September 27, 2000 4:00:20 PM GMT+01:00
 */

public final class ChatMessageStruct implements org.omg.CORBA.portable.IDLEntity
{
  public long messageTime = (long)0;
  public String messageText = null;

  public ChatMessageStruct ()
  {
  } // ctor

  public ChatMessageStruct (long _messageTime, String _messageText)
  {
    messageTime = _messageTime;
    messageText = _messageText;
  } // ctor

} // class ChatMessageStruct
```

At this point, there is an incompatibility between the existing `ChatServer/BaseServer` and `ChatClient/BaseClient` classes and the generated CORBA code. While the CORBA code is designed to use the new `ChatMessageStruct` class for transporting message data, the `ChatServer/ChatClient` implementations use the previously defined `ChatMessage` class. One simple way of addressing this problem is to create proxy classes that perform conversions between `ChatMessage` and `ChatMessageStruct`.

For example, a `ClientProxy` class can be created that defines a `displayMessage()` method that converts its `ChatMessage` argument into an equivalent `ChatMessageStruct` and uses that structure object to call the CORBA server object's `displayMessage()` method:

```
package chat.corba;

import chat.*;

public class ClientProxy implements ChatClient {

  protected CORBAChatClient delegate;

  public ClientProxy(CORBAChatClient del) {
    delegate = del;
  }

  public void displayMessage(ChatMessage message) {
    java.util.Date msgdate = message.messageDate;
    long msgtime = msgdate.getTime();
    String msgtext = message.messageText;
    ChatMessageStruct struct = new ChatMessageStruct(msgtime, msgtext);
    delegate.displayMessage(struct);
  }

}
```

Similarly, when a client calls the server's getHistory() method, the server must return an array of ChatMessageStruct objects, but the BaseClient code expects ChatMessage instances to be returned. Fortunately, it's equally simple to create a ServerProxy class that will perform a conversion from the ChatMessageStruct type into the previously defined ChatMessage type:

```
package chat.corba;

import chat.*;

public class ServerProxy implements ChatServer {

  protected CORBAChatServer delegate;

  public ServerProxy(CORBAChatServer del) {
    delegate = del;
  }

  public void broadcastMessage(String message) {
    delegate.broadcastMessage(message);
  }

  public ChatMessage[] getHistory() {
    java.util.Date msgdate;
    long timevalue;
    String msgtext;

    ChatMessageStruct[] structs = delegate.getHistory();
    ChatMessage[] messages = new ChatMessage[structs.length];
    for (int i = 0; i < messages.length; i++) {
      timevalue = structs[i].messageTime;
      msgdate = new java.util.Date(timevalue);
      msgtext = structs[i].messageText;
      messages[i] = new ChatMessage(msgdate, msgtext);
```

```
        }
        return messages;
    }


}
```

Next, we can define the CORBAServer object, which creates an instance of BaseServer and delegates most of the functionality to that object. While it would be convenient for CORBAServer to simply extend BaseServer, it's necessary it to extend the ImplBase class generated by the IDL compiler so that the server can be used as a distributed object.

Note also that when the server's getHistory() method is called, it retrieves the history information from the BaseServer object, converts the ChatMessage objects into equivalent ChatMessageStruct instances, and returns an array of those instances. The array of ChatMessageStruct objects will be retrieved by the ServerProxy, which will create an equivalent array of ChatMessage objects and return that array to the client:

```
package chat.corba;

import chat.*;

import java.io.*;
import org.omg.CosNaming.*;

public class CORBAServer extends _CORBAChatServerImplBase {

  protected BaseServer server;

  public CORBAServer() throws IOException {
    server = new BaseServer();
  }

  public boolean isValidUserInfo(String userid, String password) {
    return server.isValidUserInfo(userid, password);
  }

  public void addClient(ChatClient client) {
    server.addClient(client);
  }

  public void broadcastMessage(String message) {
    server.broadcastMessage(message);
  }

  public ChatMessageStruct[] getHistory() {
    java.util.Date msgdate;
    long timevalue;
    String msgtext;

    ChatMessage[] messages = server.getHistory();
    ChatMessageStruct[] structs = new ChatMessageStruct[messages.length];
    for (int i = 0; i < messages.length; i++) {
      msgdate = messages[i].messageDate;
      timevalue = msgdate.getTime();
```

```
        msgtext = messages[i].messageText;
        structs[i] = new ChatMessageStruct(timevalue, msgtext);
      }
    return structs;
  }


}
```

The next step is to create the `LogonManager` implementation, which we'll call `CORBALogonManager`. This class extends the generated `_LogonManagerImplBase` class and its constructor is passed a reference to a `CORBAServer` object. If the logon manager's `performLogon()` method is called with a valid userid and password combination, it will add the client to the list of active chat users and will return a reference to the server back to the calling client. The client can then use that reference to retrieve the message history information and to send chat messages to the server, which will forward those messages to all active users:

```
package chat.corba;

public class CORBALogonManager extends _LogonManagerImplBase {

  protected CORBAServer server;

  public CORBALogonManager(CORBAServer s) {
    server = s;
  }

  public CORBAChatServer performLogon(String userid, String password,
                                      CORBAChatClient client) {
    if (server.isValidUserInfo(userid, password)) {
      ClientProxy proxy = new ClientProxy(client);
      server.addClient(proxy);
      return server;
    }
    return null;
  }

}
```

Obtaining References to CORBA Objects

We've now defined the `CORBAServer` and `LogonManager` objects that will run on the server, but we must also provide the client with a way to obtain references to those objects. As mentioned earlier, the `CORBAServer` will not be made accessible directly to the client, but can be referenced only by passing a valid userid/password combination to the `LogonManager`'s `performLogon()` method. Therefore, the problem that we're faced with is not how the client obtains a reference to the server object, but how the client can obtain a reference to the `LogonManager`. Fortunately, CORBA provides a simple solution to this problem in the form of its **name service**.

CORBA's name service is one of the services provided with CORBA implementations, and the name service allows you to associate a name with some distributed object. Clients can then connect to the name service, specify the name of the object that they wish to obtain a reference to, and the name service will return a reference to the appropriate object.

We'll now add to the `CORBAServer` class a `main()` method that creates an instance of `CORBAServer` and an instance of `LogonManager` with a reference to that server. The code below shows the initial implementation of the `main()` method:

```
public static void main(String[] args) throws Exception {
  CORBAServer cs = new CORBAServer();
  CORBALogonManager manager = new CORBALogonManager(cs);
  // ...
}
```

Next, the `main()` method will add an entry to the name service for the `LogonManager` so that clients can obtain references to the `LogonManager` and use its `performLogon()` method to log on to the chat application.

Obtaining a Reference to the NameService

Before the server can add an entry to the name service for the `LogonManager`, it must first obtain a reference to the name service object. That reference is accessible through the ORB, which can be accessed by executing the following code:

```
org.omg.CORBA.ORB orb = org.omg.CORBA.ORB.init(args, null);
```

Although not previously mentioned, an **ORB (Object Request Broker)** is a very important part of CORBA. In fact, you cannot use CORBA without an ORB, but again, an implementation is provided with version 1.3 of the Java 2 SDK. Among other things, the ORB mediates calls to distributed CORBA objects' methods, ensuring that the data sent to and returned from the server is formatted in a platform-neutral manner. In other words, it's the ORB that makes it possible for a process written in one language on a given platform to call a distributed object written in a different language and running on a different operating system. For the most part, however, the ORB's role in distributed object method calls is transparent to your application.

The code shown above creates a new ORB instance when it is called, passing to that instance the parameters that were specified on the command line. Once you have a reference to the ORB, you can ask the ORB to return a reference to the service that you wish to use, which in this case is the name service. That service has a name of "NameService", and you can retrieve a reference to a service by calling the ORB's `resolve_initial_references()` method as shown below:

```
org.omg.CORBA.Object nameobj =
    orb.resolve_initial_references("NameService");
```

Before using the name service object, you must cast or "narrow" the reference that was returned from an instance of `org.omg.CORBA.Object` to `org.omg.CosNaming.NamingContext`. It might be tempting to do this by simply casting the object as shown below:

```
NamingContext nc = (NamingContext)nameobj;
```

> However, this approach may not work, since the object returned by the `resolve_initial_references()` call can be an instance of a proxy object that points to a `NamingContext` instead of actually being an instance of `NamingContext`.

The correct approach is to use the narrow() method of the helper class associated with the type of object you're attempting to access, and in this case we'll use the narrow() method of the NamingContext class:

```
NamingContext namingContext = NamingContextHelper.narrow(nameobj);
```

We now have a reference to the name service, so the only remaining step is to add an entry for the LogonManager object so that it will be accessible by clients. To do so, we must create an array of NameComponent instances that will identify the name that should be associated with the object. Conceptually, you can think of each NameComponent instance in the array as part of a hierarchical directory structure like that used to manage disk files. In other words, each object in the NameComponent array represents a level in the path that will be associated with the object being registered in the name service. In this example, however, we'll use a simple path with only a single name entry as shown in the code below:

```
NameComponent[] path = {new NameComponent("LogonManager", "Object")};
```

The first value passed to the NameComponent constructor is known as the "ID", while the second is known as the "kind". You're free to specify any String values for these two parameters, but in general, you should use the "ID" portion to uniquely identify a particular object. When specifying the "kind" value, a good rule of thumb is to use the same value for similar and/or related objects.

Now that we've created an array of NameComponent objects that identify the path of the object to be added to the name service, we can call the service object's rebind() method. That method must be passed a reference to the NameComponent array and the object that should be associated with the specified name and the name service will allow clients to obtain references to the object:

```
namingContext.rebind(path, manager);
```

The completed main() method for CORBAServer is shown below with additional code that will cause the thread that executes it to wait indefinitely:

```
public static void main(String[] args) throws Exception {
  CORBAServer cs = new CORBAServer();
  CORBALogonManager manager = new CORBALogonManager(cs);
  org.omg.CORBA.ORB orb = org.omg.CORBA.ORB.init(args, null);
  org.omg.CORBA.Object nameobj =
     orb.resolve_initial_references("NameService");
  NamingContext namingContext = NamingContextHelper.narrow(nameobj);
  NameComponent[] path = {new NameComponent("LogonManager", "Object")};
  namingContext.rebind(path, manager);
  Object o = new Object();
  synchronized (o) {
    try {
      o.wait();
    }
    catch (Exception e) {};
  }
}
```

When this code is executed, an instance of LogonManager will be created, associated with an instance of ChatServer, and the LogonManager will be registered with the name service so that it can be accessed by clients.

Implementing CORBAClient

The server portion of the CORBA-based chat application is now complete, and all that remains is to implement the client, although now that you've seen how to use the name service, the client code is actually very simple. All that's needed is for the client to obtain a reference to the naming service just as the server did, but instead of adding an entry, the client will obtain a reference to an existing entry (the LogonManager). The following code illustrates a constructor that can be used with the CORBAClient class, and that constructor is passed a number of parameters. Those parameters include the command line arguments passed to the CORBAClient's main() method, the userid and password that should be used to logon to the chat server, and the name of the LogonManager object in the name service:

```
public CORBAClient(String[] args, String userid,
    String password, String name) throws Exception {
  org.omg.CORBA.ORB orb = org.omg.CORBA.ORB.init(args, null);
  org.omg.CORBA.Object o = orb.resolve_initial_references("NameService");
  NamingContext context = NamingContextHelper.narrow(o);
  NameComponent[] path = {new NameComponent(name, "Object")};
```

Once the constructor has a reference to the name service and has constructed a NameComponent array representing the path of the LogonManager object, it can obtain a reference to that object. To do so, the naming service object's resolve() method can be called and passed a reference to the NameComponent array. However, the resolve() method will simply return an instance of org.omg.CORBA.Object, and that object must be cast/narrowed just as was done for the NamingContext object:

```
  o = context.resolve(path);
  LogonManager manager = LogonManagerHelper.narrow(o);
```

Since the client now has a reference to the LogonManager, it can call the performLogon() method, passing the userid and password values to it as arguments. If the userid/password combination is successful, a reference to the distributed server object will be returned to the client:

```
  CORBAChatServer server = manager.performLogon(userid, password, this);
```

Finally, the constructor can be completed by having the client wrap the server reference in an instance of the ServerProxy class defined earlier. In addition, the client should invoke the server's getHistory() method and display the messages that were previously issued by the chat users. The complete CORBAClient class is listed below:

```
package chat.corba;

import chat.*;

import java.awt.*;
import javax.swing.*;

import org.omg.CosNaming.*;

public class CORBAClient extends _CORBAChatClientImplBase {

  protected BaseClient client;
```

```
public static void main(String[] args) throws Exception {
  String userid = (args.length > 0 ? args[0] : "brett");
  String password = (args.length > 1 ? args[1] : "bspell");
  String name = (args.length > 2 ? args[2] : "LogonManager");
  CORBAClient cc = new CORBAClient(args, userid, password, name);
}

public CORBAClient(String[] args, String userid, String password,
                   String name) throws Exception {
  org.omg.CORBA.ORB orb = org.omg.CORBA.ORB.init(args, null);
  org.omg.CORBA.Object o = orb.resolve_initial_references("NameService");
  NamingContext context = NamingContextHelper.narrow(o);
  NameComponent[] path = {
    new NameComponent(name, "Object")
  };
  o = context.resolve(path);
  LogonManager manager = LogonManagerHelper.narrow(o);
  CORBAChatServer server = manager.performLogon(userid, password, this);
  client = new BaseClient(userid, new ServerProxy(server));
  client.displayHistory();
  JFrame f = new JFrame("Chat CORBA Client (" + userid + ")");
  f.getContentPane().add(client, BorderLayout.CENTER);
  f.setSize(400, 300);
  f.setVisible(true);
}

public void displayMessage(ChatMessageStruct struct) {
  long timevalue = struct.messageTime;
  java.util.Date msgdate = new java.util.Date(timevalue);
  String msgtext = struct.messageText;
  ChatMessage message = new ChatMessage(msgdate, msgtext);
  client.displayMessage(message);
}
}
```

Running the CORBA Chat Application

The code that's needed for the CORBA implementation of the chat application is now complete. To execute the application, you must do the following:

- ❑ Compile the IDL as described earlier using the idlj utility. This will generate Java source code, which must also be compiled using a Java compiler.

- ❑ Create and compile the CORBALogonManager, CORBAClient, and CORBAServer classes described above.

- ❑ Initialize the name service. If you're using the Java 2 Software Development Kit version 1.3, you can use the tnameserv application. For example, if you're using Windows, you can start the name service by issuing the following command from a command prompt:

  ```
  start tnameserv
  ```

- ❑ Execute the CORBAServer application, which creates a LogonManager and registers that object with the name service:

  ```
  java chat.corba.CORBAServer
  ```

❑ Execute one or more instances of the `CORBAClient` application, specifying a userid/password combination that's defined in the `userlist.txt` file:

```
java chat.corba.CORBAClient bspell brett
```

CORBA Summary

CORBA provides a valuable and important benefit by allowing a distributed object written in one language to be called by applications running on different platforms (and perhaps written in different languages). On the other hand, using CORBA can be somewhat tedious and inconvenient, and it does require the presence of an ORB and other tools that may not always be available to you. Despite that drawback, CORBA remains the best solution for the creation of distributed objects that can be called by applications written in a variety of languages. However, if you're developing applications solely in Java, it will almost certainly be more convenient for you to use Java's Remote Method Invocation (RMI), which is discussed below.

Remote Method Invocation

Remote Method Invocation (RMI) is a technology that's included with the Java core classes, and it provides a much easier way to create and use distributed objects written in Java. Creating a remote object that uses RMI is similar to creating an equivalent CORBA object, but RMI is simpler to use in many ways. It also provides greater flexibility in the types of objects that can be distributed which, as long as we're distributing Java to Java, makes RMI a superior choice. In fact, given the existing `ChatServer/BaseServer` and `ChatClient/BaseClient` classes and interfaces, there's very little more code that needs to be written to create an RMI-based chat application. To create a distributed object using RMI, you must perform the following steps:

❑ Create a **remote interface**, which is simply an interface that defines the methods to be called remotely.

❑ Create a server class that provides an implementation of the remote interface methods.

❑ If the server object is to be accessible through RMI's name service (called the **RMI registry**), you must add an entry for that object to the registry using the `Naming` class.

❑ A client must obtain a reference to the distributed object either through the registry or by calling some method that returns a reference to the object, and can then invoke the object's methods.

Just as with the CORBA implementation of the chat application, we'll create a server component that's remotely accessible, as well as a client that's also a distributed object, so that the client's `displayMesage()` method can be called. In addition, a `LogonManager` interface and implementation will be created and added to the registry, and that object will provide clients with access to the `ChatServer` implementation when they provide a valid userid/password combination during logon.

Creating Remote Interfaces

As mentioned above, the remote interface defines the methods within the distributed object that can be called remotely. A remote interface is identical to a non-remote interface, except for two minor differences: a remote interface must extend `java.rmi.Remote`, and each of its methods must be defined to throw `java.rmi.RemoteException`. As mentioned earlier in the chapter, a `RemoteException` indicates that some type of communications or network error occurred during the method invocation.

To implement the chat application using RMI, we must create three classes that will be used as remote objects: a ChatServer subclass, a ChatClient subclass, and a LogonManager implementation. The LogonManager class defined here will serve exactly the same purpose that its CORBA equivalent did: as a way for the client to gain access to the server object. In addition, the LogonManager will be added to RMI's name service (the RMI registry) just as was done with its CORBA counterpart.

The remote interfaces for the RMI-based client and server objects can be created by simply extending the existing ChatClient and ChatServer interfaces, along with the java.rmi.Remote interface. It's not necessary to explicitly declare that RemoteException can be thrown by the methods defined in those interfaces since they are already defined as being able to throw any type of Exception.

RemoteChatServer

```
package chat.rmi;

import chat.ChatServer;

import java.rmi.Remote;

public interface RemoteChatServer extends ChatServer, Remote {
}
```

RemoteChatClient

```
package chat.rmi;

import chat.ChatClient;

import java.rmi.Remote;

public interface RemoteChatClient extends ChatClient, Remote {

}
```

Since we will also define a remote LogonManager object, it's necessary to create an interface for that class as well. Note that its performLogon() method can throw RemoteException, that it's passed a reference to the ChatClient attempting to log on, and that it returns a reference to the chat server object:

```
package chat.rmi;

import chat.*;

import java.rmi.*;

interface LogonManager extends Remote {

  public ChatServer performLogon(String userid, String password,
                             ChatClient client) throws RemoteException,
                             LogonFailedException;

}
```

Creating RMIServer

With the remote interfaces defined, we can now begin to create the implementation classes, which will be named RMIServer and RMIClient. As shown below, the server can be implemented with minimal effort by extending BaseServer and implementing the remote interface. In fact, most of the code is devoted to the inner class that implements the LogonManager interface:

```java
package chat.rmi;

import chat.*;

import java.rmi.*;
import java.rmi.server.*;

public class RMIServer extends BaseServer implements RemoteChatServer {

  public static void main(String[] args) throws Exception {
    RMIServer rmis = new RMIServer();
  }

  public RMIServer() throws Exception {

    // ...
  }

  public class RemoteLogonManager implements LogonManager {

    public RemoteLogonManager() throws RemoteException {}

    public ChatServer performLogon(String userid, String password,
                            ChatClient client) throws RemoteException,
                            LogonFailedException {
      if (isValidUserInfo(userid, password)) {
        addClient(client);
        return (ChatServer) (RMIServer.this);
      }
      throw new LogonFailedException("Invalid userid and/or password");
    }
  }

}
```

The main step in completing the server portion of the chat application is to create an instance of RemoteLogonManager in the main() method and make that object available to clients through the registry. The registry can be accessed programmatically through the static methods defined in the java.rmi.Naming class, such as bind() and rebind() (which add or update entries in the registry, respectively) and lookup().

The bind() method adds a new entry to the registry if none already exists for the name specified, while rebind() adds a new entry or replaces an existing entry if one already exists. Both methods require that you pass them a String representing the name to be associated with the object being registered and a reference to the object, which must be an implementation of Remote.

For example, the RMIServer's main() method can create an instance of RemoteLogonManager and add an entry for it to the registry using the following code:

```
    public RMIServer() throws Exception {
      RemoteLogonManager rlm = new RemoteLogonManager();
      Naming.bind("chat/LogonManager", rlm);
    }
```

One final step must be taken before the RMIServer and LogonManagers can be accessed: specifically, they must be **exported**, which simply activates them, causing them to begin to wait for incoming client calls. You can either export a remote object explicitly by calling the static exportObject() method in java.rmi.server.UnicastRemoteObject, or you can have your remote object extend UnicastRemoteObject, in which case the object will automatically export itself.

The RMIServer class cannot extend UnicastRemoteObject because it already extends BaseServer, so it must be exported explicitly. However, LogonManager does not have an explicitly defined superclass, and it can be modified as shown below:

```
    package chat.rmi;

    import chat.*;

    import java.rmi.*;
    import java.rmi.server.*;

    public class RMIServer extends BaseServer implements RemoteChatServer {

      public static void main(String[] args) throws Exception {
        RMIServer rmis = new RMIServer();
      }

      public RMIServer() throws Exception {
        UnicastRemoteObject.exportObject(this);
        RemoteLogonManager rlm = new RemoteLogonManager();
        Naming.bind("chat/LogonManager", rlm);
      }

      public class RemoteLogonManager extends UnicastRemoteObject
        implements LogonManager {

      public RemoteLogonManager() throws RemoteException {}

      public ChatServer performLogon(String userid, String password,
                          ChatClient client) throws RemoteException,
                          LogonFailedException {
        if (isValidUserInfo(userid, password)) {
          addClient(client);
          return (ChatServer) (RMIServer.this);
        }
        throw new LogonFailedException("Invalid userid and/or password");
      }
    }
  }

}
```

Creating RMIClient

The RMIClient class can also be implemented easily by extending the BaseClient class and inheriting its functionality. Like RMIServer, the RMIClient class must be exported explicitly since it cannot extend UnicastRemoteObject:

```
package chat.rmi;

import chat.*;

import java.rmi.*;
import java.rmi.server.*;
import javax.swing.*;

public class RMIClient extends BaseClient implements RemoteChatClient {

  public static void main(String[] args) throws Exception {
    String user = (args.length > 0 ? args[0] : "brett");
    String password = (args.length > 0 ? args[1] : "bspell");
    String host = (args.length > 2 ? args[2] : "localhost");
    JFrame f = new JFrame("RMI Chat Client (" + user + ")");
    RMIClient rmic = new RMIClient(user, password, host);
    f.getContentPane().add(rmic);
    f.setSize(400, 300);
    f.setVisible(true);
  }

  public RMIClient(String user, String password,
                   String host) throws Exception {
    userid = user;
    UnicastRemoteObject.exportObject(this);

    // ...
  }

}
```

The client can obtain a reference to the remote LogonManager object using the lookup() method defined in the Naming class. That method returns a reference to an implementation of Remote, and you can cast that object to an instance of RemoteChatServer:

```
  public RMIClient(String user, String password,
                   String host) throws Exception {
    userid = user;
    UnicastRemoteObject.exportObject(this);
    Remote r = Naming.lookup("//" + host + "/chat/LogonManager");
    LogonManager lm = (LogonManager)(r);
    // ...
  }
```

Finally, the RMIClient constructor can be made to call the LogonManager's performLogon() method, and once it has obtained a reference to the server, it can retrieve and display the message history information:

```
    public RMIClient(String user, String password,
                     String host) throws Exception {
      userid = user;
      UnicastRemoteObject.exportObject(this);
      Remote r = Naming.lookup("//" + host + "/chat/LogonManager");
      LogonManager lm = (LogonManager)(r);
      try {
        server = lm.performLogon(userid, password, this);
      } catch (Exception e) {
        JOptionPane.showMessageDialog(null, e.getMessage(),
            "Logon Error", JOptionPane.ERROR_MESSAGE);
        System.exit(0);
      }
      displayHistory();
    }
```

Parameters, Return Values, and Exceptions with RMI

As you can see, it's much easier to create a distributed object with RMI. Once you've obtained a reference to a remote object, calling its methods is done in the same way that you would call a local object, although you must be prepared to handle a RemoteException.

When you call a remote method and pass it a parameter value, Java's object serialization mechanism is used to transmit a representation of the parameter to the server, and serialization is used to return a value to the client. In other words, any serializable item can be passed as a parameter or return value to or from a remote method. Primitive (int, float, char, boolean, etc.) values are automatically serializable, as are wrapper classes defined in java.lang (String, Integer, Boolean, etc.). In addition, a reference to a remote object (an instance of RMIServer, RMIClient, or RemoteLogonManager, say) can be passed to or returned from a method that's called remotely.

In this application, instances of ChatMessage are to be transmitted between the client and server classes, but ChatMessage is not currently serializable. However, that problem can be remedied by simply modifying the ChatMessage class so that it implements java.io.Serializable as shown below:

```
package chat;

import java.util.Date;

public class ChatMessage implements java.io.Serializable {

  public final Date messageDate;
  public final String messageText;

  public ChatMessage(Date date, String text) {
    messageDate = date;
    messageText = text;
  }

}
```

In addition to the wrapper classes, the Throwable class and all its direct and indirect subclasses (for example, Exception subclasses) are serializable. If you wish to throw an exception from a remotely invoked method, you simply throw the exception as you normally would as is done in the performLogon() method, which can throw a LogonFailedException.

rmic

The rmic utility is used to create and compile stub and skeleton classes for your remote objects, and is provided with the Java 2 Software Development Kit and most IDE applications. The stubs and skeletons serve essentially the same purpose as the stub and skeleton inner classes defined in the socket implementation of the chat application. Specifically, the stub is used by the client to convert a method call into a stream of bytes, send those bytes to the server, and process the information returned by the server that represents the return value. Similarly, the skeleton is used on the server side to read data sent from the client, convert that data into a method call, and return the results to the client.

When you execute rmic, it both creates the Java source code for the stub and skeleton classes and compiles those classes. Once they are compiled, the source files are erased and only the class files remain. However, if you wish to prevent the source files from being erased, you can use the -keepgenerated option when executing rmic.

The chat application defines three remote objects, and you must generate the stub and skeleton classes for each of them. Those classes are ChatClient and ChatServer, along with the RemoteLogonManager defined as an inner class within ChatServer. To create the necessary stub and skeleton classes, you can execute the following commands:

```
rmic chat.rmi.RMIClient
rmic chat.rmi.RMIServer
rmic chat.rmi.RMIServer$RemoteLogonManager
```

Executing the RMI-Based Chat Application

All code needed to implement the chat application using RMI has already been defined, but to execute this application, you must take the following steps:

- ❑ Compile the three remote interfaces (LogonManager, RemoteChatClient, RemoteChatServer) and the two classes (RMIClient, RMIServer).

- ❑ Generate the stubs and skeletons for the three distributed object classes (discussed above).

- ❑ Activate RMI's naming service using the rmiregistry utility, which is provided with the Java 2 Software Development Kit and most IDE applications. For example, if you're using Windows, you could issue the following command:

  ```
  start rmiregistry
  ```

- ❑ Start the RMIServer application and one or more chat clients:

  ```
  java chat.rmi.RMIServer
  ```

  ```
  java chat.rmi.RMIClient bspell brett
  ```

RMI Summary

As we've seen, RMI provides a very simple and convenient way to create distributed objects. It's easier to use than CORBA, and has been a standard part of Java since version 1.1. RMI originally used its own protocol for communications, which meant that it was only suitable for applications where both the remote object and the client using that object were written in Java. However, in Java 1.3, RMI has been modified to use CORBA's IIOP, which means that you can now use RMI in a client program that interacts with server objects written in other languages. Revising RMI so that it's built on top of CORBA also means that RMI "inherits" all of CORBA's functionality, but at the same time, it lacks most of the complexity. Therefore, RMI is an appropriate choice for many Java applications.

Enterprise JavaBeans

Like many applications, the chat program defined in this chapter uses a simple form of **authentication**. Specifically, it requires that each client provide a valid userid/password combination before allowing the client to use the chat application. In fact, authentication is just one of many "services" that are commonly implemented by software applications, and some other services include persistence, resource (thread and/or database connection) pooling, and transaction processing. In the past, it has often been necessary for developers to implement these services, but it was apparent that an off-the-shelf solution would be very useful. Although the Object Management Group attempted to provide a CORBA-based solution, that solution has evolved very slowly. In the meantime, the ORB vendors have implemented proprietary services in their ORBs that provide the same functionality, but which are incompatible with one another.

To use an off-the-shelf solution for services such as persistence and transaction processing, that solution must provide an API that your objects can use to interact with the services, and that's exactly what Enterprise JavaBeans and their related APIs provide. **Enterprise JavaBeans (EJB)** allow you to create distributed objects that you communicate with using RMI, and some or all of the services described above can be provided automatically. This capability is partially provided by encapsulating object instances in a **container** (unrelated to the `java.awt.Container` class), and invocations of the object's methods are intercepted by the container, which can impose some desired behavior. For example, an Enterprise JavaBean can be designed so that a user might obtain a reference to the EJB but be unable to call some of its methods. Since the EJB container intercepts method calls, it can determine whether the calling user should be allowed to invoke the method, and if not, can reject the invocation request.

Entity Beans and Session Beans

There are two categories of EJB: **entity beans** and **session beans**. Entity beans represent persistent data and a single entity bean instance usually corresponds to a row in some database table. Instead of requiring you to create code that queries and updates a database, Enterprise JavaBeans allow you to map instances of a class to some database table and to have an object's state stored and retrieved automatically. For example, to retrieve an existing database record as an entity bean, you can request that the application server "find" that bean without explicitly writing any database code. Once the server returns a reference to that bean, you can modify its fields and have those modifications automatically reflected in the underlying database.

Unlike entity beans, a session bean instance is not usually associated with a particular item of persistent data. Instead, session beans can be used to provide services to your application. Session beans can be either **stateful** or **stateless**, and as its name implies, a stateful session bean can maintain state information. Conceptually, you may find it helpful to think of stateful session beans as providing the type of functions you normally associate with instance (non-static) methods, while stateless beans provide services similar to those typically found in static methods.

Services such as security and transaction management are very useful, but Enterprise JavaBeans support them in a way that increases the probability that the code you write will be reusable. This is done by reducing or eliminating from your classes the code that's associated with those services and defining how an Enterprise JavaBean should behave outside of the Java source code. For example, an application that uses the traditional approach to transaction management would include explicit calls to the `commit()` and/or `rollback()` methods defined by JDBC. While you can still use that approach (called **bean-managed persistence**) with Enterprise JavaBeans, a better technique is to allow the Enterprise JavaBeans framework to handle transactions for you, referred to as **container-managed persistence**. Instead of writing Java code that controls transactions, you can simply describe how you want a bean's methods to interact with database transactions. For example, you can specify that a new transaction should be started when a given method is called and committed when it is completed.

This description of how an EJB should be used is provided in a file called a **deployment descriptor,** which is packaged with the EJB when it is deployed. By placing the information that describes how the bean is used in the deployment descriptor, the Enterprise JavaBeans architecture allows you to create distributed objects that are "pure" business logic, increasing the likelihood that you can reuse those objects. In other words, once you create an EJB, you can modify its transaction behavior by simply changing the deployment descriptor, and no changes need be made to your Java source code.

> *We're not going to explore EJBs in anymore detail as it is quite easy to write whole books on the subject.*
> *For a more complete examination of EJBs, check out Professional Java Server Programming – J2EE*
> *Edition, from Wrox Press, ISBN 1861004656*

Summary

As we've seen, there are many options available for creating distributed applications, although each option has its strengths and weaknesses:

- ❑ Sockets can theoretically be used to communicate between applications written in different languages, but using them requires you to handle many details that are concealed by CORBA or RMI.

- ❑ CORBA is robust and supports interactions between objects written in different programming languages, but it is somewhat more difficult to use than RMI.

- ❑ RMI is simple and robust, but is limited to use within Java applications.

- ❑ Enterprise JavaBeans use RMI for method invocation and add persistence capabilities, but are not as easy to use as "standalone" RMI.

In the next chapter, we will look at how to control access to system resources through the Java 2 security architecture.

Professional Java Programmin

16

Controlling Access to Resources

So far, in all our applications we have been assuming that the executing program will have full access to all the files and resources of the system in which the JVM is running. However, there may well be times when such unrestricted access is a far from ideal scenario. Fortunately, Java has always been designed with such considerations in mind, so it is quite easy to use a permission-based system of granting or denying access to local resources such as files, network connections and the runtime environment.

There are several different types of security, depending on the context that you are working in. **Authentication** refers to ensuring a user is in fact the person they claim to be, and is often done by requiring that a valid userid/password combination be entered before allowing access to an application. Closely related to authentication is **access control**, which refers to controlling which resources can be accessed by a given user or by that user's code.

A topic that's closely related to security is that of **encryption**, which is the act of modifying data so that it can't be easily interpreted by parties that should not have access to the original data. Encryption and authentication are closely related partly because it has become increasingly common to use encryption to provide a form of authentication. However, in this chapter we will only be interested in using access control to limit what an application can do in terms of use of system resources.

Therefore, in this chapter we will be covering:

❑   How to use the `SecurityManager`

❑   How to set permissions using policy files

❑   What are the standard permissions that can be set

❑   How to write your own permissions

The Java Security Model

As you know, one of the earliest uptakes of Java language was for the creation of downloadable applets over the Internet. However, the downloadable nature of the code meant that there was an inherent security risk in running foreign code locally. Therefore, early versions of Java were designed with security considerations in mind, with what is known as the **sandbox** security model.

In the sandbox model, the downloaded code ran within a specially isolated area, which prevented it from accessing valuable local resources such as files and network connections. However, this model proved to be just too restrictive so it was revised to allow remote code to be **signed** such that it could run outside of the sandbox. This process of signing was akin to saying, "I trust this bit of code to not do anything malicious". If you think about it, it's not really any different from installing any piece of software, such as the JDK, on your system.

Now with Java 2, a considerably more fine-grained approach is possible. Both local and remote code can be configured to run within specific security domains based on **security policy files** which determine which can have access to which resources.

The Java SecurityManager

At the heart of this access control lies the **SecurityManager**, a class defined in the java.lang package, which controls all access to resources on your system. Whenever a request is made to access a resource, the request is passed through the SecurityManager which checks to see if the requesting source has the correct permissions to access that resource. If the permission check fails, the SecurityManager throws a java.lang.SecurityException, if the check succeeds, execution continues as normal:

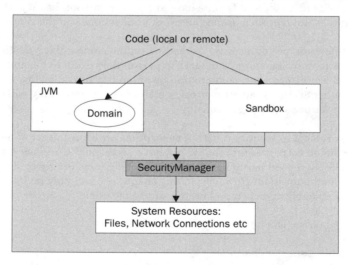

In the Java 1.x model, the **SecurityManager** class simply contained a large number of checkXXX() methods. Each of those methods was used to determine whether a particular function was allowed, such as the checkRead() and checkWrite() methods that controlled read and write access to local disk files. Before such a potentially harmful function is performed, the appropriate checkXXX() method in the current SecurityManager was called, and if the operation should be prevented, the method throws a SecurityException.

For example, let's examine the source code for one of the constructors of the FileInputStream class defined in the java.io package. Before allowing you to create an InputStream that will read a disk file, it obtains a reference to the active SecurityManager (if any) and calls its checkRead() method and returns whether it is allowed:

```
public FileOutputStream(String name, boolean append)
    throws FileNotFoundException {
  SecurityManager security = System.getSecurityManager();
  if (security != null) {
      security.checkWrite(name);
  }
  fd = new FileDescriptor();
  if (append) {
      openAppend(name);
  } else {
      open(name);
  }
}
```

Unfortunately, the early versions of SecurityManager were somewhat inflexible, as each separate security policy required the creation of a new SecurityManager subclass, which was inconvenient at best, and tedious and complex at worst. Even simple modifications to an existing policy required you to modify and recompile code, which is obviously not desirable.

However, with Java 2 the SecurityManager underwent some significant conceptual changes. Although, the SecurityManager class is still a key component in access control, the way that it works has changed substantially. Java 2 added the more generic checkPermission() method, which all the checkXXXX() methods now call. checkPermission() in turn calls the new java.security.AccessController class which performs the validation checking.

Using the SecurityManager

Under normal conditions, there is no active SecurityManager running (except for applet execution where the browser JVM automatically instantiates a SecurityManager to implement the sandbox). This means that if you simply compile and execute the following class, it will write a line of text to a disk file named test.txt without any problem:

```
import java.io.*;

public class WriteFile {

  public static void main(String[] args) throws IOException {
    FileOutputStream fos = new FileOutputStream("test.txt");
    PrintWriter pw = new PrintWriter(fos);
    pw.println("Testing");
    pw.close();
  }

}
```

However, as we saw above the FileOutputStream() constructor contains a check to the SecurityManager, but we need to activate a SecurityManager first for this to have any effect. You can cause a SecurityManager to be installed in one of two ways:

- By explicitly installing it within your application
- By specifying the `-Djava.security.manager` option when activating the JVM

For example, if you wish to execute the previously defined `WriteFile` class with the default `SecurityManager`, you could enter the command line shown below:

```
java -Djava.security.manager WriteFile
```

When this command is issued, the `WriteFile` application will fail when it attempts to write to the local drive, and the output will appear similar to the following:

```
Exception in thread "main" java.security.AccessControlException: access denied
(java.io.FilePermission test.txt write)
        at java.security.AccessControlContext.checkPermission(Unknown Source)
        at java.security.AccessController.checkPermission(Unknown Source)
        at java.lang.SecurityManager.checkPermission(Unknown Source)
        at java.lang.SecurityManager.checkWrite(Unknown Source)
        at java.io.FileOutputStream.<init>(Unknown Source)
        at java.io.FileOutputStream.<init>(Unknown Source)
        at WriteFile.main(WriteFile.java:6)
```

If you look at the stack trace you can see that `FileOutputStream` called `checkWrite()` which in turn called `checkPermission()` on the `SecurityManager` which was then delegated to `AccessController`.

You can also explicitly install a `SecurityManager` (either the default implementation or a subclass you have created) by passing an instance of it to the static `setSecurityManager()` method in `java.lang.System`. In the following example, an instance of `SecurityManager` class is created and installed:

```java
import java.io.*;

public class WriteFile {

    public static void main(String[] args) throws IOException {
        System.setSecurityManager(new SecurityManager());
        FileOutputStream fos = new FileOutputStream("test.txt");
        PrintWriter pw = new PrintWriter(fos);
        pw.println("Testing");
        pw.close();
    }

}
```

Now that we have an active `SecurityManager`, how do we re-enable the write permission to create the file? Prior to Java 2, each policy required a separate implementation of the `SecurityManager`. However, with Java 2 the policy itself has been separated from the implementation in the form of **policy files**. These are simple flat files that identify **permissions** that you wish to grant and the `checkPermission()` method compares the type of operation requested to the permissions that have been granted. If you have granted permission for that type of operation to be performed, `checkPermission()` returns quietly, but if the permission was not granted, it throws a `SecurityException`.

What this means to you is that you can create a new policy by creating a new policy file or modify an existing one by changing the appropriate file, and source code modifications and compilations are no longer necessary. In addition, it's easy to create new types of permissions and security checks, which previously would have required the creation of a new SecurityManager subclass. Finally, the Java 2 security model allows you to define permissions that apply only to classes loaded from a certain location/code base and/or only to classes signed by a particular user or group of users. We'll look at signing code in a while.

Policy Files

Although no policy file was explicitly identified or used, the SecurityManager did in fact use the permissions in a policy file to determine whether the write should be allowed.

When the Java Runtime Environment (JRE) is installed either separately or as part of the Java Development Kit (JDK), a security configuration file is installed along with a default policy file. The configuration file is java.security, and it contains a section similar to the one shown below that defines the default policy files used by the SecurityManager:

```
# The default is to have a single system-wide policy file,
# and a policy file in the user's home directory.
policy.url.1=file:${java.home}/lib/security/java.policy
policy.url.2=file:${user.home}/.java.policy
```

This list identifies the URL of policy files that are used by the SecurityManager by default. However, you can use command line options to specify policy files that will be used instead of or in addition to the ones listed in the security configuration file.

Note that policy expansion can be (and is) used in the security configuration file just as it is in the policy files. In this case, the first policy file is identified as java.policy, and is located in the /lib/security directory below the java.home directory.

If you wish to view or edit the java.policy file, you should be aware that the java.home directory corresponds to the location of the JRE and not the directory where you installed the JDK. For example, if you install the JDK 1.3 for Windows in C:\JDK1.3, the java.home directory may be set to C:\Program Files\JavaSoft\JRE\1.3. Therefore, the security configuration file will be located in the C:\Program Files\JavaSoft\JRE\1.3\lib\security directory along with the default java.policy file to which the security configuration file refers.

Perhaps the easiest way to be sure of the location of your java.home directory is to simply compile and execute the following program that retrieves the property value and displays it in standard output:

```java
public class ShowJavaHome {
  public static void main(String[] args) {
    System.out.println(System.getProperty("java.home"));
  }
}
```

If you examine the java.policy file included with the JRE, you'll find that it contains permissions that allow a program to perform only the operations that are valid within the applet sandbox. In other words, the permissions defined in the default policy file cause the Java 2 SecurityManager to behave in exactly the same way as a Java 1.x SecurityManager for most code. However, classes loaded from the /lib/ext directory below the java.home directory are allowed to execute as applications (they can perform all operations).

Creating a Custom Policy File

Policy files can be created and edited directly using a text editor or you can do so with **policytool**, a utility that is included with the Java Development Kit (JDK). To launch it, simply type `policytool` at the command prompt:

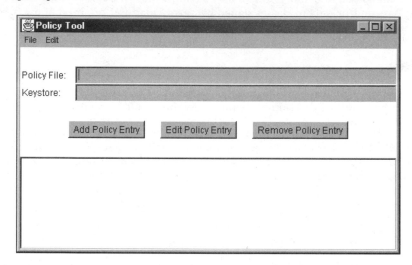

We are going to implement a fairly simple policy that allows us to write to any file. To do this, first hit the Add Policy Entry button to bring up the policy entry dialog:

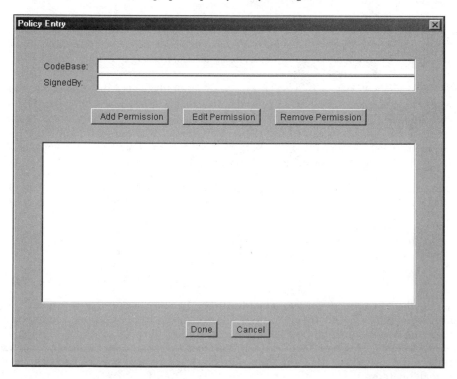

Now hit the **Add Permission** button to allow us to add a new permission to the file:

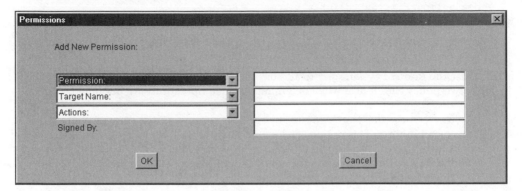

Select **FilePermission** in the top drop-down, **<<ALL FILES>>** in the middle, and **write** in the bottom drop-down:

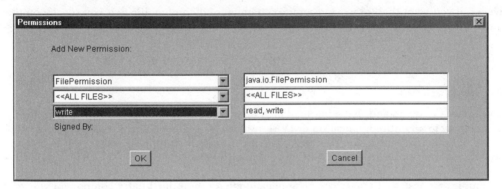

Then hit **OK** then **Done** to take you back to the initial dialog. Select **Save As** from the **File** menu and save the policy file as `WriteFile.policy` in the same place as your `WriteFile` class. Now if you open the file in a text editor you can see what the `policytool` has added to record this permission:

```
grant {
  permission java.io.FilePermission "<<ALL FILES>>", "write";
};
```

Using a Custom Policy File

Once you've created a policy file, there are two ways that you can cause the `SecurityManager` to use the file:

- ❑   By editing the security configuration file and adding an entry
- ❑   By identifying your policy file on the command line

If you wish to have your policy file used repeatedly, it may be convenient to edit the security configuration file and add an entry to it for your file. To do so, simply create an entry in the policy file section, specifying a number that's larger than the value that had been the largest number. For example, the file contains `policy.url.1` and `policy.url.2` entries by default, so the first entry you would add might appear like the one highlighted below:

```
# The default is to have a single system-wide policy file,
# and a policy file in the user's home directory.
policy.url.1=file:${java.home}/lib/security/java.policy
policy.url.2=file:${user.home}/.java.policy
policy.url.3=file:/C:/temp/WriteFile.policy
```

This will cause the SecurityManager to add the permissions in WriteFile.policy to those found in the other two policy files it uses when determining which operations are permitted.

Alternatively, you can use the java.security.policy option on the command line to identify a policy file at execution time. This option can be used to specify a policy file that will be used either in addition to or in place of the list defined in the security configuration file. To specify a file that should be used in addition to those identified in the configuration file, specify the java.security.policy option with a single equal ("=") sign as shown below:

```
java -Djava.security.manager -Djava.security.policy=WriteFile.policy WriteFile
```

However, if you want the SecurityManager to only use the policy file that you specify on the command line, use two equal signs as shown below:

```
java -Djava.security.manager -Djava.security.policy==WriteFile.policy WriteFile
```

Policy File Bounds

It's important to understand that a permission granted in a policy file applies to a class or group of classes and *not* to an entire application or JVM instance. This allows you to create an application that's made up of both classes that you consider relatively trustworthy and others that you do not, and you can do so without compromising the security of your application.

For example, suppose that you create an application that uses a third-party component you've downloaded from a web site, but you're not confident that the component does not contain malicious code. In that scenario, you can grant to the component only the permissions that it needs (if any) to function properly while allowing the code that you wrote to perform additional operations. This is possible because checkPermission() will ensure that all classes in the calling context have been granted the appropriate permission before it allows a protected operation to complete.

To understand how this works, let's suppose that you've created a class named Example1 and granted permission for it to perform some operation such as writing to a local disk file. In addition, let's assume that Example1 includes a public method called writeToTheFile() that actually performs that operation, and that you create another class called Example2 that does not have permission to write to the file. If a method in Example2 calls the writeToTheFile() method in Example1, the operation will fail, because checkPermission() requires that both Example1 and Example2 be given permission to perform the write.

The above description of how security applies to particular classes only applies to code that you supply. The classes that are included with the JVM (the "core classes") are automatically granted all permissions, and it's never necessary for you to grant permissions to those classes. For example, you do not have to grant permission to the FileOutputStream class in java.io for it to be able to write to local disk files, even when a SecurityManager is active that does not grant your code permission to perform such an operation.

764

For your own classes, and those you use from a third party vendor, permissions are granted to all the code in a directory or JAR file. This means that in the example above, `Example1` and `Example2` would have to be in different directories in order to have different security permissions.

Defining URL-Specific Permissions

Creating a permission that applies only to classes loaded from a particular location is as simple as specifying the URL that represents that location for the **codeBase**. For example, the following permission will allow only classes loaded from the local `C:/temp` directory to read the `java.version` property value:

```
grant codeBase "file:/C:/temp/" {
  permission java.util.PropertyPermission "java.version", "read";
};
```

Note that you should always use the forward slash ("/") character when specifying a URL, including a URL that represents a Windows directory even though Windows uses the back-slash ("\") character to separate directory names.

In `policytool` you can manually enter the `codeBase` in the Policy Entry screen:

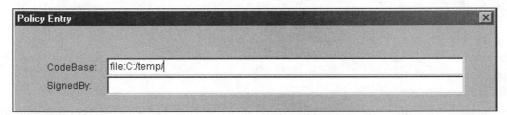

In the above example, the permission only applies to classes loaded directly from class files in the `C:\temp` directory and *will not* apply to classes loaded from a Java Archive (JAR) file stored in that directory. However, by adding an asterisk ("*") character to the end of the URL as shown below, you can cause the permission to apply in both cases:

```
grant codeBase "file:/C:/temp/*" {
  permission java.util.PropertyPermission "java.version", "read";
};
```

Similarly, the permissions described previously apply only to classes in the specified directory and they will not apply to any classes loaded from a subdirectory of `C:\temp`. However, adding a minus/dash ("-") character to the end of the URL causes the permission to apply to all classes (those stored in class files and those stored in JAR files) in the directory and all of its subdirectories:

```
grant codeBase "file:/C:/temp/-" {
  permission java.util.PropertyPermission "java.version", "read";
};
```

Note that Java 2 supports a protocol for specifying a location within a JAR file, so it's possible to define permissions that apply only to classes loaded from a particular JAR file or directory within that file. For example, the following permission applies only to the classes defined in the `/us/tx/plano/bspell` directory of the `C:/temp/MyClasses.jar` file:

```
grant codeBase "jar:file:/C:/temp/MyClasses.jar!/us/tx/plano/bspell" {
  permission java.util.PropertyPermission "java.version", "read";
};
```

If you create a permission that does not include a codeBase, the permission will apply to all classes, regardless of the location from which they are loaded.

System Property Value Substitution

A directory was explicitly identified in the above examples, but it's sometimes useful to be able to specify the name of a system property (one of the values accessible through the System.getProperty() and System.getProperties() methods) instead.

To do so, simply precede the name of the property with a dollar sign ("$") and opening brace ("{") and follow it with a closing brace ("}"). For example, the following permission only applies to classes loaded from the directory that corresponds to the value of the user.home system property:

```
grant codeBase "${user.home}" {
  permission java.util.PropertyPermission "java.version", "read";
};
```

Similarly, the following entry applies to all classes defined in the /lib/ext directory below the user.home directory or any of its subdirectories, including those loaded from JAR files:

```
grant codeBase "${user.home}/lib/ext/-" {
  permission java.util.PropertyPermission "java.version", "read";
};
```

These examples only illustrate the use of this technique (sometimes called **property expansion**) with the codeBase URL, but property expansion can also be used within the permissions themselves.

User-Specific Permissions

In addition to providing permissions that are tied to where a class was loaded from, you can also base permissions on which user(s) (if any) signed the class (see below). For example, suppose that you wish to define a permission that applies only to classes signed by a particular user:

```
grant signedBy "bspell" {
  permission java.util.PropertyPermission "java.version", "read";
};
```

If you want the permission to apply to more than one user, you must add an entry to the policy file for each user as shown below:

```
grant signedBy "dmcelwee" {
  permission java.util.PropertyPermission "java.version", "read";
};
```

```
grant signedBy "rshort" {
  permission java.util.PropertyPermission "java.version", "read";
};
```

```
grant signedBy "mvitale" {
  permission java.util.PropertyPermission "java.version", "read";
};
```

```
grant signedBy "kschwartz" {
  permission java.util.PropertyPermission "java.version", "read";
};
```

However, if you instead want the permission to apply only to classes signed by all four of the users, you could create an entry like this:

```
grant signedBy "dmcelwee, rshort, mvitale, kschwartz" {
  permission java.util.PropertyPermission "java.version", "read";
};
```

If you create a permission that does not include the signedBy parameter, the permission will be applied to all classes, regardless of which users' signatures are present.

Combination Permissions

It is valid to specify both codeBase and signedBy parameters in a permission, in which case both conditions must be met. In other words, the permission will apply only to classes that are loaded from the specified URL *and* that are signed by the specified user(s). For example, the following permission only applies to classes that are loaded from the C:\temp directory and that are signed with the digital signature associated with user bspell:

```
grant signedBy "bspell", codeBase "file:C:/temp/" {
  permission java.util.PropertyPermission "java.version", "read";
};
```

Signing Classes

The default policy file grants permissions to all classes, but when you create a custom policy file, you may want to limit the permission to classes **signed** by a specific user. As we saw earlier, you can specify a user alias with the signedBy parameter, such as in this case where only classes signed by bspell are granted all permissions:

```
grant signedBy "bspell" {

    permission java.security.AllPermission;

};
```

Now the question to be answered is where and how to define bspell and how a class can be signed by that user. To accomplish this, the person who creates and signs the code must generate a **public/private key pair**, package the class in a JAR file, and use the private key to sign the file.

> *The private and public keys are large unique numbers used to sign files and verify them respectively. Anyone can see a public key whereas a private key is kept only to that user. Therefore, only the user with a private key can sign a file but anyone can verify that it was that user who signed the file in the first place. This provides a mechanism by which you can trust that a file is signed by who it says it is.*

767

Once that's done, the JAR file and the public key can be provided to any users who wish to execute the code and grant permissions based on the identity of the signer. In other words, the users of the signed classes need the signer's public key to ensure that the code to which they're granting permissions really came from the expected source. This assumes two things: that the signer has kept their private key "secret", and that the public key that's distributed to users does indeed belong to the person that they believe it does.

To summarize the above procedure, the code signer must perform the following steps:

1. Create a private/public key pair – this is accomplished using the `keytool` utility

2. Create a JAR file containing the classes to distribute – this can be done easily using the `jar` utility

3. Sign the JAR file using the private key – the `jarsigner` utility is provided for this purpose

4. Provide the signed JAR and public key to all users of the packaged classes – to accomplish this, you must know how to use `keytool` to export the public key from the keystore. Once exported, it can be sent to other users, who will then be able to grant permissions to the code you have signed.

Note that all three utilities mentioned above (`keytool`, `jar`, and `jarsigner`) are provided as part of the JDK.

Create a Private/Public Key Pair

You can use the `keytool` utility's `-genkey` option to create a new private/public key pair and add them to a keystore. The **keystore** is simply a small database that holds private keys and their associated digital certificates, and will be created by `keytool` if the specified file does not already exist. When using the `-genkey` option, you will need to specify values for the following items :

❑   **Alias** – An alias representing the user for which the key pair is being generated.

❑   **Key password** – A password that's associated with the pair of keys.

❑   **URL** – The location of the keystore. This URL can represent either a file that already exists or one that has not yet been created.

❑   **Keystore password** – The password associated with the keystore (if it already exists). If the keystore file does not yet exist, the value you specify on this parameter will be assigned to the keystore when it is created.

The following command illustrates how you might create keys with an alias of `bspell` and a password of `secret` in a keystore file named `Creator.jks`, which has a password of `creator`:

```
keytool -genkey -alias bspell -keypass secret -keystore Creator.jks
        -storepass creator
```

When you execute this command, the `keytool` utility prompts you to enter the information shown below. The highlighted portions represent text entered by the user, while the remainder is the prompt information:

```
C:\Temp>keytool -genkey -alias bspell -keypass secret -keystore Creator.jks
-storepass creator
What is your first and last name?
  [Unknown]:  Brett Spell
What is the name of your organizational unit?
  [Unknown]:  Java Publications
What is the name of your organization?
  [Unknown]:  Wrox Press
What is the name of your City or Locality?
  [Unknown]:  Plano
What is the name of your State or Province?
  [Unknown]:  TX
What is the two-letter country code for this unit?
  [Unknown]:  US
Is <CN=Brett Spell, OU=Java Publications, O=Wrox Publishing, L=Plano, ST=TX, C=US>
correct?
  [no]:  y
```

The following table illustrates the meanings of the acronyms listed on the confirmation portion of the prompt:

Representation	Meaning
CN	Common Name
OU	Organization Unit
O	Organization
L	Locality/City
ST	State/Province
C	Country

Creating a JAR File

Creating a JAR file that contains the classes to be defined is the simplest step, and in this case can be done using the following command, which creates a file named WriteTest.jar containing WriteFile.class:

```
jar cf WriteTest.jar WriteFile.class
```

Signing a JAR File

Signing a JAR file with jarsigner requires that you specify many of the same values you entered when creating the key pair with keytool, including:

- ❑ Keystore URL
- ❑ Keystore password
- ❑ Key alias
- ❑ Key password

In addition to these four values, you should also specify the name of the JAR file to be signed and the name that will be given to the signed copy of the JAR file. The original JAR file will be overwritten if you do not specify a name for the signed copy, so you should normally specify a name for the -signedjar parameter. An example of how jarsigner might be used is shown below:

```
jarsigner -keystore Creator.jks -storepass creator -keypass secret
          -signedjar SignTest.jar WriteTest.jar bspell
```

In this case, a signed JAR file called SignTest.jar will be created from the existing WriteTest.jar, and the new JAR will be signed with the private key associated with the bspell alias.

Exporting the Public Key

When you used the -genkey option of keytool, it stores a private/public key pair in the keystore. However, for users to grant permissions only to classes that you have signed, you must first provide them with your public key so that they can verify that the classes were in fact signed by you. To make your public key available, you must export it from your keystore into a **certificate file** using the keytool utility.

*A certificate is a signed statement by one party that another party's public key belongs to them. This of course means that the certificate itself must have a public key as it is signed, so you need another certificate to validate the first certificate's public key. In order to prevent an endless chain of certificates, you use a trusted third party called a **Certificate Authority (CA)** to sign the root certificate. These CA's (such as VeriSign, Inc.) are assumed to create valid and trusted certificates as they are often legally bound to.*

The following command exports the public key associated with the bspell alias and writes that key to a disk file named BrettSpell.cer. Once that's done, this file can be sent (along with the signed JAR file) to any users who wish to use the signed classes:

```
keytool -export -alias bspell -keystore Creator.jks -storepass creator
        -file BrettSpell.cer
```

Using Signed Classes

The steps described up to this point are all performed by the creator/signer of classes being distributed, while the steps that are described below would be performed by the user(s) of those classes:

1. Import public key from certificate

2. Modify the policy file to identify the appropriate keystore

3. Identify the policy file and execute the code

Import Public Key from Certificate

Before you can grant permissions to classes signed by a specific user, you must import that user's public key into a keystore of your own and associate the public key with an alias. For example, assuming that you have access to the BrettSpell.cer file, you can create an entirely new keystore (assuming one named JARUser.jks doesn't already exist in the current directory) using the following command:

```
keytool -import -file BrettSpell.cer -alias bspell -keystore JARUser.jks
        storepass userpass
```

This command creates a new keystore file named `JARUser.jks`, assigns it a password of `userpass`, imports the public key from the `BrettSpell.cer` file, and assigns that key an alias of `bspell`. When you do this, you will be asked if you want to trust this certificate:

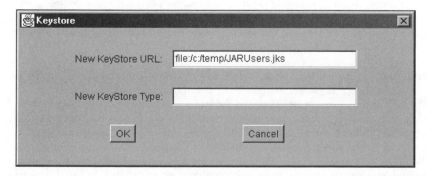

During this step, we are importing the certificate into the local keystore so we can trust all classes signed by this certificate's entity. Therefore, by accepting to trust this certificate we are saying that this user will be granted permissions for classes they have signed.

Modify the Policy File to Identify the Appropriate Keystore

The next step in this process is to modify the policy file created earlier so that it identifies the keystore containing the public keys associated with the aliases for which permissions are granted. In this case, for example, permission to perform any operation was granted to all classes signed by `bspell`, and by adding a `keystore` entry to the policy file, you allow the aliases to be mapped to their public key values:

```
keystore "file:/C:/temp/JARUser.jks";

grant signedBy "bspell" {

  permission java.security.AllPermission;

};
```

Alternatively, if you would rather use the `policytool` to do this, choose **Change Keystore** from the **Edit** menu to bring up the **Keystore** dialog:

Identify the Policy File and Execute the Code

Finally, you can execute the code using the policy file defined above by adding the file to the security configuration (`java.security`) file or by identifying the policy file on the command line.

For example, to execute the `WriteFile` application stored in a JAR file named `SignTest.jar` and use a policy file named `WriteFile.policy`, you might enter the following command:

```
java -cp SignTest.jar -Djava.security.manager
    -Djava.security.policy=WriteFile.policy WriteFile
```

Permission Types

All valid permissions defined in a policy file are represented internally in Java by an instance of some subclass of the abstract `Permission` class defined in the `java.security` package.

We've already seen that the `SecurityManager`'s `checkXXXX()` methods ultimately call the `checkPermission()` method on `AccessController`. If you look at the source for this method, you can see that the permission to be checked is passed as a `Permission` object:

```
public static void checkPermission(Permission perm)
        throws AccessControlException {
```

Some of the `Permission` subclasses are used for a single type of permission, such as in the case of `java.io.FilePermission`, which is only used to describe what type of access is allowed to a file or group of files. Other `Permission` subclasses such as `java.lang.RuntimePermission` are used in a much more general way and can be used to describe many different types of permissions.

In all cases, the `Permission` object encapsulates one or more `String` values, and those values may describe the specific type of permission represented and/or the type of access that's allowed. The type of access allowed is also referred to as the **action list**, because it identifies the actions that can be taken with respect to the resource associated with the permission.

Many of the permission classes are subclasses of `BasicPermission`, which is also defined in the `java.security` package. `BasicPermission` is a direct subclass of `Permission` and both are abstract classes, although `BasicPermission` only contains a single abstract method. That method, called `implies()`, is inherited from `Permission` and it is passed a single `Permission` object as a parameter. As its name suggests, `implies()` allows you to determine whether one permission implies another. For example, suppose that you create two separate permissions: one that allows all files in the `C:/temp` directory and its subdirectories to be read and another that allows all files in the `C:/temp/brett` directory to be read. Since `C:/temp/brett` is a subdirectory of `C:/temp`, the first permission is said to "imply" the second one.

If you're wondering why you would want to deliberately define both of these permissions, the answer is there is no reason to do so. However, `implies()` is important because it allows the `SecurityManager` to determine whether an operation should be allowed to complete. It does this by passing a `Permission` object that represents the operation your code wishes to perform to the `implies()` method of each `Permission` object created for an entry in the active policy file. In other words, it asks each `Permission` object you defined in the policy file whether or not the operation being requested should be allowed. If one of the permissions specified in the policy file implies that the operation is valid, the `SecurityManager` will not throw an exception, but will instead return quietly.

We've already seen how to create and use permission files, so it is appropriate to examine the different permissions that are available for you to use. In addition, we'll learn later in the chapter how you can create and use your own custom permission classes.

java.security.AllPermission

This permission should not normally be used because it gives the code to which it applies permission to perform all operations. In other words, granting `AllPermission` is effectively the same as executing the code without a `SecurityManager` installed. An example of how this permission would appear in a policy file is shown below:

```
grant {
  permission java.security.AllPermission;
};
```

java.io.FilePermission

You can use `FilePermission` to grant access to a file or directory, and you must provide two strings with this type of permission. The first string identifies the permission target (the file or directory to which access is being granted), while the second represents a list of the type of operations that can be performed. That list should contain one or more of the following actions:

- read
- write
- execute
- delete

In most cases, the target value will be a string that simply represents the name of the file or directory for which access is granted. For example, the following two entries grant read access to the C:\temp directory and the readme.txt file in that directory, respectively:

```
grant {
  permission java.io.FilePermission("C:/temp", "read");
  permission java.io.FilePermission("C:/temp/readme.txt", "read");
};
```

In addition to these relatively simple examples, `FilePermission` supports several variations of the target value that have special meaning. For example, if you follow a directory name with an asterisk character, the permission represents access to the directory and to all files within that directory. In the following permission, read access is granted for both the C:\temp directory and for any files that are located in that directory:

```
grant {
  permission java.io.FilePermission("C:/temp/*", "read");
};
```

Similarly, a directory name followed by a minus sign indicates that the permission represents access to the directory, to all files in that directory, and to all files and subdirectories it contains. The following permission grants access to all files and directories in and below the C:\temp directory regardless of how many levels "down" in the file hierarchy those items are:

```
grant {
  permission java.io.FilePermission("C:/temp/-", "read");
};
```

Creating a permission that simply consists of the asterisk or minus sign character will have the effect of granting the permissions described above for the current directory. For example, if the current directory is C:\temp, then the following two permissions are functionally identical:

```
grant {
  permission java.io.FilePermission("C:/temp/-", "read");
  permission java.io.FilePermission("-", "read");
};
```

Similarly, the following two permissions have the same effect if the current directory is C:\temp:

```
grant {
  permission java.io.FilePermission("C:/temp/*", "read");
  permission java.io.FilePermission("*", "read");
};
```

Finally, specifying a target value of "<<ALL FILES>>" indicates that you want the specified actions to be valid for all files and directories in the file system, regardless of their location. For example, the following entry grants read access to all files and directories:

```
grant {
  permission java.io.FilePermission("<<ALL FILES>>", "read");
};
```

As mentioned above, up to four different actions can be specified with a FilePermission, and the meanings of those actions are described below. If you do wish to specify multiple actions, you should separate them with commas as shown below:

```
grant {
  permission java.io.FilePermission("C:/temp", "read,write");
};
```

The read Action

As you would expect, when the read action is specified for a permission that applies to a file or group of files, that permission makes it possible for classes to read the contents of the file(s). However, the meaning of read when used with a directory may not be as obvious. For example, suppose that you create the following permission:

```
grant {
  permission java.io.FilePermission("C:/temp/", "read");
};
```

If no other permissions have been granted, this allows the code to obtain the names of the files contained in the directory, but it does not allow the code to read the contents of those files. In other words, it allows you to list the contents of a directory. This permission (or one that implies this permission) must be defined before the list() method in the java.io.File class can be called to obtain a list of the files in the C:\temp directory.

The write Action

In the context of a file, the write action indicates that classes granted the permission are able to modify or create the file. For a directory, the write action allows the directory to be created using either the mkdir() or mkdirs() method in java.io.File, and it allows the directory to be modified by methods such as setLastModified() and setReadOnly().

The delete Action

This action indicates that the file or directory can be deleted by the class or classes to which the permission is granted.

The execute Action

Unlike the other three FilePermission actions, this one only applies to files, and it indicates that the file(s) with which it's associated can be executed using the exec() method in the java.lang.Runtime class. The exec() method is used to activate an executable native application, and the following code might be used to activate the Netscape web browser:

```
Runtime rt = Runtime.getRuntime();
rt.exec("C:/netscape/program/netscape.exe");
```

If a SecurityManager is active when this code is executed, it will be necessary for a permission to be present that was created by an entry similar to the one shown below:

```
grant {
  permission java.io.FilePermission(
        "C:/netscape/program/netscape.exe", "execute");
};
```

java.net.SocketPermission

You probably already know that the ability of applets to create socket connections is very limited. In fact, an unsigned applet can only create socket connections to the server from which the applet was downloaded. SocketPermission allows you to specify which socket-related operations should be allowed, and consists of two items:

- ❑ A host/port value
- ❑ A list of actions that should be allowed relative to that host and port

The list of actions should contain one or more of the following: accept, connect, listen, or resolve. The meanings of each of these actions is described below.

The host/port value contained within a SocketPermission identifies a specific machine or group of machines within a domain for which the permission is intended. The host portion can be a hostname, an IP address, "localhost" (which refers to the local machine), or a domain name with an asterisk that represents a pattern-matching character. For example, the following permissions allow the associated code to create connections to the Wrox web server machine using any local port. The two permissions are equivalent because the Wrox web server's IP address is 12.34.56.78:

```
permission java.net.SocketPermission "www.wrox.com", "connect";
permission java.net.SocketPermission "12.34.56.78", "connect";
```

775

To grant permission to all machines in a particular domain, simply use the asterisk as a pattern-matching character as shown below. This entry allows connections to be made to any machine in the wrox.com domain:

```
permission java.net.SocketPermission "*.wrox.com", "connect";
```

Similarly, specifying an asterisk by itself represents a permission that allows classes to create connections to any machine accessible on the network:

```
permission java.net.SocketPermission "*", "connect";
```

If you wish to limit the local port numbers that can be used, you can specify a port number or range of numbers along with the host value by separating the two with a colon (":"). For example, the following permission only allows a connection to be made using port 1234:

```
permission java.net.SocketPermission "www.wrox.com:1234", "connect";
```

You can also specify a range of port numbers as in the following example, which allows connections to be made on any port between 1234 and 5678 (inclusive):

```
permission java.net.SocketPermission "www.wrox.com:1234-5678", "connect";
```

Finally, you can also specify a range that omits either the starting or ending value. The first permission below allows connections to be made on any port with a value of 1234 or less, while the second allows connections to be made on ports 5678 and higher:

```
permission java.net.SocketPermission "www.wrox.com:-1234", "connect";
permission java.net.SocketPermission "www.wrox.com:5678-", "connect";
```

As mentioned above, there are four different actions associated with the SocketPermission class, and their meanings are described below. As in the case of FilePermission, you can specify more than one action with a SocketPermission by separating the actions with commas:

```
permission java.net.SocketPermission "*.wrox.com", "connect,accept,listen";
```

The connect Action

As its name implies, this action allows you to specify that the local machine should be able to create socket connections to other machines, which is normally done by creating an instance of java.net.Socket.

The listen Action

This action is only meaningful when localhost is specified as the host, and is used to grant permission to listen for incoming connections (using a ServerSocket) on specific ports. Note, however, that this is different from actually being able to accept a connection on that port, which is controlled by accept as described below. For example, suppose that you create the following permission:

```
permission java.net.SocketPermission "localhost:5000-5010", "listen";
```

Although this grants permission to listen for incoming connections on ports 5000 through 5010, a call to `accept()` in `ServerSocket` will fail if no other permissions are granted and an attempt is made to create a connection. That's because the above entry only grants permission to listen for incoming connections but does not grant permission to accept them.

The accept Action

You can use this action to specify which machines should be able to create socket connections to the local machine and/or on which ports those connections can be made. `accept` is needed in addition to `listen`, because `listen` only applies to local ports whereas `accept` applies to both `local` and remote ports.

For example, if you wish to grant permission to accept incoming connections from machines in the `wrox.com` domain, but only on local ports 6000 through 6100, you could create an entry like the one shown below:

```
permission java.net.SocketPermission "wrox.com:6000-6100", "accept";
```

The resolve Action

This action controls the ability to convert a host name into an IP address or vice-versa, also known as a **DNS** (**Domain Name Server**) **lookup**. However, you won't typically need to create an entry with this action since resolve is implied by each of the other three actions (`listen`, `connect`, and `accept`). In other words, the only time you'll need to add a permission with the `resolve` action is when you want to create code that has permission to perform lookups but which cannot listen for, create, or accept socket connections.

java.awt.AWTPermission

This permission class is used to grant permission to perform operations related to the Abstract Windowing Toolkit (AWT) that could compromise your application's security. Currently, there are six operations for which you can grant permission using `AWTPermission`, each of them is represented by a **target name**. In effect, the target name is the name of the specific permission sub-type being granted, and an example of how to use `AWTPermission` appears below:

```
grant {
  permission java.awt.AWTPermission "accessClipboard";
};
```

The accessClipboard Action

Access to the system clipboard is obtained through the `getSystemClipboard()` method in `java.awt.Toolkit`. However, a malicious program could potentially retrieve sensitive information that has been left on the clipboard, so `getSystemClipboard()` will throw a `SecurityException` unless this permission has been granted.

The accessEventQueue Action

The system event queue is a queue through which all events are processed, and that event queue is accessible through the `getSystemEventQueue()` method in `java.awt.Toolkit`. If a hostile program is allowed to access the queue, it can examine or even modify the events on the queue, accessing information that should be inaccessible to it, causing the application generating the events to function incorrectly. Therefore, the `getSystemEventQueue()` method checks to see if this permission has been granted before it returns a reference to the event queue.

The listenToAllAWTEvents Action

Just as allowing a malicious program to access the system event queue is a security violation, allowing such a program to simply be notified of the events is also undesirable. The Toolkit class contains a method called addAWTEventListener() that allows the caller to register a listener that will be notified of all AWT events. If a hostile program is allowed to call this method successfully, that program might be given access to sensitive information, such as a logon password that was entered in a text field.

The readDisplayPixels Action

Just as the ability to read the information stored in the clipboard is a potential security violation, allowing all applications to access the pixels displayed on the screen also represents undesirable behavior. For this reason, you shouldn't grant this permission to code that uses functionality like that found in java.awt.Composite implementations, since they allow access to the current pixel information.

The showWindowWithoutWarningBanner Action

When a subclass of java.awt.Window such as JDialog or JFrame is displayed by a Java program that uses a SecurityManager, the default behavior is to display a warning message as a banner at the bottom of the window:

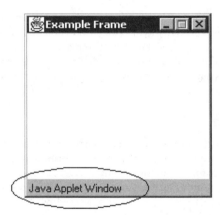

That message indicates to the user that the window was produced by an unsigned or potentially hostile applet, which is done to make the user cautious about entering sensitive information into the window's fields. However, the message may confuse users or cause unnecessary concern in some cases, so it's convenient to be able to disable the message.

The createRobot Action

One of the new features introduced in JDK 1.3 is the Robot class that's defined in java.awt. This class allows you to generate input events (mouse movement, button, and key presses) that are identical to those generated by the underlying operating system as a result of user input. This class is intended for use in creating testing tools and demo programs, but could be used by malicious code to manipulate a running application. For that reason, the Robot constructor requires that you grant this permission, and if you do not do so, a SecurityException is generated.

java.net.NetPermission

This permission class is used to grant permissions related to networking, two of which are related to the active Authenticator implementation. An Authenticator is a class that can be used to obtain authentication for a network connection.

Like `AWTPermission`, the `NetPermission` class only accepts a single parameter, which in this case is the name of the specific permission sub-type being granted:

```
grant {
  permission java.net.NetPermission "requestPasswordAuthentication";
  permission java.net.NetPermission "setDefaultAuthenticator";
};
```

The requestPasswordAuthentication Action

The `requestPasswordAuthentication()` method in `Authenticator` is responsible for requesting the authentication information, and it returns an object that contains the data received (a userid and password). Therefore, the `requestPasswordAuthentication()` method is protected by this permission to prevent hostile code from capturing authentication information.

The setDefaultAuthenticator Action

Just as there is a static `setSecurityManager()` method that allows you to set the security manager (assuming that one is not already in place), there is also a `setDefaultAuthenticator()` method in the `Authenticator` class. Once again, it's necessary to control access to that method so that malicious programs do not simply replace the existing `Authenticator` with one which will bypass the existing security check in `requestPasswordAuthentication()` that's described above.

The specifyStreamHandler Action

The `setURLStreamHandlerFactory()` method in `java.net.URL` is used to identify the object that's responsible for creating URL **stream handlers**. A stream handler is a class that performs I/O operations for a particular type of URL, and making the `setURLStreamHandlerFactory()` method accessible to all code would create a potential security problem. Specifically, it would be possible for a malicious program to make code appear to have been loaded from a trusted location when in fact the code was loaded from an untrusted URL. To prevent that from happening, the `setURLStreamHandlerFactory()` method will ensure that the code which called it has been given this permission before it performs its task.

java.util.PropertyPermission

A large number of system properties are used by Java Virtual Machines, and those properties are accessible through the `getProperty()`/`setProperty()` and `getProperties()`/`setProperties()` methods in `java.lang.System`. If a hostile program is able to modify those property values by calling `setProperty()` or `setProperties()`, it may be able to disrupt the operation of other programs running within the same JVM.

In addition, properties may even represent sensitive information that you wish to prevent some applications from reading, so it's useful to be able to control access to the system properties. Fortunately, the `PropertyPermission` class is provided specifically for that purpose, and it accepts two values:

❑ The name of the property or property group to which access is given

❑ The type(s) of access granted

The access types are specified in an action list, and there are only two valid values: `read` and `write`. As their names imply, the `read` and `write` actions allow an application to retrieve and modify a system property's value, respectively. For example, the following entry in a policy file will allow access to three different properties, with read access to the first property, write access to the second, and both read and write access granted for the third property:

```
grant {
  permission java.util.PropertyPermission "file.separator", "read";
  permission java.util.PropertyPermission "user.home", "write";
  permission java.util.PropertyPermission "user.dir", "read, write";
};
```

You can also use the asterisk character as a wildcard to grant permission for all properties in a group. For example, the first entry below grants read access to all properties in a group such as user (user.home, user.dir, etc.), while the second grants read and write access to the os group (os.name, os.arch, os.version):

```
grant {
  permission java.util.PropertyPermission "user.*", "read";
  permission java.util.PropertyPermission "os.*", "read, write";
};
```

java.lang.reflect.ReflectPermission

ReflectPermission accepts a single target name parameter, and the only parameter value that is currently supported is suppressAccessChecks, the meaning of which is described below.

Java's Reflection API allows you to dynamically access the methods and fields within an object. You can obtain a list of the methods and fields defined in a class, retrieve or update the field values, and call the methods defined in the class. Normally, however, the visibility of the fields and methods affects a program's ability to reference them. If you create private methods or fields, those items will not be accessible by other classes through the reflection API, just as they would not be accessible when accessed normally.

For example, suppose that you've created the following class that contains two fields:

```
public class TestClass {

  public String first;
  private String second;

}
```

Although the field named first is accessible from classes outside TestClass, the second field is not accessible because it is a private field. In fact, the second field will not be accessible even if you attempt to retrieve or modify it using the reflection API, because that API normally respects the field and method visibility modifiers. However, you can call the setAccessible() method of a Field, Method, or Constructor object to override this behavior as shown below. This code uses the reflection API to display the value of a field within an object even though that field is declared as private, which it does by calling the setAccessible() method before attempting to access the field's value:

```
import java.lang.reflect.*;

public class AccessTest {

  public static void main(String[] args) throws Exception {
    DataClass dc = new DataClass();
    Class cl = DataClass.class;
```

```
        Field f = cl.getDeclaredField("message");
        f.setAccessible(true);
        System.out.println(f.get(dc));
    }

}

class DataClass {

  private String message = "This is a private field";

}
```

Although the above program will execute successfully when run as a Java application, it will fail if you run the same application with the default `SecurityManager` active. That's because when a `SecurityManager` is installed, the `setAccessible()` method determines whether a `ReflectPermission` is present with a target name of `suppressAccessChecks`. In other words, specifying `suppressAccessChecks` in a `ReflectPermission` has exactly the effect that its name implies: it allows you to make fields accessible that would not otherwise be available through the reflection API. An example of how the `ReflectPermission` might be coded is illustrated below:

```
grant {

  permission java.lang.reflect.ReflectPermission "suppressAccessChecks";

};
```

java.lang.RuntimePermission

Like some of the other permission classes, `RuntimePermission` only accepts a single target name value as a parameter, and the values that can be specified are described below.

The createSecurityManager Action

When the `SecurityManager` constructor is entered, it checks for the presence of this permission before proceeding, and if the permission does not exist, it throws a `SecurityException`. There is generally not any reason to create a `SecurityManager` after one has already been created and activated, because it's not usually possible to replace one security manager with another after it is installed. However, if you need to do so, you must grant this permission to the code that creates the second (and later) `SecurityManager` instances.

The setSecurityManager Action

As mentioned earlier, a `SecurityManager` that can be replaced arbitrarily is equivalent to having no security in effect. However, since you can grant permissions to specific classes, it is possible to design a secure application that is able to replace its `SecurityManager`. Before calling the `setSecurityManager()` method in `java.lang.System`, you must grant this permission to the code to prevent the method from throwing a `SecurityException`.

The getProtectionDomain Action

A **protection domain** (represented internally by the `ProtectionDomain` class in `java.security`) is essentially an object that identifies the location from which code was loaded and the permissions granted to that code. A `getProtectionDomain()` method is defined in `java.lang.Class`, and that method returns the ProtectionDomain instance associated with the class. In other words, this permission controls access to the information that describes where a class was loaded from and which permissions it has been granted. While this information by itself does not provide a hostile program with enough information to compromise an application's security, it could potentially make it easier for a malicious user to eventually do so.

The createClassLoader Action

Class loaders extend java.lang.ClassLoader and are responsible for loading class definitions into the Java Virtual Machine, especially those not located on the classpath. Some of the most important security barriers in Java are incorporated in its class loaders, so allowing an application to create its own class loader can have severe consequences from a security perspective. For that reason, the ClassLoader constructor checks for the presence of this permission before proceeding, and will throw a SecurityException if the permission was not granted. Given the seriousness of the potential security problems that can occur, you should not normally grant this permission.

The getClassLoader Action

A getClassLoader() method is defined in java.lang.Class, and it represents a potential security threat. If hostile code is given access to a ClassLoader, it might be able to use that object to obtain access to classes which it could not normally reference, so the getClassLoader() method is protected by this permission.

The setContextClassLoader Action

A setContextClassLoader() was added to the Thread class in Java 2, and this method allows you to assign a ClassLoader on a per-thread basis. However, this permission controls access to the method, so you cannot set the ClassLoader for a thread unless the code that attempts to do so has been given this permission.

The loadLibrary Action

When you define a native method in Java, you must create a corresponding implementation for that method that is usually done in C or C++. When you create such an implementation, you'll define it as part of a "library" file, such as a Dynamic Link Library (DLL) when creating native method implementations in Windows. In addition, you must use the loadLibrary() method in java.lang.System to load the library file before you can successfully invoke the native method.

Native methods represent a potential threat to the security of your application, because native code is not constrained by the limitations imposed by Java's security features. For example, a native method might not be able to access the fields in an object through the standard Java APIs, but it is quite capable of examining memory directly to access (or even modify) sensitive information. For that reason, the loadLibrary() method will throw a SecurityException unless the code that called it has been granted this permission.

When you specify this permission, you must also specify the name of a specific library that you want to allow to be loaded, although you can use the asterisk character for pattern matching. To do so, separate the target name ("loadLibrary") from the library name or name pattern with a period (".") as in the examples below. These illustrate entries that grant the loadLibrary permission, and are accompanied by comments that describe what each one represents:

```
//  The following allows "MyLibrary" to be loaded
permission java.lang.Runtime "loadLibrary.MyLibrary";
```

```
// The following allows libraries with names that begin with
// "Secure" to be loaded
permission java.lang.Runtime "loadLibrary.Secure*";

// The following allows any library file to be loaded
permission java.lang.Runtime "loadLibrary.*";
```

The exitVM Action

The exit() method in System allows the caller to terminate the JVM, and while it does not represent a security violation in the traditional sense, it may allow hostile code to disrupt the execution of your program. To prevent this from happening, the exitVM permission has been created, and you must grant this permission for code to be able to successfully call the System.exit() method.

The queuePrintJob Action

A malicious program could monopolize a printer by submitting large and/or numerous printer jobs if not prevented from doing so. However, Java programs cannot submit printer jobs while a SecurityManager is active unless they have been given this permission.

The setFactory Action

This permission controls access to a number of different methods, most of which are used to specify the object that is responsible for creating some other type of object. For example, the ServerSocket class includes a setSocketFactory() method that is passed a SocketImplFactory object. When a new Socket is to be created by a ServerSocket, it calls the SocketImplFactory's createSocketImpl() method, and that method is responsible for creating the new Socket.

The setSocketFactory() is only one of a handful of methods for which access is controlled by this permission. Those methods are listed below, and if one of them is called from a class that has not been granted this permission, the method will throw a SecurityException.

Class	Method
java.net.ServerSocket	setSocketFactory()
java.net.Socket	setSocketImplFactory()
java.net.URL	setURLStreamHandlerFactory()
java.net.URLConnection	setContentHandlerFactory()
java.net.URLConnection	setFileNameMap()
java.net.HttpURLConnection	setFollowRedirects()
java.rmi.activation.ActivationGroup	createGroup()
java.rmi.activation.ActivationGroup	setSystem()
java.rmi.server.RMISocketFactory	setSocketFactory()

The setIO Action

The java.lang.System class defines methods that allow you to specify an instance of java.io.PrintStream that should be used for the standard output and standard error streams. In other words, you can control where the output from calls to System.out.println() and

System.err.println() are sent by calling the setOut() and setErr() methods, respectively. Similarly, the setIn() method allows you to specify the InputStream that's used to represent standard input, which normally corresponds to your console (command prompt or "DOS window" on Windows).

A hostile program could take advantage of these methods to intercept user input and/or it could conceal errors or other important messages by substituting the standard output and error streams for its own implementations. However, this permission prevents that from occurring, since it must be granted before a class can call the setOut(), setErr(), or setIn() methods in java.lang.System.

The readFileDescriptor and writeFileDescriptor Actions

A FileDescriptor is an object that's used to represent some type of system resource such as an open file or an open socket connection. Allowing all programs to read FileDescriptor instances would represent a security weakness since the descriptors may contain sensitive data. Similarly, allowing code to write FileDescriptor instances might allow a malicious program to damage or destroy important files.

The stopThread Action

When no SecurityManager is active (or this permission has been granted), it's possible for one thread to terminate another by calling the target thread's stop() method. However, this may leave the stopped thread's resources in an inappropriate state (resources may not be released). Even if that does not occur, it is still the case that hostile code is able to affect the operation of your application code, which is obviously undesirable in most cases. For that reason, the stop() method (in addition to being deprecated in Java 2) verifies that the class which called it has been granted this permission, and if it hasn't, a SecurityException is generated.

The modifyThread and modifyThreadGroup Actions

Just as it's often desirable to allow code to stop a thread, you may wish to prevent threads and/or thread groups from being modified. By default, the SecurityManager will prevent methods such as suspend(), resume(), and setPriority() in Thread from being called, as well as suspend(), resume(), and setMaxPriority() in ThreadGroup. However, you can grant the modifyThread permission to allow the Thread methods to be called and/or the modifyThreadGroup permission to allow thread groups to be modified.

The accessDeclaredMembers Action

There are many methods in java.lang.Class that allow you to access a class's fields, methods, and constructors. For example, Class includes methods such as getFields(), getField(), getDeclaredField(), getMethods(), etc. As long as the class for which you're calling these methods is loaded by the same ClassLoader as the class that calls the methods, no permissions need to be granted.

However, if one of the accessor methods in Class is called by code that was loaded by a different ClassLoader, it's necessary to grant this permission to that code. The purpose of this behavior is to prevent hostile code from being able to obtain any information about other classes. While such information does not represent a direct security threat, it could be used by a malicious user to compromise the security of an application.

The accessClassInPackage and defineClassInPackage Actions

A package name must be specified with this permission, which allows code to obtain access to other classes through the loadClass() method in ClassLoader. These are classes to which the code would not normally have access, and by accessing a class and its methods, constructors, and fields, hostile code might be able to gather information that enables it to violate an application's security.

While `accessClassInPackage` provides the ability to call `loadClass()` to gain access to a class, `defineClassInPackage` allows the `defineClass()` method in permission to be called. For that reason, `defineClassInPackage` should be used with caution, because code that is granted this permission is able to define new classes in trusted packages such as `java.security` and `java.lang`.

When you specify either of these permissions, you must specify either a specific package or group of packages (using the asterisk as a wildcard character) in the target name parameter, separating the parameter and package names with a period ("."). For example, the following permissions grant read access to the classes in all packages beginning with `bspell` and write access only to the `bspell.guest` package:

```
grant {

  java.lang.RuntimePermission "accessClassInPackage.bspell.*";
  java.lang.RuntimePermission "defineClassInPackage.bspell.guest";

};
```

The shutdownHooks Action

It's possible in Java 1.3 to define **shutdown hooks** by calling the `addShutdownHook()` and `removeShutdownHook()` methods in `java.lang.Runtime`. Shutdown hooks are threads started by the JVM when `System.exit()` is called or when the user terminates the JVM process. However, before a hook can be added or removed, the code that requests the operation must be granted this permission.

java.io.SerializablePermission

Java's serialization mechanism is convenient and flexible, but it also introduces some potential security problems. However, the `SerializablePermission` and the target names that it supports are used to limit access to the serialization features that could be used to compromise application security.

The enableSubclassImplementation Action

The `ObjectOutputStream` class in `java.io` is used to create (or "marshal") serialized representations of objects, while `ObjectInputStream` re-creates an object from its serialized representation. It's normally possible to subclass one, or both, of these classes and override their methods to modify their behavior, but doing so presents a potential security problem. For example, hostile code could intercept requests to marshal an object and store the object's content in a location that would make it accessible to users that should not have access to the data. However, the default `SecurityManager` will not allow a subclass of `ObjectInputStream` or `ObjectOutputStream` to be used unless this permission has been granted.

The enableSubstitution Action

The `enableReplaceObject()` method in `ObjectOutputStream` can be used to replace an object being marshaled with some other object. The `enableResolveObject()` method in `ObjectInputStream` similarly allows you to replace an object being unmarshaled with some other object. However, these represent another area where malicious users could create code that compromises your application's security, so a class is prevented from using those two methods unless it has been granted this permission.

java.sql.SQLPermission

This permission class currently supports a single target name value of setLog. That permission is used to allow the setLogWriter() and setLogStream() methods in DriverManager to be called. Those methods are used to specify where diagnostic messages generated by JDBC drivers should be sent, but those messages may contain sensitive information. Therefore, before a class can call either setLogWriter() or setLogStream(), it must have first been granted this permission or a SecurityException will be thrown.

java.security.SecurityPermission

This class does not support an action list, but it does support a large number of target names that correspond to different specific permissions. However, these permissions are all related to classes and methods that are used in the enforcement of security, and you'll not normally grant these permissions explicitly. Since detailed explanations of many of the permissions would require an in-depth understanding of the classes in the java.security package, they are not provided here. There is largely a one-to-one correspondence between a specific permission/target name and a method in one of the java.security classes, and those relations are described in the following table. For additional information, you should consult the JavaSoft documentation.

Permission Target Name	java.security Class	Method
createAccessControlContext	AccessControl Context	(Constructor)
getDomainCombiner	AccessControl Context	getDomainCombiner()
addIdentityCertificate	Identity	addCertificate()
removeIdentityCertificate	Identity	removeCertificate()
setIdentityInfo	Identity	setInfo()
setIdentityPublicKey	Identity	setPublicKey()
printIdentity	Identity	toString()
setSystemScope	IdentityScope	setSystemScope()
getPolicy	Policy	getPolicy()
setPolicy	Policy	setPolicy()
clearProviderProperties	Provider	checkSecurityAccess()
putProviderProperty	Provider	put()
removeProviderProperty	Provider	remove()
getProperty	Security	getProperty()
setProperty	Security	setProperty()
insertProvider	Security	insertProviderAt()
removeProvider	Security	removeProvider()
getSignerPrivateKey	Signer	getPrivateKey()
setSignerKeypair	Signer	setKeyPair()

BasicPermission Subclass and the Wildcard Character

As mentioned earlier, most of the Permission subclasses are actually direct subclasses of java.security.BasicPermission, which is a direct subclass of Permission. BasicPermission has a useful characteristic that you should be aware of, since it may allow you to more quickly and easily provide a set of related permissions. Specifically, an asterisk can be appended to the end of the target name, and that character signifies that pattern matching should be used with the permission.

For example, suppose that you wish to grant all three types of NetPermission: setDefaultAuthenticator, requestPasswordAuthentication, and specifyStreamHandler. You could specify each of these three separately, but an easier way would be to simply specify the pattern-matching character by itself, which would have the same effect:

```
grant {

  permission java.net.NetPermission "*";

};
```

Similarly, the following entry would grant all RuntimePermission capabilities for which the target name begins with "create", specifically createClassLoader and createSecurityManager:

```
grant {

  permission java.lang.RuntimePermission "create*";

};
```

Note that the pattern matching character must be specified at the end of target name, and it is not valid for it to appear at the beginning of or within the name. For example, the following *is not* a valid entry:

```
grant {

  permission java.lang.RuntimePermission "*ClassLoader";

};
```

The classes that subclass BasicPermission (those with which you can take advantage of this behavior) are:

- ❑ AWTPermission
- ❑ NetPermission
- ❑ PropertyPermission
- ❑ ReflectPermission
- ❑ RuntimePermission
- ❑ SecurityPermission
- ❑ SerializablePermission
- ❑ SQLPermission

In other words, all of the permission classes discussed in this chapter are subclasses of `BasicPermission` except for `AllPermission`, `FilePermission`, and `SocketPermission`.

Creating Custom Permission Types

Although the existing permission classes cover all potentially sensitive operations performed by Java's core classes, you may want to create your own `Permission` subclass for use in an application for enforcing application-specific security. For example, suppose that you have created the following class and wish to create a type of permission that controls access to the accessor and mutator methods:

```
public class StudentGrades {

  private String[][] allGrades = new String[1][3];

  public String[] getGrades(int studentID) {
    String[] grades;
    grades = allGrades[studentID];
    return grades;
  }

  public void setGrades(int studentID, String[] grades) {
    allGrades[studentID] = grades;
  }

}
```

Although you might be tempted to simply extend one of the existing `Permission` subclasses, you should not do so. Instead, you should create your own subclass, from either `Permission`, which we'll do for this example, or `BasicPermission`, if you don't need an event list. Specifically, we'll create a new `GradePermission` class that extends `Permission` and allows you to specify one of two target names: either `read` or `update`, both of which are associated with a constant defined in `GradePermission`. Note that the `GradePermission` constructor passes the target name to the constructor of its superclass (`Permission`), since the target name value is maintained there:

```
import java.security.*;

public class GradePermission extends Permission {

  public final static String READ_GRADES = "read";
  public final static String UPDATE_GRADES = "update";

  public GradePermission(String name, String actions) {
    super(name);
  }

  public GradePermission(String name) {
    this(name, "");
  }

}
```

The first constructor shown above (the one that accepts two `String` parameters) is required, and your `Permission` subclass will not function correctly if you do not include it, while the second one is simply provided here as a convenience.

There's no reason the second constructor couldn't call super (name) directly, but this is strictly a matter of style. The additional overhead is minimal, and this approach allows us to insert code into a single constructor (the first one) that will be executed by both constructors, which is typically what you'll want to have happen. If we were to call the superclass constructor directly, we'd have to copy the code into the second constructor or create a separate method that contains the common code and put a call to that method within both constructors. Instead, we create one "master" constructor and call it from the other constructors. In fact, this is what Sun does in most of the Java classes.

However, this class cannot be compiled successfully because Permission is an abstract class, and its concrete subclasses must provide implementations for four methods: equals(), hashCode(), getActions(), and implies(). The equals() and hashCode() methods are inherited from java.lang.Object, and are commonly overridden by user-defined classes. There are no special issues related to implementing these for a Permission subclass, and simple implementations of these methods are shown below:

```
import java.security.*;

public class GradePermission extends Permission {

    public final static String READ_GRADES = "read";
    public final static String UPDATE_GRADES = "update";

    public GradePermission(String name, String actions) {
      super(name);
    }

    public GradePermission(String name) {
      this(name, "");
    }

    public boolean equals(Object o) {
      if ((o == null) || (o.getClass() != getClass())) {
        return false;
      }
      GradePermission gp = (GradePermission)o;
      if ((gp.getName()).equals(getName())) {
        return true;
      }
      return false;
    }

    public int hashCode() {
      return getName().hashCode();
    }
}
```

Note that as always, you should strive to provide a hashCode() implementation that will return a unique value for instances that are not equal to one another, although it's not strictly required that you do so.

The getActions() method is even easier to create, since (like many of the predefined types) this type of permission does not support an action list. Therefore, that method can be implemented by simply returning an empty string:

789

```
import java.security.*;

public class GradePermission extends Permission {

  public final static String READ_GRADES = "read";
  public final static String UPDATE_GRADES = "update";

  public GradePermission(String name, String actions) {
    super(name);
  }

  public GradePermission(String name) {
    this(name, "");
  }

  public boolean equals(Object o) {
    if ((o == null) || (o.getClass() != getClass())) {
      return false;
    }
    GradePermission gp = (GradePermission)o;
    if ((gp.getName()).equals(getName())) {
      return true;
    }
    return false;
  }

  public int hashCode() {
    return getName().hashCode();
  }

  public String getActions() {
    return "";
  }

}
```

The final method that must be implemented is implies(), which indicates whether the presence of one permission implicitly means that some other permission has effectively been granted. In this case, for example, we'll assume that the ability to update grade information implies that the code should also be able to read that information and implement the implies() method accordingly:

```
import java.security.*;

public class GradePermission extends Permission {

  public final static String READ_GRADES = "read";
  public final static String UPDATE_GRADES = "update";

  public GradePermission(String name, String actions) {
    super(name);
  }

  public GradePermission(String name) {
    this(name, "");
  }
```

```
public boolean equals(Object o) {
  if ((o == null) || (o.getClass() != getClass())) {
    return false;
  }
  GradePermission gp = (GradePermission) o;
  if ((gp.getName()).equals(getName())) {
    return true;
  }
  return false;
}

public int hashCode() {
  return getName().hashCode();
}

public String getActions() {
  return "";
}

public boolean implies(Permission p) {
  if (p.getClass() != getClass()) {
    return false;
  }
  if ((p.getName()).equals(getName())
          || ((p.getName()).equals(READ_GRADES))) {
    return true;
  }
  return false;
}

}
```

Since there are only two possible target names (read and update) that can be assigned to a valid instance of GradePermission, the following table illustrates the value that will be returned from the above implies() method for each combination. The column headers represent the target name of the GradePermission object for which the implies() method is called, while the row headers represent the target name of the GradePermission passed as a parameter to that method:

Target Name	read	update
read	true	true
update	false	true

The next step in supporting this new type of permission is to add code to the methods that require its presence, which can be done very easily. All that's needed is for each method to construct an instance of the permission that it requires to be present and pass that object to the static checkPermission() method in the active SecurityManager. If there is no active SecurityManager, the operation is automatically allowed to complete:

```
public class StudentGrades {
```

```
    private String[][] allGrades = new String[1][3];

    public String[] getGrades(int studentID) {
      String[] grades;
      GradePermission gp = new GradePermission(GradePermission.READ_GRADES);
      SecurityManager sm = System.getSecurityManager();
      if (sm != null) {
        sm.checkPermission(gp);
      }
      grades = allGrades[studentID];
      return grades;
    }

    public void setGrades(int studentID, String[] grades) {
      GradePermission gp = new GradePermission(GradePermission.UPDATE_GRADES);
      SecurityManager sm = System.getSecurityManager();
      if (sm != null) {
        sm.checkPermission(gp);
      }
      allGrades[studentID] = grades;
    }

  }
```

At this point, we can test the modified `StudentGrades` class to ensure that it works correctly, but first we need to add a `main()` routine:

```
    public static void main(String[] args) {
      StudentGrades sg = new StudentGrades();
      String[] grades = {"A", "B-", "A"};
      sg.setGrades(0, grades);
      String chkGrades[] = sg.getGrades(0);
      System.out.println("Grades are: " + chkGrades[0] + ", " + chkGrades[1] +
                         ", " + chkGrades[2]);
    }
```

If you execute it as an application without an active `SecurityManager`, it will complete successfully because the security check is not performed when no manager is active. However, if you execute it with an active `SecurityManager`, an exception will be thrown.

To grant the newly created `GradePermission`, simply add an entry like the one shown below to a policy file and use that policy file when executing the code that was granted the permission:

```
  grant {

    permission GradePermission "update";

  };
```

Permission Collections

In most cases, the steps described above are sufficient for creating a custom permission type. However, there may be situations where the value that should be returned by implies() cannot be correctly determined by any single permission, but must be derived by evaluating the group of permissions. For example, let's suppose that you have created a Java application that controls access to a library of movies and that each movie is given one of the following ratings based on its content: G, PG, PG-13, R, or NC-17. You might then create a MoviePermission class such as the one shown below that allows you to grant users access to movies with specific ratings:

```java
import java.security.*;
import java.util.*;

public class MoviePermission extends Permission {

  public final static Object[][] ratings = {
     {
      "G", new Integer(1)
    }, {
      "PG", new Integer(2)
    }, {
      "PG-13", new Integer(4)
    }, {
      "R", new Integer(8)
    }, {
      "NC-17", new Integer(16)
    }
  };

  protected int targetRatings;

  public MoviePermission(String target, String action) {
    super(target);
    processTarget();
  }

  protected void processTarget() {
    String rating;
    StringTokenizer strtok = new StringTokenizer(getName(), ",");
    while (strtok.hasMoreElements()) {
      rating = (String) (strtok.nextElement());
      if (rating.equalsIgnoreCase("all")) {
        for (int i = 0; i < ratings.length; i++) {
          addRating((String) (ratings[i][0]));
        }
        return;
      } else {
        addRating(rating);
      }
    }
  }

  protected void addRating(String rating) {
    String compare;
    Integer flagValue;
```

```
      for (int i = 0; i < ratings.length; i++) {
        compare = (String) (ratings[i][0]);
        if (compare.equalsIgnoreCase(rating)) {
          flagValue = (Integer) (ratings[i][1]);
          targetRatings |= flagValue.intValue();
        }
      }
    }

    public String getActions() {
      return "";
    }

    public boolean implies(Permission p) {
      if ((p == null) || (p.getClass() != getClass())) {
        return false;
      }
      MoviePermission mp = (MoviePermission) p;
      int compare = mp.targetRatings;
      int intersection = compare & targetRatings;
      if (compare != intersection) {
        return false;
      }
      return true;
    }

    public int hashCode() {
      return targetRatings;
    }

    public boolean equals(Object o) {
      if ((o == null) || (o.getClass() != getClass())) {
        return false;
      }
      MoviePermission mp = (MoviePermission) o;
      if (mp.targetRatings != targetRatings) {
        return false;
      }
      return true;
    }

}
```

This newly created `Permission` subclass allows you to specify the ratings for which you intend to allow access, or a value of `all` to indicate that the permission provides access to movies of all ratings. For example, you might create policy file entries like those shown below:

```
keystore="file:/c:/temp/JARUser.jks";

grant signedBy "bspell" {

  permission MoviePermission "G, PG, PG-13, R";

};
```

```
   grant signedBy "mcritic" {

     permission MoviePermission "all";

   };
```

These entries grant access to movies of all ratings to the classes signed by the mcritic alias, and access to classes signed by bspell for movies with ratings of G, PG, PG-13, and R.

To test this let's create a very simple class that tries to access a movie of a particular rating:

```
public class EnterMovie {
   public static void main(String[] args) {
     MoviePermission mp = new MoviePermission("NC-17", "allow");
     SecurityManager sm = System.getSecurityManager();
     if (sm != null) {
       sm.checkPermission(mp);
     }
     System.out.println("Watching movie...");
   }
}
```

Now if you follow the steps earlier in the chapter to sign this class with the bspell and then a new mcritic alias, when you try to execute the code you should find that an exception is thrown for the bspell alias but the mcritic signed version completes perfectly.

Now let's suppose that you wish to create a somewhat different type of permission entry: one that actually *prevents* a user from accessing a movie with a particular rating. This is different from a "traditional" permission, because all of the ones that we've seen so far defined operations that are allowed, while none identified those that should be prohibited.

However, if we define a new type of entry that "disallows" certain operations, it will be possible to code permissions that effectively translate into "allow the user to view movies of all ratings except for those in this list". An example of how this could be done appears below:

```
   grant signedBy "bspell" {

     permission MoviePermission "all", "allow";
     permission MoviePermission "NC-17", "disallow";

   };
```

In other words, this policy file entry should have the same effect as the previous entry for bspell, although in that case, only a single permission was granted that explicitly identified the movie ratings that should be accessible. To support this behavior, a few simple changes should be made to the MoviePermission class:

```
import java.security.*;
import java.util.*;

public class MoviePermission extends Permission {
```

```java
public final static Object[][] ratings = {
    {
      "G", new Integer(1)
  }, {
      "PG", new Integer(2)
  }, {
      "PG-13", new Integer(4)
  }, {
      "R", new Integer(8)
  }, {
      "NC-17", new Integer(16)
  }
};

protected int targetRatings;
protected boolean allowPermission;

public MoviePermission(String target, String action) {
  super(target);
  processTarget();
  allowPermission = (action.equalsIgnoreCase("allow") ? true : false);
}

protected void processTarget() {
  String rating;
  StringTokenizer strtok = new StringTokenizer(getName(), ",");
  while (strtok.hasMoreElements()) {
    rating = (String) (strtok.nextElement());
    if (rating.equalsIgnoreCase("all")) {
      for (int i = 0; i < ratings.length; i++) {
        addRating((String) (ratings[i][0]));
      }
      return;
    } else {
      addRating(rating);
    }
  }
}

protected void addRating(String rating) {
  String compare;
  Integer flagValue;
  for (int i = 0; i < ratings.length; i++) {
    compare = (String) (ratings[i][0]);
    if (compare.equalsIgnoreCase(rating)) {
      flagValue = (Integer) (ratings[i][1]);
      targetRatings |= flagValue.intValue();
    }
  }
}

public String getActions() {
  return (allowPermission ? "allow" : "disallow");
}
```

```
      public boolean implies(Permission p) {
        if ((p == null) || (p.getClass() != getClass())) {
          return false;
        }
        MoviePermission mp = (MoviePermission) p;
        if (mp.allowPermission != allowPermission) {
          return false;
        }
        int compare = mp.targetRatings;
        int intersection = compare & targetRatings;
        if (compare != intersection) {
          return false;
        }
        return true;
      }

      public int hashCode() {
        return (allowPermission ? targetRatings : -targetRatings);
      }

      public boolean equals(Object o) {
        if ((o == null) || (o.getClass() != getClass())) {
          return false;
        }
        MoviePermission mp = (MoviePermission) o;
        if ((mp.allowPermission != allowPermission)
                || (mp.targetRatings != targetRatings)) {
          return false;
        }
        return true;
      }

    }
```

The `MoviePermission` class now supports two different types of entries: one that identifies ratings for which access should be granted, and another that identifies those that should make movies inaccessible. Now execute `EnterMovie` signed by `bspell`, which theoretically should make the call to `checkPermission` generate an exception, since NC-17 movies are not accessible by that user. However, an exception will not be thrown, and the reason for that has to do with the nature of permissions and the way that they're handled.

What happens is that the `implies()` method is called for each `MoviePermission` object, and if at least one of them returns a value of `true`, the permission is assumed to be granted. In this case, for example, the `implies()` method of the first permission entry will return `true` because it grants permission to all ratings:

```
permission MoviePermission "all", "allow";
permission MoviePermission "NC-17", "disallow";
```

What's really needed in this situation is for the permissions to be considered as a group instead of only being evaluated individually. In other words, the second (`disallow`) entry should partially (for NC-17 movies) "cancel out" the `allow` entry. It might seem that it's not possible to support this behavior without creating dependencies between the entries (allowing the `Permission` objects to "know about" one another).

However, the design of Java's security architecture makes it possible to accomplish this in an elegant (but simple way). To understand how to do so, it's first necessary to review the way in which Java manages the Permission objects that it creates from the policy file entries.

How Permissions are Managed

When a set of related permissions are loaded by Java, it creates a collection of permissions for each different Permission subclass. For example, if you define a policy file that contains FilePermission, RuntimePermission, and PropertyPermission entries, a separate collection object will be created for each of those three types:

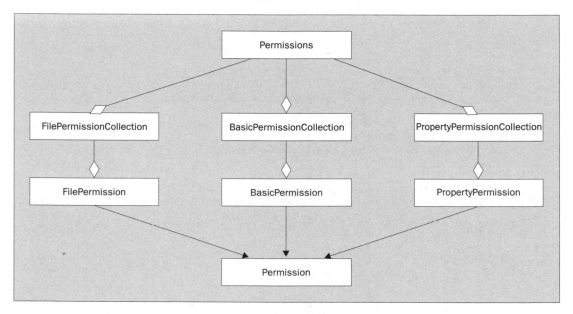

The specific class used for the collection object varies depending upon the type of Permission object, but is always a subclass of PermissionCollection. In this example, the collection objects are instances of FilePermissionCollection, BasicPermissionCollection, and PropertyPermissionCollection, respectively. Knowing this, one or both of the following questions may occur to you:

❑ What collection class is used for custom subclasses such as the MoviePermission class defined earlier?

❑ How is the mapping between a Permission subclass and its associated collection class defined?

The answer to the first question is that a class called PermissionsHash is used by default when no mapping is defined between a Permission subclass and a PermissionCollection subclass. PermissionsHash is an inner class that's defined inside the Permissions class, and Permissions is used to hold the various PermissionCollection objects. In other words, Permissions is simply a collection of collections.

The answer to the second question is that the Permission subclass itself determines which type of PermissionCollection is used, and it does this by returning an instance of the appropriate class from its newPermissionCollection() method.

For example, we will create a new PermissionCollection subclass called MoviePermissionCollection and use the new class to contain instances of MoviePermission, so we need to make the following addition to the MoviePermission class:

```
public PermissionCollection newPermissionCollection() {
  return new MoviePermissionCollection();
}
```

Now that you know how to control which PermissionCollection subclass is used to contain Permission objects, the obvious question is why do so. The answer to this question is that by creating and using your own PermissionCollection subclass you can create more complex permission structures than you can by simply allowing the default PermissionsHash to be used.

When the checkPermission() method in SecurityManager is called, that method calls implies() for the active Permissions object, which in turn calls implies() for the appropriate PermissionCollection instance. For example, this is what takes place when an instance of MoviePermission is passed to the checkPermission() method in SecurityManager:

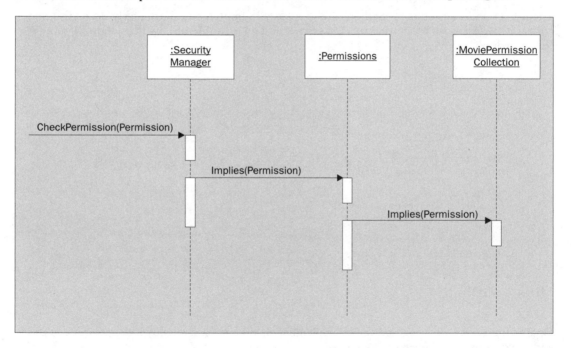

Once the collection object's implies() method is called, it in turn invokes the implies() methods of the Permission objects that it contains, and returns an appropriate result.

The behavior of the default PermissionsHash class is to return true from its implies() method if at least one of the Permission objects it contains returns a value of true from its implies() method. However, by creating your own PermissionCollection subclass, you can create a more sophisticated implementation of implies().

With that in mind, let's recall that our original goal was to allow permissions to be defined that "cancel out" parts of other permissions. Specifically, we want to be able to create a permission entry that grants access to all movies and create one or more other entries that partially or completely cancel that entry. This can be done easily by creating a `MoviePermissionCollection` subclass with the appropriate logic in its `implies()` method as described below.

Creating PermissionCollection Subclasses

Creating a `PermissionCollection` subclass is very easy since `PermissionCollection` only contains three abstract methods, two of which are normally very trivial to implement. Those methods are:

- `add(Permission)` – Adds the specified `Permission` object to the collection

- `elements()` – Returns an `Enumeration` containing the `Permission` objects that are currently in the collection

- `implies(Permission)` – Returns a `boolean` value that indicates whether the specified `Permission` is implied by one or more of the permissions currently in the collection

The `add()` and `elements()` methods are very easy to implement, particularly if you use one of the collections classes such as `java.util.Vector`, and an example of how this might be done is shown below:

```
import java.security.*;
import java.util.*;

public class MoviePermissionCollection extends PermissionCollection {

  protected Vector permissions;

  public MoviePermissionCollection() {
    permissions = new Vector();
  }

  public void add(Permission p) {
    permissions.addElement(p);
  }

  public Enumeration elements() {
    return permissions.elements();
  }

}
```

Finally, the `implies()` method can be implemented, although it is slightly more complex in this case and it performs the following tasks:

- Loop through the list of `MoviePermission` objects, keeping a record of which ratings are allowed and which ones are disallowed.

- Determine which type of `MoviePermission` (`allow` or `disallow`) was passed as an argument to the method.

- If the argument permission is a negative (`disallow`) permission, compare the ratings disallowed by that argument to the list of those disallowed by the permissions in the collection. If the parameter ratings are a subset of those disallowed in the collection, return `true`, indicating that the collection *does* imply the specified permission.

❑   If the argument permission represents a positive (allow) permission, ensure that the collection does indeed allow the specified ratings *and that it does not disallow any of those same ratings.* If both of those conditions are true, the collection does imply the argument permission, and implies() returns a value of true. Otherwise, it will return a value of false.

The code for the implementation of the implies() method just described is shown below:

```java
import java.security.*;
import java.util.*;

public class MoviePermissionCollection extends PermissionCollection {

  protected Vector permissions;

  public MoviePermissionCollection() {
    permissions = new Vector();
  }

  public void add(Permission p) {
    permissions.addElement(p);
  }

  public Enumeration elements() {
    return permissions.elements();
  }

  public boolean implies(Permission p) {
    MoviePermission mp;
    int action;
    int allow = 0;
    int disallow = 0;
    Enumeration list = elements();
    while (list.hasMoreElements()) {
      mp = (MoviePermission)(list.nextElement());
      action = mp.targetRatings;
      if (mp.getActions().equals("allow")) {
        allow |= action;
      }
      else {
        disallow |= action;
      }
    }
    mp = (MoviePermission)p;
    if (mp.getActions().equals("allow")) {
      return (((allow & mp.targetRatings) != 0) &&
          ((disallow &
          mp.targetRatings) == 0));
    }
    else {
      return ((disallow & mp.targetRatings) != 0);
    }
  }

}
```

This example may seem somewhat complex, but it illustrates an important point: by creating your own `PermissionCollection` subclass, you can easily implement complex behavior with regard to how your `Permission` objects will be evaluated. In particular, you can implement behavior that's dependent upon the presence of more than one permission.

Summary

In this chapter, we have looked at issues surrounding security in Java applications. We've seen how tight we can make the security by restricting permissions to perform various actions. Specifically, we've learned about:

- The Java Security Model and how it protects your system.

- The Java Security Manager, how it implements the Java Security Model, and how to use it.

- Policy files and how to create and use custom files.

- How to sign a class so that it can be listed in a policy file as being from a trusted source.

- Types of permission – `AllPermission`, `FilePermission`, `SocketPermission`, `AWTPermission`, `NetPermission`, `PropertyPermission`, `ReflectPermission`, `SerializablePermission`, `SQLPermission`, and `SecurityPermission`.

- The use of the wildcard character with the `BasicPermission` subclasses.

- Creating and managing custom permission types.

In the next chapter, we will be looking at how to optimize performance in your Java applications, and we'll also see ways of effective memory management.

Professional Java Programming

Online discussion at http://p2p.wrox.com

17

Performance Tuning and Memory Management

Since it came into existence, Java code has had a reputation for executing slowly, and that reputation was partially deserved. This is particularly true of the early Java Virtual Machine implementations, which offered purely interpreted execution. However, while Java is still not (and may never be) the ideal language for performing extremely CPU-intensive operations, it is entirely suitable for most software applications.

A typical application spends the majority of its time waiting for user input or for the completion of some other type of I/O operation, which is why multitasking is practical. However, some applications are CPU-bound, and advances in both hardware and software technology have allowed Java code to execute more quickly and to provide acceptable performance for those applications. Hardware improvements have come primarily in the form of faster processors, but the declining cost of memory also allows many applications to run more quickly. In addition, driven by competition among vendors, Java Virtual Machine implementations have become faster and more sophisticated, allowing Java code to execute much more quickly.

Despite the changes that have taken place, you may find your Java code running more slowly than you (or your users) would like, and it's sometimes necessary to take steps to improve its speed. Another area that's sometimes a concern to Java programmers is that of memory utilization. Java applications can sometimes use a large amount of memory, and it's sometimes difficult to determine why that occurs.

So this chapter:

- ❑   Instructs on how to diagnose problem areas in your code.
- ❑   Describes some of the many options that are available to improve the speed of execution.

❑   Provides information that describes how you can identify the portions of your code that are responsible for consuming memory, and discusses ways to reduce the amount used.

❑   Describes how to use the garbage collector effectively.

However, before we can look at how to make our code run better we need to evaluate its current performance bottlenecks.

Locating the Source of a Performance Problem

Although it may seem obvious, the first thing you should do when you detect a problem with your application's performance is to determine where most of its time is spent. It's often said that the "80/20 rule" (sometimes called the "90/10 rule") applies to how much of a processor's time is spent executing an application's code. In other words, the implication is that a large portion (say, 80%) of the processor's time will be spent executing a small portion (the other 20%) of your application code. Assuming that this is true, and it usually is, you can significantly improve your application's performance by identifying the areas of your code that consume most of the processor's time (sometimes called **hot spots**) and changing that code so that it runs more quickly.

One way to identify hot spots and other performance problems in your application is to use a commercial profiler application, such as OptimizeIt from Intuitive Systems or JProbe from Sitraka (formerly KL Group). These products are easy to use and will usually provide the functionality you need to locate the source of a performance problem. However, while reasonably priced, neither OptimizeIt nor JProbe is free, and they may not be available for the platform on which you're debugging.

Another easy way to identify hot spots is to execute your application with HPROF enabled if the Java Virtual Machine you're using supports it. This feature is currently integrated into JavaSoft's Windows and Solaris Java 2 JVM implementations, and it uses the **Java Virtual Machine Profiler Interface (JVMPI)** to collect and record information about the execution of Java code. Among other things, JVMPI allows you to profile object creation/memory utilization, monitor contention, and execution times.

HPROF Output

When HPROF is enabled, its default behavior is to write a report to a disk file named java.hprof.txt once your application terminates. As we'll see, you can control the format and contents of the report to some extent, but the output will contain some or all of the following items of information:

❑   Explanation/comments

❑   Thread information

❑   Trace entries

❑   Monitor dump

❑   Heap dump

❑   Allocation sites

❑   CPU samples/times

Before we look at the sections of the report, let's have a quick look at some of the options we have when running HPROF.

HPROF Options

To view the options that are available with HPROF, you can execute the following command:

```
java -Xrunhprof:help
```

If the virtual machine implementation you're using supports HPROF, it will produce output similar to that shown below. Note that the –X indicates that this is a non-standard option that may or may not be supported in future JVM releases:

```
Hprof usage: -Xrunhprof[:help]|[<option>=<value>, ...]

Option Name and Value    Description               Default
---------------------    -----------               -------
heap=dump|sites|all      heap profiling            all
cpu=samples|times|old    CPU usage                 off
monitor=y|n              monitor contention        n
format=a|b               ascii or binary output    a
file=<file>              write data to file        java.hprof(.txt for ascii)
net=<host>:<port>        send data over a socket   write to file
depth=<size>             stack trace depth         4
cutoff=<value>           output cutoff point       0.0001
lineno=y|n               line number in traces?    y
thread=y|n               thread in traces?         n
doe=y|n                  dump on exit?             y

Example: java -Xrunhprof:cpu=samples,file=log.txt,depth=3 FooClass
```

We'll look at the uses of the more general options here, and cover the others as we discuss individually the parts of HPROF output.

The doe Option

It's acceptable in some cases to generate profile information when your application exits, which is HPROF's default behavior, but in other cases you'll want the information to be written during execution. You can prevent the profile from being written on exit by specifying a value of "n" for the doe ("dump on exit") parameter. To generate profile information during execution, rather than after the program has finished, you can press *Ctrl-Break* on Windows or *Ctrl-* (backslash) on Solaris.

The format Option

HPROF's default behavior is to create a report in human-readable (ASCII) form, although you can store the data in binary format using this option. If you do specify format=b, you must use a utility such as the **Heap Analysis Tool** (**HAT**) provided by JavaSoft to view the output. That utility is currently unsupported, but is useful because it provides an easy way to analyze memory utilization.

When you execute the HAT utility, you must specify the name of a file that was created by HPROF and you may specify a port number or allow it to use its default (7000). When the utility runs, it creates a web server that listens on the specified port for HTTP requests, allowing you to view a summary of the HPROF data through a browser. You can do so by entering a URL of http://localhost:7000, (assuming that you're using the default port number) which will produce a display that lists the classes currently in use by the JVM. By following the various hyperlinks, you can examine different representations of the HPROF data, including one that lists the number of instances currently in existence for every class that's in use. In other words, the HAT utility provides a convenient way to easily browse the HPROF data and many different summaries of that data.

The file Option

HPROF normally sends its output to a disk file named java.hprof.txt if it's creating ASCII output or java.hprof if it's creating binary data (you specify format=b). However, you can use this option to specify that the output should be sent to a different file, as shown below:

```
java -Xrunhprof:file=myfile.txt MyTest
```

The net Option

You can use this option to have HPROF's output sent over a network connection instead of being written to a disk file. For example, it might be useful to use the net option if you wish to record profile information for an application that's running on a middleware server. An example of how to use this option is shown below, where a host name and port number are specified:

```
java -Xrunhprof:net=brettspc:1234 MyTest
```

Before the MyTest class is executed, a socket connection is established to port 1234 on the machine with a host name of brettspc, and the profile information generated by HPROF will be transmitted over that socket connection.

Explanation/Comments Section

This section is identical for every file that's created by HPROF, and it provides a brief description of how to interpret the remainder of the output generated by the utility.

Thread Summary Section

This portion of the report generated by HPROF shows a summary of the threads that were used. To illustrate how that information appears, we'll define a simple application that creates and starts two threads:

```java
public class ThreadTest implements Runnable {

  public static void main(String[] args) {
    ThreadTest tt = new ThreadTest();
    Thread t1 = new Thread(tt, "First");
    t1.setDaemon(true);
    Thread t2 = new Thread(tt, "Second");
    t2.setDaemon(true);
    t1.start();
    t2.start();
    try {
      Thread.sleep(2000);
    } catch (Exception e) {}
    ;
    synchronized (tt) {
      tt.notify();
    }
    try {
      Thread.sleep(2000);
    } catch (Exception e) {}
    ;
  }
```

```
public synchronized void run() {
  try {
    wait();
  } catch (InterruptedException ie) {}
  ;
}

}
```

This application creates two threads, each of which executes the `run()` method of a single `ThreadTest` instance, and starts those threads. It then immediately sleeps for two seconds to allow both threads to become blocked by the `wait()` method in `run()`, calls the `notify()` method to wake up one of the threads, and then sleeps for another two seconds. Therefore, one of the two threads that were created should exit prior to the `main()` method's completion (because it is removed from the wait queue when `notify()` is called), while the other should still be blocked by the `wait()` call. If we use HPROF to profile the thread activity within this application, we should see that behavior reflected in the output:

```
THREAD START (obj=7c5e60, id = 1, name="Signal dispatcher", group="system")
THREAD START (obj=7c6770, id = 2, name="Reference Handler", group="system")
THREAD START (obj=7ca700, id = 3, name="Finalizer", group="system")
THREAD START (obj=8427b0, id = 4, name="SymcJIT-LazyCompilation-PA", group="main")
THREAD START (obj=7c0e70, id = 5, name="main", group="main")
THREAD START (obj=87d910, id = 6, name="First", group="main")
THREAD START (obj=87d3f0, id = 7, name="Second", group="main")
THREAD START (obj=842710, id = 8, name="SymcJIT-LazyCompilation-0", group="main")
THREAD END (id = 6)
THREAD END (id = 5)
THREAD START (obj=87e820, id = 9, name="Thread-0", group="main")
THREAD END (id = 9)
```

This portion of the HPROF output lists each thread that was started, and if the thread ended while profiling was taking place, that fact is recorded as well. Each entry identifies the address of the `Thread` object, the identifier ("id") value assigned to the thread, the name of the thread, and the name of the associated `ThreadGroup`.

As expected, this output indicates that two threads ("First" and "Second") were started after the system-generated thread that executes the `main()` method ("main"). In addition, one of those two threads ("First" with an identifier value of 6) exits prior to the termination of the main thread as expected, while the other was still running when the profile information was created.

Note that some of the threads listed above are dependent on the particular JVM implementation used, in this case the Symantec JIT JVM.

Trace Entries Section

While profile information is being recorded, HPROF generates a number of trace entries, which are simply stack traces like those you've seen when an uncaught exception is thrown by your application. Each trace created by HPROF is assigned a unique identifier value, and as we'll see later, trace identifiers can be useful in determining which execution paths represent hot spots within your application. An example of a trace entry created by HPROF is shown overleaf:

```
TRACE 1856:
    java/lang/String.toCharArray(String.java:1899)
    java/lang/Thread.init(Thread.java:268)
    java/lang/Thread.<init>(Thread.java:398)
    ThreadTest.main(ThreadTest.java:7)
```

This particular trace entry has been assigned an identifier value of 1856, and it represents the execution of line 1899 within the String class, and that line is part of the toCharArray() method. That method was in turn called from line 268 of the Thread class, and that line is part of the init() method, which was in turn called from line 398 of a Thread constructor ("<init>"), etc.

Each line that identifies a class, method, source file, and line is called a **frame**, and there are four frames in the above example. By default, HPROF generates up to four frames for each trace entry, although as we'll see you can increase or decrease that value if it's helpful to do so.

The depth Option

You can use this option to specify the maximum number of frames that will be included in each trace entry. The default value for this parameter is four, and you will not normally need to increase that value unless four frames do not supply enough information to allow you to uniquely identify an execution path.

The lineno Option

Each frame normally includes the line number that was executed, but you can use this option to suppress the line numbers from the output listing. When you do so, each frame will contain the text "Unknown line" instead of the line number:

```
TRACE 1056:
    java/util/Locale.toUpperCase(Locale.java:Unknown line)
    java/util/Locale.<init>(Locale.java:Unknown line)
    java/util/Locale.<clinit>(Locale.java:Unknown line)
    sun/io/CharacterEncoding.aliasName(CharacterEncoding.java:Unknown line)
```

The thread Option

HPROF always records the thread summary information in its report, but by default does not associate the trace entries with a specific thread. This is not a problem if your application is single-threaded in nature, but if your code supports multiple threads, it can be helpful for the trace entries to identify the thread with which they're associated. When thread=y is specified, each trace entry contains additional text that includes the identifier value of the thread associated with the entry as shown below:

```
TRACE 1910: (thread=8)
    java/lang/Object.wait(Object.java:Native method)
    java/lang/Object.wait(Object.java:424)
    ThreadTest.run(ThreadTest.java:20)
    java/lang/Thread.run(Thread.java:479)
TRACE 1664: (thread=1)
    java/lang/StringBuffer.toString(StringBuffer.java:1063)
    java/io/BufferedReader.readLine(BufferedReader.java:Compiled method)
    java/io/BufferedReader.readLine(BufferedReader.java:329)
    java/util/Properties.load(Properties.java:179)
```

Monitor Dump Section

The monitor dump section of HPROF output displays the status of each thread and a report of the monitors that are owned by threads and for which threads have invoked the wait() method. To provide an example of this output, we'll run a slightly modified version of the ThreadTest class defined earlier. This application will start two threads that execute an object's run() method, and once inside that method, the threads will invoke wait(). After a brief delay, the main thread that started those two new threads will wake up one of the threads with a call to notify(), but in this case, that thread will call sleep() instead of exiting:

```java
public class ThreadTest implements Runnable {

    public static void main(String[] args) {
        ThreadTest tt = new ThreadTest();
        Thread t1 = new Thread(tt, "First");
        t1.setDaemon(true);
        Thread t2 = new Thread(tt, "Second");
        t2.setDaemon(true);
        t1.start();
        t2.start();
        try {
            Thread.sleep(2000);
        } catch (Exception e) {}
        ;
        synchronized (tt) {
            tt.notify();
        }
        try {
            Thread.sleep(2000);
        } catch (Exception e) {}
        ;
    }

    public synchronized void run() {
        try {
            wait();
        } catch (InterruptedException ie) {}
        ;
        sleepAWhile(5000);
    }

    protected synchronized void sleepAWhile(long time) {
        try {
            Thread.sleep(time);
        } catch (Exception e) {}
        ;
    }

}
```

If this application is run with HPROF enabled, it will produce the following thread summary:

```
THREAD START (obj=835e60, id = 2, name="Signal dispatcher", group="system")
THREAD START (obj=8367c0, id = 3, name="Reference Handler", group="system")
```

```
THREAD START (obj=83a700, id = 4, name="Finalizer", group="system")
THREAD START (obj=8b17c0, id = 5, name="SymcJIT-LazyCompilation-PA", group="main")
THREAD START (obj=8b2cb0, id = 6, name="HPROF CPU profiler", group="system")
THREAD START (obj=830e70, id = 1, name="main", group="main")
THREAD START (obj=8ece00, id = 7, name="First", group="main")
THREAD START (obj=8ec940, id = 8, name="Second", group="main")
THREAD START (obj=8b1e00, id = 9, name="SymcJIT-LazyCompilation-0", group="main")
THREAD END (id = 1)
THREAD START (obj=8edb00, id = 10, name="Thread-0", group="main")
THREAD END (id = 10)
```

Unfortunately, at the time of writing the JDK 1.3 "Hotspot" virtual machine fails with an internal error when using the monitor dump HPROF option. This problem does not occur when using the -classic option to turn off the Hotspot JVM. This bug occurs in Sun's bug database (Bug ID 4378856)

In addition, the HPROF output will include the monitor dump information listed below:

```
MONITOR DUMP BEGIN
    THREAD 11, trace 1896, status: R
    THREAD 8, trace 1897, status: CW
    THREAD 7, trace 1898, status: CW
    THREAD 6, trace 1899, status: MW
    THREAD 9, trace 1888, status: CW
    THREAD 5, trace 1900, status: CW
    THREAD 4, trace 1901, status: CW
    THREAD 3, trace 1902, status: CW
    THREAD 2, trace 1903, status: R
    MONITOR ThreadTest(8ecb50)
  owner: thread 7, entry count: 2
  waiting to be notified: thread 8
    MONITOR SymantecJITCompilationThread(8b1e00) unowned
  waiting to be notified: thread 5
    MONITOR java/lang/ref/Reference$Lock(836b00) unowned
  waiting to be notified: thread 3
    MONITOR java/lang/ref/ReferenceQueue$Lock(8392a0) unowned
  waiting to be notified: thread 4
    RAW MONITOR "_Hprof CPU sampling lock"(0x8b2f70)
  owner: thread 6, entry count: 1
    RAW MONITOR "SymcJIT Lazy Queue Lock"(0x8b1d34) unowned
  waiting to be notified: thread 9
    RAW MONITOR "_hprof_dump_lock"(0x7d0ef0)
  owner: thread 11, entry count: 1
  waiting to enter: thread 6
    RAW MONITOR "Monitor cache lock"(0x7d0df0)
  owner: thread 11, entry count: 1
    RAW MONITOR "Thread queue lock"(0x7d0cc0)
  owner: thread 11, entry count: 1
    RAW MONITOR "Monitor registry"(0x7d0c70)
  owner: thread 11, entry count: 1
MONITOR DUMP END
```

The first portion of the monitor dump identifies each active thread, its state, and the trace entry that identifies the code the thread executed. The thread's state will be one of the following four values, although you should not normally see suspended threads in Java 2 applications:

State Value	Meaning
R	Runnable
S	Suspended (should not occur, since `suspend()` is deprecated)
CW	Condition Wait (invoked `wait()` and is waiting to be notified)
MW	Monitor Wait (entered synchronized code, waiting to obtain monitor)

The second section of the monitor dump identifies the monitors that are currently owned and those that one or more threads are currently waiting on. In this case, the first thread created by our `ThreadTest` application owns the monitor of the `ThreadTest` object. The second thread had previously obtained the monitor, but implicitly released it by invoking the `ThreadTest` object's `wait()` method and is now waiting to be notified. The states of these two threads are reflected in the first entry in the monitor dump, which indicates that thread 7 owns the monitor of the `ThreadTest` object at location `8ecb50`, as shown below:

```
MONITOR ThreadTest(8ecb50)
   owner: thread 7, entry count: 2
   waiting to be notified: thread 8
```

The entry count refers to the number of nested synchronized blocks the owner thread has entered, and is used by the Java Virtual Machine to determine when a thread should release the monitor. For example, when thread 7 first entered the `run()` method and successfully obtained the monitor, the entry count value was set to one. However, once that thread executed the `sleepAWhile()` method, which is synchronized on the same object, the entry count value was incremented to two. When the thread exits `sleepAWhile()`, the entry count will be reduced to one, and when it exits the `run()` method, the count will be decremented to zero and the monitor released.

The monitor Option

While `HPROF` is capable of including a monitor dump section in its report, it does not do so by default. To include the monitor information, you must include `monitor=y` in the list of parameters.

Heap Dump Section

The heap dump is perhaps the most complex part of the output generated by `HPROF`, but in practice, you will not normally need to analyze it. However, we'll look briefly at some of the entries you'll find.

The heap dump is simply a list of the areas of memory that are allocated at the time that the profile information is recorded, and describes areas allocated for class definitions, objects, and arrays. These types are identified in the `HPROF` output with the abbreviations `CLS`, `OBJ`, and `ARR`, respectively, and each entry includes information that describes how it is used. For example, entries like those shown below are added to the output the first time an instance of `java.util.Vector` is created:

```
CLS 7b6ac0 (name=java/util/Vector, trace=10)
   super       7b8530
   constant[6]    7a58a0
   constant[10]   7b9290
   constant[13]   7a4de0
   constant[16]   7c2240
   constant[19]   7b8530
```

```
    constant[23]   7b99d0
    constant[25]   7b6ac0
CLS 7b8530 (name=java/util/AbstractList, trace=10)
    super      7b8f00
    constant[6]    7b8f00
    constant[7]    7b8530
    constant[12]   7b99d0
CLS 7b8f00 (name=java/util/AbstractCollection, trace=10)
    super      7a4de0
    constant[6]    7a4de0
    constant[11]   7b8f00
    constant[12]   7b93c0
CLS 7b93c0 (name=java/util/Collection, trace=10)
    super      7a4de0
    constant[2]    7b93c0
CLS 7b99d0 (name=java/util/List, trace=10)
    super      7a4de0
    constant[2]    7b93c0
    constant[3]    7b99d0
CLS 7b9290 (name=java/lang/Cloneable, trace=10)
    super      7a4de0
    constant[1]    7b9290
OBJ 7ba560 (sz=20, trace=11, class=java/util/Vector@7b6ac0)
    elementData    7ba6a0
ARR 7ba6a0 (sz=44, trace=12, nelems=10, elem type=java/lang/Object@7a4de0)
    [0]     83d8f0
    [1]     84b640
```

The first entry represents the Vector class definition and describes the address at which it is located. In addition, it identifies the trace entry that corresponds to this memory allocation, the address of the class definition of Vector's superclass, and points to the constants defined in Vector. Constants include string and numeric constant values defined within the Vector class, and the superclass address is simply the pointer to the class definition of Vector's superclass, which is AbstractList. The second entry in the above listing is a CLS entry for AbstractList, because that class must also be loaded before an instance of Vector can be created. In fact, the entire superclass hierarchy from Vector to Object, and all the implemented interfaces, must be loaded although no entry for the Object class definition appears in the above section because it was already loaded.

Once the hierarchy of class definitions has been loaded, the instance of Vector is created as illustrated by the OBJ entry shown above. If you examine the source code for Vector, you'll find that it has three instance fields defined like those shown below:

```
protected Object[] elementData;
protected int elementCount;
protected int capacityIncrement;
```

The two primitive values (elementCount and capacityIncrement) are stored in the area allocated for the Vector instance, but a separate area is allocated for the array of Object instances, and that fact is reflected in the ARR entry.

The report created by HPROF allows you to determine what has been allocated, and identifies the code that caused the memory to be allocated. For example, we can use these entries to determine which section of code caused this Vector to be created and all the appropriate class definitions loaded. To do so, let's review the entry that identifies the creation of the Vector object:

```
OBJ 7ba560 (sz=20, trace=11, class=java/util/Vector@7b6ac0)
    elementData   7ba6a0
```

The trace portion of this entry identifies the trace entry that is associated with the creation of this object, and by searching the file created by HPROF for the trace entry with an identifier of 11, we find the following:

```
TRACE 11:
    java/lang/ClassLoader.<clinit>(ClassLoader.java:1156)
```

This indicates that line 1156 in ClassLoader caused a Vector to be created and its associated class definitions loaded, and the <clinit> "method" indicates that the Vector was created during the initialization of the static fields in ClassLoader. By examining line 1156 of ClassLoader, we find the following code:

```
private static Vector loadedLibraryNames = new Vector();
```

As you can see from this example, the heap dump allows you to easily associate each memory allocation with a specific location within the Java code. However, as we'll see later, there's an easier way to identify which portions of your code allocate large amounts of memory.

The heap Option

You can use this option to control the type of heap information provided by HPROF, and valid values are dump, sites, and all. The dump value causes HPROF to generate only the heap dump information in its output, while sites causes it to generate only the allocation site listing, and all will result in both sections being created. The default value is all.

Allocation Sites Section

As mentioned earlier, the heap dump lists each area of storage that's allocated by your code, but it does not provide an easy way to identify which areas of your code are allocating most of the memory that's used. Fortunately, the HPROF output includes a list of allocation sites that appear in descending order based on the amount of storage each site is allocated.

To provide an example of this, we'll use the following MemoryTest application that allocates two byte arrays: one very large, and one relatively small. In this simple example, it's obvious which part of the code is responsible for allocating most of the memory. However, we'll see how HPROF's allocation site information can be used to identify the relevant section of code, and the approach illustrated here can just as easily be used with larger, more complex applications:

```
public class MemoryTest {

  private static byte[] buffer1;
  private static byte[] buffer2;

  public static void main(String[] args) {
    allocateALittle();
    allocateALot();
  }

  private static void allocateALittle() {
    buffer1 = allocateBuffer(10000);
```

```
    }

    private static void allocateALot() {
      buffer2 = allocateBuffer(1000000);
    }

    private static byte[] allocateBuffer(int length) {
      byte[] buffer = new byte[length];
      return buffer;
    }
}
```

When this application is executed, output similar to the following will appear in the allocation site section of the report generated by HPROF:

```
SITES BEGIN (ordered by live bytes) Sat Apr 15 09:43:35 2000
          percent          live        alloc'ed   stack class
 rank   self  accum    bytes objs    bytes objs  trace name
    1  84.84% 84.84% 1000004    1 1000004    1   1882 [B
    2   1.39% 86.24%   16388    1   16388    1   1228 [C
    3   1.39% 87.63%   16388    1   16388    1   1235 [C
    4   0.99% 88.61%   11628    3   11628    3    984 [C
    5   0.85% 89.46%   10004    1   10004    1   1881 [B
    6   0.70% 90.16%    8196    1    8196    1   1226 [B
    7   0.70% 90.85%    8196    1    8196    1   1233 [B
    8   0.68% 91.54%    8068    1    8068    1    987 [S
    9   0.62% 92.15%    7252    3    7252    3    981 [C
   10   0.31% 92.46%    3612    1    3612    1    763 [L<Unknown>;
   11   0.22% 92.68%    2600   70    3188   85     57 [C
   12   0.21% 92.89%    2532    1    2532    1    988 [I
   13   0.20% 93.10%    2380   17    2380   17      1 java/lang/Class
   14   0.20% 93.30%    2356    1    2356    1   1220 [C
   15   0.17% 93.47%    2052    1    2052    1     71 [B
   16   0.10% 93.57%    1236    3    1236    3     56 [L<Unknown>;
   17   0.09% 93.66%    1028    1    1028    1    986 [B
   18   0.08% 93.75%     996   83    1020   85     57 java/lang/String
   19   0.08% 93.83%     980    7     980    7   1407 java/lang/Class
   20   0.07% 93.90%     840   42     840   42     58 java/util/Hashtable$Entry
```

Each entry in this list represents storage allocations associated with a stack trace, and the entries are ordered based on most to least memory allocated. In this case, trace 1882 allocated roughly one megabyte of storage, which accounts for approximately 85% of the total storage in use. Note also that the fifth entry in the list indicates that trace 1881 allocated a much smaller 10K, which accounts for less than one percent of the storage in use.

The information provided in this report is largely self-explanatory, with the first column providing a ranking of each trace based on how much memory it allocated. The second and third columns identify the amount of storage (as a percentage of the total) allocated by that trace, and a cumulative value for the entries so far listed, respectively. The two pairs of columns containing bytes and objs represent the number of bytes and objects currently in use ("live") and the numbers originally allocated ("alloc'ed").

Finally, the last two columns identify the stack trace associated with the allocation(s) and the type of object created. In this case, most of the entries in the last column start with an open bracket, which indicates that an array of primitives was allocated, and in the case of MemoryTest, our allocation of an array of byte values is denoted [B. In other cases, however, the name of a class appears, which indicates that the allocation was due to object instantiation instead of the creation of an array. The following table identifies the "class name" that appears for each type that can be allocated:

"Class" Name	Data Type
[Z	boolean
[C	char
[B	byte
[S	short
[I	int
[J	long
[F	float
[D	double
[L	Object array

Now that we understand the information in the allocation site report, it can be used to identify the code that's responsible for allocating most of the storage in use by the application. The site report indicates that the code path associated with trace entry 1882 allocated approximately 85% of the storage in use, and by simply searching the output created by HPROF to locate trace 1882, we find the following listing:

```
TRACE 1882: (thread=1)
    MemoryTest.allocateBuffer(MemoryTest.java:20)
    MemoryTest.allocateALot(MemoryTest.java:16)
    MemoryTest.main(MemoryTest.java:8)
```

This indicates that most of the storage used by this application was allocated in the allocateBuffer() method when it was called from allocateALot(). As expected, the HPROF output identified the path that creates the large array of byte values. Similarly, trace entry 1881 identifies the execution path through the allocateALittle() method that was responsible for allocating a much smaller portion of storage:

```
TRACE 1881: (thread=1)
    MemoryTest.allocateBuffer(MemoryTest.java:20)
    MemoryTest.allocateALittle(MemoryTest.java:12)
    MemoryTest.main(MemoryTest.java:7)
```

CPU Samples and Times Section

In addition to reporting on memory allocation, HPROF is able to provide information that identifies which portions of your code the processor spends the most time executing, and it offers two different ways of doing so. You need to specify that HPROF generate one of these sections using the cpu option.

The first technique involves taking periodic samples during execution of the code and counting the number of times that the processor was found to be executing a certain code path. With a reasonably large number of samples, that approach will provide an accurate representation of time spent executing a given section of code.

The second approach that HPROF is able to use is to simply record each method call and the time it takes to complete. The times are then added together for each execution path and reported as a percentage of the total execution time of the code.

In this example, we'll use the first (sampling) approach with another simple application. As with the MemoryTest application, it's easy to identify the portion of the code that consumes the most resources, but again, the technique used here is applicable to larger and more complex applications as well:

```java
public class CPUTest {

  public static void main(String[] args) {
    executeQuickly();
    executeSlowly();
  }

  private static void executeQuickly() {
    loopAWhile(100000);
  }

  private static void executeSlowly() {
    loopAWhile(1000000);
  }

  private static void loopAWhile(int count) {
    for (int i = 0; i < count; i++) {

      // Do something to slow down this loop
      Object o = new Object();
    }
  }
}
```

If this code is executed with HPROF enabled and cpu=sample specified, it will generate a section with CPU sample information like the one shown below (though the data will vary between runs):

```
CPU SAMPLES BEGIN (total = 655) Sat Apr 15 10:57:51 2000
rank   self  accum   count trace method
   1 78.32% 78.32%     513    77 CPUTest.loopAWhile
   2  7.94% 86.26%      52    75 CPUTest.loopAWhile
   3  0.76% 87.02%       5    64 sun/net/www/protocol/file/Handler.openConnection
   4  0.46% 87.48%       3     9 sun/misc/URLClassPath$JarLoader.getJarFile
   5  0.46% 87.94%       3    50 java/io/BufferedReader.readLine
   6  0.46% 88.40%       3    62 java/lang/Class.forName0
   7  0.31% 88.70%       2    25 java/util/jar/JarFile.getManifest
   8  0.31% 89.01%       2     7 sun/misc/URLClassPath$2.run
   9  0.31% 89.31%       2    15 java/util/zip/ZipFile.getEntry
  10  0.31% 89.62%       2    48 sun/io/ByteToCharISO8859_1.convert
  11  0.31% 89.92%       2    41 java/security/Policy$1.run
  12  0.31% 90.23%       2    74 CPUTest.executeQuickly
  13  0.31% 90.53%       2    11 java/io/Win32FileSystem.canonicalize
  14  0.31% 90.84%       2    44 java/util/Properties.load
  15  0.15% 90.99%       1    28 java/util/jar/Attributes.read
  16  0.15% 91.15%       1    38 java/io/FileInputStream.open
```

Upon viewing this information, it's obvious that there is a hot spot in this application that's responsible for approximately 80% of its execution time, specifically the loopAWhile() method in CPUTest. Note, however, that there are actually two entries associated with loopAWhile(), one of which represents an execution path that was active when 513 of the 655 samples were taken, while the other was active only 52 times. By locating the trace information associated with these, we find that the first entry corresponds to loopAWhile() being called from executeSlowly(), while the second corresponds to a call from executeQuickly():

```
TRACE 77:
    CPUTest.loopAWhile(CPUTest.java:Compiled method)
    CPUTest.executeSlowly(CPUTest.java:13)
    CPUTest.main(CPUTest.java:5)

TRACE 75:
    CPUTest.loopAWhile(CPUTest.java:Compiled method)
    CPUTest.executeQuickly(CPUTest.java:9)
    CPUTest.main(CPUTest.java:4)
```

The difference in these two execution paths illustrates an important point related to identifying hot spots in your code. It's sometimes not sufficient to simply identify the methods that the processor spends the most time executing, but also where those methods were called from (the execution path) and/or the parameter values passed.

The cpu Option

This option allows you to control how HPROF gathers information about where the processor spends it time in your code, and valid values are times, samples, and old:

- ❑ times
  HPROF will record each method call and the amount of time spent executing the method each time it is called, and a "CPU Time" section will appear in the generated report.

- ❑ samples
  HPROF periodically determines what code is being executed and the execution path that resulted in the execution of that code, and counts the number of times it finds the processor in that execution path. Once the report is generated, it will contain a "CPU Samples" section that lists execution paths in descending order based on how frequently they were found to be executing. By using this option, you can easily identify hot spots within your code as was done previously with the CPUTest application.

- ❑ old
  HPROF generates profile information that's similar to that supported in earlier versions of Java. However, that information is not as detailed or useful as the new format, so you should not normally specify cpu=old.

The cutoff Option

As illustrated in this listing below, many of the samples represent an extremely small percentage of the code's total execution time:

```
CPU SAMPLES BEGIN (total = 655) Sat Apr 15 10:57:51 2000
rank   self  accum   count trace method
   1 78.32% 78.32%     513    77 CPUTest.loopAWhile
   2  7.94% 86.26%      52    75 CPUTest.loopAWhile
   3  0.76% 87.02%       5    64 sun/net/www/protocol/file/Handler.openConnection
```

```
 4  0.46% 87.48%     3      9  sun/misc/URLClassPath$JarLoader.getJarFile
 5  0.46% 87.94%     3     50  java/io/BufferedReader.readLine
 6  0.46% 88.40%     3     62  java/lang/Class.forName0
 7  0.31% 88.70%     2     25  java/util/jar/JarFile.getManifest
 8  0.31% 89.01%     2      7  sun/misc/URLClassPath$2.run
 9  0.31% 89.31%     2     15  java/util/zip/ZipFile.getEntry
10  0.31% 89.62%     2     48  sun/io/ByteToCharISO8859_1.convert
11  0.31% 89.92%     2     41  java/security/Policy$1.run
12  0.31% 90.23%     2     74  CPUTest.executeQuickly
13  0.31% 90.53%     2     11  java/io/Win32FileSystem.canonicalize
14  0.31% 90.84%     2     44  java/util/Properties.load
15  0.15% 90.99%     1     28  java/util/jar/Attributes.read
16  0.15% 91.15%     1     38  java/io/FileInputStream.open
```

By default, HPROF will include all execution paths that represent at least 0.01 percent of the processor's time, but you can increase that cutoff point using this option. For example, to eliminate all entries that represent less than one-fourth of one percent of the total execution time, you could specify cutoff=0.0025, which would have resulted in only the first 14 of the above entries being created.

Tips for Improving Performance

Once you've identified a performance problem, there are usually ways that you can address the problem. The most obvious solution is to upgrade the hardware that the application runs on, but this is often not possible, especially when large numbers of client machines are involved.

Another approach that doesn't involve changing code is to evaluate different Java Virtual Machine implementations when more than one exists for the operating system(s) onto which you will deploy your code. There is no single fastest JVM implementation for all applications, because most implementations have advantages in some areas. For example, Sun's JVM may be fastest for running the client portion of your application while IBM's implementation might be better for running the server portion. The factors that determine which JVM is the fastest for a given application are complex and difficult to predict, so the only reliable way to find out is by trying it.

If you must use a particular vendor's JVM, you should normally try to use the latest version, because as mentioned earlier in the chapter, the trend has been for JVM implementations to become faster over time. In other words, the chances are good that a later release of some vendor's JVM will execute your code more quickly than an earlier version of that same vendor's JVM.

At a minimum, you should ensure that the JVM implementation you're using includes a Just-In-Time (JIT) compiler or some other type of compiler such as JavaSoft's HotSpot, since these can greatly improve your application's performance. JIT compilers and the HotSpot compiler are described later in this chapter.

When you've identified a specific portion of your code that's responsible for a performance problem, you may be able to use one or more of the following tips to modify or rewrite that code so that it executes more quickly.

Use Native Methods

If you're unable to modify a method so that it runs quickly enough, you should consider rewriting the method using a faster language such as C or C++. By doing so, you sacrifice your application's ability to run unchanged on multiple platforms, but if you're reasonably certain that it will be run only on a single operating system this may be a worthwhile tradeoff. There is a small amount of overhead involved in transferring control from the JVM to a native code (and vice versa), but it is usually outweighed by the improved speed of the native function. See Chapter 20 for more information on using native methods.

Use Buffering on I/O Operations

As described in Chapter 13, you should use the `BufferedInputStream`, `BufferedOutputStream`, `BufferedReader`, and `BufferedWriter` classes, as these will reduce the number of I/O operations performed.

Avoid Creating New Objects

The new operation is relatively slow, so you should avoid creating objects as much as possible. In some cases, it may be possible to reuse existing objects, and it's generally preferable to do so when possible. For example, if you're performing a large number of `String` manipulations, you may have the option of reusing an instance of `StringBuffer` instead of creating more than one instance.

Use StringBuffer Instead of String Concatenations

This is really a variation on the previous recommendation, since concatenating instances of `String` together involves the creation of new objects (`String` instances). That's necessary because `String` instances are immutable, so only by creating a new instance can you concatenate two strings together. For example, suppose that you have the following code:

```
String[] lines;
// ...
String result = "";
for (int i = 0; i < lines.length; i++) {
  result += lines[i];
}
```

Each time the loop is executed, a new instance of `String` is created and its value assigned to the `result` variable. A much more efficient implementation of this same code would be one that uses a `StringBuffer` instead. Unlike `String`, `StringBuffer` is mutable, and true concatenations are possible as shown below:

```
String[] lines;
// ...
StringBuffer buffer = "";
for (int i = 0; i < lines.length; i++) {
  buffer.append(lines[i]);
}
String result = buffer.toString();
```

In practice, using `StringBuffer` in a scenario similar to this may or may not improve your application's performance, although it is very unlikely to actually make your code run more slowly. The reason it may not help is that the Java Language Specification allows Java compilers to automatically compile code that uses `String` instances into bytecodes that use `StringBuffer` instead. In other words, your compiler may already be causing your application to use `StringBuffer` even if you only use `String` in your source code.

Avoid Synchronized Methods and Blocks

A call to a synchronized method takes longer to complete than a call to an unsynchronized method. On the surface, it might seem like a good idea to simply make all methods synchronized for thread safety, but this can cause your application to run more slowly.

Use ArrayList and HashMap Instead of Vector and Hashtable

This is a variation of the previous recommendation. The Vector and Hashtable classes are heavily synchronized for thread safety, while ArrayList and HashMap (which provide similar functionality) are not. Therefore, if speed is important within your application, you should consider using the new collection classes, which are not thread-safe, instead of their older synchronized equivalents.

> *If a thread safe collection is required within your code, the* Collections *class contains static methods that create a thread-safe wrapper around a collection.*

Use Resource Pooling for Threads, Database, and Network Connections

As mentioned earlier, creating an object is a relatively time-consuming operation that should be avoided when possible. However, creating threads can also be slow, and creating network connections and database connections (which often use network connections) is usually very slow. Instead of having your application repeatedly create these types of connections, you should consider obtaining or creating a resource pool manager that allows you to reuse existing objects.

Make Methods Final, Static, or Private

To understand why final, static, and private methods execute more quickly than methods without those modifiers, let's examine how Java behaves in a simple situation. Suppose you're given the following code:

```java
public class Test {

  public static void main(String[] args) {
    First o1 = new First();
    First o2 = new Second();
    if (args.length > 0) {
      callTest(o1);
    } else {
      callTest(o2);
    }
  }

  protected static void callTest(First f) {
    f.testMethod();
  }

}

class First {

  public void testMethod() {
    System.out.println("First Implementation");
  }

}

class Second extends First {

  public void testMethod() {
    System.out.println("Second implementation");
  }

}
```

This code defines two classes called `First` and `Second`, and `Second` is a subclass of `First` and overrides `testMethod()`. The `Test` class creates an instance of each of those classes and passes one of them to its `callTest()` method based on whether any command line parameters were specified. If no parameters are specified, an instance of `Second` is created and passed to `callTest()`, while specifying parameters will result in a `First` object being used instead.

Since you're probably already familiar with inheritance and method overriding, the behavior of this class shouldn't come as a surprise to you. However, you may not have previously considered how Java is able to provide this functionality. In particular, it's worth explaining how Java is able to determine which `testMethod()` to call when an instance of `First` is passed to `callTest()`. After all, the instance of `First` can actually be an instance of `Second`, since that class is a subclass of `First`.

As you might expect, Java determines at execution time which implementation of `testMethod()` should be executed, which is necessary because there's no reliable way to know at compile time. This approach, where the method implementation is selected at runtime, is known as **dynamic binding**, and although it provides very useful functionality, it comes at a price. Specifically, dynamic binding is slower than **static binding**, where the implementation to execute is selected at compile time.

It's sometimes not appropriate to do so, but you can allow Java to use static binding (and thus speed up the method calls) by making methods `final`, `static`, and/or `private`. A method with one or more of these modifiers cannot be overridden, so there is no need for Java to determine at runtime which implementation to execute.

Minimize Subclasses and Method Overriding

An alternative approach to reducing the overhead associated with binding is to simply reduce the number of subclasses and overridden methods that your application uses, although doing so may affect the reuse potential of your code. Creating reusable code usually requires that you define classes that are loosely coupled to one another and cohesive, which in turn tends to promote the creation of small, focused classes and the implementation of extra functionality through subclasses.

Unfortunately, each superclass "level" that you add increases the overhead associated with dynamic binding, so you may need to balance your need for an effective object-oriented design with your need for an application that executes quickly. However, you should be aware that the overhead associated with dynamic binding is relatively small, and only in the most performance-critical situations should you consider sacrificing design quality for performance.

Avoid Accessors, Arrays, and Instances/Class Variables

One of the most basic guidelines of good object-oriented design is to provide access to an object's properties only indirectly through accessor methods. However, as each method call does involve some overhead, you may occasionally find it desirable to access a field directly instead of through an accessor. This is particularly acceptable if the field you're accessing is `final` and immutable, since its inability to change make its inherently thread-safe.

Although arrays are convenient and frequently necessary, there is a small amount of overhead associated with their use, so you should avoid them if it's possible to do so and performance is very critical. In addition, you should define as many variables as possible to be local variables (defined only inside a method), instead of instance or class (`static`) variables as access to these types is relatively slow in comparison to local variables.

Method Inlining

One way to improve your code's performance is to eliminate method calls completely by copying a method's code into the location from which it is called. For example, suppose that you're given the following trivial application:

```
public class Inline {

  public static void main(String[] args) {
    double value = 1d;
    for (int i = 0; i < 50; i++) {
      value = multiplyByTwo(value);
    }
    System.out.println(value);
  }

  public static double multiplyByTwo(double value) {
    return value * 2;
  }

}
```

The multiplyByTwo() method is called for each iteration of the loop in main(), and method calls can incur a significant amount of overhead. However, by copying the code inside multiplyByTwo() into main(), you can eliminate that overhead, and this is known as **method inlining**:

```
public class Inline {

  public static void main(String[] args) {
    double value = 1d;
    for (int i = 0; i < 50; i++) {
      value *= 2;
    }
    System.out.println(value);
  }

}
```

This technique can improve your code's performance, but you must balance that advantage against the need for readable code. In addition, if the method is called from more than one location, it may be necessary to make more than one copy of the code that was included in the method being eliminated. (This effectively means that the inlined method must be final.) Unfortunately, duplicate code makes an application more difficult to maintain, and you should balance that disadvantage against the performance gain made by method inlining as well.

If your code is unlikely to ever be examined or modified, inlining may be a worthwhile way to improve its performance, but if your code is modified frequently, the performance benefits gained by inlining will probably be outweighed by the disadvantages associated with duplication of code. In many cases, your code will fall somewhere between the two extremes (it is modified occasionally), and it won't be obvious which choice you should make.

Unfortunately, there is no reliable way to predict how much inlining will improve your application's performance, since it will partly depend on the optimization algorithms (if any) used by your JVM. Therefore, you may simply have to choose whether or not to use inlining by comparing the performance of two versions of your code: one with and another without inlined methods.

Use Compression to Improve Network Transmission Time

If transferring large amounts of data over a network, it may be possible for you to compress the data before it is sent and to decompress it after it is received. One way that this is commonly done is to package code and its associated resources into a JAR file, which compresses the contents and allows all the files to be downloaded simultaneously. Sending a number of files in a JAR file also avoids the significant overhead of opening and closing the network connection for each file. The `java.util.zip` and `java.util.jar` packages contain classes for writing and reading the ZIP, GZIP, and JAR formats.

Use notify() Instead of notifyAll()

Since `notifyAll()` wakes up all threads on an object's wait list, that method is less efficient than `notify()`. The choice of which method to use is often dictated by the design of your application, but when it's possible to use either method you should use `notify()`, since it will execute more quickly.

Use Batch Updates and Prefetching in Database Applications

Since network calls incur a great deal of overhead, you should attempt to minimize the number of requests that are sent across the network. One way to do this is to use a JDBC 2.x-compliant driver with your database application and take advantage of `ResultSet`'s prefetching capabilities and `Statement`'s batch update facility. These features are described in detail in Chapter 12.

Use int Instead of Other Primitive Types

Operations performed on `int` primitives generally execute faster than for any other primitive type supported by Java, so you should use `int` values whenever possible; `char` and `short` values are promoted to `int` automatically before arithmetic operations.

Cache the Results of Expensive Method Calls

Some methods are slow by nature such as those that calculate mathematical values, but it's often possible to "cache" the results of those methods when they're needed more than once. For example, the following code calls the `sqrt()` method twice:

```
double a, b, c, d, e;
// ...
a = b * Math.sqrt(e);
c = d * Math.sqrt(e);
```

Since the result of the call to `sqrt()` is used twice, it's more efficient to cache the value returned by that method and use the cached value to complete the two operations as shown below:

```
double a, b, c, d, e, f;
// ...
f = Math.sqrt(e);
a = b * f;
c = d * f;
```

Eliminate Unnecessary Code from Loop Bodies

This is a variation of the previous recommendation, but instead of multiple statements using the value returned from a method, that method may be called repeatedly when executed within a loop. For example, the following code calls the `sqrt()` method every time the loop is executed:

```
double[] a, b;
double c;
// ...
for (int i = 0; i < a.length; i++) {
  b[i] = a[i] * Math.sqrt(c);
}
```

However, as was done earlier, the value returned by the sqrt() method can be cached and used within the loop without recalculating it each time:

```
double[] a, b;
double c, d;
// ...
d = Math.sqrt(c);
for (int i = 0; i < a.length; i++) {
  b[i] = a[i] * d;
}
```

Similarly, you should avoid declaring variables unnecessarily within loops.

Use Compound Assignment Operators

You might expect that a += b; is identical to a = a + b; when the two are compiled, but that is not the case. In fact, these cause different Java bytecodes to be generated, and the second approach actually takes longer to execute. Therefore, you can make minor improvements in the speed of your code by using compound operators such as +=, -=, *=, and /=.

Avoid Throwing Unnecessary Exceptions

Creating and throwing an exception is a somewhat time-consuming process, so you should avoid throwing exceptions when it's not necessary to do so. For example, you might define a method like the one shown here that returns an object from a list until there are no more in the list. If the method is invoked when there are no objects remaining in the list, a NoMoreObjectsException is thrown:

```
public Object getNextObject() throws NoMoreObjectsException {
  // ...
}
```

Instead of throwing a NoMoreObjectsException when there are no objects remaining in the list, you might change this method so that it returns a null value instead, which will allow your code to execute more quickly when that occurs.

Use Fast Methods Provided with Java's Core Classes

By being familiar with the methods provided in Java's core classes, you will be aware of options that are available to you for performing potentially slow operations. For example, it's common to need to copy values or object references from one array to another, and you might do so using the following code:

```
int[] firstArray, secondArray;
// ...
for (int i = 0; i < firstArray.length; i++) {
  secondArray[i] = firstArray[i];
}
```

However, a much faster way to accomplish the same result is to use the arraycopy() method defined in the System class as shown below:

```
int[] firstArray, secondArray;
// ...
System.arraycopy(firstArray, 0, secondArray, 0, firstArray.length);
```

Conversely, if an operation that's implemented in the Java core classes does not execute quickly enough, you may choose to create your own implementation or locate an existing one built by a third party. For example, implementations of random number generators and string search functions exist that are much faster than those provided by JavaSoft with the Java core classes. To locate these implementations, you should search web sites such as Gamelan (http://www.gamelan.com/) and IBM's alphaWorks (http://www.alphaworks.ibm.com/).

Compilers

When you compile a Java source code file, the compiler generates a class file containing **Java bytecodes** that can be processed by a Java Virtual Machine. Other languages are usually compiled into machine code specific to one type of processor, but Java's bytecodes are not tied to a particular operating system or processor type, allowing Java programs to run on different platforms without modification.

Interpretation vs. Compilation

Most languages are compiled, meaning that their source code is converted into equivalent machine code that will run on some processor or processor family. In contrast, Java is interpreted by nature, which means that compiling it generates **bytecodes** that must be processed by some application, in this case a Java Virtual Machine.

While interpretation does allow Java to run on different platforms by implementing a JVM for each one, it also causes Java code to run more slowly than a compiled application would. Although compilation is itself a relatively slow and CPU-intensive operation, it can be done by the developer before the software is ever installed on users' machines. In contrast, Java code is compiled into platform-neutral bytecodes to make it useable on more than one platform, and that bytecode is then interpreted when it's finally executed. Some native compilers for Java are now available.

Just-In-Time Compilers

Once Java code is being executed on a specific platform, there's no reason that the bytecodes can't be temporarily converted into machine code so that it will run more quickly. In fact, that's exactly what a Just-In-Time (JIT) compiler does: creates a machine code representation of the Java bytecodes at execution time. Before a JIT-enabled JVM executes a method, it creates a machine representation of the code in that method in memory, and any calls to that method will be handled by the faster machine representation instead of by an interpreter.

Since compilation is slow, this approach may initially cause the code to run more slowly than an interpreter would, but only when the code is executed for the first time. However, a typical application executes some portion(s) of its code repeatedly, and when that is the case, a JIT compiler will usually cause the application to run much more quickly than it would when executed by a purely interpretive JVM.

Most current JVM implementations include a JIT compiler, which is also the reason that you'll often see ("Compiled Code") in stack traces like the one shown below:

```
Exception in thread "main" java.lang.NullPointerException
    at Test.doStuff(Test.java, Compiled Code)
    at Test.main(Test.java, Compiled Code)
```

This occurs because it's no longer possible to determine the line number associated with a particular method invocation once the JIT compiler has processed the code. However, some JVM implementations allow you to disable the JIT, which is usually done by specifying an option such as -nojit when executing the JVM or by setting the java.compiler system property to NONE. For example, depending on which technique your JVM supports you could use one of the following commands to execute an application named MyTest with the JIT disabled:

```
java -nojit MyTest
```

or:

```
java -Djava.compiler=NONE MyTest
```

Once the compiler is disabled, stack trace entries will normally contain the line number along with the class, method, and file name as shown below:

```
Exception in thread "main" java.lang.NullPointerException
    at Test.doStuff(Test.java:10)
    at Test.main(Test.java:5)
```

HotSpot Technology

Even with the improved performance provided by JIT-enabled JVM implementations, Java is sometimes perceived as executing too slowly, but JavaSoft's HotSpot technology provides an even greater boost to Java's speed.

Like a JIT compiler, HotSpot technology is integrated into a JVM and it performs a similar function, but it does so in a much more sophisticated way. HotSpot includes architectural improvements over previous JVM implementations, including faster and more efficient object handling, garbage collection, and thread synchronization.

For example, objects can be accessed more quickly and they occupy less memory. The garbage collector also does a better job of reclaiming unused objects and it does so without any noticeable impact upon your application's performance. In addition, monitor/synchronization processing is much faster, so there is less of a performance penalty associated with making methods and blocks of code synchronized. Lastly, HotSpot also performs runtime method inlining for you, which prevents you from having to make changes to your code that may make it less readable and more difficult to maintain.

Central to HotSpot technology is the HotSpot compiler that provides **adaptive optimization**. While a JIT compiler converts bytecodes into native code indiscriminately, the HotSpot compiler identifies hot spots within your application by "observing" its execution. The compiler then generates native code only for selected areas that are executed repeatedly, or that would benefit from compilation for some other reason. By being more selective in which portions of your code it compiles, the HotSpot compiler is able to spend less time compiling code and/or make the compiled code extremely efficient.

As of this writing, there are two different implementations of HotSpot: one that's targeted for client-side code, and another that's intended for server-side applications. The client version is called the Java HotSpot Client VM, and is integrated into version 1.3 of the Java SDK. The server edition, called the Java HotSpot Server VM, is currently available only as an early access download through the Java Developer Connection, but should be provided as a full-fledged release in the near future.

An obvious question is how much of an improvement can you expect to see by using HotSpot. The answer depends very heavily upon the nature of your application, and if your program spends most of its time waiting for user input, the answer is that you'll see little or no improvement with HotSpot. However, a CPU-intensive application could easily execute twice or even three times as quickly under a HotSpot JVM as it would with a "classic" JVM implementation.

Disassembling Code

The `javap` utility provided with the Java Software Development Kit can be used to **disassemble** a class file, which simply converts the Java bytecodes into equivalent Java source code. For example, suppose that you create and compile the following application that adds two numbers together and prints the result:

```
public class AddNumbers {

  public static void main(String[] args) throws Exception {
    int a = Integer.parseInt(args[0]);
    int b = Integer.parseInt(args[1]);
    System.out.println("Sum = " + (a + b));
  }

}
```

You can use `javap` to view the bytecodes that were generated when the file was compiled by entering the following command:

```
javap -c AddNumbers
```

When the command executes, it produces output like that shown below, with the numbered lines after the two `Method` statements representing Java bytecode instructions. The first method is the default constructor for `AddNumbers`, which was generated by the compiler since no constructor was defined explicitly. The other `Method` represents the `main()` method, and the bytecodes below it will be executed when this application is run:

```
Compiled from AddNumbers.java
public class AddNumbers extends java.lang.Object {
  public AddNumbers();
  public static void main(java.lang.String[]) throws java.lang.Exception;
}

Method AddNumbers()
   0 aload_0
   1 invokespecial #9 <Method java.lang.Object()>
   4 return

Method void main(java.lang.String[])
   0 aload_0
   1 iconst_0
   2 aaload
   3 invokestatic #13 <Method int parseInt(java.lang.String)>
   6 istore_1
   7 aload_0
   8 iconst_1
   9 aaload
```

```
10 invokestatic #13 <Method int parseInt(java.lang.String)>
13 istore_2
14 getstatic #12 <Field java.io.PrintStream out>
17 new #7 <Class java.lang.StringBuffer>
20 dup
21 ldc #1 <String "Sum = ">
23 invokespecial #10 <Method java.lang.StringBuffer(java.lang.String)>
26 iload_1
27 iload_2
28 iadd
29 invokevirtual #11 <Method java.lang.StringBuffer append(int)>
32 invokevirtual #15 <Method java.lang.String toString()>
35 invokevirtual #14 <Method void println(java.lang.String)>
38 return
```

Memory Utilization

Although Java's performance problems have often been exaggerated, it is true that Java programs sometimes use a large amount of memory. In fact, if you execute the following trivial application on Window NT 4.0 with release 1.2.2 of JavaSoft's JVM, the process uses approximately 4 megabytes of memory:

```
public class Test {

  public static void main(String[] args) {
    Object o = new Object();
    synchronized (o) {
      try {
        o.wait();
      } catch (Exception e) {};
    }
  }
}
```

Once you begin to write code that actually does something, the amount of memory used can become substantially larger. To some extent, the amount of memory your application uses is determined by its architecture, but there are ways that you can determine where memory is being used and steps that can be taken to reduce memory utilization.

For example, the HPROF utility was used earlier to identify the execution paths within an application that were responsible for allocating most of the heap space that was used. In addition, commercial software applications such as OptimizeIt provide information similar to that created by HPROF, but it can actually update the information dynamically while an application is running. You can view:

❑   Information that shows the type of object using the most space:

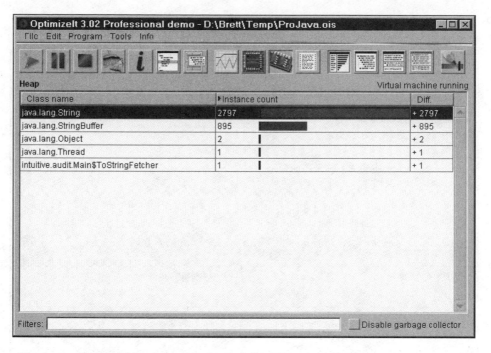

- The execution path(s) responsible for the allocations:

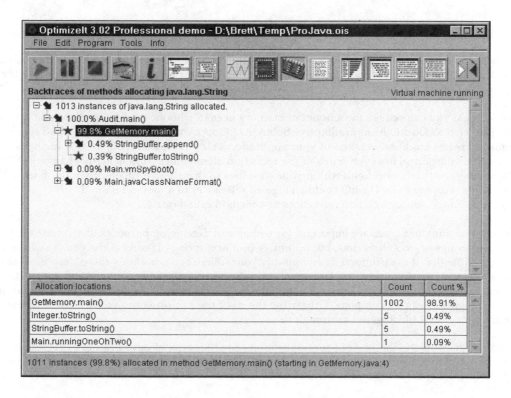

❑ A graph showing storage allocations over time:

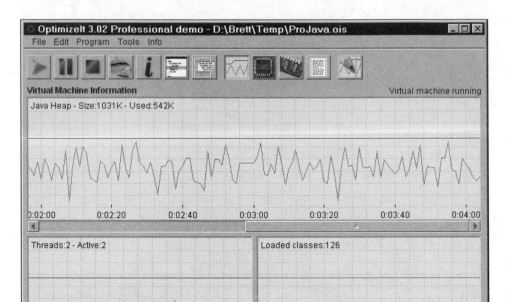

You may sometimes be surprised at how much storage certain types of objects require in Java. For example, instances of java.awt.Image tend to be much larger than the compressed GIF or JPEG files from which they're created.

One way that you can reduce the amount of memory needed without modifying your code is to use an optimizer such as DashO from preEmptive Solutions (http://www.preemptive.com/). This type of optimizer creates modified versions of your application's class files, removing unused methods, fields, classes, and constants. However, much of the reduction often comes from actually changing the names of the classes, methods, and fields within your class files so that they're smaller than those used in the source code. For example, DashO could change all references to a method named generateAnnualReport() into references to a method called gar().

Although meaningful names are important for coding and debugging purposes, they cause the JVM to use more storage at execution time, but optimizer products such as DashO allow you to reduce that problem. Note that these products do not modify your source code, but only the class files created during compilation of your source. However, since they do convert class and method names that were meaningful to you into names that are not, you normally should only use this type of optimization after your debugging is largely complete. Otherwise, the stack trace information you see when an exception is thrown may be confusing and meaningless.

In addition to reducing the size of your application code, this type of optimization provides one other advantage. Compiled Java code stored in class files is normally easy to disassemble and reverse engineer, meaning that when you distribute your application code, it's possible for the users to recreate, examine, and copy your source. Although it's not possible to prevent this entirely, the conversion of field, method, and class names into short and meaningless (or otherwise confusing) names makes it impractical. This act of making compiled Java class files more difficult to reverse engineer is called **obfuscation**, and can be accomplished using DashO or any of a number of other commercial software products.

Heap Management

When a JVM is executed, it obtains a large area of memory from the underlying operating system. That area is called the **heap**, and Java performs its own memory management by allocating areas of the heap when memory is needed. The default size of the heap varies from one JVM implementation to the next, but you can determine its current size using the `Runtime` class's `totalMemory()` method as shown below:

```
System.out.println("Heap size is " + Runtime.getRuntime().totalMemory());
```

It's similarly easy to find out how much of the heap space is unused by calling the `freeMemory()` method as in the following code:

```
System.out.println("Available memory: " +
                    Runtime.getRuntime().freeMemory());
```

At this point, you may be wondering what will happen if your Java program uses all of the memory on the heap. An easy way to find out is to deliberately create a program that does so, and an example of how this can be done is shown below:

```
public class HeapTest {

  public static void main(String[] args) {
    Runtime rt = Runtime.getRuntime();
    java.util.Vector v = new java.util.Vector();
    while (true) {
      long size = rt.freeMemory();
      System.out.println("Total memory = " + rt.totalMemory()
                          + ", free memory = " + size);
      byte[] buffer = new byte[(int) size];
      v.addElement(buffer);
    }
  }

}
```

This program loops indefinitely, displaying the amount of total and free memory and creating a `byte` array that's as large as the total amount of available memory. Each time the buffer is created, it's added to a `Vector` so that the space it uses cannot be reclaimed by the garbage collector during execution. Although the exact results will vary based on the JVM you use, this program will display output similar to that shown below:

```
Total memory = 1048568, free memory = 754944
Total memory = 2097144, free memory = 1139800
Total memory = 3403768, free memory = 1306672
Total memory = 5414904, free memory = 2011120
Total memory = 8507384, free memory = 3092464
```

```
Total memory = 12701688, free memory = 4194240
Total memory = 16895992, free memory = 4194288
Total memory = 21090296, free memory = 4194288
Total memory = 25284600, free memory = 4194288
Total memory = 29478904, free memory = 4194288
Total memory = 33673208, free memory = 4194288
Total memory = 37867512, free memory = 4192912
Total memory = 42061816, free memory = 4195624
Total memory = 46256120, free memory = 4194288
Total memory = 50450424, free memory = 4194288
Total memory = 53899256, free memory = 3448816
Exception in thread "main" java.lang.OutOfMemoryError
        at HeapTest.main(HeapTest.java, Compiled Code)
```

Since a buffer as large as the available memory is allocated each time the code within the loop is executed, you might have expected the program to terminate on the first or second iteration. What happened instead was that the total memory (the size of the heap) automatically increased so that the memory could be allocated each time. Eventually, however, no more memory could be allocated and an OutOfMemoryError was thrown.

As mentioned earlier, the initial heap size varies from one JVM implementation to the next, as does the maximum heap size. However, you can set one or both values using the −Xms and −Xmx options when starting the JVM, where the −Xms option allows you to specify the initial heap size and −Xmx the maximum heap size. For example, you can limit the heap's size to 5 megabytes by executing a command similar to the following:

```
java −Xmx5mb HeapTest
```

Since the heap size can only grow to 5MB, executing that command will cause the HeapTest application to terminate after only a few iterations as shown below:

```
Total memory = 1048568, free memory = 754944
Total memory = 2097144, free memory = 1139800
Total memory = 3403768, free memory = 1306672
Total memory = 4407288, free memory = 1003504
Exception in thread "main" java.lang.OutOfMemoryError
        at HeapTest.main(HeapTest.java, Compiled Code)
```

Note that during the last successful iteration of the loop that the total memory was approximately 4.4 megabytes. Since the heap size could not be increased to satisfy the next request for space, the application again terminated with an OutOfMemoryError.

If the documentation associated with the JVM you're using does not identify its default initial and maximum heap sizes, you may be able to learn what they are by causing it to generate an error message. For example, you might use the following option to indicate that the maximum heap size should be zero megabytes:

```
java −Xmx0m HeapTest
```

On some JVM implementations (though not Sun's JDK 1.3 "HotSpot" JVM), the error message that is produced will identify the default initial and maximum heap sizes for that JVM as shown below:

```
Incompatible initial and maximum heap sizes specified:

    initial size: 1048576 bytes, maximum size: 0 bytes

The initial heap size must be less than or equal to the maximum heap size.
The default initial and maximum heap sizes are 1048576 and 67108864 bytes.
Could not create the Java virtual machine.
```

In this case, the default initial size of the heap is 1 megabyte, while the default maximum size is 64 megabytes (64 * 1024 * 1024 = 67108864).

We'll now make a minor change to the HeapTest application and see what effect it has upon the program's execution. Specifically, we'll comment out the portions of the code that cause a reference to each byte array to be stored in a Vector:

```
public class HeapTest {

  public static void main(String[] args) {
    Runtime rt = Runtime.getRuntime();
    // java.util.Vector v = new java.util.Vector();
    while (true) {
      long size = rt.freeMemory();
      System.out.println("Total memory = " + rt.totalMemory()
                        + ", free memory = " + size);
      byte[] buffer = new byte[(int)size];
      // v.addElement(buffer);
    }
  }

}
```

If you execute this modified version of the application with the JDK 1.2.2 virtual machine, the heap size will again gradually rise to its maximum length, but the application runs indefinitely and never throws an OutOfMemoryError. In addition, it takes a much larger number of iterations for the heap to grow to its maximum size:

```
Total memory = 1048568, free memory = 756080
Total memory = 2097144, free memory = 1138976
Total memory = 3403768, free memory = 1306672
Total memory = 4452344, free memory = 1804656
Total memory = 5500920, free memory = 2187552
...
Total memory = 52559864, free memory = 17758576
Total memory = 53452792, free memory = 18034272
Total memory = 53899256, free memory = 17903072
Total memory = 53899256, free memory = 17903072
```

The explanation for this is very simple, and can easily be illustrated by specifying the -verbosegc option when executing the application. That option produces a large number of messages from the garbage collector, and the following listing provides a sample of the messages produced. Notice that the messages are sent to standard output, so they are intermixed with the messages generated by the application itself that identify the amounts of total and free memory. Those produced by the garbage collector are prefixed with <GC:

```
<GC: need to expand mark bits to cover 16384 bytes>
Total memory = 1048568, free memory = 756080
<GC: managing allocation failure: need 756088 bytes, type=1, action=1>
<GC: 0 milliseconds since last GC>
<GC: freed 1195 objects, 82792 bytes in 7 ms, 78% free (658328/838856)>
   <GC: init&scan: 1 ms, scan handles: 3 ms, sweep: 1 ms, compact: 2 ms>
   <GC: 0 register-marked objects, 6 stack-marked objects>
   <GC: 1 register-marked handles, 39 stack-marked handles>
   <GC: refs: soft 0 (age >= 32), weak 0, final 2, phantom 0>
   <GC: compactHeap: blocks_moved=1106>
   <GC: 0 explicitly pinned objects, 2 conservatively pinned objects>
   <GC: last free block at 0x0196BD54 of length 578216, is at end>
<GC: managing allocation failure: need 756088 bytes, type=1, action=2>
<GC: 10 milliseconds since last GC>
<GC: expanded object space by 1048576 to 1887432 bytes, 90% free>
<GC: need to expand mark bits to cover 16384 bytes>
Total memory = 2097144, free memory = 1138976
<GC: managing allocation failure: need 1138984 bytes, type=1, action=1>
<GC: 10 milliseconds since last GC>
<GC: freed 17 objects, 1064 bytes in 6 ms, 50% free (950848/1887432)>
   <GC: init&scan: 1 ms, scan handles: 3 ms, sweep: 1 ms, compact: 1 ms>
   <GC: 0 register-marked objects, 6 stack-marked objects>
   <GC: 1 register-marked handles, 40 stack-marked handles>
   <GC: refs: soft 0 (age >= 6), weak 0, final 0, phantom 0>
   <GC: compactHeap: blocks_moved=14>
   <GC: 0 explicitly pinned objects, 2 conservatively pinned objects>
   <GC: last free block at 0x01A246CC of length 870704, is at end>
<GC: managing allocation failure: need 1138984 bytes, type=1, action=2>
<GC: 0 milliseconds since last GC>
<GC: expanded object space by 1306624 to 3194056 bytes, 70% free>
<GC: need to expand mark bits to cover 20416 bytes>
Total memory = 3403768, free memory = 1306672
```

The second message in this listing is generated by the application code and it indicates that the heap size is 1M, while approximately 750K bytes are available for use. However, when the application attempts to create an array of that size, the garbage collector generates a message indicating that it's handling an "allocation failure":

```
<GC: managing allocation failure: need 756088 bytes, type=1, action=1>
```

Since there is memory overhead associated with each object (and array) allocation, allocating a 1000 element array of byte values will cause the JVM to allocate slightly more than 1000 bytes. Therefore, when the HeapTest application attempts to create a byte array with as many elements as there are available bytes of memory, an allocation failure occurs. In other words, the allocation request initially fails because there is not enough memory available in the heap.

The garbage collector's first response to the allocation failure is to reclaim all space that's available in the heap, which it does very quickly (7 milliseconds) as indicated by the following message:

```
<GC: freed 1195 objects, 82792 bytes in 7 ms, 78% free (658328/838856)>
```

Once it has completed its sweep, the garbage collector has managed to reclaim approximately 82K of space that was occupied by 1195 objects, which results in roughly 650K of free space being available on the heap. However, that is not sufficient to satisfy the request that was made for roughly 750K, so the garbage collector increases the heap size by 1 megabyte as indicated by the message shown below:

```
<GC: expanded object space by 1048576 to 1887432 bytes, 90% free>
```

At that point, sufficient space has been made available on the heap for the allocation request to be satisfied, and the HeapTest application is allowed to continue execution. This is why the modified code never throws an OutOfMemoryError: the garbage collector reclaims unreferenced objects and/or increases the heap size to prevent that from happening.

With the HotSpot Client JVM supplied with JDK 1.3, the results of our program are somewhat different; the total memory rapidly reaches a constant value, while free memory alternates between two values:

```
Total memory = 2031616,  free memory = 1453992
Total memory = 3485696,  free memory = 1681792
Total memory = 3342336,  free memory = 1310632
Total memory = 2818048,  free memory = 1157504
Total memory = 3190784,  free memory = 1684024
Total memory = 3719168,  free memory = 1685888
Total memory = 3719168,  free memory = 1684024
Total memory = 3719168,  free memory = 1685888
Total memory = 3719168,  free memory = 1684024
```

Running the program with the -verbosegc option also produces output somewhat different to that from the JDK 1.2.2 version:

```
[GC 509K->285K(1984K), 0.0111699 secs]
Total memory = 2031616,  free memory = 1453992
[GC 565K->349K(1984K), 0.0046168 secs]
[Full GC 349K->341K(1984K), 0.0305008 secs]
Total memory = 3485696,  free memory = 1681792
[GC 1762K->1761K(3404K), 0.0019486 secs]
[Full GC 1761K->341K(3264K), 0.0304134 secs]
Total memory = 3342336,  free memory = 1310632
[GC 1984K->1984K(3264K), 0.0021654 secs]
[Full GC 1984K->341K(2752K), 0.0301376 secs]
Total memory = 2818048,  free memory = 1157504
[GC 1622K->1621K(2752K), 0.0019380 secs]
[Full GC 1621K->341K(1984K), 0.0382456 secs]
Total memory = 3190784,  free memory = 1684024
[GC 1472K->1471K(3116K), 0.0019315 secs]
[Full GC 1471K->341K(1984K), 0.0298365 secs]
Total memory = 3719168,  free memory = 1685888
[GC 1986K->1985K(3632K), 0.0020628 secs]
[Full GC 1985K->341K(1984K), 0.0302888 secs]
Total memory = 3719168,  free memory = 1684024
[GC 1988K->1987K(3632K), 0.0019581 secs]
[Full GC 1987K->341K(1984K), 0.0304005 secs]
```

The HotSpot virtual machine is clearly being much more efficient at garbage collection than the earlier version. To better understand how to control memory utilization in your Java programs, it's helpful to closely examine how garbage collection works.

Understanding Garbage Collection

Garbage collection is used to prevent you from having to assume responsibility for explicitly allocating and releasing storage. When you create an instance of an object or an array, the necessary storage space is obtained automatically from the heap. Once the object or array is no longer **reachable** from any live thread, the storage associated with the item is eligible to be reclaimed by the garbage collector.

For an item to be "reachable" simply means that it's possible to access that item directly or directly from a given thread through some reference or series of references. For example, suppose you run the following application:

```java
public class GarbageTest {

  protected Object objectRef;

  public static void main(String[] args) {
    GarbageTest gt = new GarbageTest();
  }

  public GarbageTest() {
    objectRef = new TestClass(this);
  }

  class TestClass {

    Object testref;

    public TestClass(Object objref) {
      testref = objref;
    }

  }

}
```

The static `main()` method is called by a thread created by the Java Virtual Machine; its first line creates an instance of the `GarbageTest` class and creates a reference to that object in a local variable named `myRef`. The `GarbageTest` object's constructor in turn creates an instance of inner class `TestClass`, storing a reference to that instance in the `objectRef` field, and the `TestClass` object maintains a reference back to the `GarbageTest` instance. The figure below illustrates the chain of reachable objects and the references they maintain to one another:

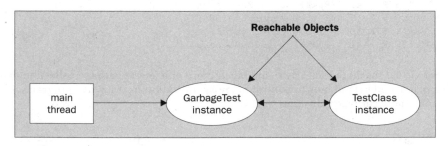

Once the thread exits the `main()` method, the `GarbageTest` object that was referenced by `myRef` becomes unreachable, because `myRef` was a local variable defined inside the `main()` method. In addition, since the `TestClass` instance was only reachable through the `GarbageTest` object, it too becomes unreachable when execution of the `main()` method completes:

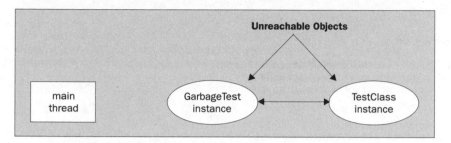

The factors that determine when the garbage collector runs are implementation-specific and the garbage collector's behavior can even vary across different releases of the same vendor's JVM implementations. For example, JavaSoft's garbage collector behavior changed significantly in Java 1.3 with the introduction of the HotSpot Client VM. Since garbage collection behavior is only loosely defined and it varies across JVM implementations, you should not make any assumptions about when unreachable objects will be reclaimed. However, as we saw earlier, the garbage collector will usually run when a space allocation cannot be satisfied by the available heap space.

Not only shouldn't any assumptions be made *when* an object will be reclaimed, but you also can't even assume that it will *ever* be collected. It's entirely possible that the JVM will terminate before the garbage collector ever gets around to reclaiming an object. In fact, the behavior of some garbage collectors makes it likely that unreachable objects *will not* be collected unless your application uses most or all of the available memory in the heap space. However, you can explicitly request that the garbage collector run by calling the static `gc()` method defined in `System` as shown below:

```
System.gc();
```

The API documentation states that once this method returns, the garbage collector will have "made a best effort to reclaim space from all discarded objects". However, there is in fact no guarantee that garbage will have been collected.

Garbage Collection and the finalize() Method

Before an object is destroyed by the garbage collector, the object's `finalize()` method is called to allow it to perform any necessary cleanup tasks. For example, if the object had used native methods to obtain resources (allocate memory, create network connections, etc.), it might be necessary to release those resources explicitly before the object is destroyed.

Just as you cannot be guaranteed that an object will ever be garbage collected, you cannot be certain that its `finalize()` method will be called. In Java 1.1, you could use the static `runFinalizersOnExit()` method in the `java.lang.System` class to force each object's `finalize()` method to be called prior to the termination of the JVM process. However, that method is deprecated in Java 2 because of problems that can occur when an object's `finalize()` method is invoked by one thread while another thread may be modifying the same object's state. In other words, `runFinalizersOnExit()` causes the `finalize()` method to be called for every object not previously finalized, even those that are still reachable.

To illustrate the fact that it's not possible to predict when or if the garbage collector will run, we can make some minor modifications to the GarbageTest class defined earlier. Specifically, we'll override finalize() in GarbageTest and TestClass so that they'll issue messages before instances are garbage collected:

```
public class GarbageTest {

  protected Object objectRef;

  public static void main(String[] args) {
    GarbageTest gt = new GarbageTest();
    System.out.println("Exiting main()");
  }

  public GarbageTest() {
    objectRef = new TestClass(this);
  }

  protected void finalize() throws Throwable {
    System.out.println("Finalizing GarbageTest");
  }

  class TestClass {

    Object testref;

    public TestClass(Object objref) {
      testref = objref;
    }

    protected void finalize() throws Throwable {
      System.out.println("Finalizing TestClass");
    }

  }

}
```

When this code is executed, neither finalize() method is called prior to termination of the JVM, so the only output produced is the message issued from the main() method as shown below:

```
Exiting main()
```

However, the main() method can be modified to force the execution of the objects' finalize() methods prior to exit by using the deprecated runFinalizersOnExit() method as shown below:

```
public static void main(String[] args) {
  GarbageTest gt = new GarbageTest();
  System.runFinalizersOnExit(true);
  System.out.println("Exiting main()");
}
```

Executing this modified version of GarbageTest produces the following output, illustrating that the finalize() methods of both the GarbageTest and TestClass instances were called prior to termination of the JVM:

```
Exiting main()
Finalizing TestClass
Finalizing GarbageTest
```

Ensuring that the `finalize()` methods are called without using the deprecated `runFinalizersOnExit()` method is slightly more complex, and as we'll see, depends upon the garbage collector implementation. For example, we can attempt to make this occur by making the `GarbageTest` instance unreachable while still executing the `main()` and then calling `System.gc()` as shown below:

```
public static void main(String[] args) {
    GarbageTest gt = new GarbageTest();
    // System.runFinalizersOnExit(true);
    gt = null;
    System.gc();
    System.out.println("Exiting main()");
}
```

Since the only reference to the `GarbageTest` instance is the local variable defined in the `main()` method, the following line makes that object unreachable:

```
gt = null;
```

Since the object is unreachable, the call to `System.gc()` should cause the garbage collector to reclaim both the `GarbageTest` object and the `TestClass` instance to which it maintains a reference, and this is what happens with the "HotSpot" JVM in JDK 1.3 on Win32. However, if you execute this code using release 1.2.2 of JavaSoft's JVM for Win32 platforms, the following output is produced:

```
Exiting main()
```

In other words, although both objects are unreachable, they are incorrectly ignored by the garbage collector, which occurs because the garbage collector in 1.2.2 is a **partially accurate** implementation. Its design makes it unable to identify some objects that are legitimate targets for collection, which can lead to memory leaks in your code. Interestingly enough, if you make the following minor change to the `GarbageTest` class and execute the modified version, the results will be different:

```
public static void main(String[] args) {
    createAndRelease();
    System.gc();
    System.out.println("Exiting main()");
}

private static void createAndRelease() {
    GarbageTest gt = new GarbageTest();
    gt = null;
}
```

Running this version of the `GarbageTest` program causes the garbage collector to correctly reclaim both the `GarbageTest` object and the `TestClass` instance to which it maintains a reference. The output produced by running the code is shown below:

841

```
Finalizing GarbageTest
Finalizing TestClass
Exiting main()
```

Perhaps even more strangely, eliminating the second line (gt = null;) in the createAndRelease() method shown above causes the garbage collector to again fail to reclaim the two unreachable objects. These variations on the GarbageTest class and the different results that they produce illustrate the unreliability of partially accurate garbage collector algorithms. In a small application that runs for only a short length of time, such omissions may not be significant. However, for an application that is expected to continue running for a long time, the failure to reclaim unused heap space can become a serious problem and even cause the application to fail with an OutOfMemoryError.

Fortunately, the HotSpot technology included in the JDK 1.3 JVM includes a **fully accurate** garbage collector. It will correctly reclaim the GarbageTest and TestClass objects with any of the implementations of the GarbageTest code described above: with or without the createAndRelease() method, and with or without assigning a null value to the gt variable.

Reference Objects

Prior to Java 2, object instances were garbage collected only when there were no more references to them from live threads. However, Java 2 includes classes that allow you to maintain special types of references to objects, and those new reference types will not prevent objects from being garbage collected.

The classes are defined in the java.lang.ref package, and the Reference class is the superclass of the three new reference types: SoftReference, WeakReference, and PhantomReference. In addition to these classes, the ReferenceQueue class allows you to determine when references to an object have been cleared. References are normally cleared by the garbage collector when it prepares to reclaim an object, but you can explicitly clear a reference by calling the Reference object's clear() method.

The traditional type of object reference provided in earlier releases of Java is referred to as a **strong reference**, and object instances with strong references cannot be garbage collected. The new reference types provide what are known collectively as **weak references**, which is somewhat confusing since the WeakReference class represents only one of these types. To create a weak reference to an object, you simply create an instance of the appropriate class, passing its constructor a reference to the object as shown below:

```
// The myObject variable represents a strong reference
Object o = new Object();
// The softRef variable represents a soft reference
SoftReference softRef = new SoftReference(o);
// The weakRef variable represents a weak reference
WeakReference weakRef = new WeakReference(o);
// The phantomRef variable represents a phantom reference
// When creating a phantom reference, you must specify a reference
// queue (discussed later)
ReferenceQueue rq = new ReferenceQueue();
PhantomReference phantomRef = new PhantomReference(o, rg);
```

SoftReference and WeakReference instances can be used to create additional (possibly strong) references to the referenced object (also known as the **referent**) through the get() method. For example, the following code illustrates how a SoftReference is created, and is later used to create a strong reference to the referent:

```
byte[] buffer = new byte[10000];
SoftReference bufferRef = new SoftReference(buffer);
// Eliminate the strong reference
buffer = null;
// ...

// Create a new strong reference
byte[] bufferData = (byte[])(bufferRef.get());
```

Note, however, that the `get()` method will return a `null` value if the reference was reclaimed by the garbage collector after the weak reference was created. Therefore, when you do use `get()` to attempt to access the referent, you should ensure that it did not return a `null` before you use the return value.

An object is classified based on the strongest type of reference that exists to that object, and will be one of the following five values:

❑ A **strongly reachable** object has strong references and may have soft, weak, or phantom references.

❑ A **softly reachable** object has soft references and may have weak or phantom references, but does not have strong references.

❑ A **weakly reachable** object has weak references and may have phantom references, but does not have strong or soft references.

❑ A **phantomly reachable** object has only phantom references; it does not have strong, soft, or weak references.

❑ An **unreachable** object is one for which there are no references of any kind.

In contrast, an object that is referenced through a chain of references is only as reachable as the weakest reference in the chain. For example, the following illustrates how a string of references can be created:

```
SoftReference sr = new SoftReference(new WeakReference(new Date()));
```

In this case, the `Date` instance is only weakly reachable, because it is referenced through a chain of two references, one of which is a `WeakReference`.

At this point, you may be wondering why there are three different types of weak references, and how their behavior differs. `SoftReference` and `WeakReference` are very similar in function and behavior, but there is one important difference. Garbage collector implementations are discouraged (but not prevented) from reclaiming softly reachable objects, especially those that have been created or accessed recently. In contrast, the garbage collector will reclaim a weakly reachable object just as if no references existed to it at all.

Phantom references are very different from the other two types, and are intended to be used specifically to allow you to determine when an object is about to be destroyed by the garbage collector. In fact, the `get()` method of a `PhantomReference` always returns `null`, even when the referent has not yet been garbage collected. After the referent's `finalize()` method has been called but before it is destroyed, any `PhantomReference` instances that refer to the referent are added to the appropriate `ReferenceQueue`.

Garbage collection of the referent will not be completed until the PhantomReference's clear() method is called, so it is the responsibility of your application to do so when using phantom references. Your code should wait for PhantomReference instances to be placed on the queue by the garbage collector, perform the appropriate cleanup for the referent, and then call the clear() method to allow the referent to be reclaimed.

The methods defined in ReferenceQueue simply allow you to retrieve Reference objects that have been placed on the queue. One implementation of the remove() method waits indefinitely until a Reference appears in the queue and returns that object. The other version of remove() allows you to specify the maximum number of milliseconds that it will wait for a Reference to be queued, and if none becomes available within that time, it returns a null value.

Finally, the poll() method always returns immediately, providing the caller with either a Reference that was queued or with a null value if none is available. In other words, the remove() method blocks the calling thread until an entry is available in queue or until the specified amount of time elapses, while poll() never blocks the caller.

How Reference Objects can be Used

Now that the behavior of the three Reference subclasses has been described, we'll briefly examine how each one can be used. Although many of the examples shown here use the java.lang.ref classes directly, you'll often find it more useful to subclass one of those when using weak references with your application. By creating a subclass, you can associate more information with the reference about how it is used and/or what action to take when you detect that its referent was cleared.

SoftReference

You can use SoftReference instances to cache information that should be discarded when your application begins to run low on memory. For example, if you're reading information from a database or files from a web browser, it may be useful to cache that data in memory as long as it does not cause your application to run out of memory. When the application needs to read information that was previously retrieved from the database or the network, it can first check the SoftReference-based cache. If the reference has not been cleared, the data can be quickly returned from the memory cache, but if it has been cleared, the data can again be retrieved from the database or network.

WeakReference

You'll sometimes wish to associate information with an object without preventing that object from being garbage collected, and you'll want the information to be destroyed when the object is reclaimed. If you were to use a "traditional" (strong) reference to associate the object with its information the object would never be garbage collected. For example, suppose that you use a Hashtable to maintain a relationship between objects and their information as shown below:

```
Hashtable ht = new Hashtable();
// ...
MyObject myObj = new MyObject();
ht.put(myObj, "This is the associated information");
```

The problem with this approach is that as long as a reference to the Hashtable exists and as long as it contains a strong reference to the MyObject instance, that object will never be reclaimed. However, by creating an association with a WeakReference, you can define a mapping that lasts only for the lifetime of the MyObject instance without affecting the garbage collector's ability to reclaim the object. In fact, that is exactly what the java.util.WeakHashMap class does, and an example of how it might be used is provided below:

```
WeakHashMap map = new WeakHashMap();
// ...
MyObject myObj = new MyObject();
map.put(myObj, "This is the associated information");
```

Each key in a WeakHashMap is an instance of a subclass of WeakReference, which allows the MyObject instance to be reclaimed by the garbage collector when there are no more strong references to it. Once that does occur, the WeakReference key entry in the map will remain, but its referent will be cleared and it will be placed on a ReferenceQueue. When an entry is added to or removed from the WeakHashMap, it checks the queue to see if any of its entries have been cleared and removes those that represent items that were garbage collected.

PhantomReference

As mentioned earlier, the purpose of the PhantomReference is to allow you to perform cleanup tasks for objects before they are destroyed by the garbage collector. Use of a ReferenceQueue with a SoftReference or WeakReference is optional, but each PhantomReference you construct must be associated with a ReferenceQueue as shown below:

```
MyObject myObj = new MyObject();
ReferenceQueue rq = new ReferenceQueue();
PhantomReference pr = new PhantomReference(myObj, rq);
```

You may wish to create a separate thread that waits for entries to be added to a ReferenceQueue, or you might design your code so that it periodically calls the poll() method. When a PhantomReference is retrieved from the queue, the appropriate cleanup should be performed for its reference and the clear() method called to allow the referent to be garbage collected.

Summary

In this chapter, we have looked at:

- ❑ Using HPROF to examine the performance of a Java application, and to locate the source of a performance problem

- ❑ Tips for improving the performance of your applications

- ❑ The various types of Java compilers that are available, including Just-In-Time compilers and Sun's HotSpot technology

- ❑ Memory management, including examination of garbage collection and reference objects

Next, we will look at internationalizing your applications, so that they support multiple languages and formatting conventions.

Professional Java Programmin

Online discussion at http://p2p.wrox.com

18
Documentation and Help

This chapter covers two important aspects of delivering an application – **Documentation** and **Help**. Documentation allows you to provide information to other developers that describes how your code should function, largely from an internal/code perspective, while help is provided for the benefit of the end users, and describes how the application works from an external/user perspective. As we'll see, Java makes it easy to provide both of these.

Aside from being very easy to use, Java's documentation capabilities have another very important characteristic: they allow you to create internal code comments and API documentation in a single step, and we'll see shortly how this is done.

Help information is an important part of all but the most trivial applications, although Java applications' help facilities have often been limited to status bars and tool tips. That was primarily due to the lack of a widely accepted standard for implementing help in Java programs, but with the introduction of **JavaHelp**, that is no longer the case. JavaHelp allows you to add robust help capabilities to your Java applications, and this chapter illustrates how to do so.

In this chapter, we'll cover:

- ❑ Adding documentation comments to your code, and using the special `javadoc` tags
- ❑ Using `javadoc` to generate API documentation from your comments
- ❑ Using JavaHelp to create online help
- ❑ Creating different views of a set of help files
- ❑ Adding help capabilities to your application

Documentation Comments

With most programming languages, adding comments to the code and creating documentation that can be used as a reference for the API must be done in two separate steps. However, with **documentation** (or "**doc**") **comments** and the **javadoc** tool, you can combine these two tasks into a single step.

> **Doc comments are simply block comments that follow some simple guidelines that make it easy for `javadoc` to process them.**

`javadoc` reads these comments from your Java source code files and generates HTML pages that describe the files and their contents. These pages provide a convenient, intuitive way to view documentation that describes your code, and provides a format that is consistent across different Java applications. In fact, the chances are that you've already seen documentation generated by `javadoc` since Sun uses it to generate the API reference information for the Java core classes. By default, `javadoc` generates the following files:

- An overview page when you run `javadoc` against more than one package. This page lists the documented packages and can include a description of each one.

- A separate page for each package processed. This includes a list of all classes defined in the package, and may include comments that describe the package.

- One page for each class or interface that was processed. This is where the detailed information on the **members** (inner classes, constructors, methods, and fields) is displayed.

In addition to these three types of documentation files, `javadoc` generates a number of index and cross-reference files that can be useful in locating a particular code element. These include:

- A single class hierarchy file that lists the class hierarchy for all classes in all packages that were processed

- A "use" file for each package that lists the other packages and classes that use the package

- A "use" file for each class that lists the other packages and classes that use the class

- A single file that lists all deprecated elements (packages, classes, interfaces, constructors, methods, and fields) in all classes

- A single file that contains an alphabetically sorted list of all members in all processed classes

Documentation Comment Guidelines

A documentation comment begins with a forward slash followed by two asterisks, and should contain a description of the element it is associated with, such as:

```
/**
 *  This is a documentation comment. It's a block comment that begins with a
 *  forward slash followed by two asterisks. A documentation comment is
 *  usually left-aligned with the CODE element that it describes, with each
 *  line after the first one indented by one additional space so that the
 *  asterisks are vertically aligned.
 */
```

Your source code should contain many documentation comments like the one shown above. In fact, `javadoc` allows you to create a documentation comment for each class and interface, as well as every inner class, field, constructor, and method:

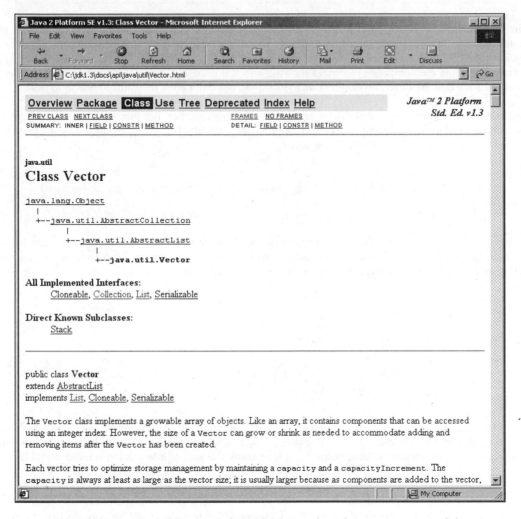

`javadoc` associates a comment with a particular code element based on its position, and the comment must immediately precede the element it is intended to describe. For example, a documentation comment that describes a class must appear just before the class definition:

```
/**
 *  This documentation comment describes the MySample class
 */
public class MySample {}
```

Similarly for members, the documentation comment should be placed just prior to the declaration of the member being documented.

> Only a single comment per element is processed by `javadoc`, so you should put all relevant information inside one block comment.

The first sentence of a doc comment should be a brief description of the element being documented. That sentence is used by `javadoc` to summarize the function of the element being described. Any additional sentences should include information that is relevant and useful, which could include a more detailed description of the element, code examples showing how it is used, etc. You should remember that the doc comments are also for other developers using your code, but don't have the source code to look at.

Java allows you to declare multiple variables of the same type together, but this will prevent you from associating a different documentation comment with each variable. For example, suppose you create the following comment for the variable declarations:

```
/**
 *  A student's test score and the total number of students in the school.
 */
public int testScore, studentCount;
```

In this case, `javadoc` uses the same comment for each of the two variables, which may be confusing or even misleading to someone reading the generated documentation. To prevent this from happening, you can define each variable separately, and create a comment for each one:

```
/**
 *  Student's test score.
 */
public int testScore;

/**
 *  Total number of students in the school.
 */
public int studentCount;
```

If you take this approach when you have a lot of variables, though, it can make the code less readable. You should think about what you include as doc comments, and whether it would be useful to someone if they read about it in the documentation. Some developers think this sort of information is too detailed for listing in `javadoc`.

You can create **overview comments** for the entire application or set of packages that are processed by `javadoc`, as well as **package-level comments**. To do so, you'll need to create files specifically to contain these comments, and in the case of the overview comments, you must use `javadoc`'s `-overview` option to identify the comment file. For package-level comments, simply create a file called `package.html` for each package that you wish to document and place the file in the directory containing the package's source files. Both overview and package comment files must be HTML files, but in practice this simply means that you are required to begin the file with the `<HTML>` and `<BODY>` tags and end it with `</BODY>` and `</HTML>`. For example:

```
<HTML>
  <BODY>
    Client-side visual components related to the student registration
    application.
  </BODY>
<HTML>
```

Using HTML Inside Documentation Comments

The doc comment examples that we've looked at so far contained plain text, which is all that's really necessary for writing javadoc-style comments. However, you can improve the readability of your comments by embedding HTML tags within them, and when a web browser processes your documentation, the tags you included will be incorporated into the output. For example, you may wish to draw the reader's attention to a point by displaying some portion of the comment in bold, italic, or underlined. The following table describes several useful HTML tags and their functions:

HTML Tag	Tag's Function
<B>	Displays the enclosed text in bold (<STRONG> in HTML 4.0)
<I>	Displays the enclosed text in italics (<EMPHASIS> in HTML 4.0)
<U>	Underlines the enclosed text (this could be confused with a URL)
<P>	Begins a new paragraph
 	Starts a new line
<UL>	Defines an unordered list, with a "bullet" for each item in the list
<LI>	Defines an item within an unordered list
<CODE>	Used with embedded program code

A sample doc comment that uses each of these tags is shown below, and the formatted output that results from running javadoc against this class declaration:

```
/**
 *  I want to emphasize that <I>you can <U>embed HTML tags</U> within
 *  <B>javadoc</B> comments.</I>
 *  <P>
 *  <UL>
 *  <LI>First list item
 *  <LI>Second list item
 *  <LI>Third list item
 *  </UL>
 *  <BR>
 *  This is what <CODE>embedded CODE</CODE> looks like
 *
 */
public class DocTest {}
```

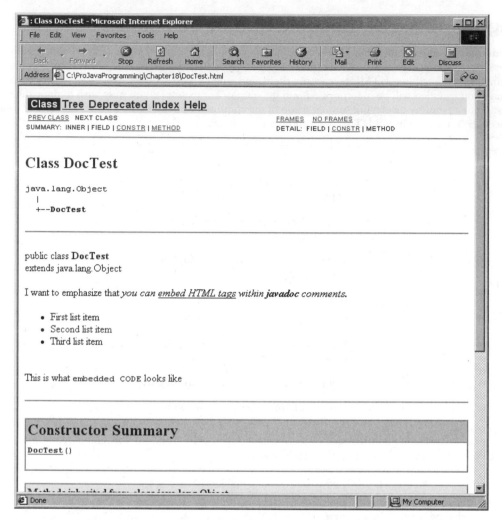

You can use any valid HTML tags, but you should avoid using tags that may not be supported by all browsers. This means that in practice you should probably stick to HTML 1.0 or 1.1. Also, keep in mind that the documentation and tags you create will be included within the set of HTML tags generated by `javadoc`. If you use tags carelessly or incorrectly, the document may not be displayed the way you intended. However, mistakes are usually obvious immediately upon viewing the generated file and are typically easy to identify and correct.

One potential problem that's not specific to `javadoc` but is always an issue when writing HTML documents is the use of characters such as the less than (<), greater than (>), ampersand (&), and double-quote (") characters. Using these in your doc comments can cause the browser to incorrectly parse the documentation file because they have special meaning within the context of an HTML file. When you do need to add these to your doc comments, you should not embed them in the comments directly. Instead, use the special sequences designed to represent these characters: `&lt;` for the less than, `&gt;` for greater than, `&amp;` for the ampersand, and `&quot;` for the double-quote. For example:

```
/**
 *   This is only valid when firstValue &lt; secondValue.
 */
```

Using javadoc Tags

Each of the documentation comment examples that we've looked at so far contained a simple description of the comment's associated element. However, the descriptive text (or **description section**) is only one of two sections that you can define in a doc comment, and the other is called the **tag section**. Here, a "tag" refers to a javadoc tag, and although somewhat similar in function to HTML tags, they are largely unrelated to one another.

While HTML tags are mainly used to specify how the data should be displayed, javadoc tags allow you to specify additional information about an element being described in a doc comment. The following example contains two javadoc tags: one that identifies the author of the class, and another that identifies its version number:

```
/**
 *   This documentation comment describes the MySample class.
 *
 *   @author  Brett Spell
 *   @version  1.0 - 11/22/1999
 */
public class MySample {}
```

With one exception, which we'll discuss later, each javadoc tag begins with the @ symbol. The first line that begins with this symbol (asterisks and spaces are ignored) marks the end of the description section and the beginning of the tag section.

Not all tags are appropriate in all types of doc comments. For example, some tags are specifically related to classes and interfaces, while others are meaningful only in the comment associated with a method or constructor. The tag section is always optional, but tags can be used to greatly improve the usefulness of the documentation generated by javadoc. The valid tags and the parameters they accept are listed below, along with how and where to use each one.

@author *name*

On programming projects, it's often helpful to record the name of the person who wrote a particular class or interface, as well as the names of those who have updated it. The @author tag allows you to do just that, and can be used in a class or interface doc comment as many times as needed. By default, this information is *not* added to the generated HTML document. However, if you specify the -author parameter when running javadoc, it includes an "Author" section for each class and interface that has at least one @author tag in its doc comment.

@version *release*

This tag allows you to specify a version for a class or interface, and can only be specified once per doc comment. The release often contains a release level and/or a date, but can be any value that's useful or meaningful to you and need not be numeric. Like @author, this tag doesn't produce any information in the generated files by default, but you can specify the -version parameter when running javadoc to add a "Version" section to the generated HTML documents.

@param *name description*

When documenting a constructor or method, use this tag to describe the parameters passed to it. You should create a separate @param tag for each parameter, where name identifies the variable name assigned to the parameter and description provides information such as the valid values for the parameter.

@return *description*

The @return tag provides a description of the value returned by a method. This could describe the values that may be returned and how they relate to the input parameters, or any other information that's useful. This tag can only be specified once per method, and should be omitted if the method does not return a value.

@throws *name description*
@exception *name description*

These two tags are synonymous, and are used to document the exceptions that can be thrown by a method or constructor. A specific class of exception is identified by name, while description should provide an explanation of when (and perhaps why) the exception is thrown. Within a method's doc comments, you can use these tags as many times as necessary to document each exception that may be thrown. Although it's possible to use both @throws and @exceptions, there's no reason to do so, and it may be confusing to someone who sees your comments in the source file. The @throws tag is a more recent addition to javadoc and is probably more intuitive for some programmers, but either tag is acceptable as long as it is used consistently throughout your documentation.

@deprecated *comments*

After you've written some code that has been used by other programmers, you may later decide to create an improved version of the code. This could take place at a package, class, constructor, method, or field level. For example, you might create a new class that performs the same functions as an existing one, but that has completely different constructors and/or methods. If you immediately delete the original class, any code that used that class would need to also be changed right away. With small applications or those where only a single programmer is involved, this may not be a problem. However, with team projects, it's usually not acceptable to abruptly eliminate or replace code that you've written when others are using it. On a larger scale, the consequences are even more serious.

For example, in Java 1.0.2, the java.util.Date class was used to represent a particular point in time and also to parse and format dates. However, in Java 1.1, the new java.util.Calendar class provided an improved version of Date's parsing and formatting capabilities. Instead of eliminating the now duplicate functionality in Date, the relevant constructors and methods were identified by Sun as having been superceded or **deprecated**. This has allowed applications that are dependent upon Date to continue to function, but also informed developers that they should avoid using the deprecated methods and constructors.

The @deprecated tag can be used within doc comments for a package, class, constructor, method, or field, and indicates that the element should not be used, and may even be deleted in the future. In some cases, an element is deprecated simply because it has been replaced by another one with a more descriptive or intuitive name, but more often, it's because a better implementation exists. In either case, you should use the comments portion of this tag to explain to the reader what replacement exists for the item and why it was deprecated.

The @deprecated tag has an interesting characteristic that's worth noting. Although Java compilers normally ignore comments, this tag is detected. The element that it's related to is marked as deprecated in the class file generated by the compiler. If you then compile some other code that references the deprecated element, the compiler generates a warning message. For example, the following code creates an instance of java.util.Date using a deprecated constructor:

```
import java.util.Date;

public class DepTest {
```

```
    public static void main(String[] args) {
      Date curdate = new Date(1999, 11, 22);
    }
  }
```

When this code is compiled using the Java 1.1 or later classes, the compiler generates a message similar to the following:

Note: DepTest.java uses or overrides a deprecated API.
Note: Recompile with -deprecation for details.

This message warns you that your code relies upon one or more deprecated elements, but does not identify them. If you then recompile with the -deprecation option, you'll receive a message like the following:

DepTest.java:5: warning: Date(int,int,int) in java.util.Date has been deprecated

Date curdate = new Date(1999, 11, 22);
              ^

1 warning

When you receive such a message, you should examine the API documentation for the deprecated element (java.util.Date in this case), determine what should be used in its place, and change your code to use the preferred interface. We'll see a sample using @deprecated in the next section.

@since *release*

It's common for applications to have multiple releases or versions, and it's often useful to know when a particular element such as a class or method was added. For example, you may want to use the API reference information generated by javadoc for Java 2 despite the fact that your application must run using the Java 1.1 core classes. In that case, it's helpful to know whether a method you see documented is available in Java 1.1, and that information is provided by the @since tag.

There is no defined relationship between the release parameter associated with this tag and the parameter of the same name used in the @version tag, but you may choose to use the same identifier in both places. The following code illustrates the use of this tag as well as several others just discussed:

```
public class Department {
  /**
   * Returns the employee number of the employee with the specified
   * first and last names.
   *
   * @param  lastName   Last name of the employee to locate.
   * @param  firstName  First name of the employee to locate.
   * @return  Numeric value that uniquely identifies the employee.
   * @throws  EmployeeNotFoundException When there is no employee
   *    with the specified first and last names.
   * @since  1.0
   * @deprecated   As of version 1.1, replaced by
   *      getEmployeeNumbers(), which can return more
   *      than one employee when there are multiple matches.
   */
  public long getEmployeeNumber(String lastName, String firstName)
```

```
      throws EmployeeNotFoundException {
    if (!(lastName.equals("Smith")))
      throw new EmployeeNotFoundException();
    return 01;
  }


  /**
   *  Returns 0 or more identification numbers of employees with
   *  the specified first and last names.
   *
   *  @param  lastName   Last name of the employee to locate.
   *  @param  firstName  First name of the employee to locate.
   *  @return  List of numbers for employees with the specified name.
   *  @since  1.1
   */
  public long[] getEmployeeNumbers(String lastName, String firstName) {
    return null;
  }


  class EmployeeNotFoundException extends Exception {}

}
```

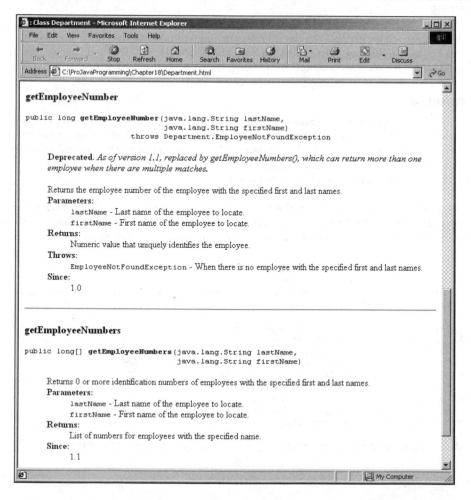

getEmployeeNumber

```
public long getEmployeeNumber(java.lang.String lastName,
                              java.lang.String firstName)
              throws Department.EmployeeNotFoundException
```

Deprecated. *As of version 1.1, replaced by getEmployeeNumbers(), which can return more than one employee when there are multiple matches.*

Returns the employee number of the employee with the specified first and last names.
Parameters:
    lastName - Last name of the employee to locate.
    firstName - First name of the employee to locate.
Returns:
    Numeric value that uniquely identifies the employee.
Throws:
    EmployeeNotFoundException - When there is no employee with the specified first and last names.
Since:
    1.0

---

getEmployeeNumbers

```
public long[] getEmployeeNumbers(java.lang.String lastName,
                                 java.lang.String firstName)
```

Returns 0 or more identification numbers of employees with the specified first and last names.
Parameters:
    lastName - Last name of the employee to locate.
    firstName - First name of the employee to locate.
Returns:
    List of numbers for employees with the specified name.
Since:
    1.1

@see *reference*

One of the most useful features of the HTML generated by javadoc is that it allows you to easily navigate from one place within the documentation to another. For example, when viewing the document that describes a particular class, you can view the document that describes its superclass with a single mouse click. This is accomplished through **hypertext links** (or "**hyperlinks**"), and many of these are generated automatically by javadoc. However, you can also use the @see tag to create additional links that would be useful to someone reading your documentation. This tag is valid within doc comments for all types of elements (for example, package, class, method, etc.), and the reference can be to any other type of element, or even to another HTML page that was not generated by javadoc. References defined by @see tags are listed in the "See Also" section of the associated element, and you can use one of the following forms to link to another code element processed by javadoc, such as a package, class, or member:

```
@see package label
@see package.Class label
@see package.Class#member label
```

The label value is optional, but if specified, identifies the text that should be displayed for this link. If it is not specified, then some form of the element name is used instead. The meaning of package and Class should be obvious, while member represents a field, constructor, or method within a class. The package name can be omitted in the second and third forms shown above if the class name can be resolved without qualifying it. For example, comments in the java.awt classes can contain links to other classes in that package without specifying the package name. The package name is also optional when the @see tag refers to a class that is imported in the source file. The following comments provide examples of the usage types, as well as a description of the rules to use when defining links:

```
package javax.swing.table;

import javax.swing.event.TableModelListener;

/**
 *  This interface's doc comments contain references to three other
 *  elements. The first one must be qualified with its package name,
 *  because JTable resides in a different package and is not imported.
 *  However, the second reference is to a class in the same package
 *  as this interface, and the third reference is valid because
 *  TableModelListener is imported.
 *
 *  @see  javax.swing.JTable
 *  @see  AbstractTableModel
 *  @see  TableModelListener
 */
public interface SeeTest {}
```

In effect, the rules that determine whether an @see tag can reference a class without specifying its package are the same rules that determine whether your executable code can reference the class. Specifically, the class must be in the same package, or must be imported. However, if you find these guidelines difficult to remember, you can simply choose to always specify the fully qualified class name when you create @see tags.

Just as you can omit the package name in certain cases, it's not always necessary to include the class name. Specifically, the class name need not be specified if the reference is to a member (constructor, method, or field) within the same class as the @see tag. For example, if you define methods that store and retrieve some property, it may be useful to link each method to its counterpart, and to create links from the methods to the associated field. An example of this is shown in the following code, in particular, notice the two links defined in the "Field Detail" section, which is the section of comments associated with the field(s) of a class:

```
public class MyClass {
  /**
   *  This represents a property value maintained by this class.
   *
   *  @see #setMyProperty(Object) Mutator method
   *  @see #getMyProperty() Accessor method
   */
  protected Object myProperty;

  /**
   *  Updates the value of 'myProperty'
   *
   *  @see #myProperty
   *  @see #getMyProperty()
   */
  public void setMyProperty(Object value)    {
    myProperty = value;
  }

  /**
   *  Returns the value of 'myProperty'
   *
   *  @see #myProperty
   *  @see #setMyProperty(Object)
   */
  public Object getMyProperty() {
    return myProperty;
  }

}
```

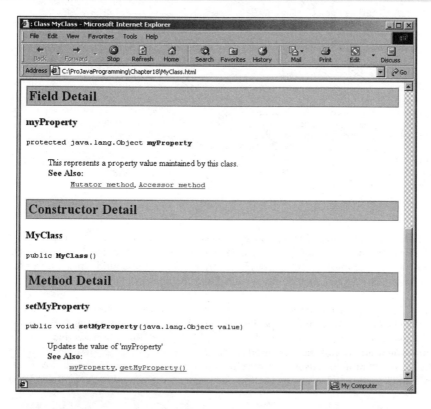

If you need to create a link to a method that has been overloaded, you should include the parameter types that the method expects on the link. The following code illustrates this point:

```
/**
 *   The first @see link in this documentation comment is a reference to the
 *   doSomething() method that accepts a String, while the second is to the
 *   one that is passed an integer. Typically, you would only reference one
 *   or the other, but references to both implementations are included here
 *   to illustrate a point.
 *
 *   @see #doSomething(String)
 *   @see #doSomething(int)
 */
public class OverloadedTest {

  public void doSomething(String stringParm) {}

  public void doSomething(int integerParm) {}

}
```

All of the examples we've discussed so far involved using @see to create links to code elements processed by javadoc. However, you can use @see to link to any HTML page, including those that were not generated by javadoc. To do so, simply create an HTML hyperlink tag, as in the following example:

```
@see <A HREF="http://www.javasoft.com">JavaSoft Home Page</A>
```

{@link *name label*}

This tag is almost identical to @see in purpose and functionality, but there is an important difference. Unlike @see, the @link tag can be used at any place within a doc comment, including the description section and within other tags. While @see allows you to add links to the "See Also" section created by javadoc, @link allows you to add in-line links anywhere within the documentation generated at the same time as that which contains the @link tag. Although you could create such links by embedding HTML tags, @link allows you to reference other javadoc pages much more easily. For example:

```
import java.util.Vector;

/**
 *   This doc comment contains two links: one within the description portion,
 *   which you're reading right now that references the
 *   {@link java.util.Vector Vector} class, and another in the tag listed
 *   below.
 *
 *   @deprecated  This comment has a link to the {@link java.lang.String}
 *        class, but doesn't contain a label, so javadoc will create
 *        one for the link using the name of the element referenced.
 *
 */
public class LinkSample {}
```

Note that if you use this tag to link to an item in the Java core classes or any other item that has already been processed by javadoc, *you'll normally want to use the* -link *option that's described later. If you do not do so, your links will not be created correctly.*

@serial *description*

This tag identifies a field that will be serialized using the default serialization mechanism. This is discussed in more depth in Chapter 13, which covers persistence and object serialization.

@serialField *name type description*

This tag describes an `ObjectStreamField` that describes a field within a serializable class. Again, this is covered in more depth in Chapter 13.

@serialData *description*

For classes that implement either `Serializable` or `Externalizable`, this tag should be used in the documentation comments for the `writeObject()`, `readObject()`, `writeExternal()`, and `readExternal()` methods. It's used to describe the data that is written and read for an instance of the class, and is discussed in detail in Chapter 13.

Running javadoc

In addition to understanding what `javadoc` creates and how to write doc comments, it's important to know how to use the tool itself. `javadoc` is among the tools provided with the Java Software Development Kit (SDK/JDK) and with most Java IDE software, such as Symantec's Visual Café, Inprise's JBuilder, and IBM's Visual Age for Java. A large number of options are supported by `javadoc`, and some of them are discussed here.

When running `javadoc`, you can identify the files that should be processed in a number of different ways. These include identifying the files by file name, by package, by identifying a file that contains a list of file and/or package names, or some combination of these. We'll look at the more frequently used options with `javadoc` in a moment. The following examples illustrate how to generate documentation by identifying specific Java source files containing classes or interfaces:

Creating documentation for a single file:

```
javadoc MyTest.java
```

Documenting multiple files:

```
javadoc MyTest.java YourTest.java HisTest.java HerTest.java
```

Creating documentation for multiple files using pattern-matching characters. In this case, all of the files in the previous example would be included:

```
javadoc *Test.java
```

You can also specify the names of packages, and all classes within those packages will be documented. If you wish to include package-level documentation in the resulting output, then you should create a `package.html` file for the package as previously described and store it in the directory that contains the package's files. An example of specifying the names of packages that should be compiled is:

```
javadoc com.pbsg.its.bussys.server com.pbsg.its.bussys.client
```

In this example, all source files in the two packages will be processed.

> **This example also illustrates an important point: that `javadoc` *does not* process packages recursively.**

In other words, you could *not* generate documentation for these packages by executing either of the following:

```
javadoc com.pbsg.its.bussys
```

or:

```
javadoc com.pbsg.its.bussys.*
```

These two commands will process only the source files in `com.pbsg.its.bussys`, which is an entirely separate and distinct package from the two **subpackages** (`server` and `client`). If you wish to generate documentation for the parent and its two subpackages, you must identify each of them on the command line.

So far, we've specified a name or pattern for each file and package that's to be included in the documentation generated by `javadoc`. However, with a large application that consists of many files and packages, the command line would become extremely long if it were necessary to list all of the items to be included. Fortunately, `javadoc` also allows you to create files that contain lists of items to be processed, and you can specify the names of those files instead of the names of packages or Java source files. For example, to process the three packages mentioned in the previous example, you could use an editor to create a text file that contains the following lines:

```
com.pbsg.its.bussys
com.pbsg.its.bussys.server
com.pbsg.its.bussys.client
```

If this is stored in a file called `mypacks.txt`, you could process all of the source files in these three packages by executing the following command:

```
javadoc @mypacks.txt
```

In this case, the "at"sign (@) identifies the file as a list of items that should be processed instead of a Java source file. Just as you can specify multiple files and packages on the command line, you can also specify multiple lists:

```
javadoc @mypacks.txt @others @somemore.lst
```

Command-Line Options for javadoc

There are many options available with `javadoc` that allow you to customize the output and to specify where certain files can be found. The following is an overview of some of the more frequently used options, and a description of when and how to use them.

–author

As previously mentioned, the @author tags do not produce any output by default. However, you can use this option to indicate that javadoc should include an "Author" section in the documentation generated for classes and interfaces that contain the tag. For example:

```
javadoc -author @mypacks.txt
```

–version

Like @author, the @version tag doesn't automatically cause its information to be included in the class and interface documentation files. However, you can specify this option to include version information in the generated output when the tags are present:

```
javadoc -version @mypacks.txt
```

–overview *path\filename*

This allows you to specify the location of the overview file that can be used to provide application-level documentation comments. This file must contain an HTML document, and javadoc uses it to generate the comments provided on the "overview" page for the entire application or set of packages. For example:

```
javadoc -overview ..\myproject\overview.html @mypacks.txt
```

Note that this, along with the following examples, uses a Windows path specification, which won't work on UNIX unless the correct directory separator character (/) is used.

–nodeprecated

When this option is specified, javadoc does not include any deprecated elements in the documentation it generates. This option also suppresses creation of the file that contains a list of all the deprecated elements within the processed packages and files.

–d *directory*

Indicates where the documentation files created by javadoc should be stored. By default, the current directory is used. The location specified by directory can be either an absolute directory, or one relative to the current working directory. For example:

```
javadoc -d .\project\docs\api @mypacks.txt
```

–sourcepath *pathlist*

This option provides javadoc with a list of paths that it should use to locate source code files when processing packages. If this option is not specified, then javadoc only searches for source files using the current directory. For example, suppose that you define a package called testpack and store its files in directory D:\brett\source\testpack. For javadoc to find those files, you must either run it from the testpack's "root directory" (D:\brett\source) or use –sourcepath to identify the directory, as in the following command:

```
javadoc -sourcepath D:\brett\source testpack
```

Note that you can specify multiple directories with this option by separating them with semicolons, or colons in the case of UNIX.

-link *url*

This option is used to link the documentation being generated with some other previously generated files. For example, you may want the documentation generated from your files to be linked to the documentation generated from the Java core classes. When you run `javadoc` without specifying this option, you'll see the names of the core classes in many places, but they won't represent links to the documentation for those classes. For example, all classes directly or indirectly subclass `java.lang.Object`, which appears in the hierarchy information generated by `javadoc`:

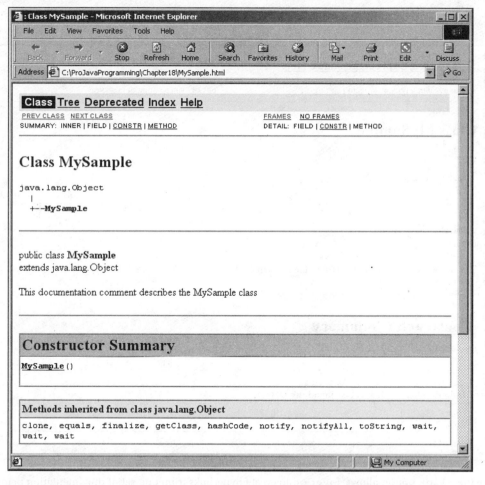

As you can see, the references to `java.lang.Object` are not hyperlinks by default, but plain text. That's because the documentation for `Object` is not usually generated when your code is processed, and `javadoc` assumes that it can't create a link to the documentation for `Object`. However, many developers do keep a copy of the core class documentation available locally and find it convenient to link their own `javadoc`-generated files to those of the core classes. To accomplish this, you must identify the location of the documentation you want to link to, which is done with the `-link` option.

For example, if the core class documentation is in `C:\jdk1.3\docs\api`, then you can link your documentation to it by entering the following command:

```
javadoc -link C:\jdk1.3\docs\api MySample.java
```

Compare the output in the following screenshot with that in the previous. Notice that instead of simply displaying the class name, `javadoc` created a link to the parent `Object` class. This makes navigation easier, and allows you to link the generated files to an existing set of `javadoc` files:

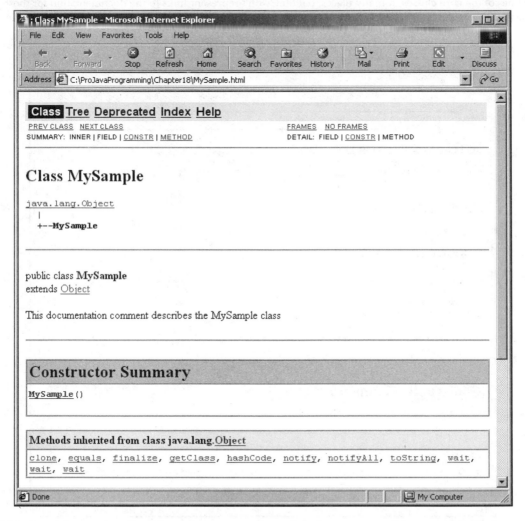

While the `-link` option allows `javadoc` to create hyperlinks from one set of documentation being generated to another that already exists, there is no way to combine two separate sets of `javadoc`-generated files into a single set. For example, you cannot create documentation for your application and merge it with the documentation for the core classes so that both sets of packages are listed together. The only way that you can create such a set of documentation is to download the source code for the Java core classes and process that code along with your own source files when you run `javadoc`.

–public
–protected
–package
–private

These options are related to the visibility of classes and members that javadoc includes in the documentation it generates. The purpose of allowing you to specify this is to remove information that isn't useful to those who read your documentation. For example, private methods and fields typically aren't of interest, because they aren't accessible outside of the class:

❑ Specifying –public specifies that javadoc should only process those elements that have public visibility

❑ Specifying –protected (the default) includes those that are public or protected

❑ Using the –package option generates documentation that includes items with public, protected, and default (package) visibility

❑ Specifying –private includes all elements, regardless of their visibility

The following code provides comments that detail what options must be specified for different elements to appear:

```
/**
 * Since this class is defined with no visibility modifier, it is considered
 * to have "package" (default) visibility, and will only be processed by
 * javadoc if either -package or -private is specified.
 */
class VisibilityTest {

  /**
   * Since this member is public, it will appear in the documentation,
   * regardless of which visiblity option (if any) is specified.
   */
  public String name;

  /**
   * This constructor will appear in the javadoc-generated documentation
   * unless the -public option is specified.
   */
  protected VisibilityTest() {}

  /**
   * Since this method is private, it will only appear if -private is
   * used.
   */
  private void doStuff () {}

}
```

Doclets

Doclets are programs that allow you to customize the behavior of the javadoc tool. For example, you can add new command line options, create your own tags and the behavior that should be associated with them, and the output that is generated. The default or "standard" doclet that is supplied with javadoc generates HTML, but you can create doclets that generate some other type of output, such as XML. In general, it should not be necessary for you to create your own doclets, but if you do need to do so, detailed information is available with the Java Software Development Kit provided by Sun.

JavaHelp

So, we've seen how you can help other developers to use your code, using documentation comments and `javadoc`. But we also need to help the user of your application, and we'll need JavaHelp for that.

JavaHelp is written entirely in Java, so it can be used on any platform for which a Java Virtual Machine exists. In addition, it can be used by applets and is compatible with Java 1.1, although with some restrictions. JavaHelp displays help files written using HTML 3.2, and those files can be created with or without a help authoring application. The examples in this chapter are simple and don't require any such tools, but a list of vendors' products that support JavaHelp is available on the JavaSoft web site.

> *Although created by Sun Microsystems, JavaHelp is a standard extension, which means that it is not included in the Java (Software) Development Kit (JDK or JSDK) or Java Runtime Environment (JRE). JavaHelp must be downloaded and installed separately, and is available on the web at http://www.java.sun.com/products/javahelp/. The download includes JAR files that allow you to easily integrate help capabilities into your application, along with utilities and examples of how to use JavaHelp. Although its primary purpose is to enable you to add help capabilities to your applications, JavaHelp's power and flexibility make it suitable for other purposes as well. For example, it can be used to view javadoc-generated API information or a document that might otherwise be provided as a Portable Document Format (PDF) file.*

To use JavaHelp, you must first define a **HelpSet**, which is simply a collection of one or more help files and some control files written in XML (see chapter 14 for information on XML). One of those files is the **HelpSet definition file**, which is normally assigned an extension of `.hs` (for example, `myhelpset.hs`). A HelpSet is represented in Java by an instance of the `HelpSet` class defined in the `javax.help` package. However, before describing how to create a `HelpSet`, we'll briefly examine the sample programs and utilities that are installed with JavaHelp.

JavaHelp Sample Programs and Utilities

When you install JavaHelp, six sample programs and utilities are created, and these are described below.

hsviewer

The `hsviewer` (help set viewer) is an application that allows you to select and view a `HelpSet`, and when executed, it initially displays the frame shown in the next screenshot. This window allows you to select a `HelpSet` definition file and clicking on the `Browse` button causes a file selection dialog to appear:

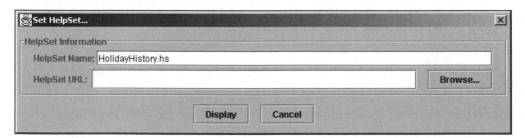

JavaHelp includes a number of sample help sets, including a collection of historical facts related to holidays. To view that information, execute `hsviewer`, navigate to the `<JavaHelp installation directory>/demos/hs/holidays/` directory, and select the `HolidayHistory.hs` file. Once you've done so, the name of the selected file and URL of its parent directory appear in the two text fields. Click on the Display button, and the `HelpSet` will be opened and displayed as shown below:

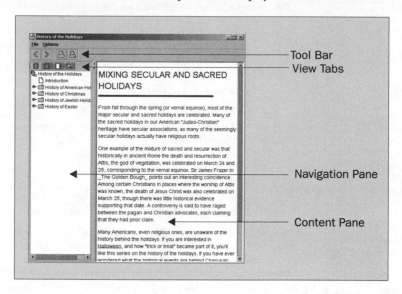

The `hsviewer` interface includes a number of useful elements that will be discussed in more detail later. Those elements include a toolbar with back/forward history, print, and print preview buttons, a set of **view tabs**, a **navigation pane**, and a **content pane**. The back and forward (left and right arrow) buttons allow you to move forward and back through the list of help files you've viewed and serve the same function as the forward and back buttons provided by most web browsers. Help information is displayed in the content pane, which is an instance of the `JEditorPane` class.

The view tabs allow you to select the type of view that should appear in the navigation panel and includes a tab for each **view** that the `HelpSet` defines. We'll examine views in more detail later, but a help set typically includes at least one table of contents and one index view, as well as a view that allows you to perform searches against the help files.

apiviewer

This provides an example of how JavaHelp can be used to browse `javadoc`-generated API information. In this case, the information is the JavaHelp API, which was generated using doclets:

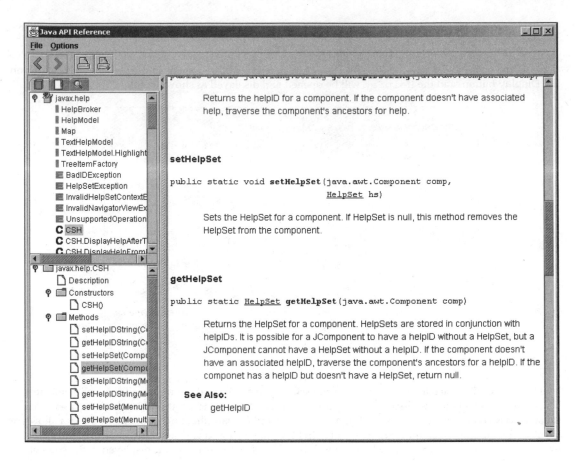

merge

This application illustrates how you can merge HelpSets together. It provides an interface that allows you to select one or more HelpSet definition files and then executes the hsviewer application to display the collection of merged help information.

object

When you request help from an application, a single window normally appears that displays some initial help file. That file typically will contain links to other, related help information, and selecting one of those links causes another file to replace the one that was originally displayed. However, when designing your help files, you'll sometimes want such a link to open a separate help window, especially if the link is associated with a very small help file. **Secondary windows** represent the JavaHelp mechanism for displaying help outside the main help window, and object provides examples of how they can be used. Secondary windows are discussed in detail later in this chapter.

UserGuide

It was mentioned earlier that JavaHelp is suitable for displaying documents that might otherwise be made available as PDF files, and UserGuide provides an example of that usage. The JavaHelp System User's Guide is provided in a form that can be browsed and searched using JavaHelp, as shown in the next screenshot:

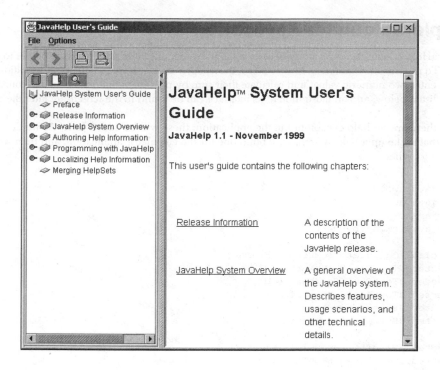

idedemo

This sample provides an illustration of how you're most likely to use JavaHelp. When you run this application, an integrated development environment (IDE) interface like the one shown in the next screenshot appears, although only the help functions actually work. For example, you can select an item from the Help menu to cause help information to appear:

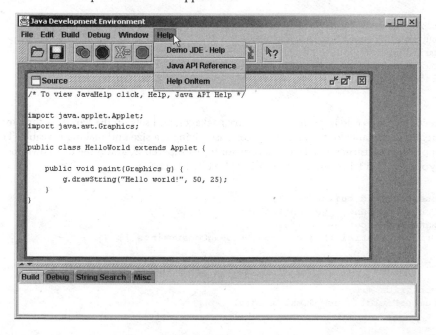

The Sample Calculator Application

Although JavaHelp is suitable for a variety of uses, you'll most often use it to add help capabilities to Java applications. To provide an example of how to do so, this chapter uses a simple calculator application that allows you to enter two numeric values and calculate their sum by pressing a button. The initial source for this application is listed below, and an illustration of its interface can be found in the screenshot after the code.

At this stage, there are no help capabilities in the application; these will be added later. As we discuss the components that make up a help system, we'll build one for the calculator application, and then we'll see how to join the two together:

```
import java.awt.*;
import java.awt.event.*;
import javax.swing.*;
import javax.swing.border.*;

public class Calculator extends JFrame {
  protected JTextField numberField1;
  protected JTextField numberField2;
  protected JTextField totalField;
  protected JButton addButton;
  protected JButton clearButton;

  protected JMenuItem appHelpItem;
  protected JMenuItem whatsThisItem;

  public static void main(String[] args) {
    Calculator c = new Calculator();
    c.setDefaultCloseOperation(JFrame.EXIT_ON_CLOSE);
    c.setSize(400, 300);
    c.setVisible(true);
  }

  public Calculator() {
    super("Calculator Application");
    buildLayout();
    buildMenuBar();
    initializeHelp();
  }
```

This first section of the code imports the necessary packages, and sets up the variables for later use. The main function creates an instance of the Calculator class, giving it a size and making it visible. The Calculator class constructor calls the constructor for its superclass, and three of its own methods – buildLayout(), buildMenuBar(), and initializeHelp():

```
protected void buildLayout() {
    Container pane = getContentPane();
    pane.setLayout(new GridBagLayout());
    GridBagConstraints gbc = new GridBagConstraints();

    gbc.fill = GridBagConstraints.HORIZONTAL;

    gbc.gridx = 0;
    numberField1 = new JTextField(5);
```

```
      pane.add(numberField1, gbc);

      numberField2 = new JTextField(5);
      pane.add(numberField2, gbc);

      totalField = new JTextField(5);
      totalField.setEditable(false);
      pane.add(totalField, gbc);

      pane.add(getButtonPanel(), gbc);
   }

   protected JPanel getButtonPanel() {
      JPanel outer = new JPanel();
      outer.setLayout(new FlowLayout());
      JPanel inner = new JPanel();
      inner.setLayout(new GridLayout(1, 2, 10, 0));
      addButton = new JButton("Add");
      addButton.addActionListener(new ActionListener() {
         public void actionPerformed(ActionEvent event) {
            onAdd();
         }
      });
      clearButton = new JButton("Clear");
      clearButton.addActionListener(new ActionListener() {
         public void actionPerformed(ActionEvent event) {
            onClear();
         }
      });
      inner.add(addButton);
      inner.add(clearButton);
      outer.add(inner);
      return outer;
   }
```

buildLayout() adds three JTextField instances, setting the third to be not editable for the total display field. It also calls getButtonPanel(), which creates a JPanel with two JButtons, each with an ActionListener. The buttons are for Add and Clear, and call onAdd() and onClear() respectively when clicked:

```
   protected void buildMenuBar() {
      JMenuBar jmb = new JMenuBar();
      JMenu jm = new JMenu("Help");
      appHelpItem = new JMenuItem("Calculator Application Help");
      jm.add(appHelpItem);
      whatsThisItem = new JMenuItem("What's This?");
      jm.add(whatsThisItem);
      jmb.add(jm);
      setJMenuBar(jmb);
   }

   protected void initializeHelp() {
   }
```

The first of these two functions, buildMenuBar(), provides little functionality at this stage in the application; it simply creates a menu for selecting help functions which have yet to be implemented. initializeHelp() does nothing yet; again, once we have implemented a help system, code will be added here to make the help system fit together with the calculator application:

```
protected void onAdd() {
  float first, second;
  String value;

  value = numberField1.getText();
  if (value.length() == 0) {
    displayError("You must specify a value for this field", numberField1);
    return;
  }
  try {
    first = Float.parseFloat(value);
  }
  catch (NumberFormatException nfe) {
    displayError("The numeric value specified is invalid", numberField1);
    return;
  }

  value = numberField2.getText();
  if (value.length() == 0) {
    displayError("You must specify a value for this field", numberField2);
    return;
  }
  try {
    second = Float.parseFloat(value);
  }
  catch (NumberFormatException nfe) {
    displayError("The numeric value specified is invalid", numberField2);
    return;
  }
  totalField.setText(Float.toString(first + second));
}
```

The onAdd() method checks the contents of the text boxes, and adds them together if they are numbers. If they are empty, or have non-numeric contents, a relevant message will be displayed by calling displayError():

```
protected void displayError(String message, JTextField comp) {
  final JDialog dialog = new JDialog(this, true);
  JButton okButton = new JButton("Ok");
  okButton.addActionListener(new ActionListener() {
    public void actionPerformed(ActionEvent event) {
        dialog.setVisible(false);
    }
  });
  JButton[] buttons = {okButton};
  JOptionPane pane = new JOptionPane(message,
      JOptionPane.ERROR_MESSAGE, 0, null, buttons);
  dialog.setContentPane(pane);
  dialog.pack();
```

```
      dialog.setVisible(true);
      comp.setSelectionStart(0);
      comp.setSelectionEnd(comp.getText().length());
      comp.requestFocus();
   }

  protected void onClear() {
    numberField1.setText("");
    numberField2.setText("");
    totalField.setText ("");
  }
}
```

The second-to-last method in the Calculator class provides error message display functionality. The message passed from onAdd() is combined with a JDialog, a JButton, and a JOptionPane to provide a display message for the user. displayError() also returns focus to the incorrectly entered text field and highlights the text. onClear() will clear the three JTextFields:

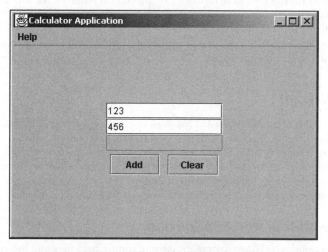

Pressing Clear causes the two value fields and the result field to be cleared, while Add attempts to add the two values together and display the sum in the result field. If one of the values is missing or if it is not a valid numeric value, an error dialog appears like the one shown here:

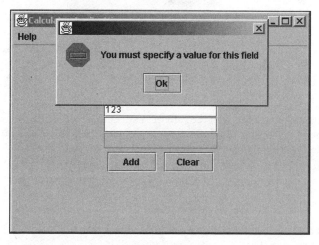

Creating a Help System

There are two steps that you must take in order to create a help system for an application:

- ❑ Create a HelpSet
- ❑ Modify your application so that it uses the HelpSet

Creating a HelpSet is in itself a three-step process:

- ❑ Create a collection of HTML files that contain the help text
- ❑ Create an XML file, which JavaHelp will use to control which HTML file is used for each item of help
- ❑ Create another XML file that defines the HelpSet; this definition specifies which XML files will be used to define the HTML files to be used, and what views will be used for navigation within the HelpSet

We'll now add support for help to the calculator application, which will allow us to examine concrete examples of each of the steps described above.

Creating a HelpSet

To create a HelpSet, you must define the HTML files containing the help information and the XML control files used by JavaHelp. Thus, a HelpSet is the set of files that JavaHelp will use to store the help information it is to display. Although there is no technical reason why you must do so, you would normally put the HTML files in a subdirectory below the root directory where the control files are stored. This makes it easier to manage your help files when there are many of them. In fact, you may even choose to create multiple subdirectories and distribute your help files across those directories based on their topics or some other criteria.

Help Files for the Calculator Application

We'll now see how to build a HelpSet by creating some simple help files and the control files needed by JavaHelp. The control files will all be placed in the same directory, while the help files will be stored in a subdirectory called /helpfiles. The following help files will need to be created for the Calculator application:

intro.html

```
<HTML>
  <HEAD>
    <TITLE>Application Overview</TITLE>
  </HEAD>
  <BODY>
    This application allows you to enter two numbers and calculate the
    results. It doesn't have much practical use, but provides an example of
    how to integrate <CODE>JavaHelp</CODE> into an application.
  </BODY>
</HTML>
```

controls.html

```
<HTML>
  <HEAD>
    <TITLE>Control Components</TITLE>
  </HEAD>
  <BODY>
    The calculator application provides a number of different components
    that you can use to add numbers together. Two of them are
    <A HREF="numfields.html">editable text fields</A> that you can enter
    numeric values into, while one is a <A HREF="result.html">field</A> that
    displays the sum of those two values. In addition, two buttons are
    provided, one of which <A HREF="addbtn.html">generates the sum</A> of
    the two values, and another <A HREF="clearbtn.html">clears the text
    fields and label</A>.
  </BODY>
</HTML>
```

numfields.html

```
<HTML>
  <HEAD>
    <TITLE>Editable Fields</TITLE>
  </HEAD>
  <BODY>
    The two editable text components displayed by the calculator application
    allow you to enter the numeric values to be added.
  </BODY>
</HTML>
```

result.html

```
<HTML>
  <HEAD>
    <TITLE>Result Field</TITLE>
  </HEAD>
  <BODY>
    When the two numeric values are added together, the result field is used
    to display the total.
  </BODY>
</HTML>
```

addbtn.html

```
<HTML>
  <HEAD>
    <TITLE>Add Button</TITLE>
  </HEAD>
  <BODY>
    You can press the <CODE>Add</CODE> button to cause the sum of the two
    values to be calculated once you have entered a value into each editable
    text field.
  </BODY>
</HTML>
```

clearbtn.html

```
<HTML>
  <HEAD>
    <TITLE>Clear Button</TITLE>
  </HEAD>
  <BODY>
    Pressing the <CODE>Clear</CODE> button causes the editable text fields
    and the result field to be cleared.
  </BODY>
</HTML>
```

future.html

```
<HTML>
  <HEAD>
    <TITLE>Future Directions</TITLE>
  </HEAD>
  <BODY>
    In the future, this application will be modified to provide additional
    arithmetic operations, including <A HREF="subtract.html">subtract</A>,
    <A HREF="multiply.html">multiply<A>, and divide.
  </BODY>
</HTML>
```

subtract.html

```
<HTML>
  <HEAD>
    <TITLE>Subtraction</TITLE>
  </HEAD>
  <BODY>
    A potential subtraction function would allow the user to subtract the
    second number entered from the first.
  </BODY>
</HTML>
```

multiply.html

```
<HTML>
  <HEAD>
    <TITLE>Multiplication</TITLE>
  </HEAD>
  <BODY>
    A multiplication operation would allow the user to multiply the two
    numbers together and would display the result.
  </BODY>
</HTML>
```

Note that each of the above files contains a `<TITLE>` tag.

Although this is not strictly required, the `<TITLE>` element is used by JavaHelp to identify a file in some cases, so you will normally want to include a `<TITLE>` element.

Map Files

When adding help capabilities to an application, there must be some way to associate a component or set of user actions with a specific help file. For example, if you press the Help key (like *F1*) to display help information for a frame or dialog, your application must be able to determine what help information should be displayed. One way to create such an association would be to explicitly identify the file by name (or by URL) inside your application. However, this approach causes your code to be tightly coupled to the name and location of the help file. If you renamed the file or simply moved it to a different directory, it would be necessary to change the reference(s) to it inside your Java program.

A better approach is to assign a unique key value to each file, define a mapping between key values and their associated files, and have your application reference only the key values. In fact, this is exactly how JavaHelp works, and a **map file** defines associations between **topic identifiers** (key values) and URLs. With this approach, you can change the name and/or location of a help file without making changes to your Java source code, since changing a file's name or location requires you to update only the map file. When an application displays help information, it will typically specify a topic identifier and JavaHelp will use the contents of the map file to translate the identifier into a URL. Map files are XML documents, and normally have an extension of .jhm.

For the Calculator application, we'll now create a file called SampleMap.jhm with the following contents. The topic identifier is specified using the target property, while the file's name and location are identified by the url property:

```
<?xml version="1.0"?>
<map>

  <mapID target="helpintro" url="helpfiles/intro.html" />
  <mapID target="futureplans" url="helpfiles/future.html" />
  <mapID target="plansub" url="helpfiles/subtract.html" />
  <mapID target="planmult" url="helpfiles/multiply.html" />
  <mapID target="ctrloverview" url="helpfiles/controls.html" />
  <mapID target="ctrlnum" url="helpfiles/numfields.html" />
  <mapID target="ctrlresult" url="helpfiles/result.html" />
  <mapID target="ctrladdbtn" url="helpfiles/addbtn.html" />
  <mapID target="ctrlclrbtn" url="helpfiles/clearbtn.html" />

</map>
```

All resources identified in this map are HTML help files, but you can also create entries for image files. For example, to assign an identifier for a file called calc.gif stored in the /images subdirectory, we can add an entry like this:

```
<mapID target="calcimage" url="images/calc.gif" />
```

HelpSet Definition Files

Besides a map file, the only other control file you must define is a HelpSet definition file, which is also created using XML and which should have an extension of .hs. The contents of the HelpSet definition file must be enclosed inside a <helpset> tag, within which four different tags are supported: <title>, <view>, <subhelpset>, and <maps>. The first three of these are optional, and we'll look at them after we've seen how the <maps> tag is used.

<maps>

This tag describes the map file associated with the `HelpSet`. Despite the fact that 'maps' implies that you may specify multiple files, JavaHelp currently only supports a single map file for each `HelpSet`. There are not known to be any plans to support multiple map files. This tag supports two embedded tags that are described below. The examples here will be combined to produce `Sample.hs`, the `HelpSet` definition file for the calculator example.

<homeID>

When creating a `HelpSet` definition file, you must specify the **home identifier**, which is simply the topic that should be displayed by default when the `HelpSet` is opened. To define the default topic for a `HelpSet`, you can use the `<homeID>` tag as shown below:

```
<homeID>helpintro</homeID>
```

In this case, the topic defined earlier that maps to the `intro.html` file was defined as the home identifier. If there is no home identifier set, when the `HelpSet` is opened the default page will be blank.

<mapref>

The `<mapref>` tag is used to identify the URL of a map file associated with a `HelpSet`. For example, to identify the previously defined map file, you might create a `mapref` tag like the one shown below:

```
<mapref location="SampleMap.jhm" />
```

In this case, only the map file's name was specified because the `HelpSet` definition file and the map file are stored in the same directory. However, if you were to store them in different directories, it would be necessary to specify either the absolute location of the map file or (preferably) a relative address. For example, if the map file is stored in a directory called `/mapdir` that's a sibling of the directory containing the `HelpSet` definition file, you could use an entry like the following:

```
<mapref location="../mapdir/SampleMap.jhm" />
```

> When specifying a URL for JavaHelp, it's usually a good idea to use a relative URL. As long as you use relative URLs, you typically won't find it necessary to modify your file references when you move **HelpSet** files from one directory to another.

Note that the forward slash (/) is used to separate a directory name from other directory names and from file names. Although some platforms (for example, Windows) use the backward slash (\) for this purpose, you should always use the forward slash when defining a URL. The backward slash character may work properly when the platform you're using supports it, but it may fail to work if you attempt to run your application on a different platform, like UNIX.

Viewing a HelpSet

It's now possible to view the `HelpSet` that's created using the map and `HelpSet` definition file previously mentioned. A complete listing of the definition `Sample.hs` file is shown below:

```
<?xml version="1.0"?>
<helpset>
```

```
      <maps>
        <homeID>helpintro</homeID>
        <mapref location="SampleMap.jhm" />
      </maps>
    </helpset>
```

This file should be created and stored in the same directory as the map file defined earlier, after which the `hsviewer` application can be used to browse this `HelpSet`'s files. As the following screenshot shows, the introduction page is displayed when the `HelpSet` is opened, but there currently is no way to view the other help topics.

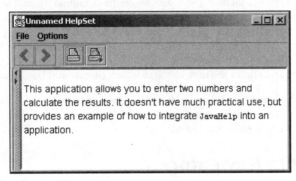

Optional HelpSet Tags

In the previous example, only the `<maps>` tag was implemented for the `HelpSet`. However, there are three other tags that you should be aware of, specifically `<title>`, `<view>`, and `<subhelpset>`.

<title>

This allows you to specify a title for the `HelpSet`, and may be displayed as part of the help user interface. "Unnamed HelpSet" appears in the title bar of the window shown above because no title was specified.

We can modify `Sample.hs` to provide one very easily:

```
<?xml version="1.0"?>
<helpset>
    <title>Calculator Application Help</title>

    <maps>
        <homeID>helpintro</homeID>
        <mapref location="SampleMap.jhm">
    </maps>
</helpset>
```

<view>

Using this tag, you can add view tabs to the user interface, and those tabs allow you to select which help topic is displayed in the content pane. No view tabs appear in the preceding screenshot because `Sample.hs` does not define any views, but in practice you'll normally create several of them. These would typically include a table of contents view, an index view, and a search view, which are all described in detail below.

<subhelpset>

This tag allows you to merge this `HelpSet` with others. Merging `HelpSets` is covered later in this chapter.

Adding Views to a HelpSet

Since the files displayed by JavaHelp are written in HTML, it's easy to embed links within them to allow users to navigate from one file to another. However, users often prefer to select a topic through more direct methods, such as by locating it in an index or a table of contents, or by searching for specific words or phrases. Although the sample `HelpSet` we have defined so far does not provide any of those capabilities, it's easy to include them. To do so, simply add a **view** to the `HelpSet` for each type of **navigator** (an index, table of contents, or search panel), and a view tab will be displayed in `hsviewer` for each navigator.

To add a navigator to a `HelpSet`, include a `<view>` tag in the definition file and specify the name of the navigator component. Three visual components are provided with JavaHelp that you can use for this purpose, and each one is a subclass of `javax.help.JHelpNavigator`. The classes are `JHelpTOCNavigator`, `JHelpIndexNavigator`, and `JHelpSearchNavigator`, and as their names imply, they provide a table of contents, an index, and a search navigator, respectively. In this context, a navigator is simply a panel that displays a list of help files and allows the user to select which one should be displayed in the content pane.

For a search navigator, the list of files is created based on the results of a search for the words specified by the user. Note that the search is performed on a database, which you create by using `jhindexer` prior to the `HelpSet` being used, a process we'll cover later.

Table of Contents Navigator

A table of contents provides a brief description of each topic and allows the user to select which topic should be displayed in the content pane, and you'll typically define at least one table of contents for a `HelpSet`. The topics in a table of contents should be listed sequentially and hierarchically. For example, the table of contents associated with the JavaHelp System User's Guide lists the major topics in the order in which they are listed in the original document. It also lists the subtopics using a tree structure as shown here:

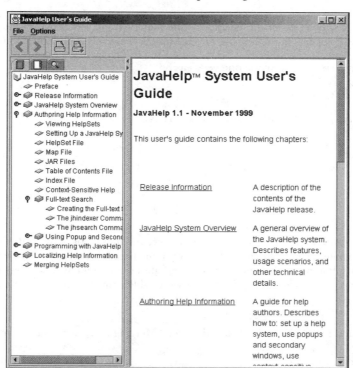

Before you can add a table of contents navigator to your HelpSet, you must first create a file that contains the information to display in the navigator.

To provide the calculator application help with a table of contents, you can use a file containing the following information, which will be named calctoc.xml and stored in the same directory as the existing map and HelpSet definition file:

```
<?xml version="1.0"?>
<toc>

  <tocitem text="Sample Calculator Application">
    <tocitem text="Introduction" target="helpintro" />
    <tocitem text="Future Additions" target="futureplans">
      <tocitem text="Subtraction" target="plansub" />
      <tocitem text="Multiplication" target="planmult" />
    </tocitem>
  </tocitem>

</toc>
```

The text attribute in the tocitem tag defines the text that is displayed for the table of contents item, while the optional target attribute identifies the topic associated with the item. If you do not specify the target attribute, the item serves as a placeholder to help organize your table of contents and will not display any help file when selected.

It's also possible to associate an image with a table of contents entry using the image attribute. In this case, the "root" item in the calctoc.xml table of contents will display the contents of the image file previously assigned a topic identifier of "calcimage":

```
<?xml version="1.0"?>
<toc>

  <tocitem image="calcimage" text="Sample Calculator Application">
    <tocitem text="Introduction" target="helpintro" />
    <tocitem text="Future Additions" target="futureplans">
      <tocitem text="Subtraction" target="plansub" />
      <tocitem text="Multiplication" target="planmult" />
    </tocitem>
  </tocitem>

</toc>
```

With the table of contents file created, you can now modify the HelpSet definition file Sample.hs so that a table of contents view is included when the HelpSet is displayed:

```
<?xml version="1.0"?>
<helpset>
  <title>Calculator Application Help</title>

  <maps>
    <homeID>helpintro</homeID>
    <mapref location="SampleMap.jhm" />
  </maps>
```

```
<view>
  <name>Table Of Contents</name>
  <label>Calculator TOC</label>
  <type>javax.help.TOCView</type>
  <data>calctoc.xml</data>
</view>

</helpset>
```

We'll now examine the tags that are embedded inside the `view` tag shown above:

<name>

This defines the name of the view.

<label>

You can use this tag to specify a label that should be associated with the view. For example, the `HelpSet` viewer sets the tool tip for the tab associated with this view, as can be seen from the next screenshot:

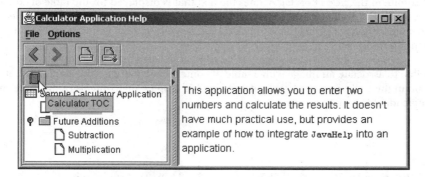

<type>

Use the `<type>` tag to identify which navigator component you wish to include, specifying the fully qualified name of the component class. Since a table of contents navigator is added in this case, the type is `javax.help.TOCView`.

<data>

To identify the location of the file containing the table of contents information, you must use the `<data>` tag. In this case, the file is `calctoc.xml`, which is stored in the same directory as the `HelpSet` definition file, so the table of contents file can be identified by its name alone without a relative URL or path.

Using a Table of Contents Navigator

If you open the `Sample.hs` HelpSet now, using `hsviewer`, you'll see a display similar to the one shown above. The navigation pane is no longer empty, but displays the table of contents navigator, which is implemented using a `JTree` so you can expand and collapse the nodes accordingly. To view the help for a particular topic, simply click on its description in the navigation pane, and the associated help file will appear in the content pane.

Index Navigator

An index navigator can be added to your help information in almost exactly the same way that a table of contents navigator is added, and you'll typically define at least one index for a HelpSet. For each index, you must define an index file and identify that file by adding another `<view>` tag to your HelpSet definition file. The information specified in that tag and the contents of the index file are almost identical to what is specified for a table of contents view.

One difference between an index and a table of contents is the way in which the topics are arranged. Specifically, they should be listed alphabetically in the index file, as opposed to being arranged by topic as they are in the table of contents. In addition, the index navigator allows you to select a topic by specifying all or part of a topic description in the Find: text field and pressing *Enter*. When you do so, the first topic with a matching description is selected and its help information displayed in the content pane.

The file listed below provides a sample index definition, and will be named `calcind.xml` and stored in the same directory as the HelpSet definition `Sample.hs`, map, and table of contents files for our calculator example:

```xml
<?xml version="1.0"?>
<index>

  <indexitem text="controls" target="ctrloverview">
    <indexitem text="Buttons">
      <indexitem text="add button" target="ctrladdbtn" />
      <indexitem text="clear button" target="ctrlclrbtn" />
    </indexitem>
    <indexitem text="number fields" target="ctrlnum" />
    <indexitem text="result field" target="ctrlresult" />
  </indexitem>

  <indexitem text="future directions" target="futureplans">
    <indexitem text="multiplication" target="planmult" />
    <indexitem text="subtraction" target="plansub" />
  </indexitem>

</index>
```

Note that just as with the `<tocitem>` tag, the `target` property is optional on the `<indexitem>` tag, so you can use items that are not associated with a help file to organize your index. An example of this is shown in the above listing, where a "Buttons" index item is defined that does not have a corresponding help file.

With the index file defined, you must identify it within the HelpSet definition file `sample.hs`:

```xml
<?xml version="1.0"?>
<helpset>
  <title>Calculator Application Help</title>

  <maps>
    <homeID>helpintro</homeID>
    <mapref location="SampleMap.jhm" />
  </maps>
```

```
<view>
  <name>Table Of Contents</name>
  <label>Calculator TOC</label>
  <type>javax.help.TOCView</type>
  <data>calctoc.xml</data>
</view>

<view>
  <name>Index</name>
  <label>Calculator Index</label>
  <type>javax.help.IndexView</type>
  <data>calcind.xml</data>
</view>

</helpset>
```

If you execute the `hsviewer` application and view this `HelpSet`, you will now be able to use the index navigator to locate help files using the newly created index:

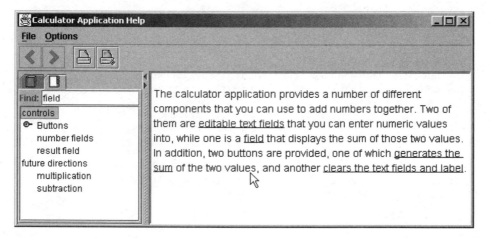

Search Navigator

The third type of view that's commonly present in a help interface is the search navigator. This tab allows you to perform a search against the help files to find those that contain the specified words, and it displays a list of the topics that contained matches.

Unlike the index and table of contents views, you do not need to create any XML files for the search navigator. Instead, you can simply add an additional view to the `HelpSet` definition file like the one shown below:

```
<?xml version="1.0"?>
<helpset>
  <title>Calculator Application Help</title>

  <maps>
    <homeID>helpintro</homeID>
```

```
      <mapref location="SampleMap.jhm" />  ,
   </maps>

   <view>
     <name>Table Of Contents</name>
     <label>Calculator TOC</label>
     <type>javax.help.TOCView</type>
     <data>calctoc.xml</data>
   </view>

   <view>
     <name>Index</name>
     <label>Calculator Index</label>
     <type>javax.help.IndexView</type>
     <data>calcind.xml</data>
   </view>

   <view>
     <name>Search></name>
     <label>Calculator Search</label>
     <type>javax.help.SearchView</type>
     <data engine="com.sun.java.help.search.DefaultSearchEngine">
       JavaHelpSearch</data>
   </view>

 </helpset>
```

The <name>, <label>, and <type> tags are all used the same way here that they were when defining the index and table of contents views, although the component is javax.help.SearchView in this case.

The only tag that is used in a different manner is <data>, which includes an engine property that identifies the class to use to perform searches. In this case, the DefaultSearchEngine class supplied with JavaHelp is specified, and you'll normally want to use that class when defining a search view. However, the ability to select the search engine class makes it easy to use a different (and perhaps more efficient) search engine if you wish to do so. As you will remember when we flagged it up earlier, you have to create a database for the search engine to use.

Finally, the value embedded in the <data> tag identifies the directory where the search database files are located. In this case, those files will be stored in a subdirectory called /JavaHelpSearch.

Creating a Search Database

If you run the hsviewer utility, open the HelpSet in its current state, and attempt to perform a search, nothing will happen. When you type words into the text field on the search page and press *Enter*, the hourglass cursor appears and no matches are ever found. This occurs because DefaultSearchEngine requires that you first create the database files that it will use to perform the search, but we have not yet done so. Fortunately, it's very easy to create the database files using the jhindexer utility provided with JavaHelp.

jhindexer

The jhindexer utility creates database files that can be used by the search navigator to determine which help files contain the word(s) you specify. jhindexer scans the help files and generates six output files:

- ❑ DOCS
- ❑ DOCS.TAB
- ❑ OFFSETS
- ❑ POSITIONS
- ❑ SCHEMA
- ❑ TMAP

By default, those six files are created in a subdirectory named /JavaHelpSearch, although you can specify a different location.

When running jhindexer, you must specify the files and/or folders that should be included in its processing. We'll come to the calculator example in a short while, once you've seen the options you can use. For example, to scan all the help files in the /helpfiles subdirectory, you could enter the following command:

```
jhindexer helpfiles
```

It's also possible to identify multiple files and folders, so if your help files are stored in more than one directory (for example, /helpfiles and /morehelpfiles), you can enter a command like the one below:

```
jhindexer helpfiles morehelpfiles
```

The jhindexer utility also supports a number of options that are described below. It is worth pointing out that jhindexer will scan all the files in the subdirectory you specify.

–db dir

This allows you to specify where the files created by jhindexer should be stored, and the default is a subdirectory called /JavaHelpSearch. For example, to have the files written to a directory called /somedir, you would execute a command similar to this one:

```
jhindexer -db somedir helpfiles
```

–locale lang_country_variant

This allows you to specify the locale to use, and should include a language, country code, and optionally a variant, with the underscore (_) character separating them. For example:

```
jhindexer -locale en_UK helpfiles
```

For more information on locales and internationalizing your application, see Chapter 19.

–logfile file

The jhindexer utility generates messages while running, but those messages may disappear too quickly for you to read them. For example, running jhindexer on Windows causes a command line window to appear, and messages are written to that window. However, it is normally destroyed immediately when jhindexer has completed execution, causing any output to be lost.

To ensure that you're able to review the messages generated by jhindexer, use the -logfile option, specifying the name of a file to which the output should be sent:

```
jhindexer -logfile messages.txt helpfiles
```

–verbose

Using this option causes `jhindexer` to issue additional messages during its processing, which may be useful when you encounter problems.

–nostopwords

Stopwords are words that `jhindexer` ignores while processing help files. In other words, it does not create index entries for these words, so they are effectively ignored when you perform a search. JavaHelp includes a default stopword list that's shown in the following table, but you can specify this option to indicate that *all* words should be indexed in the search database. Alternatively, you can create your own list of stopwords using a configuration file, which is discussed below.

JavaHelp Default StopWord List							
a	all	am	an	and	any	are	as
at	be	but	by	can	could	did	do
does	etc	for	from	goes	got	had	has
have	he	her	him	his	how	if	in
is	it	let	me	more	much	must	my
nor	not	now	of	off	on	or	our
own	see	set	shall	she	should	so	some
than	that	the	them	then	there	these	this
those	though	to	too	us	was	way	we
what	when	where	which	who	why	will	would
yes	yet	you					

–c file

This option allows you to specify the name and location of a configuration file. Configuration files allow you to customize the behavior of `jhindexer`, and examples of how they are used are provided below.

Using a Configuration File

You can customize the behavior of `jhindexer` using the `-c` parameter to identify a configuration file you've created. As previously mentioned, a configuration file allows you to create your own stopword list that `jhindexer` will use instead of its default list. In addition, you can modify the path names associated with the help files that are scanned and you can explicitly identify which files `jhindexer` should scan.

Modifying Path Names

When processing help files and creating the search database, `jhindexer` records the relative directory location of each file it processes. For example, the help files defined earlier were stored in the `/helpfiles` subdirectory, so if `jhindexer` is run from the parent of that directory, it will record that each file is stored in

/helpfiles. When an attempt is made to load a file based on the information in the search database, JavaHelp will expect the file to be in the /helpfiles subdirectory, although the parent directory is allowed to be named differently.

For example, if you're using Windows, you might initially create your JavaHelp control files in D:\project\test and store the help files in D:\project\test\helpfiles. When deploying your application, you may wish to put the JavaHelp control files in C:\deploy and the help files in C:\deploy\resources\helpfiles. However, this deployment approach will fail, since JavaHelp expects the help files to be in C:\deploy\helpfiles.

To modify the directory information associated with each help file, you can define a configuration file and add an IndexRemove or IndexPrepend entry. For example, to add /resources to the directory information, you could create the following entry in a file called samplehelp.cfg:

```
IndexPrepend resources/
```

With that entry in the configuration file, you can enter the following command:

```
jhindexer -c samplehelp.cfg helpfiles
```

This will result in each help file that's processed in the /helpfiles directory being recorded as residing in /resources/helpfiles instead of /helpfiles. Similarly, the IndexRemove can be used to delete directories from the path associated with a help file, as in the following example:

```
IndexRemove /helpfiles/
```

Identifying the Files to Index

You can add File entries to a configuration file to explicitly identify the files that should be included in jhindexer's processing. For example, to specify that only intro.html and future.html should be processed, you could add the following two entries to a configuration file:

```
File helpfiles/intro.html
File helpfiles/future.html
```

This directive can be useful when there are many help files in many different directories that you wish to process, or when a directory contains many files that you wish to process, but others that you do not. In either case, it would be difficult or even impossible to include each file's name and location on the command line when executing jhindexer.

Identifying Stopwords

As mentioned earlier, a configuration file can be used to define a custom list of stopwords, which can be done in one of two ways. You can use the StopWords directive, specifying a list of words, or you can use StopWordsFile to identify a file containing a list of stopwords. You may find it particularly useful to define a custom stopword list if you're providing a search menu for help in a language other than English.

For example, to identify the words inside the configuration file, you would create an entry similar to this one:

```
StopWords the, a, and, or, an, are, of, to, this, nor, be
```

A new line indicates the end of a `StopWords` list.

Alternatively, you can specify a file that contains one stopword on each line using an entry like the one below:

```
StopWordsFile ignore.txt
```

Unfortunately, there is not currently a way to specify that you wish to add words to or remove them from the default stopword list. Instead, the list of words that you specify when you use these options completely replaces the default list that would otherwise be used.

Running jhindexer

The `jhindexer` utility is very easy to use, although a problem exists that can prevent you from running it successfully. `jhindexer` may incorrectly create the `POSITIONS` file in the current directory and fail to create the `SCHEMA` and `DOCS.TAB` files. When this occurs, you'll encounter an exception like the one shown below, although you might need to use the `-logfile` option to view it:

```
java. io.FileNotFoundException: JavaHelpSearch\POSITIONS (The system cannot find the file
specified)
  at java.io.FileInputStream.open(Native Method)
  at java.io.FileInputStream.<init>(FileInputStream.java:64)
  at java.io.FileInputStream.<init>(FileInputStream.java:95)
  at com.sun.java.help.search.DocumentLists.<init>
(DocumentLists.java:161)
  at com.sun.java.help.search.DocumentLists.invert
(DocumentLists.java:243)
  at com.sun.java.help.search.DefaultIndexBuilder.close
(DefaultIndexBuilder.java:103)
  at com.sun.java.help.search.Indexer.compile(Indexer.java:228)
  at com.sun.java.help.search.Indexer.main(Indexer.java:76)
  at java.lang.reflect.Method.invoke(Native Method)
```

Fortunately, there is an easy workaround for this problem. Simply have `jhindexer` store all the files it creates in the current directory using the `-db` parameter and then manually move the six files to the appropriate subdirectory (for example, `/JavaHelpSearch`).

For the calculator example, the following command scans the files in the `/helpfiles` subdirectory and stores the database files in the current directory:

```
jhindexer -db . helpfiles
```

Alternatively, you can download JavaHelp 1.1.1 as a zip file from the JavaHelp website at http://java.sun.com/products/javahelp/download_binary.html#update

jhsearch

Once you've created the search database files, you can use the `jhsearch` utility to test the database, specifying the directory containing the database files as a parameter. For example:

```
jhsearch JavaHelpSearch
```

When you execute `jhsearch`, it opens a window that prompts you to enter search data, after which it searches the database files and displays the results of its search. An example of the output is shown below with the user's response displayed in bold:

```
initialized; enter query
values
query 0
0.0 helpfiles/result.html [26, 32], {values}
0.0 helpfiles/addbtn.html [62, 68], {values}
0.0 helpfiles/numfields.html [109, 115], {values}
0.0 helpfiles/controls.html [180, 186], {values}
0.0 helpfiles/controls.html [249, 255], {values}
0.0 helpfiles/controls.html [338, 344], {values}
0.1 helpfiles/addbtn.html [110, 115], {value}
170 msec search
enter next query or . to quit
```

Using the Search Navigator

Once you've created database files with `jhindexer`, you will be able to use the search navigator when viewing your help information. To perform a search, select the search tab and enter the words you wish to locate in the text field next to the Find: label. When you press *Enter*, the search is performed, and the topics containing the word(s) you entered will appear in the search panel:

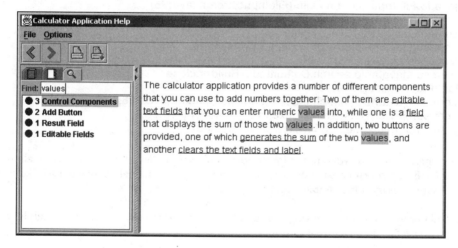

The left column of the search results display contains a circle indicating how closely each topic appeared to match your search criteria, and the value in the middle column identifies the number of matches in the file:

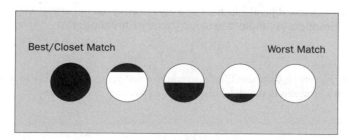

The right column of the search results display contains a single line of text that's extracted from the <TITLE> tag inside the file, which is why you should be sure to create that tag when defining help files. If a match is found for a help file that does not contain a <TITLE> tag, No Title is displayed in place of the title text.

To view a help file that matched your search criteria, click on the file's description in the search navigator pane. When you do so, the file appears in the content panel and the words you searched for are highlighted as shown in the next screenshot:

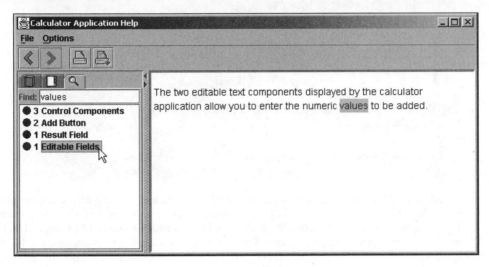

Requesting Help

In most applications, there are many ways to display help information. For example, you might request help by selecting a menu item, by clicking on a button, or by pressing the *Help* key on your keyboard. In addition, the type of help information that's presented often depends upon the way in which you requested help.

Clicking on a button or pressing the *Help* key usually displays **context-sensitive help**, which is a topic that's related to a specific task or user interface component. The user interface component is typically the window (the frame or dialog) that was active when help was requested or some individual element (for example, a text field) within that window.

For example, if you're using a word processor application and have opened a print preview window, requesting Help will usually display printing and/or print preview help information.

Another type of context-sensitive help that's often requested is field-level help, which is a topic related to a particular component within a window such as a text field. In some cases, it's possible to request field-level help for a component by pressing the *Help* key when the component has the input focus, but that approach has two limitations:

❑ Some components are not able to accept the input focus, so it's not possible to use the *Help* key to display context-sensitive help.

❑ Clicking on a component is often the easiest way (and sometimes the only way) to cause the focus to be moved to that component, but doing so usually also activates it, which may not be appropriate in some cases. For example, clicking on a button that terminates your application is not an appropriate way to assign the input focus to the button so that you can view its help information. Ideally, there should be an easy way to select a component without activating it.

JavaHelp provides support for a "help mode" that allows you to identify the component for which you wish to view context-sensitive help information. Pressing a button or selecting a menu item typically enables help mode, and it changes the cursor image to the one shown in this screenshot:

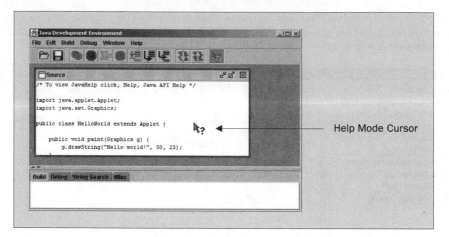

While help mode is enabled, JavaHelp intercepts mouse click events, and clicking on a component causes its context-sensitive help to be displayed instead of the component being activated. Once the help information has been displayed, help mode is automatically disabled, which returns the cursor to its original state and allows the application to again function normally. For example, if this capability is implemented in the calculator application, activating help mode and clicking on the Clear button will cause help information on that button to be displayed and the text fields will not be cleared.

A help mode trigger (a button or menu item) usually has a label such as "What's This?" or displays a cursor with a question mark next to it:

JavaHelp Library Files

Five JAR files are included with JavaHelp, and you will need to add one or more of those files to your class path before you can compile an application that includes help functionality. The five libraries are located in the /javahelp/lib subdirectory below the directory where you installed JavaHelp, and the contents of each one is described below. Once you have added help capabilities to your application, you will need to distribute one of these libraries along with your application code for the help capabilities to function. Sun allows the JavaHelp libraries to be distributed without requiring you to pay any royalty fees.

jhtools.jar

This library contains only the files needed to create a search database. In other words, these are the class files used by the jhindexer utility, and you will not usually need to make them available to your application.

jhsearch.jar

This library contains the files associated with the search engine (`DefaultSearchEngine.class`, etc.) and can be omitted if your application provides only basic help without the ability to perform searches. In most cases, however, you'll want to include this functionality in your application.

jhbasic.jar

When your application needs only basic help functions with no search capability, you can add this library to your class path. It allows you to display help information and to provide index and table of contents navigators, but does not include the search navigator or the ability to create a search database.

jh.jar

This file contains all of the classes found in `jhbasic.jar` and in `jhsearch.jar`. In other words, this library contains everything except the code for creating a search database and is the file you'll typically want to add to your class path when developing help-enabled Java applications.

jhall.jar

This file contains all the classes found in `jhbasic.jar`, `jhsearch.jar`, and `jhtools.jar`. In other words, this library contains *all* JavaHelp-related classes, including those used to create a search database.

JavaHelp Classes and Interfaces

We saw earlier that the `NavigatorView` subclasses (`IndexView`, `SearchView`, and `TOCView`) are used to provide the views available in the `hsviewer` application. Before adding the help capabilities we've just developed to the `Calculator` application, it's necessary to briefly examine some of the other classes and interfaces that are part of the JavaHelp API. If you browse the API using the `apiviewer` utility, you'll find that there are dozens of classes and interfaces defined in `javax.help` and its subpackages. However, you'll rarely need to use more than a handful of those classes, and the ones that you should be familiar with are described below.

javax.help.HelpSet

As its name implies, this class represents a `HelpSet` and contains accessor and mutator methods that allow you to retrieve and query its properties. You'll normally create an instance of `HelpSet` using the constructor that accepts two parameters: a `ClassLoader` and a URL that identifies the location of a `.hs` file. However, you can specify a `null` value for the `ClassLoader`, which causes the default loader to be used as shown in the following example:

```
URL helpSetURL = new URL("file:./Sample.hs");
HelpSet set = new HelpSet(null, helpSetURL);
```

There's rarely a reason to use a `ClassLoader` other than the default, but you may wish to do so if you need to have complete control over the loading of the help files.

javax.help.JHelp

Instances of this class display help information and they can be created using the constructor that's passed a `HelpSet` instance, as shown in the following application:

```
import java.net.*;
import javax.help.*;
import javax.swing.*;

public class JHelpTest {
  public static void main(String[] args) throws Exception {
    URL helpSetURL = new URL("file:./Sample.hs");
    HelpSet set = new HelpSet(null, helpSetURL);
    JHelp help = new JHelp(set);
    JFrame f = new JFrame();
    f.setDefaultCloseOperation(JFrame.EXIT_ON_CLOSE);
    f.setContentPane(help);
    f.setSize(400, 300);
    f.setVisible(true);
  }
}
```

If you compile and run this application (making sure the relevant JavaHelp JAR files are on your CLASSPATH), it will create a user interface like the one shown in the following screenshot. If the interface seems familiar, it's because hsviewer uses JHelp to display help information. If you're familiar with the model-view-controller concept, you may find it helpful to think of HelpSet as a model and JHelp a view of that model:

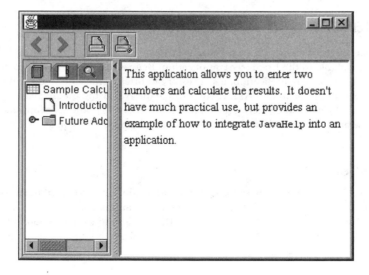

javax.help.CSH

CSH (Context Sensitive Help) provides static methods that allow you to associate a Component instance with a topic identifier and/or a HelpSet. That information can be used to display the appropriate help file when context-sensitive help is requested for the component.

In addition, CSH defines several inner classes that implement ActionListener, and each of those classes provides a constructor that's passed an instance of a HelpBroker implementation. The HelpBroker interface is described later in this chapter.

setHelpIDString()

This static method requires you to pass a reference to a `Component` instance and a `String` representing a topic identifier, and `CSH` associates the component with the specified topic. For example:

```
JTextField numberField1;
// ...

CSH.setHelpIDString(numberField1, "ctrlnum");
```

getHelpIDString()

Just as `setHelpIDString()` sets the identifier for a component, this method retrieves the identifier previously specified. Although you will not normally invoke this method directly, it's helpful to understand how it works, because it illustrates how your application will provide context-sensitive help.

If `getHelpIDString()` is called for a component that has not been assigned an identifier, it recursively traverses the component's containment hierarchy until it locates a container that is associated with an identifier. For example, suppose that you add a `JTextField` to a `JPanel` and assign an identifier to the panel but not the text field. If you then call `getHelpIDString()` and pass a reference to the text field, the panel's identifier will be returned instead.

setHelpSet()

This static method requires you to pass a reference to a `Component` instance and a `HelpSet` instance, and `CSH` associates the component with the specified help set. For example:

```
JTextField numberField1;
HelpSet helpSet;
// ...

CSH.setHelpSet (numberField1, helpSet);
```

A `JComponent` can have a `helpID` without a `HelpSet`, but it cannot have a `HelpSet` without a `helpID`. A `HelpSet` is stored in conjunction with a `helpID`.

getHelpSet ()

This method returns the `HelpSet` associated with the specified `Component`. Like `getHelpIDString()`, `getHelpSet()` will search the containment hierarchy if no `HelpSet` is associated with the specified component. For example, using the previous component:

```
CSH.getHelpSet(numberField1);
```

javax.help.CSH.DisplayHelpFromSource

This inner class implements `ActionListener`, and when `actionPerformed()` is called, it displays help information. The `actionPerformed()` method obtains the topic identifier and `HelpSet` associated with the component that generated the `ActionEvent` and uses those values to determine which help topic to display.

`DisplayHelpFromSource` is most commonly used with instances of `AbstractButton` subclasses, such as `JButton` and `JMenuItem`. To make a button display help information, you must first associate it with a `HelpSet` and topic identifier using the static methods just described. Once that's done, you can create an instance of `DisplayHelpFromSource` and register it as a listener of the button's action events. In practice, however, you won't normally use `DisplayHelpFromSource` directly, but will instead use the `enableHelpOnButton()` method in the `HelpBroker` interface described below.

javax.help.CSH.DisplayHelpFromFocus

`DisplayHelpFromFocus` is very similar to `DisplayHelpFromSource`, but with one important difference. Instead of selecting the topic identifier of the component that generated the `ActionEvent`, this class obtains the identifier associated with the component that has the input focus.

`DisplayHelpFromFocus` is most commonly used to provide context-sensitive help when the *Help* key is pressed. You will not normally use this class directly, but should instead use the `enableHelpKey()` method in the `HelpBroker` interface described below.

javax.help.CSH.DisplayHelpAfterTracking

This class is used to support the help mode described earlier, which is typically enabled using a "What's This?" menu item or button. When an application is in help mode, clicking on a component causes context-sensitive help to be displayed that describes the component. `DisplayHelpAfterTracking` provides this functionality by intercepting mouse click events until you click on a component. When you do so, `DisplayHelpAfterTracking` locates the topic identifier associated with the component, displays the appropriate help information, and returns the application to its normal state.

javax.help.HelpBroker

Just as `HelpSet` defines a model and `JHelp` provides a view of that model, `HelpBroker` represents a controller that can be used to manage the view, say a `JHelp` instance. Although `HelpBroker` contains methods that allow you to specify which `HelpSet` and topic are displayed, you won't normally call those methods directly. Instead, you'll use the convenience methods in `HelpBroker` to create listeners that will control the display of help information for you based on the events that occur.

You'll typically obtain a reference to a `HelpBroker` by requesting one from a `HelpSet` using the `createHelpBroker()` method:

```
URL helpSetURL = new URL("file:./Sample.hs");
HelpSet set = new HelpSet(null, helpSetURL);
HelpBroker broker = set.createHelpBroker();
```

There are several methods in `HelpBroker` that you'll use when adding help functions to an application, each of which is described below.

enableHelp()

This method requires you to specify a `Component`, a topic identifier, and a `HelpSet` as parameters, and it associates the specified `Component` with the `HelpSet` and topic. For example:

```
JTextField numberField1;
HelpSet helpSet;
// ...

HelpBroker broker = helpSet.createHelpBroker();
broker.enableHelp(numberField1, "ctrlnum", helpSet);
```

As you might expect, `enableHelp()` is simply a convenience method that calls the static `setHelpSet()` and `setHelpIDString()` methods in `CSH`. In other words, the two code segments:

```
CSH.setHelpSet(numberField1, helpSet);
CSH.setHelpIDString(numberField1, "ctrlnum");
```

and:

```
broker.enableHelp(numberField1, "ctrlnum", helpSet);
```

are equivalent to one another.

enableHelpOnButton()

This method requires the same three parameters as `enableHelp()`, and it too associates the specified component with the `HelpSet` and topic. However, `enableHelpOnButton()` performs an important function that `enableHelp()` does not: it causes the topic to be displayed when the component is activated. This is done by creating an instance of `CSH.DisplayHelpFromSource` and registering it as a listener of the button's events. This method is useful for creating "What's This?" buttons.

An example of how to use `enableHelpOnButton()` is provided below:

```
HelpSet helpSet;
JMenuItem appHelpItem;
// ...

HelpBroker broker = helpSet.createHelpBroker();
broker.enableHelpOnButton(appHelpItem, "helpintro", helpSet);
```

enableHelpKey()

While `enableHelpOnButton()` is used to display help when a button is pressed or a menu item activated, `enableHelpKey()` causes help to be displayed when the Help key is pressed. This is done using an instance of `CSH.DisplayHelpFromFocus`, and when the Help key is pressed, help is displayed using the topic identifier of the component that has the input focus. For example:

```
HelpSet helpSet = new HelpSet(null, helpURL);
HelpBroker broker = helpSet.createHelpBroker();
// ...

broker.enableHelpKey(this.getRootPane(), "ctrloverview", helpSet);
```

Adding Help to the Calculator Application

Now we'll see how to use the classes and methods just described to add help functionality to the `Calculator` application defined earlier. The application will initially support three different ways of requesting help information:

- ❑ Selecting the Calculator Application Help menu item
- ❑ Pressing the *Help* key while the `Calculator` application's frame is the active window
- ❑ Selecting the What's This? menu item to enable help mode

To add help capabilities to an application, you must create an instance of `HelpSet` and obtain a `HelpBroker`, so we'll add fields to `Calculator` for those objects. In addition, it's necessary to import the files defined in the `javax.help` package:

```
import java.awt.*;
import java.awt.event.*;
```

```
import javax.help.*;
import javax.swing.*;
import javax.swing.border.*;

public class Calculator extends JFrame {
  protected JTextField numberField1;
  protected JTextField numberField2;
  protected JTextField total;
  protected JButton addButton;
  protected JButton clearButton;

  protected JMenuItem appHelpItem;
  protected JMenuItem whatsThisItem;

  protected HelpSet helpSet;
  protected HelpBroker broker;

  public static void main(String[] args) {
    Calculator c = new Calculator();
    c.setDefaultCloseOperation(JFrame.EXIT_ON_CLOSE);
    c.setSize(400, 300);
    c.setVisible(true);
  }
}
```

Now we can add code to initializeHelp() to create the HelpSet and obtain a reference to a HelpBroker:

```
protected void initializeHelp() {
  try {
    java.net.URL helpURL = new java.net.URL("file:./Sample.hs");
    helpSet = new HelpSet(null, helpURL);
    broker = helpSet.createHelpBroker();
  }
  catch (Exception e) {
    JOptionPane.showMessageDialog(this,
        "Unable to initialize help:" + e.getMessage());
  }
}
```

Menu Items And Buttons

Once a HelpBroker has been created, it's easy to add help capabilities to buttons and to menu items such as the Calculator Application Help item. As described earlier, you can simply call the broker's enableHelpOnButton() method:

```
protected void initializeHelp() {
  try {
    java.net.URL helpURL = new java.net.URL("file:./Sample.hs");
    helpSet = new HelpSet(null, helpURL);
    broker = helpSet.createHelpBroker();
    enableHelpComponents();
  }
  catch (Exception e) {
```

```
        JOptionPane.showMessageDialog(this,
            "Unable to initialize help:" + e.getMessage());
    }
}
```

```
protected void enableHelpComponents() {
    broker.enableHelpOnButton(appHelpItem, "helpintro", helpSet);
}
```

Help Key

Displaying help when the Help key is pressed is equally simple, and can be done using the
enableHelpKey() method as shown below:

```
protected void enableHelpComponents() {
    broker.enableHelpOnButton(appHelpItem, "helpintro", helpSet);
    broker.enableHelpKey(getRootPane(), "ctrloverview", helpSet);
}
```

Field-Level Help

To enable field-level help, you should associate each component with a topic identifier and a HelpSet, and
then create an instance of CSH.DisplayHelpAfterTracking, adding it as a listener of the button or
menu item that enables help mode. In the case of the Calculator application, help mode is enabled using
the What's This? item on the Help menu:

```
protected void enableHelpComponents() {
    broker.enableHelpOnButton(appHelpItem, "helpintro", helpSet);
    broker.enableHelpKey(getRootPane(), "ctrloverview", helpSet);
    broker.enableHelp(numberField1, "ctrlnum", helpSet);
    broker.enableHelp(numberField2, "ctrlnum", helpSet);
    broker.enableHelp(totalField, "ctrlresult", helpSet);
    broker.enableHelp(addButton, "ctrladdbtn", helpSet);
    broker.enableHelp(clearButton, "ctrlclrbtn", helpSet);
    whatsThisItem.addActionListener(
        new CSH.DisplayHelpAfterTracking(broker));
}
```

Dialog Box Help

We can now use any of the three techniques (the *Help* key or either of the two menu items) described earlier
to display help information for the Calculator application. However, there is no way to obtain help when
it's most likely to be needed: when an error has occurred. Specifically, Calculator should be able to
provide help information when an error dialog is displayed. To add this functionality, we'll first create two
new help files: one that is displayed when the user leaves a text field empty, and another that's displayed
when one of the values entered is not a valid number.

badnumdlg.html

```
<HTML>
 <BODY>
   The value you entered is not a valid number. For example:<br>
   123<br>
```

```
   23.7<br>
   -13
 <BODY>
<HTML>
```

nonumdlg.html

```
<HTML>
  <BODY>
    You must enter a value in both text fields.
  <BODY>
<HTML>
```

Each file must be added to the HelpSet's map file (SampleMap.jhm) and associated with a topic identifier as shown below:

```xml
<?xml version="1.0"?>
<map>

  <mapID target="helpintro" url="helpfiles/intro.html" />
  <mapID target="futureplans" url="helpfiles/future.html" />
  <mapID target="plansub" url="helpfiles/subtract.html" />
  <mapID target="planmult" url="helpfiles/multiply.html" />
  <mapID target="ctrloverview" url="helpfiles/controls.html" />
  <mapID target="ctrlnum" url="helpfiles/numfields.html" />
  <mapID target="ctrlresult" url="helpfiles/result.html" />
  <mapID target="ctrladdbtn" url="helpfiles/addbtn.html" />
  <mapID target="ctrlclrbtn" url="helpfiles/clearbtn.html" />
  <mapID target="dlgbadnum" url="helpfiles/badnumdlg.html" />
  <mapID target="dlgnonum" url="helpfiles/nonumdlg.html" />

  <mapID target="calcimage" url="images/calc.gif" />

</map>
```

By making the following changes, the new help information can be accessed by pressing the *Help* key or by pressing the Help button that will now appear in the error dialogs:

```java
protected void onAdd() {
  float first, second;
  String value;

  value = numberField1.getText();
  if (value.length() == 0) {
    displayError("You must specify a value for this field",
        numberField1, "dlgnonum");
    return;
  }
  try {
    first = Float.parseFloat(value);
  }
  catch (NumberFormatException nfe) {
    displayError("The numeric value specified is invalid",
        numberField1, "dlgbadnum");
```

```
      return;
    }

    value = numberField2.getText();
    if (value.length() == 0) {
      displayError("You must specify a value for this field",
          numberField2, "dlgnonum");
      return;
    }
    try {
      second = Float.parseFloat(value);
    }
    catch (NumberFormatException nfe) {
      displayError("The numeric value specified is invalid",
          numberField2, "dlgbadnum");
      return;
    }
    totalField.setText(Float.toString(first + second));
  }

  protected void displayError(String message, JTextField comp,
                                String topic) {
    final JDialog dialog = new JDialog(this);
    JButton okButton = new JButton("Ok");
    okButton.addActionListener(new ActionListener() {
      public void actionPerformed(ActionEvent event) {
          dialog.setVisible(false);
      }
    });
    //  Enable display of help via Help key
    broker.enableHelpKey(dialog, topic, helpSet);
    JButton helpButton = new JButton("Help");
    //  Enable display of help via Help button
    broker.enableHelpOnButton(helpButton, topic, helpSet);
    JButton[] buttons = {okButton, helpButton};
    JOptionPane pane = new JOptionPane(message,
        JOptionPane.ERROR_MESSAGE,
        0, null, buttons);
    dialog.setContentPane(pane);
    dialog.pack();
    dialog.setVisible(true);
    comp.setSelectionStart(0);
    comp.setSelectionEnd(comp.getText().length());
    comp.requestFocus();
  }
```

Embedding Lightweight Components

Once you have your application with fully functional help like the calculator example, you'll sometimes want to embed a lightweight Java component inside the help files you create. To do so, simply include an <OBJECT> tag in the help file, identify the class of the component you wish to display, and use the <param> tag to initialize the component's state.

For example, the following modification to addbtn.html produces a display like the one shown in the subsequent screenshot:

```
<HTML>
  <HEAD>
    <TITLE>Add Button</TITLE>
  </HEAD>
  <BODY>
    <OBJECT classid="java:javax.swing.JButton">
      <param name="text" value="Add">
    </OBJECT>
    You can press the <CODE>Add</CODE> button to cause the sum of the two
    values to be calculated once you have entered a value into each editable
    text field.
  </BODY>
</HTML>
```

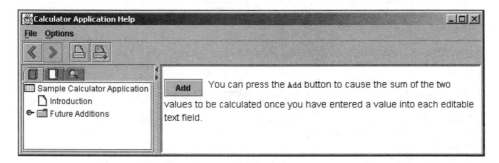

When a component is embedded this way, an instance of the class is created and each <param> tag is used to set the object's properties. In effect, a JavaBean is embedded inside the help information, and introspection is used to ensure that the parameter values specified correspond to valid bean properties.

> **This technique does have one restriction: you can only modify properties that have a pair of accessor/mutator methods that use `String` values.**

For example, suppose that you wish to include a JTextField inside the numfields.html file and you want the text field to be approximately as wide as the text fields in the Calculator application. If you add an <OBJECT> tag to the help file without any parameter values, the default JTextField constructor is used, which results in a very narrow text field like the one shown here:

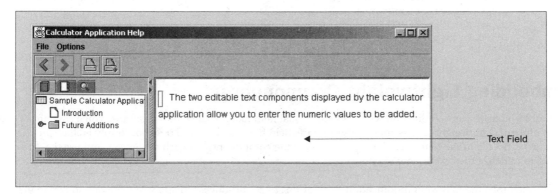

Although `JTextField` does provide the `getColumns()` and `setColumns()` methods that allow you to modify its width, those methods use primitive `int` values instead of `String`s. Therefore, you can't modify the column count directly through a `<param>` tag.

Fortunately, there is a simple solution to this problem: create a subclass that provides a `String` property counterpart for the non-`String` property you wish to modify. In other words, your accessor and mutator methods should convert `String` values to and from the property's data type. For example, since we want to change the `columns` property, we can create a `columnsString` property that converts `String` values to `int` and vice versa:

```java
import javax.swing.*;

public class JTextFieldExtended extends JTextField {

  public String getColumnsString() {
    return Integer.toString(super.getColumns());
  }

  public void setColumnsString(String columns) {
    try {
      super.setColumns(Integer.parseInt(columns));
    }
    catch (NumberFormatException nfe) {};
  }
}
```

With this class defined, you can include an instance of `JTextFieldExtended` in a help file and use its `columnsString` property to modify the underlying `columns` property in the `JTextField`. For example, you might make the following changes to `numfields.html`:

```html
<HTML>
  <HEAD>
    <TITLE>Editable Fields</TITLE>
  </HEAD>
  <BODY>
    <OBJECT classid="java:JTextFieldExtended">
      <param name="columnsString" value="10">
    </OBJECT>
    The two editable text components displayed by the calculator application
    allow you to enter the numeric values to be added.
  </BODY>
</HTML>
```

which produces results like those shown here:

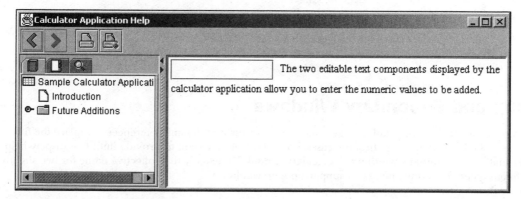

While this approach does work, it forces the programmer to use the name of the String property that corresponds to a non-String property. In this case, for example, you must remember that you can change the text field's columns property by adding a <param> tag that modifies the columnsString property.

Since the component embedded in your help information is a JavaBean, you can create a BeanInfo implementation and control not only which properties are exposed, but also the names of the accessor and mutator methods for each property. In effect, you can rename the property from columnsString to columns using a BeanInfo implementation like the one shown below:

```
import java.beans.*;

public class JTextFieldExtendedBeanInfo extends SimpleBeanInfo {

  public PropertyDescriptor[] getPropertyDescriptors() {
    PropertyDescriptor[] results = new PropertyDescriptor[2];
    try {
      results[0] = new PropertyDescriptor("text",
          JTextFieldExtended.class, "getText", "setText");
      results[1] = new PropertyDescriptor("columns",
          JTextFieldExtended.class, "getColumnsString", "setColumnsString");
    }
    catch (Exception e) {};
    return results;
  }
}
```

Note that the PropertyDescriptor array also contains an entry for the text property (which remains unchanged), although it's not used in this example. If you do create a BeanInfo class, you should be sure to expose all properties that you expect to use.

With this new BeanInfo implementation, it's now possible to modify numfields.html to refer to columns instead of columnsString:

```
<HTML>
  <HEAD>
    <TITLE>Editable Fields</TITLE>
  </HEAD>
  <BODY>
    <OBJECT classid="java:JTextFieldExtended">
      <param name="columns" value="10">
    </OBJECT>
    The two editable text components displayed by the calculator application
    allow you to enter the numeric values to be added.
  </BODY>
</HTML>
```

Popup and Secondary Windows

In most cases, clicking on a link in a help file causes the file that the link references to replace the file currently in the content pane. In some cases, however, you may want to provide links that display help information in **secondary windows**. "Secondary window" is actually the collective name for two slightly different types of window; JavaHelp supports popup windows:

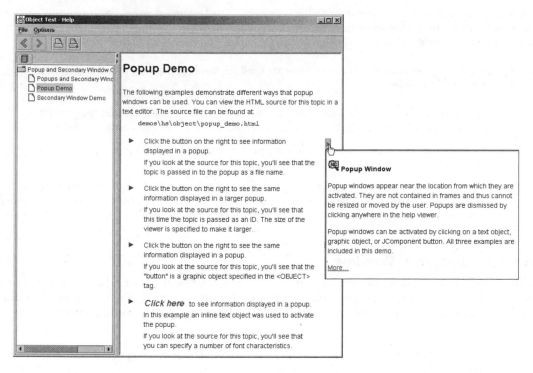

and secondary windows:

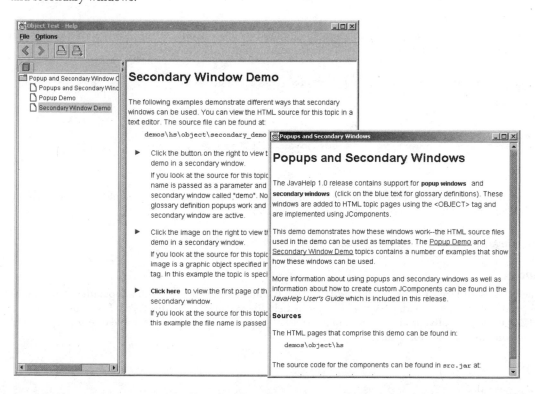

Each type allows you to display help information outside the JHelp content pane, and is typically used when more help information is needed without changing the file that's displayed. For example, you might use a popup window to provide a brief explanation of a term that's used inside your help information.

Although popup windows and secondary windows are used for similar purposes, they differ somewhat in their appearance and behavior:

- ❑ A popup window always appears, like a tooltip, adjacent to the object that triggered its appearance, while a secondary window can be displayed anywhere on the screen.

- ❑ A secondary window is represented as a frame that can be iconified, moved, and resized, while a popup menu cannot be modified in any way.

- ❑ Finally, secondary windows remain open until explicitly closed (usually by pressing the close button), while popup windows are only visible until the input focus changes. In other words, popup windows are similar to JPopupMenu instances, while secondary windows are instances of JFrame.

Creating a Secondary Window

To create a secondary window, you must embed a JHSecondaryViewer object (which is defined in the com.sun.java.help.impl package) within a help file. The JHSecondaryViewer is displayed within the help information as either a button or a label, and it creates a popup or secondary window when you click on it.

The properties supported by JHSecondaryViewer class are listed below, along with a description of how each one is used and the values that may be assigned.

viewerStyle

This property identifies the type of window, and it must be either javax.help.Popup for a popup window or javax.help.SecondaryWindow for a secondary window. For example:

```
<param name="viewerStyle" value="javax.help.Popup">
```

or:

```
<param name="viewerStyle" value="javax.help.SecondaryWindow">
```

id

This identifies the help file that will be displayed in the secondary window, and should be used when the help file has an entry in the HelpSet's map file. For example:

```
<param name="id" value="popupInfo">
```

content

When the secondary window should display a help file that isn't associated with a topic identifier, you can use the content property to identify the URL of the help file that should be displayed. If you use a relative URL, it must be relative to the location of the "parent" help file. There is an example of this property below in the continued calculator example.

viewerActivator

You can use this property to specify the type of component (label or button) that should be used to represent the JHSecondaryViewer object. Valid values for this property are javax.help.LinkLabel (to display a label) and javax.help.LinkButton (to display a button). There is an example of this property below in the continued calculator example.

text

This parameter identifies the text displayed within the button or label.

textFontFamily

When displaying text in the label or button, this property allows you to specify the font family that should be used. Valid values are:

- ❑ Serif
- ❑ SansSerif
- ❑ MonoSpaced
- ❑ Dialog
- ❑ DialogInput
- ❑ Symbol

textFontSize

When displaying text in the label or button, this property allows you to specify the font size that should be used. Valid values and their descriptions are listed in the table below:

Value	Resulting Font Size
xx-small	Extremely small ('extra-extra small')
x-small	Very small ('extra small')
small	Small
medium	Medium
large	Large
x-large	Very large ('extra large')
xx-large	Extremely large ('extra-extra large')
smaller	Base font size minus one (base - 1)
bigger	Base font size plus one (base + 1)
nnpt	Absolute point size of nn
-n	Base font size minus n (base - n)
+n	Base font size plus n (base + n)
n	Point size associated with index n

textFontWeight

When displaying text in the label or button, you can use this property to specify whether the text should be displayed using a bold font. Valid values for `textFontWeight` are `plain` and `bold`.

textFontStyle

When displaying text in the label or button, you can use this property to specify whether the text should be displayed using an italic font. Valid values for `textfontStyle` are `plain` and `italic`.

textColor

When displaying text in the label or button, you can use this property to specify the color that should be used for the text, and the valid values, which are the default colors in Java's `Color` class, are listed below:

- black
- blue
- cyan
- darkGray
- gray
- green
- lightGray
- magenta
- orange
- pink
- red
- white
- yellow

iconByName

You can use this property to identify the URL of an image file that will be displayed in the label or button. For example:

```
<param name="iconByName" value="/images/calc.gif">
```

iconByID

You can use this property to identify the topic identifier associated with an image that will be displayed in the label or button. For example:

```
<param name="iconByID" value="calcimage">
```

In both cases, `iconByName` and `iconByID`, the parameter is used in conjunction with the following parameter:

```
<param name="viewerActivator" value="javax.help.LinkLabel">
```

viewerSize

This property allows you to specify the width and height (separated by a comma) of the secondary window in pixels as shown below:

```
<param name="viewerSize" value="400, 300">
```

viewerLocation

When displaying a secondary window, you can use this property to indicate where the window should appear, and the coordinate values specified should be relative to the upper-left corner of the screen. For example:

```
<param name="viewerLocation" value="100, 100">
```

This property is only applicable to secondary windows and is ignored for popup windows.

viewerName

When displaying secondary windows and you have more than one link defined, you can use this property to reuse an existing window instead of creating a new one, by specifying the same viewer name. This property is only applicable to secondary windows and is ignored for popup windows. For example:

```
<param name="viewerName" value="calchelp">
```

Popup Window Example

An example of a popup window is shown in the next screenshot, which is produced by making the following modification to the `intro.html` page for our calculator example:

```
<HTML>
  <HEAD>
    <TITLE>Application Overview</TITLE>
  </HEAD>
  <BODY>
    This application allows you to enter two numbers and calculate the
    results. It doesn't have much practical use, but provides an example of
    how to integrate
    <OBJECT classid="java:com.sun.java.help.impl.JHSecondaryViewer">
      <param name="viewerStyle" value="javax.help.Popup">
      <param name="viewerActivator" value="javax.help.LinkLabel">
      <param name="text" value="JavaHelp">
      <param name="content" value="popup.html">
      <param name="viewerSize" value="200, 150">
    </OBJECT>
    into an application.
  </BODY>
</HTML>
```

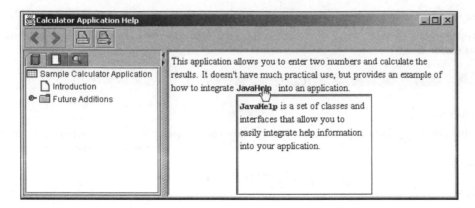

This example explicitly identifies the help file that's displayed in the content window using the `content` parameter, but in practice, you normally should instead use `id` to specify an identifier defined in the map file. The `popup.html` file used in this example is shown below:

```
<HTML>
  <BODY>
    <CODE><B>JavaHelp</B></CODE> is a set of classes and interfaces that
    allow you to easily integrate help information into your application.
  </BODY>
</HTML>
```

Supporting Multiple Locales

If your application supports more than one locale, you may wish to provide separate help information for each locale. For example, you might have two different sets of help files that are written in two different languages. When that is the case, it's easy to have JavaHelp display the appropriate `HelpSet` based on the user's locale.

In the examples provided earlier in this chapter, the URL of the `HelpSet` definition file was explicitly identified and used to create an instance of `HelpSet` as shown below:

```
URL helpSetURL = new URL("file:./Sample.hs");
HelpSet set = new HelpSet(null, helpSetURL);
```

In practice, however, you should use the static `findHelpSet` method defined in `HelpSet` to obtain the URL of a definition file. There are several versions of this method, but the simplest requires only a `ClassLoader` reference (which can be `null`) and a `String` representing a base file name:

```
URL helpSetURL = HelpSet.findHelpSet(null, "Sample.hs");
HelpSet set = new HelpSet(null, helpSetURL);
```

Using `findHelpSet()` is preferable to explicitly specify the URL because `findHelpSet()` selects a `HelpSet` definition file based on a locale. The above code will try to select the file based on your system's default locale, although another `findHelpSet()` implementation is provided that accepts a `Locale` instance as a parameter:

```
import java.util.*;              //need this to use Locale
import java.net.*;
import javax.help.*;

public class TestLocale {
  public static void main(String args[]) {
    // Language = French, Country = Canada, variant = MAC
    Locale myLocale = new Locale("fr", "CA", "MAC");

    URL helpSetURL = HelpSet.findHelpSet(null, "Sample.hs", myLocale);
    System.out.println(helpSetURL);
  }
}
```

If you execute this code on a system with a default language of en (English), country of US (United States), and variant of WIN (Windows), it returns the URL of the first file found from the following list:

```
Sample_fr_CA_MAC.hs
Sample_fr_CA.hs
Sample_fr.hs
Sample.hs
Sample_en_US_WIN.hs
Sample_en_US.hs
Sample_en.hs
```

In other words, findHelpSet() first searches for variations of the explicitly specified locale (or the system default if none is specified), then for the base file name that you specified, and finally for variations that include the system default locale. This behavior allows you to create a separate HelpSet definition file for each language that your application supports and to have the application automatically use the appropriate file when help is requested. For more information about locales, Locale, and international applications, see Chapter 19.

Combining HelpSets

You may sometimes wish to combine two or more help sets together when displaying help information, and JavaHelp does have the ability to merge sets together, although "merge" is a somewhat misleading choice of word. You might expect that the result of merging two sets is a single integrated HelpSet with all items from both sets combined and sorted. In reality, "merging" one HelpSet with another results in the index and table of contents of the **sub-HelpSet** being appended to that of the **master HelpSet**.

HelpSets can be combined in one of two ways: through the <subhelpset> tag in the HelpSet definition file (known as **static merging**), or by calling a HelpSet's add() method (**dynamic merging**). The sample merge application that's installed with JavaHelp provides an example of dynamic merging; the code segment below illustrates how to accomplish this:

```
URL masterURL = HelpSet.findHelpSet(null, "master.hs");
HelpSet masterSet = new HelpSet(null, masterURL);
URL subsetURL = HelpSet.findHelpSet(null, "subset.hs");
HelpSet subSet = new HelpSet(null, subsetURL);
masterSet.add(subSet);
```

Packaging HelpSets

You'll typically find it convenient to create a JAR file that contains the files that make up a HelpSet, although you may find it helpful to leave the HelpSet definition (.hs) file out of the archive. The definition file is the only file that's normally referenced by your application and it in turn references the map, table of contents, and index files, along with the search database directory. If you do not include the HelpSet definition file in the JAR, you can change the location of the JAR without making a corresponding change to your source code.

It's also possible to leave the map file outside of the JAR, but is not usually a good idea to do so, because you then must specify the absolute URL of each help file as shown below:

```
<mapID target="helpintro"
       url="jar:file:/C:/java/myhelp.jar!/helpfiles/intro.html" />
<mapID target="futureplans"
       url="jar:file:/C:/java/myhelp.jar!/helpfiles/future.html" />
<mapID target="plansub"
       url="jar:file:/C:/java/myhelp.jar!/helpfiles/subtract.html" />
```

In this case, the help files are stored in a JAR named myhelp.jar that's located in the C:\java directory, and the exclamation mark (!) separates the JAR file's location from the location of the help files within the JAR. However, if the map file is included in the JAR with the help files it references, you can use the more convenient relative URLs instead:

```
<mapID target="helpintro" url="helpfiles/intro.html" />
<mapID target="futureplans" url="helpfiles/future.html" />
<mapID target="plansub" url="helpfiles/subtract.html" />
```

This approach does have the disadvantage of requiring you to regenerate the JAR file each time you add a new help file to the map. In the future, however, JavaHelp will support multiple map files, so it will be possible for you to define additional topics by creating a new <mapref> entry in the HelpSet definition file.

Packaging the Calculator Application Help

To create a JAR file that contains the help files associated with Calculator, you can issue a command similar to the one below:

```
jar cf calchelp.jar SampleMap.jhm *.xml helpfiles images JavaHelpSearch
```

> Note that the **jar** protocol used here is only available in Java 1.2 and later releases.

This creates a JAR file called calchelp.jar with the following contents:

```
SampleMap.jhm
calcind.xml
calctoc.xml
META-INF/
        MANIFEST.MF
helpfiles/
        addbtn.html
```

```
              badnumdlg.html
              clearbtn.html
              controls.html
              future.html
              intro.html
              multiply.html
              nonumdlg.html
              numfields.html
              popup.html
              result.html
              subtract.html
     images/
              calc.gif
     JavaHelpSearch/
                    DOCS
                    DOCS.TAB
                    OFFSETS
                    POSITIONS
                    SCHEMA
                    TMAP
```

Note that the only file missing is the `HelpSet` definition file, which was deliberately omitted for the reasons described above. The original implementation of `Sample.hs` used relative URL entries, but to reference the entries in the newly created JAR file, those entries must be changed. For example, if the JAR file is stored in Windows directory `C:\ProJava\JavaHelp\`, you should make the following changes to `Sample.hs`:

```xml
<?xml version="1.0"?>
<helpset>
  <title>Calculator Application Help</title>

  <maps>
    <homeID>helpintro</homeID>
    <mapref
    location="jar:file:/C:/ProJava/JavaHelp/calchelp.jar!/SampleMap.jhm"/>
  </maps>

  <view>
    <name>Table Of Contents</name>
    <label>Calculator TOC</label>
    <type>javax.help.TOCView</type>
    <data>jar:file:/C:/ProJavaJavaHelp/calchelp.jar!/calctoc.xml</data>
  </view>

  <view>
    <name>Index</name>
    <label>Calculator Index</label>
    <type>javax.help.IndexView</type>
    <data>jar:file:/C:/ProJavaJavaHelp/calchelp.jar!/calcind.xml</data>
  </view>

  <view>
    <name>Search></name>
    <label>Search Navigator</label>
```

```
    <type>javax.help.SearchView</type>
    <data engine="com.sun.java.help.search.DefaultSearchEngine">jar:file:/C:
/ProJavaJavaHelp/calchelp.jar!/JavaHelpSearch</data>
  </view>

</helpset>
```

Custom Help Interface

You can easily use the JavaHelp components to create your own hsviewer-like application or to embed help information inside your application's user interface. For example, the following code creates a crude help browser like the one shown in the next screenshot:

```java
import java.awt.*;
import javax.help.*;
import javax.swing.*;

public class CustomHelp extends JFrame {

  public static void main(String[] args) throws Exception {
    CustomHelp ch = new CustomHelp();
    ch.setDefaultCloseOperation(JFrame.EXIT_ON_CLOSE);
    ch.setSize(400, 300);
    ch.setVisible(true);
  }

  public CustomHelp() throws Exception {
    super("Custom Help Viewer");
    Container contentPane = getContentPane();
    java.net.URL helpURL = HelpSet.findHelpSet(null, "Sample.hs");
    HelpSet helpSet = new HelpSet(null, helpURL);

    // Make a content pane for the helpset to be displayed in
    JHelpContentViewer viewer = new JHelpContentViewer(helpSet);
    contentPane.add(viewer, BorderLayout.CENTER);

    // Find out what navigator views are in the helpset
    NavigatorView[] views = helpSet.getNavigatorViews();
    JTabbedPane tabPane = new JTabbedPane();

    // Add a tab for each navigator view
    for (int i = 0; i < views.length; i++) {
      tabPane.add(views[i].getName(),
          views[i].createNavigator(viewer.getModel()));
    }

    // add the tab pane to left side of the content pane
    contentPane.add(tabPane, BorderLayout.WEST);
  }

}
```

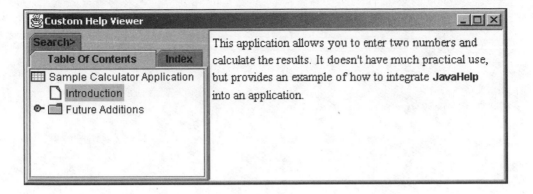

Summary

In this chapter, we have looked at two different but closely related things: documentation and help files. Documentation is your way of telling other developers what to expect from your code, and presenting it in a readable way. Help files, and implementing a help system in your applications, are ways of providing online help for people who use your applications.

We saw that providing documentation for your classes and methods is really quite easy, and Java provides `javadoc` to help. As you write your code, you can include documentation comments before each method and class you want to describe. Running `javadoc` will generate your documentation files in the same format as the API documentation files.

For help systems, we saw that you need to create a `HelpSet`, and how to implement this collection of help files and add it to your application. We also covered embedding lightweight components to make your help files look better, how you can provide support for multiple locales, packaging your application help in a JAR file, and we finished off with a quick look at defining your own help viewer.

In the next chapter, we will look at the facilities Java provides for internationalizing your applications, so that they can support more than one language and set of formatting conventions.

Professional Java Programmin

19

Internationalization

Some software applications are used only by a small number of people within a limited geographic area, but it has become increasingly common for an application to be used by many people in very different parts of the world. In some cases it's possible to require all your application's users to understand a single language and use the same symbols and formatting for items such as dates, times, and numeric values. However, most users prefer to work with the language and formatting conventions that they're most comfortable with, and by taking that into consideration when designing your application you can accommodate their wishes.

Modifying or designing an application so that it supports more than one language and set of formatting conventions is known as **internationalization** (or **i18n**, because there are 18 characters between the "i" and the "n"). As evidenced by its use of Unicode, Java was designed with internationalization in mind, and a number of classes were introduced in Java 1.1 that make it easy to internationalize your applications.

Closely related to internationalization is **localization**, which is the process of ensuring that an application will function appropriately when used in a particular region of the world. The most obvious step that must be taken to localize an application is to ensure that it displays text in the user's native language. This requires you to provide a translation for each text item that can be written or displayed by the application, and Java does not provide any facilities for automatically translating messages. However, it does provide an easy way for you to define collections of text messages, with each collection representing a particular language, and makes it easy for your application to select the appropriate translation of a text item. Where internationalization aims to create applications that can support more than one language, localization provides the extra language support for internationalized applications.

In addition to providing a translation for each message, an internationalized application should also display information using the appropriate symbols and conventions when formatting information such as dates, times, and numeric values. For example, the mm/dd/yy (two-digit month, day, and year) format for dates is appropriate for most users in the United States, but is not commonly used in other countries. Similarly, numeric values are represented in different ways in different parts of the world, especially currency values.

Just as an internationalized application must customize the output it produces, it must also handle user input appropriately. If a user is allowed to enter text that represents a number, the application must be able to parse the text and convert it into a numeric type (say, a `double` or `long` value). In addition, a date that was entered by the user will typically need to be converted into an instance of `java.util.Date` before it can be used or stored by the application. It's also sometimes necessary to parse text and isolate individual sentences, lines, words, or characters in the text, which is a very complex task to perform for some languages.

In some cases, a user's language can be implicitly identified based on the user's location. For example, a user in the United States or United Kingdom can reasonably be expected to prefer English messages. In other cases, two or more languages may be widely used in the same country, such as in Canada where both English and French are widely spoken. However, even if two different users share the same language, it cannot be assumed that they also share the same formatting conventions for dates, times, and numeric values.

In order to be able to internationalize our applications, we'll need to know about four things:

❑ Locales

❑ Using resource bundles to localize messages

❑ Formatting and parsing dates, times, and numbers

❑ Using `MessageFormat` and `ChoiceFormat` to create complex localized messages

We'll look at each of these in turn.

Locales

A user's country cannot necessarily be used to select the language that an application can use, and a language is not sufficient to determine the formatting conventions for dates, times, and numeric values. However, it is usually true that a region can be defined that has one dominant language and set of formatting conventions, and that region can be defined by geographic, political, or simply cultural boundaries. Java's `Locale` class is used to identify such a region, and each instance of `Locale` contains three property values:

❑ The language code is a two-character `String` value that's equal to one of the codes defined by the ISO-639 standard, and a list of language codes can be found at http://www.ics.uci.edu/pub/ietf/http/related/iso639.txt.

❑ Similarly, the country code is a two-character `String` that's assigned the value of an ISO-3166 country identifier, a list of which is available at http://www.chemie.fu-berlin.de/diverse/doc/ISO_3166.html.

❑ The variant value is optional and can be omitted, but may be useful in some cases. For example, multiple variations of a single language can be used within a country, and the variant allows you to identify the version that's used. For example, two different versions of the Norwegian language are used in Norway, and the variant can be used to distinguish between them. The variant can also be used to distinguish between different platforms, for example by using `WIN` for Windows, `MAC` for Macintosh, and `POSIX` for POSIX systems. (Where there are two variant values, they are separated by an underscore and the more important is put first.)

The `java.util.Locale` class by itself does not provide much functionality that's useful for internationalization, but an instance of `Locale` can be passed to some methods defined in Java's core classes, and those methods will produce the results appropriate for that `Locale`. For example, `java.text.NumberFormat` provides a `getNumberInstance()` factory method that creates an object that can be used to format numeric values. If you pass an instance of `Locale` to the factory method, it will return an object that formats numeric values in a manner that's appropriate for the `Locale` you specified. Most of those methods that accept a `Locale` parameter have a counterpart that does not accept such a parameter, and those that do not use the **default locale**. The default `Locale` is simply a static instance of `Locale` that's selected for you based on your operating system settings, and you can query and modify the default through the static `getDefault()` and `setDefault()` methods in the `Locale` class.

Although you can create an instance of `Locale`, some instances are provided for you as predefined constants in the `Locale` class. Some of those constants represent a `Locale` with only a language specified (for example, `Locale.ENGLISH`, `Locale.FRENCH`, `Locale.GERMAN`), while others represent both a language and a country (for example, `Locale.US`, `Locale.FRANCE`, `Locale.GERMANY`). In addition to those constants, Java includes the information needed to support a large number of locales, and an array of those supported can be obtained by calling the `getAvailableLocales()` method. For each `Locale` identified by that method, Java provides the ability to display dates, times, and numeric values using the conventions that are appropriate for that `Locale`. In addition, Java provides the ability to parse and compare `String` instances that consist of characters used in the `Locale`.

To create a `Locale`, you must use either the constructor that accepts country and language codes, or the constructor that accepts those values plus a variant. For example, to create a `Locale` for Cajun French used in the United States, you could use the following:

```
Locale cajunFrenchLocale = new Locale("fr", "US", "CAJUN");
```

In addition to allowing you to access its country, language, and variant values, each `Locale` provides a `getDisplayName()` method that returns the name of the locale. By default, the method returns a name in the language appropriate for the user's default locale. As with many other methods, though, `getDisplayName()` allows you to explicitly specify a `Locale`. If you do so, the name returned will be a string that's appropriate for display in the `Locale` specified. For example, suppose that your default locale is set to `Locale.US` and you execute the following line of code:

```
System.out.println(Locale.US.getDisplayName());
```

When you do so, the output will appear like that shown below:

```
English (United States)
```

However, you could instead choose to display the `Locale`'s name in a form that's appropriate for a user in France using code like this:

```
System.out.println(Locale.US.getDisplayName(Locale.FRANCE));
```

Executing this code will produce the following output:

```
anglais (États-Unis)
```

Many times, you'll want to display a representation of a `Locale` using the language that's associated with that instance, which can be done with code similar to that shown below:

```
Locale someLocale;
// Assign a reference to an instance of Locale to the variable just defined
// ...

System.out.println(someLocale.getDisplayName(someLocale));
```

Resource Bundles

Perhaps the most obvious step that must be taken to internationalize an application is to store the text it displays in an external location. For example, suppose that you have the following trivial application:

```
public class Hardcoded {
   public static void main(String[] args) {
     System.out.println("The number of arguments entered is " + args.length);
   }
}
```

This small program cannot be made to support more than one language or locale without modifying the source code, because the message text is embedded (or "hardcoded") within the source. However, Java's **resource bundles** allow you to store strings, image files, or any other type of resource in files outside your application's source code.

> Specifically, the `java.util.ResourceBundle` class allows you to create a separate resource bundle for each `Locale` you wish to support in your code, and have the appropriate bundle selected dynamically at runtime.

A `ResourceBundle` is an object that encapsulates a set of resources, each of which is associated with a unique key value that's an instance of `java.lang.String`. To access a particular resource, you simply obtain a reference to the `ResourceBundle` and call its `getObject()` method, passing a reference to the `String` that identifies the resource to which you wish to obtain a reference. Resources will often be text information that has been localized, but can be any object that's needed to internationalize your application. Since instances of `String` are the most common type of data stored in and retrieved from instances of `ResourceBundle`, a `getString()` method is provided in addition to `getObject()`. The `getString()` method simply casts the resource you retrieve to a `String` object.

Note that the resource keys are case-sensitive, so when calling `getObject()` or `getString()`, you must ensure that the `String` you specify is capitalized appropriately. If you specify a key that is not an exact match for a resource defined in the `ResourceBundle`, a `MissingResourceException` is thrown.

Once an appropriate `ResourceBundle` has been created, which you'll see how to do shortly, the `Hardcoded` application shown above could be easily modified to remove the embedded message text as shown below:

```
import java.util.*;
public class Hardcoded {
```

```
   public static void main(String[] args) {
      ResourceBundle myBundle = ResourceBundle.getBundle("MyResources");
// System.out.println("The number of arguments entered is " + args.length);
      String msg = myBundle.getString("MsgText");
      System.out.println(msg + args.length);
   }
}
```

In this case, a resource bundle named MyResources was referenced, and should contain a resource with a key of MsgText. This modified application loads the resource bundle, obtains a reference to the MsgText resource, casts it to a String, and uses that text to produce its output. With this modified design, the Hardcoded application can be made to support more than one Locale and it will display the message text in the appropriate language for each one.

> *We still need to create the resource bundle itself, though, before this will work – we'll see how to do this in a moment.*

In the above example, no Locale was specified on the call to getBundle(), but a different implementation of that method allows you to do so. For example, if you wished to load the ResourceBundle containing Canadian French messages, you could use code like that shown below:

```
   ResourceBundle myBundle = ResourceBundle.getBundle(
         "MyResources", Locale.CANADA_FRENCH);
```

When you call its getBundle() method, ResourceBundle attempts to load each class file with a variation of the name that was specified. It first looks for classes with the explicitly specified Locale values (that is, language, country, and variant codes) appended to the name and then to classes with the default Locale's values. For example, if the default Locale is Locale.US in this case, getBundle() would load each of the following files if they exist:

```
   MyResources_fr_CA.class
   MyResources_fr.class
   MyResources_en_US.class
   MyResources_en.class
   MyResources.class
```

Note that getBundle() also attempts to use the variant name if one is specified, but in this case, both the default (Locale.US) and the explicitly specified instance (Locale.CANADA_FRENCH) have a variant that's set to the empty string (""). In other words, the search order used when loading a ResourceBundle file can be summarized by the following list. In this list, (1) represents the explicitly-specified Locale, (2) represents the default locale, and basename represents the String argument passed to getBundle():

```
   basename_language(1)_country(1)_variant(1).class
   basename_language(1)_country(1).class
   basename_language(1).class
   basename_language(2)_country(2)_variant(2).class
   basename_language(2)_country(2).class
   basename_language(2).class
   basename.class
```

As we'll see shortly, there's an important reason why calling getBundle() loads each of these classes if they exist, instead of simply loading the first one that's found.

Creating a ResourceBundle

ResourceBundle is an abstract class, and although you can create your own direct subclass, you need not normally do so. Instead, you'll typically create a subclass of either ListResourceBundle or PropertyResourceBundle, which are convenience classes provided with Java that make it easier for you to create a ResourceBundle. If you are going to be using images or other objects in your ResourceBundle, then a ListResourceBundle is the one to use, while the PropertyResourceBundle is a better choice for use with text.

ListResourceBundle

Creating a subclass of ListResourceBundle is very simple, and you need to implement only a single getContents() method that returns a two-dimensional array of key/resource pairs.

To illustrate how to create a ListResourceBundle subclass, suppose that you wish to internationalize the following application that displays a dialog and requests the user to press the button corresponding to the correct answer:

```java
import java.util.*;
import javax.swing.*;

public class JavaQuestion {
  public static void main(String[] args)    {
    ImageIcon flagIcon = new ImageIcon("flags/unitedstates.gif");
    String[] options = {"Yes", "No"};
    JOptionPane pane = new JOptionPane(
        "Is Java an object-oriented programming language?",
        JOptionPane.QUESTION_MESSAGE, 0, flagIcon, options);
    JDialog dlg = pane.createDialog(null, "Java Question");
    dlg.setModal(true);
    dlg.setVisible(true);
    String selection = (String)(pane.getValue());
    boolean selectedYes = (selection == options[0]);
  }
}
```

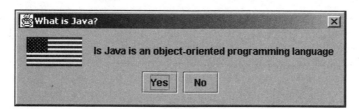

This code uses four text resources and an ImageIcon that should be localized based on the default Locale, and a ResourceBundle named MyResources can easily be created like the one below. As you can see, this class simply defines each resource and maps it to a String key, while the getContents() method returns a reference to the array containing the key/value pairs:

```java
import java.util.*;
import javax.swing.*;

public class MyResources extends ListResourceBundle {
```

```
    protected static Object[][] resources = {
        {"WhatIsJava", "What is Java?"},
        {"JavaIsLang", "Is Java is an object-oriented programming language"},
        {"LabelYes", "Yes"},
        {"LabelNo", "No"},
        {"FlagIcon", new ImageIcon("flags/unitedstates.gif")}
    };

    public Object[][] getContents()   {
      return resources;
    }
  }
```

If the application that uses these resources is intended to also be used by German-speaking people, an equivalent ResourceBundle called MyResources_de might be created like the one shown below:

```
import java.util.*;
import javax.swing.*;
```

```
public class MyResources_de extends ListResourceBundle {
  protected static Object[][] resources = {
      {"WhatIsJava", "Was ist Java?"},
      {"JavaIsLang", "Ist Java eine objektorientierte Programmiersprache?"},
      {"LabelYes", "Ja"},
      {"LabelNo", "Nein"},
      {"FlagIcon", new ImageIcon("flags/germany.gif")}
  };
```

```
  public Object[][] getContents() {
    return resources;
  }
}
```

This definition of a German-language ResourceBundle illustrates an important point. Although it may be possible for all German-speaking users to share the text in this bundle, it's not appropriate for them to share the same flag icon, since the German language is spoken in more than one country. It would not be correct, for example, to display Germany's flag for a user in Switzerland, although it might be appropriate to use the same text resources for both. Fortunately, Java's internationalization capabilities were designed to address this problem easily.

As mentioned earlier, getBundle() creates a ResourceBundle for each of the variations it finds for the specified bundle name. In this case, both MyResources_de.class and MyResources.class will be loaded if a German Locale (for example, Locale.GERMAN or Locale.GERMANY) is the default or is specified explicitly when getBundle() is called. In addition, the bundles are arranged in a logical hierarchy, and if you request a resource that is not found in the "lowest" bundle, the hierarchy will be searched until a bundle is found that does contain the resource. In this case, for example, if you request a resource that is not defined in MyResources_de.class but is defined in MyResources.class, the value from MyResources will be returned.

You can take advantage of this behavior by defining only the resources in a "lower" bundle that should be different from those in a "higher" bundle. For example, to address the issue described earlier of the German flag being returned for Swiss users, it's possible to simply define a new German Swiss (MyResources_de_CH) bundle, like the one shown overleaf:

```
import java.util.*;
import javax.swing.*;

public class MyResources_de_CH extends ListResourceBundle {
  protected static Object[][] resources = {
    {"FlagIcon", new ImageIcon("flags/switzerland.gif")}
  };

  public Object[][] getContents() {
    return resources;
  }
}
```

When a Swiss German bundle is used, the FlagIcon resource will be retrieved from that bundle. Other resources, such as the message text items, will effectively be "inherited" from the MyResources_de bundle because they are not defined in MyResources_de_CH. The results can be seen in the following screenshot:

With the base (MyResources), German (MyResources_de), and Swiss German (MyResources_de_CH) bundle classes created, the JavaQuestion application can be modified to retrieve its resources from a ResourceBundle:

```
import java.util.*;
import javax.swing.*;

public class JavaQuestion {
  protected static ResourceBundle resources =
      ResourceBundle.getBundle("MyResources");

  public static void main(String[] args) {
    ImageIcon flagIcon = (ImageIcon)(resources.getObject("FlagIcon"));
    String[] options =
        {resources.getString("LabelYes"), resources.getString("LabelNo")};
    JOptionPane pane = new JOptionPane(
        resources.getString("JavaIsLang"),
        JOptionPane.QUESTION_MESSAGE,
        0, flagIcon, options);
    JDialog dlg = pane.createDialog(null,
        resources.getString("WhatIsJava"));
    dlg.setModal(true);
    dlg.setVisible(true);
    String selection = (String)(pane.getValue());
    boolean selectedYes = (selection == options[0]);
  }
}
```

PropertyResourceBundle

The `ListResourceBundle` in the previous example included an `ImageIcon`, but in practice, your bundles will often contain only text data. In addition, it's somewhat inconvenient to recompile a `ListResourceBundle` class each time a new resource is added, updated, or deleted. However, in addition to `ListResourceBundle` Java also includes the `PropertyResourceBundle` class, which provides a more convenient way to package text resources.

Specifically, you can create a properties file, which is a flat file containing key/value pairs, with a pair on each line and the key and value separated by an equals (=) sign. For example, you could create a properties file containing the previously defined German messages:

```
WhatIsJava=Was ist Java?
JavaIsLang=Java ist eine objektorientierte Programmiersprache
LabelYes=Ja
LabelNo=Nein
```

Unlike `ListResourceBundle`, you do not need to define a new Java class to use a `PropertyResourceBundle`. Instead, you create a file with a `.properties` extension and add property information like that shown above to it. When you call `getBundle()`, it will search for properties files in addition to `ResourceBundle` subclasses, and `getBundle()` will automatically create a `PropertyResourceBundle` when it finds a `.properties` file. If it doesn't find a match after searching, it will go to the base filename if available. For example, with these messages stored in a file named `ResourceTest_de.properties`, you could access them using the following code:

```
ResourceBundle bundle = ResourceBundle.getBundle(
    "ResourceTest", Locale.GERMAN);
```

Locale-Sensitive Formatting and Parsing

Creating localized messages is only one of the tasks that you must perform to internationalize your applications. You must also ensure that dates, times, and numeric values are formatted appropriately for the `Locale` when displayed, and your applications must be able to parse these data types correctly when they're entered by a user. For example, if you provide a text field that allows a user to enter a date value, you'll typically want to convert the text entered in that field into an instance of `java.util.Date`.

Java provides the ability to format and parse date, time, and numeric values by creating instances of `java.text.NumberFormat` (for numeric values) and `java.text.DateFormat` (for dates and times). Both of those classes provide factory methods that allow you to obtain a formatter for a specified `Locale` or for the default `Locale`. For example, the following five lines of code obtain formatters that use the default `Locale`'s date, time, numeric, currency, and percent conventions respectively:

```
DateFormat dateFormatter = DateFormat.getDateInstance();
DateFormat timeFormatter = DateFormat.getTimeInstance();
NumberFormat numberFormatter = NumberFormat.getNumberInstance();
NumberFormat currencyFormatter = NumberFormat.getCurrencyInstance();
NumberFormat percentFormatter = NumberFormat.getPercentInstance();
```

These `Format` objects actually provide two types of functionality:

❑ First, they allow you to convert the value of a Java object or primitive (for example, an instance of `Date` or a `long` value) into a text string that's formatted according to the conventions of the appropriate `Locale`.

❑ Second, they allow you to perform the opposite type of conversion, where a string (perhaps one entered by your application's user) can be converted into an appropriate object or primitive type.

For example, `DateFormat` converts `java.util.Date` instances into text and can convert a text representation of a date into an instance of `Date`.

Formatting and Parsing Dates

Date values are represented very differently in various locales, even in those that use the same language. As noted earlier, the `mm/dd/yy` format is the most commonly used format in the United States, but much of the rest of the world (including other English-speaking regions) uses `dd/mm/yy` instead.

Even within a single `Locale`, different date formats are often used. For example, each of the following represents a format in which a date might be displayed in the United States:

```
03/19/00
March 19, 2000
Sunday, March 19, 2000
```

To obtain a reference to a `DateFormat` object that can be used to format and parse dates, you can call the static `getDateInstance()` method in the `DateFormat` class. When calling `getDateInstance()`, you can specify a `Locale`, and if you do not do so, a `DateFormat` object is returned that will format dates based on the conventions of your default `Locale`. In addition, `getDateInstance()` allows you to specify a **style**, which is an integer value that's equal to one of four constants defined in `DateFormat`: `SHORT`, `MEDIUM`, `LONG`, or `FULL`. The style value indicates how detailed a description of the date will be produced by the `DateFormat` instance. For example, `SHORT` generates very brief strings (for example, 03/19/00), while `MEDIUM`, `LONG`, and `FULL` each provide increasingly more detailed date representations (for example, `FULL` generates Sunday, March 19, 2000). In the following sections, you'll get to see by example what effect each of these constants has on the output.

Formatting Dates

Once you have created an instance of `DateFormat`, you can use it to convert the value of a `java.util.Date` instance into a text string by calling the `DateFormat`'s `format()` method. The following code segment creates a LONG-style `DateFormat` that will use the conventions that are appropriate for the predefined FRANCE `Locale` and uses the `Dateformat` object to display the current date:

```
DateFormat formatter = DateFormat.getDateInstance(DateFormat.LONG, Locale.FRANCE);
System.out.println(formatter.format(new java.util.Date()));
```

Running this code segment will produce this output line:

```
14 novembre 2000
```

DateFormat Example

To illustrate the different date styles and the large number of locales that Java supports, you can compile and run the following application, which produces an interface like the one shown in the screenshot after the code:

```java
import java.awt.*;
import java.awt.event.*;
import java.text.*;
import java.util.*;
import javax.swing.*;
import javax.swing.border.*;
import javax.swing.table.*;

public class DateViewer extends JPanel {
  protected JTextField valueField;
  protected JRadioButton shortButton;
  protected JRadioButton mediumButton;
  protected JRadioButton longButton;
  protected JRadioButton fullButton;

  protected AbstractTableModel tableModel;

  protected Date selectedDate = new Date();

  protected final static Locale[] availableLocales;

  static {
    availableLocales = Locale.getAvailableLocales();
  }

  public final static int LOCALE_COLUMN = 0;
  public final static int SHORT_COLUMN = 1;
  public final static int MEDIUM_COLUMN = 2;
  public final static int LONG_COLUMN = 3;
  public final static int FULL_COLUMN = 4;

  public final static String[] columnHeaders =
              {"Locale", "Short", "Medium", "Long", "Full"};

  // Create the window for the Date viewer,
  // and make it fit the later components
  public static void main(String[] args) {
    JFrame f = new JFrame("Date Viewer");
    f.setDefaultCloseOperation(JFrame.EXIT_ON_CLOSE);
    f.getContentPane().add(new DateViewer());
    f.pack();
    f.setVisible(true);
  }

  // Make the window contain a panel
  // and a table, which are defined next
  public DateViewer() {
    setLayout(new GridBagLayout());
    GridBagConstraints gbc = new GridBagConstraints();
    gbc.gridx = 0;
```

```
      gbc.insets = new Insets(5, 10, 5, 10);

      JPanel panel = getSelectionPanel();
      add(panel, gbc);

      gbc.weightx = 1;
      gbc.weighty = 1;
      gbc.fill = GridBagConstraints.BOTH;
      tableModel = new LocaleTableModel();
      JTable table = new JTable(tableModel);
      add(new JScrollPane(table), gbc);

      refreshTable();
    }

    // Create a panel with buttons to select date format
    protected JPanel getSelectionPanel() {
      JPanel panel = new JPanel();
      panel.setLayout(new GridBagLayout());
      GridBagConstraints gbc = new GridBagConstraints();
      gbc.insets = new Insets(5, 10, 5, 10);
      gbc.gridy = 0;
      JLabel label = new JLabel("Selected date:", JLabel.LEFT);
      panel.add(label, gbc);
      valueField = new JTextField(20);
      valueField.addActionListener(new ActionListener() {
        public void actionPerformed(ActionEvent event) {
          refreshTable();
        }
      });
      valueField.setMinimumSize(valueField.getPreferredSize());
      panel.add(valueField, gbc);
      JButton btn = new JButton("Refresh");
      btn.addActionListener(new ActionListener() {
        public void actionPerformed(ActionEvent event) {
          refreshTable();
        }
      });
      panel.add(btn, gbc);

      // Add the format buttons to the panel
      gbc.gridy++;
      JPanel innerPanel = new JPanel();
      innerPanel.setLayout(new GridLayout(1, 4, 10, 0));

      shortButton = new JRadioButton("Short", true);
      innerPanel.add(shortButton);

      mediumButton = new JRadioButton("Medium");
      innerPanel.add(mediumButton);

      longButton = new JRadioButton("Long");
      innerPanel.add(longButton);

      fullButton = new JRadioButton("Full");
```

```
    innerPanel.add(fullButton);

    ButtonGroup bg = new ButtonGroup();
    bg.add(shortButton);
    bg.add(mediumButton);
    bg.add(longButton);
    bg.add(fullButton);

    gbc.gridwidth = GridBagConstraints.REMAINDER;
    panel.add(innerPanel, gbc);

    BevelBorder bb = new BevelBorder(BevelBorder.RAISED);
    Locale locale = Locale.getDefault();
    TitledBorder tb = new TitledBorder(bb, locale.getDisplayName());
    panel.setBorder(tb);

    return panel;
  }

  protected void refreshTable() {
    int style = DateFormat.SHORT;

    // Work out which button is selected
    if (shortButton.isSelected()) {
      style = DateFormat.SHORT;
    }
    else if (mediumButton.isSelected()) {
      style = DateFormat.MEDIUM;
    }
    else if (longButton.isSelected()) {
      style = DateFormat.LONG;
    }
    else if (fullButton.isSelected()) {
      style = DateFormat.FULL;
    }
    // and format the date in the value field
    DateFormat parser = DateFormat.getDateInstance(style);
    try {
      selectedDate = parser.parse(valueField.getText());
      tableModel.fireTableDataChanged();
    }
    catch (ParseException nfe) {
      valueField.setText(parser.format(selectedDate));
    }
  }

  // Create a table of international date formats
  class LocaleTableModel extends AbstractTableModel {
    public int getRowCount() {
      return availableLocales.length;
    }

    public int getColumnCount() {
      return columnHeaders.length;
    }
```

```java
public Object getValueAt(int row, int column) {
  Locale locale = availableLocales[row];
  DateFormat formatter = DateFormat.getInstance();

  //For each column in the table, get the date in the right format
  switch (column) {
    case LOCALE_COLUMN:
      return locale.getDisplayName();
    case SHORT_COLUMN:
      formatter = DateFormat.getDateInstance(DateFormat.SHORT, locale);
      break;
    case MEDIUM_COLUMN:
      formatter = DateFormat.getDateInstance(DateFormat.MEDIUM, locale);
      break;
    case LONG_COLUMN:
      formatter = DateFormat.getDateInstance(DateFormat.LONG, locale);
      break;
    case FULL_COLUMN:
      formatter = DateFormat.getDateInstance(DateFormat.FULL, locale);
  }
  return formatter.format(selectedDate);
}

public String getColumnName(int column) {
  return columnHeaders[column];
}
}
}
```

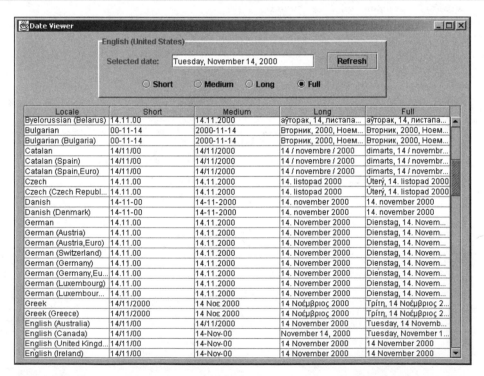

Parsing Dates

Just as you'll want your application to display dates according to the local conventions, you'll also want it to be able to convert a date string entered by a user into an instance of `java.util.Date`. To convert a string representation of a date into an instance of `Date`, simply create an instance of `DateFormat` and use its `parse()` method as shown below:

```
public static void main(String[] args) throws ParseException {
  DateFormat formatter = DateFormat.getDateInstance(DateFormat.SHORT);
  java.util.Date dateValue = formatter.parse(args[0]);
  System.out.println(dateValue);
}
```

Note that a `ParseException` is thrown if the date string passed to the `parse()` method does not represent a valid date as defined by the appropriate `Locale`'s formatting conventions. There will also potentially be an `ArrayIndexOutOfBoundsException` thrown if no argument is provided.

Parsing and DateFormat's Leniency Mode

As mentioned earlier, you can use instances of `DateFormat` to convert `String` representations of date and time values into instances of `Date`. For example, the following application converts the first command-line parameter into a `Date` value using the `SHORT` form of the default `Locale`'s date formatting conventions:

```
import java.text.*;
import java.util.Date;

public class DateTest {
  public static void main(String[] args) throws ParseException {
    DateFormat formatter = DateFormat.getDateInstance(DateFormat.SHORT);
    Date theDate = formatter.parse(args[0]);
    System.out.println(theDate);
  }
}
```

In most cases, entering an invalid date string will result in the `parse()` method throwing a `ParseException`. However, in some versions of Java, you can enter text that does not represent a valid date without an exception being thrown. For example, you might execute the application as shown below while using the Java 1.1 core classes:

```
java DateTest 02/09/hello
```

Depending upon the version of Java you're using, the invalid date (`02/09/hello`) may incorrectly produce the results shown below:

```
Mon Feb 09 00:00:00 CST 0001
```

In this case, the invalid year (`hello`) was converted to a value of `0001`. This occurs because the `DateFormat`'s leniency mode is enabled, which causes it to attempt to "guess" what date the `String` was intended to represent.

In most cases, you'll want DateFormat's parse() method to both convert and validate the date that was entered. In other words, the main purpose of parse() is to convert a String into a Date, but it's also responsible for ensuring that the text it converts represents a valid date. However, the above code segment may fail to correctly notify your application (by throwing a ParseException) that the date was invalid. To ensure that it does so, you can call the setLenient() method as shown below, specifying that lenient parsing of dates should be disabled:

```java
import java.text.*;
import java.util.Date;

public class DateTest {
   public static void main(String[] args) throws ParseException {
      DateFormat formatter = DateFormat.getDateInstance(DateFormat.SHORT);
      formatter.setLenient(false);
      Date theDate = formatter.parse(args[0]);
      System.out.println(theDate);
   }
}
```

Formatting and Parsing Times

If you wish to format and/or parse time values instead of dates, you can use the getTimeInstance() factory method defined in DateFormat as in the following code segment:

```java
DateFormat formatter = DateFormat.getTimeInstance();
```

Like getDateInstance(), the getTimeInstance() method allows you to specify a style (and optionally a Locale), and the different combinations are illustrated in the next screenshot, which is produced by running the following application.

Time Viewer

English (United States)

Selected date: `9:56:47 AM GMT+00:00`   **Refresh**

○ Short   ○ Medium   ○ Long   ● Full

Locale	Short	Medium	Long	Full
Catalan	09:56	09:56:47	09:56:47 GMT+00:00	09:56:47 GMT+00:00
Catalan (Spain)	09:56	09:56:47	09:56:47 GMT+00:00	09:56:47 GMT+00:00
Catalan (Spain,Euro)	09:56	09:56:47	09:56:47 GMT+00:00	09:56:47 GMT+00:00
Czech	9:56	9:56:47	9:56:47 GMT+00:00	9:56:47 GMT+00:00
Czech (Czech Repu...	9:56	9:56:47	9:56:47 GMT+00:00	9:56:47 GMT+00:00
Danish	09:56	09:56:47	09:56:47 GMT+00:00	09:56:47 GMT+00:00
Danish (Denmark)	09:56	09:56:47	09:56:47 GMT+00:00	09:56:47 GMT+00:00
German	09:56	09:56:47	09:56:47 GMT+00:00	9.56 Uhr GMT+00:00
German (Austria)	09:56	09:56:47	09:56:47 GMT+00:00	09:56 Uhr GMT+00:...
German (Austria,Eu...	09:56	09:56:47	09:56:47 GMT+00:00	09:56 Uhr GMT+00:...
German (Switzerlan...	09:56	09:56:47	09:56:47 GMT+00:00	9.56 Uhr GMT+00:00
German (Germany)	09:56	09:56:47	09:56:47 GMT+00:00	9.56 Uhr GMT+00:00
German (Germany,...	09:56	09:56:47	09:56:47 GMT+00:00	9.56 Uhr GMT+00:00
German (Luxembo...	09:56	09:56:47	09:56:47 GMT+00:00	9.56 Uhr GMT+00:00
German (Luxembo...	09:56	09:56:47	09:56:47 GMT+00:00	9.56 Uhr GMT+00:00
Greek	9:56 πμ	9:56:47 πμ	9:56:47 πμ GMT+00...	9:56:47 πμ GMT+0...
Greek (Greece)	9:56 πμ	9:56:47 πμ	9:56:47 πμ GMT+00...	9:56:47 πμ GMT+0...
English (Australia)	09:56	09:56:47	9:56:47	09:56:47 AM GMT+...
English (Canada)	9:56 AM	9:56:47 AM	9:56:47 GMT+00:00...	9:56:47 o'clock AM ...
English (United Kin...	09:56	09:56:47	09:56:47 GMT	09:56:47 o'clock GMT
English (Ireland)	09:56	09:56:47	09:56:47 GMT	09:56:47 o'clock GMT
English (Ireland,Eu...	09:56	09:56:47	09:56:47 GMT	09:56:47 o'clock GMT
English (New Zeala...	09:56	09:56:47	9:56:47	09:56:47 AM GMT+...
English (South Afric...	09:56	09:56:47	09:56:47	09:56:47 AM
Spanish	9:56	9:56:47	9:56:47 GMT+00:00	09H56' GMT+00:00
Spanish (Argentina)	09:56	09:56:47	9:56:47 GMT+00:00	09h'56 GMT+00:00
Spanish (Bolivia)	09:56 AM	09:56:47 AM	09:56:47 AM GMT+...	09:56:47 AM GMT+...

```java
import java.awt.*;
import java.awt.event.*;
import java.text.*;
import java.util.*;
import javax.swing.*;
import javax.swing.border.*;
import javax.swing.table.*;

public class TimeViewer extends JPanel {
  protected JTextField valueField;
  protected JRadioButton shortButton;
  protected JRadioButton mediumButton;
  protected JRadioButton longButton;
  protected JRadioButton fullButton;

  protected AbstractTableModel tableModel;

  protected Date selectedDate = new Date();

  protected final static Locale[] availableLocales;

  static {
    availableLocales = Locale.getAvailableLocales();
  }

  public final static int LOCALE_COLUMN = 0;
  public final static int SHORT_COLUMN = 1;
  public final static int MEDIUM_COLUMN = 2;
  public final static int LONG_COLUMN = 3;
  public final static int FULL_COLUMN = 4;

  public final static String[] columnHeaders =
      {"Locale", "Short", "Medium", "Long", "Full"};

  // Create the window for the Time viewer,
  // and make sure that later components will fit
  public static void main(String[] args) {
    JFrame f = new JFrame("Time Viewer");
    f.setDefaultCloseOperation(JFrame.EXIT_ON_CLOSE);
    f.getContentPane().add(new TimeViewer());
    f.pack();
    f.setVisible(true);
  }

  // Make the window contain a panel
  // and a table, which are defined next
  public TimeViewer() {
    setLayout(new GridBagLayout());
    GridBagConstraints gbc = new GridBagConstraints();
    gbc.gridx = 0;
    gbc.insets = new Insets(5, 10, 5, 10);

    JPanel panel = getSelectionPanel();
    add(panel, gbc);

    gbc.weightx = 1;
```

```
      gbc.weighty = 1;
      gbc.fill = GridBagConstraints.BOTH;
      tableModel = new LocaleTableModel();
      JTable table = new JTable(tableModel);
      add(new JScrollPane(table), gbc);

      refreshTable();
   }

   // Create a panel with buttons to select time format
   protected JPanel getSelectionPanel()    {
      JPanel panel = new JPanel();
      panel.setLayout(new GridBagLayout());
      GridBagConstraints gbc = new GridBagConstraints();
      gbc.insets = new Insets(5, 10, 5, 10);
      gbc.gridy = 0;
      JLabel label = new JLabel("Selected date:", JLabel.LEFT);
      panel.add(label, gbc);
      valueField = new JTextField(20);
      valueField.addActionListener(new ActionListener() {
        public void actionPerformed(ActionEvent event) {
          refreshTable();
        }
      });
      valueField.setMinimumSize(valueField.getPreferredSize());
      panel.add(valueField, gbc);
      JButton btn = new JButton("Refresh");
      btn.addActionListener(new ActionListener() {
        public void actionPerformed(ActionEvent event) {
          refreshTable();
        }
      });
      panel.add(btn, gbc);

      // Add the format buttons to the panel
      gbc.gridy++;
      JPanel innerPanel = new JPanel();
      innerPanel.setLayout(new GridLayout(1, 4, 10, 0));

      shortButton = new JRadioButton("Short", true);
      innerPanel.add(shortButton);

      mediumButton = new JRadioButton("Medium");
      innerPanel.add(mediumButton);

      longButton = new JRadioButton("Long");
      innerPanel.add(longButton);

      fullButton = new JRadioButton("Full");
      innerPanel.add(fullButton);

      ButtonGroup bg = new ButtonGroup();
      bg.add(shortButton);
      bg.add(mediumButton);
      bg.add(longButton);
```

```
    bg.add(fullButton);

    gbc.gridwidth = GridBagConstraints.REMAINDER;
    panel.add(innerPanel, gbc);

    BevelBorder bb = new BevelBorder(BevelBorder.RAISED);
    Locale locale = Locale.getDefault();
    TitledBorder tb = new TitledBorder(bb, locale.getDisplayName());
    panel.setBorder(tb);

    return panel;
}

protected void refreshTable() {
  int style = DateFormat.SHORT;

  // Work out which button is selected
  if (shortButton.isSelected()) {
    style = DateFormat.SHORT;
  }
  else if (mediumButton.isSelected()) {
    style = DateFormat.MEDIUM;
  }
  else if (longButton.isSelected()) {
    style = DateFormat.LONG;
  }
  else if (fullButton.isSelected()) {
    style = DateFormat.FULL;
  }
  // and format the time in the value field
  DateFormat parser = DateFormat.getTimeInstance(style);
  try {
    selectedDate = parser.parse(valueField.getText());
    tableModel.fireTableDataChanged();
  }
  catch (ParseException nfe) {
    valueField.setText(parser.format(selectedDate));
  }
}

// Create a table of international time formats
class LocaleTableModel extends AbstractTableModel {
  public int getRowCount() {
    return availableLocales.length;
  }

  public int getColumnCount() {
    return columnHeaders.length;
  }

  public Object getValueAt(int row, int column) {
    Locale locale = availableLocales[row];
    DateFormat formatter = DateFormat.getInstance();

    //For each column in the table, get the time in the right format
```

```
        switch (column) {
          case LOCALE_COLUMN:
            return locale.getDisplayName();
          case SHORT_COLUMN:
            formatter = DateFormat.getTimeInstance(DateFormat.SHORT, locale);
            break;
          case MEDIUM_COLUMN:
            formatter = DateFormat.getTimeInstance(DateFormat.MEDIUM, locale);
            break;
          case LONG_COLUMN:
            formatter = DateFormat.getTimeInstance(DateFormat.LONG, locale);
            break;
          case FULL_COLUMN:
            formatter = DateFormat.getTimeInstance( DateFormat.FULL,locale);
        }
        return formatter.format(selectedDate);
      }

      public String getColumnName(int column) {
        return columnHeaders[column];
      }
    }
  }
```

Formatting and Parsing Numeric Values

While DateFormat allows you to format and parse date and time values, NumberFormat allows you to format and parse numeric values. In this context, "numeric values" refers collectively to plain numeric values as well as currency and percentage values, although a different factory method is provided for each of the three types. To obtain a reference to a formatter/parser for plain numeric data, use the getNumberInstance() method in NumberFormat. As with DateFormat, you can specify a Locale, but NumberFormat does not support different styles.

NumberFormat provides format() methods that can be passed either a long or double value, so you can pass any numeric primitive type to those methods for formatting. For example, given the following code segment:

```
NumberFormat formatter = NumberFormat.getNumberInstance(Locale.US);
System.out.println(formatter.format(123456.78));
```

Executing that code will produce the following output:

```
123,456.78
```

There is not as much variation in the way that numbers are formatted around the world as there is variation in how dates and times are displayed, but there are some differences. For example, the United States and many other countries use the period (.) to represent the decimal point and commas (,) or a space to separate every three characters to the left of the decimal. However, other countries (for example, Germany) reverse the meaning of these two characters, using the comma to represent the decimal point and the period as the digit separator. For example, suppose that you modify the previous code segment as follows:

```
NumberFormat formatter = NumberFormat.getNumberInstance(Locale.GERMANY);
System.out.println(formatter.format(123456.78));
```

Executing this code will produce the output shown below:

```
123.456,78
```

Like DateFormat instances, NumberFormat objects can be used for both formatting and parsing, and while DateFormat's parse() method returns an instance of java.util.Date, NumberFormat's parse() returns an instance of java.lang.Number. However, Number provides convenience methods that allow you to retrieve the encapsulated value as any primitive type, so it's easy to convert a numeric String into a given type. For example, you could use the following code segment to convert the first command-line parameter into an int value:

```
public static void main(String[] args) throws ParseException {
   NumberFormat formatter = NumberFormat.getNumberInstance();
   int value = formatter.parse(args[0]).intValue();  System.out.println(value);
}
```

With Locale set to GERMANY, this code will take the figure 123,45 and return 123. As with DateFormat, NumberFormat's parse() method will throw a ParseException if the string that's parsed does not represent a valid number.

NumberFormat Example

As illustrated by the following application, the conventions used for percentage and plain numeric values do not vary much from one Locale to the next, but in contrast, the conventions used for currency values vary widely:

Locale	Numeric	Currency	Percent
Catalan	1.234.567,89	¤ 1.234.567,89	123.456.789%
Catalan (Spain)	1.234.567,89	Pts 1.234.568	123.456.789%
Catalan (Spain,Euro)	1.234.567,89	€ 1.234.567,89	123.456.789%
Czech	1 234 567,89	¤ 1 234 567,89	123 456 789%
Czech (Czech Repu...	1 234 567,89	1 234 567,89 Kč	123 456 789%
Danish	1.234.567,89	¤ 1.234.567,89	123.456.789%
Danish (Denmark)	1.234.567,89	kr 1.234.567,89	123.456.789%
German	1.234.567,89	¤ 1.234.567,89	123.456.789%
German (Austria)	1.234.567,89	öS 1.234.567,89	123.456.789%
German (Austria,Eur...	1.234.567,89	€ 1.234.567,89	123.456.789%
German (Switzerland)	1'234'567.89	SFr. 1'234'567.89	123'456'789%
German (Germany)	1.234.567,89	1.234.567,89 DM	123.456.789%
German (Germany,E...	1.234.567,89	1.234.567,89 €	123.456.789%
German (Luxembou...	1.234.567,89	1.234.567,89 F	123.456.789%
German (Luxembou...	1.234.567,89	1.234.567,89 €	123.456.789%
Greek	1.234.567,89	¤ 1.234.567,89	123.456.789%
Greek (Greece)	1.234.567,89	1.234.567,89 δρχ	123.456.789%
English (Australia)	1,234,567.89	$1,234,567.89	123,456,789%
English (Canada)	1,234,567.89	$1,234,567.89	123,456,789%
English (United King...	1,234,567.89	£1,234,567.89	123,456,789%
English (Ireland)	1,234,567.89	IR£1,234,567.89	123,456,789%
English (Ireland,Euro)	1,234,567.89	€1,234,567.89	123,456,789%
English (New Zeala...	1,234,567.89	$1,234,567.89	123,456,789%
English (South Africa)	1,234,567.89	R 1,234,567.89	123,456,789%
Spanish	1.234.567,89	¤1.234.567,09	123.456.789%

```java
import java.awt.*;
import java.awt.event.*;
import java.text.*;
import java.util.*;
import javax.swing.*;
import javax.swing.border.*;
import javax.swing.table.*;

public class NumberViewer extends JPanel {
  protected JTextField valueField;
  protected JRadioButton numberButton;
  protected JRadioButton currencyButton;
  protected JRadioButton percentButton;

  protected AbstractTableModel tableModel;

  protected double currentValue = 1234567.89d;

  protected final static Locale[] availableLocales;

  static {
    availableLocales = Locale.getAvailableLocales();
  }

  public final static int LOCALE_COLUMN = 0;
  public final static int NUMBER_COLUMN = 1;
  public final static int CURRENCY_COLUMN = 2;
  public final static int PERCENT_COLUMN = 3;

  public final static String[] columnHeaders =
        {"Locale", "Numeric", "Currency", "Percent"};

  // Create a window for the number viewer
  // and make sure that later components will fit
  public static void main(String[] args) {
    JFrame f = new JFrame("Number Viewer");
    f.setDefaultCloseOperation(JFrame.EXIT_ON_CLOSE);
    f.getContentPane().add(new NumberViewer());
    f.pack();
    f.setVisible(true);
  }

  // Make the window contain a panel
  // and a table, which are defined next
  public NumberViewer() {
    setLayout(new GridBagLayout());
    GridBagConstraints gbc = new GridBagConstraints();
    gbc.gridx = 0;
    gbc.insets = new Insets(5, 10, 5, 10);

    JPanel panel = getSelectionPanel();
    add(panel, gbc);

    gbc.weightx = 1;
    gbc.weighty = 1;
    gbc.fill = GridBagConstraints.BOTH;
```

```
      tableModel = new LocaleTableModel();
      JTable table = new JTable(tableModel);
      add(new JScrollPane(table), gbc);

      refreshTable();
   }

   // Create a panel with buttons to select number format
   protected JPanel getSelectionPanel() {
      JPanel panel = new JPanel();
      panel.setLayout(new GridBagLayout());
      GridBagConstraints gbc = new GridBagConstraints();
      gbc.insets = new Insets(5, 10, 5, 10);
      gbc.gridy = 0;
      JLabel label = new JLabel("Current value:", JLabel.LEFT);
      panel.add(label, gbc);
      valueField = new JTextField(12);
      valueField.addActionListener(new ActionListener() {
         public void actionPerformed(ActionEvent event) {
            refreshTable();
         }
      });
      valueField.setMinimumSize(valueField.getPreferredSize());
      panel.add(valueField, gbc);
      JButton btn = new JButton("Refresh");
      btn.addActionListener(new ActionListener() {
         public void actionPerformed(ActionEvent event) {
            refreshTable();
         }
      });
      panel.add(btn, gbc);

      // Add the format buttons to the panel
      gbc.gridy++;
      JPanel innerPanel = new JPanel();
      innerPanel.setLayout(new GridLayout(1, 3, 10, 0));

      numberButton = new JRadioButton("Numeric", true);
      innerPanel.add(numberButton);

      currencyButton = new JRadioButton("Currency");
      innerPanel.add(currencyButton);

      percentButton = new JRadioButton("Percent");
      innerPanel.add(percentButton);

      ButtonGroup bg = new ButtonGroup();
      bg.add(numberButton);
      bg.add(currencyButton);
      bg.add(percentButton);

      gbc.gridwidth = GridBagConstraints.REMAINDER;
      panel.add(innerPanel, gbc);

      BevelBorder bb = new BevelBorder(BevelBorder.RAISED);
```

939

```
   Locale locale = Locale.getDefault();
   TitledBorder tb = new TitledBorder(bb, locale.getDisplayName());
   panel.setBorder(tb);

   return panel;
}

protected void refreshTable() {
   NumberFormat parser = NumberFormat.getInstance();

   // Work out which button is selected
   if (numberButton.isSelected()) {
     parser = NumberFormat.getNumberInstance();
   }
   else if (currencyButton.isSelected()) {
     parser = NumberFormat.getCurrencyInstance();
   }
   else if (percentButton.isSelected()) {
     parser = NumberFormat.getPercentInstance();
   }
   // and format the number in the value field
   try {
     currentValue = parser.parse(valueField.getText()).doubleValue();
     tableModel.fireTableDataChanged();
   }
   catch (ParseException nfe) {
     valueField.setText(parser.format(currentValue));
   }
}

// Create a table of international number formats
class LocaleTableModel extends AbstractTableModel {
   public int getRowCount() {
     return availableLocales.length;
   }

   public int getColumnCount() {
     return columnHeaders.length;
   }

   public Object getValueAt(int row, int column) {
     Locale locale = availableLocales[row];
     NumberFormat formatter = NumberFormat.getNumberInstance();
     // For each column in the table, get the number in the right format
     switch (column) {
       case LOCALE_COLUMN:
         return locale.getDisplayName();
       case NUMBER_COLUMN:
         formatter = NumberFormat.getNumberInstance(locale);
         break;
       case CURRENCY_COLUMN:
         formatter = NumberFormat.getCurrencyInstance(locale);
         break;
       case PERCENT_COLUMN:
         formatter = NumberFormat.getPercentInstance(locale);
```

```
        break;
    }
    return formatter.format(currentValue);
}

public String getColumnName(int column) {
    return columnHeaders[column];
}
}
}
```

MessageFormat

The `ResourceBundle` class provides a convenient way to encapsulate messages, but it's often necessary to insert strings inside those messages before displaying them. For example, suppose that you wish to display a message describing the number of users who are logged on to an application. You might display a message like the one shown below, changing the integer at the beginning of the message to display the appropriate numeric value:

```
10 users are currently logged on.
```

On the surface, it may seem that you can simply define the non-numeric portion of the text in a message and append it to the number of users. For example:

```
ResourceBundle bundle;
int userCount;
// ...

// The ResourceBundle includes a CurrentUsers key that's associated with
// the message shown below:
//
//     users are currently logged on.
//
String msgText = (String)(bundle.getObject("CurrentUsers"));
System.out.println(userCount + msgText);
```

The problem with this approach is that when the `"users are currently logged on"` text is translated to another language, it may not be grammatically correct to simply append the message text to the numeric value. For example, the equivalent message in Spanish would be:

```
Entran a 10 utilizadores actualmente.
```

One way of addressing this would be to break the message into two segments: one that represents the text that should precede the numeric value and the other containing the text that follows it. In the English `ResourceBundle`, the text that precedes the value would be empty, while the Spanish version would be assigned a value of `"Entran a "`. However, that approach would require you to define multiple resources for each message that contains substitution parameters (for example, the numeric value). Splitting a single message into multiple resources would make your code more confusing and make the `ResourceBundle` file maintenance (updating and deleting messages) more tedious and error-prone. Fortunately, Java provides the `java.text.MessageFormat` class that allows you to format messages with substitution parameters. It does this by allowing you to format strings into pattern strings at the places you specify in your code.

To use MessageFormat, simply create an instance using the constructor that accepts a single String parameter. That String should represent message text with substitution parameters identified by numeric values in braces, as shown below:

```
{0} users are currently logged on.
```

To format this message properly, you must construct an array of objects and pass that array to the format() method of the MessageFormat you created. When you do so, the substitution parameter values embedded in the message text will be replaced by a String representation of the corresponding object in the array. In this case, there is only a single substitution parameter with a value of zero (0), so you can construct an array that contains a single object representing the number of users that are logged on:

```
Object[] values = {new Integer(userCount)};
```

The zero (0) value in the message identifies the index of the array element that should be placed in the substitution field, which in this case is an Integer representing the user count.

You can pass the array of values to the format() method and it will produce a String representing the message text with the substitution parameter values embedded within it. For example, suppose that you have defined a properties file like the one shown below that's suitable for use by a PropertyResourceBundle:

```
CurrentUsers={0} users are currently logged on.
```

To format this text with the substitution parameter, simply create an instance of MessageFormat and call its format() method, passing an array of objects that should be used for the substitution parameters. In this case, a single parameter is specified, so the array need only contain a single Object, and any additional instances are ignored:

```
ResourceBundle bundle = ResourceBundle.getBundle("FormatMessages");
int userCount;
// ...

String msgText = (String)(bundle.getObject("CurrentUsers"));
MessageFormat msgFormat = new MessageFormat(msgText);
Object[] values = {new Integer(userCount)};
System.out.println(msgFormat.format(values));
```

If the value of userCount is 15, the code segment shown above will produce the following output:

```
15 users are currently logged on.
```

Since it allows you to dynamically construct messages based on their substitution parameters, MessageFormat allows you to avoid creating code that's specific to a Locale. For example, when a Spanish equivalent of the ResourceBundle is created, the substitution parameter can simply be moved to the appropriate location within the message:

```
Entran a {0} utilizadores actualmente.
```

In effect, MessageFormat shifts the responsibility for creating grammatically correct output from the Java programmer to the person that provides message translation.

A single substitution parameter was used in this example, but it's equally simple to specify multiple parameters when using MessageFormat. For example, you might wish to create a message with the following text:

```
$123.40 was deposited at 10:49 AM on March 21, 2000.
```

In this case, a currency value, date, and time are included in the message output and the date and time should be derived from a single instance of java.util.Date. To accomplish this, you might initially create a message like the one shown below:

```
Deposit={0} was deposited at {1} on {1}.
```

Note that the second object in the array is referenced twice in this message, and in fact, MessageFormat allows you to use an object as many times as you wish. In addition, there's no requirement that you must use each object in the array within the message, so it's valid for the array to contain extraneous objects. In this example, there's no reason to add elements to the array that aren't used in the message, but in practice, you may want to format() an array that's used for other purposes within your application.

Given the message defined above, you could create code like the following to display the message:

```
ResourceBundle bundle = ResourceBundle.getBundle("FormatMessages");
float depositAmount = 123.4f;
// ...

String msgText = (String)(bundle.getObject("Deposit"));
MessageFormat msgFormat = new MessageFormat(msgText);
Object[] values = {new Float(depositAmount), new java.util.Date()};
System.out.println(msgFormat.format(values));
```

However, executing this code does not produce the desired results, but instead produces output similar to that shown below:

```
123.4 was deposited at 3/21/00 10:49 AM on 3/21/00 10:49 AM.
```

This occurs because the message text defined earlier does not contain any information that specifies how the data should be formatted. When you do not do so, the default Locale's formatting styles for numbers and date/time values are used. However, MessageFormat allows you to provide information within the message text that describes how the values should be formatted. For example, you could make the following changes to display the first parameter as a currency value, the second parameter as a SHORT-style time, and the third as a LONG-style date:

```
Deposit={0,number,currency} was deposited at {1,time,short} on {1,date,long}.
```

Making this modification to the message text results in the output being correctly formatted as shown below:

```
$123.40 was deposited at 10:49 AM on March 21, 2000.
```

The second item that can be specified in the substitution field is referred to as the **element format**, and must be one of the following: time, date, number, or choice. The third item is the **element style**, and must be short, medium, long, or full for date/time values or currency, percent, or integer for numeric values. The choice element format is useful when the message text that should be displayed is dependent upon the value of the substitution parameter, and a description of how to use choice is provided later in this chapter.

Specifying a Locale

When you create an instance of MessageFormat, it uses the default Locale to format the substitution values using instances of DateFormat, NumberFormat, and ChoiceFormat. For example, if the default Locale is equal to Locale.US, date and time values are formatted using United States formatting conventions, but you can change the Locale used by a MessageFormat instance by calling its setLocale() method. However, once you have modified the Locale, you must re-apply the message pattern, using applyPattern() as shown below:

```
ResourceBundle bundle = ResourceBundle.getBundle("FormatMessages");
float depositAmount = 123.4f;
// ...

String msgText = (String)(bundle.getObject("Deposit"));
MessageFormat msgFormat = new MessageFormat(msgText);
msgFormat.setLocale(Locale.FRANCE);
msgFormat.applyPattern(msgFormat.toPattern());
Object[] values = {new Float(depositAmount), new java.util.Date()};
System.out.println(msgFormat.format(values));
```

This code displays the same message shown earlier, but it uses French currency and date/time formatting conventions as shown below:

```
F123,40 was deposited at 10:49 AM on mars 21, 2000.
```

Specifying a Format Object

When you specify a Date object as a parameter, MessageFormat creates an instance of DateFormat that it uses to convert the Date's value to a String. Similarly, numeric values are formatted using instances of NumberFormat that are constructed automatically.

In most cases, it's appropriate to allow MessageFormat to construct DateFormat, NumberFormat, and ChoiceFormat objects for you. However, you'll sometimes wish to construct one explicitly and have it used by MessageFormat. For example, you might want to change the code shown above so that it displays dates using Italian formatting standards while still allowing other fields to be formatted using the default Locale. To accomplish this, you could use the setFormat() method as shown below:

```
ResourceBundle bundle = ResourceBundle.getBundle("FormatMessages");
float depositAmount = 123.4f;
// ...

String msgText = (String)(bundle.getObject("Deposit"));
MessageFormat msgFormat = new MessageFormat(msgText);
DateFormat timeFormat = DateFormat.getTimeInstance(
```

```
        DateFormat.LONG, Locale.ITALY);
    msgFormat.setFormat(1, timeFormat);
    DateFormat dateFormat = DateFormat.getDateInstance(
        DateFormat.LONG, Locale.ITALY);
    msgFormat.setFormat(2, dateFormat);
    Object[] values = {new Float(depositAmount), new java.util.Date()};
    System.out.println(msgFormat.format(values));
```

If your default `Locale` is equal to `Locale.US`, the output from this code segment will appear like that shown below:

```
$123.40 was deposited at 9.46.22 CST on 22 marzo 2000.
```

> Note that the index value specified on **setFormat()** corresponds to the index of a substitution field, *not* a substitution value. In other words, that index identifies the zero-based location of the substitution field within the message, where the first field corresponds to a value of zero, the second to a value of one, etc. This should not be confused with the values within the substitution fields themselves (for example, {0}, {1}, etc.), which represent indices into the array of parameter values.

In addition to the `setFormat()` method, `MessageFormat` also provides `setFormats()`, which allows you to specify an array of `Format` objects (for example, instances of `NumberFormat` or `DateFormat`). For example, the code segment below produces the same output as the previous one, but it uses a slightly different approach. It retrieves the array of `Format` objects built by the `MessageFormat` instance and overrides the second and third substitution formats with instances that use the `Locale` for Italy:

```
ResourceBundle bundle = ResourceBundle.getBundle("FormatMessages");
float depositAmount = 123.4f;
// ...
String msgText = (String)(bundle.getObject("Deposit"));
MessageFormat msgFormat = new MessageFormat(msgText);
Format[] formats = msgFormat.getFormats();
formats[1] = DateFormat.getTimeInstance(DateFormat.LONG, Locale.ITALY);
formats[2] = DateFormat.getDateInstance(DateFormat.LONG, Locale.ITALY);
msgFormat.setFormats(formats);
Object[] values = {new Float(depositAmount), new java.util.Date()};
System.out.println(msgFormat.format(values));
```

ChoiceFormat

When creating a message that contains a numeric value, it's often not sufficient to simply insert the number into the message, because the text may be grammatically incorrect for some values. For example, the message described earlier that identifies the number of logged on users can display each of the following:

```
0 users are currently logged on.
1 users are currently logged on.
2 users are currently logged on.
```

Notice that the message produced when a single user is logged on ("1 users are currently logged on.") is grammatically incorrect. In addition, a better message for the case where there are zero users would be "No users are currently logged on." Attempting to produce these results by modifying the Java source code would result in the same type of Locale-specific coding that appeared earlier, but the ChoiceFormat class provides a solution to this problem.

To create an instance of ChoiceFormat, you can use the constructor that accepts two parameters: an array of double values in ascending order, and an array of String instances. When you call ChoiceFormat's format() method and pass it an instance of a numeric wrapper class (that is, Integer, Float, Byte, etc.), it returns one of the String values from the array based on the value of that numeric object. For example, suppose that you create a ChoiceFormat using the following code.

```
double[] limits = {0d, 1d, 2d};
String[] values = {"x < 1", "1 <= x < 2", "x >= 2"};
ChoiceFormat cf = new ChoiceFormat(limits, values);
```

This ChoiceFormat defines three ranges of numbers: less than one, between one and two, and greater than or equal to two. Note that the first value in the list (in this case, zero) is effectively ignored with respect to defining ranges, but you must include it and ensure that it's less than the second value. Given this ChoiceFormat, you can call its format() method and pass it instances of a Number subclass such as Integer. Passing a value that's less than one will cause the first String to be printed, while a value greater than or equal to one but less than two causes the second value to be printed. Finally, values greater than or equal to two cause the third message to be printed. For example, you might execute code like that shown below:

```
System.out.println(cf.format(new Integer(0)));
System.out.println(cf.format(new Integer(1)));
System.out.println(cf.format(new Integer(2)));
```

Compiling and executing this output will produce the results shown below:

```
x < 1
1 <= x < 2
x >= 2
```

As you may suspect, ChoiceFormat can be used to resolve the problem with the value of a substitution parameter affecting the appropriate grammar in a message. For example, you could write the following code to generate the appropriate output based on the number of users that are logged on:

```
ResourceBundle bundle = ResourceBundle.getBundle("FormatMessages");
int userCount;
// ...

// The ResourceBundle includes a CurrentUsers key that's associated with
// the message shown below:
//
//     {0} currently logged on.

Integer countValue = new Integer(userCount);
String msgText = (String)(bundle.getObject("CurrentUsers"));
double[] borderValues = {0d, 1d, 2d};
String[] descriptions = {"No users are", "One user is", "{0} users are"};
```

```
ChoiceFormat choice = new ChoiceFormat(borderValues, descriptions);
Object[] values = {choice.format(countValue)};
MessageFormat msgFormat = new MessageFormat(msgText);
msgFormat.applyPattern(msgFormat.format(values));
values[0] = countValue;
System.out.println(msgFormat.format(values));
```

This code segment first creates a `ChoiceFormat` that contains the `String` that's appropriate for the number of logged on users. It then uses `MessageFormat` to add that `String` to the message stored in the `ResourceBundle`, and finally uses `MessageFormat` again to insert the number of users (when that number is greater than one).

Besides being somewhat confusing, this code has another serious drawback: portions of the message text are embedded within it, a problem that `ResourceBundle` and `MessageFormat` are intended to eliminate. Fortunately, `MessageFormat` provides a way to use `ChoiceFormat` objects without creating them directly as was done here. Just as it is possible to specify an element format for date, time, and numeric values, (in other words, to specify `DateFormat` and `NumberFormat` instances) it's also possible to specify one for `ChoiceFormat` values. To do so, you simply specify `choice` for the element format and create an element style that represents the limit values and the `String` that corresponds to each one as shown below:

```
CurrentUsers={0,choice,0#No users are|1#One user is|2#{0} users are} currently
logged on.
```

Notice that a substitution parameter with an index of zero appears in two places in this message. It is used first at the beginning of the message, where it identifies the `choice` value, and again within the third and final message that can be produced by the `choice`. In each case, that parameter represents the number of users that are logged on, and it is first used by the `choice` to select which of its three text strings should be used. For example, if there are 10 users logged on, `MessageFormat` uses the `choice` to create the intermediate message shown below:

```
{0} users are currently logged on.
```

Once the choice has been processed, `MessageFormat` will perform its normal processing that causes the number of users to be inserted into the message to produce the correct output as shown below:

```
10 users are currently logged on.
```

To use this new message, the previous code segment can be simplified as shown below:

```
ResourceBundle bundle = ResourceBundle.getBundle("FormatMessages");
int userCount;
// ...

String myText = (String)(bundle.getObject("CurrentUsers"));
MessageFormat mf = new MessageFormat(myText);
Object[] vals = {new Integer(userCount)};
System.out.println(mf.format(vals));
```

By implicitly using `ChoiceFormat` this way, you can ensure that your messages are grammatically correct while still maintaining the separation of message text from your application code.

Parsing Text Data

You'll often find it necessary to parse text information that has been entered by a user. For example, you may need to split text across multiple lines if it's displayed in a component that's too narrow to display the string on a single line. In other cases, you may wish to identify each word or sentence that was entered or simply process each character. These are all relatively easy operations to perform in English, but some other languages have complex rules that govern what is considered a sentence or a word. Even identifying a single character can be complex, particularly in some Asian languages, because a single logical character in one of those languages can be represented by a sequence of multiple Unicode characters. Fortunately, Java provides the BreakIterator class that can be used to parse text using the rules for a given Locale.

BreakIterator

To use a BreakIterator, you must obtain an instance of the appropriate type from one of the factory methods that are defined: getCharacterInstance(), getWordInstance(), getLineInstance(), and getSentenceInstance(). Two implementations of each of those methods are provided: one that accepts a Locale parameter, and another that uses the default Locale.

Once you have obtained a BreakIterator, you must identify the String that's to be parsed by calling the setText() method. The BreakIterator works by maintaining an index value into the text, and when you call a method to locate the next break position, that index is adjusted appropriately. The next() method is used to move the index to the next boundary in the text field and returns the position of that boundary, or BreakIterator.DONE when no more boundaries can be found. For example, the following code segments show how you can identify sentence boundaries using a BreakIterator:

```
BreakIterator bi = BreakIterator.getSentenceInstance();
String sent = "This is a sentence! Is this a sentence too? " +
    "This is the last sentence.";
bi.setText(sent);
int lastIndex = bi.first();
int currentIndex = bi.next();
while (currentIndex != BreakIterator.DONE) {
  System.out.println(sent.substring(lastIndex, currentIndex));
  lastIndex = currentIndex;
  currentIndex = bi.next();
}
```

If you compile and execute this code, it will produce the output shown below.

```
This is a sentence!
Is this a sentence too?
This is the last sentence.
```

Note that BreakIterator provides methods for moving both forward and backward through a string to identify its boundaries, although you'll typically process them in a forward direction as was done here.

You should also be aware that the white space characters (spaces in this example) are grouped with the sentence that they follow. Here, for example, the first two sentences shown above will each include a trailing space, since a space is included in the sample text between each of the three sentences.

Character Iteration

As mentioned earlier, identifying each character in a `String` is trivial in some languages, but not in others. For example, characters with accents such as the ä or ë characters that represent one logical character can be represented by two "physical" characters: the base character (for example, a or e) followed by a diacritical mark (¨). By using `BreakIterator`, you can identify each individual logical character within a `String`, regardless of how it's stored.

Word Iteration

Although relatively simple for English text, identifying word boundaries can be very complex in some languages, but `BreakIterator` allows you to do so easily. When using a word iterator, boundaries are identified on each side of punctuation characters as well as around the words themselves. For example, the following sentence will be broken into eight separate pieces:

```
This is a test.
```

The eight pieces that a word iterator will identify are the four words within the sentence, the three whitespace regions (space characters) between those words, and the period at the end of the sentence.

Line Iteration

This type of iteration is useful when you need to find an appropriate location within a `String` where the text can be split across lines. For example, you might do so if implementing word wrap behavior like that found in `JTextArea`, where a single word is not allowed to span multiple lines. In the case of English text, line boundaries occur at spaces and at hyphens, since it's considered acceptable to split a hyphenated word across two lines.

Sentence Iteration

As illustrated earlier, this type of `BreakIterator` allows you to identify the beginning and end of sentences.

BreakIterator Example

The following class provides an application that allows you to test the behavior of the various types of `BreakIterator`. It produces a user interface like the one shown opposite, which allows you to select a `Locale` and a `BreakIterator` type (character, word, line, or sentence), enter some text, and have the text parsed by a `BreakIterator`.

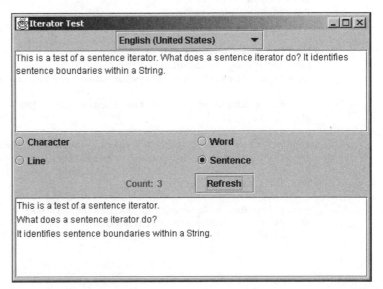

When the text is parsed by pressing the **Refresh** button, the boundaries identified by the `BreakIterator` are used to add the separate pieces of text to a `JList`, allowing you to scroll to view all of the parsed items.

```java
import java.awt.*;
import java.awt.event.*;
import java.text.*;
import java.util.*;
import javax.swing.*;

public class IteratorTest extends JPanel {
  protected JComboBox localeButton;

  protected JTextArea textArea;

  protected JRadioButton charButton;
  protected JRadioButton wordButton;
  protected JRadioButton lineButton;
  protected JRadioButton sentButton;

  protected JLabel countLabel;
  protected JButton refreshButton;

  protected JList itemList;

  // Create a window for the Iterator test
  // and make sure that later components will fit
  public static void main(String[] args) {
    JFrame f = new JFrame("Iterator Test");
    f.setDefaultCloseOperation(JFrame.EXIT_ON_CLOSE);
    f.setContentPane(new IteratorTest());
    f.pack();
    f.setVisible(true);
  }

  public IteratorTest() {
    buildLayout();
    refreshDisplay();
  }

  protected void buildLayout() {
    setLayout(new GridBagLayout());
    GridBagConstraints gbc = new GridBagConstraints();

    // Set up the contents of the Locale combo box
    gbc.gridx = 0;
    gbc.gridy = 0;
    localeButton = new JComboBox(Locale.getAvailableLocales());
    localeButton.setRenderer(new LocaleListCellRenderer());
    localeButton.setSelectedItem(Locale.getDefault());
    add(localeButton, gbc);

    gbc.gridwidth = GridBagConstraints.REMAINDER;
    gbc.fill = GridBagConstraints.BOTH;
    gbc.weightx = 1;
```

```
      // Set up the input area panel
      gbc.gridy++;
      gbc.weighty = 1;
      textArea = new JTextArea(5, 20);
      textArea.setLineWrap(true);
      textArea.setWrapStyleWord(true);
      JScrollPane jsp = new JScrollPane(textArea,
          JScrollPane.VERTICAL_SCROLLBAR_AS_NEEDED,
          JScrollPane.HORIZONTAL_SCROLLBAR_NEVER);
      add(jsp, gbc);

      // Add a panel for the choice buttons
      gbc.gridy++;
      gbc.weighty = 0;
      add(getTypePanel(), gbc);

      // Add a panel for the refresh button and the count label
      gbc.gridy++;
      add(getCountPanel(), gbc);

      // Add a panel for the parsed output
      gbc.gridy++;
      gbc.weighty = 1;
      itemList = new JList();
      add(new JScrollPane(itemList), gbc);
  }

  // Create the panel for the choice buttons
  protected JPanel getTypePanel() {
    JPanel panel = new JPanel();
    panel.setLayout(new GridLayout(2, 2, 20, 0));
    charButton = new JRadioButton("Character", true);
    panel.add(charButton);
    wordButton = new JRadioButton("Word");
    panel.add(wordButton);
    lineButton = new JRadioButton("Line");
    panel.add(lineButton);
    sentButton = new JRadioButton("Sentence");
    panel.add(sentButton);

    // Add the buttons to a group
    ButtonGroup group = new ButtonGroup();
    group.add(charButton);
    group.add(wordButton);
    group.add(lineButton);
    group.add(sentButton);
    return panel;
  }

  // Create a panel for the refresh button and the count label
  protected JPanel getCountPanel() {
    JPanel panel = new JPanel();
    JLabel label = new JLabel("Count:", JLabel.RIGHT);
    panel.add(label);
```

```
    countLabel = new JLabel("", JLabel.LEFT);
    Dimension size = panel.getPreferredSize();
    size.width = Math.min(size.width, 100);
    countLabel.setPreferredSize(size);
    panel.add(countLabel);

    // Add the refresh button
    refreshButton = new JButton("Refresh");
    refreshButton.addActionListener(new ActionListener() {
      public void actionPerformed(ActionEvent event) {
        refreshDisplay();
      }
    });
    panel.add(refreshButton);
    return panel;
  }

  protected void refreshDisplay() {
    int startIndex, nextIndex;
    Vector items = new Vector();
    // Get the input text
    String msgText = textArea.getText();
    // Set the locale and prepare the iterator
    Locale locale = (Locale)(localeButton.getSelectedItem());
    BreakIterator iterator = null;

    // Work out which button is selected and set the iterator
    if (charButton.isSelected()) {
      iterator = BreakIterator.getCharacterInstance(locale);
    }
    else if (wordButton.isSelected()) {
      iterator = BreakIterator.getWordInstance(locale);
    }
    else if (lineButton.isSelected()) {
      iterator = BreakIterator.getLineInstance(locale);
    }
    else if (sentButton.isSelected()) {
      iterator = BreakIterator.getSentenceInstance(locale);
    }
    iterator.setText(msgText);
    startIndex = iterator.first();
    nextIndex = iterator.next();

    // Find the breaks in the input text
    // and add the substrings for output
    while (nextIndex != BreakIterator.DONE) {
      items.addElement(msgText.substring(startIndex, nextIndex));
      startIndex = nextIndex;
      nextIndex = iterator.next();
    }
    countLabel.setText(Integer.toString(items.size()));
    itemList.setListData(items);              // Output the parsed input
  }

  // Combo box to select the available locales
```

```
class LocaleListCellRenderer extends DefaultListCellRenderer {
  public Component getListCellRendererComponent(
      JList list, Object value, int index,
      boolean isSelected, boolean hasFocus) {
    Locale locale = (Locale)(value);
    return super.getListCellRendererComponent(
        list, locale.getDisplayName(),
        index, isSelected, hasFocus);
  }
 }
}
```

Text Comparisons and Sorting

It's sometimes necessary for your application to compare instances of String to one another, such as when the text items in a collection are being sorted. For example, you might wish to sort a list of names alphabetically, which would be accomplished by comparing the names to one another.

Although Java's String class provides compareTo() and compareToIgnoreCase() methods, they may not return the correct results when comparing non-ASCII characters. As with parsing, the rules that govern String comparisons are simple in some cases but not in others. Fortunately, the java.text package includes the Collator class that can be used to perform Locale-specific comparisons of strings, and you can obtain an instance of Collator by calling the getInstance() method. Like many of the other methods related to internationalization, two implementations of getInstance() are available: one that accepts a Locale argument, and another that does not. The no-argument version returns a Collator that's appropriate for the default Locale, while the implementation that accepts a Locale parameter returns a Collator that sorts based on the conventions of the specified Locale.

Once you have obtained a reference to a Collator object for the appropriate Locale, you can call the compare() method that accepts two String parameters and returns an int value. The return value indicates the relative value of the first string to the second as shown in the table below:

Relative Values of the String Parameters	Value Returned by compare()
First string less than the second string	< 0
First string equal to the second string	0
First string greater than the second string	> 0

The following code segments illustrate how to perform a comparison that will work correctly regardless of the user's Locale:

```
String first, second;
// ...

Collator coll = Collator.getInstance();
int result = coll.compare(first, second);
if (result < 0) {
  System.out.println("First String is less than second");
}
```

```
    else if (result == 0) {
      System.out.println("First String is equal to the second");
    }
    else if (result > 0) {
      System.out.println("First String is greater than the second");
    }
```

Sorting the objects in a `java.util.List` implementation is even easier, since the `Collections` class in `java.util` provides a static `sort()` method that you can use. For example, if you create a `Vector` containing `String` values and you wish to sort those values, you can pass that `Vector` as a parameter to the `sort()` method in `Collections`. The only requirements for using `sort()` are that each object in the `List` must implement the `java.lang.Comparable` interface (which is true of most wrapper classes) and that a comparison between any two of the elements is meaningful. In general, for a comparison to be meaningful the two elements must be instances of the same type of object.

By default, the `sort()` method in `Collections` sorts using the rules for the default `Locale`. However, you can create a `Collator` instance and pass that to the `sort()` method along with the `List` implementation to have the items in the list sorted according to the `Locale` associated with your `Collator` object. For example, if your default `Locale` is not equal to `Locale.JAPAN` but the text to be sorted was entered by a Japanese user, you could use code like the following to ensure that the sorting is performed correctly:

```
//  This Vector will contain the items to be sorted
Vector textItems;
// ...

Collator coll = Collator.getInstance(Locale.JAPAN);
Collections.sort(textItems, coll);
```

Collator Strength

Sorting is sometimes not as simple as it may appear, even when sorting English text that contains only simple Latin characters. For example, depending upon the circumstances, it may or may not be the case that "hello" should be considered equal to "Hello". In addition, for languages where characters can be used with or without an accent (e.g. "pêche" versus "péché"), it may or may not be desirable to consider the presence or absence of accents when comparing `String` values. Fortunately, the `Collator` class allows you to select a strength value that determines which type of differences between characters (if any) will be ignored.

The four strength values supported by `Collator` are represented by constants defined in that class: `PRIMARY`, `SECONDARY`, `TERTIARY`, and `IDENTICAL`. These constants define how closely two characters must match one another for them to be considered equal. Although the specific rules for making that determination are `Locale`-specific, some generalizations can be made. For example, it's commonly the case that a **primary difference** means that two characters represent different letters of the alphabet, and the difference between "A" and "B" is primary, but the difference between "A" and "a" is not.

A **secondary difference** between two characters indicates that their accents are different or that one has an accent while the other does not. For instance, the difference between "é" and "ê" is considered a secondary difference. Finally, a **tertiary difference** in this case refers to the case of the letter, such as when comparing "e" to "E". As described in the table below, the four constants defined in `Collator` allow you to specify how closely two characters must match one another for them to be considered equal:

Collator Constant	Type of Differences Considered Significant
PRIMARY	Primary
SECONDARY	Primary and secondary
TERTIARY	Primary, secondary, and tertiary
IDENTICAL	All

IDENTICAL differs from TERTIARY in that it differentiates between pre-composed characters with accents and combined characters with accents. By setting the strength of a Collator, you can control how items are sorted, and an example of how to set the strength is shown below:

```
Collator coll = Collator.getInstance();
coll.setStrength(Collator.PRIMARY);
```

Decomposition Mode

The Collator class also supports a **decomposition mode** that determines how **composed characters** are handled by the Collator instance. Examples of composed characters are those that contain accents, which are usually broken down (or "decomposed") for comparison operations. For example, the "é" character in "péché" would be decomposed into two characters: the base letter (lower-case "e") followed by the acute character ("´"). In other words, when it is decomposed, "péché" is seven characters long instead of five, and the purpose of this decomposition is to ensure that the result of a comparison is correct.

Depending upon the language being used, it may or may not be necessary for Collator to perform decomposition. For example, decomposition is not necessary at all when comparing only English text. Since decomposition causes comparison operations to run more slowly, you may choose to disable decomposition entirely if you're certain that your application will only ever compare String values that do not require it.

If your application can be used with languages that do require some level of decomposition, you must choose between **canonical decomposition** (the default value for instances of Collator) and **full decomposition**. Canonical decomposition is appropriate for most languages, and will provide correct comparisons for all canonical variants defined in the Unicode 2.0 standard. However, if your application supports Katakana characters, for example, you may find it necessary to use full decomposition despite its relatively slow performance. For information on which character sets require full decomposition, you should visit the Unicode home page at http://www.unicode.org/. Katakana characters are traditional Japanese handwriting.

Each of the composition modes is represented by a constant defined in Collator, and you can modify and query a Collator's mode using the setDecomposition() and getDecomposition() methods. The three constants representing composition modes are NO_DECOMPOSITION, CANONICAL_DECOMPOSITION, and FULL_DECOMPOSITION, and an example of how to use them is shown below:

```
Collator coll;
String first, second;
// ...

// We may be comparing Katakana characters
coll.setDecomposition(Collator.FULL_DECOMPOSITION);
int result = coll.compare(first, second);
```

Internationalizing an Application

We'll now briefly examine the steps that must be taken to internationalize an existing application. In this case, the application is a simple program that allows the user to maintain a collection of instances of the Person class shown below:

```java
import java.util.Date;

public class Person implements java.io.Serializable {

  protected String firstName;
  protected String lastName;
  protected String address;
  protected Date dateOfBirth;

  public Person(String fn, String ln, String addr, Date dob) {
    super();
    setFirstName(fn);
    setLastName(ln);
    setAddress(addr);
    setDateOfBirth(dob);
  }

  public Person() {
    this(null, null, null, null);
  }

  public void setFirstName(String fn) {
    firstName = fn;
  }

  public String getFirstName() {
    return firstName;
  }

  public void setLastName(String ln) {
    lastName = ln;
  }

  public String getLastName() {
    return lastName;
  }

  public void setAddress(String addr) {
    address = addr;
  }

  public String getAddress() {
    return address;
  }

  public void setDateOfBirth(Date dob) {
    dateOfBirth = dob;
  }

  public Date getDateOfBirth() {
    return dateOfBirth;
  }
}
```

As illustrated below, the `EditPersonList` application allows entries to be added, updated, and deleted, and it stores those entries in a disk file named `people.ser`:

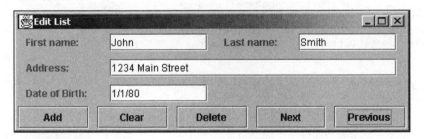

```java
import java.awt.*;
import java.awt.event.*;
import java.io.*;
import java.text.*;
import java.util.*;
import javax.swing.*;

public class EditPersonList extends JFrame {

  protected Vector personList;
  protected int currentIndex;

  protected JButton addButton;
  protected JButton deleteButton;
  protected JButton clearButton;

  protected JButton nextButton;
  protected JButton previousButton;

  protected PersonPanel personPanel;

  public static void main(String[] args) throws Exception {
    EditPersonList epl = new EditPersonList("Edit List");
    epl.setDefaultCloseOperation(JFrame.EXIT_ON_CLOSE);
    epl.setVisible(true);
  }

  public EditPersonList(String title) throws Exception {
    super(title);
    buildLayout();
    File f = new File("people.ser");
    if (f.exists()) {
      FileInputStream fis = new FileInputStream(f);
      ObjectInputStream ois = new ObjectInputStream(fis);
      personList = (Vector)(ois.readObject());
    }
    else {
      personList = new Vector();
    }
    currentIndex = 0;
    displayCurrentPerson();
    pack();
  }
```

```
protected void buildLayout() {
  Container pane = getContentPane();
  personPanel = new PersonPanel();
  pane.add(personPanel, BorderLayout.CENTER);
  pane.add(getButtonPanel(), BorderLayout.SOUTH);
}

protected JPanel getButtonPanel() {
  JPanel panel = new JPanel();
  panel.setLayout(new GridLayout(1, 5, 10, 0));

  addButton = new JButton("Add");
  panel.add(addButton);
  clearButton = new JButton("Clear");
  panel.add(clearButton);
  deleteButton = new JButton("Delete");
  panel.add(deleteButton);

  nextButton = new JButton("Next");
  panel.add(nextButton);
  previousButton = new JButton("Previous");
  panel.add(previousButton);

  addButton.addActionListener(new ActionListener() {
    public void actionPerformed(ActionEvent event) {
      Person p = new Person();
      if (personPanel.updatePerson(p)) {
        personList.addElement(p);
        currentIndex = personList.size() - 1;
        displayCurrentPerson();
      }
      savePersonList();
    }
  });

  clearButton.addActionListener(new ActionListener() {
    public void actionPerformed(ActionEvent event) {
      personPanel.clear();
    }
  });

  deleteButton.addActionListener(new ActionListener() {
    public void actionPerformed(ActionEvent event) {
      personList.removeElementAt(currentIndex);
      if (currentIndex >= personList.size()) {
        currentIndex = personList.size() - 1;
      }
      savePersonList();
      displayCurrentPerson();
    }
  });

  nextButton.addActionListener(new ActionListener() {
    public void actionPerformed(ActionEvent event) {
      currentIndex++;
```

```
        displayCurrentPerson();
      }
    });

    previousButton.addActionListener(new ActionListener() {
      public void actionPerformed(ActionEvent event) {
        currentIndex--;
        displayCurrentPerson();
      }
    });

    return panel;
  }

  protected void displayCurrentPerson() {
    if ((currentIndex >= 0) && (currentIndex < personList.size())) {
      personPanel.displayPerson((Person)
                (personList.elementAt(currentIndex)));
    }
    else {
      personPanel.clear();
    }
    previousButton.setEnabled(currentIndex > 0);
    nextButton.setEnabled(currentIndex < personList.size() - 1);
  }

  protected void savePersonList() {
    File f = new File("people.ser");
    try {
      FileOutputStream fos = new FileOutputStream(f);
      ObjectOutputStream oos = new ObjectOutputStream(fos);
      oos.writeObject(personList);
      oos.close();
    } catch (IOException ioe) {};
  }

  class PersonPanel extends JPanel {
    protected JTextField firstNameField;
    protected JTextField lastNameField;
    protected JTextField addressField;
    protected JTextField dobField;

    public PersonPanel() {
      buildLayout();
    }

    protected void buildLayout() {
      JLabel label;
      setLayout(new GridBagLayout());
      GridBagConstraints gbc = new GridBagConstraints();
      gbc.weightx = 1;
      gbc.fill = GridBagConstraints.HORIZONTAL;
      gbc.insets = new Insets(5, 10, 5, 10);

      gbc.gridy = 0;
```

```
      label = new JLabel("First name:", JLabel.LEFT);
      add(label, gbc);

      firstNameField = new JTextField(10);
      add(firstNameField, gbc);

      label = new JLabel("Last name:", JLabel.LEFT);
      add(label, gbc);

      lastNameField = new JTextField(10);
      add(lastNameField, gbc);

      gbc.gridy++;
      label = new JLabel("Address:", JLabel.LEFT);
      add(label, gbc);

      gbc.gridwidth = GridBagConstraints.REMAINDER;
      addressField = new JTextField(10);
      add(addressField, gbc);

      gbc.gridwidth = 1;
      gbc.gridy++;
      label = new JLabel("Date of Birth:", JLabel.LEFT);
      add(label, gbc);

      dobField = new JTextField(10);
      add(dobField, gbc);
   }

   public void clear() {
      firstNameField.setText("");
      lastNameField.setText("");
      addressField.setText("");
      dobField.setText("");
   }

   public void displayPerson(Person p) {
      firstNameField.setText(p.getFirstName());
      lastNameField.setText(p.getLastName());
      addressField.setText(p.getAddress());
      DateFormat formatter = DateFormat.getDateInstance(DateFormat.SHORT);
      dobField.setText(formatter.format(p.getDateOfBirth()));
   }

   public boolean updatePerson(Person p) {
      String firstName = firstNameField.getText();
      String lastName = lastNameField.getText();
      String address = addressField.getText();
      Date dateOfBirth = null;
      DateFormat parser = DateFormat.getDateInstance(DateFormat.SHORT);
      try {
         dateOfBirth = parser.parse(dobField.getText());
      }
      catch (ParseException pe) {
         JOptionPane.showMessageDialog(this, pe.getMessage(),
```

```
              "Invalid Date",
              JOptionPane.ERROR_MESSAGE);
          return false;
      }
      p.setFirstName(firstName);
      p.setLastName(lastName);
      p.setAddress(address);
      p.setDateOfBirth(dateOfBirth);
      return true;
    }
  }
}
```

Employing a ResourceBundle

No String comparisons are performed in this class, and the only parsing operation occurs when a String entered by the user is converted into a Date instance. Therefore, this class can be internationalized simply by removing the Locale-specific text that is embedded within it. Specifically, those strings are the JFrame's title, the JOptionPane's title, the JButton labels, and the text displayed within the user interface panel (PersonPanel).

> Although a **String** is specified for the name of the file that's used to store the **People** instances, that name is not visible to users of the application and need not be stored in the **ResourceBundle**.

Since all of the resources that must be isolated from the source code are text strings, a PropertyResourceBundle can be created like the one shown below named PeopleResources.properties:

```
FrameTitle=Edit List
Button_Label_Add=Add
Button_Label_Clear=Clear
Button_Label_Delete=Delete
Button_Label_Next=Next
Button_Label_Previous=Previous
Label_Text_FirstName=First name:
Label_Text_LastName=Last name:
Label_Text_Address=Address:
Label_Text_DOB=Date of Birth:
Dialog_Title_Invalid_Date=Invalid Date
Menu_Locale=Locale
```

Although you can use any identifiers/keys that you find appropriate, it's usually helpful to use names that describe how the resource is used (for example, Button_XXX for button labels, Label_XXX for JLabel text, etc.). This can provide an intuitive clue that helps you to determine how and/or where a particular resource is used within your application.

With a file defined that contains the resources, it's easy to modify the EditPersonList class so that it uses the external resources instead of embedding the messages:

```java
import java.awt.*;
import java.awt.event.*;
import java.io.*;
import java.text.*;
import java.util.*;
import javax.swing.*;

public class EditPersonList extends JFrame {

  protected Vector personList;
  protected int currentIndex;

  protected JButton addButton;
  protected JButton deleteButton;
  protected JButton clearButton;

  protected JButton nextButton;
  protected JButton previousButton;

  protected PersonPanel personPanel;

  protected static ResourceBundle resources =
      ResourceBundle.getBundle("PeopleResources");

  public static void main(String[] args) throws Exception {
    EditPersonList epl = new EditPersonList(resources.getString(
        "FrameTitle"));
    epl.setDefaultCloseOperation(JFrame.EXIT_ON_CLOSE);
    epl.setVisible(true);
  }

// ...

  protected JPanel getButtonPanel() {
    JPanel panel = new JPanel();
    panel.setLayout(new GridLayout(1, 5, 10, 0));

    addButton = new JButton(resources.getString("Button_Label_Add"));
    panel.add(addButton);
    clearButton = new JButton(resources.getString("Button_Label_Clear"));
    panel.add(clearButton);
    deleteButton = new JButton(resources.getString("Button_Label_Delete"));
    panel.add(deleteButton);

    nextButton = new JButton(resources.getString("Button_Label_Next"));
    panel.add(nextButton);
    previousButton = new JButton(resources.getString(
        "Button_Label_Previous"));
    panel.add(previousButton);

// ...

    protected void buildLayout() {
      JLabel label;
      setLayout(new GridBagLayout());
      GridBagConstraints gbc = new GridBagConstraints();
```

```
      gbc.weightx = 1;
      gbc.fill = GridBagConstraints.HORIZONTAL;
      gbc.insets = new Insets(5, 10, 5, 10);

      gbc.gridy = 0;
      label = new JLabel(resources.getString(
          "Label_Text_FirstName"), JLabel.LEFT);
      add(label, gbc);

      firstNameField = new JTextField(10);
      add(firstNameField, gbc);

      label = new JLabel(resources.getString(
          "Label_Text_LastName"), JLabel.LEFT);
      add(label, gbc);

      lastNameField = new JTextField(10);
      add(lastNameField, gbc);

      gbc.gridy++;
      label = new JLabel(resources.getString(
          "Label_Text_Address"), JLabel.LEFT);
      add(label, gbc);

      gbc.gridwidth = GridBagConstraints.REMAINDER;
      addressField = new JTextField(10);
      add(addressField, gbc);

      gbc.gridwidth = 1;
      gbc.gridy++;
      label = new JLabel(resources.getString(
          "Label_Text_DOB"), JLabel.LEFT);
      add(label, gbc);

      dobField = new JTextField(10);
      add(dobField, gbc);
    }

// ...

    public boolean updatePerson(Person p) {
      String firstName = firstNameField.getText();
      String lastName = lastNameField.getText();
      String address = addressField.getText();
      Date dateOfBirth = null;
      DateFormat parser = DateFormat.getDateInstance(DateFormat.SHORT);
      try {
        dateOfBirth = parser.parse(dobField.getText());
      }
      catch (ParseException pe) {
        JOptionPane.showMessageDialog(this, pe.getMessage(),
            resources.getString("Dialog_Title_Invalid_Date"),
            JOptionPane.ERROR_MESSAGE);
        return false;
      }
```

```
        p.setFirstName(firstName);
        p.setLastName(lastName);
        p.setAddress(address);
        p.setDateOfBirth(dateOfBirth);
        return true;
    }
  }
}
```

Changing the Locale at Runtime

In many cases, it's acceptable to always use the default `Locale` or to require the user to select a `Locale` when logging on and use that `Locale` for the duration of the user's logon session. However, you'll sometimes want to allow users to change their `Locale` preference while the application is running. Although providing this capability does require more work, it's usually not technically difficult to do so. Normally all that's necessary is to provide methods that will update the user interface components when the `Locale` selection changes. For example, the `EditPersonList` application can be changed as shown below to provide a menu with one `JRadioButtonMenuItem` for English and another for German. When one of those buttons is selected, the `ResourceBundle` is reloaded based on the selection and the messages updated, as shown in the following screenshot:

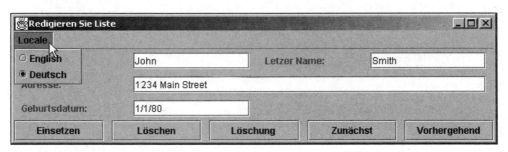

```
import java.awt.*;
import java.awt.event.*;
import java.io.*;
import java.text.*;
import java.util.*;
import javax.swing.*;

public class EditPersonList extends JFrame {

  protected Vector personList;
  protected int currentIndex;

  protected JButton addButton;
  protected JButton deleteButton;
  protected JButton clearButton;

  protected JButton nextButton;
  protected JButton previousButton;

  protected PersonPanel personPanel;

  protected JMenu localeMenu;
```

```
// ...

  protected void buildLayout() {
    JMenuItem menuItem;

    Container pane = getContentPane();
    personPanel = new PersonPanel();
    pane.add(personPanel, BorderLayout.CENTER);
    pane.add(getButtonPanel(), BorderLayout.SOUTH);

    JMenuBar jmb = new JMenuBar();
    localeMenu = new JMenu(resources.getString("Menu_Locale"));
    jmb.add(localeMenu);

    ButtonGroup group = new ButtonGroup();

    menuItem = new JRadioButtonMenuItem(
        Locale.ENGLISH.getDisplayName(Locale.ENGLISH), true);
    localeMenu.add(menuItem);
    menuItem.addActionListener(new ActionListener() {
      public void actionPerformed(ActionEvent event) {
        resources = ResourceBundle.getBundle(
            "PeopleResources", Locale.ENGLISH);
        updateLabels();
        pack();
      }
    });
    group.add(menuItem);

    menuItem = new JRadioButtonMenuItem(
        Locale.GERMAN.getDisplayName(Locale.GERMAN));
    localeMenu.add(menuItem);
    menuItem.addActionListener(new ActionListener() {
      public void actionPerformed(ActionEvent event) {
        resources = ResourceBundle.getBundle(
            "PeopleResources", Locale.GERMAN);
        updateLabels();
        pack();
      }
    });
    group.add(menuItem);

    setJMenuBar(jmb);
  }

// ...

  protected void savePersonList() {
    File f = new File("people.ser");
    try {
      FileOutputStream fos = new FileOutputStream(f);
      ObjectOutputStream oos = new ObjectOutputStream(fos);
      oos.writeObject(personList);
      oos.close();
```

```
      } catch (IOException ioe) {};
   }

   protected void updateLabels() {
     setTitle(resources.getString("FrameTitle"));
     personPanel.updateLabelText();
     localeMenu.setText(resources.getString("Menu_Locale"));
     addButton.setText(resources.getString("Button_Label_Add"));
     clearButton.setText(resources.getString("Button_Label_Clear"));
     deleteButton.setText(resources.getString("Button_Label_Delete"));
     nextButton.setText(resources.getString("Button_Label_Next"));
     previousButton.setText(resources.getString(
         "Button_Label_Previous"));
   }

   class PersonPanel extends JPanel {
     protected JTextField firstNameField;
     protected JTextField lastNameField;
     protected JTextField addressField;
     protected JTextField dobField;

     protected JLabel firstNameLabel;
     protected JLabel lastNameLabel;
     protected JLabel addressLabel;
     protected JLabel dateOfBirthLabel;

     public PersonPanel() {
       buildLayout();
     }

     protected void buildLayout() {
       // JLabel label;
       setLayout(new GridBagLayout());
       GridBagConstraints gbc = new GridBagConstraints();
       gbc.weightx = 1;
       gbc.fill = GridBagConstraints.HORIZONTAL;
       gbc.insets = new Insets(5, 10, 5, 10);

       gbc.gridy = 0;
       firstNameLabel = new JLabel(resources.getString(
           "Label_Text_FirstName"), JLabel.LEFT);
       add(firstNameLabel, gbc);

       firstNameField = new JTextField(10);
       add(firstNameField, gbc);

       lastNameLabel = new JLabel(resources.getString(
           "Label_Text_LastName"), JLabel.LEFT);
       add(lastNameLabel, gbc);

       lastNameField = new JTextField(10);
       add(lastNameField, gbc);

       gbc.gridy++;
       addressLabel = new JLabel(resources.getString(
```

```
                "Label_Text_Address"), JLabel.LEFT);
        add(addressLabel, gbc);

        gbc.gridwidth = GridBagConstraints.REMAINDER;
        addressField = new JTextField(10);
        add(addressField, gbc);

        gbc.gridwidth = 1;
        gbc.gridy++;
        dateOfBirthLabel = new JLabel(resources.getString(
            "Label_Text_DOB"), JLabel.LEFT);
        add(dateOfBirthLabel, gbc);

        dobField = new JTextField(10);
        add(dobField, gbc);
    }


    // ...

    public void updateLabelText() {
        firstNameLabel.setText(resources.getString("Label_Text_FirstName"));
        lastNameLabel.setText(resources.getString("Label_Text_LastName"));
        addressLabel.setText(resources.getString("Label_Text_Address"));
        dateOfBirthLabel.setText(resources.getString("Label_Text_DOB"));
    }


    }
}
```

Notice that the main difference between this modified version of EditPersonList and the previous implementation is the presence of methods that update the displayed text. In addition, JLabel instances that were defined locally within a method are assigned to class-level instance variables so that the labels can be modified when the Locale changes.

For this modified EditPersonList class to work, you should also define a file that contains the German language equivalent of the English text defined earlier. An example of this is shown below, which could be stored in a file called PeopleResources_de.properties:

```
FrameTitle=Redigieren Sie Liste
Button_Label_Add=Einsetzen
Button_Label_Clear=L\u00F6schen
Button_Label_Delete=L\u00F6schung
Button_Label_Next=Zun\u00E4chst
Button_Label_Previous=Vorhergehend
Label_Text_FirstName=Vorname:
Label_Text_LastName=Letzer Name:
Label_Text_Address=Adresse:
Label_Text_DOB=Geburtsdatum:
Dialog_Title_Invalid_Date=Unzul\u00E4ssiges Datum
Menu_Locale=Locale
```

Using native2ascii

As the above example illustrates, you can embed characters with a `PropertyResourceBundle` file just as with a Java source code file: using \unnnn, where nnnn is the hexadecimal value of the Unicode character that you wish to define. In fact, this may be the only way that you can enter characters that are not included in the character set supported by your keyboard. The problem with this approach is that it's not convenient if a user whose keyboard *does* support the characters is editing the file. For example, a German user editing the `PeopleResources_de.properties` file defined above would probably prefer to enter the accented character directly instead of entering each character's Unicode value.

As you can see, it's sometimes desirable to represent characters with their Unicode value, but not always. Fortunately, Java provides the **native2ascii** utility that allows you to convert files between these two formats. In addition, you should use only ASCII characters when creating class names.

By default, `native2ascii` converts a file that contains "native" (that is, non-Latin 1) characters into a format that contains the Unicode representation of those characters, but it also allows you to perform the reverse operation. For example, to convert the \unnnn characters in `PeopleResources_de.properties` file shown above into their native equivalents, you could enter the following:

```
native2ascii -reverse PeopleResources_de.properties PeopleResources_de.native
```

The `-reverse` option indicates that `native2ascii` should convert Unicode (that is, \unnnn) characters into their native equivalents, and the converted output will be stored in a file named `PeopleResources_de.native`. That file will contain the converted contents of the original `PeopleResources_de.properties` file:

```
FrameTitle=Redigieren Sie Liste
Button_Label_Add=Einsetzen
Button_Label_Clear=Löschen
Button_Label_Delete=Löschung
Button_Label_Next=Zunächst
Button_Label_Previous=Vorhergehend
Label_Text_FirstName=Vorname:
Label_Text_LastName=Letzer Name:
Label_Text_Address=Adresse:
Label_Text_DOB=Geburtsdatum:
Dialog_Title_Invalid_Date=Unzulässiges Datum
Menu_Locale=Locale
```

Similarly, this file with native characters can be re-converted using the following command that produces output identical to that found in the original `PeopleResources_de.properties` file.

```
native2ascii PeopleResources_de.native PeopleResources_de.unicode
```

You can also use the `-encoding` option with `native2ascii`, which will cause it to use the character encoding that you specify when performing conversions between native and Unicode values. If you do so, you must specify the canonical name of an encoding that's supported by Java's `InputStreamReader` and `OutputStreamWriter` classes.

Summary

In this chapter we've looked at the factors which need to be borne in mind when producing applications for an international market, and looked at the facilities provided for this purpose in Java:

❑ Locales and resource bundles

❑ The `DateFormat`, `TimeFormat`, and `NumberFormat` classes, used for formatting and parsing dates, times, and numbers

❑ `MessageFormat` and `ChoiceFormat`, used in conjunction with resource bundles to format messages in the appropriate way for the locale in which the application is run

❑ Use of `BreakIterator` for parsing text data in the appropriate manner for the locale

The final chapter considers the thorny issue of interfacing Java and native code.

Professional Java Programmin

Java Native Interface

Although Java is suitable for most programming tasks, you'll sometimes need to allow Java code to interact with software written in some other language. This might be necessary, for example, for some time-critical tasks or if you need to perform an operation that can't be accomplished at all in Java, such as accessing the Windows registry or performing assembly level instructions. In these situations, you'll need to define native methods and provide implementations for them with native (non-Java) code. In fact, JNI is built into every JVM, as this is the way that the JVM interacts with the operating system, and implements threading on the platform it is designed for.

The way that this is facilitated in Java is through the **Java Native Interface (JNI)**. JNI allows you to call native methods from Java code and to call Java methods from native code. In addition the Invocation API has been provided to allow developers to load a VM into a native application. Although it's theoretically possible to implement native methods using any language, it's easiest to use C or C++, and the examples in this chapter were created in C++.

Using native methods in your Java application should be avoided whenever possible, because it eliminates one of the biggest advantages of using Java in the first place: platform independence. The use of native methods also makes debugging your code more difficult, and can make distribution of your code more complex, since you must also ensure that the native libraries you use are available on each client machine. Lastly, the additional files and technologies in use will also make maintenance a more complex task. For these reasons, you should carefully consider whether native methods are necessary and use them only when there is no other option.

In this chapter we will cover:

- ❑ How to define and implement a native method
- ❑ How to call Java methods from native code

❑   How to create Java objects from native code

❑   How to add Java code to a native application

> **Due to the limitations imposed on the chapter size, it is assumed that you have a working knowledge of C and C++, or at least can follow C++ code. The examples were written and compiled in Visual Studio, although any compiler will do, of course.**

Defining a Native Method

Defining a native method that will be called from within Java code is extremely simple, and can be done by including the `native` keyword in a method's definition as shown below, where `printMessage()` is identified as a native method:

```
public class DisplayMessage {

  public static void main(String[] args) {
    printMessage();
  }

  public static native void printMessage();

}
```

Once you've created a class that includes native methods, you can use the `javah` utility to generate C header files that you can use to implement the native methods. The header file will include the C function definitions for the native methods declared in your class. For example, to generate a header file for the `DisplayMessage` class, you could issue the following command:

```
javah DisplayMessage
```

When used with the `-stub` option `javah` will also produce `.c` source file stubs for you to flesh out. The `javah` utility is included with the JDK, and the version shipped with Java 2 creates JNI headers by default. (There is also a non-optimized compiler `javah_g` that can be used with debuggers.) The version of `javah` included with Java 1.1, however, creates NMI headers unless you specify the `-jni` option. NMI is a now outdated system for access to native code from Java that was included in the 1.0 specification. The form for calling `javah` is shown below:

```
javah -jni DisplayMessage
```

The line above will generate an output file named `DisplayMessage.h` like the one shown below:

```
/* DO NOT EDIT THIS FILE - it is machine generated */
#include <jni.h>
/* Header for class DisplayMessage */

#ifndef _Included_DisplayMessage
```

```
#define _Included_DisplayMessage
#ifdef __cplusplus
extern "C" {
#endif
/*
 * Class:     DisplayMessage
 * Method:    printMessage
 * Signature: ()V
 */
JNIEXPORT void JNICALL Java_DisplayMessage_printMessage
    (JNIEnv *, jclass);

#ifdef __cplusplus
}
#endif
#endif
```

As indicated in the comments, this header describes a single method named `printMessage` contained in class `DisplayMessage`. The `signature` line in the comments provides an abbreviated description of the method's argument and return value types; signatures are discussed in detail later in the chapter. The most important part of this file is the section shown below:

```
JNIEXPORT void JNICALL Java_DisplayMessage_printMessage
    (JNIEnv *, jclass);
```

`JNIEXPORT` and `JNICALL` are macros provided to ensure the appropriate linkage and calling conventions for Win32 systems that require special keywords for functions exported from DLLs, and will always surround the return value type as shown here. In this case, the method does not return a value, so its return type is specified as `void`, just as in the Java code.

The method names generated by `javah` always begin with `Java`, and they include the fully qualified class name and the name of the corresponding Java method. In this case, for example, the method is named `printMessage()` and is defined in the `DisplayMessage` class, so the method name generated by `javah` is `Java_DisplayMessage_printMessage`.

No package name is included because `DisplayMessage` is assigned to the default package, which in effect means that it is not part of a specific package. To illustrate the case where the class is part of a package, if `DisplayMessage` were assigned to a package named `us.tx.plano.bspell` the name of the method definition would appear like the one shown below:

```
JNIEXPORT void JNICALL Java_us_tx_plano_bspell_DisplayMessage_printMessage
    (JNIEnv *, jclass);
```

The compiler uses a set of predefined rules to convert some non-alphabetic characters. For example, when the underscore (_) character is used in the java method name, `javah` will replace it with the underscore followed by a one (_1), while other characters such as the dollar sign ($) are replaced with a hexadecimal representation of the character, preceded by an underscore. So, if the method name was `print$Message()` instead of `printMessage()`, `javah` would generate a prototype name using the hexadecimal representation (0x0024) of the dollar sign character:

```
JNIEXPORT void JNICALL Java_DisplayMessage_print_00024Message
    (JNIEnv *, jclass);
```

Overloaded methods are distinguished from each other by appending the argument signature preceded by two underscore characters to each overloaded method.

The first argument passed to the method is a pointer to a structure representing a function table, and it is the first argument passed to all native methods. The JNIEnv structure is defined in the jni.h file included with the JDK, and it includes many functions that you'll use when implementing native methods.

The second argument passed to the method is of type jclass, and an instance of this data type is always passed to static native methods. That parameter represents the class that contains the method being called (which in this case is DisplayMessage) and is equivalent to a reference to an instance of java.lang.Class.

Native methods defined as instance methods will have a parameter of type jobject passed to them instead of a jclass, where the jobject represents the object instance whose method is being called. For example, if printMessage() were defined as an instance method instead of a static method, the prototype would differ as shown below:

```
JNIEXPORT void JNICALL Java_DisplayMessage_printMessage
    (JNIEnv *, jobject);
```

In effect, the jobject parameter passed to a native method is equivalent to the special this field accessible within instances methods defined in Java.

When a method is overloaded, it is not possible to uniquely identify an implementation from the method name alone. For example, if DisplayMessage included a printMessage() method that accepts no arguments and another that accepts a single String argument, there must be some way to distinguish between the two. As we'll see later when parameter passing is discussed, the signatures of overloaded methods are used by javah to generate a unique name for each one.

As mentioned earlier, native methods can be implemented in any language, but C and C++ offer the most convenient choices. The examples in this chapter are written using C++ partly because it provides a somewhat more concise way of invoking the methods available through the JNIEnv function table.

For example, the following code obtains a reference to the class definition for java.io.IOException using C:

```
jclass ioeClass = (*env)->FindClass(env, "java/io/IOException");
```

However, if C++ is used, the same code can be written somewhat more conveniently in the format shown below:

```
jclass ioeClass = env->FindClass("java/io/IOException");
```

Implementing a Native Method

With the Java source code and header file defined, it's now possible to create the function that implements the native method. That function must be placed in a **native library**, which is simply a collection of functions that are defined in a platform-specific fashion. For example, a Windows **Dynamic Link Library (DLL)** is an example of a native library, while Solaris supports the same concept in the form of a shared library. In other words, you must package the native methods you implement in the appropriate platform-specific manner so that the library that contains them can be loaded and its functions invoked.

If you're using Visual C++ 6.0 to create a native library for Windows, you should create a new project representing a Win32 Dynamic-Link Library:

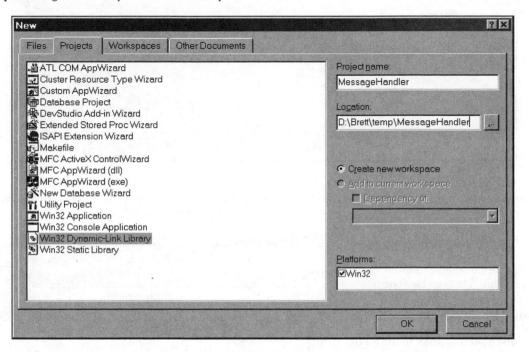

Once you've created the project, you must add a new file to the project and create an implementation like the one shown below:

```
#include <stdio.h>
#include "DisplayMessage.h"

JNIEXPORT void JNICALL Java_DisplayMessage_printMessage
    (JNIEnv *env, jclass cl)
{
  printf("Hello, Brett.");
}
```

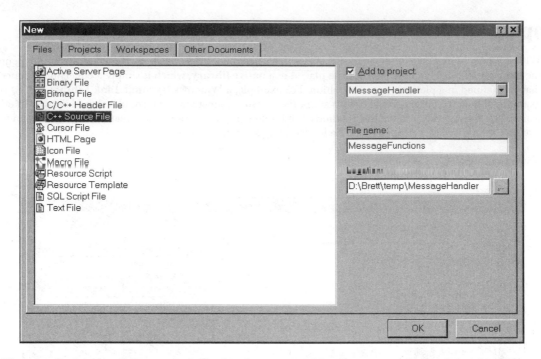

Note that the function definition is identical to that generated by the `javah` utility, and that the `DisplayMessage.h` file is included. That file in turn includes `jni.h`, which includes many definitions (for example, types and macros) that are needed, including the `JNIEXPORT` and `JNICALL` macros.

Before you can compile this file, you must ensure that the `DisplayMessage.h` file is accessible. That can be done in Visual C++ by selecting the **Options...** item on the **Tools** menu and adding the directory containing `DisplayMessage.h` to the list of include directories. In this case, for example, that directory is `D:\brett\temp`, and can be added to the directory list:

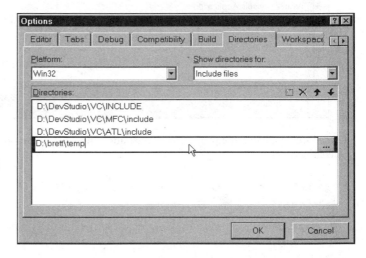

As well as including the directory containing your `javah`-generated header file, you must also include the directory that contains the `jni.h` file, along with the platform-specific definitions. The `jni.h` file is stored in the `/include` subdirectory below the directory where you installed the JDK, and the platform-specific definitions will be in a subdirectory below the `/include` directory. For example, if the JDK is installed in `D:\jdk1.3` on Windows, you should add `D:\jdk1.3\include` and `D:\jdk1.3\include\win32` to your project's include directories:

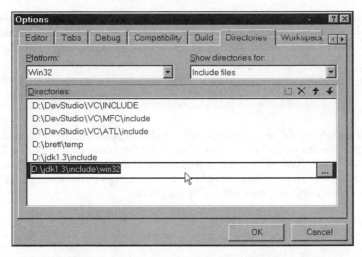

Now you will already be starting to realize one major draw back of JNI that will ensure you use it for essential purposes only, because we now have to recreate this library for every platform we wish to support. Both maintenance complexity and the workload are increased; if it can be done in a pure Java solution this is preferable.

Once you've added the include directories to your project, you can compile the file containing the native `printMessage()` function and generate a native library. For example, with Visual C++, this can be done by selecting the Build menu item from the Build menu as shown below, where a project named `MessageHandler` is used to create a file called `MessageHandler.dll`:

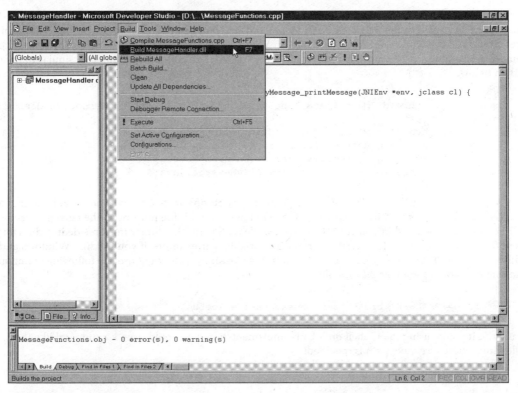

If you now attempt to execute the `DisplayMessage` application, it will generate a message like the one shown below indicating that it could not find the native implementation provided for the `printMessage()` method:

```
Exception in thread "main" java.lang.UnsatisfiedLinkError: printMessage
        at DisplayMessage.printMessage(Native Method)
        at DisplayMessage.main(DisplayMessage.java:8)
```

Although a library containing the `printMessage()` implementation has been created, the Java Virtual Machine did not load the library and it does not know about the functions it provides. To have the JVM load the library that was created, you must use the static `System.loadLibrary()` method, specifying the name of the library. A convenient place for the call to `loadLibrary()` is in the static initializer for the `DisplayMessage` class itself, as shown in the following code:

```
public class DisplayMessage {

  static {
    System.loadLibrary("MessageHandler");
  }

  public static void main(String[] args) {
    printMessage();
  }

  public static native void printMessage();

}
```

The argument passed to the `loadLibrary()` method is the name of the shared library; on Solaris this is converted to `libMessageHandler.so`, and on Win32 it is `MessageHandler.dll`. However, if you compile and attempt to execute this code, it probably will still fail, generating a message similar to the one shown below:

```
Exception in thread "main" java.lang.UnsatisfiedLinkError: no MessageHandler in
java.library.path
        at java.lang.ClassLoader.loadLibrary(Unknown Source)
        at java.lang.Runtime.loadLibrary0(Unknown Source)
        at java.lang.System.loadLibrary(Unknown Source)
        at DisplayMessage.<clinit>(DisplayMessage.java:4)
```

This message indicates that the JVM was unable to find the `MessageHandler` library that it attempted to load by calling `System.loadLibrary()`. On Windows, the DLL file must be in the current directory or in a directory that's included in your `PATH` variable, while on Solaris, the library must reside in a directory identified in the `LD_LIBRARY_PATH` environment variable. For example, if you're using Windows and the DLL is stored in `D:\brett\temp\messagehandler\debug`, you might use the following command to add that directory to your `PATH` variable:

```
set PATH=%PATH%;D:\brett\temp\messagehandler\debug
```

Similarly, if you're using the C shell on a Unix implementation, you could issue a command like the following, where a relative path is specified:

```
setenv LD_LIBRARY_PATH messagehandler/debug
```

Finally, in the Korn shell, you might use commands like those shown below:

```
LD_LIBRARY_PATH=messagehandler/debug
export LD_LIBRARY_PATH
```

Java 2 provides a somewhat easier and more generic way of setting the library path by allowing you to set a system property called `java.library.path`. For example, if the library is stored in the `messagehandler/debug` subdirectory of the current directory, you could use the following command to start the application and indicate where the JVM should expect to find library files:

```
java -Djava.library.path=messagehandler/debug DisplayMessage
```

Finally, once you have identified the location of the library file, you can execute the `DisplayMessage` application, which will produce the desired results:

```
Hello, Brett.
```

Passing Parameter Values to Native Methods

Being able to call native methods is only marginally useful if there is no way for the Java code to pass arguments to the native methods or to receive return values. Fortunately, it's very easy to pass parameters to native methods, and JNI provides direct mappings for Java's primitive types, arrays of primitive types, and for several classes to enable exchange of parameters in such a way that both Java and native code can manipulate them:

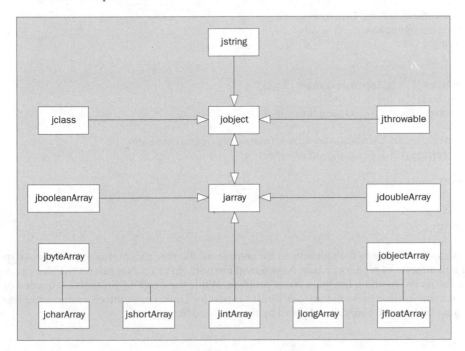

Passing Strings to Native Methods

One of the few classes that maps directly to a JNI type is `java.lang.String`. For example, suppose that we modify the `DisplayMessage` class so that the message text to be displayed is constructed in its `main()` method and passed as a parameter to the native `printMessage()` method:

```
public class DisplayMessage {

  static {
    System.loadLibrary("MessageHandler");
  }

  public static void main(String[] args) {
    String name = (args.length == 0 ? "Brett" : args[0]);
    printMessage("Hello, " + name);
  }

  public static native void printMessage(String text);

}
```

Using `javah` to generate the header file for this modified class produces a `DisplayMessage.h` file like the one shown below:

```
/* DO NOT EDIT THIS FILE - it is machine generated */
#include <jni.h>
/* Header for class DisplayMessage */

#ifndef _Included_DisplayMessage
#define _Included_DisplayMessage
#ifdef __cplusplus
extern "C" {
#endif
/*
 * Class:      DisplayMessage
 * Method:     printMessage
 * Signature: (Ljava/lang/String;)V
 */
JNIEXPORT void JNICALL Java_DisplayMessage_printMessage
    (JNIEnv *, jclass, jstring);

#ifdef __cplusplus
}
#endif
#endif
```

In addition to the change to the signature in the comments, the new `printMessage()` prototype now includes a parameter of type `jstring`. As you might expect, `jstring` represents the `String` value that's passed to the native method, but there is one problem. While the `String` contains a sequence of Unicode characters, many platforms do not provide direct support for Unicode, so the characters must be converted into a format that can be easily manipulated by the native code.

The InputStreamReader and OutputStreamWriter classes defined in java.io allow you to perform conversions between Unicode characters and various encodings. Although JNI does not provide similar functionality directly, it does allow you to convert a sequence of Unicode characters into a sequence of UTF-8 characters. As discussed in the chapter on persistence, a sequence of ASCII characters is indistinguishable from the sequence generated by representing those same characters in UTF-8. In other words, we can effectively translate two-byte Unicode character representations into one-byte UTF-8 representations as long as the Unicode characters being translated are all defined in the ASCII character set.

GetStringUTFChars() is one of the many functions available through the JNIEnv function pointer, and it allows you to create a null-terminated UTF-8 representation of a series of Unicode characters stored in a string. In the following example, the message text passed to the printMessage() function is used to create an equivalent set of UTF-8/ASCII characters that can be displayed by the native code using printf(). Note that when GetStringUTFChars() is called, it allocates a new block of memory in which to place the UTF-8 characters:

```
#include <stdio.h>
#include "DisplayMessage.h"

JNIEXPORT void JNICALL Java_DisplayMessage_printMessage
    (JNIEnv *env, jclass cl, jstring text)
{
  const char *asciiString = env->GetStringUTFChars(text, NULL);
  printf("%s", asciiString);
}
```

> If you've been programming in Java for some time, there may not seem to be anything wrong with this code, however, since the call to GetStringUTFChars() allocates a new buffer, that memory must be explicitly freed when it's no longer needed so that a memory leak will not occur.

The buffer can be released using the ReleaseStringUTFChars() function, which requires that you pass pointers to the original (Unicode) and converted (UTF-8) strings:

```
#include <stdio.h>
#include "DisplayMessage.h"

JNIEXPORT void JNICALL Java_DisplayMessage_printMessage
    (JNIEnv *env, jclass cl, jstring text)
{
  const char *asciiString = env->GetStringUTFChars(text, NULL);
  printf("%s", asciiString);
  env->ReleaseStringUTFChars(text, asciiString);
}
```

Passing Other Parameter Types to Native Methods

In the example above, we saw how easy it is to pass String parameters to native method implementations. It's equally simple to pass primitive types to native methods, since JNI defines a C data type for each Java primitive type, as shown in the following table:

Java Type	JNI Type
boolean	jboolean
byte	jbyte
char	jchar
short	jshort
int	jint
long	jlong
float	jfloat
double	jdouble

Note that when evaluating the value of a jboolean, you should use the JNI_TRUE and JNI_FALSE constants defined in jni.h, as shown below:

```
JNIEXPORT void JNICALL Java_SomeClass_testBoolean
    (JNIEnv *env, jclass cl, jboolean flagValue)
{
  if (flagValue == JNI_TRUE) {
    printf("It is true!");
  }
  else {
    printf("It is false!");
  }
}
```

As an example of how to pass primitive data type values to a native method, we'll create a new native method in DisplayMessage that adds two integer values together and prints a message that displays the result:

```
public static native void addIntegers(int first, int second);
```

When javah is run against this modified class, it will create an additional prototype:

```
/*
 * Class:      DisplayMessage
 * Method:     addIntegers
 * Signature: (II)V
 */
JNIEXPORT void JNICALL Java_DisplayMessage_addIntegers
  (JNIEnv *, jclass, jint, jint);
```

Note that two jint parameters are passed to the new addIntegers() function, and an example of how that function might be implemented is shown below:

```
JNIEXPORT void JNICALL Java_DisplayMessage_addIntegers
    (JNIEnv *env, jclass cl, jint first, jint second)
{
  jint total = first + second;
  printf("The sum of %i and %i is %i", first, second, total);
}
```

It's also very simple to return a primitive value from a native method. For example, suppose that the addIntegers() function is modified so that it adds the two values together and returns the result without printing:

```
public static native int addIntegers(int first, int second);
```

The javah utility would produce the following prototype:

```
/*
 * Class:     DisplayMessage
 * Method:    addIntegers
 * Signature: (II)I
 */
JNIEXPORT jint JNICALL Java_DisplayMessage_addIntegers
    (JNIEnv *, jclass, jint, jint);
```

Note that the signature portion of the generated comments section has changed, and the function is now defined to return a jint value. Finally, the implementation of the function can be modified slightly so that it returns the sum of the parameter values:

```
JNIEXPORT jint JNICALL Java_DisplayMessage_addIntegers
    (JNIEnv *env, jclass cl, jint first, jint second)
{
  jint total = first + second;
  return total;
  // printf("The sum of %i and %i is %i", first, second, total);
}
```

Array Parameters

The addIntegers() function can be made more generic by allowing callers to pass arrays of integers instead of only two integer values, and we'll now make that modification to illustrate how to handle arrays passed to native methods. First, the native method definition in DisplayMessage must be changed, after which the class should be recompiled:

```
public static native int addIntegers(int[] values);
```

Once the modified DisplayMessage class is compiled, javah should be executed, and it will produce results similar to the following:

```
/*
 * Class:     DisplayMessage
 * Method:    addIntegers
 * Signature: ([I)I
 */
JNIEXPORT jint JNICALL Java_DisplayMessage_addIntegers
    (JNIEnv *, jclass, jintArray);
```

The addIntegers() function now accepts a single parameter of type jintArray, which is the JNI data type that represents an array of int values.

To calculate the sum of all the integers in the array passed to addIntegers(), the first thing that must be done is to determine the size of the array. This is very easy to do, since one of the many functions available through the JNIEnv pointer is GetArrayLength(), which returns the number of elements in an array. We'll also define an integer variable named total that will contain the sum of the values that's returned by addIntegers():

```
JNIEXPORT jint JNICALL Java_DisplayMessage_addIntegers
    (JNIEnv *env, jclass cl, jintArray values)
{
  jsize count = env->GetArrayLength(values);
  jint total = 0;
  // ...
  return total;
}
```

The jsize data type used here to store the array size is used by JNI for size and index values, and is equivalent to the jint type. In fact, the definition of jsize in jni.h is shown below, where it is effectively defined as an alias for jint:

```
typedef jint jsize;
```

Now that we've identified the size of the array, we can create a loop that will calculate the sum of all its values. However, it's not possible to do that directly using the jintArray that was passed to addIntegers(), because that parameter does not represent a direct pointer to the array values. Instead, it provides a handle that can be used to retrieve a pointer to the array values by calling the GetIntArrayElements() function as shown below:

```
JNIEXPORT jint JNICALL Java_DisplayMessage_addIntegers
    (JNIEnv *env, jclass cl, jintArray values)
{
  jsize count = env->GetArrayLength(values);
  jint *value = env->GetIntArrayElements(values, NULL);
  jint total = 0;
  // ...
  return total;
}
```

The first parameter passed to GetIntArrayElements() is the array for which a pointer should be returned, while the second is a pointer to a jboolean, although in this case, a NULL value was specified. When you retrieve a pointer to an array of values, some JVM implementations will return a copy of those values, while others return a pointer to the original values.

The second parameter passed to GetIntArrayElements() represents a boolean value that is set by the function itself to indicate to the caller the type of pointer returned. If the jboolean value is equal to JNI_TRUE, a copy was returned by the function call, while JNI_FALSE indicates that the pointer location refers to the original array data. In this case, it's not significant whether the pointer refers to the original data or to a copy, but if it were relevant, the code could easily modified as shown below:

```
JNIEXPORT jint JNICALL Java_DisplayMessage_addIntegers
    (JNIEnv *env, jclass cl, jintArray values)
{
  jsize count = env->GetArrayLength(values);
```

```
    jboolean isCopy;
    jint *value = env->GetIntArrayElements(values, &isCopy);
    jint total = 0;
    // ...
    return total;
}
```

Now that a reference to the array data has been obtained, it's easy to create a loop that calculates the total of all the values stored in the array:

```
JNIEXPORT jint JNICALL Java_DisplayMessage_addIntegers
    (JNIEnv *env, jclass cl, jintArray values)
{
    jsize count = env->GetArrayLength(values);
    jint *value = env->GetIntArrayElements(values, NULL);
    jint total = 0;
    jsize i = 0;
    for (i = 0; i < count; i++) {
        total += value[i];
    }
    return total;
}
```

Finally, the native method should indicate that it no longer needs access to the array data, which it does by calling the `ReleaseIntArrayElements()` function. That function is passed a reference to the original `jintArray` reference, a reference to the pointer returned by `GetIntArrayElements()`, and a value indicating what action should be taken. This value and will be one of three values: 0, JNI_COMMIT, or JNI_ABORT.

If a copy was made of the array, changes to the array will not be reflected in the original until `ReleaseIntArrayElements()` is called. Specifying 0 or JNI_COMMIT would, in this case, save those changes to the original. Specifying 0 also causes the buffer containing the elements to be released. JNI_ABORT simply releases the buffer without copying the values to the `jintArray`. If a copy was not made, this last parameter has no effect.

The following table summarizes the behavior of `ReleaseXXXArrayElements()` for each of the three values that may be passed:

Parameter Value	Save Changes	Release Buffer
JNI_ABORT	No	Yes
JNI_COMMIT	Yes	No
0	Yes	Yes

0 is provided for fine memory management and you should only use this with care, for most cases JNI_COMMIT will suffice.

In this case, the array values were accessed without being modified, so there was no need to save them and the application can specify either 0 or JNI_ABORT:

```
JNIEXPORT jint JNICALL Java_DisplayMessage_addIntegers
    (JNIEnv *env, jclass cl, jintArray values)
{
  jsize count = env->GetArrayLength(values);
  jint *value = env->GetIntArrayElements(values, NULL);
  jint total = 0;
  jsize i = 0;
  for (i = 0; i < count; i++) {
    total += value[i];
  }
  env->ReleaseIntArrayElements(values, value, JNI_ABORT);
  return total;
}
```

Although this example only illustrates the use of an array of int values, an array data type exists for each primitive type, and GetXXXArrayElements() and ReleaseXXXArrayElements() functions are provided for each type:

JNI Type	Array Type	Get/Release Function Name
jboolean	jbooleanArray	Get/ReleaseBooleanArrayElements()
jbyte	jbyteArray	Get/ReleaseByteArrayElements()
jchar	jcharArray	Get/ReleaseCharArrayElements()
jshort	jshortArray	Get/ReleaseShortArrayElements()
jint	jintArray	Get/ReleaseIntArrayElements()
jlong	jlongArray	Get/ReleaseLongArrayElements()
jfloat	jfloatArray	Get/ReleaseFloatArrayElements()
jdouble	jdoubleArray	Get/ReleaseDoubleArrayElements()

Retrieving a Subset of Array Elements

When you use GetXXXArrayElements() to retrieve the values stored in an array, that function returns all of the elements, and as mentioned earlier, may create a copy of the elements. However, you'll sometimes want to be able to retrieve only a subset of the elements in an array, particularly when the array is very large. Fortunately, JNI also provides the GetXXXArrayRegion() functions that allow you to retrieve a portion of an array's elements instead of all of them.

To use these functions, you must define a buffer in the form of a native array and read the Java array's contents into your native array. For example, if you're accessing an array of Java int values, you must create a jint array to use as a buffer when retrieving the elements through GetIntArrayRegion(). For example, the following code segment retrieves the fourth and fifth elements of the jintArray that's passed to the native method, storing them in the array subset:

```
JNIEXPORT jint JNICALL Java_DisplayMessage_addIntegers
    (JNIEnv *env, jclass cl, jintArray values)
{
  //  Create a local jint array to hold the 4th and 5th elements
```

```
    jint subset[2];
    //  Copy values from jintArray to buffer just defined
    env->GetIntArrayRegion(values, 3, 2, subset);
    //  Add the two values together and return the result
    jint total = subset[0] + subset[1];
    return total;
}
```

This assumes that you have checked there are at least 5 values in the array. If there are not, you will get an `ArrayIndexOutOfBoundsException`. We will look at exception handling in detail later in this chapter.

The first parameter passed to `GetXXXArrayRegion()` identifies the source array from which the elements will be copied. The second and third arguments represent the starting index into the source array and the number of elements to copy, while the fourth parameter is the destination buffer into which the elements are copied.

Accessing Fields in Java Classes

When you define a native method within a class, you'll often want that method to have access to the static and/or instance fields defined within the class. For example, the `DisplayMessage` application might be modified so that it stores the message text in a static variable before calling `printMessage()`. Before the native `printMessage()` code can print the message text it must obtain a reference to the text stored in the static field and use that reference to display the message:

```
public class DisplayMessage {

  private static String messageText;

  static {
    System.loadLibrary("MessageHandler");
  }

  public static void main(String[] args) {
    messageText = "Hello, " +
        (args.length > 0 ?
        args[0] : "Brett");
    printMessage();
  }

  public static native void printMessage();

}
```

For the native method to obtain a reference to the `messageText` field, it must first obtain access to the **field ID** for that field. A field ID is simply a handle that represents a field, and is conceptually similar to an instance of the `Field` class defined in `java.lang.reflect`.

Once you've obtained the field ID for a field, you can use that value to read or modify the value stored in that field. A field ID is represented by JNI's `jfieldID` type, and the following code illustrates how to retrieve a reference to a static field named `messageText` that is an instance of `java.lang.String`:

```
JNIEXPORT void JNICALL Java_DisplayMessage_printMessage
    (JNIEnv *env, jclass cl)
{
   jfieldID field = env->GetStaticFieldID(cl, "messageText",
                                          "Ljava/lang/String;");

   // ...
}
```

The first parameter passed to GetStaticFieldID() is a reference to the jclass object that identifies the class in which the field is defined. In this case, the field is defined in the same class as the native method, so the jclass parameter passed to the native method code is used when calling GetStaticFieldID(). The second parameter is the name of the field to access, while the third and final parameter represents the **field descriptor**, which is JNI's way of identifying the data type of a field.

In the case of an object, the field descriptor is the letter L followed by the fully qualified class name with forward slash (/) character replacing the periods (.) and a semicolon (;) at the end. Each primitive type is associated with a different letter of the alphabet, and arrays use the same notation but begin with an open bracket ([) character. The following table identifies the meaning of the various characters that are used in field descriptors:

Primitive Type	Field Descriptor Character
boolean	Z
byte	B
char	C
short	S
int	I
long	J
float	F
double	D

Some examples of field descriptors and their equivalent Java code representations are shown in the table below:

Field Descriptor	Field Definition
I	int
[Ljava/lang/String	java.lang.String[]
[B	byte[]
Z	boolean
Ljava/util/Vector	java.util.Vector
[Ljava/util/Date	java.util.Date[]

Once the native method has obtained a reference to the field ID, that value can be used to access the object that the field represents which in this case is a String instance containing the message to display. Since the field is a static field and represents an object (as opposed to a primitive value), the GetStaticObjectField() function must be used to access the message text.

This method requires two parameters: a jclass representing the class in which the field is defined and a jfieldID. In this case, we'll use the jclass that was passed to the printMessage() function for the first parameter, and the jfieldID just obtained through GetStaticFieldID() for the second.

Although GetStaticObjectField() returns a reference to the String that will be printed, it is defined to return a generic jobject, so it is temporarily assigned to a variable of that type. However, we can immediately cast it to an instance of jstring as shown below:

```
JNIEXPORT void JNICALL Java_DisplayMessage_printMessage
    (JNIEnv *env, jclass cl)
{
  jfieldID field = env->GetStaticFieldID(cl, "messageText",
             "Ljava/lang/String;");
  jobject object = env->GetStaticObjectField(cl, field);
  jstring string = (jstring)object;
  // ...
}
```

Printing the text is done in exactly the same way that it was accomplished when the string was passed as a parameter to the printMessage() function: an ASCII/UTF-8 representation of the text is created and passed to printf():

```
JNIEXPORT void JNICALL Java_DisplayMessage_printMessage
    (JNIEnv *env, jclass cl)
{
  jfieldID field = env->GetStaticFieldID(cl, "messageText",
             "Ljava/lang/String;");
  jobject object = env->GetStaticObjectField(cl, field);
  jstring string = (jstring)object;

  const char *asciiString = env->GetStringUTFChars(string, 0);
  printf("%s", asciiString);
  env->ReleaseStringUTFChars(string, asciiString);
}
```

In addition to the GetStaticObjectField(), a function is provided for each primitive data type that allows you to access static field values, and the following list identifies those functions and the type of data returned by each one:

Function Name	Return Type
GetStaticObjectField	jobject
GetStaticBooleanField	jboolean
GetStaticByteField	jbyte
GetStaticCharField	jchar
GetStaticShortField	jshort
GetStaticIntField	jint
GetStaticLongField	jlong
GetStaticFloatField	jfloat
GetStaticDoubleField	jdouble

An equivalent list of functions is also provided for non-static members of your class, namely `GetObjectField`, `GetBooleanField`, and so on. You can use these functions for obtaining an ID of, and then the reference to, instance fields.

Accessing Arrays

Accessing an array is simply a combination of steps already covered in this chapter for accessing static fields. To illustrate this, we'll modify `DisplayMessage` so that it contains an array of `String` values and create a new `printNames()` native method. That method should print each of the names in the static array defined in `DisplayMessage`:

```java
public class DisplayMessage {

    private static String[] names = {"Pat", "Terry", "Lisa",
                                    "Gordon", "Lee"};

    static {
      System.loadLibrary("MessageHandler");
    }

    public static void main(String[] args) {
      printNames();
    }

    public static native void printNames();

}
```

After compiling the modified class and using `javah` to generate a header file, we can begin to implement the native `printNames()` method by obtaining a reference to the `String` array as if it's simply an object. Once that's done, you can cast the `jobject` to a `jobjectArray`, use `GetArrayLength()` to determine the number of elements it contains, and call `GetObjectArrayElement()` to retrieve each individual element:

```c
JNIEXPORT void JNICALL Java_DisplayMessage_printNames(
    JNIEnv *env, jclass cl)
{
  jfieldID field = env->GetStaticFieldID(cl, "names",
              "[Ljava/lang/String;");
  jobject object = env->GetStaticObjectField(cl, field);
  jobjectArray textArray = (jobjectArray)object;
  jsize count = env->GetArrayLength(textArray);
  jsize index;
  jobject obj;
  jstring str;
  for (index = 0; index < count; index++) {
    obj = env->GetObjectArrayElement(textArray, index);
    str = (jstring)obj;
    const char *asciiText = env->GetStringUTFChars(str, NULL);
    printf("%s\n", asciiText);
    env->ReleaseStringUTFChars(str, asciiText);
  }
}
```

Compile this code, generate the library file, and execute the new `DisplayMessage` class, using this command:

```
java -Djava.library.path=messagehandler/debug DisplayMessage
```

It should produce output like that shown below:

```
Pat
Terry
Lisa
Gordon
Lee
```

Instance Methods

All of the native methods defined and fields accessed up to this point have been static, but you'll often wish to call native instance methods and access instance variables from native code. As we'll see, however, there's very little difference between calling native static and native instance methods or between accessing static and instance variables from native code. For example, suppose that the `DisplayMessage` class is modified so that it uses instance methods as shown below:

```java
public class DisplayMessage {

    static {
        System.loadLibrary("MessageHandler");
    }

    public static void main(String[] args) {
        String name = (args.length == 0 ? "Brett" : args[0]);
        DisplayMessage dm = new DisplayMessage(name);
    }

    public DisplayMessage(String name) {
        showMessage("Hello, " + name);
    }

    private native void showMessage(String name);

}
```

When you compile this code and run the `javah` utility, it produces a header file like the one shown below, which is very similar to those previously generated:

```c
/* DO NOT EDIT THIS FILE - it is machine generated */
#include <jni.h>
/* Header for class DisplayMessage */

#ifndef _Included_DisplayMessage
#define _Included_DisplayMessage
#ifdef __cplusplus
extern "C" {
#endif
```

```
/*
 * Class:      DisplayMessage
 * Method:     showMessage
 * Signature: (Ljava/lang/String;)V
 */
JNIEXPORT void JNICALL Java_DisplayMessage_showMessage
     (JNIEnv *, jobject, jstring);

#ifdef __cplusplus
}
#endif
#endif
```

Note that the only difference between the prototype shown above and those created earlier is that the second parameter passed to showMessage() is a jobject value instead of a jclass. As mentioned previously, a jclass is equivalent to a java.lang.Class, while a jobject is effectively the same as the special this keyword that you're able to use in instance methods and constructors.

In this case, the fact that the native method is non-static does not result in any code changes, although as we'll see shortly, there are some minor differences between referencing static and instance fields. An implementation of showMessage() appears below, and will cause the specified message text to be displayed in standard output:

```
JNIEXPORT void JNICALL Java_DisplayMessage_showMessage
     (JNIEnv *env, jobject thisObj, jstring msgText)
{
   const char *asciiText = env->GetStringUTFChars(msgText, NULL);
   printf("%s", asciiText);
   env->ReleaseStringUTFChars(msgText, asciiText);
}
```

Modifying Static Fields

Field values can be modified in much the same way that they are retrieved. Just as a set of GetStaticXXXField() and GetXXXField() functions are available for retrieving values, a group of SetStaticXXXField() and SetXXXField() functions allow you to modify values. For example, DisplayMessage can be changed so that it defines a native setMessageText() method that assigns a value to the messageText field as shown below:

```
public class DisplayMessage {

  private static String messageText;

  static {
    System.loadLibrary("MessageHandler");
  }

  public static void main(String[] args) {
    setMessageText("Hello, " +
        (args.length > 0 ?
        args[0] : "Brett"));
    System.out.print(messageText);
```

```
    }

    public static native void setMessageText(String text);

}
```

To implement this method, you must again obtain the field ID for the `messageText` field, after which you can use that ID to call the `SetStaticObjectField()` function to assign a value to the field:

```
JNIEXPORT void JNICALL Java_DisplayMessage_setMessageText
    (JNIEnv *env, jclass cl, jstring text)
{
  jfieldID field = env->GetStaticFieldID(cl, "messageText",
            "Ljava/lang/String;");
  env->SetStaticObjectField(cl, field, text);
}
```

In addition to the `SetStaticObjectField()`, there is a `SetStaticXXXField()` for each primitive type, and for each `SetStaticXXXField()`, there is a `SetXXXField()` for modifying instance fields. The complete list of these functions and the data type associated with each one is listed in the following table:

Native Type	Static Field Mutator	Instance Field Mutator
jobject	SetStaticObjectField	SetObjectField
jboolean	SetStaticBooleanField	SetBooleanField
jbyte	SetStaticByteField	SetByteField
jchar	SetStaticCharField	SetCharField
jshort	SetStaticShortField	SetShortField
jint	SetStaticIntField	SetIntField
jlong	SetStaticLongField	SetLongField
jfloat	SetStaticFloatField	SetFloatField
jdouble	SetStaticDoubleField	SetDoubleField

In each of the examples we've examined, the native method retrieved or modified the value of a field in the same class in which the method is defined. This is a common scenario, and it provides a convenient example because the appropriate `jclass` is passed as an argument to the native method, but you'll sometimes want to modify a field in a different class. Before you can do so, you must obtain a reference to the `jclass` representing that class, which is accomplished by calling the `FindClass` function, passing it a string that identifies the name of the class you intend to access:

```
jclass anotherClass = env->FindClass("us/tx/plano/bspell/BookExample");
```

This code returns a `jclass` for a class named `BookExample` that's part of the `us.tx.plano.bspell` package.

Modifying Instance Fields

As you would expect, modifying an instance field is very similar to modifying a static field, although the parameters passed to SetXXXField() are slightly different from those passed to SetStaticXXXField(). Instead of specifying a jclass, which identifies the class containing the static field, you must specify a jobject that identifies the object instance containing the field to be modified. For example, suppose that the DisplayMessage class is modified as shown below so that the messageText field is an instance field instead of a static field:

```java
public class DisplayMessage {

  private String messageText;

  static {
    System.loadLibrary("MessageHandler");
  }

  public static void main(String[] args) {
    DisplayMessage dm = new DisplayMessage();
    dm.setMessageText("Hello, " +
        (args.length > 0 ?
        args[0] : "Brett"));
    System.out.print(dm.messageText);
  }

  public native void setMessageText(String text);

}
```

Once this code is compiled and the javah utility executed, the following code can be written that will provide an implementation for the setMessageText() method:

```c
JNIEXPORT void JNICALL Java_DisplayMessage_setMessageText
(JNIEnv *env, jobject instance, jstring msgText)
{
  jclass cl = env->GetObjectClass(instance);
  jfieldID field = env->GetFieldID(cl, "messageText",
            "Ljava/lang/String;");
  env->SetObjectField(instance, field, msgText);
}
```

Note that the GetObjectClass() function is used to obtain a jclass from the jobject value passed to the method implementation, and the jclass is used to retrieve a reference to the appropriate field ID using GetFieldID(). Once that's done, the jobject and jfieldID values are passed to the SetObjectField() function along with the value to assign to the field, which in this case is the message text string.

Calling Java Methods from Native Code

When implementing native methods, you'll often need to be able to call other methods that are written in Java from the native code. For example, the DisplayMessage application might be modified so that its native printMessage() method calls the getMessage() method to retrieve the message text instead of accessing the messageText field directly:

```
public class DisplayMessage {

  private static String messageText;

  static {
    System.loadLibrary("MessageHandler");
  }

  public static void main(String[] args) {
    messageText = "Hello, Brett";
    printMessage();
  }

  public static native void printMessage();

  public static String getMessage() {
    return messageText;
  }

}
```

To call a Java method from native code, you must have access to either a `jclass` (to call a static method) or a `jobject` (for an instance method), and the **method ID** associated with the method.

Method Identifiers and Signatures

Just as each field has a field ID that's obtained by identifying the name and data type of the field, every method defined in a class has a method ID that's identified by the method's name and its **signature**. The signature is simply a string that describes the data types of the arguments and the return value, although the return value may be `void`.

The same values used to represent field data types are used to represent argument and return value types. The argument type descriptors are enclosed in parenthesis and are followed by the method's return type, where "V" represents a return type of `void`. Some examples of method definitions and their signatures are shown in the following table:

Method Definition	Equivalent Signature
`private void doStuff(String text,` `int[] values)`	`(Ljava/lang/String;[I)V`
`protected String getChoice(boolean isTrue)`	`(Z)Ljava/lang/String;`
`public static int getCount()`	`()I`
`public Vector getMatch(short x, int y,` `long z)`	`(SIJ)Ljava/util/Vector;`
`public void doSomething()`	`()V`
`public int getTotal(int first, int second)`	`(II)I`

Although it's very easy to derive a method's signature "manually", you can use the `javap` utility to disassemble class files and display the signatures for the fields and methods defined within a class. That utility is provided with the JDK, and you can issue the following command to display the signatures for all fields and methods in the `DisplayMessage` class:

```
javap -s -private DisplayMessage
```

The -s option indicates that javap should print the type signatures, while -private ensures that it prints the signatures for all methods and fields regardless of their visibility (for example, private). When the above command is executed, it produces the following output:

```
Compiled from DisplayMessage.java
public class DisplayMessage extends java.lang.Object {
    private static java.lang.String messageText;
    /*   Ljava/lang/String;    */
    public DisplayMessage();
    /*   ()V   */
    public static void main(java.lang.String[]);
    /*   ([Ljava/lang/String;)V   */
    public static native void printMessage();
    /*   ()V   */
    public static java.lang.String getMessage();
    /*   ()Ljava/lang/String;   */
    static {};
    /*   ()V   */
}
```

Performing the Method Call

Now that you're familiar with method signatures, the technique for calling Java methods from native code is simply a combination of steps that have already been described. For example, if you're calling a method in the same class as the native method, you'll already have access to either a jobject or a jclass that was passed as a parameter to the native method.

To obtain a method ID, you must call either GetStaticMethodID() or GetMethodID() as shown below, and these methods will return a jmethodID value if the method is found:

```
JNIEXPORT void JNICALL Java_DisplayMessage_printMessage(
    JNIEnv *env, jclass cl)
{
    jmethodID method = env->GetStaticMethodID(cl, "getMessage",
                                     "()Ljava/lang/String;");
    // ...
}
```

The first parameter passed to GetStaticMethodID() is the jclass that represents the class in which the static method is defined, while the second parameter is the method's name, and the third parameter is the method's signature. The method signature is needed in case the method is overloaded, in which case the name alone will not be sufficient to uniquely identify the specific implementation. If the method is found, a jmethodID is returned, where a jmethodID is the native method equivalent of an instance of the Method class defined in the java.lang.reflect package.

In other words, the jmethodID serves as a sort of "handle" for the method, and it can be used to call the method from the native code. The specific function used to invoke the Java method is determined by the type of data returned from the method, and will be one of the CallStaticXXXMethod() functions for static method calls or CallXXXMethod() for instance method invocations.

The XXX portion of the function name identifies the type of value returned by the method, and will be the name of a primitive type, Object, or Void. An instance of String is returned in this case, and since String is an Object, the CallStaticObjectMethod() function is used as shown below:

```
JNIEXPORT void JNICALL Java_DisplayMessage_printMessage(
    JNIEnv *env, jclass cl) {
  jmethodID method = env->GetStaticMethodID(cl,
            "getMessage",
            "()Ljava/lang/String;");
  jobject value = env->CallStaticObjectMethod(cl, method);
  jstring text = (jstring)value;
  const char *ascii = env->GetStringUTFChars(text, NULL);
  printf("%s", ascii);
  env->ReleaseStringUTFChars(text, ascii);
}
```

The following table lists all of the CallStaticXXXMethod() and CallXXXMethod() variations that are available in JNI, along with the return type associated with each pair:

Return Type	Static Method	Instance Method
void	CallStaticVoidMethod	CallVoidMethod
java.lang.Object	CallStaticObjectMethod	CallObjectMethod
boolean	CallStaticBooleanMethod	CallBooleanMethod
byte	CallStaticByteMethod	CallByteMethod
char	CallStaticCharMethod	CallCharMethod
short	CallStaticShortMethod	CallShortMethod
int	CallStaticIntMethod	CallIntMethod
long	CallStaticLongMethod	CallLongMethod
float	CallStaticFloatMethod	CallFloatMethod
double	CallStaticDoubleMethod	CallDoubleMethod

As you would expect, calling an instance method is very much like calling a static method, and this can be illustrated by modifying DisplayMessage so that getMessage() is an instance method:

```
public class DisplayMessage {

  private String messageText;

  static {
    System.loadLibrary("MessageHandler");
  }

  public static void main(String[] args) {
    DisplayMessage dm = new DisplayMessage();
    dm.messageText = "Hello, Brett";
    dm.printMessage();
  }
```

```
public native void printMessage();

public String getMessage() {
  return messageText;
}

}
```

As illustrated below, the only difference between calling a static method and calling an instance method is that you must use GetMethodID() instead of GetStaticMethodID() and CallXXXMethod() instead of CallStaticXXXMethod():

```
JNIEXPORT void JNICALL Java_DisplayMessage_printMessage(
    JNIEnv *env, jobject instance) {
  jclass cl = env->GetObjectClass(instance);
  jmethodID method = env->GetMethodID(cl, "getMessage",
                                "()Ljava/lang/String;");
  jobject value = env->CallObjectMethod(instance, method);
  jstring text = (jstring)value;
  const char *ascii = env->GetStringUTFChars(text, NULL);
  printf("%s", ascii);
  env->ReleaseStringUTFChars(text, ascii);
}
```

Although not illustrated in this example, it's also possible for you to pass arguments to the CallXXXMethod() and CallStaticXXXMethod() functions and have those arguments passed to the Java method that's invoked. For example, suppose that DisplayMessage is again changed and that the native printMessage() implementation is responsible for displaying the message text.

In this case, however, instead of having the native method use printf(), it will use Java's println() method to display the text in standard output. In other words, the native printMessage() function will call System.out.println() to display the message, and it must pass the text as an argument to the println() method:

```
public class DisplayMessage {

  private static String messageText;

  static {
    System.loadLibrary("MessageHandler");
  }

  public static void main(String[] args) {
    messageText = "Hello, Brett";
    printMessage(messageText);
  }

  public static native void printMessage(String text);

}
```

To call System.out.println(), the native printMessage() function must do the following:

- ❑ Obtain a `jclass` reference to the `java.lang.System` class
- ❑ Obtain a `jfieldID` that represents the static field named `out` in the `System` class
- ❑ Retrieve a `jobject` reference to the `PrintStream` object that `out` represents
- ❑ Retrieve a `jmethodID` representing the `println()` method defined in the `PrintStream` class
- ❑ Use `CallVoidMethod()` to invoke the `println()` method, passing the message text as an argument to that method

The following code performs each of the steps described above, and when executed will use `System.out.println()` to display the message text:

```
JNIEXPORT void JNICALL Java_DisplayMessage_printMessage(
            JNIEnv *env,
            jclass cl,
            jstring text) {
    jclass sysClass = env->FindClass("java/lang/System");
    jfieldID outField = env->GetStaticFieldID(sysClass,
            "out",
            "Ljava/io/PrintStream;");
    jobject stream = env->GetStaticObjectField(cl,
            outField);
    jclass streamClass = env->GetObjectClass(stream);
    jmethodID println = env->GetMethodID(streamClass,
            "println",
            "(Ljava/lang/String;)V");
    env->CallVoidMethod(stream, println, text);
}
```

JNI also supports a different technique for passing parameters to a Java method by allowing you to create an array of `jvalue` objects and pass that array to the appropriate `CallXXXMethodA()` or `CallStaticXXXMethodA()` function. The `jvalue` type is a union that provides a field of each possible parameter type: one for each primitive data type, and one for object types. The definition of `jvalue` is included in `jni.h`, and is listed below:

```
typedef union jvalue {
    jboolean z;
    jbyte    b;
    jchar    c;
    jshort   s;
    jint     i;
    jlong    j;
    jfloat   f;
    jdouble  d;
    jobject  l;
} jvalue;
```

To use the `CallXXXMethodA()`/`CallStaticXXXMethodA()` functions to call a Java method, you must create an array of `jvalue` objects, with one array element for each parameter that's to be passed to the Java method. Once you've defined the `jvalue` array, you must assign a value to each element using the name of the field defined in the `jvalue` type definition shown above. For example, you might have a method like the following that you wish to call from a native method:

```
public class DisplayMessage {

  static {
    System.loadLibrary("MessageHandler");
  }

  public static void main(String[] args) {
    printMessage();
  }

  public static native void callMethod();

  public static void doSomething(short first, int second, long third) {
    System.out.println("First parameter is:  " + first);
    System.out.println("Second parameter is: " + second);
    System.out.println("Third parameter is:  " + third);
  }

}
```

To use `CallVoidMethodA()` to invoke `doSomething()`, you must create a `jvalue` array with three elements and assign `jshort`, `jint`, and `jlong` values to those elements, respectively:

```
// ...
jvalue parms[3];
jshort first = 123;
jint second = 456;
jlong third = 789;
parms[0].s = first;
parms[1].i = second;
parms[2].j = third;
// ...
```

Once the parameter list has been built, you can use `CallVoidMethodA()` just as `CallVoidMethod()` was used earlier, specifying the `jvalue` array as a parameter:

```
JNIEXPORT void JNICALL Java_DisplayMessage_callMethod(
          JNIEnv *env,
          jclass cl) {
  jmethodID doStuff = env->GetStaticMethodID(cl,
          "doSomething",
          "(SIJ)V");
  jvalue parms[3];
  jshort first = 123;
  jint second = 456;
  jlong third = 789;
  parms[0].s = first;
  parms[1].i = second;
  parms[2].j = third;
  env->CallStaticVoidMethodA(cl, doStuff, parms);
}
```

In addition to the CallXXXMethodA() and CallStaticXXXMethodA(), JNI also provides the CallXXXMethodV() and CallStaticXXXMethodV() functions. Those functions are similar to the ones just described that accept a jvalue array, but they allow you to specify a va_list, which is a C construct used to pass a variable number of arguments to functions. Other functions are also provided to call overridden methods in the superclass; refer to the documentation if you find that you need them.

Creating Java Objects in Native Methods

Up to this point, all values used in native methods were primitives or they were objects created within Java code. However, you'll sometimes want to create Java objects inside native code, perhaps to use as a return value or to use as a parameter when calling some Java method that will be invoked. Primitive values are created by simply declaring them and assigning a value, as in the following examples:

```
// Create a boolean value
jboolean myFlag = JNI_TRUE;
// Create an int value
jint myInt = 123;
```

Creating an array of primitive values is almost as simple, and can be accomplished using the appropriate NewXXXArray() function and specifying the size of the array (the number of elements). For example, to create an array of int/jint values, you could use code like the following:

```
jintArray myArray = env->NewIntArray(10);
```

As you would expect, there is a NewXXXArray() function for each of the primitive types (boolean, byte, char, etc.).

String objects are also very easy to create because the NewStringUTF() function is provided explicitly for that purpose:

```
jstring newString = env->NewStringUTF("Created in a native method");
```

You can also use the NewString() function to create a String from a sequence of Unicode characters, as shown in the following code. NewString() requires you to pass it a pointer to a set of Unicode characters and a jsize that indicates the number of characters in the sequence:

```
JNIEXPORT void JNICALL Java_DisplayMessage_printMessage
    (JNIEnv *env, jclass cl, jstring text)
{
  const jchar *ptr = env->GetStringChars(text, NULL);
  jsize length = env->GetStringLength(text);
  jstring newText = env->NewString(ptr, length);
  env->ReleaseStringChars(text, ptr);
}
```

Creating other objects is almost as simple, and is very similar to calling an instance method, although in reality, you're calling a constructor. In fact, the only differences are that the method/constructor name is always <init> and instead of using the CallXXXMethod() function, you use NewObject(). For example, suppose that you wish to create native code that creates an instance of GregorianCalendar using the constructor shown below that accepts three int values, one each for the year, month, and date:

```
// Create a GregorianCalendar initialized to October 31, 1970
GregorianCalendar gc = new GregorianCalendar(1970, 10, 31);
```

The steps needed to implement equivalent native code are as follows:

❑ Use the FindClass() function to obtain a jclass that represents the GregorianCalendar class.

❑ Call GetMethodID() to retrieve the jmethodID representing the GregorianCalendar constructor that accepts three integer values. Specifying a name of <init> indicates that the method ID should be that of a constructor

❑ Pass the jclass, jmethodID, and parameter values to NewObject(). That function returns a jobject, which in this case is a reference to the new GregorianCalendar instance.

An example of how this code can be implemented is shown below:

```
jclass gcClass = env->FindClass("java/util/GregorianCalendar");
jmethodID ymdConst = env->GetMethodID(gcClass, "<init>", "(III)V");
jint year = 1970;
jint month = 9;
jint date = 31;
jobject calendar = env->NewObject(gcClass, ymdConst, year, month, date);
```

In addition, just as there are CallXXXMethodA() functions that allow you to pass a jvalue array, the NewObjectA() function allows you to do the same thing when creating a new object. An example of how this can be used is provided in the following code segment, which is functionally identical to the previous implementation:

```
jclass gcClass = env->FindClass("java/util/GregorianCalendar");
jmethodID ymdConst = env->GetMethodID(gcClass, "<init>", "(III)V");
jvalue parms[3];
parms[0].i = 1970;
parms[1].i = 9;
parms[2].i = 31;
jobject calendar = env->NewObjectA(gcClass, ymdConst, parms);
```

Finally, the NewObjectV() function allows you to specify a va_list that contains the argument values, just as with CallXXXMethodV().

An alternative to the NewObject() functions is AllocObject(), which also creates a new object, but only requires that you specify a single parameter that identifies the object's class. While the NewObject() functions behave the same way that the new operation does in Java, AllocObject() is slightly different in that it does not invoke any of the constructors defined in the class for which you're creating an instance. In effect, AllocObject() creates an "uninitialized" instance of the class you specify. Since it's common for constructors to contain code that must be executed for an object to be initialized to an appropriate state, you should not normally use AllocObject(), but an example of how it can be invoked is shown below:

```
jclass gcClass = env->FindClass("java/util/GregorianCalendar");
jobject calendar = env->AllocObject(gcClass);
```

Creating an object array is also possible through the NewObjectArray() function that accepts three arguments: a jsize representing the number of array elements, a jclass identifying the object type and an initial value for each of the elements. For example, the following code segment creates a new array of ten GregorianCalendar objects, initializing each one to the date represented by the calendar variable:

```
jclass gcClass = env->FindClass(
    "java/util/GregorianCalendar");
jmethodID ymdConst = env->GetMethodID(gcClass, "<init>", "(III)V");
jvalue parms[3];
parms[0].i = 1970;
parms[1].i = 9;
parms[2].i = 31;
jobject calendar = env->NewObjectA(gcClass, ymdConst, parms);
jsize count = 10;
jarray newArray = env->NewObjectArray(count, gcClass, calendar);
jobjectArray calArray = (jobjectArray)newArray;
```

Native Methods and Exceptions

Although it's easiest to use JNI with C or C++ code, JNI makes no assumptions about the language in which native methods will be implemented. Therefore, it's not possible to assume that a mechanism equivalent to Java's exception handling will be available. However, since native methods interact with Java code, it's necessary to allow them to generate exceptions and to handle exceptions that have been thrown. It's not appropriate to say that native methods are able to "throw" or "catch" exceptions, because they do not do so, at least not in the traditional sense.

In fact, from the perspective of native methods, exceptions do not directly alter the flow of control at all. For example, if native code calls a Java method and that method throws an exception, the native code's execution is not automatically interrupted. Instead, the native method must explicitly check to see if an interruption was generated, and if so, it can take appropriate steps to handle the exception.

That action may involve some sort of recovery from the error, or the native code can either ignore the error completely or clear the original exception and throw a different one. Similarly, the execution of code in a native method is not interrupted when that code generates an exception, although you should normally design your native methods to return after generating an exception. That's because calling some of the JNI functions while an exception is pending can produce unpredictable results, so you should check for and clear exceptions after each function call that's capable of generating them.

As an example of how an exception can be generated from inside a native method, we'll update DisplayMessage so that it appears as shown below:

```
public class DisplayMessage {

  static {
    System.loadLibrary("MessageHandler");
  }

  public static void main(String[] args) {

    try {
      showMessage("Hello, Brett");
```

```
      } catch (IOException ioe) {
        // do something with this exception
      }

    }
    private static native void showMessage(String name)
      throws java.io.IOException;

  }
```

Next, a simple implementation of the showMessage() function can be provided that uses ThrowNew() to generate an exception. The first parameter passed to ThrowNew is a jclass representing the type of exception to generate, while the second parameter identifies the text that should be associated with the exception:

```
JNIEXPORT void JNICALL Java_DisplayMessage_showMessage(
    JNIEnv *env, jclass cl, jstring msgText) {
  // Deliberately throw an exception
  jclass exClass = env->FindClass("java/io/IOException");
  jint result = env->ThrowNew(exClass,
        "IOException thrown from native method");
}
```

Running the program produces this result:

```
Exception in thread "main" java.io.IOException: IOException thrown from
native method
        at DisplayMessage.showMessage(Native Method)
        at DisplayMessage.main(DisplayMessage.java:8)
```

Although the ThrowNew() function is adequate for most cases, you'll sometimes wish to use Exception subclass constructors that accept more than a single String parameter. In that case, you can create an instance of Exception using the NewObject() method and then invoke the Throw() function. The following native code is functionally identical to that shown above, but instead of using ThrowNew(), this implementation explicitly creates an IOException instance and passes it to the Throw() function:

```
JNIEXPORT void JNICALL Java_DisplayMessage_showMessage (
          JNIEnv *env, jclass cl, jstring text) {
  jclass ioeClass = env->FindClass("java/io/IOException");
  jmethodID ioeConst = env->GetMethodID(ioeClass,
      "<init>", "(Ljava/lang/String;)V");
  jobject ex = env->NewObject(ioeClass, ioeConst, text);
  env->Throw((jthrowable)ex);
}
```

In some cases, you may encounter an unexpected error condition from which you cannot recover, in which case simply throwing an exception is not sufficient. When that occurs, you can use the FatalError() function to indicate that an unrecoverable error has occurred. You must pass a message to the function, which will send the message to the standard error (System.err) channel and terminate the virtual machine from which the native code was invoked. An example of how this can be done is shown below:

```
env->FatalError("Unable to create a socket connection to the server");
```

Handling Exceptions In Native Code

To illustrate how a native method can process an exception thrown by a function it calls (which may in turn execute a Java method), we'll make a small modification to `DisplayMessage`. The somewhat unusual code contained in the `doSomething()` method is deliberately designed to result in a `NullPointerException` being thrown:

```java
public class DisplayMessage {

  static {
    System.loadLibrary("MessageHandler");
  }

  public static void main(String[] args) throws Exception {
    showMessage("Hello, Brett");
  }

  private static native void showMessage(String name)
      throws java.io.IOException;

  private static void doSomething () {
    Object o = null;
    o.toString();
  }

}
```

The `doSomething()` method can be called by the native code, which will also be responsible for handling the exception that's generated:

```c
JNIEXPORT void JNICALL Java_DisplayMessage_showMessage(
    JNIEnv *env, jclass cl, jstring msgText) {
  jmethodID doSomething = env->GetStaticMethodID(cl,
    "doSomething", "()V");
  env->CallStaticVoidMethod(cl, doSomething);
  // ...
}
```

When your native code wishes to determine whether an exception is pending, it can call the `ExceptionOccurred()` function. If an exception is pending, that function returns a `jthrowable`, but if no exception was pending, a `NULL` value is returned instead:

```c
JNIEXPORT void JNICALL Java_DisplayMessage_showMessage(
    JNIEnv *env, jclass cl, jstring msgText) {
  jmethodID doSomething = env->GetStaticMethodID(cl,
    "doSomething", "()V");
  env->CallStaticVoidMethod(cl, doSomething);
  jthrowable exception = env->ExceptionOccurred();
  // ...
}
```

When the native method determines that an exception has occurred, the action it takes will depend upon the design of your code. The native method can clear the exception and ignore it by simply calling the `ExceptionClear()` function as shown below:

```
JNIEXPORT void JNICALL Java_DisplayMessage_showMessage(
    JNIEnv *env, jclass cl, jstring msgText) {
  jmethodID doSomething = env->GetStaticMethodID(cl,
    "doSomething", "()V");
  env->CallStaticVoidMethod(cl, doSomething);
  jthrowable exception = env->ExceptionOccurred();
  if (exception != NULL) {
    env->ExceptionClear();
  }
}
```

Another option is to print the stack trace that indicates where the exception was thrown from, and this can be done by calling `ExceptionDescribe()`:

```
JNIEXPORT void JNICALL Java_DisplayMessage_showMessage(
    JNIEnv *env, jclass cl, jstring msgText) {
  jmethodID doSomething = env->GetStaticMethodID(cl,
    "doSomething", "()V");
  env->CallStaticVoidMethod(cl, doSomething);
  jthrowable exception = env->ExceptionOccurred();
  if (exception != NULL) {
    env->ExceptionDescribe();
  }
}
```

`ExceptionDescribe()` produces the same output that would be generated by calling the `Exception`'s `printStackTrace()` method, and an example of this output appears below:

```
Exception in thread "main" java.lang.NullPointerException
  at DisplayMessage.doSomething(DisplayMessage.java:16)
  at DisplayMessage.showMessage(Native Method)
  at DisplayMessage.main(DisplayMessage.java:8)
```

Like `ExceptionClear()`, the `ExceptionDescribe()` function results in the exception being cleared, so you should not use this method if you wish to allow the exception to remain pending.

Another function called `ExceptionCheck()` was introduced in Java 1.2 and it returns a `jboolean` that indicates whether an exception is pending. A value of `JNI_TRUE` indicates that an exception is pending, while `JNI_FALSE` is returned otherwise.

Comparisons

You'll sometimes wish to compare two references that exist within your native code, just as you compare references in Java. For example, you might implement the following code in Java and wish to provide the same functionality to a native method:

```
Object ref1, ref2;
// ...
if (ref1 == ref2) {
  System.out.println("They point to the same object instance");
}
```

To provide this functionality in a native method, you must use `IsSameObject()`, which is passed two `jobject` parameters and returns a `jboolean` that indicates whether the two references point to the same object:

```
jobject ref1, ref2;
// ...
jboolean result = env->IsSameObject(ref1, ref2);
if (result == JNI_TRUE) {
  printf("They point to the same object instance\n");
}
```

It's also often helpful to be able to determine whether an object is an instance of a particular class or if it implements an interface. When writing Java code, this test is performed using the `instanceof` keyword, and JNI provides an equivalent `IsInstanceOf()` function. For example, the following code segment tests the `jobject` to determine whether it's an instance of `java.lang.Integer`:

```
jobject testObject;
// ...
jclass intClass = env->FindClass("java/lang/Integer");
jboolean result = env->IsInstanceOf(testObject, intClass);
if (result == JNI_TRUE) {
  printf("The object is an instance of Integer\n");
}
```

Threads

No mention has been made up to this point of any issues related to using native methods in a multithread application, which is partly due to the fact that native methods don't introduce any special problems, although this can depend on the code library in use. However, just as with Java methods, you must ensure that deadlock and race conditions are avoided, and race conditions are usually prevented by synchronizing methods and/or blocks of code. JNI includes functions that provide the functionality of Java's `synchronized` keyword, allowing the currently executing thread to obtain ownership of some object's monitor.

To access a monitor, you can call the `MonitorEnter()` function, passing it a single `jobject` parameter that identifies the object associated with the monitor you wish to obtain. Just as with the `synchronized` keyword, `MonitorEnter()` will cause the current thread to become the owner of the monitor if no other thread owns it and will cause the current thread to become blocked if the monitor is already owned.

As described in Chapter 3, a thread may execute more than one section of code that's synchronized on the same object, and each time a synchronized segment is entered, a counter associated with the monitor is incremented. Only when the thread exits the first synchronized method or code block that it entered is the counter decremented to zero and the monitor released.

In a similar fashion, the counter value is incremented each time `MonitorEnter()` is called successfully, and decremented when `MonitorExit()` is invoked. Similarly, the monitor is not released until the counter value returns to zero, so you should ensure that your native code contains a `MonitorExit()` call that will be executed for each `MonitorEnter()`. If you do not do so, the thread that owns the monitor will not release it, which may prevent other threads from accessing the resource.

Reference Types

JNI provides several different reference types, although all of the references used so far have been **local references** that are valid only during the function execution in which they're defined. Once execution of a native method completes, all local references become invalid and the objects that they were associated with become eligible for garbage collection.

If you call a function that obtains a `jclass`, it is not acceptable to save the pointer so that it can be accessed by another thread or used during another invocation of the native method by the same thread. To illustrate this point, let's suppose that you have created a native method that calculates the sum of the elements in an `int` array and returns the total as an instance of `java.lang.Integer`.

```java
public class DisplayMessage {

  static {
    System.loadLibrary("MessageHandler");
  }

  public static void main(String[] args) throws Exception {
    int[] ints1 = {1, 2, 3, 4, 5};
    int[] ints2 = {6, 7, 8, 9, 10};

    System.out.println(addIntegers(ints));
    System.out.println(addIntegers(ints2));
  }

  public static native Integer addIntegers(int[] values);

}
```

The implementation of the native `addIntegers()` method might look like this:

```c
JNIEXPORT jobject JNICALL Java_DisplayMessage_addIntegers(
    JNIEnv *env, jclass cl, jintArray array) {
  jobject result;
  jsize count = env->GetArrayLength(array);
  jint *intValue = env->GetIntArrayElements(array, NULL);
  jsize i = 0;
  jint total = 0;
  for (i = 0; i < count; i++) {
    total += intValue[i];
  }
  jclass intClass = env->FindClass("java/lang/Integer");
  jmethodID constructor = env->GetMethodID(intClass,
      "<init>", "(I)V");
  result = env->NewObject(intClass, constructor, total);
  return result;
}
```

Each time this code is executed, the `FindClass()` function is called to obtain the `jclass` associated with `java.lang.Integer`, and a `jmethodID` is retrieved from the `GetMethodID()` function. It might be tempting to cache one or both of those two values to allow the function to execute more quickly, as is done in the following listing:

```
JNIEXPORT jobject JNICALL Java_DisplayMessage_addIntegers (
    JNIEnv *env, jclass cl, jintArray array) {
  static jclass intClass = NULL;
  jobject result;
  jsize count = env->GetArrayLength(array);
  jint *intValue = env->GetIntArrayElements(array, NULL);
  jsize i = 0;
  jint total = 0;
  for (i = 0; i < count; i++) {
    total += intValue[i];
  }
  if (intClass == NULL) {
    intClass = env->FindClass("java/lang/Integer");
  }
  jmethodID constructor = env->GetMethodID(intClass,
      "<init>", "(I)V");
  result = env->NewObject(intClass, constructor, total);
  return result;
}
```

With this modified implementation, FindClass() will be called the first time addNumbers() is called, and the cached value stored in the static intClass field will be used after that. The problem is that intClass represents a local reference that becomes invalid once the native method invocation in which it was created completes execution. If you write code that calls the native method twice, it will produce output like that shown below:

```
#
# HotSpot Virtual Machine Error, EXCEPTION_ACCESS_VIOLATION
# Please report this error at
# http://java.sun.com/cgi-bin/bugreport.cgi
#
# Error ID: 4F533F57494E13120E43505002D4
#

abnormal program termination
```

To maintain a reference that remains valid across invocations of a native method, you must use the NewGlobalRef() function to create a **global reference**. Global references are functionally identical to local references, but global references remain valid until explicitly released by calling DeleteGlobalRef().

Unlike local references, a global reference can also be used by a thread other than the one that created it, so global references are also useful in multithreaded applications. As shown below, the previous code can easily be modified to store the jclass reference in a global reference:

```
JNIEXPORT jobject JNICALL Java_DisplayMessage_addIntegers(
    JNIEnv *env, jclass cl, jintArray array) {
  static jclass intClass = NULL;
  jobject result;
  jsize count = env->GetArrayLength(array);
  jint *intValue = env->GetIntArrayElements(array, NULL);
  jsize i = 0;
  jint total = 0;
  for (i = 0; i < count; i++) {
```

```
      total += intValue[i];
    }
    if (intClass == NULL) {
      jclass localClass = env->FindClass("java/lang/Integer");
      intClass = (jclass)(env->NewGlobalRef(localClass));
    }
    jmethodID constructor = env->GetMethodID(intClass,
        "<init>", "(I)V");
    result = env->NewObject(intClass, constructor, total);
    return result;
  }
```

If this technique is used, the jclass object obtained during the first execution of the addIntegers() method will remain valid and cannot be garbage collected unless it is passed to the DeleteGlobalRef() function as shown below:

```
    env->DeleteGlobalRef(intclass);
```

Unlike Java code, where you can simply assign a null value to references, your native code must explicitly indicate that it wishes to release a reference. For that reason, a DeleteLocalRef() function is also provided by JNI that allows you to release local references.

Java 2 also introduced the concept of a **weak reference**, which is simply a reference that does not prevent the referenced object (the **referent**) from being reclaimed by the garbage collector. JNI supports a variation of a global reference called a **weak global reference**, and like (strong) global references, a weak global reference remains valid after the method invocation in which it is created.

A weak global reference is also like a normal global reference in that it can be used by threads other than the one that created it. Unlike normal global references, however, weak references do not prevent their referents from being garbage collected. To create a weak global reference, simply use the NewWeakGlobalRef() function as in the following example:

```
    exClass = (jclass)(env->NewWeakGlobalRef(localClass));
```

Since the referents of weak references can be garbage collected at any time, it's necessary to be able to determine when a reference is associated with an object that has been destroyed. To accomplish this in a native method, you must use the IsSameObject() function and compare the weak reference to NULL as shown below:

```
    jboolean isInvalid = env->IsSameObject(exClass, NULL);
```

The IsSameObject() function returns a value of JNI_TRUE if the weak reference was associated with an object that has been garbage collected and JNI_FALSE otherwise. When a weak reference is no longer needed, you must explicitly release it by calling DeleteWeakGlobalRef().

Caching Other Data Types

As we've just seen, it's not acceptable to use a local reference to cache a jobject or an instance of one of its subclasses (for example, jclass, jstring, jarray, jthrowable). However, it is possible to cache a method ID or a field ID as is done in the following code:

```
JNIEXPORT jobject JNICALL Java_DisplayMessage_addIntegers(
    JNIEnv *env, jclass cl, jintArray array) {
  static jclass intClass = NULL;
  static jmethodID constructor = NULL;
  jobject result;
  jsize count = env->GetArrayLength(array);
  jint *intValue = env->GetIntArrayElements(array, NULL);
  jsize i = 0;
  jint total = 0;
  for (i = 0; i < count; i++) {
    total += intValue[i];
  }
  if (intClass == NULL) {
    jclass localClass = env->FindClass("java/lang/Integer");
    intClass = (jclass)(env->NewGlobalRef(localClass));
  }
  if (constructor == NULL) {
    constructor = env->GetMethodID(intClass, "<init>", "(I)V");
  }
  result = env->NewObject(intClass, constructor, total);
  return result;
}
```

> Although it is possible to cache most values through static and/or global references, you should never cache the JNIEnv value and reuse it, especially not in a multithreaded application. Instead, simply use the value that's passed to the native method.

Adding Java Code to a Native Application

The primary purpose of JNI is to allow you to call native methods from a Java-based application, but you may sometimes find it convenient to do the opposite: call Java methods from a native application. Fortunately, JNI provides the **Invocation API** that makes it extremely easy for you to do so, and we'll now see how to call a simple Java application from a C++ program written on Windows using Visual C++.

To execute Java code from a native application, you must initialize a Java Virtual Machine, which will normally be a JVM that's installed on the machine on which you're running the native application. You should note that the Microsoft JVM only supports JNI from SDK 3.1 and above.

In this case, for example, we'll assume that Sun's Java Development Kit is installed at D:\jdk1.3. Once the JVM is installed, you can activate it using the JNI_CreateJavaVM() function that accepts three arguments: a JavaVM pointer, a JNIEnv pointer, and an instance of JavaVMInitArgs. To prepare the first two parameters (the JavaVM and JNIEnv pointers), you must simply declare a variable for each one: you are not responsible for creating an instance of JavaVM or JNIEnv. Instead, the JNI_CreateJavaVM() function creates them for you and simply uses these two arguments to return references to them to your native code.

However, we can now create the initial implementation of our C++ application with declarations for each of the three arguments. Note that jni.h is included in this application, since it contains many of the constants and other definitions that are needed to activate a JVM through the Invocation API:

```
#include <jni.h>

void main() {
  JavaVM *jvm;
  JNIEnv *env;
  JavaVMInitArgs vm_args;
  // ...
}
```

JavaVMInitArgs is used to provide information such as the JVM version and the CLASSPATH, as well as any system properties that would normally be set on the command line and is one of the structures defined inside jni.h that is required by our application, and its definition is very simple:

```
typedef struct JavaVMInitArgs {
    jint version;
    jint nOptions;
    JavaVMOption *options;
    jboolean ignoreUnrecognized;
} JavaVMInitArgs;
```

As illustrated here, the JavaVMInitArgs structure is made of up of four fields, and the usage of each field is described below.

version

JDK 1.1 and JDK 1.2/Java 2 virtual machines use slightly different initialization arguments, and this field allows you to specify the type of virtual machine you are activating. If this field is assigned a value of the JNI_VERSION_1_2 constant defined in jni.h, the third parameter passed to JNI_CreateJavaVM() is assumed to be an instance of JavaVMInitArgs. However, if the value of JNI_VERSION_1_1 is stored here, it is assumed that the structure is instead an instance of JDK1_1InitArgs. In this case, we're using a Java 2 JVM, so we'll assign a value of JNI_VERSION_1_2 to the field as shown below:

```
vm_args.version = JNI_VERSION_1_2;
```

nOptions

When you active a JVM from a command-line, you can specify options that are used during the execution of the JVM. For example, you might specify -cp or -classpath to specify the class path that should be used by the JVM or you might use -Xms and -Xmx to specify the initial and maximum heap sizes as shown below:

```
java -Xms8m -Xmx32m MyTest
```

The Invocation API also allows you to specify valid JVM options, and the nOptions field in JavaVMInitArgs indicates how many of those options you have specified. In this case, we'll use two options when activating the JVM, and the nOptions field can be initialized appropriately:

```
vm_args.nOptions = 2;
```

*options

This field represents a pointer to an array of `JavaVMOption` instances, where each of those instances represents an option that you wish to pass to the JVM. The size of the array should be equal to the value stored in the `nOptions` field as described above, and a reference to the array should be stored in this field as shown below:

```
JavaVMOption options[2];
vm_args.options = options;
```

JavaVMOption

Each instance of `JavaVMOption` represents an option that will be passed to the JVM. The definition of `JavaVMOption` is found in `jni.h`, and is shown below:

```
typedef struct JavaVMOption {
    char *optionString;
    void *extraInfo;
} JavaVMOption;
```

Since the `*extraInfo` pointer is not currently used, the only code you must write for a `JavaVMOption` definition is a statement that assigns the option text to the `*optionString` field. In this case, we'll use two options: one that will cause the JVM to display ("verbose") diagnostic messages describing JNI activity, and another that sets the class path to the current directory:

```
options[0].optionString = "-verbose:jni";
options[1].optionString = "-Djava.class.path=.";
```

ignoreUnrecognized

The last field defined in `JavaVMInitArgs` is `ignoreUnrecognized`, and when it is set to `JNI_TRUE`, it indicates that the JVM should ignore any options that were specified. However, if this field is set to `JNI_FALSE`, the JVM will exit if an unrecognized option is found. Since it will usually be the case that your native application will be somewhat tightly coupled to a given JVM, this should not normally be a problem, and in this case, the field is set to `JNI_TRUE`:

```
#include <jni.h>

void main() {
  JavaVM *jvm;
  JNIEnv *env;
  JavaVMInitArgs vm_args;

  vm_args.version = JNI_VERSION_1_2;
  vm_args.nOptions = 2;
  JavaVMOption options[2];
  vm_args.options = options;
  options[0].optionString = "-verbose:jni";
  options[1].optionString = "-Djava.class.path=.";
  vm_args.ignoreUnrecognized = JNI_TRUE;
  // ...
}
```

GetDefaultJavaVMInitArgs

There is also a function provided in jni.h that you can use to load default values into the JavaVMInitArgs structure. Before you do this you must set the version field to the JNI version you require the VM to support. This will also set default heap and stack sizes. A typical call to this function is as follows:

```
JNI_GetDefaultJavaVMInitArgs(&vm_args);
```

The argument passed to the function is a pointer to the structure to be loaded. Once we have loaded the default configuration values, we can continue to specify the remainder values as defined above.

Activating the JVM

Now that the JavaVMInitArgs structure has been completely initialized, it's possible to call the JNI_CreateJavaVM() function that will activate an instance of the JVM:

```
jint result = JNI_CreateJavaVM(&jvm, (void**)&env, &vm_args);
```

The jint value returned by JNI_CreateJavaVM() will be equal to 0 if the JVM was activated successfully or will contain a negative value if an error occurred. If the call was successful, the JavaVM and JNIEnv pointers (jvm and env respectively) will be initialized appropriately. At that point, you can use the JNIEnv value to invoke Java methods just as you would normally do from native code. For example, if the C++ method is completed as shown below, it will execute the main() method of a Java class called NativeTest that's defined in the us.txt.plano.bspell package:

```
jclass mainClass = env->FindClass("us/tx/plano/bspell/NativeTest");
jmethodID method = env->GetStaticMethodID(mainClass, "main",
                                          "([Ljava/lang/String;)V");
jclass stringClass = env->FindClass("java/lang/String");
jobjectArray args = env->NewObjectArray(0, stringClass, NULL);
env->CallStaticVoidMethod(mainClass, method, args);
```

Finally, when you wish to terminate the JVM from within your native program, you can use the DestroyJavaVM() function as shown below:

```
#include <jni.h>

void main() {
  JavaVM *jvm;
  JNIEnv *env;
  JavaVMInitArgs vm_args;

  vm_args.version = JNI_VERSION_1_2;
  vm_args.nOptions = 2;
  JavaVMOption options[2];
  vm_args.options = options;
  options[0].optionString = "-verbose:jni";
  options[1].optionString = "-Djava.class.path=.";
  vm_args.ignoreUnrecognized = JNI_TRUE;
```

```
jint result = JNI_CreateJavaVM(&jvm, (void**)&env, &vm_args);

jclass mainClass = env->FindClass("NativeTest");
jmethodID method = env->GetStaticMethodID(mainClass, "main",
    "([Ljava/lang/String;)V");
jclass stringClass = env->FindClass("java/lang/String");
jobjectArray args = env->NewObjectArray(0, stringClass, NULL);
env->CallStaticVoidMethod(mainClass, method, args);

jvm->DestroyJavaVM();
}
```

An example of the NativeTest class appears below. As you can see, there is nothing unusual about this class, and although the static main() method was invoked in this example, you could just as easily use the NewObject() function described earlier to create and initialize an instance of NativeTest directly:

```
package us.tx.plano.bspell;

public class NativeTest {

  public static void main(String[] args) {
      NativeTest nt = new NativeTest();
  }

  public NativeTest() {
    //  Initialize and execute the application code
  }

}
```

Compiling the Native Application

If you attempt to compile and link the C++ code listed above with Visual C++, you will receive an error message like the one shown below:

```
PerformCall.obj : error LNK2001: unresolved external symbol
__imp__JNI_CreateJavaVM@12
Debug/CallJVM.exe : fatal error LNK1120: 1 unresolved externals
```

This occurs because the linker could not find the function that handles the JNI_CreateJavaVM call, which is defined in the libjvm.so file on Solaris and the jvm.lib file on Windows. The file is stored in the /lib subdirectory below the location where you installed the JDK, and the screenshot overleaf illustrates how you can identify the appropriate file to Visual C++ when the JDK was installed at D:\jdk1.3:

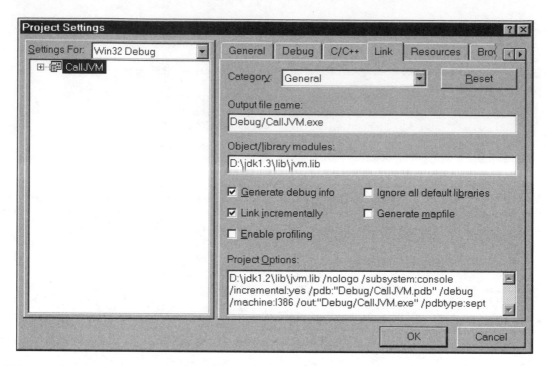

To execute the C++ program, you must also ensure that the directory containing the `jvm.dll` file (on Windows) or `libjvm.so` (on Solaris) is included in your path. If you are using Java 1.3, you will find two versions of the appropriate `jvm.dll` or `libjvm.so` file: one for the HotSpot JVM, and another for the "classic" JVM. The HotSpot file is stored in the `/jre/bin/hotspot` subdirectory below your JDK installation directory, while the "classic" file is located in `/jre/bin/classic`. For example, if you've created the C++ application on Windows and have installed the JDK into `D:\jdk1.3`, you could use the following command to add the appropriate directory to your path:

```
set PATH=%PATH%;D:\jdk1.3\jre\bin\classic
```

Once the appropriate directory is included in your path, you can execute the C++ application, and it in turn will activate a JVM and call the `main()` method in the `NativeTest` class.

The –verbose:jni Option

One of the options specified in the above example is `–verbose:jni`, and this option can be very helpful when using the Invocation API and when calling native methods from a Java application. The option causes the JVM to issue diagnostic messages that provide information describing its activities, and an example of the output produced is shown below:

```
[Dynamic-linking native method java/lang/Object.registerNatives ... JNI]
[Registering JNI native method java/lang/Object.hashCode]
[Registering JNI native method java/lang/Object.wait]
[Registering JNI native method java/lang/Object.notify]
[Registering JNI native method java/lang/Object.notifyAll]
[Registering JNI native method java/lang/Object.clone]
[Dynamic-linking native method java/lang/Thread.registerNatives ... JNI]
```

```
[Registering JNI native method java/lang/Thread.start]
 [Dynamic-linking native method java/lang/Throwable.fillInStackTrace ... JNI]
[Dynamic-linking native method java/io/FileInputStream.open ... JNI]
[Dynamic-linking native method java/io/Win32FileSystem.getLength ... JNI]
[Dynamic-linking native method java/io/FileInputStream.readBytes ... JNI]
[Dynamic-linking native method java/io/FileInputStream.close ... JNI]
[Dynamic-linking native method java/io/FileInputStream.available ... JNI]
[Dynamic-linking native method java/lang/ClassLoader.defineClass0 ... JNI]
[Dynamic-linking native method java/io/FileOutputStream.writeBytes ... JNI]
JVM activated by a native application
```

Summary

In this chapter, we've discussed the importance of native methods and when you should (and should not) use them. In addition, we've seen how easily they can be defined and invoked from Java code, as well as how to execute Java code from a native application. Examples were given of how to pass parameter values and access return values, how to handle exceptions in native code, and to create new objects, access fields, and invoke methods and constructors. With this information, you should be prepared to take advantage of JNI's capabilities when they are needed by your application.

Professional Java Programmin

Online discussion at http://p2p.wrox.com

Coding Standards

When you buy a book like this one, you usually make certain assumptions about the way that it's organized and its material presented. For example, you probably expect the book to have a table of contents, an index, and to be divided into chapters. You probably also assume that the chapters are divided into paragraphs, the paragraphs into sentences, and so on. In other words, you expect the information to be presented in a way that's at least somewhat familiar, easy to read, and consistent with the standards that are used in other books of its type.

Similarly, when it comes to software, it's helpful to follow certain conventions in the way that the software is written, formatted and documented. Doing so makes the code easier to read and maintain, especially for programmers who didn't write it and aren't as familiar with the code. This section describes the conventions commonly used in Java, and provides an explanation of why it's a good idea to follow them.

The guidelines presented here are based largely on those published by Sun (http://jsp2.java.sun.com/docs/codeconv/html/CodeConvTOC.doc.html), and for the most part have been widely adopted by Java programmers. However, it's important to realize that some of these guidelines are followed more closely than others, and that there really are no "correct" standards, and to a large degree it is down to experience and personal choice.

Naming Conventions

Naming conventions are guidelines for naming code elements such as packages, classes, fields, and methods.

There are seven different sections within a Java source file, as shown in the listing below, and we'll examine the naming and coding conventions for each of them where appropriate. The seven sections are:

- ❑ The package statement, which is optional (line 1)
- ❑ Zero or more import statements (line 3)
- ❑ The class or interface definition (line 5)
- ❑ Field definitions (lines 7-15)
- ❑ Constructors (lines 17-22)
- ❑ Methods (lines 24-26)
- ❑ Inner classes (not shown)

```
1    package com.barewood.global.busobjs;
2
3    import java.sql.Date;
4
5    public class CreditCard extends Object {
6
7        public final static int AMEX_TYPE = 3;
8        public final static int VISA_TYPE = 4;
9        public final static int MASTERCARD_TYPE = 5;
10       public final static int DISC_TYPE = 6;
11
12       protected int cardType;
13       protected long cardNumber;
14       protected Date expirationDate;
15       protected String cardHolderName;
16
17       public CreditCard(int type, long num, Date exp, String name) {
18           cardType = type;
19           cardNumber = num;
20           expirationDate = exp;
21           cardHolderName = name;
22       }
23
24       public String toString() {
25           return "CreditCard[cardNumber=" + cardNumber + "]";
26       }
27
28  }
```

The first three elements (package statement, imports, and class definition) must occur in that order for this code to be successfully compiled. On the other hand, class members (fields, constructors, methods, and inner classes) are allowed to appear in any order, and may even be interleaved. For example, you can place a field definition between two methods, although this is definitely not good coding practice. Instead, you should group elements of the same type together and place them within the class definition in the order shown above.

The Package Statement

The package statement indicates which package the class belongs to, and if included, must be the first non-comment item that appears in a source file. Although it's technically valid to use mixed case in the package name, you should use all lowercase letters and keep the name short. In fact, abbreviations and acronyms are very common, such as awt for Abstract Windowing Toolkit and util instead of utilities.

To understand how to select a package name, let's review the purpose of packages in Java. You probably already know that they allow you to group related classes together, but what may not be obvious is that choosing a package name is the key to providing the class with a unique identity.

For example, in the Java core libraries, there are two classes named Date – one in the java.util package, and another in java.sql. As we'll see shortly, it's possible for you to write code that uses both of these, but this is only possible because the classes reside in different packages. On the other hand, suppose that two different developers within your organization create two different classes with the same name and in the same package. In that case, it will be impossible for you to use both classes in your application without changing the class name and/or location of at least one of the two classes.

Actually, avoiding collisions with programmers in the same company is a relatively simple task compared to avoiding collisions with every other Java programmer in the world. It's common when building an application to use third-party software when someone else has already solved a problem you're faced with, and is willing to allow others to use their code. Such an offering may be a "shrink-wrapped" commercial product, or code that's freely downloadable from a web site. In either case, with many programmers around the globe creating Java classes independently, the potential for collisions is greatly multiplied.

Fortunately, Sun recommends an approach to selecting a package name that can virtually guarantee uniqueness for your classes. The first component of your package name should be either a top-level domain name (for example, com, org, edu, gov, etc.) or a two-letter country code (for example, us, uk, fr, etc.). These are the same identifiers used for domain names on the Internet, and they're used here for a similar purpose – to provide uniqueness. For the remainder of the package name, you should specify as many "levels" as necessary to be reasonably certain that others will not accidentally select the same name.

For example, in a large corporation, there might be many departments and several programming teams within those departments, in which case it would probably be advisable to add a number of components to the package name. Assuming that PepsiCo Business Solutions Group is your employer and you work for the Information Technology Systems (ITS) department's Business Systems team, you might use a package name like com.pbsg.its.bussys.

As you can see, this approach makes collisions unlikely, even in a very large organization with many development groups. You can also use this technique if you're creating classes for your own personal use and want to avoid conflicts when you make your work available for others to use. In that situation, an appropriate package name could be based on your geographical location and include some other information that would ensure uniqueness. For example, I might use the country, state, and city that I live in, as well as an abbreviated version of my name us.tx.plano.bspell.

The odds of some other programmer using this same package name are probably very small, but in any case, it's generally not worthwhile to spend a great deal of time trying to come up with the "correct" package name. Keep in mind that the point here is simply to provide a reasonable expectation of uniqueness, so any approach that accomplishes this is usually appropriate.

Import Statements

Importing a class or interface allows you to reference it within your source code using the simple class name instead of the fully qualified name (for example, Vector instead of java.util.Vector). There are two versions of the import statement: one that imports a single class, and another that allows you to import all classes in a package. For example:

```
import java.util.Hashtable;
import java.util.Vector;
import java.awt.*;
```

The first two statements import the Hashtable and Vector classes from the java.util package, while the third imports all classes and interfaces defined in the java.awt package.

Besides allowing you to do less typing, importing classes also provides a degree of insulation from package name changes. For example, the Swing components that now reside in javax.swing were previously included in a package called com.sun.java.swing. To migrate from the old package to the new, code that imports these components requires only that the import statements change from something like import com.sun.java.swing.* to import javax.swing.*. On the other hand, code that references these classes using their fully qualified names must be updated in every place that such a reference exists.

While the use of import provides some valuable benefits, it's better to avoid the use of the form that imports all of the classes in a package (that is, import java.util.*), for two reasons. First, if you import all classes from many packages, it can become difficult for someone reading your code to determine which package contains a particular class. Second, using this form makes it more likely that you will import two classes from different packages that have the same name, as in the following code:

```
import java.util.*;
import java.sql.*;

public class NameCollision {
  public Vector myList;
  public Date myDate;
}
```

As mentioned previously, both the java.util and java.sql packages contain a Date class, and an attempt to compile this code results in an error. The error occurs because the compiler is unable to determine which type of Date the myDate field is meant to represent. It could be either java.util.Date or java.sql.Date.

One way to resolve this problem is to declare myDate using the fully qualified name of the appropriate class, such as, public java.sql.Date myDate. An alternative solution is to change or remove one or both of the import statements, so that only one Date class is imported. For example, if you're only using the Vector class in java.util, you could replace the first import statement with one that imports that specific class:

```
import java.util.Vector;
import java.sql.*;

public class NameCollision {
  public Vector myList;
  public Date myDate;
}
```

When using a large number of classes from a package, it can become tedious to add a separate import statement for each one. However, if you're reasonably certain that you'll only use one or a few classes from the package, it's worthwhile to import only the specific class or classes that you'll reference.

Class, Method, and Field Names

The names that you assign to classes, methods, and fields are very important, since they can provide an important clue to their function for someone who's reading your code. Unlike package names, it's usually better to avoid abbreviations and acronyms, except where their meaning is likely to be very clear. For example, a class called `SQLException` is recognizable by most programmers as an exception related to the Structured Query Language (SQL). Similarly, most developers would probably guess that a component called `currencyTextField` is a text field that contains a currency value, but may not find `currTF` as intuitive. A short name is preferable to a longer one, but only when it doesn't make your code more difficult to understand. When naming classes, interfaces, methods, and fields, you should use descriptive names, but make the names only as long as they must be for their meaning to be clear.

One situation where it is common to create short, meaningless names is when defining variables that are used for a limited purpose within a method, such as a loop index:

```
for (int i = 0; i < 10; i++)
```

In this situation, the function of the variable should be obvious even without a descriptive name, and it's acceptable to use short, often single-character names for purposes such as this. However, if the variable is used in many places within the loop, you may want to consider giving it a more meaningful name.

Classes

Common practice is to capitalize the first letter of a class name, along with the first letter of each **internal word** and every letter of an acronym, as in `StringBuffer`, `SecurityManager`, and `InterruptedIOException`. A class name should generally be a noun that describes what the class represents, even if it does not have a real-world counterpart.

Variables

Variable (or "field") names follow the same guidelines that class names do, with the exception that the first letter of the name should be lowercase. For example:

```
int studentID;
float testScore;
String webPageURL;
```

However, there is an exception to the capitalization rules for variables that applies when defining constants, which are usually `final`, `static`, and often `public`. For a constant, the name should consist of all capital letters, with internal words separated by underscore characters:

```
public static final float CENTER_ALIGNMENT = 0.5f;
```

As mentioned earlier, field declarations should all be grouped together at the beginning of a class. Static (or "class") variables should be defined first and then followed by instance variables. Within these two categories (static and instance), you should define the variables from most visible to least, specifically `public`, `protected`, default (no modifier), and `private`. For example:

```
public class VariableExample {

  public static int first;
  protected static int second;
  static int third;
```

```
    private static int fourth;

    public int fifth;
    protected int sixth;
    int seventh;
    private int eight;

}
```

Note that although Java compilers allow you to define multiple variables on a single line, you should place each declaration on its own line, which will make commenting easier as we'll see later. In addition, variables defined within a method body should be defined at the beginning of the method instead of the first place within the method where they're used. This makes it easier to locate the definition and ensures that the variable is available within the entire scope of the method. For example, the following code segment would generate an error message when compiled, because the value field is defined within a try block, and is not available in the scope of the return statement:

```
public int getValue(String val) {
  try {
    int value = Integer.parseInt(val);
  } catch (NumberFormatException nfe) {
    return -1;
  }
  return value;
}
```

Methods

Method names should be capitalized using the same rules defined for variables: the first letter should be lowercase, with the first letter of each internal word and each letter of an acronym capitalized. While class names are typically nouns, a method name should be (or contain) a verb that describes the function performed by the method, such addElement(), notifyAll(), or clone(). Unlike variables, which are grouped according to visibility, methods should be grouped together based on *functionality*. In other words, instead of putting all public methods at the beginning of the class, you should put methods close together that are related in function. This makes the code easier to read for someone attempting to trace the flow of execution.

Inner Classes

Inner class names should be capitalized in the same way as outer classes, although their location should vary based on size and usage. In general, a large inner class should be placed at the end of the enclosing class to prevent confusion over whether a method is defined within the inner class or within its enclosing class. However, in the case of a small inner class, particularly one that's referenced only in a single method, defining the inner class immediately after that method is often more convenient and does not usually affect the code's readability.

Anonymous inner classes should always be small, and implement or override only one or a few methods. If you're tempted to create a larger anonymous class, consider making it a named inner class instead.

Advantages of Using Naming Conventions

Following these naming conventions makes your code easier to read and understand. For example, you can easily distinguish a class name from a variable name because a class name should begin with an uppercase letter, while a variable name should not. For example, given the following two method calls, one can be easily identified as a call to a static method, while the other is performed using an object instance:

```
String letterGrade = ScoreConverter.getLetterGrade(98);
String studentName = roster.getStudentName(1234);
```

If this code is found in an application that adheres to the coding standards described here, you can reasonably assume that `ScoreConverter` is a class name and therefore that `getLetterGrade()` is a `static` method. In contrast, `roster` begins with a lowercase letter, which suggests that it is a variable containing a reference to some object instance. Of course, you could obtain this information by spending more time looking at the application code, but by following these coding conventions, you're providing valuable information to those who read your code, including yourself.

Coding Conventions

> Coding conventions are related to how code is formatted, where white space (blank lines and spaces) is, etc.

Using White Space

White space refers to any empty space added to your source code, such as spaces, blank lines, and tab indentions. White space allows you to separate items visually, which makes it much easier for someone who's reading your code to understand it. To appreciate the importance of using white space, read the following line:

Youshouldbeabletoreadthisbutitprobablytakeslongerthanusual.

Now compare the following two lines, both of which are technically valid:

```
for(int i=0;i<10;i++)
```

```
for (int i = 0; i < 10; i++)
```

As with the earlier example, you probably found the first line more difficult to read, because there are fewer visual cues to help in **parsing** or "breaking apart" the pieces. On a larger scale, if you add a blank line between methods defined in a Java source code file, it becomes much easier to quickly identify where one method ends and another begins. Some other guidelines that will help make your code more readable are:

❑ Insert at least one blank line between the sections of a class described earlier, between each constructor, and between each method.

❑ Insert a blank line after the local variable definitions within a method, and between different sections of code.

❑ Insert a space on each side of an operator, as in the previous example where there is a space on each side of the equal (=) sign. However, you should not use spaces with the **unary operators**, such as the increment (++), decrement (--), and not (!) operators.

❑ Separate the sections of a `for` statement with spaces. That is, put a space after the semicolons that separate the initialization, test, and increment sections, as illustrated above.

❑ When a keyword is followed by an open parenthesis, such as the `for` keyword in the previous example, insert a space after the keyword so that the statement does not resemble a method call. For the same reason, you should *not* insert a space between a method name and the open parenthesis when coding method calls.

❑ Commas in method parameter lists should be followed by a space to make it obvious where each parameter begins and ends.

Code Indention

A **code block** is any code contained between a pair of open and close braces ({}) and it's common practice to indent your code each time you start a new block. For example, the code shown below contains three blocks, with each nested block indented slightly more than the previous one:

```
public class HelloWorld {
  public static void main(String[] args) {
    if (args.length > 0) {
      System.out.println("Hello, " + args[0]);
    }
  }
}
```

In this example, it might not seem very important to indent because there are so few lines in each block. However, let's see what the code looks like without any indentations:

```
public class HelloWorld {
public static void main(String[] args) {
if (args.length > 0) {
System.out.println("Hello, " + args[0]);
}
}
}
```

Both versions will compile correctly, but as you can see, indenting your code allows you to easily determine the beginning and end of a block. This simple class is much more readable when indented, and it's even more important to format your code this way when it contains more levels of blocks embedded within one another.

Now that the importance of indenting has been established, the obvious questions are which characters (tabs or spaces) to use, and how many spaces/columns to indent. The JavaSoft documentation suggests that you should indent four columns for each level, but it also states that the "construction of indentation (spaces versus tabs) is unspecified". In other words, it's left up to you to decide. The use of tabs versus spaces and even the number of spaces to indent per block are areas where there doesn't seem to be widespread agreement among Java programmers. Ultimately, it winds up being a matter of personal preference, and what really matters is that you do indent your code blocks, and do so in a consistent manner.

In some cases, the use of braces is optional, such as when creating an `if` statement or a `for` loop that executes a single statement, as shown in the following two examples:

```
for (int i = 0; i < 10; i++) System.out.println("Number " + i);

if (booleanVariable)
  System.out.println("It's true");
```

In these two cases, only a single statement is executed and the braces are not required. However, it's a good idea in these situations to enclose the statements in braces anyway to avoid problems that can occur when another statement is added. For example, if another method named `doSomeStuff()` is also to be called when the above `if` statement evaluates to `true`, an inattentive programmer might simply add a line below the existing one:

```
if (booleanVariable)
   System.out.println("It's true");
   doSomeStuff();
```

Although the intent was to execute both statements when `booleanVariable` evaluates to `true`, this code will result in the call to `doSomeStuff()` being executed regardless of the value of `booleanVariable`. The reverse happens if the new statement is added prior to the `println()` call:

```
if (booleanVariable) doSomeStuff();
   System.out.println("It's true");
```

To avoid this issue, you should always use braces with statements such as `if...then`, `for`, `do` and `while`, even when there is only a single line of code to execute.

Placement of Braces

The matter of where to put braces is another issue of some disagreement among Java programmers, and there are two popular approaches to this issue:

Place the open brace at the end of a line of code:

```
for (int i = 0; i < 10; i++) {
   System.out.println("Number " + i);
}
```

Place the open brace on its own line following a line of code:

```
for (int i = 0; i < 10; i++)
{
   System.out.println("Number " + i);
}
```

Although the JavaSoft documentation recommends the first approach, the Java community appears more or less evenly divided on this issue. Again, personal preference is usually the deciding factor, but be aware that there is no widespread agreement on this point. On the other hand, the position of the closing brace is not nearly so controversial and is usually placed on a new line by itself, aligned with the statement that began the code block.

Line Length and Breaks

Like most modern programming languages, Java imposes no restrictions on how long you can make a line of code. In practice, you'll find it awkward to write very long lines of code, and a useful guideline is to keep your lines within 80 characters. Otherwise, depending upon a variety of factors such as screen resolution, font size, and so forth, you may find yourself frequently scrolling left and right to view and edit your code. In addition, long lines may cause printed output to be truncated or printed using a small font that's difficult to read.

To keep the length of your lines below a reasonable limit, it's often necessary to split a single statement across multiple lines. Again, the "right" way to accomplish this is a matter of personal preference, but there are guidelines that can make your code more readable. Specifically, some places where lines are commonly split are the following:

- ❑ Immediately after a comma in a parameter list argument

- ❑ Before or after an operator

- ❑ Immediately after an open parenthesis

When you do split a statement across multiple lines, the remainder should either be aligned with the start of the expression on the first line or indented twice from the beginning of the first line. Both approaches are illustrated in the following code:

```
boolean isValid = cardValidator.verifyValidInformation(cardNumber,
                                                       expirationDate,
                                                       cardHolderName);

boolean isValid = cardValidator.verifyValidInformation(cardNumber,
    expirationDate, cardHolderName);
```

Which of the styles you use will depend partly on personal preference, but in some cases, the expression begins too far to the right for you to align the remainder of the expression with that column. When you do use the "double indention" approach, you should be sure and indent the code twice so that it's not aligned with any statements that follow it that are also indented. The following sample code illustrates why this is important by indenting the remainder of a statement only once:

```
if ((someReallyLongBoolean && anotherReallyLongBoolean) ||
  (thirdVeryLongBoolean && fourthAndFinalBoolean)) {
  System.out.println("Hello");
}
```

At first glance, it appears that the portion of the expression that was placed on the second line is actually part of the code block. However, indenting the statement continuation twice creates a visual separation from the code that follows, and is the recommended practice, as in the following code:

```
if ((someReallyLongBoolean && anotherReallyLongBoolean) ||
    (thirdVeryLongBoolean && fourthAndFinalBoolean)) {
  System.out.println("Hello");
}
```

This example also illustrates another guideline that you should keep in mind when breaking statements apart: when possible, you should split a statement at a "higher" level as opposed to a lower one. For example, an expression should be kept intact on a single line if possible. If it must be split, then you should attempt to divide an expression where it contains a parenthesized sub-expression as in the example shown above. Although there was enough space remaining on the first line to include thirdVeryLongBoolean, it was started on a new line so that the parenthesized expression that it's a part of would appear on a single line.

Professional Java Programmin.

Online discussion at http://p2p.wrox.com

Source Code For GridBagTester

Here is the full source code for the GridBagTester class used in Chapter 5:

```java
import java.awt.*;
import javax.swing.*;
import javax.swing.border.*;
import javax.swing.table.*;

public class GridBagTester extends JFrame {

  protected Container container;
  protected GridBagLayout manager;
  protected ColumnPanel columnPanel;
  protected RowPanel rowPanel;
  protected ComponentPanel componentPanel;

  public final static int COMPONENT_NAME = 0;
  public final static int COMPONENT_X = 1;
  public final static int COMPONENT_Y = 2;
  public final static int COMPONENT_WIDTH = 3;
  public final static int COMPONENT_HEIGHT = 4;
  public final static int COMPONENT_MINSIZE = 5;
  public final static int COMPONENT_PREFSIZE = 6;
  public final static int GRIDX = 7;
  public final static int GRIDY = 8;
  public final static int GRIDWIDTH = 9;
  public final static int GRIDHEIGHT = 10;
  public final static int FILL = 11;
  public final static int ANCHOR = 12;
  public final static int IPADX = 13;
```

```
    public final static int IPADY = 14;
    public final static int WEIGHTX = 15;
    public final static int WEIGHTY = 16;
    public final static int INSETS_TOP = 17;
    public final static int INSETS_LEFT = 18;
    public final static int INSETS_BOTTOM = 19;
    public final static int INSETS_RIGHT = 20;

    public final static int COLUMN_COUNT = 21;

    public final static Object[][] FILL_VALUES = {
        {
        new Integer(GridBagConstraints.NONE),
        new Integer(GridBagConstraints.HORIZONTAL),
        new Integer(GridBagConstraints.VERTICAL),
        new Integer(GridBagConstraints.BOTH)
      }, {
        "NONE", "HORIZONTAL", "VERTICAL", "BOTH"
      }
    };

    public final static Object[][] ANCHOR_VALUES = {
        {
        new Integer(GridBagConstraints.NORTH),
        new Integer(GridBagConstraints.NORTHEAST),
        new Integer(GridBagConstraints.EAST),
        new Integer(GridBagConstraints.SOUTHEAST),
        new Integer(GridBagConstraints.SOUTH),
        new Integer(GridBagConstraints.SOUTHWEST),
        new Integer(GridBagConstraints.WEST),
        new Integer(GridBagConstraints.NORTHWEST),
        new Integer(GridBagConstraints.CENTER)
      }, {
        "NORTH", "NORTHEAST", "EAST", "SOUTHEAST", "SOUTH",
        "SOUTHWEST", "WEST", "NORTHWEST", "CENTER"
      }
    };

    public final static Object[][] SIZE_VALUES = {
        {
        new Integer(GridBagConstraints.RELATIVE),
        new Integer(GridBagConstraints.REMAINDER)
      }, {
        "RELATIVE", "REMAINDER"
      }
    };

    public final static Object[][] POSITION_VALUES = {
        {
        new Integer(GridBagConstraints.RELATIVE)
      }, {
        "RELATIVE"
      }
    };
```

```java
public final static int NUMERIC_VALUE = 0;
public final static int STRING_VALUE = 1;

public GridBagTester(Container cont) {
  super("GridBagLayout Tester");
  setDefaultCloseOperation(JFrame.EXIT_ON_CLOSE);
  container = cont;
  manager = (GridBagLayout) (container.getLayout());
  manager.layoutContainer(container);
  buildLayout();
  pack();
  setVisible(true);
}

protected void buildLayout() {
  Container pane = getContentPane();
  pane.setLayout(new BorderLayout());
  columnPanel = new ColumnPanel();
  pane.add(columnPanel, BorderLayout.NORTH);
  rowPanel = new RowPanel();
  pane.add(rowPanel, BorderLayout.WEST);
  componentPanel = new ComponentPanel();
  pane.add(componentPanel, BorderLayout.SOUTH);
  pane.add(container, BorderLayout.CENTER);
}

class ColumnPanel extends JPanel {

  protected ColumnModel columnModel;

  public ColumnPanel() {
    super();
    setBorder(BorderFactory
      .createTitledBorder("Column Widths and Weights"));
    columnModel = new ColumnModel();
    setLayout(new BorderLayout());
    JTable table = new JTable(columnModel);
    table.setAutoResizeMode(JTable.AUTO_RESIZE_OFF);
    table.setPreferredScrollableViewportSize(new Dimension(10, 55));
    JScrollPane jsp = new JScrollPane(table);
    JTable hdrTable = new JTable(new ColumnHeaderModel());
    hdrTable.setPreferredScrollableViewportSize(new Dimension(75,
          50));
    jsp.setRowHeaderView(hdrTable);
    add(jsp, BorderLayout.CENTER);
  }

  public void refreshTable() {
    columnModel.fireTableDataChanged();
  }

}

class ColumnHeaderModel extends AbstractTableModel {

  final String[] headers = {
```

```
          "Width", "weightX", "Percent"
    };

    public int getRowCount() {
      return 3;
    }

    public int getColumnCount() {
      return 1;
    }

    public Object getValueAt(int row, int column) {
      return headers[row];
    }
}

class ColumnModel extends AbstractTableModel {

    public final int COLUMN_WIDTH = 0;
    public final int COLUMN_WEIGHT = 1;
    public final int COLUMN_DISTRIBUTION_PERCENT = 2;

    public int getRowCount() {
      return 3;
    }

    public int getColumnCount() {
      int[][] dimensions = manager.getLayoutDimensions();
      return dimensions[0].length;
    }

    public Object getValueAt(int row, int column) {
      Object value = null;
      int[][] dimensions;
      double[][] weights;
      switch (row) {
      case COLUMN_WIDTH:
        dimensions = manager.getLayoutDimensions();
        value = new Integer(dimensions[0][column]);
        break;
      case COLUMN_WEIGHT:
        weights = manager.getLayoutWeights();
        value = new Double(weights[0][column]);
        break;
      case COLUMN_DISTRIBUTION_PERCENT:
        weights = manager.getLayoutWeights();
        int count = weights[0].length;
        double total = 0;
        for (int i = 0; i < count; i++) {
          total += weights[0][i];
        }
        double percent = weights[0][column] / total * 100;
        value = new Integer((int) percent);
        break;
      }
      return value;
```

```
    }

  public String getColumnName(int column) {
    return new Integer(column).toString();
  }

}

class RowPanel extends JPanel {

  protected RowModel rowModel;

  public RowPanel() {
    super();
    setBorder(BorderFactory
      .createTitledBorder("Row Heights and Weights"));
    rowModel = new RowModel();
    setLayout(new BorderLayout());
    JTable table = new JTable(rowModel);
    table.setPreferredScrollableViewportSize(new Dimension(150,
          10));
    JScrollPane jsp = new JScrollPane(table);
    JTable hdrTable = new JTable(new RowHeaderModel());
    hdrTable.setPreferredScrollableViewportSize(new Dimension(25,
          10));
    jsp.setRowHeaderView(hdrTable);
    add(jsp, BorderLayout.CENTER);
  }

  public void refreshTable() {
    rowModel.fireTableDataChanged();
  }

}

class RowHeaderModel extends AbstractTableModel {

  public int getRowCount() {
    int[][] dimensions = manager.getLayoutDimensions();
    return dimensions[1].length;
  }

  public int getColumnCount() {
    return 1;
  }

  public Object getValueAt(int row, int column) {
    return new Integer(row);
  }

}

class RowModel extends AbstractTableModel {

  public final int ROW_HEIGHT = 0;
  public final int ROW_WEIGHT = 1;
```

```java
    public final int ROW_DISTRIBUTION_PERCENT = 2;

    final String[] headers = {
      "Height", "weightY", "Percent"
    };

    public int getRowCount() {
      int[][] dimensions = manager.getLayoutDimensions();
      return dimensions[1].length;
    }

    public int getColumnCount() {
      return 3;
    }

    public Object getValueAt(int row, int column) {
      Object value = null;
      int[][] dimensions;
      double[][] weights;
      switch (column) {
      case ROW_HEIGHT:
        dimensions = manager.getLayoutDimensions();
        value = new Integer(dimensions[1][row]);
        break;
      case ROW_WEIGHT:
        weights = manager.getLayoutWeights();
        value = new Double(weights[1][row]);
        break;
      case ROW_DISTRIBUTION_PERCENT:
        weights = manager.getLayoutWeights();
        int count = weights[1].length;
        double total = 0;
        for (int i = 0; i < count; i++) {
          total += weights[1][i];
        }
        double percent = weights[1][row] / total * 100;
        value = new Integer((int) percent);
        break;
      }
      return value;
    }

    public String getColumnName(int column) {
      return headers[column];
    }

}

class ComponentPanel extends JPanel {

  protected ComponentModel componentModel;

  public ComponentPanel() {
    super();
    setBorder(BorderFactory
      .createTitledBorder("Component Constraints"));
```

```
        componentModel = new ComponentModel();
        setLayout(new BorderLayout());
        JTable table = new JTable(componentModel);
        table.setAutoResizeMode(JTable.AUTO_RESIZE_OFF);
        table.setRowSelectionAllowed(false);
        table.setDefaultRenderer(Dimension.class,
                                new DimensionCellRenderer());
        table.setDefaultEditor(Double.class, new DoubleCellEditor());
        table.setDefaultEditor(Integer.class, new IntegerCellEditor());
        TableColumnModel tcm = table.getColumnModel();
        ConstraintDataCellRenderer cdcr =
          new ConstraintDataCellRenderer();
        ComboBoxCellEditor cbce = new ComboBoxCellEditor();
        TableColumn tc = tcm.getColumn(FILL);
        tc.setCellRenderer(cdcr);
        tc.setCellEditor(cbce);
        tc = tcm.getColumn(ANCHOR);
        tc.setCellRenderer(cdcr);
        tc.setCellEditor(cbce);
        tc = tcm.getColumn(GRIDX);
        tc.setCellRenderer(cdcr);
        tc.setCellEditor(cbce);
        tc = tcm.getColumn(GRIDY);
        tc.setCellRenderer(cdcr);
        tc.setCellEditor(cbce);
        tc = tcm.getColumn(GRIDWIDTH);
        tc.setCellRenderer(cdcr);
        tc.setCellEditor(cbce);
        tc = tcm.getColumn(GRIDHEIGHT);
        tc.setCellRenderer(cdcr);
        tc.setCellEditor(cbce);
        table.setPreferredScrollableViewportSize(new Dimension(10,
                105));
        JScrollPane jsp = new JScrollPane(table);
        add(jsp, BorderLayout.CENTER);
    }

  public void refreshTable() {
    componentModel.fireTableDataChanged();
  }

}

class ComponentModel extends AbstractTableModel {

  public final String[] headers = {
    "Name", "X", "Y", "width", "height", "minSize", "prefSize",
    "gridx", "gridy", "gridwidth", "gridheight", "fill", "anchor",
    "ipadx", "ipady", "weightx", "weighty", "top", "left",
    "bottom", "right"
  };

  public int getRowCount() {
    return container.getComponents().length;
  }
```

```java
    public int getColumnCount() {
      return COLUMN_COUNT;
    }

    public boolean isCellEditable(int row, int column) {
      switch (column) {
      case COMPONENT_MINSIZE:
      case COMPONENT_PREFSIZE:
        return false;
      }
      return true;
    }

    public Object getValueAt(int row, int column) {
      Object value = null;
      Component comp = container.getComponents()[row];
      GridBagConstraints gbc = manager.getConstraints(comp);
      switch (column) {
      case COMPONENT_NAME:
        String name = comp.getName();
        if ((name == null) || (name.length() == 0)) {
          Class cl = comp.getClass();
          name = cl.getName();
          int ind = name.lastIndexOf('.');
          value = name.substring(ind + 1);
        } else {
          value = name;
        }
        break;
      case COMPONENT_X:
        value = new Integer(comp.getLocation().x);
        break;
      case COMPONENT_Y:
        value = new Integer(comp.getLocation().y);
        break;
      case COMPONENT_WIDTH:
        value = new Integer(comp.getSize().width);
        break;
      case COMPONENT_HEIGHT:
        value = new Integer(comp.getSize().height);
        break;
      case COMPONENT_MINSIZE:
        value = comp.getMinimumSize();
        break;
      case COMPONENT_PREFSIZE:
        value = comp.getPreferredSize();
        break;
      case GRIDX:
        value = new Integer(gbc.gridx);
        break;
      case GRIDY:
        value = new Integer(gbc.gridy);
        break;
      case GRIDWIDTH:
        value = new Integer(gbc.gridwidth);
        break;
```

```
    case GRIDHEIGHT:
      value = new Integer(gbc.gridheight);
      break;
    case FILL:
      value = new Integer(gbc.fill);
      break;
    case ANCHOR:
      value = new Integer(gbc.anchor);
      break;
    case IPADX:
      value = new Integer(gbc.ipadx);
      break;
    case IPADY:
      value = new Integer(gbc.ipady);
      break;
    case WEIGHTX:
      value = new Double(gbc.weightx);
      break;
    case WEIGHTY:
      value = new Double(gbc.weighty);
      break;
    case INSETS_TOP:
      value = new Integer(gbc.insets.top);
      break;
    case INSETS_LEFT:
      value = new Integer(gbc.insets.left);
      break;
    case INSETS_BOTTOM:
      value = new Integer(gbc.insets.bottom);
      break;
    case INSETS_RIGHT:
      value = new Integer(gbc.insets.right);
      break;
    }
    return value;
}

public void setValueAt(Object value, int row, int column) {
    Component comp = container.getComponents()[row];
    GridBagConstraints gbc = manager.getConstraints(comp);
    switch (column) {
    case COMPONENT_NAME:
      comp.setName((String) value);
      break;
    case COMPONENT_X:
      comp.setLocation(((Integer) value).intValue(),
                       comp.getLocation().y);
      break;
    case COMPONENT_Y:
      comp.setLocation(comp.getLocation().x,
                       ((Integer) value).intValue());
      break;
    case COMPONENT_WIDTH:
      comp.setSize(((Integer) value).intValue(),
                 comp.getSize().width);
      break;
```

```
          case COMPONENT_HEIGHT:
            comp.setSize(comp.getSize().height,
                        ((Integer) value).intValue());
            break;
          case GRIDX:
            gbc.gridx = ((Integer) value).intValue();
            break;
          case GRIDY:
            gbc.gridy = ((Integer) value).intValue();
            break;
          case GRIDWIDTH:
            gbc.gridwidth = ((Integer) value).intValue();
            break;
          case GRIDHEIGHT:
            gbc.gridheight = ((Integer) value).intValue();
            break;
          case FILL:
            gbc.fill = ((Integer) value).intValue();
            break;
          case ANCHOR:
            gbc.anchor = ((Integer) value).intValue();
            break;
          case IPADX:
            gbc.ipadx = ((Integer) value).intValue();
            break;
          case IPADY:
            gbc.ipady = ((Integer) value).intValue();
            break;
          case WEIGHTX:
            gbc.weightx = ((Double) value).doubleValue();
            break;
          case WEIGHTY:
            gbc.weighty = ((Double) value).doubleValue();
            break;
          case INSETS_TOP:
            gbc.insets.top = ((Integer) value).intValue();
            break;
          case INSETS_LEFT:
            gbc.insets.left = ((Integer) value).intValue();
            break;
          case INSETS_BOTTOM:
            gbc.insets.bottom = ((Integer) value).intValue();
            break;
          case INSETS_RIGHT:
            gbc.insets.right = ((Integer) value).intValue();
            break;
        }
        manager.setConstraints(comp, gbc);
        refreshAllTables();
      }

      public String getColumnName(int column) {
        return headers[column];
      }

      public Class getColumnClass(int column) {
```

```java
      Class dataType = Object.class;
      switch (column) {
      case COMPONENT_NAME:
        break;
      case COMPONENT_X:
      case COMPONENT_Y:
        dataType = Integer.class;
        break;
      case COMPONENT_WIDTH:
      case COMPONENT_HEIGHT:
        dataType = Integer.class;
        break;
      case COMPONENT_MINSIZE:
      case COMPONENT_PREFSIZE:
        dataType = Dimension.class;
        break;
      case GRIDX:
      case GRIDY:
        break;
      case GRIDWIDTH:
      case GRIDHEIGHT:
        break;
      case FILL:
        break;
      case ANCHOR:
        break;
      case IPADX:
      case IPADY:
        dataType = Integer.class;
        break;
      case WEIGHTX:
      case WEIGHTY:
        dataType = Double.class;
        break;
      case INSETS_TOP:
      case INSETS_LEFT:
      case INSETS_BOTTOM:
      case INSETS_RIGHT:
        dataType = Integer.class;
        break;
      }
      return dataType;
   }
}


class DoubleCellEditor extends DefaultCellEditor {

   public DoubleCellEditor() {
     super(new NumericTextField(5, true));
   }

   public Object getCellEditorValue() {
     NumericTextField ntf = (NumericTextField) getComponent();
     return new Double(ntf.getText());
   }
```

```
  }

class IntegerCellEditor extends DefaultCellEditor {

  public IntegerCellEditor() {
    super(new NumericTextField(5, false));
  }

  public Object getCellEditorValue() {
    NumericTextField ntf = (NumericTextField) getComponent();
    return new Integer(ntf.getText());
  }

}

class DimensionCellRenderer extends DefaultTableCellRenderer {

  public void setValue(Object value) {
    Dimension size = (Dimension) value;
    super.setValue("(" + size.width + "," + size.height + ")");
  }

}

class ConstraintDataCellRenderer extends JLabel
  implements TableCellRenderer {

  public Component getTableCellRendererComponent(JTable table,
          Object value, boolean isSelected, boolean hasFocus,
          int row, int column) {
    Object cellText = getStringFromValue(column, value);
    if (cellText != null) {
      value = cellText;
    }
    if (value instanceof Number) {
      setHorizontalAlignment(RIGHT);
    } else {
      setHorizontalAlignment(CENTER);
    }
    setText(value.toString());
    return this;
  }

}

class ComboBoxCellEditor extends DefaultCellEditor {

  protected Object[][] editorValues;

  public ComboBoxCellEditor() {
    super(new JComboBox());
    JComboBox box = (JComboBox) (getComponent());
    box.setEditor(new NumericComboBoxEditor());
  }

  public Component getTableCellEditorComponent(JTable table,
```

```
          Object value, boolean isSelected, int row, int column) {
      JComboBox box = (JComboBox) (getComponent());
      Object selection;
      switch (column) {
      case GRIDX:
      case GRIDY:
        box.setEditable(true);
        break;
      case GRIDWIDTH:
      case GRIDHEIGHT:
        box.setEditable(true);
        break;
      case FILL:
        box.setEditable(false);
        break;
      case ANCHOR:
        box.setEditable(false);
        break;
      }
      editorValues = getValueArray(column);
      DefaultComboBoxModel dcbm =
        new DefaultComboBoxModel(editorValues[STRING_VALUE]);
      box.setModel(dcbm);
      Object boxValue = getStringFromValue(column, value);
      if (boxValue != null) {
        box.setSelectedItem(getStringFromValue(column, value));
      } else {
        ComboBoxEditor editor = box.getEditor();
        editor.setItem(value);
      }
      return box;
    }

    public Object getCellEditorValue() {
      Object value = null;
      JComboBox box = (JComboBox) (getComponent());
      int index = box.getSelectedIndex();
      if (index != -1) {
        return editorValues[0][index];
      } else {
        value = new Integer(box.getSelectedItem().toString());
      }
      return value;
    }

}

class NumericComboBoxEditor extends NumericTextField
  implements ComboBoxEditor {

  public NumericComboBoxEditor() {
    super(5, false);
  }

  public Component getEditorComponent() {
    return this;
```

```
      }

  public Object getItem() {
    return getText();
  }

  public void setItem(Object item) {
    if (item != null) {
      setText(item.toString());
    }
  }

}

protected Object getStringFromValue(int column, Object value) {
  Object result = null;
  Object[][] values = getValueArray(column);
  if (values != null) {
    for (int i = 0; i < values[NUMERIC_VALUE].length; i++) {
      if (values[NUMERIC_VALUE][i].equals(value)) {
        result = values[STRING_VALUE][i];
        break;
      }
    }
  }
  return result;
}

protected Object getValueFromString(int column, String value) {
  Object result = null;
  Object[][] values = getValueArray(column);
  for (int i = 0; i < values[STRING_VALUE].length; i++) {
    if (value.equals(values[STRING_VALUE][i])) {
      result = values[NUMERIC_VALUE][i];
      break;
    }
  }
  return result;
}

protected Object[][] getValueArray(int column) {
  Object[][] result = null;
  switch (column) {
  case FILL:
    result = FILL_VALUES;
    break;
  case ANCHOR:
    result = ANCHOR_VALUES;
    break;
  case GRIDX:
  case GRIDY:
    result = POSITION_VALUES;
    break;
  case GRIDWIDTH:
  case GRIDHEIGHT:
    result = SIZE_VALUES;
```

```
      break;
    }
    return result;
  }

  public void refreshAllTables() {
    container.invalidate();
    container.validate();
    container.repaint();
    columnPanel.refreshTable();
    rowPanel.refreshTable();
    componentPanel.refreshTable();
  }

}
```

Professional Java Programming

Online discussion at http://p2p.wrox.com

Index A - Methods

A Guide to the Index

There are two indexes in this book: Index A - Methods and Index B - General. Index A - Methods is a flat index intended as a quick reference. Index - B General has detailed entries arranged hierarchically, covering the entire scope of the book, including methods, at both first and subsequent levels. This is to ensure that users will find the information they require however they choose to search for it.

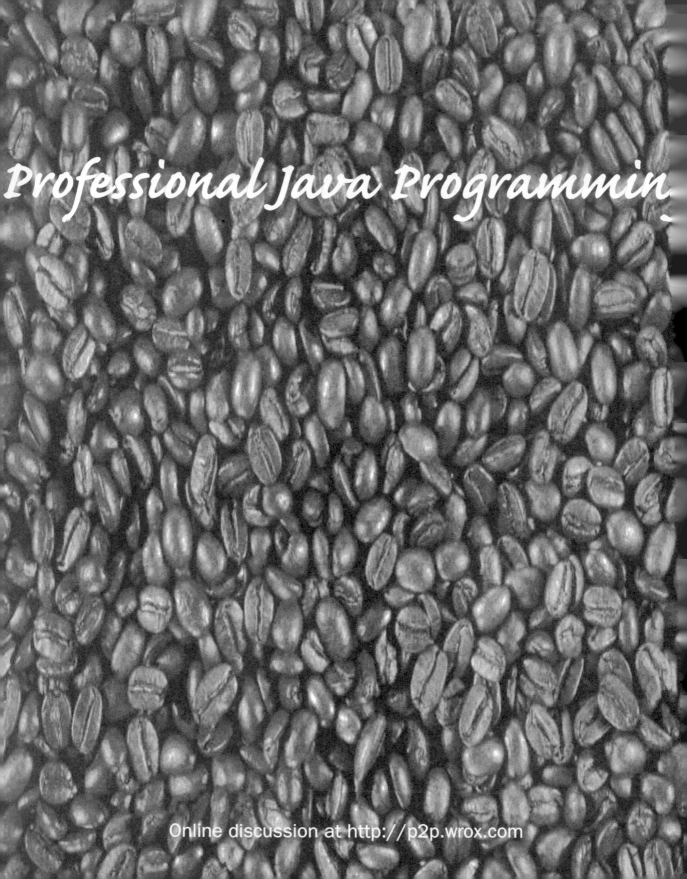

Professional Java Programming

Online discussion at http://p2p.wrox.com

Index B - General

Symbols

F

M

Professional Java Programmin

wrox

PROGRAMMER TO PROGRAMMER™

Wrox writes books for you. Any suggestions, or ideas about how you want information given in your ideal book will be studied by our team. Your comments are always valued at Wrox.

Free phone in USA 800-USE-WROX
Fax (312) 893 8001

UK Tel. (0121) 687 4100   Fax (0121) 687 4101

Professional Java Programming - Registration Card

Name _____

Address _____

_____

_____

City _____ State/Region _____

Country _____ Postcode/Zip _____

E-mail _____

Occupation _____

How did you hear about this book? _____

☐ Book review (name) _____

☐ Advertisement (name) _____

☐ Recommendation _____

☐ Catalog _____

☐ Other _____

Where did you buy this book? _____

☐ Bookstore (name) _____ City _____

☐ Computer Store (name) _____

☐ Mail Order _____

☐ Other _____

What influenced you in the purchase of this book?

☐ Cover Design

☐ Contents

☐ Other (please specify) _____

How did you rate the overall contents of this book?

☐ Excellent   ☐ Good

☐ Average   ☐ Poor

What did you find most useful about this book? _____

What did you find least useful about this book? _____

Please add any additional comments. _____

What other subjects will you buy a computer book on soon? _____

What is the best computer book you have used this year?

_____

Note: This information will only be used to keep you updated about new Wrox Press titles and will not be used for any other purpose or passed to any other third party.

382x   *Check here if you DO NOT want to receive support for this book* ▮   **382x**

wrox

PROGRAMMER TO PROGRAMMER™

NB. If you post the bounce back card below in the UK, please send it to:

Wrox Press Ltd., Arden House, 1102 Warwick Road,
Acocks Green, Birmingham B27 6BH. UK.

——— *Computer Book Publishers* ———